Foundations of Cognitive Science

Foundations of Cognitive Science

edited by
Michael I. Posner

A Bradford Book
The MIT Press
Cambridge, Massachusetts
London, England

First MIT Press paperback edition, 1993

© 1989 Massachusetts Institute of Technology

The preparation and production of this book have been aided by a grant from the Alfred P. Sloan Foundation.

This book was set in Palatino by DEKR Corporation and printed and bound in the United States of America.

Library of Congress Cataloging-in-Publication Data
Foundations of cognitive science / edited by Michael I. Posner.
    p.   cm.
"A Bradford book."
ISBN 0-262-16112-5, (HB), 0-262-66086-5 (PB)
    1. Cognitive science. 2. Cognition. I. Posner, Michael I.
BF311.F66   1989
153—dc20   89-32116
                                                                        CIP

Contents

Contributors

Alan Allport
Department of Experimental
Psychology
University of Oxford
Oxford, England

Jon Barwise
Center for the Study of Language
and Information
Stanford University
Stanford, California

E. Bizzi
Department of Brain and
Cognitive Sciences
Massachusetts Institute of
Technology
Cambridge, Massachusetts

Gordon H. Bower
Department of Psychology
Stanford University
Stanford, California

Patricia Smith Churchland
Department of Philosophy
University of California at San
Diego
La Jolla, California

John P. Clapper
Department of Psychology
Stanford University
Stanford, California

Roy G. D'Andrade
Anthropology Department
University of California at San
Diego
La Jolla, California

John Etchemendy
Department of Philosophy
Stanford University
Stanford, California

Barbara J. Grosz
Aiken Computation Lab
Harvard University
Cambridge, Massachusetts

Gilbert Harman
Department of Philosophy
Princeton University
Princeton, New Jersey

Ellen C. Hildreth
Department of Brain and
Cognitive Sciences
Massachusetts Institute of
Technology
Cambridge, Massachusetts

P. N. Johnson-Laird
MRC Applied Psychology Unit
Cambridge, England

Michael I. Jordan
Department of Brain and
Cognitive Sciences
Massachusetts Institute of
Technology
Cambridge, Massachusetts

Craig A. Kaplan
Department of Psychology
Carnegie Mellon University
Pittsburgh, Pennsylvania

John E. Laird
Department of Computer and
Electrical Engineering
University of Michigan
Ann Arbor, Michigan

F. A. Mussa-Ivaldi
Department of Brain and
Cognitive Sciences
Massachusetts Institute of
Technology
Cambridge, Massachusetts

Allen Newell
Departments of Computer
Science and Psychology
Carnegie Mellon University
Pittsburgh, Pennsylvania

Steven Pinker
Department of Brain and
Cognitive Sciences
Massachusetts Institute of
Technology
Cambridge, Massachusetts

Martha E. Pollack
AI Center
SRI International
Menlo Park, California

Alexander Pollatsek
Department of Psychology
University of Massachusetts at
Amherst
Amherst, Massachusetts

Michael I. Posner
Department of Psychology
University of Oregon
Eugene, Oregon

Zenon W. Pylyshyn
Center for Cognitive Science
The University of Western
Ontario
London, Ontario, Canada

Keith Rayner
Department of Psychology
University of Massachusetts at
Amherst
Amherst, Massachusetts

David A. Rosenbaum
Department of Psychology
University of Massachusetts at
Amherst
Amherst, Massachusetts

Paul S. Rosenbloom
Knowledge Systems Laboratory
Computer Science Department
Stanford University
Stanford, California

David E. Rumelhart
Department of Psychology
Stanford University
Stanford, California

Daniel L. Schacter
Department of Psychology
University of Arizona
Tucson, Arizona

Terrence J. Sejnowski
Department of Biophysics
Johns Hopkins University
Baltimore, Maryland

Candace L. Sidner
Harvard University and BBN
Systems and Technology, Inc.
Cambridge, Massachusetts

Herbert A. Simon
Department of Psychology
Carnegie Mellon University
Pittsburgh, Pennsylvania

Edward E. Smith
Department of Psychology
University of Michigan
Ann Arbor, Michigan

Shimon Ullman
Department of Brain and
Cognitive Science
Massachusetts Institute of
Technology
Cambridge, Massachusetts

Kurt VanLehn
Departments of Psychology and
Computer Science
Carnegie Mellon University
Pittsburgh, Pennsylvania

Thomas Wasow
Center for the Study of Language
and Information
Stanford University
Stanford, California

Preface: Learning Cognitive Science

To learn a new field, according to the cognitive science approach, is to build appropriate cognitive structures (chapter 1) and to learn to perform computations (chapter 2) that will transform what is known into what is not yet known. Despite the presence of preliminary theories of scientific induction, no one knows how to teach this over any substantial domain (chapters 12, 13). Nonetheless this book is meant to convey to a new generation of researchers what is currently known about the basic structure of cognitive science.

In this volume cognitive science deals with the nature of intelligence from the perspective of computation (chapters 1, 2). Sometimes its focus is upon symbols, those representations that stand for something else (chapter 3). The ability to manipulate symbols has allowed inanimate physical systems to solve problems and perform functions previously performed only by human beings (chapter 14). The concept of the mind as a symbol processor implies an architecture of cognition (chapter 3) that has been and is currently of great influence in the field. This architecture is then applied to the development of language (chapter 9), the construction of meaningful discourse (chapter 11), and the understanding of problems (chapters 13, 14).

Inspiration for computational ideas may come from animate systems as well as from inanimate ones. The architecture of parallel distributed (connectionist) systems is inspired by the style of computation found in nervous systems. The impressive new results in this field are reviewed in chapter 4, and methods for bridging the distance between real neurons and more abstract computational levels are introduced in chapter 8. In one way or another the chapters on reading, vision, memory, and action all relate to the theory and methods of connectionism.

Grammar was the impetus for many important developments in cognitive science. Many of the ideas for rule-based systems as the basis of computation in language came originally from transformational grammar (see chapter 5 for a review). Language involves more than syntax; it has the character of being about something that stands outside itself.

The complex of issues that relate language to the outside world raises many logical questions of semantics (discussed in chapter 6).

Syntax and semantics are both very basic to the study of the acquisition of spoken (chapter 9) and written language (chapter 10) and to its use in communication (chapter 11). The effort to develop direct communication between humans and machines (chapter 11) makes clear the centrality of real world understanding that lies outside of the formal domain of language. The nonlinguistic functions so important to the understanding and use of language include the learning of categories (chapter 13), constructing models of real world activity (chapter 12), and studying the ability to develop and employ heuristics in the process of solving problems (chapter 14). A greal deal of this book can be seen as based on the foundations of the formal analysis of grammars and semantics.

Much of cognitive science rests on empirical studies that describe the performance of human subjects in cognitive tasks. These empirical studies may involve verbal protocols (chapter 1), eye movement protocols (chapters 7, 10), or other experimental methods using response speed (chapters 2, 7), accuracy, or memory performance (chapter 7). The results of these experimental methods form the basis for the domains of reading (chapter 10), attention (chapter 16), memory (chapter 17), and action (chapters 18, 19). What makes many of these domains exciting now is the ability to summarize and extend empirical findings by the use of a variety of formal mathematical or simulation methods. Some of these methods are introduced in the foundations section in chapters 2 and 3. These methods have led to the development of expert systems, computer-assisted tutors, and other simulations based on symbolic processing. They have had their greatest impact in the study of language acquisition, induction, and problem solving.

Connectionist models have been important in tieing the findings made with cognitive methods to underlying neural systems. The use of simulation based on neural style computation directs attention to methods that connect neural systems with cognition. These methods are reviewed in chapter 8. They are having important applications in the study of language processing (chapter 10), attention (chapter 16), memory (chapter 17), and motor control (chapters 18, 19), among other areas. In order for connectionist models to make additional contact with the underlying physiology, it will be necessary to employ empirical techniques that allow for the localization of cognitive operations within the brain. Fortunately, newer methods of neural imaging and recording of time-locked electrical and magnetic signals are providing methods for making such connections (chapter 8). In some areas (chapters 16, 17, 19) the combined cognitive and neuroscience methodology makes it difficult to separate brain and mind approaches to empirical issues. It appears likely that in some areas of cognition there will be very fruitful links between neuroscience and cognitive science. In other areas only cognitive methods and simulations will be available.

Achievements in many domains of cognitive science have been impressive. Nonetheless, if the goal is no less than a verified architecture of cognition that can illuminate the full range of human intelligence, the distance yet to go is staggering. Two areas in which these distances are most notable are in the study of cultural differences in cognition and subjective mental experience and the brain. In the former area cognitive psychologists and anthropologists have both pointed the way to methods for understanding the pervasive role of culture in directing the thought processes. Although it may be convenient to suppose that a cognitive theory of representation is complete without consideration of the different contents imposed by acculturation, it seems more likely that we will understand cognitive representations better when we can consider them in the context of the cultures in which they are found (chapter 20).

Similarly, it was once fashionable to say that cognition could be implemented in any electromechanical system, so that the details of mere hardware were of no basic importance to cognitive theory. The influence of connectionist ideas (chapter 4) and the increased understanding of localization of function (chapter 8) have both worked to erode this separation. While we can now begin to talk more confidently about the neural systems involved in word reading or selective attention, this is not sufficient to explain how the brain creates and contains subjective experience. This issue is discussed from the point of view of philosophy in chapter 21. The chapter raises paradoxes that may become more critical with progress in synthesizing mind and brain.

The organization of this volume is simple. Following an overview chapter, the foundations of the field are laid in seven review chapters. These foundations are then applied to a dozen areas prominent in the current literature. The final two chapters represent critiques of the field's current state from the point of view of cultural anthropology and philosophy.

The idea for this volume arose from members of the cognitive science community who contacted Harry Stanton of Bradford Books at The MIT Press. Harry and Betty Stanton have been instrumental in all phases of the development of this project from its initiation to the production of the volume. Charlotte Golar Richie helped with assembling the manuscript. A board of editors, which included many of the authors of this volume, assembled in St. Louis to outline the chapters needed to carry forth the project. In editing the volume, I had very substantial help from George Miller, Dan Dennett, Allen Newell, Tom Wasow, Steve Pinker, Ed Smith, Richard Ivry, Barbara Tversky, Scott DeLancey, Gordon Shulman, Adele Diamond, and Steven Petersen. A generous grant from the Sloan Foundation has been vital to the development of this project.

There is no pretense that this volume contains all of cognitive science as it currently exists and still less as it will be by the time you read these words. But we hope that in these pages you will find out enough about the field to get a feeling for its methods, suppositions, and results.

Foundations of Cognitive Science

1 Foundations of Cognitive Science

Herbert A. Simon and Craig A. Kaplan

This chapter treats rather concisely a range of topics that help define the scope of cognitive science and the numerous dimensions along which the field can be explored. It focuses more on identifying issues than on providing definite answers, a task more appropriately left for the contributors on specific topics.

Since many different methods are used in cognitive science research, since several different conceptual approaches have been taken to the field, and since a number of different architectures for intelligent systems are being explored, we take some pains to recognize this diversity. At the same time we do not hesitate to express opinions about which ideas seem most correct or promising and which lines of inquiry seem most worthy of pursuit. The authors of other chapters have ample opportunity to redress our imbalances.

1.1 The Goals of Cognitive Science

Cognitive science is the study of intelligence and intelligent systems, with particular reference to intelligent behavior as computation. Although no really satisfactory intentional definition of intelligence has been proposed, we are ordinarily willing to judge when intelligence is being exhibited by our fellow human beings. We say that people are behaving intelligently when they choose courses of action that are relevant to achieving their goals, when they reply coherently and appropriately to questions that are put to them, when they solve problems of lesser or greater difficulty, or when they create or design something useful or beautiful or novel. We apply a single term, "intelligence," to this diverse set of activities because we expect that a common set of underlying processes is implicated in performing all of them.

When we wish to compare different people on a scale of intelligence, we construct batteries of tests presenting a variety of tasks that require them to solve problems or to use language appropriately. There are innumerable kinds of tests that exercise the intellectual capabilities of the test takers. Some of them call upon knowledge of very specific subject matter, but those we specifically label "intelligence tests" are usually designed to be as independent of subject-matter knowledge as possible—or at least only to draw upon subject matter that is presumed to be familiar to most members of the culture (general vocabulary, arithmetic, and the like). In this chapter we discuss both knowledge-based and (almost) knowledge-free intelligence.

Today it is quite common to attribute intelligence to both human and nonhuman systems and, in particular, to programmed computers. Not everyone accepts this usage, but we call programs intelligent if they exhibit behaviors that would be regarded as intelligent if they were exhibited by human beings. Intelligence is to be judged by the ability to perform intellectual tasks, independent of the nature of the physical system that exhibits this ability.

Cognitive science, defined as the study of intelligence and its computational processes, can be approached in several ways. We can undertake to construct an abstract theory of intelligent processes, divorced from specific physical or biological implementations. We can study human (or animal) intelligence, seeking to abstract a theory of intelligent processes from the behavior of intelligent organisms. Or we can study computer intelligence, trying to learn the computational principles that underlie the organization and behavior of intelligent programs.

In fact, cognitive science follows all of these paths. Several venerable examples of the study of intelligence in the abstract predate the computer. Formal logic is one such example; the theory of maximization of expected utility is another. For a century or more, experimental psychology has been studying organismic intelligence, especially as exhibited by people, rats, and pigeons in the laboratory. Since at least 1950 (we might take Turing's (1950) essay "Computing Machinery and Intelligence" as a convenient starting point) that branch of computer science called "artificial intelligence" has been studying the intelligence exhibited by machines. (Watt's governor or Pascal's calculating machines might be regarded as even earlier examples of machine intelligence.)

For the purposes of this chapter, then, we define cognitive science as the study of intelligence and its computational processes in humans (and animals), in computers, and in the abstract. It will be instructive to see how the communality among these three topics came to be recognized and how that recognition led to the birth of the discipline of cognitive science.

1.2 The Principal Contributing Disciplines

From a sociological standpoint, disciplines are defined less by their intellectual structure and content than by the scientists who identify with them. But more accurately, over time the intellectual content of a discipline gradually defines its boundaries and membership, whereas its membership gradually redefines its content. Therefore, if we are to understand cognitive science, we must know what disciplines have contributed to its formation (Norman 1981). Among these we must certainly count experimental and cognitive psychology, artificial intelligence (within computer science), linguistics, philosophy (especially logic and epistemology), neuroscience, and some others (anthropology, economics, and social psychology will also come in for comment).

Psychology
From its beginnings the discipline of psychology has been concerned with intelligence. The Binet–Simon intelligence test (the IQ test par excellence) dates from the turn of the century. The dominance of behaviorism during the first half of the century prevented experimental psychologists from being much interested in what was going on inside the organism, however; hence there was limited speculation and research about process. Brain research contributed to our knowledge of the location of functions witin the brain but had relatively little to say about cognitive processes. Even the precise physiological basis of memory was not (and has not yet been) unambiguously determined.

During the high tide of behaviorism, experimental psychology focused on relatively simple cognitive performance, with emphasis on sensory and motor processes such as rote verbal learning, tracking tasks requiring hand-eye coordination, memory tasks involving relatively short-term retention, and the attainment of simple concepts. The intelligence of rats and pigeons received as much attention as the intelligence of people. It was left primarily to the Gestalt psychologists to develop theories of human cognitive processes, especially for complex cognitive performances like concept formation and problem solving.

Psychology was no more monolithic than chemistry or physics: various specializations were (and are) visible, each of which has brought its particular contribution to cognitive science. Psychometrics brought its measures of intelligence and the components of intelligence. Neurophysiology brought knowledge of the biological structures that support thought. Experimental psychology brought a host of information about the speed and limitations of simple sensory, perceptual, motor, and memory processes. Gestalt psychology brought hypotheses about the processes that occur in complex thinking. Although there was some communication among these specialities, each tended to go its own way, guided by its own paradigm. A new paradigm was required to make a convincing case for their mutual relevance.

The shift came with the so-called information-processing revolution of the fifties and sixties, which viewed thinking as a symbol-manipulating process and used computer simulation as a way to build theories of thinking (Simon 1979a). A relatively new specialization, psycholinguistics, found the information-processing view congenial and opened up a line of communication between psychology and linguistics.

Mainline experimental psychology also began to adopt the information-processing point of view without necessarily embracing computer simulation, and a rough division of labor began to develop between those scientists (often computer simulators) who studied the so-called higher mental functions, such as concept formation, problem solving, and use of language, and those (less often computer simulators) who studied simpler, and more traditional, memory and perceptual tasks. The chapters by Simon (1979b) and Posner and McLeod (1982) in the *Annual Reviews of Psychology* provide a good overview of these two parts of the cognitive psychology scene in the late seventies and early eighties.

Artificial Intelligence
The very term "artificial intelligence," coined about 1956, incorporated the belief that the concept of intelligence now had to be extended beyond human and animal performance to include artificial systems—computers. Because it is by no means evident just what the intelligence of people and the intelligence of computers have in common beyond their ability to perform certain tasks, the close relation that has been maintained between research in AI and research in cognitive psychology was not preordained or even predictable.

The earliest artificial intelligence programs (for example, the Logic Theorist (Newell and Simon 1956)) are perhaps best viewed as models of abstract intelligence; but nonetheless their design was informed by psychological research on memory and problem solving—note, for example, the use of associative structures in list-processing programming languages and subsequently the frequent use of means–ends analysis for inference.

In turn AI research has made numerous contributions to cognitive psychology. For example, AI provided list-processing languages that permit the modeling of elaborate associative structures—schemas, scripts, frames—to simulate important properties of human semantic memory (Newell and Simon 1963). AI research also adapted programming languages built up from so-called productions as a sophisticated interpretation and augmentation of classical stimulus–response relations and stimulus-recognition processes (Rich 1983). Research on robotics has often turned to sensory and perceptual psychology for ideas about processing schemes, and the psychology of vision and speech recognition has borrowed many ideas from AI.

In fact, then, there has been a close continuing relation between AI and cognitive simulation during the whole thirty-odd years of the history of both subjects, and their mutual relevance and synergy was a major motivation for creating a common meeting ground in cognitive science.

Linguistics

The study of language has a long and complex history. In academia linguistics has bases in departments of classics, of biblical studies, of modern languages, and of anthropology. Until recently, it had only tenuous relations with psychology, and today it is represented in cognitive science mainly under the labels of "computational linguistics" (chapters 5, 12) and "psycholinguistics" (chapters 9, 11).

Computational linguistics, as its name implies, is concerned with the use of computers to process language, for example in parsing and translation algorithms. Within cognitive science it is most closely linked to artificial intelligence, although that linkage is of relatively recent origin. Early research on machine translation had only weak ties to either mainstream AI or mainstream linguistics.

Psycholinguistics, the psychological study of language, followed a partially autonomous path to contemporary cognitive science. A sizeable gulf in communications still exists between cognitive scientists who entered the field from AI or from the study of problem solving and concept-forming behavior, on the one side, and those who entered from a concern with language, on the other. Newell and Simon's (1972) *Human Problem Solving* is a typical example of the former viewpoint, Miller and Johnson-Laird's (1976) *Language and Perception* an example of the latter.

As we shall see, it takes rather careful inspection to verify that the group focusing on problem solving (see chapter 15) and the one focusing on language are both interested in the same process: human thinking. When linguistics is approached from a computational standpoint, the relation between the two becomes clearer. When the uniqueness of language processing as a human faculty is emphasized, as it has been by Chomsky (1965, pp. 47–59) and others, the gulf becomes wider.

Philosophy

We have already pointed to logic as a long-established domain for the study of abstract intelligence. The mathematization of logic at the turn of the twentieth century also showed how inference processes could be viewed as symbol manipulation and thereby provided some of the foundational ideas for the information processing revolution. Recently the requirements of large data bases for AI systems have stimulated new developments in modal and nonmonotonic logics for reasoning about the information stored in these bases.

In economics and statistics the twentieth century also saw the rapid development of a formal theory of "right reason" in the form of the theories of utility maximization and of Bayesian inference. We can regard these models of rationality from logic, economics, and statistics as forming an important part of a normative theory of intelligence and hence of cognitive science, although the researchers responsible for modern decision theory have had little involvement (or recognition) in the cognitive science community. The relevance of this kind of decision theory to psychology is debatable.

The relation of epistemology to cognitive science is rather different (see chapter 21). The advent of machine intelligence forced radical reconsideration of the mind–body problem. Those who rejected the idea that machines could think (for example, Searle 1980) had to forge new theories to demonstrate why the appearance of intelligence was not intelligence. Those who accepted the idea of machine thinking (for example, Turing 1950) had to establish operational criteria, such as the Turing test, to verify the presence of intelligence.

Computer simulation methods also introduced a new precision into epistemological discussion. Arguments that were often unavoidably vague when expressed in natural language lost much of their ambiguity when rephrased in terms of the behavior of actual or potential machines or computer programs.

Neuroscience
Neurophysiology, and neuroscience generally, also occupies a very complex place in cognitive science (see chapter 8). There remains today a large gap between reduction in principle and reduction in practice. Probably an overwhelming majority of psychologists believe that the processes of thinking are, in principle, explainable in terms of the electrochemical processes of the brain. Many, however, believe that theories of intermediate level—theories that take information processes and not neurological processes as their primitives—are absolutely essential to the understanding of human thinking. Just as biochemistry is not "simply" physics but must be pursued independently, thinking, in this view, is not "simply" neurophysiology but calls for levels of theory that can be linked to neurophysiology only through a sequence of connecting theories, most of which have not yet been fashioned.

Apart from this question of the relation between information processing and direct neurological explanation of thinking, neurophysiology plays a second role in cognitive science—particularly in providing hypotheses about fruitful architectures for machine intelligence (and presumably also human intelligence). Neurophysiology has, in particular, provided a strong stimulus for the connectionist architectures (see chapter 3) that we discuss.

Other Contributing Fields
The fields discussed so far all have members who are affiliated to some degree with cognitive science (for example, they belong to the Cognitive Science Society). The same is true of anthropology, possibly because of the strong representation of linguistics within anthropology. Cognitive social psychology has been more remote, with its own research agenda

focused on interpersonal perception, attribution, and self-perception (but see Abelson 1953 and chapter 20).

We have seen that economics and statistical decision theory, although their central preoccupation is with rational (intelligent?) choice, have not participated notably in the developments within cognitive science (nor are they represented in this book). Yet it would appear that their theories are quite relevant to the characterization of abstract intelligence and vice versa. One of us has argued elsewhere that the reluctance of economists and statisticians to deal systematically with the computational limits on human and machine intelligence largely accounts for their indifference to cognitive science (Simon 1977).

1.3   The Architecture of Intelligent Systems

The fundamental design specifications of an information-processing system are called its *architecture*. The components of the architecture represent the underlying physical structures but only abstractly. For example, an architecture for modeling the human brain might contain neurons as components, but the neurons might be characterized quite grossly as binary on-off elements with certain switching speeds. Another architecture might characterize the brain even more aggregately with units such as long-term memory, short-term memory, sensory organs, and so on. The amount of detail incorporated in an architecture depends on what questions it seeks to answer, as well as how the system under study is actually structured.

Levels of Abstraction
The notion that architectures may be specified at different levels is best seen in digital computers. We speak of a computer as having von Neumann architecture when it has an addressable memory capable of storing both program and data, input and output devices, and symbol-processing capabilities that operate serially, including operators for comparing symbol structures and branching. The specification does not say anything at all about the physical devices realizing this scheme, and as we know from the past four decades of computing, they may be of the most varied and disparate kinds.

At the next level of abstraction the architecture of a system may be described by defining a specific language. For example, the Lisp programming language defines an architecture for a list-processing system. Memory is organized into associative structures, lists, and property lists, and the basic operators of the language allow one to create and destroy lists, find an item on a list or property list, insert an item in a list, and so on. The elements on lists are symbols, themselves capable of indexing (denoting) other symbols or list structures of symbols.

In the contemporary practice of cognitive science, models of the human nervous system are usually defined at one of two different levels, called *connectionist* (see chapter 3) and *symbolic* (see chapter 4), respectively. The elements of connectionist systems may be conceptualized as highly simplified and schematized neurons, interconnected in a network. (Not all practitioners of connectionism regard their elements as schematic neurons. Some would describe them more neutrally as representing "features.") In connectionist systems, the operators modify the network and, in particular, modify the strengths of the connections between elements.

The elements of symbolic systems may be conceptualized as symbols held in one or more memories. The symbols are usually assumed to be stored in associative structures similar to those implemented by list-processing languages. In some architectures (for example, in Quillian's (1966) proposal for semantic memory or in the Act* system (Anderson 1983)), memories may be organized into networks as in connectionist architectures; but the elements in these networks are interpreted as symbols rather than as neurons or perceptual features. The symbolic network architecture describes the system at a higher, more abstract level than does the connectionist architecture.

If we adopt a "levels" hypothesis about the architecture of the human cognitive system, then we might postulate a basic neural level, a highly parallel connectionist level above the neural level, and a symbolic level, constrained in its processing by the bottleneck of attention (see chapter 17), above the connectionist level. Some work, but not very much, has been done to explain how symbol structures could emerge at the top level from the equilibrating activities of elements at the connectionist level.

In enumerating levels, we must keep in mind also the task environment to which a system's intelligence is to be applied. Thus in symbolic architectures that make use of heuristic search we have the level of the problem space in which the search is carried out but, above it, the level of the task domain that poses the problem to be solved. The problem representation that the system constructs and uses (its problem space) may be very different from the actual external problem situation (called by Newell (1980) the "knowledge level") from which the problem space is derived.

In evaluating the plausibility of different architectures as reasonable models of the human nervous system, it is good to keep in mind some of the parameters a system must fit if it is to claim that it describes human cognition. It takes about one millisecond for a signal to cross the synapse between two neurons, and longer, of course, for a sequence of such transmissions. A simple act of recognition takes roughly a second—about one thousand milliseconds. Hence all of the activities between simple neural events and overt behaviors emanating from a few elementary information processes must be squeezed into a time range of only three orders of magnitude. Stated otherwise, an act of recognition cannot require more than a thousand successive synaptic crossings.

When our concern is with modeling the human brain, these parameters put important constraints on the architecture of a serial system. But they also put severe constraints on the parallel systems that have been proposed, because the equilibration processes used by the connectionist systems require numerous rounds of successive approximation, or "settling down." It is not evident one way or the other whether their time requirements are greater or less than those of a serial recognition system like EPAM (Elementary Perceiver and Memorizer), a computer simulation that learns to recognize stimuli by using a discrimination net that performs a sequence of tests to sort them (Feigenbaum and Simon 1986).

The "Standard" Model

For at least the two decades from about 1960 to 1980, there existed a broad (and approximate) consensus among psychologists taking the information-processing point of view about the general architecture of the human cognitive system. There were many contributions to this "standard" model of cognition, beginning with George Miller's (1956) characterization of short-term memory with its seven chunks and Broadbent's (1958) description of the memory system and its connections with sensory inputs. There is no "official" version of the standard model, but one description of it that lies pretty well within the area of agreement can be found in chapter 14 of Newell and Simon 1972.

In the standard model there are two principal memories: a short-term memory and a long-term memory. The short-term memory is characterized by rapid access (a few hundred milliseconds) and very limited capacity (alternatively, very short retention time). The capacity has been measured as about seven *chunks*, where a chunk is anything that has become familiarized by previous learning. Thus for the readers of this book English words are chunks. In cognitive network architectures the short-term memory is simply the portion of long-term memory that is currently activated; the two memories are not separate structures.

The long-term memory is characterized by an associative organization and a virtually unlimited capacity. The time to store a new chunk is of the order of magnitude of eight to ten seconds, most of that time being used to store the information that "indexes" the chunk, permitting it to be recognized in a stimulus and accessed. The time to retrieve a chunk is of the order of two seconds for a single item and a few hundred milliseconds for succeeding items.

In some versions of the standard model, long-term memory is assumed to contain several specialized components. For example, one component may contain declarative information, another procedural information (operators). The discrimination net or "index" to the memory may be viewed as a third component. In some versions of the model, also, the elements in long-term memory can be primed by stimulation, which facilitates associative access to these elements and to elements linked with them associatively (Anderson 1983).

In the standard model the sensory organs are not connected directly with the main memories, but are buffered by small modality-specific memories. In the case of the eyes the buffer is the so-called iconic memory, revealed by Sperling's classic experiment. In the case of the ears the buffer is the "echo box," which holds auditory images for a matter of seconds. The buffers play only a limited role in most psychological phenomena and are often omitted from descriptions of the system.

In reading most of the chapters of this book that are concerned with human intelligence (except for those dealing with vision and motor control and those that proceed from a connectionist viewpoint), the reader will not be badly misled by taking the standard model as a first approximation to the architecture. Of course authors of individual chapters will have their own views as to how that model must be modifed and adapted to fit the facts.

Schemas and Productions

As we have just seen, information can be held in memories in either declarative or procedural form or both. Declarative memories may be organized in schemas, each containing information (perhaps stored in list structures and property lists) about some class of structures or about particular structures. Schemas can form parts of other schemas and, conversely, schemas can contain schemas. They may be propositionlike, picturelike, or both. They may also be accessed through some kind of discrimination net (EPAM net, "index") so that lengthy searches through memory are not required to find relevant information.

Information in procedural form can operate actively on memory. In many architectures the operators are represented as *productions*. A production, often written C → A, consists of two parts: the *conditions* and the *actions*. The conditions are tests that are applied to stored structures (say, to symbols held in a particular memory). Whenever all the tests in a production are satisfied, the actions of that production are executed. These actions may alter or destroy symbol structures or create new ones.

A *control structure* resolves conflicts between productions when the conditions of more than one are satisfied simultaneously. Of course, in a parallel system all the productions whose conditions are satisfied can execute simultaneously. Productions, like schemas, can be indexed by means of a network, similar to an EPAM net, for discriminating among different sets of conditions.

Psychological theories of the associationist and behaviorist schools postulate connections (S-R associations) between stimuli and responses.

The Würzburg school of Ach and his followers made use of more elaborate "directed associations" between the stimulus and task (Aufgabe), on the one hand, and the response, on the other (S + A → R). Productions bear a certain resemblance to both of these constructs, relating a (sometimes complex) set of conditions, possibly including a goal, to one or more actions that occur whenever these conditions are satisfied. Productions may therefore be regarded as descendants of these classical ideas, descendants that explicate and operationalize them and implement them computationally.

Control Structures
In addition to specifying the organization of memory and the elementary processes that operate on memory, an architecture generally specifies a *control structure*, which determines the conditions under which particular operators will fire. In traditional programming languages control proceeds from one instruction to the next, except where the execution of a conditional branching operation changes the order.

When a language provides for closed subroutines, as many modern programming languages do, control resides, at any given moment, with a particular routine until it relinquishes it, either by calling on one of its subroutines or by completing execution and returning control to the routine that called it. This arrangement leads to problems of control that seem not to match very well the phenomena observed in human cognition. There is no way in which higher-level routines, with a broader view of the situation than their subroutines, can force the latter to relinquish control before they finish executing. On the other hand it is sometimes difficult to transmit from lower-level subroutines to top-level routines information that would enable the latter to exercise control appropriately.

Modern architectures for cognitive simulation seek to avoid these difficulties in various ways. The two classes of control structure that provide the main alternatives to subroutine hierarchies use either production systems or networks with links of variable strength.

In early production systems productions were sometimes ordered, and conflicts (when conditions of two or more productions were simultaneously satisfied) were resolved by executing the production that came first in the order. By itself this scheme was not often satisfactory. It was usually supplemented by a rule of refractoriness, so that a production, once executed, would not execute repeatedly with the same arguments. Another rule sometimes used gave preference to matching the memory elements that were created most recently. Another gave preference to productions with strong conditions over those with weaker conditions.

To secure a still greater measure of task-relevant control, *goal symbols* were sometimes used in production systems. A goal symbol is a symbol that can be created by the action of one or more productions and whose presence in memory constitutes one of the conditions for the execution of other productions. When a goal symbol is placed in memory, the attention of the system is focused on those productions that include this goal among their conditions. It is only a short distance back from goals to traditional subroutine hierarchies; goals must be used with restraint if the "spirit" of decentralized control in production system architecture is to be retained.

In the Soar system (chapter 4) productions execute in parallel. If this creates conflict—an "impasse"—then an explicit goal is created to resolve the impasse by problem solving within an appropriate problem space.

In symbolic networks focus may be provided by specifying that conditions of productions can be matched only at nodes that are "active," and thereby serve as a momentary working memory. The procedures that cause the spreading and extinction of activation then become the main means of control.

In connectionist networks (chapter 3) the strengths of links and the levels of activity of nodes continue to change simultaneously until they match patterns that define the system goals and thereby reach equilibrium.

These brief remarks provide some picture of the problem of control of cognitive activity and of the great variety of mechanisms that have been and are being examined to accomplish control and the focusing of activity. Much more detail on a number of specific architectures is provided in the chapters that follow, especially chapter 3 and 4 on connectionist architectures and Soar, respectively.

Network Models
Only a bit more needs to be said about network models, both connectionist and symbolic. But a bit of history may cast some perspective on them. The modern history of architectures for modeling cognition can conveniently begin with Donald Hebb's (1949) proposal of a "conceptual nervous system" in the form of a complex neural network. Higher mental processes were carried out in this network through the formation of cell assemblies—organized clusters of highly interconnected neurons. Some efforts (see, for example, Rochester et al. 1956) were made to build computer models of a Hebbian system but without notable success in showing that such a network could perform complex organized activities.

The network idea had and continues to have a number of attractions. First, however schematic the "neurons" or other elements of the network, it appears to hold some promise for building an eventual bridge to the physiology of real neurons. Most neurophysiologists, looking at existing network models, conclude that the bridge is still a long way off.

A second attraction of the network model is that it offers some mechanisms for learning; learning can take the form of appropriate changes in the activations of elements and the strengths of links. It is not surprising, therefore, that many of the tasks to which network models have been applied are concept-learning tasks of one kind or another.

A third attraction of the network model is that it provides a direct means for modeling parallel processes such as those that must go on in the eye and ear and those parts of the brain closely associated with these senses. The Perceptron of Frank Rosenblatt was an early class of connectionist devices aimed at modeling perceptual processes. Contemporary connectionist systems, although they incorporate a number of important new ideas and mechanisms, may be regarded as direct descendants of the Perceptron (influenced heavily on the psychological side by Hebb's ideas).

Symbolic networks can claim some of the same ancestry, but their development was also shaped by other influences. List-processing techniques lend themselves, in the most direct way, to storing information in associative, semantic memories—that capability was, in fact, one major motivation for their invention, and they have been used in this way from their beginnings in the 1950s.

Ross Quillian, in a Carnegie Mellon University doctoral thesis (1966), was perhaps the first to explore some of the psychological implications of this kind of memory model. His work initiated an active period of development of semantic memories of this kind, the introduction of the spreading activation mechanism (Anderson 1983), and the application of these memories to the study of psychological phenomena of memory, language, and learning.

Symbolic Models
Again, because much has already been said about symbol systems, we need only provide a few additional comments on points not covered previously. Symbols are patterns with the special property that they designate or "point to" structures outside themselves. The structures designated by symbols may be other symbol structures in memory, but they may also be productions that can be used to recognize patterns in external stimuli (the objects denoted by the corresponding symbols). When symbols are organized into structures, arbitrary symbols (labels) assigned to these structures serve to designate or "name" them.

In most of the psychological models construed as symbol systems, the elementary information processes have a "grain size" that corresponds to psychological processes requiring hundreds or a few thousands of milliseconds for their operation. In a few models (for example, EPAM; Feigenbaum and Simon, 1986) some of the basic processes are at the ten-millisecond level or thereabouts. Symbolic network models incorporate a substantial amount of parallel processing, but most other symbolic models are assumed to operate serially, with an architecture not too different from the classical von Neumann architecture.

In a serial system it is an easy matter to model the limits of short-term memory and the effects of those limits on cognitive activity. On the other hand it is not as easy to model the massive parallel activity that goes on in the sensory organs and perhaps elsewhere in the nervous system. A good deal of the discussion of the relative merits of symbolic and connectionist architectures centers on the question of the respective roles of serial and parallel processes in human cognition.

1.4 Two Approaches: Reasoning and Search

In the previous section we discussed a variety of views in cognitive science on the architecture of intelligent systems. Cutting across this range of viewpoints lies another fissure that divides cognitive science and scientists into two groups that communicate with each other somewhat less than might be desirable. On the one side we have an approach that starts with language and logic and that views thinking as a process of inference or reasoning, usually using a languagelike representation. On the other side we have an approach that views thinking (especially problem solving and concept attainment) as a process of heuristic search for problem solutions, generally using representations that model, in some sense, the problem situation.

It is not surprising that such a division should exist in a domain that has been assembled from the varied disciplines named in section 1.2 or that the line of division should correspond at least roughly to the disciplinary boundaries. For the most part those who have come to cognitive science from philosophy, linguistics and psycholinguistics, and the more formal specialties within computer science find language and logic the congenial starting points for conceptualizing intelligence, whereas those who have come from artificial intelligence and most specialties within psychology are likely to use the heuristic-search paradigm as their point of departure.

For the moment we leave aside the third camp, the connectionists, who have ties with neurophysiology and whose orientation, as we have seen, is computational but whose representations are not symbolic.

The fissure between the logic/language and heuristic search viewpoints is somewhat visible in the chapter organization of this book; the chapters on semantics and logic, language acquisition, parsing, reading, and discourse mainly represent the language-and-reasoning approach, whereas the chapters on categories and induction and problem solving largely represent the heuristic-search approach. The chapter on mental models lies somewhere in between; its very title associates it with heuristic search, but it clearly has its origins in the language-and-logic–oriented literature and makes almost no reference to work using models that came out of the other tradition in cognitive psychology and artificial intelligence.

In considering how these two viewpoints are likely to relate to each other in the future, several issues must be examined. The first is whether the human language faculty is a highly specialized and separate component of the human mind, in its semantic as well as its phonetic and syntactic aspects, operating with processes and on principles different from those implicated in nonlinguistic thinking.

To the extent that language uses self-contained faculties that are independent of other parts of cognition, each paradigm might go its own way. To the extent that all modes of thinking, whether they involve language, share a common semantic representation and processes, there is a pressing need to find common ground where the two paradigms can meet.

A second issue, the central one, is to what extent "thinking" is to be identified with "reasoning," and "reasoning" with "logical inference." Is logical reasoning, in this sense, the correct metaphor for thinking, or is thinking better regarded as search? Others might prefer to state the question differently: should the "operators" that are applied in search to transform one situation into another be regarded as "inference rules"? And what are the consequences of so regarding them? To some extent the competition between the Lisp and Prolog programming languages is a competition between viewing thinking as search and viewing it as reasoning.

Here two questions are involved. First, does either one of these two paradigms give a uniquely correct picture of human thinking, or does thinking, on different occasions or in different aspects, involve both modes and perhaps others? Second, if there is both thinking in language and thinking without language (in images, say), how are these two kinds of thinking connected?

A third issue, closely linked to the second one, concerns the representation of the knowledge on which thinking operates. Is knowledge in intelligent systems to be represented in the form of propositions or networks of propositions, on the one hand, or in the form of models, imagelike or otherwise, of the problem situations, on the other? In particular, in human thinking what are the forms of mental representation? Let us consider each of these three issues.

Is Language Unique?
The hypothesis that language is a unique human faculty and the further hypothesis that the capacity to use language is innate rather than learned have been espoused strongly by Noam Chomsky (1965). At the outset several points can be accepted as beyond debate. First, children obviously have to *learn* their native languages; whatever innate language capability they have is a capacity for acquiring language and using it once acquired. And it appears that children learn any one of the several thousand native languages that exist about as easily as they learn any other. What are innate, if anything, are language universals and not the grammars of particular languages.

Second, parts of the human brain specialize in storing and processing the phonetic, syntactic, and lexical components of language, and these parts do not seem to be well represented in nonhuman mammals, even in the other primates. It is not a question of whether apes can or cannot acquire a modicum of language-using skill. Even if this has been demonstrated (it is still controversial), there is an enormous quantitative and qualitative difference between human language and the language that can be acquired by any other species. (Machine language raises other issues.)

Given these two areas of agreement, what is still in contention is whether the innate language capacity is a wholly distinct faculty or simply a gradual commitment, through learning, of part of the general human cognitive capacity to knowledge of language and language processing. The correct answer, of course, might fall somewhere between these two extremes.

On the sensory side a human being must acquire the ability to discriminate among phonemes in his or her native language, thereby to recognize lexical items, and to parse the syntax of incoming acoustical signals, so as to extract their meanings. This same human being must also have or acquire the ability to discriminate among the features of visually presented stimuli, to recognize familiar kinds of objects, and to detect and recognize the relations among objects in a visual scene. It seems parsimonious, even apart from the empirical evidence of brain localization, to postulate that there are specialized mechanisms for processing linguistic messages, on the one hand, and visual stimuli, on the other.

Accepting this specialization, the principal remaining question is how the semantic components of these two systems are related. What is the relation between the meaning that is extracted from the sentence *There is a cat in this room* and the meaning that is extracted from seeing a cat in the room? The relation must be quite intimate because a person who sees the cat will immediately (that is, in a few hundred milliseconds—see Chase and Clark 1972) conclude that the sentence is true, and a person who hears the sentence may form some expectation of seeing a cat (unless the room is supplied with the kinds of crannies in which cats love to hide).

Here parsimony appears to favor communality. That is to say, if the mental representation of the meaning of the sentence were identical, or essentially so, with the mental representation of the visual stimulus, then it would be easy to use visual sensation to test the truth of the sentence or to use the sentence to create the expectation. If there is no such common semantic representation, then there must exist a process for translating semantic knowledge acquired through the visual route into semantic knowledge acquired from language, and vice versa. A regard for Occam's razor makes that alternative seem unattractive. We prefer the hypothesis that there is only one meaning—one unified system of semantics shared by all subsystems that deal with meanings.

Another line of evidence that there is a single semantic memory comes from experiments that show that subjects store the meanings of sentences presented to them rather than storing the literal verbal strings. Thus subjects frequently report having seen a particular sentence when they have only seen a synonymous one or sentences from which the one in question could be inferred (Bransford and Franks 1971). In other experiments (Rosenberg and Simon 1977) subjects have been unable to remember whether they saw a particular sentence or a simple drawing expressing the same meaning, and bilingual subjects are frequently unable to remember whether a sentence they saw was in French or English.

That a common semantics is feasible has already been demonstrated by a number of artificial intelligence systems. Early examples include the GRANIS system of L. Stephen Coles (1972) and the ZBIE system of Laurent Siklóssy (1972), both built in the 1960s (Simon and Siklóssy 1972 and chapters 5 and 6). In Coles's system the computer is given an ambiguous sentence together with a picture of a situation to which the sentence is supposed to refer. If the sentence is found to be syntactically ambiguous, the semantic information in the picture is used to choose among the alternative parses.

Siklóssy's system proceeds in the reverse order. It starts with a structured description of a situation in what amounts to a picture language and a verbal description of the pictured situation in a natural language. As a series of such pairs is presented to it, it slowly learns to form the natural-language sentence appropriate to the situation and is then able to construct such sentences when new pictures are presented without language.

A decade later Hayes and Simon (1974) constructed the UNDERSTAND system, and Novak constructed a system called ISAAC, both of which also illustrate how semantic capabilities can be linked to natural-language inputs. The UNDERSTAND program accepts natural-language descriptions of simple, puzzlelike problems and constructs from them models of the problem situations and operators for making legal moves. ISAAC, given physics problems described in natural language, constructs a problem representation that allows an affiliated program to draw a picture of the problem situation on the terminal screen.

Three of these four programs (the exception is GRANIS) use essentially identical semantic representations: list structures in the form of networks built up of lists and description lists (property lists). These list structures may be interpreted as "pictures" because they represent objects as nodes (with descriptions of features) and link them with proximate objects. They may also be interpreted as propositions because each component can be viewed as an assertion that either a particular object has a certain property or a certain relation holds between two objects. Essentially (although quantifiers are not represented in these particular programs) they correspond to representations in the first-order predicate calculus.

The conclusion we draw from psychological experiments in which subjects compare the meanings of sentences with pictures and from artificial intelligence programs that handle both language and "diagrammatic" representations is that there is a common semantic system that contains meanings, whatever the source of information from which they are derived. Language does not have a separate and unique semantics.

Inference Rules versus Change Operators
We come now to the question of whether thinking is best regarded as reasoning or search or some combination of these. The reasoning viewpoint is closely associated with the notion that meanings are represented as propositions, whereas the search viewpoint is associated with the notion that meanings are stored as mental models of situations. It has been debated (Pylyshyn 1973, Larkin and Simon 1987) whether there is really any operational distinction between these two viewpoints—in particular whether it is possible to determine empirically whether mental semantics are propositional or diagrammatic.

The answer is surely affirmative. Even if two representations are informationally equivalent (contain exactly the same information), they may be quite different from a computational standpoint. Some information that is explicit in one representation may be implicit in the other and hence is retrievable only with the help of more or less extensive computation. Likewise information that is implicit in both representations may be much more cheaply retrievable in one than in the other. For example, it may be far easier to determine that two lines intersect by referring to a diagram than by trying to prove the existence of the intersection from the given facts, stated propositionally, together with the axioms of geometry (Larkin and Simon 1987).

When human thinking is viewed as propositional, and when the analogy of logic is used to characterize human reasoning, the resulting models of thinking usually acquire certain traits borrowed from the domain of logic. Because logic is currently concerned with rigor and verification, it generally employs only a small number of simple rules or inference—the rule of modus ponens and of replacement of variables in the system of Whitehead and Russell, for example. All other "givens" are represented by axioms. When only a small set of inference rules is admitted, it is easy to check the validity of each step of a derivation, but usually at the price of making the derivations very long. Hence the process of verification is facilitated, but the process of discovering derivations is made much more difficult than if the system is generously endowed with inference rules.

The reliance in logic on a small number of "reliable" inference rules is not an inexorable requirement, but is a habit or custom carried down from a traditional orientation toward verification rather than discovery. Any number of inference rules incorporating any number of assumptions, mathematical and empirical, can be introduced into a logic. When this is done freely, however, so that much of the knowledge of the task domain is expressed as inference rules rather than declarative assertions, the resulting system no longer looks to us like a logic but instead like a set of operators for carrying out heuristic search on a model. "Modeling" is neither more nor less logical than "reasoning." In modeling we proceduralize much of the knowledge that is represented declaratively in reasoning. Moreover in modeling we may (but need not) represent information in propositional form.

The liberal use of inference rules, especially rules incorporating semantic knowledge, blurs the distinction between the language/logic paradigm of thinking and the heuristic-search paradigm. Whatever difference remains between the paradigms must arise from the particular knowledge representations they employ. That brings us to the third issue: propositionlike versus imagelike representations.

Propositions versus Images
Almost all of us believe that we can form mental pictures of situations described to us or retain mental pictures of scenes we have actually seen. We are also all aware of the homunculus fallacy: a mental picture cannot be a photograph that is scanned by a tiny person in the brain. But there is also a homunculus fallacy associated with the idea of storing propositions in the brain—we must also exclude a homunculus who would extract the meanings from the propositions by *reading* them.

Both homonculus fallacies are avoidable in exactly the same way. A mental picture or a set of stored propositions are simply symbol structures of some kind. The information-processing system contains a variety of symbol-manipulating processes for extracting information from structures of these kinds. Thus a processor of propositions may be able to extract the predicate from a simple proposition and then access in memory a symbol structure that contains information about the meaning of that predicate. Similarly a processor of diagrams may be able to extract a feature (an intersection of lines, say) from a symbolic representation of a geometric form and then access in memory a symbol structure that contains information about that kind of feature.

There are many ways in which propositions can be stored in memory. They can be stored as strings similar to natural-language sentences. More commonly nowadays they are stored in the notation of the predicate calculus or as components of node-link networks. Each mode of storage calls for a corresponding set of processes to examine symbol structures and extract information from them.

Similarly there are many ways in which pictorial or diagrammatic images can be stored in memory. They can be stored as rectangular arrays (rasters) of points (pixels). They can also be stored as node-link structures in which spatial information is incorporated in the structure of the network, linking adjacent components so that the spatial relations can be detected. Again each of these modes of storage calls for a corresponding set of processes to extract information from it.

To say that "mental propositions" and "mental pictures" can be handled in basically the same ways is not to say that there is no significant difference between representations (Larkin and Simon 1987). On the contrary our previous discussion of the computational equivalence or inequivalence of representations tells us that our ability to extract information efficiently (or at all) from a representation depends very much on what processes are available for manipulating the representation.

Hence by studying what kinds of inferences people make easily and what kinds they make only with difficulty or not at all, we can draw conclusions about the kinds of representations and operators they are using. Kosslyn (1980), in particular, has used this strategy to argue that people use mental images extensively and has suggested the forms in which these mental images may be stored—arguing that both node-link structures and rasters are involved. His arguments seem cogent to us.

Summary: Reasoning and Search

Both the reasoning and search viewpoints on intelligence are well represented in this book. To summarize our discussion here, we need to make only three points. First, although there are clearly some mental functions (and a physiological base for them) that are specialized for handling language, the weight of evidence suggests that at the semantic level there is a single common set of mechanisms used for all forms of thinking, and this is essential for translation between propositional and imagelike inputs.

Second, the boundary between logical reasoning and heuristic search of models is a matter of degree rather than kind. Most human reasoning uses a liberal store of inference operators with substantial semantic content, and it hence more resembles searching a model than carrying out logical deductions.

Third, the knowledge on which inference rules operate may be stored in memory in a variety of ways, including propositional structures but also including structures that are better viewed as mental images. Perhaps there are others as well.

1.5 Methods of Cognitive Research

Because good science consists of asking interesting questions that give hope of being answered, good methodology is essential to good science. Not only do methods influence the types of questions we ask, they also determine what questions we can aspire to answer. Cognitive science has at its disposal a remarkably wide and varied pool of methods,

Foundations of Cognitive Science

ranging from computer simulation to naturalistic observation, from recording the electrical impulses of the brain (chapter 8) to performing linguistic analyses (chapters 5, 7), from using nonmonotonic logics to collecting reaction times (chapter 7) or verbal protocols.

Many techniques are discussed throughout the book; we have chosen to concentrate here on protocol analysis and computer simulation. In addition we discuss content analysis and meta-analysis as potentially useful methods not yet widely used in cognitive science. Content analysis serves as a generalization of protocol analysis, whereas meta-analysis provides insight into the methodology of computer simulation.

We also have something to say at the end of this section about contributions of the methods of philosophy and logic to cognitive science. Because other authors in this book have addressed most of the other standard methods of cognitive science, we do not discuss those here. In particular Bower and Clapper examine experimental methods in psychology (chapter 7), and Sejnowski and Churchland review the methods of the brain sciences (chapter 5).

Protocol Analysis

Protocol analysis, the use of verbal reports as data, has become an increasingly important (but often misunderstood) technique for studying human intelligence. Its importance stems from the fact that it is one of the few methods in cognitive science that gathers data with sufficient temporal density to test models that account for behavior nearly second by second (but not millisecond by millisecond).

Although verbal reports date back to the introspectionists, the use of such reports as *data* should not be misconstrued as introspection. Introspection took subjects' verbalizations at face value as constituting a valid theory of their own thought processes. Protocol analysis today, however, treats verbal reports as a source of data to be accounted for with an experimenter-generated theory—perhaps in the form of a computer simulation.

There are many ways of getting subjects to generate verbal reports, including questioning them, asking them to report on their mental processes, and asking them to talk or think aloud. Verbal reports of the talk- or think-aloud variety tend to be the least intrusive and to provide the most accurate records of the nature and sequence of subjects' mental processes. We focus our discussion on them.

Concurrent protocols can be obtained by asking subjects to think aloud *while* performing some task such as problem solving. Typically the verbalizations are recorded on tape, transcribed, coded from the transcript, and then subjected to a theory-based analysis.

Sometimes subjects are asked to report everything they can recall about the problem-solving episode immediately *after* solving the problem. Such *retrospective* protocols can be useful for filling the gaps in concurrent protocols and for providing the subject's overall conception of the task. They must be interpreted cautiously, however, because subjects are quite capable of reconstructing events that did not actually occur (Nisbett and Wilson 1977).

Two generalizations may be made about retrospective protocols. First, the longer a subject delays providing a report after completing a task, the more susceptible that report will be to reconstruction and distortion. Second, retrospective protocols that might constitute questionable independent evidence can nonetheless be supported and confirmed with other data such as reaction-time measures or error analysis.

Typical Procedures   In the paragraphs that follow, we discuss procedures typically used to study human information processes by protocol analysis (Ericsson and Simon 1984). Depending on how the instructions are worded, the behavior of subjects may range from simple vocalization of verbally encoded thoughts as they occur to elaborate introspections of the sort "I think I am using a perceptual process now . . ." The instructions typically discourage the latter type of reporting and encourage the former. The exact wording of the instructions depends on the nature of the task and the degree of completeness desired, but the simple instruction to talk aloud while performing the task captures the essence.

After the instructions have been given, subjects are usually allowed to practice before actually performing the task of interest. If practice effects are a concern, a different task is used as a warm-up. One task that has been used successfully is to ask subjects to take an imaginary walk through a familiar house or building, describing what they see. Another is to have them multiply a three-digit number by a two-digit number mentally while talking aloud.

If subjects fall silent (say, for 5 seconds to 1 minute, depending on the task), the experimenter may remind them to keep talking. A nondirective prompt (for example, "Keep talking") is less likely to interrupt the normal sequence of processing than a more directive prompt (for example, "What are you thinking about?").

After transcription the protocol can be segmented and encoded. Segmentation involves dividing a protocol into units that can be encoded more or less independently. Criteria for segmentation depend on the type of encoding and analysis. Typical cues for segmentation include completion of sentences or clauses, pauses, or completion of ideas.

Encoding is the process of translating the content of segments into a formal language. Determining what to encode depends largely on the nature of the task and the hypotheses of interest. Choosing the level of analysis is the first step. To test a simulation of the subject's behavior, the protocol must be coded in sufficient detail to provide data at the level of the model. For example, a simulation that accounts for individual differences between subjects requires a more detailed encoding than does a simulation that captures only behaviors common to all subjects.

Not all analyses are carried out at a fine level of detail, because one may be more interested in the overall sequence of goals and subgoals than in just how they are achieved. When aggregating the data from many subjects who have all solved a particular problem, one can simulate the general solution path first and then build more detailed variants of this general simulation to describe individual differences.

Verbal protocols generally provide explicit information about the knowledge and information heeded in solving a problem rather than about the processes used. Consequently it is usually necessary to infer the processes from the verbal reports of information heeded instead of attempting to code processes directly.

The coding formalisms can be constructed from the actual vocabulary used by subjects, economizing by defining equivalences between words used nearly synonymously. The particular words used provide powerful clues both about subjects' representations of the task and about their processing. For example, the tenses of verbs can help distinguish the planning of future actions from the retrieval of past information (for instance, the difference between *I will have* and *I had*). Function words (for example, *if, perhaps,* and *so*) can often distinguish exploring a hypothesis from drawing a conclusion, and so on.

The proper use of context in coding segments presents some perplexing problems. Inasmuch as segments sometimes refer to other segments, potentially important information may be lost if context is not taken into account. On the other hand the number of independent observations of behavior represented by an encoded protocol decreases whenever segments are not coded independently of each other. Potential loss of information must be balanced against potential gain in reliability when deciding just how much context to use in encoding.

Finally, theoretical constraints often serve to focus attention on the relevant aspects of the protocol. For example, viewing problem solving as search through a problem space suggests coding instances of goal setting, and operator application. Similarly if behavior is coded using the functional notation $R(x, y, \ldots)$, where R specifies a relation between two or more arguments, attention is thereby focused on the relations and their arguments.

Several strategies are used for determining the coding categories. First, they are often derived from a task analysis. An important advantage of this method is that the coding categories are not developed from the protocol itself, hence the categories are not ad hoc and do not subtract degrees of freedom from the data.

When it is not possible to develop coding categories solely from a task analysis, they are typically derived from the data that are to be coded (or some part of them). Because degrees of freedom are lost in this way, the goodness of fit of the theory should be judged by the number of residual degrees of freedom in the data (see Simon 1977 and Ericsson and Simon 1984 for a more complete argument). Making use of *simple* coding categories and procedures, it is quite possible to produce models that are parsimonious in relation to the amount of data explained and hence are quite credible.

Another observation concerns the derivation of categories from the protocols themselves. Using categories that are similar to the actual verbalizations both avoids loss of information and promotes reliability in coding. Reliability in protocol analysis ensures that what otherwise might be criticized as idiosyncratic interpretation can be treated as "hard" data. Reliability is secured by using a simple and precise coding scheme.

Although intercoder reliability in protocols is typically quite high (0.8 or 0.9 is not uncommon), it can probably be increased by using automated and semiautomated coding systems. Several efforts have been made in this direction with some success. PAS I and PAS II (Waterman and Newell 1971, 1973) were designed as completely automatic programs for encoding segmented protocols and producing problem-behavior graphs as output. These programs, although promising, require further development if they are to rival the performance of expert human coders.

SAPA (Bhaskar and Simon 1977) and PAW (Fisher 1988) represent a different approach to computer-aided encoding of protocols. Both of these programs interact with the human user, serving as powerful tools for protocol analysis rather than as fully automated systems. Fisher's system, for example, allows the user to devise the encoding scheme either in advance, from a task analysis, or while coding. The coding categories can be organized in schemas of a quite general kind, so that the system puts relatively few constraints on the encoding decisions. Procedures for analyzing the encoded data qualitatively and quantitatively are incorporated in the system.

The Theory of Thinking Aloud The procedures described here have been derived largely from experience. However, most of them can be induced from an information-processing theory of the processes used in thinking aloud (Ericsson and Simon 1984).

The theory starts with the assumption that the processes that generate verbal reports are a subset of the processes that generate all observable behavior and thus are amenable to an information-processing analysis. It also assumes the existence of a long-term memory (LTM) and a short-term memory (STM). STM is limited, information enters it serially, and it takes time to attend to stimuli. The additional assumption that problem solving occurs in a problem space can be included, but is not necessary for most purposes.

The key feature of this theory of verbal reports is that subjects can only report the contents of short-term memory. There are three kinds of verbal reports. The first kind, *direct verbalization,* is the simple vocalization of information that is already encoded verbally in STM. Because

Foundations of Cognitive Science

the subject is vocalizing what is already in memory, such vocalization has no significant effect on the time to perform a task or on the sequence of processing. Subjects who talk to themselves naturally while solving problems are exhibiting direct verbalization. Similarly subjects who are instructed simply to "talk aloud naturally"—while avoiding introspection, reporting on their thoughts, or striving for completeness—most likely would be engaging in direct verbalization.

The second kind of verbalization, *recording the contents of STM*, includes verbal reports describing the contents of STM when these are not encoded verbally. Thus subjects instructed to think aloud while performing a task involving imagery may have to recode some of what is in memory before being able to give a verbal report. The theory states that the recoding processes will time-share with the processes involved in performing the task. In this case we would expect verbalization to slow down task performance, but not necessarily to change the sequence of processing. Because of the time-sharing assumption the theory predicts that verbalization will cease under high processing loads that do not naturally produce verbally encoded information.

Experience with gathering protocols tends to validate this prediction. For example, in the protocols of subjects trying to find a way to cover a "mutilated" checkerboard with dominos, considerable pauses often correspond to what appears to be imaginal or visual processing. When subjects are prompted in these cases to "keep talking," they often report that they are imagining different coverings or looking at the board and waiting for something to occur to them (Kaplan and Simon 1988).

The third kind of verbalization, *explanation*, includes verbal reports that require processing beyond simple recoding. For example, asking subjects to explain their thoughts may result in their trying to synthesize a coherent explanation. When additional processes are invoked as a result of the verbalization instructions, we expect the execution time of the task to increase. We also expect that the sequence of processes normally used to perform the task will be disrupted. As for the explanation itself, it may or may not be an accurate report of the processes it is intended to describe. Much will depend on the task, the subject, and the nature of the attempted explanation.

Seemingly harmless instructions (for example, "What are you thinking now?") can by suggestion launch a subject into a bout of explanation. Although the explanations are often interesting in their own right, if our primary concern is to obtain a valid record of the sequence of information heeded (and processes used) in performing the task, verbalizations of the other two kinds are preferable.

A natural consequence of the assumption that verbal reports reflect the contents of STM is that subjects must be unable to report on processes that bypass STM (for example, the cues they use in direct recognition), although they can report the outcomes of such processes if these are stored in STM. Because information must be attended to in order to enter STM, and because we assume seriality, the contents of STM also provide a sequential record of the information attended to.

With this theory in hand it is a straightforward matter to derive several of our earlier assertions. The effects of instructions stem directly from triggering different kinds of verbalization by slight changes in wording. Warm-up trials ensure that the subject has interpreted the instructions in the desired way and is verbalizing appropriately. Knowing that verbalization reflects the contents of STM explains why protocols provide better records of information attended to than of processes used. Although many processes bypass STM, the results of these processes (that is, new knowledge) are often deposited in STM. If one *is* interested in processing, however, the theory also helps to interpret pauses and the processing deviations that can be expected with the different kinds of verbalization.

The theory helps to establish boundary conditions for the methodology. We have already noted that protocol analysis is not likely to be of use in examining processes that bypass STM such as direct recognition. We have also shown that tasks involving imagery or nonverbal processing are likely to yield incomplete protocols with intervals of silence, because STM recoding processes will have to time-share with the processes used for performing the task.

In addition to requiring recoding or the invocation of additional processes or both to form explanations, overt verbalization may affect what gets encoded in LTM or stays active in STM. The theory suggests that if only task-relevant information is verbalized, verbalization could facilitate performance on a task by improving memory. Conversely verbalization of irrelevant information might interfere with the memory of task-relevant knowledge.

In using any methodology, we must ask to what degree data can be separated from theory. What is a reaction time without a theory relating time to amount of processing? What is an image from a microscope without the optical theory that explains what a microscope does? Both the collection of reaction times and the observations made with a microscope rest on theoretical assumptions that consume degrees of freedom. When conducting a protocol analysis of a new domain, it is particularly important to minimize the degrees of freedom consumed because their loss must be balanced by the rather modest amount of data that the theory accounts for. Fortunately there are a number of ways to minimize the loss of information.

A first strategy is to keep theoretical commitments to a minimum and to be explicit about assumptions. A second strategy is to account for as much data as possible with a single set of assumptions. With regard to protocol analysis this means that the same coding procedures should be used over many segments within each protocol, and that protocols from different subjects should be coded with the same procedures. The same theory or variants of a more general theory should be used to account for data from different subjects on the same task. By keeping theories as similar as possible, one minimizes the number of degrees of freedom consumed. Converging evidence (for example, reaction-time measures, task analyses, error analyses, and the like) can lend support to the theory. None of these principles, of course, is peculiar to protocol analysis. They apply to all methodologies.

Although we have discussed protocol analysis in the context of typical psychological experiments (for example, problem solving), this method is applicable in a wide range of domains. One brief example drawn from second-language research illustrates the possibilities. Gerloff (1987) had subjects think aloud while translating a short French passage into English. Her results gave evidence for differences between good and poor translators with regard to the preferred language of analysis, the size of the units of analysis, and the characteristic patterns of movement through the text. Most interesting from a methodological perspective was her combined use of concurrent protocols with linguistic analysis in terms of morphemes, words, phrases, and so on.

Content Analysis
The strength of protocol analysis lies in providing a dense stream of data about human behavior over periods of minutes. This same principle of density of data can be used to study human behavior on even longer time scales, using *content analysis* of articles, texts, and even primary documents such as laboratory notebooks. In fact several historians of science now make systematic use of such logs in tracing the course of discoveries (Holmes 1980), and in at least one case (Kulkarni and Simon 1988) a computer simulation of a discovery process has been developed from and tested against a history extracted from laboratory logs.

In general, intellectual history would appear to be an excellent domain for increased interaction between cognitive scientists and historians. Advances in our understanding of cognitive processes should provide new ways to analyze the differences in modes of thought of different cultures and different eras. Conversely, historical texts can provide voluminous materials for testing hypotheses on how people represent and solve problems. However, cognitive scientists have yet to make full use of the methodologies that might aid in research of this type. Content analysis is one such option that has been largely overlooked.

Stone and colleagues (1966) defined content analysis as "any research technique for making inferences by systematically and objectively identifying specified characteristics within text." In practice, content analysis proceeds very much like protocol analysis but in the domain of written text.

Weber (1985) outlines some typical steps in performing a content analysis. First, one defines the size of the unit one wishes to code (for example, word, meaning of word, sentence, paragraph, and so on).

Next one defines categories for coding these units. Now one is ready to test the coding scheme on a small sample of text. After the pilot test one assesses reliability of the coding scheme and revises the procedures if necessary. After a number of loops through the revise-and-test cycle, the text is ready for final coding. The last step is to assess the reliability actually achieved.

As in our previous discussion of protocol analysis, the procedures just outlined raise a number of issues. In choosing the size of the unit to code we face the same context-versus-reliability tradeoff. As Weber (1985) stated, "Large portions of text such as paragraphs and whole texts are usually more difficult to code as a unit than smaller portions such as words and phrases, because large units typically contain more information and a greater diversity of topics." On the other hand single words or phrases often do not include enough context to disambiguate meanings. In analyzing protocols, sentences or complete ideas are often considered as segments. These criteria would seem appropriate for many content analyses as well. However, as Weber emphasized in his treatment of the subject, the resolution of such issues in each case must depend primarily on the goals of the research.

Another issue involves the scope of the categories. If the categories are too wide, one loses resolution, but if they are too narrow, the power of abstraction is lost in the proliferation of categories.

There is also the issue of the exclusivity of categories. Should a unit of information be encoded into a single category, or if it seems to fit more than one category, should it be encoded in all of them? One solution is to encode in multiple categories but to assign weights to the units based on how well they fit the categories. Other options include hierarchical coding schemes involving multiple classification in first- and second-order categories. The general disadvantages of decreased reliability and "fuzzy" categories must be set against the benefit of completeness.

Reliability is a central issue in both protocol analysis and content analysis. Weber refers to three types of reliability in content analysis: stability, reproducibility, and accuracy. Stability is essentially test-retest reliability, that is, the degree to which a given coder will code items the same way on two different occasions. A more stringent test of reliability is reproducibility or intercoder reliability: the degree to which two or more coders agree on the way items should be coded. Finally, accuracy is the degree to which human coder performance matches some established normative encoding for the items. Because most studies involve coding new information rather than coding information for which normative encodings have been established, accuracy is not often a useful test of reliability.

As with protocol analysis computer programs offer tremendous opportunities for improving reliability in content analyses, providing, in fact, a way of achieving essentially perfect coding reliability. (Validity, of course, may be more problematic.) Programs such as the General Inquirer (Stone et al. 1966) greatly facilitate the tedious process of identifying and tabulating instances of categories in text for such domains as political science, personality psychology, social psychology, clinical psychology, and anthropology. With the development of relatively cheap optical scanning procedures and artificial intelligence programs that can actually draw inferences from text (see Dyer 1983), the potential for computer-aided content analysis is enormous.

For example, to deal with the conflict between coding in unique or multiple categories the computer can efficiently code the data both ways, allowing the results to be compared. Similarly, the issue of context becomes less of a problem if one has the option of retrieving additional context and recoding at the touch of a button. Because these are issues of theoretical as well as practical import, they cannot be settled automatically. Nevertheless AI techniques have taken much of the drudgery out of content analysis, leaving a methodology with great promise for cognitive science.[1]

AI and Computer Simulation

Artificial intelligence is concerned with programming computers to perform in ways that, if observed in human beings, would be regarded as intelligent (Simon in Corsini 1987). Adding the qualification that the computer programs ought to succeed and fail in exactly those places that humans do, we can extend this definition to cover computer simulation of human behavior as well.

If we want to understand the relation between the techniques of AI and modeling of human behavior, we can compare a "pure" AI program with human behavior. Paige and Simon (1966) did exactly this in their investigation of the cognitive processes used in solving algebra word problems. Starting with STUDENT, an AI program developed by Bobrow (1968) that solves algebra word problems based on purely syntactic analysis, Paige and Simon compared STUDENT's performance with verbal protocol data collected from human subjects. They found that whereas some subjects solved the word problems in much the same way as STUDENT, others used auxiliary cues and physical representations to aid their solutions. In addition to investigating the link between protocol data and computer modeling, Paige and Simon showed that a program imported from artificial intelligence could make testable predictions about human behavior.

The overall method of computer simulation is well illustrated by a more recent computer simulation. READER (Just and Carpenter 1987) is a production system model of some of the processes involved in reading and understanding text. In particular READER simulates the time course of human reading, taking more time to process difficult words just as human readers do. READER also builds a representation of the text as it reads, with the result that it can answer text-related questions and produce summaries similar to those produced by human subjects.

The model incorporates processes that encode words, access a lexicon, perform semantic and syntactic analysis, utilize schemas, and construct a referential representation of the world described in the text. The number of cycles of production firings in READER reflects the amount of processing being done by the model. Because eye-movement studies indicate that gaze duration on a given word reflects the time needed to perceive, understand, and integrate that word, it is a relatively simple matter to compare the number of processing cycles spent by READER with the amount of time spent by human subjects on a sample passage of text. Just and Carpenter made this word-by-word comparison on a 140-word passage about flywheels. They reported that READER accounts for 67 percent of the variance in the human (mean gaze duration) data.

The strengths of the model do not rest on fit to the data alone. Rather READER's ability to simulate and coordinate several different processes in parallel must also be taken into account. It may be comparatively easy to simulate any single process, yet building a plausible *integrated* system that accounts for human behavior is a much more difficult task.

Finally Just and Carpenter make claims for the generality of the production system architecture underlying READER, named CAPS (Collaborative Activation-based Production System). In particular they point out that CAPS has been used to simulate other types of processing (for example, mental rotation tasks) in addition to those addressed by READER. Their approach reflects a growing trend in computer simulation to strive for generality of an architecture across domains (see chapter 4 for a more detailed example).

READER is instructive in typifying a number of stages in the process of building a simulation. In the case of READER Just and Carpenter had already developed a fairly well defined theory of the processes used in reading (Just and Carpenter 1980). READER sought to simulate reading in such a way as to predict gaze-duration data that their theory explained. In building it, both theoretical assumptions and constraints of the architecture were taken into account (Thibadeau, Just, and Carpenter 1982).

If READER had been simply tuned to the specific performance data, rather than to incorporating more general theoretical assumptions (for example, the immediacy of processing), then we would be less impressed by its fit to the data, because tuning consumes degrees of freedom. If models have free parameters without any theoretical means of determining their values, then tuning is unavoidable, because the parameters must be set empirically. In these cases the problem can be ameliorated if the tuning uses only a *portion* of the available data and is then tested on the remaining data.

After constructing the simulation, the performance of the model was compared with data from human experiments. In addition to quantifying the goodness of fit, it is important to pay attention to discrepancies between the model and the human data as well as to predictions of the model that cannot be tested with the current data. Discrepancies indicate how the model might be improved, whereas predictions can suggest and guide further experimental research.

One way in which READER's encoding of words differed from that of human subjects was that READER encoded almost every word. Human subjects, however, skip about 60 percent of the short function words. One explanation for the difference is that human subjects may encode short words in parafoveal vision while fixating on the preceding word. The discrepancy between READER and the human data led to development of a version of READER that can use peripheral vision in skimming a text (Thibadeau, Just, and Carpenter 1982). This research illustrates how different versions of a model, each incorporating different theoretical assumptions, can often provide more insight than can a single model.

If provided with new tasks, a simulation has the potential for responding in new ways that may then suggest experiments on human subjects to check the predictions. Trusting the model transforms computer simulation from a tool that helps refine a theory to a source of prediction that drives research. Full exploitation of computer simulation requires viewing a model not as an end product but rather as a continually evolving entity whose permutations may suggest new investigations.

The final stage in simulation is also the first. That is, once a model has been built and tested, it is time to build a revised version or a different model altogether—either to generalize the model and architecture by applying it (or variants of it) to related domains or to test its new predictions.

Many theoretical flaws can remain hidden in a verbal theory until one begins to program it. Then it becomes apparent that not any old program will fit a lengthy protocol; but that it is usually extremely difficult to build even one simulation that can account accurately for the data.

Although we have discussed what we consider to be a particularly fine example of computer simulation, not all the models being published today live up to its standards of predictive power, generality, and ability to account for human data. The techniques of meta-analysis, to which we turn next, provide a way of examining the characteristics and qualities of simulation models and experiments that are reported in the literature.

Meta-Analysis
Meta-analysis, or more generally, quantitative reviewing, attempts to bring the precision and reliability of experimental methodology to the

task of reviewing and synthesizing groups of studies. The basic procedure in meta-analysis is to define a set of questions that the analysis will address and develop a scheme for coding each relevant study in the literature. Statistical methods exist for combining the results of several different experiments addressing the same issue and taking the experimental designs, the magnitudes of effects, and other factors into account (see Wolf 1987 for a concise review). The power of meta-analysis lies not only in statistical comparison, however, but also in coding schemes that permit quantitative answers to questions about groups of studies.

As a demonstration of the applicability of the method, we conducted a small-scale meta-analysis to answer the questions raised in our previous discussion of computer modeling. (For a more complete report see Kaplan 1987.)

Because we are interested in computer simulations as psychological theories, we decided to limit out meta-analysis to simulations that refer to actual human data (although they do not always compare model with data). In keeping with the scope of our ambitions (to present a demonstration rather than a full-fledged study), we considered simulations from a single journal only, *Cognitive Science*, and from a limited time period, 1980 through 1986. Although *Cognitive Science* is probably the single richest source of computer simulations of human cognitive behavior, we recognize that our sample is quite narrow and only intend that the analysis provide some ballpark figures indicative of general trends in the use of computer simulations.

We categorized simulations according to the type of architecture used to build the model; the type of human behavior modeled; the time scale of the behavior modeled; and the degree of predictive power, generality, and fit to the data claimed by the authors.

Twenty-three articles that met the criteria for inclusion were coded along the dimensions mentioned. Table 1.1 shows the number of simulations falling into various categories. From the data in the table we reached the following conclusions: First, the majority of simulations that had actually been built were either completely tuned to the data or compared with existing data with no mention of testable predictions that might be followed up. Although some simulations appeared to meet high standards of predictive power as well as of generality or of goodness of fit to the data, it was rare to find a simulation meeting all of the normative criteria we discussed. Second, claiming a qualitative fit to the human data seemed to be the norm. Most of the authors presented neither numerical predictions nor quantitative comparisons of their model's performance with human data, yet still claimed that the model performed the task in a psychologically plausible way. There were approximately twice as many simulations claiming qualitative fits as there were simulations claiming quantitative fits. When statistics were provided comparing the models' behavior with that of human

Table 1.1 Distribution of Simulations among Various Categories

| Category | Frequency by Different Types of Simulation Architectures | | | |
	No. Serial	No. Parallel	No. Other[a]	Total (%)
Predictive Power				
Not actually built	3	3	0	6 (26)
Tuned to the data	6	1	0	7 (30)
Compared w/o tuning	4	3	1	8 (35)
Predictions made	1	0	1	2 (9)
Goodness of fit to data				
No. comp. w/human data	5	1	0	6 (26)
Qual. fit claimed	5	5	1	11 (49)
Quant. fit claimed	4	1	1	6 (26)
Generality of model				
No discussion of	1	2	1	4 (17)
General discussion of	9	3	0	12 (52)
Claims for	1	1	1	3 (13)
Demonstrations of	3	1	0	4 (17)
Generality of Architecture				
No discussion of	6	5	1	12 (52)
General discussion of	7	2	1	10 (43)
Claims for	1	0	0	1 (4)
Demonstrations of	0	0	0	0 (0)
Domain simulated				
Recognition	0	1	0	1 (4)
Skill acquisition	1	0	0	1 (4)
Skill performance	0	1	0	1 (4)
Reading	0	0	1	1 (4)
Language generation	0	2	0	2 (9)
Imagery	0	1	1	2 (9)
Perception	1	1	0	2 (9)
Memory	3	0	0	3 (13)
Language Comprehension	3	1	0	4 (17)
Problem Solving	6	0	0	6 (26)
Time scale of behavior				
0 [100 ms]	0	3	0	3 (13)
0 [1 s]	2	4	1	7 (30)
0 [10 s]	3	0	0	3 (13)
0 [min]	8	0	1	9 (39)
0 [h]	1	0	0	1 (4)

Total serial simulations = 14; total parallel simulations = 7.
[a]Other category consists of one serial–parallel hybrid and one model whose architecture was not described in sufficient detail to make the serial–parallel judgment.

subjects, the models tended to account for between 50 percent and 80 percent of the variance.

Third, the generality of the models was usually discussed only in broad terms, with only 17 percent of the models actually demonstrating generality within or across domains. As to the generality of architectures, about half of the authors did not discuss this matter, whereas the other half talked mainly in general terms.

Fourth, simulations have covered a wide range of human behavior, with concentration of effort on problem solving and language comprehension and on behavior that is executable in a matter of minutes or behavior transpiring in about one second.

Finally, although parallel simulations covered a wide range of human behavior (problem solving and memory being notable exceptions), they modeled exclusively phenomena occurring on the time scale of 100 ms to 1 s. Conversely, serial models simulated only behavior taking a second or more. The sharp division between parallel and serial models with respect to the time scale of the behavior modeled serves both to confirm intuitions about the appropriateness of these architectures for tasks at different grain sizes and to highlight the challenge that any "grand scale" serial or parallel architecture must face—breaking the time-scale barrier. Serial models scored slightly better than did parallel models on generality and goodness of fit, although the sample size is hardly large enough to draw firm conclusions.

In our meta-analysis two generalizations appear noteworthy. First, a large proportion of the computer models in our sample lack the generality and predictive power that we would hope for. The remaining minority, however, illustrate what we ought to aim for in building simulations of human data. Second, there is a striking division between the time scales of phenomena modeled by parallel and serial models, respectively. This division supports the levels argument we made previously.

We hasten to qualify these conclusions, however, because of the limited scope of our demonstration. With regard to generality our estimates may be low, because authors might subsequently publish extensions or variants of their models in other journals or may omit references to simulations published elsewhere. Further some simulations claiming only a qualitative fit to the data, but modeling several processes, might have to meet more stringent criteria than would simulations that fit less demanding data quantitatively. Although it is our impression that such factors did not play a large role in the 23 studies we considered, issues like these should be resolved before strong conclusions are drawn from the analysis.

Our main purpose has been to demonstrate that a meta-analytic review allows us to answer questions both more objectively and more precisely than a standard literature review of comparable scope allows. Quantitative reviewing techniques such as meta-analysis (see Glass 1983 and Green and Hall 1984 for others as well) are likely to become increasingly important as cognitive scientists seek to integrate knowledge from the various literatures that are their heritage.

Philosophy, Logic, and Semantics

Historically, philosophy has been wholly eclectic in its methods. Philosophers appeal to everyday observation and introspection. They use dialectical methods and seek out ambiguities and common confusions. In their search for more rigorous methods of reasoning, they have contributed to cognitive science (as well as to other disciplines) the powerful tool of modern symbolic logic.

With the very important exception of symbolic logic, however, philosophical methods of inquiry probably have less effect on the methods of cognitive science than do the substantive questions that philosophy addresses: for example, the age-old questions of the nature of mind and intelligence, of the relation of mind to body, and of how we come to know the external world.

The qualities (if any) that make humans unique in the universe have long been of interest to philosophers. Because the abilities to think and to use language intelligently have been regarded as central to the claims of human uniqueness, some philosophers have sought to establish boundaries beyond which the intelligence of machines cannot venture (Searle 1980, Dreyfus 1972). Although one need not agree with their claims about the limits of machines (as indeed we do not), the debate has been of some value in setting tasks for artificial intelligence research. If the claim is that machines cannot do X, then a computer program to do X becomes an interesting design and construction problem. One could write a good deal of the history of AI and contemporary cognitive science in terms of responses to this challenge (Simon 1988).

The debate on limits has also been of some value in forcing clear operational definitions of such terms as "thinking," "understanding," "intuition," and the like—definitions that allow unequivocal decisions to be made as to whether a particular computer program is exhibiting one or another of these qualities (or whether a human being is, for that matter). In the absence of such definitions, of course nothing can be settled.

During the brief history of AI and cognitive science, one after another of the initial philosophical distinctions between human intelligence and machine intelligence have fallen by the wayside as the technology has advanced (Simon 1979b). Thus even as philosophy contributes to cognitive science by debating the limits of machine intelligence, cognitive science has strongly affected philosophy by producing running computer programs whose performance bears on classical philosophical issues.

Additional evidence of the relevance of cognitive science to philosophy can be found in section 1.4, where we discuss such topics as the relation of language to other cognitive faculties, reasoning and search as models of thinking, and thinking in propositions versus thinking in images. As Pylyshyn (chapter 2) indicates, all of these questions are of great concern for epistemology.

Returning now to the methods of philosophy, we observe that modern symbolic logic has been absolutely fundamental in providing foundations for computer science in general and AI in particular. Apart from the use of the formalisms of logic in programming (for example, the contribution of the lambda calculus to Lisp or the role of the first-order predicate calculus in Prolog), the two key contributions have been Gödel's incompleteness theorems and Turing's (and Church's) work on computability.

The Gödel theorems have often been the basis for arguments on the limits of computers. These results show that in rich systems of logic, certain theorems, known to be true by reasoning in a metalanguage, cannot be proved within the logic itself. What is sometimes overlooked is that the Gödel theorems are wholly neutral as between people and computers, placing just as strict but no more strict limits on one as on the other. Hence the implications of the incompleteness theorems for the question of machine intelligence are still quite uncertain. The Turing machine provided a wholly new standard of precision for our examination of symbolic processing and its relation to thinking. But neither the Turing machine nor the other resources provided by symbolic logic have yet resolved all of these difficult questions.

The problem of reasoning under conditions of uncertainty is of interest to both psychologists attempting to understand human decision making and AI researchers trying to design systems that perform intelligently under real-life conditions. We alluded previously to the development in economics and statistical decision theory of an elaborate formal normative theory of decision making. In recent years a good deal of psychological research has been carried out (Kahneman, Slovic, and Tversky 1982) that shows the limitations of this normative theory as a description of actual human choice under conditions of uncertainty. Some philosophers and some psychologists have participated in these developments, but on the whole both the normative and the descriptive theories have been rather peripheral to the cognitive science endeavor.

In section 1.4 we discussed logic as a possible model for the thought process—with somewhat negative conclusions. We did not allude to efforts, both in philosophy and in AI, to develop nonstandard logics that would capture more of the properties of everyday reasoning than are captured by the predicate calculus in it usual forms. Modal logics, dealing with concepts such as causality and possibility, have been created and extensively investigated (see, for example, McCarthy and Hayes 1969), but no consensus has been reached about a form of modal logic that would be especially helpful for or appropriate to the study of intelligence.

Work has also been carried forward on nonmonotonic logics designed to deal with the fact that large data bases, built up sequentially and constantly modified, may contain numerous contradictions and the fact that it may be advantageous to reason tentatively, preserving the ability to change one's conclusions when contradictions surface. Nonmonotonic logics have not yet found wide application, but they represent an interesting area of intersection of philosophy with AI.

Themes
Before leaving our discussion of methodology we note several themes that permeate our discussion. One such theme is the principle of density of data. Protocol analysis provides a very large number of closely spaced observations on a single task. Similarly content analysis and meta-analysis find high density of data in written materials. Content analysis extracts many data points from a single text, whereas meta-analysis considers each published result as a data point and examines many such results. Computer simulation requires a dense stream of data to constrain the processes that are being modeled. Whether one is interested in a single instance of human information processing or the broader picture composed of many such instances, one seeks methodologies that provide a dense set of data points at the level of interest.

A second theme is that boundary conditions for a methodology must be established before the full potential of the method can be realized. Protocol analysis illustrates this point most clearly. Reactions against earlier introspectionist methods contained some grains of truth without a clear way of separating the wheat from the chaff. Hence many psychologists decided to avoid the methodology altogether or worse yet to condemn it. Our theory of concurrent protocols enables us to distinguish introspection from verbalization of the encoded contents of STM. The latter is likely to provide an accurate account of the information heeded during the performance of a task, whereas the former introduces all kinds of disruptive auxiliary processes that muddy the picture considerably.

The point is general. We are able to apply a method effectively to the extent that we understand its capacities and limits. The theory of protocol analysis exemplifies one approach to getting that understanding. Extending the concepts of protocol analysis to new domains (for example, linguistics) or to new levels of human behavior (for example, content analysis) is also a fruitful approach. One finds limits by pushing them. Meta-analysis can help by providing a good idea of where to start pushing.

The last theme is one of interaction and combination. Repeatedly in our discussion we have seen how methodologies from different areas have combined to create powerful new approaches. Viewing content analysis and protocol analysis as variants of the same underlying concept suggests that each might have ways of dealing with common issues (for example, reliability of coding) that the other could find useful. Applying AI to content analysis and protocol analysis has produced semiautomated encoding schemes, whose potential has just begun to be tapped. Finally, performing meta-analyses on computer simulation (or any methodology) helps provide the clear picture of a methodology that is prerequisite for fruitful interactions between the disciplines of cognitive science.

1.6 Invariance of the Laws of Cognition[2]

Intelligent behavior is adaptive and hence must take on strikingly different forms in different environments. Intelligent systems are ground between the nether millstone of their physiology or hardware, which sets inner limits on their adaptation, and the upper millstone of a complex environment, which places demands on them for change. Because they change in adapting to their environments, intelligent systems may be described as "artificial."

The task of empirical science is to discover and verify invariants in the phenomena under study. The artificiality of information-processing systems creates a problem in defining such invariants. Any accurate statement of the laws of such a system must take into account their relativity to environmental features. We often find that we are studying sociology—the effects of their past histories on our subjects—when we are seeking to study physiology—the effects of the structure of the human nervous system.

Finding invariants in artificial phenomena, then, is not easy. But the example of biology shows that it is not impossible—biological systems were also absent at the creation of the universe. They too are shaped to their environments by the forces of evolution. Biological invariants (like psychological ones) hold for limited intervals of time and bounded regions of space.

On the shortest time scale intelligent (adaptive) systems change their behavior in the course of solving each problem they encounter. A prime characteristic of effective heuristic search is that it shapes itself to the environment in which it finds itself. It tries to capture in its problem space the important features of that environment—what Allen Newell has called the knowledge level.

On a longer time scale intelligent systems make adaptations that are preserved and remain available for meeting new situations. They learn. There are many forms of learning. One important form is the accumulation of information in memories and the acquisition of access routes for retrieving it. Learning changes systems semipermanently and hence increases the difficulty of searching out invariants.

On the longest time scale intelligent systems evolve both biologically by mutation and natural selection and socially through the accumulation and transmission of new knowledge and strategies. These changes further narrow the domain of invariance.

What room is left, then, for a general science of cognition? We must seek invariants in the inner and outer environments that bound the adaptive processes. We must look for basic characteristics that might be held in common among diverse kinds of intelligent systems and also for common elements at the knowledge level, among complex problem environments.

The Outer Environment

The first source of invariance in intelligent systems stems from common characteristics of the environments to which they must adapt and in which their behavior takes place. Again, because these environments are highly diverse, the invariants will be correspondingly abstract. The environments that demand the exercise of intelligence are problem environments that do not present obvious paths to the attainment of a system's goals. Frequently, though not always, problem environments contain large, sometimes immense, numbers of alternatives, only a small fraction of which satisfies the goal requirements.

The principal mechanism of intelligence observed in people and computers operating in problem environments is heuristic search. The heuristic devices make search feasible by enabling the intelligent system to exercise great selectivity by using information stored in memory to choose more promising over less promising paths and by extracting from the problem environment new information about regularities in its structure that can similarly guide the search.

The interface between intelligent systems and their external environments—their sensory and motor organs—presents most delicate problems in the design of adaptive systems. This is because the interface must meet the requirements of both the outer and the inner environments—it must, in fact, communicate between them. It is no accident that our progress has been much slower in AI in designing effective sensors and effectors or imitating the corresponding human organs than in understanding and imitating those intelligent processes that can go on inside the human head without interaction with its environment. "Deep thinking" has proved easier to understand and simulate than hand-eye coordination.

The Inner Environment

We should not expect the invariants of the inner environment to be the same for all intelligent systems, yet there are one or two surprisingly general constraints shared by most of them.

For most purposes we are concerned with just two kinds of intelligent systems: living organisms and computers. All living organisms make use of essentially the same protoplasmic material, but exhibit a wide variety of organizations. Most of the computers that have been built in the past forty years exhibit remarkable similarity of organization, but have been assembled from a most diverse set of alternative component materials. Hence, over these two classes of intelligent systems, we do encounter a considerable diversity of both organization and material subtrate.

Computers and (in our view) human beings are symbol systems. They achieve their intelligence by symbolizing external and internal situations and events and by manipulating those symbols. They all use about the same symbol-manipulating processes. Perhaps that particular invariance arose because computers were made in the image of humans, but because only the connectionist view proposes a radically different architecture, perhaps the invariance goes deeper than imitation.

When required to do complex tasks, both people and computers exhibit vividly a severe attention bottleneck, or seriality. We may conjecture that the reason for the predominance of seriality at the level of complex processes (processes taking perhaps a half second and more in the case of human beings) is that it is very difficult to organize parallel computational systems if precise coordination is required of the computations being made simultaneously by the different components.

Where processing is basically serial, all of the relatively labile inputs and outputs of the basic processes can be handled in a working memory of limited size. (See the discussion in section 1.3 of short-term memory in the "standard model.") The need for a trade-off between flexible adaptation to the environment and coherent attention to goals also seems to point toward mechanisms for attentional focus. Hence when intelligence is implemented by production systems, a portion of memory is generally designated as working memory or as the "activated" portion of memory in which the condition sides of the productions must be tested.

In this limitation of the size of short-term memory and in the consequent seriality in behavior, we see one of the invariants we may seek to characterize and understand. As can be seen from this example; the invariant is of a relatively abstract kind, imposing constraints on the possible organizations of intelligent systems rather than on their material substrates. Intelligent systems, according to this argument, will necessarily be symbol systems, and at the level of goal-oriented activity they will be serial in operation with narrow attentional focus.

Empirically Observed Invariants
However adaptive are the intelligent systems with which we are concerned, we should not despair completely of finding invariants in their behavior. For example, the study of expertise in humans and research on the design of expert systems for computers has revealed some remarkable uniformities and generalizations. These uniformities stem

from both the limitations imposed by inner environments and the task demands of the outer environments.

Expertise, empirical research shows, generally rests on an extensive knowledge base. It has been shown for a number of fields of human endeavor that a world-class level of expertise is never attained with less than ten years of concentrated learning and practice. Here the magic number 10 represents a ratio between the amount of knowledge and skill that has to be acquired by the expert (the demand of the external environment) and the rate at which people can acquire knowledge and skill (the limits of the inner environment).

With respect to the size of the knowledge base, it has been found that thousands or tens of thousands of productions must be provided to a sophisticated expert system such as a medical-diagnosis system. Research on human world-class experts has shown that their knowledge bases are likely to amount to 50,000 or 100,000 productions or more. Numbers of the same magnitude characterize typical natural-language vocabularies of professionals. The ubiquitous presence of large knowledge bases like these is a characteristic invariant of human and mechanical expert systems.

Possessing large knowledge bases of this kind, which operate very much in the manner of production systems, experts solve a great many problems by what can equally well be called "recognition" or "intuition." Even when problem solution requires extensive heuristic search, recognition plays a major role in allowing large steps to be taken "instantaneously" and in permitting appropriate operators to be recognized and applied at each stage. Most of the AI expert systems have similar characteristics—generally depending more on ability to recognize extensive sets of cues than on the ability to model problem situations at a deep level. Powerful recognition capabilities are another common property of expert systems.

We encounter numerous invariants, too, when we get close to the sensory and motor organs that form the interface between the inner and outer environments. Perhaps one reason why many of the invariants we have discovered belong to these interfaces is that they are more accessible to study than are the deeper regions of the brain. Another possible reason is that they are more specialized, through a long period of evolution, and hence have more specific physiologically determined features than do the more central and recently evolved parts of the brain. Whatever the reasons the relevant chapters of this book testify that our knowledge of these interfaces is more precise than most of our knowledge of other aspects of cognition.

In the matter of machine intelligence the reverse is true. The sophistication of the mammalian sensory and motor capabilities has proved exceedingly difficult to match in artificial intelligence programs. Hence we go about the design of "white collar" expert systems with far more assurance and success than we show in the design of robots.

Learning

The idea that intelligent systems are highly adaptive and flexible in their behavior could well lead to the notion that a great many of their invariants are to be found not in their behavior when confronted with their usual tasks nor in the structures responsible for performance but in the long-range mechanisms that bring about adaptation—their learning mechanisms. As a matter of fact, learning was a very popular topic in the early history of artificial intelligence research and an almost dominating topic in experimental psychology during the period from World War I to the mid-1950s. The historical reasons for this domination are complex, and only one aspect needs comment here.

With respect to artificial intelligence many early workers held the view that it is easier to induce a system to organize itself from scratch by exposing it to an appropriate sequence of training experience than it is to provide it with the knowledge it would need for expert performance. It was probably also thought that learner programs avoid the charge commonly directed toward AI systems that the intelligence is really in the programmer and not in the system. If the programmer could only provide a potential for learning and not the program for the finished performance, this accusation would not stand.

For whatever reason many investigators in the early years followed the learning route but not with notable success. All of the expert systems that have been produced up to the present (except for Samuel's (1959) checker-playing program) have been given directly all or most of the knowledge and strategy on which their expertness rests.

Within the past decade there has been a revival of the learning enterprise but with viewpoints quite different from the original simple reinforcement paradigms. Connectionist architectures bring in a number of new powerful learning techniques—for example, the so-called annealing or Boltzmann methods for causing a system to settle down to an appropriate equilibrium.

Within the domain of symbolic schemes the new generation of learning programs, often using the production system architecture, are basically problem-solving systems capable of undertaking heuristic search with a reasonable armory of methods such as generate-and-test and means-ends analysis. They do not start out in the barebones fashion of the earlier generation of self-organizing systems. They also start out with a better picture of the goal of the learning: the expert performance that the learner is striving to attain. Finally, today we have clearer ideas of the mechanisms (especially adaptive production systems) needed to enable a symbolic system to bootstrap itself.

We should not suppose that it will be simple to find invariants even in learning systems. After all we must be prepared for the phenomenon of "learning to learn." The adaptive mechanisms themselves may learn from experience. In our study of performance and learning we must not imagine invariants where there are none. Because intelligent systems are programmable, we must expect to find that different systems will use quite different strategies to perform the same task.

Hence research on adaptive systems must take on a taxonomic, and even a sociological aspect. We have a great deal to learn about the variety of strategies, and describing them provides a substrate as necessary to cognitive science as the taxonomic substrate has been to modern biology. Within cognitive science only the linguists (and to some extent, the developmental psychologists) have had a tradition of detailed description, rather than a tradition of experimentation in search of generally valid truths.

In humans, moreover, performance programs are the product of social learning, and the programs of the twentieth century will not be identical with those of the nineteenth, or the first. Cognitive science must be prepared to study the respects in which the mind of the citizen of ancient Greece is the same or different from the mind of the modern Westerner or of an African villager. There is room for a greatly increased volume of cognitive science research in this sociological direction.

The social dimension of intelligence has been recognized in social psychology, where social cognition is currently a central focus of research. Yet social psychology in general and social cognition in particular have as yet had only minimal contact with cognitive science. In part this insulation may stem from the rather special cognitive concerns that social psychology has had, especially with how people perceive others (and themselves) and how they go about forming these perceptions. Whatever the reason, one may expect that social psychology will play a larger role in cognitive science in the future than it has up to now.

Conclusion

Intelligence is closely related with adaptivity—with problem solving, learning, and evolution. A science of intelligent systems has to be a science of adaptive systems with all this entails for the difficulty of finding genuine invariants. Some of the invariance in intelligence is imposed by the structure of the inner environment, for example, the limits of human short-term memory. Some of it is imposed by the outer environment—the need to search very large spaces selectively. Some of the invariance is to be found in the structure of learning systems rather than in the highly adapted performance systems they produce. But in cognitive science we must be prepared to recognize that the invariants in an adaptive system are likely to be limited to specific times and places and that in the long run almost any aspect of them can change adaptively.

Notes

This research was supported by the Personnel and Training Programs, Psychological Sciences Division, Office of Naval Research, under Contract No. N00014-86-K-0768; and by the Defense Advanced Research Projects Agency (DOD), ARPA Order No. 3597, monitored by the Air Force Avionics Laboratory under Contract F33615-78-C-1151. Reproduction in whole or in part is permitted for any purpose of the United States Government. Approved for public release; distribution unlimited.

We thank our colleague, Patricia A. Carpenter, for helpful comments and suggestions.

1. For more details on the uses of content analysis we refer the reader to the excellent reviews by Holsti (in Lindzey and Aronson 1968).

2. This section draws heavily on Simon 1980.

References

Abelson, R. P. 1953. Computer simulation of "hot" cognition. In S. S. Tompkins and S. Messick, eds. *Computer Simulation of Personality*. New York: Wiley.

Anderson, J. R. 1983. *The Architecture of Cognition*. Cambridge, MA: Harvard University Press.

Bhaskar, R., and Simon, H. A. 1977. Problem solving in semantically rich domains: An example from engineering thermodynamics. *Cognitive Science* 1:193–215.

Bobrow, D. G. 1968. Natural language input for 2 computer problem-solving system. In M. Minsky, ed. *Semantic Information Processing*, Cambridge, MA: MIT Press.

Bransford, J. D., and Franks, J. J. 1971. The abstraction of linguistic ideas. *Cognitive Psychology* 2:331–350.

Broadbent, D. E. 1958. *Perception and Communication*. New York: Pergamon Press.

Chase, W. G., and Clark, H. H. 1972. Mental operations in the comparison of sentences and pictures. In L. W. Gregg, ed. *Cognition in Learning and Memory*. New York: Wiley.

Chomsky, N. 1965. *Aspects of the Theory of Syntax*. Cambridge, MA: MIT Press.

Coles, L. S. 1972. Syntax directed interpretation of natural language. In H. A. Simon and L. Siklossy, eds. *Representation and Meaning*. Englewood Cliffs, NJ: Prentice-Hall.

Corsini, R. J. 1987. *Concise Encycopedia of Psychology*. New York: Wiley.

Dreyfus, H. L. 1972. *What Computers Can't Do*. New York: Harper & Row.

Dyer, M. G. 1983. *In-depth Understanding: A Computer Model of Integrated Processing of Narrative Comprehension*. Cambridge, MA: MIT Press.

Ericsson, K. A., and Simon, H. A. 1984. *Protocol Analysis: Verbal Reports as Data*. Cambridge, MA: MIT Press.

Feigenbaum, E. A., and Simon, H. A. 1986. EPAM-like models of recognition and learning. *Cognitive Science* 8:305–336.

Fisher, C. 1988. Advancing the study of programming with computer-aided protocol analysis. In G. Olson, E. Soloway, and S. Sheppard, eds. *Empirical Studies of Programmers: 1987 Workshop.* Norwood, NJ: Ablex.

Gerloff, P. 1987. Identifying the unit of analysis in translation: some uses of think-aloud protocol data. In C. Faerch and G. Kasper, ed. *Introspection in Second Language Research.* Philadelphia, PA: Multilingual Matters.

Glass, G. 1983. Synthesizing empirical research: meta-analysis. In S. A. Ward and L. J. Reed, eds. *Knowledge Structure and Use: Implications for Synthesis and Interpretation.* Philadelphia: Temple University Press.

Green, B., and Hall, J. 1984. Quantitative methods for literature review. *Annual Review of Psychology* 35:37–53.

Hayes, J. R., and Simon, H. A. 1974. Understanding written problem instructions. In L. W. Gregg, ed. *Knowledge and Cognition.* Potomac, MD: Erlbaum.

Hebb, D. O. 1949. *The Organization of Behavior.* New York: Wiley.

Holmes, F. L. 1980. Hans Krebs and the discovery of the ornithine cycle. *Federation Proceedings* 39:216–225.

Just, M. A., and Carpenter, P. A. 1980. A theory of reading: From eye fixations to comprehension. *Psychological Review* 87:329–354.

Just, M. A., and Carpenter, P. A. 1987. *The Psychology of Reading and Language Comprehension.* Boston, MA: Allyn & Bacon.

Kahneman, D., Slovic, P., and Tversky, A., eds. 1982. *Judgment Under Uncertainty: Heuristics and Biases.* Cambridge: Engl. Cambridge University Press.

Kaplan, C. A. 1987. *Computer Simulation: Separating Fact from Fiction.* Pittsburgh: Carnegie-Mellon University.

Kaplan, C. A., and Simon, H. A. 1988. In search of insight. [Submitted for publication in *Cognitive Science.*]

Kosslyn, S. M. 1980. *Image and Mind.* Cambridge, MA: Harvard University Press.

Kulkarni, D., and Simon, H. A. 1988. The processes of scientific discovery: The strategy of experimentation. *Cognitive Science* 12:139–175.

Larkin, J. A., and Simon, H. A. 1987. Why a diagram is (sometimes) worth 10,000 words. *Cognitive Science* 11:65–100.

Lindzey, G., and Aronson, E. 1968. *The Handbook of Social Psychology.* 2nd ed. Reading, MA: Addison-Wesley.

McCarthy, J., and Hayes, P. 1969. Some philosophical problems from the standpoint of artificial intelligence. In B. Meltzer and D. Michie, eds. *Machine Intelligence 4*. Edinburgh: Edinburgh University Press.

Miller, G. A. 1956. The magical number seven, plus or minus two. *Psychological Review* 63:81–97.

Miller, G. A., and Johnson-Laird, P. N. 1976. *Language and Perception*. Cambridge, MA: Harvard University Press.

Newell, A. 1980. Physical symbol systems. *Cognitive Science* 2:135–184.

Newell, A., and Simon, H. A. 1956. The logic theory machine. *IRE Transactions on Information Theory* IT-2(3):61–79.

Newell, A., and Simon, H. A. 1963. Computers in psychology. In R. D. Luce, R. R. Bush, and E. Galanter, eds. *Handbook of Mathematical Psychology, I*. New York: Wiley, pp. 361–428.

Newell, A., and Simon H. A. 1972. *Human Problem Solving*. Englewood Cliffs, NJ: Prentice-Hall.

Nisbett, R. E., and Wilson, T. D. 1977. Telling more than we can know: Verbal reports on mental processes. *Psychological Review* 84:231–259.

Norman, D. A., ed. 1981. *Perspectives on Cognitive Science*. Norwood, NJ: Ablex.

Paige, J. M. and Simon, H. A. 1966. Cognitive processes in solving algebra word problems. In H. A. Simon, ed. *Models of Thought*. New Haven, CT: Yale University Press.

Posner, M. I., and McLeod, P. 1982. Information processing models: In search of elementary operations. *Annual Review of Psychology* 33:477–514.

Pylyshyn, Z. 1973. What the mind's eye tells the mind's brain: A critique of mental imagery. *Psychological Bulletin* 80:1–24.

Quillian, M. R. 1966. *Semantic Theory*. Doctoral dissertation, Carnegie Institute of Technology.

Rich, E. 1983. *Artificial Intelligence*. New York: McGraw-Hill.

Rochester, N., Holland, J. H., Haibt, L. H., and Duda, W. L. 1956. Test on a cell assembly theory of the action of the brain, using a large digital computer. *IRE Transactions on Information Theory* IT-2(3):80–93.

Rosenberg, S., and Simon, H. A. 1977. Modeling semantic memory: Effects of presenting semantic information in different modalities. *Cognitive Psychology* 9:293–325.

Samuel, A. L. 1959. Some studies in machine learning using the game of checkers. *IBM Journal of Research and Development* 3:210–229.

Searle, J. R. 1980. The intentionality of intention and action. *Cognitive Science* 4:47–70.

Siklossy, L. 1972. Natural language learning by computer. In H. A. Simon and L. Siklossy, eds. *Representation and Meaning*. Englewood Cliffs, NJ: Prentice-Hall.

Simon, H. A. 1977. *Models of Discovery*. Boston, MA: D. Reidel Publishing.

Simon, H. A. 1979a. *Models of Thought*. New Haven, CT: Yale University Press.

Simon, H. A. 1979b. Information processing models of cognition. *Annual Review of Psychology* 30:363–396.

Simon, H. A. 1980. Cognitive science: The newest science of the artificial. *Cognitive Science* 4:33–46.

Simon, H. A. 1988. Creativity and Motivation: A response to Csikszentmihalyi. *New Ideas in Psychology* 6:177–181.

Stone, P. J., Dunphy, D. C., Smith, M. S., and Ogilvie, D. M. 1966. *The General Inquirer: A Computer Approach to Content Analysis*. Cambridge, MA: MIT Press.

Thibadeau, R., Just, M. A., and Carpenter, P. A. 1982. A model of the time course and content of reading. *Cognitive Science* 6:157–203.

Turing, A. M. 1950. Computing machinery and intelligence. *Mind* 59:433–460.

Waterman, D. A., and Newell, A. 1971. Protocol analysis as a task for artificial intelligence. *Artificial Intelligence* 2:285–318.

Waterman, D. A., and Newell, A. 1973. PAS-II: An interactive task-free version of an automatic protocol analysis system. In *Proceedings of the Third IJCAI*. Menlo Park, CA: Stanford Research Institute, pp. 431–445.

Weber, R. P. 1985. *Basic Content Analysis*. Beverly Hills, CA: Sage Publications.

Wolf, F. M. 1987. *Meta-Analysis: Quantitative Methods for Research Synthesis*. Beverly Hill, CA: Sage Publications.

Foundations

2 Computing in Cognitive Science

Zenon W. Pylyshyn

Nobody doubts that computers have had a profound influence on the study of human cognition. The very existence of a discipline called cognitive science is a tribute to this influence. One of the principal characteristics that distinguishes cognitive science from more traditional studies of cognition within psychology is the extent to which it has been influenced by both the ideas and the techniques of *computing*. It may come as a surprise to the outsider then to discover that there is no unanimity within cognitive science on either the nature (and in some cases the desirability) of the influence or what computing *is*, or at least on its essential character, as it pertains to cognitive science.

In this chapter I comment on both these questions. The first question brings us to a discussion of the role of computing in our understanding of human (and perhaps animal) cognition. I examine a variety of such roles—from the instrumental use of computers to express theories, through its role as a source of ideas, to the bold empirical claim that cognition is quite literally a species of computing. The latter position (which gets us into a discussion of what I call the *strong equivalence* thesis) cannot even be begun to be addressed until we have a much clearer understanding of what we mean by the term *computing*—that is, what family of processes we intend to cover by that term. This is the most contentious of the topics I cover, but one that cannot be avoided; an understanding of the assumptions underlying the discipline is a prerequisite to understanding recent proposals for a redirection of the goals of cognitive science (see, for example, chapters 4 and 8).

In the final section of this chapter, I examine the methodologies available for validating computational models as *strong* models of cognitive processes. Although many of these techniques are also discussed in other chapters of this book (for example, chapters 1 and 7), my discussion is intended to show how some of these methods relate to the notion of strong equivalence of processes.

Let us note that the view that computing is relevant to understanding cognition, or intelligent behavior in general, goes as far back as the idea of computing itself. Turing's (1937) original paper on computability contains a section in which Turing attempts to provide some intuitive motivation for his notion of a mechanically "effective procedure" by looking at what a mathematician does in the course of solving mathematical problems and distilling this process to its essentials. Later Turing (1950) argued that a properly programmed computer could in principle exhibit intelligent behavior. The argument rests on Turing's own discovery of the existence of a universal Turing machine, an abstract automation that can imitate any other formally specifiable computer. The relevance of the universal machine to cognitive science is raised briefly later.

Computers are relevant to cognition in many ways. Newell (1970; see also Newell 1973a) has discussed a range of views of the possible relation between computing and cognition. These vary all the way from the view that computers provide an interesting new metaphor, to the view—which I defend—that cognition is literally a species of computing, carried out in a particular type of biological mechanism. In the following I sketch two of the major ways in which computing is relevant to the study of cognition. Later I elaborate and defend both these general propositions and argue that they have been decisive in the development of cognitive science, even though there have been many arguments concerning the details—and even the foundational assumptions—behind them.

At the most abstract level the class of mechanisms called *computers* are the only known mechanisms that are sufficiently plastic in their behavior to match the plasticity of human cognition. They are also the only known mechanism capable of producing behavior that can be described as *knowledge dependent*. Because of such properties *computing* remains the primary candidate for meeting the dual needs of explaining cognition in mechanism terms and accounting for certain otherwise problematic aspects of cognition—in particular the fact that behavior can be systematically influenced by inducing differences in beliefs or goals.

At a more concrete level computers provide a way to deal with a number of problems that plague the attempt to understand cognition. Among them are the complexity of the processes underlying cognition and the need for a theory that bridges the gap from internal processing to actual instances of behavior. Such a theory is sometimes said to meet the *sufficiency condition*. This condition imposes a particularly stringent requirement on measures of the adequacy of a theory. It also forces the theorist to explicitly confront certain issues that could otherwise be taken for granted or presupposed. Chief among them are the architecture-process distinction (and the nature of the cognitive architecture) and the closely related question of the control structure underlying cognitive processing.

2.1 What is Computing?

Some Background: Formalisms, Symbols, and Mechanisms

The possibility of imitating life by artifact has intrigued people throughout history. But only in the second half of this century has the possibility of using the special type of artifact that we call a computer been considered seriously as a means of understanding mental phenomena. What is different about this latest interest is that the focus is not primarily on the imitation of movements (as was the case with early clockwork mechanisms) but on the imitation of certain unobservable internal processes. This notion only became conceivable with the gradual emergence, in several disparate areas of intellectual development, of a certain way of understanding mechanisms. This new and more abstract notion of mechanism is entirely divorced from the old-style "mechanical" considerations (such as those that preoccupied Descartes and that Chomsky has characterized as *contact mechanics*) and is concerned only with abstractly defined operations such as storing, retrieving, and alterating tokens of symbolic codes.

This notion of mechanism arose in conjunction with attempts to develop a completely formal, content-free foundation for mathematics. The Hilbert program was one of the most ambitious attempts to build up mathematics by purely formal means; without regard to questions of what the formalism was about. Some of this enterprise succeeded in the work of Frege and of Russell and Whitehead. On the other hand one of the greatest intellectual achievements of our age was the demonstration by purely formal means that the ultimate goal of complete formalization was in principle not achievable (this was done originally by Godel and subsequently by Turing, Church, Post, and others; see the collection of papers in Davis 1965).

The same work that provided demonstrations of particular in-principle limitations of formalization also provided demonstrations of its universality. Thus Alan Turing, Emil Post, and Alonzo Church independently developed distinct formalisms that they showed were complete in the sense that they were powerful enough to formally (that is; "mechanically") generate all sequences of expressions that could be interpreted as proofs and hence could generate all provable theorems of logic. In Turing's case this took the form of showing that there exists a universal mechanism, a particular Turing machine called the universal machine (UM), that could simulate any mechanism describable in its formalism. It does this by accepting a description of the mechanism to be simulated and then carries out a procedure whose input/output behavior is identical to that which would have been generated by the machine whose description it was given. We say that the UM computes the *same function* as the target machine, where "same function" means the same input/output pairs or the same *extension* of the function. There is no requirement that UM carry out the same steps as the target machine. That would be a stronger sense of equivalence.

What is interesting about the latter work, from our point of view, is that to derive such results (concerning the universality and incompleteness of certain formal systems), it was necessary to understand the notions of proof and of deduction in a formal system in terms of the manipulation of symbol tokens or marks on a piece of paper, where the manipulation was specified "mechanically" in a way that was entirely independent of how the symbols might be interpreted. Logic became a game played with meaningless symbol tokens according to certain formal rules (that is, syntactic rules).

It was the development of the notion of universality of formal mechanism, first introduced in the work on foundations of mathematics in the 1930s, that provided the initial impetus for viewing mind as a symbol-processing system. Universality implies that a formal symbol processing mechanism can produce *any* arbitrary input/output function that we can specify in sufficient detail. Put in more familiar terms, a universal machine can be *programmed* to compute any formally specified function. This extreme plasticity in behavior is one of the reasons why computers have from the very beginning been viewed as artifacts that might be capable of exhibiting intelligence. Many people who were not familiar with this basic idea have misunderstood the capacity of machines. For example, the Gestalt psychologist Wolfgang Kohler (1947) viewed machines as too rigid to serve as models of mental activity. The latter, he claimed, are governed by what he called *dynamic factors*,—an example of which are self-distributing field effects, such as the effects that cause magnetic fields to be redistributed when we introduce new pieces of metal—as opposed to *topographical factors*, which are structurally rigid. He wrote (Kohler 1947, p. 65):

To the degree to which topographical conditions are rigidly given, and not to be changed by dynamic factors, their existence means the exclusion of certain forms of function, and the restriction of the processes to the possibilities compatible with those conditions. . . . This extreme relation between dynamic factors and imposed topographical conditions is almost entirely realized in typical machines . . . we do not construct machines in which dynamic factors are the main determinants of the form of operation.

That computers violate this claim is one of their most important and unique characteristics. Their topographic structure is completely rigid, yet they are capable of maximal plasticity of function. It is this very property that led Turing to speculate that computers would be capable in principle of exhibiting intelligent behavior. For example, he devoted an important early philosophical paper (Turing 1950) to an exposition of this idea. Turing argued that a computer could in principle be made to exhibit intelligent activity to an arbitrary degree. He claimed that a machine should qualify as being intelligent if it could successfully play the "imitation game"—that is, fool a human observer, with whom it could communicate only through a keyboard and terminal, so that the observer could not discriminate between it and another person. The possibility of a computer being able to successfully pass what become known as the *Turing test* is based entirely on the recognition of the plasticity of behavior entailed by symbolic systems, which can be *programmed* to behave according to any finitely specifiable function.

Devices that we call computers now come in a wide variety of forms—most of which appear quite different from the one that Turing developed in his mathematical analysis. It is appropriate to ask then what makes a system a computer. This is a particularly relevant question inasmuch as a working hypothesis of much of cognitive science is that the mind is literally a type of computer. One might begin by asking, In virtue of what property does the Turing machine achieve the universality or the programmability that recommended it as a model of intelligence?

Newell (1980) provides an interesting insight into one characteristic that is essential for a device to be universal or programmable. For a mechanism to be universal, its inputs must be partitioned into two distinct components, one of which is assigned a privileged interpretation as instructions or as a specification of some particular input/output function, and the other of which is treated as the proper input to that function. Such a partition is essential for defining a universal Turing machine. Thus there can only be arbitrary plasticity of behavior if some of the inputs and outputs of the system are *interpreted* (or, as Newell puts it, if they have the power to "designate" something extrinsic).

Designation is indeed one of the core ideas of computing. In computers symbols may designate in several ways: they can provide access to other symbols, they can cause an interpreter to perform the action designated by that symbol, or they may designate other extrinsic things. For example, they may designate abstract objects called numbers, or they may designate objects of reasoning (for example, objects in the world or in the imagination, propositions, predicates, and so on), or they may even designate goals. Indeed because what symbols designate need not exist (for example, unicorns or the pot of gold at the end of the rainbow) the very notion of designation, meaning "referring to," is problematic inasmuch as people usually understand "refer" to apply only when there exists a thing being referred to. That is why we usually talk about the relation of symbols and what they symbolize as semantics, or we speak of the meaning of a symbol. In any case *semantics* and *meaning* are relevant terms used to describe properties of states of computers (and people) but not of many other complex systems that are not functioning as computers (for example, the Andromeda galaxy).

Systems that have traditionally been called computers (for example, the Turing machine) share a number of properties. The view that certain of these properties are constitutive of computing (and consequently that they are also constitutive of cognition, insofar as cognition is a species of computing) is called the *classical view* (after Fodor and Pylyshyn 1988). In the next section I consider some of these properties, acknowledging that this view is by no means unanimously held among cognitive scientists (see, for example, chapter 4).

The Classical View of Computing and Cognition

In Turing's original theoretical machine and in every real digital computer, a distinction is made between the *processor* and the *memory*. The processor "writes" symbolic expressions into memory, alters them, and "reads" them. Reading certain of these symbols causes specified actions to occur, which may change other symbols. The memory may consist of a tape, a set of registers, or any form of working storage. The expressions that are written are complex symbols that are made up of simpler symbols, just the way sentences are complex symbols made up of simpler symbols in a systematic way. The processor (or, in the case of logic, the rules of inference) then transforms the expressions into new expressions in a special kind of systematic way. The *way* such symbolic expressions are transformed in a classical computer is very important. As has already been mentioned, the symbolic expressions have a semantics, that is, they are *codes* for something, or they *mean* something. Therefore the transformations of the expressions are designed to coherently maintain this meaning or to ensure that the expressions continue to make sense when semantically interpreted in a consistent way.

For example, if the expressions are numerals like 19, 1011, XIX, or expressions in some other numeral notations, they usually serve as *codes* for *numbers*. In that case when the computer transforms these expressions, they might refer to different numbers. If you can arrange for the computer to transform them systematically in the appropriate way, the transformations can correspond to useful mathematical operations such as addition or multiplication. Consider an abacus. Patterns of beads represent numbers. People learn rules for transforming these patterns of beads in such a way that the semantic interpretation of before-and-after pairs corresponds to a useful mathematical function. But there is nothing intrinsically mathematical about the rules themselves; they are just rules for moving beads around. What makes the rules useful for doing mathematics is that we are assured of a certain continuing correspondence between the formal or syntactic patterns of beads and mathematical objects (such as numbers). The way such a correspondence can be assured is illustrated by an example in the next section.

In scientific computing, as well as in the history of computer applications up to the 1970s, the most frequently encountered domain of representation was doubtlessly that of numbers, and consequently the most common transformations over expressions were those that mirror mathematical functions over numbers. But if the symbolic expressions were codes for propositions or beliefs or knowledge, as they might be if they were expressions in some symbolic logic, then the computer might transform them in ways corresponding to proofs or inferences, or perhaps to a sequence of "thoughts" that occur during commonsense reasoning. The important thing is that, according to the classical view, certain kinds of systems, including both minds and computers, operate on *representations* that take the form of symbolic codes.

There is one more important property that such symbolic codes must have, according to the classical view. In classical symbol systems the meaning of a complex expression depends in a systematic way on the meaning of its parts (or *constituents*). This is the way ordinary language, formal logic, and even the number system works, and there are good reasons for believing that they *must* work that way in both practical computing and in modeling cognition. In the case of cognition these reasons have to do with the *productivity* and the *systematicity* of thought and reasoning, two issues discussed at length in Fodor and Pylyshyn 1988.

So to summarize, the classical view assumes that both computers and minds have at least the following three distinct levels of organization:

1. *The semantic level (or knowledge) level*[1] At this level we explain why people, or appropriately programmed computers, do certain things by saying what they know and what their goals are and by showing that these are connected in certain meaningful or even rational ways.

2. *The symbol level* The semantic content of knowledge and goals is assumed to be encoded by symbolic expressions. Such structured expressions have parts, each of which also encodes some semantic content. The codes and their structure, as well as the regularities by which they are manipulated, are another level of organization of the system.

3. *The physical (or biological) level* For the entire system to run, it has to be realized in some physical form. The structure and the principles by which the physical object functions correspond to the physical or the biological level.

This three-level organization defines what I call the *classical computational* or *cognitive architecture*.

To illustrate the claim that there are different principles that apply at each of these levels, consider the following example. Suppose you have a calculator with a square root button. If you want to explain why it gives strange answers or fails to work when the batteries are low or when you cut one of the wires in it or when the temperature is too low, you have to refer to physical properties of the calculator, the physical level. If you want to explain why certain rounding errors occur in the lower-order digits of the answer, or why it takes longer to compute the answer to some problems than to others, you have to refer to how numbers are symbolically encoded and to what particular sequence of transformations of these symbolic expressions occurs (that is, to the algorithm used). This is an explanation at the symbol level. But then if you want to show that the algorithm will always give the correct answer, you have to refer to facts and theorems of number theory, that is, to the semantics of the symbols.

One might ask how it is possible for symbolic expressions and rules to keep maintaining their semantic interpretation, to keep the semantics of the expressions coherent. It is one of the important discoveries of formal logic that one can specify rules that operate on symbolic expressions in such a way that the sequence of expressions always corresponds to a proof. In computing (and in cognitive science generally) one is interested in not only logical, or truth-preserving, sequences but also sequences that preserve such semantic properties as those exhibited in heuristic or goal-directed reasoning.

The following numerical example shows how one can define an operation over symbolic expressions and a semantic mapping (which I designate *SF*) from symbols to numbers in such a way that the operation can be consistently interpreted as addition. To emphasize the generality of the following example (so that, for example, it could apply to some system other than a conventional computer), I present it in its most abstract form. Suppose we have a certain instantiation function *IF* from equivalence classes of physical states of a certain system (perhaps only the parts of the system called its memory registers) to symbolic expressions. For concreteness let us say that the expressions consist of the atomic symbols o and x arranged in strings of arbitrary length. In this example then the states of the memory registers would correspond to such expressions as o, x, ox, xo, xx, oox, oxo, oxx, xoo, xox, xxo, xxx, xooo, and so on. Each of these expressions corresponds to some possible state of each of the machine's memory registers.[2]

Let us further suppose that when a certain pattern (which I designate by #) occurs in a portion of the machine called its instruction register, the machine's memory registers change states according to a certain specifiable regularity. For example, when the portion of the machine we call register 1 is in the state that maps onto the string xox, and register 2 is in the state that maps onto the string xxo, then register 3 changes its state from whatever it was to the state that corresponds to the string xoxx.

This sort of regularity might conceivably be used to represent addition of numbers, provided that we adopt an appropriate semantic function *SF* and that the regularity meets certain requirements. In this case the required semantic function is easy to define—it happens to be the function that maps strings of o's and x's onto numbers, using the familiar binary number system. In defining the *SF* formally, moreover, we provide a way of stating the requirements that the regularity must meet if it is to be consistently interpretable as addition of numbers.

Before defining the *SF*, however, it is necessary to give a formal definition of the set of expressions consisting of x's and o's. Because we are not assuming any bound on the number of states that a register can take (and hence on the length of the strings of x's and o's), the definition of the strings must be given recursively as

(1) o is a string,

(2) x is a string,

(3) if T is a string, then so is To (that is, string T followed by o).

(4) if T is a string, then so is Tx (that is, string T followed by x).

A simpler way to express (1) through (4) is in Backus-Nauer form as T ::= o|x|To|Tx, where ::= means "is defined to be" and | means "or."

Using the definition of the strings; the semantic function can then be defined recursively as

(1) $SF(o) = 0$ (the semantic interpretation of o is the number zero),

(2) $SF(x) = 1$ (the semantic interpretation of x is the number one),

(3) $SF(To) = 2*SF(T)$ (the semantic interpretation of a string T followed by o is twice the semantic interpretation of T alone),

(4) $SF(Tx) = 2*SF(T) + 1$ (the semantic interpretation of a string T followed by x is twice the semantic interpretation of T alone plus one).

This constitutes an example of a semantic function, defined recursively on the structure of the strings of symbols. It is analogous to Tarski's method for defining the semantics of sentences in some formal calculus in terms of their combinatorial properties. This mapping function is nontrivial. In fact it defines the semantic interpretation of a *place-value* numeral notation.

For this semantic function to be useful, however, there must be regularities in the state transitions in the computer that correspond to mathematical operations defined over the interpretations of the symbols in the intended domain. In other words there must be state transitions that *preserve the intended interpretation SF*. One such regularity, which was associated with the occurrence of # in the instruction register, has already been proposed. For # to correspond to addition (or alternatively for it to be consistently interpretable as addition), state transitions must preserve the semantic interpretation of the symbol strings under the mathematically defined operation of addition (defined, say, in terms of

Peano's axioms). In other words something like the following must be true:

If the computer is in the state characterized by the description
1. Register 1 "contains" (or *IF* maps it onto) string T_1,
2. Register 2 "contains" (or *IF* maps it onto) string T_2,
3. The instruction register "contains" (or *IF* maps it onto) #;
then the computer goes into the state characterized by
4. Register 3 "contains" (or *IF* maps it onto) the string T_3, where the relation $SF(T_3) = SF(T_1) + SF(T_2)$ holds.

In other words the (mathematically defined) sum of the semantic interpretations of the two register states must always correspond to the semantic interpretation of the state of the third register. Note that the interpretation is in the abstract domain of *numbers*, where operations such as addition are mathematically defined, whereas the symbols being interpreted (the domain of the *SF* function) are functional states, defined by *IF* as equivalence classes of physical states of the computer.

These ideas and distinctions arise in clear form in the case of conventional computers. They apply equally however, in the case of cognition, even though our subjective experience suggests that what is going on in the mind may be different. The empirical facts and the requirement of explanatory adequacy, however, demand all three distinct levels (physical, symbolic, and semantic) in the case of human cognition, just as we needed them in the computer case. Although the arguments are beyond the scope of this chapter (see Pylyshyn 1984), it appears that to explain intelligent human behavior, we need to appeal to all three levels of organization.

1. We need the knowledge level to explain why certain goals and beliefs tend to lead to certain behaviors, and why the behaviors can be changed in rational ways when new beliefs are added by telling things. For example, to explain why I am sitting here at this moment striking these particular keys of my keyboard, one must mention my beliefs about cognitive science, my beliefs about what will become of this manuscript, and my general goals of conveying true information to those who might read the book in which this chapter is intended to appear. Without this level we could not capture such regularities as, for example, the fact that if I were to have the belief that publication of the book had been canceled, I would exhibit quite different behavior *regardless of the particular "stimuli" that might have led me to have this (presumably false) belief*. This sort of semantically characterizable malleability of behavior is referred to as *cognitive penetrability* and has been used as diagnostic of behavior requiring knowledge-level explanation (for more on this see the section 2.3, as well as Pylyshyn 1984).

2. We need the symbol level to explain such things as why some tasks take longer or result in more errors than other tasks. Information-

processing psychology is full of examples of discovering that the form of the representation makes a difference to their behavior in experiments. For example, in problem-solving experiments it makes a difference whether subjects encode the fact that all the objects in a box are red or the equivalent fact that none of the objects is blue.

3. We obviously need the biological level to explain such things as the effects of drugs or jet lag or brain damage on behavior. It is also possible that we may need the biological level to explain other things as well, such as possibly the nature of cognitive development or maturation or psychopathology, and perhaps some changes that are now called learning; exactly what facts fall at each of the three levels remains to a large extent an open empirical question.

Objections to the Classical View

There has always been opposition to the view that we have symbol structures in our heads. The idea that the brain thinks by writing symbols and reading them sounds absurd to many. It suggests to some people that we have been influenced too much by the way current electronic computers work. The basic source of uneasiness seems to come from the fact that we do not have the subjective experience that we are manipulating symbols. But subjective experience has been a notoriously misleading source of evidence for what goes on in the mind. Research in human information processing reveals countless processes that clearly must be occurring (for example, parsing, inference) of which we have little or no subjective awareness.

Arguments for the necessity of positing symbol structures in human reasoning—for a "language of thought"—are given elsewhere (Fodor 1975, Pylyshyn 1984, Fodor and Pylyshyn 1988). Details of these arguments are beyond the scope of this chapter. For the present purposes, the following summary will suffice.

If the knowledge-level description is correct, then we have to explain how it is possible for a physical system, like a human being, to behave in ways that correspond to the knowledge-level principles while at the same time being governed by physical laws. The content of knowledge is related to the state of a system by a *semantic* relation, which is quite a different relation from the ones that appear on natural laws (for one thing the object of the relation need not exist). At present there is only one candidate explanation for how knowledge-level principles can be causally realized, and that is the one that builds on a set of ideas going back to the insights of Boole, Hilbert, Turing, Frege, and other logicians. It says that knowledge is *encoded* by a system of symbolic codes, which themselves are physically realized, and that it is the physical properties of the codes that cause the behaviors in question.

What Fodor and Pylyshyn (1988) have added to this general statement is an argument that the system of codes must be *structured* much like a language (as indeed it is in the various logical calculi that have been developed). The argument stems in part from the observation that both representational capacity and inferential capacity in intelligent systems is *systematic*. Representational or inferential capacities are not punctate—they do not occur in isolation; the capacity for representing certain things or for drawing certain inferences goes along with the capacity for representing other things and for drawing other inferences. For example, an intelligent system that is capable of representing certain situations (for example, that John loves Mary, or that a small red ball is in a large blue box) must also be capable—whether or not this capacity is exercised—of representing other situations involving the same conceptual components (for example, that Mary loves John or that a large blue ball is in small red box). Similarly any intelligent system that can draw certain inferences (for example, can infer from knowing that it is sunny and warm and humid that it is sunny; that is, infer P from P and Q and R) can also draw other related inferences (for example, can infer from knowing that it is sunny and warm that it is sunny; that is, infer P from P and Q).

This sort of systematicity follows automatically from the use of structured symbolic expressions to represent knowledge and to serve as the basis for inference. In other words it is a side effect of a classical architecture.[3] In contrast it is a property that must be stipulated and enforced by the theorist (that is, it is a free empirical parameter) in other nonsymbolic architectures, such as the so-called connectionist architectures.

It must be stressed that at present there exists no alternative to what Newell (1980) has called the *physical symbol system* assumption for dealing with reasoning in a mechanical way, even though there are many speculative discussions of how one might eventually be able to do without symbols. Therefore even if one does not accept the various arguments that have been given for the ultimate necessity of symbol structures, the rational strategy is to continue with the classical assumption until some better alternative comes along. At least that is the strategy adopted in every other mature science.

2.2 Computational Methodologies in Cognitive Science: The High Road and the Low Road

As I have already suggested, computers can enter into the detailed process of constructing models of cognitive processes at several levels. In practice the more fine-grained the correspondence match, the narrower the range of phenomena the model is able to cover. For this reason experimental psychologists, who have traditionally been more concerned with models that can be tested in quite specific detail against laboratory data, have generally worked with models that are relatively narrow in scope. On the other hand investigators working within the artificial intelligence tradition have been more concerned with explaining the general abilities or capacities in question and postponing the detailed empirical validation of the mechanisms and algorithms actually used in the model. These have sometimes been referred to as the "low road" and the "high road," respectively, to understanding cognitive processes. They represent different strategies for arriving at the same ultimate end: modeling human cognitive processes.[4]

David Marr was one of the most influential champions of the high road, or at least of the strategy that begins at the high end of the road. He has proposed that there are three levels at which cognitive processes may be studied. He referred to these as the level of the *computation*, the level of the *algorithm*, and the level of the *mechanism*. A theory at the first level was called a type I theory. Although the notion of a type I theory is not very well defined, Marr did give some examples, chiefly from his own work or that of his colleagues.

Any domain that has a closed formal characterization of the task or of the input/output function being carried out has a type I theory. Frequently cited examples involve the recovery of 3-D structure from a variety of types of visual cues. Thus, for example, there are at least partial theories concerning what is entailed in recovering structure from motion, stereopsis, shading, or contour information. Such theories give a precise characterization of the conditions under which the "inverse mapping" from the data in question (for example, motion of points or contours on a 2-D surface) to a 3-D structure is possible, and they formally characterize the mapping. Such theories invariably rely on recognizing certain "natural constraints" that exist in the world and are exploited by the visual system in recovering the 3-D structure.

In those cases in which there is a type I theory of some particular cognitive skill, it might be possible to determine the conditions under which that skill will succeed or fail to accomplish some particular task. For example, if we had a mathematical characterization of the relations between certain features of the light and the percepts that they engendered (that is, a type I theory of certain aspects of visual perception), then we might be able to relate the light features in question to the scene layout (via projective geometry) and determine the conditions under which perception mediated by those features would be veridical.

This in fact is what was done in modeling such processes as those involved in the perception of form from motion (Ullman 1979), of surface orientation from texture (Stevens 1981), or of stereopsis (Marr and Poggio 1979). In the first of these, for example, Ullman showed mathematically that the unambiguous recovery of 3-D shape from the motion of certain visual features on the retina (for example, random dots in the case of the kinetic depth effect studied by Wallach and O'Connell (1953)) can only be done if certain conditions are met. The mathematical function relating moving proximal features to the 3-D scene from which the features are projected is unique only if (a) there are enough distinct views and distinct features (three views and four features for orthographic projection or two views and five features for perspective projection), and (b) if the process is constrained in the possible interpretations it considers. Without (b) a unique function is not possible because the same proximal feature movements can originate from arbitrarily many different distal configurations. If the interpretation is constrained by what Ullman calls the rigidity assumption, however, then a unique interpretation is possible in very nearly just those cases where people give the true interpretation. The constraint is that the process attempts to provide an interpretation of the features as originating from points on a rigid body in motion and fails to provide any interpretation if that is not possible—it does not consider other logically possible interpretations. Although this is not yet a completely adequate type I theory (for example, it fails for biological motion, such as studied by Johansson (1975), and for perceived elastic deformations), it provides an original *computational* account of the kinetic depth effect.

Note that such a mathematical result is not based on a detailed study of the process of human perception, only on the fact that it has a certain capacity, namely, the capacity to perceive a unique 3-D structure from the motion of certain feature points (that is, on the existence of the kinetic depth effect). The mathematical result tells us the conditions under which such an accomplishment is possible. Thus it tells us something about the intrinsic requirements of that task; requirements that the visual system must somehow meet. In Ullman's case the function was also described in a constructive manner—that is, in a manner that allowed it to be computed from the sort of information that is available to a computer equipped with appropriate transducers. The latter property is also an important part of the computationalist program. Of course how the human visual system does in fact compute that function is a question whose answer depends on further empirical considerations. Notice, however, that simply knowing some of the properties of the function that the visual system computes allows one to understand why perception is generally veridical even though, contrary to Gibson, we know that the step from activating sensors to perception involves a fallible process (an inferencelike process that, however, is insensitive to general knowledge of the world). The reason it is generally veridical is that the conditions under which this quasi-inferential inverse mapping is valid, are ones that happen in fact to be frequently met in our kind of world—that is, the rigidity assumption is generally true, at least to a first approximation, in our world (though it may well not be generally true in, say, the world inhabited by fish).

What Marr was advocating is a special case of a top-down research strategy, wherein one proceeds by attempting to discover the broader outlines of a problem domain before solving some of the detailed subproblems. This sort of approach is practiced systematically in computer science, where—sometimes under the name "structured programming"—it is considered the strategy of choice in the design of computer systems. Consequently it is the strategy that characterizes artificial intelligence approaches to understanding cognition. Marr went even further to advocate that one should not worry about developing a system that exhibits the performance in question until one has at least attempted to develop a theory of the task (a type I theory), and consequently that one should work first in domains (such as perhaps vision) that lend themselves to a type I theory, rather than in domains like commonsense reasoning where there may not be such a theory. He argued that if one begins by hypothesizing a particular algorithm used by an organism without first understanding exactly what the algorithm is supposed to be computing, one runs the danger of simply mimicking fragments of behavior without understanding its principles or the goals that the behavior is satisfying.[5] This is similar to Chomsky and others' methodological injunction not to hypothesize learning mechanisms for the acquisition of certain skills until one has a good theory of the steady-state skill itself.

Although few people in cognitive science take a position as extreme as Marr's, there continue to be differences in style of approach in cognitive science research. There are differences between people who are concerned with generality and with the search for general principles, as opposed to those who wish to account for experimental variance. There are also differences between approaches that place top priority on the sufficiency criterion, and hence construct working programs that cover some domain of skill, as opposed to those who are concerned with deciding between one or two general options (for example, deciding whether a certain phenomenon, say, the recognition that a stimulus is a member of a previously memorized set, is the result of a parallel search, a serial self-terminating search, or a serial exhaustive search).

To some extent which of these strategies is followed depends on the area of research or the particular empirical phenomena being investigated. Thus the study of early vision is frequently pursued by attempting to implement algorithms and explore their entailments. Problems associated with language understanding and discourse processes are often pursued within that tradition as well. On the other hand the study of learning, memory, and problem solving has been successfully approached by both the high road and the low road. Insofar as the empirical phenomenon of interest can be attributed to some particular isolated mechanism or process, it may be possible to establish empirically the nature of that process by carrying out a series of experiments. But to the extent that the phenomenon arises from the interaction of many processes, it may not be possible to explain it without a more general model that embodies the entire set of relevant processes. The pitfalls of attempting to answer general questions by isolating effects and by attributing phenomena to particular features of the process have been well documented by Newell (1973c), who argued (as the title of his paper says) that "You can't play twenty questions with nature and win."

Despite these pitfalls it appears to be possible to study certain specific subprocesses in detail in some cases without building large-scale models. Indeed the area of cognitive science sometimes known as information-processing psychology has been dominated by the empirical validation of minimodels. The analysis of cognitive processes into stages using mental chronometry (see, for example, Posner 1978) is a good example. The methodology for such fine-grained analysis of cognitive processes is discussed in chapter 7. To take a specific example, it appears to be possible to study aspects of short-term memory without developing large-scale models (see, for example, Sperling 1967). Indeed because the models are so small-scale, theorizing in this area has typically not involved implementing models in the form of computer programs.

But even here one must be cautious in concluding that there is nothing to be gained by actually implementing small-scale models. Newell (1973b) provided an excellent example of how the attempt to design a computer model to account for certain empirical phenomena of short-term memory can itself lead to new hypotheses that might otherwise not have arisen. In that particular example the attempt to implement a model in an independently motivated architecture led to a particular way of accounting for Sternberg's (1970) short-term-memory–scanning results, the so-called decoding hypothesis, which involves neither exhaustive nor self-terminating search (the two options that had been under investigation in much of the experimental research) and contains both parallel and serial components (two options that also had been assumed to exhaust the possibilities).

The Control Issue

The commitment to the construction of a model meeting the sufficiency condition, that is, one that actually generates token behaviors, forces one to confront the problem of how and under what conditions the internal representations and the rules are invoked in the course of generating actions. These are question that concern the *control* of the process. Although they form a central topic of study in computer science, they were virtually never raised in a cognitive psychology that was not constrained by computational sufficiency. Indeed one of the main criticisms that was leveled against the early work by cognitive psychologists like Tolman was that their theories dealt only with the organism's representations (mental maps), but had no way of saying how these representations would lead to action. For example, in an early critique of this cognitivist approach Guthrie (1935, p. 172) wrote, "In his concern for what goes on in the rat's mind, Tolman has neglected to predict what the rat will do. So far as the theory is concerned, the rat is left buried in thought; if he gets to the food-box at the end, that is his concern, not the concern of the theory."

There is much more to understanding control structures than knowing how operations are sequenced. We are so used to thinking of procedures as sequences of instructions that continue their fixed course until some conditional branch operation detects a specified condition that alternative organizations do not readily spring to mind. Yet this is just one type of organization of control—one in which control is *passed* along a linear sequence from operation to operation; when one operation finishes it passes control to the next operation in line. In computer science and artificial intelligence, however, there is a great deal of interest in very different control schemes—ones that may change psychologists' thinking about the range of possibilities available for converting representations into actions.

In what follows I briefly survey some of the issues that arise when one considers the problem of controlling the way that processes unfold in response to representations, rules, and the contingencies of the environment. My purpose is not to describe the range of control structures that are currently being studied in computer science, but merely to provide some intuitive sense of what some of the distinctions are in this field and to suggest that cognitive science has much to learn from this area of development. Considerations such as these are not likely to be raised without a commitment to the realization of the process model on a computer. And because control issues are one of the central areas of study in computer science, progress in developing computational models of cognitive processes will very likely depend on technical ideas originating in computer science (and more particularly in artificial intelligence).

One of the earliest breakthroughs in understanding the nature of control was the articulation of the idea of feedback from the environment to be controlled. With this a certain balance was restored between a device and its environment: Although only the device is credited with having a goal, the responsibility for its behavior is shared. At times when the environment is passive, the initiative appears to come primarily from the device, whereas at other times the environment appears to intervene, and the initiative seems to go in the opposite direction. This notion of the responsibility for initiation of different actions is fundamental to the understanding of control. In the case of most computer programs, the most common idea has been that of control moving from point to point, or from instruction to instruction, in a largely predetermined way. Such sequencing of instructions makes the notion of *flow* of control quite natural, and branch instructions make it equally natural to think of *passing* or *sending* control to another locus. When control passing is combined with a primitive message-passing facility (for passing arguments), *subroutines* become possible. And because subroutines can be nested—that is, subroutines can themselves send control to still lower subroutines with the assurance that control will eventually find its way back—the notion of a *hierarchy* of control also emerges. Miller, Galanter, and Pribram (1960) saw the psychological importance of the idea of hierarchical subroutines; they called them test-operate-test-exit, or TOTE, units and suggested that they should be viewed as the basic theoretical unit of psychology, replacing the ubiquitous reflex arc. This idea has been very influential in shaping psychologists' thinking about cognition.

There are a number of good reasons why a hierarchical system of control is such a powerful concept. By keeping the interactions between routine and subroutine simple (in terms of both when control is passed and what messages are sent along with it), it becomes easier to think of each routine as a nearly independent subsystem; and that makes the whole system easier to add to, modify, and understand (see the classical discussion of the importance of hierarchical organization in nature in Simon 1969). Each routine in the hierarchy can be thought of as defining some (sub)goal in an overall *goal-directed* system. Passing control to a subroutine amounts to activating a subgoal, and control is returned when that subgoal is consummated. So powerful an idea is this that its shortcomings were largely overlooked for many years.

As early as 1962, however, Allen Newell (Newell 1962) pointed out some of the rigidity in such an organization. So long as each subroutine is a narrow "specialist," such as a routine for searching a list, the usual highly restricted communication between routine and subroutine works well; you can just pass the arguments and a return address to that routine and give it control. It will then return with an answer when it is finished. But if the subroutine is not such a narrow specialist, it might help to be able to communicate each task in more flexible terms. Furthermore it might help if the subroutine's progress could be monitored along the way to prevent it from using up an unwarranted amount of time and resources (for example, memory) on some relatively minor task or on a task that some other process might be able to determine was doomed to fail. Likewise it would help if the subroutine could report its results more flexibly; especially if it could report what went wrong in cases where it failed. How to convert these desiderata into efficient computational form has been one of the main design concerns in developing artificial intelligence programming languages.

A variety of different control structures can be characterized in terms of two distinctions: (1) between *sending* control (where the initiative lies with the *old* locus) and *capturing* control (where the initiative lies with the *new* locus), and (2) between *directing* a message to one specified recipient and *broadcasting* it to all routines or "modules" at once. For example, in the standard subroutine-hierarchy case, control is always *sent* (by the routine that already has it), and a message (containing parameters and a return address) is *directed* specifically to the routine that is being given control; and when the subgoal is achieved, control is *sent* back, along with a result message. In pattern-invoked procedure calls, such as used in Planner or Prolog, when a task needs to be done, a message describing the goal is broadcast, and control is then captured by some module designed to respond to that particular goal message. This is also the basic idea of what is sometimes called a *blackboard* control structure, of which the old Pandemonium system (see, for example, Lindsay and Norman 1977) and the newer Hearsay-II speech recognition system (Erman, Hayes-Roth, Lesser, and Reddy 1980) are examples.

Production systems are special cases of pattern invoked procedure calls. In production systems messages are also broadcast, and control is captured. But when the production finishes, it again just broadcasts a message. Its basic control cycle is called a *recognize-act* cycle, in contrast with the more traditional *fetch-executive* cycle of conventional computing. The current work on production systems is described in chapter 3.

The distinction between whether processes are invoked explicitly by commands, indirectly by the occurrence of other events, or implicitly by certain conditions being met is important in computer science. The distinction is closely related to the difference between a test and an "interrupt" (the latter of which can occur in arbitrary relation to a process). The distinction between data-invoked, or event-invoked, processes (characteristic of so-called demon procedures, which include "if-added" or "if-altered" or "if-examined" procedures that are evoked by various distinct types of computational events), and explicit process-invoked procedures (characteristic of what are sometimes called servant or if-needed procedures) is an important recurring theme in the study of control regimes.

Many of the concerns in designing new architectures reduce to the following three questions: (1) how to enable flexible and effective communication among different processes or modules, (2) how to ensure that all relevant information (and as little as possible irrelevant information) is brought to bear in making decisions or inferences, and (3) how to withhold and release the making of decisions until the appropriate times. The second question has received a great deal of research and has led to some proposals for organizing knowledge so that its relevance to particular topics is easily determined (for example, "Frames," "Scripts," "schemas"). The third question is also of special concern to psychologists (see, for example, Bransford and Johnson 1973) who have demonstrated experimentally that many inferences are carried out in advance of being required for some particular task (for example, at the time utterances are heard, as opposed to at the time their content is needed for some decision). Making decisions or executing procedures must sometimes be withheld until the appropriate context is available. Several proposals for dealing with such linguistic problems as referential opacity rely on this notion of withholding execution pending the appropriate context. For instance, Davies and Isard's (1972) discussion of language comprehension places considerable emphasis on the importance of withholding the evaluation of procedures that attempt to identify the referents of various parts of an utterance until the appropriate time. Thus there is a growing recognition among investigators interested in the problems of cognitive psychology that a variety of questions related to control must play a more prominent role.

For psychologists it has primarily been the attempt to provide a running system that has forced such issues to the fore. Without the need to think in terms of a running system, people have typically focused on what are sometimes called "permissive" rules—such as the rules of logic or of grammar—which specify the relations among representations that are permissible. In that case there is no need to be concerned with the conditions under which particular rules are invoked or with the implications of such control issues for the cognitive architecture.

There is no denying that the system of permissive rules is important. Without a distinction between what Chomsky calls a competence theory and a performance theory, or what McCarthy and Hayes (1969) refer to as the epistemological and the heuristic problems of intelligence, we can find ourselves simply mimicking the most frequent behavior rather than inferring the underlying mechanisms. Yet according to the computational view, understanding a process also requires having a theory of what makes the process unfold as it does on particular occasions, and that in turn requires that issues of control and of the appropriate cognitive architecture be addressed as well.

The Empirical Status of Computational Models: Levels of Correspondence and Strong Equivalence

Regardless of whether one takes the high road or the low road, in cognitive science one is ultimately interested in whether the computational model is empirically valid—whether it corresponds to human cognitive processes. "Corresponding," however, is not a straightforward notion; correspondence can occur at many levels. If a computational process is to be a serious candidate as an explanatory model of mental processing, one is owed some account, as explicit as possible, of how this model relates to the domain of phenomena it is to explain. Specifying the empirical claims entailed by the model is the task of the theory that the model instantiates. Such a theory might, for example, simply claim that the model realizes the same input/output function as the organism being modeled, that it is perhaps a theory of that function, or a type I theory in Marr's terms. As we have seen in discussing the high-road methodology in the previous section, even at this most general level of correspondence, such a theory can make a substantial contribution to understanding the process by providing a theory of the demands of the task.

A stronger claim might be that the model realizes some particular function using the same *method* as the person being modeled. The notion of a method is not very well defined nor consistently used, even among computer scientists. However, it generally entails something more specific than just input/output equivalence. For example, we talk of the relaxation method for solving equations of interacting constraints, Newton's method for locating minima and maxima of a function, the Fourier transform method of computing the effect of a certain filter on a waveform, and so on. These provide a more specific indication of the nature of the process than we would get if we knew only the input/output function.

To specify in greater detail what sequence of steps the system went through would be to provide something like an *algorithm* for the process. The notion of algorithm is somewhat better established in computer science than is the notion of method. For example, there are a variety of well-known algorithms for various kinds of numerical approximations to functions (which are in fact cataloged and published), for parsing context-free languages (for example, the Early algorithm), and so on. Algorithms for sorting and merging lists are another major area of study (see, for example, Knuth 1968), as are algorithms for table lookup.

There are of course even finer levels of comparison between computational processes. For example, an even more specific level of comparison for computational models is that of a *program*: the encoding of a particular algorithm in some programming language. Even finer levels of comparison between computational systems are possible when implemented on actual computers. For example, we could have identical programs that were run on physically different computers, and so on. Thus there is plenty of scope in the possible claims that a theory might make about the level of correspondence between model and empirical domain, or about what properties of the model could be said to have "psychological reality." Clearly, if the computational system is to be viewed as a model of the cognitive *process*, rather than as a simulation of cognitive behavior, it must correspond to the mental process in more detail than is implied by weak equivalence. On the other hand it is equally clear that because computers are not only made of quite different stuff from brains, but the details of how they realize particular operations (say by certain register transfer paths, and by using binary mechanisms and bit-shifting operations) are different from the ways brains work. The correspondence between computational models and cognitive processes seems to fall somewhere in between these extremes.

The general assumption in cognitive science has been that the appropriate level of comparison corresponds roughly to the intuitive notion of algorithm. From our point of view we can think of two computational systems as strongly equivalent, or as being different realizations of the same algorithm or the same cognitive process, if they can be represented by the same program in some theoretically specified computer. A simple way to put this is to say that we individuate cognitive processes in terms of their expression in the canonical language of this theoretical machine.

The functional (as opposed to anatomical) structure of the machine—or what we call its *functional architecture* or just simply its *architecture*—represents our theoretical definition of the right level of specificity (or level of aggregation) at which to view cognitive processes. It is the level at which data structures (or states) of the model are semantically interpreted, with the semantic domain being the cognitive one (that is, in which the states represent the things that are the objects of thought and reasoning, what subjects are thinking *about*). A description of the functional architecture also sets out the functional properties of the cognitive system that are determined by its structure (rather than by the instantaneous contents of its memory), properties such as the functional resources that the brain makes available (for example, which operations are primitive, how memory is organized and accessed, what sequences are allowed, what limitations exist on the passing of arguments and on the capacities of various buffers, and so on). Specifying the functional architecture of a system is very much like providing a manual defining some particular programming language.

Thus one way to address the issue of the appropriate level of comparison between a model and a cognitive process—or the notion of strong equivalence of processes—is by providing a specification of the functional architecture of a "cognitive computer," which I will henceforth refer to as the *cognitive architecture*. Much of the work described in Pylyshyn 1984 is concerned with developing this idea—with providing constraints on an adequate cognitive architecture and showing its relevance to the computational view of mind. For the present purpose the notion of functional architecture will be introduced by discussing the role that this idea plays in computer science and by introducing the closely related, though in many ways unique, role it is required to play in cognitive science. The following discussion illustrates the point that *any* notion of correspondence stronger that weak equivalence *must* presuppose some underlying functional architecture. Thus the question is not whether we need to worry about the cognitive architecture in developing computational models. Rather the issue is whether we can be content to leave it as an implicit assumption—largely conditioned by the functional architecture of currently available computers—or whether we ought to make it explicit and endeavor to bring empirical criteria to bear in constraining it.

Algorithms and Cognitive Architecture

Cognitive algorithms, the central concept in computational psychology, are understood to be executed by the cognitive architecture. According to the strong realism view that many of us have advocated, a valid cognitive model must execute the *same algorithm* as that carried out by subjects. But now it turns out that *which* algorithms can be carried out in a direct way depends on the functional architecture of the device. Devices with different functional architectures cannot in general *directly* execute the same algorithms.[6] But typical commercially available computers are likely to have a functional architecture that differs significantly in detail from that of brains.[7] Hence we would expect that in constructing a computer model of the mental architecture will first have to be *emulated* (that is, itself modeled) before the mental algorithm can be implemented.

For an algorithm to serve as a model of a cognitive process, it must be presented in some standard or canonical form or notation, for example, as a program in some programming language. What is typically overlooked when we do this is the extent to which the class of algorithms that can be considered is conditioned by the assumptions we make regarding what basic operations are possible, how these may interact, how operations are sequenced, what data structures are possible, and so on. Such assumptions are an intrinsic part of our choice of descriptive formalism because descriptive formalism defines what I have been calling the functional architecture of the system.

Yet the range of programming languages or functional architectures that are conveniently available is actually quite narrow. Most available architectures are register-based, in which symbols are stored and retrieved by their numerical or symbolic "addresses," control is transferred sequentially through a program (except for "branching" instructions), and operations on symbols are accomplished by retrieving them from memory, placing them in a designated register, applying one of the primitive commands to them, and then storing the resulting symbol back into memory. Although there are variants of this basic pattern, the main idea of a sequential process proceeding through a series of "fetch," "operate," and "store" operations has been dominant since the beginning of digital computation (see the previous section for a discussion of alternatives being examined in computer science research). This goes for both hardware and software (see a discussion of the latter in Backus 1978).

Because our experience has been with such a narrow range of architectures, we tend to associate the notion of computation, and hence of algorithm, with the particular class of algorithms that can be executed by architectures in this limited class. However, this is misleading because, as I noted, different architectures permit different algorithms to be executed.

This point is best illustrated by considering examples of several simple architectures. Perhaps the most primitive machine architecture is the original binary-coded Turing machine. Although this machine is universal, in the sense that it can be programmed to compute any computable function, anyone who has tried to write procedures for it will have noticed that most computations are extremely complex. More important, however, the complexity of the sequence of operations it must go through varies with such things as the task and the nature of the input in ways that are quite different from that of machines with a more conventional architecture. For example, the number of basic steps required to look up a string of symbols in such a Turing machine increases as the square of the number of strings stored.

In contrast to this architecture, in what is called a register architecture (an architecture that has what is usually referred to as random access memory, in which retrieving a symbol by name or by "reference" is a primitive operation), the time complexity for looking up a symbol in a table can, under certain conditions, be made independent of the number of strings stored. Because of this a register architecture can directly execute certain algorithms (for example, the hash-coding lookup algorithm) which are impossible in the Turing machine—in spite of the fact that the Turing machine is universal and therefore can compute the *same function* as the algorithm or be programmed to be "weakly equivalent" to the algorithm. In other words it can compute the same lookup function, but not with the same complexity profile and hence not by using the same hash-coding algorithm.

Now of course a Turing machine could be made to mimic the sequence of states that the register machine goes through by first arranging for the Turing machine to compute the functions realized by *each individual operation* of the register machine or in other words to simulate each individual step that the register machine takes in executing its algorithm. But in that case the Turing machine would first be *emulating* the architecture of the register machine and then executing the algorithm in the emulated architecture, a very different matter from computing it directly by the Turing machine.

The distinction between directly executing an algorithm and executing it by first emulating some other functional architecture is crucial to cognitive science. It bears on the central question of which aspects of the computation can be taken literally as part of the model and which aspects are to be considered as mere implementation details (like the color and materials out of which a physical model of the double helix of DNA is built). We naturally expect that we shall have to have ways of implementing primitive cognitive operations in computers, and that the details of how this is done may have little empirical content.

From the point of view of cognitive science, it is important to be explicit about *why* a model works the way it does and to independently justify the crucial assumptions about the cognitive architecture. That is, it is important for the use of computational models as part of an explanation, rather than merely to mimic some performance, that we not take certain architectural features for granted simply because they happen to be available in our computer language. We must first explicitly acknowledge that certain noncomputational properties originate with certain assumed properties of the cognitive architecture, and then we must attempt to empirically motivate and justify such assumptions. Otherwise important features of our model may be left resting on adventitious and unmotivated assumptions.

This issue frequently arises in connection with claims that certain ways of doing intellectual tasks, for example, by the use of mental imagery, bypasses the need for explicit representation of certain logical or even physical properties of the represented domain and bypasses the need for inefficient combinatorially explosive processes like logical inference. The issue is frequently stated in terms of hypotheses that one or another mental function is carried out by an "analog" process. The whole issue of analog versus digital processing is complex and has not in general been well understood (see the discussion in chapter 7 of Pylyshyn 1984). For the present I consider only simple cases involving the claim that some process was carried out by "direct readout" or otherwise noncognitive or noninferential means. From the present perspective this would be interpreted as the claim that some cognitive function was actually part of the cognitive architecture.

Consider cases such as the following: People have occasionally suggested that subjects do not need to have knowledge of relational properties such as, say, transitivity, in making certain inferences, such as in three-term series problems (for example, "John is taller than Mary and John is shorter than Fred. Who is tallest?"). According to this view, all subjects have to do is arrange the three items in order (either in a list or in an image) and read the answer off—they simply *notice* which object is first (or last) in the list. But of course even if a subject can solve the problem in this way, that does not mean that tacit knowledge[8] of formal properties (for example, transitivity) of the relation "taller than" is not needed.

There are at least two reasons why one might have to postulate knowledge of formal relations. First, the decision to represent "taller" by something like "further on the list" must have been based on the tacit recognition that the two relations were of the same formal type (a list would not, for example, have been suitable for representing the relation "is married to"). Second, although ordering three names in a list and then examining the list for the position of a particular name may seem straightforward and free from logical deduction, a little thought will show that the ability to carry out this operation mentally, as distinct from physically, presupposes a great deal about the available primitive mental operations. In particular, appealing to the existence of a "mental list" (or some such structure) involves certain assumptions about the properties that such a structure *intrinsically* possesses. For example, if the subject has a mental representation of items A, B, and C and reasons (according to the theory) by placing A and B in a certain order and then adding C next in the sequence, the model must assume that placing C next to B leaves the relation between A and B unchanged and the relation of A to C (with B between them) remains the same with respect to the relevant represented relation (that is, tallness) as that between A and B.

Assumptions such as these are justifiable only if there exists an operation in the cognitive architecture that has the same formal mathematical properties (that is, falls under the same system of logical axioms) as the relations "taller" and "further along the ordering." Furthermore even if such an operation is part of the cognitive architecture, one is still not entitled to assume that the use of this capacity requires no further appeal to tacit knowledge of logical constructs like transitivity, as the first point shows. To take another timely example, matrix data structures have frequently been used to represent the spatial properties of images (see, for example, Kosslyn and Shwartz 1977, Funt 1980). This is a convenient way to represent spatial layout, partly because we tend to think of matrices in spatial terms anyway. In addition, however, this structure seems to make certain consequences available without any apparent need for certain deductive steps involving reference to knowledge of geometry. For example, when we represent the locations of imagined places in our model by filling in cells of a matrix, we can "read off" such facts as which places are adjacent, which places are left of, right of, above, or below a given place, and which places are in between a given pair of places. Furthermore when a particular object is moved to a new place, its spatial relations to other places need not be recomputed. In an important sense this is implicit in the data structure. Such properties make the matrix a much more natural representation than, say, a list of assertions specifying the shape of objects and their locations relative to other objects.

But, as in the example of solving the three-term series problem without apparently using logical inference rules (by using a list), such properties of matrices arise from the existence of certain formal properties that are part of the architecture of virtually all contemporary computers. Such properties are not, however, constitutive of computing. They would not, for instance, be available in a Turing machine architecture. For a matrix data structure with the desired properties to be realizable, the architecture must provide at least the primitive capacity to address the content of a representation by place—that is, it must be possible to name a location and to ask for the content of a named location. This itself requires what is called a register architecture (or some other kind of location-addressable store).

Furthermore in this architecture it must also be possible to primitively generate the names of places adjacent to a given place (that is, it must be possible to do this without appealing to other representations or to tacit knowledge of geometry or anything else that would involve intermediate inferential steps). This is necessary if we want "scanning" of the representation to be a (nondeductive) primitive operation. In addition there must be primitive predicates that, when applied to names, evaluate the relative directions of places corresponding to those names (for example, two-place predicates such as *right-of* must be primitive in the architecture). This in turn implies that there are at least two independent total orderings over the set of names. In addition if the relative distance between places is to be significant in this representation, then there might have to be further primitive operations that can be applied to place names so as to evaluate, say, relative size (for example, the predicate *larger-than*).

This whole array of formal properties is available in all common computer architectures because they all use numerical expressions for register (that is, place) names and have built-in primitive arithmetic operations. But these properties are part of such architectures for reasons that have nothing to do with the theoretical needs of cognitive science. When these features are exploited in building cognitive models, we tacitly assume that such operations are part of the cognitive architecture of the mind—an assumption that clearly needs to be independently motivated and justified. Arguments have rarely been provided for any such proposals. Among the few suggestions for such abstract architectural features that I have seen are due to Brouwer (1964) and Nicod (1970), who for quite different reasons proposed that *succession* be viewed as a cognitive primitive, and G. Spencer Brown (1969), who proposed that drawing a (binary) distinction (a sort of universal figure-ground conceptual separation) is a primitive operation of the mind. Of course a great deal of the recent cognitive science research program— at least since Newell's seminal paper on production systems (Newell 1973b)—has been concerned with proposing specific features of the cognitive architecture (see, for example, chapter 3).

In choosing a particular architecture, one makes a commitment concerning which functions are the free parameters that can be tailored to fit specific situations, and which are fixed over a certain range of influences or are primitive subfunctions shared by all processes in a certain class. Restrictions on the availability of certain primitive computational functions is a virtue if our goal is to provide an explanation. The more constrained a notation or architecture, the greater the explanatory power of resulting models.

This is exactly the problem of reducing the degrees of freedom available for fitting a model to observations. Each function that can be attributed to the functional architecture, rather than to the flexibly alterable program, attains the status of a constant rather than that of a free empirical parameter in the model. It provides a principled rationale for why on some particular occasion the model takes one particular form as opposed to other logically possible ones. It is precisely the lack of such a rationale that makes some computational models ad hoc. One goal in developing explanatory cognitive models then would be to fix as many properties as possible by building them into the fixed cognitive architecture. Opposing this goal, however, is the need to account for the remarkable flexibility of human cognition. This in turn leads us to attribute the behavioral regularities to the way in which the architecture is used—that is, to the programs and knowledge that allow the relatively rigid architecture to be exploited in generating behavior that is highly plastic. The stimulus-independence of cognition provides one of the strongest reasons for attributing much of its manifest behavior to tacit knowledge of various kinds rather than to the sorts of fixed functional properties that have frequently been proposed.

2.3 Methodologies for Assessing Strong Equivalence

How does one distinguish between regularities that are attributable to properties of the cognitive architecture and those attributable to the nature of the cognitive process and its representations? Twenty-five years ago many of the techniques for assessing strong equivalence (for example, mental chronometry) were not available—or rather their use in this context was not understood. If someone had undertaken to analyze the notion of strong equivalence at that time, much of what we now believe is germane would not have been included. Although we can expect such techniques to continue to evolve, it may be useful to list a few provisional methods that are pervasive in the work of information-processing psychologists.

Intermediate State Evidence
As an example, recall that strong equivalence requires that a model be expressed at a level of aggregation in which all the basic representation states are revealed, because each such state is essential in the representational story. Thus the transitions between representational states must themselves not involve any representational states; these transitions must be realized directly by the cognitive architecture. Hence any evidence for the existence of such intermediate representational states is evidence for the nonprimitiveness of the subprocess in question. There are various methods for obtaining such evidence.

One of the earliest methods for discovering intermediate states in problem solving involves the recording of subjects' expressed thoughts while solving the problem (Duncker 1935). Newell and Simon (1972) developed this technique, which they call *protocol analysis*, to a high level of precision. Although the method can only be used with certain slow and deliberate types of problem-solving tasks (including problems involving visual imagery; compare Baylor 1972, Farley 1974, Moran 1973), it does provide evidence for intermediate states that might otherwise be unavailable for constraining the model. When combined with additional intermediate observations, such as protocols of movements obtained from video recordings (Young 1973) and records of eye movements (Just and Carpenter 1976), this method can yield extremely useful data. The use of this method is discussed in greater length in chapter 1.

The existence of intermediate representational states can sometimes also be inferred in more indirect ways. A good example occurs in psycholinguistics, in the study of real-time sentence processing. There is some indirect evidence for the availability of certain components of syntactic analysis in the course of sentence comprehension (Frazier and Fodor 1978, Marslen-Wilson and Tyler 1980, Forster 1979). Any evidence of the availability of intermediate states of a process to any other process (that is, any evidence that the workings of the process are "transparent" to another part of the system) can be taken as evidence that such a process is not primitive but has a further cognitive decomposition.

In the remainder of this section I consider two other empirically based criteria for deciding whether certain aspects of behavior regularities ought to be attributed to properties of mechanisms—that is, to the cognitive architecture—or to the representations and processes operating on them. Both are, as suggested, sufficient though not necessary conditions—that is, they can ideally tell you when a function requires a more complex cognitive analysis, but cannot tell you that you have gone far enough because there may be various sources of indirect evidence for the need for further decomposition. The *first* of these criteria derives from computational considerations and defines a notion of strong equivalence of processes referred to as *complexity-equivalence*. This criterion is frequently associated with the use of reaction-time measures, or with such on-line measures as those that assess the attention demand of tasks (for example, measuring the performance on a secondary task).

The *second* criterion helps us to decide whether a particular empirical phenomenon ought to be attributed to the architecture or to goals and beliefs. It relies on the assumption that we can identify certain clear cases of phenomenon that should be accounted for at the knowledge level, that is, in terms of the representations alone, rather than in terms of properties of the cognitive architecture. Phenomena that depend in a rational way on subjects' goals, beliefs, and utilities are a case in point. For example, in psychophysics we assume that if a measure (such as a threshold) changes systematically as we change the payoffs (that is, the relative cost of errors of commission and of omission), then the explanation of that change must be given at the knowledge level—in terms of decision theory—rather than in terms of properties of sensors or other mechanisms that are part of the architecture. In general showing that certain empirical phenomena are sensitive to goals and beliefs (or are what I call *cognitively penetrable*) is prima facie evidence that they should not be attributed to properties of the architecture.

Relative Complexity Evidence and Complexity-Equivalence

Recall that in the example discussed previously, there was at least one property of the hash-coding algorithm that needs to be preserved by any strongly equivalent process—and which would not be preserved if the same function were to be realized on a traditional Turing machine. That property is the *relation* between (or the form of the function that characterizes the relation between) the number of steps that it would take to look up a symbol in a table and the total number of symbols stored there. The hash-coding algorithm, implemented on an architecture with a primitive facility to retrieve symbols by name (what is commonly referred to as a random access or register architecture), is able to look up symbols with a number of steps that is (to a first approximation) independent of the number of entries in the table. By contrast if this algorithm were emulated on a Turing machine, the number of steps that it would take would increase as the square of the number of strings stored on the tape (so that the function relating the number of steps and the number of items stored would be a second order polynomial).

The relation between number of primitive steps taken and certain properties of the symbolic input is generally considered to be an essential invariant property of what one intuitively thinks of as different realizations of the same algorithm. For example, one would clearly not count two processes as realizing the same algorithm if one of them computed a function in some fixed time, independent of the size of its input, whereas the other was combinatorially explosive—so that the time it took increased exponentially as some property (for example, length) of the input was varied. The total amount of time or the total number of steps taken is not important for assessing equivalence of algorithms, because that depends on the particular machine on which the algorithm is running. What is important is the nature of the relation between such things as time or number of steps taken and properties of the input, such as its length. Because of this there are certain apparent differences among programs that do not matter for purposes of what I have called their *complexity-equivalence* (Pylyshyn 1984).

In cognitive science the most common way of assessing relative complexity is by measuring relative reaction times, that is, by observing the form of the function relating the time taken for a task and certain parametric properties of the task (for example, size of the input). Although the utility of this measure also rests on methodological assumptions, it has turned out to be one of the most valuable sources of relative complexity evidence in the cognitive science toolbox. Examples of its use are discussed in chapter 7, as well as in many other chapters. In a following section of this chapter, I return to a consideration of the status of measures such as reaction time when I take up the question of whether it is possible in principle to decide on the correct computational models by using behavioral data alone.

The set of programs that are complexity-equivalent clearly represents a refinement of the set of programs that compute the same input/output function, and hence complexity-equivalence represents a restriction of the weak equivalence relation. Although complexity-equivalence captures an important aspect of the intuitive notion of "same algorithm," it is not by itself sufficient to define strong equivalence. It is in other words a necessary but not sufficient condition for strong equivalence.

Cognitive Penetrability

A second class of methods for studying strong equivalence assumes that what I have been calling cognitive phenomena are a natural scientific domain that can be explained entirely in terms of the nature of the representations and the structure of programs running on the cognitive architecture. If that is to be true, then the cognitive architecture itself must not vary in ways that demand the same sort of *cognitive* explanation. It must in other words form a cognitive "fixed point," so that differences in cognitive phenomena might be explained by appeal to the arrangements (sequences of expressions and of basic operations) among the fixed set of operations and to the basic resources provided by this architecture. Though the architecture might vary as a function of physical or biochemical conditions, it should not vary directly and in logically coherent ways with changes in the content of the organisms' goals and beliefs. If the cognitive architecture were to change in ways requiring a cognitive rule-governed explanation, it could itself no longer serve as the basis for explaining how changes in rules and representations produce changes in behavior. Consequently the input/output behavior of the hypothesized primitive operations of the cognitive architecture must not itself depend on goals and beliefs, and hence on conditions that change the organism's goals and beliefs, it must be what I refer to as *cognitively impenetrable*.

This is usually a straightforward criterion to apply in practice. To determine whether certain empirical evidence favors certain hypothesized architectural properties of the cognitive system, the natural question to ask is whether the evidence is compatible with some other, different, architectural properties. One way to do this is to see whether the empirical phenomena in question can be systematically altered by changing subjects' goals or beliefs. If they can, then this suggests that the phenomena tell us not about the architecture but rather about some representation-governed process—something that in other words would remain true even if the architecture were different from that hypothesized.

For example, this appears to be the case with certain kinds of imagery phenomena, such as the linear relation between reaction time and the distance on a mental image that is mentally "scanned" (for more on this case, see Pylyshyn 1981). That is because the linear increase can be made to disappear by changing the instructions, for example, by asking subjects to imagine a situation in which they do not believe there would be any increase in reaction time as a function of distance (that is, in which they believe there would be no relation between time and distance in the *real* situation that they are to imagine).

In general, showing that a certain phenomenon is cognitively penetrable provides strong reason to interpret that phenomenon as arising from the nature of the representations and from cognitive processes operating over these representations. In practice there is always the question of exactly which stage of the process is affected by the instructions, but this is not a problem unique to the penetrability criterion. Being able to determine whether some phenomenon is due to properties of the architecture or of the representation-governed process is critical to assessing strong equivalence because it gives us a way of determining whether we have broken down the processing steps into the right primitive elements.

Can We Decide which Model is Correct from Behavioral Data? The Behavioral Indeterminacy Claim

Finally, I end this section on methodology with a brief discussion of the claim that strong equivalence may in principle not be possible in psychology (or that it can only be achieved by appealing to the facts of biology or by the gratuitous importation of esthetic or other sorts of subjective judgments). Weak equivalence is, by definition, equivalence with respect to input/output behavior. Consequently one might suppose that if all we had in cognitive science was observed behavior, one could not hope to determine which computational model is the correct one beyond choosing one of the weakly equivalent ones. Indeed this point of view has frequently been advocated (compare Anderson 1978, Townsend 1974). Note that this is supposed to be indeterminism beyond the usual scientific indeterminism, wherein a finite body of data never uniquely determines the true theory.

First, it should be pointed out that nobody wishes to exclude psychobiological data as a source of evidence in evaluating theories of cognition (see, for example, the discussions by Sejnowski and Churchland in chapter 8). But whether or not they are included has no bearing on the indeterminism arguments because cognitive models are not models of how the brain realizes processes in neural tissue, they are theories that describe *cognitive* mechanisms that process *cognitive representations*. Neurophysiological evidence can and sometimes does help to decide psychological issues, but contrary to what some people appear to believe, this sort of evidence is just as indirect and fallible as the measurement of reaction times; we can no more directly observe a cognitive mechanism by the methods of biology than we can by the methods of psychophysics (or for that matter by introspection). If that is the case, how can we hope to do better than selecting one of the set of models that are weakly equivalent (other than perhaps by appeal to such external criteria as parsimony and elegance—as some have suggested (Anderson 1978))?

The answer that I have suggested (Pylyshyn 1978b) for this sort of indeterminability claim is this: Although in a sense all we have is behavior, not all behavior is of the same kind from the point of view of theory construction. By distinguishing between different kinds of behavioral measures and by interpreting these measures in different ways that are independently motivated, we can do very much better than weak equivalence.

Notice that placing different interpretations on observed behavior is routine in all experimental psychology. For example, an investigator may collect primary observations in a certain domain—say, concerning the behavior of a person in solving a problem. There are observations that a constructive theory of that domain might be expected to account for by generating similar behavior as its output. But the investigator typically also collects observations of a secondary kind (which might even be called, without too serious a distortion of terminology, meta-behavioral observations), from which certain properties of the problem-solving process itself might be inferred. This is the case, for example, when subjects provide "thinking-out-loud" protocols. It is also the case when observations are made that are interpreted as *indexes* of such things as processing complexity or the attention demand of the task. In such a case it is not expected that a theory or a model would actually generate such behavior as part of its *output*. Rather the idea is that the model should generate the primary (output) behavior in a manner that reflects certain real-time processing properties indexed by observations in the secondary class.

Consider the following example in which the developing methodology of cognitive science has led to a gradual shift in the way an important aspect of observed behavior is interpreted. The example concerns what is probably the most widely used dependent measure in cognitive psychology, namely, reaction time. This measure has sometimes been interpreted as just another response, to be accounted for by a cognitive model in the same way that the model accounts for such response records as the sequence of the buttons that were pressed. Since Donders's pioneering work (carried out in the 1860s and reprinted as Donders 1969) it has also been widely interpreted as a more-or-less direct measure of the duration of mental processes (Wasserman and Kong 1979). I have argued (Pylyshyn 1979a, 1984) that neither of these interpretations is correct in general; reaction time can be viewed in general as neither the computed output of a cognitive process itself nor a measure of the duration of a mental event or mental operation.[9]

If reaction time were thought of as simply another response, then it would be sufficient if our computational model simply calculated a predicted value for this reaction time, given the appropriate input. But that would not be sufficient if the computation is to be viewed as a literal model of the cognitive *process*. Contemporary cognitive scientists would not view a system that generated pairs of output strings, interpreted as the response and a number designating the time taken, as being an adequate model of the underlying process, no matter how well these outputs fit the observed data. That is because they wish to interpret the model as computing the output *in the same way* as the subject (that is, by using the same algorithm).

It has become customary in cognitive science to view reaction time the same way that measures such as galvanic skin response or plethysmograph records, or measures of distractibility (see, for example, Brown 1962) are viewed, namely as an *index*, or an observable correlate, of some aggregate property of the process. In particular reaction time is frequently viewed as an index of what I call *computational complexity*, which is usually taken to correspond to such properties of the model as the number of operations carried out. A process that merely computed time as a parameter value would not account for reaction time viewed in this particular way because the parameter would not express the computational complexity of the process.

I have discussed several cases in which it is possible to decide which of two different algorithms is being used by examining the relative number of primitive steps that they took when given different inputs. Now if there is some reason to believe that the amount of (real) time it takes is proportional to (or at least a monotonically increasing function of) the number of such primitive steps of the algorithm, then measures of relative time taken might provide the evidence needed to decide between the putative algorithms. But in this case we need to have independent reason to believe that reaction time is a valid index of the number of primitive steps of the cognitive architecture. Such independent reasons are frequently available, as, for example, when regularities inferred on the basis of the assumption that reaction time is a reliable indicator of processing complexity are corroborated by other methods. When such patterns of consistency keep showing up under converging methodologies, we then have a prima facie reason to expect such methods to be valid, other things being equal (compare Posner 1978).

Nonetheless it should be kept in mind that when we draw inferences about the nature of the algorithm from reaction-time data (or any other *physical* measurement), we always depend on the validity of ancillary hypotheses. Such hypotheses could in principle be false. There are many situations in which measurements of properties of the underlying physical events may tell us little about the algorithm. They might instead tell us either about the way in which the process is physically (that is, neurophysiologically) instantiated on some particular occasion or in one particular individual, or they might tell us about subjects' tacit knowledge or about the nature of the task itself. For example, I have argued (Pylyshyn 1981, 1984) that many of the phenomena of mental imagery research (for example, the so-called mental scanning results of Kosslyn 1980) are of just this sort. In these cases it appears that the particular reaction-time patterns observed are the direct result not of properties of the architecture but of subjects' tacit knowledge of what would happen in the imagined situations and their ability to duplicate aspects of these situations (for example, their duration) imaginally. The argument for this is based on the cognitive penetrability criterion: if the pattern of behavior can be altered in a rational way by changing subjects' beliefs about the task, then we have prima facie evidence that the process involves inference. Moreover we have little reason to hypothesize special-purpose architectural properties if we can account for the pattern of reaction times merely in terms of subjects' beliefs together with their psychophysical ability to generate the relevant time intervals. This of course does not apply in cases where it is clear that subjects' performance is not explicable in terms of their beliefs—as, for example, when they are operating at the limits of their ability, as is the case with most studies carried out in the information-processing tradition, including some of the imagery manipulation experiments, such as those involving "mental rotation" (as in Shepard and Cooper 1982).

There are other sorts of cases where observed reaction times do not tell us much about the nature of the cognitive architecture. For example, Ullman (1984) has suggested that the reason certain kinds of visual processes (which he calls *visual routines*) are carried out serially is not because of the nature of the cognitive architecture but because the nature of the task itself requires it. In that case the fact that the process is serial cannot be attributed to requirements imposed by the architecture (at least not entirely), though it does show that the architecture is capable of serial operation.

2.4 Conclusion: The Domain of Cognitive Science

What makes some area of study a natural scientific domain is the *discovery* (not the stipulation) that some relatively uniform set of principles can account for phenomena in that domain. It is never the case that we can stipulate in advance precisely what will fall into that natural domain. Nor can we stipulate in advance what the class of principles is that will define the domain; the evolution of the boundaries of a scientific domain is a gradual process, requiring provisional conjectures as one proceeds.

Cognitive science has been viewed as the study of the natural domain of cognition, where cognition includes prototypical phenomena of perception, problem solving, reasoning, learning, memory, and so on. At present the working hypothesis appears to be that what these have in common is that they involve intelligent activity in some general sense.

A bolder hypothesis is that cognition is the domain of phenomena that can be viewed as natural information processing, which in current terms means that it is computational, that being the only notion of autonomous mechanistic information processing we have. This in turn means that phenomena in this domain can be explained on at least three distinct levels, as suggested by what I call the classical view. According to this hypothesis (which we might call the *computational realist* view), we cannot stipulate in advance which empirical phenomena will turn out to be cognitive in the technical sense (meaning susceptible to a computational explanation). It would be both surprising and troublesome if too many of what we pretheoretically took to be clear cases of cognition ended up being omitted in the process. But it would also not be entirely surprising if some of our favorite candidate cognitive phenomena got left out. For example, it could turn out that consciousness is not something that can be given a computational account. Similarly certain kinds of statistical learning, aspects of ontogenetic development, the effect of moods and emotions, and many other important and interesting phenomena could simply end up not being amenable to a computational account. Substantial components of such phenomena could, for example, require a noncomputational explanation, say, in terms of biochemistry or some other science.

In that regard it *could* turn out that certain phenomena might not arise from symbol processing, contrary to earlier assumptions. In that case connectionists' claims that symbol systems are not needed (see, for example, Rumelhart, McClelland, et al. 1986) could turn out to be right for those phenomena. On the other hand there are very good reasons for maintaining that *reasoning* and other *knowledge-dependent* or rational process require symbol processing, and moreover that these processes are extremely pervasive in the phenomena that have been studied in cognitive science. Only time and further research will tell which phenomena might be better explained by models that do not conform to the classical notions of computing.

Notes

I thank Allen Newell for his extensive comments on a draft of the manuscript.

1. Although the cognitive science community tends to use the term *knowledge* quite freely in discussing semantic level principles, it is sometimes worth distinguishing those semantic entities that are knowledge, from those that are goals, percepts, plans, and so on. The more general term *semantic level* is used in contexts where such distinctions are important. Philosophers even talk about the "intentional" level or "intentional" objects, but because the use of that terminology tends to raise a large, ancient, and not entirely relevant set of issues, we shun that term here.

2. Note that although no bounds are assumed on the length of the expressions, the arguments presented hold even if the expressions are bounded—so long as the length is sufficiently great that the expressions have to be treated as though they were not atomic, which is true in any useful computer. Because of this *IF* instantiates the expressions *by means of* instantiations of the elementary symbols o and x and the concatenation relation. Similarly operations on expressions (such as the operation *#*) are defined in terms of operations on individual symbols.

3. I use the term *architecture* here somewhat loosely because it has not yet been defined. In a following section this notion is discussed in greater detail because it is one of the central computational ideas in cognitive science.

4. Of course there are also those studying cognition who deny any concern with modeling human cognitive processes; they wish only to create computer systems that carry out some intelligent task. Yet there is reason to think that such people are also implicitly developing theories of human cognition, inasmuch as facts about human cognition are being brought in as part of the task definition (see the discussion of implicit empirical constraints in artificial intelligence research in Pylyshyn 1978).

5. Although in discussing the distinction between a computational theory and an algorithm Marr draws the analogy between mathematical theories, such as the theory of Fourier analysis, and particular algorithms, such as the fast Fourier transform (FFT) algorithm, the examples from his own work in vision do not appear to fit that analogy. In fact what is called a "theory of the computation" (or a type I theory) is typically a theory that links a function (such as computing structure from motion or shading) to a teleological story. Marr was preoccupied with the question What is this computation *for*? or What useful information about the world does it provide the organism? This, however, does not provide the basis for a principled distinction between levels. It is clearly just a useful heuristic for encouraging the theorist to look for independent motivations and broader functional units when formulating a theory in some domain.

6. We can take this claim as a point of definition for present purposes, although there are some technical issues here that would have to be addressed in a more detailed discussion. The criterion for being the same algorithm is closely linked to the idea of *direct* execution. For example, we can trivially change an algorithm (say, by adding a fixed number of redundant operations such as "no ops" to each original operation), yet for our purposes we may not want to count this variant as a distinct algorithm—that is, we may want to count any machine executing the variant as carrying out the same process as the original machine executing the original algorithm. To develop this idea, we may need concepts such as that of a canonical description of a process (for example, along the lines that I have sketched in Pylyshyn 1984).

7. Although, as I have already suggested, the working hypothesis of most of cognitive science is that whatever the functional architecture turns out to look like in detail, it will continue to fall into the class of symbol-processing, or classical, architectures as originally envisaged by Turing and as is true of all systems we call digital computers today. The reason is that to have sufficient representational power as well as the right kind of semantically coherent behavioral plasticity, the computational system must read, write, and transform structured symbolic expressions that have combinatorial semantic properties (these points are argued at some length in Fodor and Pylyshyn 1988).

8. The term *tacit knowledge* is used here in the usual way to refer to real knowledge that subjects have even though they are not aware of having and using it—an unproblematic idea in contemporary cognitive science, where it is taken for granted that subjects need not have awareness or "metaaccess" to most cognitive structures and processes. The term has nothing to do with Polanyi's (1964) use of the same phrase.

9. The reason that reaction times cannot be viewed as measuring the duration of a mental operation is simply that when one speaks of a certain mental operation, such as comparing a stimulus with an item in memory, one is referring not to any one particular occurrence of this operation in the brain but in general to the class of all occurrences—all event *tokens*—that would constitute the same event-*type*—for example, the event-type "compare stimulus S with item X in memory." Thus in referring to the CAR function in Lisp, one is not referring to any particular occasion on which that function is evaluated. Because we distinguish between the operation as a *computational* event and the particular *physical* events that carry it out on particular occasions, all occurrences of a particular operator

need not (by definition) have a unique duration associated with them, just as they need not have a unique size or location in the brain (or a computer) associated with them. Because of this, one does not in general speak of the duration of a CAR operation, although of course each particular event-token that constitutes the execution of a CAR operation does have a unique duration on each occasion. For some reason the idea of distinguishing token events from event types is alien to many psychologists, so this point is frequently lost (see, for example, Wasserman and Kong 1979).

References

Anderson, J. R. 1978. Arguments concerning representations for mental imagery. *Psychological Review* 85:249–277.

Backus, J. 1978. Can programming be liberated from the von Neumann style? A functional style and its algebra of programs. *Communications of the Association for Computing Machinery* 21:613–641.

Baylor, G. W. 1972. A treatise on the mind's eye: An empirical investigation of visual mental imagery. Ph.D. diss., Carnegie Mellon University, Pittsburgh, PA. Ann Arbor, MI: University Microfilms, no. 72-12,699.

Bransford, J. D., and Johnson, M. K. 1973. Considerations of some problems of comprehension. In W. Chase, ed. *Visual Information Processing*. New York: Academic Press.

Brouwer, L. E. J. 1964. Intuitionism and formalism. In P. Benacerraf and H. Putnam, eds. *Philosophy of Mathematics*. Englewood Cliffs, NJ: Prentice-Hall.

Brown, G. S. 1969. *Laws of Form*. London: Allen Unwin.

Brown, I. D. 1962. Measuring the "spare mental capacity" of car drivers by a subsidiary auditory task. *Ergonomics* 5:247–250.

Davies, D. J. M., and Isard, S. D. 1972. Utterances as programs. In B. Meltzer and D. Michie, eds. *Machine Intelligence 7*. Edinburgh: Edinburgh University Press.

Davis, M., ed. 1965. *The Undecidable: Basic Papers on Undecidable Propositions, Unsolvable Problems and Computable Functions*. Hewlett, NY: Raven Press.

Donders, F. C. 1969. On the speed of mental processes (1868–1869). *Acta Psychologica* 30:412–431.

Duncker, K. 1935. On problem solving. *Psychological Monographs* 58(270):5.

Erman, L. D., Hayes-Roth, F., Lesser, V. R., and Reddy, D. R. 1980. The HEARSAY-II speech understanding system: Integrating knowledge to resolve uncertainty. *Computing Surveys* 12:213–253.

Farley, A. 1974. A visual imagery and perception system. Ph.D. diss., Carnegie Mellon University, Pittsburgh, PA.

Fodor, J. A. 1975. *The Language of Thought*. New York: Crowell.

Fodor, J. A., and Pylyshyn, Z. W. 1988. Connectionism and cognitive architecture: A critical analysis. *Cognition* 28:3–71.

Forster, K. I. 1979. Levels of processing and the structure of the language processor. In W. E. Cooper and E. C. T. Walker, eds. *Sentence Processing: Psycholinguistic Studies Presented to Merrill Garrett*. Hillsdale, NJ: Erlbaum.

Frazier, L., and Fodor, J. D. 1978. The sausage machine: A new two-stage parsing model. *Cognition* 6:291–325.

Funt, B. V. 1980. Problem-solving with diagrammatic representations. *Artificial Intelligence* 13(3):201–230.

Guthrie, E. R. 1935. *The Psychology of Learning*. New York: Harper.

Johansson, G. 1975. Visual motion perception. *Scientific American* 232:76–88.

Just, M. A., and Carpenter, P. A. 1976. Eye fixations and cognitive processes. *Cognitive Psychology* 8:441–480.

Knuth, D. E. 1968. *Fundamental Algorithms. The Art of Computer Programming*. Vol. 1. Reading, MA: Addison-Wesley.

Kohler, W. 1947. *Gestalt Psychology, An Introduction to New Concepts in Modern Psychology*. New York: Liveright.

Kosslyn, S. M. 1980. *Image and Mind*. Cambridge, MA: Harvard University Press.

Kosslyn, S. M., and Shwartz, S. P. 1977. A data-driven simulation of visual imagery. *Cognitive Science* 1:265–296.

Lindsay, P. H., and Norman, D. A. 1977. *Human Information Processing: An Introduction to Psychology*. 2d ed. New York: Academic Press.

Marr, D., and Poggio, T. 1979. A computational theory of human stereo vision. *Proceedings of Royal Society, London B* 204:301–328.

Marslen-Wilson, W., and Tyler, L. K. 1980. The temporal structure of spoken language understanding. *Cognition* 8(1):1–71.

McCarthy, J., and Hayes, P. 1969. Some philosophical problems from the standpoint of artificial intelligence. In B. Meltzer and D. Michie, eds. *Machine Intelligence 4*. Edinburgh: Edinburgh University Press.

Miller, G. A., Galanter, E., and Pribram, K. H. 1960. *Plans and the Structure of Behavior*. New York: Holt, Rinehart and Winston.

Moran, T. 1973. The symbolic imagery hypothesis: A production system model. Ph.D. diss., Carnegie Mellon University, Pittsburgh, PA.

Newell, A. 1962. Some problems of basic organization in problem-solving programs. In A. Yovitts, G. T. Jacobi, and G. D. Goldstein, eds. *Self-Organizing Systems*. New York: Spartan.

Newell, A. 1970. Remarks on the relationship between artificial intelligence and cognitive psychology. In R. Banerji and M. D. Mesarovio, eds. *Theoretical Approaches to Non-Numerical Problem Solving*. New York: Springer-Verlag.

Newell, A. 1973a. Artificial intelligence and the concept of mind. In R. C. Schank and K. Colby, eds. *Computer Models of Thought and Language*. San Francisco: W. H. Freeman.

Newell, A. 1973b. Production systems: Models of control structures. In W. Chase, ed. *Visual Information Processing*. New York: Academic Press.

Newell, A. 1973c. You can't play twenty questions with nature and win. In W. Chase, ed. *Visual Information Processing*. New York: Academic Press.

Newell, A. 1980. Physical symbol systems. *Cognitive Science* 4(2):135–183.

Newell, A., and Simon, H. A. 1972. *Human Problem Solving*. Englewood Cliffs, NJ.: Prentice-Hall.

Nicod, J. 1970. *Geometry and Induction*. Berkeley: University of California Press.

Polanyi, M. 1964. *Personal Knowledge*. London: Routledge and Kegan Paul.

Posner, M. I. 1978. *Chronometric Explorations of Mind*. Hillsdale, NJ: Erlbaum.

Pylyshyn, Z. W. 1978. Computational models and empirical constraints. *Behavioral and Brain Sciences* 1:93–99.

Pylyshyn, Z. W. 1979a. Do mental events have durations? *Behavioral and Brain Sciences* 2(2):277–278.

Pylyshyn, Z. W. 1979b. Validating computational models: A critique of Anderson's indeterminacy of representation claim. *Psychological Review* 86(4):383–394.

Pylyshyn, Z. W. 1981. The imagery debate: Analogue media versus tacit knowledge." *Psychological Review* 88:16–45.

Pylyshyn, Z. W. 1984. *Computation and Cognition: Toward a Foundation for Cognitive Science*. Cambridge, MA: MIT Press. A Bradford Book.

Rumelhart, D. E., and McClelland, J. L., and the PDP Research Group. 1986. *Parallel Distributed Processing*. Cambridge, MA: MIT Press. A Bradford Book.

Shepard, R. N. and Cooper, L. A. 1982. *Mental Images and Their Transformations*. Cambridge, MA: MIT Press. A Bradford Book.

Simon, H. A. 1969. *The Sciences of the Artificial*. Cambridge, MA: MIT Press.

Sperling, G. 1967. Successive approximations to a model for short-term memory. *Act Psychologica* 27:285–292.

Sternberg, S. 1970. Mental scanning: Mental processes revealed by reaction time experiments. In J. S. Antrobus, ed. *Cognition and Affect*. Boston: Little, Brown.

Stevens, K. A. 1981. The visual interpretation of surface contours. *Artificial Intelligence* 17:47–74.

Townsend, J. T. 1974. Issues and models concerning the processing of a finite number of inputs. In B. H. Kantowitz, ed. *Human Information Processing: Tutorials in Performance and Cognition*. Hillsdale, NJ: Erlbaum.

Turing, M. A. 1937. On computable numbers, with an application to the Entscheidungs-problem. *Proceedings of the London Mathematical Society* 42:230–265.

Turing, M. A. 1950. Computing machinery and intelligence. In *Mind*; reprinted in 1964 in A. R. Anderson, ed. *Minds and Machines*. Englewood Cliffs, NJ: Prentice-Hall.

Ullman, S. 1979. *The Interpretation of Visual Motion*. Cambridge, MA: MIT Press.

Ullman, S. 1984. Visual routines. *Cognition* 18:97–159.

Wallach, H., and O'Connell, D. N. 1953. The kinetic depth effect. *Journal of Experimental Psychology* 45:205–217.

Wasserman, G. S., and Kong, K. L. 1979. Absolute timing of mental activities. *Behavioral and Brain Sciences* 2(2):243–304.

Young, R. M. 1973. Children's seriation behavior: A production system analysis. Ph.D. diss., Department of Psychology, Carnegie Mellon University, Pittsburgh, PA.

3 Symbolic Architectures for Cognition

Allen Newell, Paul S. Rosenbloom, and John E. Laird

In this chapter we treat the fixed structure that provides the frame within which cognitive processing in the mind takes place. This structure is called the *architecture*. It will be our task to indicate what an architecture is and how it enters into cognitive theories of the mind. Some boundaries for this chapter are set by the existence of other chapters in this book. We will not address the basic foundations of the computational view of mind that is central to cognitive science, but assume the view presented by Pylyshyn in chapter 2. In addition to the groundwork Pylyshyn also deals with several aspects of the architecture. Chapter 1, the overview by Simon and Kaplan, also touches on the architecture at several points and also in the service of the larger picture. Both treatments are consistent with ours and provide useful redundancy.

This chapter considers only *symbolic architectures* and, more particularly, architectures whose structure is reasonably close to that analyzed in computer science. The space of all architectures is not well understood, and the extent and sense to which all architectures must be symbolic architectures is a matter of contention. Chapter 4 by Rumelhart covers nonsymbolic architectures, or more precisely the particular species under investigation by the connectionists.

First, we sketch the role the architecture plays in cognitive science. Second, we describe the requirements the cognitive architecture must meet. Third, we treat in detail the nature of the cognitive architecture. Fourth, we illustrate the concepts with two cognitive architectures: Act* and Soar. Fifth, we indicate briefly how theories of the architecture enter into other studies in cognitive science. We close with some open questions.

3.1 The Role of the Architecture in Cognitive Science

Viewing the world as constituted of *systems of mechanisms* whose *behavior* we observe is part of the common conceptual apparatus of science. When the systems are engineered or teleological, we talk about *structure* and *function*—a system of a given structure producing behavior that performs a given function in the encompassing system. The term *architecture* is used to indicate that the structure in question has some sort of primary, permanent, or originating character. As such one can talk about the architecture of the mind or a part of the mind in a general and descriptive way—the architecture of the visual system, an architecture for the conceptual system, and so on.

In cognitive science the notion of architecture has come to take on a quite specific and technical meaning, deriving from computer science. There the term stands for the hardware structure that produces a system that can be programmed. It is the design of a machine that admits the distinction between hardware and software.[1] The concept of an architecture for cognitive science then is the appropriate generalization and abstraction of the concept of computer architecture applied to human cognition: the fixed system of mechanisms that underlies and produces cognitive behavior. As such, an appropriate starting place is a description of an ordinary computer architecture.

The Architecture of Computers

Consider a simple (uniprocessor) digital computer. The top of figure 3.1 shows the gross physical configuration of the system. There is a set of components—a processor, a primary memory, and so on—joined by communication links (the link connecting almost everything together is called the bus). Over the links flow streams of bits. A look inside the processor (the lower-left portion of the figure) reveals more anatomical detail of components connected by links—a number of register memories; a data unit for carrying out various operations such as addition, intersection, shifting, and the like; and an interpreter unit for carrying out the instructions of the program. The primary memory contains a few instructions from a program. The address in the program address register points to one of them, which is brought into the program register and decoded. The left part of the instruction is used to select one of the basic operations of the computer, and the right part is used to address a cell of the primary memory, whose content is retrieved to become an argument for the operation. The repeated acts of obtaining the next instruction, interpreting it, and performing the operation on the argument are called the *fetch-execute cycle*.

Figure 3.1 specifies the architecture of a digital computer (given literary license). It describes a mechanistic system that behaves in a definite way. The language used to describe it takes much for granted, referring to registers, links, decoders, and so on. These components and how they operate require further specification—to say how they are to be realized in circuit technology and ultimately in electron physics—all of which can be taken for granted here.

The behavior of this machine depends on the program and data stored in the memory. Indeed the machine can exhibit essentially any behavior whatsoever depending on the content. By now we are all well ac-

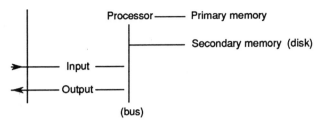

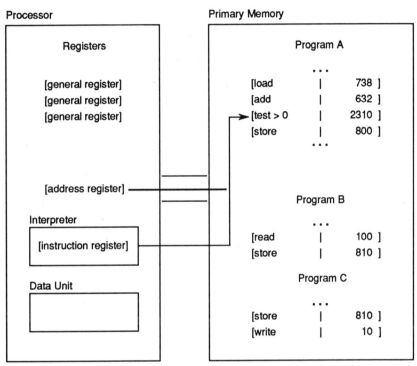

Figure 3.1 Structure of a simple digital computer

Symbolic Architectures for Cognition

quainted with the amazing variety of such programs—computing statistics, keeping inventories, playing games, editing manuscripts, running machine tools, and so on—but also converting the machine's interaction with its environment to occur by a wide variety of languages, graphic displays, and the like. All this happens because of three things taken jointly: the computer architecture, which enables the interpretation of programs; the flexibility of programs to specify behavior, both for external consumption and for creating additional programs to be used in the future; and lots of memory to hold lots of programs with their required data so that a wide variety of behavior can occur.

Figure 3.1 is only the tip of the iceberg of computer architectures. It contains the essential ideas, however, and serves to introduce them in concrete form.

The Architecture of Cognition

Figure 3.1 epitomizes the invention of the computer, a mechanism that can exhibit indefinitely flexible, complex, responsive, and task-oriented behavior. We observe in humans flexible and adaptive behavior in seemingly limitless abundance and variety. A natural hypothesis is that systems such as that of figure 3.1 reveal the essential mechanisms of how humans attain their own flexibility and therefore of how the mind works.

A chief burden of chapter 2 (and a theme in chapter 1) is to show how this observation has been transformed into a major foundation of cognitive science. The empirical basis for this transformation has come from the immense diversity of tasks that have been accomplished by computers, including, but not limited to, the stream of artificial intelligence (AI) systems. Compelling force has been added to this transformation from the theory of computational mechanisms (Hopcroft and Ullman 1979), which abstracts from much that seems special in figure 3.1 and shows both the sufficiency and the necessity of computational mechanisms and how such mechanisms relate to systems having representations of their external world (that is, having semantics). The architectures that arise from this theory are called symbolic architectures.

As laid out in chapter 2, the human can be described at different system levels. At the top is the *knowledge level*, which describes the person as having goals and knowing things about the world, in which knowledge is used in the service of its goals (by the principle of rationality). The person can operate at the knowledge level only because it is also a *symbol level* system, which is a system that operates in terms of representations and information-processing operations on these representations. The symbol level must also be realized in terms of some substrate, and the architecture is that substrate defined in an appropriate descriptive language. For computers this turns out to be the *register-*

transfer level, in which bit-vectors are transported from one functional unit (such as an adder) to another, subject to gating by control bits. For humans it is the neural-circuit level, which currently seems well described as highly parallel interconnected networks of inhibitory and excitatory connections that process a medium of continuous signals. Below that of course are other levels of description—neurons, organelles, macromolecules, and on down.

This arrangement of system levels seems very special—it is after all the eye of the needle through which systems have to pass to be able to be intelligent. Nevertheless there is an immense variety of architectures and an immense variety of physical substrates in which they can be implemented. No real appreciation exists yet for this full double variety or its consequences, except that they are exceedingly large and diverse. It is relatively easy to understand a given architecture when presented, though there may be a fair amount of detail to wade through. However, it is difficult to see the behavioral consequences of an architecture, because it is so overlaid by the programs it executes. And it is extremely difficult to compare different architectures, for each presents its own total framework that can carve up the world in radically different ways. Despite these difficulties cognitive science needs to determine the architecture that underlies and supports human cognition.

The architecture does not by itself determine behavior. The other main contributors are the goal the person is attempting to attain, the task environment within which the person is performing, and the knowledge the person has. The first is not only the knowledge of the conditions or situation desired, but also the commitment to govern behavior to obtain such conditions. The second is the objective situation, along with the objective constraints about how the person can interact with the situation. The third is the subjective situation of the person in relation to the task. The knowledge involved in accomplishing any task is diverse and extensive and derives from multiple sources. These sources include the statement or presenting indications of the task, the immediately prior interaction with the task situation, the long-term experience with analogous or similar situations, prior education including the acquisition of skills, and the socialization and enculturation that provide the background orientation. All these sources of knowledge make their contribution.

The goal, task, and knowledge of course constitute the knowledge-level characterization of a person. The architecture's primary role is to make that possible by supporting the processing of the symbolic representations that hold the knowledge. If it did so perfectly, then the architecture would not appear as an independent factor in the determination of behavior any more than would acetylcholine or sulfur atoms. It would simply be the scaffolding that explains how the actual determinants (task and knowledge) are realized in our physical world.

But the knowledge-level characterization is far from perfect. As the linguists used to be fond of saying, there can be a large gap between competence and performance. The architecture shows through in many ways, both large and small. Indeed much of cognitive psychology is counting these ways—speed of processing, memory errors, linguistic slips, perceptual illusions, failures of rationality in decision making, interference effects of learned material, and on and on. These factors are grounded in part in the architecture. Aspects of behavior can also have their source in mechanisms and structure defined at lower levels—neural functioning, properties of muscle, imperfections in the corneal lens, macromolecular structure of drugs, the effects of raised temperature, and so on. When the architecture fails to support adequately knowledge-based goal-oriented behavior, however, it gives rise by and large to characteristics we see as psychological. Viewed this way, much of psychology involves the investigation of the architecture.

What the notion of the architecture supplies is the concept of the *total* system of mechanisms that are required to attain flexible intelligent behavior. Normally psychological investigations operate in isolation, though with a justified sense that the mechanisms investigated (memory, learning, memory retrieval, whatever) are necessary and important. The architecture adds the total system context within which such separate mechanisms operate, providing additional constraints that determine behavior. The architecture also brings to the fore additional mechanisms that must be involved and that have received less attention in experimental psychology, for instance, elementary operations and control. This requirement of integration is not just a pleasant condiment. Every complete human performance invokes most of the psychological functions we investigate piecemeal—perception, encoding, retrieval, memory, composition and selection of symbolic responses, decision making, motor commands, and actual motor responses. Substantial risks are incurred by psychological theory and experimentation when they focus on a slice of behavior, leaving all the rest as inarticulated background.

A theory of the architecture is a proposal for the total cognitive mechanism, rather than for a single aspect or mechanism. A proposed embodiment of an architecture, such as a simulation system, purports to be a complete mechanism for human cognition. The form of its memory embodies a hypothesis of the form of human symbolic specifications for action; the way its programs are created or modified embodies a hypothesis of the way human action specifications are created or modified; and so on (Newell 1987).

To summarize, the role of the architecture in cognitive science is to be the central element in a theory of human cognition. It is not the sole or even the predominant determinant of the behavior of the person, but it is the determinant of what makes that behavior psychological rather than a reflection of the person's goals in the light of their knowledge. To have a theory of cognition is to have a theory of the architecture.

3.2 Requirements on the Cognitive Architecture

Why should the cognitive architecture be one way or the other? All architectures provide programmability, which yields indefinitely flexible behavior. Why wouldn't one architecture do as well as another? We need to address this question as a preliminary to discussing the nature of the cognitive architecture. We need to understand the requirements that shape human cognition, especially beyond the need for universal computation. The cognitive architecture must provide the support necessary for all these requirements. The following is a list of requirements that could shape the architecture (adapted from Newell 1980):

1. Behave flexibly as a function of the environment
2. Exhibit adaptive (rational, goal-oriented) behavior
3. Operate in real time
4. Operate in a rich, complex, detailed environment
   a. perceive an immense amount of changing detail
   b. use vast amounts of knowledge
   c. control a motor system of many degrees of freedom
5. Use symbols and abstractions
6. Use language, both natural and artificial
7. Learn from the environment and from experience
8. Acquire capabilities through development
9. Live autonomously within a social community
10. Exhibit self-awareness and a sense of self

These requirements express our common though scientifically informed knowledge about human beings in their habitat. There is no way to know how complete the list is, but many relevant requirements are certainly included.

(1) We list first the requirement to behave flexibly as a function of the environment, since that is the central capability that architectures provide. If a system cannot make itself respond in whatever way is needed, it can hardly be intelligent. The whole purpose of this list, of course, is to go beyond this first item. (2) Flexibility by itself is only a means; it must be in the service of goals and rationally related to obtaining the things and conditions that let the organism survive and propagate. (3) Cognition must operate in real time. This demand of the environment is both important and pervasive. It runs directly counter to the requirements for flexibility, where time to compute is an essential resource. (4) The environment that humans inhabit has important characteristics

beyond just being dynamic: it is combinatorially rich and detailed, changing simultaneously on many fronts, but with many regularities at every time scale. This affects the cognitive system in several ways. (a) There must be multiple perceptual systems to tap the multiple dynamic aspects; they must all operate concurrently and dynamically, and some must have high bandwidth. (b) There must be very large memories because the environment provides the opportunity to know many relevant things, and in an evolutionary, hence competitive, world opportunity for some produces requirements for all. (c) For the motor system to move around and influence a complex world requires continual determination of many degrees of freedom at a rate dictated by the environment.

(5) Human cognition is able to use symbols and abstractions. (6) It is also able to use language, both natural and artificial. These two requirements might come to the same thing or they might impose somewhat distinct demands. Both are intimately related to the requirement for flexibility and might be redundant with it. But there might be important additional aspects in each. All this need not be settled for the list, which attempts coverage rather than parsimony or independence.

(7) Humans must learn from the environment, not occasionally but continuously and not a little but a lot. This also flows from the multitude of regularities at diverse time scales available to be learned. (8) Furthermore many of our capabilities are acquired through development. When the neonate first arrives, it is surely without many capabilities, but these seem to be exactly the high-level capabilities required to acquire the additional capabilities it needs. Thus there is a chicken-and-egg constraint, which hints at a significant specialization to make development possible. As with the requirements for symbols and language, the relation between learning and development is obscure. Whatever it turns out to be, both requirements belong in the list.

(9) Humans must live autonomously within a social community. This requirement combines two aspects. One aspect of autonomy is greater capability to be free of dependencies on the environment. Relative to the autonomy of current computers and robots, this implies the need for substantially increased capabilities. On the other hand much that we have learned from ethology and social theory speaks to the dependence of individuals on the communities in which they are raised and reside (von Cranach, Foppa, Lepinies, and Ploog 1979). The additional capabilities for low-level autonomy do not negate the extent to which socialization and embedding in a supportive social structure are necessary. If humans leave their communities, they become inept and dysfunctional in many ways. (10) The requirement for self-awareness is somewhat obscure. We surely have a sense of self. But it is not evident what functional role self-awareness plays in the total scheme of mind. Research has made clear the importance of metacognition—considering the capabilities of the self in relation to the task environ-

ment. But the link from metacognition to the full notion of a sense of self remains obscure.

Human cognition can be taken to be an information-processing system that is a solution to all of the listed requirements plus perhaps others that we have not learned about. Flexibility, the grounds for claiming that human cognition is built on an architecture, is certainly a prominent item, but it is far from the only one. Each of the others plays some role in making human cognition what it is.

The problem of this chapter is *not* what shape cognition as a whole takes in response to these requirements—that is the problem of cognitive science as a whole. Our problem is what is implied by the list for the shape of the architecture. For each requirement there exists a body of general and scientific knowledge, more or less well developed. But cognition is always the resultant of the architecture plus the content of the memories, combined under the impress of being adaptive. This tends to conceal the inner structure and reveal only knowledge-level behavior. Thus extracting the implications for the architecture requires analysis.

Several approaches are possible for such analyses, although we can only touch on them here. The most important one is to get temporally close to the architecture; if there is little time for programmed behavior to act, then the architecture has a chance to shine through. A good example is the exploration of immediate-response behavior that has established an arena of *automatic* behavior, distinguished from an arena of more deliberate *controlled* behavior (Schneider and Shiffrin 1977, Shiffrin and Schneider 1977). Another approach is to look for universal regularities. If some regularity shows through despite all sorts of variation, it may reflect some aspect of the architecture. A good example is the power law of practice, in which the time to perform repeated tasks, almost no matter what the task, improves according to a power law of the number of trials (Newell and Rosenbloom 1981). Architectural mechanisms have been hypothesized to account for it (Rosenbloom and Newell 1986). Yet another approach is to construct experimental architectures that support a number of the requirements in the list. These help to generate candidate mechanisms that will meet various requirements, but also reveal the real nature of the requirement. Many of the efforts in AI and in the development of AI software tools and environments fit this mold (a recent conference (VanLehn 1989) provides a good sampling).

Functional requirements are not the only sources of knowledge about the cognitive architecture. We know the cognitive architecture is realized in neural technology and that it was created by evolution. Both of these have major effects on the architecture. We do not treat either. The implications of the neural structure of the brain are treated in other chapters of this volume, and the implications of evolution, though tantalizing, are difficult to discern.

3.3 The Nature of the Architecture

We now describe the nature of the cognitive architecture. This is to be given in terms of functions rather than structures and mechanisms. In part this is because the architecture is defined in terms of what it does for cognition. But it is also because, as we have discovered from computer science, an extremely wide variety of structures and mechanisms have proved capable of providing the central functions. Thus no set of structures and mechanisms has emerged as sufficiently necessary to become the criterial features. The purely functional character of architectures is especially important when we move from current digital computers to human cognition. There the underlying system technology (neural circuits) and construction technology (evolution) are very different, so we can expect to see the functions realized in ways quite different from that in current digital technology.

In general the architecture provides support for a given function rather than the entire function. Because an architecture provides a way in which software (that is, content) can guide behavior in flexible ways, essentially all intellectual or control functions can be provided by software. Only in various limiting conditions—of speed, reliability, access to the architectural mechanisms themselves, and the like—is it *necessary* to perform all of the certain functions directly in the architecture. It may, of course, be *efficient* to perform functions in the architecture that could also be provided by software. From either a biological or engineering perspective there is no intrinsic reason to prefer one way of accomplishing a function rather than another. Issues of efficiency, modifiability, constructibility, resource cost, and resource availability join to determine what mechanisms are used to perform a function and how they divide between architectural support, and program and data.

The following list gives known functions of the architecture.

1. Memory
   a. Contains structures that contain symbol tokens
   b. Independently modifiable at some grain size
   c. Sufficient memory
2. Symbols
   a. Patterns that provide access to distal symbol structures
   b. A symbol token in the occurrence of a pattern in a structure
   c. Sufficient symbols
3. Operations
   a. Processes that take symbol structures as input and produce symbol structures as output
   b. Complete composibility

4. Interpretation
    a. Processes that take symbol structures as input and produce behavior by executing operations
    b. Complete interpretability
5. Interaction with the external world
    a. Perceptual and motor interfaces
    b. Buffering and interrupts
    c. Real-time demands for action
    d. Continuous acquisition of knowledge

We stress that these functions are only what are known currently. Especially with natural systems such as human cognition, but even with artificial systems, we do not know all the functions that are being performed.[2] The basic sources of our knowledge of the functions of the architecture is exactly what was skipped over in the previous section, namely the evolution of digital computer architectures and the corresponding abstract theory of machines that has developed in computer science. We do not ground the list in detail in this background, but anyone who wants to work seriously in cognitive architectures should have a fair acquaintance with it (Minsky 1967, Bell and Newell 1971, Hopcroft and Ullman 1979, Siewiorek, Bell, and Newell 1981, Agrawal 1986, Fernandez and Lang 1986, Gajski, Milutinovic, Siegel, and Furht 1987). We now take up the items of this list.

Symbol Systems
The central function of the architecture is to support a system capable of universal computation. Thus the initial functions in our list are those required to provide this capability. We should be able to generate the list simply by an analysis of existing universal machines. However, there are many varieties of universal systems. Indeed a striking feature of the history of investigation of universal computation has been the creation of many alternative independent formulations of universality, all of which have turned out to be equivalent. Turing machines, Markov algorithms, register machines, recursive functions, Pitts-McCulloch neural nets, Post productions, tag systems, plus all manner of digital computer organizations—all include within them a way of formulating a universal machine. These universal machines are all equivalent in flexibility and can all simulate each other. But like architectures (and for the same reasons) each formulation is a framework unto itself, and they often present a quite specific and idiosyncratic design, such as the tape, reading head, and five-tuple instruction format of a Turing machine. Although not without a certain charm (special but very general!), this tends to obscure the general functions that are required. The formulation we choose is the *symbol system*[3] (Newell 1980), which is equivalent

to all the others. The prominent role it gives to symbols has proved useful in discussions of human cognition, however, and its avoidance of specific details of operation makes it less idiosyncratic than other formulations.

The first four items of the list of functions provide the capability for being a symbol system: *memory, symbols, operations,* and *interpretation.* However, none of these functions (not even symbols) is the function of *representation* of the external world. Symbols do provide an internal representation function, but representation of the external world is a function of the computational system as a whole, so that the architecture supports such representation, but does not itself provide it. (See chapter 2 for how this is possible, and how one moves from the knowledge level, which is *about* the external world, to the symbol level, which contains the mechanisms that provide *aboutness*.)

Memory and Memory Structures   The first requirement is for *memory,* which is to say, structures that persist over time. In computers there is a memory hierarchy ranging from working registers within the central processor (such as the address register) to registers used for temporary state (such as an accumulator or operand stack), to primary memory (which is randomly addressed and holds active programs and data), to secondary memory (disks), to tertiary memory (magnetic tapes). This hierarchy is characterized by time constants (speed of access, speed of writing, and expected residency time) and memory capacity, in inverse relation—the slower the memory the more of it is available. The faster memory is an integral part of the operational dynamics of the system and is to be considered in conjunction with it. The larger-capacity, longer-term memory satisfies the requirement for the large amounts of memory needed for human cognition.

Memory is composed of structures, called *symbol structures* because they contain *symbol tokens*. In computers all of the memories hold the same kinds of structures, namely, vectors of bits (bytes and words), although occasionally larger multiples of such units occur (blocks and records). At some sufficiently large grain size the memory structures must be independently modifiable. There are two reasons for this. First, the variety of the external world is combinatorial—it comprises many independent multivalued dimensions located (and iterated) throughout space and time. Only a combinatorial memory structure can hold information about such a world. Second, built-in dependencies in the memory structure, while facilitating certain computations, must ultimately interfere with the ability of the system to compute according to the dictates of the environment. Dependencies in the memory, being unresponsive to dependencies in the environment, then become a drag, even though it may be possible to compensate by additional computation. Within some limits (here called the grain size) of course structures may exhibit various dependencies, which may be useful.[4]

Symbols and Symbol Tokens   Symbol tokens are patterns in symbol structures that provide *access* to distal memory structures, that is, to structures elsewhere in memory.[5] In standard computer architectures a symbol is a memory address and a symbol token is a particular string of bits in a particular word that can be used as an address (by being shipped to the memory-address register, as in figure 3.1). The need for symbols[6] arises because it is not possible for all of the structure involved in a computation to be assembled ahead of time at the physical site of the computation. Thus it is necessary to travel out to other (distal) parts of the memory to obtain the additional structure. In terms of the knowledge level this is what is required to bring all of the system's knowledge to bear on achieving a goal. It is not possible generally to know in advance all the knowledge that will be used in a computation (for that would imply that the computation had already been carried out). Thus the ingredients for a symbol mechanism are some pattern within the structures being processed (the token), which can be used to open an access path to a distal structure (and which may involve search of the memory) and a retrieval path by means of which the distal structure can be communicated to inform the local site of the computation.[7]

Operations   The system is capable of performing *operations* on symbol structures to compose new symbol structures. There are many variations on such operations in terms of what they do in building new structures or modifying old structures and in terms of how they depend on other symbol structures. The form such operations take in standard computers is the application of an operator to a set of operands, as specified in a fixed instruction format (see figure 3.1). Higher-level programming languages generalize this to the full scope of an applicative formalism, where $(F\ x_1, x_2, \ldots, x_n)$ commands the system to apply the function F to operands $x_1, \ldots, x_n$ to produce a new structure.

Interpretation   Some structures (not all) have the property of determining that a sequence of symbol operations occurs on specific symbol structures. These structures are called variously *codes, programs, procedures, routines,* or *plans*. The process of applying the operations is called *interpreting* the symbol structure. In standard computers this occurs by the fetch-execute cycle (compare figure 3.1), whereby each instruction is accessed, its operands decoded and distributed to various registers, and the operation executed. The simplicity of this scheme corresponds to the simplicity of machine language and is dictated by the complexity of what can be efficiently and reliably realized directly in hardware. More complex procedural (high-level) languages can be compiled into an elaborate program in the simpler machine language or executed on the fly (that is, interpretively) by the microcode of a simple subcomputer. Other alternatives are possible, for example, constructing a specific special-purpose machine that embodies the operations of the program and then activating the machine. All these come to the same thing—the ability to convert from symbol structures to behavior.

The Integrated System We now have all the ingredients of a symbol system. These are sufficient to produce indefinitely flexible behavior (requirement 1 in the first list). Figure 3.2 gives the essential interaction. Operations can construct symbol structures that can be interpreted to specify further operations to construct yet further symbol structures. This loop provides for the construction of arbitrary behavior as a function of other demands. The only additional requirements are some properties of sufficiency and completeness. Without sufficient memory and sufficient symbols the system will be unable to do tasks demanding sufficiently voluminous intermediate references and data, just because it will run out of resources. Without completeness in the loop some sequences of behavior will not be producible. This has two faces: complete composability, so operators can construct any symbol structure, and complete interpretability, so interpretable symbols structures are possible for any arrangement of operations. Under completeness should also be included reliability—if the mechanisms do not operate as posited (including memory), then results need not follow.

Universality is a simple and elegant way to state what it takes to be flexible, by taking flexibility to its limit.[8] Failures of sufficiency and completeness do not necessarily threaten flexibility in critical ways. In a finite world all resources are finite, but so is the organism's sojourn on earth. Failures of completeness are a little harder to assess because their satisfaction can be extremely devious and indirect (including the uses of error-detecting and correcting mechanisms to deal with finite reliability). But in general there is a continuum of effect in real terms with the severity and extent of the failure. However, no theory is available to inform us about approximations to universality.

In addition to providing flexibility, symbol systems provide important support for several of the other requirements in the first list. For adapt-

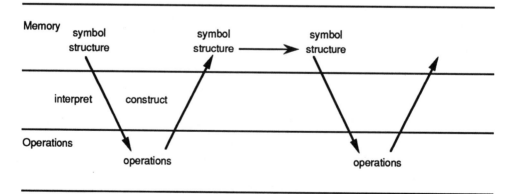

Figure 3.2 The basic loop of interpretation and construction

ability (requirement 2) they provide the ability to represent goals and to conditionalize action off of them. For using vast amounts of knowledge (requirement 4.b), they provide symbol structures in which the knowledge can be encoded and arbitrarily large memories with the accompanying ability to access distal knowledge as necessary. For symbols, abstractions, and language (requirements 5 and 6) they provide the ability to manipulate representations. For learning (requirement 7) they provide the ability to create long-term symbol structures.

Interaction with the External World
Symbol systems are components of a larger embedding system that lives in a real dynamic world, and their overall function is to create appropriate interactions of this larger system with that world. The interfaces of the large system to the world are sensory and motor devices. Exactly where it makes sense to say the architecture ends and distinct input/output subsystems begin depends on the particular system. All information processing right up to the energy transducers at the skin might be constructed on a common design and be part of a single architecture, multiple peripheral architectures of distinct design might exist, or multiple specialized systems for transduction and communication might exist that are not architectures according to our definition. Despite all this variability several common functions can be identified: The first is relatively obvious—the architecture must provide for the interfaces that connect the sensory and motor devices to the symbol system. Just what these interfaces do and where they are located is a function of how the boundary is drawn between the central cognitive system (the symbol system) and the peripheral systems.

The second arises from the asynchrony between the internal and external worlds. Symbol systems are an interior milieu, protected from the external world, in which information processing in the service of the organism can proceed. One implication is that the external world and the internal symbolic world proceed asynchronously. Thus there must be *buffering* of information between the two in both directions. How many buffer memories and of what characteristics depends on the time constants and rates of the multiple inputs and outputs. If transducers are much slower than internal processing, of course the transducer itself becomes a sufficiently accurate memory. In addition there must be *interrupt* mechanisms to cope with the transfer of processing between the multiple asynchronous sources of information.

The third function arises from the real-time demand characteristics of the external world (requirement 3 in the first list). The environment provides a continually changing kaleidoscope of opportunities and threats, with their own time constants. One implication for the architecture is for an interrupt capability, so that processing can be switched in time to new demands. The mechanics of interruption has already been posited, but the real-time demand also makes clear a requirement for precognitive assessment, that is, for assessment that occurs before assessment by the cognitive system. A demand that is more difficult to specify sharply, but is nonetheless real, is that processing be oriented toward getting answers rapidly. This cannot be an unconditional demand, if we take the time constants of the implementation technology as fixed (neural circuits for human cognition), because computing some things faster implies computing other things slower, and more generally there are intrinsic computational complexities. Still, architectures that provide effective time-limited computation are indicated.

The fourth function arises from an implication of a changing environment—the system cannot know in advance everything it needs to know about such an environment. Therefore the system must continually acquire knowledge from the environment (part of requirement 7) and do so at time constants dictated by the environment (a less obvious form of requirement 3). Symbol systems have the capability of acquiring knowledge, so in this respect at least no new architectural function is involved. The knowledge to be acquired flows in from the environment in real time, however, and not under the control of the system. It follows that learning must also occur essentially in real time. In part this is just the dynamics of the bathtub—on average the inflow to a bathtub (here encoded experience) must equal the outflow from the bathtub (here experience processed to become knowledge). But it is coupled with the fact that the water never stops flowing in, so that there is no opportunity to process at leisure.

Summary

We have attempted to list the functions of the cognitive architecture, which is to provide the support for human cognition, as characterized in the list of requirements for shaping the architecture. Together the symbol-system and real-time functions cover a large part of the primitive functionality needed for requirements 1 through 7. They do not ensure that the requirements are met, but they do provide needed support.

There is little to say for now about architectural support for development (requirement 8). The difficulty is our minimal knowledge of the mechanisms involved in enabling developmental transitions, even at a psychological level (Klahr 1989). It makes a significant difference whether development occurs through the type of general learning that is supported by symbol systems—that is, the creation of long-term symbol structures—or by distinct mechanisms. Even if development were a part of general learning after the first several years, it might require special architectural mechanisms at the beginning of life. Such requirements might shape the architecture in many other ways.

Autonomy in a social environment is another requirement (number 9 in the list) where we cannot yet pin down additional functions for the architecture to support. On the more general issue of autonomy, however, issues that have proved important in computer architecture include protection, resource allocation, and exception handling. Protection enables multiple components of a system to behave concurrently without interfering with each other. Resource allocation enables a system to work within its finite resources of time and memory, recycling resources as they are freed. Exception handling enables a system to recover from error situations that would otherwise require intervention by a programmer (for example, a division by zero or the detection of an inconsistency in a logic data base).

Issues of self-awareness (requirement 10) have recently been an active research topic in computer science, under the banner of metalevel architecture and reflection (the articles in Maes and Nardi 1988 provide a good sampling). Functionalities studied include how a system can model, reason about, control, and modify itself. Techniques for exception handling turn out to be a special case of the ability of a system to reason about and modify itself. On the psychological side the work on metacognition has made us aware of the way knowledge of a person's own capabilities (or lack of) affects performance (Brown 1978). As yet this work does not seem to have clear implications for the architecture, because it is focused on the development and use of adaptive strategies that do not seem to require special access to the instantaneous running state of the system, which is the obvious architectural support issue.

3.4 Example Architectures: Act* and Soar

We now have an analysis of the functions of a cognitive architecture and the general way it responds to the requirements of our first list. To make this analysis concrete, we examine two cognitive architectures, Act* (Anderson 1983) and Soar (Laird, Newell, and Rosenbloom 1987). Act* is the first theory of the cognitive architecture with sufficient detail and completeness to be worthy of the name. It represents a long development (Anderson and Bower 1973, Anderson 1976), and further developments have occurred since the definitive book was written (Anderson 1986, Anderson and Thompson 1988). Soar is a more recent entry as a cognitive theory (Newell 1987, Polk and Newell 1988, Rosenbloom, Laird, and Newell 1988). Its immediate prior history is as an AI architecture (Laird, Rosenbloom, and Newell 1986, Steir et al. 1987), but it has roots in earlier psychological work (Newell and Simon 1972, Newell 1973, Rosenbloom and Newell 1988). Using two architectures provides some variety to help clarify points and also permits a certain amount of comparison. Our purpose is to make clear the nature of the cognitive architecture, however, rather than to produce a judgment between the architectures.

Overview

Let us start with a quick overview of the two systems and then proceed to iterate through the functions in the second list. Figure 3.3 gives the

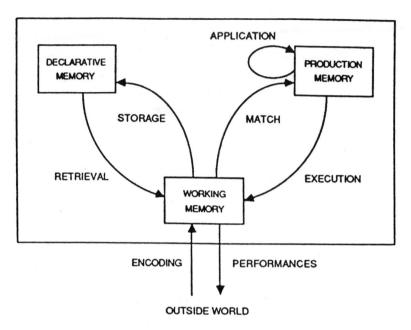

Figure 3.3 Overview of the Act* cognitive architecture (Anderson 1983)

basic structure of Act*. There is a long-term declarative memory in the form of a semantic net. There is a long-term procedural memory in the form of productions. Strengths are associated with each long-term memory element (both network nodes and productions) as a function of its use. Each production has a set of conditions that test elements of a working memory and a set of actions that create new structures in the working memory. The working memory is activation based; it contains the activated portion of the declarative memory plus declarative structures generated by production firings and perception.[9] Activation spreads automatically (as a function of node strength) through working memory and from there to other connected nodes in the declarative memory. Working memory may contain goals that serve as large sources of activation. Activation, along with production strength, determines how fast the matching of productions proceeds. Selection of productions to fire is a competitive process between productions matching the same data. New productions are created by compiling the effects of a sequence of production firings and retrievals from declarative memory so that the new productions can move directly from initial situations to final results.[10] Whenever a new element is created in working memory, there is a fixed probability it will be stored in declarative memory.

Figure 3.4 provides a corresponding overview of Soar. There is a single long-term memory—a production system—that is used for both declarative and procedural knowledge. There is a working memory that contains a goal hierarchy, information associated with the goal hierarchy, preferences about what should be done, perceptual information, and motor commands. Interaction with the outside world occurs via

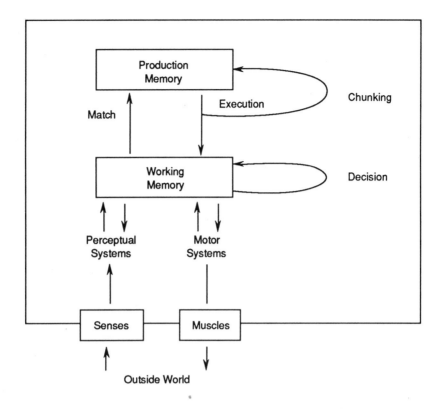

Figure 3.4 Overview of the Soar cognitive architecture

interfaces between working memory and one or more perceptual and motor systems. All tasks are formulated as searches in problem spaces, that is, as starting from some initial state in a space and finding a desired state by the application of the operators that comprise the space. Instead of making decisions about what productions to execute—all productions that successfully match are fired in parallel—decisions are made about what problem spaces, states, and operators to utilize. These decisions are based on preferences retrieved from production memory into working memory. When a decision proves problematic (because of incomplete or inconsistent knowledge), a subgoal is automatically created by the architecture and problem solving recurses on the task of resolving the impasse in decision making. This generates a hierarchy of goals and thus problem spaces. New productions are created continuously from the traces of Soar's experience in goal-based problem solving (a process called chunking).

Memory
Memory is to be identified by asking what persists over time that can be created and modified by the system. Both Act* and Soar have memory hierarchies that range in both time constants and volume. At the small, rapid end both have working memories. Working memory is a

temporary memory that cannot hold data over any extended duration. In Act* this is manifest because working memory is an activated subset of declarative memory and thus ebbs and flows with the processing of activation. In Soar working memory appears as a distinct memory. Its short-term character derives from its being linked with goals and their problem spaces, so that it disappears automatically as these goals are resolved.

Beyond working memory both architectures have permanent memories of unbounded size, as required for universality. Act* has two such memories—declarative memory and production memory—with strengths associated with each element in each memory. The normal path taken by new knowledge in Act* is from working memory to declarative memory to production memory. Declarative memory comes before production memory in the hierarchy because it has shorter storage and access times (though it cannot lead directly to action). Soar has only one permanent memory of unbounded size—production memory—which is used for both declarative and procedural knowledge. Soar does not utilize strengths.

The above picture is that Act* has two totally distinct memories, and Soar has one that is similar to one of Act*'s memories. However, this conventional surface description conceals some important aspects. One is that Act* and Soar productions do not function in the same way in their respective systems (despite having essentially the same condition-action form). Act* productions correspond to problem-solving operators. This is essentially the way productions are used throughout the AI and expert-systems world. Soar productions operate as an associative memory. The action side of a production contains the symbol structures that are held in the memory; the condition side provides the access path to these symbol structures. Firing a Soar production is the act of retrieval of its symbol structures. Operators in Soar are implemented by collections of productions (or search in subgoals). Another hidden feature is that Act*'s production memory is realized as a network structure similar in many ways to its semantic net. The main effect is that activation governs the rate of matching of productions in the same way that activation spreads through the declarative network. Thus these two memories are not as distinct as it might seem.

In both Act* and Soar the granularity of long-term memory (the independently modifiable unit) is relatively fine, being the individual production and, for Act*'s declarative memory, the node and link. This is a much larger unit than the word in conventional computers (by about two orders of magnitude) but much smaller than the frame or schema (again by about two orders of magnitude). This is an important architectural feature. The frame and schema have been introduced on the hypothesis that the unit of memory organization needs to be relatively large to express the organized character of human thought (Minsky 1975). It is not easy to make size comparisons between units of memory organization because this is one place where the idiosyncratic world-view character of architectures is most in evidence, and all memory organization have various larger and smaller hierarchical units. Nevertheless both Act* and Soar are on the fine-grained side.

The memory structures of both Act* and Soar are the discrete symbolic structures familiar from systems such as Lisp. There are differences in detail. Soar has a uniform scheme of objects with sets of attributes and values. Act* has several primitive data structures: attributes and values (taken to be the abstract propositional code), strings (taken to be the temporal code), and metric arrays (taken to be the spatial code). The primary requirement of a data structure is combinatorial variability, and all these structures possess it. The secondary considerations are on the operations that are required to read and manipulate the data structures, corresponding to what the structures are to represent. Thus standard computers invariably have multiple data structures, each with associated primitive operations, for example, for arithmetic or text processing. Act* here is taking a clue from this standard practice.

Symbols
Symbols are to be identified by finding the mechanisms that provide distal access to memory structures that are not already involved in processing. For both Act* and Soar this is the pattern match of the production system, which is a process that starts with symbolic structures in working memory and determines that a production anywhere in the long-term memory will fire. The symbol tokens here are the combinations of working memory elements that match production conditions. Each production's left-hand side is a symbol.

For Soar this is the only mechanism for distal access (working memory being essentially local). For Act* there is also a mechanism for distal access to its declarative memory, in fact a combination of two mechanisms. First, each token brought into working memory by firing a production (or by perception) makes contact with its corresponding node in the declarative semantic net. Second, spreading activation then operates to provide access to associated nodes.

It is useful to identify the pair of features that gives symbolic access in production systems its particular flavor. The first feature is the context-dependent nature of the production match. Simple machine addresses act as context-independent symbols. No matter what other structures exist, the address causes information to be retrieved from the same location.[11] In a production system a particular pattern can be a symbol that results in context-independent access to memory structures, or (more typically) it can be conjoined with additional context patterns to form a more complex symbol that constrains access to occur only when the context is present.

The second feature is the recognition nature of the production match. Traditional computers access memory either by pointers to arbitrary memory locations (random access) or by sequential access to adjacent locations (large secondary stores). In production systems symbols are constructed out of the same material that is being processed for the task, so memory access has a *recognition, associative,* or *content-addressed* nature. All schemes can support universality; however, the recognition scheme is responsive to two additional cognitive requirements. First, (approximately) constant-time access to the whole of memory is responsive to the real-time requirement. This includes random-access and recognition memories, but excludes sequential access systems such as Turing machines. But specific task-relevant accessing schemes must be constructed, or the system is doomed to operate by generate and test (and might as well be a tape machine). Recognition memories construct the accessing paths from the ingredients of the task and thus avoid deliberate acts of construction, which are required by location-pointer schemes. This may actually be an essential requirement for a learning system that has to develop entirely on its own. Standard programming involves intelligent programmers who invent specific accessing schemes based on deep analysis of a task.[12]

Operations

The operations are to be identified by asking how new structures get built and established in the long-term memory. In standard computer systems the form in which the operations are given is dictated by the needs of interpretation, that is, by the structure of the programming language. Typically everything is fit within an operation-operand structure, and there is a single, heterogeneous set of all primitive operation codes—load, store, add, subtract, and, or, branch-on-zero, execute, and so on. Some of these are operations that produce new symbol structures in memory, but others affect control or deal with input/output.

Production systems, as classically defined, also operate this way. The right-hand-side actions are operation-operand structures that can specify general procedures, although a standard set of operations are predefined (make, replace, delete, write . . .). In some it is possible to execute a specified production or production system on the right-hand side, thus providing substantial right-hand-side control. But Act* and Soar use a quite different scheme.

The right-hand-side action becomes essentially just the operation of creating structures in working memory. This operation combines focusing, modifying, and creating—it brings existing structures into working memory, it creates working memory structures that relate existing structures, and it creates new structures if they do not exist. This operation is coextensive with the retrieval of knowledge from long-term memory (production firing). The dependence of the operation on existing structures (that is, its inputs) occurs by the matching of the production conditions. It is this matching against what is already in working memory that permits the multiple functions of focusing, modifying, and creating to be distinguished and to occur in the appropriate circumstances, automatically, so to speak. Along with this the act of retrieval from long-term memory (into working memory) does not happen as a distinct operation that reproduces the content of long-term memory in working memory. Rather each retrieval is an act of computation (indeed computation takes place only in concert with such retrievals), so that working memory is never the same as stored memory and is always to some extent an adaptation of the past to the present.

In Act* and Soar storing information in long-term memory is separated from the act of computation in working memory. It is incorporated as learning new productions, called *production compilation* in Act* and *chunking* in Soar, but similar operations nonetheless. The context of production acquisition is the occasion of goal satisfaction or termination, and the constructed production spans from the conditions holding before the goal to the actions that caused the final resolution. The production is simply added to the long-term production memory and becomes indistinguishable from any other production. Such a production is functional, producing in one step what took many steps originally. It also constitutes an implicit form of generalization in that its conditions are extracted from the total context of working memory at learning time, and so can be evoked in situations that can be arbitrarily different in ways that are irrelevant to these conditions. Production compilation and chunking go considerably beyond the minimal support for experiential learning provided by a standard symbol system. Without deliberate effort or choice they automatically acquire new knowledge that is a function of their experiences.

Act* has other forms of memory aside from the productions and necessarily must have operations for storing in each of them. They are all automatic operations that do not occur under deliberate control of the system. One is the strength of productions, which governs how fast they are processed and hence whether they become active in an actual situation. Every successful firing of a production raises its strength a little and hence increases the likelihood that if satisfied it will actually fire (another form of experiential learning). The second is storage in declarative memory. Here there is simply a constant probability that a newly created element will become a permanent part of declarative memory. Declarative learning is responsive to the requirement of learning from the environment. In Soar chunking performs this function in addition to its function of learning from experience.

Interpretation
Interpretation is to be identified by finding where a system makes its behavior dependent on the symbolic structures in its long-term memory, in particular, on structures that it itself created earlier. A seemingly equivalent way is to find what memory structures correspond to the program in typical computer systems, namely, the symbol structures

that specify a sequence of operations: do this, then do that, then do this, although also admitting conditionals and calls to subprocedures. Namely, one seeks compact symbol structures that control behavior over an extended interval.

One looks in vain for such symbol structures in the basic descriptions of the Act* and Soar architectures. (Program structures can exist of course, but they require software interpreters.) Memory-dependent behavior clearly occurs, however, and is derived from multiple sources—production systems, problem-solving control knowledge, and goal structures.

The first source in both systems is the form of interpretation inherent in production systems. A production system shreds control out into independent fragments (the individual productions) spread out all over production memory, with data elements in working memory entering in at every cycle. This control regime is often referred to as *data directed*, in contrast to *goal directed*, but this characterization misses some important aspects. Another way to look at it is as a *recognize-act cycle* in contrast to the classical *fetch-execute cycle* that characterizes standard computers. According to this view, an important dimension of interpretation is the amount of decision making that goes on between steps. The fetch-execute cycle essentially has only a pointer into a plan and has to take deliberate steps (doing tests and branches) to obtain any conditionality at all. The recognize-act cycle opens up the interpretation at every point to anything that the present working memory can suggest. This puts the production match *inside* the interpretation cycle.

The second source is the control knowledge used to select problem-solving operators. In Act* the productions are the problem-solving operators. As described in the previous paragraph, production selection is a function of the match between working memory elements and production conditions. Several additional factors, however, also come into play in determining the rate of matching and thus whether a production is selected for execution. One factor is the activation of the working memory elements being matched. A second factor is the strength of the production being matched. A third factor is the competition between productions that match the same working memory elements in different ways.

In Soar problem-solving operators are selected through a two-phase *decision cycle*. First, during the elaboration phase the long-term production memory is accessed repeatedly—initial retrievals may evoke additional retrievals—in parallel (there is no conflict resolution) until quiescence. Any elements can be retrieved, but among these are *preferences* that state which of the operators are acceptable, rejectable, or preferable to others. When all the information possible has been accumulated, the decision procedure winnows the available preferences and makes the next decision, which then moves the system to the next cycle.

In fact Soar uses this same basic interpreter for more than just selecting what operator to execute. It is always trying to make the decisions required to operate in a problem space: to decide what problem space to use, what state to use in that problem space, what operator to use at that state, and what state to use as the result of the operator. This is what forces all activity to take place in problem spaces. This contrasts with the standard computer, which assumes all activity occurs by following an arbitrary program.

The third source of memory-dependent behavior is the use of goal structures. Act* provides special architectural support for a goal hierarchy in its working memory. The current goal is a high source of activation, which therefore operates to focus attention by giving prominence to productions that have it as one of their conditions. The architecture takes care of the tasks of popping successful subgoals and moving the focus to subsequent subgoals, providing a depth-first traversal of the goal hierarchy. Thus the characterization of data- versus goal-directed processing is somewhat wide of the mark. Act* is a paradigm example of an AI system that uses goals and methods to achieve adaptability (requirement 2 in the first list). Complex tasks are controlled by productions that build up the goal hierarchy by adding conjunctions of goals to be achieved in the future.

Soar uses a much less deliberate strategy for the generation of goals. When the decision procedure cannot produce a single decision from the collection of preferences that happen to accumulate—because, for example, no options remain acceptable or several indistinguishable options remain—an impasse is reached. Soar assumes this indicates lack of knowledge—given additional knowledge of its preferences, a decision could have been reached. It thus creates a subgoal to resolve this impasse. An impasse is resolved just when preferences are generated, of whatever nature, that lead to a decision at the higher level. Thus Soar generates its own subgoals out of the impasses the architecture can detect, in contrast to Act*, which generates its subgoals by deliberate action on the part of its productions. The effect of deliberate subgoals is achieved in Soar by the combination of an operator, which is deliberately generated and selected, and an impasse that occurs if productions do not exist that implement the operator. In the subgoal for this impasse the operator acts as the specification of a goal to be achieved.

Interaction with the External World

Act*, as is typical of many theories of cognition, focuses on the central architecture. Perception and motor behavior are assumed to take place in additional processing systems off stage. Input arrives in working, which thus acts as a buffer between the unpredictable stream of environmental events and the cognitive system. Beyond this, however, the architecture has simply not been elaborated on in these directions.

Soar has the beginnings of a complete architecture, which embeds the central architecture within a structure for interacting with the external world. As shown in figure 3.4, Soar is taken as a controller of a dynamic system interacting with a dynamic external environment (located across the bottom of the figure). There are processes that transduce the energies in the environment into signals for the system. Collectively they are called *perception*, although they are tied down only on the sensory side (transduction from the environment). Similarly there are processes that affect the environment. Collectively they are called the *motor system*, although they are tied down only on the physical action side. As in Act* working memory serves as the buffer between the environment and central cognition.

The total system consists of more than perception to central cognition to the motor system. There are productions, called *encoding productions* and *decoding productions*. These are identical in form and structure to the productions of central cognition. They differ only in being independent of the decision cycle—they just run free. On the input side, as elements arrive autonomously from the perceptual system, encoding productions provide what could be termed perceptual parsing, putting the elements into a form to be considered by central cognition. On the output side decoding productions provide what could be called motor-program decoding of commands produced by the cognitive system into the form used by the motor system. The motor system itself may produce elements back into the working memory (possibly parsed by encoding productions), permitting monitoring and adjustment.

All this activity is not under control; these productions recognize and execute at will, concurrently with each other and central cognition. Control is exercised by central cognition, which can now be seen to consist essentially of just the architecture of the decision mechanism, from which flows the decision cycle, impasses, the goal stack, and the problem-space organization. Further, central cognition operates essentially as a form of localized supervisory control over autonomous and continuing activities in working memory generated by the perception systems, the motor systems, and their coupled encoding and decoding productions.

This permits an understanding of an architectural question that has consumed a lot of attention, namely, wherein lies the serial character of cognition? Central cognition is indeed serial, which is what the decision mechanism enforces, and so it can consider only some of what goes on in the working memory. The serial system is imposed on a sea of autonomous parallel activity to attain control, that is, for the system to be able to prevent from occurring actions that are not in its interests. Thus seriality is a designed feature of the system. Seriality can occur for other reasons as well, which can be summarized generally as resource constraints or bottlenecks. Such bottlenecks can arise from the nature of the underlying technology and thus be a limitation on the system.

Interrupt capabilities are to be identified by finding where behavior can switch from one course to another that is radically different. For Act* switching occurs by the basic maximum-selecting property of an activation mechanism—whatever process can manage the highest activation can take over the control of behavior. For Soar switching occurs by the decision cycle—whatever can marshal the right preferences compared with competing alternatives can control behavior. Switching can thus occur at a fine grain. For both Act* and Soar their basic switching mechanism is also an interrupt mechanism, because alternatives from throughout the system compete on an equal basis. This arises from the open character of production systems that contact all of memory at each cycle. Thus radical changes of course can occur at any instant. This contrasts with standard computers. Although arbitrary switching is possible at each instruction (for example, branch on zero to an arbitrary program), such shifts must be determined deliberately and by the (pre-constructed) program that already has control. Thus the issue for the standard computer is how to be interrupted, whereas the issue for Soar and Act* (and presumably for human cognition) is how to keep focused.

Learning from the environment involves the long-term storage of structures that are based on inputs to the system. Act* stores new inputs into declarative memory with a fixed probability, from which inputs can get into production memory via compilation, a process that should be able to keep pace with the demands of a changing environment. Soar stores new inputs in production memory via chunking. This implies that an input must be used in a subgoal for it to be stored, and that the bandwidth from the environment into long-term memory will be a function of the rate at which environmental inputs can be used.

Summary
We have now instantiated the functions of the cognitive architecture for two architectures, Soar and Act*, using their commonalities and differences to make evident how their structures realize these functions. The communalities of Act* and Soar are appreciable, mostly because both are built around production systems. We have seen that production systems, or more generally, recognition-based architectures, are a species of architecture that is responsive to the real-time requirement, which is clearly one of the most powerful shapers of the architecture beyond the basic need for symbolic computation.

The move to production systems, however, is only the first of three major steps that have moved Act* and Soar jointly into a very different part of the architecture space from all of the classical computers. The second step is the abandonment of the application formalism of applying operations to operands. This abandonment is not an intrinsic part of production systems, as evidenced by the almost universal use of application on the action side of productions. This second step locks the operations on symbolic structures into the acts of memory retrieval.

The third step is the separation of the act of storing symbolic structures in long-term memory—the learning mechanisms of Act* and Soar—from the deliberate acts of performing tasks.

There are some architectural differences between Act* and Soar, though not all appear to be major differences when examined carefully. One example is the dual declarative and procedural memory of Act* versus the single production memory of Soar. Another is the use of activation in Act* versus the use of accumulated production executions (the elaboration phase) in Soar. A third is the commitment to multiple problem spaces and the impasse mechanism in Soar versus the single-space environment with deliberate subgoals in Act*. Thus these architectures differ enough to explore a region of the architecture space.

The downside of using two closely related architectures for the exposition is that we fail to convey an appreciation of how varied and rich in alternatives the space of architecture is. With a slight stretch we might contend we have touched three points in the architecture space: classical (von Neumann) architectures, classical production systems, and Act* and Soar. But we could have profitably examined applicative languages (for example, Lisp; see Steele 1984), logic programming languages (for example, Prolog; see Clocksin and Mellish 1984), frame (or schema) systems (for example, KLONE; see Brachman 1979), blackboard architectures (for example, BB1; see Hayes-Roth 1985), and others as well. Also we could have explored the effect of parallelism, which itself has many architectural dimensions. This was excluded because it is primarily driven by the need to exploit or compensate for implementation technology, although (as has been pointed out many times) it can also serve as a response to the real-time requirement.

3.5 The Uses of the Architecture

Given that the architecture is a component of the human cognitive system, it requires no justification to spend scientific effort on it. Understanding the architecture is a scientific project in its own right. The architecture, however, as the frame in terms of which all processing is done and the locus of the structural constraints on human cognition, would appear to be the central element in a general theory of cognition. This would seem to imply that the architecture enters into all aspects of cognition. What keeps this implication at bay is the fact (oft noted, by now) that architectures hide themselves beneath the knowledge level. For many aspects of human cognitive life, what counts are the goals, the task situation, and the background knowledge (including education, socialization, and enculturation). So the architecture may be critical for cognition, just as biochemistry is, but with only circumscribed consequences for ongoing behavior and its study.

How then is a detailed theory of the architecture to be used in cognitive science, other than simply filling in its own part of the picture?

There are four partial answers to this question, which we take up in turn.

Establishing Gross Parameters

The first answer presupposes that the architecture has large effects on cognition, but that these effects can be summarized in a small set of gross parameters. The following list assembles one set of such parameters, which are familiar to all cognitive scientists—the size of short-term memory, the time for an elementary operation, the time to make a move in a problem space, and the rate of acquisition into long-term memory:

1. Memory Unit: 1 chunk composed of 3 subchunks
2. Short-term memory size: 3 chunks plus 4 chunks from long-term memory
3. Time per elementary operation: 100 ms
4. Time per step in a problem space: 2 s
5. Time to learn new material: 1 chunk per 2 s

It is not possible to reason from parameters alone. Parameters always imply a background model. Even to fill in the list it is necessary to define a unit of memory (the chunk), which then already implies a hierarchical memory structure. Likewise to put a sequence of elementary operations together and sum their times is already to define a functionally serial processing structure.

The block diagrams that have been a standard feature in cognitive psychology since the mid-1950s (Broadbent 1954) express the sort of minimal architectural structure involved. Mostly they are too sketchy, in particular, providing only a picture of the memories and their transfer paths. A somewhat more complete version, called the *model human processor* (Card, Moran, and Newell 1983), is shown in figure 3.5, which indicates not only the memories but a processor structure of three parallel processors—perceptual, cognitive, and motor. Perception and motor systems involve multiple concurrent processors for different modalities and muscle systems, but there is only a single cognitive processor. The parameters of the two figures have much in common. Figure 3.5 is of course a static picture. By its very lack of detail it implies the simplest of processing structures. In fact it can be supplemented by some moderately explicit general principles of operation (Card, Moran, and Newell 1983), such as that uncertainty always increases processing time. These principles provide some help in using it, but are a long way from making the scheme into a complete architecture. In particular the elementary operations and the details of interpretation remain essentially undefined.

If the way the architecture influences behavior can be summarized by a small set of parameters plus a simple abstract background model,

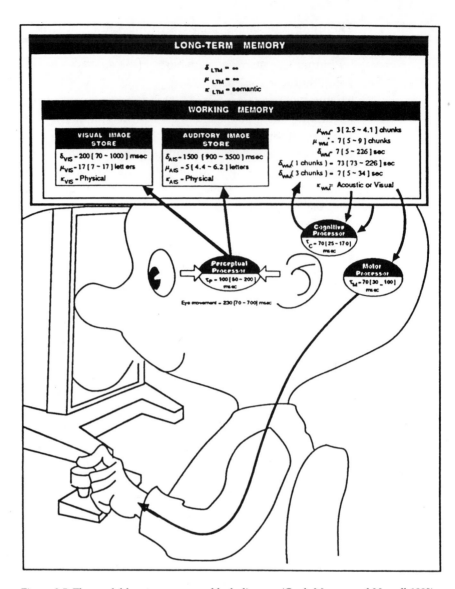

Figure 3.5 The model human processor block diagram (Card, Moran, and Newell 1983)

then the contribution from studying the architecture is twofold. First, given an established scheme such as figure 3.5, the parameters need to be pinned down, their variability understood, their mutability discovered, their limits of use assessed, and so on. Second, the gross processing model can be wrong, not in being a gross approximation (which is presumed) but in being the wrong sort of formulation. If it were replaced with a quite different formulation, then inferences might become easier, a broader set of inferences might be possible, and so forth. One such example from the mid-1970s is the replacement of the multistore model of memory with a model containing only a single memory within which information is distinguished only by the depth to which it has been processed (Craik and Lockhart 1972).

The Form of Simple Cognitive Behavior
To perform a complex task involves doing a sequence of basic operations in an arrangement conditional on the input data. Much of psychological interest depends on knowing the sequence of operations that humans perform for a given task, and much psychological effort, both experimental and theoretical, is focused on finding such sequences. This is especially true for tasks that are primarily cognitive, in which perceptual and motor operations play only a small role in the total sequence.

The architecture dictates both the basic operations and the form in which arrangements of operations are specified, namely, the way behavior specifications are encoded symbolically. Thus the architecture plays some role in determining such sequences. For tasks of any complexity, however, successful behavior can be realized in many different ways. At bottom this is simply the brute fact that different methods or algorithms exist for a given task, as when a space can be searched depth first, breadth first, or best first, or a column of numbers can be added from the top or the bottom. Thus writing down the sequence of operations followed by a subject for a complex task, given just the architecture and the task, is nearly impossible. It is far too underdetermined, and the other factors, which we summarize as the subject's knowledge, are all important.

As the time to perform the task gets shorter, however, the options get fewer for what sequences could perform a task. Indeed suppose the time constant of the primitive data operations of the architecture is about 100 ms, and we ask for a task to be performed in about 0.1 ms, then the answer is clear without further ado: it cannot be done. It makes no difference how simple the task is (for example, are two names the same?). Suppose the task is to be performed in about 100 ms. Then a scan of the architecture's basic processes will reveal what can be done in a single operation time. If the performance is possible at all, it is likely to be unique—there is only one way to test for name equality in a single basic operation, though conceivably an architecture might offer some small finite number of alternatives. As the time available grows, what can be accomplished grows and the number of ways of accomplishing a given task grow. If 100 s is available, then there are probably several ways to determine whether two names are the same. The constraint comes back, however, if the demands of the performance grow apace.

Thus there is a region in which knowing the architecture makes possible plausible guesses about what operation sequences humans will use on a task. Consider the memory-scanning task explored by Sternberg and discussed by Bower and Clapper in chapter 7 in connection with the additive-factors methodology. The subject first sees a set of items H, P, Z and then a probe item Q and must say as quickly as possible whether the probe was one of the sequence. Three regularities made this experiment famous. First, the time to answer is linear in the size of the test set (response time $= 400 + 3 \cdot 40 = 520$ ms for the case above), strongly suggesting the use of a serial scan (and test) at 40 ms per item. Second, the same linear relation with the same slope of 40 ms per item holds whether the probe is or is not in the list. This contradicts the obvious strategy of terminating the scan when an item is found that matches the probe, which would lead to an apparent average search rate for positive probes that is half as large as that for negative probes—on average only half of the list would be scanned for a positive probe before the item is found. Third, the scan rate (40 ms per item) is *very* fast—humans take more than 100 ms per letter to say the alphabet to themselves.

As Bower and Clapper (chapter 7) report, this experimental situation has been explored in many different ways and has given rise to an important experimental method (*additive factors*) to assess how different factors entered into the phenomena. For us the focus is on the speed with which things seem to happen. Speeded reaction times of about 400 ms already get close to the architecture, and phenomena that happen an order of magnitude faster (40 ms per item) must be getting close to the architecture floor. This is especially true when one considers that neurons are essentially 1-ms devices, so that neural circuits are 10-ms devices.

Just given the Sternberg phenomena, including these tight bounds, one cannot infer the mechanisms that perform it. In fact the Sternberg situation has been studied to show that one cannot even infer whether the "search" is going on in series or in parallel. Given an architecture, however, the picture becomes quite different. For instance, given Act*, the time constants imply that productions take a relatively long time to fire, on the order of 100 ms. Thus the Sternberg effect cannot be due to multiple production firings. Hence it must be a spreading activation phenomenon. Indeed the explanation that Anderson offers for the Sternberg effect is based on spreading activation (Anderson 1983, pp. 119–120). Two productions, one to say yes if the probe is there and one to say no if the probe is not, define the subject's way of doing the task, and then a calculation based on the flow of activation shows that it approximates the effect. The important point for us is that the two productions are the obvious way to specify the task in Act*, and there are few if any alternatives.

If we turn to Soar, there is an analogous analysis. First, general timing constraints imply that productions must be 10-ms mechanisms, so that the decision cycle is essentially a 100-ms mechanism, although speeded tasks would force it down (Newell 1987). Thus selecting and executing operators will take too long to be used to search and process the items of the set (at 40 ms each). Thus the Sternberg effect must be occurring within a single decision cycle, and processing the set must occur by executing a small number of productions (one to three) on each item. The fact that the decision cycle runs to quiescence would seem to be related to all items of the set being processed, whether the probe matches or not. These constraints do not pin down the exact program for the memory-scanning task as completely as in Act*, but they do specify many features of it. Again the important point here is that the closer the task is to the architecture, the more the actual program used by humans can be predicted from the structure of the architecture.

Hidden Connections

An architecture provides a form of unification for cognitive science, which arises, as we have seen, from all humans accomplishing all activities by means of the same set of mechanisms. As we have also seen, these common mechanisms work through content (that is, knowledge), which varies over persons, tasks, occasions, and history. Thus there is immense variability in behavior, and many phenomena of cognitive life are due to these other sources.

One important potential role for studies of the architecture is to reveal hidden connections between activities that on the basis of content and situation seem quite distant from each other. The connections arise, of course, because of the grounding in the same mechanisms of the architecture, so that, given the architecture, they may be neither subtle nor obscure. One such example is the way chunking has turned out to play a central role in many different forms of learning—such as the acquisition of macrooperators, the acquisition of search-control heuristics, the acquisition of new knowledge, constraint compilation, learning from external advice, and so on—and even in such traditionally non-learning behaviors as the creation of abstract plans (Steier et al. 1987). Previously, special-purpose mechanisms were developed for these various activities.

In addition to the joy that comes directly from discovering the cause of any scientific regularity, revealing distal connections is useful in adding to the constraint that is available in discovering the explanation for phenomena. An example—again from the domain of Soar—is how chunking, whose route into Soar was via a model of human practice, has provided the beginnings of a highly constrained model of verbal learning (Rosenbloom, Laird, and Newell 1988). Using chunking as the basis for verbal learning forces it to proceed in a reconstructive fashion—learning to recall a presented item requires the construction of an internal representation of the item from structures that can already be recalled—and is driving the model, for functional reasons, to where it has many similarities to the EPAM model of verbal learning (Feigenbaum and Simon 1984).

Removing Theoretical Degrees of Freedom

One of the itches of cognitive scientists ever since the early days of computer simulation of cognition is that to get a simulation to run, it is necessary to specify many procedures and data structures that have no psychological justification. There is nothing in the structure of the simulation program that indicates which procedures (or more generally which aspects) make psychological claims and which do not.

One small but real result of complete architectures is to provide relief for this itch. A proposal for an architecture is a proposal for a complete operational system. No additional processes are required or indeed even possible. Thus when a simulation occurs within such an architecture, all aspects of the system represent empirical claims. This can be seen in the case of Soar—the decision cycle is claimed to be how humans make choices about what to do, and impasses are claimed to be real and to lead to chunking. Each production is claimed to be psychologically real and to correspond to an accessible bit of knowledge of the human. And the claims go on. A similar set of claims can be made for Act*. Many of these claims (for Act* or Soar) can be, and indeed no doubt are, false. That is simply the fate of inadequate and wrong theories that fail to correspond to reality. But there is no special status of aspects that are not supposed to represent what goes on in the mind.

All this does is remove the somewhat peculiar special status of simulation-based theory and return such theories to the arena occupied by all other scientific theories. Aspects of architectures are often unknown and are covered by explicit assumptions, which are subject to analysis. Important aspects of a total theory are often simply posited, such as the initial contents of the mind resulting from prior learning and external conditions, and behavior is invariably extremely sensitive to this. Analysis copes as best it can with such uncertainties, and the issue is not different with architectures.

3.6 Conclusions

An appropriate way to end this chapter is by raising some issues that reveal additional major steps required to pursue an adequate theory of the cognitive architecture. These questions have their roots in more general issues of cognitive science, but our attention is on the implications for the cognitive architecture.

The list of requirements that could shape the architecture contains a number of items whose effects on the architecture we do not yet know, in particular the issues of acquiring capabilities through development, of living autonomously in a social community, and of exhibiting self-awareness and a sense of self (requirements 8 through 10).

Another issue is the effect on the architecture of its being a creation of biological evolution that grew out of prior structures shaped by the requirements of prior function. Thus we would expect the architecture to be shaped strongly by the structure of the perceptual and motor systems. Indeed we know from anatomical and physiological studies that vast amounts of the brain and spinal cord are devoted to these aspects. The question is what sort of architecture develops if it evolves out of the mammalian perceptual and motor systems, existing as sophisticated controllers but not yet fully capable of the flexibility that comes from full programmability. Beneath the level of the organization of the perceptual and motor systems, of course, is their realization in large, highly connected neural circuits. Here with the connectionist efforts (chapter 4) there is a vigorous attempt to understand what the implications are for the architecture.

An analogous issue is the relationship of emotion, feeling, and affect to cognition. Despite recent stirrings and a long history within psychology (Frijda 1986), no satisfactory integration yet exists of these phenomena into cognitive science. But the mammalian system is clearly constructed as an emotional system, and we need to understand in what way this shapes the architecture, if indeed it does so at all.[13]

We close by noting that the largest open issue with respect to the architecture in cognitive science is not all these phenomena whose impact on the architecture remains obscure. Rather it is our almost total lack of experience in working with complete cognitive architectures. Our quantitative and reasonably precise theories have been narrow; our general theories have been broad and vague. Even where we have approached a reasonably comprehensive architecture (Act* being the principal existing example), working with it has been sufficiently arcane and difficult that communities of scientists skilled in its art have not emerged. Thus we know little about what features of an architecture account for what phenomena, what aspects of an architecture connect what phenomena with others, and how sensitive various explanations are to variations in the architecture. About the only experience we have with the uses for architectures described in section 3.5 is analysis using gross parameters.

Such understandings do not emerge by a single study or by many studies by a single investigator. They come from many people exploring and tuning the architecture for many different purposes until derivations of various phenomena from the architecture become standard and understood. They come, as with so many aspects of life, from living them.

Notes

1. This technical use of the term is often extended to include combinations of software and hardware that produce a system that can be programmed. This broad usage is encouraged by the fact that software systems often present a structure that is meant to be fixed, so that the computer plus software operates just as if it were cast in hardware. In this chapter, however, we always take *architecture* in the narrow technical sense.

2. In part this is because functions are conceptual elements in an analysis of natural systems, and so what functions exist depends on the scheme of analysis.

3. They have been called *physical symbol systems* (Newell and Simon 1976) to emphasize that their notion of symbol derives from computer science and artificial intelligence, in contradistinction to the notion of symbol in the arts and humanities, which may or may not prove to be the same. The shorter phrase will do here.

4. Note, however, that it has proved functional in existing computers to drive the independence down as far as possible, to the bit.

5. Access structures can be (and are in plenitude) built up within the software of a system; we discuss the basic capability in the architecture that supports all such software mechanisms.

6. Note that the term *symbol* is used here for a type of structure and mechanism within a symbol system and not, as in *to symbolize*, as a synonym for something that represents. This notion of symbol, however, does at least require internal representation—addresses designate memory structures, input stimuli must map to fixed internal structures, and operator codes designate operations.

7. Conceivably this could be extended to include the external world as a distal level in the system's memory hierarchy (beyond the tertiary level). Symbol tokens would specify addresses in the external world, and the access and retrieval paths would involve perceptual and motor acts.

8. As the famous results of Turing, Church, and others have shown, this limit does not include all possible functional dependencies but only a large subclass of them, called the *computable functions*.

9. Another way to view the relationship of working memory to the long-term declarative memory is as two manifestations of a single underlying declarative memory. Each element in this underlying memory has two independently settable bits associated with it: whether the element is active (determines whether it is in working memory), and whether it is permanent (determines whether it is in long-term declarative memory).

10. In Anderson 1983 Act* is described as having two additional methods for creating new productions—generalization and discrimination—but they were later shown to be unnecessary (Anderson 1986).

11. *Virtual addressing* is a mechanism that introduces a small fixed amount of context, namely, a base address.

12. As always, however, there is a trade-off. Recognition schemes are less flexible compared with location-pointer schemes, which are a genuinely task-independent medium for constructing accessing schemes, and hence can be completely adapted to the task at hand.

13. Feelings and emotions can be treated as analogous to sensations so they could affect the content of the cognitive system, even to including insistent signals, but still not affect the shape of the architecture.

References

Agrawal, D. P. 1986. *Advanced Computer Architecture.* Washington, DC: Computer Society Press.

Anderson, J. R. 1976. *Language, Memory and Thought.* Hillsdale, NJ: Erlbaum.

Anderson, J. R. 1983. *The Architecture of Cognition.* Cambridge, MA: Harvard University Press.

Anderson, J. R. 1986. Knowledge compilation: The general learning mechanism. In R. S. Michalski, J. G. Carbonell, and T. M. Mitchell, eds. *Machine Learning: An Artificial Intelligence Approach.* Vol. 2. Los Altos, CA: Morgan Kaufmann Publishers, Inc.

Anderson, J. R., and Bower, G. 1973. *Human Associative Memory.* Washington, DC: Winston.

Anderson, J. R., and Thompson, R. 1988. Use of analogy in a production system architecture. In S. Vosniadou and A. Ortony, eds. *Similarity and Analogical Reasoning.* New York: Cambridge University Press.

Bell, C. G., and Newell, A. 1971. *Computer Structures: Readings and Examples.* New York: McGraw-Hill.

Brachman, R. J. 1979. On the epistemological status of semantic networks. In N. V. Findler, ed. *Associative Networks: Representation and Use of Knowledge by Computers.* New York: Academic Press.

Broadbent, D. E. 1954. A mechanical model for human attention and immediate memory. *Psychological Review* 64:205.

Brown, A. L. 1978. Knowing when, where, and how to remember: A problem in metacognition. In R. Glaser, ed. *Advances in Instructional Psychology.* Hillsdale, NJ: Erlbaum.

Card, S., Moran, T. P., and Newell, A. 1983. *The Psychology of Human-Computer Interaction.* Hillsdale, NJ: Erlbaum.

Clocksin, W. F., and Mellish, C. S. 1984. *Programming in Prolog.* 2nd ed. New York: Springer-Verlag.

Craik, F. I. M., and Lockhart, R. S. 1972. Levels of processing: A framework for memory research. *Journal of Verbal Learning and Verbal Behavior* 11:671–684.

Symbolic Architectures for Cognition

Feigenbaum, E. A., and Simon, H. A. 1984. EPAM-like models of recognition and learning. *Cognitive Science* 8:305–336.

Fernandez, E. B., & Lang, T. 1986. *Software-Oriented Computer Architecture.* Washington, DC: Computer Society Press.

Frijda, N. H. 1986. *The Emotions.* Cambridge, Engl.: Cambridge University Press.

Gajski, D. D., Milutinovic, V. M., Siegel, H. J., and Furht, B. P. 1987. *Computer Architecture.* Washington, DC: Computer Society Press.

Hayes-Roth, B. 1985. A blackboard architecture for control. *Artificial Intelligence* 26:251–321.

Hopcroft, J. E., and Ullman, J. D. 1979. *Introduction to Automata Theory, Languages, and Computation.* Reading, MA: Addison-Wesley.

Klahr, D. 1989. Information processing approaches to cognitive development. In R. Vasta, ed. *Annals of Child Development.* Greenwich, CT: JAI Press, pp. 131–183.

Laird, J. E., Newell, A., & Rosenbloom, P. S. 1987. Soar: An architecture for general intelligence. *Artificial Intelligence* 33(1):1–64.

Laird, J. E., Rosenbloom, P. S., and Newell, A. 1986. Chunking in Soar: The anatomy of a general learning mechanism. *Machine Learning* 1:11–46.

Maes, P., and Nardi, D., eds. 1988. *Meta-Level Architectures and Reflection.* Amsterdam: North-Holland.

Minsky, M. 1967. *Computation: Finite and infinite machines.* Englewood Cliffs, NJ: Prentice-Hall.

Minsky, M. 1975. A framework for the representation of knowledge. In P. Winston, ed. *The Psychology of Computer Vision.* New York: McGraw-Hill.

Newell, A. 1973. Production systems: Models of control structures. In W. C. Chase, ed. *Visual Information Processing.* New York: Academic Press.

Newell, A. 1980. Physical symbol systems. *Cognitive Science* 4:135–183.

Newell, A. 1987 (Spring). Unified theories of cognition. The William James lectures. Available in videocassette, Psychology Department, Harvard University, Cambridge, MA.

Newell, A., and Rosenbloom, P. S. 1981. Mechanisms of skill acquisition and the law of practice. In J. R. Anderson, ed. *Cognitive Skills and their Acquisition.* Hillsdale, NJ: Erlbaum.

Newell, A., and Simon, H. A. 1972. *Human Problem Solving.* Englewood Cliffs, NJ: Prentice-Hall.

Newell, A., and Simon, H. A. 1976. Computer science as empirical inquiry: Symbols and search. *Communications of the ACM* 19(3):113–126.

Polk, T. A., and Newell, A. 1988 (August). Modeling human syllogistic reasoning in Soar. In *Proceedings Cognitive Science Annual Conference—1988*. Cognitive Science Society, pp. 181–187.

Rosenbloom, P. S., and Newell, A. 1986. The chunking of goal hierarchies: A generalized model of practice. In R. S. Michalski, J. G. Carbonell, and T. M. Mitchell, eds. *Machine Learning: An Artificial Intelligence Approach*. Vol. 2. Los Altos, CA: Morgan Kaufmann Publishers, Inc.

Rosenbloom, P. S., and Newell, A. 1988. An integrated computational model of stimulus–response compatibility and practice. In G. H. Bower, ed. *The Psychology of Learning and Motivation*. Vol. 21. New York: Academic Press.

Rosenbloom, P. S., Laird, J. E., and Newell, A. 1988. The chunking of skill and knowledge. In H. Bouma and B. A. G. Elsendoorn, ed. *Working Models of Human Perception*. London: Academic Press, pp. 391–440.

Schneider, W., and Shiffrin, R. M. 1977. Controlled and automatic human information processing: I. Detection, search and attention. *Psychological Review* 84:1–66.

Shiffrin, R. M., and Schneider, W. 1977. Controlled and automatic human information processing: II. Perceptual learning, automatic attending, and a general theory. *Psychological Review* 84:127–190.

Siewiorek, D., Bell, G., and Newell, A. 1981. *Computer Structures: Principles and Examples*. New York: McGraw-Hill.

Steele, G. L., Jr., ed., with contributors Fahlman, S. E., Gabriel, R. P., Moon, D. A., and Weinreb, D. L. 1984. *Common Lisp: The Language*. Marlboro, MA: Digital Press.

Steier, D. E., Laird, J. E., Newell, A., Rosenbloom, P. S., Flynn, R. A., Golding, A., Polk, T. A., Shivers, O. G., Unruh, A., and Yost, G. R. 1987 (June). Varieties of learning in Soar: 1987. In *Proceedings of the Fourth International Workshop on Machine Learning*. Los Altos, CA: Morgan Kaufmann.

VanLehn, K., ed. 1989. *Architectures for Intelligence*. Hillsdale, NJ: Erlbaum.

von Cranach, M., Foppa, K., Lepinies, W., and Ploog, D., eds. 1979. *Human Ethology: Claims and Limits of a New Discipline*. Cambridge, Engl.: Cambridge University Press.

4 The Architecture of Mind: A Connectionist Approach

David E. Rumelhart

Cognitive science has a long-standing and important relationship to the computer. The computer has provided a tool whereby we have been able to express our theories of mental activity; it has been a valuable source of metaphors through which we have come to understand and appreciate how mental activities might arise out of the operations of simple-component processing elements.

I recall vividly a class I taught some fifteen years ago in which I outlined the then-current view of the cognitive system. A particularly skeptical student challenged my account with its reliance on concepts drawn from computer science and artificial intelligence with the question of whether I thought my theories would be different if it had happened that our computers were parallel instead of serial. My response, as I recall, was to concede that our theories might very well be different, but to argue that that wasn't a bad thing. I pointed out that the inspiration for our theories and our understanding of abstract phenomena always is based on our experience with the technology of the time. I pointed out that Aristotle had a wax tablet theory of memory, that Leibniz saw the universe as clockworks, that Freud used a hydraulic model of libido flowing through the system, and that the telephone-switchboard model of intelligence had played an important role as well. The theories posited by those of previous generations had, I suggested, been useful in spite of the fact that they were based on the metaphors of their time. Therefore, I argued, it was natural that in our generation— the generation of the serial computer—we should draw our insights from analogies with the most advanced technological developments of our time. I don't now remember whether my response satisfied the student, but I have no doubt that we in cognitive science have gained much of value through our use of concepts drawn from our experience with the computer.

In addition to its value as a source of metaphors, the computer differs from earlier technologies in another remarkable way. The computer can be made to *simulate* systems whose operations are very different from the computers on which these simulations run. In this way we can use the computer to simulate systems with which we *wish* to have experience and thereby provide a source of experience that can be drawn upon in giving us new metaphors and new insights into how mental operations might be accomplished. It is this use of the computer that the connectionists have employed. The architecture that we are exploring is not one based on the von Neumann architecture of our current generation of computers but rather an architecture based on considerations of how brains themselves might function. Our strategy has thus become one of offering a general and abstract model of the computational architecture of brains, to develop algorithms and procedures well suited to this architecture, to simulate these procedures and architecture on a computer, and to explore them as hypotheses about the nature of the human information-processing system. We say that such models are *neurally inspired*, and we call computation on such a system *brain-style computation*. Our goal in short is to replace the computer metaphor with the brain metaphor.

4.1 Why Brain-Style Computation?

Why should a brain-style computer be an especially interesting source of inspiration? Implicit in the adoption of the computer metaphor is an assumption about the appropriate level of explanation in cognitive science. The basic assumption is that we should seek explanation at the *program* or *functional* level rather than the implementational level. It is thus often pointed out that we can learn very little about what kind of program a particular computer may be running by looking at the electronics. In fact we don't care much about the details of the computer at all; all we care about is the particular program it is running. If we know the program, we know how the system will behave in any situation. It doesn't matter whether we use vacuum tubes or transistors, whether we use an IBM or an Apple, the essential characteristics are the same. This is a very misleading analogy. It is true for computers because they are all essentially the same. Whether we make them out of vacuum tubes or transistors, and whether we use an IBM or an Apple computer, we are using computers of the same general design. When we look at essentially different architecture, we see that the architecture makes a good deal of difference. It is the architecture that determines which kinds of algorithms are most easily carried out on the machine in question. It is the architecture of the machine that determines the essential nature of the program itself. It is thus reasonable that we should begin by asking what we know about the architecture of the brain and how it might shape the algorithms underlying biological intelligence and human mental life.

The basic strategy of the connectionist approach is to take as its fundamental processing unit something close to an abstract neuron. We imagine that computation is carried out through simple interactions among such processing units. Essentially the idea is that these processing elements communicate by sending numbers along the lines that connect the processing elements. This identification already provides some interesting constraints on the kinds of algorithms that might underlie human intelligence.

The operations in our models then can best be characterized as "neurally inspired." How does the replacement of the computer metaphor with the brain metaphor as model of mind affect our thinking? This change in orientation leads us to a number of considerations that further inform and constrain our model-building efforts. Perhaps the most crucial of these is time. Neurons are remarkably slow relative to components in modern computers. Neurons operate in the time scale of milliseconds, whereas computer components operate in the time scale of nanoseconds—a factor of 10^6 faster. This means that human processes that take on the order of a second or less can involve only a hundred or so time steps. Because most of the processes we have studied— perception, memory retrieval, speech processing, sentence comprehension, and the like—take about a second or so, it makes sense to impose what Feldman (1985) calls the "100-step program" constraint. That is, we seek explanations for these mental phenomena that do not require more than about a hundred elementary sequential operations. Given that the processes we seek to characterize are often quite complex and may involve consideration of large numbers of simultaneous constraints, our algorithms *must* involve considerable parallelism. Thus although a serial computer could be created out of the kinds of components represented by our units, such an implementation would surely violate the 100-step program constraint for any but the simplest processes. Some might argue that although parallelism is obviously present in much of human information processing, this fact alone need not greatly modify our world view. This is unlikely. The speed of components is a critical design constraint. Although the brain has *slow* components, it has *very many* of them. The human brain contains billions of such processing elements. Rather than organize computation with many, many serial steps, as we do with systems whose steps are very fast, the brain must deploy many, many processing elements cooperatively and in parallel to carry out its activities. These design characteristics, among others, lead, I believe, to a general organization of computing that is fundamentally different from what we are used to.

A further consideration differentiates our models from those inspired by the computer metaphor—that is, the constraint that all the knowledge is *in the connections.* From conventional programmable computers we are used to thinking of knowledge as being stored in the state of certain units in the system. In our systems we assume that only very short-term storage can occur in the states of units; long-term storage takes place in the connections among units. Indeed it is the connections—or perhaps the rules for forming them through experience—that primarily differentiate one model from another. This is a profound difference between our approach and other more conventional approaches, for it means that almost all knowledge is *implicit* in the structure of the device that carries out the task rather than *explicit* in the states of units themselves. Knowledge is not directly accessible to interpretation by some separate processor, but it is built into the processor itself and directly determines the course of processing. It is acquired through tuning of connections as these are used in processing, rather than formulated and stored as declarative facts.

These and other neurally inspired classes of working assumptions have been one important source of assumptions underlying the connectionist program of research. These have not been the only considerations. A second class of constraints arises from our beliefs about the nature of human information processing considered at a more abstract, computational level of analysis. We see the kinds of phenomena we have been studying as products of a kind of constraint-satisfaction procedure in which a very large number of constraints act simultaneously to produce the behavior. Thus we see most behavior not as the product of a single, separate component of the cognitive system but as the product of large set of interacting components, each mutually constraining the others and contributing in its own way to the globally observable behavior of the system. It is very difficult to use serial algorithms to implement such a conception but very natural to use highly parallel ones. These problems can often be characterized as *best-match* or *optimization* problems. As Minsky and Papert (1969) have pointed out, it is very difficult to solve best-match problems serially. This is precisely the kind of problem, however, that is readily implemented using highly parallel algorithms of the kind we have been studying.

The use of brain-style computational systems, then, offers not only a hope that we can characterize how brains actually carry out certain information-processing tasks but also solutions to computational problems that seem difficult to solve in more traditional computational frameworks. It is here where the ultimate value of connectionist systems must be evaluated.

In this chapter I begin with a somewhat more formal sketch of the computational framework of connectionist models. I then follow with a general discussion of the kinds of computational problems that connectionist models seem best suited for. Finally, I will briefly review the state of the art in connectionist modeling.

The Connectionist Framework

There are seven major components of any connectionist system:

· a *set of processing units;*

· a *state of activation* defined over the processing units;

· an *output function* for each unit that maps its state of activation into an output;

· a *pattern of connectivity* among units;

· an *activation rule* for combining the inputs impinging on a unit with its current state to produce a new level of activation for the unit;

· a *learning rule* whereby patterns of connectivity are modified by experience;

· an *environment* within which the system must operate.

Figure 4.1 illustrates the basic aspects of these systems. There is a set of processing units, generally indicated by circles in my diagrams; at each point in time each unit u_i has an activation value, denoted in the diagram as $a_i(t)$; this activation value is passed through a function f_i to produce an output value $o_i(t)$. This output value can be seen as passing through a set of unidirectional connections (indicated by lines or arrows in the diagrams) to other units in the system. There is associated with

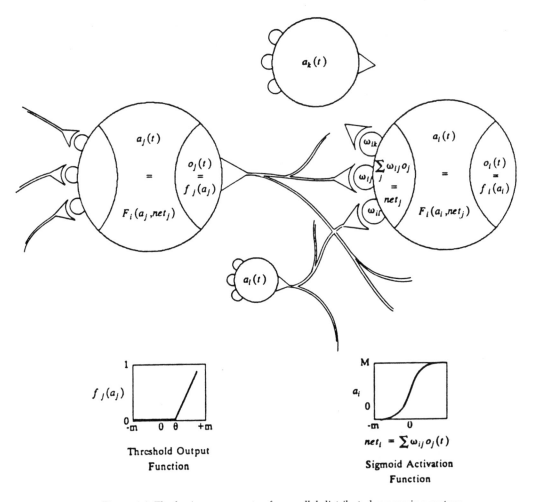

Figure 4.1 The basic components of a parallel distributed processing system

The Architecture of Mind: A Connectionist Approach

each connection a real number, usually called the *weight* or *strength* of the connection, designated w_{ij}, which determines the affect that the first unit has on the second. All of the inputs must then be combined, and the combined inputs to a unit (usually designated the *net input* to the unit) along with its current activation value determine its new activation value via a function F. These systems are viewed as being plastic in the sense that the pattern of interconnections is not fixed for all time; rather the weights can undergo modification as a function of experience. In this way the system can evolve. What a unit represents can change with experience, and the system can come to perform in substantially different ways.

A Set of Processing Units Any connectionist system begins with a set of processing units. Specifying the set of processing units and what they represent is typically the first stage of specifying a connectionist model. In some systems these units may represent particular conceptual objects such as features, letters, words, or concepts; in others they are simply abstract elements over which meaningful patterns can be defined. When we speak of a distributed representation, we mean one in which the units represent small, featurelike entities we call *microfeatures*. In this case it is the pattern as a whole that is the meaningful level of analysis. This should be contrasted to a *one-unit–one-concept* or *localist* representational system in which single units represent entire concepts or other large meaningful entities.

All of the processing of a connectionist system is carried out by these units. There is no executive or other overseer. There are only relatively simple units, each doing its own relatively simple job. A unit's job is simply to receive input from its neighbors and, as a function of the inputs it receives, to compute an output value, which it sends to its neighbors. The system is inherently parallel in that many units can carry out their computations as the same time.

Within any system we are modeling, it is useful to characterize three types of units: *input, output,* and *hidden* units. Input units receive inputs from sources external to the system under study. These inputs may be either sensory inputs or inputs from other parts of the processing system in which the model is embedded. The output units send signals out of the system. They may either directly affect motoric systems or simply influence other systems external to the ones we are modeling. The hidden units are those whose only inputs and outputs are within the system we are modeling. They are not "visible" to outside systems.

The State of Activation In addition to the set of units we need a representation of the state of the system at time t. This is primarily specified by a vector $\mathbf{a}(t)$, representing the pattern of activation over the set of processing units. Each element of the vector stands for the activation of one of the units. It is the pattern of activation over the set of units that captures what the system is representing at any time. It is useful to see processing in the system as the evolution, through time, of a pattern of activity over the set of units.

Different models make different assumptions about the activation values a unit is allowed to take on. Activation values may be continuous or discrete. If they are continuous, they may be unbounded or bounded. If they are discrete, they may take binary values or any of a small set of values. Thus in some models units are continuous and may take on any real number as an activation value. In other cases they may take on any real value between some minimum and maximum such as, for example, the interval [0,1]. When activation values are restricted to discrete values, they most often are binary. Sometimes they are restricted to the values 0 and 1, where 1 is usually taken to mean that the unit is active and 0 is taken to mean that it is inactive.

Output of the Units   Units interact by transmitting signals to their neighbors. The strength of their signals and therefore the degree to which they affect their neighbors are determined by their degree of activation. Associated with each unit u_i is an output function $f_i(a_i(t))$, which maps the current state of activation to an output signal $o_i(t)$. In some of our models the output level is exactly equal to the activation level of the unit. In this case f is the identity function $f(x) = x$. Sometimes f is some sort of threshold function so that a unit has no affect on another unit unless its activation exceeds a certain value. Sometimes the function f is assumed to be a stochastic function in which the output of the unit depends probabilistically on its activation values.

The Pattern of Connectivity   Units are connected to one another. It is this pattern of connectivity that constitutes what the system knows and determines how it will respond to any arbitrary input. Specifying the processing system and the knowledge encoded therein is, in a connectionist model, a matter of specifying this pattern of connectivity among the processing units.

In many cases we assume that each unit provides an additive contribution to the input of the units to which it is connected. In such cases the total input to the unit is simply the weighted sum of the separate inputs from each of the individual units. That is, the inputs from all of the incoming units are simply multiplied by a weight and summed to get the overall input to that unit. In this case the total pattern of connectivity can be represented by merely specifying the weights for each of the connections in the system. A positive weight represents an excitatory input, and a negative weight represents an inhibitory input. It is often convenient to represent such a pattern of connectivity by a weight matrix **W** in which the entry w_{ij} represents the strength and sense of the connection from unit u_j to unit u_i. The weight w_{ij} is a positive number if unit u_j excites unit u_i; it is a negative number if unit

u_j inhibits unit u_i; and it is 0 if unit u_j has no direct connection to unit u_i. The absolute value of w_{ij} specifies the *strength of the connection*.

The pattern of connectivity is very important. It is this pattern that determines what each unit represents. One important issue that may determine both how much information can be stored and how much serial processing the network must perform is the *fan-in* and *fan-out* of a unit. The fan-in is the number of elements that either excite or inhibit a given unit. The fan-out of a unit is the number of units affected directly by a unit. It is useful to note that in brains these numbers are relatively large. Fan-in and fan-out range as high as 100,000 in some parts of the brain. It seems likely that this large fan-in and fan-out allows for a kind of operation that is less like a fixed circuit and more statistical in character.

Activation Rule We also need a rule whereby the inputs impinging on a particular unit are combined with one another and with the current state of the unit to produce a new state of activation. We need function **F**, which takes $\mathbf{a}(t)$ and the net inputs, $net_i = \Sigma_j w_{ij}o_j(t)$, and produces a new state of activation. In the simplest cases, when **F** is the identity function, we can write $\mathbf{a}(t+1) = \mathbf{W}\mathbf{o}(t) = \mathbf{net}\ (t)$. Sometimes **F** is a threshold function so that the net input must exceed some value before contributing to the new state of activation. Often the new state of activation depends on the old one as well as the current input. The function **F** itself is what we call the activation rule. Usually the function is assumed to be deterministic. Thus, for example, if a threshold is involved it may be that $a_i(t) = 1$ if the total input exceeds some threshold value and equals 0 otherwise. Other times it is assumed that **F** is stochastic. Sometimes activations are assumed to decay slowly with time so that even with no external input the activation of a unit will simply decay and not go directly to zero. Whenever $a_i(t)$ is assumed to take on continuous values, it is common to assume that **F** is a kind of sigmoid function. In this case an individual unit can *saturate* and reach a minimum or maximum value of activation.

Modifying Patterns of Connectivity as a Function of Experience Changing the processing or knowledge structure in a connectionist system involves modifying the patterns of interconnectivity. In principle this can involve three kinds of modifications:

1. development of new connections;
2. loss of existing connections;
3. modification of the strengths of connections that already exist.

Very little work has been done on (1) and (2). To a first order of approximation, however, (1) and (2) can be considered a special case of (3). Whenever we change the strength of connection away from zero to some positive or negative value, it has the same effect as growing a new connection. Whenever we change the strength of a connection to zero, that has the same effect as losing an existing connection. Thus we have concentrated on rules whereby *strengths* of connections are modified through experience.

Virtually all learning rules for models of this type can be considered a variant of the *Hebbian* learning rule suggested by Hebb (1949) in his classic book *Organization of Behavior*. Hebb's basic idea is this: If a unit u_i receives a input from another unit u_j, then, if both are highly active, the weight w_{ij} from u_j to u_i should be *strengthened*. This idea has been extended and modified so that it can be more generally stated as

$$\delta w_{ij} = g\ (a_i(t), t_i(t))h(o_j(t), w_{ij}),$$

where $t_i(t)$ is a kind of *teaching* input to u_i. Simply stated, this equation says that the change in the connection from u_j to u_i is given by the product of a function $g()$ of the activation of u_i and its teaching input t_i and another function $h()$ of the output value of u_j and the connection strength w_{ij}. In the simplest versions of Hebbian learning, there is no teacher and the functions g and h are simply proportional to their first arguments. Thus we have

$$\delta w_{ij} = \epsilon a_i o_j,$$

where ϵ is the constant of proportionality representing the learning rate. Another common variation is a rule in which $h(o_j(t), w_{ij}) = o_j(t)$ and $g(a_i(t), t_i(t)) = \epsilon(t_i(t) - a_i(t))$. This is often called the *Widrow-Hoff*, because it was originally formulated by Widrow and Hoff (1960), or the *delta rule*, because the amount of learning is proportional to the *difference* (or delta) between the actual activation achieved and the target activation provided by a teacher. In this case we have

$$\delta w_{ij} = \epsilon(t_i(t) - a_i(t))o_j(t).$$

This is a generalization of the *perceptron* learning rule for which the famous *perception convergence theorem* has been proved. Still another variation has

$$\delta w_{ij} = \epsilon a_i(t)(o_i(t) - w_{ij}).$$

This is a rule employed by Grossberg (1976) and others in the study of *competitive learning*. In this case usually only the units with the strongest activation values are allowed to learn.

Representation of the environment   It is crucial in the development of any model to have a clear representation of the environment in which this model is to exist. In connectionist models we represent the environment as a time-varying stochastic function over the space of input patterns. That is, we imagine that at any point in time there is some probability that any of the possible set of input patterns is impinging on the input units. This probability function may in general depend on the history of inputs to the system as well as outputs of the system. In practice most connectionist models involve a much simpler characterization of the environment. Typically the environment is characterized by a stable probability distribution over the set of possible input patterns independent of past inputs and past responses of the system. In this case we can imagine listing the set of possible inputs to the system and numbering them from 1 to M. The environment is then characterized by a set of probabilities p_i for $i = 1, \ldots , M$. Because each input pattern can be considered a vector, it is sometimes useful to characterize those patterns with nonzero probabilities as constituting *orthogonal* or *linearly independent* sets of vectors.

To summarize, the connectionist framework consists not only of a formal language but also a perspective on our models. Other qualitative and quantitative considerations arising from our understanding of brain processing and of human behavior combine with the formal system to form what might be viewed as an aesthetic for our model-building enterprises.

Computational Features of Connectionist Models
In addition to the fact that connectionist systems are capable of exploiting parallelism in computation and mimicking brain-style computation, connectionist systems are important because they provide good solutions to a number of very difficult computational problems that seem to arise often in models of cognition. In particular they are good at solving constraint-satisfaction problems, implementing content-addressable memory-storage systems, and implementing best match; they allow for the automatic implementation of similarity-based generalization; they exhibit graceful degradation with damage or information overload; and there are simple, general mechanisms for learning that allow connectionist systems to adapt to their environments.

Constraint Satisfaction Many cognitive-science problems are usefully conceptualized as constraint-satisfaction problems in which a solution is given through the satisfaction of a very large number of mutually interacting constraints. The problem is to devise a computational algorithm that is capable of efficiently implementing such a system. Connectionist systems are ideal for implementing such a constraint-satisfaction system, and the trick for getting connectionist networks to solve difficult problems is often to cast the problem as a constraint-satisfaction problem. In this case we conceptualize the connectionist network as a *constraint network* in which each unit represents a hypothesis of some sort (for example, that a certain semantic feature, visual feature, or acoustic feature is present in the input) and in which each connection represents constraints among the hypotheses. Thus, for example, if feature B is expected to be present whenever feature A is present, there should be a positive connection from the unit corresponding to the hypothesis that A is present to the unit representing the hypothesis that B is present. Similarly if there is a constraint that whenever A is present B is expected *not* to be present, there should be a negative connection from A to B. If the constraints are weak, the weights should be small. If the constraints are strong, then the weights should be large. Similarly the inputs to such a network can also be thought of as constraints. A positive input to a particular unit means that there is evidence from the outside that the relevant feature is present. A negative input means that there is evidence from the outside that the feature is not present. The stronger the input, the greater the evidence. If such a network is allowed to run, it will eventually *settle* into a locally optimal state in which as many as possible of the constraints are satisfied, with priority given to the strongest constraints. (Actually, these systems will find a *locally* best solution to this constraint satisfaction problem. *Global* optima are more difficult to find.) The procedure whereby such a system *settles* into such a state is called *relaxation*. We speak of the system *relaxing* to a solution. Thus a large class of connectionist models contains constraint satisfaction models that settle on locally optimal solutions through the process of relaxation.

Figure 4.2 shows an example of a simple 16-unit constraint network. Each unit in the network represents a hypothesis concerning a vertex in a line drawing of a Necker cube. The network consists of two interconnected subnetworks—one corresponding to each of the two global interpretations of the Necker cube. Each unit in each network is assumed to receive input from the region of the input figure—the cube—corresponding to its location in the network. Each unit in figure 4.2 is labeled with a three-letter sequence indicating whether its vertex is hypothesized to be front or back (F or B), upper or lower (U or L), and right or left (R or L). Thus, for example, the lower-left unit of each subnetwork is assumed to receive input from the lower-left vertex of the input figure. The unit in the left network represents the hypothesis that it is receiving input from a lower-left vertex in the front surface of the cube (and is thus labeled FLL), whereas the one in the right subnetwork represents the hypothesis that it is receiving input from a lower-left vertex in the back surface (BLL). Because there is a constraint that each vertex has a single interpretation, these two units are connected by a strong negative connection. Because the interpretation of any given vertex is constrained by the interpretations of its neighbors, each unit in a subnetwork is connected positively with each of its neighbors within the network. Finally there is the constraint that there can be only one vertex of a single kind (for example, there can be only one lower-left vertex in the front plane FLL). There is a strong negative connection between units representing the same label in each subnetwork. Thus each unit has three neighbors connected positively, two competitors connected negatively, and one positive input from the stim-

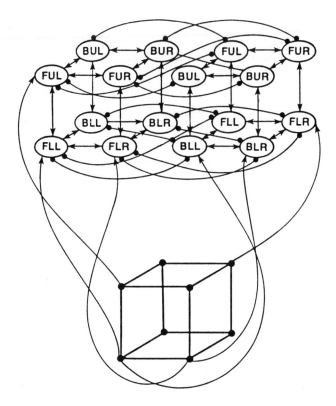

Figure 4.2 A simple network representing some constraints involved in perceiving a Necker cube

ulus. For purposes of this example the strengths of connections have been arranged so that two negative inputs exactly balance three positive inputs. Further it is assumed that each unit receives an excitatory input from the ambiguous stimulus pattern and that each of these excitatory influences is relatively small. Thus if all three of a unit's neighbors are on and both of its competitors are on, these effects would entirely cancel out one another; and if there were a small input from the outside, the unit would have a tendency to come on. On the other hand if fewer than three of its neighbors were on and both of its competitors were on, the unit would have a tendency to turn off, even with an excitatory input from the stimulus pattern.

In the preceding paragraph I focused on the individual units of the networks. It is often useful to focus not on the units, however, but on entire *states* of the network. In the case of binary (on-off or 0-1) units, there is a total of 2^{16} possible states in which this system could reside. That is, in principle each of the 16 units could have either value 0 or 1. In the case of continuous units, in which each unit can take on any value between 0 and 1, the system can in principle take on any of an infinite number of states. Yet because of the constraints built into the network, there are only a few of those states in which the system will settle. To see this, consider the case in which the units are updated asynchronously, one at a time. During each time slice one of the units is chosen to update. If its net input exceeds 0, its value will be pushed toward 1; otherwise its value will be pushed toward 0.

Imagine that the system starts with all units off. A unit is then chosen at random to be updated. Because it is receiving a slight positive input from the stimulus and no other inputs, it will be given a positive activation value. Then another unit is chosen to update. Unless it is in direct competition with the first unit, it too will be turned on. Eventually a coalition of neighboring units will be turned on. These units will tend to turn on more of their neighbors in the same subnetwork and turn off their competitors in the other subnetwork. The system will (almost always) end up in a situation in which all of the units in one subnetwork are fully activated and none of the units in the other subnetwork is activated. That is, the system will end up interpreting the Necker cube as either facing left or facing right. Whenever the system gets into a state and stays there, the state is called a *stable state* or a *fixed point* of the network. The constraints implicit in the pattern of connections among the units determine the set of possible stable states of the system and therefore the set of possible interpretations of the inputs.

Hopfield (1982) has shown that it is possible to give a general account of the behavior of systems such as this one (with symmetric weights and asynchronous updates). In particular Hopfield has shown that such systems can be conceptualized as minimizing a global measure, which he calls the *energy* of the system, through a method of *gradient descent* or, equivalently, maximizing the constraints satisfied through a method of *hill climbing*. In particular Hopfield has shown that the system operates in such a way as to always move from a state that satisfies fewer constraints to a state that satisfies more constraints, where the measure of constraint satisfaction is given by

$$G(t) = \sum_i \sum_j w_{ij} a_i(t) a_j(t) + \sum_i \text{input}_i(t) a_i(t).$$

Essentially the equation says that the overall goodness of fit is given by the sum of the degrees to which each pair of units contributes to the goodness plus the degree to which the units satisfy the input constraints. The contribution of a pair of units is given by the product of their activation values and the weights connecting them. Thus if the weight is positive, each unit wants to be as active as possible—that is, the activation values for these two units should be pushed toward 1. If the weight is negative, then at least one of the units should be 0 to maximize the pairwise goodness. Similarly if the input constraint for a given unit is positive, then its contribution to the total goodness of fit is maximized by being the activation of that unit toward its maximal value. If it is negative, the activation value should be decreased toward

0. Of course the constraints will generally not be totally consistent. Sometimes a given unit may have to be turned on to increase the function in some ways yet decrease it in other ways. The point is that it is the sum of all of these individual contributions that the system seeks to maximize. Thus for every state of the system—every possible pattern of activation over the units—the pattern of inputs and the connectivity matrix **W** determine a value of the goodness-of-fit function. The system processes its input by moving upward from state to adjacent state until it reaches a state of maximum goodness. When it reaches such a *stable state* or *fixed point*, it will stay in that state and it can be said to have "settled" on a solution to the constraint-satisfaction problem or alternatively, in our present case, "settled into an interpretation" of the input.

It is important to see then that entirely *local* computational operations, in which each unit adjusts its activation up or down on the basis of its net input, serve to allow the network to converge toward states that maximize a *global* measure of goodness or degree of constraint satisfaction. Hopfield's main contribution to the present analysis was to point out this basic fact about the behavior of networks with symmetrical connections and asynchronous update of activations.

To summarize, there is a large subset of connectionist models that can be considered constraint-satisfaction models. These networks can be described as carrying out their information processing by climbing into states of maximal satisfaction of the constraints implicit in the network. A very useful concept that arises from this way of viewing these networks is that we can describe the behavior of these networks not only in terms of the behavior of individual units but also in terms of properties of the network itself. A primary concept for understanding these network properties is the *goodness-of-fit landscape* over which the system moves. Once we have correctly described this landscape, we have described the operational properties of the system—it will process information by moving uphill toward goodness maxima. The particular maximum that the system will find is determined by where the system starts and by the distortions of the space induced by the input. One of the very important descriptors of a goodness landscape is the set of maxima that the system can find, the size of the region that feeds into each maximum, and the height of the maximum itself. The states themselves correspond to possible interpretations, the peaks in the space correspond to the best interpretations, the extent of the foothills or skirts surrounding a particular peak determines the likelihood of finding the peak, and the height of the peak corresponds to the degree to which the constraints of the network are actually met or alternatively to the goodness of the interpretation associated with the corresponding state.

Interactive Processing   One of the difficult problems in cognitive science is to build systems that are capable of allowing a large number of knowledge sources to usefully interact in the solution of a problem. Thus in language processing we would want syntactic, phonological, semantic, and pragmatic knowledge sources all to interact in the construction of the meaning of an input. Reddy and his colleagues (1973) have had some success in the case of speech perception with the Hearsay system because they were working in the highly structured domain of language. Less structured domains have proved very difficult to organize. Connectionist models, conceptualized as constraint-satisfaction networks, are ideally suited for the blending of multiple-knowledge sources. Each knowledge type is simply another constraint, and the system will, in parallel, find those figurations of values that best satisfy all of the constraints from all of the knowledge sources. The uniformity of representation and the common currency of interaction (activation values) make connectionist systems especially powerful for this domain.

Rapid Pattern Matching, Best-Match Search, Content-Addressable Memory   Rapid pattern matching, best-match search, and content-addressable memory are all variants on the general best-match problem (compare Minsky and Papert 1969). Best-match problems are especially difficult for serial computational algorithms (it involves exhaustive search), but as we have just indicated connectionist systems can readily be used to find the interpretation that best matches a set of constraints. It can similarly be used to find stored data that best match some target. In this case it is useful to imagine that the network consists of two classes of units, with one class, the *visible* units, corresponding to the content stored in the network, and the remaining, *hidden* units are used to help store the patterns. Each visible unit corresponds to the hypothesis that some particular feature was present in the stored pattern. Thus we think of the content of the stored data as consisting of collections of features. Each hidden unit corresponds to a hypothesis concerning the *configuration* of features present in a stored pattern. The hypothesis to which a particular hidden unit corresponds is determined by the exact *learning rule* used to store the input and the characteristics of the ensemble of stored patterns. Retrieval in such a network amounts to turning on some of the visible units (a retrieval probe) and letting the system settle to the best interpretation of the input. This is a kind of pattern completion. The details are not too important here because a variety of learning rules lead to networks with the following important properties:

· When a previously stored (that is, familiar) pattern enters the memory system, it is amplified, and the system responds with a stronger version of the input pattern. This is a kind of recognition response.

· When an unfamiliar pattern enters the memory system, it is dampened, and the activity of the memory system is shut down. This is a kind of unfamiliarity response.

· When part of a familiar pattern is presented, the system responds by "filling in" the missing parts. This is a kind of recall paradigm in which the part constitutes the retrieval cue, and the filling in is a kind of memory-reconstruction process. This is a content-addressable memory system.

· When a pattern similar to a stored pattern is presented, the system responds by distorting the input pattern toward the stored pattern. This is a kind of assimilation response in which similar inputs are assimilated to similar stored events.

· Finally, if a number of similar patterns have been stored, the system will respond strongly to the central tendency of the stored patterns, even though the central tendency itself was never stored. Thus this sort of memory system automatically responds to prototypes even when no prototype has been seen.

These properties correspond very closely to the characteristics of human memory and, I believe, are exactly the kind of properties we want in any theory of memory.

Automatic Generalization and Direct Representation of Similarity
One of the major complaints against AI programs is their "fragility." The programs are usually very good at what they are programmed to do, but respond in unintelligent or odd ways when faced with novel situations. There seem to be at least two reasons for this fragility. In conventional symbol-processing systems similarity is indirectly represented and therefore are generally incapable of generalization, and most AI programs are not self-modifying and cannot adapt to their environment. In our connectionist systems on the other hand, the content is directly represented in the pattern and similar patterns have similar effects—therefore generalization is an automatic property of connectionist models. It should be noted that the degree of similarity between patterns is roughly given by the inner product of the vectors representing the patterns. Thus the dimensions of generalization are given by the dimensions of the representational space. Often this will lead to the right generalizations. There are situations in which this will lead to inappropriate generalizations. In such a case we must allow the system to *learn* its appropriate representation. In the next section I describe how the appropriate representation can be learned so that the correct generalizations are automatically made.

Learning A key advantage of the connectionist systems is the fact that simple yet powerful learning procedures can be defined that allow the systems to adapt to their environment. It was work on the learning aspect of these neurally inspired models that first led to an interest in them (compare Rosenblatt, 1962), and it was the demonstration that the learning procedures for complex networks could never be developed that contributed to the loss of interest (compare Minsky and Papert 1969). Although the *perceptron convergence procedure* and its variants have been around for some time, these learning procedures were limited to simple one-layer networks involving only input and output units. There were no hidden units in these cases and no internal representation. The coding provided by the external world had to suffice. Nevertheless these networks have proved useful in a wide variety of applications. Perhaps the essential character of such networks is that they map similar input patterns to similar output patterns. This is what allows these networks to make reasonable generalizations and perform reasonably on patterns that have never before been presented. The similarity of patterns in the connectionist system is determined by their overlap. The overlap in such networks is determined outside the learning system itself—by whatever produces the patterns.

The constraint that similar input patterns lead to similar outputs can lead to an inability of the system to learn certain mappings from input to output. Whenever the representation provided by the outside world is such that the similarity structure of the input and output patterns is very different, a network without internal representations (that is, a network without hidden units) will be unable to perform the necessary mappings. A classic example of this case is the exclusive-or (XOR) problem illustrated in table 4.1. Here we see that those patterns that overlap least are supposed to generate identical output values. This problem and many others like it cannot be performed by networks without hidden units with which to create their own internal representations of the input patterns. It is interesting to note that if the input patterns contained a third input taking the value 1 whenever the first two have value 1, as shown in table 4.2, a two-layer system would be able to solve the problem.

Table 4.1 XOR Problem

Input Patterns		Output Patterns
00	→	0
01	→	1
10	→	1
11	→	0

Table 4.2 XOR with Redundant Third Bit

Input Patterns		Output Patterns
000	→	0
010	→	1
100	→	1
111	→	0

The Architecture of Mind: A Connectionist Approach

Minsky and Papert (1969) have provided a careful analysis of conditions under which such systems are capable of carrying out the required mappings. They show that in many interesting cases networks of this kind are incapable of solving the problems. On the other hand, as Minsky and Papert also pointed out, if there is a layer of simple perceptronlike hidden units, as shown in figure 4.3, with which the original input pattern can be augmented, there is always a recoding (that is, an internal representation) of the input patterns in the hidden units in which the similarity of the patterns among the hidden units can support any required mapping from the input to the output units. Thus if we have the right connections from the input units to a large enough set of hidden units, we can always find a representation that will perform any mapping from input to output through these hidden units. In the case of the XOR problem, the addition of a feature that detects the conjunction of the input units changes the similarity structure of the patterns sufficiently to allow the solution to be learned. As illustrated in figure 4.4, this can be done with a single hidden unit. The numbers on the arrows represent the strengths of the connections among the units. The numbers written in the circles represent the thresholds of the units. The value of +1.5 for the threshold of the hidden unit ensures that it will be turned on only when both input units are on. The value 0.5 for the output unit ensures that it will turn on only when it receives

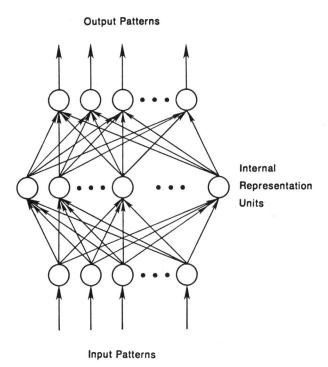

Figure 4.3 A multilayer network in which input patterns are *recoded* by internal representation units

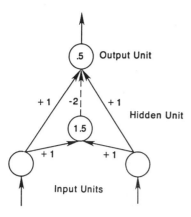

Figure 4.4 A simple XOR network with one hidden unit

a net positive input greater than 0.5. The weight of -2 from the hidden unit to the output unit ensures that the output unit will not come on when both input units are on. Note that from the point of view of the output unit the hidden unit is treated as simply another input unit. It is as if the input patterns consisted of three rather than two units.

The existence of networks such as this illustrates the potential power of hidden units and internal representations. The problem, as noted by Minsky and Papert, is that whereas there is a very simple guaranteed learning rule for all problems that can be solved without hidden units, namely, the perceptron convergence procedure (or the variation reported originally by Widrow and Hoff 1960), there has been no equally powerful rule for learning in multilayer networks.

It is clear that if we hope to use these connectionist networks for general computational purposes, we must have a learning scheme capable of learning its own internal representations. This is just what we (Rumelhart, Hinton, and Williams 1986) have done. We have developed a generalization of the perceptron learning procedure, called the *generalized delta rule*, which allows the system to learn to compute arbitrary functions. The constraints inherent in networks without self-modifying internal representations are no longer applicable. The basic learning procedure is a two-stage process. First, an input is applied to the network; then, after the system has processed for some time, certain units of the network are informed of the values they ought to have at this time. If they have attained the desired values, the weights are unchanged. If they differ from the target values, then the weights are changed according to the difference between the actual value the units have attained and the target for those units. This difference becomes an error signal. This error signal must then be sent back to those units that impinged on the output units. Each such unit receives an error measure that is equal to the error in all of the units to which it connects times the weight connecting it to the output unit. Then, based on the error, the weights into these "second-layer" units are modified, after

The Architecture of Mind: A Connectionist Approach

which the error is passed back another layer. This process continues until the error signal reaches the input units or until it has been passed back for a fixed number of times. Then a new input pattern is presented and the process repeats. Although the procedure may sound difficult, it is actually quite simple and easy to implement within these nets. As shown in Rumelhart, Hinton, and Williams 1986, such a procedure will always change its weights in such a way as to reduce the difference between the actual output values and the desired output values. Moreover it can be shown that this system will work for any network whatsoever.

Minsky and Papert (1969, pp. 231–232), in their pessimistic discussion of perceptrons, discuss *multilayer machines*. They state that

The perceptron has shown itself worthy of study despite (and even because of!) its severe limitations. It has many features that attract attention: its linearity; its intriguing learning theorem; its clear paradigmatic simplicity as a kind of parallel computation. There is no reason to suppose that any of these virtues carry over to the many-layered version. Nevertheless, we consider it to be an important research problem to elucidate (or reject) our intuitive judgment that the extension is sterile. Perhaps some powerful convergence theorem will be discovered, or some profound reason for the failure to produce an interesting "learning theorem" for the multilayered machine will be found.

Although our learning results do not *guarantee* that we can find a solution for all solvable problems, our analyses and simulation results have shown that as a practical matter, this error propagation scheme leads to solutions in virtually every case. In short I believe that we have answered Minsky and Papert's challenge and *have* found a learning result sufficiently powerful to demonstrate that their pessimism about learning in multilayer machines was misplaced.

One way to view the procedure I have been describing is as a parallel computer that, having been shown the appropriate input/output exemplars specifying some function, programs itself to compute that function in general. Parallel computers are notoriously difficult to program. Here we have a mechanism whereby we do not actually have to know how to write the program to get the system to do it.

Graceful Degradation Finally connectionist models are interesting candidates for cognitive-science models because of their property of graceful degradation in the face of damage and information overload. The ability of our networks to learn leads to the promise of computers that can literally learn their way around faulty components because every unit participates in the storage of many patterns and because each pattern involves many different units, the loss of a few components will degrade the stored information, but will not lose it. Similarly such memories should not be conceptualized as having a certain fixed capacity. Rather there is simply more and more storage interference and blending of similar pieces of information as the memory is overloaded. This property of graceful degradation mimics the human response in many ways and is one of the reasons we find these models of human information processing plausible.

4.2 The State of the Art

Recent years have seen a virtual explosion of work in the connectionist area. This work has been singularly interdisciplinary, being carried out by psychologists, physicists, computer scientists, engineers, neuroscientists, and other cognitive scientists. A number of national and international conferences have been established and are being held each year. In such environment it is difficult to keep up with the rapidly developing field. Nevertheless a reading of recent papers indicates a few central themes to this activity. These themes include the study of learning and generalization (especially the use of the backpropagation learning procedure), applications to neuroscience, mathematical properties of networks—both in terms of learning and the question of the relationship among connectionist style computation and more conventional computational paradigms—and finally the development of an implementational base for physical realizations of connectionist computational devices, especially in the areas of optics and analog VLSI.

Although there are many other interesting and important developments, I conclude with a brief summary of the work with which I have been most involved over the past several years, namely, the study of learning and generalization within multilayer networks. Even this summary is necessarily selective, but it should give a sampling of much of the current work in the area.

Learning and Generalization
The backpropagation learning procedure has become possibly the single most popular method for training networks. The procedure has been used to train networks on problem domains including character recognition, speech recognition, sonar detection, mapping from spelling to sound, motor control, analysis of molecular structure, diagnosis of eye diseases, prediction of chaotic functions, playing backgammon, the parsing of simple sentences, and many, many more areas of application. Perhaps the major point of these examples is the enormous range of problems to which the backpropagation learning procedure can usefully be applied. In spite of the rather impressive breadth of topics and the success of some of these applications, there are a number of serious open problems. The theoretical issues of primary concern fall into three main areas: (1) The architecture problem—are there useful architectures beyond the standard three-layer network used in most of these areas that are appropriate for certain areas of application? (2) The scaling problem—how can we cut down on the substantial training time that

seems to be involved for the more difficult and interesting problem application areas? (3) The generalization problem—how can we be certain that the network trained on a subset of the example set will generalize correctly to the entire set of exemplars?

Some Architecture

Although most applications have involved the simple three-layer backpropagation network with one input layer, one hidden layer, and one output layer of units, there have been a large number of interesting architectures proposed—each for the solution of some particular problem of interest. There are, for example, a number of "special" architectures that have been proposed for the modeling of such sequential phenomena as motor control. Perhaps the most important of these is the one proposed by Mike Jordan (1986) for producing sequences of phonemes. The basic structure of the network is illustrated in figure 4.5. It consists of four groups of units: *Plan units*, which tell the network which sequence it is producing, are fixed at the start of a sequence and are not changed. *Context units*, which keep track of where the system is in the sequence, receive input from the output units of the systems and from themselves, constituting a memory for the sequence produced thus far. *Hidden units* combine the information from the plan units with that from the context units to determine which output is to be produced next. *Output units* produce the desired output values. This basic structure, with numerous variations, has been used successfully in producing sequences of phonemes (Jordan 1986), sequences of movements (Jordan 1989), sequences of notes in a melody (Todd 1989), sequences of turns in a simulated ship (Miyata 1987), and for many other applications. An analogous network for *recognizing* sequences has been used by Elman (1988) for processing sentences one at a time, and another variation has been developed and studied by Mozer (1988). The architecture used by Elman is illustrated in figure 4.6. This network also

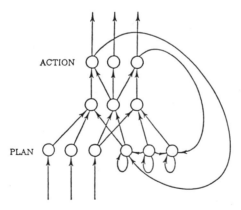

Figure 4.5 A recurrent network of the type developed by Jordan (1986) for learning to perform sequences

involves three sets of units: *input units,* in which the sequence to be recognized is presented one element at a time; a set of *context units* that receive inputs from and send inputs to the hidden units and thus constitute a memory for recent events; a set of *hidden units* that combine the current input with its memory of past inputs to either name the sequence, predict the next element of the sequence, or both.

Another kind of architecture that has received some attention has been suggested by Hinton and has been employed by Elman and Zipser (1987), Cottrell, Munro, and Zipser (1987), and many others. It has become part of the standard toolkit of backpropagation. This is the so-called method of autoencoding the pattern set. The basic architecture in this case consists of three layers of units as in the conventional case; however, the input and output layers are identical. The idea is to pass the input through a small number of hidden units and reproduce it over the output units. This requires the hidden units to do a kind of nonlinear-principle components analysis of the input patterns. In this case that corresponds to a kind of extraction of critical features. In many applications these features turn out to provide a useful compact description of the patterns. Many other architectures are being explored. The space of interesting and useful architecture is large and the exploration will continue for many years.

The Scaling Problem

The scaling problem has received somewhat less attention, although it has clearly emerged as a central problem with backpropagationlike learning procedures. The basic finding has been that difficult problems require many learning trials. For example, it is not unusual to require tens or even hundreds of thousands of pattern presentations to learn moderately difficult problems—that is, those whose solution requires tens of thousands to a few hundred thousand connections. Large and

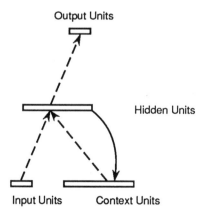

Figure 4.6 A recurrent network of the type employed by Elman (1988) for learning to recognize sequences

fast computers are required for such problems, and it is impractical for problems requiring more than a few hundred thousand connections. It is therefore a matter of concern to learn to speed up the learning so that it can learn more difficult problems in a more reasonable number of exposures. The proposed solutions fall into two basic categories. One line of attack is to improve the learning procedure either by optimizing the parameters dynamically (that is, change the learning rate systematically during learning) or by using more information in the weight-changing procedure (that is, the so-called second-order backpropagation in which the second derivatives are also computed). Although some improvements can be attained through the use of these methods, in certain problem domains the basic scaling problem still remains. It seems that the basic problem is that difficult problems require a large number of exemplars, however efficiently each exemplar is used. The other view grows from viewing *learning* and *evolution* as continuous with one another. On this view the fact that networks take a long time to learn is to be expected because we normally compare their behavior to organisms that have long evolutionary histories. On this view the solution is to start the system at places that are as appropriate as possible for the problem domain to be learned. Shepherd (1989) has argued that such an approach is critical for an appropriate understanding of the phenomena being modeled.

A final approach to the scale problem is through modularity. It is possible to break the problem into smaller subproblems and train subnetworks on these subproblems. Networks can then finally be assembled to solve the entire problem after all of the modules are trained. An advantage of the connectionist approach in this regard is that the original training needs to be only approximately right. A final round of training can be used to learn the interfaces among the modules.

The Generalization Problem
One final aspect of learning that has been looked at is the nature of generalization. It is clear that the most important aspect of networks is not that they learn a set of mappings but that they learn the function implicit in the exemplars under study in such a way that they respond properly to those cases not yet observed. Although there are many cases of successful generalization (compare the learning of spelling with phoneme mappings in Sejnowski and Rosenberg's Nettalk (1987), there are a number of cases in which the networks do not generalize correctly (compare Denker et al. 1987). One simple way to understand this is to note that for most problems there are enough degrees of freedom in the network that there are a large number of genuinely different solutions to the problems, and each solution constitutes a different way of generalizing to the unseen patterns. Clearly not all of these can be correct. I have proposed a hypothesis that shows some promise in promoting better generalization (Rumelhart 1988). The basic idea is this:

The problem of generalization is essentially the induction problem. Given a set of observations, what is the appropriate principle that applies to all cases? Note that the network at any point in time can be viewed as a specification of the inductive hypothesis. I have proposed that we follow a version of Occam's razor and select the *simplest, most robust* network that is consistent with the observations made. The assumption of robustness is simply an embodiment of a kind of continuity assumption that small variations in the input patterns should have little effect on the output and on the performance of the system. The simplicity assumption is simply—of all networks that correctly account for the input data—to choose that net with the fewest hidden units, fewest connections, most symmetries among the weights, and so on. I have formalized this procedure and modified the backpropagation learning procedure so that it prefers simple, robust networks and, all things being equal, will select those networks. In many cases it turns out that these are just the networks that do the best job generalizing.

References

Cottrell, G. W., Munro, P. W., and Zipser, D. 1987. Learning internal representations from grey-scale images: An example of extensional programming. In *Proceedings of the Ninth Annual Meeting of the Cognitive Science Society*. Hillsdale, NJ: Erlbaum.

Denker, J., Schwartz, D., Wittner, B., Solla, S., Hopfield, J., Howard, R., and Jackel, L. 1987. Automatic learning, rule extraction, and generalization. *Complex Systems* 1:877–922.

Elman, J. 1988. *Finding Structure in Time*. CRL Tech. Rep. 88-01, Center for Research in Language, University of California, San Diego.

Elman, J., and Zipser, D. 1987. *Learning the Hidden Structure of Speech*. Rep. no. 8701. Institute for Cognitive Science, University of California, San Diego.

Feldman, J. A. 1985. Connectionist models and their applications: Introduction. *Cognitive Science* 9:1–2.

Grossberg, S. 1976. Adaptive pattern classification and universal recoding: Part I. Parallel development and coding of neural feature detectors. *Biological Cybernetics* 23:121–134.

Hebb, D. O. 1949. *The Organization of Behavior*. New York: Wiley.

Hinton, G. E., and Sejnowski, T. 1986. Learning and relearning in Boltzmann machines. In D. E. Rumelhart, J. L. McClelland, and the PDP Research Group. *Parallel Distributed Processing: Explorations in the Microstructure of Cognition. Volume 1: Foundations*. Cambridge, MA: MIT Press, A Bradford Book.

Hopfield, J. J. 1982. Neural networks and physical systems with emergent collective computational abilities. *Proceedings of the National Academy of Sciences, USA* 79:2554–2558.

Jordan, M. I. 1986. Attractor dynamics and parallelism in a connectionist sequential machine. In *Proceedings of the Eighth Annual Meeting of the Cognitive Science Society*. Hillsdale, NJ: Erlbaum.

Jordan, M. I. 1989. Supervised learning and systems with excess degrees of freedom. In D. Touretzky, G. Hinton, and T. Sejnowski, eds. *Connectionist Models*. San Mateo, CA: Morgan Kaufmann.

Minsky, M., and Papert, S. 1969. *Perceptrons*. Cambridge, MA: MIT Press.

Miyata, Y. 1987. *The Learning and Planning of Actions*. Ph.D. thesis, University of California, San Diego.

McClelland, J. L., Rumelhart D. E., and the PDP Research Group. 1986. *Parallel Distributed Processing: Explorations in the Microstructure of Cognition. Volume 2: Psychological and Biological Models*. Cambridge, MA: MIT Press, A Bradford Book.

Mozer, M. C. 1988. *A Focused Book-Propagation Algorithm for Temporal Pattern Recognition*. Rep. no. 88-3, Departments of Psychology and Computer Science, University of Toronto, Toronto, Ontario.

Reddy, D. R., Erman, L. D., Fennell, R. D., and Neely, R. B. 1973. The Hearsay speech understanding system: An example of the recognition process. In *Proceedings of the International Conference on Artificial Intelligence*. pp. 185–194.

Rosenblatt, F. 1962. *Principles of Neurodynamics*. New York: Spartan.

Rumelhart, D. E. 1988. *Generalization and the Learning of Minimal Networks by Backpropagation*. In preparation.

Rumelhart, D. E., Hinton, G. E., and Williams, R. J. (1986). Learning internal representations by error propagation. In D. E. Rumelhart, J. L. McClelland, and the PDP Research Group. *Parallel Distributed Processing: Explorations in the Microstructure of Cognition. Volume 1: Foundations*. Cambridge, MA: MIT Press. A Bradford Book.

Rumelhart, D. E., McClelland, J. L., and the PDP Research Group 1986. *Parallel Distributed Processing: Explorations in the Microstructure of Cognition. Volume 1: Foundations*. Cambridge, MA: MIT Press. A Bradford Book.

Sejnowski, T., and Rosenberg, C. 1987. Parallel networks that learn to pronounce English text. *Complex Systems* 1:145–168.

Shepherd, R. N. 1989. Internal representation of universal regularities: A challenge for connectionism. In L. Nadel, L. A. Cooper, Calicover, P., and Harnish, R. M., eds. *Neural Connections, Mental Computation*. Cambridge, MA: MIT Press. A Bradford Book.

Smolensky, P. 1986. Information processing in dynamical systems: Foundations of harmony theory. In D. E. Rumelhart, J. L. McClelland, and the PDP Research Group. *Parallel Distributed Processing: Explorations in the Microstructure of Cognition. Volume 1: Foundations.* Cambridge, MA: MIT Press. A Bradford Book.

Todd, P. 1989. A sequential network design for musical applications. In D. Touretzky, G. Hinton, and T. Sejnowski, eds. *Connectionist Models.* San Mateo, CA: Morgan Kaufmann.

Widrow, G., and Hoff, M. E. 1960. Adaptive switching circuits. In *Institute of Radio Engineers, Western Electronic Show and Convention, Convention Record, Part 4.* pp. 96–104.

5 Grammatical Theory

Thomas Wasow

The use of language is arguably the most pervasive and uniquely human characteristic of the species. The ways people put sounds together to convey meanings has always fascinated scholars, and many have argued that the study of language provides an especially clear window into the workings of the human mind. In recent decades linguistic issues have played a central role in the development of cognitive science, and conversely progress in cognitive science has had a profound effect on the investigation of language. In particular the rise of cognitive science has been inextricably linked to a revolution in the theory of grammar.

Grammar—the study of the structure of words, phrases, and sentences—is millennia old, but an introduction to contemporary grammatical theory can begin with the situation in the midtwentieth century. American linguistics at the time concerned itself primarily with refining methods of data collection and classification. Postulation of abstract or "mentalistic" constructs was regarded as unscientific and hence to be avoided. This descriptivist bias had two sources: first, it was a reaction to earlier attempts to impose the categories of traditional Latin and Greek grammars on radically different languages (especially Native American languages); and second, it reflected the dominance of behaviorism in American psychology at the time. (See Newmeyer 1980, ch. 1, for further discussion and Joos 1958 for examples of such work.)

A number of factors led to a radical change in this picture. Developments in logic and the foundations of mathematics in the first half of the twentieth century had provided powerful tools for the analysis of the artificial languages of mathematics—tools that some were naturally tempted to apply to the study of natural languages as well (see, for example, Reichenbach 1952 and Bar-Hillel 1964). This temptation was greatly reinforced by the advent of digital computers, leading to the invention of high-level programming languages and hopes of someday interacting with machines using natural languages. Among the applications early computer scientists envisioned for their devices were several that involved natural language, including voice typewriters and translating machines. Such concerns, together with a growing skepticism about the dominant behaviorist paradigm in psychology, paved the way for a radical reorientation in theoretical linguistics.

The leading figure in grammatical theory in recent decades has been Noam Chomsky, whose 1957 book *Syntactic Structures* is usually cited as the beginning of the generative revolution in linguistics. Although Chomsky's theories have changed considerably over the years (especially in their more technical aspects), there are a number of general features that distinguish all of his work (and that of his followers) from the earlier tradition.

Central to all of Chomsky's work is a concern with what he has called "the creative aspect" of language use—that is, the fact that normal language use involves putting together combinations of words that are novel in the sense that the speaker has never before heard the combinations. This observation provides a powerful argument that grammarians must go beyond providing a taxonomy of utterances they may have collected; instead they must provide theories that make predictions about which combinations of words are possible and which are not.

Moreover, Chomsky argued, natural languages contain infinitely many sentences. If they did not, each language would have a fixed bound on sentence length; but any such bound can easily be exceeded by multiple conjunction. Thus, to pick a particularly simple example, the following sentence can be continued to an arbitrarily finite length without becoming ill formed: *This sentence goes on and on and on and on . . .* For this reason as well, grammars should be *generative* in the sense that they provide a finite characterization of an infinite set, making predictions about the well-formedness of examples that are not in any predetermined corpus.

To make such predictions, it is necessary for grammars to be more precise and explicit than traditional descriptive grammars. According to Chomsky (1957, p. 5),

Precisely constructed models for linguistic structure can play an important role, both negative and positive, in the process of discovery itself. By pushing a precise but inadequate formulation to an unacceptable conclusion, we can often expose the exact nature of this inadequacy and, consequently, gain a deeper understanding of the linguistic data. More positively, a formalized theory may automatically provide solutions for many problems other than those for which it was explicitly designed. Obscure and intuition-bound notions can neither lead to absurd conclusions nor provide new and correct ones, and hence they fail to be useful in two important respects.

Toward this end Chomsky (1963) investigated the mathematical properties of certain grammatical formalisms. This work laid the foundations for much subsequent work in the branch of theoretical computer science now known as *formal language theory,* while at the same time setting a standard of rigor for subsequent work in the theory of grammar.

Another feature of Chomsky's work that is intimately related to his concern with the "creative aspect" of language is mentalism. Rejecting behaviorism (see especially Chomsky 1959), he argued that human linguistic abilities could only be explained by reference to a complex system of rules and principles represented in the minds of speakers.

Moreover he maintains that the most remarkable fact about human language is that people can acquire such a rich system on the basis of the meager data to which language learners are exposed. This gulf between knowledge of language and the experience it is based on, he argues, strongly suggests that knowledge of language is largely not learned but biologically determined. Chomsky's nativism and the "argument from the poverty of the stimulus" on which it is based have aroused a great deal of controversy among linguists, psychologists, and philosophers. They have nevertheless provided the stimulus for much important research. To the extent that knowledge of language is part of our common biological endowment, all languages must be alike. Hence if Chomsky is right, there must be substantive universal principles governing the structure of all languages; the search for such principles has been an important and productive avenue of investigation in recent decades. Another fruitful line of research stemming from the poverty-of-stimulus argument is the study of language learnability, discussed by Pinker in chapter 9.

Related to mentalism is the importance of meaning in Chomsky's work. From the earliest days of generative grammar, semantic judgments have played an important role in shaping analyses. Over the decades semantic representations of one sort or another have come to have an increasingly central role in the technical apparatus of generative theories. Although Chomsky has often been criticized for not going far enough in this direction, it is important to recognize that it was his break with his immediate predecessors in legitimizing appeals to meaning that opened the door to much of the dramatic progress that has been made in semantics (see chapter 6).

In the remainder of this chapter I present a greatly abridged introduction to a few of the central issues and constructs of generative grammar. I begin with a brief sketch of some results in formal language theory that have been of interest to people working on natural language. I then review some key ideas that played a role in the establishment and growth of generative grammar and follow with a survey of the situation in grammatical theory in the late 1980s.

5.1 Relevant Aspects of Formal Language Theory

Most work in generative grammar takes languages to be sets of sentences (but see Chomsky 1986, ch. 2, for a radically different perspective). For much of the mathematical work on languages, sentences are taken to be finite strings of words. A grammar, on this highly oversimplified view, is a finite system of rules for characterizing the membership of some language—that is, for specifying all and only the sentences of the language.

One very general family of formalisms for expressing grammars, whose mathematical properties have been extensively studied, is called *rewriting systems*. Each rule of a rewriting system is of the form $\varphi \rightarrow \psi$ and is read "φ can be rewritten as ψ" or "φ consists of ψ." φ and ψ are strings of symbols drawn from two vocabularies: the *terminal vocabulary*, that is, the finite set of words out of which the sentences of the language are composed; and the *nonterminal vocabulary*, which comprises auxiliary symbols used in the rules (analogous to such notions as "noun," "clause," or "prepositional phrase" from traditional grammar).

A rewriting system permits one string to be derived from another if the first can be obtained from the second by some finite sequence of rule applications. More precisely we can recursively define "can be derived from" for a rewriting system as follows:

Let G be a rewriting system.

If $\varphi \rightarrow \psi$ is a rule of G, then $\sigma\psi\tau$ can be derived from $\sigma\varphi\tau$ in G, for any strings σ and τ.

If ψ can be derived from ω in G, and ω can be derived from φ in G, then ψ can be derived from φ in G.

A string is generated by a rewriting system G if it can be derived from the distinguished nonterminal symbol S in G.[1] The *language* generated by a rewriting system G is the set of all terminal strings (that is, strings containing only terminal symbols) generated by G.

The very general form of rewriting systems just presented, known as "unrestricted rewriting systems" or "type 0 grammars," are exceedingly powerful. Indeed they are provably equivalent to Turing machines and therefore are capable of encoding any arbitrary algorithm (assuming Church's thesis—see, for example, Rogers 1967). This excess power diminishes their linguistic interest for two reasons. First, it means that nothing inherent in the rewriting system formalism distinguishes between natural languages (or possible natural languages) and arbitrary (recursively enumerable) sets of strings. Second, systems of this power are computationally intractable (and hence, arguably, psychologically implausible) in various ways, most obviously in lacking a decision procedure (that is, an effective procedure for determining whether a given string can be generated by a given grammar).[2] Consequently most of the work on rewriting systems has concentrated on special subclasses in which the form of the grammar rules is more constrained.

Three such subclasses have received particularly careful attention:

· *type 1* or *context-sensitive grammars,* in which every rule is of the form $\sigma A\tau \rightarrow \sigma\varphi\tau$, where A is a nonterminal symbol and σ, τ, and φ are arbitrary strings of terminals and nonterminals, with φ nonempty;

· *type 2* or *context-free grammars,* in which every rule is of the form
A → φ, where A is a nonterminal and φ is an arbitrary nonempty string
of terminals and nonterminals;

· *type 3* or *finite-state grammars,* in which every rule is of one of the
following two forms: A → x B or A → x, where A and B are single
nonterminals, and x is an arbitrary string of terminals.

Underlying these definitions are certain intuitions. Behind types 1 and
2 is a picture of sentences being made up of phrases, which are themselves made up of smaller phrases, and so on, until one eventually
reaches individual words.[3] The nonterminal symbol (A) singled out on
the left side of the rules corresponds to the type of a phrase (prepositional phrase, clause, and the like); φ on the right side corresponds to
the words and phrases it is composed of. This conception of sentence
structure is manifest in the tree diagrams that linguists employ, such
as in figure 5.1 (adapted from Chomsky 1957, p. 27).

Such trees correspond rather straightforwardly to equivalence classes
of derivations in type 1, 2, or 3 grammars, and they are often used to
illustrate how a given string could be derived using a certain grammar.
The groupings of words into phrases that are indicated in tree diagrams
play a very important role in most recent theories of natural-language
syntax.

In the definition of type 1 grammar σ and τ can be used to indicate
that a certain type of phrase (A in this case) exhibits a certain constituency (φ in this case) only in certain contexts (σ on its left and τ on its
right). Imagine, for example, a hypothetical language just like English,
except that nouns precede articles in subjects but follow them in other
noun phrases. This could be characterized using type 1 rules such as.[4]

NP VP → N ART VP,
V NP → V ART N,
P NP → ART N,

and so on.

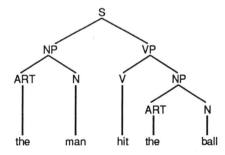

Figure 5.1 A tree diagram

Type 2 grammars are simply type 1 grammars in which σ and τ (the left and right contexts) are always empty. That is, in a type 2 grammar the constituency of a phrase depends only on what type of phrase it is, not what context it appears in.

Behind type 3 grammars is a rather different sort of intuition. Type 3 derivations generate sentences left to right, just as people speaking produce and hear sentences sequentially. At any point in a sentence, what constitutes an acceptable continuation depends on what has already been said. The nonterminals of a type 3 grammar encode information about what has come before in the sentence and they determine what can come later. A simplistic psychological model of language use might identify these nonterminals with states of mind in the speaker (or hearer), dependent on the preceding sequence of stimuli and determining the following responses.

A language is said to be of type n if it can be generated by some type n grammar. In practice, "L is a type n language" is often used to mean not only that there is a type n grammar for L but also that there is no type $n + 1$ grammar for L.

The four classes of languages characterized by these four types of grammars are mathematically quite robust in the sense that each of them admits a wide range of different formal characterizations. For example, it turns out that the type 0 grammars whose rules are nonshortening in the sense that their left sides are no longer than their right sides generate all and only the type 1 languages. Similarly the type 3 languages are precisely the "regular sets," that is, the sets that can be generated from finite sets using the operations of set union, set product, and Kleene star.[5]

A very different looking method for specifying membership in a formal language is to characterize an automaton that will accept just the strings in the language. It turns out that there is a hierarchy of types of automata that serves to define the same hierarchy of languages as the types of grammars discussed here (see Hopcroft and Ullman 1979 for details of the relevant results, or Wall 1972, ch. 10, for an overview).

In this context an automaton should be thought of as a hypothetical machine with the following components:

· an input tape of unbounded length on which a finite string of (terminal) symbols is written;

· a reading head that scans the input on the tape, one symbol at a time, from left to right;

· a finite set of internal states, a subset of which are designated as "final states";

· some internal memory structure (which will differ for different types of automata);

· a finite set of instructions stipulating how the internal state and memory structure are to be altered, based on the input symbol being scanned, the state, and what is in memory.

An automaton accepts a string if it halts (that is, reaches a situation in which there are no applicable instructions) in a final state at the end of scanning the string.

Four types of automata of special interest in the present context are:

Turing machine There are no constraints on the size or mode of access of the memory. It can be thought of as an infinite tape that the machine can write on, read from, and move in either direction.

Linear bounded automaton The amount of memory available is a linear function of the length of the input string. That is, it is like a Turing machine that can use only some of its memory, the amount being determined by the size of the input.

Pushdown automaton There is no bound on the size of the memory but it functions as a stack—that is, information in memory must be accessed according to a last-in–first-out pattern.

Finite-state automaton There is no internal memory structure.

These four types of automata characterize exactly the same classes of languages as the four types of grammars. In other words the grammars and automata are in a sense equivalent, with the following pairing:

Unrestricted rewriting system	Turing machine
Context-sensitive grammar	Linear bounded automaton
Context-free grammar	Pushdown automaton
Finite-state grammar	Finite-state automaton

It follows from the definitions of the types of grammars that every type n grammar is a type $n - 1$ grammar ($1 \leq n \leq 3$). Hence the class of type n languages is a subset of the class of type $n - 1$ languages, for each n from 1 to 3. It is true but not obvious that this inclusion is proper—that is, there are type n languages that are not type $n + 1$, for each n for 0 to 2 (see Wall 1972, ch. 9, or Hopcroft and Ullman 1979 for proof of this assertion).

There are certain standard examples of languages that are not finite state and others that are not context free, and it is illustrative to look at some of their properties.

Consider first the language $L_1 = \{a^n b^n | n \geq 1\}$ whose sentences consist of some number of a's followed by the same number of b's. L_1 is not finite state because, generating sentences left to right, a finite-state grammar would have to keep track of how many a's had been generated so as to ensure that the same number of b's were generated. The only mechanism for such bookkeeping would be the choice of nonterminal symbols, but then there would have to be a different nonterminal for each choice of n. Because n can be any positive integer there would have to be infinitely many nonterminals, which the definition of rewriting systems does not permit. For essentially the same reason, infinite palindrome languages (that is, languages whose sentences all read the same backward as forward) are not finite state. Such languages are easy to generate using context-free grammars. For example, the following is a simple context-free grammar for L_1:

$S \rightarrow aSb,$

$S \rightarrow ab.$

The inability of finite-state grammars to handle such dependencies provides an argument that most familiar languages, both natural and artificial, are not finite state. The propositional calculus, for example, in its standard notation, requires that left and right parentheses be paired; and as formulas get more complex the number of parentheses required grows without limit. Hence this is not a finite-state language. Many natural languages contain similar bracketing devices, for example, *either . . . or*, *both . . . and*, and *if . . . then* in English. On the basis of this observation, Chomsky (1957, pp. 22–23) concluded that finite-state grammar (and, by implication, any psychological model associated with it) should be rejected as a theory of natural-language structure.

Similar arguments have been advanced regarding context-free grammars, though these have been more controversial. Two standard examples of languages that are not context free are $L_2 = \{a^n b^n c^n | n \geq 1\}$ and $L_3 = \{xx | x$ is a string of a's and b's$\}$. Context-free grammars can deal with languages such as L_1 or palindrome languages because dependencies between elements can be expressed by generating them with a single rule, adjacent to an intervening nonterminal symbol. This mechanism readily handles dependencies between two lists, so long as the dependencies are nested. Matching of three or more lists (as In L_2) or cross-serial dependencies (as in L_3), however, is provably beyond the power of context-free grammars.

In the early 1960s a number of arguments were published purportedly demonstrating that natural languages exhibit dependencies of a kind that context-free grammars cannot deal with. The most celebrated of these was Postal's (1964a) claim that Mohawk exhibits the type of dependency found in L_3 and that it thus could not be generated by any context-free grammar. Postal (1964b) argued, further, that several leading nontransformational grammatical theories of that era were (if properly formalized) equivalent to context-free grammar. He concluded that these theories must be rejected. This and similar arguments played a significant role in establishing transformational grammar as the dominant syntactic paradigm.[6]

5.2 Transformational Grammar

Arguments for Transformations

Even more influential than the mathematical arguments against the context freeness of natural languages were considerations of simplicity and generality. Attempts to analyze natural-language syntax using only the machinery of phrase-structure grammars (see note 3), it was claimed, would result in redundant and unrevealing analyses, whereas many languages with simple phrase-structure grammars bear little resemblance to natural languages. To "capture linguistically significant generalizations," Chomsky and others proposed that phrase-structure grammars should be augmented with a set of transformational rules that operate on the output of the rewriting rules, moving, deleting, or inserting material.

Before looking at such arguments it will be useful to consider the question of how distinctions such as that between transitive and intransitive verbs might be dealt with. Consider, for example, *devour* and *dine*. There are good reasons to treat these as members of the same grammatical category (namely, verb), the most obvious of which is the parallelism of their inflections (*devours/dines*, *devoured/dined*, *devouring/dining*). Their distribution, however, is different because *devour* is transitive and *dine* is intransitive:[7]

(1) a. After the game, the team devoured a hearty supper.

    b. After the game, the team dined.

    c. *After the game, the team devoured.

    d. *After the game, the team dined a hearty supper.

In a rewriting system such examples might be taken as arguments for context sensitive rules like V NP → *devour* NP and V # → *dine* # (where # denotes the end of the clause). Chomsky (1965) proposed that such context sensitivity could be confined. He argued that the basic structure of simple sentences, minus the words, should be generated by means of context-free rewriting rules. In addition, there would be a lexicon containing the idiosyncratic information about particular words, including their grammatical categories and specification of the contexts in which they can appear (or "cooccurrence restrictions," as these are often called). The lexical entry for *devour*, for example, might stipulate V, [__NP], meaning it is a verb that must be followed by a noun phrase.

Now consider examples such as

(2) a. The supper was devoured (by the team).

    b. *The supper was devoured dessert (by the team).

    c. *The supper was dined (by the team).

In (2a) *devoured* does not demand a following noun phrase; indeed, (2b) shows that the passive participle *devoured* forbids a following noun phrase. In (2c) *dined* cannot appear in this construction, even though it is not followed by a noun phrase. The environment in (3) exhibits a similar pattern.

(3) a. What did the team devour?

    b. *What did the team devour a hearty supper?

    c. *What did the team dine?

One might attempt to deal with such examples by complicating the statement of the cooccurrence restrictions on lexical entries, saying, for example, that *devour* must be followed by a noun phrase except when it is in the passive voice or in a *wh*-question, in which case it cannot be followed by a noun phrase. Aside from the fact that this would not be quite right factually (for example, it would rule out *Who devoured the dessert?*), it is unsatisfactorily complex and stipulative. Intuitively what is going on is the following: *devour*, unlike *dine*, requires explicit mention of what it is that is eaten. In simple sentences this is accomplished by means of a noun phrase immediately following the verb; in passives and some questions, the requisite noun phrase appears elsewhere.

Transformational grammar explicates this intuition by positing multiple levels of representation for sentences. At one level (called "deep structure" in the theories of the 1960s and 1970s and "d-structure" in more recent work) a verb like *devour* requires an immediately following noun phrase. These structures take the form of trees that are generated by means of a context-free grammar (with context-sensitive information in the lexicon). They are then modified by transformational rules that may move elements from the positions in which they were generated.

Transformations then are rules that map tree structures into other tree structures; the output of the transformational component is referred to as "surface structure" ("s-structure" in more recent work). Various formalizations of transformations have been developed (see, for example, Chomsky 1955, Peters and Ritchie 1973, and Lasnik and Kupin 1977), but they go beyond the scope of this chapter. For present purposes, what is important is that passivization is accomplished by a transformation that moves an underlying postverbal noun phrase into subject position and that *wh*-phrases are transformationally moved to the front of questions. The inputs to the transformations need not be (trees for) well-formed sentences.[8]

Notice that the primary motivation for transformations was to account for facts about the distribution of certain forms—facts that have no obvious semantic explanation. In addition to simplifying the statement of the cooccurrence restrictions on transitive verbs like *devour*, however, transformations provide appealing accounts of a variety of types of facts. The analysis of passives sketched above, for instance, captures the intuition that the subject of a passive clause plays the same semantic role as the object of the corresponding active clause. This is true in a variety of grammatical contexts, as illustrated in (4).

(4) a. Pat gave Chris a book./Chris was given a book by Pat.

    b. Pat put the book on the table./The book was put on the table by Pat.

c. Pat considers Chris charming./Chris is considered charming by Pat.

d. Pat persuaded Chris to leave./Chris was persuaded to leave by Pat.

e. Pat bet Chris $5 that the Mets would win./Chris was bet $5 by Pat that the Mets would win.

The simplest formulation of the transformation in question will apply in all of these contexts. Moreover it will account for the fact that the highly idiosyncratic cooccurrence restrictions found in idioms are preserved under passivization. That is, in many cases, verb-object active idioms can appear in the passive as subject-verb idioms, as in (5a) versus (5b):

(5) a. The FBI keeps tabs on leftists./Tabs are kept on leftists by the FBI.

b. *The FBI holds tabs on leftists./*Tabs are held on leftists by the FBI.

Tabs (in its idiomatic usage) only occurs in the presence of *keep:* in the active it must be the object and in the passive, the subject. This relationship between the active object and the passive subject is captured directly by the passive transformation.

The transformational account of *wh*-questions helps to explain a variety of observations. Specifically certain normally "local" dependencies between parts of sentences can hold between *wh*-words and elements arbitrarily far away. Subject-verb agreement and case marking are two of these: in simple clauses, verbs agree with their subjects (the noun phrases immediately preceding them), and pronouns exhibit nominative or accusative case depending on whether they precede or follow the verb:

(6) a. The children were enjoying the show.

b. The child was enjoying the show.

c. *The children was enjoying the show.

d. *The child were enjoying the show.

e. She was talking to him.

f. *Her was talking to him.

In *wh*-questions agreement and case marking facts depend on what in transformational terms is the premovement position of the *wh*-phrase. In the following examples blanks indicates the location of the "gaps"— that is, where the *wh*-phrase would be moved from, on a transformational account.

(7) a. Which children did you think the teacher said _____ were enjoying the show?

b. Which child did you think the teacher said _____ was enjoying the show?

c. *Which children did you think the teacher said _____ was enjoying the show?

d. *Which child did you think the teacher said _____ were enjoying the show?

e. Who did you think the teacher said _____ was talking to him?

f. Whom did you think the teacher said she was talking to _____ ?

g. *Whom did you think the teacher said _____ was talking to him?

As an examination of the distribution of gaps in these examples indicates, the locality of agreement and case marking can be maintained under a transformational analysis if *wh*-phrases are fronted after agreement and case marking.

Even the contraction of *want to* to *wanna*, which one would expect to be a purely local operation on surface strings, exhibits reflexes of the premovement position of *wh*-phrases:

(8) a. Who do you want to meet _____ ?

b. Who do you want _____ to meet your parents?

c. Who do you wanna meet _____ ?

d. *Who do you wan _____ na meet your parents?

In short by positing multiple levels of representation for the syntactic structures of sentences, transformational grammar manages to simplify the statement of cooccurrence restrictions on particular words, while at the same time making possible highly intuitive accounts of a variety of complex and subtle dependencies between parts of sentences. During the first decade of generative grammar a great deal of work went into motivating and formulating transformational analyses of various constructions in natural languages and into exploring the rich interactions among the rules posited. See Baker 1978 and Newmeyer 1980 for surveys of some of the main results of this research.

Constraining Transformational Grammar
Beginning in the late 1960s and continuing into the present, the central focus of transformational grammarians has been to make their theory more restrictive. What is meant by this will become clearer after a brief discussion of just why it came to be such an important goal.

Chomsky's argument for nativism, based on "the poverty of the stimulus," suggests that not every logically possible language is a humanly possible language.[9] That is, Chomsky's position predicts that all natural languages will have significant commonalities—properties that reflect the character of the human language faculty. To many nonlinguists this is the most interesting aspect of Chomsky's program, because it suggests that work in grammatical theory can provide indirect insights into the nature and organization of the human cognitive apparatus. Once transformational grammar had become firmly entrenched as the dominant paradigm within linguistics (by the mid-1960s), this more general issue took on an increased importance to generative grammarians. This is reflected in the attention devoted to it in the literature since then.

One manifestation of this issue is concern with restricting the power of transformational theory. Linguistic universals, it was reasoned, ought to be incorporated into the theory of grammar, either in the design and interpretation of formalisms, or in a set of general constraints or laws governing the use of the formalisms. Formulating, testing, and refining hypotheses regarding universals have thus been the central activities of generative grammarians in recent years. The term "universal grammar" has come to be used for the collection of constraints that all natural languages must conform to, and it is often taken as an abstract characterization of the innate (and unconscious) knowledge of language that children bring to the task of language acquisition.

The need for constraints on transformational grammar was highlighted by the results of Peters and Ritchie (1973), who developed a rigorous formalization of transformational theory as described by Chomsky (1965), and proved that the resulting system was equivalent to Turing machines.[10] They showed that this result was stable under several different sets of assumptions about the character of the base (rewriting) component and of the transformational component. They also investigated in a preliminary way what it would take to make transformational grammar less powerful. Given Church's thesis, Peters and Ritchie's work entails that any formal procedure at all can be expressed by using a transformational grammar. In other words, transformational grammar in its first decade did nothing to distinguish humanly possible languages from arbitrary formal systems.[11]

This conclusion was particularly striking in light of the fact that many linguists at the time were arguing that the descriptive apparatus of transformational grammar needed to be *enhanced* to deal with certain kinds of complex data (see Newmeyer 1980, chs. 4 and 5, for a survey of some of these arguments). Linguists began to realize that clever use of a more constrained system might be preferable to the sort of work that they had been pursuing.

One of the first and most influential works dealing with constraints on transformations was John R. Ross's (1967) dissertation. Ross distinguished a class of transformations he called "chopping rules," which, he claimed, could move elements to the front of a clause from positions arbitrarily deeply embedded in that clause. A paradigm example of such a rule is the one fronting *wh*-phrases in questions.

(9) Which child did the teacher say she thought we wanted someone to take a picture of _____ ?

Ross noted that there are a number of constructions that appear to be "islands" with respect to chopping rules, in the sense that it is impossible to move an element from inside one of these constructions to a position outside of it. These constructions include relative clauses, coordinate constructions, clausal subjects, and several others. Thus the following are all ill formed (where square brackets indicate the island):

(10) a. *Which child did you criticize the teacher [who spanked _____]?
     b. *Which child did you see [Pat and a friend of _____]?
     c. *Which child did [that the teacher spanked _____] upset you?

Ross noticed that several such restrictions applied to a variety of chopping rules not only in English but also in other languages he looked at.[12] Consequently he postulated several universal constraints on the operation of transformations, each of which specified a phrase-structure configuration that constitutes an island for chopping rules. The proper formulation of island constraints is an issue that has been much discussed, and we will return to it below.

A rather different sort of constraint on transformational grammar was proposed by Joseph Emonds (1976). A number of linguists had observed that some transformations produced outputs that looked structurally very much like sentences that had not undergone the transformation. For example, there appears to be no reason to distinguish the tree structure assigned to a passive sentence such as *Pat was hit by a rock* from that assigned to an active sentence such as *Pat was standing by a rock,* though transformational analysis would assign them very different derivations. Emonds noticed that such "structure-preserving" transformations could quite generally apply entirely within subordinate clauses, whereas other rules that transformed sentences in more radical ways had to involve the main clause in their operation. An example of this latter sort of transformation is the rule that inverts a tensed auxiliary verb with the subject in English questions (for example, *Has Pat been sleeping?,* derived from a deep structure in which *Pat* precedes *has*). Notice that it cannot apply in embedded questions: *Chris questions whether has Pat been sleeping.* Passives, by contrast, can appear freely in subordinate clauses: *Chris questions whether Pat was hit by a rock.* Emonds proposed a general constraint on the theory of transformations to the effect that nonstructure-preserving transformations could only apply to main clauses.[13] This entailed extensive reanalysis of phenomena that had been studied by transformational grammarians, because many proposed transformations (for example, the rule preposing *wh*-words) had been formulated in ways not conforming to this constraint. In a number of cases the new analyses proved to be better (that is, either more elegant or covering a wider range of data) than the earlier treatments that violated Emonds's constraint.

It is interesting to note that none of the early proposals for constraints on transformational grammar solved the problem of excess formal power, as is evident from the fact that the grammar used in Bach and

Marsh's (1978) proof of Peters and Ritchie's theorem conforms to both Ross's and Emonds's constraints. Later developments, which involved much more radical alterations of standard transformational grammar, however, did result in theories with reduced generative capacity.

Semantics in Transformational Grammar

The role of meaning in transformational theory has changed considerably over the years. Although Chomsky's earliest work broke with the behaviorist tradition of the time in admitting semantic judgments (for example, intuitions of ambiguity) as legitimate evidence for syntactic analyses, transformationalists initially expressed skepticism about the possibility of developing a theory of meaning comparable in rigor to their syntactic theory. According to Chomsky (1957, pp.103–104), "Part of the difficulty with the theory of meaning is that 'meaning' tends to be used as a catch-all term to include every aspect of language that we know very little about. Insofar as this is correct, we can expect various aspects of this theory to be claimed by other approaches to language in the course of their development."

In the 1960s a good deal of attention was devoted to the problem of adding a semantic component to transformational grammar. The seminal paper was by Katz and Fodor (1963), who suggested that the syntactic structures proposed by transformational analysis could serve as the basis for a precise characterization of how the meanings of words get combined into the meanings of phrases and ultimately of sentences. The meanings of words were themselves decomposed into more primitive elements, called "semantic markers." Representations of sentence meanings in terms of markers were built up by means of "projection rules"—rules for constructing semantic representations for complex expressions out of those for their constituent parts.

Little attention was devoted to the question of the interpretation of the markers themselves. For this reason some people (see, for example, Lewis 1972) dismissed the whole enterprise as mere translation from one language into another without providing anything that could legitimately be called semantics. Although this complaint has some substance, the "markerese" research program had some perfectly legitimate goals. In particular it sought to explicate certain robust semantic intuitions that fluent speakers of a language have, including intuitions of paraphrase, semantic anomaly, analyticity, entailment, and the like. The idea was that these properties of sentences (or pairs of sentences) could be rigorously defined as formal properties of their semantic representations in terms of markers, without appeal to the denotations of the representations. This program was clearly spelled out by Katz (1972), and parallels, in obvious ways, the syntactic goal of transformational theory. The fruitfulness of this enterprise is perhaps debatable, but it is clear in retrospect that its influence was primarily on developments in syntactic theory. Hence reflecting the literature of the time, the discussion here will concentrate on the question of the relationship between semantic and syntactic representations.

Katz and Postal (1964) put forward a hypothesis about the place of semantics in transformational grammar that set the direction of research and debate in the field for nearly a decade. Their idea was simple: The semantic interpretation of a sentence is fully determined by its deep structure. In other words, two different sentences with the same deep structure (differing only in that some optional transformation had applied in the derivation of one but not the other) must be synonymous.

This proposal had great intuitive appeal. It suggested the organization of a grammar depicted in figure 5.2.

Deep structures were straightforwardly mapped onto semantic representations, or meanings; surface structures were mapped onto phonetic representations, or sounds. If a language is thought of as a system that pairs sounds with meanings, then the transformations constitute the crucial link. The simplicity and symmetry of this picture attracted the attention not only of linguists but also of psychologists, philosophers, and others interested in the structure of language. The version of transformational grammar conforming to the Katz-Postal hypothesis became known as the "standard theory" and served as the point of departure for grammatical research for many years.

Nevertheless general acceptance of the Katz-Postal hypothesis was short lived. Prima facie counterexamples (some taken from earlier literature) were quickly cited. Many of these consisted of active-passive pairs that, it was claimed, had different truth conditions. Such pairs were presumed to differ only in the application of an optional passivization transformation, and, of course, two sentences could not have the same meaning if conditions could be imagined under which one was true and the other false. On these assumptions (the former of which later came to be challenged), pairs like (11) were offered as counterexamples to the Katz-Postal hypothesis.[14]

(11) a. Everyone in the room knows at least two languages./At least two languages are known by everyone in the room. (Chomsky 1957, pp. 100–101)

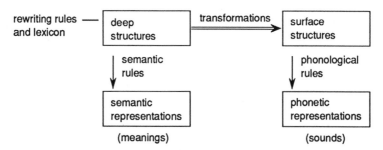

Figure 5.2 Organization of the standard theory

b. Many of the arrows didn't hit the target./The target wasn't hit by many of the arrows. (Jackendoff 1972, p. 326)

c. Beavers (characteristically) build dams./Dams are (characteristically) built by beavers. (Chomsky 1975, p. 97)

Similar pairs were constructed using other purported optional transformations.

In the face of apparent counterexamples to the Katz-Postal hypothesis were two natural reactions: either abandon the hypothesis or modify the analysis of the crucial examples to bring them into conformity with the hypothesis. In the late 1960s transformational grammarians divided into two warring camps, one adopting the former option and the other taking the latter. Chomsky and a number of his students argued that whereas some aspects of meaning were a function of deep structure, others—including pairing of pronouns with antecedents and determining the scope of logical elements like quantifiers and negation—had to take derived structure into account. This position was known as "interpretivism." Another faction, including Postal, Ross, and many others, adopted the Katz-Postal hypothesis as a methodological principle; whenever they found a meaning difference between two sentences, they posited a difference in underlying structure. The converse—the idea that any two synonymous sentences had the same underlying structure—was also widely invoked. This approach was quickly carried to its logical conclusion: it was argued that the input to the transformational component of a grammar simply *was* the semantic representation. This position was labeled "generative semantics" and for a few years was the dominant paradigm in grammatical research.

The generative semantics movement died out surprisingly quickly,[15] and the idea that some semantic rules apply to derived structures has been undisputed in transformational grammar in recent years. In fact changes in syntactic theory in the early 1970s (to which I will return) made it possible to maintain that *all* semantic interpretation is done on the basis of s-structure.

One legacy of the debate over the Katz-Postal hypothesis is that most subsequent work on meaning in generative grammar has been concentrated on the scoping of *logical elements* (for example, quantifiers and negation) and the assignment of antecedents to pronouns. As a consequence there is rarely any mention in modern transformational work of semantic representations. There has been, however, a great amount of work (see Chomsky 1981) that invokes of a level of representation known as *logical form* (LF), at which the linear order of logical elements corresponds to their scoping, and pronouns are identified with their antecedents by giving them identical subscripts. Discussion of lexical meaning or of the interpretation of LF is rare in this literature, suggesting that some of the early skepticism about the tractability of semantics has returned; see Higginbotham 1985 for an influential view of these topics.

The work of Richard Montague (see Montague 1970 and chapter 6), applying model theoretic techniques taken from mathematical logic to the analysis of natural language, has had a profound effect on subsequent work in semantics. Many linguists adopted Montague's approach or adapted it to their syntactic analyses (see, among others, Partee 1975, Dowty 1979, and Gazdar et al. 1985); they too have tended to focus on problems of scope (quantifiers) and coreference (pronouns), rather than on translations into markerese.[16]

5.3 Major Schools of Generative Grammar

After the interpretive/generative semantics split, generative grammar never regained the unity it had in the 1960s. Standard transformational grammar has spawned a number of descendants. Differing widely in terminology, notation, and emphasis, they nevertheless share certain features, including a commitment to accounting for infinite languages with finite grammars, concern with discovering linguistic universals, and reliance on native-speaker judgments as the primary source of data. Of the dozens of such theories that have been proposed, only a few have had any substantial following. In this section I present a very superficial overview of five of the most important theories.[17]

Government-Binding Theory

Research in transformational grammar in the 1970s introduced a series of changes that altered the theory almost beyond recognition. The effect of most of them was to reduce the role of language-particular transformations, putting more and more of the descriptive burden onto conditions in the general theory. The end result of these changes was the theory of government and binding (GB), first laid out by Chomsky (1981), and described in more accessible terms by van Riemsdijk and Williams (1986). Before we turn to GB itself, it will be useful to consider some of the developments that led up to it.

Chomsky's 1970 paper "Remarks on Nominalization" steered generative research in new and important directions. Chomsky argued that the relationship between clauses and their corresponding nominalizations (for example, *The enemy destroyed the city* and *the enemy's destruction of the city*) should not be accounted for by means of a transformation turning sentences into noun phrases, as had been assumed in earlier work in generative grammar. Instead Chomsky proposed two innovations:

First, he argued that the relationship between a verb (*destroy*) and its corresponding noun (*destruction*) should be handled lexically by means of a category neutral lexical entry or a disjunctive lexical entry.[18] Such an analysis differs from a transformational one in that it only needs to be concerned with capturing relationships within a finite lexicon and hence it need not be generative. The tendency to unburden the syntactic rules in favor of a richer lexicon is one that has continued and has manifested itself in several theories, as we shall see below.

Second, to capture structural parallelisms between the clause and the noun phrase Chomsky proposed the idea of schematizing the rewriting rules in a manner that has come to be known as *X-bar theory*. The idea is that the grammatically significant properties of phrases (such properties as plurality, case, tense, and even major category—that is, noun, verb, and so on) can be largely projected from the properties of the words that head them; further, the gross structure of phrases is generally the same across noun phrases, verb phrases, and adjective phrases. These ideas were embodied in the proposal that the rewriting rules of a transformational grammar should conform to the general schemata (12).

(12) a. $S \rightarrow \bar{\bar{N}} \, \bar{\bar{V}}$

 b. $\bar{\bar{X}} \rightarrow$ SPECIFIER $\bar{X}$

 c. $\bar{X} \rightarrow X$ COMPLEMENT

Here X ranges over N, V, A (for adjective), and possibly P (for preposition). SPECIFIER and COMPLEMENT are essentially placeholders for such things as articles and prepositional phrases, which occur before and after the heads of phrases. Although this is quite vague as presented, it does embody the important idea of schematizing the rewriting component of a transformational grammar in ways that apply across major grammatical categories and possibly even across languages. This idea has been retained and developed in a great deal of subsequent grammatical research (see Jackendoff 1977 for the most detailed attempt to work out an explicit version of X-bar theory). Likewise, though linguists have debated how many distinct levels of phrases (how many bar levels) the theory should permit, the idea of regarding phrases as projections of lexical heads has persisted, and the notion of "maximal projection" has played an important role in GB, as will become evident in what follows.

GB theorists have claimed that the X-bar schemata, together with the increased lexicalization of syntactic information, make it possible to eliminate language-particular rewriting rules altogether. All that is needed, it is argued, is a specification of whether phrases in the language put the head at the beginning of the phrase (as in English) or at the end of the phrase (as in Japanese). This is a simple illustration of one of the principal characteristics of GB: it attempts to reduce differences between languages (aside from differences in vocabulary) to differences in a small number of parameters, each of which has only a few possible values. This idea has an obvious appeal from the point of view of learnability, for it reduces the problem of language acquisition to the setting of parameters.

Returning to the genesis of GB, a major turning point was the publication in 1973 of Chomsky's "Conditions on Transformations," his first detailed proposal concerning island constraints. The crucial difference between Chomsky's approach and Ross's earlier work on the same topic was the generality of the constraints. Whereas Ross had listed certain grammatical constructions that functioned to block the applicability of one class of grammatical rules, Chomsky formulated conditions that cut across the usual taxonomies of constructions and rules.

For example, to rule out extractions from relative clauses, Ross posited the "complex NP constraint," which says that nothing may be extracted by a chopping rule from a clause that is directly dominated by a noun phrase with a lexical head noun.[19] This covers little other than the data that motivated the original constraint (except of course that it was purported to apply to all languages, and Ross could only check a very few). Chomsky, on the other hand, proposed the "subjacency condition," saying (approximately) that no grammatical rule could involve elements separated by more than one "bounding node."[20] The bounding nodes may vary from language to language (another parameter), but in English would include NP and S. Because elements inside a relative clause are under an S node that is under an NP node, any rule that extracted them would violate subjacency.

Chomsky's analysis makes many more novel predictions than Ross's. Indeed it required extensive reanalysis of a number of phenomena whose standard analyses violated subjacency. For example, to account for extractions from multiply embedded clauses, Chomsky had to argue that *wh*-phrases moved up the tree one clause at a time. That is, in a sentence like (13), *which book* would first have to be moved to a position between *think* and *the teacher* before it could be moved to the front of the main clause.[21]

(13) Which book did the students think [the teacher said [they should read _____ ?]]

This idea engendered much controversy at first; however, it is now widely accepted that filler-gap dependencies are mediated by the intervening structures.[22]

Moreover Chomsky's constraint is not limited to chopping rules. Whereas Ross had assumed that different classes of rules (for example, clause-bound rules such as passivization, chopping rules, rules of semantic interpretation, and so on) would each be subject to their own constraints, subjacency was initially posited as a perfectly general condition. This lends it a certain plausibility from a psychological point of view: both acquisition and processing of language would be simplified if structural dependencies are highly local, that is, if the analysis at any point in the string depends only on elements sufficiently "close" (in some well-defined sense) to that point. Subjacency is a natural candidate for a very general locality constraint. An example of a nonchopping (indeed nontransformational) rule purportedly subject to subjacency is the rule marking certain pairs of noun phrases as disjoint in reference. This predicts the following distribution of data:

(14) a. *I saw me.

    b. I saw [the story about [the picture of me]]

The tendency to replace construction-specific constraints with more general principles has been a hallmark of GB. The inventory and specificity of transformations was likewise reduced, to the point where GB posits only one transformation. This rule, known as "move α," simply says that constituents can be moved. Which elements get moved, in which contexts, and where they get moved to need not be stipulated because, according to GB, such specifics follow from general principles.

Another crucial modification of transformational grammar was what came to be called "trace theory." To account for certain technical problems concerning the interactions among transformations (see Chomsky 1975, ch. 3, for a summary), it was proposed that when an element is transformationally moved, an empty (that is, unpronounced) copy (or "trace") of it is left behind. The link between a moved element and its trace is marked by coindexing—that is, assigning them identical indices as subscripts. Coindexing is also used for pairing pronouns of various sorts with their antecedents. Under trace theory, it is therefore natural to expect that the structural constraints on filler-gap pairings will include the structural constraints on pairs of antecedents and pronouns. This idea has been extensively refined and developed, and a version of it forms the heart of the "binding" part of GB, to which I will return.

From a surface structure with coindexed traces it is possible to reconstruct most of the transformational history of the sentence. Hence those aspects of deep structure that were deemed essential for semantic interpretation can be computed at surface structure. Trace theory thus led to the claim that surface structure was the sole input to the rules of semantic interpretation.

Empty categories also came to be used for a number of other purposes in addition to trace theory. Certain phenomena that were handled by deletion rules in standard transformational grammar were reanalyzed by positing empty nodes and appropriate interpretive rules. One such is what is often called "control," that is, accounting for the interpretation of the "missing" subject in constructions like infinitives and gerunds in English (see the sub section Lexical-Functional Grammar for examples and further discussion). In standard transformational grammar this was handled by a rule deleting the subject "under identity" with a noun phrase in the superordinate clause, but this approach has serious problems. In more recent analyses an empty element (referred to as "PRO") is generated as the subject of such constructions and interpreted as if a special sort of pronoun. Another use of empty categories is as "landing sites" for movement rules: Emonds's structure-preserving constraint was implemented by requiring that transformations move elements only into positions where an empty node of the same category is already present.

Thus empty categories came to play an important role in transformational theory, to the point where Chomsky (1981, p. 55) could write:

The question of the nature of empty categories is a particularly interesting one . . . [T]here is an intrinsic fascination in the study of properties of empty elements. These properties can hardly be determined inductively from observed phenomena, and therefore presumably reflect inner resources of the mind. If our goal is to discover the nature of the human language faculty, abstracting from the effects of experience, then these elements offer particularly valuable insights.

Given this centrality of empty categories in GB and the importance of coindexing them properly, it is not surprising that one crucial component of this theory is a set of principles for coindexing various kinds of noun phrases (including empty ones). These principles, known as the "binding theory," make use of several key notions; because the GB literature contains numerous alternative definitions for several of them, the following characterizations should not be taken as definitive:

c-command Intuitively, α c-commands β if α is at least as high in the tree as β (but not on the same branch); a more precise definition is that α c-commands β if α does not dominate β, but every maximal projection[23] dominating α dominates β.

governor α governs β (and is thus its governor) if α is a noun, verb, adjective, preposition, or tense (which is assumed to be separate from the verb at d-structure), and α and β c-command each other.

governing category The governing category of a node α is the smallest S or NP containing both α and a governor of α.

binding α binds β if α c-commands β and they are coindexed.

The GB binding theory consists of three principles, each for a different type of element. Although the types of elements are not precisely defined, the standard examples make the classification fairly clear.

anaphors include reflexive pronouns (for example; *herself, themselves*) and reciprocals (*each other*); they are noun phrases requiring linguistic antecedents.

pronominals include nonreflexive third-person pronouns (*he, she, it, them*).

R-expressions include nonpronominal noun phrases (names and descriptions).

These categories are also used to classify empty noun phrases, as will become clear.

The binding theory can now be stated quite simply:

- *Principle A:* An anaphor must be bound in its governing category.
- *Principle B:* A pronominal must be free in its governing category.
- *Principle C:* An R-expression must be free.

There are a great many consequences of the binding theory. For the case of overt noun phrases they include[24]

(15) a.　The men think that [John is deceiving himself].

　　 b.　*The men think that [John is deceiving themselves]. [A]

　　 c.　The men$_i$ think that [John is deceiving them$_i$].

　　 d.　*The men think that [John$_i$ is deceiving him$_i$]. [B]

　　 e.　*They$_i$ think that John is deceiving the men$_i$.[C]

　　 f.　*The men think that [himself$_i$ is deceiving John$_i$]. [A & C]

As noted, the binding theory also applies to empty categories. Traces are divided into two types: traces of movements into subject or object (for example, the trace of the underlying object in passives) are considered anaphors, and traces of movements into complementizer position (for example, the fronting of *wh*-phrases) are analyzed as R-expressions. These classifications rule out the indicated analyses of the following examples (where *e* is used to designate an empty category):

(16) a.　*The men$_i$ think that [John was deceived e_i]. [A]

　　 b.　*Who does he$_i$ like e_i? [C]

　　 c.　*Who does he$_i$ think that I like e_i? [C]

PRO, the empty category posited as the subject of infinitives, is analyzed as being both an anaphor and a pronominal. It follows from principles A and B that PRO has to be both bound and free in its governing category. This would appear to be a contradiction but it is in fact possible if PRO has no governing category. That is, the dual classification of PRO entails that PRO cannot have a governing category. There is only one noun phrase position that does not have a governing category, namely, subject position of a tenseless subordinate clause. Objects are governed by the verb of preposition of which they are objects, and subjects of tensed clauses are governed by tense. Thus the highly restricted distribution of PRO is entirely accounted for by independently motivated principles of the binding theory. In contrast, the earlier deletion analysis of subjectless infinitives had to stipulate the contexts in which the relevant transformation applied, and the distribution of "missing" subjects was treated as unrelated to anything else.

Analyses such as those sketched above have given GB an extremely wide following, resulting in a very considerable literature. This work is characterized by its reliance on general principles and simple parameters rather than detailed rule systems. There are of course a great many more such principles and parameters in GB than could be presented in this chapter. The theory consists of a number of modules (of which the binding principles constitute one example), each one quite simple, whose interactions produce the diversity and apparent complexity that are evident in natural languages. GB analyses typically exhibit what has been called "rich deductive structure," that is, intricate argumentation from simple premises to unexpected conclusions, with the goal of minimizing what has to be stipulated. GB's success at approaching this goal has, to a certain extent, been purchased at the expense of decreased attention to details of linguistic description and formal rigor. Consequently GB has many critics, though it is clearly the current dominant paradigm in grammatical theory.

Relational Grammar
Transformational grammar, with its roots in formal language theory, is based on the manipulation of strings and trees. Rules and principles are expressed in terms of the geometry of tree structures. This is a departure from traditional grammars (and informal statements by transformationalists), which make extensive use of what are sometimes called "grammatical relations" or "grammatical functions," that is, notions such as "subject" and "object." Chomsky (1965) suggested a means of defining grammatical relations in terms of tree configurations, but these definitions have met with considerable skepticism.

The central premise of relational grammar is that transformational grammar has adopted the wrong set of primitives, and that rules and principles should be formulated in terms of grammatical relations, not tree structures.

The clearest example of this is probably passivization. In transformational analyses the key operation in the English passive rule is movement of the postverbal noun phrase into preverbal position. Perlmutter and Postal (1977) argue that this does not generalize well to other languages with freer word order than English. In some languages (for example, Russian) actives and passives are distinguished by the inflections on the verb and the case marking on the nouns, not by word order. If the notion of "passive" is to be characterized cross-linguistically, it cannot be done in terms of word order. Similarly it cannot be done in terms of verbal inflection or case marking because there are languages (for example, Mandarin Chinese) in which active and passive verbs look the same and languages (for example, Basque) in which the case marking on actives and passives is not differentiated. In spite of these differences, relational grammarians claim that a general definition of passivization is possible: passive is the rule that turns a direct object into a subject. In different languages, the rule may manifest itself in different ways, because the mechanisms used to express grammatical relations in different languages differ, including at least word order, case marking, and verbal agreement. Universal properties of this and other constructions are best stated, it is argued, in terms of grammatical relations that are taken to be primitive notions, not reducible to anything configurational.

Relational grammarians have provided detailed analyses of clause structure in a wide variety of languages, discovering a great many fascinating and important generalizations. They have also formulated a number of "laws," that is, general constraints on the form and functioning of their relational rules. Both the rules and the laws are formulated in terms of an inventory of grammatical relations that is somewhat richer than that found in traditional grammars. See Perlmutter 1983 and Perlmutter and Rosen 1984 for examples of this research.

Relational grammar can be illustrated more concretely by considering what is probably its most influential contribution to grammatical theory, namely, "the unaccusative hypothesis" (see Perlmutter and Postal 1984 for a fuller exposition). According to this hypothesis; intransitive clauses (that is, clauses with only one obligatory noun phrase) can be divided into two types: those with an underlying subject but no object and those with an underlying object but no subject. The former are called "unergative" and the latter "unaccusative." A law requires that clauses have subjects in derived structure, so the objects of unaccusative clauses will normally be advanced to subject. In underlying structure, however, it is postulated that a large class of predicates are unaccusative including those in which the (superficial) subject is involuntarily affected by the event described by the verb. Examples include *melt, accumulate, fall,* and many others. Verbs with volitional subjects such as *play, jump,* and *speak* are unergative.

A law called "the 1-advancement exclusiveness law" states that at most one advancement to subject is possible in any given clause. In conjunction with the unaccusative hypothesis this law predicts that advancements to subject that are possible in unergative clauses will not be possible in unaccusative clauses. This can be illustrated in English by considering the "pseudopassive," that is, the construction that looks just like a passive, except that the surface subject corresponds not to the direct object of the active, but to the object of a preposition. Examples of pseudopassives (with unergative verbs) are given in (17).

(17) a. This auditorium has been played in by some great orchestras.

b. The bed should not be jumped on.

c. I have never been spoken to so rudely.

As predicted, pseudopassives are impossible with unaccusatives.

(18) a. *This oven was melted in by many ice cubes.

b. *The table was accumulated on by dust.

c. *This lake has been fallen into by many large boulders.

Some verbs are ambiguous between unergative and unaccusative interpretations, but the pseudopassives only permit the unergative.

(19) a. Burglars broke into the shed.

    b. The window broke into many pieces.

    c. The shed was broken into by burglars.

    d. *Many pieces were broken into by the window.

Several other correlates of the unaccusative/unergative distinction have been found in a variety of languages. A great deal of recent syntactic research has gone into investigation of these phenomena and into providing accounts of them within various theories. Versions of the unaccusative hypothesis have been proposed within several different theories.

The unaccusative hypothesis is illustrative of research in relational grammar. It is concerned with relations among the noun phrases in a single clause, and it has been tested against data from diverse languages. This sort of work has uncovered interesting data and generalizations; consequently relational grammar has had a pervasive influence on grammatical theory for a number of years. On the other hand relational grammar has been criticized because it has little to say about long-distance dependencies (like the filler-gap relations in *wh*-questions), semantics, or grammatical phenomena not involving relations among noun phrases (for example, the position of verbal auxiliaries). Hence the number of adherents to relational grammar is not commensurate with its influence.

Lexical-Functional Grammar

Lexical-functional grammar (LFG) shares with relational grammar the idea that grammatical relations (or functions, as they are called in LFG) are primitives, not definable in terms of tree configurations. LFG shares with transformational grammar the idea that surface constituent structure, formalizable in terms of tree diagrams, constitutes a linguistically significant level of representation.

LFG differs from both transformational grammar and relational grammar in positing only two levels of representation, known as functional structure (f-structure) and constituent structure (c-structure). Their roles are very roughly analogous to the roles of deep and surface structure in standard tranformational grammar (Bresnan 1982b, p. 4): "The constituent structure represents the superficial constituency of the sentence (which is phonologically interpreted), and the functional structure is the representation of its meaningful grammatical relations (which is semantically interpreted)."

Instead, however, of generating sentences through a derivational process involving a sequence of many levels, each related to the next by a rule, LFG assigns to each sentence two formally quite different representations, providing principles governing the pairings of c-structures and f-structures.

Aside from some minor differences that need not concern us here, the c-structure of a sentence is its (surface) phrase-structure tree. The grammar of a language includes a set of context-free phrase-structure rules generating the c-structures.[25]

Functional structures look quite different. They consist of sets of attributes paired with values. Attributes include grammatical-function names such as "Subject" and the like, grammatical-feature names such as "Definite" or "Case," and a special attribute called "Pred," whose values are "semantic forms"—that is, representations of the predicate-argument relations of that f-structure. Values (for attributes other than Pred) may be atomic symbols such as "+," or "Nominative," or they may be f-structures themselves. The standard notation for an f-structure consists of two columns enclosed in square brackets: the first column lists the attribute names with the value for each one listed across from it in the second column. In some cases two distinct attributes will have the same value. Under those circumstances it is impossible to write the common value across from both attributes, so it is written in only one place and connected to the other by a curved line. Such "reentrancy" is the critical formal difference between f-structures and trees, and it plays an important role in the analysis of certain natural-language phenomena, as will become evident in the following.

Several important properties of LFG representations can be illustrated by considering the sentence *Pat tried to leave* (figure 5.3).[26]

Notice, first of all, that though there is a correspondence between c-structure constituents and f-structures, it is not one to one. Thus the NP *Pat* corresponds rather directly to the value of the SUBJ attribute,

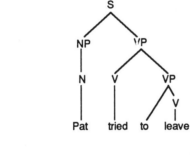

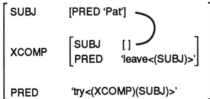

Figure 5.3 C-structure and f-structure

but the only f-structure corresponding to the VP *tried to leave* is the one that also corresponds to the whole sentence. Second, note that the value of the SUBJ attribute is also the value of the SUBJ attribute of the XCOMP. This expresses the fact that the understood subject of the verb *leave* is the same as the subject of *tried*.

A lexical-functional grammar of a language must provide mechanisms for assigning an appropriate f-structure to each sentence of that language. There are two principle sources of functional information; tree configurations and the lexicon. The phrase-structure rules that generate c-structures are annotated to indicate, for example, that in the English rule S → NP VP the f-structure corresponding to the NP will be the value of the SUBJ attribute in the f-structure corresponding to the S. Particular lexical entries will also contribute to the construction of the f-structure. An entry for a verb, for example, will contain a specification for PRED, indicating the grammatical function that is paired with each of the verb's logical arguments. It may also impose syntactic restrictions on those arguments. The functional information from lexical entries and from rule annotations can be merged (or "unified") to construct f-structures, so long as there is no incompatibility. See Kaplan and Bresnan 1982 for a detailed description of this aspect of LFG.

This unification operation (originally used in linguistic research by Kay 1979) can be illustrated by considering the phenomenon of subject–verb agreement in English. The noun *fish* has no lexical specification for the attribute Number (that is, it can be singular or plural). The verb *swims* requires that the Number attribute in the f-structure of its SUBJ have the value Singular. These are compatible, so they can unify, yielding an f-structure with a Singular SUBJ. Hence *The fish swims* is grammatical; likewise *The fish swim,* in which the verb's entry specifies that its subject must not be third-person singular, is possible. By contrast, *The men swims* is ungrammatical because *men* is lexically marked as plural and thus cannot unify with the f-structure for *swims*.[27]

As this example illustrates, a great deal of the grammatical information in LFG resides in lexical entries. In this it is like much other recent work in generative grammar and unlike early versions of transformational grammar. Many of the rules that earlier theories treated as mappings between (representations of) full sentences are handled in LFG as lexical rules—that is, rules generating new lexical entries on the basis of old ones. The clearest case of this is the passive rule, which can be treated entirely internal to the lexicon, given that the association of grammatical functions with semantic arguments is specified in the entries for verbs. Such an approach has the immediate advantage of predicting the fact, noted above, that passive clauses look on the surface just like active clauses, because the phrase-structure rules that generating c-structures do not distinguish between actives and passives. See Bresnan 1982b for a detailed discussion of the passive in LFG.

One research area in which LFG has been particularly successful is in the analysis of control—that is, in providing principles to account for the choice of understood subject in constructions (such as infinitives) that may lack overt subjects. Unlike both standard transformational grammar and GB, LFG can handle control neatly in the f-structure, without either deletion rules or empty elements in the c-structure.

Bresnan (1982c) identifies two fundamentally different types of control. "Functional control" requires an explicit linguistic antecedent for the missing subject in the same sentence. "Anaphoric control" can apply across sentence boundaries, or even without a linguistic controller.

Functional control is analyzed as reentrancy in f-structure, as illustrated above. The determination of which other grammatical function will determine the value of the controlled SUBJ may be a property of the configuration or of the lexical items in it.

In lexically induced functional control the lexical entry of a predicate (typically a verb) specifies the identity of its complement's subject with one of its own grammatical functions. In the vast majority of cases, if the predicate in question is a transitive verb, the controller is its object, and if the predicate is intransitive, the controller is its subject. Bresnan (1982c, p. 322) states a universal rule to this effect.[28] Her rule gives only the default assignments, allowing for lexically stipulated exceptions, such as *promise*, whose complement is controlled by the subject, not the object:

(20) a. Pat tried to leave. [SUBJ of *leave* is Pat]

    b. Pat persuaded Chris to leave. [SUBJ of *leave* is Chris]

    c. Pat promised Chris to leave. [SUBJ of *leave* is Pat]

Constructionally induced functional control is given by means of annotations on the phrase-structure rule that generates the configuration that results in control. These specify a set of grammatical functions that can serve as controllers; which functions are in the set will be fixed for each language but may vary across languages. Hence constructionally induced functional control will be ambiguous and it will permit obliques (that is, in English, prepositional objects) to be controllers, though not all noun phrases can be controllers. Thus in (21) the one who is drunk must be Mary or John's father; it cannot be John or someone not mentioned.

(21) Mary bumped into John's father in the hall yesterday drunk as usual.

Anaphoric control is treated quite differently. Because the controller need not be in the sentence (or even explicitly mentioned in the discourse), reentrancy cannot be used. Instead PRED can take a special value (called "PRO") that is interpreted essentially as a pronoun; the c-structure is not required to have a corresponding node. Anaphoric control in English is illustrated by a sentence such as *Pat was uncertain about how to proceed*. Here the subject of *proceed* may be Pat, but it also may be someone else not mentioned in this sentence who has consulted Pat about how to proceed.

This brief sketch of the LFG approach to control is intended to illustrate the manner in which this theory makes use of its various components to account for complex linguistic data. By adopting a rich set of descriptive tools (including phrase-structure trees, grammatical functions, and lexical rules), LFG is able to partition grammatical information in ways that facilitate elegant and comprehensive analyses.

Whereas LFG has served as the vehicle for a number of important studies of syntactic phenomena in various languages, much of its research deals with psychological and computational issues. Indeed the theory was designed with these concerns in mind. Earlier attempts to embed transformational grammar into models of linguistic processing had met with serious difficulties. In particular, the data simply did not support what has come to be called "the derivational theory of complexity," namely, the hypothesis that the psychological complexity of a sentence (in terms of such measures as recall and reaction time) would correlate with the number of transformations involved in its derivation (see Fodor, Bever, and Garrett 1974 for a survey of the relevant research). Bresnan (1978) argued that this constituted a serious shortcoming and sought to design a more "realistic" theory of grammar. Drawing on ideas developed by computational linguists in the context of a formalism known as "augmented transition networks" (see, for example, Wanner and Maratsos 1978), Bresnan and Kaplan proposed LFG as a theory that would simultaneously serve as a basis for elegant linguistic descriptions, a realistic psychological processing model, and efficient computational implementations. A substantial body of research now exists to lend plausibility to these ambitious goals (see part III of Bresnan 1982a for examples).

Generalized Phrase-Structure Grammar
In addition to LFG several other nontransformational theories of natural-language syntax have garnered substantial followings. Particularly notable among these is generalized phrase-structure grammar (GPSG), which is, in essence, simply an augmented version of context-free grammar. Underlying linguists' renewed interest in context-free grammar was the observation that the strongest arguments against context-free analyses of natural languages were based on parsimony, not on generative capacity. This left open the possibility that there might be alternative formalisms generating only context-free languages that nonetheless could capture linguistically significant generalizations efficiently. Whereas transformational grammar responded to the inadequacies of phrase-structure grammar by adding hugely powerful formal devices and then seeking constraints, GPSG attempted to find the minimal extensions that would handle the known problems. A very strong initial hypothesis was that this could be accomplished by means of

purely notational modifications without any increase of generative capacity–in other words, that natural languages are context free. As mentioned, this hypothesis has by now been abandoned even by the advocates of GPSG, but the definitive formulation of GPSG (Gazdar, Klein, Pullum, and Sag 1985) permits generation only of context-free languages.

A very important mechanism used in GPSG is one that was originally proposed by Chomsky (1965), namely, the decomposition of grammatical categories. The nonterminal symbols of rewriting systems are unanalyzed primitives whose relations to one another are defined entirely by the rewriting rules. The categories used in descriptions of natural languages, however, fall naturally into classes; further a given word or phrase will typically be in several of these classes. For example, the noun phrase *the child* is singular, definite, common (that is, not a proper noun), third person, animate, and soon. These properties are (at least partially) independent in the sense that for each of them there are phrases sharing that property but not some other property with *the child*. Following older work in phonology Chomsky proposed that this sort of cross-classification could be expressed by introducing syntactic features, which are assigned values, and treating grammatical categories simply as sets of feature-value pairs. For example, the category *the child* would be a collection including the following elements: [NOUN +], [VERB −], [NUMBER SINGULAR], [DEFINITE +], [PROPER −], [PERSON 3], [ANIMATE +], and the like. This makes it possible to make reference to natural classes of grammatical categories very succinctly, simply by mentioning a feature and its value. Of course if there are only finitely many features and values, there are still only finitely many categories, so features enhance notational economy without changing the generative capacity of the theory.

Although syntactic features have been part of generative grammar for many years their use was greatly expanded in GPSG. A great deal of syntactic information is encoded into the features making up grammatical categories. Universal principles are posited for propagating this information within phrase-structure trees. For example, the "foot-feature principle" says, very roughly, that there is a designated class of features (called "foot features"), whose values get passed up in trees, node by node. That is, any value for a foot feature on a node in a tree must be shared by the immediately dominating node, unless a rule specifies another value for that feature. Other feature-passing principles apply to different sets of features and different propagation algorithms.

A crucial extension of the use of features in GPSG is the idea that the values of features might themselves be categories.[29] Category-valued features are used in the analyses of several linguistic phenomena. One such is what Gazdar termed "unbounded dependencies"—that is, what had earlier been called chopping rules. GPSG posits a category-valued feature called "SLASH"; in constituents containing gaps (for example, in *wh*-questions), the value of SLASH is the category (that is, the set of features) one would normally expect to find in the position of the gap. The value of SLASH must be consistent with the category of any purported filler.[30]

Thus in a sentence such as (22), *whom* is licensed because the value of SLASH includes something like [CASE ACCUSATIVE], as does the lexical entry for *whom*.

(22) Whom did you want to talk to?

A simplified version of the tree for (22) would be something like figure 5.4.

Slash is a foot feature, introduced by a special null element in the position of the gap and propagated by the foot-feature principle. A rule saying something like S → α S[SLASH α] accounts for the top of the tree. In this way GPSG is able to represent in a single tree information that would be divided between different levels of representation in the other theories considered here.

This analysis interacts in an interesting way with GPSG treatments of coordinate conjunction.[31] Coordinate structures are unusual in that they are possible with almost any type of phrase. The following is only a small sample:

(23) a. Pat and Chris left. (NP CONJ NP)

b. Pat went out and took a walk. (VP CONJ VP)

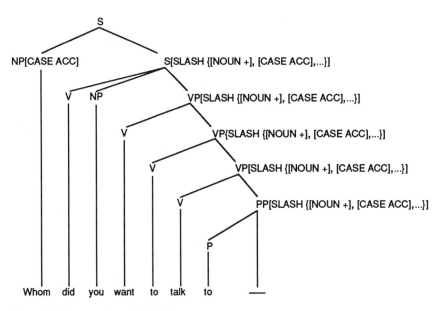

Figure 5.4 Propagation of SLASH

c. Pat thinks that Chris is lying and Sandy is telling the truth. (S CONJ S)

d. Pat walked around the block and to the store. (PP CONJ PP)

This can be schematized in GPSG by means of a rewriting rule schema of the form (24), where α is a variable over categories.

(24) α → α CONJ α

Informally this rule claims that like categories can conjoin. Now consider what happens when one tries to conjoin a category containing a specification for SLASH. By (24) two phrases may conjoin only if they are of the same category,[32] and by the definition of grammatical categories, phrases are of the same category only if they have the same value for SLASH. It follows that phrases with gaps in them may be conjoined only with other phrases containing identical gaps. This is borne out by the facts:

(25) a. Pat talked about Chris and made fun of Sandy.
(VP CONJ VP)

b. Who did Pat talk about and make fun of?
(VP[SLASH NP] CONJ VP[SLASH NP])

c. *Who did Pat talk about Chris and make fun of?
(VP CONJ VP [SLASH NP])

d. *Who did Pat talk about and make fun of Sandy?
(VP[SLASH NP] CONJ VP)

Precisely this pattern of data had been noted by Ross (1967), who proposed a constraint (known as the coordinate-structure constraint) prohibiting chopping out of coordinate structures and a special exception (known as the across-the-board exception) for cases in which extraction is uniform across conjuncts. The elegance of the GPSG analysis contrasts strikingly with the stipulative character of Ross's treatment, especially because Ross was working within a far more permissive theory.

GPSG extended the normal context-free grammar formalism in a number of additional ways, each of which has interesting consequences for the analysis of natural-language data (though they do not affect the context-freeness of the languages generated). Two of these extensions have occasioned considerable interest and study. The first (developed by Gazdar and Pullum (1981) on the basis of many earlier suggestions in the literature) is the idea of factoring information about linear precedence out of the rewriting rules. That is, the rewriting rules in GPSG only provide information about constituency (what dominates what in the phrase-structure tree); information about left-to-right order of constituents is provided by a separate set of rules. This permits GPSG to capture succinctly certain general facts about the order of constituents in natural languages (for example, that verbs are initial in verb phrases in English), without having them repeated in numerous rewriting rules. Other redundancies across rewriting rules are captured by positing "metarules"—statements to the effect that if a grammar contains a rule of form f, then it will contain a rule of form f', where f' is some function of f. Without careful constraints metarules greatly increase the formal power of GPSG (see Uszkoreit and Peters 1986), so their use must be greatly restricted. Gazdar and colleagues (1985) allow each metarule to apply at most once in the derivation of any rule, and more recent work in the tradition of GPSG eliminates metarules altogether (see especially Pollard 1985).

One additional difference between GPSG and ordinary context-free grammar deserves mention. Every rewriting rule in GPSG is paired with a semantic rule that specifies how the meanings of the daughter constituents are combined to yield the meaning of the mother. Most GPSG work adopts a version of the semantic theory of Montague (1970), and although the primary emphasis is clearly on syntax, this work tends to be quite explicit about how the structures it generates are to be interpreted. Some of the literature, including Gazdar et al. 1985, argues that in most cases the rules of semantic composition can be predicted on the basis of the form of the rewriting rule and hence need not be stipulated. Thus GPSG takes the position that syntax and semantics are very closely linked, and it contains explicit proposals about the connection.

Unlike Chomsky, Bresnan, and others, the developers of GPSG have studiously avoided attributing any psychological significance to their theory. Gazdar and colleagues (1985) are quite explicit: "[W]e feel it is possible, and arguably proper, for a linguist (*qua* linguist) to ignore matters of psychology." They go on to cite approvingly some psycholinguistic research (see Crain and Fodor 1985) based on GPSG. The computational implications of GPSG, on the other hand, have been a major concern from its inception. There have been numerous references to the fact that "Sentences of a context-free language are provably parsable in a time which is, at worst, proportional to less than the cube of the sentence length" (Gazdar 1982, p. 133). This compares favorably with exponential parsing times for some richer classes of languages (but see Barton, Berwick, and Ristad 1987 for a critical discussion of such comparisons). GPSG-based computer systems for processing natural-language input have been developed at a number of universities and industrial labs in the United States, Great Britain, Germany, and Japan.

While computational work based on GPSG continues to thrive, its following in linguistics proper seems to have peaked with the publication of Gazdar et al. 1985. The influence of GPSG, however, is evident in much ongoing grammatical research. In particular head-driven phrase-structure grammar (see Pollard and Sag 1987) and contemporary versions of categorial grammar incorporate many ideas about linguistic structures and their formal representation that were advanced and developed within the framework of GPSG. What these theories do *not* take over from GPSG is the heavy reliance on rewriting rules to express syntactic information. Instead they posit a more structured lexicon so that most of the information about how words and phrases combine into larger phrases can be located there. This emphasis on the role of the lexicon in syntax is shared by GB and LFG and represents one area of genuine convergence in recent grammatical research.

Categorial Grammar

The logical endpoint of the movement toward lexicalization of syntactic information is to put into the lexicon even the information about how words combine into phrases. Interestingly a grammar formalism embodying this idea, known as *categorial grammar*, actually predates the development of rewriting systems. Categorial grammar was first developed by Ajdukiewicz (1935) and explored further by several logicians over the next two decades. Bar-Hillel, Gaifman, and Shamir (1960) proved that a simple version of categorial grammar was equivalent in generative capacity to context-free grammar. Consequently when linguists in the early 1960s argued that natural languages were not context free, this was taken as proof that categorial grammars were inadequate for linguistic analysis. Montague's work on natural language used a greatly enhanced version of categorial grammar for its syntactic rules, bringing this formalism once again to the attention of linguists. In the late 1980s categorial grammar has enjoyed a renaissance among linguists, especially those with a computational bent (see Bach, Oehrle, and Wheeler 1987 for a collection of recent papers on the subject).

The central idea of categorial grammar is that the combinatory possibilities of a word or phrase are inherent in its grammatical category. For example, we might take sentence and noun phrase (S and NP) to be primitive categories. We could then define verb phrase as a category that combines with a noun phrase to make a sentence (notated S/NP). An intransitive verb would be a lexical S/NP. A transitive verb could be defined as something that combines with a noun phrase to make a verb phrase (that is, (S/NP)/NP). A verb such as *tell* (in constructions such as *We tell children the earth is round*) would be of category ((S/NP)/NP)/S. In this way, most of the task of specifying which elements can combine with each other can be handled by general schemata such as (26), without the need for construction-specific rewriting rules.[33]

(26) a. $\alpha \cdot \beta/\alpha \rightarrow \beta$

    b. $\beta/\alpha \cdot \alpha \rightarrow \beta$

The above sketch of how categorial grammar works ignores the issue of the left-to-right order of constituents, but natural languages clearly must take this into account. Order can be introduced by introducing directionality into the categories and the rules of combination. For example, we could distinguish between β/α and $\beta\backslash\alpha$, requiring that the former combine with an α on its right to make a β, whereas the latter combines with an α on its left to make a β. Other systems permit a form of "composition" by including a rule of combination like $\alpha/\beta\ \beta\gamma \rightarrow \alpha/\gamma$, and still others allow categories to be combined in ways more complex than simple concatenation. The formal and linguistic properties of such variants are being investigated by a number of researchers.

Others have examined how categorial grammars might be enhanced by importing ideas from other theories of natural-language grammar, especially the use of syntactic features and unification. Groups of researchers in several locations in Europe and the United States have been developing categorial unification grammars, that is, systems in which the slashes (forward and/or backward) connect categories that are feature complexes of the sort used in GPSG, and in which the matching required in schemata such as (26) is formalized as unification. For an introduction to this approach, see Uszkoreit 1986.

One area of linguistic research in which categorial analyses have been particularly successful is coordinate conjunction of what appear to be strings of constituents. Most treatments of coordination concentrate on a conjoined phrases; indeed, the ability to coordinate is often employed as a test for constituency. Examples such as (27) constitute a problem for such approaches, because (under normal assumptions about phrase structure) it is impossible to have two overlapping constituents like *gave Randy* and *Randy enough money to buy a car* in a single phrase (that is, *gave Randy enough money to buy a car*).

(27) a. Pat loaned Chris and gave Randy enough money to buy a car.

    b. Pat gave Chris the down payment on a house and Randy enough money to buy a car.

Categorial grammarians have devised analyses that permit *Randy* to combine either with the verb *gave* on its left, or the noun phrase *enough money to buy a car* on its right (see Dowty 1987). This makes it possible to treat *all* coordination as conjunction of constituents, thereby solving a major problem for most other theories.

The investigation of augmented versions of categorial grammar is too new an enterprise to assess its long-term impact on grammatical theory. It has spawned a number of empirical investigations, as well as several computational implementations, and it appears to be one of the most promising current trends in syntax.

5.4 Conclusion

The revolution in grammatical theory surveyed in this chapter has not been without its problems. A perennial point of controversy is the relationship between the constructs of generative grammarians and the operations taking place in the minds (or brains) of actual language users.

This issue, often called the question of "psychological reality," has naturally been of concern to many cognitive scientists, especially in light of the outspoken positions Chomsky has taken with respect to some psychological questions, notably the nativism issue.

Generative linguists have based their theories almost exclusively on the sort of data presented in this chapter, that is, native-speaker judgments of the acceptability of isolated sentences. Psycholinguists concerned with the psychological reality question have, at various times, sought to develop other experimental methods that would permit a finer-grained testing of the processes going on in the minds of language users and the sorts of representations used in these processes (see Fodor, Bever, and Garrett 1974 for a survey of early research on this question, and Fodor 1990 for discussion of some more recent work).

Such investigations have produced few conclusive results, largely because grammars purport to represent linguistic *competence*, "the speaker-hearer's knowledge of his language," not *performance*, "the actual use of language in concrete situations" (Chomsky 1965, pp. 3–4):

Linguistic theory is concerned primarily with an ideal speaker-listener . . . who . . . is unaffected by such grammatically irrelevant conditions as memory limitations, distractions, shifts of attention and interest, and errors (random or characteristic) in applying his knowledge of the language in actual performance . . . To study actual linguistic performance, we must consider the interaction of a variety of factors, of which the underlying competence of the speaker-hearer is only one.

The other factors contributing to linguistic performance are not well understood; existing theories of language use are not nearly so well developed as the theories of grammar described above. Consequently the use of such data as reaction times, recall rates, or slips of the tongue to test the psychological reality of grammars is open to the charge that they do not reflect linguistic competence but the functioning of those poorly understood mechanisms that utilize the knowledge of language in actual production and comprehension.[34]

Although the competence–performance distinction is certainly necessary, the asymmetry between sophisticated competence theories and fairly rudimentary performance theories has had the effect of insulating linguistic theory from decisive testing for psychological reality. Many cognitive scientists see this as a serious shortcoming in the research program of generative grammar.

Moreover the competence–performance distinction is by no means as clear as the discussion makes it out to be. In the extensive literature on this topic, competence has been taken to mean a variety of things, from whatever is systematic about linguistic behavior to an abstract characterization of language unconnected to observable behavior. This ambiguity has been a source of confusion regarding the psychological relevance of generative theories.

Another criticism that has been raised against this program over the years is that it underestimates the role of context in language. It has been repeatedly noted that examples that generative linguists have starred in their papers can be made to sound perfectly natural in the appropriate context. This raises the question of whether it even makes sense to talk about isolated sentences being grammatical or ungrammatical. Perhaps instead we can only evaluate discourses (possibly including nonlinguistic context) for coherence. If this is so, then the methodology (and hence the results) of generative grammar are thrown into doubt.

A closely related criticism is that generative grammar shortchanges the social aspects of language by treating it strictly as a matter of individual psychology. Many features of natural languages are neither innate nor arbitrary but, rather, conventional. For example, the factors determining the choice of familiar or polite forms of address in languages (such as French or German) that make this distinction grammatically cannot be explicated without reference to social conventions. More generally, by ignoring the communicative function of language, generative grammarians may complicate the descriptions of linguistic structure and overlook potential explanations.

These and similar criticisms have been leveled against generative grammar since its inception. Although they are not without substance, they should not obscure its enormous contributions both to progress in linguistics and to the development of cognitive science. Chomsky's ideas played a vital role in the demise of behaviorism and in the establishment of models of human cognition based on abstract representations and operations. The conception of mind as a collection of specialized faculties whose general properties are biologically determined has received its strongest support from generative linguistics. Finally and most importantly, the work reported on in this chapter has provided the most elaborate and detailed proposals in existence regarding the nature and structure of one mental faculty.

Notes

I am grateful to John Etchemendy, Steven Pinker, and Peter Sells for helpful comments on an earlier draft of this chapter, and to Emma Pease for extensive help in preparing the manuscript. Most of the writing was done while I was Director of the Center for the Study of Language and Information at Stanford, and I owe much to the resources, both human and electronic, of that institution.

My work at CSLI was supported by a gift from the System Development Foundation and NSF grant number BNS-851168.

1. Most definitions of rewriting systems allow for more than one "initial" symbol, but almost all examples make use of only one and call it S.

2. There has been considerable debate over the years regarding the question of whether natural languages actually are decidable (that is, have decision procedures). Among the more celebrated arguments on this issue were Putnam's (1961) claim that speakers' ability

to distinguish sentences from nonsentences suggests that natural languages are decidable, and Hintikka's (1977) argument that the distribution of the word *any* made English nonrecursively enumerable (that is, beyond the descriptive power of Turing machines).

3. Type 1 and type 2 grammars are sometimes called "phrase-structure grammars," though this term is also sometimes used to mean only type 2 grammars.

4. The symbols NP, VP, ART, N, V, and P here are meant to stand for noun phrase, verb phrase, article, noun, verb, and preposition, respectively.

5. I am assuming the following definitions of set product and Kleene star:
$A \cdot B = \{\widehat{x\,y} \mid x \in A \text{ and } y \in B\}$, where $\widehat{}$ represents concatenation;
$A^* = \{x \mid x \text{ is a finite string of elements of A}\}$.

6. In 1979 Gerald Gazdar reopened the question of whether natural languages were in fact beyond the generative capacity of context-free grammars. Pullum and Gazdar (1982) reviewed the published literature on the question, concluding that it was riddled with mathematical errors and questionable linguistic claims. This led to a flurry of papers arguing more carefully that certain natural languages are not context free (see Pullum 1986 for a quick tour of the renewed debate). There appears once again to be consensus that not all natural languages are context free.

7. An asterisk preceding a string indicates that it is not a well-formed sentence.

8. This feature of Chomsky's theory of transformational grammar constitutes a break with his teacher, Zellig Harris, who had earlier developed the idea of transformations as relations between sentences.

9. This literature is actually somewhat equivocal on the question of whether it is only the class of grammars, not the class of languages, that must be restricted. See Chomsky 1981 (ch. 1) and Wasow 1977 for two different views on this issue.

10. See Bach and Marsh 1978 for an elementary proof of this theorem.

11. Chomsky (1965), anticipating the possibility of such a result, argued that it would not matter, if linguistic theory included a metric for evaluating grammars that gave preference to grammars for possible human languages. No such metric has yet been developed, though informal judgments of elegance and notational economy play a significant role in syntactic argumentation.

12. More recent research has indicated that there is more cross-rule and cross-language variability in island constraints than Ross thought. Much attention has been devoted to the question of how to deal with such variability in the theory of grammar.

13. Emonds actually allowed for a third class of transformations, which he called "minor movement rules," but they will not be considered here.

14. There was some debate about whether each of these sentences was actually ambiguous, with passivization changing only the order of preference of the readings, not the set of possible interpretations. In spite of the plausibility of this position, such examples were widely taken as serious problems for the standard theory.

15. See Newmeyer 1980, ch. 5, for discussion of the reasons.

16. One important exception is the work of Jackendoff (1976, 1983), which has kept alive the idea of decomposing the meanings of words into more primitive components.

17. See Sells 1985 for an excellent survey of three of the five theories.

18. Subsequent work along similar lines (for example, Jackendoff 1975) suggested that rules internal to the lexicon would be preferable. That is, a rule would map the lexical entry for a verb onto the entry for its nominal form.

19. The stipulation about a lexical head noun was added to make the constraint consistent with certain widely accepted analyses of Ross's day. It need not concern us here.

20. Chomsky (1973) used the term "cyclic node" not "bounding node," but the latter term is more descriptive and has been used in more recent literature.

21. Square brackets indicate clause boundaries.

22. This change was in part due to the discovery of phenomena in a number of languages indicating that positions between the filler and the gap can show signs that such a dependency obtains. See Zaenen 1983 for summaries of several such phenomena, analyzed in nontransformational terms.

23. A maximal projection is a phrase with the maximal number of bars; see the discussion of (12) in the text.

24. The square brackets in some examples indicate the governing category of the anaphor or pronominal, and the letters in square brackets following starred examples indicate which principle has been violated.

25. The rules may overgenerate because a sentence will be grammatical only if its c-structure can be legally paired with a well-formed f-structure. Hence LFG is perfectly consistent with the claim of Bresnan and colleagues (1982) that no context-free grammar can generate all and only the c-structures for the sentences of Dutch.

26. These figures are somewhat simplified, but will suffice for present purposes.

27. Essentially this analysis is employed in several related linguistic theories. See Shieber 1985 for more details.

28. Bresnan's rule is actually both more comprehensive and more precise than the informal statement in the previous sentence.

29. To maintain context freeness it is necessary to prevent recursion in category valued features. This can be accomplished by prohibiting any category valued feature [F] from appearing embedded within the value of an occurrence of [F].

30. That is, no grammatical feature may have conflicting values in the filler and in the value of SLASH. In other words the filler and the value of SLASH must be able to unify.

31. There are several GPSG analyses of coordination. Probably the most thorough is that of Sag and colleagues (1985). The one presented here is closer to that of Gazdar (1981), but the interaction with SLASH is similar in all of them.

32. This is clearly too restrictive because it rules out cases such as *Pat is a Communist and proud of it* (where a noun phrase and an adjective phrase are conjoined) and even cases such as *The woman and her children left* (where singular and plural noun phrases are conjoined). Such problems are dealt with in detail in recent versions of this analysis (for example, those of Sag et al. (1985) and Gazdar et al. (1985)).

33. The arrows in such schemata have a different interpretation from those in the rules of rewriting systems. They mean that constituents of the types given on the left side may be concatenated (in the indicated order) to yield a constituent of the type given on the right side.

34. Of course the same could be said of judgments of acceptability, but it almost never is.

References

Ajdukiewicz, K. 1935. Die Syntaktische Konnexität. *Studia Philosophica* 1:1–27.

Bach, E., and Marsh, W. 1978. An elementary proof of the Peters and Ritchie theorem. In *Papers from the Eighth Annual Meeting of the Northeastern Linguistics Society.* Department of Linguistics, University of Massachusetts, Amherst.

Bach, E., Oehrle, R. T., and Wheeler, D., eds. 1987. *Categorial Grammars and Natural Language Structures.* Dordrecht: Reidel.

Baker, C. L. 1978. *Introduction to Generative-Transformational Syntax.* Englewood Cliffs, NJ: Prentice-Hall.

Bar-Hillel, Y. 1964. *Language and Information.* Reading, Mass.: Addison-Wesley.

Bar-Hillel, Y., Gaifman, C., and Shamir, E. 1960. On categorial and phrase structure grammars. In Bar-Hillel 1960.

Barton, E., Berwick, R., and Ristad, E., 1987. *Computational Complexity and Natural Language.* Cambridge, MA: MIT Press.

Bresnan, J. W. 1978. A realistic transformational grammar. In M. Halle, J. Bresnan, and G. Miller, eds. *Linguistic Theory and Psychological Reality.* Cambridge, MA: MIT Press.

Bresnan, J. W., ed. 1982a. *The Mental Representation of Grammatical Relations.* Cambridge, MA: MIT Press.

Bresnan, J. W. 1982b. The passive in lexical theory. In Bresnan 1982a.

Bresnan, J. W. 1982c. Control and complementation. In Bresnan 1982a.

Bresnan, J. W., Kaplan, R. M., Peters, S., and Zaenen, A. 1982. Cross-serial dependencies in Dutch. *Linguistic Inquiry* 13:613–635.

Chomsky, N. 1955. *The Logical Structure of Linguistic Theory.* (Mimeograph.) Published in 1975 (with a new introduction), New York: Plenum.

Chomsky, N. 1957. *Syntactic Structures.* The Hague: Mouton.

Chomsky, N. 1959. Review of B. F. Skinner, *Verbal Behavior*. In J. A. Fodor and J. J. Katz, eds. *The Structure of Language*. Englewood Cliffs, NJ: Prentice-Hall.

Chomsky, N. 1963. Formal properties of grammars. In D. Luce, R. Bush, and E. Galanter, eds. *Handbook of Mathematical Psychology II*. New York: John Wiley & Sons.

Chomsky, N. 1965. *Aspects of the Theory of Syntax*. Cambridge, MA: MIT Press.

Chomsky, N. 1970. Remarks on nominalization. In R. Jacobs and P. Rosenbaum, eds. *Readings in English Transformational Grammar*. Waltham, MA: Ginn & Company.

Chomsky, N. 1973. Conditions on transformations. In S. R. Anderson and P. Kiparsky, eds. *A Festschrift for Morris Halle*. New York: Holt, Rinehart and Winston.

Chomsky, N. 1975. *Reflections on Language*. New York: Pantheon.

Chomsky, N. 1981. *Lectures on Government and Binding*. Dordrecht: Foris.

Chomsky, N. 1986. *Knowledge of Language: Its Nature, Origin and Use*. New York: Praeger.

Crain, S., and Fodor, J. D. 1985. How can grammars help parsers? In D. Dowty, L. Karttunen, and A. Zwicky, eds. *Natural Language Parsing: Psychological, Computational, and Theoretical Perspectives*. New York: Cambridge University Press.

Dowty, D. 1979. *Word Meaning and Montague Grammar*. Dordrecht: Reidel.

Dowty, D. 1987. Type raising, functional composition, and nonconstituent coordination. In Bach, Oehrle, and Wheeler 1987.

Emonds, J. 1976. *A Transformational Approach to English Syntax*. New York: Academic Press.

Fodor, J. D. 1990. Sentence processing and the mental grammar. In P. Sells, S. Shieber, and T. Wasow eds. *Foundational Issues in Natural Language Processing*. Cambridge, MA: MIT Press.

Fodor, J. A., Bever, T., and Garrett, M. F. 1974. *The Psychology of Language*. New York: McGraw-Hill.

Gazdar, G. 1981. Unbounded dependencies and coordinate structure. *Linguistic Inquiry* 12:155–84.

Gazdar, G. 1982. Phrase structure grammar. In P. Jacobson and G. Pullum, eds. *The Nature of Syntactic Representation*. Dordrecht: Reidel.

Gazdar, G., Klein, E., Pullum, G. K., and Sag, I. A. 1985. *Generalized Phrase Structure Grammar*. Cambridge, MA: Harvard University Press.

Gazdar, G., and Pullum, G. K. 1981. Subcategorization, constituent order and the notion of "head." In M. Moortgat, H. v. d. Hulst, and T. Hoekstra, eds. *The Scope of Lexical Rules*. Dordrecht: Foris.

Higginbotham, J. 1985. On semantics. *Linguistic Inquiry* 16:547–594.

Hintikka, J. 1977. Quantifiers in natural language: Some logical problems. *Linguistics and Philosophy* 2:153–72.

Hopcroft, J., and Ullman, J. 1979. *Introduction to Automata Theory, Languages, and Computation*. Reading, MA: Addison-Wesley.

Jackendoff, R. 1972. *Semantic Interpretation in Generative Grammar*. Cambridge, MA: MIT Press.

Jackendoff, R. 1975. Morphological and semantic regularities in the lexicon. *Language* 51:639–671.

Jackendoff, R. 1976. Toward an explanatory semantic representation. *Linguistic Inquiry* 7:89–150.

Jackendoff, R. 1977. *X-bar Syntax: A Study of Phrase Structure*. Cambridge, MA: MIT Press.

Jackendoff, R. 1983. *Semantics and Cognition*. Cambridge, MA: MIT Press.

Joos, M., ed. 1958. *Readings in Linguistics*. Washington: American Council of Learned Societies.

Kaplan, R. M., and Bresnan, J. W. 1982. Lexical-functional grammar: A formal system for grammatical representation. In Bresnan 1982a.

Katz, J. J. 1972. *Semantic Theory*. New York: Harper & Row.

Katz, J. J., and Fodor, J. A. 1963. The structure of a semantic theory. In J. A. Fodor and J. J. Katz, eds. *The Structure of Language*. Englewood Cliffs, NJ: Prentice-Hall.

Katz, J. J., and Postal, P. 1964. *An Integrated Theory of Linguistic Descriptions*. Cambridge, MA: MIT Press.

Kay M. 1979. Functional grammar. In *Proceedings of the Fifth Annual Meeting of the Berkeley Linguistics Society*. Department of Linguistics, University of California, Berkeley.

Lasnik, H., and Kupin, J. J. 1977. A restrictive theory of transformational grammar. *Theoretical Linguistics* 4:173–96.

Lewis, D. 1972. General semantics. In D. Davidson and G. Harman, eds. *Semantics of Natural Language*. Dordrecht: Reidel.

May, R. 1985. *Logical Form: Its Structure and Derivation*. Cambridge, MA: MIT Press.

Montague, R. 1970. *Formal Philosophy*. R. H. Thomason, ed. New Haven, CT: Yale University Press.

Newmeyer, F. J. 1980. *Linguistic Theory in America*. New York: Academic Press.

Partee, B. 1975. Montague grammar and transformational grammar. *Linguistic Inquiry* 6:203–300.

Perlmutter, D., ed. 1983. *Studies in Relational Grammar 1*. Chicago: University of Chicago Press.

Perlmutter, D., and Postal, P. 1977. Toward a universal characterization of passivization. In *Proceedings of the Third Annual Meeting of the Berkeley Linguistics Society*. Department of Linguistics, University of California, Berkeley.

Perlmutter, D., and Postal, P. 1984. The 1-Advancement Exclusiveness Law. In Perlmutter and Rosen 1984.

Perlmutter, D., and Rosen, C., eds. 1984. *Studies in Relational Grammar 2*. Chicago: University of Chicago Press.

Peters, S., and Ritchie, R. 1973. On the generative power of transformational grammars. *Information and Control* 18:483–501.

Pollard, C. J. 1985. Phrase structure grammar without metarules. In *Proceedings of the Fourth West Coast Conference on Formal Linguistics*. Stanford, CA: Center for the Study of Language and Information.

Pollard, C., and Sag, I. A. 1987. *Head-driven Phrase Structure Grammar*. Chicago: CSLI Lecture Notes, distributed by University of Chicago Press.

Postal, P. 1964a. Limitations of phrase structure grammars. In J. A. Fodor and J. J. Katz, eds. *The Structure of Language*. Englewood Cliffs, NJ: Prentice-Hall.

Postal, P. 1964b. *Constituent Structures*. The Hague: Mouton.

Pullum, G. K. 1986. Footloose and context-free. *Natural Language and Linguistic Theory*. 4:409–414.

Pullum, G. K., and Gazdar, G. 1982. Natural languages and context-free languages. *Linguistics and Philosophy* 4:471–501.

Putnam, H. 1961. Some issues in the theory of grammar. *Proceedings of the Twelfth Symposium in Applied Mathematics*. New York: American Mathematical Society.

Reichenbach, H. 1952. *Elements of Symbolic Logic*. New York: Macmillan.

Rogers, H., Jr. 1967. *Theory of Recursive Functions and Effective Computability*. New York: McGraw-Hill.

Ross, J. R. 1967. *Constraints on Variables in Syntax*. Ph.D. thesis, MIT, Cambridge, MA.

Sag, I. A., Gazdar, G., Wasow, T., and Weisler, S. 1985. Coordination and how to distinguish categories. *Natural Language and Linguistic Theory* 3:117–71.

Sells, P. 1985. *Lectures on Contemporary Syntactic Theories*. Chicago: CSLI Lecture Notes, distributed by University of Chicago Press.

Shieber, S. M. 1985. *An Introduction to Unification-based Approaches to Grammar*. Chicago: CSLI Lecture Notes, distributed by University of Chicago Press.

Uszkoreit, H. 1986. *Categorial Unification Grammars*. Report No. CSLI-86-66. Center for the Study of Language and Information, Stanford, CA.

Uszkoreit, H., and Peters, S. 1986. On some formal properties of metarules. *Linguistics and Philosophy* 9:477–494.

van Riemsdijk, H., and Williams, E. 1986. *Introduction to the Theory of Grammar.* Cambridge, MA: MIT Press.

Wall, R. 1972. *Introduction to Mathematical Linguistics.* Englewood Cliffs, NJ: Prentice-Hall.

Wanner, E., and Maratsos, M. 1978. An ATN approach to comprehension. In M. Halle, J. Bresnan, and G. Miller, eds. *Linguistic Theory and Psychological Reality.* Cambridge, MA: MIT Press.

Wasow, T. 1977. On constraining the class of transformational languages. *Synthese* 39:81–104.

Zaenen, A. 1983. On syntactic binding. *Linguistic Inquiry* 14:469–504.

6 Model-Theoretic Semantics

Jon Barwise and John Etchemendy

6.1 The Challenge of Semantics

As long as scholars have been talking about thinking, they have found themselves thinking about talk, about humans' ability to use language. The relationship between language and thought is a classic chicken-and-egg problem in the study of cognition. The use of language clearly requires an ability to think. Some have argued, however, that thought itself seems to presuppose some sort of language. But if they are right, then an account of thought requires an account of language. Whichever way it goes, it seems important to come to an understanding of the relation between thought and language.

The most striking similarity between thought and language is their "semantic reach," that both are typically *about* something. This contrasts with most of what science sets out to explain. There is much about the motion of the planets that needs explanation—the period of that motion, the forces involved, the shape of the trajectories. But we do not need to explain what that motion is about. Indeed the motion of the planets is not about anything. Neither is an earthquake or a toothache. But if someone *says* "The earth revolves around the sun," what has been said and the thought that gave rise to it are both about the solar system. So there seems to be an entirely new type of property—"aboutness" or "semantic content"—in need of explanation. This property is sometimes called the "intentionality" of language and thought. The study of semantics is about this commonplace but fascinating property.

To understand the challenge of semantics, though, we must go beyond the simple observation that statements and thoughts have semantic content. Signs and symbols used in animal communication can also have content. What seems to distinguish human communication from animal communication is the combinatory character of the symbolic system, a feature that allows users to combine the basic elements in novel and unlimited ways, and to know, somehow, what the resulting combinations mean.

It is obvious upon a moment's reflection that we express, hear, and read sentences every day that we have never encountered before. For example, it is extremely unlikely that you have ever encountered this particular sentence before, yet you understand what it means. Somehow, by knowing the meanings of the words involved and the ways they are put together you can understand the meaning of the whole.

What makes this truly impressive, and a challenge to the theorist, is the infinite character of human language that results from its combinatory nature. Using a very few words and grammatical constructions, we can generate an infinite set of different sentences, each of which is perfectly meaningful and, in principle, easy to understand. Consider, for instance, the following list:

My friend won.

My friend's friend won.

My friend's friend's friend won.

[and so on]

It is unlikely that many of these sentences would ever be very useful. But it also seems clear that they are perfectly good sentences of English, each with a definite meaning.

The combinatory richness and infinitude of human languages contrasts sharply with animal communication systems, with their relatively fixed stock of signs and symbols. To see just how different they are, imagine the following task: Suppose we wanted to train an animal, say a dog, to "understand" decimal notation. Say that when we show the dog a "10," we want it to emit ten short barks. Now if we only had to train our dog to do this trick for some fixed, relatively small set of small numbers, the task would probably not be too difficult. But suppose we had to teach the dog how to do this *in general*, for an arbitrary decimal expression. This is clearly a task of a different order of magnitude. It may even be impossible, given the dog's cognitive capacities.

How do humans manage to stuff an infinite language into their finite brains? In some sense the answer is obvious: there is a systematic relation between the meanings of complex expressions and those of their parts. For example, if we replace "friend" by "neighbor" or "boss" in the above list, we get a systematic change in the meanings of all the sentences. This observation—that there is a systematic relation between the meaning of the whole and that of its parts—is known as the Principle of Compositionality. The assumption that drives the study of semantics is that some form of this principle is what makes human languages, with their infinite character, possible. The accepted wisdom is that the only way for finite agents such as ourselves to master a language is by having knowledge (implicit or explicit) of the *relations between* the meaning and structure of complex expressions and the meaning and structure of simpler expressions, in addition to knowledge of the meanings of a stock of basic items like "friend," "my," and "won." Only such knowledge would allow them to determine the meanings of the unbounded set of novel sentences they may encounter.

This view of the relation between language and the mind raises three tasks. One task is simply that of explaining how signs and symbols can ever be about anything at all, how they come to *have* semantic content. This is not generally considered part of the field of semantics proper, but it is the topic of closely related work in the philosophy of language.[1] Rather semanticists presuppose that symbols somehow acquire content and take their task to be that of characterizing the semantic content of arbitrary complex expressions, given the content of their basic constituents. This is usually broken into two related parts. One is to describe the meanings of the semantically basic items of the language. This is called *lexical* semantics and deals with the meanings of expressions such as "friend" and "my."[2] The other part is to give a precise characterization of how the meanings of complex expressions depend on the meanings of their constituent parts. This is called *compositional* semantics and deals with the meanings of expressions such as "my friend" and "my friend's friend won." The third task is a task for the cognitive scientist. It is to explain in detail how knowledge of the semantics of a language is actually achieved by its speakers and to give an account of the cognitive processes and structures involved.

These tasks are not, of course, unrelated. Indeed it is widely acknowledged that a solution to the first task—giving an account of how signs come to have conventional meaning—must draw heavily on basic psychological and cognitive concepts. Communication is, after all, a species of intelligent activity, and the devices used to carry it out cannot be fully understood in isolation from a broader account of our cognitive capacities. So too the semanticist's study of the complex systems of communication involved in natural language must be guided by the recognition that these languages are used by finite agents. Finally, the cognitive scientist's account of how complex languages are learned will require an understanding of how those languages work, an understanding of the complex syntactic and semantic systems that relate sounds and meaning.

To get some idea of how the second, semantic, task might be accomplished, and how it relates to the task of the cognitive scientist, let us go back to our decimal-notation problem. Here one task for the semanticist would be to specify a function, call it den_{10}, that gives the denotation of each numeral in the base-ten notation. This is pretty easy. The lexical component of the semantics would specify the denotations of the ten basic Arabic numerals "0," "1," "2," . . . , "9." We could simply list these denotations with statements such as

The base-ten denotation of the numeral "5" is the number five.

Or more compactly

$den_{10}("5") = 5$.

We then need to explain the relation between the denotation of complex numerals (that is, those that contain more than one basic symbol) and the denotations of their parts. There are various ways we could do this. The most elegant is to give the following recursive clause. In it, α varies over arbitrary base-ten numerals, for example "273" and "46," and n varies over the basic numerals "0" through "9":

$$den_{10}(\alpha n) = den_{10}(\alpha) \times 10 + den_{10}(n).$$

Our ten basic clauses, plus this one recursive equation, completely determine the infinite function den_{10}. This is quite characteristic of what goes on in semantics. The technique of recursion is used to assign meaning to an infinite number of expressions.

This is a classic example of how we can specify the relation between an infinite family of symbols and the things they represent. As we will see later, though, there are some very special properties of the example that make it quite misleading, especially for the semanticist interested in cognitive aspects of human language. One of these is the abstract nature of numbers, the values of the function den_{10}. Another is the independence of the denotation from contingent facts about the things referred to (contrast the denotation of "2014" with the denotation of "the current president of the United States"). Yet another is the independence of the denotation from any facts about the speaker, or user, of the symbol (contrast this with the denotation of "the leader of my country"). However, let us stick with this example for now and see what we can learn from it about the logician's approach to semantics.

There is a very basic question about the relation between semantics and cognitive science that should immediately be addressed. Cognitive science tries to understand what is going on, so to speak, "in the head." But notice that the above example characterizes a function from expressions to numbers, neither of which is in any obvious sense "in the head." So what relevance can such an account possibly have for a cognitive scientist, even one interested in our ability to understand base-ten numbers? Isn't it missing the crucial ingredient, namely, some reference to the mental structures that people use to represent numbers?

To answer this objection, let us look in a little more detail at our account of the function den_{10}. Our first characterization uses what might be called a right-to-left recursion. For example, the denotation of "2014" is described in terms of the denotation of "201" and the denotation of "4," and the denotation of "201" is then described in terms of the denotation of "20" and the denotation of "1," and so forth. This is not, however, the only way to describe the semantics of the base-ten notation system. For example, we can give an alternative description of this same function, using a left-to-right recursion. Let us use $length(\alpha)$ for the length of the string α. Thus $length("2014")$ is four. We could now substitute the following recursive clause for the earlier one:

$$den_{10}(n\alpha) = den_{10}(n) \times 10^{length(\alpha)} + den_{10}(\alpha)$$

From the point of view of mathematical semantics these two descriptions are equivalent because they describe the same denotation function. However, they suggest quite different ways in which people might actually understand and process decimal notation. Interestingly enough the more complicated description (the second) is closer to the way we are taught decimal notation in grade school and seems introspectively to model more accurately the way we understand complex numerals.[3] Thus the *cognitive* semanticist, the semanticist concerned with how we actually process decimal numerals, might well judge the second account preferable to the first. Of course the question of whether this is or is not a better model of our understanding of numerals cannot be answered in isolation from an account of other, related cognitive processes, such as counting, adding, and the like.

One way to understand what is going on here is by analogy with the computer modeling of cognitive processes. The practitioner of AI constructs a computer program to model a specific cognitive process, one that gives rise to certain outputs when given certain inputs. The cognitive processes modeled may be as diverse as pattern recognition, chess playing, or medical diagnosis, but in each case the overall goal is for the program to mimic or match, at some level of abstraction, the I/O behavior associated with the process. The fact that this is to be done with a finite program running on a finite machine makes a successful program of obvious interest to the cognitive scientist. Of course it does not follow that the specific algorithm embodied in the program corresponds to the way humans carry out the same task, but it does provide one method where we had none before.

There are two features of AI modeling that are relevant for our analogy. The first is that the interest in this modeling arises from the tension between the need to do a certain complicated task and the requirement that it be done on a finite device of a reasonably limited sort. For example, in the case of chess it is impractical for the computer to search through all possible continuations of the game and choose a play guaranteed to win. Rather the algorithm must compute its function from chessboard states to chessboard states using highly limited resources. The second feature is the cut AI takes on any particular problem. For instance, in the chess example we abstract away from many of the details of actual chess play, such as the problem of recognizing the chess pieces or of physically moving them around the board. Rather it isolates a certain important aspect of actual chess games as the one it tries to model.

The way the logician approaches semantics is analogous to the AI approach to modeling intelligence. First, the logician abstracts away from many details of actual language use such as phonetic issues, the effects of intonation, and metaphorical uses of language. And, as in the case of AI, the interest lies largely in the tension between the need to specify a complicated object, the semantics of a potentially infinite language, and the requirement that it be done in a finite way. For example, we managed to describe the infinite function den_{10} with two very simple finite theories, and both of these suggest algorithms that might be involved in understanding decimal notation. Here we are in the fortunate position of being able to compare the theories in terms of mathematical elegance and cognitive or computational plausibility.

Again the situation is analogous to AI modeling, in which there will in general be more than one algorithm for carrying out a given task. It may well happen that of two algorithms, one is more elegant or efficient, whereas the other is a better cognitive model of how people carry out the task. In such a case the interests of the AI researcher and the cognitive scientist may well diverge. Of course it is well known that the problems in AI have proved to be extremely difficult. For this reason the AI practioner is mainly interested in coming up with *some* program that approximates the desired behavior. Once that is achieved, the researcher can try to find more than one and compare them to see which is the most elegant, efficient, or cognitively plausible.

The task of the natural-language semanticist has similarly proved to be extremely difficult. The semanticist is concerned with coming up with at least one finite, mathematically precise theory that characterizes the meanings of expressions in an infinite language. When we have two or more such theories, we may want to judge between them on the basis of various criteria, depending on our objectives. The person interested in building a natural-language interface for computers will focus on issues of elegance and efficiency. The cognitive semanticist will in contrast focus on the account's plausibility as a cognitive model. These different interests may end up pulling in quite different directions.

In this chapter we will consider several approaches to the semantic task that have grown out of the tradition in logic, approaches known generically as model-theoretic semantics. Our goal is not just to survey these approaches or to point the reader toward the relevant literature. Rather, we hope to give the reader a feel for some of the important techniques that are common to model-theoretic approaches. To do this in the space available, we illustrate, in some detail, one quite traditional semantic account, known as extensional model-theoretic semantics. We then discuss, much more briefly, additions and emendations to this theory that result in its principal competitors. However, the rival theories we will consider do not differ from one another in the way our two descriptions of den_{10} do. There we had one function that was characterized in two different ways. But it is not obvious that this is even the function that the cognitive semanticist would be most interested in describing. For example, an alternative approach to the semantics of the numerals might characterize a relation, $Count(\alpha, B)$, that holds between a numeral α and any set B that has the appropriate number of objects. One could imagine an argument that the relation *Count* gets at something more directly relevant to the use of numerals by people. Of course this is not something that can be finally judged in isolation from the remainder of our semantic and cognitive accounts.

6.2 Dimensions of Semantic Analysis

Before looking at our sample semantic theory, it will be helpful to make a few observations about the general project of model-theoretic semantics. What can we reasonably expect of a semantic account of this sort? What will such an account look like and what sorts of things will it explain?

Because we are aiming at a scientific theory of language, our account should first and foremost be clear and mathematically rigorous, in just the way that both our accounts of the denotation function den_{10} are. Many people, confronted with the idea of a mathematically precise account of language, raise the following objection. How can we hope for such a theory when so much of language is by its very nature ambiguous, imprecise, and vague? What would such an account say about a vague and ambiguous sentence such as "The bank is somewhere over there," or about a sentence used for its poetic force?

This objection is ill conceived. It does not follow from the fact that much of ordinary language is, for example, vague that one can say only vague things about it. Similarly it is certainly possible to give an unambiguous account of various forms of ambiguity. A vague and ambiguous semantic theory is every bit as unsatisfactory as a vague and ambiguous theory of physics, and for exactly the same reasons. To be sure, phenomena such as vagueness, ambiguity, and so forth provide additional challenges to the semanticist, but these are challenges that need to be met by developing suitable mathematical tools to apply to these phenomena, not by simply abandoning precise methods of inquiry.

What sorts of things might a semantic theory explain? Language is an extremely subtle and flexible tool, and consequently there is a multitude of phenomena that we might hope to account for with such a theory. We observed that the semanticist is forced to take some cut or other on the rather amorphous phenomenon of language, paying attention to certain phenomena in isolation from others. What cut has model-theoretic semantics typically taken? In point of fact, semanticists have focused on ten or twelve key concepts, including

· linguistic meaning of expressions,

· propositional content of utterances,

· cognitive significance of utterances,

· reference,

· indexicality and context sensitivity,

- compositionality,
- truth,
- entailment,
- ambiguity,
- presupposition.

These concepts are easily illustrated with a simple example. Consider the first words spoken by Alexander Graham Bell over the telephone, "Come here, Watson. I need you." We see that there are two different kinds of sentences here, an imperative expressing a command, and a declarative expressing a claim. To date, most work in semantics has focused on the meaning of declarative sentences. This is not from lack of interest in other sorts of sentences, say imperatives and questions, or in other types of "speech acts," say commanding, requesting, and promising. The reason for this focus is primarily historical. As we have noted, logicians have played a central role in the development of model-theoretic semantics, and a large part of their interest stems from the desire to understand entailment relations between declarative sentences. Because most of the work we survey deals with declarative sentences, let us focus on Bell's second sentence.

At a naive level the very least we would expect of a semantic account of this sentence is an account of its meaning. But what exactly is its meaning? Does it mean that Bell needs (or needed) Watson? In some sense it does, because this is the claim Bell made by uttering the sentence. But of course in another sense the meaning has nothing to do with Bell and Watson; the very same sentence with its same meaning has been uttered countless times by other speakers, to other addressees, to make entirely different claims. Thus if some other speaker, say Watson, were to say "I need you" to some other addressee, say Bell, the claim made would be a different one. But the meaning of the sentence would not have changed.

So right off the bat we have to distinguish two senses of the term "meaning." On the one hand there is meaning as it applies to expressions themselves, regardless of who uses them. It is the meaning in this sense that remains the same whether our sentence is spoken by Bell to Watson or by Watson to Bell. On the other hand there is the meaning of a particular use of an expression—the sense in which Bell's use of "I need you" meant that Bell needed Watson. We will call this latter the *content* of the utterance. Thus we will say that the *meaning* of our sentence remains the same in the two cases, though the *content* differs.

One thing we might reasonably hope for a semantic theory to explain is the relation between the meaning of an expression and the content of a particular use of it. Presumably this will bring in features of the context in which the expression is used. For example, facts about who is speaking, when the utterance takes place, and who is being addressed are all important factors in determining the content and cognitive significance of a given use of the sentence "I need you."

As we noted in section 6.1, the main challenge of model-theoretic semantics is to give an account of the systematic relation between the meanings of complex expressions and the meanings of their parts. In our example we need to explain how the meaning of the sentence "I need you" is related to the meanings of its parts, for example, to the meaning of the word "you." But here we have the same kind of split as above. The word itself has a certain fixed meaning that allows different speakers to refer to different addressees on different occasions. But if we were to ask who Bell meant by his particular use of "you," the answer would be Watson—the person he was referring to. We will say that the *meaning* of "you" is what remains the same through different uses, though the *referent* may change from use to use.

Two concepts that have proved pivotal in model-theoretic semantics are the related notions of truth and entailment. The semanticist's interest in the notion of truth may seem a bit surprising at first glance. After all, specifying which sentences or uses of sentences are in fact *true* is not part of the semanticist's business; if it were, the task would obviously be hopeless. The way the notion of truth figures into many semantic theories is the following. It seems reasonable to suppose that a crucial part of what we understand when we know the meaning of a declarative sentence is not whether it is in fact true but rather *under what conditions* it can be used to make a true claim. For example, a fluent speaker of English knows that any particular use of the sentence "I need you" will be true when and only when the speaker of the sentence needs the person to whom the sentence is addressed. It is this knowledge, plus the assumption that Bell is speaking the truth, that allows Watson to conclude that he is needed and to act accordingly. Thus a major thrust in semantics has been to try to characterize the meaning of declarative sentences in terms of the conditions under which they are true or, more accurately, the conditions under which they can be used to make true claims.

This concern with the "truth conditions" of sentences is related to entailment in a straightforward way. The idea is that one sentence entails a second just in case any condition under which the first would be true is also a condition under which the second would be true. For example, Bell's claim that he needed Watson entails that he needed someone. If the former was true, so was the latter. This characterization of entailment in terms of truth conditions provides us with an important way to test semantic theories. Thus one common criterion of a semantic theory is that it yield predictions that square with our pretheoretic semantic judgments about entailment relations in the language under study. If our semantic theory predicted that Bell's claim entails, say, that he needs *everyone*, then our theory has clearly gone awry.

Two other notions that have received considerable attention in current semantic theories are ambiguity and presupposition. We want a theory that explains why "A student spoke in every course" could be used to mean two quite different things—that there is a particular student who spoke in all the courses, or that each course had at least one student who spoke. Our theory should explain why this sort of ambiguity arises here, but does not arise with, say, the sentence "A student from every course spoke." Similarly we want to account for the intuition that the use of "both" in "I need both of you" presupposes that there are exactly two addressees, in a way that "I need two of you" does not. Just what is it about the meanings of "both" and "two" that has this effect?

These are some of the questions that semanticists have devoted a great deal of effort toward answering. There are many other semantic phenomena that could also be studied but have received less attention. In this chapter we discuss various approaches that have been taken to these phenomena.

6.3 Designed Languages

The approaches to semantics we discuss differ in some of the phenomena they try to explicate, but they share certain methodological features. The most striking of these is the use of simple, designed languages, rather than a full-fledged natural language or even fragments of one. To the uninitiated, designing and studying an artificial language may seem a puzzling way to approach the study of human languages. But in fact there is a straightforward rationale. Semanticists design simple languages that display the semantic features of current concern while suppressing those features they want to hold fixed or otherwise ignore in their account. This is part of the cut semanticists take on their subject matter. The designed languages are treated as a simplifying model of human language or, at any rate, of some of its features. Just as AI approaches to chess set aside many details of people's chess-playing skills, so too the use of designed languages allows semanticists to set aside many subtle syntactic and morphological issues that would otherwise overwhelm the enterprise.[4]

To motivate our particular choices for our artificial language, let us recall the famous incident in which Galileo is called before the pope to discuss his ideas about the place of Earth in the solar system. Simplifying history a bit, let us suppose things go this way. Galileo says to the pope, "It does revolve around the sun." The pope does not believe Galileo, but he does form one true belief, namely, that Galileo does not believe that the Earth is the center of the universe. What about this interaction can we expect to be explained by a semantic theory? Certainly it will not explain how Galileo came to believe what he believes, that is, what got him into the state of mind that led him to make his heretical claim. It should explain, however, why Galileo's chosen sentence is appropriate for expressing the claim he wanted to express, whereas most sentences he could have uttered would have been inappropriate. Part of this explanation will involve an account of how this sentence managed to express a *true* claim. But that cannot be the whole explanation. Many true sentences would have failed to express Galileo's belief. Finally, the account should also say something about the relation between Galileo's claim and the pope's inference about Galileo's beliefs.

The Syntax of Old Zealandish

Let us begin by designing a simple language to use in modeling interactions such as the above. This language, which we dub Old Zealandish, is a hybrid of first-order logic and English. It will be similar enough to familiar languages that you should be able to guess the intended meanings of most of its expressions. On the other hand it will be different enough to remind you that it is not English.

In designing our language, we set aside issues of time and tense, at least for the time being. Because the solar system is relatively stable, this is not too serious. Further it allows us to lump together the treatment of verb phrases such as "moves around the sun," and common nouns such as "planet that moves around the sun," and to call them both *predicate phrases*. Our language will have predicate phrases, noun phrases (including names and variables), and sentences. We will also need some connectives such as "or" and "and" to form compound sentences, and some determiners such as "every" and "neither" to form complex noun phrases. Here are the syntactic rules for our language, followed by some examples of Old Zealandish sentences.

1. Predicate phrases

(a) Basic predicate phrases:

`Planet, Center, Thing, MovesAround, LargerThan`[5]

The first three of these are called *unary* predicates; the last two are called *binary* predicates.

(b) Complex predicate phrases: if S is a sentence containing a variable v, then $\hat{v}[S]$ is a (unary) predicate.

2. Noun phrases

(a) Basic noun phrases:

`Earth, Mars, Sun, Moon,` x, y, z, x_1, y_1, z_1, . . .

The first four noun phrases are *names*; the remainder are called *variables*.

(b) Complex noun phrases: if P is a unary predicate phrase, and `Det` is a determiner, then `Det` P is a noun phrase.[6]

3. Sentences

(a) Basic sentences: if P is a unary predicate and t is a basic noun phrase, then (t P) is a sentence. Similarly if R is a binary predicate and t, t' are basic noun phrases, then (t R t') is a sentence.

(b) Complex sentences: If NP is a complex noun phrase and P is a unary predicate phrase, then NP P is a sentence.

(c) Compound sentences: If S_1 and S_2 are sentences, then so are $\neg S_1$, $(S_1 \wedge S_2)$, $(S_1 \vee S_2)$. The symbols $\neg$, $\wedge$, $\vee$ are read, respectively, *not, and,* and *or.*

4. Determiners

We will have three sets of determiners, corresponding to three increasingly large fragments of Old Zealandish.

(a) The determiners of fragment A:

```
Every, Some, No, Most
```

(b) The determiners of fragment B:

```
Every, Some, No, Most, Neither, Both, The
```

(c) The determiners of fragment C:

```
Every, Some, No, Most, Neither, Both, The, Many, Few
```

This definition is a mutually recursive definition of the sets of expressions of the various categories mentioned. For those more familiar with phrase-structure grammars, this definition could be stated using rules such as

$$
S \rightarrow \left\{ \begin{array}{l} \text{BasicSentence} \\ \text{ComplexSentence} \\ \text{CompoundSentence} \end{array} \right.
$$

$$
\text{ComplexSentence} \rightarrow \text{NP Pred}
$$

$$
\text{NP} \rightarrow \text{Det Pred}
$$

Because we have designed our language from scratch, we are of course free to stipulate the meanings in any way we want. Because our semantic account is meant to say something significant about natural language, however, we will stipulate the meanings of our sentences so that they reflect the way corresponding English sentences work, at least along those dimensions of concern in the account.

Let us look at some examples. The expression

```
(Earth MovesAround Sun) ∨ (Earth Center)
```

is a compound sentence formed from the basic sentence (`Earth MovesAround Sun`) and the basic sentence (`Earth Center`) using rule 3c. We will use it to model the English sentence "The planet Earth moves around the sun or is the center of the solar system." Similarly the expression

```
No Planet x̂[x MovesAround Sun]
```

is a complex sentence formed from the complex noun phrase `No Planet` and the complex predicate `x̂[x MovesAround Sun]` using rule 3b. To understand what this complex predicate is supposed to mean, note that $\hat{x}[\ .\ .\ .\ x\ .\ .\ .\ ]$ can be read "is such that . . . *it* . . ." Thus the sentence corresponds to the English sentence "No planet is such that it moves around the sun," or better to the more natural sentence "No planet moves around the sun."

For a final example consider this moderately complicated sentence:

```
No Planet x̂[Every Planet ŷ[x MovesAround y]]
```

This sentence is formed from the complex noun phrase No Planet and the complex predicate x̂[Every Planet ŷ[x MovesAround y]]. This complex predicate is in turn formed from the complex sentence Every Planet ŷ[x MovesAround y], which says "Every planet is such that x moves around it," or simply "x moves around every planet." Our original sentence, then, corresponds to the English sentence "No planet moves around every planet."

This last example brings out an idealization that we have incorporated into our language. In English, sentences with multiple-quantified noun phrases—for example, "Every planet moves around something"—are frequently ambiguous. (Does this sentence mean that there is some particular thing that every planet moves around, or does it simply mean that every planet moves around something or other?) Our designed language will have no corresponding semantic ambiguity. We simply note that the two readings of the above sentence correspond to two distinct sentences in Old Zealandish, namely,

```
Some Thing ŷ[Every Planet x̂[x Moves Around y]],
Every Planet x̂[Some Thing ŷ[x Moves Around y]].
```

6.4 Extensional Model-Theoretic Semantics

Let us now construct a sample semantics for Old Zealandish. As we noted previously, one of the foremost concerns of model-theoretic semantics is to spell out the truth conditions of sentences in the target language and to do so in a mathematically precise way. Of course it is not entirely obvious how to approach such a task. Indeed semanticists in this tradition have pursued a variety of different approaches. Extensional model-theoretic semantics was the first approach tried; others were developed in reaction to a variety of perceived difficulties with it. We discuss it in some detail and then briefly discuss some of the alternatives that are currently being pursued.

It is obvious that sentences are not true or false all on their own. This is so in at least two respects. First, as we observed previously, languages contain a multitude of contextually relative expressions, such as "I," "you," "many," and so forth. It clearly makes little sense to talk about the truth of a sentence containing these expressions without bringing in details about a particular utterance of that sentence. But even when we set aside such contextual dependencies, which we will do for a while, sentences are not true all on their own. Whether or not a sentence (or the claim made by some use of a sentence) is true has *something* to do with the world, with the way things actually are. For example, in the case of Galileo's claim that the earth revolves around the sun, a fact about the solar system is responsible for the claim's truth. Had the solar system been configured differently, say the way the pope thought it was, then Galileo's claim would have been false.

Part of what our semantic theory aims to capture is the content of a speaker's knowledge of the truth conditions of the sentences of his or her language. That is, it should give an explicit account of the relationship between sentences and nonlinguistic facts about the world that would support the truth of a claim made with the sentence. What all competent English speakers know about the meaning of "The sun moves around the earth" is the conditions under which it would be true. What some English speakers know, in addition, is that the sentence is false. But that is not part of their semantic competence. Thus what we are after is an explicit account of the dependence of the truth of a sentence on typically nonlinguistic states of affairs.

To provide a rigorous analysis of this dependence, model-theoretic semantics first develops some machinery for representing these nonlinguistic states of affairs. A variety of techniques for doing this have been used, but they all agree in general methodology. Specifically they all use the resources provided by set theory to build simple models of the world, or portions thereof. Extensional model theory takes the most straightforward approach. It models properties of and relations among things in the same way that set theory models mathematical properties and relations: sets model properties, sets of ordered pairs model binary relations, sets of triples model ternary relations, and so forth. Thus the fact that an object has a particular property is modeled by the object's membership in the set taken to represent that property. Of course sets are "extensional," that is, the identity of a set is entirely determined by its members. Thus in extensional model theory two properties are represented as distinct only if there are objects that have the one but not the other.

To provide such a framework for our semantics, we introduce the notion of a model w of the world. Because our language is designed for use in talking about the solar system, we could think of these models as mathematical models of the solar system, much as an orrery is a physical model of the solar system. To get at the dependence mentioned above, we want models not only of the way the solar system is actually configured but also of all other possible configurations. One of these models will be singled out as the intended model, the one that represents the solar system as it actually is.

A model w will consist of an ordered pair $\langle D, f \rangle$, where D is some set, and f is a function defined on the basic lexical items of Old Zealandish. We will impose various conditions on D and f in a moment. The set D represents a domain of discourse and so is often called the *domain* or *universe* of the model. We can think of the objects in D as representing the totality of celestial bodies in (some possible configuration of) the solar system. The function f will assign various sorts of things to the basic expressions of Old Zealandish. For example, it will assign a subset of the domain D to the unary predicate Planet. The set $f(\text{Planet})$ will be thought of as representing the "extension" of the predicate in this model, that is, as representing the collection of planets (as opposed to moons, asteroids, and the like) in the solar system. Similarly the function f will assign an element of D to the name Earth, and this element will be taken as our representative of the Earth.[7] For convenience we write D^w for the domain of a model w. Similarly, given a lexical item Abc, we write Abc^w for the value that the function f assigns to Abc, that is, for the value $f(\text{Abc})$.

We now impose some natural conditions on these models. First, we require that P^w be a subset of D^w for each basic unary predicate phrase P. Further we require that Thing^w be the set D^w itself. Next, for a binary predicate R we require that R^w be a set of pairs $\langle a,b \rangle$, where both a and b are members of D^w. Finally, we require that for each name t of the fragment, t^w be some object in D^w.

This takes care of all the simple lexical items in our language except the determiners. How should we handle these? The basic idea is that determiners express a relation between the extensions of two unary predicate phrases. Thus the sentence No Planet Center claims that the extentions of Planet and Center are disjoint. Because our models assign sets to unary predicates, we assign to determiners a binary relation on sets. Given our way of modeling relations, this just boils down to using a set of pairs $\langle A, B \rangle$, where A and B are subsets of D^w. Thus to each determiner Det we assign a (set-theoretic) relation Det^w between subsets A and B of our domain of discourse D^w. The idea is that a sentence of the form Det P Q will be true in the model w, just in case the pair $\langle A, B \rangle$, consisting of the extensions of P and Q respectively, is in Det^w.

The determiners of fragment A are Every, Some, No, and Most. For these determiners we specify their extensions (given a domain D^w of discourse) as follows. Here "A" and "B" vary over subsets of D^w.

$\text{Every}^w = \{\langle A, B \rangle \mid A \subseteq B\}$
$\text{Some}^w = \{\langle A, B \rangle \mid A \cap B \neq \varnothing\}$
$\text{No}^w = \{\langle A, B \rangle \mid A \cap B = \varnothing\}$
$\text{Most}^w = \{\langle A, B \rangle \mid card(A \cap B) > card(A - B)\}$[8]

To relate truth in a model to the ordinary concept of truth we need the notion of a standard model. With this language the *standard* model is the model w_0 whose domain D^{w_0} consists of the heavenly bodies in our solar system. The names are assigned the usual referents, for example, Earth^{w_0} is the planet Earth and Moon^{w_0} is Earth's moon. Similarly each predicate is assigned its usual extension. For example, Planet^{w_0} is the set of all planets in our solar system and Center^{w_0} is the set of things at the center of the solar system, that is, the set whose only element is the sun. MovesAround^{w_0} is the set of pairs $\langle a, b \rangle$ such that a orbits around b—and so forth.

Given this setup, we can begin to give a semantics for fragment A. As noted, one main goal is to spell out the conditions on an arbitrary model w under which an arbitrary sentence S is true. However, we also need to assign semantic values to certain other complex expressions of the language. Thus we need to assign an extension to *every* predicate phrase, not just the basic ones. For example, in the analysis of the sentence

(1) Some Thing $\hat{x}$[No Planet $\hat{y}$[x MovesAround y]]

we will need to have an extension for the predicate phrase

(2) $\hat{x}$[No Planet $\hat{y}$[x MovesAround y]].

Suppose A is the set of all things in w and B is the extension of (2), intuitively, the set of things that move around no planet. As we mentioned, sentence (1) will be true in a model w just in case the pair $\langle A, B \rangle$ is in Some^w, that is, just in case some member of A is also a member of B. Thus we clearly need to assign extensions to complex predicate phrases like (2).

This brings up a couple of problems. Intuitively the extension of (2) is determined in turn by looking at the sentence

(3) No Planet $\hat{y}$[x MovesAround y].

This in turn leads us to the predicate phrase

(4) $\hat{y}$[x MovesAround y],

which leads us finally to the sentence

(5) x MovesAround y.

Thus it seems that the analysis of sentences presupposes the analysis of predicates, and the analysis of predicates presupposes the analysis of sentences. What this means is that we are not able to give a simple recursive analysis of either one in isolation. Rather we have to give a recursive analysis of both simultaneously.

The second problem emerges when we examine the expressions (3) through (5). For example, sentence (3) contains a "free variable," namely, x. Thus the sentence is somewhat similar to the sentence "It moves around no planet." This English sentence is not true or false per se, but is true of some objects and false of others. We need to represent the notion of a sentence with one or more free variables being true of certain objects. Then what we want is for the predicate phrase (2) to stand for the set of objects that sentence (3) is true of.

The way this is done is with the notion of a *variable assignment* and the companion notion of a variable assignment *satisfying* a sentence S. In the case in which a sentence has no free variables, a variable assignment will satisfy the sentence if and only if the sentence is true; if the sentence has free variables, the assignment will satisfy the sentence if the sentence is true of the objects assigned to the corresponding variables. Formally we define a variable assignment g to be a function from the variables x, y, z, ..., into the domain D^w of a given model w. We write $Val(S, w, g) = true$, if S is satisfied in w by the variable assignment g.[9] Examples such as (4) show that we must also take the notion of the extension of a predicate to be relative to a variable assignment. Intuitively the extension of (4) should be the set of objects that move around whatever x stands for. We write $Ext(P, w, g) = E$, if E is the extension of the predicate phrase P in w relative to the variable assignment g.

By now the main idea of our semantics should be fairly clear. For the record we give the definition in all its detail. To simplify our statement of some of the clauses, we use $den(t, w, g)$ for the denotation of the simple noun phrase t in w relative to g; that is,

$$den(t, w, g) = \begin{cases} t^w & \text{if t is a name,} \\ g(t) & \text{if t is a variable.} \end{cases}$$

We also use $g(x \rightsquigarrow b)$ for the variable assignment just like g except that it assigns the object b to the variable x.

The Semantics of Fragment A

1. Extensions of predicate phrases

(a) Basic predicate phrases: Let Abc be a basic predicate phrase. Then its extension is given by

$$Ext(\text{Abc}, w, g) = \text{Abc}^w.$$

(b) Complex predicate phrases: Given a predicate phase $\hat{v}[S]$, its extension is given by

$$Ext(\hat{x}[S], w, g) = \{c \in D^w \mid Val(S, w, g(v \rightsquigarrow c)) = true\}.$$

2. Truth-values of sentences

(a) Basic sentences: Given a basic sentence of the form (t P), its truth value is given by

$$Val((\text{t P}), w, g) = \begin{cases} true & \text{if } den(t, w, g) \in Ext(P, w, g), \\ false & \text{if } den(t, w, g) \notin Ext(P, w, g), \end{cases}$$

The value of a basic sentence of the form (t_1 R t_2) is given by

$$Val((t_1 \text{ R } t_2), w, g) = \begin{cases} true & \text{if } \langle den(t_1, w, g), den(t_2, w, g) \rangle \in Ext(R, w, g), \\ false & \text{if } \langle den(t_1, w, g), den(t_2, w, g) \rangle \notin Ext(R, w, g). \end{cases}$$

(b) Complex sentences: Let S be a sentence of the form Det P Q, where P and Q are unary predicate phrases. Let $A = Ext(P, w, g)$ and $B = Ext(Q, w, g)$. Then the value of S is given as follows:

$$Val \text{ (Det P Q, } w, g) = \begin{cases} true & \text{if } \langle A, B \rangle \in \text{Det}^w, \\ false & \text{if } \langle A, B \rangle \notin \text{Det}^w. \end{cases}$$

(c) Compound sentences: The truth values of $S_1 \wedge S_2$, $S_1 \vee S_2$ and $\neg S_1$ are defined as follows:

$$Val(S_1 \wedge S_2, w, g) = \begin{cases} true & \text{if } Val(S_1, w, g) = Val(S_2, w, g) = true, \\ false & \text{otherwise;} \end{cases}$$

$$Val(S_1 \vee S_2, w, g) = \begin{cases} false & \text{if } Val(S_1, w, g) = Val(S_2, w, g) = false, \\ true & \text{otherwise;} \end{cases}$$

$$Val(\neg S_1, w, g) = \begin{cases} true & \text{if } Val(S_1, w, g) = false, \\ false & \text{otherwise.} \end{cases}$$

We will say that a sentence of Old Zealandish (with no free variables) is true just in case it is true in the standard model, relative to some variable assignment. This turns out to be equivalent to its being true in the standard model relative to every variable assignment, because the choice of variable assignment is irrelevant in the case of an expression with no free variables.

Let us look at an example. Consider the sentence

No $\hat{x}$[x MovesAround Mars] $\hat{y}$[y LargerThan Mars].

Let us compute its truth value, that is, its truth value in the standard model w_0. The denotation of Mars in w_0 is Mars. Then, by the above definition, the extension of the predicate phrase $\hat{x}$[x MovesAround Mars] is the set A of all objects in the domain that move around Mars, which is the set of Mars's two moons. Similarly the extension of $\hat{y}$[y LargerThan Mars] is the set B of objects in the domain of discourse that are larger than Mars. The sentence as a whole is true if and only if the pair $\langle A, B \rangle$ is in No^{w_0}, that is, just in case nothing in A is in B. Because neither of Mars's moons is in B, the sentence is true.

Entailment One of the driving forces behind model-theoretic semantics has been the desire for an account of entailment. Just what is it for one statement to "follow logically" from another? Intuitively a sentence is logically true if it is true in virtue of the semantic properties of the language, independent of how other facts happen to fall out. Similarly one sentence logically entails another just in case the second is true if the first is—again, simply in virtue of the semantic properties of the language.

These intuitions give rise to the following definition. Let $\mathcal{W}$ be some collection of models, representing various ways the world might have been. We say that sentence S is *logically true* with respect to $\mathcal{W}$ provided that for every $w \in \mathcal{W}$ and every g, $Val(S, w, g) = true$. Similarly we say that sentence S *logically entails* sentence S' (with respect to $\mathcal{W}$) provided that for every $w \in \mathcal{W}$ and every g, if $Val(S, w, g) = true$, then $Val(S', w, g) = true$.

As an example we see that if S is any sentence of fragment A, then $S \lor \neg S$ is logically true, regardless of what collection $\mathcal{W}$ we happen to take. Similarly, according to our definitions, we see that $S_1 \land S_2$ entails S_2, and that Every P Q $\land$ Some Thing P entails Most P Q. Many people think that the notions of logical truth and logical entailment are exactly captured by the above definitions when $\mathcal{W}$ is the collection of all models. We discuss this in more detail in the section on the factorization problem. In the meantime we keep $\mathcal{W}$ as a parameter in our account. Let us look at some specific entailments involving determiners. First, consider a class of entailments that hold for all determiners. The kind of entailment we have in mind can be illustrated by the following example:

Most planets are larger than Neptune.
Most planets are planets that are larger than Neptune.

This is a valid inference. That is, any situation that is truly described by the former must be truly described by the latter. And note that the validity of the inference does not depend on the fact that we used the determiner "most." It would be equally valid had we used, say, "every," "no," "few," "both," or "exactly three." Further, the inference works the other way around as well:

Most planets are planets that are larger than Neptune.
Most planets are larger than Neptune.

Again the validity of the entailment does not depend on which determiner is used.

If our semantics for fragment A is an adequate model of English, it should predict that for any determiner Det and any two predicate phrases P and Q the sentences Det P Q and Det P (P $\land$ Q) are logically equivalent.[10] To see that it does, we first note an important set-theoretic property of our determiner extensions. If R is an extensional relation on subsets of D, then R is said to *live on its first coordinate* (or to be a *conservative* relation) provided that for all $A, B \subseteq D$, $\langle A, B \rangle \in R$ if and only if $\langle A, A \cap B \rangle \in R$.

The reader can easily verify that for each determiner Det of fragment A (that is, every, some, no, and most), the extension Det^w lives on its first coordinate. This simple set-theoretic observation shows that the sentences in question are logically equivalent on the current account. Thus the semantics does make the correct prediction. Furthermore we would expect that as we expand the semantics to other determiners, the extensions assigned to them will always live on their first coordinate.

Now consider an inference that is logically valid for some determiners but not for others. For which determiners of Old Zealandish will Det P (Q∧R) logically entail Det P Q? Consider a couple of English examples.

Most planets are gaseous and larger than Earth.

Most planets are larger than Earth.

Here it seems that any situation truly described by the former is truly described by the latter. Note though that in this case the validity is dependent on the particular determiner we have used. For example, the following is not valid:

Few planets are rocky and larger than Earth.

Few planets are larger than Earth.

The following English determiners support this sort of inference: *each, every, some, (at least) two, (at least) three, most, many, both*. By contrast the following do not support the inference: *few, no, neither, at most two, exactly two*. What is it that accounts for the difference? Again our semantic theory predicts the right valid inferences, and it is easy to isolate the property that accounts for their validity. We say that a relation R on subsets of D is *monotone (increasing) in its second coordinate* provided that for all $A, B \subseteq D$, if $\langle A, B \rangle \in R$ and $B \subseteq B'$ then $\langle A, B' \rangle \in R$. The inference in question is a logical entailment in exactly those cases in which the determiner is monotone increasing in its second argument. For each of the determiners Every, Some, and Most of fragment A, their extension in any model is monotone in its second coordinate, and for these the inference is valid. In contrast the extension of No is not monotone increasing and the inference is not valid. These simple results are examples of the explanatory power of the model-theoretic approach, the kind of clear, crisp answers it can provide about entailment relations in the language under study.

Inference We introduced a parameter in our account of logical truth and entailment for a collection 𝒲 of models. We can exploit this parameter to make a few comments on the relevance of this account to the study of the cognitive architectures that underlie *inference*, the psychological counterpart of entailment.

According to the model-theoretic account of entailment, to know that a sentence S is logically true is to know that it is true no matter how the nonlinguistic world is configured. Similarly to know that S logically entails S′ is to know that S′ is true if S is true, no matter how the nonlinguistic world is configured. No attempt was made to describe a mechanism whereby a speaker of the language might come to know this. In particular the account did not give anything like an algorithm a speaker might use to determine whether or not a sentence is logically true.

There is a good reason for this. There simply *is* no algorithm for determining of an arbitrary sentence of fragment A whether it is logically true. This is known as Church's theorem.[11] If the model-theoretic account is a good mathematical model of logical truth, then no particular algorithmic process will ever completely capture this notion. This is not to say that we cannot determine whether a particular sentence is logically true. It just means there is no fixed algorithm that will always work.

By itself this result says nothing in particular about cognitive science. But if we assume that all cognitive processes are essentially algorithmic, we end up with a mildly surprising conclusion, namely, that we can know what it means for sentences to be logically true or for arguments to be logically valid but we cannot in general recognize whether they are. You might say that the human cognitive capacity has managed to create a rock it cannot lift.

There is of course a related empirical question. How do people in fact try to determine that a sentence is logically true or that one sentence entails another? The model-theoretic account says nothing directly about this problem. But this is not to say that the account cannot be turned to some advantage in cognitive science. Some cognitive scientists, most notably Johnson-Laird, have found it suggestive of an underlying architecture, which Johnson-Laird calls "mental models."[12] Mental models are taken to be similar to mathematical models in two respects. First, as with our mathematical models they are taken to represent the world in a fairly direct "structural" way. This is why they are called mental "models" rather than, say, mental "sentences." Second, mental models are viewed as having the kind of structure that makes it sensible to ask whether an arbitrary sentence is true in a given model.

Whereas Johnson-Laird's idea was inspired by model-theoretic semantics, we can turn this historical relationship on its head. Though we have been thinking of our mathematical models as models of the world, we could reinterpret the theory and think of them as models of the kind of cognitive architecture proposed by Johnson-Laird. This gives us a nice framework in which to compare two approaches to the notion of entailment.

Suppose that we could, through empirical means, isolate a collection of models $\mathcal{W}_m$ as the natural set-theoretic counterparts of mental models. For example, one might well want to restrict attention to models with finite domains. We could then define the notion of a *cognitive truth* as a sentence true in all models in $\mathcal{W}_m$. We could define the notion of cognitive entailment in a similar way. Having done this, we would be in a position to compare systematically the notions of logical truth and logical entailment with cognitive truth and cognitive entailment. The one mathematical apparatus would serve both functions.

Let us give one very simple example of how this approach might provide some guidance in cognitive science. There are well-known examples of sentences that are true in all finite structures but not true in all structures, for example, a sentence that asserts "If *larger than* is a linear ordering, then there is a largest object." This sentence is true in every finite domain but false in many infinite domains, say, where *larger than* is modeled by the usual > relation on natural numbers. If we limit $\mathcal{W}_m$ to finite structures, such sentences would come out as cognitive truths even though they are not logical truths. However, such sentences do not in fact seem to be cognitive truths, because we easily recognize that they could be false. This shows that either the mental-model approach is not the right way to think about inference or that we must admit that some mental models are best represented by infinite set-theoretic models. Still another possibility is that the mathematical models we are using do not correspond well to mental models in that they are assumed to be "first-order" and "total." By contrast, mental models are in general higher-order and inherently partial. This would suggest using something more similar to the models of situation semantics, discussed below.

6.5 Other Approaches

Extensional model-theoretic semantics is a useful approach to some phenomena, but it has its limitations. These limitations have prompted extensions and modifications of the approach along various dimensions. In this section we describe one extension of the theory and two modifications of it. We motivate these alterations with three well-known shortcomings of the extensional approach. Our discussions in the following sections are necessarily quite brief. They should be taken as mere glimpses into the subjects discussed.

Adding a Parameter for Context
The first problem concerns the effect of context on the content of an utterance. This dependence is clearly illustrated by Bell's utterance of "I need you" to Watson. Similarly when Galileo said "It revolves around the sun," the content of the claim depended on the fact that Galileo was referring to Earth. Expressions such as "I," "you," "here," "now," "today," "this," and the like are called *indexicals*. What they denote depends in a very systematic way on features of their context of use. Expressions such as "it," "he," "she," "that," and the like are also context sensitive, but the dependence is not so systematic. These expressions are often called *demonstratives*. Neither indexicals nor demonstratives fit very well into the previous framework. The problem is that the ordinary extensional approach does not provide a mechanism to reflect the dependence of content, and hence truth, on the context in which the expression is used.

The effect of context becomes especially important when we consider the cognitive significance of an assertion. Suppose a child A says "I am hungry" to her mother B, and B says "She is hungry," referring to her child A. There is a clear sense in which they have made the same claim. However, the cognitive significance of the two claims, that is, what the claims tell us about the speakers' cognitive states, is quite different. We expect A to try to eat, whereas we expect B to try to find something for A to eat. A semantic framework that systematically ignores context is ill suited to give any account of the cognitive significance of utterances.

When we take context seriously, a certain confusion in the notions of logical truth and logical entailment becomes evident. This was observed in the work of David Kaplan (1978) on what he called the logic of demonstratives. Let us focus on the concept of logical truth and consider sentences such as

I am here now.

I am speaking English.

Kaplan observed that sentences such as these have an interesting property. Whenever they are used (in the normal way) to make a statement, that statement is true. However, the claim made by such a statement is only contingently true. The fact that we are speaking English is an accident of history, not a logical truth.

Only when we ignore context does the assignment of truth values to sentences seem reasonable. Hence it is only under this idealization that the notion of a logically true *sentence* really makes any sense at all. Once we bring in context as an explicit parameter in the semantic account, it becomes clear that neither truth nor logical truth are properties of sentences but rather of something else—something like statements, propositions, claims, or sentences in context. The traditional notion of entailment as a relation between sentences is equally called into question.

Additional problems of context arise with the determiners of fragments B and C: The, Both, Neither, Many, and Few. For example, if we assert "Neither planet is as warm as Earth," in a discussion of Uranus and Neptune, then we are clearly making a claim about these two planets. Notice, though, that this cannot be accounted for by simply limiting the domain of discourse to include these and no other planets, because Earth must be part of the domain of discourse. Even more serious problems emerge with determiners such as "many" and "few." Obviously what counts as *many* depends on context. If we say that many people were late with their homework, in a class of 50, it means one thing, whereas if we say that many people regret voting for Reagan, it means something quite different.

What is clearly missing in the previous account is a parameter for the context of an utterance. We need to add a parameter u to our semantics that will in some ways be analogous to the parameter w. Just as we developed tools for studying the dependence of truth on facts about the world w, so too we need tools for studying the dependence of truth on facts about the utterance u in which the claim was made.

As long as we restrict attention to indexicals, we can take a fairly straightforward approach to context. Because any given language has only a finite number of indexical elements, we can simply list them in a some given order and then use a finite sequence of objects to model the values assigned to these items by a given context. Suppose, for example, that we were only concerned with the indexicals I, you, here, and now. We could let u range over sequences $\langle s, a, l, t \rangle$, thought of as representing the speaker, addressee, location, and time of the utterance, respectively. We could then add these indexicals to Old Zealandish and make the parameter $u = \langle s, a, l, t \rangle$ explicit in giving the semantics of our language. So, for example, we would now define the value of sentence S relative to *three* things: a context u, a model w of the world, and a variable assignment g. To say that $Val(S, u, w, g) =$ *true* would mean that the claim expressed by S in the context u would be satisfied by the assignment g if the world were arranged as modeled by w. Because the variable assignment can be thought of as akin to a contextual assignment of values to pronouns, it is often absorbed into the context parameter u, giving us $Val(S, u, w)$.

This same idea can be pushed further. Suppose we wanted to represent the dependence on context of the determiners Both, Neither, and The. Intuitively what is going on is that an utterance comes not just with a domain D^w but also with a subdomain of objects that have been made especially salient in the discourse. We might call this the resource domain d and add it to the sequence u used to model context. Thus a model of context would now consist of a sequence $u = \langle s, a, l, t, d \rangle$, where $s, a, l, t \in D^w$ and $d \subseteq D^w$. This parameter would feature in the characterization of the extensions of the determiners as follows:

$$Both^w = \{\langle A, B, d \rangle \mid card(d \cap A) = 2 \text{ and } d \cap A \subseteq B\},$$
$$Neither^w = \{\langle A, B, d \rangle \mid card(d \cap A) = 2 \text{ and } d \cap A \cap B = \varnothing\},$$
$$The^w = \{\langle A, B, d \rangle \mid card(d \cap A) = 1 \text{ and } d \cap A \subseteq B\}.$$

Using this, we could give a systematic characterization of the semantics of fragment B of Old Zealandish. Such a semantics would allow us to account for the presuppositions associated with sentences containing the above determiners. Space does not permit us to go into the details here.

One of the chief advantages of making explicit the parameter for context is that it allows us to distinguish the meaning of a sentence from the content of a given use. This distinction goes back to Kaplan's work. In the above framework we can model the *meaning* of a sentence S with a set-theoretic relation between contexts u and models w defined as

$$meaning(S) = \{\langle u, w \rangle \mid Val(S, u, w) = true\}.$$

Then for any particular u we can model the *content* of the sentence in context u with the set of w such that $\langle u, w \rangle \in$ *meaning*(S).

For several years work on context took this tack, adding more terms to a sequence representing the relevant aspects of context. However, some semanticists believe this approach is too unsystematic and does not square well with the enormously wide range of contextual dependence found in natural language. For example, although the approach works well for the determiners of fragment B, it is not adequate for the determiners Many and Few of fragment C. There is much more to the context dependence of these determiners than just a resource domain d. Or consider a sentence such as *The enemy destroyed my local grocery store at 3 PM*. This has at least five contextually sensitive elements. Most obvious is the indexical expression "my," whose semantic content depends on who is speaking. But the interpretations of the expressions "the," "enemy," "local," and "3 PM" each involve contextual dependence of one sort or another, as well.

Once one appreciates the extraordinary influence of context on content, the idea of using longer and longer sequences to represent the former becomes unworkable. There is no way in advance to guess what we need to represent, so there is no way to assign in advance an interpretation to the various elements of the sequence. Current work in semantics, especially in connection with discourse,[13] is still grappling with the problem of modeling the context of an utterance.

Possible-Worlds Semantics

The most striking difference between the extensional approach to semantics and that pursued in much of the semantic literature is the addition of so-called possible worlds. To understand the motivation for this move, we discuss another problem with the ordinary extensional account.

The Problem of Grain Extensional models are notoriously inadequate representations of the way things are. This is due in large part to its coarse-grained representation of properties and relations. The most blatant, if not the most pressing, form of the problem has to do with properties that are not actually instantiated. For example, there exist neither unicorns nor centaurs, so both of these properties are represented by the empty set. But if an account uses the same set to model the semantic contribution of both "unicorn" and "centaur," then the account predicts that these words are interchangeable, which of course they are not. The sentence "Claire dressed up for Halloween as a unicorn" could be true, whereas "Claire dressed up for Halloween as a centaur" would be false.

The inadequacy of the extensional model of properties and relations is apparent when we look at adjectives and adverbs. Consider, for example, the phrase "Max's best friend." Linguistically the noun "best friend" is obtained by combining the adjective "best" and the noun "friend." Intuitively the friend relation is modified to pick out the best friend. So we would like the semantics to work in that way. But it can't, given our extensional models of properties and relations. If we represent the extension of the friend relation with a set of pairs of people, then Max's friends would be represented by a certain set of people. The question is, how should we model the semantic content of the modifier "best"?

There are two ways we might try to model this extensionally. We might represent the meaning of "best" with a choice function that assigns to any nonempty set B an element $b \in B$, intuitively its best element. This won't work though. Suppose, for example, that Max's friends were also Claire's friends, and vice versa. It does not follow that Max's best friend is Claire's best friend, as this strategy would predict. Another strategy would be to model the meaning of "best" by means of a uniformization function, a function that assigns to any binary set-theoretic relation R a subrelation $R_0 \subseteq R$ such that R_0 is a function. The idea is that $\langle a, b \rangle \in R_0$ if and only if b is the best member related to a by R. But this won't work either. For example, it could happen that two distinct relations had the same extension, say, the friend relation and the neighbor relation. But it would not follow that your best friend was your best neighbor, as the strategy would predict, because we expect different things of neighbors and friends. Max's best friend could well be a lousy neighbor.

The same problem would arise in Old Zealandish if we had the predicate modifier Large and so could form the predicate phrases Large Planet and Large Thing. Even if the extension of Planet and Thing happened to be the same in a particular model, we would probably not want the extensions of Large Thing and Large Planet to be the same, since every planet is a large thing but not every planet is a large planet. The problem again is that the set-theoretic objects used to represent properties are simply too coarse grained.

Another version of the grain problem, and one that played a bigger historical role, becomes apparent when we consider so-called propositional attitude verbs: "believes," "knows," "sees," "claims," "proves," and the like. These verbs take sentential complements and say something about the cognitive state of an agent. If we augment our fragment to allow such verbs, there is no way to extend the semantics given above to anything approaching an adequate account. Consider the pope's true claim "Galileo does not believe that the earth is at the center of the universe." All our theory gives us for classifying the sentential complement here is its truth-value, *false*. Thus the theory would predict that if we replace the sentential complement with any other false sentence, we should get a true statement. This would be tantamount, however, to the claim that Galileo has no false beliefs. Although the latter *might* be true, it certainly does not follow from facts about language and the truth of the original claim.

Adding Another Parameter   The most popular strategy for tackling the problem of grain has been the introduction of a parameter for alternative "possible worlds." The idea is that whereas two properties might happen to have the same extension, if they are different properties, they *could* have had different extensions. For example, although it happens to be the case that there are neither unicorns nor centaurs, this need not have been so. We can envision other ways the world might have been, say, in which there were unicorns but no centaurs. Once we incorporate this range of possible variation, the two properties are no longer represented by the same thing.

The seed of this idea is already present in the extensional approach, where we employ a range of models in some collection $\mathcal{W}$. This suggests representing the property of being a unicorn not with one set, $\mathrm{Unicorn}^w$, but with a family of sets $\mathrm{Unicorn}^{\mathcal{W}} = \{\mathrm{Unicorn}^w | w \in \mathcal{W}\}$. Here the property of being a unicorn and the property of being a centaur will be represented by different objects, because there will be models in which $\mathrm{Unicorn}^w$ and $\mathrm{Centaur}^w$ are distinct sets.

For technical reasons this approach must be modified somewhat. Instead of working with a collection of models of the old sort, we need to introduce a set $\mathcal{I}$ of new primitives. The objects $i \in \mathcal{I}$ are usually called "possible worlds." By saying they are primitives, we mean that the members of $\mathcal{I}$ are assumed not to have any set-theoretic structure of their own. One of these members, $i_{@}$, is viewed as representing the actual world. In addition we assume that to each $i \in \mathcal{I}$ there is a domain D^i of individuals that are "actual in" i.

Using this framework, we get finer-grained representations of properties and relations. For example, we can represent a property P with a function f_P that assigns to each $i \in \mathcal{I}$ a subset of D^i, thinking of $f_P(i)$ as the set of things that have property P in world i. Similarly a two-place relation R will be represented by a function f_R from $\mathcal{I}$ to subsets of $D^i \times D^i$. Let us call these representations p.w. properties and p.w. relations, respectively, the "p.w." standing for possible worlds.[14]

Defining the notion of a model in this framework is a bit complex, so we must omit the details.[15] The basic idea is that a model $\mathcal{M}$ consists of a set of possible worlds $\mathcal{I}$, each with a domain D^i, a distinguished possible world $i_{@}$, and a function that assigns to basic lexical items appropriate objects. For example, the model will assign to a unary predicate P a p.w. property $P^{\mathcal{M}}$, and to a binary predicate R some p.w. relation $R^{\mathcal{M}}$.

Let us see how this setup will model the meanings of the expressions Friend, Best Friend, Max's Best Friend, and so forth. Associated with the word Friend we have a binary p.w. relation, that is, a function $\text{Friend}^{\mathcal{M}}$ that assigns to each world $i \in \mathcal{I}$ some subset $\text{Friend}^{\mathcal{M}}(i)$ of $D^i \times D^i$. Intuitively $\langle a, b \rangle \in \text{Friend}^{\mathcal{M}}(i)$ if and only if b is a friend of a in world i. The meaning of the word Best should take us from a relation to a function, for example, from the *friend* relation to the single-valued *best friend* relation. Thus the semantic value of Best can be modeled by means of a p.w. function $\text{Best}^{\mathcal{M}}$ from p.w. relations to p.w. functions, where the value is always a subfunction of the argument. That is, $\text{Best}^{\mathcal{M}}$ will be a function that assigns to each possible world i and binary p.w. relation f_R a p.w. function f_{R0}, which is a subfunction of f_R.

What sorts of semantic values do we assign to noun phrases of the form α's Best Friend? For notational ease, let us use F and B as abbreviations of $\text{Friend}^{\mathcal{M}}$ and $\text{Best}^{\mathcal{M}}$, respectively. Our definition of $den(\alpha, \mathcal{M}, i)$, the denotation of α in world i of model $\mathcal{M}$, would contain something like

$$den(\alpha\text{'s Best Friend}, \mathcal{M}, i) = (B(i)(F))(i)(den(\alpha, \mathcal{M}, i)).$$

Let us look at what this means, intuitively, for the noun phrase Max's Best Friend. According to the definition, the denotation of this term in possible world i (relative to the model $\mathcal{M}$) is obtained as follows: First, $B(i)$ is the way we go from relations to their "best parts" in world i. Thus $(B(i)(F))$ is the best-friend relation. Consequently $(B(i)(F))(i)$ is the extension of the best-friend relation in the world i. And hence $B(i)(F)(i)(\text{Max})$ is Max's best friend in i.

How does this solve the problem of grain? Suppose our language also included terms such as $\text{Max's Best Neighbor}$. The unary predicates Friend and Neighbor will be assigned distinct p.w. properties, even if the extension of the *friend* relation happens to be the same as the extension of the *neighbor* relation in the actual world, that is, even if $\text{Friend}^{\mathcal{M}}(i_@) = \text{Neighbor}^{\mathcal{M}}(i_@)$. But the function B does not look at just the extension of these relations in $i_@$ and so can assign distinct subfunctions as desired.

How might this same strategy be used to solve other aspects of the problem of grain?[16] Recall the problem posed by propositional attitude verbs. We noted that truth values were too coarse grained to serve as contents of sentential complements of "Galileo believes that." The most natural move, given the p.w. framework, is to model contents not by truth values, but by functions from possible worlds to truth values. Call such a function a p.w. proposition. The idea is that a p.w. proposition p represents how the truth of that same claim depends on the way the world is. Such a p.w. proposition is *true* provided $p(i_@) = true$. The claim that Earth is at the center of the universe could be represented by a different p.w. proposition than the claim that Mars has only one moon, even though both are actually false, that is, false in $i_@$. These propositions can then be the objects of belief, and we can have Galileo believing one while failing to believe the other.

The most prevalent approach to model-theoretic semantics today is a hybrid of the accounts we have sketched so far; it uses the possible-worlds framework, with the addition of an explicit parameter for context. The resulting semantics gives an explicit account of an impressive list of semantic phenomena, including meaning, context, content, truth, entailment, and presupposition. Although it may not give a definitive account of these phenomena, we certainly know much more about all of them and how they fit together than we did 50 or even 25 years ago. This progress is a tribute to the vision of the founders of model-theoretic semantics and to those like Montague who pushed the development forward into uncharted waters. Still many researchers believe that the approach fails to solve the problem that motivated it in the first place, the problem of grain. The problem is that many sentences that are true in the same possible worlds do not have the same content. For example, all sentences expressing mathematical truths are true in all possible worlds. We do not have room to go into this problem in any detail here but refer the reader to the literature, in which it is known as the problem of logical equivalence.[17]

Situation Semantics

Finally, let us turn to an alternate approach to semantics being pursued by a number of researchers, including ourselves. Situation semantics arose around 1980, when the pervasive influence of context was beginning to be recognized and with it the inadequacy of the ordered-sequence approach to modeling context. It arose partly in response to this inadequacy and partly in response to the failure of the possible-worlds approach to solve the problem of grain.

Perhaps the best way to understand how situation semantics differs from either extensional semantics or possible-worlds semantics is to go back to our previous attempt to characterize the meaning of a declarative sentence S:

$$meaning(S) = \{\langle u, w\rangle | Val(S, u, w) = true\}.$$

In this equation u ranges over contexts of utterance, and w ranges over extensional models of the world. In practice the set D^w of the model w is not taken to be everything there is but rather to be some limited set of things: witness the terminology "domain of discourse." Thus in practice we do not think of w as a model of the whole world but rather as a model of that portion of the world under discussion in the context u.

Let us admit this up front and call w a parameter for the *described* situation. So we can think of our equation as an attempt to characterize the meaning of a sentence in terms of a relation between two limited portions of the world, the *utterance* situation, and the *described* situation. This way of looking at things suggests that we adopt a uniform technique for modeling these two parameters. The question is how to develop sufficiently fine-grained models of situations.

To solve the problem of grain, situation semantics takes a quite different approach from possible-worlds semantics. Rather than introduce a set of primitive possible worlds, it abandons the attempt to model properties and relations with anything else and treats *them* as primitive. To see the reason for this move, we turn to the third of our three problems with the extensional approach.

The Factorization Problem In the extensional approach we used models to represent different ways the world might be, and in defining logical truth, we relativized this to a collection W of models. But just what dimension of variation is being signified by the members of W? The problem in a nutshell is that we have only one parameter w to represent two sorts of variation. For example, there are two contingent facts that are involved in getting us from a word, say, a noun like `Planet`, to its extension, the set of planets. One is a linguistic fact, the fact that we are using `Planet` to express the property of being a planet. Had the history of English been different, we might have used the same word to express some other property. The second is an astronomical fact, the fact that the planets are the ones they are. But our extensional models only give us one object to represent these two dimensions of variation. We call this the *factorization problem*. As a consequence of it, our theory is ambiguous: Do different models represent different ways the linguistic facts might have been or do they represent ways the astronomical facts might have been?

One finds both construals in the literature. We call the first view the "interpretational reading" of the semantics. From this perspective different models represent different possible interpretations of the language; indeed what we have called models are frequently called "interpretations." The second view we call the "representational reading" of the semantics. On this reading, different models represent different ways the world might have been, given that the words mean what they do.

To see how this ambiguity presents a serious practical problem for the theory, consider the following three sentences:

Every moon of Mars is a moon of Mars.

Every moon of Mars moves around Mars.

Every moon of Mars is smaller than Mercury.

First, note that on pretheoretic grounds it seems like the first two make true statements solely in virtue of their meanings, whereas the truth of the third is contingent on facts about the solar system. We would like our account to predict these facts, say, by the first two coming out logically true, true in all $w \in W$.

On the interpretational reading of the semantics, it is unreasonable to restrict the collection W at all. But then the first sentence comes out a logical truth, whereas the second does not. Indeed the first sentence is logically true with respect to any collection W of models. But the same is not so with the second and third. Some collections will declare the second a logical truth, some will not. (For example, if we let $\text{MovesAround}^w = \{\langle a, b \rangle | a$ is larger than $b\}$, then it will come out false.) Similarly with the third sentence. On the representational reading of the above theory we need a way to restrict attention to those models that respect the actual meanings of the lexical items. This is what the factorization problem keeps us from doing. The extensional account lumps the latter two sentences together, offering no explanation for the intuition that the second is true simply in virtue of meaning whereas the third is not.

We believe it is the representational reading that captures the intent of semantic theorizing. But the mathematical tradition, with its emphasis on the axiomatic method, squares better with the interpretational view. Consequently the account does not make the correct semantical predictions.

We can solve the problems of grain and factorization with one stroke by giving up the idea of modeling properties and relations with set-theoretic constructs. Semantic theory needs an account of properties and relations: they are among the most basic things that expressions in language are used to express. But rather than model them in terms of other things, why not take *them* as primitives rather than possible worlds? This idea is not unique to situation semantics but it is used in it to provide a finer-grained way of modeling situations.

Notice that this move, though motivated by the problem of grain, also solves the factorization problem. If we take properties and relations as basic, we can represent the two sorts of facts that must be kept distinct. We can represent the linguistic fact that the word Planet expresses the property of being a planet, not the property of being an asteroid, and also the nonlinguistic facts about which objects are planets and which are not. This allows us to distinguish the two sorts of variations.

Taking properties and relations as primitive suggests an obvious way of modeling situations. For simplicity assume that R is a binary relation and that a and b are objects. We could use the four-tuple $\langle\!\langle R, a, b; 1 \rangle\!\rangle$ to represent the fact that a stands in relation R to b, and the tuple $\langle\!\langle R, a, b; 0 \rangle\!\rangle$ to represent the dual fact that a does not stand in R to b. We can think of such tuples as representing atomic states of affairs, or "possible facts." Following a suggestion of Keith Devlin, let us call these "basic infons," because they represent basic informational units. We can then represent the world, or some part of it, by a collection s of such basic infons. We will think of such collections as representing "possible situations," ways part of the world might be or might have been. We write $s \models \sigma$ if $\sigma \in s$, for basic infon σ and situation s.[18]

Context as Situation   Situations can be used to represent both the part of the world being described by an utterance and the part that provides the context of the utterance itself. One of the chief advantages of this viewpoint is that there is no need to restrict the facts in the utterance situation to facts directly tied to one of the words used in the utterance, as was the case in the previous approach.

Consider how we might describe the meanings of the Old Zealandish expressions Me, My Friend, My Friend's Friend, ... We will analyze the semantics of one of these expressions, say NP, in terms of a three-place relation $[\![NP]\!](u, s, b)$. Intuitively $[\![NP]\!](u, s, b)$ holds if and only if in the utterance u, the speaker is referring to b by the use of NP, and in the situation s, the speaker is a friend of a friend of . . . b. We assume our stock of relations contains the following: *speaking* (a property of individuals), *referring to* (a three-place relation relating a speaker, an expression, and an object being referred to), *expressing* (a three-place relation relating a speaker, an expression, and a relation being expressed by the expression), and *describing* (a binary relation that holds between a speaker and a situation being described). By an *utterance situation u* we mean a situation in which there is a unique speaker, that is, a unique individual a satisfying $u \models \langle\!\langle speaking, a; 1 \rangle\!\rangle$. We also impose the following constraint on utterances: if $u \models \langle\!\langle referring\ to, a, \alpha, b; 1 \rangle\!\rangle$, then a is the speaker of u, and similarly if $u \models \langle\!\langle expressing, a, \alpha, b; 1 \rangle\!\rangle$, then a is the speaker of u.

Because one of our aims is to address the factorization problem head on, we want to take account of the fact that the noun Friend has several senses. Our own dictionary lists six. We shall consider two of these, the most common and the least common. Thus we associate with the word Friend two distinct relations, *friend* and *Friend*. The former is the expected relation between individuals, so that $s \models \langle\!\langle friend, a, b; 1 \rangle\!\rangle$ if, in s, a is attached by personal regard to b. By contrast, *Friend* is simply a property, and $s \models \langle\!\langle Friend, b; 1 \rangle\!\rangle$ if, in s, b is a Quaker. We associate with the word Friend a meaning $[\![Friend]\!](u, R)$ as follows: $[\![Friend]\!](u, R)$ holds if and only if $u \models \langle\!\langle expressing, a, Friend, R; 1 \rangle\!\rangle$, where R is one of the two previously mentioned relations and a is the speaker in u.

It would be possible to use the English expression "my friend" to mean "my Quaker," but it would require a very unusual context. Because we want to make a different point, let us suppose that this is not possible in Old Zealandish. That is, we will set things up so that it is possible to say things like A Friend to describe a Quaker, but that the only way to use NP's Friend is when Friend is used in the primarily relational sense. Here are our rules for the expressions in question:

- $[\![\text{Me}]\!](u, s, a)$ iff $u \models \langle\!\langle speaking, a; 1\rangle\!\rangle \wedge \langle\!\langle describing, a, s; 1\rangle\!\rangle$;
- $[\![\text{NP's Friend}]\!](u, s, b)$ iff there are a, b', R such that
  1. $u \models \langle\!\langle referring\ to, a, \text{NP's Friend}, b; 1\rangle\!\rangle$,
  2. $u \models \langle\!\langle describing, a, s; 1\rangle\!\rangle$,
  3. $[\![\text{NP}]\!](u, s, b')$,
  4. $[\![\text{Friend}]\!](u, R)$,
  5. $s \models \langle\!\langle R, b', b; 1\rangle\!\rangle$.

This characterization may seem complicated for such simple expressions. But the complications are all required by facts about the language that need to be captured. Indeed it is easy to see that each of these clauses must be a consequence of any theory that gets the semantic facts right. Consider the five conditions in the second, recursive clause:

1. The requirement that $u \models \langle\!\langle referring\ to, a, \text{NP's friend}, b; 1\rangle\!\rangle$ incorporates our recognition that the speaker must be referring to one person by the use of this complex noun phrase, even though individuals may have more than one friend.

2. The condition $u \models \langle\!\langle describing, a, s; 1\rangle\!\rangle$ makes explicit the contextual fact that determines just what the described situation is.

3. The condition $[\![\text{NP}]\!](u, s, b')$ guarantees that b' is the person referred to by the use of NP.

4. The requirement that $[\![\text{Friend}]\!](u, R)$ guarantees that the speaker is using the word Friend to express one of the two relations it can express in Old Zealandish.

5. Finally, the fact that the person b (referred to by NP's Friend) must indeed be a friend of the person b' (referred to by the constituent noun phrase NP) is required by the condition $s \models \langle\!\langle R, b', b; 1\rangle\!\rangle$. Note that because the relation R here requires two objects, this rules out one of the two readings of Friend.

How would we extend this to expressions such as My Best Friend? Again we would not try to model the meaning of Best with any set theoretic object. Rather we would view its (preferred) meaning as expressing a relation between properties.[19] Intuitively there is a situation c of background circumstances, and $c \models \langle\!\langle best, P_0, P; 1\rangle\!\rangle$ if c supports the fact that P_0 is the property of being among the best of the objects b satisfying $s \models \langle\!\langle P, b; 1\rangle\!\rangle$. To model the working of *best* correctly, we also impose the condition that if $s \models \langle\!\langle best, P_0, P; 1\rangle\!\rangle$, and $s \models \langle\!\langle P_0, b; 1\rangle\!\rangle$, then $s \models \langle\!\langle P, b; 1\rangle\!\rangle$.[20]

Possible Worlds as Situations One way to appreciate the difference between possible worlds and situations is to see how the former are treated using the latter. How do we model possible worlds within situation semantics? The natural way is with maximal, consistent collections w of infons.[21] These capture the idea of a possible world as a way things might have been. But although we can model possible worlds as certain sorts of situations, we do not model propositions as sets of possible worlds. Space does not permit us to go into this here, so we refer the reader to our book (Barwise and Etchemendy 1987) for a discussion of modeling propositions in situation semantics.

There are several ways in which situations are more flexible than possible worlds. First, they need not be consistent. This is not of much use in characterizing parts of the world, but it is useful for modeling mental states, which are not consistent, in general. Second, they need not be maximal. This feature is useful in modeling both real situations, which are usually limited portions of the world, and in modeling mental states, which are inherently partial. In addition the use of higher-order relations, and facts involving them, provides additional flexibility needed for natural-language semantics.

Notes

1. See, for example, the papers by H. P. Grice (1957, 1968), and David Lewis (1969).

2. Unfortunately the work in semantics reported here by and large assumes that words rather than morphemes form the smallest meaningful units. For a detailed treatment of lexical semantics, see, for example, Dowty (1979).

3. For example, we are taught that "2014" stands for 2 thousands, 0 hundreds, 1 ten, and 4 ones, that is, $2 \times 10^3 + 0 \times 10^2 + 1 \times 10^1 + 4$. Our second recursion is also known as a "tail recursion," a type of recursion that is computationally more manageable.

4. Of course in using this technique there is a danger, because simplifying assumptions made at either the syntactic or semantic level may prejudge semantic issues in unforeseen ways. A case in point is the once-popular treatment of tense as involving a sentential operator, which flies in the face of natural-language syntax. It turns out that this is not just an innocuous syntactic simplification, but makes a viable treatment of tense impossible.

5. Because we always talk *about* Old Zealandish, but never speak the language ourselves, all occurrences of Zealandish expressions in this chapter should be quoted. But to make things more readable, we omit the quotation marks and use a different style of type instead. Thus we write LargerThan instead of "LargerThan."

6. Thus the complex noun phrase Every Thing functions like the quantifier symbol ∀ of first-order logic, and Some Thing functions like ∃.

7. The function f is often called an "interpretation function." We think this is unfortunate terminology, for reasons that emerge later in the text, having to do with the factorization problem.

8. By *card(A)* we mean the cardinality of the set A. The reader unfamiliar with the notion of cardinality need only note that it is a measure of the size of sets. Note, though, that this account of `Most` is almost certainly an overly simple model of the English determiner "Most."

9. This is often written $w \models S\ [g]$.

10. Two sentences are logically equivalent if each entails the other. Because we have not included conjoined predicates in Old Zealandish, the reader should take P $\wedge$ Q as shorthand for $\hat{v}[(v\ P) \wedge (v\ Q)]$, where v is some variable not free in P or Q.

11. There are many subtleties on this matter that we cannot go into here. For fragment A it so happens that there is a complete axiomatization of the logical truths, if one takes $\mathcal{W}$ to be the collection of all models, finite and infinite. This entails that the collection of logical truths of the language is "recursively enumerable." What this means, roughly, is that there is an algorithm that will tell you of logical truths and only logical truths that they *are* logical truths, but the algorithm may never give any answer at all if the sentence is not a logical truth. There are very simple extensions of fragment A, however, for which even this weak result is false.

12. We refer the reader to chapter 12 by Johnson-Laird.

13. See chapter 11 by Grosz, Sidner, and Pollack.

14. Notice, for future reference, that the subrelation relation is no longer modeled by the subset relation, as in the extensional case. Rather, one p.w. relation f_R will be a subrelation of another p.w. relation f_S just in case for every $i \in \mathcal{I}$, $f_R(i) \subseteq f_S(i)$. Similarly, a binary p.w. relation f_R will be single-valued (or functional) provided, for each world i, the set $f_R(i)$ is a function. We call such a p.w. relation a p.w. function.

15. See Kripke 1963, Montague 1974, or Lewis 1972 for details.

16. This approach has been applied to the study of modalities, conditionals, propositional attitudes, and other phenomena. See, for example, Kripke 1963, Montague 1974, Lewis 1972, Hintikka 1969, and Stalnaker 1984.

17. It is discussed in, for example, Lewis 1972 and Stalnaker 1984.

18. In addition to the basic infons that are used to form our models of situations, situation semantics uses an algebra of information. For example, there is a meet operation on infons with the condition that $s \models \sigma_1 \wedge \sigma_2$ iff $s \models \sigma_1$ and $s \models \sigma_2$.

19. As with `Friend` we could accommodate the fact that the word `Best` can express more than one relation when, for example, it is used as a transitive verb.

20. Note, however, that we would not impose such a condition for the relation expressed by a word such as "fake." Indeed we want just the contrary: if $s \models \langle\!\langle fake, P_0, P; 1 \rangle\!\rangle$; and $s \models \langle\!\langle P_0, b; 1 \rangle\!\rangle$, then $s \models \langle\!\langle P, b; 0 \rangle\!\rangle$.

21. The notion of consistent used here includes the constraint that no infon $\langle\!\langle R, \ldots ; 1 \rangle\!\rangle$ and its dual $\langle\!\langle R, \ldots ; 0 \rangle\!\rangle$ are both in w. But there would be additional constraints as well. For example, if we use *NO* for the relation on properties of having disjoint extensions, we would require that if $\langle\!\langle NO, P, Q; 1 \rangle\!\rangle \in w$ and $\langle\!\langle P, c; 1 \rangle\!\rangle \in w$, then $\langle\!\langle Q, c; 0 \rangle\!\rangle \in w$. To account for the facts discussed under the factorization problem, we also impose con-

straints such as the following: if $\langle\!\langle moon\ of,\ a,\ b;\ 1 \rangle\!\rangle \in w$ then $\langle\!\langle moves\ around,\ a,\ b;\ 1 \rangle\!\rangle \in w$. By a *maximal* consistent collection of infons we mean one that is not properly contained in any other consistent collection.

References

Barwise, J. and Etchemendy, J. 1987. *The Liar: An Essay on Truth and Circularity*. New York: Oxford University Press.

Dowty, D. 1979. *Word Meaning and Montague Grammar*. Dordrecht: Reidel.

Grice, H. P. 1957 Meaning. *Philosophical Review* 66:377–388.

Grice, H. P. 1968. Utterer's meaning, sentence-meaning, and word-meaning. *Foundations of Language* 4:1–18.

Hintikka, J. 1969. *Models for Modalities*. Dordrecht: Reidel.

Kaplan, D. 1978. On the logic of demonstratives. *J. Philosophical Logic* 8:81–98.

Kripke, S. 1963. Semantical considerations on modal logic. *Acta Philosphica Fennica* 16:83–94.

Lewis, D. 1969. *Convention*. Cambridge, MA: Harvard University Press.

Lewis, D. 1972. General semantics. In D. Davidson and G. Harman; ed. *Semantics of Natural Language*. Dordrecht: Reidel, pp. 169–218. Reprinted in B. Partee, ed. 1976. *Montague Grammar*. New York: Academic Press, pp. 1–50.

Montague, R. 1974. *Formal Philosophy: Selected Papers of Richard Montague*. R. Thomason, ed. New Haven, CT: Yale University Press.

Stalnaker, R. 1984. *Inquiry*. Cambridge, MA: MIT Press.

Further Reading

Barwise, J., and Perry, J. 1983. *Situations and Attitudes*. Cambridge, MA: MIT Press.

Barwise, J., and Cooper, R. 1981. Generalized quantifiers and natural language. *Linguistics and Philosophy* 4:159–220.

Cooper, R. 1983. *Quantification and Syntactic Theory*. Dordrecht: Reidel.

Dowty, D., Wall, R., and Peters, S. 1981. *Introduction to Montague Semantics*. Dordrecht: Reidel.

Etchemendy, J. 1990. *The Concept of Logical Consequence*. Cambridge, MA: Harvard University Press.

Fenstad, J. E., Halvorsen, P-K, Langholm, T., and van Benthem, J. 1987. *Situations, Language and Logic*. Dordrecht: Reidel.

Gärdenfors, P. 1987. *Generalized Quantifiers*. Dordrecht: Reidel.

Kamp, H. 1979. Instant, events and temporal discourse. In R. Bauerle et al., eds. *Semantics from Different Points of View*. New York: Springer Verlag.

Martinich, A. P., ed. 1985. *The Philosophy of Language*. Oxford University Press.

7 Experimental Methods in Cognitive Science

Gordon H. Bower and John P. Clapper

7.1 General Introduction

Cognitive science is a multidisciplinary field with diverse goals and intellectual agenda. Of the fields contributing to cognitive science, it is cognitive psychology that makes primary use of experimental methods to answer its questions. We do not argue that reliable knowledge can only be obtained through experimentation. Science is not identical with experimentation; otherwise astronomy or anthropology could not be sciences, which they manifestly are. Rather each intellectual discipline has its own rules for justifying its claims, hypotheses, and theories. Cognitive science is a somewhat uneasy marriage of the differing methodologies and styles of justification of its contributing disciplines. The relevance of experimental observations to cognitive science largely depends on what *claims* are being made for the "psychological reality" of the principles under discussion—that is, whether the authors propose their claims as descriptions of human mentation.

The goal of sciences is to build theories that enable the explanation, prediction, and control of events in their domain of inquiry. Such theories are like mental models of their empirical domain; they postulate an interlocking network of theoretical concepts to explain and unify known facts and occasionally guide the discovery of new, previously unobserved regularities. Theories are systems of abstract concepts whose properties and rules of operation *correspond* (are analogous) to some empirical system. For us to have confidence in this correspondence, the observations on which the theory is based should be accurate and reliable. Evaluating a theory depends on checking whether its implications are true.

Many facts about the human mind are apparent from introspection, and no special methods seem necessary to uncover them. But introspection alone has had a dismal record of failure as a primary method in psychology, a field that began with only the introspective method a hundred years ago and then abandoned it after years of frustration because of its variability, reactive unreliability, and frequent invalidity. Much of the data obtained by introspection are heavily influenced by the observers' theoretical preconceptions (Nisbett and Wilson 1977, Nisbett and Ross 1980). Moreover many cognitive processes go on outside of awareness (Lewicki 1986) or occur far too rapidly to be available for conscious report. Thus a science of human cognition can benefit from special techniques for observing, recording, and interpreting mental events. There are a variety of empirical techniques that can yield quite reliable knowledge. We briefly discuss two of them before moving on to experimental methods.

Naturalistic Observation
Naturalistic observation refers to the systematic observation and recording of the behavior of some organism (or social unit) as it occurs in a somewhat "natural setting" without any attempt by the observer to intervene. Developmental psychologists, for example, have conducted many naturalistic studies of infants to describe the normative (average) maturation sequence of physical abilities—at what average age infants can sit up, walk, babble, and so on. Computer-simulation theorists who try to recreate in their program introspections of their own problem-solving (or question-answering) activities are doing a sort of naturalistic observation. So is the linguist who tries to generate a set of counter-example sentences to some proposed linguistic generalization and then tries to formulate a more adequate generalization to cover all the examples.

Although naturalistic observations can provide descriptive generalizations about a class of phenomena (say, the formation of plurals in English nouns), they are weak in supplying evidence for *cause-effect* relations. For instance, we might hypothesize that as the days grow shorter, a species of bird begins to migrate south. But simple observation alone cannot allow us to untangle all the factors other than day-length that might contribute to migration, such as temperature changes, the azimuth of the sun, and so on. Experiments could try to check for the causal power of length of daylight by *controlling* these other *confounding* factors.

Correlational Studies
Correlational studies have a more formal character than naturalistic observations in that they usually try to measure the degree of association (relatedness) of two or more events or attributes. A well-known example is the correlation of cigarette smoking with lung cancer: the amount and duration of smoking correlates with the likelihood of developing lung cancer. The weakness of the correlational approach is that correlation provides no clear evidence for inferring a cause-effect relationship.

A major problem is that one cannot rule out the possibility of an unknown third variable that is causing both of the other two factors to vary together. The tobacco industry has repeatedly argued that the smoking-cancer correlation provides no evidence for causation, because there may be certain kinds of people who are both cancer prone and also readily addicted to cigarettes and would get cancer at the same rate whether or not they smoked. Even assuming that the correlated variables are causally related, the correlation itself goes both ways and does not itself provide any hint as to the *direction* of the causation. For example, elementary-school students who get better grades are liked more by their teachers, but which is cause and which is effect? Each cause-effect link is plausible on its own merits, or the two might reciprocally cause one another, or both might be caused by a third variable, such as the child's social skills. The point is that correlation does not imply causation, whereas causation almost always implies correlation.

Controlled Experiments

The deficiencies of correlational studies for arriving at conclusions about cause-effect relationships are rectified by the use of experiments. The basic idea of an experiment is very simple: one group of subjects is treated in one fashion, another group in a different fashion, and we measure whether their behavior differs as a consequence. If the two groups were equivalent in all other respects at the beginning of the experiment, then we can justifiably claim that any difference in their behavior at the end of the experiment can be viewed as an effect caused by the different treatments they received. This basic idea is so simple that it bears repetition: in experiments we compare observations under two conditions—an "experimental" condition, which has the crucial procedure, treatment, or factor introduced, versus a "control" condition, identical in all respects to the first group except that the experimental procedure, treatment, or factor is omitted. The comparison of the two conditions enables us to infer whether the experimental treatment causes a difference in behavior in the experimental group.

Experiments are usually conducted to test a specific *hypothesis* about the relation between two variables. The factor that the experimenter manipulates is referred to as the *independent variable*, whereas the behavior that is measured to detect any effects of this manipulation is called the *dependent variable*. Many experiments use several independent and dependent variables in complex arrangements, but the experiments can all be reduced to the same simple reasoning. The hypothesis is a *generalization* or universal statement about the causal relations between variables in the world and the conditions under which these relations can be expected to hold. In a cognitive-science experiment the hypothesis is usually a prediction that a particular change in the conditions under which subjects are observed will cause a specific change in their behavior. If the prediction fails, then the hypothesis should be rejected. On the other hand if the results accord with the hypothesis, then our confidence in that hypothesis will increase (although it is still open to disconfirmation from further experiments).

Measuring Experimental Effects As indicated, experiments are set up to measure changes in people's behavior (cognitive performances) caused by manipulating a particular independent variable. To measure this influence on behavior, we should be able to describe the behavior quantitatively in countable units such as the number of milliseconds required to make a decision or the proportion of answers of a given type. Although qualitative observations (for example, introspective protocols) are useful preliminaries, they should be replaced whenever possible by quantitative measures that can be statistically summarized and compared across experimental conditions. Anyone who has ever confronted the Herculean task of content coding and comparing a large number of unstructured "think-aloud" protocols will appreciate the utility of having behaviors classified into countable categories.

Isolating Causal Effects It is a blunt fact of life that even with constant conditions human behavior is quite variable, both within a given subject as well as between subjects. Consequently it is usually not very informative to compare single observations, either from different subjects or even from the same subject in different conditions. In the face of statistical variability between subjects and conditions, a single subject's behavior provides little assurance of the causal impact of the treatment. Investigators are therefore often forced to examine the behavior of groups of subjects (say, ten to twenty or so subjects). In a *between-subjects* experimental design different subjects are tested in each condition and the average scores obtained from the different groups are compared. In *within-subjects* designs each subject is run in all conditions, then the differences in subjects' performance across conditions are examined to see whether the subjects perform better under some conditions than they do under other conditions. (Which type of experimental design is best for a particular situation depends on many practical factors; see Winer 1971 for details.) By testing groups of subjects in either of these arrangements, extraneous sources of variability such as individual differences in abilities or strategies may be expected to cancel out overall, allowing valid comparisons to be made.

But even when groups of subjects are tested, it is not enough to simply observe that the average performance in one condition exceeds that in another, because any such outcome might also have arisen simply by chance. For instance, in a highly variable performance such as reading comprehension or text memory, the fact that subjects score slightly higher in one condition than another could easily be a random, chance outcome. To cope with the difficulties introduced by such variability, social scientists rely on statistical procedures that evaluate observed differences with respect to that behavioral measure's baseline variability. Statistical procedures allow a precise estimate to be made of how likely an apparent effect is to have occurred by chance alone. Only if the probability of a difference that large occurring by chance is very small (by convention less than 5 percent) will investigators reject the null hypothesis of "no effect" and report a "positive" finding (for details see statistics texts such as Winer 1971).

The goal of an experiment is to so arrange circumstances that when interpreting the findings one can exclude all plausible alternative hypotheses (or causes of the effect). Thus to conclude that an observed difference between groups is caused by the experimental manipulation rather than some other, extraneous factor, it is important that the conditions differ *only* in the level of the independent variable. (In the world outside the laboratory of course many factors will vary together, which is why it is difficult to justify causal arguments from informal observations alone.) Experimenters go to great lengths to arrange circumstances so that they can be sure that only the independent variable changes across conditions. Standard precautions include randomly assigning subjects to conditions (or testing each subject in all conditions, when this is possible), not informing subjects fully about the experimenter's hypotheses, using equivalent tests in each condition, and so on. Equating groups can often be difficult simply because we may not know all the factors that might vary and cause experimental subjects' behavior to differ from the control condition. As we learn more about important causative factors for a given performance, the complexity and kinds of controls experimenters must arrange to study a *new* variable grow.

The important factors to control differ somewhat across content areas (language, memory, perception, and the like), and accordingly each has its own standard task configurations and experimental designs. An experimental design is a procedure for assigning treatments (procedures or potential causes) to subjects in such a way that we can reach valid inferences about causal relationships. Designs differ along many dimensions, such as the number of causal factors being studied at once, how many "levels" (or values) of each factor are being studied, and whether subjects are tested in all, some, or only one condition. In turn each standard experimental design calls for a particular type of statistical analysis with which to evaluate its results (for details see Winer 1971).

Coordinating Theory with Observables

Experiments examine the relationships between categories of *observable* events, such as the effects of consuming a stimulant on reading comprehension or the influence of just prior colors on perception of a current color. Many lawful generalizations simply relate categories of observable events; examples of such descriptive laws abound in the physical sciences and are occasionally found in the biological and social sciences. Obviously such empirical regularities are useful for controlling and predicting some behavioral phenomena.

A more cherished goal of most scientists, however, is to be able to explain why the empirical law holds. They usually do this by postulating theoretical constructs that do *not* correspond directly to categories of observable events. For instance, mentalistic constructs such as goals, beliefs, and intentions are not directly observable, but they have strong intuitive appeal and are used frequently in cognitive theorizing. Other common theoretical constructs are memory stores such as short-term and long-term memory, various data structures such as propositions and images, mental processes such as encoding and retrieval, or syntactic and semantic analysis during parsing. None of these are simply "categories of observable events."

Such theoretical constructs provide simple and coherent explanations for a diverse range of empirical phenomena. The goal is to achieve a simpler and more elegant theory than would be possible were scientists to restrict themselves to discussing only categories of observable events. To take just one example, a broad range of cognitive performances are powerfully influenced by the extent to which subjects *attend* to the task at hand. As subjects "pay more attention" to a given task, they usually perform it better. We cannot directly observe attention. However, the construct of attention simplifies a large number of observable relationships. It captures common effects resulting from many dissimilar categories of observable operations, such as orienting instructions, payoffs for good performance, time of day, stimulant drugs, and any other factors that might influence attention.

Positing a link between a theoretical construct and a set of outcomes is obviously more parsimonious than enumerating separate links between many observable independent variables and many dependent variables. It also provides a more *coherent* theory, because the single construct of attention captures the relationship between many categories of observable operations that would not be apparent by simply enumerating them separately. Further the theoretical construct invites extensions; once we learn that some new independent variable affects attention in a particular way, we already know how it will affect the whole range of other behaviors that depend on attention.

Most of the variables of interest to cognitive scientists are unobservable, perhaps because human behavior is so complex that simple descriptive laws are not easily achieved. This fact creates a gap when we wish to check the correspondence between our cognitive theory and human cognition in the laboratory. Because experiments deal with observable events, terms in the theory must be coordinated to observable stimuli, responses, and events in the experimental setting. We can indirectly manipulate a theoretical variable by altering observable factors that are presumed to affect it (for example, induce "thirst" by having the subject eat salty crackers); similarly a theoretical variable can be measured indirectly through the observable behaviors that it affects (for example, the amount of water subjects drink indexes their thirst). In this way observable variables can be used as proxies for unobservable variables in experiments, making experimental testing possible.

To illustrate this process of "operationalizing" theoretical variables, we review a study by Gluck and Bower (1988). They applied a "connectionist" model to the behavior of human subjects learning to examine the medical symptoms displayed by patients and then diagnose them as having one of several diseases. Connectionist models consist of an interconnected collection of neuronlike computing units, typically divided into a sensory input layer, a motor output layer, and zero, one, or more intermediate layers (see figure 7.1). Information in the form of stimulus activation of units passes forward from the input to the output layer via a set of connections. The response of the system to a given input is determined by the weights (amplifier values) of the connections among the various units. The system is trained to respond properly to a set of stimulus patterns by repeatedly presenting the stimuli one at a time and adjusting the weights between units so that the network gives the correct response to that input pattern.

In Gluck and Bower's experiments 20 college-student subjects saw a series of 250 patients, each characterized by one to four medical symptoms (such as runny nose, stomach cramps, or high fever). The subject first classified each patient as having one or the other of two fictitious diseases ("burlosis" or "mydosis"), was next told the correct disease for that patient, and then proceeded to the next patient. Over the course of the experiment the subjects learned the degree to which the four symptoms were more or less diagnostic of the two diseases. At the end of the experiment the subjects directly estimated the conditional probability of each disease given only knowledge that a patient had a specific symptom (without knowing about any other symptoms).

In applying the connectionist theory Gluck and Bower chose the simplest correspondences possible (see figure 7.1). Presentation of each medical symptom in a given patient was coordinated to activation of a corresponding single element in the sensory input layer, so there were four input units in total. Two response output units were postulated,

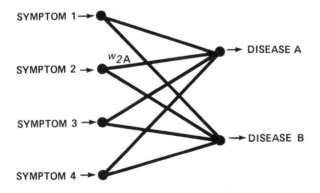

Figure 7.1 A simple connectionist network that learns to diagnose patterns of up to four symptoms as having one of two diseases. The specific w shown denotes the weight of evidence that presence of symptom 2 contributes toward disease A. (From Gluck and Bower 1988. Used with permission.)

corresponding to the two disease categories in the experiment. Each sensory unit was connected directly to both output units, so no intermediate units were assumed. The weights were interpreted as the association strengths from each input unit to each output unit. Each patient corresponded to a pattern of activation (1 or 0) on the four sensory units, which led in turn to a weighted sum of activation on the two response-output ("disease") units. The probability of the subject choosing to classify the patient as having a given disease was assumed to be a logistic function of the difference in activation of the two output units. The more activation on output unit 1 versus 2, the greater the supposed probability that subjects would classify the patient as having disease 1 rather than 2. The theory of Gluck and Bower specified how the connection weights would change trial by trial in adjusting to the corrective feedback. Thus for given symptom-to-disease correlations the theory implied differing strengths for the specific symptom-to-disease connections depending on the training conditions. Gluck and Bower found that the theoretically predicted ordering of association weights was quite accurate across several experiments. That success increased the plausibility of the theory as a whole.

Suppose, however, that the predictions had failed. Then one could question parts of either the theory or the correspondences between theoretical and observable terms set up when applying the theory. Perhaps one sensory unit for each symptom is too simplistic, and we could do better by identifying a symptom with a pattern of activation over a large set of sensory-input units, with different symptoms sharing some input units. Perhaps we need a different output rule or need to postulate one or more layers of hidden units intermediate between the input and output units. Or perhaps the learning rule for adjusting weights trial by trial is wrong and needs to be corrected. Clearly there are many places in the total system where we could assign credit for the failed predictions. Sometimes the misfit can be remedied by altering one coordination. At other times no simple modification in the application seems to rectify the problem, at which point we conclude that the theory is simply not applicable to this situation. Such misfits are often extremely informative, however, in telling us in what way the actual behavior deviates from the idealized system of our model. In any event the applicability of the theory becomes narrowed and its credibility as a whole will be weakened.

The symptom-disease coordination has been described because it illustrates a relatively transparent case. More typical examples of theoretical constructs in cognitive science may seem more complex at first glance (for example, the situational model for a text), but usually reduce upon analysis to similar identifications. All such theoretical concepts must lead to some observational consequences; otherwise they have no empirical cash value. Usually observable indicators relate to a particular theoretical construct; we then try to validate inferences about a theoretical construct or a scenario of unobservable events by searching for *converging evidence* from several indicators or consequences of the construct or event. The more that different indicators agree, the more confidence is justified in our inferences about these unobservable events.

Experiments on Human Cognitive Processes

Experiments on cognition generally observe people's behavior as they are performing a specific task, such as perceiving, learning, judging, or remembering something. Many different tasks are used, but a conventional vocabulary has evolved for describing them. Subjects are presented with a *stimulus* in a particular *task context* and must *respond* to that stimulus in some way. For example, an experimenter might present subjects with line drawings of common objects and instruct them to name each object as rapidly as they can. Each picture serves as a "stimulus" and the subject's "response" is to produce a label for the picture; the instructions subjects have received, as well as background factors such as how fast the stimuli are presented, the method of presentation, and so on, can be regarded as part of the task context. The subjects' responses are jointly determined by the stimulus and the task context; if either of these is changed, say, by presenting a picture of a different object or using different instructions, then the subjects' responses change accordingly.

Since the inception of the information-processing approach, performance in cognitive tasks is commonly described by analogy to a computer program that carries out computations on input data and returns some output as a response. The presented stimulus corresponds to the program input, and the subject's response corresponds to the program output; the subject executes a mental "program" to compute the response from the stimulus. The task context is instrumental in determining the particular program the subject runs on the input. For instance, under one set of instructions a subject might respond to a picture of a dog with the corresponding verbal label; under another set of instructions he or she might judge whether it was the same as or different from some stimulus presented earlier.

Assuming cognitive performance can be represented as a kind of program, several types of questions can be asked about it (see, for example, J. R. Anderson 1987, Marr 1982). First, one can simply ask what *function* the program computes (that is, to characterize its input/output relations) or what are the properties of that function. For example, subjects in a typical psychophysics experiment might be presented with tones of various intensities and be asked to give direct magnitude estimates of the loudness of each. The aim of such experiments is to characterize the function that relates physical intensity to perceived loudness (in fact it is a simple power function; see Stevens 1957). A second question asks about the particular algorithm by which a program function is computed. For example, when subjects multiply two three-digit numbers in their heads, we know that they are computing a multiplication function; what we wish to find out is the mental algorithm by which they compute it and how this algorithm changes with such factors as memory capacity, age, expertise, or intelligence. Because a given function could be computed by any of several algorithms, the cognitive scientist wants to discover which particular algorithm subjects use. For instance, researchers investigating the development of problem-solving skill in such domains as geometry or computer programming usually focus on the particular procedures subjects use to solve problems. Their actual solutions are interesting only to the extent that frequently occurring mistakes provide clues about which problem-solving strategies subjects of a given level of experience tend to use, and what their limitations are. A third question suggested by the computer-program analogy asks about the physical implementation of a given cognitive process in the nervous system. This question has traditionally been regarded as outside the province of cognitive science. As several authors in this book attest, however, cognitive scientists are now beginning to take questions of neural implementation more seriously and to investigate constraints this may place on theorizing at the cognitive level (see, for example, chapter 8 and J. A. Anderson 1983).

Cognitive psychologists believe that, by observing subjects' performance in various laboratory tasks, they can investigate basic properties of human cognition in situations sufficiently simple and transparent that those properties can be revealed. This approach rests on the assumption that humans have a reasonably small set of powerful, general-purpose cognitive operations and capabilities that are applied across a wide variety of situations (see, for example, chapter 2 and Newell and Simon 1972). Probably anyone who thinks that we can have a "science of the mind" must believe something like this. By using relatively simple tasks, it is hoped that these various abilities or operations can be isolated and studied systematically.

It is important, however, to understand that performance in some laboratory tasks often reflects the particular *strategies* subjects use to guide their behavior in that situation, as well as more fundamental cognitive processes. A strategy is like a special-purpose program or sequence of mental operations that the subject constructs to optimize performance in a specific situation. Although the mental components from which such internal programs are built might be basic cognitive structures, the strategies themselves may be quite idiosyncratic and their details may only be relevant to a particular laboratory setting. Because detailed investigation of particular strategies often yields little of general interest, investigators usually attempt to focus on those aspects of task performance that are controlled by basic, or nonstrategic, factors. In such cases the objective is not to fully characterize people's behavior in a specific task situation but to use the task as a window to more fundamental properties of cognition. This approach is similar to analyzing the performance of a particular computer program to discover properties of the language in which it was written or the machine on which it is running, rather than to characterize that program per se.

Interest in strategies can be illustrated with an example. Much of what people do to solve anagram problems and similar brainteasers is highly strategic; to the extent that these strategies are specific to a particular problem domain, they tell us little about human behavior in general. Nevertheless experimenters may use such tasks to investigate general issues in problem solving. For example, people have severe limitations on how much information they can maintain in active memory. These memory limitations are a major cause of subjects' errors; they also constrain the set of acceptable strategies that subjects can use. Anagrams solved "in the head" can be used to study the role of working memory in problem solving by examining which factors affect the number and types of memory-based errors subjects make, how memory aids improve performance, and so on. We can sometimes identify general heuristics subjects use to solve a variety of problems, and these may generalize beyond the simple situations studied in the laboratory.

In some cases cognitive scientists are interested in studying a specific task itself (for example, text editing) rather than merely using it as a means for studying cognition. Educational research on math, reading, human/computer interaction, or applied memory might be seen as attempting to understand and improve skilled performance in particular task domains. Strategies can be of central interest in applied areas because they play such a large role in determining subjects' performance. A variety of techniques for the analysis of strategies has been developed; a detailed treatment is beyond the scope of this chapter, but see Ericsson and Simon 1980 or Sperling and Dosher 1986.

Characterizing Psychological Processes

Decomposing an empirical system into a set of hypothetical related components and then validating this decomposition through experiments is part of the goal of cognitive science. Most cognitive scientists treat the mind as a system that can be decomposed into a collection of more or less separable subsystems. At a general level this decomposition is reflected in the subdisciplines within the field, for example, the study of memory, language, attention, visual perception, reasoning, and emotion. In turn each of these subdisciplines can be decomposed into subdomains within which more elementary theoretical constructs play prominent roles.

Given some proposed theoretical distinction, say, between short-term and long-term memory or between encoding and comparison stages in a recognition memory task, how is one to evaluate the validity of this distinction? The basic criterion, of course, is that two things are meaningfully different if they have different properties. To take an obvious case, it is useful to distinguish between visual and auditory sensory memories because they have different characteristics and function somewhat independently. Unfortunately most of the distinctions that cognitive scientists worry about are considerably less transparent than this example.

It is often difficult to decide whether constructs in two similar theories have the same or different implications. Often the theories are too vague for this issue to be sharply decided. The basic *empirical* criterion is whether or not the proposed components behave sufficiently differently in experiments to justify distinguishing them. This is ascertained by observing whether they are affected by different independent variables or whether they are affected in different ways by the same independent variable. For instance, psychologists often distinguish between recognition and recall as involving different retrieval processes. Part of the argument for this distinction is that the two memory indices are affected in different ways by certain independent variables. For instance, people show better recall for common words but better recognition memory for rare words (Crowder 1976).

A number of experimental methods have evolved for evaluating theoretical constructs and claims in cognitive psychology. To familiarize the reader with the basic logic that underlies these methods, we briefly discuss several of them.

Analyzing Representational Types   A standard issue in cognitive science is to specify the form in which particular information is represented in the mind. One small aspect of this general issue that has been heavily investigated is the way in which a discrete stimulus (such as a word or letter) is represented in memory immediately following its presentation and how the form of this representation changes over time. These analyses assume that perception of a stimulus can be analyzed into a series (or cascade) of successive stages of encoding, with each stage providing a temporary "internal record" of the stimulus that can be read or utilized by other processes. The internal record (or representation) at each stage of the stimulus analysis is called a "code"; the major goal of this research is to describe these internal codes and their properties.

A typical theory (see, for example, Posner 1969) is that a discrete stimulus event first gives rise to a specific sensory code in the affected modality (visual, acoustic, and so forth) and that, depending on instructions, this initial encoding can later give rise to associated secondary or tertiary codes. Thus a visually presented form such as an alphabetic letter may be represented (coded) initially as a visual form, then by its name in a phonemic code, and then perhaps by some further classification (for example, as a type of consonant or vowel). Several codes may simultaneously coexist, but some codes typically become available at an earlier stage of stimulus analysis than do others. Interest usually focuses on discriminating among the various codes that are formed and determining the time at which a particular coding of the stimulus becomes available.

Several techniques have been devised for attacking such questions. Although we will describe their application to simple letter stimuli, the reader should keep in mind that more complex stimuli, such as language samples or pictures of natural scenes, can also be studied using these techniques. A basic method asks subjects to make speeded recognition judgments of identity—that two stimuli are identical (match) at a specified level of description or categorization. Recognition of identity (under a given description) is a basic operation involved in many cognitive tasks. Regardless of the level of description the matching task can always be cast as a question that yields a simple Yes or No answer. By recording how long it takes subjects to answer such questions, we can make inferences about components of the overall recognition process.

One version of the matching task is to decide whether two successive forms are physically identical (for example, AA are, whereas Aa or Ba are not). A second task is to decide whether the two successive forms have the same name (for example, Bb do, whereas AB do not). In the name-identity task the "same" letters can either by physically identical (AA) or not (Aa). In this "same-name" task response time to physically identical pairs (AA's) averages about 70 to 100 milliseconds faster than to pairs having only the same name (Aa's) (Posner and Mitchell 1967). It was thus concluded that subjects were forming a code for the stimulus letters that preserved their physical features and could be used for carrying out a rapid physical match of the second letter to the first.

If the name code becomes available only after the physical code, then it should not affect the speed of processes that use the earlier, physical code. This independence was confirmed in that deciding whether two stimuli are physically different (versus identical) required the same amount of time for same-name letters (Aa, Bb) as for different-name letters (Ab, Ba). Thus the fact that two visual forms had the same name caused no interference whatsoever in deciding that they were not physically identical. Another bit of evidence that the name-code becomes available some time after the physical code comes from examining the kind of similarity that slows down the decisions. Chase and Posner (1965) found that physical-letter-matching speed is much slowed when the nonmatching lures are visually similar (OQ, GC, PR) but not when they have similar-sounding names (BC, DE, VT).

How long is a particular code maintained in active memory? This question can be investigated using the name-matching task. Posner and Keele (1967) imposed a brief delay (from 0 to 2 seconds) between presentation of the first and second letter. The advantage for the physically identical pair, which was about 90 milliseconds when the two letters occurred together (0-second delay), rapidly declines to only a 10-milli-

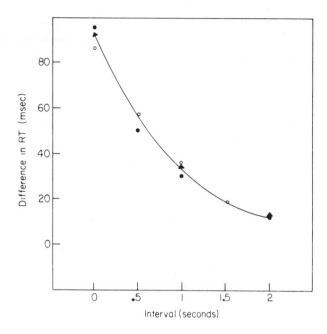

Figure 7.2 Difference in reaction time between name and physical identity "same" responses as a function of the interval between the two letters. The different point symbols represent results obtained under slightly different conditions of presentation of the letter stimuli. (From Posner 1969. Used with permission.)

second advantage by 2 seconds after the presentation of the first stimulus (figure 7.2). The interpretation is that in a name-matching task the subject converts the physical code as quickly as possible into a name code; because it is then no longer being actively maintained, the physical code decays rapidly. Presumably only the name of the first letter remains for comparison with the second letter, so that the advantage for the physical-identity match disappears. Furthermore, if subjects are required to rehearse a short list of letters that are phonemically similar to the first letter of the pair to be tested, then their decision times are slowed substantially. On the other hand this same interfering task produces no impairment when subjects are making physical-identity decisions (Boies, cited in Posner 1969). Thus holding irrelevant phonetic information active in memory interferes with short-term memory for the name of a probe letter but not with its physical code.

These cases illustrate several methods used in analyzing the nature of the memory code (representation) for simple stimulus events. Let us summarize them. We have discussed *judgment times* (for example, that B name-matches b) to infer codes; this method is based on the assumption that retrieval and matching is quicker the more closely the internal representation of the second stimulus matches the memory representation of the first stimulus.

A second set of methods are direct or indirect means of assessing the *similarity* of two or more stimuli after they have been coded in a particular form. Internal representations are selective, leaving out some features of the full stimulus pattern (for example, a city map does not tell us the height and color of buildings). Two stimulus patterns that differ in features that are ignored (or squashed) by the coding scheme will have internal representations that appear more similar than the original full patterns. The trademark of similar stimuli is that they may be confused with one another. Thus one method for studying coding uses *confusion errors* in recall or recognition. For example, letters that have been coded phonemically will be confused in recall with other letters that sound like them. Encoding words and statements in terms of their meaning can lead to *false recognitions* of synonyms or paraphrases similar in meaning.

A third set of techniques exploits the fact that material that is encoded similarly to the target material will create greater *interference* in processing, or in accurately remembering, the target material. For example, people's ability to "shadow" (repeat immediately) one message and ignore a second, simultaneous message depends on their similarity along many perceptual and semantic dimensions, such as their voicing, pitch, source, ear of arrival, and topical overlap. Similarly people's ability to retain a set of target items in short-term memory despite attending to other material is better the more dissimilar the modality and encoding of the interfering material is to the target items.

A fourth method occasionally used to infer similarity of encoding is *clustering* of items in free recall. Free recall refers to unconstrained recall of a set of items in any order as they come to mind. When subjects freely recall a list of presented words that belong to taxonomic categories (names of furniture items, animals, cities, and so on), they tend to cluster (recall together) items belonging to different categories. The assumption is that these words were encoded during the learning phase of the experiment in terms of their meaning and category membership and that these relationships are then used to guide later recall. The method is quite general; in practically any unconstrained recall task subjects will tend to recall and cluster together items that they have encoded in similar ways. This method can be used to detect how subjects have subcategorized different domains of their topical knowledge.

Additive Factors Method
In Posner and Keele's (1967) task, subjects see an item, then after a variable delay they see a second item, which they compare with their memory of the first item. Saul Sternberg (1966, 1967) used a similar task in which a small *set* of items (say, H, P, Z) must be held in memory before the probe item is presented. The subject's task is to compare the probe item to the memory set and decide whether it matches some one of the items in a specified way (for example, has the same name). Sternberg found a nearly linear increase in decision time as the memory

set was increased from 1 to 6 elements. (This number of elements can be maintained errorlessly in short-term memory; with more than 6 elements significant errors occur for once-presented lists.) Much is known about this "memory-scanning" task.

Almost more important than the specific task that he introduced, Sternberg suggested a general experimental logic or method for dissecting the different processes involved in such performances. This is the "additive-factors" method, illustrated in figure 7.3. This schematic diagram depicts a series of stages in the processing of a probe item: first, the probe is encoded in a form suitable for comparison to the memory set, then the items in the memory set are retrieved and compared with the probe, with match or mismatch being decided according to a criterion specified by the experimenter (for example, "same name"). Finally, the response (match or no match) is determined on the basis of the accumulated comparisons. If the stages are executed independently and in series, then the total reaction time (RT) should be the additive sum of the times for each of the stages, that is, total RT = encoding time + comparison time + response time.

The additive-factors method provides a way to decide whether two independent variables that influence overall reaction time do so by affecting the same or different components of the model depicted in figure 7.3. The investigator attempts to manipulate independently the duration of different stages by using several independent variables, each of which affects only a single stage. This should be possible if the stages are really independent in terms of their processing times. Variables that affect the same stage may interact, but variables that affect different stages should have additive effects on total reaction time. (A computer analogy would be that the time to search computer memory for a given datum should be independent of how that statement was input to the CPU, whether from a keyboard, magnetic tape, or from memory.)

Sternberg used the additive-factors method to demonstrate that the several stages in his item-recognition task were independent, in the

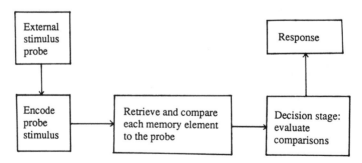

Figure 7.3 A proposed series of mental events that occur during each trial of Sternberg's memory-scanning experiment.

sense that the time required to complete each stage was independent of the time to complete any other stage. As an example, blurring the probe item by presenting it in visual noise increased total reaction times but did so by making the probe harder to encode. The critical point is that this encoding effect was independent of the effect of another variable, namely, memory-set size: degrading the probe had the same slowing effect regardless of how many items were in the memory set; similarly increasing the size of the memory set increased RTs the same amount regardless of whether the probe item was degraded. In other words degrading the probe elevated the intercept of the reaction-time function (by about 100 milliseconds), but did not affect the slope of that function relating reaction time to set size.

On the other hand the presence of interactions among variables signals that they are influencing the same stage in the model. For instance, visual degradation and stimulus probability (of a Yes versus No test probe) interact in their effects on the encoding stage, but neither variable interacts with memory load (Miller and Pachella 1973). This pattern of dissociations supports Sternberg's (1969) claim that probe encoding and memory comparison represent separate, independent stages in the overall recognition process. He argued that the existence of independent stages is empirically established by finding variables that affect each stage: variables from the same set should interact, but those from different sets should have additive effects. This method can be used generally in research on reading or memory retrieval, whenever a theory suggests a serial-stage analysis of some cognitive task.

The additive-factors method is particularly interesting because it provides an elegant and powerful technique for disentangling the component stages of a serial process. But its power carries the price of specialization, which is its somewhat limited applicability; many processes of interest do not fit the simple model of a sequence of clearly independent mental operations. Other methods have been devised for studying concurrent processes; we now discuss one of them.

Dual Tasks One of the fundamental propositions of cognitive science is that the *processing resources* of the mind (or any other cognitive system) are *limited*. The attention (processing resources) required by a task depends on its complexity, its points of decisional uncertainty, and how well practiced it is. It is assumed that the mind has available only a fixed amount of processing resources (analogous to computing cycles per second), and that we allocate more or less to the several tasks in which we are concurrently engaged so as to optimize the utility of our overall performance (see Sperling and Dosher 1986). The resource-allocation models are similar to schedules for prioritizing and assigning CPU cycles to different jobs in a time-sharing computer system.

Dual-task experiments are used to investigate how much processing capacity is required for particular tasks, and how people allocate resources among tasks depending on payoffs. If performance on a given task gets worse the less attention is allotted to it, then we can use that task as an *indirect* measure of how much processing is required by another, concurrent task. Consider an example: as subjects read a text on which their comprehension will be tested, they may be asked simultaneously to listen for a soft tone that comes on at random, unpredictable intervals as they read. When they hear the tone, they are to press a button as quickly as possible. Their detection and average reaction time to the probe tone while reading are compared with those measures obtained when subjects are not reading but only listening for the tone. The increased RT during reading is presumed to be an indirect measure of the processing resources required to read and comprehend the text. If the text is difficult, involving many unfamiliar ideas and complex arguments, people will have to process it more deeply for comprehension, and consequently their signal-detection performance will suffer, as measured by their reaction times to a probe tone (see Kahneman 1973). Such dual-task experiments are common because cognitive scientists are often interested in how much "mental effort" is required by a given task. The logic and pitfalls of the procedure are detailed in Sperling and Dosher 1986.

Signal-Detection Theory In the aforementioned tasks the subject is trying to detect a weak signal, such as a soft tone or faint light. Accordingly this is an appropriate place to mention the standard theory of signal detection, which is widely used in studies of perception, discrimination, and memory. The theory best applies to experiments using discrete trials, on each of which a specified signal is either presented or not; the subject indicates at the end of each trial whether he or she thinks the signal was presented. In the paradigmatic case the signal is a simple tone added to white noise; on no-signal trials the white noise is presented alone. The experimental variables in such tasks are the intensity of the signal relative to the noise, the proportion of signal versus no-signal trials, the payoffs for correct responses, and the penalties for errors.

The theory of signal detection derives from statistical decision theory (Chernoff and Moses 1959, Wald 1950): each trial type, either signal-plus-noise or noise-alone, is assumed to give rise to a collection of internal sensory samples that are distributed according to normal bell-shaped probability curves, with the signal-plus-noise distribution having the higher mean. Subjects are presumed to reach their decision on a given trial by comparing their sensory sample to a criterion and deciding "Yes; signal" if the sample exceeds the criterion and "No; no-signal" otherwise. For given signal and noise distributions the choice of a criterion determines both the probability that a signal will be detected and that no-signal trials will be correctly identified. The criterion is under the subject's control. As the subject shifts the criterion, the probabilities of correct hits and rejections are constrained to covary; for instance, if the criterion is lowered to detect weaker signals, the person will perforce begin making more "false positives," misidentifying noise-alone trials as "signal" trials. The important point is that perceptual sensitivity (the difference between the means of the two underlying distributions) depends on both performance indices (correct Yes and No responses), and the theory tells us how to carry out this estimation. For details, see Green and Swets (1966).

The framework of signal-detection theory is quite general, and it has been applied to a large number of judgment tasks in which subjects must discriminate among two or more classes of stimuli. Included would be discriminating any property of two auditory or two visual stimuli, the length of two time intervals, the correct pronunciation of two syllables, the genuine versus counterfeit nature of an author's writings, suicide notes, paintings, and so on. The framework has been extended especially to recognition-memory judgments, in which after exposure to a list of learning items, the subject judges a series of other items, deciding whether each is a repeat (or copy) of one of the learning items or is just a distracting lure (Parks 1966). In those cases the extent to which certain lures are "falsely recognized" as repeated old items tells us much about the way the initially learned items were coded and represented in memory.

Having introduced several general methods, we now look in detail at more specific methods in particular content areas. The major content areas of cognitive science comprise studies of perception, attention, learning, memory, skill learning, categorization, language processing, semantic (or world) knowledge, and problem solving. For specific experimental techniques in each one, see Kling and Riggs 1971 and Puff 1982, for example. We limit our discussion to just two of the domains, namely, studies of memory and of language processing because these comprise major foci of interest within cognitive science. Many of the issues and techniques from these two research domains can also be applied to other content areas.

7.2 Experimental Methods I: Learning and Memory

Key Issues in Memory Research

One set of research questions about memory concerns "implementational" issues (following J. R. Anderson 1987)—that is, the fundamental nature of the brain's basic memory mechanisms, regardless of the type of task or materials. Such research focuses on the basic processes for *encoding* information into memory and later *retrieving* it when needed, the nature of the *representational codes* in which this information is stored, whether memory is a unitary system or a collection of separate, more specialized subsystems, and similar issues. Also included here is the general topic of inductive learning, covering such diverse topics as classical (Pavlovian) and instrumental (operant) conditioning, category learning, and social perception, all of which focus on discovering principles that determine how people abstract general knowledge from individual experiences.

A second major research area aims to characterize people's *knowledge* of the world—the organization of that knowledge in memory; how it is derived from experience; how sensory, motor, and conceptual features of the knowledge are interrelated; and so on. Much recent research on such topics as the structure of natural categories (see, for example, Rosch 1973, Smith and Medin 1981), schemas (see, for example, Bartlett 1932, Rumelhart and Ortony 1977, Brewer and Treyens 1981), and scripts (see, for example, Schank and Abelson, 1977, Bower, Black, and Turner 1979, Graesser, Woll, Kowalski, and Smith 1980) falls under this heading.

A third set of topics relates to more "applied" issues, such as educational tutoring, strategies for improving memory performance, the effects of various drugs on learning and memory, aging and memory, and so on. Of course findings in these areas frequently have strong theoretical implications.

Characterizing Memory Experiments

Memory tasks generally involve three phases: (1) an *acquisition* or encoding phase, during which the person first encounters the material to be remembered, with or without an intention to remember it; (2) a *retention* phase, during which the material must be maintained in memory, often while the subject is engaged in some other activity; and (3) a testing or *retrieval* phase, during which the subject may retrieve the material from memory to perform some task, for example, to judge whether a particular test item had occurred in a set studied during the acquisition phase.

A typical memory task that illustrates these three phases is the "list-learning" task. Here subjects are presented with a series of items—words, pictures, number-letter pairs, and the like—and are asked to commit them to memory. They then rest or engage in some distracting activity for awhile, after which they are tested on their memory of the original list. This test can take a variety of forms, depending on the experimenter's aims and the nature of the stimuli being used. Common examples are *recall* tests, in which subjects are asked to reproduce the items from the list, and *recognition* tests, in which they are asked to discriminate those test items that were present on the original list from some lures (distractor items) that were not.

A surprising number of issues can be studied with different variations on this simple task. Consider just a few examples. One task, called context discrimination, is the experimental analog of remembering where or in what context one has experienced overlapping collections of objects (for example, which friends were met at which parties, which furniture was seen at which houses). In the laboratory several different lists of items are presented, and subjects are later asked to judge in which list or lists a given test item had occurred (see Anderson and Bower 1974). By varying such factors as the similarity of the list contexts, how closely in time they were presented, and in how many contexts a given item occurred we can learn much about how people reconstruct contexts in which they learned something. A second illustration examines people's learning of words or statements of differing emotional connotations, depending on the learner's current emotional state. Thus when presented with a mixed list of pleasant and unpleasant words or statements, people who are feeling temporarily happy or sad will learn more of those items that are congruent with their emotional state (see Bower 1981). As a third illustration, list learning has been a useful method for comparing the efficacy of various "mnemonic strategies." We can compare memory performance of subjects who have studied the same list of items using different mnemonic techniques (see Bower 1970).

These examples illustrate the versatility of the simple list-learning task. Moreover the basic acquisition-retention-retrieval schema can be varied to produce many useful tasks. Let us consider some of these.

Memory Tasks

Recall Tasks In a recall test subjects are asked to *reproduce* the items they encountered during the acquisition period, in response to some cue. This cue may range in specificity from quite vague to a modest hint, up to one that is highly detailed and specific. In general the more specific the cue, the better subjects' performance will be. Cue specificity can be illustrated by experiments in which subjects learn lists containing words grouped by taxonomic categories (for example, several names of fruit, followed by several names of animals, city names, and so on). When later asked to write all the items they can remember, subjects will perform more poorly than if they are provided with specific category names as cues (so-called cued recall; see Crowder 1976). The effect of cue specificity is similarly illustrated by the beneficial effect of hints on our performance in memory-based brainteasers such as crossword puzzles.

The most straightforward way to analyze recall is simply to compare subjects' overall performance (that is, mean percent of items correctly recalled) across the different experimental conditions and note whether they differ significantly. But a variety of more subtle analytic techniques is often required to interpret the results. One such procedure (mentioned previously) analyzes subjects' recall for their tendency to recall together in sequence ("cluster") items on the basis of their thematic or taxonomic relations. This tendency can be exploited to discover the kinds of interitem relations subjects find most obvious, because meaningful relations often serve as a basis for clustering. Another informative class of errors, as mentioned previously, are recall *confusions*. For example, subjects may mix up the serial order of two list items or mistakenly produce a synonym of a word or a paraphrase of a statement from the acquisition list. The nature of these confusions can reveal much about how subjects represent the stimulus materials in memory.

An often informative by-product of recall tests is a set of items that subjects have mistakenly produced that were not presented during acquisition. Such *intrusion* errors often result from subjects' guessing strategies; having forgotten, they then produce items that seem likely to have been on the original list but were not in fact presented there. When witnesses to crimes (real or staged) are asked to recall the events they saw, their intrusion errors can create serious complications (Loftus 1979). Intrusions in an experiment can similarly complicate comparisons across different conditions, because frequent intrusions make it difficult to estimate subjects' memory merely by counting the number of list items they reproduce at testing. To obtain an accurate estimate of subjects' memory, the intrusions must be subtracted from the overall score to correct for guessing. Intrusions are not all bad news, however, they are often a useful source of information in themselves. Frequently they reflect the background knowledge subjects use to reconstruct the earlier learning episode. For instance, when subjects recall stories about scripted event sequences, such as doing laundry or eating in a restaurant, they often intrude descriptions of events that are central to the goal of the script but were not mentioned in the text (Bower et al. 1979; Graesser et al. 1980). This indicates that people's memory for scripted events is organized around the characters' goals satisfied by the scripted activities.

Recognition Tasks   In recognition-memory tests subjects are presented with a series of test items and for each item must judge whether it was presented during an earlier acquisition period. In other words they must *discriminate* probe items that were originally presented ("targets") from those that were not ("distractors" or "foils"). Whereas in recall tasks subjects are asked to produce the previously learned items in response to some contextual cue, such as "recall all the words from the first list" or "recall the name of the man married to Sally," this situation is reversed in recognition. In recognition subjects are provided with an item and must attempt to remember its association to the acquisition context. This yes-no decision is often supplemented with a confidence rating, say, on a three-point scale. The subjects indicate whether they have high, moderate, or low confidence in the accuracy of their yes-no decisions. Such confidence ratings often provide more differentiating information than the simple yes-no decision alone.

A related format uses multiple-choice recognition tests: presented with a set composed of the old item and N distractors, subjects try to select the one that they remember as having been presented during the acquisition phase. Even more discriminating information can be obtained by having subjects rank order all the alternatives in the set in terms of their likelihood of being the old item. The experimenter can then calculate the average rank of the old items in subjects' rememberings.

Several factors influence how well subjects perform in recognition tests. One of these is the similarity of the distractor foils to the targets; the more similar the incorrect alternatives are to the correct one, the more difficult the test becomes. It is much easier, for example, to pick out the correct value of pi from the set 48.0, 3.1416, and 6.3842 than from the set 3.4116, 4.3146, and 3.1416.

Performance in yes-no recognition is also influenced by subjects' beliefs about the proportion of old (target) versus new (distractor) items on the test and the relative payoffs for positive versus negative responses (Parks 1966). These factors mainly influence subjects' tendency to guess old or new when they are uncertain about a test item. Obviously if a subject is unsure about an item but knows that most of the items on the test are targets, a positive response is the best bet. Similarly if a larger reward is given for every correct old response, whereas incorrect old responses receive less penalty, a bias toward old responses would be justified. Such factors must be controlled or equated across conditions when designing recognition tests.

As noted before, when intrusion errors are plentiful on recall tests we cannot use the "percent correctly recalled" as a direct index of subjects' memory. A similar problem exists with recognition tests. Subjects' positive responses will be composed of both correct olds ("hits") and erroneous olds ("false alarms"). Similarly the set of negative responses will consist of both correct and incorrect negatives ("correct rejections" and "misses," respectively). None of these response categories, taken alone, tells the whole story about subjects' memory because they are all determined both by subjects' actual memory for the material and their guessing strategies. The mere fact that a subject has a very high hit rate, for example, is not in itself an indication of good memory; it may just reflect the subject's bias to respond old to any item he or she is uncertain about.

This situation requires a method for separating the contributions of subjects' guessing strategies from their actual memory for the material. One such procedure is based on signal-detection theory, which was introduced previously (Parks 1966). Given that some assumptions about underlying familiarity distributions of old and new items are satisfied, signal-detection theory can be used to obtain separate estimates of each subject's response bias and memory sensitivity. For a detailed treatment of signal-detection theory, see Green and Swets 1966.

In addition to analyzing subjects' *accuracy* in recognition tasks, it is useful to measure the *speed* with which they respond to each test item.

This reaction time (RT) measure makes it possible to detect differences among conditions even when subjects are near ceiling levels (100 percent) on accuracy. If subjects respond more rapidly to one type of item than to another, we can assume that these items are more accessible in memory. This property makes the RT measure ideal for studying memory retrieval. If subjects perform with 100 percent recognition accuracy across all experimental conditions, then we know that differential RTs are not caused by subjects' having failed originally to encode more of the items in one condition than another. Rather the difference must be caused by one type of item being easier to retrieve from memory.

Whenever accuracy is less than perfect, however, the experimenter must be alert to the possibility of speed-accuracy trade-offs, in which subjects tolerate more errors in one condition to go faster. This trade-off, familiar to all typists, is suspected whenever subjects are faster in condition 1 than in condition 2, but show greater accuracy in condition 2 than in condition 1. Such trade-offs can occur if subjects adopt a more conservative response strategy for probes in condition 2, causing them to slow down and exercise greater care than they do with probes from condition 1. Speed-accuracy trade-offs can make the results of an experiment considerably more difficult to interpret. Sperling and Dosher (1986) provide an introductory discussion of correcting for speed-accuracy trade-offs.

Judgment Tasks   In addition to recognition-memory judgments, several other judgment tasks are commonly used to study memory issues. For instance, subjects can be asked to judge which of two items occurred more *recently* or more *frequently* during an acquisition period, whether the items were printed in uppercase or lowercase letters, were in French or English, what *order* they were presented in, and so on. Such memory judgments can be used to uncover facts about subjects' memory not easily obtainable by recognition or recall measures. For example, the factors that affect subjects' ability to keep track of an item's frequency of occurrence can reveal much about how separate presentations of an item are represented in memory (Hintzman 1976).

Judgment tasks are often used to study the structure of people's world knowledge. For instance, Rosch (1973, 1975, 1977) and Rosch and Mervis (1975) studied the structure of people's knowledge of natural categories (for example, plants, animals) by asking subjects to judge which instances are more representative or *typical* members of these categories. They found that membership in most natural categories appears to be a matter of graded degree rather than an all-or-none relation; this result challenges the Aristotelian view that categories have rigid definitions in terms of necessary and sufficient attributes (see, for example, Rosch 1973, Smith and Medin 1981). Judgments of the *similarities* of pairs of stimuli drawn from a larger set can be subjected to various analyses, such as multidimensional scaling (see, for example, Shepard 1980, Shepard and Arabie 1979) or cluster analyses (see, for example, Sattath and Tversky 1977), which help investigators identify the major features or dimensions in subjects' internal representations of these stimuli. These topics comprise large research areas of their own, and a detailed treatment of them is beyond the scope of this chapter.

So far we have described several important performance indexes used to assess subjects' knowledge during the retrieval phase of a memory experiment. We now turn to discussion of task factors that operate before testing, that have their influence during the acquisition and retention periods.

Transfer Tasks It is a truism that all learning takes place within a context of knowledge previously acquired, and that this strongly influences how various events are interpreted and remembered. The main purpose of *transfer* tasks is to study the effects of knowledge acquired before (or after) a given learning episode on what is learned during that episode, and how well this learning is retained over time. Because transfer from previous or subsequent learning is an important factor in any learning or retention situation, psychologists have devoted much time to the careful study of this topic.

One situation that illustrates many transfer issues is learning to use a new computer text editor (Anderson and Singley 1987). Imagine recruiting a group of subjects (say, from a secretarial school) with no prior experience with text editors and teaching them first to use one editor (say, Wordstar) to a satisfactory degree of proficiency and then training them to use a second editor (say, E-macs). What performance could we expect on the second transfer task? First, the time subjects require to learn the second editor should be greatly reduced relative to the time they took to learn the first. This is because much of what was learned in mastering the first editor could be directly "transferred" to the second. These common components include not only commands to achieve specific goals but also an entire superordinate goal structure shared by the two text editors—what an editor can do, how to sequence parts of an editing plan, what plans to use in familiar situations such as deleting or adding pieces of text, concepts such as accessing and saving a file, and so on. These are the components common to any text editor because they characterize the general problem of generating and revising text. Not only would learning a first editor prepare learners for the second (a "proactive" effect in the sense that the influence acts forward in time), but practicing the second editor should maintain or improve the retention of those features it shares with the first (a "retroactive" effect).

Not all of the influences are expected to be mutually beneficial, however. If the two editors require different keystrokes or different sequences of basic commands to achieve the same goal, then specific *negative transfer* is likely to arise at just those points of conflict during learning of the second editor. It is as though the specific habits learned with the first editor come to mind at the moment the learner wants to achieve a certain goal (for example, "delete the right side of this line"), and these habits get in the way and interfere with learning and performing the correct habits for the second editor. This negative transfer at the level of specific keystrokes, however, is usually not sufficient to overcome the large positive transfer at the global level of goal-structures common to the two text editors.

If sufficient time is allowed to pass after learning the second editor, subjects who are brought back to the laboratory and tested will demonstrate forgetting for certain aspects of both editors, especially those different commands or procedures that gave rise to negative transfer during learning of the second editor. The forgetting of some previously learned material caused by learning similar (but not identical) material later is called *retroactive interference;* the forgetting of later material caused by prior learning of similar material is called *proactive interference.* If we examine only the specific parts of the two editors that differ, then the forgetting of these parts would probably be far greater in a group learning both editors than in a control group learning only one. Such interference-caused forgetting has been much studied by psychologists, especially in the so-called verbal learning tradition (see Cofer 1971, Postman 1971).

This example illustrates several points. The first is simply the important role of transfer in any learning situation, especially the effects of prior knowledge on new learning. Even learning of the first editor was doubtless influenced by subjects' general knowledge about how to achieve editing goals, write papers, use computer terminals, and so on. A second point is that transfer can occur at many levels of abstraction, from high-level goal or plan structures to specific microlevel details. Third, transfer can either facilitate learning or impair it, and both effects can operate at different levels simultaneously (for example, global versus detailed). On one hand using prior knowledge as "scaffolding" for new learning underlies our ability to learn efficiently. On the other hand negative transfer (interference) is considered by many to be the primary cause of forgetting in humans. Fourth, transfer tends to operate mainly across corresponding "roles" in different knowledge systems. For instance, changing the "line-delete" command across text editors will affect performance on just that command but not on other commands such as saving a file or advancing the cursor. In fact because the pattern of transfer observed between two (or more) bodies of knowledge depends on how they are represented in memory, transfer studies can be used as diagnostic "microscopes" for studying knowledge representation.

Whereas readers may be personally familiar with phenomena alluded to in the text-editing example, psychologists studying transfer have focused on simpler cases of associative learning to obtain a clearer view of the phenomena. Thus transfer has been studied most intensively at the level of specific associations (relations) between pairs of explicitly presented, unrelated items. This is usually done using a task in which subjects learn sets of such pairs and are later asked to recall the second item in each pair given the first as a cue. An example is recalling the specific key that must be pressed to execute a particular text-editing command. By presenting several such sets (lists) of pairs and manipulating how the pairs in each list relate to those in the others, one can study many aspects of associative transfer.

To illustrate this, one might ask subjects to learn a list of carefully controlled text-editing commands, such as "line delete → f12" and "cursor right → control-r." Let us denote the pairings learned on the first list generically as A-B pairs, where A is the abstract command goal and B refers to the particular key or keys that must be pressed to execute it. After this list of pairs is learned to a satisfactory level, a second list of commands, supposedly from a different editor, would be learned. The pairs on the second list may bear one of several relations to the pairs on the first list: (1) A-B pairs, consisting of repetitions of items from the first list; (2) A-D pairs, in which a cue term (command goal) from the first list is retained but the response (keys to be pressed) is altered (for example, "line delete → f4"); and (3) C-D pairs, in which neither the cue nor the response terms were presented on the first list; both are unique to the second list. After second-list learning and a specified retention interval have been completed, memory for either list can be tested by asking questions such as, How do you execute a line delete in the first editor?

Most of the forms of transfer that would result from learning two text editors could be studied with this task, although the units of transfer would be simple keystroke associations rather than high-level structural elements. When commands from the first list are repeated on the second (A-B, A-B condition), positive transfer should result. In the A-B, A-D condition, learning the A-D command on the second list should cause retroactive interference in recalling the A-B association from the first list. Prior learning of A-B should also cause negative transfer in how rapidly A-D is learned and proactive interference with subjects' ability to recall A-D later on. Novel commands in the second list (C-D condition) and first-list commands not repeated on the second list would serve as control associations against which transfer would be judged negative or positive by comparison.

The items used in such "paired-associate" experiments can be any material that subjects perceive and encode into memory as units or "chunks." We used text-editing commands in our example, but practically any items can be used—words, letters, pictures, numbers, subjects and predicates of sentences, and so forth (Cofer 1971).

The advantage of having subjects learn associations between explicitly presented items is that we remove uncertainty about *what* subjects are learning and thus can focus attention on how such learning takes place and how it is affected by transfer. By studying transfer in situations in which it is clear what the cue and response items are, psychologists acquire basic information helpful in studying transfer in cases in which it is not completely obvious how to characterize what subjects are learning. Many realistic learning situations are examples of such cases.

Transfer tasks can also be used to study the acquisition of generalized schemas, which are clusters of interrelated properties. As an illustration suppose that subjects view a series of photographs of unfamiliar insectlike creatures that vary in their size, color, wing markings, shape and so on. After examining a given instance for several seconds, subjects would try to draw it accurately from memory. Over a series of trials we would find two distinct trends in their recalls. First, across trials subjects will improve because they are learning the "conceptual macrostructure" or "slots" that characterize the population of insects. For example, they would learn to include legs, wings, and antennae drawn in particular relationships, as well as constant values of any of the attributes from this set (for example, these insects have six legs, orange wings, and so on). Figure 7.4 depicts an illustrative memory schema. Second, as subjects examine successive exemplars that differ

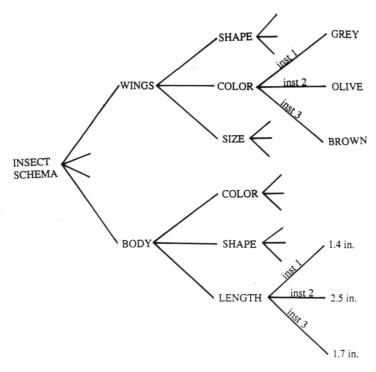

Figure 7.4 Part of a schema representing some of the commonalities and differences among several instances. Exposure to multiple instances (denoted inst 1, inst 2, and inst 3) increases the availability from memory of the superordinate attributes (for example, wings, body) and their interrelations, but causes interference among multiple values of the same attribute (for example, brown or gray wings).

in the values of various attributes, the potential for proactive interference increases so that subjects become more likely to err in recalling the specific details of the most recent insect they have seen (see figure 7.4, Bellezza and Bower 1986, Bower 1974, Thorndyke and Hayes-Roth 1979).

Variations of this schema-abstraction experiment could be conducted with materials from many interesting domains, such as routinized procedures or event sequences, pictures or descriptions of scenes or objects, software packages, series of physics problems that share a common "solution algorithm," and so forth. Many training factors can be varied in such domains to note how the schema acquired becomes attuned to the conditions of learning. Such experiments provide a window to the processes by which people learn and use complex domain knowledge.

Concept-Learning Tasks So far we have mainly discussed rote memory, that is, people's ability to retrieve information from memory in more or less the same form in which it was originally encoded. Although rote memorization is an important topic, it hardly exhausts interesting methods used in studies of learning and memory. We now turn to the topic of *induction* or *generalization*, especially as it has been studied experimentally in *concept-learning* tasks.

A *concept* can be thought of as an internal summary or model that captures some of the commonalities that exist across a particular collection of stimulus patterns or situations. A concept can also be thought of as a "decision rule" for discriminating members from nonmembers. We will use the term *category* to refer to the set of stimuli that are instances of a particular concept. Thus our concept of dogs is our model of what dogs are like; the category "dogs" is the set of objects to which this model applies. Philosophers refer to these as the intension and extension of the concept, respectively.

In concept-learning experiments we examine how subjects learn and apply fairly simple artificial concepts in the laboratory. The goal is to identify general principles that characterize inductive learning across a variety of situations. The prototypical concept-learning experiment has two phases. During the *training* phase subjects are taught to classify a set of stimuli into members and nonmembers of the category. (Actually subjects are usually taught two or more concepts at once, but for simplicity we restrict discussion to the single-concept case). In the *transfer* phase subjects are given new stimuli to classify. The way subjects classify the stimuli in the transfer phase can reveal much about the concept model (or rule) they learned during the training phase. The training and transfer phases need not be explicitly separated. They can be combined by presenting unfamiliar stimuli at several points during the training phase so that subjects' knowledge of the concept is tested as they progress toward learning it.

As noted, training usually involves presenting subjects with a series of stimuli, some of which are members of the category and some not. On each trial subjects decide whether or not the stimulus is a member of the category. The experimenter then gives the subjects "feedback" telling them whether their judgment was correct. Such trials are repeated until the subject achieves some criterion level of performance, or until the entire stimulus set has been presented for a specified number of cycles. The usual performance indexes for this task are the number of errors before learning and the number of training instances required before a subject learns the concept; a derivative index is the proportion of subjects who learn the concept within the allotted trials. These indicators of learning difficulty are influenced by many variables in the induction situation, allowing us to draw inferences about the learning process.

Practically any type of concept can be studied using some variation of this basic procedure. For instance, many studies have investigated how people infer concepts based on simple rules such as (for geometric shapes) "all members are blue and square, with other attributes free to vary." One can also investigate concepts that are probabilistic or "fuzzy," which specify a set of characteristics that most instances will possess, but none of which are individually necessary for category membership. Most "natural" concepts of everyday experience are of this type (Rosch 1973, Wittgenstein 1953). A common type of stimulus used to study fuzzy concepts in the laboratory are categories of fictitious diseases; such diseases are characterized by a typical set of diagnostic symptoms, but not all of these symptoms are necessarily present in any particular case of the disease.

Depending on the aspect of inductive learning under investigation, the features or attributes by which subjects classify the stimuli can be made more or less obvious. For instance, when teaching subjects to classify hypothetical patients as instances or noninstances of a particular disease, the features of each patient are obvious, namely, his or her symptoms. But in other cases the features can be made quite inconspicuous. Subjects can learn to classify abstract paintings on the basis of their style or the artist who created them, they can learn to discriminate the age of different types of wines, and so on. People have remarkable and little-understood abilities to learn categories of such stimuli, even though the cues they use to do so may be extremely subtle. This type of research often focuses on how subjects discover diagnostic cues with sufficient experience, despite the fact that naive observers are at a loss to identify them (for a review of perceptual learning, see Gibson 1969). Often the experts themselves cannot identify or describe the subtle cues that control their discriminative responses (see Lewicki 1986).

One topic of theoretical interest is to characterize what sort of training is required to learn different kinds of concepts. Some types of concepts are learned easily, even in the absence of explicit feedback from a teacher; these concepts simply "pop out" of one's experience with instances. These concepts have the sort of regularities or correlated features that our mental apparatus is designed to pick up easily. Other concepts are learned only with great difficulty or not at all. For example, people are poor at learning *exclusive disjunctive* concepts, which are defined by such rules as "all members have either feature X or feature Y but not both." Characterizing which factors make a concept easy or hard to learn tells us much about our inductive mechanisms.

During the transfer phase subjects see series of stimuli, some from the training phase and some not previously presented, and are asked to decide whether each stimulus is a member of the category. These are usually designed to test various hypotheses regarding what subjects learned about the category during the previous training phase. For example, by comparing how subjects respond to new versus old instances of the category, one can evaluate the contributions of rote memory for specific instances versus the induction of a general concept. If subjects can classify familiar training instances, but perform at chance when attempting to classify new stimuli, it is reasonable to infer that during training they simply memorized which stimuli were members and which were not. On the other hand if subjects are equally proficient at classifying both new and old stimuli, then it is plausible that they induced a general concept or classification rule during the training phase. Now one can argue in such cases that subjects respond to new examples not by a rule but by their similarity to preceding examples stored in memory, (see, for example, Hintzman 1986, Medin and Schaffer 1978). Nonetheless, the ability to classify new stimuli at least demonstrates subjects' ability to *apply* to novel cases whatever they learned during training.

For some types of concepts measures other than classification may be used. For instance, if subjects learned some procedural concept during the training phase, such as a programming construct like FOR or WHILE loops in Pascal, we might test subjects' ability to apply these concepts to solve actual programming problems rather than test the subjects' ability to classify program-examples of WHILE loops.

Sometimes it is useful to ask subjects to report verbally on any learning strategies they might have used, the attributes they attended to, and so on. The more reliable verbal reports refer to concurrent mental processes; retrospective reports suffer from distortions created by forgetting and hindsight rationalizations (Ericsson and Simon 1980). Verbal reports cannot be taken as a direct readout of what subjects are actually doing to learn the concept; often people believe they are responding to completely different factors than those that are actually affecting their behavior (see Lewicki 1986 and Nisbett and Wilson 1977 for some interesting examples). Often people simply don't know how they have learned something. For instance, when learning a tennis forehand (which we might consider a "motor concept"), we might not really have much explicit, verbalizable knowledge of what is being learned; the same is probably the case for expert wine tasters, art critics, medical X-ray interpreters, and so on. But it may be just as important to know that people *do not* have introspective access to their inductive learning processes in some circumstances as to know that they do have in other circumstances. This information would allow inferences to be made about what other factors (for example, conscious learning strategies) would affect learning.

Studies of categorization share many features with perceptual studies of pattern recognition. In such studies interest often centers on how accurately or rapidly the subject can identify or categorize a given stimulus pattern when it is presented under degraded conditions—for example, for short durations with low signal-noise contrast. For review of experimental methods specific to investigations of pattern recognition, the reader should consult such texts as Sekular and Blake 1985 or Kling and Riggs 1971.

Knowledge-Based Learning Tasks   The previous section described techniques for studying how people induce simple concepts under controlled laboratory conditions. We now discuss methods for investigating the structure of people's knowledge about *real-world* categories of objects, events, social groups, and so on. Because many performances of interest to cognitive scientists (for example, language use, reasoning, inference, and the like) depend on the application of such knowledge, advances here can help advance these other areas as well.

By investigating knowledge that subjects already have rather than studying artificial laboratory concepts, investigators surrender control over many important variables relating to the conditions under which the knowledge was acquired, the nature of that knowledge, and so on. Although this increases the difficulty of designing and interpreting such research, these difficulties can sometimes be offset by the advantages gained by analyzing complex concepts that people have learned in realistic contexts. Despite the difficulties and the newness of this research area, several useful experimental methods have already evolved.

Research in this area usually involves two or more steps. First, subjects' intuitive knowledge about the concepts under study are systematically collected. For example, a group of subjects might be asked to list the events that typically occur during routine activities, such as doing their laundry or eating at a restaurant (Bower et al. 1979, Graesser et al. 1980). Alternatively subjects might be asked to rate a number of such events along various dimensions such as their probability of occurrence or their centrality to the activity, their distinctiveness, and so on (see, for example, Galambos and Rips 1982). These ratings can then be used to establish different categories of materials—say, low-centrality versus high-centrality events in the script—which can be correlated with differences in subjects' performance in later memory tasks using these materials.

A typical experiment of this type would present subjects with several passages describing different stereotyped event sequences, social groups, personality types, physical layouts, and the like and later test their memory for these passages. Subjects might be asked to recall the passages or to write summaries of them. Recognition tests are also frequently used; here the subject reads some statements and judges whether each one appeared in the original passage (one can test either verbatim or gist memory).

In such experiments the errors subjects make on the memory test are often of primary interest. To illustrate this, consider a task in which subjects read narratives describing characters eating at a restaurant (a "script" of Schank and Abelson 1977). When their memories are inexact, people believe that events rated as highly central or "typical" for a given script (such as ordering a meal when eating in a restaurant) were probably presented in the original passage. Thus they will often produce or falsely recognize such highly typical items even when they were not actually mentioned in the passages (see, for example, Graesser et al. 1980). In contrast memory discrimination is much better for "low-typicality" items or (especially) for items that violate subjects' expectations about the topic of the passage. Such findings provide clues about what subjects attend to as they read the passages, how the new information is integrated into previous knowledge, and how this knowledge is applied to reconstruct the episode later during testing.

After finding that some factor such as the "typicality" or "centrality" of events in a script-based passage affects subjects' memory, a next likely project might be to determine the locus of this effect. It could arise during encoding, for example, by subjects attending more to one type of event than another; or the performance difference could arise at retrieval, when subjects use general knowledge to reconstruct gaps in their memory. If the phenomenon is multiply determined, then the factors operating during different stages of memory can be teased apart.

Several techniques can help determine which stage an independent variable influences. One of these is to measure subjects' reading speed for each line of text. If subjects spend more time reading one type of statement than another (say, sentences describing unpredictable versus predictable events), then we may infer that they are paying more attention to, thus encoding more deeply, that type of item. Such an attentional bias could easily influence later memory performance.

A second method for detecting attentional biases at encoding involves *forcing* one group of subjects to attend equally to all items and comparing their memory performance to another group of subjects who are allowed to allocate attention to different parts of the material in any way they

Experimental Methods in Cognitive Science

wish. If this manipulation eliminates (or reduces) memory differences observed in the "free-choice" condition, we would infer that differences were wholly or partly due to attentional factors.

Other methods can be used to assess factors at work during retrieval when the subject tries to reconstruct the original stimuli. Retrieval effects can be examined by manipulating the retention interval between study and test. For instance, one group of subjects might be tested immediately after they read each passage, whereas another group might be tested after, say, an hour's delay. If subjects from the immediate-test condition remember both types of items equally well (say, typical versus atypical events in a script-based passage), then we could infer they have at least encoded both types of items. If differences then appear on the delayed test—that is, if subjects forget one type of item more rapidly than another—then we could infer that the effect of materials occurs *after* subjects have initially encoded the passage. For instance, typical items may suffer great interference and forgetting because of previously encountered instances than do atypical items.

In general memory for material based on naturalistic schemas reflects not only the nature of the underlying schema but also the material presented, its conditions of presentation, and other factors. Therefore one is well advised to examine how a schema influences performances across a variety of situations, using different materials, testing procedures, and the like, so that the effects of particular situations can be "cancelled out" and stable theoretical constructs can be identified. The procedures we have described can be combined to help untangle several factors that might be contributing to performance. Brewer and Treyens (1981) provide an especially clear set of methods for doing so.

The goal of all such experimental investigations of course is to obtain empirical findings that one can relate to a theory's predictions. Moreover a good theory helps specify which factors should be investigated and helps interpret experimental results, especially in complex research areas. In turn experimental results force a theory to stay in close correspondence with its empirical domain and provide a check on theorists' intuitions. Every experimenter has a long, expanding list of "blatantly obvious" predictions that turned out to be disconfirmed by his or her results. In trying to explain unexpected results, we are forced to consider important new possibilities that would not otherwise have been entertained. In the end empirical testing may be the only antidote we have to perpetual self-delusion.

We now conclude our discussion of methods for studying the learning of laboratory-presented materials. Our review has omitted several techniques (including autobiographic memory, implicit or unconscious memory tasks, skill acquisition) for brevity. For further information, interested readers may consult a methodology book by Puff (1982) or any of several textbooks on human memory (for example, Baddeley 1976, Crowder 1976, Wickelgren 1977).

7.3 Experimental Methods II: Language Processing

Key Issues in Language Research

The fundamental questions in language research concern the mechanisms by which language is understood and produced. How is a first language acquired and how is it represented in the brain? How is language used to get things done in social communications? Language studies focus not only on speech but also on written language. A dominant trend is the analysis of language understanding on-line, in real time, either for the listener or for the reader. A second trend analyzes speech production, usually for the speaker (not the writer).

Characterizing Studies of Language Processing

Laboratory studies of language processing can be loosely partitioned into three types of tasks, which we discuss in turn:

1. *Judgment* tasks, in which word strings are presented to a supposedly knowledgeable subject who judges the strings according to some criterion specified by the investigator. This is the standard method of linguists who ask their subjects (or themselves) to judge the "linguistic acceptability" of sample sentences. Subjects' judgments in such tasks can reveal much about their linguistic knowledge—for example, their internalized semantic distinctions or syntactic rule systems.

2. Speech *production* experiments, which deal with the processes by which people plan and execute various types of utterances. Here one might examine the pause structure and intonation of phrases as subjects either compose a narrative, recount some episode, or repeat aloud sentences they have just read. A second class of investigations would look for particular types of "slips of the tongue" (for example, spoonerisms such as "bad-cat" spoken as "cad-bat") when the speaker performs under time pressure.

3. *Reception* tasks, in which subjects listen to spoken utterances or read text and then indicate in some manner their understanding of the message. An example might have college students read a short story and then a day later write a summary or abstract of the story from memory. The aim of this research is to characterize the processes and knowledge sources that people use to understand various types of linguistic messages.

Judgment Tasks

Judgment tasks are commonly used to study speakers' linguistic knowledge and their expectations about how the language would be used in various communicative situations. Many types of judgments have been investigated. For example, subjects might be asked to judge what class of words will fit into a sentence frame to make an acceptable sentence. Or they might judge how similar in meaning two sentences are. For

Experimental Methods in Cognitive Science

example, if you believe that syntactic transformations should preserve meaning, then you can ask people whether a transform (*Wasn't that John?*) means the same as a base sentence (*Was that John?*). Another common task is to judge the grammaticality of single sentences. A standard procedure for collecting judgments is to ask the subject to rate directly (say, on a seven-point rating scale) the degree to which the stimulus satisfies the specified criterion. A related method is to rank order a set of stimuli from best to worst in terms of the degree to which they satisfy the criterion. Thus subjects might be asked to rank several metaphors on their "aptness."

By observing how subjects judge various stimuli, it is possible to test hypotheses about the subjects' linguistic knowledge or communicative expectations. For instance, a theory of English syntax could be tested by asking subjects to decide whether each of a series of word strings forms a grammatically correct sentence. The stimuli should be chosen such that different syntactic theories will disagree in their predictions about which word strings subjects will find more or less acceptable. This procedure is often applied with only a single subject (usually the investigator), but it is better to use multiple subjects to ensure that the judgments are reliable across speakers. The intuitions of experts are often contaminated by their theoretical preconceptions; the data obtained from naive subjects are sometimes more useful for theorizing about language users in general.

Such judgments can be made in or out of a linguistic context. Many sentences that appear meaningless out of context become acceptable in an appropriate context or when interpreted metaphorically. For example, *Ideas breed papers* is literal nonsense but acceptable as a metaphor. Similarly assertions of connections between events may appear non-sensical (for example, *The notes were sour because the seams split*) until a contextual cue activates a relevant knowledge structure (for example, *bagpipe*). An example of judgments in context would have subjects rate the importance, centrality, or relatedness of a given text statement to the "overall meaning" of a short text or story. Subjects agree reasonably well in the ranking of text statements in their degree of importance; such judgments are determined by aspects of text structure (for example, degree of causal connectedness of the event described by the statement to the other events in the narrative) and are positively correlated with such performance indices as the likelihood of the statement's recall or inclusion in a summary of the text.

Production Tasks
Production tasks are used to study how people plan and execute their utterances. For instance, when we are planning our next sentence in a conversation, do we usually plan out the whole sentence before executing it, or do we just plan a phrase at time? Do people plan a unit of

speech in its totality before execution, or do planning and execution occur in parallel? How much does this process depend on global discourse knowledge, our beliefs about where the conversation is going, and the topic we are discussing? How do we establish convenient ways to refer to the entities we are discussing, especially in cases where these do not have familiar labels? Ideally one would like to answer questions like these with a computational theory that is able to plan and execute speech just as humans do.

In most production tasks subjects' vocal responses are either elicited on cue (and the reaction time to initiate speaking is recorded) or are tape recorded for later analysis of such prosodic features as speech rate, pauses, dysfluencies, intonation contours, and so on. Any way in which the subject departs from an "ideal delivery" (continuous, error-free execution) provides us with information about the production process. For instance, subjects usually pause during execution when they are heavily involved in planning a new constituent; therefore pauses can be used as an index to help researchers identify speakers' "units of planning." We should find that their performance on a secondary dual task is especially poor at just those points in composing their utterance.

Language-production tasks come in several varieties. One task has the subject say as rapidly as possible different word series or sentences in response to different cues. Such tasks have been used in research by Cooper and Paccia-Cooper (1980) and by Sternberg, Monsell, Knoll, and Wright (1978). Here the interest is in how the time to start producing speech increases with the length of the series to be produced. A second task, studied by Motley and Baars (1981), tries to create slips of the tongue in the laboratory. A subject silently reads a pair of words and is then cued to say the words aloud either in the order written or in the reverse order. When driven at a rapid pace, subjects make a small percentage (about 10 to 20 percent) of speech errors such as spoonerisms or perseverations. One can then investigate factors that promote more errors. For example, over a short series of trials one can create a temporary set for subjects to pronounce *ba-* then *fay-* by presenting a series such as *bat fake* and *bad fate;* thus when subjects are pressed to hurriedly pronounce the written pair *fag base,* they are likely to slip and say *bag face.* Phonetic switches that make real words are more likely to occur than are similar switches that do not make words.

In the tasks reviewed so far, the person's productions are strictly controlled. However, subjects can be given more liberty to generate speech at their "natural" rate. One useful task requires subjects to describe a known spatial layout; for instance, Linde and Labov (1975) asked apartment dwellers to describe their living quarters. Interest focused on the way subjects organized and planned their description. This was typically achieved by the speaker taking the listener on a verbal "walking tour" of the apartment, beginning with entering the front door and proceeding through adjacent rooms with their contents and fixtures. Other investigators have studied recitals of everyday hassles and cooking recipes. The focus of these studies is on how people organize their recitals and how they pause as they finish generating one segment and plan the next segment.

Another class of studies investigates children's abilities to compose and generate coherent stories. Story generation requires considerable linguistic skill, conceptual knowledge, and familiarity with story conventions. The storyteller must introduce a central character (or group) who has a goal and then compose and relate a plan of action for the character to overcome obstacles and achieve his or her goal. Developmental psychologists track the way in which these component abilities improve as children develop greater levels of competence at the whole task (see, for example, Stein 1987).

A final class of speech production tasks studies social communication in controlled laboratory situations. One of the more fruitful tasks, devised by Krauss and Weinheimer (1966), studies how two subjects come to agree on a common ground of novel referring expressions. The subjects are separated by a screen; both have a collection of ten or so similar but unfamiliar nonsense figures on scrambled cards before them. One subject serves as the "sender," who is asked to verbally communicate a specified serial order of the ten figures to the "receiver" subject. Interest focuses on how the sender chooses to label or describe each of the figures; this is typically initiated by the sender describing what the figure resembles (for example, "the man with the top hat who's kicking out behind him"). Investigators study the "negotiating exchanges" by which the sender and receiver check, confirm, and eventually come to agree on a unique figure as the referent of a given description. The task is usually repeated many times, with the experimenter specifying on each trial a new random order of the same figures (cards) to be communicated by the sender. At issue is how subjects come to agree on an abbreviated shorthand to refer to each figure (for example, "The top hat" or "the kicker"), and how this substantially reduces the time they require to communicate each new order accurately. This communication game has been taken as a model of how two participants in a conversation search for common ground and effective referring expressions for their conversation. A variant of this task, devised by Wilkes-Gibbs (1986), has two subjects in separated cubicles planning a route through a city's streets by sharing knowledge gleaned from city maps that have large areas blacked out, different for the two subjects. At issue is how the subjects compare and coordinate their respective partial knowledge bases so as to compose a complete route through the patched-together maps. The performance is presumed to bring into prominence and model several *coordination* processes that are presumed to underlie social communication.

Reception Tasks

Reception tasks are used to study the processes by which people understand what they read or hear. Many aspects of comprehension have been investigated; these include recognizing individual words, constructing syntactic and semantic descriptions of an input sentence, and relating a statement to the ongoing discourse and to one's general knowledge about the world. In all such tasks subjects are presented with some sort of linguistic stimulus and are asked to respond in some way that will inform the investigator about either the process by which the material was understood or the resulting mental representation. Generally the investigator will vary some structural property of the stimulus material or its conditions of presentation. For instance, one might ask subjects to read sentences that vary in their grammatical complexity (according to a particular syntactic theory) and see if it takes subjects longer to understand more complex sentences (as indicated by the amount of time they spend reading them). We organize our review of reception tasks by first discussing various types of stimuli and stimulus manipulations and then describing several performance indices.

Language Stimuli   Virtually every kind of language fragment has been used as stimuli in reception tasks. Discourse units vary in their length or inclusiveness—from single sounds or phonemes to syllables, words, phrases, sentences, and larger pieces of discourse such as complete stories or expository texts. People can be said to "comprehend" at each of these levels; they identify phonemes, retrieve word meanings, and interpret sentences and larger discourse units. Researchers have developed theories of how comprehension is achieved at each level. These theories specify relevant factors to investigate and the expected nature of their effects.

Words, for example, vary in their familiarity to the average subject, their length, number of meanings, visual or semantic confusability with other words, relation to the context in which they occur, and countless other dimensions. Any of these factors might affect comprehension. Research in this area attempts to identify those factors that do have an effect, and to establish where in the overall comprehension process these effects occur. For instance, longer words might be recognized more slowly because they take longer to read; on the other hand, infrequent words may not take longer to read than common words but they may require more time for their meanings to be looked up in our mental lexicon. Different performance indexes, such as reading versus paraphrasing, may be sensitive to these different types of effects.

At the sentence level investigators are usually interested in how people construct syntactic or semantic descriptions of the sentences they read or hear. One question that has occupied researchers is whether extraction of these two descriptions are really separate processes that occur independently of one another (see, for example, Fodor 1983, Forster and Olbrei 1973). Do semantic or pragmatic factors affect the initial syntactic analysis, or is syntax a separate "module" in the language-understanding system? Given that it makes sense to sharply distinguish these processes, what is the "correct" description of each?

Although the questions at the sentence level are different from the major issues in word comprehension, the logic for answering them is essentially the same. Structural factors and their expected effects are specified by one's theory; the investigator then selects materials that differ on some factor of interest and tests whether this difference has the predicted effect. For instance, a syntactic theory might be used to rank order sentences in terms of their "syntactic ambiguity." One could then see whether this ranking accurately predicts how rapidly subjects read the sentences, how well they can paraphrase or recall them later, and so on.

The study of larger discourse units such as narratives or expository passages is currently a burgeoning research area. One practical aim of some investigators is to describe what makes texts easy to understand, easy to recall, or both. One of the stronger determinants of comprehensibility is the reader's familiarity with the ideas in the text, the words by which they are expressed, and the syntactic simplicity of the sentences. A good predictor of a word's familiarity is the frequency of its occurrence in English texts; Kucera and Francis (1967) have published tables of word-frequency counts that are often used in language research. The familiarity of "idea units" in text is often judged intuitively and reflects the "expertise" of the readers regarding the topics of the text. A text on organic chemistry is highly readable to professional chemists but not to elementary-school children. The most direct way to assess comprehensibility of texts is to have subjects from the target population read and rate a variety of experimental texts; investigators then select a sample of texts that have the desired comprehensibility level to use in further studies.

In studies of comprehension and recall of longer texts (say, 250 to 500 words), a critical variable is the organization of ideas in the text—how they are laid out, sequenced, interrelated, and signalled by rhetorical words and phrases. Texts can be designed that vary in logical coherence (for example, number of illustrations, amount of support for general assertions) and that vary in explicit signalling of the underlying organization of the ideas (see Grimes 1975, Meyer 1975, 1985). These factors influence how much a reader can comprehend and remember from the text. A volume edited by Britton and Black (1985) has many papers illustrating different analyses of expository prose. Mandler and Johnson (1977, Johnson and Mandler 1980) describe hypotheses regarding the structure of narratives (simple folk tales). Having in hand a hypothesis about what constituents (theme, goal, setting, embedded episodes, and the like) comprise a coherent story, the investigator may design stories that either delete the constituents or rearrange the canonical order of the constituents in a story and then note how this influences people's comprehension and recall of the texts.

A different level of analysis of narratives is provided by identifying the several strands of causal connections that course through the events described by a story. Starting with work by Schank (1975), the analysis of texts for causal connections has been further developed by Black and Bower (1980), Trabasso and van den Broek (1985), and Trabasso and Sperry (1985). Because stories typically describe people's problems and their plans to solve their problems, successive events can be viewed as causing or enabling subsequent events, either by physical or psychological causation. Causal analysis is relevant because it is associated with several psychological indicators: for instance, story events that are multiply connected by causal linkages to other story events are more likely to be judged as "centrally important" events, more likely to be recalled, and more likely to be included in a summary of the story (see the Trabasso papers for details). An acknowledged weakness of this approach is that because texts are often cryptic, important cause-effect linkages within the story's actions may not be explicitly stated; thus a causal chain analysis either must infer unmentioned links or tolerate broken chains in the description of the narrative.

In investigating text understanding, researchers must remember that people can adopt alternative strategies for reading a text. They will choose a strategy appropriate to their own goal or to whatever goal has been set for them. For a competent adult each goal initiates a reading (or listening) plan that is designed to focus on the text information judged most relevant to the goal. Of course people best remember what they focus on and react to in a text. Other information that is given only passing attention will be quickly forgotten. Thus a person who proofreads a paragraph for typing errors may show relatively little understanding or memory for the content of the material; conversely a person who reads to summarize a text may not notice or recollect which words were misspelled.

A word of caution is needed concerning the use of language materials to test psychological hypotheses. The hypotheses are usually abstract in the sense of referring to the behavioral differences that should arise when people process linguistic inputs of type A versus those of type B, all other things being equal. The A-B inputs might be ambiguous versus nonambiguous words, abstract versus concrete words, causally ordered versus temporally ordered narratives, and so forth. To test the generality of such hypotheses, one should select sizeable samples of many language units that exemplify the theoretical variable and are otherwise roughly equivalent. Obviously the larger the sample, the more generalizable the result. To generalize a given result (based on a sample of linguistic units) to the population of all possible units of that type, the investigator should try to demonstrate that the effect holds up consistently when comparing individual items of the same type. An important methodological paper by Clark (1973) argues for the need to test the consistency of effects across language samples. Psycholinguistics researchers now routinely follow Clark's injunctions regarding experimental design and statistical hypothesis testing with multiple language samples.

Performance Indexes   The index of linguistic performance chosen by an investigator varies according to the purpose and object of study. In studies of language reception investigators are usually interested in the subject's comprehension and how it varies with properties of the text and the subject. The measures may be divided into those that track a serial reception task as it unfolds in real time, versus those that examine the resultant memory established by a reader or listener after having comprehended some text. We call these "on-line" versus "memory" measures of language reception.

On-Line Performance Measures

Repeating Back   Perhaps the simplest reception task is one commonly used in studies of speech perception, namely, requiring subjects to repeat the speech sounds they think they heard over noisy earphones. The presentation and response units involved may be of any size, from a phoneme to a syllable, word, or full sentence. It is well known that performance in such tasks is better the higher the intensity of the signal (speech sounds) relative to the noise, the fewer the confusable alternatives in the choice set, and the more probable (or expected) the signal item is in the given context (see, for example, Licklider and Miller 1951).

Reading Time   Probably the most widely used method for studying on-line comprehension is to measure the time a subject requires to read a language unit such as a word, phrase, sentence, or fixed block of text. With the widespread use of microcomputers that display text, the typical laboratory arrangement is to visually present words, phrases, or sentences on a CRT screen for a duration controlled by the reader. The reader presses an advance button on the keyboard to indicate when he or she has finished reading (and comprehending) the presented unit and is ready to view the next unit of text. One method, called rapid serial visual presentation (RSVP), presents only single words (from sentences) in this manner. Successive words may appear either at the same location on the CRT screen or may march across the screen as though one were reading a line of text from left to right.

The basic measure taken in RSVP is the time to read each word, indicated by the time between successive button presses. Slower times are taken to reflect greater underlying difficulty of "processing" the unit. Slower times are typically observed for longer words, for relatively unfamiliar words, semantically unexpected words, words involved in unexpected syntactic constructions, and words that mark the end of major constituents.

The same reading-time measure can be used for whole phrases or sentences presented all at once on the CRT. Here the subjects' button presses control how long they take to read each phrase or sentence. Such reading times are sensitive to structural variables such as the length of a sentence in syllables, familiarity of the words or relations, and syntactic complexity of the sentence. Reading times are also affected by the expectedness of the sentence given the preceding linguistic context. The more easily a statement can be linked to the reader's current representation of the text, the more quickly it can be read and understood. The RSVP method is most often used in on-line psycholinguistic experiments because it is very sensitive to experimental variables and is also quite easy and inexpensive to set up.

Eye Tracking The RSVP method disrupts the normal reading process, introduces several problems, and fails to capture certain aspects of normal reading (such as going back over material read previously). More normal reading can be studied by recording readers' eye movements as they fixate on successive words or groups of words on a page (or screen) of text. Elaborate optical equipment can accurately determine and record exactly where a subject's eyes are looking at each moment. By superimposing this gaze location onto a copy of the text, the investigator can obtain a precise record of where the subject was looking and for how long. People read by successive fixations (of 20 to 5000 milliseconds), jumping across a standard line of text in 2 to 5 seconds. Actual reading occurs only for the word or two in the center of foveal vision; our ability to discriminate words more than a few degrees off center is very poor. To a first approximation, then, we may assume that the eyes fixate on a word (or cluster of words) until it has been integrated into the unfolding representation of the text (Just and Carpenter 1987). Thus fixation times provide a sensitive measure of how difficult particular words are to understand in context. As one might expect, poor readers have longer fixations, more fixations per sentence, and more eye regressions than do good readers.

Eye-movement records have provided a rich array of information about the "mechanics" of reading. They tell us that people look longer at content words than function words; longer at unfamiliar, unusual, or unexpected words; and longer at words that terminate and wrap up a phrase. The records also tell us when a reader's eyes "regress," or go back to reread difficult parts of the text. For example, when readers encounter that point in a "garden path" sentence where they realized they have been tricked, their eyes will regress to a previous part of the sentence, from which point they will start over with a different interpretation. Thus in reading the sentence *The boat floated down the river sank*, readers get into trouble when they get to *sank*, at which point they stop, move their eyes back to the beginning, reread the sentence, and recategorize "floated" as the beginning of a complement phrase that modifies *boat*. Eye regressions are also frequent when readers encounter pronouns with indeterminate or ambiguous referents. The readers' eyes scan rapidly over the preceding text, looking for a proper antecedent for the problematic pronoun.

The main difficulty with eye-movement recordings is that the investigator is in danger of becoming buried in mounds of data as well as details of the technical apparatus. Therefore scientists considering the use of eye-movement recordings are advised to become familiar with the costs in time and money before they embrace such an expensive and data-rich source. Also they will need a set of practical data-reduction programs to help them deal with the huge volume of eye-fixation data generated by a few subjects reading just a few passages.

Probe Reaction Time A reasonable hypothesis is that readers' processing resources are more engaged (or used up) during their intake of certain difficult parts of a sentence. For instance, we might hypothesize that it takes extra mental effort (attentional "resources" or "capacity") for a person to understand syntactically complex or semantically ambiguous sentences or to find the referent of opaque pronouns in the sentence. Cognitive psychologists often use dual-task methods for measuring how much attentional capacity is engaged by such performances. In such procedures the subject performs a primary task (say, reading words by the RSVP method), while at the same time performing a second task. Of course frequent testing of subjects' comprehension of the primary-task material is required to ensure that they attend to it as much as required. A typical secondary task is to have subjects listen for an occasional soft tone (or look for a dim light) and to press a key as soon as they hear (or see) it. The probe stimulus appears only infrequently, in an unpredictable pattern. People's reaction time to a probe stimulus is presumed to be slower the more absorbing the primary task is at the moment the probe appears. In terms of an energy-reserve metaphor, the more processing resources are absorbed by the primary task at a given moment, the less capacity there is for performing the secondary task, resulting in a less efficient (slower) performance on the secondary task. These effects are usually quite small, however, relative to the baseline variability in the RT measure. Thus fairly large samples (about 50 observations per condition) are usually required to obtain reliable results.

Phoneme Monitoring A similar monitoring task asks the subjects to listen for a particular phoneme (such as *ba*) as they listen to a continuous stream of speech and to press a key as soon as they detect it. Thus hearing a sentence such as *The emperor went to the royal baths*, subjects should press the key upon hearing the initial *ba* in baths. A visual analog can be arranged wherein subjects look for a target pair of letters (*ba*) in an RSVP reading task. The idea behind the phoneme-monitoring task is similar to that of the probe RT task: the more engrossing and difficult the primary task (of comprehension) just before the target phoneme is presented, the slower the subject should be in detecting and reacting to the target. Thus people will react more slowly to target probes that occur just after ambiguous words or just after words signalling a syntactically ambiguous construction (see Foss 1969, 1970, 1982). Unfortunately performance in phoneme monitoring itself is a complex affair and is affected by many "nuisance" variables such as the frequency and distribution of targets across sentences, the discriminability and voicing of the target phoneme, and the frequency (familiarity) of the word in which the target phoneme occurs and of the preceding word (see Newman and Dell 1978). Thus investigators must exercise some care in using the phoneme-monitoring task to reach conclusions about the mental effort involved in parsing and comprehending different parts of a sentence.

Interrupting Questions   A simple way to catch some of the processes of comprehension in nearly real time is to interrupt subjects' reception of text and ask them a question. The question may or may not refer directly to elements in the antecedent text. An example is to ask subjects to name the referent of a pronoun in a sentence they are just hearing (or have just heard) and measure the time required to reply as well as the accuracy of the response. Another example is to have the reader answer who-what-where-when questions immediately after hearing or reading a sentence. Various hypotheses can be tested in this way—for example, that elements in syntactically complex constructions will be harder to retrieve as answers. Thus the agent can be shown to be more accessible immediately after presentation of an active rather than a passive sentence (Wright 1969).

Other types of interrupting questions are used to examine the way in which the preceding sentence or passage *primes* and speeds up the retrieval of semantically related information from long-term memory. An example is the so-called *lexical decision* task, in which the person decides whether or not a probe string of letters forms a word. Half the probes form words and half are near-miss nonwords (for example, *order* and *ordar*). The time to decide that an item is a real word depends on how much that word is expected, activated, or primed by the preceding context. Thus following a sentence describing a character entering a restaurant to eat, the word *order* will elicit a fast decision whereas a control word like *older* would be slower by about 50 milliseconds (Sharkey and Mitchell 1985). The lexical decision task has been used as a tool to collect information relevant to many issues in psycholinguistics. For example, it has been used to demonstrate that immediately after hearing or reading a polysemous word in context, it primes *several* of its related meanings, not just the one appropriate to that context. After hearing

John deposited his money in the bank, people are speeded in lexical decisions for words related to the contextually irrelevant meaning of *bank* (*river, water, ground*) as much as they are for words related to the contextually relevant meaning (*office, saving, teller*). This effect is time dependent, however; the irrelevant priming is measurable immediately following the polysemous word, but after a pause of a second or more, the relevant meaning becomes dominant and the activation of the irrelevant meaning decays to the control baseline (Swinney 1979).

A related interrupted technique is the Stroop interference task. In the Stroop task a probe word is presented in colored letters (such as red or green), and the subject is instructed to name the letters' color as quickly as possible. This requires inhibiting the strong tendency to read the word, which is harder the more the word is primed by the context. Thus a strongly primed word such as *lamb* in *Mary had a little* _____ would require more time to name the color of its letters than would the same word in an unprimed context. Thus the degree of Stroop interference is a derived measure of priming.

We mention a final probe test that allows the investigator to trace the effect of a text on the accessiblity of different parts of a knowledge structure in long-term memory. Morrow, Greenspan, and Bower (1987) had subjects first memorize the spatial layout of a building composed of four rooms, each containing four named objects. Subjects then read a story about a character carrying out a plan that required him to move from room to room. The question of interest was whether objects near the reader's focus of attention in the mental map would be activated and more accessible to retrieval than objects outside the focus of attention. To assess this, as subjects were reading one statement at a time on a CRT screen they were interrupted just after reading any statement describing the character moving between rooms, say, from room A to room B. The interruption consisted of a probe test of two objects from the building (for example, *projector, computer*), and subjects were to indicate as rapidly as possible whether the two objects were located in the same or different rooms. Morrow and colleagues found that access to objects' locations was very fast for objects in the current-focus room, somewhat slower for objects in the room just exited, and slowest for objects in other rooms of the building. The value of this technique is that it allows us to assess moment-by-moment changes in the activation of information in long-term memory as the story moves the reader's attention to different parts of the building and the corresponding mental map.

Verification Tests of Comprehension A simple test of comprehension of a declarative statement asks subjects to decide whether the statement is true or false with respect either to general knowledge or a specific visual display. Thus the subject might read and answer quickly statements such as *Six isn't an odd number* or *Four isn't larger than seven*. The response times tell us something about the difficulty of understanding and untangling negatives (for example, *isn't odd* means *even*) as well as marked comparative adjectives. Such statements can also be tested against a continually changing display, such as (true or false) *The B doesn't precede the A . . . BA*. Clark (1974) has made ingenious use of this technique for testing a range of hypotheses about the comprehension of implicitly negative verbs. For example, subjects take longer to respond to a question such as *If John forgot to let the dog out, is the dog now in?* than a related question such as *If John remembered to let the dog out, is the dog now in?* The different response times presumably reflect the time required to decompose the implicitly negative verb, *forgot*.

Memory-Based Measures of Comprehension   It is understood that comprehension is an aid to memory but distinct from it. A person with organic amnesia will fully understand a conversation, but will totally forget it within a few minutes if distracted. Similarly a person can memorize a passage verbatim (say, in a foreign language) yet understand none of it. Despite these caveats the correlation between comprehension and memory is normally so high that answering questions from memory is often taken as an index of comprehension of the material.

Question Answering   The verification task noted previously asks a true-or-false question about information that is immediately available to the subject or is presumed to be common knowledge. This method can be extended to ask questions about a collection of statements that has recently been read for comprehension or for memorization. Lehnert (1978) enumerated the different categories of questions that might be asked about simple narratives and has provided a computer-simulation model of how people answer such questions from a memory representation of the text. In addition to true-or-false questions, there are fill-in-the-blank questions about events involving the who-why-when-where-how slots in a typical event frame. One can also ask for answers to *What happened after event X? Did event X precede Y? Why didn't such and so happen?* Lehnert's simulation program produces impressively human-like answers to such questions. The theory has not yet been tested in psychological laboratories, perhaps because it makes few if any predictions about the speed with which subjects could answer the different types of questions.

Recognition-Memory Tests   The most commonly used tests of comprehension (in the "classroom" sense) require subjects to decide whether a test sentence is true or plausible in light of the sentences (text) they just read. The instructions may ask the subject to answer "yes" only if the test statement is an exact verbatim match to one of the studied sentences and to say "no" otherwise. In such cases the investigator focuses on the accuracy of verbatim memory in different conditions and how often false-positive answers are given to paraphrases of the presented statements.

Speed of recognition-memory judgments is often used to investigate associative priming between two different statements from the text (see, for example, McKoon and Ratcliff 1980). In such experiments the test statements are presented singly on a CRT screen and the computer records how fast the subject presses the true or false key. In priming, when a given test statement queries (and thus activates) a particular episode from the studied narrative, then the very next test statement is answered more quickly if it also queries the same or an associatively related episode.

More commonly the subject is asked not for verbatim memory but for judgments of whether a test statement is plausible or probably true given the information in the text. The main interest in such cases is usually the availability in memory of different types of inferences about the text statements. Many kinds of inferences are plausible (for a classification of several, see Rieger 1975), and a few of these have been studied experimentally (see, for example, Singer 1986). Inferences about probable instruments, locations, consequences, and actions are common. For example, a *hammer* is commonly used to pound nails, a kiss is usually placed on the *lips,* people who fall out of sailboats usually get *wet,* and pythons who catch mice usually *eat* them. By checking the frequency and speed with which subjects assent to a particular test inference, investigators can test hypotheses about which inferences are normally made during initial comprehension and which are only derived as they are needed, in response to later queries.

Cued Recall Tests In contrast to true-or-false tests, cued recall tests require the subjects to fill in the blank or blanks in a series of test statements. The Cloze technique used in school tests is an example: subjects receive the original text they read previously except that a number of content words are missing and replaced by blanks; the subjects try to fill in the blanks with the correct word or one similar in meaning. Often in sentence-memory experiments the cue for recall is a single content word, such as the subject or object of the sentence. Scoring involves simply recording the percentage of content words filled in correctly.

Ordered Recall The most difficult memory test is to recall the original text (or sentences) in its original order and as close to verbatim as possible. The subjects either write or tape record their recall and are usually given sufficient time to reproduce the entire passage. The investigator may be interested in the temporal character of the subjects' recall; for example, people tend to recall a story in an initial burst, then pause while they retrieve the next episode, recall that episode rapidly, then pause again, and so on.

Scoring subjects' protocols for gist or substance recall presents formidable problems. One obviously needs a means of identifying idea units in the text, as well as some conventions for coding and scoring recall to give credit for paraphrases, confabulations or blends of two or more ideas, generalizations over several ideas, and plausible inferences from the text statements. With the recent advent of propositional scoring systems (see the papers in Britton and Black 1985), the way has been cleared for extensive studies of comprehension by means of recall. When applied to a medium-sized text (say, of more than 200 words), the full propositional scoring system is quite laborious and time consuming to apply. Its output is a recall score (of yes, no, or partial credit) for each of the text's propositional (idea) units for each subject, and this suffices to permit statistical analyses by subject conditions or type of items. Fortunately a far simpler measure, namely the number of content words recalled, turns out to be very highly correlated (in the 0.90s) with the more complex propositional scores (Paul 1959, Voss, Tyler, and Bisanz 1982). Thus for most purposes the number of content words recalled can be used as an easily obtainable measure of recall.

Summarization One of the most demanding tests of peoples' comprehension of a text is to have them summarize it, distilling and abstracting it into a few statements. A summary supposedly tells only the centrally important points of the text and shows their global interrelations. Summarization presumably reveals some kind of macrostructure that holds the various parts of the text together in memory.

Summarization is a difficult task. Typically it is done from memory, imposing an added burden on the performer; this can be relieved by letting people inspect the text as they compose their summary of it. To add to the difficulty, a summary is an ill-defined and fuzzy concept: for a given text there is not a well-specified "correct" summary that everyone will recognize. Thus investigators can ask their subjects to write summaries under different constraints; for example, subjects may be asked to write a summary of a text using no more than (say) 25 content words or to use only phrases from the text itself or to produce a distillation of the text's main points at a level more abstract than the text itself (for example, the moral of a folktale). Because subjects have differing notions of what comprises a summary, investigators would be well advised to explicitly instruct them on the kind of summary they want; otherwise subjects' summaries will hardly be comparable. Despite the fuzziness of the summary concept, people are fairly reliable in rank ordering a set of summaries of a text according to their quality.

Once summaries are produced within certain constraints, they are usually analyzed in terms of propositions, and if possible these are then identified with their source in the text. Often this identification requires the scorer to understand how several text propositions could have been combined to imply the summary statement. There are no mechanical rules for doing this, although Rumelhart (1977) and Lehnert (1981) provide some techniques for analyzing narrative summaries, and the papers in the collection edited by Britton and Black (1985) provide analyses of summaries of expository text.

Perhaps because of these scoring difficulties, relatively few studies of summarization per se have been published. We know that propositions that are important to the text's global structure are likely to appear in summaries, as are narrative events that have high causal connectivity to other events in a story (Trabasso and van den Broek 1985). In narratives these elements are usually the main character's primary goal (or an event that instigated it), a penultimate successful plan of action, and the final upshot or outcome of the narrative. Any abnormal constraint or condition of the actor and his or her plan may also be mentioned in the summary. Although data collection on summarization is still relatively sparse, the simulation programs of Lehnert (1981) and DeJong (1979) provide useful starting theories of the on-line processes by which subjects might construct summaries of simple narratives. We may expect to see more empirical development of such theories in the future.

7.4 Concluding Comments

In our recital of specific techniques in experimental cognitive science we have been able to review in moderate detail only research methods for memory and language processing. Although these areas comprise a large portion of cognitive science research, we are fully aware of other important areas (including pattern recognition and problem-solving) whose procedures we have not been able to cover.

To recapitulate, we have touched briefly on the role of empirical investigation in justifying our beliefs and guiding our actions and reviewed several empirical methods including introspection, naturalistic observations, and correlational studies. But we argued that intuitive introspection is often a weak, uninformative, even biased, measuring instrument for rapid, nonconscious cognitive processes. And our powers of naturalistic observation are seriously limited; even if we could get beyond our blinding preconceptions to observe things carefully, nature rarely conveniently arranges the exact observational conditions we need to infer causal relationships.

The history of humankind is one of increasing use of tools for extending our power, expanding or amplifying our physical senses, and more recently for amplifying our intellectual senses, our mental powers. Experimentation is a *conceptual prosthetic*, an intellectual tool that allows us to create in the laboratory possible microworlds never seen before and then observe how specific cognitive subsystems operate in those microworlds.

Experimentation provides a generate-and-test heuristic for checking the validity of our causal theories, for testing theoretical predictions. We presented a few general methods used in experimental studies of cognition and indicated how analogical theories can be placed in correspondence to observable, experimental events. We then reviewed some specific techniques used in studies of memory and language processing, trying in most cases to indicate a few substantive issues addressed by them.

Obviously these substantive theoretical issues are the meat and potatoes of the scientist's diet, whereas the experimental methods we have reviewed comprise only the metaphorical pots and pans used to prepare that intellectual feast. The later, substantive chapters in this book serve up various feats prepared with the help of these tools.

References

Anderson, J. A. 1983. Cognitive and psychological computation with neural models. *IEEE Transactions on Systems, Man, and Cybernetics* 5:799–815.

Anderson, J. R. 1987. Methodologies for studying human knowledge. *Behavioral and Brain Sciences* 10:467–505.

Anderson, J. R., and Bower, G. H. 1974. Interference in memory for multiple contexts. *Memory and Cognition* 2:509–514.

Anderson, J. R., and Singley, M. K. 1987. An identical-productions model of transfer. Paper given at the Ninth Annual Conference of the Cognitive Science Society, Seattle, WA.

Baddeley, A. D. 1976. *The Psychology of Memory.* New York: Basic Books.

Bartlett, F. C. 1932. *Remembering: A Study in Social Psychology.* Cambridge, Engl.: Cambridge University Press.

Bellezza, F. S., and Bower, G. H. 1986. *The Formation of Verbal Schemata: Mediation and Interference Processes.* Stanford University Psychology Department, Stanford, CA.

Black, J. B., and Bower, G. H. 1980. Story understanding as problem-solving. *Poetics* 9:223–250.

Bower, G. H. 1970. Analysis of a mnemonic device. *American Scientist* 58:496–510.

Bower, G. H. 1974. Selective facilitation and interference in retention of prose. *Journal of Educational Psychology* 66:1–8.

Bower, G. H. 1981. Mood and memory. *American Psychologist* 36:129–148.

Bower, G. H., Black, J. B., and Turner, T. J. 1979. Scripts and memory for text. *Cognitive Psychology* 11:177–220.

Brewer, W. F., and Treyens, J. C. 1981. The role of schemata in memory for places. *Cognitive Psychology* 13:207–230.

Britton, B. K., and Black, J. B. 1985. *Understanding Expository Text: A Theoretical and Practical Handbook for Analyzing Explanatory Text.* Hillsdale, NJ: Erlbaum.

Chase, W. G., and Posner, M. I. 1965. *The Effect of Visual and Auditory Confusability on Visual and Memory Search Tasks.* Paper presented at the meetings of the Psychonomic Society, Chicago.

Chernoff, H., and Moses, L. E. 1959 *Elementary Decision Theory.* New York: Wiley.

Clark, H. H. 1973. The language-as-fixed-effect fallacy: A critique of language statistics in psychological research. *Journal of Verbal Learning and Verbal Behavior* 12:335–359.

Clark, H. H. 1974. Semantics and comprehension. In T. A. Sebeok, ed. *Current Trends in Linguistics, Volume 12: Linguistics and Adjacent Arts and Sciences.* The Hague: Mouton Publishers, pp. 1291–1498.

Cofer, C. N. 1971. Properties of verbal materials and verbal learning. In J. W. Kling and L. A. Riggs, eds. *Experimental Psychology.* 3rd ed. New York: Holt, Rinehart & Winston; pp. 847–904.

Cooper, W. E., and Paccia-Cooper, J. 1980. *Syntax and Speech.* Cambridge, MA: Harvard University Press.

Crowder, R. G. 1976. *Principles of Learning and Memory.* Hillsdale, NJ: Erlbaum.

DeJong, G. F. 1979. *Skimming Stories in Real-Time: An Experiment in Integrated Understanding.* Doctoral dissertation, Research Report No. 158, Department of Computer Science, Yale University, New Haven, CT.

Ericsson, K. A., and Simon, H. A. 1980. Verbal reports as data. *Psychological Review* 87:215–251.

Fodor, J. A. 1983. *The Modularity of Mind.* Cambridge, MA: MIT Press.

Forster, K., and Olbrei, J. 1973. Semantic heuristics and syntactic analysis. *Cognition* 2:319–347.

Foss, D. J. 1969. Decision processing during sentence comprehension: Effects of lexical item difficulty and position upon decision times. *Journal of Verbal Learning and Verbal Behavior* 8:457–462.

Foss, D. J. 1970. Some effects of ambiguity upon sentence comprehension. *Journal of Verbal Learning and Verbal Behavior* 9:699–706.

Foss, D. J. 1982. Discourse on semantic priming. *Cognitive Psychology* 14:590–607.

Galambos, J. A., and Rips, L. J. 1982. Memory for routines. *Journal of Verbal Learning and Verbal Behavior* 21:260–281.

Gibson, E. J. 1969. *Principles of Perceptual Learning and Development.* New York: Appleton Publishers.

Gluck, M. A., and Bower, G. H. 1988. Evaluating an adaptive network model of human learning. *Journal of Memory and Language* 27:166–195.

Graesser, A. C., Woll, S. B., Kowalski, D. J., and Smith, D. A. 1980. Memory for typical and atypical actions in scripted activities. *Journal of Experimental Psychology: Human Learning and Memory* 6:503–513.

Green, D. M., and Swets, J. 1966. *Signal Detection Theory and Psychophysics*. New York: Wiley.

Grimes, J. E. 1975. *The Thread of Discourse*. The Hague: Mouton.

Hintzman, D. L. 1976. Repetition and memory. In G. H. Bower, ed. *The Psychology of Learning and Motivation* New York: Academic Press, pp. 47–93.

Hintzman, D. L. 1986. Schema abstraction in a multiple trace memory model. *Psychological Review* 93:411–428.

Johnson, N. S., and Mandler, J. M. 1980. A tale of two structures: Underlying and surface forms in stories. *Poetics* 9:51–86.

Just, M. A., and Carpenter, P. A. 1987. *The Psychology of Reading and Language Comprehension*. Boston, MA: Allyn and Bacon.

Kahneman, D. 1973. *Attention and Effort*. Englewood Cliffs, NJ: Prentice-Hall.

Kling, J. W., and Riggs, L. A., eds. 1971. *Experimental Psychology*. 3rd ed. New York: Holt, Rinehart & Winston.

Krauss, R. M., and Weinheimer, S. 1966. Concurrent feedback, confirmation, and the encoding of referents in verbal communication. *Journal of Personality and Social Psychology* 4:343–346.

Kucera, H., and Francis, W. N. 1967. *Computational Analysis of Present Day American English*. Providence, RI: Brown University Press.

Lehnert, W. G. 1978. *The Process of Question Answering*. Hillsdale, NJ: Erlbaum.

Lehnert, W. G. 1981. Plot units and narrative summarization. *Cognitive Science* 4:293–331.

Lewicki, P. 1986. *Nonconscious Social Information Processing*. Orlando, FL: Academic Press.

Licklider, J. C. R., and Miller, G. A. 1951. The perception of speech. In S. S. Stevens, ed. *Handbook of Experimental Psychology*. New York: Wiley, pp. 1040–1074.

Linde, C., and Labov, W. 1975. Spatial networks as a site for the study of language and thought. *Language* 51:924–939.

Loftus, E. S. 1979. *Eyewitness Testimony*. Cambridge, MA: Harvard University Press.

Mandler, J. A., and Johnson, N. S. 1977. Remembrance of things parsed: Story structure and recall. *Cognitive Psychology* 9:111–151.

Marr, D. 1982. *Vision*. San Francisco: W. H. Freeman.

McKoon, S., and Ratcliff, R. 1980. Priming in item recognition: The organization of propositions in memory for text. *Journal of Verbal Learning and Verbal Behavior* 18:369–386.

Medin, D. L., and Schaffer, M. M. 1978. Context theory of classification learning. *Psychological Review* 85:207–238.

Meyer, B. J. F. 1975. *The Organization of Prose and its Effects on Memory.* Amsterdam: North-Holland.

Meyer, B. J. F. 1985. Prose analysis: Purposes, procedures, and problems. In B. K. Black and J. B. Black, eds. *Understanding Expository Text* Hillsdale, NJ: Erlbaum, pp. 11–64.

Miller, J. O., and Pachella, R. G. 1973. Locus of the stimulus probability effect. *Journal of Experimental Psychology* 101:227–231.

Morrow, D. G., Greenspan, S. L., and Bower, G. H. 1987. Accessibility and situation models in narrative comprehension. *Journal of Memory and Language* 26:165–187.

Motley, M. T., and Baars, B. J. 1981. Syntactic criteria in pre-articulatory editing: Evidence from laboratory-induced slips of the tongue. *Journal of Psycholinguistic Research* 105:503–522.

Newell, A., and Simon, H. A. 1972. *Human Problem Solving.* Englewood Cliffs, NJ: Prentice Hall.

Newman, J. E., and Dell, G. S. 1978. The phonological nature of phoneme monitoring: A critique of some ambiguities studies. *Journal of Verbal Learning and Verbal Behavior* 17:359–374.

Nisbett, R. E., and Ross, L. 1980. *Human Inferences: Strategies and Shortcomings of Social Judgment.* Englewood Cliffs, NJ: Prentice Hall.

Nisbett, R. E., and Wilson, T. D. 1977. Telling more than we can know: Verbal reports on mental processes. *Psychological Review* 84:231–259.

Parks, T. E. 1966. Signal detectibility theory of recognition memory performance. *Psychological Review* 73:44–58.

Paul, I. H. 1959. Studies in remembering: The reproduction of connected and extended verbal material. *Psychological Issues.* Monograph no. 2, vol. 1. New York: International Universities Press.

Posner, M. I. 1969. Abstraction and the process of recognition. In G. H. Bower and J. T. Spence, eds. *The Psychology of Learning and Motivation.* Vol. 3. New York: Academic Press, pp. 44–100.

Posner, M.I., and Keele, S. W. 1967. Decay of visual information from a single letter. *Science* 158:137–139.

Posner, M. I., and Mitchell, R. F. 1967. Chronometric analysis of classification. *Psychological Review* 74:392–409.

Postman, L. 1971. Transfer, interference, and forgetting. In J. W. Kling and L. A. Riggs, eds. *Experimental Psychology.* 3rd ed. New York: Holt, Rinehart & Winston, pp. 1019–1132.

Puff, C. R. 1982. *Handbook of Research Methods in Human Memory and Cognition.* New York: Academic Press.

Rieger, C. G. 1975. Conceptual memory and inference. In R. C. Schank, ed. *Conceptual Information Processing*. Amsterdam: North-Holland, pp. 157–288.

Rosch, E. 1973. On the internal structure of perceptual and semantic categories. In T. E. Moore, ed. *Cognitive Development and the Acquisition of Language*. New York: Academic Press, pp. 111–144.

Rosch, E. 1975. Cognitive representation of semantic categories. *Journal of Experimental Psychology: General* 104:192–233.

Rosch, E. 1977. Human categorization. In N. Warren, ed. *Advances in Cross Cultural Psychology*. Vol. 1. New York: Academic Press.

Rosch, E., and Mervis, C. B. 1975. Family resemblance studies in the internal structure of categories. *Cognitive Psychology* 7:573–605.

Rumelhart, D. E. 1977. Understanding and summarizing brief stories. In D. LaBerge and S. Samuels, eds. *Basic Processes in Reading, Perception, and Comprehension*. Hillsdale, NJ: Erlbaum.

Rumelhart, D. E., and Ortony, A. 1977. The representation of knowledge in memory. In R. C. Anderson, R. J. Spiro, and W. E. Montague, eds. *Schooling and the Acquisition of Knowledge*. Hillsdale, NJ: Erlbaum.

Sattath, S., and Tversky, A. 1977. Additive similarity trees. *Psychometrika* 42:319–345.

Schank, R. C. 1975. *Conceptual Information Processing*. Amsterdam: North-Holland.

Schank, R. C., and Abelson, R. P. 1977. *Scripts, Plans, Goals, and Understanding*. Hillsdale, NJ: Erlbaum.

Sekular, R., and Blake, R. 1985. *Perception*. New York: Random House.

Sharkey, N. E., and Mitchell, D. C. 1985. Word recognition in a functional context: The use of scripts in reading. *Journal of Memory and Language*. 84:253–270.

Shepard, R. N. 1980. Multidimensional scaling, tree-fitting, and clustering. *Science* 210:390–398.

Shepard, R. N., and Arabie, P. 1979. Additive clustering: Representation of similarities as combinations of discrete overlapping properties. *Psychological Review* 30:87–123.

Singer, M. 1986. Answering wh____ questions about sentences and text. *Journal of Memory and Language*. 25:238–254.

Smith, E. E., and Medin, D. L. 1981. *Categories and Concepts*. Cambridge, MA: Harvard University Press.

Sperling, G., and Dosher, B. 1986. Strategy and optimization in human information processing. In K. Boff, L. Kaufman, and J. Thomas, eds. *Handbook of Perception and Performance*. Vol. 1. New York: Wiley.

Stein, N. L. 1987. The development of children's story-telling skill. In M. B. Franklin and S. Bartan, eds. *Child Language: A Book of Readings*. New York: Oxford University Press.

Sternberg, S. 1966. High-speed scanning in human memory. *Science* 153:652–654.

Sternberg, S. 1967. Two operations in character recognition: Some evidence from reaction time experiments. *Perception and Psychophysics* 2:45–53.

Sternberg, S. 1969. Memory-scanning: Memory processes revealed by reaction-time experiments. *American Scientist* 57:421–457.

Sternberg, S., Monsell, G. S., Knoll, R. L., and Wright, C. E. 1978. The latency and duration of rapid movement sequences: Comparisons of speech and typewriting. In G. E. Stelmach, ed. *Information Processing in Motor Control and Learning*. New York: Academic Press, pp. 117–152.

Stevens, S. S. 1957. On the psychophysical law. *Psychological Review* 64:153–181.

Swinney, D. A. 1979. Lexical access during sentence comprehension: Reconsideration of context effects. *Journal of Verbal Learning and Verbal Behavior* 18:645–659.

Thorndyke, P. W., and Hayes-Roth, B. 1979. The use of schemata in the acquisition and transfer of knowledge. *Cognitive Psychology* 11:82–106.

Trabasso, T., and van den Broek, P. 1985. Causal thinking and the representation of narrative events. *Journal of Memory and Language* 24:612–630.

Trabasso, T., and Sperry, L. L. 1985. Causal relatedness and importance of story events. *Journal of Memory and Language* 24:595–611.

Voss, J., Tyler, S. W., and Bisanz, G. L. 1982. Prose comprehension and memory. In C. R. Puff, ed. *Handbook of Recent Methods in Human Memory and Cognition*. New York: Academic Press, pp. 349–395.

Wald, A. 1950. *Statistical Decision Functions*. New York: Wiley.

Wickelgren, W. A. 1977. *Learning and Memory*. Englewood Cliffs, NJ: Prentice-Hall.

Wilkes-Gibbs, D. 1986. *Collaborative Processes of Language Use in Conversation*. Doctoral dissertation, Stanford University, Stanford, CA.

Winer, B. J. 1971. *Statistical Principles in Experimental Design*. 2nd ed. New York: McGraw-Hill.

Wittgenstein, L. 1953. *Philosophical Investigations*. New York: Macmillan.

Wright, P. 1969. Transformations and the understanding of sentences. *Language and Speech* 12:156–166.

8 Brain and Cognition

Terrence J. Sejnowski and Patricia Smith Churchland

The hope that biological and cognitive levels of investigation might be integrated has had a long history. Once it became evident that the operations of the brain were essential for thoughts and actions, discovering the biological basis for mental functions was an abiding objective (see, for example, Hippocrates (trans. 1949), Gall and Spurzheim 1968, von Helmholtz 1948, Cajal 1937, and Jackson 1958). Translating that goal into reality has been far from straightforward, however, because nervous systems are notoriously difficult to study. Until quite recently the hope often seemed frustratingly remote and unattainable.

A number of developments have improved the prospects that some of the biological mechanisms underlying cognition may be discovered in this century. In particular, important new techniques for investigating the functions of the brain have been invented in the last several decades that make possible a much more detailed structural and functional description of the brain than was previously available. Additionally we have a much better understanding of the components and dimensions of cognitive abilities (see chapter 1), and more systematic and sophisticated methods for determining the behavioral parameters of cognition have evolved (see chapter 7). Finally, the vast increases in the speed and availability of computers, together with new computational approaches to modeling in neuroscience (Sejnowski, Koch, and Churchland 1988), have allowed some problems of information processing in the nervous system to be approached effectively and have suggested new ways for thinking about cognitive operations (see chapter 4). These developments suggest that it is now possible to begin to integrate levels and to construct theories to explain functional properties of neural tissue (Churchland and Sejnowski 1988b).

The general organization of this book reflects the belief that cognitive abilities such as perception, language, memory, and attention are somehow related to brain systems. It is by no means clear, however, at what structural levels these correspondences will be made, so that the general issue of levels of organization is crucial to the enterprise from the outset. For example, it may turn out that a particular aspect of attention depends on a variety of mechanisms, some of which can be found at the level of local neural networks and others at the level of larger neural systems that reside in many different locations within the brain. Other cognitive capacities, such as planning and problem solving, may involve a complex interplay between several neural systems.

Collaborations between researchers working at different levels of investigation on common problems is often difficult. Results from one level are not always understandable or usable by researchers addressing other levels. Normally experiments are designed to address questions at a single level of organization, and the significance of the results for other levels is often not obvious. One solution is to design experiments specifically to link different levels of investigation. However, this requires an understanding of the available methodologies and knowledge of the relevant facts at both levels.

The main purpose of this chapter is to make techniques and central principles of neuroscience accessible to those who are not already immersed in the neurosciences. We do not intend to review all of the literature in neuroscience concerning the biological substrate of cognition. In particular we have not surveyed the large literature on animal behavior, which is highly pertinent. Rather, this chapter is meant to be a guide for the cognitive reader to the methods and techniques available in neuroscience for addressing cognitive issues, together with some representative examples.

8.1 Levels of Investigation

Two types of levels will be distinguished in this section—*levels of analysis* and *levels of organization*. In general it is possible to characterize a phenomenon under investigation according to its physical scale—for example, whether it is at the level of an entire perceptual system or at the level of single neurons. However, another characterization is by the level of analysis. Thus one can study a specific task performed by a particular neural structure, or one can analyze a problem in a general way that applies to all systems. In this section the relationship between these two different types of levels is explored.

Levels of Analysis
A framework for a theory of levels articulated by Marr (1982) provided an important and influential background for thinking about levels in the context of computation by nervous structures.[1] This framework drew on the concept of levels in computer science, and accordingly Marr characterized three levels: (1) the computational level of *abstract problem analysis*, decomposing the task (for example, determining structure from motion) into its main constituents; (2) the level of the algorithm, specifying a *formal procedure* to perform the task by providing the correct output for a given input; and (3) the level of *physical implementation*, constructing a working device using a particular technology.

An important element in Marr's view was that a higher level was largely independent of the levels below it, and hence computational problems of the highest level could be analyzed independently of understanding the algorithm that performs the computation. Similarly, the algorithmic problem of the second level was thought to be solvable independently of understanding its physical implementation.

Unfortunately, two very different issues were confused in the doctrine of independence. The first concerns whether, as a *matter of discovery*, one can figure out the relevant algorithm and the problem analysis independently of facts about implementation. The other concerns whether, as a *matter of formal theory*, a given algorithm that is already known to perform a task in given machine (for example, the brain) can be implemented in some other machine that has a different architecture. So far as the latter is concerned, computational theory tells us that algorithms can be run on different machines, and in that sense and that sense alone the algorithm is independent of the implementation. The formal point is straightforward: because an algorithm is formal, no specific physical parameters (for example, "vacuum tubes," "Ca^{++}") are part of the algorithm. That said, it is important to see that the purely formal point cannot speak to the issue of how best to *discover* the algorithm in fact used by a given machine, nor how best to arrive at the neurobiologically adequate task analysis. Certainly it cannot tell us that the *discovery* of the algorithms relevant to cognitive functions will be independent of a detailed understanding of the nervous system. Moreover it does not tell us that any implementation is as good as any other—and it had better not because different implementations display enormous differences in speed, size, efficiency, elegance, and so on. The formal independence of algorithm from architecture is something we can exploit to build other machines once we know how the brain works, but it is no guide to discovery if we do not know how it works.

The issue of independence of levels marks a major conceptual difference between Marr (1982) and the current generation of researchers studying neural and connectionist models. In contrast to the doctrine of independence, current research suggests that considerations of implementation are vital in the kinds of algorithms that are devised and the kind of computational insights available to the scientist. Knowledge of brain architecture, so far from being irrelevant to the project, can be the essential basis and invaluable catalyst for devising likely and powerful algorithms that have a reasonable shot at explaining how in fact the job gets done.

Levels of Organization

Marr's three-level division treats computation monolithically, as a single kind of level of analysis. Implementation and task description/decomposition are likewise each considered as a single level of analysis. Yet when we measure Marr's three *levels of analysis* against *levels of organi-*

zation in the nervous system, the fit is poor and confusing at best (Crick 1979, Churchland and Sejnowski 1988a, Shepherd 1989). To begin with, there is organized structure at different scales: molecules, synapses, neurons, networks, layers, maps, and systems. At *each* structurally specified stratum we can raise the computational question: what does that organization of elements do? What does it contribute to the wider, computational organization of the brain? In addition there are physiological levels: ion movement, channel configurations, EPSPs (excitatory postsynaptic potentials), IPSPs (inhibitory postsynaptic potentials), action potentials, evoked-response potentials, and probably other intervening levels that we have yet to learn about and that involve effects at higher anatomical levels such as networks or systems.

The range of structural organization implies, therefore, that there are many levels of implementation, and that each has its companion task description. But if there are as many types of task descriptions as there are levels of structural organization, this diversity will probably be reflected in a multiplicity of *algorithms* that characterize how the tasks are accomplished. This in turn means that the notion of *the* algorithmic level is as oversimplified as the notion of *the* implementation level.

Note also that the same level can be viewed computationally (in terms of functional role) or implementationally (in terms of the substrate for the function), depending on what questions you ask. For example, the details of how an action potential is propagated, from the point of view of communication between distant areas, might be considered an implementation because it is an all-or-none event and only its timing carries information. However, from a lower structural level—the point of view of ionic distributions—the propagating action potential is a computational construct because its regenerative and repetitive nature is a consequence of several types of nonlinear voltage-dependent ionic channels spatially distributed along an axon.

Structural Levels

Structure at every scale in the nervous system—molecules, synapses, neurons, networks, layers, maps, and systems (figure 8.1)—is separable conceptually, but not detachable physically. What is picked out as a level is actually a boundary imposed on the structure that depends on the techniques available to understand the phenomenon at hand. In the brain, they are all part of one integrated, unified biological machine. That is, the function of a neuron depends on the synapses that bring it information, and in turn the neuron processes information by virtue of its interaction with other neurons in local networks, which themselves play a particular role by virtue of their place in the overall geometry of the brain.

Accordingly, which structures really constitute a level of organization in the nervous system is an empirical, not an a priori, matter. We cannot tell in advance of studying the nervous system how many levels there

Levels of Investigation

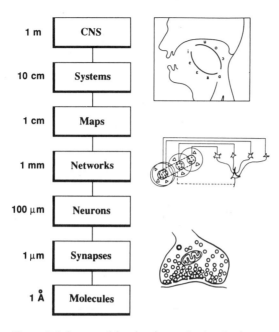

Figure 8.1 Structural levels of organization in the nervous system. The spatial scale at which anatomical organization can be identified varies over many orders of magnitude. Schematic diagrams to the right illustrate an articulatory system that produces speech sounds, a small network model for receptive fields of simple cells in visual cortex (Hubel and Wiesel 1962), and the structure of a chemical synapse (Kandel and Schwartz 1984). Relatively little is known about the properties at the network level in comparison with the detailed knowledge of synapses and the general organization of pathways in sensory and motor systems.

are nor what is the nature of the structural and functional features of any given level. The techniques that are used to study the levels are surveyed in the next section. In the next section seven general categories of structural organization are discussed (figure 8.1). The count is imprecise for several reasons. Further research may lead to the subdivision of some categories, such as "systems," into finer-grained categories, and some categories may be profoundly misdrawn and may need to be completely reconfigured. As we come to understand more about the brain and how it works, new levels of organization may be postulated. This is especially likely at higher levels where much less is known than at the lower levels.

Systems   Using tract-tracing techniques, neuroanatomists have identified many *systems* in the brain. Some of the systems, such as the visual system, correspond to sensory modalities; others, such as the autonomic system, respect general functional characteristics (figures 8.2a,b). Yet others, such as the limbic system, are difficult to define and may turn

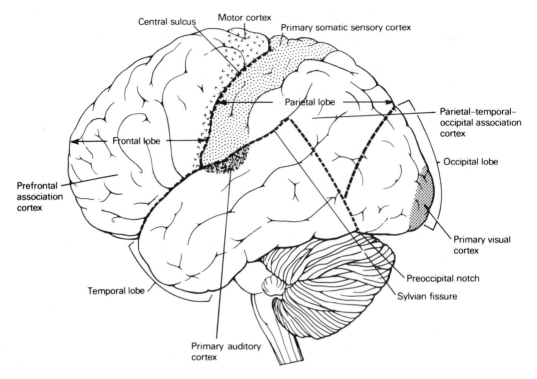

Figure 8.2a Side view of the cerebral cortex with the major divisions identified. In addition to the primary visual cortex in the occipital lobe and the primary auditory cortex near the junction of the parietal and temporal lobes, two large association areas are visible: the prefrontal-association cortex and the parietal-temporal-occipital–association cortex. The central sulcus separates the primary somatic sensory cortex from the motor cortex. The Sylvian fissure is the most prominent cleft visible in this view. (From Kandel and Schwartz 1985.)

out not to be one system with an integrated or cohesive function. The components of these systems are not neatly compartmentalized, but are distributed widely in the brain and are connected by long fiber tracts. For example, a particular brain system for long-term memory may involve such diverse structures as the hippocampus, the thalamus, the frontal cortex, and basal forebrain nuclei (Mishkin 1982). In this respect brain systems contrast quite vividly, and perhaps discouragingly, with systems designed by an engineer, in which components are discrete and functions are compartmentalized (figure 8.3).

One of the earliest systems concepts was that of a reflex arc, such as the monosynaptic reflex in the knee-jerk response (Sherrington 1906) (figure 8.4). The pathways of some reflexes have now been traced in great detail, for example, as in the vestibuloocular reflex, which stabilizes images on the retina when the head is moving (Robinson 1981), and the gill withdrawal reflex in *Aplysia*, which has been a focus for research into the molecular mechanisms of plasticity (Kandel et al. 1987). The reflex arc is not a useful prototype for brain systems in general—

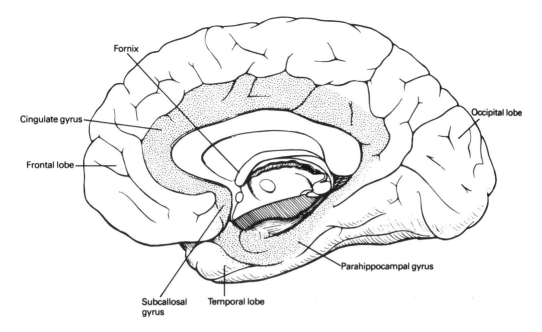

Figure 8.2b Medial view of the brain (split down the midline) showing some of the structures in the limbic system. The stippled regions of cortex that encircle the upper brainstem are primitive areas of cortex that project to the hippocampus, which is even more primitive in morphology. The hippocampus has the form of a horn and is near the arc of the fornix, which is a bundle of fibers joining the hippocampus to cortical and subcortical areas. This part of the limbic system has an important role in storing information about facts (Squire 1987). The amygdala, an olive-shaped nucleus, is located at the temporal pole of the hippocampus and has extensive connections with the hypothalamus. The emotional aspects of cortical processing are mediated by this brain region. (From Kandel and Schwartz 1985.)

or even, it appears, for most reflexes, such as the stepping reflex in the cat or the nociceptive reflex (withdrawal of limb from a painful stimulus). Take, for example, the smooth pursuit system for tracking visual targets, in which one pathway originates in the retina, leads to the lateral geniculate nucleus (LGN), to the cortex and through distinct visual topographic areas, down to the pons, and eventually to the oculomotor nuclei (Lisberger et al. 1987). Despite the machinelike quality of smooth pursuit, it is to some extent under voluntary control and depends on expectation as well as the visual stimulus. Behaviors more sophisticated than simple reflexes probably exploit more complex computational principles.

In this regard, two important features of brain systems should be mentioned. First, there are almost always reciprocal (feedback) connections between brain areas, at least as rich in number as the feedforward connections. For example, the recurrent projections from the visual cortical area V1 back to the LGN are about ten times as numerous as those from the LGN to V1. Second, although the simple models of

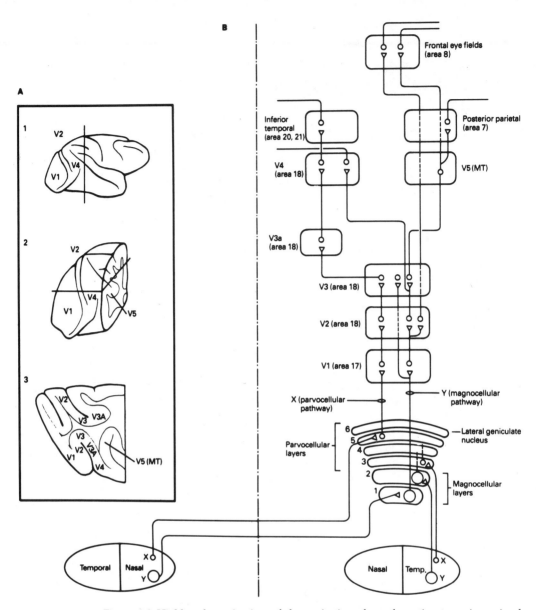

Figure 8.3 Highly schematic view of the projections from the retina to various visual areas of the cerebral cortex. (A) Visual cortical areas of the macaque monkey seen from the side (1) and through two slices, first in the coronal plane (2) and in the horizontal plane (3). The approximate location of the cortical areas V1, V2, V3, V4, and V5 are indicated (although some of these areas can be further subdivided into multiple maps of the visual field. (B) Diagram of the connections between areas in the visual pathway emphasizing three key factors in their organization. First, there are discrete levels, suggesting a hierarchy in the processing of visual information. Second, there are streams within single pathways, such as the magnocellular and parvocellular pathways. Third, there are two major divisions of higher visual processing, one following a ventral route to the inferotemporal cortex, which specializes in visual pattern recognition, and the other following a dorsal route to the posterior cortex, which specializes in processing spatial information. (From Kandel and Schwartz 1985.)

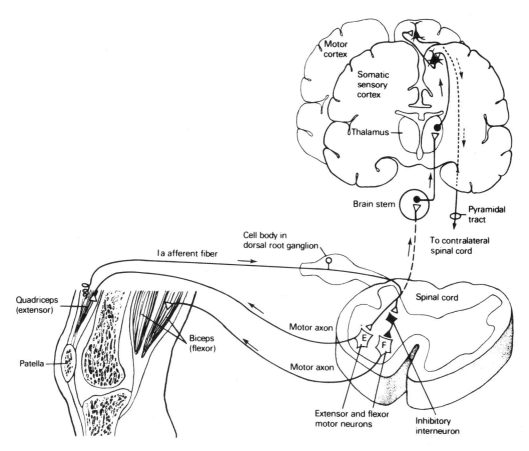

Figure 8.4 Schematic diagram of the pathways for the stretch reflex. Stretch receptors in muscle spindles react to changes in length of the muscle and afferent fibers carry this information along the dorsal roots to the spinal cord, where they synapse on extensor motoneurons, which extend the knee, and the inhibitory interneurons, which reduce activity in motoneurons that produce contractions of the antagonistic flexor muscles. Both of these actions combine to produce a coordinated expression of the knee-jerk reflex. This information is also conveyed to higher brain centers, which in turn can modify the reflex behavior through descending pathways to the spinal cord. (From Kandel and Schwartz, 1985.)

reflex arcs suggest that a single neuron may be sufficient to activate the neuron on which it synapses, in fact a large number of neurons are almost always involved, and the effect of any single neuron on the next is typically quite small. For example, an important feature in the visual system is that input from a specific neuron in the LGN generally makes relatively weak synaptic contacts on a large population of cortical cells rather than a strong synaptic effect on just one or a few neurons (Martin 1984). This implies that cortical neurons rely on a convergence of many afferents, and correlations between pairs of neurons tend to be relatively weak (Fetz and Cheney 1980, Ts'o et al. 1986). There may be interesting exceptions to this; for example, chandelier cells in cortex make inhibitory connections on the axon hillocks of their targets, and they may, as single cells, have a strong, decisive effect on their target cells. Another exception is the strong influence that single climbing fibers have on single Purkinje cells in the cerebellum.

Topographic Maps   A major principle of organization within many sensory and motor systems is the topographic map. For example, neurons in visual areas of cortex, such as V1, are arranged topographically, in the sense that adjacent neurons have adjacent visual receptive fields and collectively they constitute a map of the retina. In the visual systems of monkeys physiologists have found more than twenty distinct areas, most of which are topographically mapped, though some maps are distorted and properties are unevenly represented over the surface of the map (Allman 1982, De Yoe and Van Essen 1988, Hubel and Livingstone 1987, Livingstone and Hubel 1987a,b). A similar hierarchy of multiple topographic maps are found for body location in the somatosensory system (Kaas et al. 1979; see figure 8.5), for frequency in the auditory system (Merzenich and Brugge 1973), and for muscle groups in the motor system (Ferrier 1876, Asanuma 1975). One possible exception is the olfactory system, but even odors may be spatially organized at the level of the olfactory bulb (Adrian 1953, Stewart et al. 1979). To some extent the different sensory maps can be distinguished by differences in the fine details in the laminations of neurons (see the next subsection) and their cellular properties, but often these are so subtle that only physiological techniques can distinguish boundaries between different cortical areas.

Some brainstem structures, such as the superior colliculus, also display this organization. The cerebellum appears to have patches of partial maps, though the principles do not seem clear, and these areas may not be maps in any real sense at all. Some areas seem to lack a strong topographic organization, and for other areas the topographic organization is quite complex, for example the basal ganglia (Goldman-Rakic and Selemon 1986). Cortical areas anterior to the central sulcus seem sparser in topographic maps, but research may show that what they map are abstract, not sensory, representations, and hence they cannot

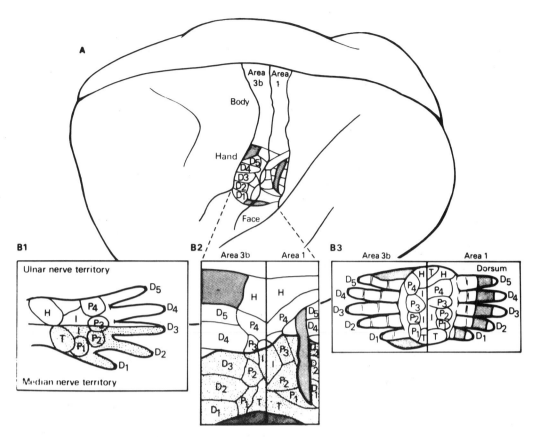

Figure 8.5 Schematic drawing of the multiple representations of the body surface in the primary somatic sensory cortex of the owl monkey. Because the cortex of the owl monkey is relative flat, most of the body representation is located on the surface rather than in the convolutions found in the species of most other primates. (A) Two representations of the hand are shown in areas 3b and 1. (B) The hand of the owl monkey is innervated by the median and ulnar nerves, which have different territory on the ventral surface (B1) and are represented in adjacent areas of cortex in each of the two maps (B2). The topographical organization of the cortical map for the ventral surface of the hand is highly ordered (B3) in both areas. Cortex devoted to the ventral surface is indicated in white; that devoted to the dorsal surface is in dark shading. D_1 to D_5 represent the five digits, P_1 to P_4 the four palmar pads, I the insular pad, H the hypothenar pads, and T the thenar pads. (From Kandel and Schwartz 1985.)

be discovered by methods used to establish response patterns to peripheral stimuli (P. M. Churchland 1985). For example, in bat auditory cortex there are topographic mappings of abstract properties such as frequency differences and time delays between emitted and received sounds, properties that may help the bat to echolocate prey (Suga 1984), and in the barn owl internal spatial maps are synthesized from binaural auditory inputs (Konishi 1986, Knudsen et al. 1987). There are some areas of cortex, such as association areas, parietal cortex, and some parts of frontal cortex, for which it has not yet been possible to find properties that form orderly mappings. Nonetheless projections between these areas remain topographic. For example, Goldman-Rakic (1987) has shown that in the monkey projections from parietal cortex to target areas in the prefrontal cortex, such as the principal sulcus, preserve the topographic order of the source neurons.

Maps of the surface of the body in the brain are formed during development by projections that become ordered, in part, through competitive interactions between adjacent fibers in the target maps (Sejnowski 1987). Some of the neurons undergo cell death during this period, and with a few rare exceptions, no new neurons are formed in the mature animal (Cowan et al. 1984). However, competitive interactions between neurons continue to some extent even in adulthood because the territory in cortex devoted to a particular part of the body surface can shift up to two millimeters, but not much farther, weeks after injury to sensory nerves or after excessive sensory stimulation (Merzenich and Kaas 1982). Thus regions in somatosensory cortex that are silenced following denervation of a sensory nerve will eventually become responsive to nearby regions of the body. It is not yet known how much of this rearrangement is due to plasticity in cerebral cortex or perhaps in subcortical structures that project to cortical maps. Nonetheless this evidence, and further evidence for synaptic plasticity, summarized below, makes it difficult to think of the machinery in the adult brain as "hardwired" or static. Rather, the brain has a remarkable ability to adapt to changes in the environment at many different structural levels and over a wide range of time scales.

Layers and Columns Many brain areas display not only topographic organization but also a laminar organization (figure 8.6a). Laminae are layers (sheets) of neurons in register with other layers, and a given lamina conforms to a highly regular pattern of where it projects to and from where it receives projections. For example, the superior colliculus receives visual input in superficial layers, and tactile and auditory input in deeper layers. Neurons in an intermediate layer of the superior colliculus represent information about eye movements. In the cerebral cortex specific sensory input from the thalamus typically projects to layer 4, the middle layer, whereas output to subcortical motor structures issues from layer 5, and intracortical projections originate mainly in

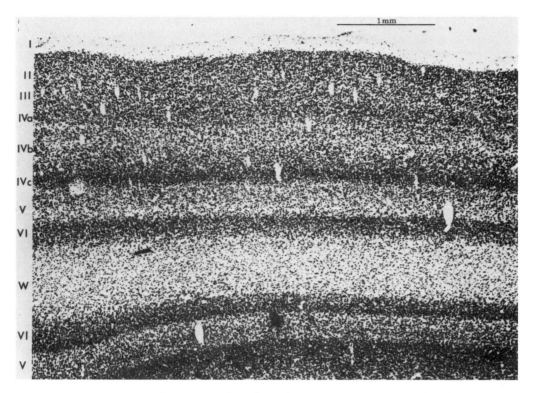

Figure 8.6a Cross-section through monkey striate cortex using cresyl violet to stain cell bodies. Laminations are clearly visible, and the layers are numbered on the left margin (W = white matter). Deeper layers of the buried fold of cortex are shown in the lower part of the figure. (From Hubel and Wiesel 1977.)

layers 2 and 3 (superficial) layers. Layer 6 mainly projects back to the thalamus. The basal ganglia do not have a laminar organization, but instead have a patchwork of islands that can be distinguished by developmental and chemical markers (Graybiel and Hickey 1982).

As well as the horizontal organization seen in laminae, cortical structures also display vertical organization. This organization consists of a high degree of commonality between cells in vertical columns, crossing laminae, and is reflected both anatomically in terms of local connections between neurons (Martin 1984, Lund 1987) and physiologically in terms of similar response properties (Hubel and Wiesel 1962). For example, a vertical penetration of an electrode in visual cortex reveals cells that share a preference for stimuli with the same orientation (for example, a bar of light oriented at about 20° from the horizontal). Another vertical penetration nearby will show cells that prefer a different orientation. Inputs and outputs are also organized columnarly, such as the eye dominance columns in V1 and inputs into the principal sulcus that alternate between parietal projections from the same side and projections from the principal sulcus in the opposite hemisphere (Goldman-Rakic 1987).

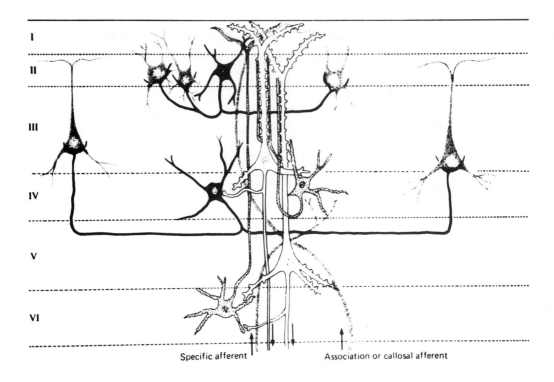

I

II

III

IV

V

VI

Specific afferent   Association or callosal afferent

Figure 8.6b Schematic diagram of laminae and principal types of neurons in cerebral cortex. Two large pyramidal cells (white) shown in layers 3 and 5 receive synaptic contacts from the star-shaped stellate cell (stippled) in layer 4. The stellate interneuron receives specific input from principal neurons located in the thalamus. The basket cell (black) has inhibitory synaptic contacts on the somata of cortical neurons. Most of the thalamic inputs (specific afferents) are directed to cells in layer 4; association and callosal inputs from other parts of the cortex mainly terminate in the more superficial layers. (From Kandel and Schwartz 1985.)

Typically the vertically organized connectivity patterns do not result in columns with sharp boundaries, and the response properties tend to vary continuously across the cortex. Hence the expression "vertical column" may be slightly misleading. Thus for cells in visual area V1, orientation varies over the cortex smoothly, save for some fractures and singularities (Blasdel and Salama 1986), and a similar organization can be found in area V2 (Swindale et al. 1987), which receives a topographically mapped projection from V1. There are, however, places where vertical, cross-laminar columns with quite sharp boundaries are seen—for example the ocular dominance columns in layer 4 of area V1 and the "barrels" in the rodent somatosensory cortex, each of which contains cells preferentially sensitive to stimulation of a particular whisker (Woolsey and Van der Loos 1970). Sharp anatomical boundaries are, however, the exception rather than the rule. Also, the spatial scale of columnar organization can vary from about 0.3 mm for ocular dominance columns to 25 μm for orientation columns in monkey visual cortex.

Topographic mapping, columnar organization, and laminae are special cases of a more general principle, namely exploitation of geometric properties in information processing design. Spatial proximity may be an efficient way for biological systems to assemble in one place information needed to solve a problem. To consider a simple case, suppose it is necessary to compare differences between stimuli at neighboring locations, where comparison requires that signals be brought together. Then topographic organization may achieve this efficiently while minimizing the total length of the connections. This is desirable because most of the volume of the brain is already filled with axonal processes, and there are limitations on how big the brain can be as well as temporal tolerances that must be met. Lateral inhibitory interactions within the spatial maps are used to make comparisons, enhance contrast at borders, and perform automatic gain control. Mutual inhibition within a population of neurons can be used to identify the neuron with the maximum activity, a type of "winner-take-all" circuit (Feldman and Ballard 1982).

Local Networks Within a cubic millimeter of cortical tissue there are approximately 10^5 neurons and about 10^9 synapses, with the vast majority of these synapses arising from cells located within cortex (see figure 8.6b). These local networks have been very difficult to study owing to the complexity of the tangled mass of axons, synapses, and dendrites called the neuropil. Nevertheless some general features of local networks are beginning to emerge. For example, the orientation tuning of cells in V1 must emerge from nonoriented inputs and activity in local networks in ways that we are just beginning to understand (Ferster and Koch 1987).

Most of the data available on local networks are based on single-unit recordings, and to achieve a deeper understanding of the principles governing networks, it will be necessary to monitor a large population of neurons (see discussion of recording techniques in section 8.2). Even a local network involves many cells, but only small populations can be studied by exhaustive sequential recordings from single cells. Consequently we run the risk of generalizing from an atypical sample and of missing circuit properties that can be inferred only from a richer profile. Therefore, to understand the principles of local networks, much more work has to be done to determine the dynamical traffic within a larger population of cells over an extended period of time.

Computer simulations may help to interpret single-unit data by showing how a population of cells could represent properties of objects and perform coordinate transformations. For example, network models of spatial representations have been constructed that help to explain the response properties of single cells in parietal cortex (Andersen and Mountcastle 1983, Zipser and Andersen 1988; see figure 8.17). Another network model has been used to explain how the responses of single neurons in visual cortex area V4 could compute color constancy (Zeki 1983, Hurlbert and Poggio 1988). Network simulations can also suggest alternative interpretations for known response properties. For example, there are certain oriented cells in V1 whose response summates with the length of the slit or edge of light up to the borders of the receptive field, but then the response diminishes as the length increases. This property, called "end-stopping," has recently been related to the extraction of the one-dimensional curvature of contours (Dobbins et al., 1987) and the two-dimensional curvature of shapes in shaded images (Lehky and Sejnowski 1988). As we learn more about the distributed representation of information in local networks, we may achieve a better understanding of the style of computation in the brain (Sejnowski 1986, 1988, Hinton 1986).

Computers can also help in the analysis of experiments that use multielectrode recordings and optical techniques for recording. Even though the anatomical reconstruction of local networks may be prohibitive, it may be possible to reconstruct the functional properties of these networks with computer simulations (Gerstein and Aertsen 1985, Koch and Segev 1989).

Neurons Ever since Cajal's work in the late nineteenth century, the neuron has been taken as an elementary unit of processing in the nervous system (see figure 8.7). In contrast to Golgi, who believed neurons formed a continuous "reticulum" or network, Cajal argued that neurons were distinct individual cells, separated from each other by a spatial gap, and that mechanisms additional to those operating intracellularly would need to be found to explain how the signal passed from neuron to neuron. Physiological studies have borne out his judgment, though in some areas, such as the retina, syncytia of cells that are electrically coupled have been found. As it turns out, these are rather more like the structures Golgi predicted because the cells are physically joined by conducting "gap junctions." These electrical synapses are faster and more reliable than chemical transmission, but are more limited in their flexibility.

There are many different types of neurons, and different parts of the nervous system have evolved neurons with specialized properties. There are five general types of cells in the retina, for example, each with highly distinctive morphology, patterns of connectivity, physiological properties, and embryological origin. In recent years, however, physiological and chemical differences have been found within classes. For example, 23 different types of ganglion cells (whose axons project to the brain through the optic nerve) have been identified as well as 22

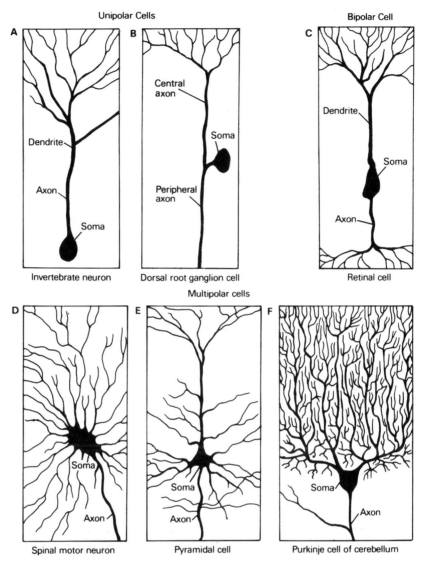

Figure 8.7 Examples of neurons illustrating the variety of shapes in different areas of the brain. The neurons are classified according to the number of processes that originate from the soma, or cell body. A unipolar cell has only a single process leaving the soma. In invertebrates (A) different segments of the unipolar process can have a receptive surface (dendrite) or transmitting regions (axons). Neurons in the dorsal root ganglion of the spinal cord (B) belong to a subclass of unipolar cells in which the soma is not directly involved with the transmission of information from the dendrites to the axon terminals. Bipolar cells (C) have two processes: the dendrite carries information toward the soma, and the axon transmits information away from the cell. Multipolar cells usually have many dendritic processes emerging from the cell body and are common in the mammalian nervous system. The spinal motoneuron (D) innervates muscle fibers and is the final common pathway for the nervous system. A pyramidal cell (E) from the hippocampus is named after the shape of the cell body. Dendrites emerge from both the apex (apical dendrites) and the base (basal dendrites). Similar pyramidal cells are found in cerebral cortex. A Purkinje cell (F) from the cerebellum has a highly branched dendritic tree that is confined to a plane. (From Kandel and Schwartz 1985.)

different types of amacrine cells (which provide lateral interactions and temporal differentiation) (Sterling 1983). There are 7 general types of neurons in the cerebellum and about 12 general types in the neocortex, with many subtypes distinguishable by their chemical properties, such as the neurotransmitters that they contain. The definition of a neuronal type is somewhat arbitrary because judgments are often made on the basis of subtle morphological differences, which can be graded rather than categorical. As more chemical markers are found, however, it is becoming clear that the diversity of neurons within cerebral cortex has been vastly underestimated. The number of subtypes of neurons in neocortex is not known, but there are at least 50 and probably less than 500 (Sereno 1988).

On the basis of their effects, neurons divide into two general classes: excitatory and inhibitory. Some neurons also have modulatory effects on other neurons, principally by releasing peptides or monoamines. Another useful classification concerns projections: some cells ramify only within an area, for example, stellate cells in cortex; and other neurons, such as pyramidal cells, have long-range projections out of an area, where the route goes via the white matter rather than directly through the cortex itself. Research on the properties of neurons shows that neurons are much more complex processing devices than previously imagined. For example, dendrites of neurons are themselves highly specialized, and some parts can probably act as independent processing units (Shepherd et al. 1985, Koch and Poggio 1987).

Synapses Chemical synapses are found in nervous systems throughout phylogeny, and they are a basic unit of structure that has been highly conserved during evolution. A synaptic bouton has a surface area of a few square microns and forms a highly stereotyped apposition with the postsynaptic membrane, which itself is highly specialized (figure 8.8). Synapses are the primary gateways by which neurons communicate with one another and consist of specialized presynaptic structures for the release of neurochemicals and postsynaptic structures for receiving and responding to those neurochemicals. Evidence is accumulating that signaling between neurons at synapses is selectively altered by experience (Alkon 1987). Nevertheless, there are other structural components of neurons that might also be modified through experience, such as the shapes and topology of dendrites as well as the spatial distribution of membrane channels (Purves and Voyvodic 1987).

The understanding of the nervous system at the subcellular level is changing rapidly, and it is becoming apparent that neurons are very dynamic and complex entities whose computational properties cannot be approximated by static response functions, a common idealization. It remains an open scientific question how the integrity of memories that span decades can remain intact if the neural substrate is as fluid

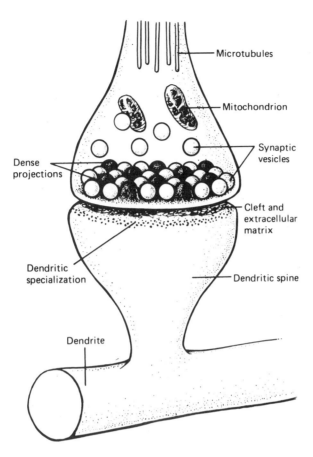

Figure 8.8 Schematic diagram of a synapse on a dendritic spine. Dense projections in the presynaptic membrane are surrounded by vesicles that presumably contain neurotransmitter molecules. This morphology characterizes a type I synapse, which is excitatory. Type II synapses (not shown) display flattened vesicles in the electron microscope after glutaraldehyde fixation and are often inhibitory. (From Kandel and Schwartz 1985.)

as preliminary reports indicate, especially if, as it seems, networks of neurons both process and store information.

Molecules   The integrity of neurons and synapses depends on the properties of membranes and the internal cytoskeleton of the neuron. The membrane serves as a barrier about 10 nm thick separating the intracellular and extracellular aqueous compartments. The membrane itself is a two-dimensional fluid medium in which integral membrane proteins and other molecules form associations. Some integral membrane proteins are important in maintaining the ionic milieu inside and outside the cell. For example, membrane proteins that serve as ionic channels can be voltage-sensitive, chemically activated, or both. They may thus permit or prevent the passage of ions across the membrane, which in turn can affect the propagation of a signal down the length of the axon or neurotransmitter release at the presynaptic terminal (figure

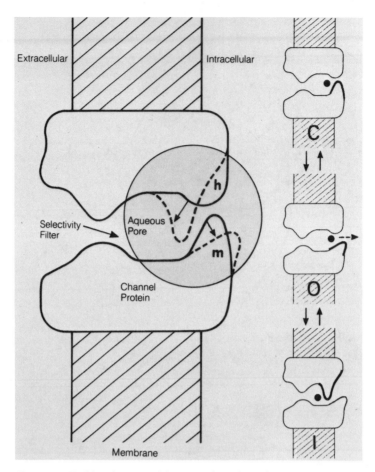

Figure 8.9 Highly schematized drawing of a sodium channel. The transmembrane protein is shown with a pore that allows sodium ions to flow between the extracellular and intracellular sides of the membrane when the gate is open. The standard Hodgkin-Huxley model of the sodium channel has two voltage-sensitive gates: The first gate (m) is normally closed at the resting potential, but opens when the cell is depolarized; the second gate (h) is normally open at the resting potential, but closes when the cell depolarizes, which inactivates the flow of ions. These two gates allow the channel to be open for only a brief period. The transitions between the closed (C) and open (O) states of the channel and the inactivated state (I) are shown on the right side of the diagram. (From Ritchie 1987.)

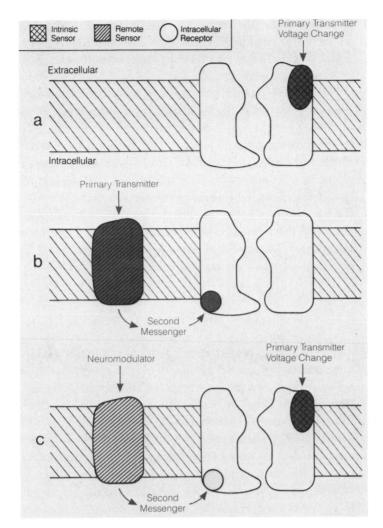

Figure 8.10 Three classes of ion channels. (a) The channel is controlled directly by voltage change or binding of a neurotransmitter molecule to a receptor. (b) The effect of the primary signal on the channel is mediated by another molecule acting as a second messenger. (c) The channel can be activated directly by the primary signal, but the response of the channel can be modulated by a neuromodular acting through a second messenger. (From Ritchie 1987.)

8.9). In a sense, the membrane allows the intracellular compartment of a neuron to respond selectively to extracellular signals, and it is this selectivity that endows different neurons with specialized information-processing capabilities.

Electrical signaling in neurons is achieved by ionic currents that are regulated by ionic channels and ionic pumps in the cell membrane. Signaling between neurons is mediated by neurotransmitter receptors in the postsynaptic membrane that respond to particular neurotransmitter molecules by transiently and selectively changing the ionic conductance of the membrane. In addition, some receptors can activate one or more second-messenger molecules that can mediate longer-term changes (figure 8.10). Second messengers in neurons can be activated by more than one receptor. Hence there is a network of interacting chemical systems within a neuron, which can itself be considered a chemical parallel-distributed processor.

8.2 Anatomical and Physiological Techniques

Nervous systems are dynamic, and physiological observations at each structural level can be arranged in a hierarchy of time scales. These scales range from microseconds, in the case of opening of single ionic channels, to days or weeks for biophysical and biochemical events underlying memory, such as long-term potentiation (McNaughton and Morris 1987, Brown et al. 1989). A large battery of techniques has been developed to try to address physiological events and processes occurring at different time scales, and by understanding what kinds of observations a given technique permits, we can begin to piece together hypotheses concerning the nature of information processing in a given structure, and how that structure contributes to the ongoing business of the brain.

Lesions

Human Studies Sometimes the brain is damaged as a result of stroke, gunshot wound, tumors, or other illnesses. Neurological assessments of the deficits and residual capacities of brain-damaged patients are an important source of information about specialization of function. When behavioral observations are correlated with a determination of the site of the lesion(s), for example, at autopsy or by magnetic resonance imaging (MRI) or positron emission tomography (PET), hypotheses can be generated concerning the brain areas that are particularly critical for certain functions. On this basis, left-hemisphere lesions have been strongly implicated in language deficits, even in most left-handed humans; bilateral lesions of the medial temporal lobe typically result in anterograde amnesia (Milner 1966, Squire et al. 1988), and lesions of the posterior parietal cortex have been implicated in loss of capacity to attend to the opposite side of the body and to the opposite hemispace (Mesulam 1985). Some lesions produce surprisingly specific perceptual and linguistic deficits (McCarthy and Warrington 1988, Damasio 1985).

Although data from clinical neurology have traditionally been and continue to be very important, they do have well-known limitations. For example, the size and exact location of lesions, which are difficult to determine, vary considerably from patient to patient. Another factor relevant in using clinical data is that patients may display some recovery of function that varies over time and that also depends on such things as the age and the gender of the patient. Additionally, the data are often difficult to interpret because a lesion may result in loss of function, not because it interferes with the specific information-processing task of a given structure, but because it interrupts fibers of passage to and from areas crucial for the function in question or some biochemical system that has a widespread influence. Moreover a lesion may affect a number of functionally distinct areas and may affect other areas through secondary degeneration. Further interpretive complications derive from other premorbid neurological and psychiatric factors, such as epilepsy, schizophrenia, and so forth. Finally, it is often difficult to find animal models for experimentation that are comparable to human cases. Despite these difficulties, important findings have been made that help to generate hypotheses concerning functional specialization of structures such as the hippocampus (see, for example, Squire, Shimamura, and Amaral 1988).

Special mention should be given in this context to split-brain studies because they involved a fairly precise surgical intervention in which any significant sparing of callosal fibers can now be detected by MRI. The disconnection effects discovered in split-brain patients (Sperry and Gazzaniga 1967) demonstrated the fragmentation of experience and awareness and confirmed the lateralization of certain functions, particularly speech production and spatioconstructive capacities, in some patients. Even in these studies, however, there are interpretive complications because all the subjects were epileptic (as opposed to normal), and there were nontrivial differences in surgical technique and in the completeness of the commissural sections. Nonetheless, studies on split-brain patients can provide a unique source of information about the global organization of processing in the brain for perceptual and cognitive phenomena such as color constancy (Land et al. 1983) and mental imagery (Kosslyn et al. 1985).

Animal Models Because humans cannot be the subjects of experimental lesions and recordings, it is essential to approach many questions concerning the human brain indirectly, via animal models. For example, the discovery in human patients that lesions to the hippocampus and related structures result in anterograde amnesia but selectively spare learning of certain skills and priming sparked the search for an animal model fitting essentially the same profile (see chapter 17). Studies on monkeys (Zola-Morgan and Squire 1984) have revealed important similarities to the human cases and, in conjunction with anatomical, pharmacological, and physiological research on the hippocampus and related structures in a variety of animals (turtles, rats, and rabbits), permit a convergence on the principles of declarative long-term memory. They also suggest new hypotheses about human memory that can be tested behaviorally. Animal studies have also been crucial to research on the neurobiological basis of sleeping and dreaming (Hobson et al. 1985).

Virtually everything we know about the microorganization of nervous systems derives from work on animal brains, and such research is absolutely indispensable if we are to have any hope of understanding the human brain. Of course there are limitations, inasmuch as there are nontrivial differences between the brains of different species, and we cannot blithely generalize from cat and monkey brains to a human brain. Even the problem of identifying homologous structures in different species can be vexing (Campbell and Hodos 1970). Nevertheless, it may be that fundamental principles can be discovered in animal models and that knowing these will provide the scaffolding for answering questions concerning those aspects of the human brain that make it unique.

Reversible Lesions and Microlesions
Some of the shortcomings of the lesion technique are being overcome by recent technical advances that make more selective intervention possible. For example, kainic acid and ibotenic acid are neurotoxic substances that destroy neurons but not fibers of passage. Additionally, the size and placement of the lesion can be carefully controlled by adjusting the amount and location of the injection. This new lesion method has been used to localize specific deficits in motion processing in MT, an extrastriate visual area in cerebral cortex (Newsome et al. 1985, Newsome and Pare 1986, Siegel and Andersen 1986).

Permanent lesions are often difficult to interpret for the reasons given above. Temporary lesions can also be made, for example, by locally cooling a region of the brain or applying local anesthetics such as lidocaine that produce measurable changes in the behavior of the animal or in the responses of neurons in other areas of the brain. Thus it is possible to separate short-term changes specific to the lesion from general or long-term alterations.

Pharmacological agents are available that can selectively interfere with particular neurons or pathways. For example, 6-hydroxydopamine, when administered to newborn rat pups, selectively destroys all the neurons in the brain that use catecholamines, such as dopamine and norepinephrine, as neurotransmitters. Even more specific lesions are possible by taking advantage of pharmacological agents that block specific synapses. The substance 4-amino-phosphonobutyric acid (APB) has been used to selectively block a class of glutamate receptors at synapses between photoreceptors and the on-center bipolar cells in the vertebrate retina (Horton and Sherk 1984, Schiller 1982). When administered to the vitreous humor, this drug reversibly blocks the entire on-center pathway to the visual system and allows the contribution of the off-center pathway to be assessed in isolation. This is very useful because it allows us to test hypotheses about the interaction of the on-center and off-center pathways and to construct models for the origin of orientation selectivity of cells in visual cortex. Another important pharmacological agent used to investigate functional properties is amino-phosphonovaleric acid (APV), which selectively blocks N-methyl-D-aspartic acid (NMDA) receptors. This selective blocking is fortunate because NMDA receptors are involved in the generation of long-term potentiation in the hippocampus, which is a change in the strengths of certain synapses when they are stimulated at a high rate (McNaughton and Morris 1987, Brown et al. 1989). The selective blocking of NMDA receptors may make it possible to dissect out components of some memory systems (Squire 1987).

One of the most important inhibitory neurotransmitters in the brain is gamma-aminobutyric acid (GABA). It can be applied exogenously in cerebral cortex and other areas to hyperpolarize certain neurons and thereby silence the generation of action potentials. This technique effectively lesions the cells from the local networks, and the lesion is reversible. It has been used to show that neurons in layer 6 of striate cortex contribute to the end-stop inhibition observed in the upper layers of the cortex (Boltz and Gilbert 1986). It is also possible to chronically apply GABA and look for long-term effects of the activity of neurons on the effectiveness of synapses. For example, if the eye of a kitten is sutured shut during its critical period of development, the geniculate afferents from the closed eye normally diminish in strength with the result that afterward, with both eyes open, cortical neurons respond only to stimulation of the previously open eye. Reiter and Stryker (1987) have reported that if the visual cortex of a kitten is chronically silenced by GABA and the same experimental conditions (above) are maintained, then the responses from the closed eye are preserved, whereas the responses from the open eye are abolished, reversing the normal finding. These experiments provide valuable information about the rules for synaptic plasticity (Sejnowski and Tesauro 1988).

As evidence about the composition of the brain at the molecular levels accumulates, more selective and more powerful techniques will become available for dissecting out specific neural circuits and assessing their functional significance. In particular, monoclonal antibodies, which bind specifically to particular molecules; genetic cloning techniques, which can be used to identify particular genes; and retroviruses, which can be used to insert particular genes into cells, may soon make it possible to target specific classes of cells and subclasses of synapses (Kandel 1983). Already many neurotransmitter receptors have been identified and their amino-acid sequences determined by cloning their genes. Clearly these new techniques cannot by themselves provide a deeper understanding of the function of the brain. But they can provide the answers to more detailed questions than was previously possible, though the questions must themselves evolve to exploit the potential of the techniques.

Imaging Techniques

Sherrington (1940) has described his imaginary vision of what the nervous system might look like if only the electrical activity in the brain could be seen: "Millions of flashing shuttles weave a dissolving pattern, though never an abiding one; a shifting harmony of subpatterns." With the advent of imaging techniques in the last decade, Sherrington's "enchanted loom" fantasy for large-scale visualization of the nervous system is becoming a reality, though by devices and with results that would have amazed and delighted him. Techniques for producing images of physiological activity depend on the introduction of tracers and dyes that are sensitive to physiological variables. Imaging also relies on computer power to handle the enormous flow of information, which is typically several orders of magnitude greater than that collected with traditional techniques such as single-unit recording. Some imaging techniques are noninvasive and can be safely used on a routine basis for studying normal processing in humans.

The first noninvasive mapping of brain structure was made possible by tomographic techniques that reconstructed a two-dimensional cross-section through the brain from a series of measurements on one-dimensional rays. Computed tomography (CT) uses differences in X-ray opacity of tissue as revealed on the reconstructed images to differentiate between major structures and to determine whether nervous tissue contains abnormalities. It has a spatial resolution of about 1 mm in the plane of section, which is good enough to distinguish brain regions such as the hippocampus from the amygdala. More recently MRI has been developed, and the most common maps are of hydrogen density. MRI maps have a much higher spatial resolution (about 0.1 mm in the plane of section, which is good enough to distinguish the line of Gennari, layer 4 of striate cortex), a better signal-to-noise ratio, and involve no conditions harmful to the subject, thus permitting studies of normal brains. The principle of the MRI depends on placing the tissue in strong magnetic fields and inducing and measuring changes in the magnetic orientation of the nuclei of atoms that make up the tissue. Patients are merely required to lie still in a magnetic field for about fifteen minutes. These two techniques are very useful for localizing lesions, tumors, and developmental abnormalities, but are thus far limited in not being able to assess functional damage that leaves the brain structures intact. They have provided only static images of brain anatomy, not dynamic information about brain activity. They can, however, be used in conjunction with techniques for measuring dynamic changes in brain activity (figure 8.11).

It is also possible to map other chemical elements in the brain using MRI, especially elements such as sodium and phosphorus whose concentrations vary with the functional state of the brain (Bachus et al. 1987). The concentration of sodium, phosphorus, and other chemical elements in living tissue, however, is much less than that of hydrogen, and hence the signal-to-noise ratio and the resolution with which a chemical element can be mapped using MRI are much lower.

The link between electrical activity and metabolism is exploited in the 2-deoxyglucose (2-DG) technique (Sokoloff 1984), in which a radioactively labeled sugar analog is injected into the blood and is selectively absorbed by neurons that have elevated levels of metabolic activity. In animals it is possible to section brain tissue and expose the brain tissue to X-ray film, thereby producing an image of local glucose metabolism with about a 0.1-mm resolution. Figure 8.12 is an image of responses in monkey visual cortex produced after presentation of a visual stimulus (Tootell et al. 1982), which was a flickering bull's-eye pattern. This is the first image to portray the remarkable correspondence between features in the world and activity patterns in a topographically mapped area of cortex. In humans PET can be used to image 2-DG metabolism with about a 10-mm resolution (Phelps and Mazziotta 1985).

One of the disadvantages of the 2-DG technique is that the activity must be averaged over 45 minutes, which is a very long time when we consider that a visual recognition task can be performed in under 500 ms. The time required to process the brain tissue and to expose it to X-ray film can be many months. Too much brain activity will saturate the response over large brain regions, reducing the visible differences between the areas. Moreover, it is not possible to match the experiment with a control run in the same animal because it must be killed to produce an image on film, and humans are limited to a single PET scan in one session. Because of variability between individuals, and even the same human on different sessions, averages over many subjects must be obtained. Also there is the complication of an uncertain link between glucose metabolism and electrical activity. The presumption is that they are tightly coupled in the neuropil, but although this is reasonable, it is not known with certainty in all brain areas. Nonetheless, comparisons between the 2-DG mapping and conventional electrical recordings provide a more comprehensive view of global processing (Jones, Juliano, and Whitsel 1987) and have revealed important data about topographical organization of neuronal properties within brain areas and projections between regions.

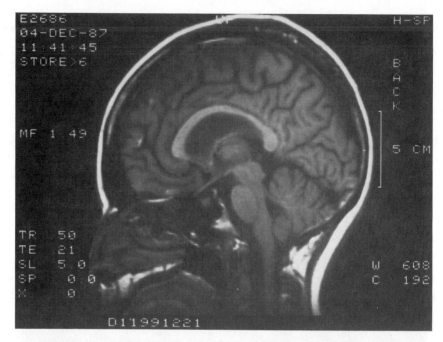

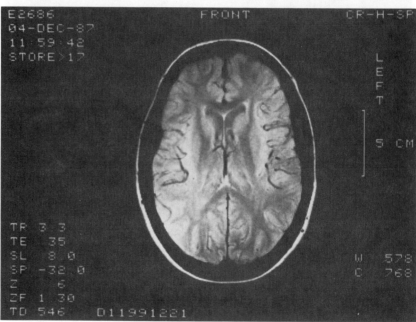

Figure 8.11 MRI (magnetic resonance imaging) of human brain. *Top*: sagittal section; *bottom*: horizontal section. (Courtesy of Bruce Crosson.)

Figure 8.12 Pattern of activity in layer 4 of primary visual cortex of a monkey visualized using the 2-deoxyglucose technique. About half of the total surface area of V1 in one hemisphere can be seen in this flattened map. The visual stimulus, presented to only one eye, was a flickering target, centered on the fovea, consisting of 8 radial lines and 5 concentric circles equally spaced on a logarithmic scale. This visual cortex responds best at the onset or offset of the stimulus. The pattern of elevated brain activity is shown in this autoradiogram by the dark regions. The stripes on the dark lines are interruptions from the ocular dominance columns of the unstimulated eye. (From Tootell et al. 1982.)

Regional blood flow can be used to monitor variable metabolic demands resulting from electrical activity (Ingvar and Schwartz 1974, Roland 1984a, Raichle 1986). Blood flow is measured by following the clearance of a bolus of xenon-133 injected into the carotid artery monitored with external radiation detectors. A related method is to measure the changes in blood flow with PET following the injection of oxygen-15–labeled water into the blood. One great advantage of these methods is that several different conditions can be studied in a single session because the clearance times and half-lives are only several minutes. These techniques have been used to study voluntary motor activity (Fox et al. 1985) and selective attention to somatosensory stimuli (Roland 1984b). The current spatial resolution of PET scanning is around 10 mm, and the ultimate resolution, limited by the range of positrons, is estimated to be 2 to 3 mm. Using an averaging technique that is applicable to point sources, however, it has been possible to map the visual field in the primary visual cortex of humans with a resolution of 1 mm (Fox et al. 1987).

PET recording offers significant opportunity to investigate the localization of higher functions, including language abilities in humans. For example, cognitive tasks such as reading single words have been studied using a subtractive technique to localize individual mental operations (Petersen et al. 1988, Posner et al. 1988; see figure 8.13). There are, however, a number of confounding variables that have to be carefully separated, such as subvocal motor activity that often accompanies mental activity.

A promising approach for use on animals is the optical recording of electrical and ionic changes in the brain by direct observation. New optical dyes have been developed for noninvasive monitoring of changes in the membrane potential of neurons (Salzberg et al. 1983, Grinvald 1985, Grinvald et al. 1986). This technique has recently been used to visualize the ocular dominance and orientation columns in visual cortex (Blasdel and Salama 1986; see figure 8.14). It also appears that small changes in the absorption of red light in visual cortex can be recorded, and that these changes are correlated with electrical responses of neurons even in the absence of dyes (Grinvald et al. 1986). Ion-sensitive fluorescent dyes, such as the calcium-sensitive dye Fura-2, have also been developed that can monitor the change in intracellular ion concentration (Tsien and Poenie 1986, Connor et al. 1987). These optical techniques could be used with confocal microscopy to produce three-dimensional images of physiological activity in vivo (Boyde 1985).

Lest the beauty and remarkable achievements of these new imaging techniques inspire uncritical enthusiasm, it should be emphasized that these techniques introduce potential artifacts as well as many new problems of interpretation, and it may be some time before they can be used routinely and with confidence. Also, none of the imaging techniques is yet nearly as flexible or has as good spatial and temporal resolution *in vivo* as recording from single neurons with microelectrodes. Despite such problems, the prospects are good that we may someday obtain global views of processing in the nervous system under conditions that are close to normal.

Gross Electrical and Magnetic Recording

The earliest electrical recordings from the scalps of humans were obtained in 1929 by Hans Berger, who recorded the microvolt changes in potential with a string galvanometer. Significant differences in the electrical activity could easily be seen depending on whether the subject was awake, in deep sleep, or dreaming (Penfield and Jasper 1954; see also figure 8.15). The electroencephalogram (EEG) has also been useful in determining the general regions of the brain specialized for certain modalities and thus in locating auditory cortex, somatosensory cortex,

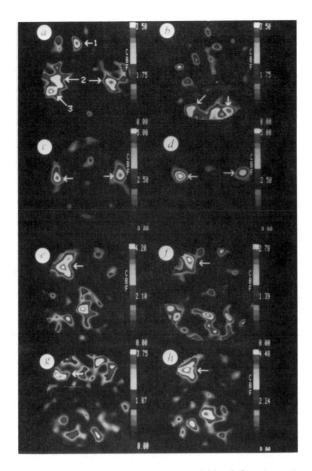

Figure 8.13 Images showing increased blood flow in regions of the brain during word processing of auditory and visual stimuli using positron emission tomography (PET). Each panel shows a horizontal slice through a human brain. The averaged difference in blood flow between two states of the brain is shown using false coloring (see scale for cerebral flow, CBF). Each of the first three pairs of panels shows tasks with auditory presentations of words at one per second (left side), and for tasks in which the words were visually presented (right side). (a, b) Average subtraction images of blood-flow change when the blood flow during rest was subtracted from blood flow during the passive response to words. The arrows indicate foci of activity in known visual and auditory sensory-processing areas. (c, d) Average subtraction images of blood-flow change when the blood flow during passive sensory presentation was subtracted from blood flow during active vocal repetition of presented words. The arrows indicate foci of activity in motor cortex. (e, f) Average subtraction images of blood-flow change when the blood flow during repetition of presented words was subtracted from blood flow during vocalization of an appropriate use for the presented word (for example, the presentation of "cake" might elicit the response "eat"). The arrows indicate strongly lateralized foci of activity in frontal cortex. (g, h) Comparison of activation on two semantic tasks. The right slice (h) is under the same condition as in e. The left slice is for change of blood flow when blood flow during passive presentation of words is subtracted from blood flow during a condition when the subject is asked to monitor the string of words for a semantic category. No motor output was required. The similar foci of activity (arrows) implicate this region of frontal cortex in semantic processing. (From Petersen et al. 1988)

Brain and Cognition

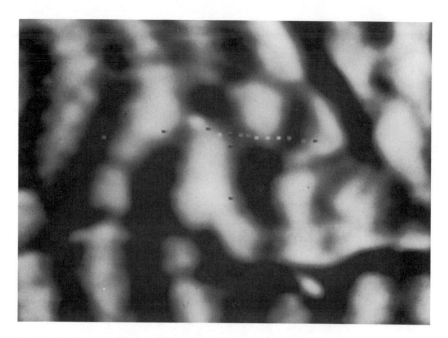

Figure 8.14 Computer-enhanced visualization of ocular dominance columns of monkey striate cortex revealed using optical recordings. A voltage-sensitive dye was applied to the cortex. One eye was closed, and the open eye was visually stimulated. Elevated activity among the neurons in alternating bands on the cortex (around 0.3 mm wide) represent ocular-dominance columns. Electrode penetrations were made into cortex tangential to layer 4, and the responses of single neurons were recorded (dots). The eye dominance recorded physiologically was consistent with the optical recording. (From Blasdel and Salama 1986.)

and so forth. A major advantage of the technique is that it is noninvasive, and it can be used on alert, behaving, normal humans.

Although the EEG has been helpful in diagnosing diseases of the brain, it has been less useful in uncovering brain mechanisms than was initially hoped. One serious difficulty in relating waveforms to underlying processing activities of neurons is that the EEG recording is a composite signal from volume conduction in many different parts of the brain, and it is far from clear what a signal means in terms of how neurons in the relevant networks are behaving. In animals, depth electrodes can be inserted and used to sort out the locations of the strong sources, but in humans this technique can be used only under special conditions where there is clear clinical justification. But even under the most favorable circumstances the localization of EEG sources is difficult and problematic.

The evoked response potential (ERP) can be extracted from the EEG recordings by signal-averaging scalp potentials that are time locked to a particular sensory stimulus or motor event, as shown in figure 8.16. (For a review see Hillyard and Picton 1987.) For example, the experimenter might present a subject with a visual stimulus, take an EEG

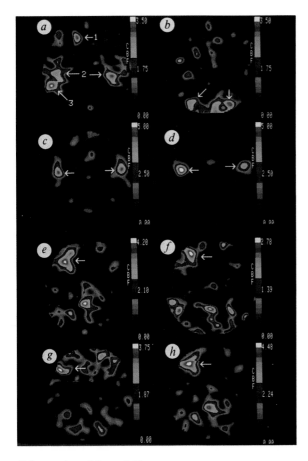

Color version of figure 8.13

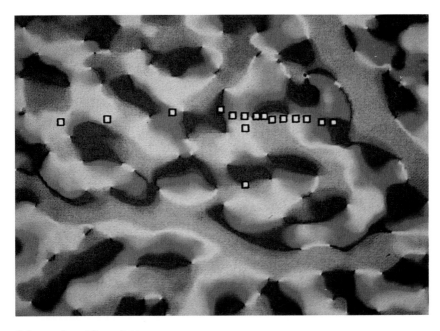

Color version of figure 8.14

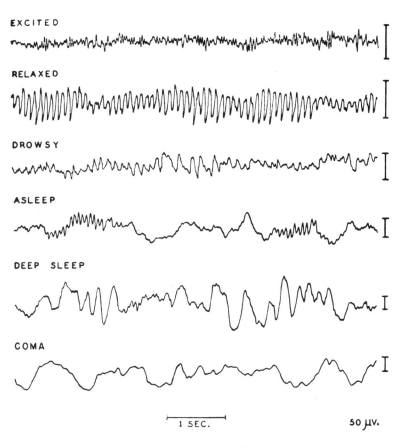

EXCITED

RELAXED

DROWSY

ASLEEP

DEEP SLEEP

COMA

1 SEC.   50 μV.

Figure 8.15 Characteristic electroencephalographic traces during variations in state of consciousness. (From Penfield and Jasper 1954.)

recording on each of ten trials, and then average those traces. Significant progress has been made in relating specific components of the ERP trace to different aspects of sensory perception. For example, reliable patterns in waveform are produced in the first 50 ms after the stimulus has been presented, and these vary reliably as a function of whether or not the stimulus was sufficiently long or intense to be conciously experienced. Other waveforms occurring later appear to reflect higher-level information processing. At about 300 ms after the stimulus, a large positive wave (P300) is produced if the stimulus was surprising or unpredicted by the subject (Donchin et al. 1983), and this has been replicated in monkeys (Paller et al. 1989). The discovery of a large negative wave (N400) under conditions where a subject is presented with a semantic incongruity (Kutas and Van Petten 1988) suggests that this technique can be used to study certain aspects of language processing. Other characteristics of the wave forms have been useful in arbitrating hypotheses about language processing and in addressing questions concerning the temporal sequence of language-processing events (Van Petten and Kutas 1987). Unfortunately, some of the com-

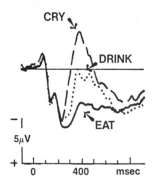

THE PIZZA WAS TOO HOT TO

BEST COMPLETIONS
RELATED ANOMALIES
UNRELATED ANOMALIES

Figure 8.16 Results of an experiment using the evoked-response potential (ERP) to study language processing in humans. Ten subjects were presented with 160 different seven-word sentences, with one word presented every 700 ms via a slide projector. All subjects were presented with the same first six words (for example, *He hung it out on the line to*), but for the final word saw one of three different words (in this example, either *sing*, *wet*, or *dry*). Recording electrodes were placed on the scalp at the midline in the parietal zone. The figure shows the grand average ERPs to the most expected sentence completions (for example, *dry*), anomalous completions (for example, *sing*), and anomalous completions that were related to the most expected word (for example *wet*). The grand average for the final word is achieved by averaging waveforms across sentences (80 expected completions, 40 anomalous completions, and 40 anomalous but related completions) and across subjects. The N400 waveform is largest when the final word presented is an unrelated anomaly, as in *He hung it out on the line to sing*, and flattest when the final word is fitting, as in *He hung it out on the line to dry*. (Courtesy of Marta Kutas and Cyma Van Petten.)

ponents of the ERP are probably not unitary, but have several sources that have different magnitudes under different experimental conditions. For example, P300 appears to have both cortical and subcortical sources. It may be possible to model sources of evoked potentials in the brain and localize the origin of each component (Scherg and Von Cramon 1986).

The currents in neurons give rise to magnetic as well as electrical fields. These magnetic fields are not affected by volume conduction, as is the EEG, so that current sources are more easily localized than the electrical fields and can be measured with sensitive superconducting magnetometers (Williamson and Kaufman 1987). One strategy, therefore, is to try to correlate magnetic-field properties with aspects of information processing. However, it is not possible to reconstruct the internal current sources from the magnetoencephalogram (MEG) without making additional assumptions about the spatial distribution of the sources. Nonetheless, it has been possible to map parts of the visual cortex in humans and to show that primary auditory cortex is tonotopically mapped with a logarithmic frequency scale. The MEG technique is still very new and its potential has not been fully explored. In particular, arrays of magnetic sensors will soon be available that will speed up the process of producing magnetic brain maps.

Single-Unit Recording

Most of our knowledge of the response properties of single neurons has been derived from the method of single-unit recording. In this technique a microelectrode with a sharp tip is inserted into the brain and used to record local extracellular potentials. Intracellular potentials can also be recorded using extremely fine glass micropipettes; stable intracellular recordings in vivo are only possible for a few minutes, however, compared with many hours for extracellular recordings (figure 8.17). One major advantage of recording from single units is high spatial and temporal resolution, and many groundbreaking results have been achieved using the technique. For example, we have learned much about the architecture of visual cortex in anesthetized animals following the pioneering work of Hubel and Wiesel (1962). The discoveries concerning topographically mapped areas of cortex all depended on using single-unit recordings.

More recently it has become possible to study the changes in single-unit responses in the visual cortex of awake behaving animals to directed visual attention (Moran and Desimone 1985) and task-dependent variables, such as whether the animal is searching for a specific visual pattern to match a presented tactile pattern (Hanny, Maunsell, and Schiller 1988, Maunsell and Newsome 1987). The higher in the visual hierarchy one looks, however, the more difficult it is to find the adequate visual stimulus for a neuron, though there are tantalizing reports of neurons selective for hands and faces (Barlow 1985, Perrett, Mistlin, and Chitty 1987) and of neurons in the hippocampus selective for spatial location of the animal (O'Keefe and Nadel 1978). In the higher visual areas and in association cortex it is not at all clear that the stimuli chosen are the appropriate ones to use, or even how the responses should be interpreted. For example, it may someday be discovered that cells that were thought selective for faces may in fact also respond to more abstract stimuli, such as a particular class of fractal shapes (Mandelbrot 1983, Pentland 1984). Furthermore, there is always the worry that we are missing an important population of neurons because of low yield and selective sampling.

Many response properties of single neurons are highly correlated with properties of sensory stimuli and movements, but the responses of relatively few cells have been correlated with what an organism

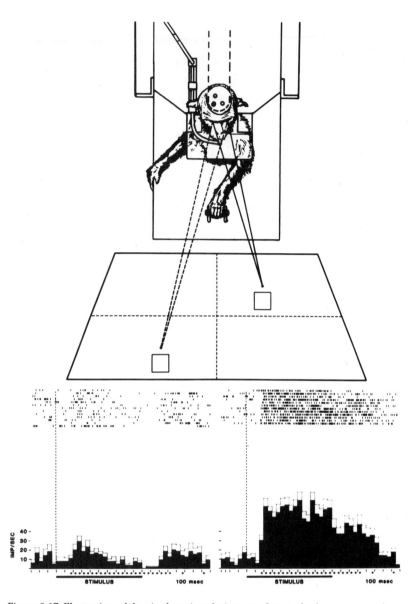

Figure 8.17 Illustration of the single-unit technique used to study the response of neurons in the parietal cortex of an awake, behaving monkey. The animal fixated a small target light placed at a series of positions on the screen, with its head fixed. The results obtained at two positions are shown here. At each fixation position a square was flashed for one second at 10° above the point of fixation. Recordings from a single neuron are shown below the screen. Each line represents a single trial and each small nick made on the line represents the discharge of an impulse by the neuron. The impulses were summed in the histograms. The right side of the figure shows the responses for the fixation to the left and down, and the responses on the left side are for fixation to the right and up. This and other experiments show that this class of neurons in parietal cortex has receptive fields that are fixed to the retina, but the degree of activation of the neuron to a visual stimulus within the receptive field is modulated by the position of the eye. Zipser and Andersen (1988) have shown that these responses can be accurately modeled by a network of neurons that transforms the location of an object from a retinal-centered coordinate system to a head-centered coordinate system. This is an example of a distributed representation of a spatial relationship. (From Andersen and Mountcastle 1983.)

perceives. For example, many neurons in our visual system respond differentially to the wavelength of light. However, the perception of color dépends more on the reflectance properties of surfaces than on wavelength, so that the perception of color is roughly constant under varying illumination. Only a small subset of neurons in the visual cortex respond similarly to the perceptual report of color (Zeki 1983). If most neurons in the visual cortex respond to the spectral composition of a scene, why do we not have perceptual awareness of this information? For that matter, most neurons in V1 have an ocular preference, and some cells respond only to one eye, but when a spot of light is randomly shined into the one of the eyes, an observer cannot report which eye was stimulated despite all the information contained in single-unit responses. In general the higher a neuron in a sensory system the more likely that its response can be related to perceptual responses. For example, some neurons in V2 but not in V1 respond to illusory contours, such as Kanizsa figures (von der Heydt et al. 1984). A further problem is that responses correlated with behavior may not be causally necessary and sufficient for that behavior. For example, there is a massive change in the firing rate of hippocampal neurons in a rabbit during conditioning of an eye-blink response, but lesion of the hippocampus after training does not affect the acquired response, and rabbits without a hippocampus show normal conditioning (Berger and Thompson 1978).

Properties of networks of neurons cannot be simply inferred on the basis of the properties of small samples of cells, yet determining network properties is probably essential for understanding perceptual mechanisms. Therefore, to understand the principles of spatiotemporal coding in networks of neurons, much more work has to be done to discover what is happening in a larger population of cells. Methods for obtaining simultaneous multiunit recordings are being developed, and it is already evident that network properties to which we are blind when restricted to single-unit methods become accessible when behavior of a larger population is observed, such as synchronous firing (Llinas 1985, Reitboeck 1983, Gerstein et al. 1983). Desirable though these methods are, the technical problems in developing them are immense. Optical techniques for recording cellular responses may also prove useful in addressing population properties, but they have not yet achieved single-unit resolution in cortical structures.

A useful way to get an overview of the assorted techniques is to graph them with respect to temporal and spatial resolution. This permits us to spot spatiotemporal domains where there do not yet exist techniques to access levels of organization and to compare the strengths and weaknesses of various methods (see figure 8.18). For example, it is apparent that we lack detailed information about processing in cortical layers and columns over a wide range of time scales, from milliseconds to hours. There is also a pressing need for experimental techniques designed to address the dendritic and synaptic level of investigation in

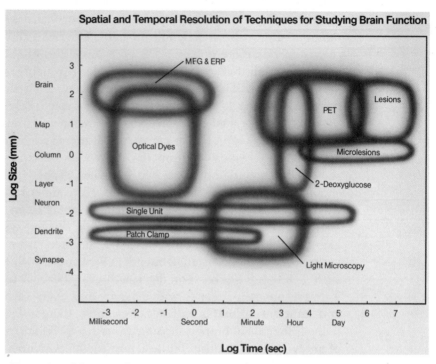

Spatial and Temporal Resolution of Techniques for Studying Brain Function

Figure 8.18 Schematic illustration of the ranges of spatial and temporal resolution of various physiological techniques for studying the function of the brain. The vertical axis represents the spatial extent of the technique, with the boundaries indicating the largest and smallest sizes of the region from which the technique can provide useful information. Thus single-unit recording can only provide information from a small region of space, typically 10 to 50 μm on a side. The horizontal axis represents the minimum and maximum time interval over which information can be collected with the technique. Thus action potentials from a single neuron can be recorded with millisecond accuracy over many hours. Patch recording allows the iconic currents through single channels to be recorded. Optical dyes have been used with cellular resolution in tissue culture, where it is possible to obtain a clear view of single cells. Recordings from the central nervous system are limited in resolution, however, by the optical properties of nervous tissue, and only about 0.1-mm resolution has been achieved. ERP (evoked-response potential) and MEG (magnetoencephalography) record the average electrical and magnetic activity over large brain regions and are limited to events that take place over about one second. The temporal resolution of PET (positron emission tomography) depends on the lifetime of the isotope being used, which ranges from minutes to an hour. It may be possible to achieve a temporal resolution of seconds with oxygen-15 to study fast changes in blood flow using temporal binning of the gamma-ray events (equivalent to the poststimulus time histogram for action potentials). The 2-deoxyglucose technique has a time resolution of about 45 minutes and a spatial resolution of 0.1 mm with large pieces of tissue and 1 μm with small pieces of tissue. Lesions allow the interruption of function to be studied both immediately after and for a long period of time following the ablation. Microlesion techniques make possible much more precise and selective interruptions of particular regions of the brain. Confocal microscopy, a promising technique for the study of nervous tissue, is a recent improvement of the light microscope for use with three-dimensional specimens. All of the boundaries here show rough regions of the spatiotemporal plane where these techniques have been used, and are not meant to indicate fundamental limitations. Purely anatomical techniques are not included. Major advances in MRI (magnetic resonance imaging) could lead to the in vivo dynamical imaging of structural modifications and chemical reaction rates (Luyten and den Hollander 1986).

cerebral cortex. Finally, every technique has its limitations, so that more than one technique may be needed at a given resolution to validate results.

8.3 General Neurobiological Constraints on Cognitive Mechanisms

A central part of the basic strategy for figuring out how a novel device works is reverse engineering. That is, when a new camera or chip appears on the market, competitors will take it apart to find out how it works. Typically, of course, competitors already know quite a lot about devices of that general kind, so the problem can be manageable. Although we have to use reverse engineering to study the brain, our starting point is much further back because we know so little about devices of that general kind. From our vantage point the brain is essentially a bit of *alien* technology, and hence it is especially difficult to know, among the available facts, which are theoretically important and which are theoretically uninteresting. We may actually misunderstand some aspects of brain organization and consequently be blocked from having some important insight into mechanisms crucial for cognition. For example, some divisions made in gross anatomy may turn out to conceal close relationships between distant brain regions. Moreover, it may turn out that the functional properties of some synapses in the central nervous system are very different from peripheral synapses in autonomic ganglia and neuromuscular junctions, on which most of our knowledge of synaptic mechanisms is based.

It would be an interesting and useful exercise to have a survey of neuroscientific opinion on this question: What are twelve basic organizational constraints on brain function from neuroscience? Or in another version: If a cognitive neuroscientist can have only twelve organizational constraints from neurobiology before being locked in a room to develop functional hypotheses, which twelve would they be? Short of having formally conducted such a survey, we conjecture that the following dozen are among those likely to be on such a list, although we recognize that opinion can diverge in considerable and surprising ways, and also that any current list would undoubtedly be quickly outdated (for comparable lists see Shepherd 1988 and Crick and Asanuma 1986):

1. It is estimated that in the human nervous system there are about 10^{12} neurons and about 10^{15} synapses.

2. An action potential lasts about 1 ms; synaptic transmission, including electronic conduction in dendrites, takes about 5 ms. Transmission velocity in myelinated axons is about 10 to 100 m/s; in unmyelinated axons it is less than 1 m/s. These are general ranges, not precise values.

3. Synapses are excitatory or inhibitory and synaptic potentials can last from a millisecond to many minutes (Kuffler 1980). The integration of synaptic potentials can be additive or multiplicative depending on the ionic conductances and the synaptic geometry. Certain neurotrans-

mitters, such as some peptides and monoamines, act at several tenths of a millimeter from their release sites, though with a delay and a long-lasting effect (Kuffler 1980). It has also been discovered that at some synapses the same transmitter can activate several different receptors on the postsynaptic membrane and different neurotransmitters can be released from a single bouton under different stimulus conditions (Kuffler 1980). Peptide neurotransmitters, for example, almost always co-localize with at least one other neurotransmitter (Hokfelt 1987). Hormones in the general circulation can alter neural activity.

4. Typically, cell-to-cell interactions are weak (amounting to 1 to 5 percent of the firing threshold), and cells receive inputs from thousands of other cells. There may be some interesting exceptions to this, such as the chandelier cells in cerebral cortex (Martin 1984).

5. The brain appears to be highly parallel in that there are many parallel streams of input for a given function. For example, in the monkey two parallel streams from the retina, starting with different types of ganglion cells, project to two distinct sets of layers of the lateral geniculate nucleus, the parvocellular and magnocellular layers respectively, which in turn project to distinct sublaminae in layer 4 of cortical area V1 of the visual cortex (Hubel and Livingstone 1987; Livingstone and Hubel 1987a,b). The system also appears to be hierarchical, insofar as there are multiple feedforward stages. The latency of response to a sensory stimulus, such as a flashing light, reveals a temporal hierarchy of processing within each processing stream.

6. Not everything is directly connected to everything else, and connectivity appears to be highly specific. Most connections are between, not within, cell classes (Sereno 1988). Within certain limits there is considerable plasticity in connectivity, as demonstrated by the changes in ocularity of cortical cells of kittens induced by keeping one of the eyes closed during the critical period of development.

7. Cortical layers in sensory areas display considerable regularity in projection profiles: feedforward connections are mainly from layer 4, feedback connections are mainly non-4, namely 2, 3, and 5, and are made via white matter (Maunsell and Van Essen 1983). Pyramidal cells in layers 5 and 6 mainly project to subcortical structures such as the basal ganglia, superior colliculus, claustrum and thalamus (see figure 8.6b). Cortical connections from one topographically mapped area to another are strictly excitatory.

8. In addition to the specific system projecting to the neocortex via the thalamus, such as is seen in the visual, auditory, and somatosensory systems, there are five sources of widely projecting neurons, each associated with a specific neurotransmitter, which may be important in the sleep-dream-wake cycle, in memory, and in awareness and attention. The five sources are the locus coeruleus in the brain stem (norepinephrine), the raphe nucleus in the midbrain (serotonin), the substantia

nigra in the midbrain (dopamine), the nucleus basalis in the basal forebrain (acetylcholine), and special groups of cells in the mammillary region of the hypothalamus (GABA). The neurotransmitter receptors for these systems belong to a superfamily of receptors whose effects are mediated by second-messenger effects (see figure 8.10). The effects are longer lasting than those produced by neurotransmitters acting on receptors from other superfamilies, such as the class of glutamate receptors.

9. Under the classical definition, the receptive field of a cell is that region of the sensory field from which an adequate sensory stimulus will elicit a response. Receptive field properties in higher areas of visual cortex differ from the early stages, where receptive fields are quite small (one-sixth of a degree in the foveal region of V1), and cells are tuned to respond to quite simple stimuli (spot of light, bar of light). In inferotemporal cortex, for example, the fields are much larger (10° to the whole visual field), and the stimuli evoking responses are more complex (a hand, a face).

10. Neurons are rather coarsely tuned, and the receptive fields of cells overlap. This suggests that precision is achieved through overlapping redundancy and population coding. It is not known to what extent particular objects and single items are coded by small sets of neurons ("grandmother cells"). It is not generally possible to characterize correctly the tasks of neurons in a particular area, even when something is known about the response properties from single cells in that area. More precisely, models show that the *function* of a sensory neuron depends on its output "projective" field as well as its receptive field (Lehky and Sejnowski 1988).

11. Events outside the classical receptive field of a cell have been found to selectively modulate the responses of the cell (Allman et al. 1985). The effects are selective since they vary as a function of the type of surrounding stimuli. For example, certain wavelength-dependent neurons in V4 are influenced by the color balance in the surroundings (Zeki 1983). The surrounding effects of cells in the middle temporal area (MT), where receptive fields are typically 5° to 10°, can extend from 40° to 80°.

12. Last, but of fundamental importance, the nervous system is the product of a long evolution. The original functions of some parts have been altered by layer upon layer of modifications. For example, our ability to mentally image complex objects depends on visual processing systems that probably evolved for other functions (Kosslyn 1987, 1988). We cannot expect the design of the brain to resemble anything that a human would consider optimal. Much of our intuition must be guided therefore by biological facts rather than by logical assumptions. This may doom forever someone who wants to understand brain function but does not have access to more of the relevant experimental literature.

8.4 Models

While we need experimental data concerning the properties of neurons, we also need to find models that explain how neural networks manage to represent such things as surfaces, optical flow, and color constancy; how networks learn, store, and retrieve information; how they accomplish sensorimotor integration; and so forth. Ideally, modeling and experimental research have a symbiotic relationship, such that each informs, corrects, and inspires the other.

To treat a mechanism as a black box is equivalent to deciding to ignore certain details of the mechanism in order to find the properties that play a prominent role in the function. Such simplifying and idealizing is essential to theorizing in science in general, though it is notoriously difficult to determine which properties one can safely ignore in constructing the theory of the function, and certainly no decision procedure exists for that problem.

We could treat the brain as a whole as a black box, but the trouble with this strategy is that there are indefinitely many computational models one might dream up, and none might be even close to how the brain in fact achieves solutions to difficult computational problems. The more profitable strategy would be to treat the brain as a lot of little black boxes. For example, one could take an individual neuron as a black box, thereby deciding not to worry for the nonce about such matters as types of single channels in neuronal membranes, the details of dendritic responsivity, the role of microtubules, and so on. One could choose a slightly larger size of black box, taking, say, cortical columns as units, where the details of connectivity within the column are ignored in the model but intercolumn connectivity is analyzed and incorporated. Or, going larger yet again, one could treat the visual areas as wholes, or the hippocampus or cerebellar cortex as the level of organization one tries to address.

Although diverse kinds of things are presented as models for some part of the nervous system, it is useful to distinguish between ideas that are genuinely and strongly predictive of some aspect of nervous system dynamics or anatomy and ideas that, though not so predictive, demonstrate that the nervous system *could be* governed by the principles specified in the idea. The first—genuinely predictive hypotheses—we call *models*, and the second we call *demonstrations*.[2] *Connectionist network models* (see chapter 4) are typically motivated by cognitive phenomena and are governed primarily by computational constraints, while figuring in the background are very general neurobiological constraints such as number of processing units and time required to perform a task. Accordingly they are more properly considered demonstrations than models, in the sense defined above. *Models of real neural networks,* by contrast, are primarily motivated by biological constraints, such as the physiological and anatomical properties of specific cell types (Arbib and George

1987, MacGregor 1987a,b, Sejnowski, Koch, and Churchland 1988, Koch and Segev 1989). Despite their different origins and sources of dominant constraints both connectionist models and neural models are based on the mathematics of nonlinear dynamical systems in high-dimensional spaces (Abraham and Shaw 1982). As a consequence, there is a common conceptual and technical background that allows researchers in both fields to communicate with each other. Such communication provides links between two rich sources of experimental data, and consequently connectionist and neural models have the potential to coevolve toward an integrated, coherent account of information processing in the mind-brain.

The ultimate goal of a unified account does not entail that it be a *single* model that spans all the levels of organization seen in nervous systems, or that the highest level be explained directly in terms of events at the molecular level. Instead it is more probable that the integration consist of a chain of theories and models that links adjacent levels. The unifying connections would derive, therefore, from the chain of interlocking theories in virtue of which phenomena at one level are explained in terms of phenomena at a lower level, and those in turn by phenomena at yet lower levels. Notice also that should one level be explained in terms of a lower level, this does not mean that the higher-level theory is no longer useful, or that the phenomena at that level no longer exist, or that if they do, they are no longer worth studying. On the contrary, such levels, and the theories pertinent to those levels, will persist. As in genetics and embryology, explanations coexist at all levels, from the molecular to the systems level.

8.5 Conclusions

It would be very convenient if we could understand the nature of cognition without understanding the nature of the brain itself. Unfortunately, it is very difficult if not impossible to theorize effectively on these matters in the absence of neurobiological constraints. The primary reason is that computational space is consummately vast, and there are many conceivable solutions to the problem of how a cognitive operation could be accomplished. Neurobiological data provide essential constraints on computational theories, and they consequently provide an efficient means for narrowing the search space. Equally important, the data are also richly suggestive of hints concerning what might really be going on and what computational strategies evolution might have chanced upon. Moreover, it is by no means clear or settled yet what exactly are the functional categories at the cognitive levels, and theories of lower-level function may well be crucial to the discovery of the nature of higher-level organization. Accordingly, despite the fact that the brain is experimentally demanding, neurobiology is indispensable to the discovery of theories that explain how we perform such tasks as seeing, thinking, and being aware.

On the other hand, the possibility that cognition will be an open book once we understand the details of each and every neuron and its development, connectivity, response properties, and so forth is likewise misconceived. Even if we could simulate, synapse for synapse, our entire nervous system, that accomplishment, by itself, would not be the same as understanding how it works. The simulation might be just as much of a mystery as the function of the brain currently is, for it may reveal nothing about the network and systems properties that hold the key to cognitive effects. Genuine theorizing about the nature of neurocomputation is therefore essential.

Assuming that there are a number of levels of organization in nervous systems, such that cognitive science specifically addresses higher levels whereas neuroscience typically addresses lower levels, we can acknowledge this joint effort by saying that the goal is to figure out how the *mind-brain* works. In this sense, an ultimate goal is the *reductive integration* of the psychological and neurobiological sciences, and thus cognitive neuroscience is a genuinely interdisciplinary undertaking (LeDoux and Hirst 1986). Reduction here does not entail elimination, any more than the reduction of chemistry to physics entails the elimination of chemical principles. On the contrary, an integrative reduction between theories at different levels can provide insights that enrich the principles at both levels (Churchland 1986).

Remarkable developments in the seventies and eighties in cognitive science, computational theory, and neuroscience have engendered a new, if cautious, optimism for achieving some measure of integration and explanatory unification of the various levels of organization in nervous systems. Until quite recently the immediate goals of neuroscientists and cognitive scientists were sufficiently distant from each other that their discoveries often seemed of merely academic significance to the other. The third element, computer science, was unpromising as a means of bridging the gap because the dominant model of computation, based on the Turing machine and the von Neumann architecture, did not relate at all to what was known about nervous systems at the level of signal processing. All this has begun to change quite dramatically, and there is gathering conviction among scientists that the time is especially propitious for a fruitful convergence of research from hitherto isolated fields. In light of these considerations, the prospects favor genuine progress in generating theories that honor neurobiological and psychological constraints to explain how networks of neurons achieve high-level effects.

The social and institutional background for studying the relationship between mind and brain is rapidly evolving. Cross-disciplinary contact and collaboration is increasing, there are meetings on such topics as computational neuroscience and biological cognition, new journals for cognitive neuroscience and neural computation are being founded, and departments of cognitive science and institutes for the study of the mind-brain are coming into existence. These developments signify the need for stable scientific institutions to enable further cross-disciplinary research, and they are enormously important if the integrative program is to succeed. For it is not enough that researchers in one field read the journals and attend the meetings of the other field. Rather it will be through working together on common projects that the major break-throughs will most likely come.

Notes

We are indebted to Francis Crick, whose insights as well as critical judgments were a major resource in writing this chapter. We are grateful to Michael Posner and William Lytton for thoughtful readings of the manuscript.

1. The original concept of levels of analysis can be found in Marr and Poggio (1976, 1977). Although Marr (1982) emphasized the importance of the computational level, the notion of a hierarchy of levels grew out of earlier work by Reichardt and Poggio (1976) on the visual control of orientation in the fly. In a sense the current view on the interaction between levels is not so much a departure from the earlier views as a return to the practice that was previously established by Reichardt, Poggio, and even by Marr himself, who published a series of papers on neural-network models of the cerebellar cortex and cerebral cortex (see, for example, Marr 1969, 1970). The emphasis on the computational level has nonetheless had an important influence on the problems and issues that concern the current generation of neural and connectionist models (Sejnowski, Koch, and Churchland 1988).

2. We owe this analysis to Francis Crick, who sees demonstrations as "don't-worry theories," inasmuch as they address only the possibility that something could be done in a certain way, not the further question of whether it is in fact done in that way.

Selected Annotated Readings

Other chapters in this book touch on specialized aspects of brain and cognition including vision (chapter 15), attention (chapter 16), memory (chapter 17), and motor control (chapters 18 and 19). In this annotated bibliography we list some accessible books, journals, and reviews that can provide the reader with an entry into the literature. The list is selective and by no means exhaustive.

Arbib, M. A., 1987. *Brains, Machines and Mathematics*. 2nd ed. New York: Springer-Verlag. Historical survey of brain modeling.

Changeux, J.-P., 1985. *Neuronal Man*. Oxford: Oxford University Press. Sweeping view of the brain and behavior in the light of developmental and molecular neurobiology.

Churchland, Patricia Smith. 1986. *Neurophilosophy: Toward a Unified Science of the Mind-Brain*. Cambridge, MA: MIT Press. Exploration of the rapprochement of the cognitive and neural sciences.

Dowling, J. E. 1987. *The Retina: An Approachable Part of the Brain*. Cambridge, MA: Harvard

University Press. Though separate from the brain, the retina is part of the central nervous system, and it is one of the few parts some of whose functions we may already understand.

Groves, Philip M., and Rebec, George V. 1988. *Introduction to Biological Psychology.* 3rd ed. Dubuque, IA: William C. Brown Co. Publishers. Comprehensive and very readable basic introduction.

Hubel, D. H. 1988. *Eye, Vision and Brain.* New York: Freeman. Masterly survey of what is currently known about the structure and function of the visual systems of cats and monkeys.

Jeannerod, M. 1985. *The Brain Machine.* Cambridge, MA: Harvard University Press. Thoughtful historical account of the development of ideas on the neurophysiology of higher mental functions, particularly of action systems.

LeDoux, Joseph E., and Hirst, William, eds. 1986. *Mind and Brain: Dialogues in Cognitive Neuroscience.* Cambridge, Engl.: Cambridge University Press. Topics such as memory and attention are addressed by both psychologists and neuroscientists, with each commenting on the other. Illustrates the problems and prospects for interactions between neuroscientists and cognitive scientists.

Kandel, E., and Schwartz, J. 1985. *Principles of Neural Science.* 2nd ed. New York: Elsevier. Comprehensive introduction to all levels of brain organization including topics from neurology.

Kuffler, S. W., Nicolls, J. G., and Martin, A. R. 1984. *From Neuron to Brain: A Cellular Approach to the Function of the Nervous System.* 2nd ed. Sunderland, MA: Sinauer. Reliable, well-written introduction to cellular neurobiology.

Plum, F., and Mountcastle, V., eds. 1987. Higher functions of the brain. In *Handbook of Physiology.* Vol. 5, sec. 1. See especially chapters by R. Andersen on parietal cortex, P. Goldman-Rakic on frontal cortex, and S. Hillyard and T. Picton on evoked-responses potentials.

Rumelhart, D. G., and McClelland, J. L. 1986. *Parallel Distributed Processing: Explorations in the Microstructure of Cognition. Volume 1: Foundations. Volume 2: Psychological and Biological Models.* Cambridge, MA: MIT Press. Seminal collection of papers on connectionist modeling.

Schwartz, E., ed. 1990. *Computational Neuroscience.* Cambridge, MA: MIT Press. Collection of papers on modeling the nervous system, from the biophysical to the systems level.

Shepherd, G. M. 1987. *Neurobiology.* 2nd ed. Oxford: Oxford University Press. Broadly based survey of cellular and systems-level neuroscience, including invertebrate neurobiology.

Squire, L. R. 1987. *Memory and Brain.* Oxford: Oxford University Press. Accessible and sound entry to the literature on the biological basis of memory and learning.

Cognitive Neuroscience. Quarterly journal. Cambridge, MA: MIT Press. Research articles on neural mechanisms that underlie cognitive processing.

Neural Computation. Quarterly journal. Cambridge, MA: MIT Press. Short research papers on brain models in computational neuroscience and neural information processing systems in neurocomputing. Also contains reviews that are accessible to a general reader.

Trends in Neuroscience. Monthly journal (Elsevier). Contains brief but very useful technical reviews and is a good place to get up-to-date references to the literature on topics of current interest.

Annual Reviews of Neuroscience. Palo Alto, CA: Annual Reviews Inc. Comprehensive reviews of the literature on special topics.

Daedalus: Journal of the American Academy of Arts and Sciences. Winter 1988 Special Issue on Artificial Intelligence. Includes many interesting essays on the relationship between brains and computers. See especially "Neural Nets and Artificial Intelligence," by J. D. Cowan and D. H. Sharp; "The New Connectionism: Developing Relationships Between Neuroscience and Artificial Intelligence," by J. T. Schwartz; "Real Brains and Artificial Intelligence," by G. N. Reeke Jr. and G. M. Edelman; "The Prospects for Building Truly Intelligent Machines," by D. L. Waltz; and "Making Machines (and Artificial Intelligence) See," by A. Hurlbert and T. Poggio.

References

Abraham, R. F., and Shaw, C. D. 1982. *Dynamics, the Geometry of Behavior.* Santa Cruz: Aerial Press.

Adrian, E. D. 1953. The mechanism of olfactory stimulation in the mammal. *Adv. Sci. (Lond.)* 9:417–420.

Alkon, D. L. 1987. *Memory Traces in the Brain.* Oxford: Oxford University Press.

Allman, J. 1982. Reconstructing the evolution of the brain in primates through the use of comparative neurophysiological and neuroanatomical data. In E. Armstrong and D. Falk, eds. *Primate Evolution.* New York: Plenum, pp. 13–28.

Allman, J., Miezin, F., and McGuiness, E. 1985. Stimulus specific response from beyond the classical receptive field: Neurophysiological mechanisms for local–global comparisons in visual neurons. In W. M. Cowan, E. M. Shooter, C. F. Stevens, and R. F. Thompson, eds. *Annual Review of Neuroscience.* Palo Alto: Annual Reviews, Inc., pp. 407–430.

Andersen, R. A., and Mountcastle, V. B. 1983. The influence of the angle of gaze upon the excitability of light-sensitive neurons of the posterior parietal cortex. *Journal of Neuroscience* 3:532–548.

Arbib, M., and George, S. A. 1987. *1987 Short Course Syllabus: Computational Neuroscience.* Washington, DC: Society for Neuroscience.

Asanuma, H. 1975. Recent developments in the study of the columnar arrangement of neurons within motor cortex. *Physiological Review* 55:143–156.

Bachus, R., Mueller, E., Koenig, H., Braeckle, G., and Weber, H. 1987. Functional imaging using NMR. In V. R. McCready, M. Leach, and P. J. Ell, eds. *Functional Studies Using NMR.* New York: Springer-Verlag, pp. 43–60.

Barlow, H. B. 1985. The Twelfth Bartlett Memorial Lecture: The role of single neurons in the psychology of perception. *Quart. J. Exp. Psych.* 37A: 121–145.

Berger, T. W., and Thompson, R. F. 1978. Neuronal plasticity in the limbic system during classical conditioning of the rabbit nictitating membrane response. 1. The hippocampus. *Brain Research* 145:323–346.

Blasdel, G. G., and Salama, G. 1986. Voltage-sensitive dyes reveal a modular organization in monkey striate cortex. *Nature* 321:579–585.

Boltz, J., and Gilbert, C. D. 1986. Generation of end-inhibition in the visual cortex via interlaminar connections. *Nature* 320:362–365.

Boyde, A. 1985. Stereoscopic images in confocal (tandem scanning) microscopy. *Science* 230:1270–1272.

Brown, T. H., Ganong, A. H., Kariss, E. W., and Keenan, C. L. 1989. Hebbian synapses— Computations and biophysical mechanisms. *Ann. Rev. Neurosci.* 12: (in press).

Cajal, S. R. 1937. *Recollections of My Life.* Philadelphia: American Philosophical Society.

Campbell, C. B. G., and Hodos, W. 1970. The concept of homology and the evolution of the nervous system. *Brain, Behavior and Evolution* 3:353–367.

Churchland, P. M. 1985. Some reductive strategies in cognitive neurobiology. *Mind* 95:279–309.

Churchland, P. S. 1986. *Neurophilosophy: Toward a Unified Science of the Mind-Brain.* Cambridge, MA: MIT Press.

Churchland, P. S., and Sejnowski, T. J. 1988a. Neural representations and neural computations. In L. Nadel, ed. *Neural Connections and Mental Computation.* Cambridge, MA: MIT Press.

Churchland, P. S., and Sejnowski, T. J. 1988b. Perspectives in cognitive neuroscience. *Science* 242:741–745.

Connor, J. A., Tseng, H. S., and Hockberger, P. E. 1987. Depolarization- and transmitter-induced changes in intracellular calcium of rat cerebellar granule cells in explant cultures. *Journal of Neuroscience* 7:1384–1400.

Cowan, W. M., Fawcett, J. W., O'Leary, D. D. M., and Stanfield, B. B. 1984. Regressive events in neurogenesis. *Science* 225:1258–1265.

Crick, F. H. C. 1979 (September). Thinking about the brain. *Scientific American* 241(3):219–232.

Crick, F. H. C., and Asanuma, C. 1986. Certain aspects of the anatomy and physiology of the cerebral cortex. In J. L. McClelland, and D. E. Rummelhart, eds. *Parallel Distributed Processing: Explorations in the Microstructure of Cognition: Psychological and Biological.* Cambridge, MA: MIT Press, pp. 333–371.

Damasio, A. R. 1985. Disorders of complex visual processing: Agnosias, achromotopsia,

Balint's syndrome, and related difficulties of orientation and construction. In M.-M. Mesulam, ed. *Principles of Behavioral Neurology.* Philadelphia: F.A. Davis, pp. 259–288.

DeYoe, E. A., and Van Essen, D. C. 1988. Concurrent Processing Streams on monkey visual cortex. *Trends in Neuroscience* 11:219–226.

Dobbins, A., Zucker, S. W., and Cynader, M. S. 1987. Endstopped neurons in the visual cortex as a substrate for calculating curvature. *Nature* 329:438–441.

Donchin, E., McCarthy, G., Kutas, M., and Ritter, W. 1983. Event-related potentials in the study of consciousness. In G. E. Schwartz and D. Shapiro, eds. *Consciousness and Self-Regulation.* New York: Plenum, pp. 81–121.

Feldman, J. A., and Ballard, D. H. 1982. Connectionist models and their properties. *Cognitive Science* 6:205–254.

Ferrier, D. (1876). *The Function of the Brain.* London: Smith, Elder.

Ferster, D., and Koch, C. 1987. Neuronal connections underlying orientation selectivity in cat visual cortex. *Trends in Neurosciences* 10:487–492.

Fetz, E. E., and Cheney, P. D. 1980. Postspike facilitation of forelimb muscle activity by primate corticomotoneural cells. *Journal of Neurophysiology* 44:751–772.

Fox, P. T., Fox, J. M., and Raichle, M. E. 1985. The role of the cerebral cortex in the generation of voluntary saccades: A positron emission tomographic study. *Journal of Neurophysiology* 54:348–369.

Fox, P. T., Miezin, F. M., Allman, J. A., Van Essen, D. C., and Raichle, M. E. 1987. Retinoptic organization of human visual cortex mapped with positron emission tomography. *Journal of Neuroscience* 7:913–922.

Gall, F. J., and Spurzheim, J. C. 1968. Anatomie et physiologie du system nerveux en general, et du cerveau en particulier, avec des observations sur la possibilité de reconnaître plusieurs dispositions intellectuelles et morales de l'homme et des animaux, par la configuration de leurs têtes. In E. Clark, and C. D. O'Mally, eds. *The Human Brain and Spinal Cord: A Historical Study Illustrated by Writings from Antiquity to the Twentieth Century.* Berkeley and Los Angeles: University of California Press, pp. 476–480.

Gerstein, G. L., and Aertsen, A. M. H. J. 1985. Representation of cooperative firing activity among simultaneously recorded neurons. *Journal of Neurophysiology* 54:1513–1528.

Gerstein, G. L., Bloom, M. J., Espinosa, I. E., Evanczuk, S., and Turner, M. R. 1983. Design of a laboratory for multineuron studies. *IEEE Transactions on Systems, Man, and Cybernetics* SMC-13:668–676.

Goldman-Rakic, P. S. 1987. Circuitry of primate prefrontal cortex and regulation of behavior by representational knowledge. In F. Plum, and V. Mountcastle, eds. *Higher Cortical Function: Handbook of Physiology.* Washington, DC: American Physiological Society, pp. 373–417.

Goldman-Rakic, P. S., and Selemon, L. D. 1986. Topography of corticostriatal projections in nonhuman primates and implications for functional parcellation of the neostriatum. In E. G. Jones, and A. Peters, eds. *Cerebral Cortex.* New York: Plenum Press, pp. 447–466.

Graybiel, A. N., and Hickey, T. L. 1982. Chemospecificity of ontogenetic units in the striatum: Demonstration by combining [^{3}H]thymidine neuronography and histochemical staining. *Proc. Natl. Acad. Sci. USA* 79:198–202.

Grinvald, A. 1985. Real-time optical mapping of neuronal activity: From single growth cones to the intact mammalian brain. In W. M. Cowan, E. M. Shooter, C. F. Stevens, and R. F. Thompson, eds. *Annual Review of Neuroscience*. Palo Alto: Annual Reviews, Inc., pp. 263–305.

Grinvald, A., Lieke, E., Frostig, R. D., Gilbert, C. D., and Wiesel, T. N. 1986. Functional architecture of cortex revealed by optical imaging of intrinsic signals. *Nature* 324:361–364.

Hanny, P. E., Maunsell, J. H. R., and Schiller, P. H. 1988. State-dependent activity in monkey visual cortex: II. Visual and nonvisual factors in V4. *Experimental Brain Research* 69:245–259.

Hillyard, S. A., and Picton, T. W. 1987. Electrophysiology of cognition. In F. Plum, ed. *Handbook of Physiology Section 1: Neurophysiology*. New York: American Physiological Society, pp. 519–584.

Hinton, G. E. 1986. Learning distributed representations of concepts. In *Proc. 8th Ann. Conf. Cog. Sci. Soc.* Hillsdale, NJ: Lawrence Erlbaum Assoc., pp. 1–12.

Hippocrates. 1949. *Ancient Medicine and Other Treatises*. F. Adams, trans. Chicago: Regnery.

Hobson, J. A. 1985. The neurobiology and pathophysiology of sleep and dreaming. *Discussions in Neuroscience* 2:9–50.

Hokfelt, T. 1987. Neuronal communication through multiple coexisting messengers. In G. M. Edelman, W. E. Gall, and W. M. Cowan, eds. *Synaptic Function*. New York: John Wiley & Sons, pp. 179–211.

Horton, J. C., and Sherk, H. 1984. Receptive field properties in the cat's lateral geniculate nucleus in the absence of on-center retinal input. *Journal of Neuroscience* 4:374–380.

Hubel, D. H., and Livingstone, M. S. 1987. Segregation of form, color, and stereopsis in primate area 18. *Journal of Neuroscience* 7:3378–3415.

Hubel, D. H., and Wiesel, T. N. 1962. Receptive fields, binocular interaction and functional architecture in the cat's visual cortex. *J. Physiol. (Lond.)* 160:106–154.

Hubel, D. H., and Wiesel, T. N. 1977. Functional architecture of macaque monkey visual cortex. *Proc. R. Soc. Lond. B* 198:1–59.

Hurlbert, A., and Poggio, T. 1988. Synthesizing a color algorithm from examples. *Science* 239:482–485.

Ingvar, D. H., and Schwartz, M. S. 1974. Blood flow patterns induced in the dominant hemisphere by speech and reading. *Brain* 97:273–288.

Jackson, J. H. 1958. *Selected Writings of John Hughlings Jackson*. New York: Basic Books.

Jones, E. G., Juliano, S. L., and Whitsel, B. L. 1987. A combined 2-deoxyglucose and neurophysiological study of primate somatosensory cortex. *Journal of Comparative Neurology* 263:514–525.

Kaas, J. H., Nelson, R. J., Sur, M., and Merzenich, M. M. 1979. Multiple representations of the body within the primary somatosensory cortex of primates. *Science* 204:521–523.

Kandel, E., and Schwartz, J. 1985. *Principles of Neural Science.* 2nd ed. New York: Elsevier.

Kandel, E. R. 1983. Neurobiology and molecular biology: The second encounter. In *Cold Spring Harbor Symposia on Quantitative Biology.* Cold Spring Harbor: Cold Spring Harbor Laboratory, pp. 891–908.

Kandel, E. R., Klein, M., Hochner, B., Schuster, M., Siegelbaum, S. A., Hawkins, R. D., Glanzman, D. L., and Castellucci, V. F. 1987. Synaptic modulation and learning. New insights into synaptic transmission from the study of behavior. In G. M. Edelman, W. E. Gall, and W. M. Cowan, eds. *Synaptic Function.* New York: John Wiley and Sons, pp. 471–518.

Knudsen, E. I., du Lac, S., and Esterly, S. D. 1987. Computational maps in the brain. In W. M. Cowan, E. M. Shooter, C. F. Stevens, and R. F. Thompson, eds. *Annual Review of Neuroscience.* Palo Alto: Annual Reviews, Inc., pp. 41–65.

Koch, C., and Poggio, T. 1987. Biophysics of computation: Neurons, synapses, and membranes. In G. M. Edelman, W. E. Gall, and W. M. Cowan, eds. *Synaptic Function.* New York: John Wiley & Sons, pp. 637–697.

Koch, C., and Segev, I. 1989. *Methods in Neuronal Modeling: From Synapse to Networks.* Cambridge, MA: MIT Press.

Konishi, M. 1986. Centrally synthesized maps of sensory space. *Trends in Neurosciences* 9:163–168.

Kosslyn, S. M. 1987. Seeing and imaging in the cerebral hemispheres: A computational approach. *Psych. Rev.* 94:148–175.

Kosslyn, S. M. 1988. Aspects of cognitive neuroscience of mental imagery. *Science* 240:1621–1626.

Kosslyn, S. M., Holtzman, J. D., Gazzaniga, M. S., and Farrah, M. J. 1985. A computational analysis of mental imagery generation: Evidence for functional dissociation in split brain patients. *J. Exp. Psych.: General* 114:311–341.

Kuffler, S. W. 1980. Slow synaptic responses in autonomic ganglia and the pursuit of a peptidergic transmitter. In: E. A. Kravitz and J. E. Treherne, eds. *Neurotransmission, Neurotransmitters, and Neuromodulators.* Cambridge, Engl.: Cambridge University Press, pp. 257–286.

Kutas, M., and Van Petten, C. 1988. Event-related brain potential studies of language. In P. K. Ackles, J. R. Jennings, and M. G. H. Coles, eds. *Advances in Psychophysiology.* Greenwich, CT: JAI Press.

Land, E. H., Hubel, D. H., Livingstone, M. S., Perry, S. H., and Burns, M. M. 1983. Colour-generating interactions across the corpus callosum. *Nature* 303:616–618.

LeDoux, J., and Hirst, W. 1986. *Mind and Brain: Dialogues in Cognitive Neuroscience*. Cambridge, Engl.: Cambridge University Press.

Lehky, S. R., and Sejnowski, T. J. 1988. Network model of shape-from-shading: Neural function arises from both receptive and projective fields. *Nature* 333:452–454.

Lisberger, S. G., Morris, E. J., and Tychsen, L. 1987. *Ann. Rev. Neurosci.* 10:97–129.

Livingstone, M. S., and Hubel, D. H. 1987a. Connections between layer 4B of area 17 and the thick cytochrome oxidase stripes of area 18 in the squirrel monkey. *Journal of Neuroscience* 7:3371–3377.

Livingstone, M. S., and Hubel, D. H. 1987b. Psychophysical evidence for separate channels for the perception of form, color, movement, and depth. *Journal of Neuroscience* 7:3416–3468.

Llinas, R. R. 1985. Electronic transmission in the mammalian central nervous system. In M. E. L. Bennett, and D. C. Spray, eds. *Gap Junctions*. Cold Spring Harbor: Cold Spring Harbor Laboratory, pp. 337–353.

Lund, J. S. 1987. Local circuit neurons of macaque monkey striate cortex: I. Neurons of laminae 4C and 5A. *Journal of Comparative Neurology* 257:60–92.

Luyten, P. R., and den Hollander, J. A. 1986. Observation of metabolites in the human brain by MR spectroscopy. *Radiology* 161:795–798.

MacGregor, R. J. 1987a. Simplified models of single neurons. In *Neural and Brain Modeling*. New York: Harcourt Brace Jovanovich, pp. 220–260.

MacGregor, R. J. 1987b. Synaptic bombardment in model neurons. In *Neural and Brain Modeling*. New York: Harcourt Brace Jovanovich, pp. 261–288.

Mandelbrot, B. B. 1983. *The Fractal Geometry of Nature*. San Francisco, W. H. Freeman.

Marr, D. 1969. A theory of cerebellar cortex. *J. Physiol. (Lond.)* 202:437–470.

Marr, D. 1970. A theory for cerebral neocortex. *Proc. R. Soc. Lond. B* 176:161–234.

Marr, D. 1982. Vision. San Francisco: W. H. Freeman.

Marr, D., and Poggio, T. 1976. *From Understanding Computation to Understanding Neural Circuitry*. MIT Artificial Intelligence Laboratory Technical report. AI Memo 357, MIT AI Laboratory, Cambridge, MA.

Marr, D., and Poggio, T. 1977. From understanding computation to understanding neural circuitry. *Neurosciences Res. Prog. Bull.* 15:470–488.

Martin, K. A. C. 1984. Neuronal circuits in cat striate cortex. In E. G. Jones, and A. Peters, eds. *Cerebral Cortex*. New York: Plenum Press.

Maunsell, J. H. R., and Newsome, W. T. 1987. Visual processing in monkey extrastriate cortex. In W. M. Cowan, E. M. Shooter, C. F. Stevens, and R. F. Thompson, eds. *Ann. Rev. Neurosci.* Palo Alto: Annual Reviews Inc., pp. 363–401.

Maunsell, J. H. R., and Van Essen, D. C. 1983. The connections of the middle temporal visual area (MT) and their relationship to a cortical hierarchy in macaque monkey. *Journal of Neuroscience* 3:2563–2586.

McCarthy, R. A., and Warrington, E. K. 1988. Evidence for modality-specific meaning systems in the brain. *Nature* 334:428–430.

McNaughton, B. L., and Morris, R. G. 1987. Hippocampal synaptic enhancement and information storage within a distributed memory system. *Trends in Neurosciences* 10:408–415.

Merzenich, M. M., and Brugge, J. F. 1973. Representation of the cochlear partition on the superior temporal plane in the macaque monkey. *Brain Research* 50:275–296.

Merzenich, M. M., and Kaas, J. H. 1982. Reorganization of mammalian somatosensory cortex following peripheral nerve injury. *Trends in Neurosciences* 5:434–436.

Mesulam, M. M. 1985. Attention, confusional states, and neglect. In M. M. Mesulam, ed. *Principles of Behavioral Neurology*. Philadelphia: F. A. Davis, pp. 125–168.

Milner, B. 1966. Amnesia following operation on the temporal lobes. In C. W. M. Whitty and O. Zangwill, ed. *Amnesia*. London: Butterworth, pp. 109–133.

Mishkin, M. 1982. A memory system in the monkey. *Phil. Trans. R. Soc. Lond. B* 298:85–95.

Moran, J., and Desimone, R. 1985. Selective attention gates visual processing in the extrastriate cortex. *Science* 229:782–784.

Newsome, W. T., and Pare, E. B. 1986. MT lesions impair visual discrimination of direction in a stochastic motion display. *Society of Neuroscience Abstracts* 12:1183.

Newsome, W. T., Wurtz, R. H., Durtsteler, M. R., and Mikami, A. 1985. Deficits in visual motion processing following ibotenic acid lesions of the middle temporal visual area of the macaque monkey. *J. Neurosci.* 5:825–840.

O'Keefe, J., and Nadel, L. 1978. *The Hippocampus as a Cognitive Map*. Oxford: Clarendon Press.

Paller, K. A., Zola-Morgan, S., Squire, L. R., and Hillyard, S. A. 1984. Monkeys with lesions of hippocampus and amygdala exhibit event-related brain potentials that resemble the human P300 view. *Soc. Neurosci. Abstr.* 10:849.

Paller, K. A., Zola-Morgan, S., Squire, L. R., and Hillyard, S. A. 1989. P-3 like brain waves in normal monkeys and monkeys with medial temporal lesions. *Behavioral Neuroscience* 102:714–725.

Penfield, W., and Jasper, H. 1954. *Epilepsy and the Functional Anatomy of the Human Brain*. Boston: Little, Brown.

Pentland, A. P. 1984. Fractal-based description of natural scenes. *IEEE Transactions on Pattern Analysis and Machine Intelligence* PAMI-6:661–674.

Perrett, D. I., Mistlin, A. J., and Chitty, A. J. 1987. Visual neurones responsive to faces. *Trends in Neurosciences* 10:358–364.

Petersen, S. E., Fox, P. T., Posner, M. I., Mintun, M. A., and Raichle, M. E. 1988. Positron emission tomographic studies of the cortical anatomy of single-word processing. *Nature* 331:585–589.

Phelps, M. E., and Mazziotta, J. C. 1985. Positron emission tomography: Human brain function and biochemistry. *Science* 228:799–809.

Posner, M. I., Petersen, S. E., Fox, P. T., and Raichle, M. E. 1988. Localization of cognitive operations in the human brain. *Science* 240:1627–1631.

Purves, D., and Voyvodic, J. T. 1987. Imaging mammalian nerve cells and their connections over time in living animals. *Trends in Neurosciences* 10:398–404.

Raichle, M. E. 1986. Neuroimaging. *Trends in Neurosciences* 9:525–529.

Reichardt, W., and Poggio, T. 1976. Visual control of orientation behavior in the fly. *Quarterly Reviews of Biophysics* 9:311–375.

Reitboeck, H. J. P. 1983. A 19-channel matrix drive with individually controllable fiber microelectrodes for neurophysiological applications. *IEEE Transactions on Systems, Man, and Cybernetics* SMC-13:676–683.

Reiter, H. O., and Stryker, M. P. 1987. A novel expression of plasticity in kitten visual cortex in the absence of postsynaptic activity. *Society for Neuroscience Abstracts* 13:1241.

Ritchie, J. M. 1987. Ion channels in neural membranes. *Discussions in Neurosciences* 4:11–55.

Robinson, D. A. 1981. The use of control systems analysis in the neurophysiology of eye movements. *Annual Review of Neuroscience* 4:463–503.

Roland, P. E. 1984a. Organization of motor control by the normal human brain. *Human Neurobiology* 2:205–216.

Roland, P. E. 1984b. Somatotopic tuning of postcentral gyrus during focal attention in man. *Journal of Neurophysiology* 46:744–754.

Salzberg, B. M., Obaid, A. L., Senseman, D. M., and Gainer, H. 1983. Optical recording of action potentials from vertebrate nerve terminals using potentiometric probes provides evidence for sodium and calcium components. *Nature* 306:36–40.

Scherg, M., and Von Cramon, D. 1986. Evoked dipole source potentials of the human auditory cortex. *Electroenceph. Clin. Neurophys.* 65:344–360.

Schiller, P. 1982. The central connections of the retinal on and off pathways. *Nature* 297:580–583.

Sejnowski, T. J. 1986. Open questions about computation in cerebral cortex. In: J. L. McClelland and D. E. Rumelhart, eds. *Parallel Distributed Processing: Explorations in the Microstructure of Cognition.* Vol. 2. Cambridge, MA: MIT Press, pp. 372–389.

Sejnowski, T. J. 1987. Computational models and the development of topographic projections. *Trends in Neurosciences* 10:304–305.

Sejnowski, T. J. 1988. Neural network learning algorithms. In R. Eckmiller, and C. von der Malsberg, eds. *Neural Computers*. New York: Springer-Verlag.

Sejnowski, T. J., Koch, C., and Churchland, P. S. 1988. Computational neuroscience. *Science* 241:1299–1306.

Sejnowski, T. J., and Tesauro, G. J. 1988. The Hebb rule for synaptic plasticity: Implementations and applications. In J. Byrne and W. O. Berry, eds. *Neural Models of Plasticity*. New York: Academic Press.

Sereno, M. I. 1988. The visual system. In I. W. V. Seelen, U. M. Leinhos, G. Shaw, eds. *Organization of Structure and Function in the Brain*. Basel: VCH Verlagsgesellschaft.

Shepherd, G. M. 1988. The basic circuit of cortical organization. In M. S. Gazzaniga, ed. *Perspectives in Memory Research*. Cambridge, MA: MIT Press.

Shepherd, G. M. 1989. The significance of real neuron architectures for neural network simulations. In E. Schwartz, ed. *Computational Neuroscience*. Cambridge, MA: MIT Press.

Shepherd, G. M., Brayton, R. K., Miller, J. P., Segev, I., Rinzel, J., and Rall, W. 1985. Signal enhancement in distal cortical dendrites by means of interactions between active dendritic spines. *Proceedings of the National Academy of Sciences USA* 82:2192–2195.

Sherrington, C. 1940. *Man and his Nature*. Cambridge, Engl.: Cambridge University Press.

Sherrington, C. S. 1906. *The Integrative Action of the Nervous System*. New Haven: Yale University Press.

Siegel, R. M., and Andersen, R. A. 1986. Perceptual deficits following ibotenic acid lesions of the middle temporal area (MT) in the behaving rhesus monkey. *Society for Neuroscience Abstracts* 12:1183.

Sokoloff, L. 1984. *Metabolic Probes of Central Nervous System Activity in Experimental Animals and Man*. Sunderland, MA: Sinauer Associates.

Sperry, R. W., and Gazzaniga, M. 1967. Language following surgical disconnection of the hemispheres. In C. Millikan, and F. Darley, eds. *Brain Mechanisms Underlying Speech and Language*. New York: Grune and Stratton, pp. 108–115.

Squire, L. R. 1987. *Memory and Brain*. Oxford: Oxford University Press.

Squire, L. R., Shimamura, A. P., and Amaral, D. G. 1988. Memory and the hippocampus. In J. Byrne, and W. Berry, eds. *Neural Models of Plasticity*. New York: Academic Press.

Sterling, P. 1983. Microcircuitry of the cat retina. In W. M. Cowan, E. M. Shooter, C. F. Stevens, and R. F. Thompson, eds. *Annual Review of Neuroscience*. Palo Alto: Annual Reviews, Inc., pp. 149–185.

Stewart, W. B., Kauer, J. S., and Shepherd, G. M. 1979. Functional organization of rat olfactory bulb analyzed by the 2-deoxyglucose method. *Journal of Comparative Neurology* 185:715–734.

Suga, N. 1984. The extent to which biosonar information is represented in the bat auditory cortex. In G. M. Edelman, W. E. Gall, and W. M. Cowan, eds. *Dynamic Aspects of Neocortical Function.* New York: John Wiley & Sons, pp. 315–373.

Swindale, N. V., Matsubara, J. A., and Cynader, M. S. 1987. Surface organization of orientation and direction selectivity in cat area 18. *Journal of Neuroscience* 7:1414–1427.

Tootell, R. B. H., Silverman, M. S., Switkes, E., and De Valois, R. L. 1982. Deoxyglucose analysis of retinotopic organization in primate striate cortex. *Science* 218:902–904.

Ts'o, D. Y., Gilbert, C. D., and Wiesel, T. N. 1986. Relationship between horizontal interactions and functional architecture in cat striate cortex as revealed by cross-correlation analysis. *Journal of Neuroscience* 6:1160–1170.

Tsien, R. Y., and Poenie, M. 1986. Fluorescence ratio imaging: A new window into intracellular ionic signaling. *Trends in Biochemical Sciences* 11:450–455.

Van Petten, C., and Kutas, M. 1987. Ambiguous words in context. An event-related potential analysis of the time course of meaning activation. *Journal of Memory and Language* 26:188–208.

von Helmholtz, H. 1948. On the rate of transmission of the nerve impulse. In W. Dennis, ed. *Readings in the History of Psychology.* New York: Appleton-Century-Crofts, pp. 197–198.

von der Heydt, R., Peterhans, E., and Baumgartner, G. 1984. Illusory contours and cortical neuron responses. *Science* 224:1260–1262.

Williamson, S. J., and Kaufman, L. 1987. Analysis of neuromagnetic signals. In: A. Gevins and A. Rémond, eds. *Handbook of Electroencephalography and Clinical Neurophysiology.* Amsterdam: Elsevier.

Woolsey, T. A., and Van der Loos, H. 1970. The structural organization of layer IV in somatosensory region (SI) of mouse cerebral cortex. *Brain Research* 17:205–242.

Zeki, S. 1983. Colour coding in the cerebral cortex: The reaction of cells in monkey visual cortex to wavelengths and colours. *Neuroscience* 9:741–765.

Zipser, D., and Andersen, R. 1988. Back propagation programmed network that simulates response properties of a subset of posterior parietal neurons. *Nature* 331:679–684.

Zola-Morgan, S., and Squire, L. R. 1984. Preserved learning in monkeys with medial temporal lesions. *Journal of Neuroscience* 4:1072–1085.

Domains

9 Language Acquisition

Steven Pinker

9.1 The Importance of Understanding Language Acquisition

Language acquisition has always been a crucial topic in cognitive science; every major theoretical framework has tried to account for it in some way. There are many reasons for its preeminence. Possessing a language is the quintessentially human trait: all normal humans speak, no nonhuman animal does. Language is the main vehicle by which we know about other people's thought processes, and the two must be intimately related. Data about language structure are easy to come by, and they hint at a system of extraordinary complexity. With language so close to the core of what it means to be human, it is not surprising that children's acquisition of language has received so much attention. For better or worse, anyone with strong views about the human mind would like to show that children's first few steps are steps in the right direction.

Explaining language acquisition means providing answers to many of the central recurring issues in cognitive science:

Task Specificity (Modularity) and Species Specificity

Is language a distinct "mental organ," with principles of organization not shared with other cognitive systems such as perception, motor control, or reasoning (Chomsky 1975, 1986, Fodor 1983)? Or does language arise from general principles of intelligence applied to the problem of communicating with other humans over an auditory channel (Anderson 1983, Minsky 1975)?

A related question is whether language is unique to humans or whether homologous systems can be seen in other organisms. The two questions are, strictly speaking, logically independent. Modularity could be false while species specificity is true: other organisms could fail to speak because they were simply not smart enough. Conversely species specificity could be false while modularity is true: organisms closely related to humans could display rudiments of languagelike skill because they had special-purpose brain structures that were precursors or homologues to those structures subserving language in people (see Osherson and Wasow 1976). But the two issues are linked in practice. Other organisms don't naturally use anything like a human language; their communication systems tend to involve a fixed repertoire of behaviors rather than a generative rule system (Seidenberg 1986). If they can be taught to communicate, it is unlikely that they would communicate using a special-purpose mental organ that has lain dormant for millions of years; communication would have to be by general-purpose intelligence.

Language and Thought

Is language simply grafted on top of cognition as a way of overtly expressing thoughts that occur independently of it (Fodor 1975, Piaget 1926)? Or does learning a language mean learning to think in that language (Whorf 1956)? Within modern cognitive science there is a vast consensus for the former position. This consensus is inspired by a number of factors: the existence of complex nonlinguistic forms of thought in normal adults; demonstrations of complex thought processes in those deaf people that lack any form of language, in prelinguistic infants, and in nonhuman animals; the unsuitability of natural language as a medium of computation because of its widespread ambiguity; the logical problem of how a language could be acquired without there being complex thought processes in place first; the failure of empirical demonstrations that differences in language cause differences in thought; and the acceptance of theories that have language as a module either independent of cognition or built on top of it (see Fodor 1975 and Shepard and Cooper 1982 for discussion of the evidence). Given that different languages require speakers to attend to very different aspects of the world, however, learning a particular language must involve learning to recruit cognitive abilities in particular ways, and so the influence of language on cognition cannot be null (Bowerman 1985).

Learning and Innateness

Language offers an unparalleled opportunity for understanding precise interactions between heredity and environment. All humans talk, but no house pets do, so heredity must be involved; but a child growing up in Japan speaks Japanese, whereas the same child brought up in California would speak English, so the environment is also crucial. This much is uncontroversial. Though not much else in this debate is, all proposals are accountable to an extremely stringent base of evidence. The linguistic abilities of adults have been studied in unusual detail among cognitive processes, and theories of adult knowledge of language are quite complex (see chapter 4). Any theory of language learning that cannot account for this complex linguistic knowledge must be false. Similarly the crucial input to language acquisition—parents' sentences—can be easily characterized, at least in its essentials. Thus both the input and the output to language acquisition can be specified precisely, unlike other domains of learning such as social skills or concepts, and proposals about specific language-learning mechanisms can be unusually focused and precise (see, for example, Wexler and Culicover 1980), potentially offering lessons about the nature of learning and heredity in other domains.

Historically language acquisition became a prime testing ground for these three questions in the late 1950s, when Noam Chomsky (1959) published his review of Skinner's *Verbal Behavior*. At that time Anglo-American natural science, social science, and philosophy had come to a virtual consensus about the answers to these questions: psychological processes consisted of sensorimotor abilities plus a few simple laws of learning governing gradual changes in an organism's behavioral repertoire. Therefore language must be learned, it cannot be a module, and thinking must be a form of verbal behavior because verbal behavior is the prime manifestation of "thought" that can be observed externally. Chomsky argued that the facts of language acquisition falsified these beliefs in a single stroke: children learn languages that are governed by highly subtle and abstract principles, and they do so without explicit instruction or any other environmental clues to the nature of such principles. Hence language acquisition depends on an innate, species-specific module that is distinct from general intelligence. Much of the research in language acquisition has attempted to test various aspects of this once-revolutionary conjunction of ideas, with implications extending to the rest of human cognition.

9.2 Language Acquisition and Cognitive Science

Language acquisition is perhaps the most interdisciplinary of the topics within cognitive science, with essential contributions from several areas.

Linguistics
Linguistic theory (see chapter 5) is an essential part of the theory of language acquisition for three reasons. First, the goal of linguistic theory is a theory of the adult's knowledge of a particular language, or a *grammar*. (This is a technical sense of the term, to be distinguished from prescriptive guidelines for language use or general summaries of grammatical patterns.) Thus any theory of language acquisition must show how the child eventually attains such a grammar. Many of the fiercest controversies in language-acquisition research stem from disagreements, often unacknowledged, over how this criterion should be applied. Linguists and researchers sympathetic to them point out that many nonnativist and nonmodular theories of language acquisition evade their responsibility to show how the child grows into an adult with full mastery of language, including the kinds of phenomena characterized by linguistic theory; these theories leave the subtleties of adult

knowledge a mystery. Moreover languages contain innumerable opportunities for a learner to make reasonable, but false, generalizations. For instance in each of the following examples, a learner who heard sentences a and b could quite sensibly extract a generalization that when applied to the sentence c yields version d. Yet in each of these cases the result is actually not the kind of sentence anyone would say or hear without a sense of oddness.

(1) a. John saw Mary with her best friend's husband.
  b. Who did John see Mary with?
  c. John saw Mary and her best friend's husband.
  d. *Who did John see Mary and?

(2) a. Irv drove the car into the garage.
  b. Irv drove the car.
  c. Irv put the car into the garage.
  d. *Irv put the car.

(3) a. I expect the fur to fly.
  b. I expect the fur will fly.
  c. The fur is expected to fly.
  d. *The fur is expected will fly.

(4) a. The baby seems to be asleep.
  b. The baby seems asleep.
  c. The baby seems to be sleeping.
  d. *The baby seems sleeping.

(5) a. John liked the pictures of Bill that Mary took.
  b. John liked Mary's pictures of Bill.
  c. John liked the pictures of himself that Mary took.
  d. *John liked Mary's pictures of himself.

These judgments constitute one kind of fact that plays an important role in arguments for the innateness and modularity of grammar; theories that ignore them are failing to be responsible for an important empirical data base. That is, many of the facts relevant to language acquisition can be gathered without an experimental laboratory; they are empirical data about human psychology in the same way as the perception of an illusory contour or of a reversing Necker cube.

The second contribution of linguistics is in the area of *language universals* (Comrie 1981, Greenberg 1978, Shopen 1985). Children are not predisposed to learn English or any other particular language, and catalogues of universal, prevalent, rare, and nonexistent patterns across languages bear on what language-acquisition mechanisms find easy or hard to learn.

The third and possibly most important contribution is in the theory of *universal grammar* (Chomsky 1965, 1981; see chapter 4). This specifies the allowable representations and operations that all languages are confined to use; a theory of universal grammar must be consistent with grammars for particular languages and with language universals. The theory of universal grammar is closely tied to the theory of the mental mechanisms children use in acquiring language; their hypotheses about language must be couched in structures consistent with universal grammar.

Computer Science

Intuitions about what kind of learning device can learn what kinds of abilities are notoriously unreliable, yet knowledge about learning powers are crucial if the criteria mentioned in the previous section are to be applied. Computer science can provide such knowledge in two ways. An important recently developed subdiscipline of the theory of computation called *learnability theory* or *formal learning theory* (Gold 1967, Osherson, Stob, and Weinstein 1985, Pinker 1979) consists of models of learning, each with four parts: a class of languages, one of which is the target of learning; a learning environment providing information to a learner relevant to selecting the corrent language; a learning strategy that maps sequences of environmental inputs onto hypotheses about the target language; and a success criterion defining the correspondence between the learner's conjectures and the actual target language. Theorems in formal learning theory show how assumptions about any of the three components impose logical constraints on the fourth. In principle they can, given the right empirical premises, rule out certain theories of language acquisition on logical grounds (Osherson et al. 1985, Wexler and Culicover 1980). In practice the applications of learnability theory have been more heuristic than formal (see Anderson 1977, Berwick 1986, Pinker 1979, 1982, 1984, Wexler and Culicover 1980). A key contribution is the role of *negative evidence*, or information about which strings of words are not sentences in the language to be acquired. According to one of the first and most important theorems proved in this field, none of the classes of languages in the "Chomsky hierarchy" of formal languages is learnable, according to one criterion, without negative evidence. Though this result narrowly applies to one paradigm of learning and hence should not be misinterpreted to mean literally that no interesting classes of language are learnable without negative evidence, the rationale for the result has broad applicability to the problem of language acquisition (Baker 1979, Pinker 1984). Without negative evidence there is no direct information from the environment telling a learner when he or she has hypothesized a language that properly includes the target language (see figure 9.1).

A second way in which computer science can sharpen intuitions about which learning mechanisms are capable of which feats comes from artificial intelligence and cognitive simulation, wherein computers are programmed to acquire languages based on linguistic input either as a

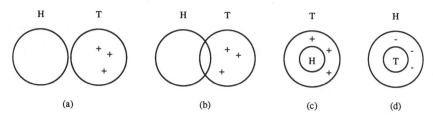

Figure 9.1 Four states that a child could be in during language acquisition. (a) The child's hypothesis language (H) is disjoint from the language to be acquired (the "target language" T). (b) The child's hypothesis and the target language intersect. (c) The child's hypothesis language is a subset of the target language. (d) The child's hypothesis language is a superset of the target language. In cases a through c the child can realize that his or her hypothesis is incorrect by hearing sentences ("positive evidence," indicated by +) that are in the target language but not the hypothesized one. This is impossible in case d; negative evidence would be needed.

practical end in itself (AI) or as a model of how children do so (simulation) (Anderson 1977, Berwick 1986; see also Pinker 1979).

Biology
Many findings in biology and neurology are relevant to language acquisition, though the application of such findings has been piecemeal since Lenneberg's (1967) landmark effort. Direct anatomical and physiological studies of neural maturation (Huttenlocher 1979, Thatcher, Walker, and Guidice 1987) are relevant to specifying the onset, rate, and possible termination of natural language-acquisition abilities. Possible dissociations between language and cognition, relevant to the modularity issue, can be assessed by studying focal brain lesions or other observable neurological abnormalities (Studdert-Kennedy 1983), linguistic savants (Cromer 1986, Curtiss, Yamada, & Fromkin 1979, Gardner 1983), and heritable disorders that differentially spare linguistic and cognitive functioning (Lenneberg 1967). Though the differentiation of linguistic from cognitive deficits is invariably tricky, good prima facie cases for their dissociability have been made using each of these techniques. Finally, there have been attempts to teach sign languages to chimpanzees and other primates (Gardner and Gardner 1969, Premack and Premack 1983). Though once heralded as one of psychology's crowning achievements and a refutation of the species specificity and modularity of language, these efforts have since been reinterpreted as showing exactly the opposite if they show anything at all (Terrace, Petitto, Sanders, and Bever 1979, Seidenberg and Petitto 1979, Seidenberg 1986). Early studies suffered from methodological problems in that data were reported selectively, and experimenter cueing was not unambiguously eliminated. But more important, careful analyses have documented that chimpanzees usually require massive regimented teaching sequences to acquire quite rudimentary linguistic abilities, mostly limited to a small number of signs strung together in long,

repetitive, quasi-random sequences, used almost exclusively to request things and containing nothing resembling syntax except for occasional rough statistical probabilities on sign ordering. This contrasts sharply with human children, who pick up thousands of words spontaneously, combine them in structured sequences in which every word has a determinate role, respect the word order of the adult language, and use sentences for a variety of purposes such as commenting on interesting objects. (Experiments teaching symbolic systems to apes, however, can serve as valuable contributions to comparative cognitive psychology; see Premack and Premack 1983.)

Developmental Psycholinguistics

Developmental psycholinguistics, a branch of developmental psychology, specifies the nature of parental speech to children learning language and children's linguistic abilities at a variety of stages of development (Brown 1973, Maratsos 1983, Gleitman and Wanner 1982). Hence it is relevant to characterize the input to language acquisition and the nature of the child's interim hypotheses about the language he or she is in the process of learning, inasmuch as they can be teased apart from other developmental changes such as cognitive, perceptual, and social skills. Methods are numerous, but can be divided into two groups: *Naturalistic studies* of children's spontaneous speech are uncontrolled, but extremely rich and informative and free from experimental artifact; recently they have become far more accessible because of the dissemination of computer-based transcripts of the standardly referenced corpora of children's speech and of simple text-manipulation tools designed to analyze them (MacWhinney and Snow 1985). *Experimental methods* have the complementary set of advantages and disadvantages and can be subdivided according to their dependent variables. In *production* tasks children utter sentences to describe pictures or scenes, in response to questions, or in imitation of target sentences; in *comprehension* tasks children listen to sentences and then point to pictures or act out events with toys; in *judgment* tasks children indicate whether or which sentences provided by an experimenter sound "silly."

Most experiments on children's language bear only indirectly on language acquisition because no actual learning takes place in the laboratory. This is a crucial limitation on our ability to understand the process; it is for this reason alone that most theories of language acquisition have been neither confirmed nor disconfirmed. The obvious tests of such theories would be to design careful, extended input sequences, bring children up so that they hear the sequences exclusively, and then test their abilities. The crucial experiments are ruled out for ethical and practical reasons of course, and researchers have made do with imperfect but often informative substitutes. Children may be taught new words in the laboratory, and the extent of their generalizations based on that novel input can be measured (see, for example, Berko 1958,

Pinker, Lebeaux, and Frost 1987). This technique is limited, however, by how quickly and with how little evidence children are willing to master a new form in the laboratory.

A complementary source of evidence can come from crosslinguistic studies of language development, which define a set of natural experiments. Each of the world's 5,000 languages, in a sense, contains a set of values of independent variables (that is, any of the differences among the grammars of those languages), so differences in the acquisition of analogous structures across a variety of languages provide crucial tests of the generality of putative acquisition mechanisms (Slobin 1973, 1985a,). Of course no two languages differ from one another along only one dimension, so the design of this "natural experiment" is massively nonorthogonal, but this has not prevented interesting generalizations from arising.

There are other empirical wedges into the learning mechanism. Naturally occurring variation among parents can be correlated with differences in children's rate of development (Newport, Gleitman, and Gleitman 1977), or parents or caretakers can deliberately adjust their speech in certain ways, and the results can be observed (Nelson, Carskaddon, and Bonvillian 1973). Such manipulations can occur only within a fairly narrow range, unfortunately. More extreme natural variations, such as severe neglect, are often accompanied by a variety of other confounding variables (Curtiss 1977), though some, such as blindness or deafness, can provide interesting data on otherwise untestable hypotheses (Goldin-Meadow and Feldman 1977, Newport 1981, Petitto 1989). One intriguing set of natural experiments was conducted until the early part of this century, when plantations staffed by slaves or indentured servants brought up their children in a milieu in which an impoverished pidgin was the primary input. Children in such settings seem to have invented complex languages, called creoles, in a single generation, and the properties of creoles, especially properties shared across creoles with radically different pidgins serving as their sources, can illuminate children's inherent propensities for creating language (Bickerton 1981). Finally, adults can be taught entire miniature artificial languages (Moeser 1977), though the extent to which this taps natural language-acquisition processes is probably small (Miller 1967, Schlesinger 1977).

Developmental Studies Related to Linguistic Issues: Three Examples
To make the discussion more concrete, let us consider three examples of studies from developmental psycholinguistics. I choose them to illustrate some of the common methodologies and some of the important theoretical questions that these methodologies provide answers to. Furthermore they illustrate aspects of language acquisition that I return to frequently in the subsequent discussion.

A Study of Productivity One of the earliest and most famous experiments on language development was done by Jean Berko in 1958. A common naive conception of language acquisition is that it is a form of "imitation" of parental speech. Berko showed that on the contrary children had the ability to create completely new forms, by applying some internal mechanism that captured the effects of a rule of language. The technique was a very simple elicited production task. Children between the ages of four and seven years were shown a picture of a cartoon bird and told that it was a "wug." Then they were shown a second picture with two cartoon birds. "Now there are two of them," the children were told; "there are two ＿＿＿ ." Most of the time the children completed the sentence with the word "wugs." Similarly they were shown a picture of a man swinging an instrument and were told "Here is a man who likes to rick. Yesterday he did the same thing. Yesterday he ＿＿＿ ." (Children's response: "ricked.") Clearly children had never said nor heard the words *wugs* or *ricked* beforehand because they are not part of English. Therefore their performance cannot be explained by any straightforward notion of "imitation" (nor of reinforcement because they had never uttered the words beforehand and so could not have been reinforced for uttering them). Instead they had clearly internalized the relevant regularities of English, which they could apply *productively*. Where and when children will apply a regularity productively is a crucial issue in language acquisition, because children must go beyond the finite sample of information in the input and generalize to the infinitely large language of their community.

The laboratory results were nicely confirmed by the naturalistic studies of Susan Ervin (1964), who showed that children's spontaneous speech contained many examples of the overapplication of these regularities to irregular verbs that don't take the ending, resulting in errors such as *bringed*, *goed*, or *foots*. Interestingly before children make these errors, they use the irregulars correctly, saying *brought*, *went*, and *feet*. At some point they get worse, using the correct forms and errors side by side. Slowly the errors begin to drop out during the late preschool and early school-age years.

The phenomenon's simplicity is deceptive. The traditional interpretation, captured in the learning mechanisms proposed in, say, Pinker 1984, is that children first simply memorize stem and past-tense forms directly from the input. They correctly use irregular forms because the overregularized forms do not appear in the input, and all they are doing is reproducing what they have heard. Regular past tenses are acquired in the same way, with no analysis of them into a stem plus an inflection. In the meantime the child has recorded the fact that, say, *walked* is used reliably to refer to past instances of walking, whereas *walk*, similar in phonological substance to *walked*, is used in nonpast circumstances to refer to the same kind of action. The child juxtaposes *walk* and *walked*, notes that the second is created by adding *d* to the first, and creates the corresponding rule "To form the past, add *d* to the stem." This rule can then be applied to other stems, including (mistakenly) irregulars such as *go*. At some point though the child has to realize that *goed* is not allowable. He or she might do so by applying a *uniqueness principle*, a constraint from universal grammar that has the effect of ensuring roughly that every verb has no more than one past-tense form. When the child realizes that *went* corresponds exactly to the past tense form of *go*, he or she can begin to get rid of *goed*.

Rumelhart and McClelland (1986) have proposed a very different model, however, for the same phenomena. In their connectionist, or parallel distributed processing, model (see chapter 4), no words are stored, and no rules are coined. Rather the child records the input frequency of any of a huge number of possible mappings between phonological patterns in the stem and phonological patterns in the past version. Regularities are extended to new stems on the basis of their similarity to these phonological patterns. The differences between these two models has become an important controversy in psycholinguistics and cognitive science in general, and is discussed again in section 9.6.

A Study of Structure Dependence   Sentences are linearly ordered strings of words. No child could fail to notice word order in learning and understanding language. Most regularities of language, however, are couched in terms of hierarchically organized phrase structures (see chapter 5). If the structures of linguistic theory correspond to the hypotheses that children formulate in learning a language, children should create rules and processes that are defined over hierarchical structures, not simple properties of linear order such as which word comes before which other word or how close two words are in a string.

Another classic experiment in developmental psycholinguistics is due to Carol Chomsky (1969). Languages often have embedded clauses missing a subject, such as *John told Mary to leave*, where the clause *to leave* has no subject. The phenomenon of *control* governs how the missing subject is interpreted; in this sentence it is Mary who is understood as fulfilling the missing subject role of the person doing the leaving. We say that the phrase *Mary* "controls" the missing subject position of the lower clause. For most verbs in the top-level clause, there is a simple principle defining control. If the first verb has no object, then the subject of the first verb controls the missing subject of the second verb. For example, in *John tried to leave*, the phrase *John* is interpreted as the subject of both *try* and *leave*. If the first verb has a subject and an object, then it is the object that controls the missing subject of the second verb, as we see in *John told Mary to leave*. Chomsky showed that children apply this principle quite extensively, even for the handful of verbs that are exceptions to it. In act-out comprehension experiments with children between the ages of five and ten years, she showed that even relatively old children were prone to this kind of mistake. When told *Mickey promised Donald to jump; make him jump*, the children would make *Donald*, the object of the first verb, do the jumping, in accord with the general principle. The "right answer" in this case would have been *Mickey*, because *promise* is an exception to the principle, calling for an unusual kind of control where the subject of the first verb should act as controller.

But what is the principle that children are overapplying? One possibility can be called the surface minimal-distance principle: the controller of the second verb is the noun phrase nearest to it in the linear string of words in the sentence. If children analyze sentences in terms of linear order, this should be a natural generalization. However, it isn't right for the adult language. Consider the sentence *Mary was told by John to leave*. The phrase *John* is closest to the subject position for *leave*, but adult English speakers understand the sentence as meaning that Mary is the one leaving. The surface minimal-distance principle gives the wrong answer here. Instead we need a principle sensitive to grammatical structure. Such a structural-control principle would say that the controller is a grammatical object if one exists; otherwise it is a grammatical subject. The object of a preposition is never a controller, basically because it is embedded "too deeply" in the sentence's tree structure. That's why *Mary was told by John to leave* has *Mary* as the controller. (It is also why, incidentally, the sentence *Mary was promised by John to leave* is virtually uninterpretable—it would require a prepositional phrase to be the controller, which is ruled out by the structural principle.)

It would certainly be understandable if children were to follow the surface minimal-distance principle; not only is it easily stated in terms of surface properties of sentences that children can easily perceive, but sentences that would disconfirm it such as *Mary was told by John to leave* are extremely rare in parents' speech. Michael Maratsos (1974) did the crucial experiment. He gave children such sentences and asked them who was leaving. Of course on either account children would have to be able to understand passive sentences in general to interpret these sentences, and Maratsos gave them a separate test of comprehension of simple passive sentences to select out only those children who could. Indeed such children interpreted passive sentences with missing embedded subjects just as adults would. In accord with the structural principle and in violation of the surface minimal-distance principle, they interpreted *Mary was told by John to leave* as having the subject (Mary) as the controller.

A similar demonstration comes from Crain and Nakayama (1986), based on an example frequently used by Noam Chomsky to illustrate how language acquisition should work. The sentence *The man is in the room* can be turned into a question: *Is the man in the room?* Two versions of this rule are possible. A linear rule would say: "Find the first instance of *is* and move it to the front." A structural rule would say: "Find the instance of *is* that is in the top layer of the phrase structure tree and move it to the front." The two rules behave differently in sentences such as *The man who is tall is in the room.* The linear rule yields an incorrect version: *Is the man who tall is in the room?* The structural rule yields the correct version: *Is the man who is tall in the room?* Crain and Nakayama did an experiment where children played a game in which they had to convert an experimenter's sentences into questions. Even though the linear rule is in some sense "simpler," Crain and Nakayama showed that children never would ask questions such as *Is the man who tall is in the room?*—therefore they must have formed their answers by using a structural rule, not a linear rule. Furthermore, the rule pertains to syntactic structure, not semantic structure: children had no trouble converting *It is raining* to *Is it raining?* despite the fact that *it* and *is* carry little meaning.

A Study of Innate Constraints Arguments that the child must come to the language-learning task with inborn constraints about the possible form of linguistic rules are usually defended by comparing the facts of adult grammar with the facts of parental input to children and inferring what children must possess to go from the latter to the former. Sometimes it is possible to corroborate such theories with evidence of a different sort, namely, children's behavior in experimental settings.

An elegant illustration of how this might be done comes from Gordon (1985a). According to a prominent theory of word structure (Kiparsky 1982), words are built in layers. To build a word, one starts with a root, (for example, *red*) and one can apply one series of rules to it, called "level 1 rules," to yield a more complex word. For example, there is a rule adding the suffix *-ish*, turning the word into *reddish*. Level 1 rules, according to the theory, can affect the sound of the stem; for example, someone from Spain is *Spanish*, not *Spainish*. Furthermore level 1 rules can yield words with unpredictable meanings; for example, a *bookish* person is not like a book but is a kind of person who likes to read books. Level 2 rules can apply to the output of level 1 rules. An example of a level 2 rule is the one that adds the suffix *-ness*, yielding, for example, *redness*. Level 2 rules generally do not affect the pronunciation of the words they apply to; they just add material onto the word, leaving it intact. They also have predictable semantic effects; *Xness* is the state or quality of being *X*. Finally, level 3 rules apply the product of level 2 rules. Many regular rules of inflectional morphology are examples of level 3 rules; for example, the rule that adds an *-s* to the end of a noun to form its plural, in this case *rednesses*. Crucially, if several kinds of rule apply to a word they must apply in order: the output of the level 1 rules is the input to the level 2 rules, and the output of the level 2 rules is the input to the level 3 rules. That constraint yields predictions about what kinds of words are possible and which are impossible. For example, the order I gave for these three rules makes it possible to derive *reddishness* or even *reddishnesses*, but impossible to derive *rednessish, rednessesish, redsness, redsish,* and so on.

Within this theory irregular inflectional rules, such as the one that relates *mouse* to *mice*, belong to level 1, whereas regular inflectional rules, such as the one that relates *rat* to *rats*, belong to level 3. Compounding is in between. This predicts that *a rat-eater* and *a mouse-eater* are possible words as is *a mice-eater* because the rule forming *mice* comes before the rule combining it with *eater*. However, *a rats-eater*, even though it is cognitively quite similar to *mice-eater*, sounds strange, at least to adult ears, as the theory predicts. Gordon had children between the ages of three and five years participate in an elicited-production experiment in which he would say, "Here is a puppet who likes to eat _____ . What would you call him?" The experimenter provided a response for several singular nouns beforehand, so that the children were aware of the existence of the "x-eater" compound form. By and large, children behaved just like adults: a puppet who likes to eat a mouse was called a *mouse-eater*, a puppet who likes to eat a rat was called a *rat-eater*, a puppet who likes to eat mice was called a *mouse-eater* or a *mice-eater*, but a puppet who likes to eat rats was called a *rat-eater* but virtually never a *rats-eater*. Interestingly children treated their own overregularizations, such as *mouses*, exactly as they treated legitimate regular plurals: they would never call the puppet a *mouses-eater*, even if they used *mouses* in their own speech.

Even more interesting, Gordon examined how children could have acquired the constraint. Perhaps, he reasoned, they had learned the fact that compounds can contain either singulars or irregular plurals, never regular plurals. It turns out that they would have no way of learning that fact. Although there is no grammatical reason why compounds cannot contain irregular plurals, in fact the speech that children hear probably does not contain any. Compounds like *toothbrush* abound (there is no word *teethbrush*, though there could be); compounds like *people-mover* containing irregular plurals are extremely rare, according to the standardized frequency data that Gordon examined, and he found none that was likely to appear in the speech children hear. Therefore children were willing to say *mice-eater* and unwilling to say *rats-eater* with no good evidence from the input that that is the pattern required in English. Gordon suggests that some version of the level-ordering constraints may be innate.

Now that we have seen some examples of how research in developmental psycholinguistics can provide answers to key questions concerning the language-acquisition task, we can take a closer look at what those questions are.

9.3 Input to Language Acquisition

The Significant Issues
The input to language-acquisition mechanisms relevant to acquiring the grammar of a particular language consists of the speech of parents or other caretakers. Thus the nature of parental speech—how reliable, informative, or transparent it is with respect to the target language—is an important empirical question. The issue essentially is whether language is *learned* or *taught*. It is easy to lose sight of this issue, however, and for the study of parental speech to become a study of the psychology of the parent instead of that of the child. For any aspect of parental behavior (such as special baby-talk forms or various kinds of parent-child interactions) to be relevant to the psychology of language acquisition, the following questions must be asked: First, is the special kind of information *present* in the speech of all caretakers? All children learn to talk, so if a feature is used only by some doting middle-class parents, it is unlikely to play a key role in acquisition. Second, does the child *use* that information? Third, if children use a special kind of information at all, is that information *sufficient* to teach a construction, or must there be some other mechanism in the child's mind that does not require that special input for the learning to take place? Fourth, if a special aspect of parental speech is sufficient to teach some construction to a child, is the feature *necessary*? Certain parental behaviors—such as explicit language lessons, to take an extreme example—might indeed help any child lucky enough to get them, but if the child would succeed at learning without them, independent learning mechanisms capable of generating such success must exist. Because such questions are rarely asked, let alone answered, the discovery of special features of parental speech has often led to premature dismissals (see, for example, Snow 1972) of the need for language-acquisition mechanisms designed to account for the robustness of acquisition. (Another impediment to characterizing the role of linguistic input properly is the myth, surprisingly common among academics, that the grammar acquired in non-middle-class households is simpler or more concrete than that acquired in middle-class environments. See Labov 1970.)

Several aspects of parental speech have been studied:

Positive Evidence
In the study of formal learning theory, the term *positive evidence* or *text* is used to refer to an infinite sequence of sentences drawn from the target language, every sentence appearing at least once in the sequence. Less formally it refers to input that informs the child which strings of words are grammatical sentences of the target language. Contrary to the belief of many linguists, the vast majority of speech to children during the language-learning years is fluent, complete, and grammatically well formed: 99.93 percent, according to one estimate (Newport,

Gleitman, and Gleitman 1977). (This assumes that elliptical utterances, such as when the question *Where are you going?* is answered with *To the store*, are considered "well formed," a reasonable assumption given that children must learn a language's rules of ellipsis as part of its grammar.) Of course "well formed" also must be taken to refer to colloquial spoken English, not to the prescriptively sanctioned prestige dialect. Thus the child can confidently assume that if a parent utters a string, it is part of the language to be learned.

Negative Evidence

Negative evidence refers to information about which strings of words are not grammatical sentences in the language; the usual psychological version of what such evidence would be is corrections or other forms of feedback from a parent that tell the child whenever one of his or her utterances is ungrammatical. Whether children get and need negative evidence is of crucial importance. In the absence of negative evidence any learner who hypothesizes a rule that generates a superset of the language will have no way of knowing that he or she is wrong (Baker 1979, Gold 1967). So if children don't receive negative evidence (or don't use it), any theory of the learning mechanisms they possess must explain how the child avoids or recovers from overgeneration. A variety of mechanisms have been proposed that do exactly that (see, for example, Pinker 1984, Wexler and Manzini 1987, Baker 1979, Berwick 1986). If children do use negative evidence, in contrast, none of these mechanisms would be necessary.

The classic studies of negative evidence come from Brown and Hanlon (1970). In careful quantitative analyses of naturalistic dialogues between parents and children, they found that parents do not differentially express approval or disapproval contingent on whether the child's prior utterance was well formed. Approval depends instead on whether the child's utterance was true. Brown and Hanlon also analyzed parents' responses to children's questions and found that parents do not answer their children's syntactically well-formed questions better than their ill-formed ones. This shows that systematic comprehension failure, another possible form of negative evidence, is unlikely to be available to children either.

Brown and Hanlon's results have been replicated, but it was found that there are differences in the frequency with which mothers repeat, alter, question, or continue their child's well-formed versus ill-formed utterances (Hirsh-Pasek, Treiman, and Schneiderman 1984, Demetras, Post, and Snow 1986, Penner 1987). If we ask the questions raised at the beginning of this section, however, we find that the answers to them are almost certainly "no," and so it is unlikely that such parental behaviors will obviate the need for mechanisms regulating overgeneration. First of all, the forms of feedback that have been discovered are not "negative evidence" in the technical sense: correct information about the grammaticality of any string of words. The feedback is extremely noisy, inconsistent across mothers and age ranges, and unselective as to whether the child's utterance was deviant for syntactic, phonological, semantic, or pragmatic reasons (see Pinker 1989, Grimshaw and Pinker 1989, Morgan and Travis 1989, and Gordon 1989 for discussions of the data). Thus the parental behavior examined in these studies could not tell the child whether it is the grammar and lexicon that needs fixing, or pronunciation or conversational skills, and any child who changed his or her grammar to rule out an utterance on the basis of parental reactions would be making the grammar worse almost as often as he or she would be making it better. Second, there is no evidence that feedback is used, necessary, or sufficient for the acquisition of any part of language. Though we lack the experimental results that would establish whether children would profit from negative evidence even if they were to receive it, there are many case studies showing examples of children being oblivious to overt corrections of their speech (see, for example, Braine 1971, McNeill 1966) and no evidence of any sort showing effects of negative evidence. Finally, there is empirical evidence of a different sort, from the facts of adults' judgments of sentences. Virtually any study in linguistics contains examples of sentences that most speakers of English immediately perceive to be odd or ill-formed—*I dripped the floor with paint, Ten pounds were weighed by the boy, I murmured John the answer, I cried the baby, The boy seems sleeping, Went she to the store?*—and thousands of other types. Why do most people have these perceptions? Is it because every one of them has at some point uttered such sentences and has benefited from negative feedback? Given that people don't often make these errors (many of them are never even made by children; see Pinker 1984, Maratsos 1983), and that corrections and other negative feedback are extremely elusive if they exist at all, the uniformity of adults' judgments of many rare ungrammatical sentence types is itself a strong indirect empirical argument that negative evidence is not required in language acquisition.

Parental Speech Register
There is evidence that caretakers in many societies modify their speech when talking to young children. This is an example of how people in general use several "registers" in different social settings. Speech to children is slower, shorter, in some ways (but not all) simpler, higher pitched, more exaggerated in intonation, more fluent and grammatically well formed, and more directed in content to the present situation than speech among adults (Snow and Ferguson 1977). Some investigators have concluded that this register serves as a set of "language lessons" to children, obviating the need for powerful inborn acquisition mechanisms containing information about the structure of language. This position is now considered unlikely, however. In many ways parental

speech is quite complex and opaque—for example, much of the speech of American parents consists of questions, which are some of the most grammatically complex structures in English or any other language (Newport el al. 1977). Furthermore several studies have actually attempted to measure the influence of special features of parental speech on children's language development. When appropriate methodological safeguards are imposed, such as disentangling the effects of the mother's speech on the linguistic abilities of the child from the effects of the linguistic abilities of the child on the mother's speech, no correlation between the use of "Motherese" and the general level of linguistic sophistication, as measured by a number of indices of sentence complexity, has been found (Newport et al. 1977, Gleitman, Newport, and Gleitman 1984). Perhaps the most dramatic evidence that special parental registers are not necessary for language learning comes from recent studies of communities where parents do not use baby-talk when interacting with their children, but model adult sentences for them to repeat (Kaluli, studied by Schieffelin 1979), and where parents do not talk to their children at all until the children, by overhearing adult speech, can converse (Piedmont Carolinas, studied by Heath 1983). There is no systematic typological difference between the languages spoken in these communities and languages spoken in communities where parental baby-talk is used, so language acquisition is clearly not dependent on any one kind of modified input.

Prosodic Information
In English syntactic structure influences a number of the prosodic properties of the speech wave, such as lengthening, intonation, and pausing (Cooper and Paccia-Cooper 1980). Though the effect of syntactic structure is combined with other influences that are many times stronger (such as hesitations resulting from planning, effects of word frequency and syllabic structure, illocutionary force, and the emotion felt by the speaker), the exaggerated intonations, slow rate, and clear demarcation of sentence boundaries in parental speech could be informative to a child in the effort to find significant units in it (Morgan 1986, Gleitman and Wanner 1984). Little is known about the systematicity or children's usage of such patterns, but it has been shown that children prefer to listen to speech that displays such correlations than speech that violates them (Fernald 1984, Hirsh-Pasek et al. 1987).

Contextual and Semantic Information
Mere exposure to sentences from a language is not enough for language learning to occur. Ervin-Tripp (1973) studied hearing children of deaf parents whose only access to English was from radio or television broadcasts. The children did not learn language from that input. The language input that children do seem to process consists of speech uttered in nonlinguistic contexts that children can encode via perception

(Macnamara 1972, Schlesinger 1971). Furthermore even before children have learned syntax, they know the meaning of many words and can make good guesses as to what speakers might be saying based on their knowledge of how the referents of these words typically act (for example, people tend to eat apples, but not vice versa).

Many models of language acquisition within a variety of frameworks assume that the effective input to the child consists of a sentence and a full encoding of the meaning of that sentence, inferred from context and from the child's knowledge of the meanings of individual words (see, for example, Anderson 1977, Berwick 1986, Pinker 1982, 1984, Wexler and Culicover 1980). Although no one believes that this is literally true—children don't hear every word of every sentence, and surely don't, to begin with, perceive the entire meaning of a sentence from context—it is a reasonable first idealization that can later be complicated once we understand how mechanisms that learn grammars from input might work at all. Usually the contextual information is thought to be represented by the child in a format appropriate for the semantic component of a theory of grammar; this simplifies the task of language acquisition, sometimes in indispensible ways, reducing it to the learning of the mapping from semantic to syntactic representations. Such a reduction does not render the language-acquisition problem trivial in any case because the nature of the mapping is still quite complex and opaque.

It is difficult to test the critical assumption about the presence and use of contextual information. On the one hand some version of it is called for in the acquisition of meaning itself; nothing in the sound of the word *dog*, for example, can inform a learner that it means "dog"; some extraneous information, presumably the presence or memory of a dog in situations in which the word is used, is crucial. Furthermore it has been found that much of parental speech to young children is so redundant with its context that a person with no knowledge of the order in which parents' words are spoken, only the words themselves, can infer with high accuracy what was being said (Slobin 1977). On the other hand we know that children do not need so rich a perceptual encoding of their current situations that blindness would impede language development: blind children learn language without problems except for some specifically visual words and are often unimpaired even in these (Landau and Gleitman 1985). Furthermore although a child can perceive the *referents* of a sentence, he or she cannot literally perceive its *meaning* or invariably construct an accurate semantic representation before language acquisition is accomplished, because in many cases semantic representations must themselves be learned as part of the language. For example, when a parent fills a glass with water from a pitcher, no perceptual information can tell the child whether the verb the parent is using means *pour* or *fill* (see Pinker 1989, for a discussion of how contextual and linguistic information could interact in fixing such meanings).

9.4 Bootstrapping into Language

The input to language acquisition consists of sounds and situations; the output is a formal grammar, specifying for that language the order and arrangement of abstract entities and relations such as nouns, verbs, subjects, phrase structures, and government. Adults command these abstract entities and relations, and the experiments on structure dependence show that young children do too. But how does a child discover particular examples of abstract structural entities and relations in the input? Innate knowledge of grammar itself is not sufficient; the child must have a way of determining which aspects of his or her perceptual input are relevant to tuning the innate knowledge so that it conforms to the particular language spoken by the community (Fodor 1966). Nativist theories posit a "rich deductive structure," whereby a child who knows that a phrase is a subject, for example, can predict without further evidence that it cannot be extracted from, or that it can be missing in an embedded clause and controlled. But deductions need premises—how does a child know that a phrase is a subject to begin with, given that subjects do not universally have any perceptual property that would help a learner pick it out? There have been a number of proposed solutions to this "bootstrapping problem" (see Pinker 1982, 1984, 1987, 1989).

Correlational Bootstrapping
One possibility is that the child records the degree of correlation between every serial, morphological, or semantic property and every other such property over the set of words heard in the input (Hanson and Kegl 1987, Maratsos and Chalkley 1981). Syntactic categories would arise as the child discovered that certain sets of properties are mutually intercorrelated in large sets of words (for example, many words occur sentence-initially, are inflected with -s when referring to plural entities, and occur after words such as *a* and *the*; this set of words would be grouped together as the equivalent of the noun category (Maratsos and Chalkley 1981)). This proposal has the advantage that it is consistent with the fact that children often acquire purely formal grammatical properties such as grammatical gender and case with few errors, even in instances where semantic properties might be thought to seduce the child into making errors. For example, French children seldom use feminine gender when using a masculine noun referring to a female person; see Karmiloff-Smith 1979 and Levy 1983. The problems with the proposal include the following: First, there is a combinatorial explosion of possible intercorrelations among linguistic properties for the

child to test (such as whether a sentence containing the word "cat" in third position must have a plural word at the end; see Pinker 1984 for discussion). Second, many of the properties that the child would have to test for cannot be observed within input sentences until after a large amount of language learning has already taken place. Therefore finding these correlations cannot be what gets language learning started. For example, noting whether a word has a suffix that agrees with the subject in number, gender, and person cannot be done until the child determines whether the word contains a suffix and what it is, how to find the subject of the sentence, and whether the subject and the suffix correspond to a particular number, person, or gender. But that is exactly what must be explained to begin with. Some linguistic properties, such as that "a phrase cannot be extracted from X," are not recordable from input sentences at all because their function is to cause certain kinds of sentences *not* to occur, requiring negative evidence. Finally, many possible correlations among features (with no obvious liabilities in terms of usefulness or excessive complexity) never even occur in natural languages (Grimshaw 1981, Pinker 1984). For example, tense is not marked on nouns; nor does the first verb in a sentence ever have to agree across the board with the last phrase. It would be a mystery, then, why children are built with complex machinery designed to test for such correlations; another way of putting it is that it would be a mystery why there are no languages exhibiting certain kinds of correlations given that children are capable of finding them.

Prosodic Bootstrapping

A second way in which the child could begin syntax learning would be to exploit the prosodic properties of input sentences and to posit phrase boundaries at points in the acoustic stream marked by lengthening, pausing, and drops in fundamental frequency. This proposal, defended by Morgan (1986), Morgan and Newport (1981), and Gleitman and Wanner (1984), is consistent with experiments showing that adults easily learn artificial languages if phrase boundaries are explicitly labeled (Morgan and Newport 1981). Its chief problems are: (1) there is a multiplicity of factors other than phrase structure that influence the prosodic contour of a sentence (syllabic structure, emotion, illocutionary force, word frequency, planning hesitations) and no known way for the child to subtract them from inputs before attempting to derive phrase boundaries, and (2) it is unlikely that correlations of this sort hold universally; if they don't, the child could not rely on them to begin his or her analysis of the phrase structure of a language.

Semantic Bootstrapping

A third possibility, proposed in various forms by Pinker (1982, 1984), Macnamara (1982), Grimshaw (1981), and Wexler and Culicover (1980), is that the child assumes that semantic and syntactic categories are correlated in restricted ways in the early input and uses semantic properties of words and phrases as evidence that they belong to certain syntactic categories. For example, the child could infer that a word that designated a person, place or thing was a noun, that a word designating an action was a verb, that a word expressing the agent argument of an action predicate was the subject of its sentence, and so on. Once an initial set of rules was learned in this manner, items that violate the correlation between syntax and semantics could be learned via their distribution in already-learned structures: in *Ideas interest Mary*, for example, the child could deduce that *ideas* is a noun because it occurs in a position that the child previously learned was a noun position, as in sentences like *The dog chewed the bone*. The advantages of this proposal include the following: (1) it accounts for the "semantic look" of early child speech, whereby children often restrict their use of syntactic forms to express a small set of semantic notions like "agent-action-patient" (Brown 1973, Slobin 1985b), while avoiding the problematic assumption that the child makes a qualitative transition from a semantic to a syntactic rule system; (2) it allows the child to infer the kinds of formal abstract entities that natural language requires; and (3) it accounts for the fact that natural languages exhibit contingencies between semantics and syntax in basic structures to begin with. The chief disadvantages are that it is difficult to formulate the canonical correlations in a way that is valid for all languages, and it is problematic to assume that the child can invariably infer exact correct meanings from context.

Most likely all of these sources of information are used in some manner, perhaps combined in a way that would allow the child to arrive at the grammatical analysis of the input that is most consistent with all of the sources. Constraint-satisfaction networks might be a way of implementing this suggestion (Pinker 1987); they might also give the learner a degree of robustness against exceptions, noise in the input, or misconstrual of aspects of the input.

9.5 The Course of Language Acquisition

Many aspects of the course of language development have been documented in great detail (see, for example, Brown 1973, MacWhinney 1982, Maratsos 1983, Menyuk 1969, Slobin 1985a,b, Gleitman and Wanner 1982). Beyond the earliest word combinations, however, no general characterization of the child's grammatical abilities has been offered. The problem is that children are often not reflective enough to offer stable judgments of what kinds of strings are ill formed according to their current state of linguistic knowledge (de Villiers and de Villiers 1974). This removes a crucial source of evidence for the psycholinguist who aims to characterize this state of knowledge precisely, leaving the form of children's spontaneously produced sentences as the main source of evidence. For early states where sentences tend to be confined to one- and two-word sequences, near-exhaustive accounts are possible, but beyond that children's speech becomes so complex so quickly that precise characterizations do not exist. On top of this the *causes* of change in children's abilities over time have remained obscure.

Early Development
Children's early language development shows considerable variation in terms of the absolute ages at which different skills are attained, but far more uniformity in terms of the order of attainment of skills and the kinds of errors made at different stages (Brown 1973).

Children typically begin to utter single words in a "holophrastic" stage beginning around the child's first birthday. However, a parameter of individual variation that manifests itself in a number of ways over an extended time is whether a child analyzes the input into distinct words and learns their referents in the world or memorizes larger phrases and uses them for social purposes, gradually breaking them down into their constituents (Bretherton, McNew, Snyder, and Bates 1983, Nelson 1981, Peters 1983). The transition to the first word combinations and sentences takes place around the eighteenth month. Children usually pass through a stage in which they combine words into strings no more than two items long, typically expressing one of a dozen or so semantic relations, including agent-action, agent-object, action-object, object-location, object-attribute, possessor-object, recurring object or event, disappearing or absent object or event, and notice of an object or event (Brown 1973, Braine 1976, Bloom, Lightbown, and Hood 1975). Some of the two-word utterances are correctly ordered two-word subsets of a three-item relation (for example, agent-action, action-object, and agent-object, drawn from the hypothetical full sequence agent-action-object; see Bloom 1970). Sequences are almost always in one of the orders that would be correct in the adult language (Brown 1973, Braine 1976). Often a pattern will be used at first only with a small number of words filling one of the roles rather than any word in the child's vocabulary (Braine 1976). Unstressed morphemes are usually absent entirely; in many languages this has the effect of making this stage and later ones "telegraphic," lacking closed-classed morphemes such as prepositions, auxiliaries, and complementizers.

Though there is often a one- and a two-word stage, there is no three-word stage; at a certain point children begin to use sentences ranging from three to eight words, with the mean length of their utterances increasing steadily until well into the fourth year. These longer utterances begin with combinations that are similar to the two-word combinations except for two differences: three-term and longer sequences (for example, agent-action-object) are uttered in toto, or else one of the terms is itself expanded into a two-word combination; thus rather than simply saying *doggie run* (agent-action), children say *big doggie run* (agent-action where agent = (attribute-object); see Brown 1973, Bloom 1970).

These early utterances contain no syntactic reflexes of interrogation or other semantic modifications of the entire proposition (for example, inversion in English); questions are indicated by rising intonation (Bowerman 1973), even though inverted sentences are as common or more common in parental speech (Newport, Gleitman, and Gleitman 1977). Likewise relativization and coordination are rare, emerging in the fourth year (Brown 1973). A variety of structures containing complements to verbs, however, blossom around the same time as the first three-word utterances, such as "equi" forms (for example, *I want to go* and *I let her eat*) and "raising" forms (for example, *I have to leave*) (Limber 1973, Bloom, Lahey, Hood, Lifter, and Fiess 1980, Pinker 1984). The first auxiliaries, usually *can, can't,* and *don't,* emerge at this time as well, and most of the others soon follow.

Later Development
Shortly after children progress to three-word and longer utterances, their speech undergoes an explosion in complexity that no one has characterized systematically. It has been easier to catalogue the ways in which their speech differs from adults (that is, their systematic error patterns). Many errors arise from children's formulation of a general rule for which there are complex conditioning factors or lexical exceptions in the adult language. Two such examples that have already been discussed are past and plural inflections, and control in exceptional verbs like *promise.* Similarly, general alternations among verbs' argument structures (for example, the causative rule relating *The glass broke* and *He broke the glass*) are used in too general a form, applying to intransitive verbs inappropriately (hence children say *Don't giggle me!* (Braine 1971, Bowerman 1974, 1982a,b)). In adult English this rule applies to causation of change of state (*The ice melted / I melted the ice*) and to causation of particular ways that objects can move (*The ball bounced / I bounced the ball*) but not to actions, such as *giggle,* or moving in particular directions, such as *go* or *fall* (Pinker 1989). Apparently children do not acquire these restrictions instantaneously, first using a rule that applies to *any* kind of causation.

At the level of clausal interactions some of the common errors include the failure to invert subject and auxiliary in English *wh*-questions, such as *why he can go* rather than *why can he go* (Brown 1968, Kuczaj and Brannick 1979); this may be an example of a larger pattern whereby children in general often fail to permute or deform the constituent orders of main clauses to signal sentence modalities such as questions, negations, conditionals, and so on (Slobin 1973, 1985b).

Some errors seem to betray the overapplication of general linkages between syntax and semantics, perhaps reflecting a universal core of notions that children expect to be expressed in consistent grammatical fashion. For example, children may "expect" their language, whatever it is, to give them a standard grammatical way of expressing basic concepts such as objects moving to locations, agents acting on objects, and the distinction between bounded events and boundariless states (Slobin 1985b). Thus in Russian there are accusative case markers (suffixes on nouns indicating that they are direct objects) that must be used for all direct objects. But very young children use them to refer to objects affected by actions alone; they use them with verbs like *hit* or *move*, but omit them when using verbs like *read* or *like*. In other cases languages make finer distinctions than those that a child expects, and children may use a morpheme in a semantic class that is *broader* than the one used in the language. For example, some languages use one marker for a goal of a physical transfer (for example, *go TO₁ the store*) and another to mark the goal of a transfer of possession (for example, *give it TO₂ Bill*). Children lump the two kinds of goals together, however, and use the first one in the second kind of usage as well (Slobin 1985b), as if transfer of possession was seen as a kind of physical movement of an object. Similar overextensions can be seen in English when children fail to select the proper preposition to accompany a verb, using one that fits some general conceptualization of a type of event. Children frequently say things such as *The ice cream was melted FROM the sun* as if causality "flowed from" the sun, or *Can I have any reading BEHIND dinner?* as if time was spread out in space like a line (Maratsos and Abramovitch 1974, Bowerman 1982a,b). These errors, in other words, seem to show the use of a spatial metaphor to represent nonspatial events such as causation, transfer of possession, changes of state, or the passage of time, with the causal force or the object undergoing the change described as if it were moving from one location to another.

9.6 Causes of Developmental Changes

It is far easier to document change in children than to explain it. Several kinds of mechanisms are presumably at work.

Maturation
Maturation surely plays a role in development: the onset of language and differences in rate among children bear no systematic relation to properties of the input. Similarly there is evidence that the ability to attain native competence levels in speaking a language actually declines at a certain point, usually around adolescence: the ability to speak a second language without an accent severely diminishes (Lieberman 1984), and the ability to master morphological systems (and possibly other fine points of grammar) deteriorates as well. This can be shown most clearly in the acquisition of American Sign Language, one of the few languages that is ever acquired by some of its speakers as a first language in adulthood. On a variety of measures people who acquire

it as adults have poorer mastery than those who first learn it as children (Newport and Supalla 1989). Furthermore immigrants learning English as a second language also do poorly if they begin learning in adulthood, even if they work at it for an equal or greater length of time than people who begin to learn it as children (Johnson and Newport 1989). Obviously there is learning outside of childhood, but it usually plateaus far short of the level of mastery found in people who have acquired a language beginning in early childhood. Furthermore onset and decline are correlated roughly with observable maturational factors: cerebral metabolic rate and synaptic density attain a peak around the age of two, then undergo a steep decline between the ages of ten and fifteen (Huttenlocher 1979). Maturational effects can also be corroborated by natural experiments. For example, Gleitman and Landau (1989) studied a group of children born prematurely by various amounts to see whether their language development was better correlated with number of months since conception (reflecting a maturational schedule) or number of months in the world (reflecting the accumulation of experience). They were able to document both kinds of effects. Pinpointing specific milestones in grammatical development that have maturational causes is of course far more difficult; see Borer and Wexler 1987 and Pinker et al. 1987 for discussions of one such hypothesis.

General Information Processing Abilities: Attention, Memory, Input, and Output Buffers

General information processing abilities leave their mark on a number of features of child language. Information at the ends of words (Slobin 1973) and at the beginnings and ends of sentences (Newport et al. 1977) is preferentially extracted, presumably reflecting serial position effects in holding strings of segments in short-term memory. Stressed elements have been found to be acquired before analogous elements that are unstressed in comparisons within and across languages, reflecting their auditory salience (Slobin 1973, Gleitman and Wanner 1982, 1984). As mentioned in the preceding section, early word combinations are two words long, though there is reason to believe that these sequences are subsets drawn from underlying patterns containing three or four elements (Bloom 1970, Brown 1973); an output buffer with two slots is a common explanation (Pinker 1984). When one element in a sentence constrains the form of another, the interdependence is enforced more consistently when they are adjacent or proximal (for example, *Can the boy ran?* is a more common error than *The boy can ran*; see Maratsos and Kuczaj 1978, Slobin 1973). This apparent short-term memory phenomenon appears to affect both the on-line enforcement of the constraint during sentence production and the acquisition of the constraint itself (Pinker 1984). Moreover limitations in forming behavioral plans may be the cause of some of children's difficulties in acting out the meanings of complex sentences (Hamburger and Crain 1984). Thus much of the increasing complexity and completeness in children's speech might be due to increases in their information-processing capacities.

Pattern Extraction

Children clearly must notice similarities holding across many pairs of related items and abstract such similarities out as general rules. For example, the discussion of productivity in the acquisition of inflection shows that words like *jog/jogged, play/played, turn/turned*, acquired as six independent forms, eventually lead to a rule "past (x)= x + /d/." There is good evidence that variables shown to affect rate of pattern learning in traditional studies of concept attainment and verbal learning, such as word frequency and consistency of mapping, have effects on the rate of learning these patterns across different items in the same domain (Bates and MacWhinney 1987, Bybee and Slobin 1982, MacWhinney 1982, Slobin 1973). However, the predictive power of statistical pattern learning is quite small. For one thing many developmental changes do not correlate at all with frequency in parental speech. One example is general measures of development such as overall complexity of children's speech (Newport et al. 1977, Gleitman et al. 1984), possibly because it is entrained to a maturational schedule; another is the order of acquisition of the fourteen principal closed-class morphemes in English, presumably because the semantic, morphological, and phonetic properties of the set are so heterogeneous that they are the rate-limiting steps (Brown 1973, de Villiers and de Villiers 1973, Pinker 1981).

The most dramatic demonstration of the limitations of statistical factors comes from an examination of a parallel distributed processing model designed to extract any combination of over 200,000 regularities relating phonological properties of English verbs and phonological properties of their past-tense forms (Rumelhart and McClelland 1986). At first glance the model appears to duplicate the behavior of children, progressing from a stage at which irregular pasts such as *broke* are used correctly to a stage at which they are overregularized (*breaked*). This performance was a direct consequence of the input statistics. In written English high-frequency verbs tend to be irregular and vice versa. Children, Rumelhart and McClelland reasoned, are likely to learn a few high-frequency verbs first, then a large number of verbs, of which an increasing proportion would probably be regular. So they first fed their model a few high-frequency verbs, almost all of them irregular, and the model, lacking much evidence for the regular pattern, reproduced the past-tense forms of all the verbs correctly. Then they fed it a much larger collection of high- to medium-frequency verbs, the majority of them regular, and the model, picking up this overwhelming pattern, began to overregularize. A change in input statistics, however, cannot be the explanation for the onset of regularization in children. In an examination of transcripts of children's spontaneous speech, Pinker and Prince (1988) found that the ratio of irregular to regular verbs in parents' speech and in children's own vocabularies does not change during the developmental stages at which overregularizations begin to occur, and it contains neither a large preponderance of irregular verbs during the first, conservative stage, nor a large preponderance of regular verbs during the overregularization stage. The key event is not in the environment, as the model assumes, but in the head of the child. This is also shown by the fact that across a sample of children, use of the regular pattern correlates with a general measure of grammatical sophistication, mean length of utterance, though not with chronological age (Kuczaj 1977). The use of irregular past forms, in contrast, correlates with chronological age. This is what one would expect if rote (for the irregulars) and rule (for the regulars) were distinct mechanisms, the former depending on input frequency, perhaps, but the latter depending on other factors tied to mastery of the grammatical system in general, perhaps maturation, perhaps acquisition of the notion "past tense" (Pinker and Prince 1988).

Most important, the key factor in the explanation of how children extract patterns must be which patterns they are capable of extracting. For language acquisition to succeed, these "patterns" must be surprisingly subtle and abstract. A properly formulated theory of language universals should delimit the possible ones: the kinds of rules or structures that a theory of grammar allows in the characterization of linguistic knowledge (see chapter 4) define precisely the kinds of patterns the child looks for in the input. Turning again to the case of the past tense in English (see Pinker and Prince 1988 for detailed analyses), it might first appear that the relevant patterns are correlations between phonological properties of the stem and phonological patterns of the past-tense form (for example, *sting* goes to *stung*, *fling* to *flung*, *stick* to *stuck*). However, such patterns cannot be recorded and then applied willy-nilly. Phonological similarity is not enough: *come* goes to *came*, and *become* goes to *became*, but *succumb* does not go to *succame* (basically an irregular verb counts as an irregular if it is the root of a verb containing a legitimate though meaningless prefix, but not if it is simply a part of a phonological sequence containing it.) Likewise two verbs with the same sound can have different past-tense forms: *ring the bell* / *rang the bell*; *ring the table with flowers* / *ringed the table with flowers*; *wring the shirt out* / *wrung the shirt out*. Semantic factors play no systematic role; for example *hit* goes to *hit* (no change), *strike* goes to *struck* (vowel change), and *slap* goes to *slapped* (regular suffix). The crucial "patterns" consist of lexical items in and of themselves, which are abstract entities; phonological patterns are secondary. Less obviously, phonological similarity must be shelved entirely if a verb is derived from a noun, no matter how similar the form may be to an irregular: you get *high-sticked*, not *high-stuck*, *braked the car*, not *broke the car*, and so on. (This is because irregularity is a property of verb *roots*, not verbs in general, and because it makes no sense for a noun to be marked in a person's lexicon as having an irregular past tense. Thus whenever a verb is derived from a noun root, it gets a regular past-tense form.) Generalization of inflections requires arriving at and applying "patterns" that are defined in terms of abstract morphological entities such as root, stem, prefix, suffix, and lexical item; and the experiment by Gordon (1985a) suggests that even young children analyze words in those terms. It is largely the specification of which "patterns" of this sort the child records, a responsibility of theories of morphology and phonology (see, for example, Chomsky and Halle 1968, van der Hulst and Smith 1982), that does the work in explaining their acquisition of the system, not the notion of "pattern extraction" itself or the statistical factors affecting it.

Conceptual Development

Conceptual development in domains other than language itself must affect language development. To take just the simplest case, if a child has not yet mastered a subtle semantic distinction (for example, different forms of possession or implication), he or she will be unable to use different constructions dedicated to expressing it correctly. Fifteen years ago nonlinguistic cognitive development was seen as a primary pacesetter for language acquisition (see Bever 1970, Brown 1973, Bowerman 1973, Schlesinger 1971, Slobin 1973). Constructions were thought to be acquired in the order of the development of the underlying semantic distinctions; syntactic rules that correlated in one-to-one fashion with semantic notions were thought to be acquired more easily than abstract rules; even the form of the linguistic rules was thought to be constrained to be consistent with the kinds of mental operations available to the child during that stage of development (for example, passivization was thought to depend on reversability in the Piagetian sense). Though the idea that cognitive development will account for trends in linguistic development was once a widespread belief among developmental psychologists (and still is among those working in the Piagetian framework), cognitive development must be now seen as a minor factor. There are a number of reasons for this change. First, the evidence that cognitive development is a pacesetter for language development (see, for example, Johnston 1985) is surprisingly weak. Virtually all the examples where conceptually complex constructions are held to be acquired later than conceptually more basic ones are either (a) seriously confounded with grammatical or phonological differences between the constructions, (b) lacking an independent motivation for the supposed conceptual difference, (c) nonreplicable across children or languages (see Bowerman 1985, Maratsos and Chalkley 1981); or (d) orthogonal to grammar altogether, involving only the mastery of the concept itself (logically analogous to the fact that children don't master the expression *differential equation* until they study calculus). Second, children seem to respect formal distinctions such as that between verb and adjective even when the conceptual categories that words belong to would seem to obscure the distinction. For example, verbs usually denote activities, but *noisy*, which usually denotes an activity, is an adjective. This lack of correlation with cognitive categories does not seem to trouble children: errors like *he noisied* are virtually nonexistent in their speech (Maratsos and Chalkley 1981). Similarly purely formal inflectional rules can be acquired very rapidly and with no regression in the direction of some associated cognitive distinction (for example, grammatical gender and biological sex; count/mass and object/substance) (Levy 1983, Maratsos and Chalkley 1981, Gordon 1985b). Third, when more complex grammatical structures are examined, the role of preexisting cognitive categories in language development is seen as even smaller. The kinds of distinctions and operations needed in constructing a language system are often eccentric with respect to salient cognitive and perceptual distinctions; in fact they are usually abstract and without cognitive and perceptual counterparts at all (Chomsky 1986, Pinker 1984, Wexler and Culicover 1980). The Gordon experiment provides an example: in terms of cognitive categories there is no relevant conceptual difference between *mice* on the one hand and *rats* and *mouses* on the other, but the children somehow unconsciously knew that the linguistic difference between them was relevant to the compounding rule.

Complexity
Simpler rules and forms are applied before more complex ones; complex forms are first applied in simpler approximations. This can be seen in the fact that the order of acquisition of English closed-class morphemes is a function of their semantic and syntactic complexity, measured in any of a number of ways (Brown 1973, de Villiers and de Villiers 1973, Pinker 1981, 1984). In addition many morphemes or phrase orders that are sensitive to a conjunction of features are first used respecting only one of those features (for example, a suffix marking masculine gender and accusative case might first be used correctly for case but indiscriminately for both genders; see Slobin 1973, 1985b). Presumably this reflects a process whereby children "sample" from a space of hypotheses, one feature or constraint at a time, eliminating features that are contradicted by future inputs, and retaining those that survive. As more features are sampled, the number of surviving ones grows (for complex structures), and the complexity of the child's system begins to approach that of the adult's (Pinker 1982, 1984).

Parameter Setting and the Subset Principle
One goal of theories of generative grammar is to show that the child need only set a small number of "parameters" on the basis of parental input, and the full richness of a grammar for a natural language will ensue when those parameterized rules interact with one another and with universal principles. For example, whether a language allows one to omit the subject in a tensed sentence with an inflected verb (the null

subject parameter) is predictive of whether a host of superficially un-related phenomena are also admissible in that language (for example, free inversion of subject and verb in simple sentences, certain types of questioning and relativization of subjects, empty resumptive pronouns in embedded clauses, appearance of *that* in subject questions, and several others; see Chomsky 1981). As such they can help explain the universality and rapidity of language acquisition: when the child learns one such phenomenon about his or her language, the others can be deduced by applying principles of grammar, without the child having to learn them from the input one by one.

This raises the question of how the child sets the parameters. An influential hypothesis is that parameter settings are ordered, with children assuming a particular "unmarked" setting as the default case, moving to less and less "marked" parameter settings as input evidence forces them to (Chomsky 1981). More specifically it has been proposed that there is a principle governing the markedness order: for every case in which setting A generates a subset of the sentences generated by setting B, the child would first hypothesize A, then abandon it for B only if a sentence generated by B but not by A was encountered in the input (Baker 1979, Berwick 1986, Osherson et al. 1985). The motivation for the "subset principle" is that the child would have no need for negative evidence; he or she would never guess too large a language. (For settings that generate languages that intersect or are disjoint, it doesn't matter which one the child picks first, because either setting can be discarded as incorrect when it fails to generate some sentence that turns up in parental speech; see figure 9.1.) Many interesting arguments hinge on whether children do guess the smallest subset among a set of nested possible languages first. In some cases this seems to be true: children are reluctant to use free word order without evidence that their language allows it, for example (Pinker 1984); they are likely to assume that words have single part-of-speech categorizations rather than to assume without direct evidence that they are syntactically ambiguous (Maratsos and Chalkley 1981), and they assume that auxiliaries are morphologically unproductive, even though the productive patterns of verbs could easily be extended to auxiliaries (Pinker 1984). Furthermore there is evidence (Wexler and Manzini 1987) that in some domains children acquire binding relations between certain kinds of pronouns and their antecedents in an order that corresponds to increasing size of resulting languages. Specifically, in English a set of principles discussed in chapter 4 are set to a parameter that allows one to say *John thinks that Bill likes himself* but not *John thinks that Mary likes himself*; in other languages the translations of both such sentences are allowable. (The relevant parameter here is how "close" an "anaphor" like *himself* has to be to its antecedent; in English it must be in the same clause; in Japanese it can also be in a higher clause.) Experiments on children's interpretation of these sentences show that children learning both kinds of languages start off assuming that the languages are like English, allowing only the "smaller" of the two possibilities (Chien and Wexler 1987, Lee and Wexler 1987). In general, formulating markedness hierarchies and testing them against the facts of development are important goals of current research.

Eliminating Errors through the Application of Principles

The strictest version of the subset hypothesis would predict that children would *never* generate an incorrect form and its correct counterpart simultaneously, because that would define a superset of the target language, which contains only the correct form. Unfortunately children do exactly that in several domains. One example we have already discussed is their use of regularized and irregular past-tense forms (for example, *breaked, broke*) side by side for a number of years (Kuczaj 1977). Another is their application of the intransitive-causative alternation across the board rather than restricting it to semantically delineated subsets of the verbs (Bowerman 1982b, Pinker 1987, 1989). This rules out the strongest version of the subset hypothesis, but leaves it a mystery how the child recovers from the error patterns in the absence of negative evidence. There must be some combination of positive data and an endogenous process that uses the positive data as evidence that some rule should be delimited or in some form discarded.

Though all sorts of arbitrary schemes for eliminating errors could be posited, the most plausible ones invoke some general principle that the child at first does not realize applies to a particular word or construction. As the child's knowledge increases, the relevance of the principle to the errant form manifests itself, and the form can be ruled out so as to make the grammar as a whole simpler or more consistent with the principle. One clear example of such a principle is the uniqueness principle in morphology, which says that for every stem there is a single form for any of its inflectional categories (for example, a single past-tense form in English). Thus hearing *broke* in the input, and realizing that it was the past tense form of *break,* would be sufficient to discard *breaked* even in the absence of negative evidence (Pinker 1984). But then why do children persist in using the incorrect and correct form side-by-side, usually for several years? One hypothesis is that the child has not yet realized that the irregular form is the past version of its stem; the child might misconstrue it as an independently existing verb. To test this hypothesis, one can check to see if there is any other evidence that children misconstrue irregular pasts as being independent verbs. Indeed such evidence exists. First, children have been documented to use irregular pasts as if they were separate stems; they say, *to broke; Did he broke it?; They were broking it; She broked it* side by side with *to break; Did he break it?, They were breaking it; She breaked it* (Kuczaj 1977, 1981). Second, the transparency of the morphological relation between stem and past has been found to affect the amount of overregularization:

verbs with dissimilar pasts (for example, *went*) are overregularized more than verbs with similar pasts (for example, *hit;* see Bybee and Slobin 1982).

Despite the importance of formulating and testing mechanisms that are capable of leading the child from a state in which errors are made to the adult state, there are few other concrete suggestions in the literature, and this remains an important gap in our understanding.

9.7 Conclusion

Though the scientific study of language acquisition is as old as modern cognitive science, it has recently entered a new phase. Only twenty-five years ago our ignorance of the facts of language development was nearly total. Until about twenty years ago theories of generative grammar were complex and unconstrained systems, with the stated goal of specifying principles of universal grammar rarely achieved in practice. As recently as fifteen years ago talk about specific algorithms capable of acquiring detailed grammatical structures could have been dismissed as pipe dreams; no one could even state in careful terms what the problem of language learning was. It is no wonder that claims about language acquisition were metaphorical and vague, and that debates over its nature were highly emotional and usually ended with participants going off to study completely different kinds of phenomena.

Language acquisition today is no less contentious a topic, but the nature of the controversies has changed considerably (for an example, see the proceedings of the recent Carnegie Mellon Symposium on Cognition, dedicated to "Mechanisms of Language Acquisition"; Mac-Whinney 1987). Linguists and psychologists routinely collaborate and exchange ideas; a conference or book on the nature of acquisition without contributions from both fields is virtually unthinkable. Explicit mechanisms for the acquisition of grammatical knowledge can be tested in terms of their actual performance and in terms of their fidelity to a cumulative body of data on children's development from a variety of languages. As a result, when researchers disagree, the disagreement can be over the truth of a concrete proposal about the psychology of the child rather than about the attractiveness of a certain approach, the interest of a particular topic, or the aptness of a favored metaphor. Though the obstacles to understanding are still formidable, the opportunities for scientific progress have never been better.

References

Anderson, J. 1977. Induction of augmented transition networks. *Cognitive Science* 1:125–157.

Anderson, J. R. 1983. *The Architecture of Cognition*. Cambridge, MA: Harvard University Press.

Baker, C. 1979. Syntactic theory and the projection problem. *Linguistic Inquiry* 10:533–581.

Bates, E., and MacWhinney, B. 1987. Competition, variation, and language learning. In B. MacWhinney, ed. *Mechanisms of Language Acquisition*. Hillsdale, NJ: Erlbaum.

Berko, J. 1958. The child's learning of English morphology. *Word*. 14:150–177.

Berwick, R. C. 1986. *The Acquisition of Syntactic Knowledge*. Cambridge, MA: MIT Press.

Bever, T. G. 1970. The cognitive basis for linguistic structures. In J. R. Hayes, ed. *Cognition and the Development of Language*. New York: Wiley.

Bickerton, D. 1981. *The Roots of Language*. Ann Arbor, MI: Karoma.

Bloom, L. 1970. *Language Development: Form and Function in Emerging Grammars*. Cambridge, MA: MIT Press.

Bloom, L., Lahey, M., Hood, M., Lifter, K., and Fiess, K. 1980. Complex sentences: Acquisition of syntactic connectives and the semantic relations they encode. *Journal of Child Language* 7:235–261.

Bloom, L., Lightbown, P., and Hood, M. 1975. Structure and variation in child language. *Monographs of the Society for Research in Child Development* 40:1–78.

Borer, H., and Wexler, K. 1987. The maturation of syntax. In T. Roeper and E. Williams, eds. *Parameter-Setting and Language Acquisition*. Dordrecht: Reidel.

Bowerman, M. 1973. Structural relationships in children's utterances: syntactic or semantic? In T. Moore, ed. *Cognitive Development and the Acquisition of Language*. New York: Academic Press.

Bowerman, M. 1974. Learning the structure of causative verbs: A study in the relationship of cognitive, semantic and syntactic development. In E. Clark, ed. *Papers and Reports on Child Language Development*. No. 8. Stanford, CA: Stanford University Committee on Linguistics, pp. 142–178.

Bowerman, M. 1982a. Reorganizational processes in lexical and syntactic development. In E. Wanner and L. Gleitman eds. *Language Acquisition: The State of the Art*. New York: Cambridge University Press.

Bowerman, M. 1982b. Evaluating competing linguistic models with language acquisition data: Implications of developmental errors with causative verbs. *Quaderni di Semantica* 3:5–66.

Bowerman, M. 1985. What shapes children's grammars? In D. I. Slobin, ed. *The Crosslinguistic Study of Language Acquisition. Volume 2: Theoretical issues*. Hillsdale, NJ: Erlbaum.

Braine, M. D. S. 1971. On two types of models of the internalization of grammars. In D. I. Slobin, ed. *The Ontogenesis of Grammar: A Theoretical Symposium*. New York: Academic Press.

Braine, M. D. S. 1976. Children's first word combinations. *Monographs of the Society for Research in Child Development* 41.

Bretherton, I., McNew, S., Snyder, L., and Bates, E. 1983. Individual differences at 20 months: Analytic and holistic strategies in language acquisition. *Journal of Child Language* 10:293–320.

Brown, R., and Hanlon, C. 1970. Derivational complexity and order of acquisition in child speech. In J. R. Hayes, ed. *Cognition and the Development of Language.* New York: Wiley.

Brown, R. 1968. The development of *wh* questions in child speech. *Journal of Verbal Learning and Verbal Behavior* 7:279–290.

Brown, R. 1973. *A First Language: the Early Stages.* Cambridge, MA: Harvard University Press.

Bybee, J. L., and Slobin, D. I. 1982. Rules and schemes in the development and use of the English past tense. *Language* 58:265–289.

Chien, Y.-C., and Wexler, K. 1987 (23–25 Oct). A comparison between Chinese-speaking and English-speaking children's acquisition of reflexives and pronouns. Paper presented at the Twelfth Annual Boston University Conference on Language Development.

Chomsky, C. 1969. *Acquisition of Syntax in Children from 5–10.* Cambridge, MA: MIT Press.

Chomsky, N. 1959. A review of B. F. Skinner's "Verbal Behavior." *Language* 3:26–58.

Chomsky, N. 1965. *Aspects of the Theory of Syntax.* Cambridge, MA: MIT Press.

Chomsky, N. 1975. *Reflections on Language.* New York: Random House.

Chomsky, N. 1981. *Lectures on Government and Binding.* Dordrecht: Foris Publications.

Chomsky, N. 1986. *Knowledge of Language.* New York: Fontana.

Chomsky, N., and Halle, M. 1968. *The Sound Pattern of English.* New York: Harper and Row.

Comrie, B. 1981. *Language Universals and Linguistic Typology.* Chicago: University of Chicago Press.

Cooper, W. E., and Paccia-Cooper, J. 1980. *Syntax and Speech.* Cambridge, MA: Havard University Press.

Crain, S., and Nakayama, M. 1986. Structure dependence in children's language. *Language.* 63:522–543.

Cromer, R. 1986 (17–19 Oct). Case studies of dissociations between language and cognition. Paper presented at the Eleventh Annual Boston University Conference on Language Development.

Curtiss, S. 1977. *Genie: A Psycholinguistic Study of a Modern Day "Wild Child."* New York: Academic Press.

Curtiss, S., Yamada, J., and Fromkin, V. 1979. How independent is language? On the question of formal parallels between grammar and action. *UCLA Working Papers in Cognitive Linguistics* 1:131–157.

de Villiers, J., and de Villiers, P. 1973. A cross-sectional study of the acquisition of grammatical morphemes. *Journal of Psycholinguistic Research* 12:267–278.

de Villiers, J., and de Villiers, P. 1974. Competence and performance in child language: are children really competent to judge? *Journal of Child Language* 1:11–22.

Demetras, M. J., Post, K. N., and Snow, C. E. 1986. Feedback to first language learners: The role of repetitions and clarification questions. *Journal of Child Language* 13:275–292.

Ervin, S. 1964. Imitation and structural change in children's language. In E. Lenneberg, ed. *New Directions in the Study of Language*. Cambridge, MA: MIT Press.

Ervin-Tripp, S. 1973. Some strategies for the first two years. In T. E. Moore, ed. *Cognitive Development and the Acquisition of Language*. New York: Academic Press.

Fernald, A. 1984. The perceptual and affective salience of mothers' speech to infants. In L. Feagans, C. Garvey, and R. Golinkoff, eds. *The Origins and Growth of Communication*. Norwood, NJ: Ablex.

Fodor, J. A. 1966. How to learn to talk: some simple ways. In F. Smith and G. Miller, eds. *The Genesis of Language*. Cambridge, MA: MIT Press.

Fodor, J. A. 1975. *The Language of Thought*. New York: T. Y. Crowell.

Fodor, J. A. 1983. *Modularity of Mind*. Cambridge MA: MIT Press. A Bradford Book.

Gardner, R. A., and Gardner, B.T. 1969. Teaching sign language to a chimpanzee. *Science* 165:664–672.

Gardner, H. 1983. *Frames of Mind: The Theory of Multiple Intelligences*. New York: Basic Books.

Gleitman, L. R., and Landau, B. 1989. Effects of gestational age on language onset and development. Unpublished manuscript, University of Pennsylvania.

Gleitman, L. R., Newport, E. L., and Gleitman, H. 1984. The current status of the motherese hypothesis. *Journal of Child Language* : 43–80.

Gleitman, L. R., and Wanner, E. 1982. Language acquisition: the state of the state of the art. In E. Wanner and L. R. Gleitman, eds. *Language Acquisition: The State of the Art*. New York: Cambridge University Press.

Gleitman, L. R., and Wanner, E. 1984. Richly specified input to language learning. In O. Selfridge, E. L. Rissland, and M. Arbib, eds. *Adaptive Control of Ill-Defined Systems*. New York: Plenum.

Gold, E. 1967. Language identification in the limit. *Information and Control* 10:447–474.

Goldin-Meadow, S., and Feldman, S. 1977. The development of language-like communication without a language model. *Science* 197:401–403.

Gordon, P. 1985a. Level ordering in lexical development. *Cognition* 21:73–93.

Gordon, P. 1985b. Evaluating the semantic categories hypothesis: the case of the count-mass distinction. *Cognition* 20:209–242.

Gordon, P. 1989. Learnability and feedback: A commentary of Bohannon and Stanowicz. *Developmental Psychology.*

Greenberg, J., ed. 1978. *Universals of Human Language. Volume 4: Syntax.* Stanford, CA: Stanford University Press.

Grimshaw, J. 1981. Form, function, and the language acquisition device. In C. L. Baker and J. McCarthy, eds. *The Logical Problem of Language Acquisition.* Cambridge, MA: MIT Press.

Grimshaw, J., and Pinker, S. 1989. Positive and negative evidence in language acquisition. (Commentary on D. Lightfoot's "The child's trigger experience: 'Degree-0' learnability.") *Behavioral and Brain Sciences.*

Hamburger, H., and Crain, S. 1984. Acquisition of cognitive compiling. *Cognition* 17:85–136.

Hanson, S. J., and Kegl, J. 1987. PARSNIP: A connectionist network that learns natural language grammar from exposure to natural language sentences. *Proceedings of the Ninth Annual Cognitive Science Society Meeting.* Hillsdale, NJ: Erlbaum.

Heath, S. B. 1983. *Ways with Words: Language, Life and Work in Communities and Classrooms.* New York: Cambridge University Press.

Hirsh-Pasek, K., Nelson, D. G. N., Jusczyk, P. W., Cassidy, K. W., Druss, B., and Kennedy, L. 1987. Clauses are perceptual units for young infants. *Cognition* 26:269–286.

Hirsh-Pasek, K., Treiman, R., and Schneiderman, M. 1984. Brown and Hanlon revisited: Mothers' sensitivity to ungrammatical forms. *Journal of Child Language* 11:81–88.

Huttenlocher, P. R. 1979. Synaptic density in human frontal cortex during developmental changes and the effects of aging. *Brain Research* 163:195.

Johnson, J. S., and Newport, E. L. 1989. Critical period effects in second language learning: The influence of maturational state on the acquisition of English as a second language. *Cognitive Psychology* 21:60–99.

Johnston, J. 1985. Cognitive prerequisites: The evidence from children learning English. In D. I. Slobin, ed. *The Crosslinguistic Study of Language Acquisition. Volume 2: Theoretical Issues.* Hillsdale, NJ: Erlbaum.

Karmiloff-Smith, A. 1979. *A Functional Approach to Child Language: A Study of Determiners and Reference.* Cambridge: Cambridge University Press.

Kiparsky, P. 1982. From cyclical to lexical phonology. In H. van der Hulst and N. Smith, eds. *The Structure of Phonological Representations.* Dordecht: Foris.

Kuczaj, S. A., II. 1977. The acquisition of regular and irregular past tense forms. *Journal of Verbal Learning and Verbal Behavior* 16:589–600.

Kuczaj, S. A., II. 1977. The acquisition of regular and irregular past tense forms. *Journal of Verbal Learning and Verbal Behavior* 16:589–600.

Kuczaj, S. A., II. 1981. More on children's initial failure to relate specific acquisitions. *Journal of Child Language* 8:485–487.

Kuczaj, S. A., II, and Brannick, N. 1979. Children's use of the *wh* question modal auxiliary placement rule. *Journal of Experimental Child Psychology* 28:43–67.

Labov, W. 1970. *The Study of Nonstandard English*. Urbana, IL: National Council of Teachers of English.

Landau, B., and Gleitman, L. R. 1985. *Language and Experience*. Cambridge, MA: Harvard University Press.

Lee, H., and Wexler, K. 1987 (23–25 Oct). The acquisition of reflexives and pronouns in Korean. Paper presented at the Twelfth Annual Boston University Conference on Language Development.

Lenneberg, E. H. 1967. *Biological Foundations of Language*. New York: Wiley.

Levy, Y. 1983. It's frogs all the way down. *Cognition* 15:75–93.

Lieberman, P. 1984. *The Biology and Evolution of Language*. Cambridge, MA: Harvard University Press.

Limber, J. 1973. The genesis of complex sentences. In T. E. Moore, ed. *Cognitive Development and the Acquisition of Language*. New York: Academic Press.

MacWhinney, B., and Snow, C. 1985. The child language data exchange system. *Journal of Child Language* 12:271–296.

MacWhinney, B. 1982. Basic processes in syntactic acquisition. In S. A. Kuczaj, II, ed. *Language Development. Volume 1: Syntax and Semantics*. Hillsdale, NJ: Erlbaum.

MacWhinney, B., ed. 1987. *Mechanisms of Language Acquisition*. Hillsdale, NJ: Erlbaum.

Macnamara, J. 1972. Cognitive basis of language learning in infants. *Psychological Review* 79:1–13.

Macnamara, J. 1982. *Names for Things: A Study of Child Language*. Cambridge, MA: MIT Press. A Bradford Book.

Maratsos, M. P. 1974. How preschool children understand missing complement subjects. *Child Development* 45:700–706.

Maratsos, M. P. 1983. Some current issues in the study of the acquisition of grammar. In P. Mussen, ed. *Carmichael's Manual of Child Psychology*. 4th ed. New York: Wiley.

Maratsos, M. P., and Abramovitch, R. 1975. How children understand full, truncated and anomalous passives. *Journal of Verbal Learning and Verbal Behavior* 14:145–157.

Maratsos, M. P., and Chalkley, M. 1981. The internal language of children's syntax: The ontogenesis and representation of syntactic categories. In K. Nelson, ed. *Children's Language.* Vol. 2. New York: Gardner Press.

Maratsos, M. P., and Kuczaj, S. A., II. 1978. Against the transformationalist account: A simpler analysis of auxiliary overmarkings. *Journal of Child Language* 5:337–345.

McNeill, D. 1966. Developmental psycholinguistics. In F. Smith and G. Miller, eds., *The genesis of language.* Cambridge, MA: MIT Press.

Menyuk, P. 1969. *Sentences Children Use.* Cambridge, MA: MIT Press.

Miller, G. A. 1967. Project grammarama. In G. A. Miller. *The Psychology of Communication.* New York: Penguin Books.

Minsky, M. 1975. A framework for representing knowledge. In P. H. Winston, ed. *The Psychology of Computer Vision.* New York: McGraw-Hill.

Moeser, S. D. 1977. Semantics and miniature artificial languages. In J. Macnamara, ed. *Language Learning and Thought.* New York: Academic Press.

Morgan, J. L. 1986. *From Simple Input to Complex Grammar.* Cambridge, MA: MIT Press. A Bradford Book.

Morgan, J., and Newport, E. 1981. The role of constituent structure in the induction of an artificial language. *Journal of Verbal Learning and Verbal Behavior* 20:67–85.

Morgan, J. L., and Travis, L. L. 1989. Limits on negative information in language learning. *Journal of Child Language* (in press).

Nelson, K. 1981. Individual differences in language development: Implications for development and language. *Developmental Psychology* 17:170–187.

Nelson, K. E., Carskaddon, G., and Bonvillian, J. D. 1973. Syntax acquisition: Impact of experimental variation in adult verbal interaction with the child. *Child Development* 44:479–504.

Newport, E. 1981. Constraints on structure: Evidence from American Sign Language and language learning. In W. A. Collins, ed. *Aspects of the Development of Competence: Minnesota Symposia on Child Psychology.* Vol. 14. Hillsdale, NJ: Erlbaum.

Newport, E., Gleitman, H., and Gleitman, E. 1977. Mother, I'd rather do it myself: Some effects and noneffects of maternal speech style. In C. E. Snow and C. A. Ferguson, eds. *Talking to Children: Language Input and Acquisition.* New York: Cambridge University Press.

Newport, E. L. 1986 (17–19 Oct). The effect of maturational state on the acquisition of language. Paper presented at the Eleventh Annual Boston University Conference on Language Development.

Newport, E. L., and Supalla, T. 1989. A critical period effect in the acquisition of a primary language. *Science.*

Osherson, D. N., Stob, M., and Weinstein, S. 1985. *Systems That Learn.* Cambridge, MA: MIT Press. A Bradford Book.

Osherson, D. N., and Wasow, T. 1976. Task-specificity and species-specificity in the study of language: A methodological note. *Cognition* 4:203–214.

Penner, S. 1987. Parental responses to grammatical and ungrammatical child utterances. *Child Development* 58:376–384.

Peters, A. 1983. *The Units of Language Acquisition*. New York: Cambridge University Press.

Petitto, L. A. 1987. On the autonomy of language and gesture: Evidence from the acquisition of personal pronouns in American Sign Language. *Cognition* 27:1–52.

Piaget, J. 1926. *The Language and Thought of the Child*. New York: Routledge & Kegan Paul.

Pinker, S. 1979. Formal models of language learning. *Cognition* 7:217–283.

Pinker, S. 1981. On the acquisition of grammatical morphemes. *Journal of Child Language* 8:477– 484.

Pinker, S. 1982. A theory of the acquisition of lexical interpretive grammars. In J. Bresnan, ed. *The Mental Representation of Grammatical Relations*. Cambridge, MA: MIT Press.

Pinker, S. 1984. *Language Learnability and Language Development*. Cambridge, MA: Harvard University Press.

Pinker, S. 1987. The bootstrapping problem in language acquisition. In B. MacWhinney, ed. *Mechanisms of Language Acquisition*. Hillsdale, NJ: Erlbaum.

Pinker, S. 1989. *Learnability and Cognition: The Acquisition of Argument Structure*. Cambridge, MA: MIT Press.

Pinker, S., Lebeaux, D. S. and Frost, L. A. 1987. Productivity and constraints in the acquisition of the passive. *Cognition* 26:195–267.

Pinker, S., and Prince, A. 1988. On language and connectionism: Analysis of a parallel distributed processing model of language acquisition. *Cognition* 28:73–193.

Premack, D., and Premack, A. J. 1983. *The Mind of an Ape*. New York: Norton.

Rumelhart, D. E., and McClelland, J. L. 1986. On learning the past tenses of English verbs. In J. L. McClelland, D. E. Rumelhart, and the PDP Research Group. *Parallel Distributed Processing: Explorations in the Microstructure of Cognition*. Vol. 2. Cambridge, MA: MIT Press. A Bradford Book.

Schieffelin, B. 1979. How Kaluli children learn what to say, what to do, and how to feel: An ethnographic study of the development of communicative competence. Doctoral dissertation, Columbia University.

Schlesinger, I. M. 1971. Production of utterances and language acquisition. In D. I. Slobin, ed. *The Ontogenesis of Grammar*. New York: Academic Press.

Schlesinger, I. M. 1977. Miniature artificial languages as research tools. In J. Macnamara, ed. *Language Learning and Thought*. New York: Academic Press.

Seidenberg, M. S. 1986. Evidence from great apes concerning the biological bases of language. In W. Demopoulos and A. Marras, eds. *Language Learning and Concept Acquisition*. Norwood, NJ: Ablex.

Seidenberg, M. S., and Petitto, L. A. 1979. Signing behavior in apes: A critical review. *Cognition* 7:177–215.

Shepard, R. N., and Cooper, L. A. 1982. *Mental Images and their Transformations*. Cambridge, MA: MIT Press.

Shopen, T., ed. 1985. *Language Typology and Syntactic Description. Volume II: Complex Constructions*. New York: Cambridge University Press.

Skinner, B. F. 1957. *Verbal Behavior*. New York: Appleton-Century Crofts.

Slobin, D. 1973. Cognitive prerequisites for the development of grammar. In C. Ferguson and D. I. Slobin, eds. *Studies in Child Language Development*. New York: Holt, Rinehart and Winston.

Slobin, D. I. 1977. Language change in childhood and in history. In J. Macnamara, ed. *Language Learning and Thought*. New York: Academic Press.

Slobin, D. I. 1982. Universal and particular in the acquisition of language. In E. Wanner and L. R. Gleitman, eds. *Language Acquisition: The State of the Art*. New York: Cambridge University Press.

Slobin, D. I. 1985a. *The Crosslinguistic Study of Language Acquisition. Volume I: The Data*. Hillsdale, NJ: Erlbaum.

Slobin, D. I. 1985b. Crosslinguistic evidence for the language-making capacity. In D. I. Slobin, ed. *The Crosslinguistic Study of Language Acquisition. Volume II: Theoretical Issues*. Hillsdale, NJ: Erlbaum.

Snow, C. E. 1972. Mothers' speech to children learning language. *Child Development* 43:549–565.

Snow, C. E., and Ferguson, C. A. 1977. *Talking to Children: Language Input and Acquisition*. Cambridge: Cambridge University Press.

Studdert-Kennedy, M., ed. 1983. *Psychobiology of Language*. Cambridge, MA: MIT Press.

Terrace, H., Petitto, L. A., Sanders, R. J., and Bever, T. G. 1979. Can an ape create a sentence? *Science* 206:891–902.

Thatcher, R. W., Walker, R. A., and Guidice, S. 1987. Human cerebral hemispheres develop at different rates and ages. *Science* 236:1110–1113.

van der Hulst, H., and Smith, N., eds. 1982. *The Structure of Phonological Representations*. Dordrecht: Foris.

Wexler, K., and Culicover, P. 1980. *Formal Principles of Language Acquisition*. Cambridge, MA: MIT Press.

Wexler, K., and Manzini, R. 1987. Parameters and learnability in binding theory. In T. Roeper and E. Williams, eds. *Parameters and Linguistic Theory*. Dordecht: Reidel.

Whorf, B. 1956. *Language, Thought, and Reality*. Cambridge, MA: MIT Press.

10 Reading

Alexander Pollatsek and Keith Rayner

Reading is a topic far too vast to be sensibly covered in a chapter of this length. As a result we select three topics within the field of reading that seem particularly relevant to cognitive science and virtually ignore the rest of reading. Before we do, however, let us place these topics in some context by listing the central questions in the psychology of reading (as we see them):

1. How are written words identified?

2. How does the system of oral language interact with word identification and reading?

3. Are words identified in text differently than in isolation?

4. In reading, the eyes move across the page. How does this process shape the answers to the above questions?

5. How does the reader go beyond the meaning of individual words? (For example, how are sentences parsed, the literal meaning of a sentence constructed, anaphoric links established, inferences made, and so on?)

6. What is the end product of reading? (That is, what new mental structures are formed or retained as a result of reading?)

7. How does the skill of reading develop?

8. How can we characterize individual differences among readers in the same culture and differences in readers across cultures?

9. How can we characterize and remediate reading disabilities?

10. Can we improve on "normal reading" (for example, is "speedreading" possible)?

Elsewhere we discuss all of these topics and present a model of the reading process that we believe encompasses many of the details that are known about reading (Rayner and Pollatsek 1989). For a more complete presentation of reading, we invite you to consult our book or one of the other recent books on the psychology of reading (for example, Crowder 1982, Just and Carpenter 1987, Mitchell 1982).

The three topics that we discuss here have been studied intensively in the last fifteen years, mainly by cognitive psychologists. The first is word identification. In particular we focus on two aspects of word identification: the relationship between the identification of words and letters, and the role of recoding to sound in word identification. The second topic is how visual information is extracted from the text in reading; our discussion deals with eye movements in two ways: both the function of eye movements in reading and the use of eye movements as a tool for studying reading. The third topic is the effects of prose context on the identification of individual words; again the use of eye movements is discussed.

A full discussion of the broader implications of the research on these topics makes more sense after the research is discussed. However, a few preliminary comments are in order. First, the research that we discuss concentrates on understanding the *process* of reading. Accordingly the methods discussed employ *on-line* measures, such as reaction-times or the pattern of eye movements. Such methods are much more direct for revealing the moment-to-moment processing in reading than more traditional methods that examine the *products* of reading using measures such as recall and comprehension. As a result of this emphasis a central question in the research is the relationship between various forms of internal representations as the reader goes through the text converting arbitrary visual forms to complex meanings.

Length considerations force us to restrict our discussion largely to the level of words (and questions 1 through 4). However, similar methods offer major insights into higher level processes (questions 5 and 6) such as syntactic parsing and construction of discourse structure (see, for example, chapters 7 and 8 in Rayner and Pollatsek 1989). In addition, space considerations force us to concentrate on the adult skilled reader (and to largely ignore questions 7 through 10). Fortunately some of the slack is taken up by other chapters in this book: the processing of discourse is discussed by Grosz, Sidner, and Pollack (chapter 11), some of the developmental issues are discussed by Pinker (chapter 9), and cross-cultural issues are discussed by D'Andrade (chapter 20).

10.1   Visual Word Identification

It should be obvious that the identification of words is a major component of the reading process. Children learning to read are already able to identify many spoken words and to put these words together to form phrases, clauses, and sentences and to construct meaning from relatively complex spoken utterances. Thus a simple view of learning to read is that the child must learn to decipher the written words in order to insert them into the routines already in place for understanding spoken words in discourse. Of course it may not be quite that simple because new routines may have to be developed for fluently combining written words. The bulk of the evidence does indicate, however, that dysfunction in the word-identification process is the major stumbling block in learning to read (Perfetti 1985, Rayner and Pollatsek 1989).

Letters and Words

Three Classes of Models   Obviously a basic issue concerning the identification of words is the relationship between letter identification and word identification. In particular, researchers have sought to understand whether letter identification is a preliminary stage of word identification and if so the nature of the mechanism that combines the information from component letters. Much of the research has been guided by three classes of simple models of word recognition that have taken different stances on the two issues. To simplify future discussion, we assume that there are representations in the brain called *letter detectors* and *word detectors* (that is, some reproducible pattern of neural activity that occurs when a given letter or word is identified) and rephrase the questions in terms of the relationship between letter detectors and word detectors.

In the first class of models, which we term *direct word-recognition models* (see figure 10.1), letter recognition is irrelevant to word recognition (that is, the letter detectors and word detectors are independent of each other). Models of this class differ as to whether the word as a whole is recognized by a visual "template" or by a set of visual "features" that defines the word (Smith 1971).

In the second class of models, which we term *serial letter models,* letter recognition is a stage before word recognition, and the letters in a word are processed serially (usually hypothesized going from left to right in languages like English). Often models of this type posit that the serial process of letter lookup activates sound units such as phonemes, so that the process of word recognition goes through two stages: letters leading to a sound representation of the word followed by the sound representation activating the meaning (see, for example, Gough 1972). In other versions, however, serial processing of letters does not entail an intervening sound stage (see, for example, Mewhort and Beal 1977).

In the third class of models, *parallel letter models,* letter detectors are activated, and the letter information is fed in parallel into word detectors. When the excitation from component letter detectors is sufficiently strong, the appropriate word detector is activated. Of course such a model must assume that the spatial position of letters is somehow registered so that *loop* can be distinguished from *pool* (see figure 10.1).

In the following discussion we argue that the parallel-letter model is closest to the truth. Some data indicate that word recognition may be more complex, however, than an automatic parallel registration of the component letters, and that sound codes are also involved.

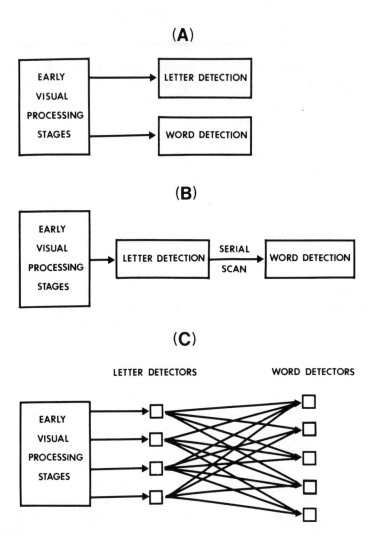

Figure 10.1 Three alternative classes of models of the relationship between the identification of letters and the identification of words. (A) The identification of words is assumed
to go on independently of and in parallel with the identification of letters (*direct word
recognition models*). (B) The identification of words proceeds by a serial scan of previously
identified letters (*serial letter models*). (C) Letters in the word are activated in parallel, and
the activation from these letter detectors is sent in parallel to the word detectors in the
lexicon (*parallel letter models*). In some parallel letter models there is also feedback from
the word detectors to the letter detectors. (See the text for additional detail.)

The "Word-Superiority Effect" and Related Phenomena   An experimental method that has been relied on heavily to distinguish between these models is the *tachistoscopic presentation* of words. In this type of experiment either a letter or a string of letters is presented briefly (50 ms or less) for a controlled duration (originally in a tachistoscope, but now often on cathode ray tubes or CRTs). Usually either the subject's accuracy in identifying a word or letter is measured as a function of the exposure duration, or the accuracy for two different kinds of stimuli are compared at the same exposure duration. Often the brief presentation of the *target* (the letter or letter string) is immediately followed by a *mask* (a patterned stimulus in the same location) in order to terminate or interfere with visual processing of the target. This is because prior research (Sperling 1960) demonstrated that a visual memory of a briefly presented stimulus persists for about 300 ms even when the stimulus is presented for 50 ms or less. There is still controversy about whether a mask does serve the function of completely terminating visual processing of the target stimulus; however, this controversy is peripheral to most of the research discussed here.

One of the major findings from this research is that when the exposure duration of the stimulus is controlled, letters in words are actually identified better than letters in isolation. Although such findings were reported about 100 years ago (Cattell 1886), modern interest in the phenomenon stemmed from an experiment by Reicher (1969) in which many of the potentially uninteresting reasons for the phenomenon were eliminated. In Reicher's experiment the subject was shown either a word (for example, *WORK*), a nonword (for example, *ORWK*), or a single letter (for example, *K*) for about 30 ms. In each case the *K* appeared in the same location on the screen and the same location relative to where the subject's eyes were fixating (see table 10.1) The stimulus was masked immediately upon its offset, and two letters appeared, one above and one below a target location, and the subject indicated which of the two letters he or she believed had been in the

Table 10.1 Examples of Conditions in Reicher's Experiment

	Condition		
	Word	Nonword	Letter
Target stimulus	W O R K	O R W K	K
	D	D	D
Mask and probe	# # # #	# # # #	# # # #
	K	K	K

The target stimulus is presented for about 30 to 40 ms (durations are adjusted for each subject to achieve overall performance of about 75 percent correct), and the mask and probe are typically presented for much longer periods of time.

target location. In this example a *D* and a *K* would appear above and below the *K* in the target stimulus (see table 10.1).

Reicher's major finding (called the *word-superiority effect*) was that a letter in a word (for example, *K* in *WORK*) was correctly identified a greater percent of the time than when it appeared in isolation. An important feature of the experiment was that guessing was controlled. All of the stimuli were constructed as the example in table 10.1 in which either *D* or *K* together with the rest of the presented letters would spell a word. Thus subjects could not guess which of the two letters was in the final location simply by knowing that it was a word. Reicher's finding has been replicated dozens if not hundreds of times (see, for example, Wheeler 1970, Baron and Thurston 1973, Johnston and Mc-Clelland 1974). A second finding (that has also been replicated many times) was that accuracy was about the same when the target letter appeared in a nonword that is very unwordlike (for example, *ORWK*) as when it appeared in isolation.

Let's consider the effect of these data on the models. First, the findings indicate that the serial-letter model cannot be true. If letters in words are processed one at a time, then the *K* in *WORK* would only be processed after *W, O,* and *R* are processed, whereas the *K* in isolation would be processed first. A letter in isolation should be processed as rapidly as the first letter processed in the word; therefore the accuracy of reporting the isolated letter should be better than reporting the letter in a word. In addition, the fact that *K* is processed as well in *ORWK* as in isolation is evidence that even patternless strings of letters are not processed in series. Although it is possible that serial identification of letters is very rapid and other factors in addition to visual information extraction are producing errors in this task, it seems unlikely because exposure durations of about 60 to 80 ms are usually sufficient to ensure 100 percent correct identification in all conditions (Adams 1979).

The fact that letter identification is better for letters in words than for letters in isolation indicates either that words are recognized as wholes, independent of and before letter identification, or that letters in words are processed in parallel leading to word identification and that word identification somehow facilitates letter identification. How can we distinguish between the two explanations? The general method that has been used is to examine what happens when stimuli are used that are wordlike but not actually familiar word patterns. One direction this has taken is using *pseudowords:* strings of letters such as *MARD* that are pronounceable and obey the orthographic constraints of the written language, but are not words (Baron and Thurston 1973, Carr, Davidson, and Hawkins 1978, McClelland and Johnston 1977). A replicable finding is that letters in pseudowords are identified more accurately than letters in isolation (the *pseudoword-superiority effect*). This causes problems for a model that posits independent word and letter detectors. In such a model the word-superiority effect is presumably due to the word detectors being activated faster than the letter detectors. One would then have to posit a separate mechanism to explain the pseudoword superiority effect, however, unless one wanted to posit "word detectors" not only for words but for all conceivable pseudowords.

Another problem for models that posit word detectors independent of letter detectors is that the visual form doesn't appear to matter. That is, when text is presented in which every word is in aLtErNaTiNg CaSe LiKe ThIs, people can, with a little bit of practice, read almost as well as they normally do (Smith, Lott, and Cronnell 1969, Coltheart and Freeman 1974). Thus the word detectors cannot be tuned to specific visual forms of the word. Although it is conceivable that a "visual feature" version of such a model might be viable (see, for example, Smith 1971), it is hard to know exactly what these visual features of words would be that are impervious to case changes. Instead it appears that words are sequences of *abstract letters* (that is, case- and font-independent letters), and that the most likely model of word recognition is one in which abstract representations of letters are encoded in parallel and combined to form words. (We ignore special cases such as proper names, where the uppercase representation of the first letter is probably an important feature of identification.)

At this point you may justifiably be wondering whether this discussion is fair. We have pointed out the problems with models in which the recognition of words does not proceed through the recognition of letters without discussing potential problems with the third class of models, in which word detectors are activated by the parallel input from letter detectors. After all, doesn't the word-superiority effect rule out this class of models? How can it be that letters are activated first, but letters in words are recognized better than letters in isolation? There are two ways we could answer the question. The first is that there are two simulations of such a model (McClelland and Rumelhart 1981, Paap, Newsome, McDonald, and Schvaneveldt 1982) that can in fact predict both the word- and pseudoword-superiority effects. The second is to try to give you an intuitive feeling for how such models work.

Two Parallel Letter Models There are some details on which these two models differ, which we discuss in the following. Because Paap and colleagues' model is a bit simpler to explain than McClelland and Rumelhart's model (see also Rumelhart and McClelland 1982), we focus on it. In both models, letter detectors are conceived of as a stage prior to the word detectors. (Both models are fairly vague about stages before letter detection.) The way that the word- and pseudoword-superiority effects are handled in both models is by the redundancy of English; that is, only a restricted set of the combinations of letters can be words (or pseudowords) in any given language. However, neither model posits rules: rulelike behavior emerges from the contents of the lexicon. In addition, both models work on the principle that excitation at the letter level does not have to reach the threshold of identification in order to affect the word detectors. Let's return to our example to give a feeling for how this all works.

Because the stimulus *WORK* is exposed briefly and then masked, the visual information of the component letters is not fully registered. For the purpose of argument, assume that this degraded visual information causes each of the component letters to reach an excitation state that is 60 percent of maximum. Also assume that 80 percent of maximum is needed for letter identification to reach threshold. However, it is possible (because of redundancy in written English) that 60 percent excitation of each component letter is enough to cause the word detector for *WORK* to cross threshold. If the word detector reaches threshold, then the component letters (*K* in this example) can be identified. This kind of mechanism explains the word-superiority effect in both models.

What about the pseudoword-superiority effect? The models differ a bit in their explanation. The subject's task, identification of the target letter, can be accomplished in one of two ways in Paap and colleagues' model: either it can be "read off" the letter detectors or it can be read off the word detectors (for example, the stimulus was *work*, thus the fourth letter was *k*). Actually for pseudowords the read-off mechanism from the word detectors is a bit more complicated than that. For most words and pseudowords not only is one word detector excited, but a "neighborhood" of visually similar word detectors is excited. Thus if *MARD* is presented, detectors for *MARK*, *HARD*, *MAID*, *CARD*, and other words visually similar to *MARD* become activated, with the degree of activation dependent on the difference between the actual stimulus and the sequence of letters that the word detector is tuned for. The identification of any individual letter is then accomplished by polling the excited word detectors, letter by letter (the polling process, however, is in parallel). That is, if the subject is asked what the last letter was, most of the excited detectors would have a *D* in the last position, and so the subject would be likely to respond "d." (Letters in words are actually also read off by this mechanism because a neighborhood of detectors would be activated for them as well.)

We should point out that not only do each of these models predict both the word- and pseudoword-superiority effects, they also make good quantitative predictions of the data. Thus the two models appear to be sufficient in the sense that the mechanisms proposed appear not only to explain the word-superiority effect, but to model word and pseudoword perception in these circumstances. Because we have seen that the competing classes of models (the direct-word-recognition and serial-scanning models) appear to be flawed, the parallel-letter models appear to be by far the best explanation of word identification. Before going on, it might be of some value to compare the model by Paap and colleagues with McClelland and Rumelhart's model.

Although they differ on certain minor technical aspects, the major difference is that McClelland and Rumelhart's model is explicitly interactive, whereas Paap and colleagues' model is not. That is, in the former model the word detectors actually send excitation back to the letter detectors to enhance the excitation of letters in words (or pseudowords), whereas in the latter model they do not. Thus in McClelland and Rumelhart's model, the enhanced performance of identifying letters in words and pseudowords is explained directly by enhanced excitation of the letter detectors. In contrast Paap and colleagues posit that the enhanced performance in words and pseudowords results from an attentional mechanism being able to read out letter information from the word level by a polling process. (The feedback mechanism in McClelland and Rumelhart's model not surprisingly works fairly similarly to this polling process.)

Is this a fundamental difference between the models or just a difference in modeling style? We are not certain, but we think that the difference is largely one of style. Even though there is no explicit interaction between letter and word detectors in Paap and colleagues' model, the fact that letter information can be read off of the word detectors makes the end product, letter identification, at least in part a result of word detectors.

Which model is better? On the one hand McClelland and Rumelhart's model is more parsimonious because it predicts the probability of letter detection directly from the level of activation of letter detectors, whereas Paap and colleagues' model allows strategies to enter that determine whether the subject reads letter information off the letter detectors or off the word detectors. On the other hand we view the flexibility of the latter to be a positive factor because it appears to explain certain changes in performance as a function of expectation more naturally. For example, in an experiment by Carr, Davidson, and Hawkins (1978), it was found that biasing subjects to expect nothing but unpronounceable nonwords caused much of the pseudoword-superiority effect to go away, but left the word-superiority effect intact. Paap and colleagues' model explains this effect fairly naturally in terms of biasing subjects to attend to the letter level unless excitation at the word level exceeds some threshold (which would be reached when words were presented). In contrast McClelland and Rumelhart explain the phenomenon by positing that certain inhibitory weights between certain connections would be altered.

Paap and colleagues' explanation seems more satisfactory for two related reasons. First, the way in which the model changes from task to task seems more understandable and would make it easier to use the model as a heuristic device for prediction. Second, Paap and colleagues' model makes a clearer distinction between what in the system is "hard wired" and not easily changeable from what is changeable by instruction or "set."

The Relationship of Word Identification to Object Identification   A question that naturally arises is whether the identification of words is fundamentally different from the identification of other visual objects. Unfortunately there are little data on the issue, partly because most psychological studies on object recognition have used words.

Why have cognitive psychologists been so preoccupied with words? There are several related reasons for this. The first is practical. It is much easier to create word stimuli than pictorial stimuli. With words, stimuli can be created with a typewriter (and used in a tachistoscope) or with simple computer programs (and displayed on monitors or other display screens). Pictorial stimuli usually need the help of a trained artist or draftsman or much more sophisticated programming and display hardware. Moreover with words it is usually believed (justifiably) that if the letters are reasonably clear, other details of the stimulation, such as the color, luminance, and font style, are of minor importance psychologically and thus do not have to be tightly controlled.

A second reason is that it is far easier to separate systems of coding with words than with other visual stimuli. This allows the psychologist great freedom in independently manipulating variables. For most visual stimuli the form is closely related to the meaning, whereas in alphabetic or syllabic languages the visual form of a word is independent of its meaning. Even though the form of words in alphabetic languages is closely related to the sound of their names, languages like English that have irregularities allow the experimenter some freedom to vary the visual form independent of the sound and vice versa.

Moreover studying the recognition of words seems to be a more manageable problem than studying the recognition of objects because many of the levels of analysis are clear. First, it seems clear that the basic unit of interest is the word. In addition it is probably uncontroversial that an account of word identification prominently features the following subunits: letters, syllables, morphemes, phonemes, and letter clusters. Although all of these subunits may not be identified before the identification of a word, a reasonable model of word identification would be expected to explain just how the analysis of these entities is related to word identification. In contrast a major problem in studying the recognition of line drawings, photographs, or three-dimensional images is to discover the representations that are involved. For most objects it is not at all clear what the components or features are, and it is often unclear what one wants to take as the basic "object." Although there are interesting claims made for the necessity of certain systems of representation (for example, Marr's (1982) claims for the necessity of coding systems such as the "primal sketch" and "2 1/2-dimensional sketch"), there is generally little common ground in most pattern-recognition research on what the forms of representations are (see chapter 15).

In fact the work on visual word recognition finesses many of the problems that plague people studying the more general question of pattern recognition (see chapter 15). That is, much of the work on pattern recognition is concerned with how people can "parse" the visual field into separable surfaces and objects. In contrast the visual stimulus is already naturally "parsed" in reading because there are spaces between words and smaller spaces to demarcate letters. (Of course the visual information provides only some hints, such as commas and periods, about syntactic parsing.) Second, most of the work on visual word recognition is not concerned with the basic question of how a form can be recognized when it is seen in many different sizes, orientations, positions, and so on. As illustrated in the research discussed in this chapter, it is usually assumed that the pattern-recognition problem is somehow solved for some basic unit (usually the letter), and that the question one focuses on is how the system works from that point on (for example, how letters are combined to form words).

A priori it would thus appear that the word-identification literature has little applicability to pattern recognition in general because the patterns involved in reading are special in many ways. They are symbolic, two-dimensional, clearly demarcated from the background and each other, independent of important features of normal perception such as color, size, and texture, but closely related to the sounds of language. Certain recent theories of pattern recognition suggest, however, that word identification may not be that different from the identification of other patterns. An important thread that goes through a lot of the theorizing is that "parts" of objects may be subcomponents of objects the way that letters are components of words. One interesting direction has been procedures for identifying parts in natural objects; an interesting suggestion is that concavity is an indicator of a border between two parts (Hoffman and Richards 1985). A second direction is theories of what the "letters" of objects may be (Biederman 1987). Of course the relationship between parts of natural objects is far more complex than the linear ordering of letters, and theories of recognition by part have not adequately specified how the parts of natural objects would be related.

Visual Words and Sound

An issue that has been central to word recognition for over 100 years is the role of sound coding in the process of identifying visual words. Because a skilled reader can name a word aloud in under a half a second, it is clear that the sound of a visual word can be accessed rapidly. What is less clear is how much faster an internal representation of the sound is accessed, and whether this internal sound representation is accessed before identifying the word's meaning, the meaning is accessed first, or the two are accessed independently. In Paap and colleagues' and McClelland and Rumelhart's models, access to the lexicon (and presumably meaning) proceeds directly from the letters, and hence accessing sound is irrelevant to accessing meaning. The data that we discuss indicate that lexical access is more complex, and that sound codes are involved in the access of meaning. The role of internal sound representations in lexical access, however, is still a matter of controversy, and there are no data that convince everyone. We present some relevant data briefly and then sketch what the issues are.

Access of Sound Codes   Perhaps the issues can be approached best by asking a slightly different question: how is the sound of a pronounceable letter string accessed? Consider three cases. If the letter string is an *irregular word* such as *ONE* (that is, a word whose pronunciation cannot be derived by spelling-to-sound "rules" of the language), then it would appear that the sound could only be looked up from a *lexical entry*. That is, the letters *O, N,* and *E* would fire off a visual "word detector" or lexical entry, and then the lexical entry would in turn activate another entry, which would be the appropriate pronunciation /wun/. In contrast if the string of letters was a pseudoword such as *MARD*, there would be no lexical entry for it. Hence its pronunciation could not be looked up from a single lexical entry; it thus would have to be constructed in some way, either by using rules, by drawing analogies from the pronunciation of lexical entries, or some combination of the two processes. Finally, the sound of a regular word such as *WON* could in principle be produced by either a direct *lexical lookup route*, an indirect *constructive route*, or both. An important issue is how the sound of a regular word is in fact accessed when fluently pronounced in about half a second.

A line of evidence for the reality of these two routes to the pronunciation of a word comes from research on people with *acquired dyslexia*, who could once read normally, but can no longer do so due to a stroke or injury to part of the brain (Coltheart, Patterson, and Marshall 1980, Patterson, Marshall, and Coltheart 1985). The dramatic finding is that there are such patients who appear to have a selectively impaired direct lexical route (*surface dyslexics*) and others who have a selectively impaired indirect constructive route (*deep dyslexics* and *phonemic dyslexics*). Surface dyslexics can pronounce both real words and pseudowords and often "regularize" irregular words (for example, pronouncing *ISLAND* as /*iz-land*/). In contrast deep and phonemic dyslexics are usually unable to pronounce pseudowords, but pronounce words (both regular and irregular) correctly. Initially it was conjectured that surface dyslexics had a normal indirect route with a severed direct route, whereas deep and phonemic dyslexics had an intact direct route and a severed indirect route (Marshall and Newcombe 1966, 1973). Recent work has made clear, however, that the syndromes in both cases are more complex (Coltheart et al. 1980, Patterson et al. 1985). Some have used this complexity to argue against there being two separable routes (see, for example, Humphreys and Evett 1985), whereas others have argued that the most parsimonious explanation involves damage to one of two separable routes but with other malfunctioning aspects of the system as well (see, for example, Coltheart 1981). We find the dual-route explanation more convincing and assume it throughout the subsequent discussion.

The data suggest that both of these routes are used in parallel when naming a word. Many experiments (for example, Baron and Strawson 1976, Forster and Chambers 1973, Perfetti and Hogaboam 1975) indicate that regular words are named faster than irregular words. (In these experiments other variables such as the length of the words and their frequency in the language are carefully matched for the regular and irregular words.) If the sound of words is only accessed by the direct lookup route (or if the constructive route is used only when the direct route failed), the regularity of the word should make no difference. Another finding in these studies is that irregular words are named faster than pseudowords, indicating that the direct route is faster than the constructive route. A popular model to explain this pattern of data is a "horse-race" model (Coltheart 1978, Meyer and Gutschera 1975). In the standard version of the horse race model of dual access, the two access routes act in parallel, and the "horse" that accesses the name faster "wins" the race and selects the pronunciation. Because the correct pronunciation is almost always selected for irregular words, but with naming time being a bit slower than for regular words, the direct-route "horse" must always win the race, but the indirect constructive "horse" must come close enough to winning to slow down the response (perhaps by creating conflict between the two pronunciations).

The regularity effect (the difference between naming times for regular and irregular words) is smaller for high-frequency words (that is, words that are common in the language) than for low-frequency words (Seidenberg, Waters, Barnes, and Tannenhaus 1984). (In fact there is often no regularity effect observed for high-frequency words.) This finding is explained by the race model given some natural additional assumptions. First, the direct lookup route should be faster for high-frequency words than low-frequency words. In contrast the speed of the indirect constructive route should be relatively independent of the frequency of the word because it is dependent on some sort of constructive process that does not depend on accessing the lexical entry of the word presented. Thus the direct horse would easily beat the indirect horse for high-frequency words (and thus there would be no regularity effect), but would narrowly beat it for low-frequency words (and thus there would be a regularity effect).

Access of Word Meanings So far we have been talking about how words access their names. But the key question is how words access their meanings. Again we can think of two routes: one a direct route to the lexicon as in Paap and colleagues' or McClelland and Rumelhart's models, and the other an indirect route going through rules or analogies to a sound code, and then the sound code looking up the meaning (just as an auditory word would). Here again the data suggest a dual-route model. One paradigm that has been employed to investigate the issue is the *lexical decision task;* subjects view letter strings (usually words and pseudowords) and decide whether the string is a word or not as fast as they can. Here again the usual finding is a regularity effect (Bauer and Stanovich 1980, Parkin and Underwood 1983, but see Coltheart, Besner, Jonasson, and Davelaar 1979). Similar to our above reasoning, if lexical access merely proceeded through the component letters, one would expect no regularity effect (assuming that all other aspects of the component words were properly controlled).

The regularity effects observed in all these experiments are relatively small, suggesting that although sound coding is not irrelevant to either naming or lexical access of words, it may not be particularly important in most cases. However, some recent evidence from experiments involving the categorization of visual words (Van Orden 1987) suggests a more central place for sound coding. In the experiments, subjects judged whether words were members of a certain category or not. For example, subjects saw a category label such as *FOOD,* and then a word that was either a category member (*MEAT*) or a nonmember (*ROCK*). Of central interest in the experiments was how subjects would respond when a homophone of a member was presented (for example, *MEET*).

Van Orden found that subjects incorrectly classified "pseudomembers" such as *MEET* as category members 25 percent of the time. In contrast they incorrectly classified nonmembers that also differed from a category member by only one letter (for example, *MELT*) less than 10 percent of the time. Because the words were exposed for a half a second, and because the distribution of latencies for incorrectly classified pseudomembers was similar to that for legitimate category members, Van Orden argued that the sound-based processing involved in misclassifying pseudomembers was part of the normal process of accessing the meaning of printed words.

Van Orden's finding is strong evidence that sound coding is involved in accessing the meaning of printed words. There are two issues, however, that are still shrouded in controversy. The first is the level at which sound coding is involved. One reaction to Van Orden's data (and others that show sound coding to be involved in the reading of prose) is to argue that sound coding is involved, but only after lexical access. That is, it would be argued that *MEET* accesses the appropriate "meet" detector in the lexicon by direct access, and only then is the sound /meet/ activated, which excites the meaning "meat." A piece of data against this argument is that similar effects have been obtained by Van Orden, Johnston, and Hale (1988) even when pseudowords were used (for example, *SUTE* was a pseudomember of the category *clothing*).

The second controversy (which spills over into the first) is how the indirect sound route works. The early work (for instance, Gibson 1971) assumed that the ability to exhibit rulelike behavior in pronouncing nonwords was in fact due to the application of rules. Recently the hypothesis that application of rules accounts for the fluent access of sound codes from words or pseudowords has come under attack from several directions. One is the argument that the pronunciation of English is too variable to sensibly be explained by rules, with estimates ranging from about 25 percent to 75 percent of the pronunciation of words being accounted for by rules. (The percentage varies of course with the complexity and number of rules hypothesized.) A second is that it is not clear how such a rule-application process would work in real time. Moreover if it was serial and was part of the process of lexical access, it would contradict much of the work discussed previously; suggesting that lexical access operated in parallel across the component letters.

As a result an alternative parallel mechanism called "analogical" has been proposed (see, for example, Brooks 1977, Glushko 1979, Marcel 1980). This mechanism actually works quite similarly to Paap and colleagues' model, except that component sounds (rather than letters) are read from a neighborhood of lexical entries. That is, if *BAVE* is seen, the lexical entries in the neighborhood (for example, *HAVE, WAVE, BANE*) excite their constituent phonemes (for example, /b/, /a/, /ay/, /v/, /h/), and the most "popular" phoneme in each position is selected. Such a model predicts the finding that a nonword with an "inconsistent" pronunciation, such as the *A* in this example, is harder to pronounce than one in which there is not an inconsistent pronunciation, because there would be conflict among candidate phonemes in the former case.

Such a model is an attractive theory about how rulelike behavior can be produced rapidly and without conscious knowledge of the "rules." However, there are two problems with the model as sketched. The first is that there are many nonwords that are easily pronounceable (for example, *JOOV*) that have virtually no near neighbors (for example, there are no words that end in *OOV*). The response to this problem (pointed out by Coltheart 1981) has been to posit items in the "lexicon" that are not words but represent letters and clusters of letters that commonly appear (for example, one for *OO* and one for *V*). Such an extension of the analogy model (see, for example, Glushko 1979) pushes it close to having components that are rules (for example, *OO* activates the sound /u/ and *V* activates the sound /v/). Another problem for the analogy model is that it is not clear how the component sounds are supposed to "line up." That is, if one pronounces *VELOP* by analogy to *DEVELOP* or *ENVELOP*, one needs guidelines that establish that the first two letters are a syllable, and thus the rest can be pronounced as if the syllable weren't there.

Let us briefly summarize what we know and do not know about word identification. First, it appears that letters in words are processed in parallel. We have to add the cautionary note, however, that the research that this is based on has employed short words (for the most part four-letter words). It is possible that a different answer might be obtained with longer words because the identification of longer words is still largely unexplored (however, see Taft 1985). Second, it appears that sound codes are involved in some way in the identification of visual words. The fact that irregular words are correctly identified indicates that irregular words such as *ONE* cannot be identified *only* by going through rules or analogies to access sound and then the sound to access meaning. On the other hand sound codes do appear to be involved in the access of meaning of a word because the regularity of the spelling of a word affects lexical decision time, and homophones are confused in a categorization task. What is significantly less clear is the process by which sound is accessed other than a direct lookup process in the lexicon. Current "analogical" models are a promising attempt to model the access of sound, but unlike the models of the "word-superiority effect" we discussed, they are currently largely "hand waving": few of the details have been spelled out.

A final issue worth discussing briefly is whether the "horse-race" metaphor is the best way to describe dual access. If each route simply produced a single "horse," then the system would not make much functional sense: because the indirect "horse" is often the wrong sound representation and never faster than the direct "horse," it would appear to interfere with lexical access without producing compensatory bene-fits. We believe that a better alternative metaphor (Carr and Pollatsek 1985) is one more closely related to that of Paap and colleagues' and McClelland and Rumelhart's models. In it each route is seen as activat-ing a "neighborhood" of lexical entries, with the combined activation from the two routes determining the lexical entry selected. Thus even though the indirect route may be "wrong," it is not wrong by much and thus should help to activate the appropriate lexical entry. As with much of the theorizing on this issue, however, it remains to be seen whether such a model would in fact produce the desired behavior if actually simulated.

10.2 Visual Processing in Reading Text

So far we have discussed experiments in which words are processed in isolation. We move now to experiments that investigate visual process-ing of words in meaningful text. Much of the research that we review involves techniques that use eye movements to monitor and control cognitive processing. As mentioned previously, a major reason for monitoring eye movements is to obtain an on-line measure of the cognitive processes in reading. Accordingly we need to review some basic facts about eye movements.

Some Basic Facts about Eye Movements

When people read text, their introspection is that their eyes are moving continuously across the line of text. However, this is an illusion. During reading (or viewing any static visual display), the eyes move in a series of "jumps," rapid eye movements known as *saccades*. Between these saccades the eyes stay more-or-less fixed on a point for relatively long periods of time, known as *fixations*. Functionally no useful information comes in during the saccades, so that the reader's visual information when reading text consists of a discrete series of "snapshots" from the fixations (Rayner 1978a, Rayner and Pollatsek 1987). The fixations last for about 200 to 250 ms, although there is considerable variability in the duration of a fixation. Similarly there is considerable variation in the length of the saccades, with the average saccade length being about 7 to 9 character spaces. (The duration of the saccade depends on its length, with a typical saccade taking about 25 to 50 ms.)

The Perceptual Span in Reading

A central question about reading that has been of interest for at least 100 years is how much information is actually extracted from a printed page during a single fixation. The fact that the eye is moving to new locations every quarter of a second or so suggests that the visual information available on a fixation is quite limited. There are also psychophysical data indicating that visual acuity rapidly decreases as one goes away from the point at which the eyes are directed (the *fixation point*). These data suggest that the area from which useful information is being extracted during reading is limited.

This conclusion appears to contradict the phenomenological impression that one can continually see the entire page during reading. The feeling that the entire page is continuously visible has led to many schemes for "speedreading" that claim that proper training allows the reader to extract useful information from a large region of the page on a single fixation. According to these claims, the typical pattern of eye movements is largely a bad habit and is not necessary to extract all the visual information needed during reading. The data we present clearly indicate, however, that the area from which useful information is extracted during reading is in fact quite limited, and that the claims for "speedreading" based on extraction of visual information from a broad region of text are unfounded.

The principal technique that has been used to uncover *the perceptual span* (the area of text around the fixation point that is of functional importance in reading) is known as the *moving-window technique* (Mc-Conkie and Rayner 1975, Rayner and Bertera 1979, Underwood and

McConkie 1985). In this technique the subject's eyes are monitored, and the eye position is being continuously sent to a computer. The computer also displays the text that the subject is reading and changes the text contingent on where the reader is looking. The basic idea of the moving window technique is to present a "window" of normal text around the fixation point, but to present mutilated versions of the text outside this window (for example, random letters). The logic is the following: if readers can read normally with a window of a given size, then they cannot be extracting useful information outside this window region on any fixation.

Figure 10.2 presents an example. A reader is presented with a window that extends from 4 characters to the left of fixation to 14 characters to the right of fixation. The succession of "snapshots" a reader might see is illustrated in figure 10.2 (lines 2 through 4) with the sequence of fixation points indicated by the series of asterisks over the letters. We must emphasize that the sequence of windows is "tailored" to the reader. If the reader makes a different sequence of fixations, the windows presented would be different. Moreover if the reader makes a backward saccade (a *regression*) the position of the window would move backward to follow the eyes. It's also important to realize that the display changes are made very quickly; within 5 ms after the eye movement ends, the new window is in place.

```
By far the single most abundant substance in the biosphere   (1)



            *
XXXXXXXXXe single most abundXXXXXXXXXXXXXXXXXXXXXXXXXXXXXXXXX   (2)

                 *
XXXXXXXXXXXXXXXle most abundant suXXXXXXXXXXXXXXXXXXXXXXXXXXX   (3)

                      *
XXXXXXXXXXXXXXXXXXXXXX abundant substance XXXXXXXXXXXXXXX   (4)



            *
XX XXX XXe single most abundXXX XXXXXXXXX XX XXX XXXXXXXXX   (5)

            *
Nw oqm kxe single most abundzif ewjpsldyf vr upq copzmwlhg   (6)
```

Figure 10.2 Examples of the moving window technique. Line 1 represents a normal line of text. Lines 2 through 4 represent three windows that a reader might see on three consecutive fixations in reading the line of text. In this case the window area extends from 4 letter spaces to the left of fixation (indicated by the *) to 14 letter spaces to the right of fixation. Lines 5 and 6 represent alternative types of windows that have been used. In both cases the fixation point is as in line 2 and the extent of the window region is the same. In both lines 5 and 6, however, space information is preserved even outside the window, and in line 6 the letters are replaced by random letters rather than Xs.

The major finding is that reading is perfectly normal under these conditions. That is, both comprehension and reading speed are unaffected by the window. If the window is made any smaller than this, however, reading speed is diminished, though reading comprehension usually is undiminished. Thus useful information only appears to be extracted from a region extending from 4 characters to the left of fixation (McConkie and Rayner 1976, Rayner, Well, and Pollatsek 1980) to 14 to 15 characters to the right of fixation (McConkie and Rayner 1975, Rayner and Bertera 1979).

Although the perceptual span of readers is limited, it extends beyond the word that is fixated on. For example, Rayner, Well, Pollatsek, and Bertera (1982) presented subjects with either a one-word window (that encompassed only the fixated word), a two-word window (that encompassed the fixated word and the next word), and a three-word window (that encompassed the fixated word and the next two words). In this experiment subjects' average reading rate was about 330 words per minute (wpm) with normal text, but was reduced to about 200 wpm with a one-word window and about 300 wpm with a two-word window. With a three-word window the reading rate was about 330 wpm. That is, if skilled readers are only allowed to see the fixated word, they read reasonably fluently but at only two-thirds of normal speed. Hence the reader is reading more than one word per fixation (but not much more).

Before we explore the details of what is going on here, a few key points about the technique must be made clear. One standard reaction to a casual description of the technique is: "Of course the reader is slowed down when the window is made smaller; that's because the reader is seeing all these changes in the display and gets distracted and confused." The actual situation, however, is quite different. When the material outside the window is all Xs (as in lines 1 through 5 of figure 10.2), the reader is aware of where the normal text is and where the Xs are. In contrast if the "text" outside the window is random letters (and the spaces between the words are preserved), readers are almost always unaware of any display changes (as in line 6 of figure 10.2). For example, in a one-word window condition your introspection is that you can't see anything peculiar about the display, but you may become aware that you are reading more slowly than usual and have the feeling that something is holding you back. This comment even applies to the authors who know exactly what the computer program is doing and yet are unable to "see" the funny text extending beyond the fixated word on most fixations. (Occasionally one will see that the first letter of the next word is wrong, especially if it is a short-word such as "a" or a two-letter preposition.) Thus the perceptual span (the area of useful information extraction) extends beyond the area from which one can consciously perceive details of stimulation. Moreover one's conscious awareness of change does not relate to reading speed: subjects read faster in the condition where Xs are outside the window than where random letters are outside the window (presumably because the random letters lead to misidentification of letters or words whereas the Xs don't). Thus the technique is getting at the information that is extracted rather than an epiphenomenal awareness of change.

We now return to the details of how a reader extracts information on a fixation. Sometimes a reader appears to process not only the fixated word (word n) but the next word (word n + 1) as well. This conclusion is supported by the finding that readers frequently skip words, especially words that are either frequent in the language, highly predictable by the prior text, or both (O'Regan 1979, Ehrlich and Rayner 1981). However, skipping word n + 1 is not necessarily an indicator that the reader visually processed it; perhaps the reader merely guessed it on the basis of context. Although guessing may account for some skipping behavior, it does not account for all of it because the probability of skipping word n + 1 depends on whether the correct visual form was presented while word n was fixated (Balota, Pollatsek, and Rayner 1985, Ehrlich and Rayner 1981).

The fact that words are more likely to be skipped if they are predictable suggests that the perceptual span may be variable. Perhaps on some fixations one word is processed, on others two are processed, and on a few fixations three are processed. In fact data (to be discussed) indicate that context may affect the size of the perceptual span. In addition the situation seems even more complex as many words appear to be partially processed in parafoveal vision on one fixation with processing completed when they are subsequently fixated.

The evidence for partial processing of words in the parafovea (that is, those near fixation but not directly fixated) comes from several sources. Perhaps the clearest evidence comes from an experiment by Rayner, Well, Pollatsek, and Bertera (1982) in which word n + 1 was never fully exposed, only its first three letters were (and fewer than three letters if the entire word was three letters or less), with the other letters replaced by visually similar letters. In these conditions subjects read significantly faster than in conditions in which only the fixated word was exposed (a one-word window), and at about the same rate as when the entire word n + 1 was exposed. This indicates that partial information about a word can be used to speed reading. (Remember that in most conditions the subjects were unaware of the visual aspects of these window conditions.) Moreover it has been shown that a parafoveal preview of a word decreases the time spent fixating the word (for example, Blanchard, Pollatsek, and Rayner 1989).

Integration of Information across Fixations

Many experiments have been conducted to diagnose the levels of coding that are involved that allow information from word n + 1 to be extracted on one fixation and then integrated with the information extracted when it is fixated. A variation of the moving window technique called the *boundary technique* (Rayner 1975) has been used to investigate this issue. Within a passage a critical word location is identified, but the word that should normally be in that location is generally replaced by a word (or nonword). For example, in figure 10.3 the word *bomb* is initially in the passage, but when the reader's eye crosses an invisible boundary location, *bomb* is replaced by the target word (in this case *cake*). Because the change occurs during the saccade when vision is suppressed, the subject does not perceive and is not aware of the change. By examining how long the reader looks at the target word as a function of the relationship between the initially displayed stimulus and the target word, inferences can be made about what kind of information is integrated across eye movements.

Although the boundary technique has been influential in determining what kind of information is integrated, much of the diagnostic work has been done with a simpler naming paradigm intended to simulate the visual aspects of reading text (Balota and Rayner 1983, McClelland and O'Regan 1981, Rayner 1978b, Rayner, McConkie, and Ehrlich 1978, Rayner, McConkie, and Zola 1980). In this paradigm the subject sees a single word in the parafovea, moves his or her eyes to fixate that spatial location, and then names the fixated word. What is of interest is how naming times are affected when the string of letters exposed in the parafovea is not identical to the word that is fixated. (Again we point out that subjects are virtually never aware of a display change nor what the parafoveal letter string was in either the boundary technique or in the naming paradigm.)

A major finding is that significant facilitation accrues when the first two or three letters of the word are the same, even if all the other letters are changed (Rayner, McConkie, and Zola 1980). This finding reinforces our conclusion that subjects can extract partial information on one fixation to use in identification of a word on a subsequent fixation. This contrasts with the finding that there is virtually no facilitation when the first letter of the parafoveal string is different from that of the fixated word, even though all the other letters are the same. Perhaps the most surprising finding (Rayner, McConkie, and Zola 1980) is that the facilitation obtained from a parafoveal preview is undiminished when the case of all the letters changes (for example, *chest* changes to *CHEST*).

```
                                          *   |
Fixation n          the baker rushed the wedding bomb to the reception.


                                              |   *
Fixation n + 1      the baker rushed the wedding cake to the reception.
```

Figure 10.3 Example of the boundary technique. On fixation n the reader is fixated on the letter *e* in wedding. However, as soon as the eye movement crosses over the boundary location (in this case the letter *n* in *wedding*), the computer replaces *bomb* with the target word *cake*. The asterisks mark the location of the fixations, and the bar marks the location of the boundary. (The boundary location is invisible to the subject.)

This finding indicates that the integration of information from one fixation to the next is not at the level of visual features but at a more abstract letter level. A similar finding of case irrelevance was obtained in a reading experiment (McConkie and Zola 1979) in which the text was presented in aLtErNaTiNg CaSe LiKe ThIs. In one condition the text was changed on each fixation so that the case of each letter was reversed (for example, aLtErNaTiNg was changed to AlTeRnAtInG and then back to the first form), whereas in a control condition alternating text was presented, but the case of each letter remained the same. As with the naming study, changing the case of the letters had no effect.

These studies indicate that subjects sometimes extract abstract (that is, case-independent) letter information from the parafovea and sometimes identify the entire word. Subsequent experiments have investigated whether other subword units are activated in the parafovea and aid subsequent word identification. So far the results are negative.

An experiment by Rayner, McConkie, and Zola (1980) indicated that preserving the first phoneme of the parafoveal word was irrelevant, suggesting that sound coding was not involved. (Merely preserving the first letter, however, also produced no facilitation; thus this was not a powerful test of sound coding.) In addition boundary-technique experiments designed to show that *morphemes* are involved also came up with negative findings. Lima (1987) found that a preview of a prefix (for example, *misxxxxx* for *mistrust*) produced no greater benefit than preview of a meaningless unit of equal length (for example, *misxxxxx* for *mistress*). Similarly Inhoff (1989) found that preview of a meaningful subcomponent (for example, *cowxxx* as a preview for *cowboy*) had no greater benefit than a meaningful unit that was not a subcomponent (for example, *carxxx* as a preview for *carpet*) or a nonmeaningful unit (for example, *shaxxx* as preview for *shadow*). Moreover at present there is no evidence that seeing a related word in the parafovea facilitates subsequent identification of the word. For example, in a boundary experiment a preview of *tune* caused *song* to be fixated as long as if the preview was *door* (Rayner, Balota, and Pollatsek 1986). Thus at present there is no indication that any level of representation other than abstract letters (when word n + 1 is not identified) or words (when word n + 1 is identified) is of any functional significance in encoding parafoveal information. It is possible, however, that more sensitive tests will cause a change in this conclusion.

Summary
The region of text that is actually being used by a reader on a given fixation is limited. That region encompasses more than the word being fixated, however, including the next word or two to the right. We should note that the asymmetry of the perceptual span depends on the language being read. In Hebrew, which is written from right to left, the perceptual span is asymmetric to the left of fixation (Pollatsek, Bolozky,

Well, and Rayner 1981). Moreover the asymmetry is flexible: these readers, when reading English, showed the same right asymmetry as native English speakers.

The details of the extraction of information are complex, however, because some words are processed even though they are not fixated, and other words are processed on more than one fixation. The experiments on levels of coding indicate that the physical reality of the parafoveal word is not preserved from one fixation to the next, only the letter information (in an abstract code) is preserved, and possibly lexical information as well. In fact one way to view the facilitating effect of seeing the first three letters in the parafovea is in terms of a model similar to Paap and colleagues' model. That is, the first three letters excite a neighborhood of lexical entries (including the correct one), but not up to the threshold of identification. When the eye then fixates the word, this partial excitation of the lexical entries allows the word to be identified faster than if no preview had been present.

We return to some of these issues in the next section, where we consider how context affects the identification of words. Let us close this section with a brief comment on speedreading. The data we have presented so far indicate that the perceptual span is small for normal readers. Perhaps it is larger for people who have been trained in speedreading. To test this hypothesis, Just and Carpenter (1987) studied a group of graduates of a speedreading course. Instead of using contingent display changes, they measured the perceptual span with comprehension questions. Subjects read passages of text (during which eye movements were recorded) and were then asked to answer comprehension questions. A variety of questions were asked, but some required a certain word in the text (for example, a person's name) to be processed for the question to be answered correctly. In fact the speedreaders were no better than chance at answering these questions unless the key word had actually been fixated. Thus there is no evidence that speedreaders can extract lexical information from a wider region than can other readers.

10.3 Word Identification in Context

In this section we discuss whether sentential context affects the speed of identifying a word. We have already touched on it in the prior section by indicating that a parafoveal word is more likely to be skipped if it is predictable from the prior sentence context. In addition it has been shown that a word that is more predictable is also fixated for a shorter time when it is fixated (Ehrlich and Rayner 1981, Schustack, Ehrlich, and Rayner 1987, Zola 1984). Thus it appears that less time is needed to process a word if it is predictable. It is less clear, however, what aspect of processing is affected by the prior context: is it the access of the word in the lexicon that is facilitated, or is it a later stage such as fitting the word into the context of the sentence?

The research on this topic bears on the general issue of "modularity" (Fodor 1983), which has received a great deal of attention in the past few years. Fodor's claim is that different "modules" (for example, those that handle lexical access, syntactic processing, thematic processing) do not communicate directly with each other. (There are in fact interesting results (Ferreira and Clifton 1986, Rayner, Carlson, and Frazier 1983) that suggest that initial syntactic parsing is somewhat independent of other modules.) In particular Fodor and others have claimed that lexical access is a "module," in the sense that lexical access could not be affected by "postlexical" processes. Thus if lexical access were affected by the predictability of the word in sentence context, it might be evidence against modularity, because the predictability of a word is presumably computed by a higher-order mechanism that is constructing the overall meaning of the text.

Before plunging ahead, we need to say a few words about "predictability." In the studies discussed in this section, predictability is usually assessed by giving a group of people a sentence up to but not including the target word of interest and asking them to guess what the next word is. In these experiments a word is termed "predictable" if a substantial majority of these subjects (usually greater than 70 percent) guesses the target word based on the prior context. In contrast, "unpredictable" words are usually guessed less than 5% of the time (although they are not anomalous).

Although "predictability" is operationally defined by a procedure involving conscious guessing, it should not be presupposed that the effects observed when people are actually reading the passages are due to such a guessing process. An important consideration is that when subjects guess to produce the predictability norms, their guesses take several seconds. In contrast, words are fixated for about a quarter of a second. Thus on the face of it a much different process is likely to go on when subjects are reading text. Furthermore most people's introspection is that they are not usually consciously guessing words when they read. For ease of discussion we call the manipulation "predictability" but without presupposing that the facilitation mechanism is either a conscious or unconscious prediction. We return to the issue of what is causing the facilitation after examining what processes are facilitated.

What Processes are Facilitated by Context?
As mentioned previously, a major tool for studying reading of text has been the measurement of eye movements. We have so far primarily focused on their use to manipulate text. We now turn to the use of eye movements in monitoring cognitive processes, and more specifically, lexical access. The most obvious candidate from the eye-movement record to measure the speed of lexical access is the fixation time on a

word. Unfortunately there are several problems with assuming that the fixation time on a word is a valid index of the time to access the word. The first is that there is not one measure of fixation time because words are sometimes fixated once, sometimes more than once, and sometimes not at all. The two measures most commonly used are the average first fixation duration on a word and average *gaze duration* (Just and Carpenter 1980). The gaze duration is the total time spent fixating on a word before the eye moves on to the next word. Both averages usually only include instances when a word is fixated (that is, a skip is not counted as a 0-ms fixation).

Our discussion of preview effects in the previous section indicates that either of the above fixation time measures is bound to be a flawed estimate of lexical access time because the reader processes more than the fixated word on many fixations. Moreover processing the next word has been shown to affect fixation time. For example, people fixate longer on a word if the next word is skipped than if it is not (Hogaboam 1983, Pollatsek, Rayner, and Balota 1986). In addition there is no guarantee that the time to fixate on a word is merely indexing the time it takes to access its lexical entry. Reading involves more than the identification of words: the sentence structure must be constructed, and an overall meaning to the sentence arrived at (see chapters 11 and 12). Nonetheless there is reason to believe that fixation times are indeed sensitive indices of lexical access. For example, Inhoff and Rayner (1986) and Rayner and Duffy (1986) showed that first fixation duration and gaze duration on a word were both affected by the frequency of the word in the language in normal reading conditions, even when word length was controlled.

We have already established that predictive context decreases fixation times on words and increases the probability that they are skipped. The question is whether this decrease in fixation time can plausibly be due to lexical access. As we just indicated, fixation time on a word is strongly influenced by a variable (word frequency) widely assumed to influence lexical access. It therefore is plausible that context effects on fixation times are also due to variations in the time to access words. The problem is that there is also evidence that fixation time on a word is influenced by text integration processes (Schustack et al. 1987, Duffy, Morris, and Rayner 1988). Thus it is difficult to determine just by examining the fixation time on a word whether context affects lexical access or text-integration processes.

Given the difficulty of coming up with an unambiguous measure of the speed of lexical access, Balota and colleagues (1985) asked a slightly different question: does the predictability of the word interact with the visual aspects of the stimulation? If so, then it would appear that context is modulating the extraction of visual information (Sternberg 1969), and hence influencing a relatively early stage of processing that would be part of lexical access. The experiment involved the use of the boundary technique and was quite complex. However, the basic idea is that there was a key target location in which there could be either a highly predictable word or an unpredictable word. For example, there was a sentence about weddings in which either the predictable word *cake* or the nonpredictable word *pies* could appear. In addition the visual similarity of the preview of the word was varied, so that the preview was either the identical word, a visually similar nonword (for example, *cahc* or *picz*), or a visually dissimilar word or nonword.

There were two key findings. First, a visually similar preview reduced fixation times for the predictable word more than for the unpredictable word. Thus readers benefitted from the parafoveal information more when it was identical to or visually similar to a predictable word. Second, there was a difference between the benefit for *cake* and *cahc*, whereas there was no difference between the benefit for *pies* and *picz*. That is, the letters at the end of the "word" in the parafovea made a difference when it was predictable, but not when it was unpredictable. Thus in some sense readers were extracting visual information from a wider region when the word was predictable than when it was not. Both results thus indicate that context is affecting the flow of visual information extraction and therefore is affecting lexical access. In addition the latter finding indicates that the size of the perceptual span may not be constant. In this case it is affected by the predictability of the word in the parafovea. Other experiments indicate that the size of the perceptual span is also affected by the difficulty of the text (Rayner 1986), the legibility of the foveal stimulus (Inhoff, Pollatsek, Posner, and Rayner 1989), and the frequency or syntactic complexity of the foveal word (Henderson and Ferreira 1987).

Is Modularity Disconfirmed?
Balota and colleagues' (1985) experiment thus appears to be evidence against the hypothesis that lexical access is a module, because the speed of lexical access appears to be modulated by "predictability," an index of higher-level discourse processes. As indicated earlier, however, the manipulation of "predictability" may be varying factors other than predictability. In particular, people who have presented evidence for modularity of lexical access in other circumstances (Seidenberg et al. 1984, Stanovich and West 1983) have argued that context effects, when observed, may be due to "lexical priming," which they argue is a mechanism working within the lexical module rather than being imposed from without.

Let us clarify the point by using our cake-pies example. One of the prior words in the sentence was *wedding*. An advocate of modularity would argue that the speeded processing of *cake* observed in Balota and colleagues' experiment is due not to its predictability but to automatic "spreading activation" from one lexical node or word detector (for example, "wedding") to all related lexical nodes (for example, "cake"). In fact this argument could plausibly explain the predictability effect in

Balota and colleagues' experiment, because it is hard to create a highly predictable context for a target word without using highly associated prior words.

Although more carefully controlled experiments are needed for a full resolution of the modularity issue, a result that makes it somewhat implausible that all predictability effects are due to lexical priming is that predictable function words (such as articles and prepositions) are often skipped over (O'Regan 1979). It would be stretching the meaning of "priming" to argue that *the* is primed by a standard noun or verb. This finding is also not unambiguous, however, because these words may be skipped not because they are predictable but because they are very common in the language. Perhaps the clearest test of the priming hypothesis would be a study in which the predictability of function words was varied. If predictability has a clear effect on the visual processing of these words, a strong version of modularity could be rejected.

10.4 Simulations of the Reading Process

Cognitive science relies on both experimental data and on simulations of the phenomena of interest. Although we have drawn our conclusions about how the reading process works chiefly from experimental evidence, we have discussed some impressive simulations of the word-superiority effect. We think that the extent to which we relied on experimental evidence reflects the current state of the field of reading. At this point, however, it might be of value to examine the extent to which various types of simulations have influenced the way researchers think about the reading process.

As indicated previously, the simulation work by McClelland and Rumelhart (1981; Rumelhart and McClelland 1982) and by Paap and colleagues (1982) nicely captured the basic findings of ten years of research on the word-superiority effect. There were a great many experiments that followed up the original findings reported by Reicher (1969). However, the flurry of experimental work declined with the appearance of these simulations. We think that the reason for the decline is that the simulations accounted for virtually all of the relevant findings, so that new experiments would just be "filling in details" as opposed to finding out something new and interesting.

In addition, simulation work is also able to account for the parafoveal preview effect results. Brady (1981) and McClelland (1986) have reported simulations of an experiment by Rayner (1975) dealing with parafoveal preview effects, and it is clear that these simulations could be extended to account for the fact that much of the preview effect comes from the first few letters of a parafoveal word. Seidenberg and McClelland (1988) have also recently reported simulation work modeling the relationship between word frequency and regularity in word perception.

In each of these limited domains that we have discussed, simulations have proved to be effective in accounting for existing data. In principle (and sometimes in practice) these simulations are constrained enough to make unique and interesting predictions of outcomes in experimental situations. In our view, however, these simulations have been so successful because there has been clear experimental evidence to draw on. Effective simulations cannot be done in a vacuum; experimental data are needed to constrain the simulations so that they are manageably precise. Otherwise the strength of computer simulations—that formalisms can be completely spelled out—is wasted.

When we move to the more comprehensive and complex skill of reading, the simulations are not so impressive. Current simulations of the reading process via production systems (Thibadeau, Just, and Carpenter 1982) or connectionist systems (McClelland 1986) seem far less attractive. We do not wish to demean these efforts to simulate a complex process; they are interesting first attempts. Our sense, however, is that there is a fundamental limitation imposed on these attempts. Although we understand certain components of the reading process fairly well (for example, lexical access), we do not understand others very well at all (for example, discourse processes), nor do we understand in any detail how the various subcomponents are orchestrated to yield the skill of fluent reading. It will be interesting to see in the coming years how well cognitive scientists are able to grapple with the complex skill of reading. Will breakthroughs in understanding this complex process come from large-scale simulations of the entire reading process or from continued investigation into various aspects of the subcomponent processes? It is difficult to answer this question, but if the example of the word-superiority effect is representative, then we suspect that considerably more experimental evidence will need to accumulate before there are impressive simulations of the entire reading process.

10.5 Summary

We have covered just a small part of the process called "reading," namely the visual processes that lead to word identification both in isolation and in context. Although there are still many unresolved issues, the experimental data that have accumulated in the last twenty years have resolved many issues that have been speculated on for at least a hundred years. Moreover precise computer-simulation models exist that plausibly can explain many of the phenomena and can also explain the data from selected experiments precisely.

In particular the data are quite clear that words are accessed through a level best termed "abstract letter identities" (Coltheart 1981, Rayner, McConkie, and Zola 1980), and that the letters (for short words at least) are processed in parallel. Moreover computer simulations exist that predict the results of certain word-perception experiments in great detail. We should add, however, that these simulations are quite incomplete in the sense that they do not explain how abstract letters are perceived in the first place. We should also point out that the experimental work has exclusively dealt with printed words. It is possible that the process by which handwriting is perceived could be quite different.

It is also quite clear that sound coding is involved in the process of getting to the meaning of a word. The details of this involvement are far less clear. It seems likely that some sort of parallel dual-route mechanism is involved, however, in which one route is something like Paap and colleagues', or Rumelhart and McClelland's "direct" letter to lexical lookup, and the other is mediated by some sort of constructive mechanism that is "rulelike" in some sense. Currently the consensus seems to be that this rulelike behavior is likely to be due to a parallel mechanism that activates words and word parts, automatically generates the sound codes of the entries in this expanded "lexicon," and then somehow computes a sound from this pattern of activation. Many of the details of such a process are far from clear.

We have also discussed data that imply that the region of text that is analyzed on any fixation is small, but encompasses more than one word. Moreover the process of information extraction during a fixation in reading is complex, in the sense that not only can more than one word be extracted on a given fixation, but many words are processed on more than one fixation. The integration of information across fixations appears to be relatively abstract, involving abstract letters rather than visual features.

It is interesting that the answers to the questions "What codes are used in the access of words on a single fixation?" and "What codes are used in the integration of information across fixations?" are quite similar. In principle a variety of codes could be used to access words in the lexicon, but only a small set of these codes might survive the movement of the eye. The models of lexical access based on the tachistoscopic presentation data concluded, however, that lexical access proceeded chiefly using input from abstract letter detectors with a modicum of help from sound-based codes, whereas the work on integration of information across fixations concluded that only abstract letter detectors were involved in the integration process (although the negative evidence against sound coding is weak).

The effect of predictive context on the speed of word identification in reading argues that the visual information from predictable words is extracted more efficiently than from unpredictable words, and thus that context can affect lexical access. However, it is not clear at present whether the effect of predictability is because of a (likely unconscious) prediction being made on the basis of prior context or a "lexical priming" mechanism. We should note that these context effects are relatively small, even in the case when a word is almost completely predictable (a relatively rare instance for nouns, verbs, and adjectives in text (Gough, Alford, and Holley-Wilcox 1981)). Most of the work on word perception in and out of context suggests that the visual information in text can be processed rapidly even without context, and that predictability (and other context effects) play a minor role in word identification. Balota and colleagues' data in fact indicate that most of the effects of context are on the extraction of parafoveal information. This is consistent with the notion that context plays a larger role when the visual information is poorest.

A cautionary note is in order, however. The bulk of the work on word identification has been done on simple short words. There are data that suggest that access to more complex polymorphemic words such as *UNDELIVERABLE* may not be explained by a direct visual access model, but instead proceed through stages (Taft 1985). In fact many words whose meanings are clear may not have ever been seen by the reader in the current form (for example, a verb may not have been seen in the past tense). If so, then unless lexical entries exist for words not actually seen, the meanings of these words must be constructed rather than accessed using rules of formation (Selkirk 1982) or analogies. At present the work on this question is still in its infancy.

Notes

Preparation for this chapter was partially supported by Grant BNS86-09336 to the authors from the National Science Foundation. This chapter was written while Keith Rayner was a Fellow at The Netherlands Institute for Advanced Study. We thank Michael Posner and two anonymous reviewers for their comments on the chapter.

References

Adams, M. J. 1979. Models of word recognition. *Cognitive Psychology* 11:133–176.

Balota, D. A., Pollatsek, A., and Rayner, K. 1985. The interaction of contextual constraints and parafoveal visual information in reading. *Cognitive Psychology* 17:364–390.

Balota, D. A., and Rayner, K. 1983. Parafoveal visual information and semantic contextual constraints. *Journal of Experimental Psychology: Human Perception and Performance* 5:726–738.

Baron, J., and Strawson, C. 1976. Use of orthographic and word-specific knowledge in reading words aloud. *Journal of Experimental Psychology: Human Perception and Performance* 2:386–393.

Baron, J., and Thurston, I. 1973. An analysis of the word superiority effect. *Cognitive Psychology* 4:207–228.

Bauer, D. W., and Stanovich, K. E. 1980. Lexical access and the spelling-to-sound regularity effect. *Memory and Cognition* 8:424–432.

Biederman, I. 1987. Recognition by components: A theory of human image understanding. *Psychological Review* 94:115–147.

Blanchard, H. E., Pollatsek, A., and Rayner, K. 1989. Parafoveal processing during eye fixations in reading. *Perception and Psychophysics* (in press).

Brady, M. 1981. Toward a computational theory of early visual processing in reading. *Visible Language* 15:183–215.

Brooks, L. 1977. Visual pattern in fluent word identification. In A. S. Reber and D. Scarborough, eds. *Toward a Psychology of Reading*. Hillsdale, NJ: Erlbaum.

Carr, T. H., Davidson, B. J., and Hawkins, H. L. 1978. Perceptual flexibility in word recognition: Strategies affect orthographic computation but not lexical access. *Journal of Experimental Psychology: Human Perception and Performance* 4:674–690.

Carr, T. H., and Pollatsek, A. 1985. Recognizing printed words: A look at current models. In D. Besner, T. G. Waller, and G. E. MacKinnon, eds. *Reading Research: Advances in Theory and Practice*. Vol. 5. Orlando, FL: Academic Press.

Cattell, J. M. 1886. The time it takes to see and name objects. *Mind* 11:63–65.

Coltheart, M. 1978. Lexical access in simple reading tasks. In G. Underwood, ed. *Strategies of Information Processing*. New York: Academic Press.

Coltheart, M. 1981. Disorders of reading and their implications for models of normal reading. *Visible Language* 15:245–286.

Coltheart, M., Besner, D., Jonasson, J. T., and Davelaar, E. 1979. Phonological recoding in the lexical decision task. *Quarterly Journal of Experimental Psychology* 31:489–508.

Coltheart, M., and Freeman, R. 1974. Case alternation impairs word recognition. *Bulletin of the Psychonomic Society* 3:102–104.

Coltheart, M., Patterson, K., and Marshall, J., eds. 1980. *Deep Dyslexia*. London: Routledge and Kegan Paul.

Crowder, R. G. 1982. *The Psychology of Reading: An Introduction*. New York: Oxford University Press.

Duffy, S. A., Morris, R., and Rayner, K. 1988. Lexical ambiguity and fixation times in reading. *Journal of Memory and Language* 27:429–446.

Ehrlich, S. F., and Rayner, K. 1981. Contextual effects on word perception and eye movements during reading. *Journal of Verbal Learning and Verbal Behavior* 20:641–655.

Ferreira, F., and Clifton, C. 1986. The independence of syntactic processing. *Journal of Memory and Language* 25:348–368.

Fodor, J. A. 1983. *Modularity of Mind*. Cambridge, MA: MIT Press.

Forster, K. I., and Chambers, S. M. 1973. Lexical access and naming time. *Journal of Verbal Learning and Verbal Behavior* 12:627–635.

Gibson, E. J. 1971. Perceptual learning and the theory of word perception. *Cognitive Psychology* 2:351–368.

Glushko, R. J. 1979. The organization and activation of orthographic knowledge in reading aloud. *Journal of Experimental Psychology: Human Perception and Performance* 5:674–691.

Gough, P. B. 1972. One second of reading. In J. F. Kavanagh and I. G. Mattingly, eds. *Language by Ear and by Eye*. Cambridge, MA: MIT Press.

Gough, P. B., Alford, J. A., Jr., and Holley-Wilcox, P. 1981. Words and contexts. In O. L. Tzeng and H. Singer, eds. *Perception of Print: Reading Research in Experimental Psychology*. Hillsdale, NJ: Erlbaum.

Henderson, J. M., and Ferriera, F. 1987. Visual attention and the perceptual span in reading. Paper presented at the Joseph R. Royce Research Conference, University of Alberta.

Hogaboam, T. W. 1983. Reading patterns in eye movement data. In K. Rayner, ed. *Eye Movements in Reading*. New York: Academic Press.

Hoffman, D. D., and Richards, W. A. 1985. Parts of recognition. In S. Pinker, ed. *Visual Cognition*. Cambridge, MA: MIT Press, pp. 65–96.

Humphreys, G. W., and Evett, L. J. 1985. Are there independent lexical and nonlexical routes in word processing? An evaluation of the dual-route theory of reading. *Behavioral and Brain Sciences* 8:689–740.

Inhoff, A. W. 1989. Lexical access during eye fixations in sentence reading: Are word access codes used to integrate lexical information across interword fixations? *Journal of Memory and Language* (in press).

Inhoff, A. W., Pollatsek, A., Posner, M. I., and Rayner, K. 1989. Covert attention and eye movements in reading. *Quarterly Journal of Experimental Psychology* 41a:63–89.

Inhoff, A. W., and Rayner, K. 1986. Parafoveal word processing during eye fixations in reading: Effects of word frequency. *Perception and Psychophysics* 40:431–439.

Johnston, J. C., and McClelland, J. L. 1974. Perception of letters in words: Seek and ye shall not find. *Science* 184:1192–1193.

Just, M. A., and Carpenter, P. A. 1980. A theory of reading: From eye fixations to comprehension. *Psychological Review* 87:329–354.

Just, M. A., and Carpenter, P. A. 1987. *The Psychology of Reading and Language Comprehension*. Newton, MA: Allyn and Bacon.

Lima, S. D. 1987. Morphological analysis in sentence reading. *Journal of Memory and Language* 26:84–99.

Marcel, A. J. 1980. Surface dyslexia and beginning reading: A revised hypothesis of pronunciation of print and its impairments. In M. Coltheart, K. Patterson, and J. C. Marshall, eds. *Deep Dyslexia*. London: Routledge & Kegan Paul.

Marr, D. 1982. *Vision: A Computational Investigation into the Human Representation and Processing of Visual Information*. San Francisco: W.H. Freeman.

Marshall, J. C., and Newcombe, F. 1966. Syntactic and semantic errors in paralexia. *Neuropsychologia* 4:169–176.

Marshall, J. C., and Newcombe, F. 1973. Patterns of paralexia: A psycholinguistic approach. *Journal of Psycholinguistic Research* 2:175–200.

McClelland, J. L. 1986. The programmable blackboard model of reading. In J. L. McClelland and D. E. Rumelhart, eds. *Parallel Distributed Processing: Explorations in the Microstructure of Cognition.* Vol. 2. Cambridge, MA: MIT Press.

McClelland, J. L., and Johnston, J. C. 1977. The role of familiar units in the perception of words and nonwords. *Perception and Psychophysics* 22:249–261.

McClelland, J. L., and O'Regan, J. K. 1981. Expectations increase the benefit derived from parafoveal visual information in reading words aloud. *Journal of Experimental Psychology: Human Perception and Performance* 7:634–644.

McClelland, J. L., and Rumelhart, D. E. 1981. An interactive activation model of context effects in letter perception: Part 1. An account of basic findings. *Psychological Review* 88:375–407.

McConkie, G. W., and Rayner, K. 1975. The span of the effective stimulus during a fixation in reading. *Perception and Psychophysics* 17:578–586.

McConkie, G. W., and Rayner, K. 1976. Asymmetry of the perceptual span in reading. *Bulletin of the Psychonomic Society* 8:365–368.

McConkie, G. W., and Zola, D. 1979. Is visual information integrated across successive fixations in reading? *Perception and Psychophysics* 25:221–224.

Mewhort, D. J. K., and Beal, A. L. 1977. Mechanisms of word identification. *Journal of Experimental Psychology: Human Perception and Performance* 3:629–640.

Meyer, D. E., and Gutschera, K. 1975. *Orthographic Versus Phonemic Processing of Printed Words.* Paper presented at the annual meeting of the Psychonomic Society, Denver, CO.

Mitchell, D. C. 1982. *The Process of Reading.* Chichester, Engl.: John Wiley & Sons.

O'Regan, J. K. 1979. Eye guidance in reading: Evidence for linguistic control hypothesis. *Perception and Psychophysics* 28:112–117.

Paap, K. R., Newsome, S. L., McDonald, J. E., and Schvaneveldt, R. W. 1982. An activation-verification model for letter and word recognition: The word superiority effect. *Psychological Review* 89:573–594.

Parkin, A. J., and Underwood, G. 1983. Orthographic vs. phonological irregularity in lexical decision. *Memory and Cognition* 11:351–355.

Patterson, K. E., Marshall, J. C., and Coltheart, M. 1985. *Surface Dyslexia: Neuropsychological and Cognitive Studies of Phonological Reading.* Hillsdale, NJ: Erlbaum.

Perfetti, C. A. 1985. *Reading Ability.* New York: Oxford University Press.

Perfetti, C. A., and Hogaboam, T. 1975. Relationship between single word decoding and reading comprehension skill. *Journal of Educational Psychology* 67:461–469.

Pollatsek, A., Bolozky, S., Well, A. D., and Rayner, K. 1981. Asymmetries in the perceptual span for Israeli readers. *Brain and Language* 14:174–180.

Pollatsek, A., Rayner, K., and Balota, D. A. 1986. Inferences about eye movement control from the perceptual span in reading. *Perception and Psychophysics* 40:123–130.

Rayner, K. 1975. The perceptual span and peripheral cues in reading. *Cognitive Psychology* 7:65–81.

Rayner, K. 1978a. Eye movements in reading and information processing. *Psychological Bulletin* 85:618–660.

Rayner, K. 1978b. Foveal and parafoveal cues in reading. In J. Requin, ed. *Attention and Performance VII.* Hillsdale, NJ: Erlbaum.

Rayner, K. 1986. Eye movements and the perceptual span in beginning and skilled readers. *Journal of Experimental Child Psychology* 41:211–236.

Rayner, K., Balota, D. A., and Pollatsek, A. 1986. Against parafoveal semantic preprocessing during eye fixations in reading. *Canadian Journal of Psychology* 40:473–483.

Rayner, K., and Bertera, J. H. 1979. Reading without a fovea. *Science* 206:468–469.

Rayner, K., Carlson, M., and Frazier, L. 1983. The interaction of syntax and semantics during sentence processing: Eye movements in the analysis of semantically biased sentences. *Journal of Verbal Learning and Verbal Behavior* 22:358–374.

Rayner, K., and Duffy, S. A. 1986. Lexical complexity and fixation times in reading: Effects of word frequency, verb complexity, and lexical ambiguity. *Memory and Cognition* 14:191–201.

Rayner, K. McConkie, G. W., and Ehrlich, S. F. 1978. Eye movements and integrating information across fixations. *Journal of Experimental Psychology: Human Perception and Performance* 4:529–544.

Rayner, K., McConkie, G. W., and Zola, D. 1980. Integrating information across eye movements. *Cognitive Psychology* 12:206–226.

Rayner, K., and Pollatsek, A. 1987. Eye movements in reading: A tutorial review. In M. Coltheart, ed. *Attention and Performance 12.* London: Erlbaum.

Rayner, K., and Pollatsek, A. 1989. *The Psychology of Reading.* Englewood Cliffs, NJ: Prentice Hall.

Rayner, K., Well, A. D., and Pollatsek, A. 1980. Asymmetry of the effective visual field in reading. *Perception and Psychophysics* 27:537–544.

Rayner, K., Well, A. D., Pollatsek, A., and Bertera, J. H. 1982. The availability of useful information to the right of fixation in reading. *Perception and Psychophysics* 31:537–550.

Reicher, G. M. 1969. Perceptual recognition as a function of meaningfulness of stimulus material. *Journal of Experimental Psychology* 81:275–280.

Rumelhart, D. E., and McClelland, J. L. 1982. An interactive activation model of context effects in letter perception: Part 2. *Psychological Review* 89:60–94.

Schustack, M. W., Ehrlich, S. F., and Rayner, K. 1987. The complexity of contextual facilitation in reading: Local and global influences. *Journal of Memory and Language* 26:322–340.

Seidenberg, M. S., and McClelland, J. L. 1988. A distributed, developmental model of visual word recognition and naming. Paper presented at the 28th Annual Meeting of the Psychonomic Society, Seattle, WA.

Seidenberg, M. S., Waters, G. S., Barnes, M. A., and Tanenhaus, M. K. 1984. When does irregular spelling or pronunciation influence word recognition? *Journal of Verbal Learning and Verbal Behavior* 23:383–404.

Selkirk, L. 1982. *The Syntax of Words*. Cambridge, MA: MIT Press.

Smith, F. 1971. *Understanding Reading: A Psycholinguistic Analysis of Reading and Learning to Read*. New York: Holt, Rinehart and Winston.

Smith, F., Lott, D., and Cronnell, B. 1969. The effect of type size and case alternation on word identification. *American Journal of Psychology* 82:248–253.

Sperling, G. 1960. The information available in brief visual presentations. *Psychological Monographs* 74 (498).

Stanovich, K. E., and West, R. F. 1983. On priming by a sentence context. *Journal of Experimental Psychology: General* 112:1–36.

Sternberg, S. 1969. The discovery of processing stages: Extensions of Donders method. In W. G. Koster, ed. *Attention and Performance II. Act Psychologica* 30:276–315.

Taft, M. 1985. The decoding of words in lexical access: A review of the morphological approach. In D. Besner, T. G. Waller, and G. E. MacKinnon, eds. *Reading Research: Advances in Theory and Practice*. Vol. 5. New York: Academic Press.

Thibadeau, R., Just, M. A., and Carpenter, P. A. 1982. A model of the time course and content of reading. *Cognitive Science* 6:157–203.

Underwood, N. R., and McConkie, G. W. 1985. Perceptual span for letter distinctions during reading. *Reading Research Quarterly* 20:153–162.

Van Orden, G. C. 1987. A rows is a rose: Spelling, sound, and reading. *Memory and Cognition* 15:181–198.

Van Orden, G. C., Johnston, J. C., and Hale, B. L. 1988. Word identification in reading proceeds from spelling to sound to meaning. *Journal of Experimental Psychology: Learning, Memory, and Cognition* 14:371–386.

Wheeler, D. D. 1970. Processes in word recognition. *Cognitive Psychology* 1:59–85.

Zola, D. 1984. Redundancy and word perception during reading. *Perception and Psychophysics* 36:277–284.

11 Discourse

Barbara J. Grosz, Martha E. Pollack, and Candace L. Sidner

Research in discourse analysis, discourse structure, and discourse processing considers discourses, rather than isolated sentences, to be the basic units of language. Central to all endeavors is a desire to uncover the mechanisms that make certain sequences of utterances coherent and others not and to understand how context affects the use and understanding of various kinds of linguistic expressions. In this chapter we focus on three collections of discourse problems: those that arise in trying to determine discourse structure, those relating to phrase-level phenomena (for example, pronouns, definite descriptions, ellipsis), and those that concern how the meaning or effect of a discourse or discourse segment is derived. Because more research has been done in the cognitive sciences than could be reported in this chapter, we focus on work that has taken computational or processing questions to be central.

We begin with a survey of early approaches to discourse within artificial intelligence. These early approaches made evident the problems in existing theories, the need to determine the role of nonlinguistic information (including domain knowledge, differences among beliefs of speaker and hearer, reader and writer, and cognitive state) in discourse processing, and the need for computationally tractable theories adequate to support discourse processing. Next we describe approaches to discourse structure, discussing various ideas about the kinds of discourse segments that exist and the kinds of relations that join them. Following previous work (Grosz and Sidner 1986), we distinguish the linguistic structure of the discourse from its intentional structure and its evolving attentional state.

In section 11.3 we examine different kinds of information about discourse structure that is carried explicitly in the linguistic signal itself. In section 11.4 we describe research on the effects of discourse structure and discourse context on the interpretation of various phrase-level phenomena, including definite descriptions, pronouns, quantified noun phrases (for example, *every girl on the block*), event reference, and ellipsis. Section 11.5 describes various formulations of plans and techniques that have been developed for plan recognition. Once we take seriously the idea that language is used by agents to affect their world, it becomes crucial to understand the effects an individual utterance can have (this was the initial purview of speech-act theory), and the ways in which utterances can combine to form larger actions (research on plan recognition in discourse). Linguistic actions can thus be seen to affect discourse structure and discourse meaning.

11.1 Early Approaches to Discourse Processing

The earliest attempts to deal directly with the computational problems of discourse were carried out within the context of building complete computer-based natural-language processing systems in the early 1970s. These systems maintained no model of discourse structure in the sense that it is now understood. However, system creators experimented with techniques for pronoun understanding and a limited form of intention recognition. The LUNAR system (Woods et al. 1972, Woods 1978) provided mechanisms for resolving pronouns, but because each question-and-answer pair was an independent exchange, the discourse model was simple: only a list of previously mentioned entities were maintained for use in pronoun understanding. Charniak (1977) attempted to identify the referents of definite descriptions and pronouns in the process of "understanding" children's stories by encoding domain information in rules of inference and associated triggering programs. The most extensive dialogue system, Winograd's SHRDLU system (Winograd 1971, 1972) participated in a dialogue with a user about constructions of toy blocks. SHRDLU interpreted the user's intentions as programs to perform actions on its part and kept a history of actions it had performed. It could interpret some of the personal pronouns, some definite descriptions, and "the one"-type anaphoric expressions using "word specialists," that is, programs that determined reference based on heuristics of plausibility for the objects most recently mentioned in the previous sentence.

The next generation of natural-language systems, built toward the end of the 1970s, concentrated either on the use of domain knowledge in discourse or on methods of incorporating discourse phenomena other than pronoun understanding. Most systems dramatically limited the domain of the discourse to one small class of actions or events and focused on interactions that conformed to a narrow range of discourse behavior (for example, SAM (Cullingford 1977, 1981) and GUS (Bobrow et al. 1977)). However, Lehnert (1977) experimented with a system to capture the nonliteral meaning of questions posed to a story-understanding program. Grosz and colleagues (Grosz 1977, Walker 1978) developed the Task Dialogue Understanding System, in which distinctions were made among domain knowledge (represented in a task model), discourse information (represented in the global focus and associated algorithms for interpreting references), and intention recognition (treatment of questions about and updates to the task model).

This system was the first to consider the interaction between the (linguistic) structure of a discourse and the interpretation of expressions in the discourse. It did not distinguish with sufficient clarity, however, the different roles of a task model in discourse processing.

Early approaches to discourse processing taught researchers that discourse processing could not be viewed as an agglomeration of procedures for reference understanding, intention recognition, and manipulation of domain knowledge. It requires a means of distinguishing among these processes and providing mechanisms for each as well for their interaction.

11.2 Discourse Structure

The utterances a discourse comprises are not random sequences, but rather have structure much in the way that the words in an individual sentence have syntactic structure. Analysis of a variety of types of discourse has established that discourses divide into discourse segments, and that these segments may bear different kinds of relations to one another. Among the types of discourse that have been analyzed are task-oriented dialogues (see, for example, Grosz 1978a, Mann et al. 1975, Sidner 1982), descriptions of complex objects (Linde 1979), narratives (Polanyi 1985, Schiffrin 1982), arguments (both informal (Reichman-Adar 1984) and formal (Cohen 1984)), negotiations (Linde and Goguen 1978), and explanations (Reichman-Adar 1984).

An understanding of discourse structure is important both for theories of discourse meaning and for language processing. Theories of discourse meaning depend in part on a specification of the basic units of a discourse and the relations that can hold among them. Discourse processing requires an ability to determine to which portions of a discourse an individual utterance relates. Thus the role of discourse structure in discourse processing derives both from its role in delimiting units of discourse meaning and from constraining the units of discourse considered to be relevant to the interpretation of any individual utterance.

Furthermore an account of the interpretation of a variety of linguistic expressions depends on an explanation of the role of some of these expressions in determining discourse structure as well as on an understanding of the effect of discourse structure in constraining the interpretation of others. Section 11.3 discusses the use of cue phrases and intonation to mark discourse structure. Section 11.4 describes research on the interaction between discourse structure and the interpretation of anaphoric expressions.

Although there is general agreement on the fact that discourses are composed of segments, and on the interaction between discourse structure and the interpretation of various classes of linguistic expressions, theories of discourse structure postulate different types of information as central to the computation of discourse structure. Furthermore theories differ in the kinds of relations between segments considered important. Early work on text understanding (vanDijk 1972, Rumelhart 1975) proposed text (or story) grammars analogous to sentence grammars;[1] the earliest work on dialogue (Grosz 1974) argued that task-oriented dialogues had a structure that depended on the structure of the task being done. Subsequent work has taken one of the following approaches: (1) adaptions of the notion of grammar, (2) specification of a small set of rhetorical or textual relations as the basis of discourse structure, (3) investigation of domain-specific or commonsense knowledge as the source of discourse structure, or (4) examination of intentions broadly construed (a generalization of task structure) and relations among them as the foundation of discourse structure.

Segmentation and Structure of Utterances

Research on the possible relationships among the utterances that a discourse comprises has addressed such questions as which utterances group together into a segment, and what relations may hold between these segments (Polanyi 1985, Hobbs 1979, Linde 1979, Mann and Thompson 1986). In previous work (Grosz and Sidner 1986) we have referred to this structuring of the discourse into groups of utterances as the linguistic structure of the discourse. Our terminology reflects the focus placed on the structure of the language behavior itself. In theories that primarily consider linguistic structure, discourse structure is typically represented by a tree with clause-level utterances or groups of them as the nodes.[2]

Theories differ with respect to the information on which they base decisions about the embedding relationships encoded in the tree, and with respect to the kinds of specific embedding relationships they consider possible. Although some differences stem from the types of discourse treated (for example, narratives as opposed to arguments), others reflect disparate views of the goals of discourse processing.

Linde (1979) and Polanyi (1986) propose models derived in part from the sociolinguistic tradition, in which explanations are expressed solely in terms of surface behavior. They are thus concerned with providing an explanation of discourse structure in terms of the surface connections that obtain among utterances. Polanyi claims that the hierarchical structure of discourse "emerges from the structural and semantic relationships obtaining among the linguistic units which speakers use to build up their discourses" (Polanyi 1986, p. 4). In her model a discourse tree is constructed using a set of discourse grammars. The nodes of the tree are clauses (in some cases with their associated semantics). That is, the discourse structure is taken to be a tree structure with linguistic elements as the nodes.

Research in this paradigm typically takes full interactions (for example, extended personal conversations, doctor-patient interactions) as the largest unit of discourse, and clauses, perhaps grouped by coordinating or subordinating relations (for example, lists, expansions), as the smallest unit. Intermediate units of explanation may be socially motivated units (for example, service encounters, medical examinations), or linguistically motivated ones (for example, stories). Frequently labels are applied at these levels (for example, question/answer) that indicate the intentions of the discourse participants, but the theories avoid any reference to intention in their explanations.

Rhetorical Relations

Reichman-Adar (1984) studied informal arguments; the structure she proposed is based on a grammar for arguments that is analogous to story or text gammars (vanDijk 1972, Rumelhart 1975). For example, she claims an argument consists of a claim followed by support, and that support decomposes into an authority citation or a narrative or a proposition. Although the relations she posits between utterances and discourse segments combine semantic, pragmatic, and intentional properties, Reichman's analysis of processing is focused at the linguistic level.

Other research that builds a tree structure with linguistic nodes has focused on the relationships that can hold among meanings of utterances (that is, on semantic relationships). Cohen (1987) has analyzed a variety of arguments and investigated the problem of inferring evidence relations among the propositions expressed in them. She presents a processing model for arguments that uses a combination of cue-phrase information and (an initial set of) methods for inferring evidence relations to determine argument structure.

Much of the research described so far, as well as work by Hobbs (1979), Lehnert (1981), Mann and Thompson (1986), and McKeown (1985), offers an underlying stratum of rhetorical relations as the basis for deriving relationships among utterances and segments. Each such relation requires processing of domain information to determine how a relation could be recognized or produced in discourse processing. For example, Hobbs (1979) defines a set of coherence relations (for example, parallel, enablement, contrast; a complete list may be found in Hobbs 1983) that hold between discourse segments. Determination of the relation that holds between two successive utterances depends in inferences drawn on the basis of domain facts. Lehnert's relations derive from an underlying model of mental states and events. A set of primitive configurations, which she dubs *plot units*, describes the permissible transitions between states or events and thereby directly encodes domain information. These plot units then serve as the relations among utterances of segments. In McKeown's work on generation of discourses, a collection of rhetorical predicates (including, for example, attribution, identification, and comparison) are organized into schemas that abstractly define the set of acceptable discourse types; one or more individual utterances are produced as instantiations of the predicates in a schema.

Intentions and Attention in Discourse Structure

Levy (1979) and Grosz and Sidner (1986) have argued that plan-based or intentional relations are the root of discourse structure and postulate only an embedding relationship in the linguistic structure. The embedding relationships between segments depend in part on certain linguistic features of the segment (such as intonation or cue phrases), and in part on the intentions conveyed by the utterances of the segment. The segment-level intention is not a simple function of the utterance-level intentions, however, but a complex function of utterances, domain facts, utterance-level intentions, and inferences about these.

We argue further (Grosz and Sidner 1986) that discourse structure is a composite of three interrelated structures; in addition to linguistic structure there are a structure of intentions and an attentional state. The intentional structure comprises discourse-segment purposes and relationships between them. Discourse-segment purposes are intentions of the discourse participants that lead in part to the discourse and are, like Gricean utterance-level intentions (1957, 1968), intended to be recognized. Unlike the rhetorical relations discussed previously, discourse-segment purposes are not drawn from any special set of intentions; almost anything that can be intended can be a discourse-segment purpose. However, two relations among intentions are defined as common in many discourses: *domination* and *satisfaction precedence*. These relations represent, respectively, the fact that satisfaction of one intention contributes to the satisfaction of a second, and the fact that one intention needs to be satisfied before another. Recognition of these two relations plays the same role in our theory that recognition of rhetorical relations plays in the theories described previously. Determination of discourse-segment purposes depends in part on recognition of these relationships, in part on domain knowledge, and in part on other features of the discourse context.

Attentional state reflects the focus of attention of discourse participants as the discourse progresses. It is modeled as a (pushdown) stack of focus spaces, one for each segment of the discourse. The focus spaces contain representations of the discourse-segment purpose and the entities referred to in the segment. The stack grows when segments are introduced into a discourse and shrinks as the intentions of the segments are satisfied. Following standard terminology, we say that a new space is *pushed* onto the stack when a new segment is introduced, and that a space is *popped* when its purpose is satisfied. The focus space model of attentional state constrains processing as the discourse unfolds. Those entities and purposes represented in the stack are most salient to the discourse. Constraints may use this fact to stipulate when various linguistic expressions can be used and to help determine when a given discourse-segment purpose may dominate or satisfaction-precede another.

11.3 Linguistic Indicators of Discourse Structure

The moral of this chapter should by now be clear: discourses exhibit structure. Every discourse can be intuitively partitioned into segments, and discourse segments can embed and be embedded in other discourse segments, resulting in a hierarchical structure. Recognizing the structure of a discourse is an essential part of comprehending it.

But how is it that the structure of a discourse is recognized? As we noted in the preceding section, the answer to that question is still widely debated—not surprisingly because it is the central motivating question in research on discourse. Virtually all researchers agree, however, that speakers have available certain powerful linguistic devices for assisting hearers in recognizing the structure of an ongoing discourse. These devices, such as cue phrases, intonational patterns, and gesture, can indicate both where a discourse segment begins and ends, and how it is related to other segments.

Cue Phrases

The most widely studied class of linguistic indicators of discourse structure are the *cue phrases* (sometimes called *clue words, discourse markers,* or *discourse particles*). Cue phrases are expressions such as *now, in the first place,* and *by the way,* which do not make a direct semantic contribution to an utterance, but instead convey information about the structure of the discourse containing the utterance. Of course because different theories make different claims about what the structure of a discourse amounts to, there are also variations among theories about precisely what structural information is signalled by a cue phrase.

Researchers who view the structure of a discourse as solely a linguistic structure maintain that cue phrases provide a direct indication of how distinct segments are related in the hierarchy (Cohen 1984). Those who argue that the structure of a discourse consists of an underlying stratum of rhetorical relations linking discourse segments view cue phrases as suggesting the particular relation that holds between two discourse segments. For example, Hobbs (1985, p. 31) claims that "'That is' or 'i.e.' suggests *elaboration,* 'similarly' suggests *parallel,* 'for example' suggests *exemplification,* and 'but' suggests *contrast* or *violated expectation.*"[3] Similar claims have been made in Rhetorical Structure Theory (Mann and Thompson 1986) and in accounts of discourse parsing (Polanyi and Scha 1984, Reichman-Adar 1984).

A contrasting claim about the role of cue phrases has been made by Grosz and Sidner (1986). As already noted, we have argued that the structure of a discourse actually comprises three interrelated structures. In this view cue phrases can provide information about one or more components of the overall (three-part) structure (Grosz and Sidner 1986, pp. 196–199). For instance, certain cue phrases, such as *that reminds me* and *anyway*, indicate changes to the attentional state—the former indicating a push to a new focus space and the latter a pop to a previously established space. Notice that although the change to attentional state signalled by *that reminds me* is accompanied by the addition of new components to the intentional structure, the cue phrase itself does not specify what this change is. With *anyway* there is no change to the intentional structure at all. In contrast other cue phrases directly indicate changes to the intentional structure. The expression *incidentally* provides information that the speaker is embarking on a digression, and consequently the intentional structure is to be extended with a new intentional hierarchy distinct from the existing one. The expression *for example* indicates that the intention underlying the upcoming discourse segment—the one whose starting boundary is marked with the cue phrase—is dominated in the intentional structure by the intention underlying the preceding discourse segment.

Most researchers, regardless of their stance on what discourse structure actually constitutes, believe that cue phrases are in general neither necessary nor sufficient for determining discourse structure. There are many cases in which it is quite possible to determine the structure of a discourse, or a portion of one, that lacks any cue phrases. Likewise there are many discourses, or portions thereof, containing cue phrases that only suggest the underlying structure or, put another way, provide constraints on the range of possible structures. Ultimately the structure of a discourse depends on the information conveyed by the utterances it comprises and the way in which that information is interconnected. Cue phrases simplify the task of determining those connections. It has been shown that the process of determination of intersentential semantic relationships (Cohen 1984) and plan recognition (Litman and Allen 1988) can be constrained by taking into account cue phrases.

Intonation and Gesture
Intonation is another powerful tool for indicating discourse structure. Studies of spontaneously produced discourses have shown that changes in pause length (Chafe 1979, 1980) and speech rate (Butterworth 1975) correlate with discourse-segment boundaries. Hirschberg, Pierrehumbert, Litman, and Ward have provided evidence of a close correspondence between particular intonational features and specific components of the three-part discourse structure proposed by Grosz and Sidner (Hirschberg et al. 1987, Hirschberg and Pierrehumbert 1986). *Pitch range* can indicate discourse segment boundaries (Silverman (1987) came to the same conclusion); *accent* can provide information about the attentional state, and *tune* can mark intentional structure. In addition phrasing and accent can help distinguish the use of an expression such as

now as a cue phrase from a use in which the expression contributes directly to sentence meaning (Hirschberg and Litman 1987).

Gesture is another device that is useful, at least in face-to-face conversation, for signalling discourse structure. Studies have shown that gesture tends to be coincident with discourse-segment boundaries (Kendon 1972, Marslen-Wilson et al. 1982) and can provide information about focus of attention and about intentional structure (McNeill 1979, McNeill and Levy 1982).

11.4   Phrase-Level Phenomena

Discourse context affects the interpretation of individual phrases and clauses within a single utterance. The meaning of pronouns and definite descriptions is quite obviously influenced by the context in which they are used; among the most widely studied problems in discourse processing are those concerning the influences of context on the processes of generating and interpreting such phrases. The related problem of appropriately representing quantified noun phrases has also been addressed. We discuss a range of approaches to these problems of noun-phrase reference in the following subsection. Reference may be made to events as well as objects, raising problems discussed in the second subsection. Other phrase-level problems that have received treatment from the perspective of discourse processing are modifier attachment and discourse ellipsis.

Of the three components of discourse structure, attentional state has the greatest effect on problems of phrase-level interpretation. Research on referring expressions has most directly used attentional models, whereas approaches to modifier attachment and discourse ellipsis have only begun to make use of them. Although there is as yet no full account of the range of discourse constraints (nor of perceptual ones) relevant to any of these phrase-level problems, researchers have identified and experimented with a range of representations and algorithms central to them.

Pronouns and Definite Descriptions

The primary concern of computational theories and models of the use of referring expressions has been with determining the entity (or entities) to which a pronoun or definite description refers.[4] Both the problem of specifying the range of possible referents an initial description makes available and the problem of choosing among possibilities have been investigated.

Two approaches have been taken to the problem of identifying the referent of an anaphoric[5] phrase. In one approach (Hobbs 1979) referent identification is subsumed by more general processes of inference. In the other approach questions of how referring expressions interact with attentional state are considered primary (Grosz 1977, Sidner 1981, Reichman-Adar 1984, Grosz and Sidner 1986). Research following the first approach considers only problems of interpreting referring expressions, whereas research following the second is concerned as well with specifying constraints on generation of appropriate referring expressions.

For the second approach the concepts of focus and the process of focusing (Grosz 1977, Grosz 1978b, Grosz 1981, Grosz and Sidner 1986) have played central roles in the treatment of definite descriptions, used both for first reference and as anaphoric noun phrases. In this work focusing is defined as the movement of the focus of attention of the discourse participants as the discourse progresses. Two levels of focusing, global and local, have been identified (Grosz 1977, Grosz and Sidner 1986). Global focusing is modeled by a stack of focus spaces; it affects the use and interpretation of definite descriptions. Focusing at the local level is modeled with centers and centering. The center of a given segment is an element of the attentional state, and at the beginning of each new segment a new center is introduced. Centering affects the use and interpretation of pronouns.

Each individual space on the global focus stack contains representations of the entities that the participants focus on during a corresponding discourse segment, as well as the discourse-segment purpose. The entities currently in focus (that is, in some space on the focus stack) are the primary candidates for referents of definite descriptions; they are also the source of implicitly focused entities (that is, a phrase may refer to an item related to something in a current focus space; for example, *the cover* may be used to refer to the cover of a book when that book is in focus). The set of entities in the global focus also provides constraints on the content of subsequent definite descriptions; for example, a speaker must include sufficient descriptors to distinguish the entity to which he wishes to refer from other entities in focus.

Grosz (1977) devised a set of focusing mechanisms for the interpretation of definite noun phrases in a system that participated in a dialogue about a task.[6] The mechanisms brought entities into focus as the discourse moved to a subtask of the overall task and moved them from global focus when the subtask was completed. Position in global focus was relative to the most immediate subtask; other incomplete subtasks and their associated entities were in global focus, but were less salient than those associated with the most immediate subtask. Procedures for the interpretation of anaphoric definite noun phrases and of implicitly focused first references chose items from among those in global focus. The focusing techniques could predict the anaphoric referent of a definite noun phrase such as *the screw* when the screw in the wheelpuller had been brought into focus. They also limited the search necessary to find the representation of a previously mentioned entity—those entities not in focus were unavailable, and those in focus and associated with the most immediate subtask were searched before less salient ones. For example, *the screw* would be understood as a referent to the screw of the wheelpuller only when the wheelpuller was more salient than some other screw (for example, the drill screw) in the global focus; otherwise the drill screw would be chosen as the referent.

Appelt and Kronfeld (1987) have used the mechanisms for focusing in the generation of first-use referring expressions. In addition Kronfeld (1986) has provided the concepts of functionally relevant descriptions (that is, those whose content is needed to distinguish the referent) and conversationally relevant descriptions (that is, those whose content provides information about the referent's relation to other aspects of the conversation). These concepts redefine Donnellan's (1966) classical distinction between referential and attributive descriptions in terms of the role a phrase plays as a referring tool and as a contributor to the content of discourse.

Immediate focus (Sidner 1979) guides the interpretation and generation of third-person pronouns as well as the anaphoric uses of *this* and *that*. Immediate focusing operates within individual discourse segments; it tracks the entity most relevant at any utterance within the segment, based on features of the preceding context, especially properties of the preceding utterance. Sidner (1979, 1981, 1983) developed a set of algorithms for predicting the choice of local foci in discourse and their movement as the discourse progressed. Her algorithms used the concepts of a discourse focus and an actor focus, that is, entities mentioned in an utterance that were locally in focus because of the syntactic structure and thematic relations of the utterance. A set of rules, using the immediate foci and a set of potential new foci, predicted the intended interpretation of pronouns in subsequent utterances. McKeown (1985) and McDonald (1983) adapted the focusing algorithms to generate pronouns in text.

The centering theory of Grosz, Joshi, and Weinstein (Joshi and Weinstein 1981, Grosz et al. 1983) replaced the notion of immediate foci with that of centers: a backward-looking center (Cb) that corresponds roughly to the discourse focus, and several forward-looking centers (Cf) corresponding to the potential new foci. As in Sidner's theory the centers shift according to the behavior of referring expressions in each utterance of discourse. The theory differs in having no correlate of actor focus and accounting for multiple uses of the same pronoun by allowing entities other than the Cb to be pronominalized so long as the Cb is. The centering theory simplifies Sidner's account of local focusing by eliminating the need for both actor and discourse foci and by providing an explanation of particular instances of pronoun interpretation that are problematic in the immediate focus theory.

Although the focus of attention is crucial in the understanding of anaphora, the form and content of the phrases and utterances that first evoke the entities to which anaphora refer vitally contribute to their understanding as well. Webber (1980, 1983) introduced the notion of phrases "evoking discourse entities." By this she meant that phrases brought into the discourse, or *naturally evoked*, a well-structured collection of representations of the (actual) entities referred to. Discourse entities were available for interpretation of definite anaphora and verb phrase ellipsis. She defined the concept of *discourse entity invoking description* (ID) to formalize her notion and posed a set of specific representations and rules for creating these IDs by successive application of the rules.

Webber's rules operated on complex semantic representations, which included embedded quantifiers and quantification over sets of individuals. The rules produced IDs for each possible interpretation of the noun phrases and verb phrases of an utterance, but Webber did not explore how to determine computationally which interpretation was intended on the basis of subsequent anaphoric descriptions. Sidner (1983), however, sketched an account of how focusing might provide the necessary information. In subsequent work Kamp (1981) and Heim (1982) have proposed similar alternative formalisms; Guenthner and colleagues (1986) report on a system using Kamp's formalism. Two system-building efforts have investigated methods for computing the representations of complex noun phrases as part of the process of determining (a representation of) the meaning of a sentence (Dahl 1987, Pollack and Pereira 1988).

Among the referring expressions least investigated in computational discourse research is the use of deixis.[7] Fillmore (1975) subcategorized four types of deixis: spatial, temporal, social, and discourse. Discourse structure may constrain the latter two types as is exemplified by the phrases *the former*, used to refer to the first of two items in a list (an instance of discourse deixis), and *we* (an instance of social deixis). Sidner (1979) explored instances of discourse deixis, but a general treatment remains to be provided.

Reference to Events
Discourse research has considered two problems caused by references to events: identifying to which event an anaphoric reference refers, and determining the relative temporal ordering of the events described in the discourse.

Anaphoric references typically use pronominal forms either bare (*it, this, that*) as in example 1, or with the proverb do (*do so, do it, do that*), as in example 2. The *do* form and the bare pronoun appear to behave differently. Although some research treats *do* forms (Sidner 1979, Sidner 1981, Robinson 1981), a comprehensive account of all directly anaphoric references to events remains to be given.

(1) John runs every day of the week.
   That's his main form of exercise.
   that = John's running every day.

(2) John runs every day of the week.

   He *does it* to stay healthy.

   does it = act of running every day of the week.

Relative temporal ordering is affected by verb tense and aspect, as well as by adverbial modifiers; it also depends on attentional state changes. In the following discourse (from Webber 1987) the event described in utterance 1, E1, occurs at some point in the past, utterance 2 describes an event E2 that occurs before E1, the event E3 of utterance 3 occurs after E2 and before E1 and is situated in the location described in utterance 2, and the event E4 in utterance 4 occurs after E1.

(1) John went over to Mary's house.

(2) On the way, he stopped by the flower shop for some roses.

(3) He picked out 5 red ones and 3 white ones.

(4) Unfortunately they failed to cheer her up.

Two major proposals for a theory of event reference, that of Webber (1987) and that of Hinrichs (1986) and Partee (1984), each provide an account of the relative order of events. Webber also provides an account for the recognition of the ordering of events based on temporal focus and focus movement, concepts analogous to the immediate-focus treatment (Sidner 1983, Grosz et al. 1983) for definite anaphora.

Modification Relations in Noun Phrases

Modification relations among parts of a complex noun phrase pose two problems for the interpretation or generation of reference. The first concerns the choice of a single underlying (intended) description of the structural and functional relations among the entities described by the complex noun phrase; this single description must be chosen from a number of possible such descriptions. For example, the intended description of the phrase *the pump dispenser* rests on uncovering the functional relationship between the two objects: pump and dispenser. The second problem for interpreting modification relations is identifying the entity referred to (using of course some technique for determining possible relationships). Identification problems can be quite difficult for complex noun phrases with prepositional modifiers used in a context that includes several possible referents for each simple part of the noun phrase. The problem is illustrated by the phrase *the cat in the hat* used in a context in which there are two cats, two hats, but only one cat in a hat (one of *the* hats). Although the referent is clear here, no simple search for either a unique cat or a unique hat in context can serve as the basis of the search for the referent.

Research on nominal compounds has explored frameworks for using linguistic information to predict the possible structure of complex noun phrases (compare Isabelle 1984). Computational approaches to these problems (Finin 1980, Hobbs and Martin 1987) have addressed the joint problems of appropriately representing the domain knowledge needed to determine the intended interpretation and defining processes for searching this knowledge. Although attentional state obviously affects the identification of appropriate interpretation, this issue has not yet been explored computationally.

By contrast recent approaches (Mellish 1982, Haddock 1987) to identifying the referent (which have considered prepositional phrase attachment rather than nominal compounds) have concentrated on the concept of incremental reference evaluation using constraint-satisfaction techniques. These techniques assume that the head noun, noun phrase embedded in the prepositional phrase, and the relation specified by the preposition form a set of constraints on the choice of candidate referents for the whole phrase; these constraints may be applied incrementally as the phrase is constructed to search for the intended referent. These approaches assume some representation of attentional state that delineates a small set of possible referents and serves to limit the search undertaken by incremental constraint satisfaction. A theory that incorporates aspects of incremental evaluation with the search methods proposed for nominal compounds previously discussed has only recently been explored (Pollack and Pereira 1988).

Discourse Ellipsis

Discourse ellipsis is the omission (or *elision*) from an utterance of a syntactically required phrase when the content needed to determine the interpretation of the elided utterance can be recovered from a previous utterance. An adequate treatment of discourse ellipsis requires that a discourse (rather than a sentence) be considered the primary unit of communication. Two kinds of discourse ellipsis have been investigated. In the first type the elided material can be recovered directly from a representation of the meaning of the previous utterance. In the second the intentional structure provides the source of the elided material; in this case the elided content may not appear directly in any prior utterance.

Approaches to the first type (Hendrix et al. 1978, Webber 1983) have considered both noun-phrase and verb-phrase ellipsis. They have viewed ellipsis as similar to discourse anaphora because an ellipsis is also interpreted by locating previously mentioned phrases and their discourse representations as the source of the material to be reconstructed. Unlike discourse anaphora elided phrases need not refer to the same act or entity as the previously mentioned phrase, as shown in the following example:

(1) Fred kissed his mother.
    John did 0 too.
    0 = kissed his own mother or, alternatively, kissed Fred's mother.

Rather the discourse representation of the previously mentioned phrase provides material to construct the representation for the elided phrase.[8]

Approaches to the second type have used the intentional structure as the source of elided material. Elliptical utterances are presumed to be intended to contribute to the overall purpose of a discourse or discourse segment. As long as the discourse environment contains sufficient information, a full utterance need not be used; a phrase or portion of a sentence will contribute just as well. Elliptical fragments such as (1) (from Allen 1979) and (2) (from Carberry 1985) below can be seen to contribute directly to the discourse purpose; no reconstruction is needed of a full sentence in which the fragment is embedded.

(1) (said to information booth clerk at a railroad station) The train to Windsor?

(2) I want to get a degree. CS major. No courses at night.

Allen (1979) demonstrated that such phrases can be directly associated with a speech act which in turn identifies a portion of a speaker's plan to act in a domain of interest. The plan recognition models of Allen and Perrault (1980), Carberry (1985), and Litman (1985) underscored Allen's position and related the fragment to speech acts and the plans of speakers (that is, plans in a domain of action). By viewing action as a root of the explanation for why discourse occurs, these researchers illustrated that some forms of ellipsis could be viewed in terms of the intentional structure of discourse rather than in terms of a set of relations to other utterances.

11.5 Plan Recognition

Contemporary accounts of plan recognition in discourse understanding derive largely from two major theories of the philosopher Grice: his theory of *nonnatural meaning*[9] (Grice 1957, 1968) and his theory of *implicature* (Grice 1975, 1978). In Grice's theory of nonnatural meaning what speakers mean when they use language depends crucially on what they intend. The theory of implicature rests on the observation that much of what is intentionally conveyed during language use is not explicitly expressed; the theory itself shows how speakers can convey more than they explicitly express in their utterances. In both theories speakers are seen as producing utterances with the intention that their hearers recognize the intentions underlying those utterances. The collection of intentions underlying any utterance will thus include, but will not be limited to, an intention to have at least some portion of the collection itself recognized.

Understanding language thus requires determining what intentions speakers have: figuring out what plans they are pursuing in part by making an utterance. Plan recognition in conversation is a feasible task precisely because the speaker intends the hearer to perform it. The speaker cannot achieve her intended effect unless the hearer recognizes the speaker's plan; hence the speaker will include in the utterance what she believes to be sufficient information to make plan recognition possible for the hearer. This characteristic of plan recognition in conversation distinguishes it from the problem of determining the plans of an agent merely by observing the agent's actions without interacting with her. The latter problem, dubbed "keyhole recognition" because of its similarity to the problem of watching an agent through a keyhole and inferring the next action, is in general much more difficult.[10]

In constructing detailed models of the process of plan recognition in discourse, researchers have drawn not only on the work of Grice but also on the related insight of Austin (1962) and of Searle (1969, 1975) that language is used not merely to "say" things but also to "do" things. In other words communicative behavior should be viewed primarily as purposeful action. It follows that to a large extent the same tools that are used to analyze nonlinguistic action can be applied to the analysis of linguistic action—an idea originally developed largely in the work of Cohen and Perrault (1979), Allen (1983), and Perrault and Allen (1980). In particular, AI models of plan recognition in discourse have made use of techniques for representing and reasoning about action originally developed by those interested in the problem of automatic plan formation.[11] Before turning to a discussion of these models, however, it is worthwhile noting the range of discourse phenomena for which plan recognition is important.

Consider a person who walks up to the attendant at a train-station information booth and says, "Do you know when the next train to Detroit leaves?" with the intention that the attendant tell her the departure time of the next train to Detroit.[12] The speaker's communicative plan is to make a request—to be told when the next train to Detroit leaves—and to make this request by uttering her query. If the attendant recognizes this plan, she can cooperatively respond by performing the requested action (assuming of course that she is able to do so and has no reason to prefer not doing so). That is, she may reply by saying "At 12:30" rather than by saying simply "Yes."

Usually communicative plans are performed as part of larger plans, and it is often necessary for a hearer to infer these larger plans as well. In the current example if the attendant recognizes that the speaker's communicative plan is likely to be part of a plan to go to Detroit, she may be able to provide the speaker with additional information that will facilitate her goal. She may, for example, tell her what gate the train departs from or she may critique her plan, telling her that although the next train to Detroit leaves in 15 minutes, it is a local train, and the express that leaves in 45 minutes will get her to her destination sooner.

Plan recognition is thus important to responding appropriately to a speaker's utterances in interactive discourse.[13] It is also important to understanding the coherence of multiclause utterances. Consider a different person, who says to the information-booth attendant, "I'm going to Detroit. Where's gate 7?" It is by recognizing what plan the speaker may have that the attendant can determine why the speaker's utterance is coherent; indeed plan recognition enables the attendant to understand the utterance fully. It is essential to be able to understand the coherence of multiclause utterances in noninteractive as well as in interactive discourse. In fact several studies of plan recognition have focused on story understanding, an essentially noninteractive form of discourse (Bruce 1981, Wilensky 1983).

The Basic Technique
As noted in the previous subsection, the idea that language use should be viewed as purposeful action led to models of discourse that make use of techniques already developed for reasoning about (nonlinguistic) actions. In particular the representation of plans and actions used in most plan-recognition systems is a direct outgrowth of the representation first developed in the STRIPS system (Fikes and Nilsson 1971) and later expanded in the NOAH system (Sacerdoti 1977). Because the STRIPS representation has certain limitations in expressiveness, there has been since the mid-1980s a resurgence in interest in the plan formation process, and a number of alternative representation schemes have been devised.[14] However, the basic plan recognition techniques have been developed for STRIPSlike representations of actions.

In these representations states of the world are modeled as sets of propositions, and actions are modeled with *operators* that map one state of the world to another. Each operator has a *header*, which names the action being represented, a *precondition list*, which describes what propositions must be true for the action to be performed, and an *effect list*, which describes what becomes true as a result of performing the action. A *plan* is analyzed as a sequence of actions and states of the world. Specifically $[\alpha_1, S_1, \ldots, S_{n-1}, \alpha_n]$ is a plan to transform a state S_0 to a state S_n provided that

· all the preconditions of α_1 are true in S_0;

· all the effects of α_n are true in S_n;

· in each intermediate state S_i all the effects of α_i and all of the preconditions of α_{i+1} are true.

Plan formation is the process of finding a plan that transforms the current state of the world into a state in which some set of goals are true. In the simplest case plan formation can be cast as a *graph-search* process, in which the nodes of the graph represent actions or states of the world, and legal connections between nodes are determined by the relations between states and actions specified in the set of operators (see chapter 7 of Nilson 1980).

This simple view can be refined by allowing each operator to include a *body* as well as a precondition and an effect list. The body of an operator may be either a list of subactions whose performance constitutes performance of the action named in the header or a list of subgoals whose achievement constitutes performance of the header action. When operators include bodies, the plan formation process may be *hierarchical*: a sequence of actions and intermediate states that are relatively abstract can first be sought and then elaborated into more and more detailed plans. Hierarchical plan formation is often much more efficient than linear plan formation (Sacerdoti 1977, Stefik 1981, Tate 1984, Wilkins 1984).[15]

In plan recognition one agent observes another agent perform some action or sequence of actions and then attempts to determine what plan the latter agent is carrying out. In discourse the observed actions are the utterances of a speaker;[16] thus we can let S (for speaker) denote the actor whose plan is being inferred, and H (for hearer) denote the agent who is inferring S's plan. Suppose H observes S perform some action α in a state S_1 in which all of the preconditions of α are true. Then H may conclude that S's purpose in performing α is to bring about one or more of α's effects. Indeed H may be able to reason further. If some effect of α, say e, is a precondition of some other action β, then H may conclude that S intends to perform β. The process may again be iterated: H may conclude that S intends to achieve some effect of β, and so on. Typically this reasoning process terminates when H determines that S intends to achieve some typical domain goal.

One of the earliest and most influential formulations of plan recognition was by Allen (1979, 1983). Allen provided a set of plan-recognition rules, along with a heuristic strategy for controlling their application. A typical plan-recognition rule is the Action-Effect Rule:

$\text{Bel}(H, \text{Int}(S,\alpha)) \rightarrow \text{Bel}(H, \text{Int}(S,e))$ if e is an effect of α.

This rule can be glossed as "if the hearer (or more generally the inferring agent) believes that the speaker (or more generally the actor) intends to perform some action α, then the hearer may decide that the speaker intends to make some proposition e be true, if e is an effect of performing α (in the state of the world in which α will be performed)."[17]

An assumption of intentionality is necessary for the plan-recognition process to begin. That is, given that H observes S perform some action α, the Action-Effect Rule only applies if H concludes that S did α intentionally. An assumption of intentionality is not problematic in cases in which the plan recognition is being performed in conversation: if S says something to H, it is quite reasonable for H to suppose that S's utterance was intentional.

Other rules link propositions to actions of which they are preconditions and link subactions to actions containing them. These rules, plus the rule discussed, are used for so-called *forward-chaining*: reasoning from an observed action to effects of that action, and from those effects to further actions that are thereby made possible, and so on. Plan-recognition systems typically also include rules for *backward-chaining*. An inferring agent can also reason about what goals an actor is likely to have and backward from that to reason about what actions would achieve those goals, what the preconditions of those actions are, and so forth. Allen's Effect-Action Rule is one example of a plan inference rule to be used in backward-chaining:

$$\text{Bel}(H, \text{Int}(S,e)) \rightarrow \text{Bel}(H, \text{Int}(S,\alpha)) \qquad \text{if } e \text{ is an effect of } \alpha.$$

In addition to the simple forward- and backward-chaining rules, many plan-recognition systems have additional rules that apply only to information-seeking actions. For example, many systems relate the action of "finding out whether p," for some proposition p, to the action of "achieving p." These rules, along with rules for handling so-called nested plan inference, however, can be viewed as special cases of the simpler rules (Kautz 1985).

It is important to note that the plan-inference rules are not to be construed as logical entailments but rather as descriptions of "likely" but nondeductive inferences that an agent may make in performing plan recognition. Kautz (1988) presents a precise formalization of the process of using these likely inference principles to perform plan recognition, providing model, proof, and algorithmic theories that are founded on McCarthy's theory of circumscription (McCarthy 1980, 1984).

The application of plan-inference rules is typically controlled by a set of heuristics, which are designed both to make the recognition process more efficient and to ensure that more plausible plans are found before less plausible ones. Some of the control heuristics are based on commonsense notions about the nature of plans and apply equally well to the process of inferring the plans of one's conversational partner and inferring the plans of another agent whom one is merely observing. For example, one such heuristic biases a plan-recognition system against consideration of candidate plans that contain actions whose effects are true at the time that the action is to be performed. This heuristic is reasonable whether or not the plan-recognition process is taking place in discourse: in general plans do not contain superfluous actions.

In contrast a number of important control heuristics are only justified for plan recognition in conversation because they are founded on the Gricean notion of *intended recognition*: that speakers intend for their hearers to recognize at least some subset of their intentions. This idea motivates plan-recognition heuristics such as the *forking heuristic*, which asserts that the likelihood that a candidate plan is the one that the speaker actually intends is inversely proportional to the number of alternatives into which it can be expanded (Allen 1983), and the *single-branch assumption*, which asserts that if the speaker believes that more than one plan might be inferred at some stage of the discourse, it is her responsibility to make known the one she intends—hearers need only infer to the point of a potential split (Sidner 1985). Such heuristics mediate against difficult inferences on the assumption that speakers in general attempt to produce utterances that facilitate relatively simple plan recognition.

As just one example of the application of the basic technique for plan recognition in discourse, consider a traveler who says, "When does the next train to Detroit leave?" Following Allen, we can encode this utterance action as

REQUEST(S, H, INFORM-REF(S, H, time1)).

That is, S has requested H to inform her of the reference of some constant time1, which happens to denote the departure time of the next train to Detroit.[18] By applying the Action-Effect Rule to the REQUEST operator

Header: REQUEST(Agent1, Agent2, Action)

Effect: WANT(Agent2, DO(Agent2, Action))

H can conclude that S may want H to want to inform S of the Detroit train's departure time. Further reasoning allows H ultimately to infer the entire plan shown in figure 11.1.[19]

The arcs of the plan graph have been labeled with forward-chaining plan-inference rules, but of course some portion of the graph might actually have been found using backward-chaining. A number of additional operators are also necessary for inferring this plan. One is the BOARD operator; construction of the others is left as an exercise for the reader.

Header: BOARD(Agent, Train, Station)

Precondition: AT(Agent, dept-loc(Train), dept-time(Train))

Effect: ON-BOARD(Agent, Train)

Extensions to the Basic Technique
The basic technique for plan recognition has several limitations. Perhaps most striking is the fact that it is restricted to cases in which the inferring agent makes a single observation. When applied to discourse, this means that the basic technique is useful for reasoning only about single-clause utterances. But one of the defining features of discourses is that they are extended in time. Speakers convey information using several clauses and in interactive discourse using several utterances (or "turns").

Incremental recognition techniques have been developed to extend the basic technique for plan recognition to deal with sequences of utterances (Carberry 1988, Sidner 1983, 1985). In incremental recognition the sys-

AT (S,detroit)

↑ action-effect

TRAVEL-TO (S,detroit,train1)

↑ precondition-action

ON-BOARD (S,train1)

↑ action-effect

BOARD (S,train1,detroit)

↑ precondition-action

AT (S,locl,time1)

↑ action-effect

GOTO (S,loc1,time1)

↑ precondition-action

KNOW-REF (S,time1)

↑ action-effect

INFORM-REF (S,H,time1)

↑ precondition-action

WANT (H,INFORM-REF(S,H,time1))

↑ action-effect

REQUEST (S,H,INFORM-REF(S,H,time1))

time1 = dept-time (train 1)

loc1 = dept-loc (train 1)

Figure 11.1 A plan to board a train

tem playing H's role, begins by using the basic technique to infer as much as possible from S's first (discourse-initial) utterance. It may not be possible yet to determine which of several plans S is pursuing, and it may not be possible to determine what S's plan is to a level of detail sufficient to respond appropriately. The interim result thus may be a set of candidate partial plans. Once these have been computed, processing is suspended. Upon hearing each subsequent utterance, the system attempts to expand as many of the already constructed partial plans as possible. The expansion process again makes use of the basic technique: plan-inference rules are used to relate some node of an existing subgraph to the action performed by making the utterance and then to reason from that action to other actions. It may prove impossible to expand certain of the existing subgraphs: these are then eliminated from consideration.

Incremental plan recognition can be made more efficient by taking into account the speaker's focus of attention. As we noted in section 11.2, in task-oriented dialogues at least, the structure of the task influences the structure of the discourse. When a speaker is talking about a plan to perform some task, she is not likely to skip around in the presentation, talking first about some subtask, then about another, then returning to the first, and so on. Rather at each point in the discourse, some portion of the speaker's overall plan will be more salient than others, and the speaker's utterances are most likely to concern the salient portion. This idea can be used to constrain the plan-recognition process: H can prefer to expand those portions of candidate subplans that are in focus to those that are not (Carberry 1988, Litman and Allen 1989).[20]

It is often necessary in discourse processing to recognize several related plans that a speaker is executing. In particular speakers often interrupt their discussion of some domain plan to execute a discourse plan, for example, inviting clarification or correcting an earlier misconception, with the execution of domain plans. In the following dialogue, adapted from one in Litman and Allen 1989, the passenger engages in a plan to clarify the information he has already received in the midst of carrying out his plan to determine the departure time and location of a particular train:

Passenger: The train to Montreal?

Clerk: Gate seven.

Passenger: Where is it?

Clerk: Down this way. Second one on the left.

Passenger: And what time does it leave?

Clerk: Nine o'clock.

Additional operators that represent discourse plans can be introduced. Litman has proposed the use of a stack of partial plans in plan recognition: representations of discourse plans are to be stacked on top of the representations of the domain plans on which they depend (Litman and Allen 1989).

A further difficulty arises when the observed behavior is the result of two or more interacting domain plans. Wilensky (1983) has proposed handling such cases by providing the inferring agent with a set of *metaplans* that operate on other domain plans to construct more complex plans: *resolve-conflicts* is one example of such a meta-plan.[21] In noninteractive text there is also a problem in reasoning about the interactions among the separate plans of multiple agents, for example, the characters in a story; this problem has been studied in detail by Bruce and colleagues (Bruce 1981).

Another kind of restriction inherent in the standard model of plan recognition has been pointed out by Pollack (1986, 1988): it assumes that the inferring agent (*H*) and the actor (*S*) have extremely similar beliefs about the domain of action. Consider again the Action-Effect plan-inference rule. It was glossed as "if the *H* believes that the *S* intends to perform some action α, then the *H* may decide that the *S* intends to make some proposition *e* be true, if *e* is an effect of performing α." Note that this rule leaves unstated precisely who it is—*H* or *S*—that believes that *e* is a precondition of α. If we take this to be a belief of *H*, it is not clear that *H* will infer *S*'s plan; on the other hand if we consider it to be a belief of *S*, it is unclear how *H* comes to have direct access to it. In practice there is only a single set of operators relating preconditions and actions in standard models of plan recognition; the belief in question is regarded as being both *H*'s and *S*'s.

In many situations an assumption that the relevant beliefs of *S* are identical to those of *H* results in failure not only of the plan-recognition process but also of the communicative process that plan recognition is meant to support. In particular it precludes the principled generation of appropriate responses to queries that arise from invalid plans. Pollack (1986, 1988) has proposed a model of plan recognition in conversation that distinguishes between the beliefs of *S* and those of *H*. The model rests on an analysis of plans as mental phenomena: "having a plan" is analyzed as having a particular configuration of beliefs and intentions. The plan-recognition process can take advantage of diverse techniques of belief ascription. Judgments that a plan is invalid are associated with particular discrepancies between the beliefs that *H* ascribes to *S*, when *H* believes that *S* has some plan, and *H*'s own beliefs.

Furthermore discourse participation may require an ability to represent the joint plans of multiple agents. Grosz and Sidner (1989) have shown that such plans cannot be defined solely in terms of the private plans of individual agents. They have proposed a representation that extends Pollack's definition of a plan to the plans of two or more agents as they collaborate on a task and communicate in discourse.

One other recent trend in plan recognition in discourse has been to relate more closely speech-act theories with fundamental theories of rational action. Cohen and Levesque (1989) have shown that illocutionary acts, such as requesting or promising, need not be treated as primitives in a model of plan recognition in discourse; instead the proper behavior of the discourse participants can be analyzed in terms of a model of rational principles of belief and intention adoption. Similarly Perrault (1989) has shown how an account of speech acts can be based on a simple theory of belief adoption and action observation. Like Cohen and Levesque, Perrault avoids the need for treating illocutionary acts as primitives in the model. His theory differs in making use of Reiter's (1980) default logic, which allows him to present axioms that are more context independent.

Notes

1. Story grammars as the basis of processing have been widely criticized; Levy's (1979) article on discourse structure and syntax contains a good summary.

2. The tree is taken to be analogous to parse trees for individual sentences. In a previous paper (Grosz and Sidner 1986) we argue that the embedding (or constituency) relationships represented in the tree are derived from the stack behavior of attentional state.

3. Hobbs (1985) argues that not only are cue phrases used by speakers to signal discourse structure, but that attempts to insert them in a complete discourse can prove useful for an analyst attempting to discern its structure.

4. This emphasis differs from that of much of American linguistics, in which the constraints that prevent cospecification of pronouns have been central (see, for example, Reinhart's (1983) and Lasnik's (1976) research on pronominal anaphora).

5. We use *anaphora* and *anaphoric* here to refer to those phrases that refer to entities that have been mentioned previously in the discourse and that cospecify (compare Sidner 1983) with some phrase occurring previously in the discourse.

6. For this system discourse-segment purposes were approximated by tasks and subtasks.

7. *Deixis*, from the Greek for "pointing," is used to refer to demonstrative phrases (for example, *this book* and *that*) and to other linguistic constructs whose interpretation similarly involves pointing at some circumstance of the utterance (for example, *here* and *now*).

8. This view contrasts with that of Halliday and Hasan (1976), who view ellipsis as a form of textual substitution.

9. Nonnatural meanings include the sort of meanings conveyed in language and are to be distinguished from natural meanings, for example, that smoke "means" fire.

10. For examples of systems attempting keyhole recognition, see Fischer et al. 1985, Genesereth 1979, McCue and Lesser 1983, and Schmidt et al. 1978.

11. The work of Austin and of Searle has also been tremendously influential outside of AI, inspiring an entire field of research called *speech-act theory*, with practitioners in each of the major disciplines of cognitive science. Levinson (1983, chapter 5) provides a good overview of work in speech act theory. See also the papers in Cohen, Morgan, and Pollack (1989).

12. Examples from the "train-station" domain have been widely discussed in the literature. They were inspired by a set of dialogues recorded at the Toronto train-station information booth (Horrigan 1977). The particular example described here was first analyzed by Allen (1983).

13. Appropriate response generation may also depend on distinguishing between intended responses and unintended (though still helpful) responses (Sidner 1983, 1985).

14. Georgeff (1987) provides a good overview of these recent developments; Georgeff and Lansky (1986a) have edited a collection of relevant papers.

15. Rosenschein (1981) provides a logical analysis of hierarchical plans; Wilkins (1985)

clarifies a number of important distinctions that should be made among hierarchical planning processes.

16. Of course here, as throughout this chapter, we mean by "speaker" any agent who is producing language, whether that language is spoken or written.

17. Actually a rule such as the Action-Effect Rule is used to infer not just that S intends to make e true, but that S intends to bring about e by doing α—that is, that S's plan includes the subsequence $[\alpha,e]$.

18. Allen's encoding of speech acts derives largely from Cohen's formalization of speech-act theory using AI planning notions (Cohen and Perrault 1979).

19. Most of the operators shown in figure 11.1 should be self-explanatory. KNOW-REF (agent, value) should be understood as "the agent knows the reference of (or the value of) the constant." Arguments to the operators that are capitalized (except S and H) are variables; arguments in lowercase are constants.

20. Linguistic indicators of discourse structure, such as *cue phrases,* can also be used to constrain incremental recognition; see section 11.3 for a discussion of such indicators.

21. Recent work in plan formation has also incorporated the idea of meta-plans such as these; see, for example, Georgeff and Lansky 1986b.

References

Allen, J. F. 1979. *A Plan-Based Approach to Speech Act Recognition.* Technical report 131, University of Toronto, Toronto, Canada.

Allen, J. F. 1983. Recognizing intentions from natural language utterances. In M. Brady and R. C. Berwick, eds. *Computational Models of Discourse.* Cambridge, MA: MIT Press, pp. 107–166.

Allen, J. F., and Perrault, C. R. 1980. Analyzing intention in dialogues. *Artificial Intelligence* 15(3):143–178.

Appelt, D., and Kronfeld, A. 1987. A computational model of referring. In *Proceedings of the Tenth International Joint Conference on Artificial Intelligence,* Milan, pp. 640–647.

Austin, J. L. 1962. *How to Do Things with Words.* 2nd ed. Cambridge, MA: Harvard University Press.

Bobrow, D., and the PARC Understander Group. 1977. Gus, a frame driven dialog system. *Artificial Intelligence* 8:155–173.

Bruce, B. 1981. Plans and social action. In *Theoretical Issues in Reading Comprehension.* Hillsdale, NJ: Lawrence Erlbaum.

Butterworth, B. 1975. Hesitation and semantic planning in speech. *Journal of Psycholinguistic Research* 4:75–87.

Carberry, M. S. 1985. A pragmatics based approach to understanding intersentential ellipsis. In *Proceedings of the 23rd Annual Meeting of the Association for Computational Linguistics*, Chicago, pp. 188–197.

Carberry, M. S. 1988. Pragmatic modeling: Toward a robust natural language interface. *Computational Intelligence* 3.

Chafe, W. L. 1979. The flow of thought and the flow of language. In T. Givon, ed. *Syntax Semantics 12: Discourse and Syntax*. New York: Academic Press, pp. 159–182.

Chafe, W. L. 1980. The deployment of consciousness in the production of a narrative. In *The Pear Stories: Cognitive, Cultural and Linguistic Aspects of Narrative Production*. Norwood, NJ: Ablex, pp. 9–10.

Charniak, E. 1977. A framed painting: The representation of commonsense knowledge fragment. *Cognitive Science* 1(4).

Cohen, P. R., and Levesque, H. 1989. Rational interaction as the basis for communication. In P. R. Cohen, J. L. Morgan, and M. E. Pollack, eds. *Intentions in Communication*. Cambridge, MA: MIT Press.

Cohen, P. R., Morgan, J. L., and Pollack, M. E., eds. 1989. *Intentions in Communication*. Cambridge, MA: MIT Press.

Cohen, P. R., and Perrault, C. R. 1979. Elements of a plan-based theory of speech acts. *Cognitive Science* 3:177–212.

Cohen, R. 1984. A computational theory of the function of clue words in argument understanding. In *Proceedings of COLING84*, Stanford, CA.

Cohen, R. 1987. Analyzing the structure of argumentative discourse. *Computational Linguistics* 13(1–2).

Cullingford, R. E. 1977. Script application: Computer understanding of newspaper stories. Doctoral dissertation, Yale University, New Haven, CT.

Cullingford, R. E. 1981. Sam. In *Inside Computer Understanding: Five Programs Plus Miniatures*. Hillsdale, NJ: Erlbaum, pp. 75–119.

Dahl, D. A. 1987. Nominalizations in *PUNDIT*. In *Proceedings of the 25th Annual Meeting of the Association for Computational Linguistics*, Stanford, CA, pp. 131–139.

Donnellan, K. S. 1966. *Reference and Definite Descriptions*. Vol. 75. Reprinted in Steinberg and Jacobovits, eds. *Semantics*. Cambridge, Engl.: Cambridge University Press.

Fikes, R. E., and Nilsson, N. J. 1971. STRIPS: a new approach to the application of theorem proving to problem solving. *Artificial Intelligence* 2:189–208.

Fillmore, C. J. 1975. *Santa Cruz Lectures on Deixis*. Technical report, Indiana Linguistics Club, Bloomington, IN.

Finin, T. 1980. *The Semantic Interpretation of Compound Nominals*. Ph.D. thesis, University of Illinois, Urbana, IL.

Fischer, G., Lemke, A., and Schwab, T. 1985. Knowledge-based help systems. In *Pro-

ceedings of the CHI'85 Conference on Human Factors in Computing Systems, ACM SIGCHI, San Francisco, pp. 161–167.

Genesereth, M. R. 1979. The role of plans in automated consultation. In *Proceedings of the 6th International Joint Conference on Artificial Intelligence*, Tokyo, pp. 311–319.

Georgeff, M. P. 1987. Planning. In J. Traub, ed. *Annual Review of Computer Science*. Palo Alto, CA: Annual Reviews.

Georgeff, M. P., and Lansky, A. L. 1986a. *Reasoning about Actions and Plans: Proceedings of the 1986 Workshop*. Los Altos, CA: Morgan Kaufmann.

Georgeff, M. P., and Lansky, A. L. 1986b. Procedural knowledge. *Proceedings of the IEEE, Special Issue on Knowledge Representation*, pp. 1383–1398.

Grice, H. P. 1957. Meaning. *Philosophical Review 67*.

Grice, H. P. 1968. Utterer's meaning, sentence-meaning, and word-meaning. *Foundations of Language*, 4:1–18.

Grice, H. P. 1975. Logic and conversation. In P. Cole and J. L. Morgan, eds. *Syntax and Semantics Vol. 3: Speech Acts*. New York: Academic Press, pp. 41–58.

Grice, H. P. 1978. Further notes on logic and conversation. In P. Cole, ed. *Syntax and Semantics Vol. 9: Pragmatics*. New York: Academic Press, pp. 113–128.

Grosz, B. [Deutsch]. 1974. The structure of task oriented dialogs. In *IEEE Symposium on Speech Recognition: Contributed Papers*, IEEE. Pittsburgh: Carnegie Mellon University, Computer Science Dept.

Grosz, B. J. 1977 (July). The representation and use of focus in a system for understanding dialogs. In *Proceedings of the Fifth International Joint Conference on Artificial Intelligence*, Cambridge, MA.

Grosz, B. J. 1978a. Discourse analysis. In D. Walker, ed. *Understanding Spoken Language*. Ch. IX. New York: Elsevier North-Holland, pp. 235–268.

Grosz, B. J. 1978b. Focusing in dialog. In *Proceedings of Workshop on Theoretical Issues in Natural Language Processing-2*, Urbana, IL.

Grosz, B. J. 1981. Focusing and description in natural language dialogues. In A. K. Joshi, I. Sag, and B. Webber, eds. *Elements of Discourse*. Cambridge, Engl.: Cambridge University Press.

Grosz, B. J., Joshi, A. K., and Weinstein, S. 1983. Providing a unified account of definite noun phrases in discourse. In *Proceedings of the 9th International Joint Conference on Artificial Intelligence*, Cambridge, MA.

Grosz, B. J., and Sidner, C. L. 1986. Attention, intentions, and the structure of discourse. *Computational Linguistics* 12(3).

Grosz, B. J., and Sidner, C. 1989. Plans for discourse. In Cohen, Morgan, and Pollack, eds. *Intentions in Communication*. Cambridge, MA: MIT Press.

Guenthner, F., Lehmann, H., and Schoenfeld, W. 1986. A theory for the representation of knowledge. *IBM Journal of Research and Development* 30(1):39–56.

Haddock, N. J. 1987. Incremental interpretation and combinatory categorial grammar. In N. Haddock, E. Klein, and G. Morril, eds. *Edinburgh Working Papers in Cognitive Science, Vol. 1: Categorial Grammar, Unificiation Grammar and Parsing*. Edinburgh, Scotland, pp. 71–84.

Halliday, M., and Hasan, R. 1976. *Cohesion in English*. English Language Series, Title No. 9. London: Longman's.

Heim, I. 1982. The semantics of definite and indefinite noun phrases. Ph.D. dissertation University of Massachusetts, Amherst, MA.

Hendrix, G., Sarcedoti, E., Sagalowicz, D., and Slocum, J. 1978. Developing a natural language interface to complex data. *ACM Trans. on Database Sys.* 3(2).

Hinrichs, E. 1986. Temporal anaphora in discourses of English. *Linguistics and Philosophy* 1(9).

Hirschberg, J. B., and Pierrehumbert, J. 1986. The intonational structuring of discourse. In *Proceedings of the 24th Annual Meeting of the Association for Computational Linguistics*, New York, pp. 136–144.

Hirschberg, J. B., and Litman, D. J. 1987. Now let's talk about now: Identifying cue phrases intonationally. In *Proceedings of the 25th Annual Meeting of the Association for Computational Linguistics*, Stanford, CA, pp. 163–171.

Hirschberg, J. B., Litman, D. J., Pierrehumbert, J., and Ward, G. L. 1987. Intonation and the intentional structure of discourse. In *Proceedings of the Tenth International Joint Conference on Artificial Intelligence*, Milan, Italy, pp. 636–639.

Hobbs, J. 1979. Coherence and co-reference. *Cognitive Science* 1:67–82.

Hobbs, J. 1983. Why is discourse coherent? In F. Neubauer, ed., *Coherence in Natural Language Texts*. Hamburg: H. Buske Verlag.

Hobbs, J. R. 1985. *On the Coherence and Structure of Discourse*. Technical report CSLI-85-37, Center for the Study of Language and Information, Stanford, CA.

Hobbs, J., and Martin P. 1987. Local pragmatics. In *Proceedings of the 10th International Conference on Artificial Intelligence*, Milan, Italy.

Horrigan, M. K. 1977. *Modelling simple dialogues*. Technical report TR 108, Dept. of Computer Science, University of Toronto, Toronto, Ontario.

Isabelle, P. 1984. Another look at nominal compounds. In *Proceedings of the Tenth International Conference on Computational Linguistics*, Stanford, CA, pp. 509–516.

Joshi, A., and Weinstein, S. 1981. Control of inference: Role of some aspects of discourse structured-centering. In *Proceedings of International Joint Conference on Artificial Intelligence*, Vancouver, BC, pp. 385–387.

Kamp, H. 1981. A theory of truth and semantic representation. In J. Groenendijk, T.

Janssen, and M. Stokhof, eds. *Formal Methods in the Study of Language*. MC TRACT 135, Amsterdam, The Netherlands.

Kautz, H. A. 1985. *Toward a Theory of Plan Recognition*. Technical report TR162, University of Rochester, Rochester, NY.

Kautz, H. A. 1988. A circumscriptive theory of plan recognition. In P. R. Cohen, J. L. Morgan, and M. E. Pollack, eds. *Intentions in Communication*. Cambridge, MA: MIT Press.

Kendon, A. 1972. Some relationships between body motion and speech. In *Studies in Dyadic Communication*. New York: Pergamon.

Kronfeld, A. 1986 (June). Donnellan's distinction and a computational model of reference. In *Proceedings of the 24th Annual Meeting of the Association for Computational Linguistics*. New York: Association for Computational Linguistics.

Lasnik, H. 1976. Remarks on co-reference. *Linguistic Analysis* 2(1):1–22.

Lehnert, W. 1977. A conceptual theory of question answering. In *Proceedings of the Fifth International Joint Conference on Artificial Intelligence*. Palo Alto, CA: Morgan Kaufman.

Lehnert, W. G. 1981. Plot units and narrative summarization. *Cognitive Science* 5(4):291–331.

Levinson, S. C. 1983. *Pragmatics*. Cambridge, Engl.: Cambridge University Press.

Levy, D. M. 1979. Communicative goals and strategies: Between discourse and syntax. In T. Givon, ed. *Discourse and Syntax*. New York: Academic Press, pp. 183–210.

Linde, C. 1979. Focus of attention and the choice of pronouns in discourse. In T. Govon, ed. *Syntax and Semantics*. New York: Academic Press, pp. 337–354.

Linde, C., and Goguen, J. 1978. Structure of planning discourse. *J. Social Biol. Struct.* 1:219–251.

Litman, D. 1985. *Plan Recognition and Discourse Analysis: An Integrated Approach for Understanding Dialogues*. Technical report TR170, University of Rochester, Rochester, NY.

Litman, D. J., and Allen, J. F. 1987. A plan recognition model for subdialogues in conversations. *Cognitive Science* 11:163–200.

Litman, D. J., and Allen J. F. 1989. Discourse processing and commonsense plans. In P. R. Cohen, J. L. Morgan, and M. E. Pollack, eds. *Intentions in Communication*. Cambridge, MA: MIT Press.

Mann, W. C., Moore, M. A., Levin, J. A., and Carlisle, J. H. 1975. *Observation Methods for Human Dialogue*. Technical report, Information Services Institute, Marina del Rey, CA.

Mann, W. D., and Thompson, S. A. 1986. Relational propositions in discourse. *Discourse Processes* 9(1):57–90.

Marslen-Wilson, W., Levy, E., and Tyler, L. K. 1982. Producing interpretable discourse: The establishment and maintenance of reference. In *Speech, Place, and Action*. Chichester, Engl.: Wiley.

McCarthy, J. 1980. Circumscription—a form of non-monotonic reasoning. *Artificial Intelligence* 13:27–39.

McCarthy, J. 1984. Applications of circumscription to formalizing common sense knowledge. In *Proceedings of the AAAI Workshop on Nonmonotonic Reasoning*, New Paltz, NY, pp. 295–324.

McCue, D., and Lesser, V. 1983. *Focusing and Constraint Management in Intelligent Interface Design*. Technical report COINS 83-36, University of Massachusetts, Amherst, MA.

McDonald, D. D. 1983. Natural language generation as a computation problem. In *Computational Models of Discourse*, Cambridge, MA: MIT Press.

McKeown, K. 1985. *Text Generation*. New York: Cambridge University Press.

McNeill, D. 1979. *The Conceptual Basis of Language*. Hillsdale, NJ: Erlbaum.

McNeill, D., and Levy, E. 1982. Conceptual representations in language activity and gesture. In *Speech, Place, and Action*. Chichester, Engl.: Wiley.

Mellish, C. S. 1982. *Incremental Evaluation: An Approach to the Semantic Interpretation of Noun Phrases*. Technical Report, University of Sussex Cognitive Studies Programme, Sussex, Engl.

Nilsson, N. J. 1980. *Principles of Artificial Intelligence*. Palo Alto, CA: Tioga.

Partee, B. H. 1984. Nominal and temporal anaphora. *Linguistics and Philosophy* 7:243–286.

Perrault, C. R., and Allen, J. F. 1980. A plan-based analysis of indirect speech acts. *American Journal of Computational Linguistics* 6:167–182.

Perrault, C. R. 1989. An application of default logic to speech act theory. In P. R. Cohen, J. L. Morgan, and M. E. Pollack, eds. *Intentions in Communication*. Cambridge, MA: MIT Press.

Polanyi, L. 1986. *The Linguistic Structure of Discourse: Towards a Formal Theory of Discourse Structure*. Technical report 6489, Bolt, Berenek and Neuman, Cambridge, MA.

Polanyi, L., and Scha, R. 1984. A syntactic approach to discourse semantics. In *Proceedings of the 10th International Conference on Computational Linguistics*, Stanford, CA: pp. 413–419.

Polanyi, L. 1985. A theory of discourse structure and discourse coherence. In W. Eilfort, P. Kroerber, and K. Peterson, eds. *Proceedings of the 21st Regional Meeting of the Chicago Linguistics Society*. Chicago: University of Chicago Press, pp. 306–322.

Pollack, M. E. 1986 (June). A model of plan inference that distinguishes between the beliefs of actors and observers. In *Proceedings of the 24th Annual Meeting of the Association for Computational Linguistics*, Association for Computational Linguistics, New York, pp. 207–214.

Pollack, M. E. 1988. Plan as complex mental attitudes. In P. R. Cohen, J. Morgan, and M. E. Pollack, eds. *Intentions in Communication*. Cambridge, MA: MIT Press.

Pollack, M. E., and Pereira, F. C. N. 1988. An integrated framework for semantic and pragmatic interpretation. In *Proceedings of the 26th Annual Meeting of the Association for Computational Linguistics*, Buffalo, NY.

Reichman-Adar, R. 1984 (Mar). Extended person-machine interface. *Artificial Intelligence* 22(2):157–218.

Reinhart, T. 1983. Co-reference and bound anaphora: A restatement of the anaphora question. *Linguistics and Philosophy* 6:47–88.

Reiter, R. 1980. A logic for default reasoning. *Artificial Intelligence* 13:81–132.

Robinson, A. 1981. Determining verb phrase referents in dialogs. *Computational Linguistics* 7(1).

Rosenschein, S. J. 1981. Plan synthesis: a logical perspective. In *Proceedings of the 7th International Joint Conference on Artificial Intelligence*. IJCAI, Vancouver, BC, pp. 331–337.

Rumelhart, D. E. 1975. Notes on a schema for stories. In D. G. Bobrow and A. Collins, eds. *Representation and Understanding*. New York: Academic Press.

Sacerdoti, E. D. 1977. *A Structure for Plans and Behavior*. New York: American Elsevier.

Schiffrin, D. 1982. *Discourse Markers: Semantic Resource for the Construction of Conversation*. Ph.D. thesis, University of Pennsylvania, Philadelphia, PA.

Schmidt, C. F., Sridharan, N. S., and Goodson, J. L. 1978. The plan recognition problem: An intersection of artificial intelligence and psychology. *Artificial Intelligence* 10:45–83.

Searle, J. R. 1969. *Speech Acts*. Cambridge, Engl.: Cambridge University Press.

Searle, J. R. 1975. Indirect speech acts. In P. Cole and J. L. Morgan, eds. *Syntax and Semantics Vol. 3: Speech Acts*. New York: Academic Press, pp. 59–82.

Sidner, C. L. 1979 (June). *Towards a Computational Theory of Definite Anaphora Comprehension in English Discourse*. Ph.D. thesis. Technical report 537, Artificial Intelligence Laboratory, Massachusetts Institute of Technology, Cambridge, MA.

Sidner, C. L. 1981. Focusing for interpretation of pronouns. *Computational Linguistics* 7(4):217–231.

Sidner, C. L. 1982. *Protocols of Users Manipulating Visually Presented Information With Natural Language*. Technical report, Bolt, Berenek and Newman, Cambridge, MA.

Sidner, C. L. 1983. What the speaker means: The recognition of speakers' plans in discourse. *International Journal of Computers and Mathematics* 9(1):71–82.

Sidner, C. L. 1985 (Feb). Plan parsing for intended response recognition in discourse. *Computational Intelligence* 1(1):1–10.

Silverman, K. 1987. *Natural Prosody for Synthetic Speech*. Ph.D. thesis, Cambridge University, Cambridge, Engl.

Stefik, M. 1981. Planning with constraints. *Artificial Intelligence* 16:111–140.

Tate, A. 1984. Goalstructure-capturing the intent of plans. In *Proceedings of the Sixth European Conference on Artificial Intelligence*, Pisa, Italy, pp. 273–276.

vanDijk, T. A. 1972. *Some Aspects of Text Grammars*. The Hague: Mouton.

Walker, D. 1978. *Understanding Spoken Language*. New York: Elsevier North-Holland.

Webber, B. L. 1980. *A Computational Approach to Discourse Anaphora*. New York: Garland.

Webber, B. L. 1983. So what can we talk about now. In M. Brady, ed. *Computational Approaches to Discourse*. Cambridge, MA: MIT Press.

Webber, B. L. 1987. The interpretation of tense in discourse. In *Proceedings of the 25th Annual Meeting of the Association for Computational Linguistics*, Association for Computational Linguistics, Stanford, CA, pp. 147–154.

Wilensky, R. 1983. *Planning and Understanding*. Reading, MA: Addison-Wesley.

Wilkins, D. E. 1984. Domain-independent planning: Representation and plan generation. *Artificial Intelligence* 22:269–301.

Wilkins, D. E. 1985. *Hierarchical Planning: Definition and Implementation*. Technical report 370, Artificial Intelligence Center, SRI International, Menlo Park, CA.

Winograd, T. 1971. *Procedures as a Representation for Data in a Computer Program for Understanding Natural Language*. Ph.D. thesis. Report no. TR-84, Project MAC, Massachusetts Institute of Technology, Cambridge, MA.

Winograd, T. 1972. *Understanding Natural Language*. New York: Academic Press.

Woods, W. A. 1978. Semantics and quantification in natural language question answering. In M. Yovits, ed. *Advances in Computers*. New York: Academic Press, pp. 1–87.

Woods, W. A., Kaplan, R. M., and Nash-Webber, B. L. 1972 (June). *The Lunar Sciences Natural Language Information System: Final Report*. BBN Report 2378, Bolt, Beranek and Newman, Cambridge, MA.

12   Mental Models

P. N. Johnson-Laird

The modern formulation of the concept of a mental model is due to Kenneth Craik (1943). In his remarkably prescient book, *The Nature of Explanation*, he argued that human beings translate external events into internal models and reason by manipulating these symbolic representations. They can translate the resulting symbols back into actions or recognize a correspondence between them and external events. Although Craik died before the invention of the programmable digital computer, he would have recognized the computer metaphor. He argued that the physical substrate of the brain is less pertinent than the way it functions. He wrote (Craik 1943, p. 51), "By a model we thus mean any physical or chemical system which has a similar relation-structure to that of the processes it imitates. By 'relation-structure' I do not mean some obscure physical entity which attends the model, but the fact that it is a physical working model which works in the same way as the processes it parallels, in the aspects under consideration at any moment. . . ." Hence for Craik a mental model was preeminently a dynamic representation or simulation of the world. He had little to say about the form of such representations or about the processes that manipulate them. It was bold enough to postulate representations in the heyday of Behaviorism.

Most cognitive scientists following Craik have adopted the basic tenet that the mind is a symbolic system (see, for example, Miller, Galanter, and Pribram 1960, Newell and Simon 1976). And during the 1980s there has been an enormous growth in studies of mental models. These studies are so extraordinarily diverse, however, that they seem to have little in common beyond the bare appeal to symbolic representations of some sort. Thus explanations of visual perception, the comprehension of discourse, reasoning, and the representation of knowledge and expertise have all invoked versions of the mental-model hypothesis. My aim in this chapter is to bring some order to this diversity. Although many writers have gone out of their way to draw distinctions between alternative concepts of mental models, the theories may differ more than they ought to because they nearly all concern the same underlying reality. It is as though explorers keep reporting the existence of a hitherto unknown animal, but their fragmentary glimpses of it convince them that they are observing different creatures.

I begin by sketching the role of models in perception and discourse, but only briefly to avoid trespassing on other chapters in this volume. Next I consider reasoning as a process of manipulating models and then their role as representations of knowledge. Finally I present a critique of the theory of mental models and outline some of the major problems in its development.

12.1 Perception as a Source of Mental Models

A primary source of mental representations is perception. As I argue in my book on mental models (Johnson-Laird 1983), the simplest creatures, such as single-cell organisms, merely react physically to their immediate environment. Paramecia, for instance, bump into an obstacle, and the ensuing chemical changes cause their cilia to beat in the opposite direction. But evolution has produced creatures with a nervous system that detects energy from distant objects and that directly modulates the activity of the neurons controlling stereotyped responses. More complicated creatures use the information impinging on the sensorium to compute an internal representation that in turn is used by the processes controlling action. These internal representations may encode relatively superficial features of the world. The housefly's visual system, for example, controls its flight pattern by way of a representation that probably makes explicit only certain features of the visual field, such as a rapid expansion as the fly approaches a surface (see Reichardt and Poggio 1981). Human vision, as David Marr and his colleagues have emphasized, depends on the construction of a series of symbolic representations culminating in a three-dimensional *model* of the spatial relations among objects (see Marr 1982 and chapter 15). This model makes explicit *what* is *where* to our conscious processes of judgment and thereby enables us to navigate our way through the world avoiding obstacles and hazards.

Our models need to integrate the information from all the senses and from general knowledge—the sights, sounds, smells, and possibilities of the world. Our capacity to envisage different situations appears to be limitless, but the brain cannot contain an infinite number of preexisting symbols no more than a library can contain an infinite number of books. The vast range of mental models must be constructed out of finite means—out of primitive symbols and the basic processes that operate on them. In the case of vision, computational procedures carried out by the brain convert the retinas' response to light into a model of the objects reflecting that light, and these procedures embody constraints based on the nature of the world (Marr 1982). Our phenomenological experience of the world is a triumph of natural selection. We seem to perceive the world directly, not a representation of it. Yet this phenomenology is illusory: what we perceive depends on both what is in the world and what is in our heads—on what evolution has "wired" into our nervous systems and what we know as a result of experience. The limits of our models are the limits of our world.

12.2 Mental Models of Discourse

Wittgenstein (1922, section 4.01) in his celebrated "picture" theory of meaning wrote, "The proposition is a model of reality as we imagine it." When I tell you, say, that there is a table in front of the stove in my kitchen, you can imagine the arrangement even if you cannot see it. A major function of language is thus to enable us to experience the world by proxy, because we can envisage how it is on the basis of a verbal description. The assertion "A table is in front of the stove" establishes a relation between two entities. Hence its model contains two mental tokens, corresponding to the table and the stove, interrelated in a way that corresponds to the spatial relation between them. In short, discourse models make explicit the structure *not* of sentences but of situations as we perceive or imagine them (Johnson-Laird 1983, p. 419).

One reason for believing that people construct models is that the hypothesis explains a central feature of comprehension. The explicit content of a discourse is usually only a blueprint for a state of affairs: it relies on the reader or listener to flesh out the missing details. Such "bridging" inferences are rapid and automatic, and people are seldom aware of them though they may show up in recalling the discourse (see Clark 1977). These inferences sometimes depend on general knowledge, as a number of cognitive scientists have argued (for example, Schank and Abelson 1977, Sanford and Garrod 1981). But the key fact is that they yield conclusions of a sort that would be explicit only in models of situations. Bransford and his colleagues have demonstrated this phenomenon in a number of studies. For example, Bransford, Barclay, and Franks (1972) observed that when subjects were presented with the sentence

Three turtles rested on a floating log and a fish swam beneath them.

they later confused it with

Three turtles rested on a floating log and a fish swam beneath it.

If the subjects had imagined the situation described in the original sentence, constructing a model in which the turtles are on the log and the fish swims beneath it, then the model would also represent the fish as swimming beneath the log. This explanation is corroborated by the lack of any such error when the original sentence yields no such model:

Three turtles rested beside a floating log and a fish swam beneath them.

There is also abundant evidence that the coherence of discourse depends in part on how easy it is to construct a single mental model from it (see Garnham, Oakhill, and Johnson-Laird 1982, Ehrlich and Johnson-Laird 1982, Oakhill and Garnham 1985). Kannan Mani and I have similarly shown that passages calling for a single model of a spatial layout are easier to remember than indeterminate descriptions that are consistent with more than one layout (Mani and Johnson-Laird 1982). Thus the description

The spoon is to the left of the knife.

The plate is to the right of the knife.

The fork is in front of the spoon.

The cup is in front of the knife.

describes the following arrangement of objects:

spoon knife plate
fork   cup

But a change of one word in the second sentence,

The plate is to the right of the spoon.

yields an indeterminate description consistent with two quite different layouts:

spoon knife plate   spoon plate knife
fork   cup   fork   cup

After our subjects had classified a series of determinate and indeterminate descriptions as true or false of diagrams of layouts, they were given an unexpected recognition test of their memory for the descriptions. They retained the gist of the determinate descriptions very much better than the gist of the indeterminate descriptions. Yet they were better at recognizing verbatim details of the indeterminate descriptions. This pattern of results bore out our hypothesis that the subjects would construct a model of a determinate description to compare with a diagram, but try to commit an indeterminate description to memory rather than construct its alternative possible models. It is difficult to see how subjects could even be sensitive to the difference between the two sorts of descriptions unless they attempt to construct models of them.

The existence of two forms of representation—linguistic representations and discourse models—has been corroborated in a number of other experiments. Thus where two expressions with different meanings, such as

the man with the martini

the man standing by the window

occur in contexts in which they refer to the same individual, then as Garnham (1987) has shown, subjects readily confuse the two in an unexpected recognition test of the passage. But subjects who are warned about the recognition test retain their memory for the particular expressions used to refer to individuals. As Garnham points out, the outcome of this experiment is at odds with the idea that discourse is encoded solely in a semantic network or in any other format that represents merely the meanings of expressions. Referents and, in particular, tokens corresponding to individuals, must be independently represented in a discourse model based on the meanings of the expressions, general knowledge, and the prior context established in the model.

The distinction between linguistic representations and discourse models accounts for a variety of linguistic phenomena, notably anaphoric reference (see Sag and Hankamer 1984 and chapter 11). Linguistic representations are expressions in a mental language (Kintsch 1974, Kintsch and van Dijk 1978, Fodor 1975), which can cope with those anaphora that depend on meanings or forms of words. For example, in the discourse

The cats were biting the dogs.

The fleas were too.

the interpretation of the second elliptical sentence requires access to the surface form of the previous sentence. (Compare its interpretation with the one that would occur if the previous sentence had a different surface form: "The dogs were being bitten by the cats." Unless the listener has retained a linguistic representation, these sorts of anaphora are indeed difficult to understand (see Garnham and Oakhill 1987). Other anaphoric expressions, however, refer to entities that have been introduced earlier in the discourse (or by extralinguistic means, such as a gesture). In the discourse

There's a large wooden table in front of the stove.

It has four chairs, one on each side.

the pronoun "it" harks back, not to some form of words but to a particular referent that has been introduced earlier. There is therefore a need to go beyond the linguistic representation of discourse to a model of the situation.

A further reason for postulating discourse models concerns the vexed issue of truth. Theories based solely on linguistic representations do not say anything about how words relate to the world (Johnson-Laird, Herrmann, and Chaffin 1984). Until such relations are established, the question of whether a description is true or false cannot arise. Mental models are symbolic structures, and the relation of a model to the world cannot simply be read off from the model. So how is the truth or falsity of an assertion judged in relation to the world? The answer is that a discourse will be judged true if its mental model can be embedded in the model of the world. Thus, for example, you will judge my remark about the table being in front of the stove as true if it corresponds to your perception of the world, that is, a model based on the assertion can be embedded within a perceptual model of the situation (Johnson-Laird 1983, pp. 247, 441). (You may be in a position to relate the linguistic representation directly to a perceptual model of the world.) The notion of embedding means that the same individuals with the same properties and relations are preserved from one model to the other (see Kamp 1981). Hence when you judge an assertion to be true, you have related either its initial linguistic representation, or a model based on that representation, to a model of the world. And, more important, you know that it is true: you are aware of having made a comparison, and such an awareness in turn depends on a model of your own performance.

Of course much of language goes beyond the perceptible. Some expressions refer directly to mental states, processes, and feelings; there is a vocabulary for referring to one's own internal milieu. Other expressions refer to abstract matters such as possibility, permissibility, and causation (Miller and Johnson-Laird 1976). These abstract concepts relate to scenarios, that is, models of a course of hypothetical or future events (Tversky and Kahneman 1973; Johnson-Laird 1983, pp. 410 et seq), and to conventions that regulate interactions between members of a society (Johnson-Laird 1983, pp. 415 et seq).

The case for discourse models has been advanced in formal semantics (Kamp 1981, Spencer-Smith 1987), in linguistics (Karttunen 1976, Reichgelt 1982, Shadbolt 1983, Fauconnier 1985), in artificial intelligence (Webber 1978, Wilks and Bien 1979), and in psycholinguistics (Stenning 1978, 1986, Johnson-Laird and Garnham 1980, Garnham 1981, 1987, Garnham and Oakhill 1989, van Dijk and Kintsch 1983, Glenberg, Meyer, and Lindem 1987). But there is a major problem for psychological theories. An assertion such as "A table is in front of the stove" can be true of an infinite number of different possible situations. Hence in formal semantics theorists postulate that an assertion has an infinite number of models, or "possible worlds," in which it would be true (see chapter 6). Granted that the mind has only a finite capacity, then an infinite number of models, as Partee (1979) has observed, cannot fit inside anyone's head. One solution to this problem is to assume that the initial linguistic representation of an assertion is used to construct just *one* model (Johnson-Laird 1983, ch. 11), but this model can serve as a representative and provisional sample from the infinite set of all possible models of the assertion. It can stand in for the correct model, presuming that the speaker has a specific state of affairs in mind, because it can be revised in the light of subsequent discourse. I will describe in the next section how the inferential procedure for such revisions could work.

In summary the theory of discourse models is based on three principal ideas:

1. A mental model represents the *reference* of a discourse, that is, the situation that the discourse describes.

2. The initial linguistic representation of a discourse, together with the machinery for constructing and revising discourse models from it, captures the *meaning* of the discourse, that is, the set of all possible situations that it could describe.

3. A discourse is judged to be true if there is at least one model of it that can be embedded in a model of the real world.

12.3 Reasoning and Mental Models

Three Theories of Reasoning

Inference is a systematic process of thought that leads from one set of propositions to another. Granted that the premises may be mentally represented in the form of a model, it is natural to ask how models might enter into inferential processes. The nature of these processes, however, is highly controversial in both artificial intelligence and cognitive psychology. The arguments in the two disciplines are largely independent of one another, but they run in parallel to a remarkable degree. There are the same three main points of view.

The first class of theories assumes that reasoning depends on formal rules of inference, like those of a logical calculus. The use of logic in artificial intelligence has been defended by Hayes (1977), and a variety of formal systems have been implemented (see, for example, Robinson 1979, Reiter 1973). The programming language Prolog is based on the same philosophy (Kowalski 1979). In psychology too there are many theories of reasoning that postulate a "mental logic" consisting of formal rules of inference (see, for example, Inhelder and Piaget 1958, Osherson 1975, Braine 1978, Rips 1983). Formal rules work in a purely syntactic way, and so they are blind to the content of a premise, depending solely on its so-called logical form—a notion that also has currency in linguistic theory (see Chomsky 1977, Hornstein 1986). Unlike such rules, however, people are highly sensitive to the content of premises when they make inferences. Such effects on the inferences of daily life have been independently discovered by workers in both artificial intelligence and cognitive psychology.

On the one hand psychologists have found that the difficulty of a deductive problem, and the nature of the responses to it, can be profoundly affected by its content (see, for example, Wason and Johnson-Laird 1972, Evans 1982). On the other hand there is a hiatus between what is valid in logic and in daily life. Logic, for example, warrants the inference from

If patients have cystitis, then they are given penicillin.

to the conclusion

If patients have cystitis and are allergic to penicillin, then they are given penicillin.

which is clearly an inference that runs counter to common sense. In logic, however, a conditional is treated as true whenever its antecedent is false (or its consequent is true), and so if the premise here is true, the conclusion must be true. Logic is indeed "monotonic" in that the validity of an inference is unaffected no matter what additional premises are added. Various attempts have been made to formulate "nonmonotonic" logics that tally with the inferences of daily life (see, for example, McDermott and Doyle 1980). The problem usually arises from the content of premises, however, not their logical form, and so it is unlikely to be patched up by a formal remedy (Davis 1980). Still worse, many verbal inferences in daily life are not derivable within a formal calculus at all. Some depend on the particular situation to which the premises refer (Johnson-Laird 1983, pp. 240, 261); some are plausible on the basis of general knowledge, but may be overruled by specific information to the contrary (see Minsky 1975, Schank and Abelson 1977); some derive from premises that can never be rendered sufficiently complete to ensure validity (Johnson-Laird 1987); and some are inductions (see chapter 13). The fact that so much reasoning is not deductive has lead one former adherent of formal rules to abandon them (McDermott 1986).

The second class of theories directly recognize the importance of content. They postulate *content-specific* rules of inference. One origin of such theories lies in programming languages, such as PLANNER (Hewitt 1971), and production systems (Newell 1973) that enable general assertions to be expressed in the form of conditional rules, such as

If x is a dog, then x is an animal.

If someone asserts that Fido is a dog, then this rule will be triggered because the assertion matches its antecedent, and it will spring to life to make the further assertion that Fido is an animal. Another rule can be formulated so that given the goal of showing that Fido is an animal, it yields the subgoal of showing that Fido is a dog. Such rules are commonplace in the representation of the knowledge used in so-called expert systems (see chapter 14). These are computer programs that embody human expertise and that are designed to help their users to reach sensible decisions about such matters as medical diagnosis, chemical analysis, or where to drill for minerals. They rely on a large knowledge-base of rules that have been culled from interrogating human experts and on procedures that use these rules to make inferences about specific cases (see, for example, Buchanan and Feigenbaum 1978, Michie 1979, Davis and Lenat 1982, Feigenbaum and McCorduck 1984).

The idea of basing psychological theories of reasoning on content-specific rules was discussed by Johnson-Laird and Wason (1977), and various sorts of such theories have been proposed (see, for example, Anderson 1983, E. R. Smith 1984, Cheng and Holyoak 1985, and Holland, Holyoak, Nisbett, and Thagard 1986). A related idea is that reasoning depends on the accumulation of specific examples within a connectionist framework, where the distinction between inference and recall is blurred (see chapter 4).

The main case for formal rules is that they explain how in principle people can reason about anything regardless of its content, including abstract and unfamiliar domains. The main case for content-specific rules is that they explain how the content of premises affects reasoning. But of course it is necessary to explain both these phenomena, as well as nondeductive inferences, and most relevant here is the third class of theories—those based on mental models. They do not employ rules of inference of any sort, either formal or content-specific, but assume instead that reasoning depends on the manipulation of mental models.

Such theories have been formulated for a variety of domains (see, for example, de Kleer and Brown 1981, Kahneman and Tversky 1982, Johnson-Laird 1983, ch. 5). Some rare individuals appear to have developed a conscious strategy that relies on the technique. As the late Richard Feynman explained (Feynman and Leighton 1985),

I had a scheme, which I still use today when somebody is explaining something that I'm trying to understand: I keep making up examples. For instance, the mathematicians would come in with a terrific theorem, and they're all excited. As they're telling me the conditions of the theorem, I construct something that fits all the conditions. You know, you have a set (one ball)—disjoint (two balls). Then the balls turn colors, grow hairs, or whatever, in my head as they put more conditions on. Finally they state the theorem, which is some dumb thing about the ball which isn't true for my hairy green ball thing, so I say, 'False!'"

The same idea informs theories of reasoning based on mental models, which I illustrate first in terms of syllogistic inference.

Mental Models in Syllogistic Reasoning

Some syllogisms are so easy that even nine-year-old children can draw correct conclusions from them. Thus given the premises

None of the athletes is a beachcomber.

All the clerks are beachcombers.

most people correctly deduce the conclusion

None of the athletes is a clerk.

or its equally valid converse. Other syllogisms, however, are very much harder—so hard in fact that the majority of adults fail to draw a correct conclusion. Given the premises

None of the athletes is a beachcomber.

Some of the clerks are beachcombers.

most people make one of the following erroneous responses:

None of the athletes is a clerk.

None of the clerks is an athlete.

There's no valid conclusion.

Only a few draw the valid conclusion

Some of the clerks are not athletes.

The theory of mental models proposes that the reasoners' first task is to understand the premises and in particular to construct a model of them. Various proposals have been made about the form of such models. Some theorists assume that they are Euler circles, where sets are represented by circles that may or may not overlap (see Erickson 1974, Guyote and Sternberg 1981). One feature of this proposal is that there is no need to introduce a special symbol for negation. Other theorists concur that abstract notions such as negation should be encoded only in linguistic representations (Inder 1987, Jackendoff 1987). Euler circles, however, cannot represent assertions containing more than one quantifier, for example, "*Some* of the athletes know *all* the artists," and they can lead to combinatorial explosions because many premises call for several separate representations. Moreover there is a decisive objection to models that lack abstract elements. They cannot represent such assertions as "Ben knows that his presents weren't left by Santa Claus," because such "propositional attitudes" as the example shows often have a negative content. Another version of mental-model theory therefore makes the important assumption that any propositional attitude can itself be represented by a corresponding component within a mental model (Johnson-Laird 1983, ch. 15). To represent a negative proposition, for example, a special symbol for negation is directly introduced into a model. There is nothing improper about such a maneuvre provided that the routines for evaluating the truth of models have an appropriate procedure for the symbol (see Kamp 1981; Johnson-Laird 1983, pp. 423–442). Indeed Venn diagrams are a traditional notation exploiting just such a device, that is, regions within three overlapping circles are shaded to represent the nonexistence of certain sets (see Newell 1981 for an algorithm for reasoning with Venn diagrams, and Polk and Newell 1988 for a defense of models containing propositional elements).

My colleagues and I have argued that the models used in reasoning are neither Euler circles nor Venn diagrams, because they are remote from the perceived structures of situations. We assume that the models are instead the discourse models discussed in the previous section. The premise

None of the athletes is a beachcomber.

is represented by a model containing an arbitrary number of tokens for athletes and an arbitrary number of tokens for beachcombers that are mentally tagged in some way to indicate that they are disjoint, for example,

athlete
athlete
_____
       beachcomber
       beachcomber
       beachcomber

where the barrier separates the two sets of tokens. (An alternative and perhaps equally plausible representation would tag each individual athlete as not a beachcomber, and vice versa.) The information from the premise

All the clerks are beachcombers.

can be directly added to the model

athlete
athlete
_____
       beachcomber = clerk
       beachcomber = clerk
       (beachcomber)

where the beachcomber who is not a clerk has been tagged with parentheses to represent the possible existence of such individuals.

The second stage of the process is the formulation of a putative conclusion: the model is scanned to determine what relation, if any, holds that is not explicitly stated in the premises. In the present case the procedure readily establishes the conclusion

None of the athletes is a clerk.

or its converse, depending on which direction the model is scanned.

The third stage consists of a search for a counterexample to the putative conclusion. An inference is valid if its conclusion cannot be false, given that its premises are true. Hence validity can be tested by searching for counterexamples—a procedure that has been exploited in logic (see, for example, Beth 1971). There is no need to manipulate the number of individuals for its own sake because it has no bearing on the conclusion. The model has only a finite number of tokens, and there are only a finite number of possible rearrangements of them. Because there is no way of establishing identities between athletes and clerks that does not also violate the premises, the present conclusion is valid. In fact even if no attempt to test it is made, it remains the correct answer.

Matters are very different in the case of the problem in which the second premise is

Some of the clerks are beachcombers.

If the information in this premise is added to the model in the following way:

athlete
athlete
_____
       beachcomber = clerk
       beachcomber = clerk
       (beachcomber) (clerk)

then the model supports the erroneous conclusions

None of the athletes is a clerk.

None of the clerks is an athlete.

which the majority of subjects draw. A search for a counterexample can produce the following model:

athlete   =   (clerk)
athlete   =   (clerk)
_____
       beachcomber = clerk
       beachcomber = clerk
       (beachcomber) (clerk)

Subjects who succeed in constructing it may nevertheless err by deciding that the premises fail to support any definite conclusion. It is necessary to scan the model from clerks to athletes to appreciate that all the possible models of the premises support the conclusion

Some (at least) of the clerks are not athletes.

Can we be certain that subjects follow such principles in reasoning? Higher cognitive processes tend to occur in many different ways, and some individuals may construct an initially misleading model and then revise it, whereas others may appreciate the existence of different possible models right from the start. One point is certain: without a training in logic, ordinary individuals do not have a simple standard procedure for dealing with syllogisms. Hence those premises that lead only to a single model are reliably easier than those that offer a choice of models. The precise number of distinct models that a subject constructs on any occasion is uncertain. My colleagues and I have developed a number of computer programs that model syllogistic reasoning and that differ on this point (see, for example, the two programs described in Johnson-Laird and Bara 1984). We can be sure, however, that many subjects do construct initially erroneous models—they draw invalid conclusions.

Similarly when subjects are given the chance to think again after they have had only a brief interval (10 s) in which to formulate a conclusion, they often change their minds (Johnson-Laird and Bara 1984). An unpublished experiment by Ruth Byrne and myself is relevant here: when subjects are given an unexpected recognition test of the conclusions that they have drawn to a series of different syllogisms, one common error is to select the conclusion predicted by the initial model in place of the subjects' actual (and correct) conclusion. This error is of course predicted if subjects draw an initial conclusion according to one model, which they then revise after they have constructed another model.

There is no doubt that people are able to search for counterexamples to conclusions, but the process is affected by the cognitive load of the task (see Oakhill and Johnson-Laird 1985). What is much harder to identify are the actual processes by which such models are constructed. Allen Newell in his William James Lectures at Harvard University in 1987 argued that mental models can be treated as state representations within a problem space. Thus when someone solves, say, the missionaries and cannibals problem, he or she applies a series of operations to transform a model of the initial state of affairs through a succession of models representing intermediate states until the goal is reached. This formulation is useful in characterizing the sequence of conscious states that an individual is aware of in solving a problem. One of the oddities of deductive reasoning, however, is that people have little conscious access to how they come up with a conclusion. Unless they are using visual images, they have no conscious access to the models themselves—an introspective deficiency that critics of mental models cite as contrary to the theory (Martin Braine, personal communication, 1988). Because the representation of individuals to whom anaphoric reference can be made is equally inaccessible—and there must be such a representation—I do not think that inaccessibility counts decisively against the theory. What remains true, however, is that little is known about the nature of the processes that generate counterexamples. A number of processes may occur in parallel and thus violate a direct analysis in terms of Newell's problem space, which assumes that only single operations lead from one state to the next within the space.

The crux is whether a valid conclusion calls for more than one model to be constructed. Whenever there is a choice of models, ordinary individuals are in serious danger of falling into error, because they lack a systematic inferential procedure.

Models and Other Forms of Reasoning
Reasoning on the basis of mental models depends, as shown in the previous subsection, on three semantic procedures:

1. The construction of a mental model of the state of affairs described in the premises, taking into account any relevant general and specific

knowledge. This procedure corresponds to the ordinary comprehension of discourse.

2. The formulation of a novel conclusion based on the model, unless of course a conclusion is already present for evaluation. This procedure corresponds to the description of a state of affairs with the proviso that the description should establish a relation not explicitly stated in the premises.

3. A search for alternative models that refute the putative conclusion. Only this search for counterexamples is peculiar to the process of inference. If there is no such model then the conclusion is valid. If there is such a model, then the reasoner must return to the second step and try to construct a new conclusion true in all the models so far constructed. If it is not clear whether there is such a model, then the conclusion can be accepted tentatively or expressed with some modal or probablistic qualification (see Kahneman and Tversky 1982), but it may be subject to revision in the light of subsequent information.

The search for counterexamples solves the puzzle of how one model can stand in for an infinite number of different possible situations. Whenever an assertion is interpreted it may be necessary to make an arbitrary assumption to construct a single model. If a subsequent assertion is false in relation to this model, then it may be false because it conflicts with something depending on the arbitrary assumption. Hence an attempt can be made to revise the model so that it is consistent with the new assertion while still remaining an accurate model of the previous discourse. In this way earlier arbitrary assumptions can be corrected, or, should the revision be impossible, a genuine inconsistency can be detected between the latest assertion and the earlier discourse. This procedure is of course closely related to the search for counterexamples in deductive reasoning: there the aim is to render a currently true assertion false to check its validity; here the aim is to render a currently false assertion true to check its consistency. The same mechanism can be used to reason nonmonotonically. If an assumption is embodied in a model on the basis of default or prototypical information (see chapter 13), for example, that a dog has four legs, then a subsequent assertion may conflict with the model, for example, "my dog has three legs." In this case an attempt is made to revise the model. Such revisions can undo default assumptions (as well as arbitrary ones), but they cannot undo those conditions that are necessary to a concept.

The theory of inference based on mental models has been explored in a variety of domains. Indeed the study of three-term series problems, such as

Alice is taller than Bill.

Bill is taller than Charles.

Therefore Alice is taller than Charles.

led to one of the earliest versions of the theory. Various researchers, notably Huttenlocher (1968), proposed that reasoners form a mental arrangement of the individuals in the appropriate serial order. Other research revealed a more complicated picture. Thus Clark (1969) showed that a term such as "taller" is easier to understand than its converse "shorter," because the former is essentially neutral and affirmative in tone, whereas the latter is contrastive and negative in tone. A further complication is that subjects appear to develop different strategies to cope with the experimental task (compare Sternberg and Weil 1980, Egan and Grimes-Farrow 1982).

Spatial reasoning depends on more complex relations than three-term series problems. Consider, for example, the following inference:

The black ball is directly beyond the cue ball.

The green ball is on the right of the cue ball, and there is a red ball between them.

Hence if I move so that the red ball is between me and the black ball, then the cue ball will be to the left (of my line of sight).

Rules of inference for it would be complicated, and it is more likely to be drawn by manipulating a model of the spatial arrangement (see Johnson-Laird 1983, ch. 11, for the description of a spatial-reasoning program based on models).

One central point to make clear is that the logical properties of a term are emergent properties of its meaning rather than an explicit part of that meaning. For instance, the relation "greater than" has the logical property of transitivity, that is, any inference of the form

$x > y$ and $y > z$, therefore $x > z$

is valid. Yet there is no need to postulate a mental logic containing such a rule. Granted the concept of the successor of a number, for example, the successor of 2 is 3, the relation can be defined recursively (see Rogers 1967).

$x > y$ if x is the successor of y, or there is some number z such that x is the successor of z and z is greater than y.

It follows from this definition that, say, $4 > 2$, because there is a number, 3, such that 4 is its successor and $3 > 2$ (because 3 is the successor of 2). The principle of transitivity is plainly not part of the definition, but any model based on the meaning of the premises $a > b$ and $b > c$ yields the conclusion $a > c$.

The emergence of logical properties from meanings is a general principle. It applies to relations that hold between propositions, including simple relations such as "and" and "or," and more complicated conditional and causal relations. As in negation the key to the representation of these abstract relations is the introduction of appropriate procedures for interpreting special elements within models. A discourse may describe an actual situation, a possible situation, or a hypothetical or fictitious situation. There must be therefore some way of representing the status of a discourse and of symbolizing it within a model. A conditional assertion, such as

If John is here, then Mary has left.

accordingly calls for a model in which the antecedent situation is represented as a possible state of affairs in which the consequent situation holds (see Johnson-Laird 1986).

Recent results suggest that conditional reasoning may call for a search for counterexamples rather than the manipulation of linguistic representations according to formal rules of inference. It is well known that people are inclined to commit certain fallacies. Thus given the premises

If it rains, she get wet.
It doesn't rain.

they conclude fallaciously *She does not get wet*. Why not postulate a corresponding fallacious formal rule? Because, say the defenders of mental logic, the inference can be suppressed by providing an appropriate additional premise suggesting that there are other ways in which to get wet, for example, if it snows, she gets wet (Rumain, Connell, and Braine 1983). Byrne (1989) has shown, however, that an additional premise can also suppress the use of the central rule of formal logic, modus ponens. Thus given the following sort of premises:

If it rains, she gets wet.
If she goes out, she gets wet.
It rains.

there is a striking suppression in the percentage of people who conclude *She gets wet*. The explanation, Byrne argues, is that people construct a model of the situation described by the premises, taking into account their general knowledge. They can readily find a counterexample to the putative conclusion that she gets wet, that is, they assume she does not go out. Thus they treat the original conditional, "If it rains, she gets wet," as at best an elliptical description of the state of affairs.

Any form of deductive reasoning in a finite domain can be based on semantic procedures for constructing, interpreting, and manipulating mental models. These procedures will obviously be sensitive to the content of premises. Likewise stress, emotionality, prejudice, or frank psychopathology may lead to a failure at any stage and particularly to a failure to confront counterexamples. On the one hand the theory allows for rationality in principle—the complete and correct performance of all the procedures; on the other hand it provides a natural explanation for errors.

12.4 Models as the Representation of Knowledge

Whenever you understand some phenomenon, such as how an electronic calculator operates, how a hydrogen bomb detonates, or how Gödel's theorem works, you have a mental representation of it that is like a working model. Expertise rests on such knowledge, and cognitive scientists have undertaken a massive investigation of systems that represent knowledge and retrieve it when it is needed. There have been studies of models in many domains, including the movement of objects (de Kleer 1977, de Kleer and Brown 1981, Forbus 1983), electrical circuits (Gentner and Gentner 1983, de Kleer 1985), propulsion systems (Williams, Hollan, and Stevens 1983), medical diagnosis (Meyer, Leventhal, and Gutmann 1985), navigation (see, for example, Oatley 1977, Hutchins 1983), and, above all, computing systems (see, for example, Du Boulay, O'Shea, and Monk 1981, Soloway, Ehrlich, Bonar, and Greenspan 1982).

Theorists have used the term "mental model" in these contexts to refer primarily to the *content* of a mental representation. But, although mental models may differ markedly in their content, there is no evidence to suggest that they differ in representational format or in the processes that construct and manipulate them. What is at issue is how such models develop as an individual progresses from novice to expert, and whether there is any pedagogical advantage in providing people with models of tasks they are trying to learn.

The Development of Expertise

In the study of intellectual development there has been a shift away from the traditional Piagetian emphasis on a change in structures and processes toward the view that what really changes is the content of knowledge (see, for example, Carey 1985, Keil 1979, 1989). Similarly as adults become more competent in a particular domain, they develop a richer model of that domain. As Young (1983) has argued, your model of an electronic calculator may represent merely a simple causal link from pushing certain keys to the execution of certain mathematical functions:

You type in an expression. The machine examines it, analyzes it, and calculates the answer according to the rules of arithmetic.

But to exploit the calculator fully, you need a rather richer model that maps specifications of particular arithmetic tasks onto specifications of particular sequences of actions—a so-called task-action model (Moran 1981, Young 1983, Green, Schiele, and Payne 1988). The model that you need to diagnose a malfunction will be still different again, perhaps incorporating the notion of binary adders, logic gates, and so on.

An important difference between the way a novice and an expert reason about a physical situation is that the novice's model represents objects in the world and simulates processes that occur in real time, whereas a trained scientist can construct a model that represents highly abstract relations and properties, such as forces and momenta (Larkin 1983). The novice reasons qualitatively because appropriate quantitative reasoning calls for the more abstract model. A similar moral can be drawn from Tversky and Kahneman's work on judgments of probability. Naive individuals reason on the basis of mental simulations that call for the construction of models representing typical sequences of affairs (Kahneman and Tversky 1982); appropriate quantitative reasoning demands a more abstract model that embodies such factors as the a priori probabilities of events, the variances of distributions, and so on.

A model of a domain may be incomplete or inaccurate, and yet it can still be useful (Norman 1983; Johnson-Laird 1983, ch. 1)—just as a clock can be useful even though it is neither wholly accurate nor a complete representation of the earth's rotation. An erroneous model can obviously lead to erroneous conclusions and to certain persistent cognitive illusions. Thus, for example, many people believe that if a coin is rolled round the side of another fixed coin from top to bottom, it will end up inverted (see diSessa 1983). Many students believe that if an object is rotated on the end of a string, and the string snaps, then the trajectory of the object (ignoring gravity) is a spiral (see McCloskey, Caramazza, and Green 1980). Yet erroneous models are not always sources of error, and sometimes they may be a better guide than more sophisticated models. Kempton (1986) reports that there are two common models of thermostats. One model assumes that a thermostat acts as a feedback device that senses temperature and turns the furnace on or off to maintain a given temperature. The other, more primitive, model treats the thermostat as a valve that directly controls the furnace as the knob on a gas cooker. A "feedback" model can lead to a failure to set the thermostat low at night, if it implies that the fuel saved is balanced by the extra expense of reheating the house in the morning. This error is not made with the "valve" model because it implies that a lower setting always reduces the use of the furnace.

The source of error in a model may be mere ignorance, as in many misconceptions about force in physical systems. Sometimes, however, the error arises from a failure to envisage the situation properly or to hold in mind various possibilities, particularly in difficult deductive inferences. A nice example of the failure to envisage a situation has been described by Hinton (1979). The task is to imagine a cube balanced on one corner with the diametrically opposed corner vertically above it and then to indicate the locations of the other corners of the cube. Correct performance is rare without considerable previous experience with cubes. Many people consider that there are only four other corners that lie on the same horizontal plane.

Pedagogy, Analogy, and the Source of Models

One source of mental models is observation (aided by knowledge), another is other people's explanations, and still another is our ability to construct models for ourselves either from a set of basic components or from analogous models that we already possess. The whole of mathematics can be constructed from a small set of primitive ideas; any computational procedure can be constructed from a small set of building blocks; and most surprisingly explanations of the physical world, it seems, also rest on a foundation of basic ideas. Once we have a grasp of some of these ideas, a verbal explanation of a phenomenon enables us to construct a model of it. (Certain aspects of quantum physics elude such models; see Feynman 1985.)

A pedagogical precept, laid down by Wertheimer (1961), is that information should be presented to students in a way that enables them to cope with novel problems. This precept has also emerged from modern studies: an outline of the causal model of a machine, as opposed to its operating principles alone, enables novices to make inferences about novel problems (Halasz and Moran 1983, Kieras and Bovair 1984).

In situations where there is no teacher, people are reasonably adept at constructing causal models of their own. They already possess a rich knowledge of the variety of causal relations (Miller and Johnson-Laird 1976, sec. 6.3). They understand three important principles: first, in a deterministic domain all events have causes; second, causes precede their effects; and third, an action on an object is the likely cause of any change that occurs in it. These principles suffice, as Lewis (1986) has demonstrated in a computer program, for the construction of simple causal models of a physical system.

When a causal model fails to explain some phenomenon, a person is likely to search for a useful analogy, for example, the model of a thermostat as a valve. Gentner (1983, 1989) argues that the mere similarity of features between one domain and another cannot possibly account for the use of one as an analogy for the other. What has to be carried over are higher-order semantic relations, such as a causal framework. Thus in Rutherford's analogy between the solar system and the atom, the sun maps onto the nucleus of the atom, and the planets map onto the electrons. The properties of the sun, such as its heat, are dropped, but the higher-order relations are carried over. Hence the relation

the sun's attraction of the planets causes them to revolve around it

yields the inference

the nucleus's attraction of the electrons causes them to revolve around it.

In fact the computer implementation of Gentner's theory establishes the best global mapping of systematic structure and then sets up the mappings between the objects (Falkenhainer, Forbus, and Gentner 1986).

Holyoak and his colleagues have argued that the critical step in the mobilization of an analogy is the failure to solve a problem (Gick and Holyoak 1983, Holyoak 1985, Holyoak and Thagard 1989). The failure triggers an attempt to find an analogous problem to which the solution *is* known—a procedure that depends on finding existing links from the concepts active in the unsolved problem to those in another domain. Once sufficient links have been established, the actions contributing to the earlier solution can be transferred to the new problem. Analogical thinking is almost certainly not a unitary process, however, but, as Keane (1988) emphasizes, a set of different processes that depend on what an individual knows about a particular domain. In the case of profound scientific analogies, the search for links between one domain and another seems likely to be beyond the scope of any general algorithm.

12.5 A Critique of Mental Models

Theories of mental models have generated considerable interest, and inevitably they have also excited criticism, particularly from those committed to mental logic. One frequent objection is voiced in the form of a question: What exactly is a mental model? If the questioner requires a working definition, then a mental model can be defined as a representation of a body of knowledge—either long-term or short-term that meets the following conditions:

1. Its structure corresponds to the structure of the situation that it represents.

2. It can consist of elements corresponding only to perceptible entities, in which case it may be realized as an image, perceptual or imaginary. Alternatively it can contain elements corresponding to abstract notions; their significance depends crucially on the procedures for manipulating models.

3. Unlike other proposed forms of representation, it does not contain variables. Thus a *linguistic* representation of, say, *All artists are beekeepers* might take the form

For any x, if x is an artist, then x is a beekeeper.

In place of a variable, such as "x" in this expression, a model employs tokens representing a set of individuals.

Another major thrust against mental models is that they are an unnecessary explanatory concept. This criticism is similar to a familiar argument against imagery. Various authors, including Pylyshyn (1973, 1981) and Rips (1986), argue that everything can be represented by *propositional representations*, that is, structured strings of symbols in a mental language. Any mental representation ultimately depends on neural events, and these, like the machine code of a computer, may well be computations on strings of symbols. But such symbols do not make explicit to consciousness the high level "relation structures" of which we are normally aware—the fact that the table is in front of the stove, and so on—and thus it seems that mental computations must have higher levels of organization. Indeed in another, narrower sense, the expression "propositional representation" is used to refer to high-level representations, namely, linguistic representations made up from symbols corresponding to lexical items in the language (see Kintsch 1974, Fodor 1975). In this case, as we have seen, there is a need to supplement them with mental models to account for reasoning and the comprehension of discourse.

The great danger for theories of representation is that they perpetrate the "symbolic fallacy" that meaning is merely a matter of relating one set of symbols to another. As Lewis (1972) said, to translate a sentence into a linguistic representation provides no more of an account of the conditions in which it is true than does a translation into Latin. One extreme reaction here is to say, in effect, so much the worse for truth conditions. Thus Rips (1986) wrote: "Cognitive psychology has to do without semantic notions like truth and reference that depend on the relationship between mental representations and the outside world." Alas, if we give up truth and reference, not much of mental life remains, and we cannot even account for the comprehension and verification of discourse. Contrary to Rips's methodological prescription many authors have urged that a major problem for cognitive science is to explain how symbols refer to the world (compare Hofstadter and Dennett 1981, Haugeland 1985, Russell 1987). The theory of mental models proposes a solution to this problem, though some commentators wrongly believe that it treats the interpretation of language as nothing more than the translation of utterances into models and neglects the question of how models are related to the world (see Oden 1987). As we have seen, however, the solution is that models of the world can also be constructed as a result of perception, internal experience, and social interaction. A discourse is deemed true if a model based on its linguistic representation can be embedded within such a model (Johnson-Laird 1983, pp. 247, 441).

A major problem with theories that invoke mental models as a representation of knowledge is their radical incompleteness. Indeed is it really possible to render overt our common sense about the everyday world, our knowledge of the meanings of words, and the competence underlying our expertise? A chorus of skeptics has argued to the contrary. Thus Dreyfus (1972), a persistent critic of artificial intelligence, says that the intractable problem in the simulation of human behavior is that "all alternatives must be made explicit." Even Winograd, an erstwhile advocate of artificial intelligence, has recently argued that background knowledge cannot be represented as a set of explicit propositions (Winograd and Flores 1986). The overwhelming nature of knowledge may make it difficult—even impossible—for us to construct intelligent machines (other than by the original biological method). But it has no direct bearing on the feasibility of cognitive science, because a scientific account of how knowledge is acquired, retained, and used in interpreting the world does not necessarily call for a complete specification of all knowledge. Moreover, as Hayes (1979, 1985) and other like-minded theorists have argued, it may be possible to spell out intuitive knowledge in a completely explicit way. The enterprise is enormously time consuming, but if there are any insuperable barriers to it, they have yet to be discovered.

A more serious form of incompleteness concerns the theories of mental models themselves. Thus theories of vision do not yet give a full explanation of how retinal stimuli are mapped into rich dynamic models of the sort that the human perceptual system constructs. Theories of discourse account only for how fragments of language can be translated into models. Theories of reasoning have been advanced only for finite domains. And only a small number of expert sytems have exploited model-based reasoning despite its apparent advantages for coping with nondeductive inferences. One reason for such deficiencies is the sheer difficulty of formulating theories, especially where the theorist is forced to analyze the truth conditions of expressions—a matter that can be finessed within semantic networks or other forms of linguistic representation.

12.6 Conclusion

In some domains theorists have emphasized the *content* of mental models. Thus studies of our everyday theories of the world have concentrated on what we know, and theorists have used a variety of representational formats—semantic networks, logical calculi, production systems—to represent such knowledge. In other domains, such as perception, discourse, and reasoning, theorists have emphasized the *structure* of models and how they are constructed by mental processes. Yet the theorists are talking about the same beast. Human beings create models of the world from both perceptual acquaintance with it and descriptions of it. These two forms of knowledge must be commensurable, otherwise we would never know what we were talking about or whether what we were saying was true. We retain such knowledge in long-term memory as the basis of our expertise in dealing with the world; and we can reason about any of our knowledge whether its source is perception, discourse, or memory.

In short, despite the diversity of theories, if we are to do justice to mental representations, the evidence suggests that those that we build from discourse are akin in structure to those that we build by other means, and that reasoning exploits the same sort of models. Mental models are internal symbols, and so one question remains: What other sorts of symbols are there? Images, as I remarked, are a special sort of model—a two-dimensional representation that is projected from an underlying three-dimensional model. Hence the theory invokes a simple three-part inventory: linguistic representations, models, and procedures for manipulating them.

When Craik (1943) argued that people reason by carrying out thought experiments on internal models, the idea seemed dangerously heterodox. Now the range of phenomena that mental models are used to explain is growing rapidly. They include metacognition (Gilhooly 1986), consciousness and the self (Oatley 1981), intentional behavior and free will (Johnson-Laird 1988), and psychopathy (Power and Champion 1986). What remains as perhaps the major puzzle is how an entity can have recursive access to a model of its own performance (Weyrauch 1980; Johnson-Laird 1983, ch. 16; Smith 1984; Hayes-Roth, Garvey, Johnson, and Hewett 1987), and how it can exploit that knowledge in dealing with the world.

Note

I am grateful to my former colleague Alan Garnham, whose own ideas on mental models (see, for example, Garnham 1987) have had a major effect on my thinking. I thank Phil Barnard, Alan Garnham, Ed Smith, Mark Keane, and Michael Posner for many useful comments. Finally, I am grateful to Ruth Byrne for detailed criticisms of a previous draft and for other help in preparing this chapter.

References

Anderson, J. R. 1983. *The Architecture of Cognition*. Cambridge, MA: Harvard University Press.

Beth, E. W. 1971. *Aspects of Modern Logic*. Dordrecht: Reidel.

Braine, M. D. S. 1978. On the relation between the natural logic of reasoning and standard logic. *Psychological Review* 85:1–21.

Bransford, J. D., Barclay, J. R., and Franks, J. J. 1972. Sentence memory: A constructive versus interpretive approach. *Cognitive Psychology* 3:193–209.

Buchanan, B. G., and Feigenbaum, E. A. 1978. DENDRAL and Meta-DENDRAL: Their applications dimension. *Artificial Intelligence* 11:5–24.

Byrne, R. M. J. 1989. Suppressing valid inferences with conditionals. *Cognition* 31:61–83.

Carey, S. 1985. *Conceptual Change in Childhood*. Cambridge, MA: MIT Press.

Cheng, P. N., and Holyoak, K. J. 1985. Pragmatic reasoning schemas. *Cognitive Psychology* 17:391–416.

Chomsky, N. 1977. *Essays on Form and Interpretation.* New York: North Holland.

Clark, H. H. 1969. Linguistic processes in deductive reasoning. *Psychological Review* 79:387–404.

Clark, H. H. 1977. Bridging. In P. N. Johnson-Laird and P. C. Wason, eds. *Thinking: Readings in Cognitive Science.* Cambridge, Engl.: Cambridge University Press.

Craik, K. 1943. *The Nature of Explanation.* Cambridge, Engl.: Cambridge University Press.

Davis M. 1980. The mathematics of non-monotonic reasoning. *Artificial Intelligence* 13:73–80.

Davis, R., and Lenat, D. B. 1982. *Knowledge-based Systems in Artificial Intelligence.* New York: McGraw-Hill.

de Kleer, J. 1977. Multiple representations of knowledge in a mechanics problem solver. *International Joint Conference on Artificial Intelligence* 5:299–304.

de Kleer, J. 1985. How circuits work. In D. G. Bobrow, ed. *Qualitative Reasoning about Physical Systems.* Cambridge, MA: MIT Press.

de Kleer, J., and Brown, J. S. 1981. Mental models of physical mechanisms and their acquisition. In J. Anderson, ed. *Cognitive Skills and their Acquisition.* Hillsdale, NJ: Erlbaum.

diSessa, A. 1983. Phenomenology and the evolution of intuition. In D. Gentner and A. L. Stevens, eds. *Mental Models.* Hillsdale, NJ: Erlbaum, pp. 15–33.

Dreyfus, H. L. 1972. *What Computers Can't Do: A Critique of Artificial Reason.* New York: Harper and Row.

Du Boulay, B., O'Shea, T., and Monk, J. 1981. The black box inside the glass box: Presenting computer concepts to novices. *International Journal of Man-Machine Studies* 14:237–249.

Egan, D. E., and Grimes-Farrow, D. D. 1982. Differences in mental representations spontaneously adopted for reasoning. *Memory and Cogniton* 10:297–307.

Ehrlich, K., and Johnson-Laird, P. N. 1982. Spatial descriptions and referential continuity. *Journal of Verbal Learning and Verbal Behavior* 21:296–306.

Erickson, J. R. 1974. A set analysis theory of behaviour in formal syllogistic reasoning tasks. In R. Solso, ed. *Loyola Symposium on Cognition.* Vol. 2. Hillsdale, NJ: Erlbaum.

Evans, J. St. B. T. 1982. *The Psychology of Deductive Reasoning.* London: Routledge and Kegan Paul.

Falkenhainer, B., Forbus, K. D., and Gentner, D. 1986. The structure-mapping engine. University of Illinois, Technical Report No. UIUCDS-R-86-1275.

Fauconnier, G. 1985. *Mental Spaces: Aspects of Meaning-Construction in Natural Language.* Cambridge, MA: MIT Press.

Feigenbaum, E. A., and McCorduck, P. 1984. *The Fifth Generation: Artificial Intelligence and Japan's Computer Challenge to the World*. London: Pan Books.

Feynman, R. P. 1985. *QED: The Strange Theory of Light and Matter*. Princeton: Princeton University Press.

Feynman, R. P., and Leighton, R. 1985. *"Surely You're Joking, Mr. Feynman!"* New York: W. W. Norton.

Fodor, J. A. 1975. *The Language of Thought*. Hassocks, Sussex: Harvester Press.

Forbus, K. D. 1983. Qualitative reasoning about space and motion. In D. Gentner and A. L. Stevens, eds. *Mental Models*. Hillsdale, NJ: Erlbaum, pp. 53–73.

Garnham, A. 1981. Anaphoric reference to instances, instantiated and non-instantiated categories: A reading-time study. *British Journal of Psychology* 72:377–384.

Garnham, A. 1987. *Mental Models as Representations of Discourse and Text*. Chichester: Ellis Horwood.

Garnham, A., and Oakhill, J. V. 1987. Interpreting elliptical verb phrases. *Quarterly Journal of Experimental Psychology* 39A:611–627.

Garnham, A., and Oakhill, J. V. 1989. The everyday use of anaphoric expressions: Implications for the 'Mental Models' theory of text comprehension. In N. E. Sharkey, ed., *Modelling Cognition: An Annual Review of Cognitive Science*. Vol. 2. Norwood, NJ: Ablex.

Garnham, A., Oakhill, J. V., and Johnson-Laird, P. N. 1982. Referential continuity and the coherence of discourse. *Cognition* 1:29–46.

Gentner D. 1983. Structure-mapping: A theoretical framework for analogy. *Cognitive Science* 7:155–170.

Gentner, D. 1989. The mechanisms of analogical learning. In S. Vosniadou and A. Ortony, eds. *Similarity and Analogy in Reasoning and Learning*. Cambridge, Engl.: Cambridge University Press.

Gentner, D., and Gentner, D. R. 1983. Flowing waters or teeming crowds: Mental models of electricity. In D. Gentner and A. L. Stevens, eds. *Mental Models*. Hillsdale, NJ: Erlbaum, pp. 99–129.

Gick, M. L., and Holyoak, K. J. 1983. Schema induction and analogical transfer. *Cognitive Psychology* 15:1–38.

Gilhooly, K. J. 1986. Mental modelling: A framework for the study of thinking. In J. Bishop, J. Lochhead and Perkins, D. N. eds. *Thinking: Progress in Research and Teaching*. Hillsdale, NJ: Erlbaum.

Glenberg, A. M., Meyer, M., and Lindem, K. 1987. Mental models contribute to foregrounding during text comprehension. *Journal of Memory and Language* 26:69–83.

Green, T. R. G., Schiele, F., and Payne, S. J. 1988. Formalisable models of user knowledge in human-computer interaction. In T. R. G. Green, G. C. van der Veer, J.-M. Hoc, and

D. Murray, eds. *Working with Computers: Theory versus Outcome*. New York: Academic Press.

Guyote, M. J., and Sternberg, R. J. 1981. A transitive-chain theory of syllogistic reasoning. *Cognitive Psychology* 13:461–525.

Halasz, F. G., and Moran, T. P. 1983. Mental models and problem solving in using a calculator. *Proceedings of CHI '83: Human Factors in Computing Systems*. New York: Association for Computing Machinery.

Haugeland, J. 1985. *Artificial Intelligence—The Very Idea*. Cambridge, MA: MIT Press.

Hayes, P. J. 1977. In defense of logic. *Proceedings of the Fifth International Joint Conference on Artificial Intelligence*, pp. 559–565.

Hayes, P. J. 1979. Naive physics 1—ontology for liquids. Memo, Centre pour les etudes Semantiques et Cognitives, Geneva. Reprinted in J. Hobbs and R. Moore, eds., 1985. *Formal Theories of the Commonsense World*. Hillsdale, NJ: Ablex, pp. 71–107.

Hayes, P. J. 1985. The second naive physics manifesto. In J. Hobbs and R. Moore, eds. 1985. *Formal Theories of the Commonsense World*. Hillsdale, NJ: Ablex, pp. 1–20.

Hayes-Roth, B., Garvey, A., Johnson, M. V., and Hewett, M. 1987. A modular and layered environment for reasoning about action. Knowledge Systems Laboratory Report No. KSL 86-38, Cognitive Science Department, Stanford University, Stanford, CA.

Hewitt, C. 1971. PLANNER: A language for proving theorems in robots. *Fourth International Joint Conference on Artificial Intelligence*, pp. 115–121.

Hinton, G. 1979. Some demonstrations of the effects of structural descriptions in mental imagery. *Cognitive Science* 3:231–250.

Hofstadter, D. R., and Dennett, D. C., eds. 1981. *The Mind's I: Fantasies and Reflections on Self and Soul*. New York: Basic Books.

Holland, J., Holyoak, K. J., Nisbett, R. E., and Thagard, P. 1986. *Induction: Processes of Inference, Learning, and Discovery*. Cambridge, MA: MIT Press. A Bradford Book.

Holyoak, K. J. 1985. The pragmatics of analogical transfer. In G. H. Bower, ed. *The Psychology of Learning and Motivation: Advances in Research and Theory*. Vol. 19. New York: Academic Press.

Holyoak, K. J. and Thagard, P. R. 1989. Rule-based spreading activation and analogical transfer. In S. Vosniadou and A. Ortony, eds. *Similarity and Analogy in Reasoning and Learning*. Cambridge, Engl.: Cambridge University Press.

Hornstein, N. 1986. *Logic as Grammar*. Cambridge, MA: MIT Press.

Hutchins, E. 1983. Understanding Micronesian navigation. In D. Gentner and A. L. Stevens, eds. *Mental Models*. Hillsdale, NJ: Erlbaum, pp. 191–225.

Huttenlocher, J. 1968. Constructing spatial images: A strategy in reasoning. *Psychological Review* 75:550–560.

Inder, R. 1987. The computer simulation of syllogism solving using restricted mental models. Ph.D. thesis, Cognitive Studies, Edinburgh University.

Inhelder, B., and Piaget, J. 1958. *The Growth of Logical Thinking from Childhood to Adolescence*. New York: Basic Books.

Jackendoff, R. 1987. On beyond Zebra: The relation of linguistic and visual information. *Cognition* 26:89–114.

Johnson-Laird, P. N. 1983. *Mental Models: Towards a Cognitive Science of Language, Inference, and Consciousness*. Cambridge, MA: Harvard University Press. Cambridge, Engl.: Cambridge University Press.

Johnson-Laird, P. N. 1986. Conditionals and mental models. In E. C. Traugott, A. ter Meulen, J. S. Reilly and C. A. Ferguson, eds. *On Conditionals*. Cambridge, Engl.: Cambridge University Press.

Johnson-Laird, P. N. 1987. Reasoning, imagining, and creating. *Bulletin of the British Psychological Society* 40:121–129.

Johnson-Laird, P. N. 1988. Freedom and constraint in creativity. In Sternberg, R. J., ed. *The Nature of Creativity*. New York: Cambridge University Press.

Johnson-Laird, P. N., and Bara, B. G. 1984. Syllogistic inference. *Cognition* 16:1–61.

Johnson-Laird, P. N., and Garnham, A. 1980. Descriptions and discourse models. *Linguistics and Philosophy* 3:371–393.

Johnson-Laird, P. N., Herrmann, D. J., and Chaffin, R. 1984. Only connections: A Critique of semantic networks. *Psychological Bulletin* 96:292–315.

Johnson-Laird, P. N., and Wason, P. C., eds. 1977. *Thinking: Readings in Cognitive Science*. Cambridge, Engl.: Cambridge University Press.

Kahneman, D., and Tversky, A. 1982. The simulation heuristic. In D. Kahneman, P. Slovic, and A. Tversky, eds. 1982. *Judgement Under Uncertainty: Heuristics and Biases*. Cambridge, Engl.: Cambridge University Press, pp. 201–208.

Kamp, J. A. W. 1981. A theory of truth and semantic representation. In J. A. G. Groenendijk, T. Janssen and M. Stokhof, eds. *Formal Methods in the Study of Language*. Amsterdam: Mathematical Center Tracts, pp. 277–322.

Karttunen, L. 1976. Discourse referents. In J. McCawley, ed. *Syntax and Semantics, Vol. 7: Notes from the Linguistic Underground*. New York: Academic Press.

Keane, M. 1988. *Analogical Problem Solving*. Chichester, Engl.: Ellis Horwood.

Keil, F. 1979. *Semantic and Conceptual Development: Ontological Perspective*. Cambridge, MA: Harvard University Press.

Keil, F. 1989. *Concepts, Word Meanings, and Cognitive Development*. Cambridge, MA: Harvard University Press.

Kempton, W. 1986. Two theories of home heat control. *Cognitive Science* 10:75–90.

Kieras, D. E., and Bovair, S. 1984. The role of a mental model in learning to operate a device. *Cognitive Science* 8:255–273.

Kintsch, W. 1974. *The Representation of Meaning in Memory*. Hillsdale, NJ: Erlbaum.

Kintsch, W., and van Dijk, T. A. 1978. Towards a model of text comprehension and reproduction. *Psychological Review* 85:363–394.

Kowalski, R. A. 1979. *Logic for Problem Solving*. Amsterdam: Elsevier North-Holland.

Larkin, J. H. 1983. The role of problem representation in physics. In D. Gentner and A. L. Stevens, eds. *Mental Models*. Hillsdale, NJ: Erlbaum, pp. 75–98.

Lewis, C. 1986. A model of mental model construction. *Proceedings of CHI '86 Conference on Human Factors in Computer Systems*. New York: Association for Computing Machinery.

Lewis, D. K. 1972. General semantics. In D. Davidson and G. Harman, eds. *Semantics of Natural Language*. Dordrecht: Reidel.

McCloskey, M., Caramazza, A., Green, G. 1980. Curvilinear motion in the absence of external forces: Naive beliefs about the motion of objects. *Science* 210:1139–1141.

McDermott, D. 1986. A critique of pure reason. Mimeo, Artificial Intelligence, Yale University, New Haven, CT.

McDermott, D., and Doyle, J. 1980. Non-monotonic logic I. *Artificial Intelligence* 13:41–72.

Mani, K., and Johnson-Laird, P. N. 1982. The mental representation of spatial descriptions. *Memory and Cognition* 10:181–187.

Marr, D. 1982. *Vision: A Computational Investigation in the Human Representation of Visual Information*. San Francisco: Freeman.

Meyer, D., Leventhal, H., and Gutmann, M. 1985. Common-sense models of illness: The example of hypertension. *Health Psychology* 4:115–135.

Michie, D., ed. 1979. *Expert Systems in the Micro-Electronic Age*. Edinburgh: Edinburgh University Press.

Miller, G. A. 1972. English verbs of motion: a case study in semantics and lexical memory. In A. W. Melton and E. Martin, eds. *Coding Processes in Human Memory*. Washington, DC: Winston.

Miller, G. A., Galanter, E., and Pribram, K. 1960. *Plans and the Structure of Behavior*. New York: Holt, Rinehart, and Winston.

Miller, G. A., and Johnson-Laird, P. N. 1976. *Language and Perception*. Cambridge, MA: Harvard University Press. Cambridge, Engl.: Cambridge University Press.

Minsky, M. 1975. A framework for representing knowledge. In P. H. Winston, ed. *The Psychology of Computer Vision*. New York: McGraw-Hill.

Moran, T. P. 1981. The Command Language Grammar: A representation for the user interface of interactive computer systems. *International Journal of Man-Machine Studies* 15:5–30.

Newell, A. 1973. Production systems: Models of control structures. In W. G. Chase, ed. *Visual Information Processing*. New York: Academic Press.

Newell, A. 1981. Reasoning, problem solving and decision processes: The problem space as a fundamental category. In R. Nickerson, ed. *Attention and Performance*. Vol. 8. Hillsdale, NJ: Erlbaum.

Newell, A., and Simon, H. A. 1976. Computer science as empirical inquiry: Symbols and search. *Communications of the Association for Computing Machinery* 19:113–126.

Norman, D. A. 1983. Some observations on mental models. In D. Gentner and A. L. Stevens, eds. *Mental Models*. Hillsdale, NJ: Erlbaum, pp. 7–14.

Oakhill, J. V., and Garnham, A. 1985. Referential continuity, transitivity, and the retention of spatial descriptions. *Language and Cognitive Processes* 1:149–162.

Oakhill, J. V., and Johnson-Laird, P. N. 1985. Rationality, memory, and the search for counterexamples. *Cognition* 20:79–94.

Oatley, K. G. 1977. Inference, navigation, and cognitive maps. In P. N. Johnson-Laird and P. C. Wason, eds. *Thinking: Readings in Cognitive Science*. Cambridge, Engl.: Cambridge University Press, pp. 537–547.

Oatley, K. G. 1981. Representing ourselves: Mental schemata, computational metaphors, and the nature of consciousness. In G. Underwood and R. Stevens, eds. *Aspects of Consciousness, vol. 2: Structural Issues*. New York: Academic Press.

Oden, G. C. 1987. Concept, knowledge, and thought. *Annual Review of Psychology* 38:203–227.

Osherson, D. N. 1975. Logic and models of logical thinking. In R. J. Falmagne, ed. *Reasoning: Representation and Process in Children and Adults*. Hillsdale, NJ: Erlbaum.

Partee, B. H. 1979. Semantics—mathematics or psychology? In R. Baurle, U. Egli, and A. von Stechow, eds. *Semantics from Different Points of View*. Berlin: Springer.

Polk, T., and Newell, A. 1988. Modeling human syllogistic reasoning in Soar. *Proceedings of the Tenth Annual Conference of the Cognitive Science Society*. Hillsdale, NJ: Erlbaum, pp. 181–187.

Pylyshyn, Z. 1973. What the mind's eye tells the mind's brain: A critique of mental imagery. *Psychological Bulletin* 80:1–24.

Pylyshyn, Z. 1981. The imagery debate: Analogue media versus tacit knowledge. In N. Block, ed. *Imagery*. Cambridge, MA: MIT Press.

Power, M. J., and Champion, L. A. 1986. Cognitive approaches to depression: A theoretical critique. *British Journal of Clinical Psychology* 25:201–212.

Reichardt, W. E., and Poggio, T. 1981. Visual control of flight in flies. In W. E. Reichardt and T. Poggio, eds. *Theoretical Approaches in Neurobiology*. Cambridge, MA: MIT Press.

Reichgelt, H. 1982. Mental models and discourse. *Journal of Semantics* 1:371–386.

Reiter, R. 1973. A semantically guided deductive system for automatic theorem-proving. *Third International Joint Conference on Artificial Intelligence*, pp. 41–46.

Rips, L. J. 1983. Cognitive processes in propositional reasoning. *Psychological Review* 90:38–71.

Rips, L. J. 1986. Mental muddles. In M. Brand and R. M. Harnish, eds. *Problems in the Representation of Knowledge and Belief*. Tucson, AZ: University of Arizona Press.

Robinson, J. A. 1979. *Logic: Form and Function, The Mechanization of Deductive Reasoning*. Edinburgh: Edinburgh University Press.

Rogers, H. 1967. *Theory of Recursive Functions and Effective Computability*. New York: McGraw-Hill.

Rumain, B., Connell, J., and Braine, M. D. S. 1983. Conversational comprehension processes are responsible for reasoning fallacies in children as well as adults: IF is not the biconditional. *Developmental Psychology* 19:471–481.

Russell, J. 1987. Rule-following, mental models, and the developmental view. In M. Chapman and R. A. Dixon, eds. *Meaning and the Growth of Understanding: Wittgenstein's Significance for Developmental Psychology*. New York: Springer.

Sag, I., and Hankamer, J. 1984. Toward a theory of anaphoric processing. *Linguistics and Philosophy* 7:325–345.

Sanford, A., and Garrod, S. 1981. *Understanding Written Language: Explorations of Comprehension Beyond the Sentence*. Chichester, Engl.: Wiley.

Schank, R. C., and Abelson, R. P. 1977. *Scripts, Plans, Goals and Understanding*. Hillsdale, NJ: Erlbaum.

Shadbolt, N. 1983. Processing reference. *Journal of Semantics* 2:63–98.

Smith, B. C. 1984. Reflection and semantics in LISP. Conference Record of the Eleventh Annual Association for Computing Machinery Symposium on Principles of Programming Languages, Salt Lake City, Utah, pp. 23–35.

Smith, E. R. 1984. Models of social inference processes. *Psychological Review* 91:392–413.

Soloway, E., Ehrlich, K., Bonar, J., and Greenspan, J. 1982. What do novices know about programming? In A. Badre and B. Schneiderman, eds. *Directions in Human-Computer Interactions*. Norwood, NJ: Ablex, pp. 27–54.

Spencer-Smith, R. 1987. Survey: Semantics and discourse representation. *Mind and Language* 2:1–26.

Stenning, K. 1978. Anaphora as an approach to pragmatics. In M. Halle, J. Bresnan and G. A. Miller, eds. *Linguistic Theory and Psychological Reality*. Cambridge, MA: MIT Press.

Stenning, K. 1986. On making models: A study of constructive memory. In T. Myers, K. Brown and B. McGonigle, eds. *Reasoning and Discourse Processes*. London: Academic Press.

Sternberg, R. J., and Weil, E. M. 1980. An aptitude x strategy interaction in linear syllogstic reasoning. *Journal of Educational Psychology* 72:226–239.

Tversky, A., and Kahneman, D. 1973. Availability: A heuristic for judging frequency and probability. *Cognitive Psychology* 4:207–232. Reprinted in Kahneman, D., Slovic, P., and Tversky, A., eds. 1982. *Judgement under Uncertainty: Heuristics and Biases*. Cambridge, Engl.: Cambridge University Press.

van Dijk, T. A., and Kintsch, W. 1983. *Strategies of Discourse Comprehension*. New York: Academic Press.

Wason, P. C., and Johnson-Laird, P. N. 1972. *Psychology of Reasoning: Structure and Content*. Cambridge, MA: Harvard University Press. London: Batsford.

Webber, B. L. 1978. Description formation and discourse model synthesis. In D. L. Waltz, ed. *Theoretical Issues in Natural Language Processing, 2*. New York: Association for Computing Machinery.

Wertheimer, M. 1961. *Productive Thinking*. London: Tavistock.

Weyrauch, R. W. 1980. Prolegomena to a theory of mechanized formal reasoning. *Artificial Intelligence* 13:133–170.

Wilks, Y., and Bien, J. S. 1979. Speech acts and multiple environments. *Sixth International Joint Conference on Artificial Intelligence*, pp. 451–455.

Williams, D., Hollan, J. D., and Stevens, A. L. 1983. Human reasoning about a simple physical system. In D. Gentner and A. L. Stevens, eds. *Mental Models*. Hillsdale, NJ: Erlbaum, pp. 131–153.

Winograd, T., and Flores, F. 1986. *Understanding Computers and Cognition: A New Foundation for Design*. Norwood, NJ: Ablex.

Wittgenstein, L. 1922. *Tractatus Logico-Philosophicus*. London: Routledge and Kegan Paul.

Young, R. 1983. Surrogates and mappings: Two kinds of conceptual models for interactive devices. In D. Gentner and A. L. Stevens, eds. *Mental Models*. Hillsdale, NJ: Erlbaum, pp. 35–52.

13 Concepts and Induction

Edward E. Smith

The study of concepts is central to every discipline of cognitive science. In cognitive psychology and philosophy of mind, concepts are assumed to be the basic constituents of thought and belief. In linguistics the study of word meanings or lexical representations often involves the study of those concepts that are coded by single words. And in artificial intelligence, more often than not, proposals about knowledge representations *are* proposals about concepts. Moreover in each of these disciplines concepts are intimately linked to the process of drawing inductive inferences.

The centrality of concepts is due to their playing major functional roles in any intelligent system, including human beings. One function is that concepts promote "cognitive economy" (Rosch 1978). By partitioning the world into classes, concepts allow us to decrease the amount of information that we must perceive, learn, remember, communicate, and reason about. Thus if we had no concepts, we would have to refer to each individual entity by its own name, and the mental lexicon required would be so enormous that communication as we know it might collapse.

A second major function of concepts is that they allow us to bring to bear our past experience on present concerns. Because the same situation never repeats itself exactly, past experience is useful to the extent that it is partitioned into classes that *do* reoccur. For example, if a child has the concepts *stove* and *burn*, (italics indicate concepts), he or she is able to relate experience with one particular stove and one particular burn to a subsequent experience with another stove and another possible burn.

A third major function of concepts is that they permit inductive inferences, particularly about properties that are not perceptible. Upon coming across a growling dog, for example, you have direct knowledge only of its appearance, yet once you have used this information to categorize it as a *dog*, you can infer many of its properties that are not then visible, such as the possibility that it will bite if its territory is invaded. Concepts thus permit categorizations, which in turn license inferences, which in turn direct our actions. This is one way in which concepts and inductions are intimately related.

In what follows discussion of concepts and induction divides into two parts. The first part focuses on the "basic picture" of concepts and categorization. It presupposes that a concept is a mental representation of a class or individual and deals with *what* is being represented and *how* that information is typically used during categorization. I briefly consider the view that what is being represented is a definition, and that categorizing an item amounts to instantiating a definition. This view seems to correctly characterize only a limited set of concepts. Then we take up the idea that what is represented is a "prototype," or description, of the best examples, and that categorizing an item involves determining its similarity to a prototype. This view seems to characterize a large set of concepts. In the second part of the chapter, I discuss the relation between categorization and induction, focusing on concepts that represent prototypes. First, I consider some recent experiments that indicate that sometimes people consider more than similarity to prototype in categorizing an item. Then I show that these findings fit within a framework in which categorization is treated as a kind of induction problem, and in which modes of induction other than similarity can be used for categorization. Finally, I extend the framework to include some well-known experiments on estimating the probability of category membership (for example, Tversky and Kahneman 1974).

13.1   The Basic Picture of Concepts and Categorization

Typically to have a concept of X is to know something about the properties of X's instances. Hence what is represented in a concept is presumably information about properties. The nature of these properties is the topic of concern.

Concepts as Definitions

The Classical View   An old and influential idea is that the properties that comprise a concept are singly necessary and jointly sufficient to define the concept. For a property to be singly necessary, every instance of the concept must have it; for a set of properties to be jointly sufficient, every entity having that set must be an instance of the concept. We can illustrate this with the concept of *grandmother*, whose two critical properties include being female and being a parent of a parent. Each property is necessary—someone cannot literally be a grandmother if he is a man, or if she has no children. And the two properties are jointly sufficient—someone who is female and the parent of a parent must be a grandmother. The position that proposes the concepts consist of definitions is called the *classical view*; according to it, an object is categorized as an instance of a concept if and only if it contains the defining properties of the concept (Smith and Medin 1981).

Clearly there are some concepts that conform to the classical view. These include kin concepts like *grandmother* and *uncle*, concepts that belong to axiomatic theories like *even number* and *triangle*, legal concepts like *contract* and *robber*, and other concepts that are part of a technical field. Such concepts are often tailor-made or invented for some specialized system, and are referred to as *nominal-kind* concepts (Schwartz 1979). Nominal-kind concepts appear to differ markedly from most of the concepts that make up our mental life, such as *natural-kind* concepts like *dog* and *daisy*, which seem more discovered than invented.

Currently the classical view seems viable only for nominal-kind concepts, but historically the view was applied to all concepts. Indeed it dominated theories of mind for many years (for examples in linguistics see Katz and Fodor 1963, and in psychology see Bruner, Goodnow, and Austin 1956). Since the early 1970s, though, the generality of the classical view has been seriously challenged by the collective work of linguists, philosophers, and psychologists. This work is reviewed in detail in a number of sources, including Schwartz (1979), Fodor, Garrett, Walker, and Parkes (1980), and Smith and Medin (1981). In what follows I summarize briefly a few of the major criticisms of the classical view as applied to natural-kind concepts, with an emphasis on those points that have led to the development of an alternative view.

Failure to Specify Defining Properties   The severest problem for the classical view is that decades of analyses by linguists, philosophers, and psychologists have failed to turn up definitions of most natural-kind concepts. Consider *tiger*. For most people its properties include striped and carnivorous. If you came across a tiger, however, whose stripes had been painted over and whose digestive system had been altered surgically so that it could eat only vegetables, likely you would still categorize it as a *tiger*. Hence striped and carnivorous cannot be defining properties. But if not them, then what? Arguments like this have led scholars to conclude that many natural kinds are not mentally represented as definitions.

Typicality Effects   A number of experimental findings about how people use natural-kind concepts are also problematic for the classical view. The first of these findings is that people can reliably order the instances of any concept with respect to how "typical" or "representative" they are of the concept. Table 13.1 presents typicality ratings for the concepts *fruit* and *bird* (ratings were made on a 7-point scale, with 7 corresponding to the highest typicality and 1 to the lowest; see Malt and Smith 1984). *Apple* and *peach* are considered typical fruits, *raisin* and *fig* less typical, and *pumpkin* and *olive* atypical. There are similar variations among the instances of *bird*. Ratings like these have been obtained for

Table 13.1 Typicality Ratings for Fifteen Instances of *Fruit* and *Bird*

Fruit	Rating	Bird	Rating
Apple	6.25	Robin	6.89
Peach	5.81	Bluebird	6.42
Pear	5.25	Seagull	6.26
Grape	5.13	Swallow	6.16
Strawberry	5.00	Falcon	5.74
Lemon	4.86	Mockingbird	5.47
Blueberry	4.56	Starling	5.16
Watermelon	4.06	Owl	5.00
Raisin	3.75	Vulture	4.84
Fig	3.38	Sandpiper	4.47
Coconut	3.06	Chicken	3.95
Pomegranate	2.50	Flamingo	3.37
Avocado	2.38	Albatross	3.32
Pumpkin	2.31	Penguin	2.63
Olive	2.25	Bat	1.53

From Malt and Smith 1984

numerous natural-kind concepts and have been shown to be relatively uncorrelated with the frequency or familiarity of the instances (Rosch and Mervis 1975, Mervis, Catlin, and Rosch 1976).[1]

What is most important about these ratings is that they predict performance in a wide variety of tasks. One task is categorization. If subjects are asked to decide as quickly as possible if an item is an instance of a concept (for example, *Is a fig a fruit?*), they are faster the more typical the instance is (see, for example, Smith, Shoben, and Rips 1974). Another task is memory retrieval. If asked to generate from memory all instances of a concept, subjects retrieve typical before atypical instances (for example, Rosch 1978). A third "task" is vocabulary development. Children learning to name concept members master the typical instances before the atypical ones (see, for example, Rosch 1978). Still another task is deductive reasoning. When asked to determine the validity of incomplete deductive arguments (for example, *All birds have property P. Therefore all robins have property P.*), subjects are faster when the missing premise (*All robins are birds.*) involves a typical rather than an atypical instance (Cherniak 1984). Yet another task is inductive reasoning. When told that an "initial" instance of a concept has a novel property P and asked to estimate the likelihood that another instance also has P, subjects' estimates are higher the more typical the initial instance (Rips 1975). In short whenever we categorize, remember, name, or reason about a concept's instances, we do better with typical than atypical members.

These typicality effects seem inhospitable to the classical view—they show that not all instances of a natural-kind concept are equal, yet equality is what one might expect if every instance met the same definition.[2] This argument is considerably strengthened by the additional finding that typicality effects are due to unnecessary properties. In an experiment by Rosch and Mervis (1975), subjects listed properties of instances of a number of concepts. For each concept (for example, *fruit*) virtually all of the properties listed were nonnecessary (for example, the property of being sweet). Some instances had properties that occurred in many other instances (for example, sweet), whereas other instances had properties that occurred less frequently among concept members (for example, green); the more frequent its properties, the more typical the instance was rated by another group of subjects. The typicality of an instance is therefore a matter of the frequency of its nonnecessary properties among other concept instances. Because definitions are restricted to necessary properties, the classical view cannot account for typicality effects.

Concepts as Prototypes

Similarity to Prototype   The typicality findings have led to a new view of concepts. Instead of offering defining conditions, the properties of a natural-kind concept are assumed to occur in some instances—the best examples—but not all, and to be perceptually salient. A collection of such properties is called a *prototype*.[3] Under the prototype view an object is categorized as an instance of a concept if it is sufficiently similar to the prototype, similarity being determined in part by the number of properties that the object and prototype share.

It is easy to see that this view can accommodate the phenomena that challenged the classical view. There need be no defining properties for natural kinds. Furthermore the typicality of an instance may be taken to be a.direct measure of the instance's similarity to the concept's prototype, and similarity to prototype is assumed to be involved in categorization, memory, naming, reasoning, and so forth. For example, typical instances are categorized faster than atypical instances because categorization involves determining that an item exceeds some critical level of similarity to the prototype, and the more similar the item to the prototype the faster this determination can be made (see Smith and Medin 1981 for discussion).

The problem with this proposal is that it is vague and unconstrained. To put more substance in it we need to be able to identify the properties in a prototype and specify how these properties are used in computing similarity to the prototype. A straightforward approach to identifying prototype properties is to ask people to list them, for example, "List all the properties of *bird* you can think of in 90 seconds." Table 13.2 contains a small subset of property listings obtained by this technique (Malt and Smith 1984). In this experiment thirty subjects were each presented fifteen instances of *bird*; the subjects collectively produced more than

Table 13.2 Illustrations of How to Use Listed Properties to Calculate an Instance's Similarity to Prototype

Properties	Robin	Bluebird	Swallow	Starling	Vulture
Flies	+	+	+	+	+
Sings	+	+	+	+	−
Lays eggs	+	+	+	−	−
Is small	+	+	+	+	−
Nests in trees	+	+	+	+	+
Eats insects	+	+	+	+	−
Similarity to bird	6−0−0=6	6−0−0=6	6−0−0=6	5−1−0=4	2−4−0=−2

Properties	Sandpiper	Chicken	Flamingo	Penguin	Bird
Flies	+	−	−	−	+
Sings	+	−	−	−	+
Lays eggs	+	+	−	+	+
Is small	+	−	−	−	+
Nests in trees	−	−	−	−	+
Eats insects	+	−	−	−	+
Similarity to bird	5−1−0=4	1−5−0=−4	0−6−0=−6	1−5−0=−4	

fifty distinct properties, each property being produced by more than one subject. Table 13.2 considers only nine of the instances and six of the properties—flies, sings, lays eggs, is small, nests in trees, and eats insects. The rows of the table list the six properties; the columns give the instances in order of decreasing typicality, with the last column representing the concept *bird*. Each entry in the resulting matrix is a + or a −, where + indicates that at least two subjects listed the property for that instance and − means that either one or no subjects did. To determine the entries for *bird*, a property was assigned a + only if a majority of the instances had a + for that property. The prototype for *bird* thus contained the frequent or modal properties of the instances.

One way to use these properties to compute the similarity between an instance and a prototype is Tversky's (1977) "contrast" rule. The similarity between the set of properties characterizing an instance (labeled I) and the set of properties of a prototype (labeled P) is given by

$$\text{Sim } (I,P) = af(I \cap P) - bf(P - I) - cf(I - P).$$

Here $I \cap P$ designates the set of properties common to the instance and prototype, $P - I$ designates the set of properties distinct to the prototype, and $I - P$ designates the set of properties distinct to the instance. In addition f is a function that measures the salience of each set of properties, and a, b, and c are parameters that determine the relative contribution of the three property sets. The basic idea is that similarity is an increasing function of the properties common to the prototype and instance and a decreasing function of the properties distinct to the prototype and of those distinct to the instance.

Let us use the equation to determine the similarity of each instance in table 13.2 to *bird*. In making the calculations (given directly below the table), we assume that all properties are equally salient (that is, f assigns 1 to each property), and that distinctive properties count as much as common ones (specifically, a = b = c = 1). For the instances in table 13.2, the contrast rule correctly segregates the instances into three levels of typicality (3 high, 3 medium, and 3 low), though it makes few distinctions among the instances within each level. Finer distinctions can readily be made by assuming that properties differ in their salience.[4]

The analysis in table 13.2 is not without its problems. First, requiring subjects to list properties produces a biased estimate of an object's properties. People are likely to favor properties that are codable (that is, require only brief descriptions) and that discriminate among the instances presented (see Armstrong, Gleitman, and Gleitman 1983 for further discussion). A second problem is that there are alternatives to the contrast rule for computing similarity, including geometric approaches that view similarity as proximity in some underlying psychological space rather than as a matter of common and distinctive properties (see, for example, Shepard 1974). In defense of the analysis in table 13.2, we note that properties that are codable and discriminating may be salient and hence likely to be in a prototype, and that property approaches like the contrast rule may capture similarity better than geometric approaches when the items involved are semantic rather than perceptual (Tversky and Hutchinson 1986). Although hardly definitive, this analysis is plausible and at least demonstrates how the prototype view can lead to testable proposals.

Other Concepts The similarity-to-prototype approach has been generalized to concepts other than natural kinds, especially artifact concepts like *furniture* and *clothing*. The phenomena for natural kinds hold for artifacts as well: (1) people do not have fixed definitions of most artifacts; (2) the instances of any artifact concept vary in typicality (for example, for *furniture*, *chair* is more typical than *rug*), with typical instances being easier to categorize, remember, name, and reason about; and (3) more typical instances of an artifact concept have nonnecessary properties that occur frequently in other instances (Rosch and Mervis 1975). These findings fit nicely with the view that an artifact concept consists of a prototype, that typicality reflects an instance's similarity to its prototype, and that similarity to prototype is involved in categorization, memory, naming, and reasoning. As before, this proposal may be fleshed out by identifying the properties in a prototype and using these properties to compute an item's similarity to the prototype.

The similarity-to-prototype approach has also been extended to social and personality concepts, though in a more sketchy fashion. Some of the concepts investigated denote personality types, such as *extrovert* and *introvert*. For example, Cantor and Mischel (1979) showed that the extent to which an "instance"—that is, a description of an individual—was judged typical of *extrovert* increased with the number of properties that the individual shared with extroverts in general. This suggests that, just as in natural-kind concepts, instances of a personality concept vary in typicality, where typicality increases with the number of properties common to the instance and concept. There are comparable results for the concept of *emotion*. Its instances—including *happiness, anger, fear, awe, respect,* and *envy*—can be reliably ordered with respect to typicality, and these typicality rankings predict the ease with which the instances can be categorized as well as the order in which they are retrieved from memory (Fehr and Russel 1984; see also Shaver, Schwartz, Kirson, and O'Connor 1987).

A similar story holds even for personality concepts of a technical nature, such as *paranoid schizophrenia* and *involutional depression*. For such concepts psychiatrists can reliably rate patients for typicality, and these ratings predict important aspects of the patient's categorization (diagnosis). For example, the more typical of *paranoid schizophrenia* a patient is, the more likely he or she will receive that diagnosis by two independent assessors (Cantor, Smith, French, and Mezzich 1980).

This list of generalizations of the similarity-to-prototype approach could be extended. For virtually every concept that has been considered, there is a typicality gradient among its instances. And in many of these cases, there is evidence that typicality predicts ease of categorization. There is something right about the idea of prototypes.[5]

On-line Computation of Prototypes Let us refer to the concepts that I have been discussing—natural kinds, artifacts, personalities, and so on—as "ordinary" concepts. We have been assuming that the prototypes of ordinary concepts are prestored. This assumption seems reasonable for the simple concepts we have been considering, but it may not be plausible for certain complex concepts. To illustrate this, suppose you were asked if a new neighbor is typical of other people on your block. Answering this question would likely involve your forming on-line the concept *people on my block*. Presumably your computation of the prototype would include retrieving remembered descriptions of individuals on your block and abstracting the more frequent properties of these individual instances (Kahneman and Miller 1986). Such an on-line prototype leads to the same typicality effects as a prestored prototype: an on-line and a prestored prototype of *people on my block* both contain roughly the same properties (middle-class, polite, aloof, and so on), and overlap with these properties is what determines an instance's typicality.

The notion of on-line prototypes allows us to extend the similarity-to-prototype approach to a variety of complex concepts. This much seems relatively straightforward. What is more controversial is the claim that prototypes may be computed on line even for simple concepts (see, for example, Hintzman 1986, Kahneman and Miller 1986). When asked whether a particular object is a *bird*, for example, we may use remembered *bird*-exemplars to compute a prototype on line rather than retrieve a prestored abstraction. Alternatively we may compare the object directly to the retrieved exemplars without even bothering to form a prototype (see, for example, Estes 1986, Medin and Schaffer 1978, Nosofsky 1987). This procedure yields roughly the same results as a comparison to an on-line prototype because the prototype is a summary of the retrieved exemplars.

These exemplar-based proposals have received detailed support from experiments using artificial concepts (for example, a set of schematic faces varying in eye height, nose length, and mouth curvature). On the other hand these proposals cannot account for some general aspects of ordinary concepts. In particular we are frequently taught facts about a general class rather than specific instances, such as "all birds lay eggs," and intuitively it seems that we associate each such fact with a single summary—a prestored prototype—rather than store it multiple times with a host of exemplars. Perhaps the safest conclusion is this: For simple, ordinary concepts like *bird*, prestored prototypes play the dominant role in categorization, reasoning, and other processes; however, exemplars may play some role in these processes as when we decide that a novel animal is a *bird* based on its similarity to an *ostrich*. For complex concepts like *people on my block*, exemplars likely play a critical role, being used either to derive the prototype on line or to directly classify the input. In what follows I continue to emphasize simple, ordinary concepts and their prestored prototypes.

The Prototype-Core Distinction   The proposal that an ordinary concept includes only a prototype turns out to be too simple. A more defensible claim is that an ordinary concept contains two components—a prototype and a *core*. The prototype contains properties that are useful for a "quick and dirty" categorization of objects, where such properties tend to be perceptually salient and easy to compute, though not very diagnostic of concept membership. In contrast the properties that comprise the core are more diagnostic of concept membership, but tend to be relatively hidden and less accessible for rapid categorization (Smith, Medin, and Rips 1984). Consider *bird* again. Our prototype includes the following properties: flies, is small, sings, perches in trees, and eats insects. Our core includes those properties that are most diagnostic of being a *bird*, say, that is has bird-genes (or that it was born of bird-parents).

This example makes it clear why we use prototype properties for categorization—they are far more accessible than core properties, even though less diagnostic.

Note that the core of an ordinary concept is not a definition. For one thing a core is not fixed the way a definition is. Your core for many animal concepts may involve some mention of genes, but someday scientists may change their theories and genes may be out and something else in. Thus you can entertain the possibility that penguins may not be birds after all but not the possibility that grandmothers may not be female. Another important difference is that cores are often too sketchy to qualify as definitions. Your core for *bird* may involve some notion of genes, but it is likely to be very vague. Rather than trying to precisely specify *bird*, most of us are content with some vague biological knowledge plus an indication that there are experts out there who can fill in the gaps (Putnam 1975).

If cores are not used for rapid categorizations, what purposes do they serve? One is that they "ground" our concepts—they give concepts stability. Though your core for *bird* may involve only some vague biological beliefs, those beliefs will likely be shared by other people, thereby providing some interpersonal stability of the concept. Similarly your core for *bird* is unlikely to undergo any radical shift (for example, believing that genes are irrelevant), which provides some intrapersonal stability of the concept (Smith et al. 1984). Another purpose of cores is that they may be used as the ultimate arbiters of categorization in special cases. For example, if you want to know whether the expensive pet dog you are thinking of buying is truly a terrier, you will inquire about its parentage rather than relying on properties such as its coloring. Still another function of cores is their role in reasoning. If you know that something is a *tiger*, for example, you can infer that it is more related (biologically) to cats than dogs, that it has internal organs, and that it will produce tiger offspring. These inferences and others like them follow from your core knowledge about *tiger* and, in particular, from the connection of this core to your general knowledge of biology (see Osherson and Smith 1981, Armstrong et al. 1983, and Carey 1985 for further discussion of the function of cores).[6]

Some Computational Considerations

Given some idea of *what* is represented in an ordinary concept, now we can ask *how* it is represented and processed. In what follows I focus on prototypes. (Presumably cores are represented just like prototypes except for an indication of greater diagnosticity of properties.)

Schema Representations   The most prevalent proposal is that a prototype is represented as a "schema" or "frame" (see, for example, Minsky 1975, Rumelhart and Ortony 1977). A possible schema for *bird* is illustrated in figure 13.1. Several aspects of this representation are

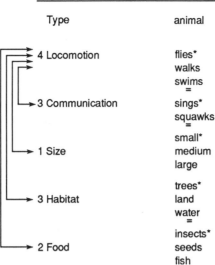

Bird	
Type	animal
→ 4 Locomotion	flies* walks swims =
→ 3 Communication	sings* squawks =
→ 1 Size	small* medium large
→ 3 Habitat	trees* land water =
→ 2 Food	insects* seeds fish =

Figure 13.1 An illustration of a possible schema for *bird*. The left-most terms designate attributes (type, locomotion, and so on), the terms on the right designate possible values (flies, sings, and so on), and the asterisks specify which values are the defaults. The number to the left of an attribute indicates its diagnosticity, and an arrow between two attributes indicates they are related.

critical. Note first that it has an attribute-value (or "slot-filler") format. For each attribute (for example, locomotion) there is a list of the possible values that instances of the concept can assume (for example, flies and walks). A second critical aspect is that one value of each attribute is designated as a default (as indicated by an asterisk). Any instance of the concept is assumed to have that default in the absence of information to the contrary; for example, instances of *bird* are assumed to fly unless one is informed otherwise. A third critical aspect is that relations between attributes are specified (as indicated by the arrows); for example, being able to locomote by air makes it possible to have a habitat in trees. For ease of exposition figure 13.1 gives only the relations involving the locomotion attribute and does not specify the exact relation involved (*causal, enablement,* and so forth).

A fourth aspect of our schema representation is that there is an indication of the type, or superset, that the concept is a member of (*animal* in this case). This type information connects the representation of interest to other schemas in a semantic network. A fifth aspect is that each attribute is marked for its importance, as given by the number to the attribute's left. Presumably an attribute's importance is determined partly by its diagnosticity, or usefulness in discriminating concept instances from noninstances; locomotion, for example, is an important attribute for *bird* because flying is useful for discriminating *birds* from *mammals*.

Each aspect of our schema representation can be justified by considering the kinds of questions that people can answer about various concepts. To see that we encode the attributes of a concept (not just its values), note that we might complete the statement *If a bird doesn't fly, it _____ "* with *walks* but not with *eats insects;* this is because we know that *flies* and *walks* are values on the same attribute, whereas *flies* and *eats insects* are not. With regard to the assumption of default values, intuition suggests that we would have no difficulty answering questions such as *Are birds more likely to fly or just walk?* As further support for defaults there is the widespread intuition that when we think of a concept, we tend to concretize it—that is, think of a best example of it—where the values that we fill in are the defaults. To see that we encode relations between attributes, note that we can answer questions such as *Which birds are more likely to sing, small ones or large ones?* (which queries the relation between vocalization and size) and *Which birds are more likely to fly, those that live in trees or those that live in water?* (which queries the relation between locomotion and habitat). The claim that each concept is linked to its superset is supported by our ability to answer questions about novel concept-property pairings, such as *Does a bird have internal organs?* Presumably we deduce the answer from the stored facts that (1) *Birds are animals* and (2) *Animals have internal organs,* where fact 1 is the link between *bird* and its superset (this idea was originally proposed by Collins and Quillian 1969). Finally, the assumption about attribute importance is supported by our ability to answer questions such as *Which is more important in telling birds from mammals, shape or color?*[7]

One reason why schema representations are so prevalent is that they foster the kinds of computations that people presumably execute. Compared with simple property representations such as those considered previously, the schema representation in figure 13.1 provides (1) a far greater· set of potential inductive inferences, (2) a richer means for computing similarity to prototypes, and (3) a clearcut means for combining simple concepts into composite concepts.

Point 1 is obvious—the extra inferences available from the schema are those having to do with attribute-value relations, default values, relations between attributes, links between concepts and their supersets, and differential importance of attributes. Point 2 requires a bit more elaboration. Previously we determined an instance's similarity to its prototype simply by counting matching and mismatching properties or values (see table 13.2). Now in computing similarity, we can weight each matching or mismatching value by the importance of its underlying attribute; furthermore we can consider whether the relations between an instance's attributes parallel those between the concept's attributes. There is experimental evidence that weighting the matches and mismatches of values improves the prediction of typicality ratings (Smith, Osherson, Rips, and Keane 1988), as well as evidence that considering relations between attributes further increases predictive accuracy (Medin and Shoben 1988).

Point 3—that a schema provides a means for combining concepts— also needs elaboration. One fundamental case of conceptual combination involves adjective-noun compounds like *large bird*, where the adjective concept modifies the noun concept. Modification is readily explicable in terms of schemas, as illustrated in figure 13.2. The left side of the figure repeats our schema for *bird* (save that relations between attributes have been suppressed), whereas the right side contains a schema for *large bird*. A comparison of the two schemas indicates that the adjective concept *large* has three direct effects: (1) it selects the critical attribute, size, in the prototype of the noun concept; (2) it boosts the diagnosticity of this attribute; and (3) it replaces the default on the critical attribute *small* with the value named by the adjective *large*. There may also be an indirect effect of adjective modification: the values on attributes related to the critical one (locomotion, communication, and so on) may be changed (this is not shown in figure 13.2). Roughly this modification process has been proposed by Smith and Osherson (1984; see also Smith, Osherson, Rips, and Keane 1988), who showed that it does a reasonable job of accounting for typicality ratings for conjunctive concepts, for example, the typicality of chicken in *large bird*.

Other Representations for Prototypes There are other possible representations for prototypes, two of which deserve brief mention. One is a production system, which has been used to model many aspects of

Bird		Large Bird	
Type	animal	Type	animal
4 Locomotion	flies* walks swims =	4 Locomotion	flies* walks swims =
3 Communication	sings* squawks =	3 Communication	sings* squawks =
1 Size	small* medium large	5 Size	small* medium large
3 Habitat	trees* land water =	3 Habitat	trees land water* =
2 Food	insects* seeds fish =	2 Food	insects* seeds fish =

Figure 13.2 An illustration of adjective modification. The left side contains a schema for *bird*, and the right side contains a schema for the modified concept *large bird*.

cognition (see, for example, Newell and Simon 1972, Anderson 1983, Holland, Holyoak, Nisbett, and Thagard 1986). A production system is composed of condition-action rules, each of which has the form "*If* such-and-such conditions prevail, *then* perform such-and-such action."

Different kinds of rules would be needed to model categorization and induction. For purposes of categorization we need rules that have attributes and values as their conditions and the assignment of a concept as their actions. Examples include

(1) *If* an animal's means of locomotion is flying, *then* (0.6) it's a bird.

(2) *If* an animal's means of locomotion is flying, *then* (0.1) it's a bat.

(3) *If* an animal's means of communication is singing, *then* (0.9) it's a bird.

(The numbers in parentheses indicate the extent to which the conditions support the categorization action.) In some systems all rules with satisfied conditions are activated simultaneously, and a final categorization occurs when there is a critical level of support for a particular concept (see, for example, Holland et al. 1986).

For drawing inferences, we need another kind of rule, one that has a concept as its condition and an attribute-value pair as its action, for example,

(4) *If* an animal is a bird, *then* (0.8) its means of locomotion is flying.

It seems likely that these rule types and others can be used to capture all the knowledge contained in a schema.

Another representation for concepts is a connectionist network. Although many such networks have a "distributed memory" (for example, the meaning of a term is distributed throughout the network), for our purpose it suffices to consider a network in which a single node represents a single concept or value (as in McClelland and Rumelhart 1981 and Feldman and Ballard 1982). In such a network the paths between nodes represent either excitatory or inhibitory relations. Thus the fact that wings are diagnostic of *bird* would be represented by an excitatory link leading from the *wings* node to the *bird* node; any time the *wings* node is activated (by the presence of a winged object), the activation spreads to the *bird* node. If enough value nodes that are excitatorily linked to *bird* are activated within a brief time period, the total activation culminating at *bird* should pass some categorization threshold. Conversely drawing an inference such as *birds fly* involves activation moving along an excitatory path from the *bird* node to the *wings* node. This kind of network can also capture the notion of an attribute by having inhibitory links between values of the same attribute. An inhibitory link between the *sings* node and the *squawks* node, for example, means that one cannot infer both that *birds sing* and that *birds squawk*.

Given the ingenuity with which connectionist nets have been developed recently, these representations can probably also capture all the knowledge contained in a schema (see, for example, Rumelhart, Smo-lensky, McClelland, and Hinton 1986). It seems then that the choice of which representation is best for concepts will be decided not by considerations of expressive power but rather by ease of accounting for empirical phenomena.

13.2 Categorization and Induction

Though the basic picture of categorization accounts for a mass of results about ordinary concepts (see Smith and Medin 1981), some recent findings indicate that there is more to categorization than determining an item's similarity to a prototype. A broader framework is therefore needed. The framework advanced here views categorization as a case of induction and considers modes of induction other than similarity to prototype.

Beyond Similarity

A recent study by Rips (1989) provides a clearcut example of people going beyond similarity in categorization judgments. On each trial of the experiment, a subject was presented a description of an object that mentioned only a value on a single dimension (say, an object's diameter). Then the subject decided which of two categories the object belonged to, where prior work had determined that the object was between the subject's average values for the two categories. For example, one item was "an object three inches in diameter," and the associated categories were *pizzas* and *quarters*. Although the object was if anything closer to the average diameter of a quarter (indeed another group of people had judged it more similar to a quarter), subjects judged it more likely to be a pizza than a quarter presumably because there is a constraint on the size of quarters but not on the size of pizzas. This kind of situation prevailed on all trials, because one category always allowed more variability on the relevant dimension than did the other, and subjects consistently chose the high-variability categories. These results indicate that subjects' categorization consider variability as well as similarity, and suggest that categorization is some form of inductive inference.

For another challenge to the basic picture of categorization, consider a thought experiment due to Murphy and Medin (1985). Suppose that you are at a party and see a man jump into a swimming pool with all his clothes on. You would probably categorize the man as *drunk*. This categorization is almost certainly not based on similarity—your prototype for *drunk* is not likely to include any mention of jumping into swimming pools clothed. Again the categorization seems to be some kind of inductive inference.

There are other relevant studies that deserve mention, but before considering them, I flesh out the suggestion that categorization is a form of induction.

Modes of Induction

For clarification let us think of an inductive inference as equivalent to a strong inductive argument, where the latter is standardly defined as an argument whose conclusion is unlikely to be false if its premises are true (Skyrms 1986). By this definition categorizing an object *is* an inductive argument, where the observed properties play the role of premises, and the claim about concept membership plays the role of conclusion. Categorizing a particular object as a *bird*, for example, might amount to believing the following argument:

(1) This object flies.
    This object perches in trees.
    This object sings.
    _____
    This object is probably a bird.

Thus the basic picture that we presented earlier amounts to the claim that inductive arguments about categorization are evaluated in terms of similarity, whereas Rips's pizza-quarter experiment and Murphy and Medin's *drunk* example amount to the claim that people can evaluate arguments by modes of induction other than similarity. What is needed then are descriptions of these other modes.

Osherson, Smith, and Shafir (1986) provide descriptions for several modes of induction, three of which are relevant here. One is the "similarity" mode. According to it, an argument is considered strong to the extent that the objects and relations mentioned in the premises are similar to those mentioned in the conclusion, where one includes typical properties of mentioned objects in determining similarity. In evaluating argument 1 by similarity, one notes that flying, perching, and singing (the premises) are very similar to the typical properties of *bird* (the conclusion) and therefore judges the argument strong.

Argument 1, however, would also be judged strong when evaluated by another mode of induction considered by Osherson and colleagues, which I refer to as "forward deduction" (Osherson and colleagues call it "enthymeme"). According to it, people judge an inductive argument strong to the extent that they can add to the premises a belief that turns the argument into a deductive one (that is, an argument whose conclusion cannot possibly be false if its premises are true). In argument 1 if we add to the premises the belief that *All flying, singing objects that perch in trees are probably birds,* then the conclusion of probable birdhood follows deductively. Osherson and colleagues also consider a third mode of induction, called "reverse deduction," which is relevant to our concerns. According to it, an inductive argument is judged strong to the extent that adding a belief to the conclusion allows one to deduce the premises. This mode does not work with argument 1, but it does with the very next example that we consider.

Although Osherson and colleagues (1986) showed that no single mode of induction suffices for all cases of induction, it is possible that each mode works for some situations, and that collectively the proposed modes come close to "covering the board." For our purposes these modes of induction provide a framework for interpreting Rips's pizza-quarter experiment, Murphy and Medin's *drunk* example, and many other empirical findings. Consider first Rips's experiment. On each trial subjects essentially had to decide which of two arguments was stronger, for example,

(2) This object is three inches in diameter.
   This object is a pizza.

(3) This object is three inches in diameter.
   This object is a quarter.

One way subjects could have discriminated between these arguments is by using forward deduction. If one adds to the premises of argument 3 the belief *If any object is three inches or more in diameter, it cannot be a quarter,* one can deduce that the object is not a quarter, which directly contradicts the conclusion. This shows that argument 3 is weaker than argument 2, which means that the object is more likely to be a pizza than a quarter.

Alternatively subjects could have used reverse deduction to choose between arguments 2 and 3. They could have added to the conclusion of argument 3 the belief *If an object is a quarter, it cannot be as large as three inches in diameter,* which would allow them to deduce that the object is not three inches in diameter, which leads to a contradiction of the premise. Thus what Rips's results show is that sometimes people us a deduction-type rather than similarity-type mode of induction in categorization decisions, and that they do this by adding beliefs about variability.[8,9]

Deduction-type modes also help make sense of Murphy and Medin's *drunk* example. Deciding that jumping into a pool clothed is an indicator of being drunk amounts to making the following argument:

(4) The man jumped into the swimming pool clothed.
   The man is probably drunk.

Presumably this categorization is based on forward deduction. If one adds to the premise the beliefs *Jumping into water clothed is an instance of erratic behavior* and *Anyone who behaves erratically (at a party) is probably drunk,* one can deduce the conclusion *The man is probably drunk.* Note that this argument does not seem as strong as the argument corresponding to Rips's pizza-quarter experiment. This difference in strength is likely due to our having less conviction in our added beliefs in the *drunk* example than in the pizza-quarter experiment. More generally the strength of an argument that is evaluated by deduction-based induction should increase with the strength of the added beliefs (Osherson et al. 1986).

In the preceding case the critical added belief was diagnostic of a causal condition (*behaving erratically is diagnostic of being drunk*), whereas in Rips's pizza-quarter study the added beliefs concerned variability. In other experiments on the limits of similarity, the added beliefs concern the nature of categorization itself. Another study by Rips (1989) illustrates this. Subjects were told about an animal that had typical bird properties, but suffered an accident that caused many of its properties to resemble those of an insect. Subjects were further told that eventually this animal mated with a normal female of its species, who produced normal young. Subjects rated this creature as more likely to be a *bird* than an *insect* but more similar to an *insect* than a *bird*. Hence we have another demonstration that categorization need not be based on similarity. Once more it is instructive to view the categorization as an inductive argument:

(5) The animal originally had typical bird properties.
The animal accidentally acquired typical insect properties.
<u>The animal produced offspring with typical bird properties.</u>
This animal is probably a bird.

Presumably subjects used forward deduction to evaluate argument 5, where a critical added belief may have been of the sort *If an animal produces offspring of a particular natural category, then that animal is probably in that natural category.* (See Keil 1986 for similar findings with children.)

In sum the studies reviewed in this section show that when faced with a categorization problem, people can go beyond similarity and use deduction-type modes that involve accessing additional beliefs. We do not yet know what aspects of the categorization problem trigger the use of deduction-type modes. Nor do we know much about the diversity of the added beliefs that are brought into play. The latter is particularly important. For as a number of philosophers have pointed out, developing a theory of categorization may be feasible to the extent that there are limits on what beliefs may figure in decisions about concept membership (see, for example, Fodor 1983, Rey 1983).

Estimating Probabilities
The inductive tasks in which people routinely participate include not only determining whether an item belongs to a particular category but also estimating the probability that an item belongs to a particular category or has a particular property. The strategies that people use in probability estimation turn out to be the same as those used in categorization. And analyzing probability-estimation studies in terms of

these strategies sheds some new light on why people's estimates of probability often violate fundamental principles of probability theory.

The extent to which people's probability estimates accord with probability theory has been ingeniously and extensively studied by Tversky and Kahneman. In one of their best-known experiments (Tversky and Kahneman 1973), subjects read personality descriptions of various men and estimated the probability that each one was an engineer rather than a lawyer. Some descriptions were more typical of engineers than lawyers, for example, ". . . spends most of his free time on his many hobbies, which include home carpentry, sailing, and mathematical puzzles," whereas other descriptions were nondiagnostic with respect to the engineer-lawyer contrast, for example, "a man of high ability and high motivation." In addition one group of subjects was told that 70 percent of the men being described were engineers (the rest being lawyers), and a second group was told that 30 percent of the men described were engineers (the rest being lawyers). This frequency information is terribly relevant to the subject's task—according to probability theory, the higher the prior probability of an engineer the higher the subject's estimate should be—and this information is what distinguishes the study from a standard experiment on categorization.

However, subjects in this experiment made little use of the frequency information. Instead they based their probability estimates primarily on the similarity of the descriptions to the prototype of an engineer. For example, given a nondiagnostic description, subjects in both the "70 percent engineers" and "30 percent engineers" groups estimated the probability that the man was an engineer as roughly 0.5. In the terminology of our modes of induction, subjects were using the similarity mode, and there is no obvious way for relative-frequency information to enter such a process (see Smith and Osherson 1989 for discussion).

The failure to use relative-frequency information is not the only error that people commit when estimating probabilities. In another of Tversky and Kahneman's (1983) experiments, subjects first read a brief description of a person and then decided which of two possible categories the person was more likely to belong to. For instance, subjects read about "Linda, who is outspoken and concerned with issues of social justice" and had to decide whether she was more likely to be a *bankteller* or a *feminist bankteller*. Most subjects thought Linda was more likely to be a *feminist bankteller* than a *bankteller*, which is a flagrant violation of the principle that a conjunction of events can never be more probable than one of its constituents. As Tversky and Kahneman note, presumably subjects commit such "conjunction fallacies" because they base their decisions on Linda being more similar to a prototypical *feminist bankteller* than to a prototypical *bankteller*.

With regard to the preceding experiment, it is again instructive to consider the arguments that subjects were essentially evaluating:

(6) <u>Linda is outspoken and . . . issues of social justice.</u>
Linda is a bankteller.

(7) <u>Linda is outspoken and . . . issues of social justice.</u>
Linda is a feminist bankteller.

Clearly the similarity mode declares argument 7 to be stronger than argument 6, which is why subjects judged *feminist bankteller* to be more likely than *bankteller*. It is of further interest to ask what kind of argument subjects would have had to consider to ensure a correct answer. Presumably subjects needed something such as

(8) <u>The two arguments about Linda are identical except that the first one's conclusion is a part of the second one's conclusion.</u>
The first argument is stronger.

Argument 8 would be judged strong by the forward-deduction strategy to the extent that one can access the belief corresponding to the probability principle *A conjunction can never be more probable than one of its constituents.*

The preceding analysis indicates that people's failure to use probability principles could reflect a difficulty with metaarguments (like argument 8), a preference for similarity over deductive-type modes, or a difficulty in accessing the probability beliefs that would be used in a deduction-type mode. Another experiment by Tversky and Kahneman (1983) suggests that inaccessibility of beliefs is a key factor. In this study subjects read a description of a man, "John P. . . . convicted once for smuggling [but is] meek [and] . . . mildmannered." When presented with possible actions of John P., subjects judged it less probable that "John P. killed one of his employees" than that "John P. killed one of his employees to prevent him from talking to police." Again subjects erroneously judged a conjunction to be more probable than one of its constituents. This time, however, the conjunction fallacy may have arisen even though subjects were using a deduction-type mode.

That is, subjects were essentially evaluating the arguments

(9) <u>John P. . . . convicted of smuggling . . . meek . . . mildmannered.</u>
John P. killed his employee.

(10) <u>John P. . . . convicted of smuggling . . . meek . . . mildmannered.</u>
John P. killed his employee to prevent him from talking to the police.

Although it is unclear how subjects evaluated argument 9, they may have evaluated argument 10 by forward deduction where the added belief was a causal rule such as, *Even a meek criminal will kill to prevent an informant from talking to the police.* To the extent this analysis is correct, we have evidence that people fail to use statistical principles even when they use a deductive mode, presumably because statistical beliefs are less accessible than causal ones. (I hedge about the correctness of this analysis because it is possible that subjects used similarity to evaluate arguments 9 and 10, where the information added to the conclusion of argument 11 somehow increased John P.'s similarity to the prototype of a murderer.)

Finally, it is worth noting that my interpretation of the above experiments bears some correspondences to the analysis that Tversky and Kahneman themselves offer. They talk of "decision heuristics" rather than induction modes, which fits with their construing the modes as common procedures for estimating probabilities. All told, Tversky and Kahneman (see, for example, 1974) identify four distinct heuristics, where two of them, *representativeness* and *causal analysis*, correspond roughly to similarity and deduction-type modes, respectively. Their other two heuristics, *availability* and *anchoring and adjustment*, correspond less to induction modes than to variations in how a particular mode may be executed. In anchoring and adjustment, for instance, people may first use a particular mode of induction to obtain a general estimate of a desired probability and then use that or another mode to refine the estimate.

Summary

The similarity mode corresponds to what I call similarity to prototype in the basic picture of categorization. In this picture similarity plays the major role in explaining findings obtained with ordinary concepts in standard categorization tasks. Although similarity continues to play an important role in some of the probability-estimation studies, the major burden of this section has been to show that similarity alone cannot provide a complete picture of categorization with ordinary concepts. Other modes of induction must be considered, where these modes correspond to different ways of doing induction. In the bigger picture then categorization is best thought of as a case of induction.

Notes

1. Although the frequency with which we think of a specific instance, say *apple*, may have little to do with its related typicality, the frequency with which we think of *apple* as a *fruit* may have some effect on typicality (Barsalou 1985).

2. This argument against the classical view is not very strong because even nominal-kind concepts, which conform to the view, can manifest typicality effects. For example, clearly some instances of *grandmother* seem more typical than others.

3. The term "prototype" has also been used by some investigators to refer to a particular instance (for example, Rosch and Mervis 1975).

4. Note that this analysis also explains the Rosch and Mervis's (1975) result that instances with frequent properties are rated as more typical than instances with less frequent properties. Properties that occur frequently among a concept's instances are likely to be properties of the concept itself; hence an instance with frequent properties is one that shares many features with the concept, which means it is highly similar to the concept.

5. This is not to say that the different kinds of concepts we have been considering—natural kinds, artifacts, personalities—do not differ in other important respects. As examples: (1) natural-kind concepts may support more inductive inferences about invisible properties than do artifact concepts (Gelman and O'Reilly 1988), and (2) both natural-kind and artifact concepts are organized in "tighter" taxonomies than are personality concepts (for example, it is more difficult to imagine that the same object can be both *cat* and *dog* than that the same person can be both *extrovert* and *introvert*). See Lakoff 1987 for an extended discussion of differences among concepts that share a basic prototype structure.

6. I have been making the case that ordinary concepts, which lack definitions, contain a core as well as a prototype. It should be noted that even nominal-kind concepts like *grandmother* and *even number* may contain both a core and a prototype. The cores of such concepts are their definitions. That these concepts also contain prototypes is suggested by the findings that instances of such concepts can be reliably rated for typicality (see note 2), where these ratings predict the speed with which the instances can be categorized (Armstrong et al. 1983).

7. By using question-answering evidence, we assume that people "read-off" the answers from the prototypes mentioned in the question. Sometimes, however, people may have to compute the answer, and in doing so they may use knowledge other than that presented in the mentioned concepts.

8. A caveat is in order here. The critical added belief—for example, *If an object is a quarter, it cannot be as large as three inches in diameter*—is unlikely to be prestored; rather, when needed, it is probably inferred from other beliefs. That is, the critical belief may itself be a conclusion from another inductive argument, one whose premises include prestored beliefs such as *A quarter has to be a specific size* and *The quarters I can think of are less than three inches in diameter*.

9. Beliefs about variability also play a role in inductive situations other than categorization, as illustrated in an experiment by Nisbett, Krantz, Jepson, and Kunda (1983). Subjects were asked to imagine they were exploring a remote South Pacific island and encountered a member of the Barratos tribe who was brown-skinned. When asked what percent of all Barratos are brown-skinned, subjects' estimates were close to 100 percent. In contrast if told the Barratos man was obese, subjects estimated that less than 40 percent of all Barratos are obese. Presumably this substantial difference in the inductive power of a property (brown-skinned versus obese) is being mediated by beliefs about variability (for example, roughly, *Members of a tribe are alike in skin color, but vary considerably in weight*).

References

Anderson, J. R. 1983. *The Architecture of Cognition.* Cambridge, MA: Harvard University Press.

Armstrong, S. L., Gleitman, L. R., and Gleitman, H. 1983. What some concepts might not be. *Cognition* 13:263–308.

Barsalou, L. W. 1985. Ideals, central tendency, and frequency of instantiation as determinants of graded structure in categories. *Journal of Experimental Psychology: Learning, Memory, and Cognition* 11:629–654.

Bruner, J. S., Goodnow, J., and Austin, G. 1956. *A Study of Thinking.* New York: Wiley.

Cantor, N., and Mischel, E. 1979. Prototypes in person perception. In L. Berkowitz, ed. *Advances in Experimental Social Psychology.* Vol. 12. New York: Academic Press.

Cantor, N., Smith, E. E., French, R., and Mezzich, J. 1980. Psychiatric diagnosis as prototype categorization. *Journal of Abnormal Psychology* 89:181–193.

Carey, S. 1985. *Conceptual Change in Childhood.* Cambridge, MA: MIT Press.

Cherniak, C. 1984. Prototypicality and deductive reasoning. *Journal of Verbal Learning and Verbal Behavior* 23:625–642.

Collins, A. M., and Quillian, M. R. 1969. Retrieval time from semantic memory. *Journal of Verbal Learning and Verbal Behavior* 8:240–247.

Estes, W. K. 1986. Array models for category learing. *Cognitive Psychology* 18:500–549.

Fehr, B., and Russel, J. A. 1984. Concepts of emotion viewed from a prototype perspective. *Journal of Experimental Psychology: General* 113:464–486.

Feldman, J. A., and Ballard, D. H. 1982. Connectionist models and their properties. *Cognitive Science* 6:205–254.

Fodor, J. 1983. *The Modularity of Mind.* Cambridge, MA: MIT Press.

Fodor, J., Garrett, M., Walker, E., and Parkes, C. M. 1980. Against definitions. *Cognition* 8:263–367.

Gelman, S. A., and O'Reilly, A. W. 1988. Children's inductive inferences with superordinate categories: The role of language and category structure. *Child Development* 59:876–887.

Hintzman, D. L. 1986. "Schema abstraction" in a multiple trace memory model. *Psychological Review* 93:411–428.

Holland, J. H., Holyoak, K. J., Nisbett, R. E., and Thagard, P. R. 1986. *Induction: Processes of Inference, Learning, and Discovery.* Cambridge, MA: MIT Press.

Kahneman, D., and Miller, D. T. 1986. Norm theory: Comparing reality to its alternatives. *Psychological Review* 93:136–153.

Katz, J. J., and Fodor, J. A. 1963. The structure of a semantic theory. *Language* 39:170–210.

Keil, F. C. 1986. The acquisition of natural-kind and artifact terms. In W. Demopoulos and A. Marras, eds. *Language Learning and Concept Acquisition.* Norwood, NJ: Ablex.

Lakoff, G. 1987. *Women, Fire, and Dangerous Things*. Chicago: University of Chicago Press.

McClelland, J. L., and Rumelhart, D. E. 1981. An interactive activation model of context effects in letter perception: Part 1. An account of basic findings. *Psychological Review* 88:375–407.

Malt, B. C., and Smith, E. E. 1984. Correlated properties in natural categories. *Journal of Verbal Learning and Verbal Behavior* 23:250–269.

Medin, D. L., and Shoben, E. J. 1988. Context and structure in conceptual combination. *Cognitive Psychology* 20:158–190.

Medin, D. L., and Schaffer, M. M. 1978. A context theory of classification learning. *Psychological Review* 85:207–238.

Mervis, C. B., Catlin, J., and Rosch, E. 1976. Relationships among goodness-of-example, category norms and word frequency. *Bulletin of the Psychomic Society* 7:268–284.

Minsky, M. 1975. A framework for representing knowledge. In P. H. Winston, ed. *The Psychology of Computer Vision*. New York: McGraw-Hill.

Murphy, G. L., and Medin, D. L. 1985. The role of theories in conceptual coherence. *Psychological Review* 92:289–316.

Newell, A., and Simon, H. A. 1972. *Human Problem Solving*. Englewood Cliffs, NJ: Prentice-Hall.

Nisbett, R. E., Krantz, D. H., Jepson, D., and Kunda, Z. 1983. The use of statistical heuristics in everyday inductive reasoning. *Psychological Review* 90:339–363.

Nosofsky, R. M. 1987. Attention, similarity, and the identification-categorization relationship. *Journal of Experimental Psychology: General* 115:39–57.

Osherson, D. N., and Smith, E. E. 1981. On the adequacy of prototype theory as a theory of concepts. *Cognition* 9:35–58.

Osherson, D. N., Smith, E. E., and Shafir, E. B. 1986. Some origins of belief. *Cognition* 24:197—224.

Putnam, H. 1975. The meaning of "meaning." In K. Gunderson, ed. *Language, Mind, and Knowledge*. Minneapolis: University of Minnesota Press.

Rey, G. 1983. Concepts and stereotypes. *Cognition* 15:237–262.

Rips, L. J. 1975. Inductive judgements about natural categories. *Journal of Verbal Learning and Verbal Behavior* 14:665–681.

Rips, L. J. 1989. Similarity, typicality, and categorization. In S. Voisniadou and A. Ortony, eds. *Similarity, Analogy, and Thought*. New York: Cambridge University Press.

Rosch, E. 1978. Principles of categorization. In E. Rosch and B. B. Lloyd, eds. *Cognition and Categorization*. Hillsdale, NJ: Erlbaum.

Rosch, E., and Mervis, C. B. 1975. Family resemblances: Studies in the internal structure of categories. *Cognitive Psychology* 3:382–439.

Rumelhart, D. E., and Ortony, A. 1977. The representation of knowledge in memory. In R. C. Anderson, R. J. Spiro, and W. E. Mongatue, eds. *Schooling and the Acquisition of Knowledge.* Hillsdale, NJ: Erlbaum.

Rumelhart, D. E., Smolensky, P., McClelland, J. L., and Hinton, G. E. 1986. Schematic and sequential thought processes in PDP models. *Parallel Distributed Processing.* Vol. 2. Cambridge, MA: MIT Press.

Schwartz, S. P. 1979. Natural kind terms. *Cognition* 7:301–315.

Shaver, P., Schwartz, J., Kirson, D., and O'Connor, C. 1987. Emotion knowledge: Further exploration of a prototype approach. *Journal of Personality and Social Psychology* 52:1061–1086.

Shepard, R. N. 1974. Representation of structure in similarity data: Problems and prospects. *Psychometrika* 39:373–421.

Skyrms, B. 1986. *Choice and Change: An Introduction to Inductive Logic.* 3rd ed. Belmont: Wadsworth.

Smith, E. E., and Medin, D. L. 1981. *Categories and Concepts.* Cambridge, MA: Harvard University Press.

Smith, E. E., Medin, D. L., and Rips, L. J. 1984. A psychological approach to concepts: Comments on Rey's "Concepts and Stereotypes." *Cognition* 17:265–274.

Smith, E. E., and Osherson, D. N. 1984. Conceptual combination with prototype concepts. *Cognitive Science* 11:337–361.

Smith, E. E., and Osherson, D. N. 1989. Similarity and decision making. In S. Voiniadou and A. Ortony, eds. *Similarity, Analogy, and Thought.* New York: Cambridge University Press.

Smith, E. E., Osherson, D. N., Rips, L. J., and Keane, M. 1988. Combining prototypes: A selective modification model. *Cognitive Science* 12:485–527.

Smith, E. E., Shoben, E. J., and Rips, L. J. 1974. Structure and process in semantic memory: A featural model for semantic decisions. *Psychological Review* 81:214–241.

Tversky, A. 1977. Features of similarity. *Psychological Review* 84:327–352.

Tversky, A., and Hutchinson, J. W. 1986. Nearest neighbor analysis of psychological spaces. *Psychological Review* 93:3–22.

Tversky, A., and Kahneman, D. 1974. Decision making under uncertainty: Heuristics and biases. *Science* 185:1124–1131.

Tversky, A., and Kahneman, D. 1973. On the psychology of prediction. *Psychological Review* 80:237–251.

Tversky, A., and Kahneman, D. 1983. Extensional versus intuitive reasoning. The conjunction fallacy in probability judgment. *Psychological Review* 90(4):293–315.

14 Problem Solving and Cognitive Skill Acquisition

Kurt VanLehn

Although virtually any human activity can be viewed as the solving of a problem, throughout the history of the study of problem solving, most research has concerned tasks that take minutes or hours to perform. Typically subjects make many observable actions during this period, and these actions are interpreted as the externally visible part of the solution process. Even if subjects are required to solve problems in their heads (for example, to mentally multiply 135×76), they are usually asked to talk aloud as they work, and the resulting verbal protocol is interpreted as a sequence of actions (see chapter 1). Thus the tasks studied are not only long tasks but also *multistep* tasks.

The earliest experimental work on human problem solving was done by Gestalt psychologists, notably Kohler, Selz, Duncker, Luchins, Maier, and Katona (see Duncan 1959 for a review). They concentrated on multistep tasks in which only a few of the steps to be taken were crucial and difficult. Such problems are called *insight problems* because the solution follows rapidly once the crucial steps have been made. An example of such a task is construction of a wall-mounted candleholder from an odd assortment of materials, including a candle and a box of tacks. The materials are chosen in such a way that the only solution involves using the box as a support for the candle by tacking it to the wall. To find this solution, subjects must change their belief that the box is only a container for the tacks and instead view the box as construction material. This belief change is the crucial, insightful step. Once it is made, the solution is soon reached.

In contrast most problem-solving research in the past three decades has concerned multistep tasks in which no single step is the key. In these tasks finding a solution depends on making a number of correct steps. An example of such a task is solving an algebraic equation. The solution is a sequence of proper algebraic transformations, correctly applied. The difficulty in the problem lies in deciding which transformations to apply, remembering them accurately, and applying them correctly. Thus the responsibility for the solution is spread over the whole solution process rather than falling on the discovery of one or two key steps. This choice of tasks caused research to focus on how people organize the solution process, how they decide what steps to make in what circumstances, and how their knowledge of the task domain determines their view of the problem and their discovery of its solution. These topics are emphasized in this chapter.

In the 1950s and 1960s most research concerned tasks that require no special training or background knowledge. Everything that the subject needs to know to perform the tasks is presented in the instructions. A classic example of such a task is the "Tower of Hanoi." The subject is shown a row of three pegs. On the leftmost peg are three disks: a large one on the bottom, then a medium sized one, and a small disk on top. The subject is told that the goal of the puzzle is to move all three disks to the rightmost peg, but only one disk may be moved at a time, and a larger disk may never be placed on top of a smaller one. There are many variations of this basic puzzle. For instance, there can be more than three disks, and the starting and finishing states can be arbitrary configurations of disks. All these variants of the puzzle are called a *task domain*, and each specific version is called a *task*, that is, one element of the task domain. "Task" and "problem" are virtually synonymous. The Tower of Hanoi and other simple, puzzlelike task domains are called *knowledge-lean*, because it takes very little knowledge (that is, just what one reads in the instructions) to solve problems in the task domain. Of course some subjects may have a great deal of knowledge about the task domain—puzzle fanatics, for instance. Possession of such knowledge, however, is not essential for obtaining a solution. Someone with very little knowledge can blunder through to a solution.

The study of knowledge-lean tasks led to the formulation of Newell and Simon's landmark theory. Their 1972 book, *Human Problem Solving*, is still required reading for anyone seriously interested in the field. This theory became the foundation for many detailed models of problem solving in specific task domains. The models are able to explain not only the steps taken by the subjects but also their verbal comments (see, for example, Newell and Simon 1972, chs. 6, 9, 12), the latencies between steps (see, for example, Karat 1982), and even their eye movements (see, for example, Newell and Simon 1972, ch. 7). The early seventies marked a high point for theoretical work in the field of knowledge-lean problem solving.

In the late 1970s attention shifted to studying *knowledge-rich* task domains, in which many pages of instructions are required for presenting even the minimal knowledge necessary for solving the problem. Knowledge-rich task domains that have been studied include algebra, physics, thermodynamics, chess, bridge, geometry, medical diagnosis, public-policy formation, and computer programming.

Much early empirical research into knowledge-rich tasks concerned the differences between experts and novices. Varying the level of expertise while holding the task domain constant helped investigators separate the effects of expertise from the influence of the task domain. The typical study gave the same set of problems to experts and novices and used protocol analysis (see chapter 1) to examine differences in the performance of the two groups. Of course the novices found the problems quite hard and the experts found them quite easy. If one assumes that the experts had encountered the same or similar problems many times in the past, one would expect them to simply recognize the problem as an instance of a familiar problem type, retrieve the solution template from memory, and generate the problem's solution directly. Novices on the other hand might have no such knowledge, so they would have to blunder about, searching for a solution just as the subjects in the knowledge-lean task domains do. To put it briefly, the hypothesis is that expertise allows one to substitute recognition for search.

Although the mid-1970s saw development of computer programs that could model the steps, latencies and even eye movements of subjects solving puzzles, no such models have been developed for experts solving problems in knowledge-rich task domains. Partly this is because it has proved difficult to build computer programs that contain a great deal of knowledge, and only recently has the technology for building such expert systems begun to bear fruit. There are an increasing number of programs that can competently solve problems in knowledge-rich task domains, although they often resort to methods that human experts do not seem to use (for example, extensive combinational searches).

However, there are also scientific reasons for *not* just building an expert system as a model of expert problem solving. Expert behavior, whether generated by people or programs, is a product of their knowledge, so any explanation of that behavior must rest on postulating a certain base of knowledge. But what explains that knowledge? Although it could be measured or formally constrained in various ways, the ultimate explanation for the form and content of the human experts' knowledge is the learning processes that they went through in obtaining it. Thus the best theory of expert problem solving is a theory of learning. Indeed learning theories may be the only scientifically adequate theories of expert problem solving.

Thus the focus of attention in the 1980s has been on the acquisition of expertise. There has been a revival of interest in traditional topics in skill acquisition, such as practice effects and transfer, and many of the regularities demonstrated with perceptual-motor skills have been found to govern cognitive skills as well. There are also novel experimental paradigms. For instance, much has been learned from taking protocols of students as they learn. A number of learning mechanisms have been developed and are discussed herein, but we still have incomplete knowledge about their respective roles in the total picture of cognitive skill acquisition.

Because this is a time of transition, a coherent theory of problem solving and skill acquisition cannot be presented here, so the ingredients for developing such a theory are presented instead. First, the 1972 theory of Newell and Simon is presented using as illustrations the knowledge-lean task domains that are its forte. Second, the idea of a *schema* is introduced because it has played an important role in explaining the long-term memory structures of experts. Third, a list of major empirical findings is presented.

14.1 Knowledge-Lean Problem Solving

This section discusses a theory of problem solving that was introduced by Newell and Simon (1972) in *Human Problem Solving* and has come to dominate the field. It forms a framework or set of terms that have proved useful for constructing specific analyses and models of human cognition.

The theory begins by making idealizations that distinguish between types of cognition. These distinctions are often difficult to define in objectively measurable terms. For instance, the first idealization is to distinguish between problem solving that involves learning and problem solving that does not. "Learning" in this context means resilient changes in the subject's knowledge about the task domain that are potentially useful in solving further problems (see Simon 1983 for a discussion of this definition of learning). Early work (for example, Newell and Simon 1972) assumed that there is little or no learning during problem solving. This idealization allowed formulation of a theory that is still useful. Moreover it provided the foundation for accounts of problem solving *with* learning. As usual in science oversimplification is not necessarily a bad thing.

The first several subsections present a discussion of problem solving under the idealization that learning is not taking place. In the last subsection the oversimplification is amended, and learning mechanisms are discussed.

A second important idealization is that the overall problem-solving process can be analyzed as two cooperating subprocesses, called *understanding* and *search*. The understanding process is responsible for assimilating the stimulus that poses the problem and for producing mental information structures that constitute the person's understanding of the problem. The search process is driven by these products of the understanding process rather than the problem stimulus itself. The search process is responsible for finding or calculating the solution to the problem. To put it differently, the understanding process generates the person's internal representation of the *problem*, whereas the search process generates the person's *solution*.

It is tempting to think that the understanding process runs first, produces its product, and then the search process begins. However, the two processes often alternate or even blend together (Hayes and Simon 1974, Chi, Glaser, and Rees 1982). If the problem is presented as text, then one may see the solver read the problem (the understanding process), make a few moves toward the solution (the search process), then reread the problem (understanding again). Although some understanding is logically necessary before search can begin, and indeed most understanding does seem to occur toward the beginning of the problem solving session, it is not safe to assume that understanding always runs to completion before search begins.

The first subsection will discuss the understanding process, and the second will discuss the search process. A third, brief subsection deals with a common type of problem solving that has some of the characteristics of both understanding and search.

The Understanding Process in Knowledge-Lean Task Domains
The understanding process converts the problem stimuli into the initial information needed by the search process. The early stages of the understanding process depend strongly on the media in which the problem is presented: text or speech, diagrams or pictures, physical situations or imaginary ones. Presumably a variety of perceptual processes can be involved in the early stages of understanding. Because perceptual processes are studied in other fields of cognitive science, problem-solving research has concentrated on describing the later stages of understanding and, in particular, on specifying what the output of the understanding process is.

In knowledge-lean task domains there is widespread agreement on what the product of understanding is. It follows almost logically from constraints on the type of material being understood. By definition the instructions for a problem in a knowledge-lean task domain contain all the information needed for solving the problem, although they may have to be supplemented and interpreted by commonsense knowledge. When this definition is combined with the fact that problem solving tasks are, almost by definition, multistep tasks, then it follows that the minimal information that the subject needs to obtain from the problem instructions consists of three components: (1) the initial problem state, (2) some operators that can change a problem state into a new state, and (3) some efficient test for whether a problem state constitutes a solution. These three components, along with some others that can be derived from them, are collectively called a *problem space*. Thus a major assumption about the understanding process for knowledge-lean task domains is that it yields a problem space.

The name "problem space" comes from the fact that the conjunction of an initial state and a set of operators logically implies a whole space of states (that is, a state space). Each state can be reached from the initial state by some sequence of operator applications. An incontestable principle of cognition is that people are not necessarily aware of all the deductive consequences of their beliefs, and this principle applies to problem spaces as well. Although the state space is a deductive consequence of the initial state and the operators, people are not aware of all of it. For instance, a puzzle solver may not be able to accurately estimate the number of states in the state space even after solving the puzzle several times. On the other hand the size and topology of the state space has played an important role in theoretical analyses where, for instance, the difficulty of a problem is correlated with the topology of the state space (Newell and Simon 1972).

As an illustration of the concept of a problem space, the problem spaces of two subjects are compared. Both subjects heard the following instructions:

Three men want to cross a river. They find a boat, but it is a very small boat. It will only hold 200 pounds. The men are named Large, Medium, and Small. Large weighs 200 pounds, Medium weighs 120 pounds, and Small weighs 80 pounds. How can they all get across? They might have to make several trips in the boat.

One subject was a nine-year-old girl, who asked me to refer to her as "Cathy" in describing her performance. Upon hearing the instructions, Cathy immediately asked "The boat can hold only 200 pounds?" and the experimenter answered affirmatively. Thereafter almost all of Cathy's discussion of the puzzle used only "sail" as a main verb and "Large," "Medium," "Small," "the boat," and pronouns as noun phrases. It is apparent from the protocol that Cathy solves this problem by imagining the physical situation and the actions taken in it, as opposed to, say, converting the puzzle to a directed graph then finding a traversal of the graph. Thus we can formally represent her belief about the current state of the imagined physical world as a set of propositions of the form $(On\ X\ Y)$, where X is in the set $\{L, M, S, B\}$, and Y is in the set $\{Source, Destination\}$. For instance, the set of propositions

$(On\ L\ Source)$ $(On\ M\ Source)$ $(On\ S\ Source)$ $(On\ B\ Source)$

represents the initial situation, where Large, Medium, Small, and the boat are all on the source bank of the river. Notice that Cathy could have a much richer description of the situation in mind that includes, for instance, propositions describing how much weight is in the boat and on each of the banks. Such descriptions never appear in her protocol, however, so it can be assumed (justified by simplicity and parsimony, and subject to refutation by further experiments) that Cathy maintains *only* descriptions of the $(On\ X\ Y)$ type while she solves the puzzle.

Similarly we can ask what types of operators Cathy believes are permitted in solving this puzzle. Apparently she infers it is not permitted that the three men can swim across the river or take some other transportation than the boat. Moreover she must have inferred that the 200-pound limit implies that only certain combinations of passengers are possible, because she only mentions legal boat rides. Thus Cathy seems to have just one legal operator, which can be formally represented as (*Sail X Y Z*), which stands for sailing passenger set X from bank Y to bank Z. The argument X is either $\{L\}$, $\{M,S\}$, $\{M\}$, or $\{S\}$, and Y and Z are either *Source* or *Destination*.

Cathy immediately recognizes when she has reached the desired final state, and moreover she shows signs throughout the protocol of being aware of it. So we can safely assume that Cathy's understanding of the LMS puzzle contains at least an initial state, the *Sail* operator, and the desired final state.

It is clear that Cathy's problem state is a very coarse representation of the actual physical situation of some men and a boat. Apparently she does not believe that the river's current, the weight of a boatload, and other factors are relevant to solving the puzzle. To highlight the subject's beliefs about what aspects of the puzzle's situations are relevant, most definitions of "problem space" (see, for example, Newell and Simon 1972) specify a fourth component, a *state-representation language*. Every state in the problem space, including the initial and final states, should be representable as some expression in this formal language. The state-representation language in Cathy's case is simply all possible conjunctions of (*On X Y*) propositions.

It is important to note that not all subjects derive the same problem space from the instructions. For instance, another subject, a 60-year-old man, first understood the instructions given to Cathy as an arithmetic problem. After hearing the instructions, the subject immediately answered that it would take two trips, because only 200 pounds could be moved per trip, and there were 400 pounds of men to move. He generated a different problem space from Cathy's, even though he received the same instructions. He was asked to describe exactly what those two trips were. He indicated that first Large could row across, then Medium and Small. The experimenter asked him how the boat was gotten back across. The subject replied that there must be a system of ropes or something. The experimenter asked him to assume instead that someone would have to row the boat back. This added instruction caused the subject to change his problem space. His new problem space was similar to Cathy's. This second subject's behavior shows that the understanding of simple knowledge-lean puzzles can interact with commonsense knowledge in interesting and nonobvious ways and can proceed differently with different subjects.

This example also shows that subjects can change their problem space to accommodate added information from the experimenter. Sometimes information garnered by the subjects themselves in the course of problem solving also causes them to change their problem space. Some investigators (Duncker 1945, Ohlsson 1984) have hypothesized that the "insights" of subjects solving insight problems are often changes of problem spaces.

There are problems that do not fit neatly into the problem-space mold, mostly because the solution states are not well defined. For instance, one can ask a subject to draw a pretty picture. Although minimal competence in this task requires no special knowledge, and therefore the task domain qualifies as knowledge-lean, it is difficult to characterize the subject's test for the final state. Indeed it is likely that some subjects themselves may not know what the final state will be until the picture is half-drawn. In these cases finding a set of constraints that qualify a problem state as a solution is just as important as generating a solution state. For knowledge-lean task domains a problem is *well-defined* if the subject's understanding of the problem produces a problem space, that is, an initial state, a set of operators, and a solution-state description. Problems whose understanding is not readily represented as a problem space are called *ill-defined*. Sketching pretty pictures is an ill-defined problem. A definition of well-defined for knowledge-rich task domains would be equivalent in spirit, but is not so easily stated because the understanding process for knowledge-rich task domains is considerably more complicated. There have been only a few studies of ill-defined problem solving. Reitman (1965) studied a composer writing a fugue for piano. Akin (1980) studied architectural design. Voss and his colleagues have studied agricultural policy formulation (Voss, Greene, Post, and Penner 1983, Voss, Tyler, and Yengo 1983). Simon (1973) provides a general discussion of ill-defined problem solving. This chapter concentrates exclusively on well-defined problems because that is where most of the research has been focused.

Although the output of the understanding process in knowledge-lean task domains is well understood (albeit by fiat), less is known about the process itself. In part this is because the understanding process for typical puzzles takes very little time. Cathy's protocol was two minutes long, but the understanding process seems to have run to completion during the first twenty seconds. The only behavior to observe during that brief time was Cathy's posing a question to the experimenter. To magnify the understanding process, Hayes and Simon (1974) studied a puzzle, called the tea ceremony, whose instructions are quite difficult to understand:

In the inns of certain Himalayan villages is practiced a most civilized and refined tea ceremony. The ceremony involves a host and exactly two guests, neither more nor less. When his guests have arrived and have seated themselves at his table, the host performs five services for them. These services are listed in the order of the nobility which the Himalayans attribute to them: (1) Stoking the Fire, (2) Fanning the Flames, (3) Passing the Rice Cakes, (4) Pouring the Tea, and (5) Reciting Poetry. During the ceremony, any of those present may ask another, "Honored Sir, may I perform this onerous task for you?" However, a person may request of another only the least noble of the tasks which the other is performing. Further, if a person is performing any tasks, then he may not request a task which is nobler than the least noble task he is already performing. Custom requires that by the time the tea ceremony is over, all the tasks will have been transferred from the host to the most senior of the guests. How may this be accomplished?

Hayes and Simon took a protocol of a subject interpreting these instructions and solving the puzzle. The subject read the text many times before he began to solve the puzzle. From the protocol it appears that the subject first built up an understanding of the objects in the initial state, then of the relationships between the objects, and finally of the legal operators. The subject proceeded statement by statement, trying to reconcile each statement with his current understanding.

The subject's major problem lay in interpreting the sentence, "During the ceremony, any of those present may ask of another, 'Honored Sir, may I perform this onerous task for you?'" The correct interpretation of this sentence, which the subject eventually discovered, is that the responsibility and ownership of the onerous task is transferred from one person to another. The subject's initial interpretation of the sentence, however, was that one person asks to do the task for the benefit of the other without actually relieving the other of the responsibility and ownership of the task. This benefactive reading is arguably the default interpretation for the English "perform for" construction, so it is no surprise that the subject's initial interpretation was benefactive. He only changed his interpretation when he noticed that the desired solution state requires that ownership of the onerous tasks have been transferred, and yet he has no operator that will effect such transfers. To make the problem solvable, he reexamines his interpretation of the "perform for" sentence and discovers its other reading.

This study and others (Hayes and Simon 1976, Kotovsky, Hayes, and Simon 1985) indicate that understanding of well-defined problems in knowledge-lean task domains is a rather direct translation process whose character is determined mostly by the type of stimulus used and the need for an internally consistent initial problem space. As will be discussed, this is not an apt characterization of the understanding process in knowledge-rich domains, nor does it explain why different subjects sometimes generate different problem spaces from the same instructions.

The Search Process

Suppose that problem spaces had not yet been invented, and we set out to formally describe the process of searching for problem solutions. We would soon discover that it is often quite easy to represent the subjects' current assumptions, postulations, or beliefs about the problem as a small set of assertions. For example, in the midst of trying to extrapolate the sequence ABMCDM, the subject might have the beliefs that the sequence has a period of three, and the third element of the period is always M. Thus the subject's current beliefs could be notated formally as including the assertions *Period = 3* and *For all p, Third (p) =*

"M", where p indexes periods. The search process consists of small, incremental changes in the subject's beliefs that can be modeled as small changes to the set of assertions. For instance, the next step in the search for the pattern of ABMCDM might produce just one new assertion about the problem, say, that the first and second elements in a period are consecutive letters in the alphabet. (Put formally, the new assertion is *For all p, Second(p) = Next(First(p))*.) This formal description of the problem-solving process, as a sequence of incremental changes to a set of assertions, is exactly the same as the problem-space notation. A state in a problem space corresponds to a set of assertions. The application of an operator to a state corresponds to the incremental changes in the subject's set of assertions. The operators themselves correspond to the heuristic rules that the subject uses to modify assertions (for example, "If the same letter occupies both positions i and $i + x$, then assert that *Period = x*"). This demonstrates the naturalness of problem spaces as a formal notation for the behavior that subjects exhibit while problem solving.[1]

The assertions that populate a problem state can represent beliefs that arise directly from perception. For instance, if the subject sees that the leftmost peg of the Tower of Hanoi puzzle has no disks on it at this time, then one could include the assertion *Disks (leftmost-peg) = {}* in the set that represents the subject's beliefs. Similarly moving a disk can be represented as an incremental change in the set of assertions. Thus the problem-space framework serves both to represent changes of the subject's internal state as well as changes in the physical state of the world.[2]

For most problem spaces there are usually several operators that can be applied to any given state. For instance, instead of inferring that *Second(p) = Next(First(p))*, which relates A with B and C with D in ABMCDM, it could be inferred that *First (p + 1) = Next(Second(p))*, which relates B with C. In this case it does not matter which operator is chosen. Some operator applications, however, lead to dead ends. For instance, if it is decided that the period of the sequence defgefghfghi is three, then a correct solution cannot be found by adding more assertions to the resulting state, because the correct period is actually four. These facts—that multiple operators apply at most states, and that some sequences of operator applications lead to dead ends—follow logically from the definition of the problem space. Any intelligence, human or artificial, must cope with these facts to find a solution path.

Suppose it is assumed that only one operator can be applied at a time, and that an operator can only be applied to an *available* state, where a state is available only if it is mentioned in the statement of the problem or it has been generated by application of an operator to an available state.[3] These assumptions logically imply that any solution process must be a special case of the algorithm template shown in table 14.1. The "slots" in this template are the functions for choosing a state, choosing an operator, and pruning states from the set of active states.

Table 14.1 A General Search Procedure

Let active-states be a set of states that initially contains only the states
mentioned in the problem statement.

1. Choose a state from active-states. If there are no states left in active-states,
   then stop and report failure.

2. Choose an operator that can be applied to the state. If no operator applies,
   then go to step 5.

3. Apply the operator to the state, producing a set of new states. If the set is
   empty, go to step 5.

4. Test whether any of the new states is a desired final state. If one is, then
   stop and report success. If none are, then place them in active-states and
   go to step 5.

5. Choose a subset of the states in active-states and remove them from active-
   states. Go to step 1.

A variety of specific algorithms can be formed by instantiating these
slots with specific computations. The class of algorithms formed this
way are called *state space search* algorithms. Much work has been done
on the properties of these algorithms.[4]

Although the search-algorithm template of table 14.1 is simple, it
does not have quite the right structure for describing human problem
solving. People seem to distinguish between new states and old states,
where a new state is one produced by the most recent operator application. In selecting a state (step 1 of the algorithm), choosing a new
state is viewed as proceeding along the current path in the search,
whereas choosing an old state is viewed as failing and backing up. For
people different principles of operation seem to apply to these two
kinds of selections. To capture this distinction, the work of search can
be allocated among two collaborating processes:

1. the *backup strategy*, which maintains the set of old states and chooses
one when necessary, and

2. the *proceed strategy*, which chooses an operator to apply to the current
state, applies it, and evaluates the resulting states. If one of them is a
desired, final state, the search stops and reports success. On the other
hand if none of them seems worth pursuing, then the backup strategy
is given control. Otherwise this process repeats.

Although this algorithm template is logically equivalent to the one of
table 14.1, it has different slots, namely, one for the backup strategy
and one for the proceed strategy (the latter is not a standard term in
the field).

Both the backup strategy and the proceed strategy are viewed as
potentially nondeterministic procedures, in that there are a number of
choice points (for example, choosing an operator) where the procedure
does not specify how the choice is to be made. However, some subjects

seem to apply simple, efficient criteria, called *heuristics*, to narrow the set of choices. Sometimes the heuristics are so selective that they narrow the options to just a single, unambiguous choice. In short this general template for search algorithms has three slots: (1) the backup strategy, (2) the proceed strategy, and (3) heuristics for the backup and proceed strategies.

It is generally held that there is a handful of distinct *weak methods* that novice subjects use for knowledge-lean task domains (Newell and Simon 1972, Newell 1980, Laird, Newell, and Rosenbloom 1987). Most of these methods are proceed strategies. The simplest weak method is a proceed strategy called *forward chaining*. Search starts with the initial state. Heuristics are used to select an operator from among those that are applicable to the current state. The selected operator is applied, and the strategy repeats. Another strategy, called *backward chaining*, can be used only when a solution state is specific and the operators are invertible; it starts at the solution state, heuristically chooses an operator to apply, and applies it inversely. Thus it builds a solution path from the final state toward the initial state. A third strategy is *operator subgoaling*. It heuristically chooses an operator without paying attention to whether that operator can be applied to the current state. If the operator turns out to be inapplicable because some precondition—a condition that the operator requires—is not met, then a subgoal is formed, which is to find a way to change the current state so that the precondition is true. The strategy recurses, using the new subgoal as if it were the solution state specified by the problem space.[5]

All these strategies may usefully incorporate *heuristics* (rules of thumb) to narrow the guesswork. Often heuristics are specific to the particular task domain. A particularly general heuristic, however, is based on having the ability to simply calculate the difference between a state and the description of a desired state. If states are notated as sets of assertions, then set difference can be used to calculate interstate differences. The *difference reduction* heuristic is simply to choose operators such that the differences between the current state and the desired state are maximally reduced.[6]

There is a very general method, called *means-ends analysis*, that is so widely used that it is worth examining in some detail. Table 14.2 shows the basic strategy. It subsumes two common strategies: forward chaining and operator subgoaling. For instance, if there are never any unsatisfied preconditions in step 3 of table 14.2, the method will do forward chaining. Thus means-ends analysis is a generalization of several other weak methods. (Such incestuous relationships among weak methods make it difficult to give crisp definitions, so the terminology is rather fluid. Indeed some authors would take issue with the definitions given in this chapter.)

Table 14.3 shows means-ends analysis as a model for Cathy's solving of the LMS puzzle. Note that the heuristics used in this task mention

Table 14.2 The Method of Means-Ends Analysis

Let State hold the current state and Desired hold a description of the desired state. Let Goal and Op be temporary variables.

1. Calculate the differences between State and Desired. If there are no differences, then succeed. Otherwise set the differences into Goal.
2. See which operators will reduce the differences in Goal. If there are none, then fail. Otherwise use heuristics to select one and set it into Op.
3. Calculate the differences between State and the preconditions of Op. If there are any, set Goal to the differences and go to step 2. Otherwise apply Op to State and update State accordingly.
4. Use heuristics to evaluate State. If it seems likely to lead to Desired, then go to step 1. Otherwise fail.

specific information in the task, such as men and river banks. This is typical. The heuristics are task-specific, whereas the methods are general. Note also that means-ends analysis does not specify what happens when a failure occurs. It is only a proceed strategy and not a backup strategy. Means-ends analysis alone suffices to model Cathy's behavior, however, because she never backs up during the solution of this puzzle.

Backup strategies are determined mostly by the types of memory available for storing old states. If external memory is used, such as a piece of scratch paper, then more old states may be available than when only internal memory is used. Also some tasks place physical constraints on backup strategies. For instance, there are puzzles, such as the eight-puzzle, Rubik's cube, or the Chinese Ring puzzle, in which the goal is to rearrange the puzzle's parts into a certain configuration. The parts are constructed, however, so only some kinds of moves are physically possible. Thus one cannot backup to arbitrary states, even if one writes them down.

Elaboration: Search or Understanding?

There is a special type of problem solving that deserves some extra discussion because it blurs the distinction between understanding and search. It concerns a certain class of beliefs, called *elaborations*, that subjects often develop about problems. Suppose as usual that subjects' current beliefs about a problem are viewed as a set of assertions. As subjects work on the problem, they could add new assertions, take old ones away, or modify old assertions. They could even add assertions that, although not causing any of the old assertions to be removed, cause them to become irrelevant to subsequent problem solving. An elaboration is an assertion that is added to the state without removing any of the old assertions or decreasing their potential relevance. Consider the following problem: "Al is bigger than Carl. Bob is smaller than Carl. Who is smallest?" Such problems are called series problems (see Ohlsson 1987 for a recent model of problem solving in this task domain

Table 14.3 Protocol and Simulation of Cathy Solving the LMS Puzzle

Problem space:

   (1) A state is a pair consisting of two sets, representing the contents of the source and destination banks, respectively. Both sets are subsets of {L,M,S,B}, which stand for Large, Medium, Small, and the Boat. The union of the two sets is {L,M,S,B}. (2) There is only one operator, Sail. It takes a set of men and a bank as arguments. It only applies if the men are only the bank and if their weight sums to 200 or less. It has a precondition that the boat be on the bank. (3) The initial state is LMS on the source bank. (4) The final state is LMS on the destination bank.

Heuristics:

   (1) Choose an operator that maximizes the number of men on the destination bank. (2) Choose an operator that maximizes the weight of the men on the destination bank.

Line Number		Protocol	Simulation
0			Goal = LMS on destination bank
1	S:	The boat can only hold 200 pounds?	Op = ...
2	E:	The boat can only hold 200 pounds.	
3	S:	Okay...first...	
4		Small and medium go back,	Op = Sail MS to destination bank
5	E:	Uh-huh.	
6	S:	...go across the river on it.	Apply Op
7		and then, um, ... Oh	Goal = L on destination bank
8		Large... /3 second pause/	Op = Sail L to destination Bank
9	E:	Yeah, go on... talk out loud.	
10	S:	... and... um...	
11		Large... um... /3 sec. pause/	
12	E:	Talk out loud.	
13		Tell me everything you're thinking.	
14	S:	But, I can't do it	Goal = Boat on source bank
15		because someone has to sail the boat back.	
15	E:	Ok... That's right.	
16		Somebody has to sail the boat back.	
18	S:	Oh! Ok... so... /4 sec. pause/	Op = Sail S to source bank
19		Small sails the boat back	Apply Op
20			Goal = LS on destination bank
21		and gets off,	Op = Sail L to destination bank
22		and lets Large sail the boat back.	Apply Op
23	E:	Um-hmm. And then what happens.	Goal = S on destination bank
24	S:	Uh... /3 sec. pause/	Op = Sail S to destination bank
25	E:	Talk out loud...	
26	S:	And then small...	
27		small...	Goal = boat on source bank
28		can't think of anything...	
29	E:	Keep talking.	Op = Sail M to destination bank
30	S:	So... Medium... sails back.	Apply Op
31		and...	Goal = MS on destination bank
32			Op = Sail MS to destination bank
33		Medium and small sail back.	Apply Op
34	E:	Keep talking.	
35	S:	And they're all across!	
36	E:	Very good!	

and an introduction to the rather large literature on series problems). Suppose a subject reads this problem and immediately says "I guess it has to be one of the three of them." The subject apparently had some initial understanding of the problem, which could be modeled as a set of assertions. This statement indicates a reasoning process of some kind has run, producing a new assertion. The new assertion qualifies as an elaboration because it does not negate, remove, or obviate any of the older assertions.

It is not clear what kind of reasoning produced this elaboration. On the one hand the subject's behavior seems similar to the behavior of Cathy, who understood the LMS puzzle by assuming that the only transportation was a boat. This similarity suggests that the elaboration is a product of the understanding process. However, suppose the subject's next statement is "It can't be Carl because Bob is smaller." This inference also qualifies as an elaboration. Indeed there is nothing to distinguish it formally from the earlier elaboration. It is clear, however, that the subject could go on to find a solution of the puzzle by making only elaborations of this sort. If all of them are considered to be products of understanding instead of operator application, then it follows that this problem can be solved by just understanding it. Search is not needed.

Clearly elaborations can be classified either as part of the understanding process or as part of the search process. This might seem like a pointless terminological quibble. However, the search process is currently better understood than the understanding process. If elaboration is classified as search, then it inherits hypotheses (for example, means-ends analysis, the paucity of backup) that might shed light on its organization and occurrence. Whether these hypotheses hold for elaboration remains to be seen.

Learning during Problem Solving

If subjects are given a knowledge-lean task, their initial performance may be stumbling and slow, but improves rapidly with practice. Mechanisms of practice-driven learning may be needed to give a sufficient explanation of such behavior. Several mechanisms have been proposed. Although this is a part of the field that is developing rather rapidly, its importance makes it worthwhile to describe some of the more widely known mechanisms. The mechanisms need not be used exclusively, but may be combined and thus account for more phenomena than each can explain individually.

Compounding is a process that takes two operators in the problem space and combines them to form a new operator, often called a macrooperator (Fikes, Hart, and Nilsson 1972). Macrooperators are just operators, so they can be compounded with other operators to form even larger operators. To illustrate this, suppose that a subject's algebraic equation–solving problem space originally has an operator for subtracting a constant from both sides of the equation and a second operator for performing arithmetic simplifications. The following lines show an application of each operator:

$$3x + 5 = 20$$
$$3x = 20 - 5$$
$$3x = 15$$

Compounding can create a macrooperator that would produce the third line directly from the first line. When there are preconditions or heuristics associated with operators, then some bookkeeping is necessary to create the appropriate preconditions and heuristics for the macrooperator. This is easiest to see when operators are notated as productions so that the preconditions and heuristics appear in the condition of the operator's production. The two algebra operators can be represented as:

If "+ ⟨constant⟩" is on the left side of the equation,
then delete it and put "− ⟨constant⟩" on the right side of the equation.
If "⟨constant1⟩ ⟨arithmetic operation⟩ ⟨constant2⟩" is in the equation,
then replace it with "⟨constant3⟩," where ⟨constant3⟩ is . . . etc.

The second production's condition cannot be added verbatim to the macroproductions left side, because it would not be true at the time the macroproduction should be applied. Thus the correct formulation of the macroproduction is:

If "+ ⟨constant1⟩" is on the left side of the equation, and
"⟨constant2⟩" is on the right side of the equation,
then delete both and put "⟨constant3⟩" on the right side, where ⟨constant3⟩ is . . . etc.

This demonstrates that compounding is not always a trivial process. Fikes, Hart, and Nilsson (1972) give a general algorithm. Lewis (1981) and Anderson (1982) have investigated the special case of production compounding.

Heuristics are often used in deciding which operator to select while moving forward. *Tuning* is the process of modifying the operator selection heuristics. Suppose for the sake of illustration that there are two applicable operators, A and B, in a certain situation. The heuristic conditions associated with A are false, say, so A is deemed a poor choice in this situation. The heuristics associated with B are true, which makes it a good choice, so it is selected. Suppose that the application of B leads immediately to failure, so backup retreats, A is chosen instead, and success occurs immediately. Obviously the two heuristics gave poor advice, so they should be tuned. A's condition was too specific: it was false of the situation and should have been true. The appropriate tuning is to generalize A's condition. Conversely B's condition was too general: it was true of the situation and should have been false, so its condition needs to be specialized. Generalization and specialization are the two most common forms of condition tuning. A variety of cognitive models have used one or both of them (Anderson 1982, Langley 1987, VanLehn 1987).

Newell and Rosenbloom (1981) invented a mechanism that serves the function of both compounding and tuning. The mechanism, called *chunking,* requires that operators and heuristics be represented as productions that read and modify only the temporary information storage buffer called working memory. It also requires that there be a bookkeeping mechanism that keeps track of which working memory items were read or modified (or both) over a sequence of production applications. Given a sequence of production applications, chunking creates a new production by putting on the condition side all the pieces of information that were read and on the action side all the pieces that were modified. This creates a production that does the work of several smaller productions. In this respect it is just like compounding. Because the chunking mechanism builds the new production directly from the working memory elements that were accessed, however, it builds very specific productions that incorporate all the detail of those elements. Thus chunking "specializes" productions in a sense. In some circumstances it can also generalize productions (Laird, Rosenbloom, and Newell 1986). For this reason chunking is a form of tuning as well as compounding.

Another learning mechanism, called *proceduralization,* is applicable only in models such as Act* (Anderson 1983) or Understand (Hayes and Simon 1974) that distinguish between procedural and declarative knowledge. Such models view the mind as analogous to a program that employs both a data base (declarative knowledge) and some functions for manipulating it (procedural knowledge). Procedural knowledge is usually represented as a production system. Act* and Understand assume that when subjects encode the problem stimulus, a declarative knowledge representation of it is built. In order to explain how subjects solve problems initially, it is assumed that they have general-purpose productions that can read the declarative representation of the problem, infer what actions to take, and take them. Thus the problem is solved initially by this slow interpretive cycle. Proceduralization gradually builds specific productions from the general interpretive ones. It copies a general production and fills in parts of it with information from the declarative knowledge. Thus proceduralization creates task-specific productions by instantiating the general-purpose productions.

Another common learning mechanism is *strengthening* (Anderson 1982). It is assumed that each operator has a strength, and that the operator selection process prefers stronger operators over weaker ones.

The learning mechanism is simply to increment an operator's strength whenever it is used successfully. In order to keep strengths from growing indefinitely, some kind of strength decay is usually assumed.

Another learning mechanism is *rule induction* (Sweller 1983). When the sequence of moves along a solution path has a salient pattern, such as two operators being applied alternately, then subjects may notice the pattern and induce a rule that describes it. Several mechanisms for such *serial pattern learning*, as it is sometimes called, have been described (Kotovsky and Simon 1973, Levine 1975). Sweller and his colleagues (Sweller 1983, Mawer and Sweller, 1982, Sweller and Levine 1982, Sweller, Mawer, and Ward 1983) showed that this type of learning is rare when subjects employ means-ends analysis as their problem-solving strategy, but that various experimental manipulations can reduce the use of that strategy and increase the occurrence of rule induction.

Notorious Technical Problems and a Standard Solution Several of the mechanisms (tuning and strengthening at least, perhaps also compounding and chunking) require knowing whether the application of a given operator led to success or failure. This presents problems. Often the operator application may occur quite some time before the problem is successfully solved, so substantial memory capacity may be required to remember which operators contributed to the success. Moreover making learning conditional on success means that no learning will occur until the problem has been solved, but it is quite clear that people can learn in the middle of problem solving. This set of difficulties is sometimes called the *credit assignment problem.*

Another problem common to several mechanisms is that they can build highly idiosyncratic operators. Not only do these idiosyncratic operators waste storage space, they can sometimes grab control of the model and cause it to predict absurd behaviors of the subjects. This problem is sometimes called the *mental clutter problem.*

To handle the assignment of credit problem, the mental clutter problem, and others, it is standard to embed the learning mechanisms in a processing architecture that allows severe constraints to be placed on their operation. A common approach is to assume that the architecture is *goal-based*. All processing is done in the context of the current goal; goals may be pushed and popped, as in the method of operator subgoaling. Goals help solve the credit assignment problem by allowing success to be defined relative to the given goal, thus providing earlier feedback. Mental clutter is avoided by combining operators only when they contribute directly to the success of the current goal.

This completes the description of problem spaces, understanding, search, and learning—the major components of contemporary as well as past theorizing about problem solving.

14.2   Schema-Driven Problem Solving

If one gives subjects the same set of problems many times, they may learn how to solve them and cease to labor through the understanding and search processes described in section 14.1. Instead they seem to recognize the stimulus as a familiar problem, retrieve a solution procedure for that problem, and follow it. The collection of knowledge surrounding a familiar problem is called a *problem schema*, so this style of problem solving could be called *schema-driven*. It seems to characterize experts who are solving problems in knowledge-rich domains. This section describes it by first discussing how schemas are used to solve familiar problems, then how they are adapted in solving unfamiliar problems. The last subsection describes how schemas can be explained as the products of the learning mechanisms presented previously.

Word Problems in Physics, Mathematics, and Engineering
In many of the knowledge-rich task domains that have been studied, problems are presented as a brief paragraph that describes a situation and asks for a mathematical analysis of it (Paige and Simon 1966, Bhaskar and Simon 1977, Hinsley, Hayes, and Simon 1977, Simon and Simon 1978, McDermott and Larkin 1978, Larkin et al. 1980, Larkin 1981, Chi, Feltovich, and Glaser 1981, Silver 1981, Chi, Glaser, and Rees 1982, Schoenfeld and Herrmann 1982, Larkin 1983, Sweller, Mawer, and Ward 1983, Anzai and Yokoyama 1984, Sweller and Cooper 1985, Reed, Dempster, and Ettinger 1985). Because so much work has been done with word problems, and schemas are so prominent in subjects' behavior when solving word problems, such problems make a good starting place for the examination of schema-driven problem solving.

For purposes of exposition let us distinguish two types of problem solving. If the subjects are experts, and the problem given is an easy, routinely encountered problem, then the subjects will not seem to do any search. Instead they will select and execute a solution procedure that they judge to be appropriate for this problem. For these subjects the understanding process consists of deciding what class of problem this is, and the search process consists of executing the solution procedure associated with that class. Let us call this case *routine problem solving*. Of course experts can solve nonroutine problems as well, but on those problems their performance has a different character. Routine problem solving is discussed first; a discussion of nonroutine problem solving follows.

Schemas   In order to explain routine problem solving, it is usually assumed that experts know a large variety of problem schemas, where a *problem schema* consists of information about the class of problems the schema applies to and information about their solutions. Problem sche-

Table 14.4 A Schema for River Problems

Problem Type: There is a river with a current and a boat that travels at a constant velocity relative to the river. The boat travels downstream a certain distance in a certain time and travels upstream a certain distance in the same amount of time. The difference between the two distances is either given or desired.

Solution information: Given any two of (a) the difference between the upstream and downstream distances, (b) the time, and (c) the river current's speed, the other one can be calculated because the boat's speed drops out. First write the distance-rate-time equations for the upstream and downstream trips, then subtract them, then solve the resulting equations for the desired in terms of the givens.

---

mas have two main parts: one for describing problems and the other for describing solutions. Table 14.4 shows a schema that an expert in high-school algebra might have.[7] This schema applies to a very specific class of problems and contains the "trick" for solving problems in that class. If upstream-downstream problems are solved in a general way, they translate into a system of six linear equations in nine unknowns. Thus given any three quantities, all the others can be calculated. But the trick upstream-downstream problems give only two quantities, not three. The quantities given, however, just happen to be such that subtracting the distance-rate-time equations yields a solution. Thus this schema encodes expert knowledge about how to recognize and solve this special "trick" class of river problems.

Routine problem solving consists of three processes: selecting a schema, adapting (instantiating) it to the problem, and executing its solution procedure. These three processes are discussed in this order.

Schema selection often begins when a particular schema suddenly pops into mind. This *triggering* process is not well understood. It seems to occur early in the processing of the problem stimulus. For instance, when Hinsley, Hayes, and Simon (1977) read algebraic word problems slowly to their subjects, more than half the subjects selected a schema after hearing less than one-fifth of the text. Hinsley and colleagues (1977, p. 97) gave the following example:

For example, after hearing the three words, "A river steamer . . ." from a river-current problem, one subject said, "It's going to be one of those river things with upstream, downstream, and still water. You are going to compare times upstream and downstream—or if the time is constant, it will be the distance." Another subject said, "It is going to be a linear algebra problem of the current type—like it takes four hours to go upstream and two hours to go downstream. What is the current—or else it's a trig problem—the boat may go across the current and get swept downstream."

These quotes indicated that the triggering process seems to happen very early in the perception of the problem. Experts reading physics problems (Chi, Feltovich, and Glaser 1981) and X-ray pictures (Lesgold et al. 1988) also tend to trigger schemas early.

Once an initial schema has been triggered, it guides the interpretation of the rest of the problem. In this case it appears that both subjects have selected a general river-problem schema that has several subordinate schemas, representing more specific river-problem schemas. The first subject seems to know about the schema of table 14.4 and considers whether this problem might be an instance of it or of a different schema (constant-distance river schema). The second subject also considers several special cases of the generic river crossing problem. In this case triggering the general river-crossing schema could guide subsequent processing by setting up some expectations about what kinds of more specific, subordinate schemas to look for. The subjects probably used these expectations to read the problem statement selectively, looking for information that would tell them which of their expectations is met. This strategy of starting with a general schema and looking for specializations of it may be common in understanding because it appears in physics problem solving as well (Chi, Feltovich, and Glaser 1981).

Selection of a schema goes hand in hand with *instantiating* it to the given problem. Instantiation means adapting the schema to the specific problem. For instance, to adapt the schema of table 14.4 to this problem:

A river steamer travels for 12 hours downstream, turns around, and travels upstream for 12 hours, at which point it is still 72 miles from the dock that it started from. What is the river's current?

requires noting which two quantities are given and which is desired. In the standard terminology the variable parts of a schema (that is, the three quantities in this case) are called *slots,* and the parts of the problem that instantiate the slots are called *fillers.* So instantiating a schema, in the simplest cases at least, means filling its slots. Often occasions of slot filling are mingled with occasions of specialization, where a schema is rejected in favor of a subordinate schema. Indeed it is sometimes not easy to distinguish, either empirically or computationally, between instantiation and specialization.

Experts seem to derive features of problem situations that novices do not and to use the derived features during selection and instantiation. Such features are called *second-order features* (Chi, Feltovich, and Glaser 1981) because they seem to be derived by some kind of elaboration process rather than being directly available in the text. An example of this is found in the remark of a subject of Hinsley and colleagues, who said, "If the time is constant, it will be the distance." But the problem states "A river steamer travels for 12 hours downstream, turns around, and travels upstream for 12 hours . . ." The problem does not state that the time is constant, but as that seems to be the feature that the subject looks for, it is likely that the subject will notice the equality of the two given times, and immediately infer that the temporal second-order feature that he seeks is present. Chi and colleagues (1981, 1982) provide evidence that experts in physics notice second-order features, but novices do not.

The whole process of selecting and instantiating a schema is a form of elaboration because it does not actually change the problem state, but augments it with a much richer description. Section 14.1 indicated that elaboration could be viewed equally well as search or understanding.

Following the Solution Procedures Once a schema has been selected and instantiated, the subject must still produce a solution to the problem. For routine problem solving this is can be accomplished by simply following step by step the solution procedure that constitutes the second half of the schema. For instance, the algebraic schema of table 14.4 contains a three-step solution procedure: write the two distance-rate-time equations, subtract them, and solve for the desired quantity in terms of the givens. Following such procedures is the third and final process in schema-driven problem solving.

Procedure following is not always trivial. Sometimes the execution of a step may present a subproblem that requires the full power of schema-driven problem solving for its solution. For instance, the first step requires the subject to write distance-rate-time equations, but it does not say how. Schema-driven problem solving can easily solve this subproblem, provided that subject knows schemas such as

Problem There is a boat moving downstream on a river at a constant rate. A distance-rate-time equation is desired.

Solution The equation is the standard distance-rate-time equation, with the rate equal to the sum of the boat's speed and the river current's speed.

These simple examples illustrate that the overall process of schema-driven problem solving is *recursive*, in that executing one small part of the process can potentially cause complete, recursive invocation of the problem-solving process.

There is yet another complexity involved in following solution procedures. It is quite likely that some subjects do not follow the procedure's steps in their standard order. They prefer to use a permutation of the standard order, and sometimes these permutations produce effects different from the standard one. This particular complexity is difficult to demonstrate experimentally, because it is difficult to find out exactly what the subjects' solution procedures are. Thus one cannot be certain whether they are following a standard-order procedure in a nonstandard way, or whether they simply have a procedure with permuted steps. Perhaps the best evidence so far comes from the task domain of subtraction calculation, where children are asked to work problems such as

$$\begin{array}{r} 3\ 4\ 5 \\ -\ 0\ 7\ 9 \\ \hline \end{array}$$

Although this is not at all a knowledge-rich task domain, it is a task in which the subjects follow procedures (VanLehn 1989), so the findings there might generalize to experts' following the solution procedures of their schemas. Even if the results do not generalize in any detail, subtraction still serves as a convenient illustration for how procedures can be followed flexibly.

VanLehn, Ball and Kowalski (1990) discovered 8 students (out of a biased sample of 26) who used nonstandard orders. All of the orders standardly taught in the United States have the student finish one column before moving on to the next, even if that column requires extensive borrowing from other columns. However, the 8 students did not always exhibit a standard order. For instance, some students did all of the problem's borrowing first, moving right to left across the columns, then returned, left to right, answering the columns as they went. It was also found that students would often shift suddenly from one order to another. This is consistent with the hypothesis that these students' underlying procedures were stable, but they chose to permute the order of steps during execution. This conclusion is bolstered by the authors' demonstration that a small set of standard-order procedures excellently fits the observed orders when they are executed by a simple queue-based interpreter. Moreover that set of standard-order procedures can all be produced by an independently motivated learning model when it is instructed with the same lessons that the subjects received (VanLehn 1983, 1989). These results led VanLehn and his colleagues to conclude that their 8 students were indeed executing standard-order procedures in a nonstandard way. Whether this same flexibility in execution will turn up in expert behavior remains to be seen.

Nonroutine Solving of Word Problems

The preceding subsection dealt with the routine case of problem solving wherein a single schema matches the whole problem umambiguously, and its solution procedure can be followed readily, encountering at worst only routine subproblems. This subsection describes some of the many ways that schema-driven problem solving can be nonroutine. Research is just beginning in this area, so many of the proposed processes are based only on a rational extension of the basic ideas of routine problem solving and as yet have not been scrutinized experimentally.

Perhaps the most obvious source of complexity in expert problem solving occurs when more than one schema is applicable to the given situation. Because the subjects do not know which schema to select (by definition), they must make a tentative decision and be prepared to change their mind. That is, they must search. Such cases illustrate that

Problem Solving and Cognitive Skill Acquisition

schema selection can be usefully viewed as the result of applying an operator that produces a new state in a problem-space search. The new state differs from the old one only in that it contains an assertion marking the fact that the schema has been selected. Redoing a schema selection becomes a case of the usual backing up in search of a problem space. As noted, schema selection and instantiation are forms of elaboration and thus can be viewed either as search or understanding. When the subject is uncertain which schema to select, it is useful to view schema selection as search.

Larkin (1983) provides a nice example of such a search. She gave five expert physicists a straightforward but difficult physics problem. Although two subjects immediately selected the correct schema, and one even said, "I know how to do this one. It's virtual work." (Larkin 1983, p. 93), the other three subjects tried two or more schemas. Each schema was instantiated, and its solution was partially implemented. Usually the solution reached a contradiction (for example, a sum of forces that should be zero is not). Only the final schemas selected by these subjects led to a contradiction-free solution. Thus schema selection plays a crucial role in these subjects' search for a solution.

Another type of difficulty occurs when no schema will cover the whole problem, but two or more schemas each cover some part of the problem. The problem is to combine the schemas so that they cover the whole problem. Larkin (1983) gives some examples of experts combining schemas.

A third type of difficulty occurs when execution of a solution procedure halts because the procedure mandates an impossible action or makes a false claim about the current state. Such an event is called an *impasse* (Brown and VanLehn 1980, VanLehn 1982). Although this notion was originally invented to explain the behavior of children executing arithmetic procedures (Brown and VanLehn 1980), it readily applies to experts executing solution procedure. For instance, Larkin's (1983) three experts reached impasses during their initial solving of the physics problems because their selected schema's solution procedure claimed, for instance, that the balance of forces should be zero when it was not. The subject's response to an impasse is called a *repair*, because it fixes the problem of being stuck. In the case of Larkin's experts, the repairs were always to reject the currently selected schema and to select another. Such backing up may be a frequent type of repair, but it is certainly not the only type (Brown and VanLehn 1980, VanLehn, 1982, 1989).

This subsection has enumerated several processes that seem to occur regularly in nonroutine problem solving: ambiguity in selecting a schema, schema combination, impasses, and repairs. However, these are probably just a few of the many interesting types of behavior that occur when experts solve difficult problems. Much research remains to be done.

Expert Problem Solving in Other Task Domains

It may be unsurprising that schemas provide the basis for a natural account of word-problem solving, because the schemas have long been used in psychology to explain how people process paragraph-sized pieces of text (Bartlett 1932). In this view the prominence of schemas in expert solutions of word problems is because of the task domain rather than the expertise of the subjects. There is some evidence, however, that schemas or something much like schemas are used by experts in other task domains as well.

For instance, research on programming and algorithm design (Adelson 1981, Jeffries, Turner, Polson, and Atwood 1981, Anderson, Farrell and Saurers 1984, Pirolli 1985, Pirolli and Anderson 1985, Kant and Newell 1984) has shown that experts know many schemas such as the one shown in table 14.5. This schema is midway between a schema for coding and a schema for algorithm design. Coding schemas often mention language-specific information. For instance, schemas for recursion in Lisp may mention positions in Cond clauses where one should place the code for the recursive step and the terminating step (Pirolli 1985, Pirolli and Anderson 1985). Algorithm design schemas mention more general techniques, such as dividing a set of data points in half, recursively performing the desired computation on each half, and combining the solutions for each half into a solution for the whole (Kant and Newell 1984).

In many respects the use of such schemas resembles the use of word-problem schemas. In particular they must be selected and instantiated before their solution halves are implemented. Moreover the problem-solving process is recursive in that doing a small part of the process, such as filling a slot in a selected schema, may create a subproblem whose solution requires more schemas to be selected and implemented (Kant and Newell 1984).

In some task domains schema-driven problem solving does not seem to play a prominent role in expert behavior. For instance, Lewis (1981)

Table 14.5 A Schema for Programming

Problem: Given a list of elements and a predicate, remove the elements of which the predicate is false.

Solution: Use a trailing-pointer loop. The initialization of the loop puts a new dummy element on the front of the list, and it sets two variables. One variable (called the trailing pointer) points to the list, and the other points to the second element of the list (that is, the first element of the original list). The main step of the loop is to call the predicate on the element, and if the predicate is false, then the element is spliced out of the loop, using the trailing pointer. If the predicate is true, then both pointers are advanced by one element through the list. The loop terminates after the last element has been examined. At the conclusion of the loop, the list must have the dummy first element removed.

studied algebraic equation solving using rather tricky problems in high-school algebra, such as solving for x in

$$x + 2(x + 2(x + 2)) = x + 2$$

Lewis compared expert professional mathematicians with high-school and college students. If the experts were doing schema-driven problem solving, one might expect them to say, "Oh, one of those," and produce the answer in one step. This almost never occurred. In fact Lewis concluded that "the expert's performance was not sharply different from that of the students," (1981, p. 85) except that the experts made fewer mistakes.

There is no space in this chapter for a thorough review of the expertise literature. Fortunately there is a recent review (Riemann and Chi 1989) and a recent collection of articles (Chi, Glaser, and Farr 1988). The major purpose of this section is to introduce an analytical idea—schema-driven problem solving—that has sometimes proved useful in understanding problem solving. The last task of this section is to show how this notion relates to the standard theory of problem solving.

Relationship to the Standard Theory

It is quite plausible that schemas are acquired via the learning mechanisms of the standard theory. Although there is some disagreement about the exact nature of the learning mechanisms, they all predict that experts acquire many large, specialized pieces of knowledge, regardless of whether they are called chunks, macrooperators, or compounded productions. Each piece is highly tuned, in that it only applies to a small class of problems, and yet it is quite effective in solving those problems. At a rough qualitative level the assumptions about the products of learning fit nicely with the assumptions about schemas.

Closer examination yields more points of agreement. In particular the increased size of the units of knowledge can be expected to change the character of the problem solving somewhat. To demonstrate this, suppose that compounding glues together several operators that make physical changes in the world, and these actions cannot be performed simultaneously. This means that application of the macrooperator results in execution of a single action plus an intention (plan) to perform some others. Thus the macrooperator is more like a procedure (or stored plan) than an operator per se. Thus it is likely that the solution procedures of schemas correspond to the products of compounding, chunking, or similar learning mechanisms.

Operator selection can also be expected to change character as learning proceeds. When a notice searches a problem space, operator selection is taken care of by a proceed strategy and some heuristics. But the experts' macrooperators/schemas are very specialized, so it might take some extra work to analyze the current state well enough to be able to discriminate among the relevant operators to find the appropriate one.

Elaborations may be needed to build a case for selecting one operator over the others. Thus increases in the number of available units of knowledge and in their specificity is consistent with the complicated selection processes that seem to characterize schema-driven problem solving.

Although it certainly seems that schema-driven problem solving is the product of learning during the course of problem-space search, there are many technical details that stand in the way of demonstrating this. No computer program yet exists that can start off as a novice in some knowledge-rich task domain and slowly acquire the knowledge needed for expert performance. Thus we lack even a computationally explicit account of the novice-expert transition, let alone one that compares well with the performance of human learners. Needless to say, many theorists are hard at work on this project, so progress can be expected to be quite rapid.

This concludes the discussion of theoretical concepts. The remainder of the chapter reviews empirical findings and their relationship to theory.

14.3 Major Empirical Findings

Recent work in artificial intelligence has dispelled much of the mystery surrounding human problem solving that was once called "inventive" (Stevens 1951), "creative" (Newell, Shaw, and Simon 1962), or "insightful" (Weisberg and Alba 1981). Computer programs now exist that can easily solve problems that were once considered so difficult that only highly intelligent, creative individuals could solve them. The new mystery of human problem solving is to find out *which* of the now-plentiful solution methods for creative or inventive problems are used by subjects. Thus experimental findings in problem solving have taken on a new importance. This section reviews the experimental findings that seem most robust.

Practice Effects
The literature on practice effects goes back to the turn of the century (see Fitts and Posner 1967 for a dated but still relevant review). Most of the earlier work, however, dealt with perceptual-motor skills, such as sending Morse code. This subsection discusses only the practice effects that have been demonstrated explicitly on problem-solving tasks (also called *cognitive skills*). It starts with effects seen during the early stages of practice and progresses toward effects caused only by years of practice.

Reduction of Verbalization   It has often been noted that during the initial few minutes of experience with a new task, the subjects continually restate the task rules, but as practice continues, these restatements of rules diminish. For instance, Sweller, Mawer, and Ward (1983) tracked naive subjects as they learned how to solve simple kinematics problems that require knowing a half-dozen equations relating velocity, distance, and acceleration. They found that the number of times a subject wrote one of the equations without substituting any quantities for its variables decreased significantly over the practice period. Similar findings have been reported by Simon and Simon (1978), Anderson (1982), and Krutetskii (1976). Reduction of verbalization can be explained as the result of proceduralization (Anderson 1982).

Tactical Learning On some knowledge-lean tasks subjects quickly improve in their ability to select moves. Greeno (1974) showed that on average only 3.6 repetitions of the Missionaries and Cannibals puzzle were required before subjects met a criterion of two successive error-free trials.[8] Reed and Simon (1976) and Anzai and Simon (1979) presented similar findings. Rapid tactical learning is consistent with several of the learning mechanisms mentioned. Tuning, chunking, and strengthening all suffice to explain the finding, provided that they are assumed to happen rapidly (for example, at every possible opportunity). Atwood, Polson, and their colleagues have also shown that simply remembering what states have been visited also suffices for modeling rapid tactical-learning solution paths (Atwood and Polson 1976, Jeffries, Polson, Razran, and Atwood 1977, Atwood, Masson, and Polson 1980).

The Power Law of Practice A great deal of experimental evidence shows that there is a power-law relationship between the speed of performance on perceptual-motor skills and the number of trials of practice (Fitts and Posner 1967). If time per trial and number of trials are graphed on log-log coordinate axes, a straight line results. Recently the power law has been shown to govern some cognitive skills as well (Newell and Rosenbloom 1981, Neves and Anderson 1981).

The power law of practice does not fall out naturally from any single one of the learning mechanisms discussed. Both chunking and compounding accelerate performance, but they tend to produce exponential practice curves instead of power-law curves (Lewis 1979, Neves and Anderson 1981, Newell and Rosenbloom 1981). That is, they learn too fast. Various proposals have been put forward for slowing the mechanisms down (Anderson 1982, Rosenbloom 1983), but the experiments that split these hypotheses have yet to be performed.

The biggest theoretical problem presented by the power-law finding is that the effects of practice never stop. Crossman (1959) showed that a subject who rolled cigars for a living was still getting faster after several years of practice. Chunking, compounding, and other such mechanisms will have long since built a single huge operator for the task, so they cannot readily explain how performance continues to improve.

Other Possible Effects Not Yet Demonstrated From the perceptual-motor literature it seems likely that the following findings also apply to problem solving: (1) Within limits, subjects can trade speed for accuracy, reducing one at the expense of increasing the other. No theoretical work has tried to model this. (2) If exactly the same task is practiced for hundreds of trials, it can be automatized, that is, it will be very rapid, cease to interfere with concurrent tasks, and run to completion once started even if the subject tries to stop it. If the task varies beyond certain limits during training, however, even hundreds of practice trials do not suffice for automatization (Schneider and Shiffrin 1977, Shiffrin and Schneider 1977). Although chunking, compounding, and similar mechanisms are consistent with the general quality of automatization, it is not yet clear whether they can explain why some types of practice cause automatization and others do not. (3) The distribution of practice makes a difference in the speed of learning, but the effect depends on the structure of the skill being practiced. Practicing parts of the skill before the whole is sometimes better and sometimes not. Many short practice sessions are sometimes better than a few long ones and sometimes not. Current cognitive theory has not yet tried to explain these effects. Also experimental work is needed to check that these effects are not limited to perceptual-motor skills, but are found with cognitive skills as well.

Problem Isomorphs

Many knowledge-lean tasks have an "intended" problem space, which is the problem space assigned by people who are very familiar with the problem. The LMS puzzle is a case in point. The intended problem space is the one used by Cathy. Of course a subject's problem space is not necessarily the intended one, as illustrated by the 60-year-old subject who initially interpreted the LMS puzzle as an arithmetic word problem.

Two problems are said to be *isomorphic* if their intended problem spaces are isomorphic. Two problem spaces are isomorphic if there is a one-to-one correspondence between states and operators such that whenever two states are connected by an operator in one problem space, the corresponding states are connected by the corresponding operator in the other problem space. This section compares problem solving behaviors on isomorphic problems.

Varying the Cover Story Does Not Affect Difficulty A simple way to create an isomorphic puzzle is to change the cover story. For instance, the Missionaries and Cannibals puzzle has three missionaries and three cannibals trying to cross a river subject to certain restrictions. Several investigators (Greeno 1974, Jeffries, Polson, Razran, and Atwood 1977) created problem isomorphs by substituting elves and men (or other pairs of creatures) for the missionaries and cannibals. This change in the cover story of the puzzle had no measurable effect on the solution times or patterns of moves. This result tends to support the idea that subjects really are thinking of the puzzle as a formal problem space and in fact as the intended problem space.

Other Variations Significantly Affect Difficulty Although changing the cover story does not seem to affect problem-solving behavior, other manipulations of puzzles can have a very significant effect on the relative difficulty of problem isomorphs. It is not yet clear how these manipulations differ from the cover-story manipulation. For instance, Kotovsky, Hayes, and Simon (1985) studied isomorphs of the Tower of Hanoi, such as the tea ceremony puzzle, and found that some isomorphs took 16 times as long to solve as other isomorphs (29.39 min versus 1.83 min). Reed, Ernst, and Banerji (1974) obtained similar but less dramatic results with isomorphs of the Missionaries and Cannibals puzzle.

Kotovsky and colleagues developed a model that exhibits good qualitative agreement with their data. They assume that subjects search in a problem space but not the intended problem space. Rather they search in a finer-grained problem space where it takes several operator applications to achieve the same effect as one operator application in the intended problem space.

Transfer and Problem Solving by Analogy
Before presenting some findings concerning transfer and analogy, a brief introduction to this rather complex subfield is in order. It is clear that complete transfer of expertise between domains never occurs (for example, going to medical school does not make one a good lawyer). However, it may be that incomplete transfer occurs. There are two possibilities: (1) The domain-specific knowledge of two task domains may overlap. For instance, chemists and physicists overlap in their knowledge of mathematics and fundamental properties of matter and energy. Thus there should be *specific transfer* of expertise from one domain to another. (2) If two task domains seem to have no overlap in their requisite knowledge, there still may be *general transfer* because problem solving in both domains may require an organized, methodical style of thinking, so training in that type of thinking in one task domain may give a subtle advantage in another task domain. For instance, learning to program a computer is often thought to increase one's ability to do logical and quantitative problem solving of all types (see, for example, Papert 1980).

General transfer is difficult to study, however, and as a consequence there is some doubt as to whether general transfer even exists. For a recent review of the general transfer literature, see Pea 1987. The rest of the remarks here concern specific transfer.

The existence of specific transfer has been amply demonstrated

(Thorndike and Woodworth 1901, Singley and Anderson 1985, Singley and Anderson 1989, Singley 1986, Kieras and Bovair 1986, Kieras and Polson 1985, Reed, Ernst, and Banerji 1974, Kotovsky, Hayes, and Simon 1985). However, the exact nature of specific transfer is still being investigated. One leading theory, originated by Thorndike and rendered more precise by Kieras, Singley, Anderson and their colleagues, is that transfer is accomplished by actually sharing (or copying) relevant units of knowledge. For instance, it is possible to notate knowledge of procedural skills as production systems in such a way that the degree of transfer is directly proportional to the number of shared productions (Keiras and Bovair 1986, Kieras and Polson 1985, Singley and Anderson 1985, Singley 1986, Singley and Anderson 1989).[9] This theory is called the *identical-elements theory* of transfer.

In the identical-elements theory, knowledge is viewed as a set, so calculating the overlap between two tasks' knowledge structures amounts to simply taking a set intersection. Another common view, however, has knowledge structured as a semantic net. Because a semantic net is a labeled directed graph rather than a set, there are multiple ways to calculate the overlap of two semantic nets. See Gentner (1989) and Holyoak (1985) for two contrasting views on how people do it. The identical-elements view and the mapping view of transfer can be seen as compatible hypotheses that examine the same phenomenon at different levels of description. Identical-elements theory counts the number of units transferred, whereas mapping theories explain exactly what parts of an element are transferred.

Having presented a few basic concepts about specific transfer and analogy, a few findings from this large and rapidly growing literature will be discussed.

Asymmetric Transfer Occurs When One Task Subsumes Another The identical-elements theory of transfer predicts that when one task's productions are a subset of another's, transfer appears to be asymmetric even though it is implicitly symmetric. Training on the harder task— the one with more productions—causes complete competence in the easier task because all the units for the easier task will have been learned. On the other hand training in the easy task causes only partial competence in the harder task. Thus although the same number of units is being transferred in either case (that is, the underlying transfer is symmetric), the measured transfer is asymmetric. This prediction is consistent with several findings of asymmetric transfer where competence in the more difficult task transfers to the easier task but not vice versa (Reed, Ernst, and Banerji 1974, Kotovsky, Hayes, and Simon 1985, Singley 1986)

Negative Transfer is Rare Negative transfer occurs when prior training on one task slows down the learning of another task or blocks its performance completely. The identical-elements theory predicts that there will never be negative transfer. Singley and Anderson (1985, 1989) tested this implication by using two versions of the same text editor. The only difference between the editors was the assignment of keys to commands. They trained two groups of subjects on the two editors for six hours, then switched one group to the other editor and trained that group for six hours. If negative transfer occurs, then the learning curve of the transfer group after it had been switched over should start lower or rise more slowly than the learning curve of the control group during its first six hours of training. This did not occur. Instead the learning curve for the transfer group started higher than the learning curve for the control group, thus indicating substantial positive transfer. Moreover the transfer group's curve paralleled the control group's curve, indicating that there was no detrimental effect of the prior training on subsequent learning. Thus the experimental results fit the predictions of the identical-elements theory quite well. Kieras and Bovair (1986) found a similar lack of negative transfer.

Singley and Anderson (1985) point out that editor users probably hope for total positive transfer when they switch editors. That is, they anticipate being able to use the new editor just as well as they used the old. Because their actual performance on the new editor is not as fluid as their old performance, they say they have suffered "negative transfer." Because their actual performance is much better than a novice, however, they actually are enjoying a large degree of positive transfer, even though it is not the total transfer hoped for.

Set Effects   The lack of negative transfer contradicts intuition. For instance, Fitts and Posner (1967, p. 20) give the following rather compelling examples of negative transfer:

If you drive in a country in which traffic moves on the opposite side of the road from the side on which you are accustomed to driving, you are likely to find it difficult and confusing to reverse your previous learning; similarly, in cases where the faucets which control hot and cold water are reversed from their usual positions, months of learning are often required before their operation is smooth.

The first example probably does not constitute true negative transfer, because it probably takes less time to learn to drive on the opposite side of the road than it takes to learn to drive initially. This is another case of frustrated expectations for massive positive transfer. On the other hand it does not take months to learn the positions of the hot- and cold-water controls initially, so the last example constitutes a clear case of negative transfer. How does this example differ from Singley and Anderson's experiments?

In a more fine-grained analysis of their data, Singley and Anderson (1989) found that subjects would sometimes choose a less efficient method during the transfer task for achieving certain of their text-editing goals, presumably because the chosen method was more familiar to them from their prior training. This is similar to the set effects observed by Luchins, Duncker, and others (Luchins, 1942, Duncker, 1945, Greeno, Magone, and Chaiklin 1979, Sweller and Gee 1978). *Set effects* occur when there are alternatives in a problem-solving task, and some of the alternatives are more familiar than others. The set effect is that the subjects tend to pick the familiar alternative, even if it is not the best. The hot- and cold-water controls are an example of a set effect. In short set effects are a special kind of negative transfer that does seem to take place. Moreover its existence is not predicted by the identical-elements theory.

There are two major kinds of set effects in the literature. *Functional fixity* refers to a familiarity bias in the choice of functions for an object. In Duncker's famous task of constructing a wall-mounted candle holder, the subjects tend to view the box as a container for tacks rather than as a platform for the candle (Duncker 1945, Weisberg and Alba 1981, Greeno, Magone, and Chaiklin 1979). *Einstellung* refers to a familiarity bias in the choice of a plan. In Luchin's water-jug task the subjects are given a series of problems that can all be solved with the same sequence of operations. Presumably this induces the person to formulate this repetitive sequence as a plan and reuse it on the later problems in the series. The Einstellung effect occurs when the subject is given a problem that can be solved two ways. The plan will solve it, but so will a sequence of operations that is much shorter than the plan. Although the short sequence of operations is the best choice, many subjects use the plan instead (Luchins 1942).

Spontaneous Noticing of a Potential Analogy is Rare   In the experiments on negative transfer, the stimuli were identical in the training and transfer phases, but the responses were supposed to be different. In experiments on problem solving by analogy, there are also training and transfer phases, but it is the stimuli (tasks) that are different across the two phases. The responses are supposed to be the same or at least analogous. For instance, a subject might be given one puzzle to solve then another isomorphic puzzle. If they use the solution of the first puzzle in solving the second, then they are said to have done problem solving by analogy. Problem solving by analogy can be detected by a number of means, such as verbal protocols or decreases in solution times compared with a control.

In some analogy experiments the subjects are not told that the two tasks are related. Instead they are simply given training on one task then switched to another task without comment. In such circumstances it is common to find that no transfer occurs. For instance, Reed, Ernst, and Banerji (1974) had subjects solve two problem isomorphs in the same thirty-minute experiment. They demonstrated that transfer occurred only when subjects were told the relationship between the two puzzles, otherwise the subjects did not seem to notice that the two tasks were analogous. Similar findings are reported by Gick and Holyoak (1980, 1983), Gentner (1989), and others.

This result is consistent with the common finding that problem solving by analogy is often used by students working problems in an instructional setting (Anderson, Farrell, and Saurers 1984, Pirolli and Anderson 1985, LeFevre and Dixon 1986, Chi, Bassok, Lewis, Reimann, and Glaser 1989). For instance, students working physics problems at the end of a chapter expect that problems solved as examples in the chapter use the same methods, so they actively page through the chapter seeking such solved problems to use them as analogs (Chi, Bassok, Lewis, Reimann, and Glaser 1989). Although students may not have been explicitly told that the chapter's examples are similar to the exercises, experienced students make that assumption anyway.

Spontaneous Noticing is Based on Superficial Features Even in experiments where subjects are neither told to look for analogies nor led by their past experience to look for them, spontaneous noticing of analogies does sometimes occur. When it does, it seems to be based most frequently on noticing superficial similarities between the tasks. Ross (1984, 1987) taught subjects several methods for solving probability problems. Each method was taught with the aid of an example. The example contents varied (dice, car choice, exam scores, and the like). Subjects were tested with problems whose contents were either new, superficially similar to some training example for the appropriate method for solving that problem, or superficially similar to an inappropriate example. Subjects often chose to use the method whose example is similar to the test problem, even if that method is inappropriate. Thus subjects seem to have been cued by the surface similarities, rather than the deep structures of the examples. Similar effects have been found for text editing (Ross 1984), algebraic story problems (Reed 1987), and simple stories (Gentner and Toupin 1986).

Noticing that an analogy is useful is only part of the process of solving problems by analogy. In some cases, it is quite nontrivial to map the solution from the analog over to the target problem. Several studies (Reed, Dempster, and Ettinger 1985, Catrambone and Holyoak 1987) have shown that even when subjects are told about the existence of the analogy, they sometimes have difficulty making use of them. The conditions that facilitate and inhibit such transfers, however, are not yet entirely clear.

Expert-Novice Differences: Problem-Solving Studies
The next few sections contrast expert and novice problem solvers. The term "expert" is usually reserved for subjects with several thousand hours of experience (there are 2000 working hours in a year). Hayes (1981) argues that no one, not even a child prodigy, becomes a world-

class expert without at least 20,000 hours of experience. Although the term "expert" is used in a fairly uniform way, there is substantial variation in the literature on the use of "novice." For some experiments subjects who know nothing about the task domain are selected, given an hour or two of training, and then asked to solve the experimental problems. In other experiments the novices are students who have taken one or two college courses in the subject. These substantial differences in training explain many of the apparent contradictions in the findings. To keep things straight in this chapter, "prenovice" is defined to mean someone with only a few hours training, and "novice" means someone with several hundred hours of training (approximately a college course's worth). Given these definitions, there are several unsurprising findings to mention before bringing out the findings that could really be called discoveries.

Experts Can Perform Faster than Novices   If required to perform quickly, an expert can generally perform faster than a novice. For instance, a master chess player can play lightning chess, but a novice cannot (de Groot 1965). Somewhat surprisingly if experts are not required to perform quickly, they often take about as long to solve a task as do novices (Chi, Glaser, and Rees 1982).

Experts are More Accurate than Novices   Expertise is correlated with the quality of the solution given by the subject. With one exception all the expert-novice studies cited in this section show that experts perform much better than novices.[10] The exception is making decisions based on uncertain evidence. In a recent review Johnson (1988) summarizes the evidence as follows:

In many studies, experts have not performed impressively at all. For example, many expert judges fail to do significantly better than novices who, at best, have slight familiarity with the task at hand. This result has been replicated in diverse domains such as clinical psychology, graduate admissions, and economic forecasting. Not surprisingly, this has led to strong recommendations. Consider the following recommendation about experts' forecasts: "Expertise beyond a minimal level in the subject area is of almost no value . . . The implication is obvious and clear cut: Do not hire the best expert you can—or even close to the best. Hire the cheapest expert."

Note that these authors, although denigrating the performance of experts, never claim that experts perform *worse* than novices. In fact Johnson goes on to show that experts are usually better than novices, although they are sometimes substantially worse than simple mathematical decision-making models.

Strategy Differences   In as much as general strategy can be characterized, it appears that experts and novices tend to use the same general strategy for a given problem, but prenovices sometimes use quite different strategies. For instance, Jeffries, Turner, Polson, and Atwood (1981) contrasted the protocols of expert, novice, and prenovice software engineers as they solved a complex design problem. Both experts and novices used a top-down, breadth-first, progressive-refinement design strategy. They decomposed the overall system into a few big modules, refined each module into submodules, then refined each submodules into subsubmodules, and so on until the design was detailed enough that they could begin writing program code. The prenovice, however, began writing code almost immediately, with no sign of a top-down design strategy. Similarly in the solution of physics problems, no strategic differences were found between experts and novices (Chi, Glaser, and Rees 1982), but prenovices were found to use a different strategy than either novices (Sweller, Mawer, and Ward 1983) or experts (Simon and Simon 1978). Several other investigators (de Groot 1965, Charness 1981, Lewis 1981) found no major strategic differences between experts and novices. In short at a general level of description, the strategies of experts and novices are the same, whereas prenovices may have a quite different strategy.

Self-Monitoring Skill Experts seem better at monitoring the progress of their problem solving and allocating their effort appropriately. Schoenfeld (1981) analyzed protocols of experts and novices who were solving unusual mathematical problems. Both experts and novices had to search; the problems were not routine even for the expert. However, the experts' search was more closely monitored. Approximately once a minute the experts would make some comment that either evaluated their current direction (for example, "Isn't that what I want?"), assessed the likelihood of a contemplated approach (for example, "Knock this off with a sledgehammer" meaning that the approach is too high-powered and unlikely to work), or assessed the difficulty of a subproblem before attempting it (for example, "This is going to be interesting. . . ."). In contrast the novices would generally adopt a single approach with little assessment of the likelihood of success, then follow it for ten or twenty minutes, without considering abandoning it. Schoenfeld concludes that metacognitive or managerial skills are of paramount importance in human problem solving. The same sort of managerial monitoring is also evident in Larkin's (1983) protocols of physicists and Jeffries and colleagues' (1981) protocols of programmers.

A related finding is that experts are able to estimate the difficulty of a task with higher accuracy than novices. For instance, Chi, Glaser, and Rees (1982) found that experts are more accurate than novices at rating the difficulty of physics problems. Chi (1978) found that expert chess players are better than novices at estimating how many times they will need to see a given board position before being able to reproduce it correctly. This ability to estimate the difficulty of subtasks is probably important for allocating effort.

The hypothesis that experts have more schemas than do novices is consistent with their superior self-monitoring ability. Suppose that subjects estimate the difficulty of a subproblem by first finding the best-fitting schema, then combining its known difficulty with an estimate of the quality of the fit. The estimated quality of fit is needed because a poorly fitting schema means some extra work may be required to derive the information the schema needs from the problem. If this is how subjects estimate difficulty, then experts should be better at it because their schemas are more plentiful and more specialized so the fits are better. Thus their estimates of difficulty are dominated by the known difficulties of the schema, which is presumably more accurate than the process that estimates the quality of the fit.

Expert-Novice Differences: Memory Studies
As indicated in the preceding subsection, the speed and accuracy of experts is not accomplished by major, qualitative changes in their problem-solving strategies. The effects of expertise are more subtle. For instance, whenever an expert and a novice are deciding which chess move to make, both consider the same number of moves and investigate each move for about the same amount of time. The difference is that the expert considers only the good moves and usually chooses the best one, whereas the novice considers mediocre moves as well, and often does not choose the best move from those considered (de Groot 1965, Charness 1981). Thus expertise lies not in having a more powerful overall strategy or approach but rather in having better knowledge for making decisions at the points where the overall strategy calls for a problem-specific choice.

Protocol data are excellent for studying overall strategies because the strategies can be inferred from the patterns of observable moves. Protocols of even the most articulate subjects, however, are too often silent at the points where the subject is making a problem-specific decision. When subjects do talk, they often say that the choice was obvious (de Groot 1965). In short protocols have not proved a rich source of data about how experts make decisions. Other types of experiments, however, have been much more illuminating. In this subsection I discuss some of the more robust findings.

Classification of Problems   Chi, Feltovitch, and Glaser (1981) pioneered the use of a card-sorting technique for assessing differences in how experts and novices classify problems. In the study each card holds the text and diagram for a single elementary physics problem. The subject is asked to sort 24 cards into piles, placing problems that "seem to go together" into the same pile. Subjects could sort at their own rate. The novices tended to sort problems on the basis of literal, surface features, such as the types of objects involved (that is, inclined planes, pulleys, and so on). On the other hand the experts tended to sort problems on the basis of the physics principles used to solve the problem (for example, Newton's second law, or work-energy). Moreover the names for the piles given by the experts and novices reflected these observational characterizations. A specially constructed set of problems that crossed surface features with solution principles replicated the result. Similar results have been found in mathematics (Silver 1979, Schoenfeld and Herrmann 1982) and programming (Weiser and Shertz 1983).

It is possible that the classification difference is because of some between-subjects factor. For instance, a natural aptitude for mathematics or physics might cause both the classification difference and the career choice of the subject. Schoenfeld and Herrmann (1982) and Silver (1979) showed that this could not be the case. They tested mathematics students before and after courses in mathematical problem solving. The training causes students' classifications to become more expertlike.

These results led Chi and the other authors to hypothesize that experts have problem schemas that novices lack. Roughly put, subjects would put problems into the same category if those problems could be solved using the same problem schema.

However, it could be that the classifications/schemas of experts are not causally related to their improved problem-solving ability. Although this is difficult to test unequivocally, Chi, Feltovitch, and Glaser (1981) found that experts could give an abstract "basic approach" to a physics problem (for example, "I'd use dynamics, $F = ma$"), whereas novices could not. Instead the novices would either give very global statements (for example, "First, I figured out what was happening . . . then I started seeing how these different things were related to each other . . ." (Chi et al. 1981, p. 142)), or they would launch into a detailed solution of the problem. Voss and his colleagues (Voss, Tyler, and Yengo 1983) also found that experts but not novices tended to state basic approaches as they solved problems in governmental policy formation.

In short it seems that experts but not novices are able to classify problems according to problem schemas, and that these same schemas are used to solve problems.

Association Structures A variety of experimental techniques have been used in memory research to find out about the connectivity of the semantic network of concepts that is assumed to constitute people's declarative knowledge base (see chapter 7). Some of these have been used to try to differentiate the associative structures of experts and novices. For instance, Schvaneveldt and colleagues (1985) asked expert and novice fighter pilots to rate the similarities of pairs of technical terms from combat flying (for example, "high yo yo," "switchology"). They used two multidimensional scaling algorithms to uncover how the underlying association structures of experts differed from those of novices. McKeithen, Reitman, Rueter, and Hirtle (1981) and Adelson (1981) used item order in free recall; Pennington (1985) used priming; and Chi, Feltovitch, and Glaser (1981) used an elaboration technique to contrast the knowledge structures of experts and novices. All these studies showed that traditional methods for measuring semantic distance or connectedness succeeded in uncovering expert-novice differences in knowledge structure, and in most cases these differences are readily interpretable in terms of their utility in solving problems.

Episodic Memory for Problems and Solutions   Since Tulving's work (1972), it is customary to distinguish between semantic memory, which contains generic knowledge applicable to many situations, and episodic memory, which contains specific episodes in the subject's history. The preceding findings concerned differences in the semantic memory of expert and novices. There are also differences in the episodic memory of experts and novices.

A typical experiment on episodic memory presents a stimulus to the subject for a certain length of time, then occupies the subject in various ways for another interval of time, then asks the subject either to recall the stimulus, sometimes with the aid of a cue (hint), or to recognize the stimulus from among a set of similar items. Sometimes these three phases are repeated until the subject is able to recall the stimulus perfectly.

The general finding is that experts outperform novices in all versions of this paradigm that have been used so far, but only if the stimuli are ones that the expert would normally encounter in the course of problem solving.

The first experiment of this type was de Groot's (1965) demonstration that chess masters could recall almost all the pieces and positions of a chess board after having seen the board for only five seconds. Novices could recall only a few pieces. Moreover if the stimulus was a chess board with the pieces arranged randomly, the recall of the expert sank to the level of a novice. This finding has been replicated many times with stimuli consisting of chess boards (Chase and Simon 1973a, Charness 1976, Frey and Adesman 1976), Go boards (Reitman 1976), electronic circuit diagrams (Egan and Schwartz 1979), and bridge hands (Engle and Bukstel 1978, Charness 1979). In all these experiments the subject was tested almost immediately after the stimulus was presented. Thus it seems that experts have better short-term memory for problems.

Long-term memory for problems and solutions has also been measured. Chiesi, Spilich, and Voss (1979) demonstrated that experts have better long-term recognition and recall of episodes of baseball games. The experts' long-term memory is also better for chess games (Chase and Simon 1973b), bridge hands (Engle and Bukstel 1978, Charness 1979), and mathematics problems (Krutetskii 1976).

These results on episodic memory present a puzzle. Suppose it is assumed that the major knowledge difference between experts and novices is that experts have more schemas. This assumption is quite compatible with the finding that experts have better long-term episodic memory for problems and solutions. As Bartlett (1932) and many others have shown, stimuli that fit well into an existing schema are recalled better than stimuli that fit poorly. Because experts have more schemas than do novices, chances are better that they can select a schema that fits the problems or solutions well, and hence they have better long-term recall. However, it is not so easy to see how schemas facilitate short-term memory. The next subsection is devoted to this important issue.

Recall Structures   It is common to try to account for observed differences in episodic memory performance in terms of an underlying difference in the contents of the subjects' semantic memory. A standard technique for showing the influence of semantic memory contents on episodic memory performance is to use a stimulus consisting of several items and allow the subject to recall the items in any order. Subjects often reorder the items from their original presentation and recall them in runs of items, separated by pauses. The usual interpretation is that a run of items corresponds to the contents of an instantiated semantic memory structure. In particular the longer the run, the larger the unit of semantic memory (see, for example, Chase and Simon 1973a). Thus recall structure is important for determining the influence of semantic memory on episodic recall.

A common experiment is to contrast recall structure with some measure of semantic relatedness. Often semantic relatedness is obtained by a classification task, such as asking experts to circle the stimulus items that go together (Reitman 1976, Egan and Schwartz 1979). Sometimes a copying task is used, where the subject glances back and forth between the stimulus array and a blank array, copying the items seen in the stimulus onto the response array (Chase and Simon 1973a, Reitman 1976). The items copied with each glance are interpreted as being semantically related. Another technique is to use an expert or textbook to obtain a list of important relationships that one item can have to another (for example, in chess, whether one piece defends another). The semantic relatedness of two items can be equated with the number of relationships connecting them (Chase and Simon 1973a).

In experiments of this sort the major finding is that recall *orders* can be predicted by the expertise and semantic relatedness of items, but the recall *pauses* cannot. In particular for experts but not novices, items that have strong semantic relationships to each other are more likely to be recalled consecutively than items that have little semantic relationship (Chase and Simon 1973a, Reitman 1976, Egan and Schwartz 1979, Engle and Bukstel 1978). On the other hand pause times do not correlate strongly with the degree of semantic relatedness (Reitman 1976, Egan and Schwartz 1979). Thus item order seems to be a function of the underlying knowledge structures, but interitem retrieval times do not. This finding turns out to play an important role in the discussion of the next subsection.

Expert-Novice Differences: Chunking

It is well accepted that human perceptual processes are driven by knowledge in the form of *chunks*. (Note that although previous sections used "chunking" for the learning mechanism developed by Newell and his collaborators (Newell 1987, Laird, Rosenbloom, and Newell 1986, Laird, Newell, and Rosenbloom 1987, Newell and Rosenbloom 1981, Rosenbloom 1983), this section uses the term as in the general psychological literature.) For instance, an AI expert will perceive SHRDLU as a single chunk because it is the name of a famous AI program, whereas nonexperts will see it as a string of six letters. On the other hand someone who is unfamiliar with the Roman alphabet will see it as a configuration of lines because he or she does not have chunks for the letters. The chunking assumption is that the perceptual system will rapidly parse the stimulus, forming a hierarchical structure of instantiated chunks that covers as much of the stimulus as possible given the set of chunks known by the subject. The result is a set of instantiated chunk trees. The roots of these chunk trees are what the subject "notices." Thus the AI expert will have one tree/chunk, whose decendents are trees/chunks corresponding to each of the letters of SHRDLU. The nonexpert will see only six trees/chunks corresponding to the letters.

Chunks rose to prominence as the unit of measurement for memory capacity with Miller's (1956) hypothesis that short-term memory was limited to 7 ± 2 chunks. Although Miller's simple hypothesis is no longer tenable, chunks still play an important role in contemporary theories of short-term memory (Baddeley 1986, Zhang and Simon 1985) as well as other memory phenomena.

Chunks have played an important role in the development of theories of expert-novice differences. In particular a leading hypothesis, first proposed by Chase and Simon (1973a), is that at least some of the second-order features of experts are chunks. Thus an expert looking at a situation literally *sees* more than a novice does because the expert has more chunks. Chase and Simon pointed out that the hypothesis that experts have larger chunks than do novices would explain de Groot's (1965) result that chess masters could recall many more pieces from a briefly exposed chess position than novices. Assuming that both the novices and the experts have a short-term memory capacity of 7 ± 2 chunks, if the experts have an average chunk size of three or more, they could recall 20 to 30 chess pieces. On the other hand if novices have only one piece per chunk, then they can recall only a few pieces.

To test this prediction of their hypothesis, Chase and Simon needed some independent measure of chunk size. They used recall structure. Unfortunately they hypothesized that pauses represented the boundaries between chunks. By this measure the chunk size of experts was only a little larger than that of novices (2.5 pieces versus 1.9 pieces). Moreover the experts recalled more chunks than the novices, contrary to the assumed constant capacity of short-term memory. The support for Chase and Simon's hypothesis was weakened further by Charness's (1976) demonstration that immediate memory for chess positions was not affected by the kinds of interference manipulations that were known to affect short-term memory for other types of stimulus material. Also Reitman (1976) demonstrated that pauses were not a reliable indicator of chunk structure in the recall of Go positions, and Egan and Schwartz (1979) demonstrated that increased study time led to larger "chunks," as determined by pause structure. These results undermined the support for the chunk-size effect of expertise.

A few years later Chase and Ericsson (1981) proposed a new explanation for the expert's short-term memory. They showed that training could increase the apparent short-term memory capacity to 22 or more chunks. The primary device used by subjects is a version of the venerable pattern of loci device used by mnemonists. The idea is to form a schema with specific slots that can be filled in with the stimulus material. The material can be recalled (in fact in any order) by visiting the slots and reading out their contents. Chase and Ericsson named this device a *retrieval structure*. They showed that their digit-span expert's schema/retrieval structure was a specific three-level tree whose 22 leaves constituted the slots in which stimulus material could be stored.

Chase and Ericsson hypothesized that the superior memory of chess masters and other experts is due to possession of schemas/retrieval structures. This hypothesis is consistent with the findings that familiar stimuli permitted the expert to exhibit superior memory, because they can be used to select and instantiate schemas, whereas random stimuli do not. Moreover Chase and Ericsson's hypothesis can be used to make sense of Chase and Simon's finding that experts' runs were only a little larger than novices, and that experts tended to have more runs than novices. If one assumes that pauses in recall protocols correspond to moving from one slot to another, then the number and size of the runs is a function of the instantiated retrieval structure, rather than the subject's chunks. Chase and Ericsson's hypothesis is also consistent with the findings of Charness (1976) and Egan and Schwartz's (1979) assumption that instantiated schemas are held in long-term memory rather than short-term memory.

Chase and Ericsson's hypothesis has thus far survived empirical challenges. It is consistent with all the major short-term memory findings in the expert-novice literature. Moreover there is independent evidence for schemas from several sources mentioned previously in this chapter:

(1) categorization studies, (2) protocol studies, and (3) learning mechanisms. Thus it looks as though schemas are the key to understanding expertise.

Because Chase and Ericsson's hypothesis explains everything that Chase and Simon's hypothesis explains, however, there is currently no direct evidence that experts have larger chunks than novices. But it still remains an extremely plausible hypothesis, given all the evidence for chunking from experiments on verbal learning and perception (see chapter 7).

14.4 Summary

Three ingredients of any future theory of problem solving have been presented. They are: (1) the existing theory of problem solving in knowledge-lean task domains, (2) ideas for analyzing expert problem solving in knowledge-rich task domains, and (3) some robust experimental findings. Comments on the contact between theory and findings are sprinkled throughout the preceding sections, so this summary can be mercifully brief. Table 14.6 lists the robust experimental findings, or-

Table 14.6 Robust Empirical Findings

Practice Effects
  1. Reduction of verbalization
  2. Tactical learning
  3. The power law of practice

Problem Isomorphs
  4. Varying the cover story does not affect difficulty
  5. Other variations significantly affect difficulty

Transfer and Problem Solving by Analogy
  6. Asymmetric transfer
  7. Negative transfer
  8. Set effects
  9. Spontaneous noticing of potential analogies is rare
  10. Spontaneous noticing is based on superficial features

Expert-Novice Differences: Problem-solving Studies
  11. Experts perform faster than novices
  12. Experts are more accurate than novices
  13. Strategy differences
  14. Self-monitoring

Expert-Novice Differences: Memory Studies
  15. Classification of problems
  16. Association structures
  17. Episodic memory for problems and solutions
  18. Recall structures

Expert-Novice Differences: Chunking
  19. Experts may have larger chunks than novices have

Table 14.7 Major Theoretical Terms

The Standard Theory

Problem spaces
  States
  Operators

Understanding

Search
  Backup strategies vs. proceed strategies
  Heuristics
  Weak methods: forward and backwards chaining, operator subgoaling, etc.
  Means-ends analysis

Elaboration

Learning Mechanisms
  Compounding
  Tuning
  Chunking
  Proceduralization
  Strengthening

Schema-Driven Problem Solving

Schemas
  Problem half
  Solution half

Selection and instantiation
  Triggering
  Slot filling
  Second-order features

Following solution procedures
  Recursion
  Flexibility

Non-routine problem solving
  Search
  Schema compounding
  Impasses and repairs

ganized as presented in section 14.3. Table 14.7 lists most of the major theoretical concepts, organized as presented in sections 14.1 and 14.2.

Notes

I would like to thank John Anderson, Dirk Ruiz, Herbert Simon and especially Micki Chi for their comments. This work was supported by the Personnel and Training Research Program, Psychological Sciences Division, Office of the Naval Research, under contract N00014-86-K-0349 and by the Information Sciences Division, Office of Naval Research, under contract N00014-K-0678.

1. Sequence extrapolation has the expository advantage of being a simple task domain that most readers are familiar with. It is not a knowledge-lean task domain, however, because subjects are usually not told what types of patterns are legal. Thus the subjects must use their common sense or their prior experience with the task to decide what kinds of patterns are legal and hence what kinds of states and operators to use in the problem space. For sequence extrapolation the understanding process is just as important as the search process. See Kotovsky and Simon (1973) for a serious treatment of this task domain.

2. Many specific models of problem solving in the literature do not distinguish between assertions generated by perception and assertions generated by inference. The models sometimes produce a state with several dozen assertions in it, and this worries students who are familiar with the limitations of human short-term memory. Some of these assertions, however, may represent information that does not reside in the subject's short-term store. Rather it is information that the subject once saw in the external environment and could easily see again just by directing his or her gaze to the appropriate location. Although the limitations of short-term memory obviously do place some constraints on human problem solving, it would be far too simple to equate the contents of a problem state with the contents of short-term memory. Section 14.3 deals with the issue of short-term memory limitations in more detail.

3. In principle the initially available states could be much larger. The problem statement could mention final states or have hints that mention intermediate states. The subjects could even derive intermediate states deductively from their state-representation language.

4. Often courses on human problem solving include discussions of the major types of state-space search algorithms, such as depth-first search, breadth-first search, or even A*. Although it is doubtful that these types of search occur in human performance, they are nonetheless an important part of the conceptual vocabulary of a well-trained cognitive scientist. Fortunately these terms are almost always covered in introductory courses on AI, so a discussion of them is not included in this chapter.

5. Backward chaining and operator subgoaling are similar and often confused with each other. Backward chaining computes with concrete problem states, however, whereas operator subgoaling computes with descriptions of desired problem states. Backward chaining requires invertible operators, but operator subgoaling does not.

6. A special case of this strategy is called *hillclimbing*. It is applicable when the differences between the current and desired states can be estimated numerically. In this case the heuristics simply choose the operator that minimizes that numerical distance.

7. The algebraic examples used in this section have the advantage that they come from a

Problem Solving and Cognitive Skill Acquisition

task domain that most readers know quite well, so they make easily understood illustrations. Much less is known about specific schemas in algebra, however, than in physics where more work with detailed computer simulations has been done. No claim about the actual existence of this particular algebraic schema or the others mentioned herein is intended.

8. The Missionaries and Cannibals puzzle is: "Three missionaries and three cannibals wish to cross a river. There is a boat, but it holds only two people. Find a schedule of crossing that permits all six people to cross the river in such a way that at no time do the cannibals outnumber the missionaries on either bank." This version of the puzzle, with three missionaries, three cannibals, and a boat that holds two, is the most common. Other versions vary the number of people, the size of the boat, and other constraints. The mathematics of river-crossing puzzles is explored by Fraley, Cooke, and Detrick (1966) and others.

9. Although the knowledge is notated as productions, Kieras and Singley have argued that the type of knowledge transferred in some experiments is actually declarative rather than procedural, because these subjects had too little practice to allow them to proceduralize their declarative knowledge before the transfer task was given.

10. This finding must be qualified slightly for some domains, such as political science, where there is no objective measure of solution correctness or quality, so the experts' solutions are defined to be the correct ones.

References

Adelson, B. 1981. Problem solving and the development of abstract categories in programming languages. *Memory and Cognition* 9(4):422–433.

Akin, O. 1980. *Models of Architectural Knowledge*. London: Pion.

Anderson, J. R. 1982. Acquisition of cognitive skill. *Psychological Review* 89:369–406.

Anderson, J. R. 1983. *The Architecture of Cognition*. Cambridge, MA: Harvard University Press.

Anderson, J. R., Farrell, R., and Saurers, R. 1984. Learning to program in LISP. *Cognitive Science* 8:87–129.

Anzai, Y., and Simon, H. A. 1979. The theory of learning by doing. *Psychological Review* 86:124–140.

Anzai, Y., and Yokoyama, T. 1984. Internal models in physics problem solving. *Cognition and Instruction* 1:397–450.

Atwood, M. E., and Polson, P. G. 1976. A process model for water jug problems. *Cognitive Psychology* 8:191–216.

Atwood, M. E., Masson, M. E. J., and Polson, P. G. 1980. Further explorations with a process model for water jug problems. *Memory and Cognition* 8(2):182–192.

Baddeley, A. 1986. *Working Memory*. Oxford: Clarendon Press.

Bartlett, F. C. 1932. *Remembering: A Study in Experimental and Social Psychology*. Cambridge, Engl.: Cambridge University Press.

Bhaskar, R., and Simon, H. A. 1977. Problem solving in a semantically rich domains: An example from engineering thermodynamics. *Cognitive Science* 1:193–215.

Brown, J. S., and VanLehn, K. 1980. Repair theory: A generative theory of bugs in procedural skills. *Cognitive Science* 4:379–426.

Catrambone, R., and Holyoak, K. J. 1987. Transfer of training as a function of procedural variety of training examples. In *Proceedings of the Ninth Annual Conference*. Hillsdale, NJ: Cognitive Science Society, pp. 36–49.

Charness, N. 1976. Memory for chess positions; resistance to interference. *Journal of Experimental Psychology* 2:641–653.

Charness, N. 1979. Components of skill in bridge. *Canadian Journal of Psychology* 33(1):1–16.

Charness, N. 1981. Search in chess: Age and skill differences. *Journal of Experimental Psychology* 7(2):467–476.

Chase, W. G., and Ericsson, K. A. 1981. Skilled memory. In J. R. Anderson, ed. *Cognitive Skills and Their Acquisition*. Hillsdale, NJ: Erlbaum.

Chase, W. G., and Simon, H. A. 1973a. Perception in chess. *Cognitive Psychology* 5:55–81.

Chase, W. G., and Simon, H. A. 1973b. The mind's eye in chess. In W. G. Chase, ed. *Visual Information Processing*. New York: Academic.

Chi, M. T. H. 1978. Knowledge Structures and Memory Development. In R. S. Siegler, ed., *Children's Thinking: What Develops?* Hillsdale, NJ: Erlbaum.

Chi, M. T. H., Bassok, M., Lewis, M., Reimann, P., and Glaser, R. 1989. Learning problem solving skills from studying examples. *Cognitive Science*.

Chi, M. T. H., Feltovich, P. J., and Glaser, R. 1981. Categorization and representation of physics problems by experts and novices. *Cognitive Science* 5(2):121–152.

Chi, M. T. H., Glaser, R., and Farr, M. 1988. *The Nature of Expertise*. Hillsdale, NJ: Erlbaum.

Chi, M. T. H., Glaser, R., and Rees, E. 1982. Expertise in problem solving. In R. J. Sternberg, ed. *Advances in the Psychology of Human Intelligence*. Hillsdale, NJ: Erlbaum.

Chiesi, H. L., Spilich, G. J., and Voss, J. F. 1979. Acquisition of domain-related information in relation to high and low domain knowledge. *Journal of Verbal Learning and Verbal Behavior* 18:257–273.

Crossman, E. R. F. W. 1959. A theory of the acquisition of speed-skill. *Ergonomics* 2:159–166.

de Groot, A. D. 1965. *Thought and Choice in Chess*. The Hague: Mouton.

Duncan, C. P. 1959. Recent research on human problem solving. *Psychological Bulletin* 56(6):397–429.

Duncker, K. 1945. On problem-solving. *Psychological Monographs* 58(270):1–113.

Egan, D. E., and Schwartz, B. J. 1979. Chunking in recall of symbolic drawings. *Memory and Cognition* 7(2):149–158.

Engle, R. W., and Bukstel, L. 1978. Memory processes among bridge players of differing expertise. *American Journal of Psychology* 91:673–689.

Fikes, R. E., Hart, P. E., and Nilsson, N. J. 1972. Learning and executing generalized robot plans. *Artificial Intelligence* 3:251–288.

Fitts, P. M., and Posner, M. I. 1967. *Human Performance.* Belmont, CA: Brooks/Cole.

Fraley, Cooke, and Detrick. 1966. Graphical solution of difficult crossing problems. *Mathematics Magazine* 39:151–157.

Frey, P. W., and Adesman, P. 1976. Recall memory for visually presented chess positions. *Memory and Cognition* 4:541–547.

Gentner, D. 1989. Mechanisms of analogical learning. In S. Vosniadou and A. Ortony, eds. *Similarity and Analogical Reasoning.* London: Cambridge University Press.

Gentner, D., and Toupin, C. 1986. Systematicity and surface similarity in the development of analogy. *Cognitive Science* 10:277–300.

Gick, M. L., and Holyoak, K. J. 1980. Analogical problem solving. *Cognitive Psychology* 12:306–355.

Gick, M. L., and Holyoak, K. J. 1983. Schema induction and analogical transfer. *Cognitive Psychology* 15:1–38.

Greeno, J. G. 1974. Hobbits and orcs: Acquisition of a sequential concept. *Cognitive Psychology* 6:270–292.

Greeno, J. G., Magone, M. E., and Chaiklin, S. 1979. Theory of constructions and set in problem solving. *Memory and Cognition* 7:445–461.

Hayes, J. R. 1981. *The Complete Problem Solver.* Philadelphia, PA: Franklin Institute Press.

Hayes, J. R., and Simon, H. A. 1974. Understanding written problem instructions. In L. W. Gregg ed. *Knowledge and Cognition.* Hillsdale, NJ: Erlbaum. Reprinted in Simon, H. A., 1979. *Models of Thought.* New Haven, CT: Yale University Press.

Hayes, J. R., and Simon, H. A. 1976. The understanding process: Problem Isomorphs. *Cognitive Psychology* 8:165–190. Reprinted in Simon, H. A. 1979. *Models of Thought.* New Haven, CT: Yale University Press.

Hinsley, D. A., Hayes, J. R., and Simon, H. A. 1977. From words to equations, meaning and representation in algebra word problems. In M. A. Just, ed. *Cognitive Processes in Comprehension.* Hillsdale, NJ: Erlbaum.

Holyoak, K. 1985. The pragmatics of analogical transfer. In G. H. Bower, ed. *The Psychology of Learning and Motivation*. New York: Academic.

Jeffries, R., Polson, P. G., Razran, L., and Atwood, M. E. 1977. A process model for missionaries-cannibals and other river-crossing problems. *Cognitive Psychology* 9:412–440.

Jeffries, R., Turner, A. A., Polson, P. G., and Atwood, M. E. 1981. The processes involved in designing software. In J. R. Anderson, ed. *Cognitive Skills and Their Acquisition*. Hillsdale, NJ: Erlbaum.

Johnson. 1988. Expertise and decision under uncertainty: Performance and process. In M. T. H. Chi, R. Glaser, and M. Farr, eds. *The Nature of Expertise*. Hillsdale, NJ: Erlbaum.

Kant, E., and Newell, A. 1984. Problem solving techniques for the design of algorithms. *Information Processing and Management* 20(1,2):97–118.

Kieras, D. E., and Bovair, S. 1986. The acquisition of procedures from text: A production-system analysis of transfer of training. *Journal of Memory and Language* 25:507–524.

Kieras, D. E., and Polson, P. G. 1985. An approach to the formal analysis of user complexity. *International Journal of Man-Machine Studies* 22:365–394.

Kotovsky, K., and Simon, H. A. 1973. Empirical tests of a theory of human acquisition of concepts for sequential patterns. *Cognitive Psychology* 4:399–424.

Kotovsky, K., Hayes, J. R., and Simon, H. A. 1985. Why are some problems hard? Evidence from tower of Hanoi. *Cognitive Psychology* 17:248–294.

Krutetskii, V. A. 1976. *The Psychology of Mathematical Abilities in Schoolchildren*. Chicago, IL: University of Chicago Press.

Laird, J. E., Newell, A., and Rosenbloom, P. S. 1987. Soar: An Architecture for General Intelligence. *Artificial Intelligence* 33:1–64.

Laird, J. E., Rosenbloom, P. S., and Newell, A. 1986. Chunking in Soar: The anatomy of a general learning mechanism. *Machine Learning* 1(1):11–46.

Langley, P. 1987. A general theory of discrimination learning. In D. Klahr, P. Langley, and R. Neches, eds. *Production System Models of Learning and Development*. Cambridge, MA: MIT Press.

Larkin, J. H. 1981. Enriching formal knowledge: A model for learning to solve problems in physics. In J. R. Anderson, ed. *Cognitive Skills and Their Acquisition*. Hillsdale, NJ: Erlbaum.

Larkin, J. H. 1983. The role of problem representation in physics. In D. Gentner and A. Collins, eds. *Mental Models*. Hillsdale, NJ: Erlbaum.

Larkin, J. H., McDermott, J., Simon, D. P., and Simon, H. A. 1980. Expert and novice performance in solving physics problems. *Science* 208:1335–1342.

Lesgold, A., Robinson, H., Feltovitch, P., Glaser, R., Klopfer, D., and Wang, Y. 1988. Expertise in a complex skill: Diagnosing X-ray pictures. In M. T. H. Chi, R. Glaser, and M. J. Farr, eds. *The Nature of Expertise*. Hillsdale, NJ: Erlbaum.

LeFevre, J., and Dixon, P. 1986. Do written instructions need examples? *Cognition and Instruction* 3(1):1–30.

Levine, M. 1975. *A Cognitive Theory of Learning: Research on Hypothesis Testing*. Hillsdale, NJ: Erlbaum.

Lewis, C. H. 1979. *Production System Models of Practice Effects*. Doctoral dissertation, University of Michigan, Department of Psychology, Ann Arbor, MI.

Lewis, C. 1981. Skill in algebra. In J. R. Anderson, ed. *Cognitive Skills and Their Acquisition*. Hillsdale, NJ: Erlbaum.

Luchins, A. S. 1942. Mechanization in problem solving. *Psychological Monographs* 54(248).

Mawer, R. F., and Sweller, J. 1982. Effects of subgoal density and location on learning during problem solving. *Journal of Educational Psychology* 8(3):252–259.

McDermott, J., and Larkin, J. H. 1978. Representing textbook physics problem. In *Proceedings of the 2nd National Conference*. Canadian Society for Computation Studies of Intelligence.

McKeithen, K. B., Reitman, J. S., Rueter, H. H., and Hirtle, S. C. 1981. Knowledge organization and skill differences in computer programmers. *Cognitive Psychology* 13:307–325.

Miller, G. A. 1956. The magic number seven plus or minus two: Some limits on our capacity for processing information. *Psychological Review* 63:81–97.

Neves, D. M., and Anderson, J. R. 1981. Knowledge compilation: Mechanisms for the automatization of cognitive skills. In J. R. Anderson, ed. *Cognitive Skills and Their Acquisition*. Hillsdale, NJ: Erlbaum.

Newell, A. 1980. Reasoning, problem solving and decision processes: The problem space as a fundamental category. In R. Nickerson, ed. *Attention and Performance VIII*. Hillsdale, NJ: Erlbaum.

Newell, A. 1987. Unified Theories of Cognition: The 1987 William James Lectures. On video tape, available from Harvard University, Department of Psychology.

Newell, A., and Rosenbloom, P. S. 1981. Mechanism of skill acquisition and the law of practice. In J. R. Anderson, ed. *Cognitive Skills and Their Acquisition*. Hillsdale, NJ: Erlbaum.

Newell, A., and Simon, H. A. 1972. *Human Problem Solving*. Englewood Cliffs, NJ: Prentice-Hall.

Newell, A., Shaw, J. C., and Simon, H. A. 1962. The process of creative thinking. In H. E. Gruber, G. Terrell, and M. Wertheimer, Eds. *Contemporary Approaches to Creative Thinking*. New York: Lieber-Atherton. Reprinted in H. A. Simon's (1979) *Models of Thought*. New Haven, CT: Yale University Press.

Ohlsson, S. 1984. Restructuring revisited, II: An information processing theory of restructing and insight. *Scandinavian Journal of Psychology* 25:117–129.

Ohlsson, S. 1987. Truth versus appropriateness: Relating declarative to procedural knowledge. In D. Klahr, P. Langley, and R. Neches, eds. *Production System Models of Learning and Development*. Cambridge, MA: MIT Press.

Paige, J. M., and Simon, H. A. 1966. Cognitive processes in solving algebra word problems. In B. Kleinmuntz, ed. *Problem Solving: Research, Method and Theory*. New York, NY: Wiley.

Papert, S. 1980. *Mindstorms: Children, Computers and Powerful Ideas*. New York, NY: Basic Books.

Pea, R. D. 1987. Socializing the knowledge transfer problem. *International Journal of Educational Research* 11(6):639–663.

Pennington, N. 1985. *Stimulus structures and mental representations in expert comprehension of computer programs*. Technical report 2-ONR, Graduate School of Business, The University of Chicago, Chicago, IL.

Pirolli, P. L. 1985. *Problem solving by analogy and skill acquisition in the domain of programming*. Doctoral dissertation, Carnegie-Mellon University, Department of Psychology, Pittsburgh, PA.

Pirolli, P. L., and Anderson, J. R. 1985. The role of learning from examples in the acquisition of recursive programming skills. *Canadian Journal of Psychology* 39(2):240–272.

Reed, S. K. 1987. A structure-mapping model of word problems. *Journal of Experimental Psychology: Learning, Memory and Cognition* 13(1):124–139.

Reed, S. K., and Simon, H. A. 1976. Modeling strategy shifts in a problem-solving task. *Cognitive Psychology* 8:86–97.

Reed, S. K., Dempster, A., and Ettinger, M. 1985. Usefulness of analogous solutions for solving algebra word problems. *Journal of Experimental Psychology: Learning, Memory and Cognition* 11:106–125.

Reed, S. K., Ernst, G. W., and Banerji, R. 1974. The role of analogy in transfer between similar problem states. *Cognitive Psychology* 6:436–450.

Reimann, P., and Chi, M. T. H. 1989. Human expertise in complex problem solving. In Gilhooly, ed. *Human and Machine Problem-Solving* (in press).

Reitman, J. S. 1976. Skilled perception in Go: Deducing memory structures from inter-response times. *Cognition Psychology* 8:336–356.

Reitman, W. R. 1965. *Cognition and Thought: An Information-Processing Approach*. New York: Wiley.

Rosenbloom, P. S. 1983. *The chunking of goal hierarchies: A model of practice and stimulus-response compatibility*. Doctoral dissertation, Carnegie-Mellon University, CMU Computer Science Technical Report #83-148.

Ross, B. H. 1984. Remindings and their effects in learning a cognitive skill. *Cognitive Psychology* 16:371–416.

Ross, B. H. 1987. This is like that: The use of earlier problems and the separation of similarity effects. *Journal of Experimental Psychology: Learning, Memory, and Cognition* 13(4):629–639.

Schneider, W., and Shiffrin, R. M. 1977. Controlled and automatic human information processing: I. Detection, search and attention. *Psychological Review* 84(1):1–66.

Schoenfeld, A. H. 1981. Episodes and executive decisions in mathematical problem solving. Paper presented at the 1981 AERA Annual Meeting, Los Angeles, CA.

Schoenfeld, A. H., and Herrmann, D. J. 1982. Problem perception and knowledge structure in expert and novice mathematical problem solvers. *Journal of Experimental Psychology: Learning, Memory, and Cognition* 8(5):484–494.

Schvaneveldt, R. W., Durso, F. T., Goldsmith, T. E., Breen, T. J., and Cooke, N. M. 1985. Measuring the structure of expertise. *International Journal Man-Machine Studies* 23:699–728.

Shiffrin, R. M., and Schneider, W. 1977. Controlled and automatic human information processing: II. Perceptual learning, automatic attending, and a general theory. *Psychological Review* 84(2):127–190.

Silver, E. A. 1979. Student perceptions of relatedness among mathematical verbal problems. *Journal for Research in Mathematics Education* 10:195–210.

Silver, E. A. 1981. Recall of mathematical problem information: Solving related problems. *Journal for Research in Mathematical Education* 12:54–64.

Simon, H. A. 1973. The structure of ill-structured problems. *Artificial Intelligence* 4:181–201.

Simon, H. A. 1983. Why should machines learn? In R. S. Michalski, J. G. Carbonell, and T. M. Mitchell, eds. *Machine Learning: An Artificial Intelligence Approach.* Palo Alto, CA: Tioga.

Simon, D. P., and Simon, H. A. 1978. Individual difference in solving physics problems. In R. Siegler, ed. *Children's Thinking: What Develops?* Hillsdale, NJ: Erlbaum.

Singley, M. K. 1986. *Developing models of skill acquisition in the context of intelligent tutoring systems.* Doctoral dissertation, Department of Psychology, Carnegie-Mellon University, Pittsburgh, PA.

Singley, M. K., and Anderson, J. R. 1985. The transfer of text-editing skill. *International Journal of Man-Machine Studies* 22:403–423.

Singley, M. K., and Anderson, J. R. 1989. *The Transfer of Cognitive Skill.* Cambridge, MA: Harvard University Press.

Stevens, S. S. 1951. *Handbook of Experimental Psychology.* New York: Wiley.

Sweller, J. 1983. Control mechanisms in problem solving. *Memory and Cognition* 11(1): 32–40.

Sweller, J., and Cooper, G. A. 1985. The use of worked examples as a substitute for problem solving in learning algebra. *Cognition and Instruction* 2(1):59–89.

Sweller, J., and Gee, W. 1978. Einstellung, the sequence effect and hypothesis theory. *Journal of Experimental Psychology: Human Learning and Cognition* 4:513–526.

Sweller, J. and Levine, M. 1982. Effects of goal specificity on means-ends analysis and learning. *Journal of Experimental Psychology: Learning, Memory and Cognition* 8(5):463–474.

Sweller, J., Mawer, R. F., and Ward, M. R. 1983. Development of expertise in mathematical problem solving. *Journal of Experimental Psychology: General* 112(4):639–661.

Thorndike, E. L., and Woodworth, R. S. 1901. The influence of improvement in one mental function upon the efficiency of other functions. *Psychological Review* 8:247–261.

Tulving, E. 1972. Episodic and semantic memory. In E. Tulving and W. Donaldson, ed. *Organization and Memory.* New York: Academic Press.

VanLehn, K. 1982. Bugs are not enough: Empirical studies of bugs, impasses and repairs in procedural skills. *The Journal of Mathematical Behavior* 3(2):3–71.

VanLehn, K. 1983. Human skill acquisition: Theory, model and psychological validation. In *Proceedings of AAAI-83.* Los Altos, CA: Morgan Kaufman, pp. 420–423.

VanLehn, K. 1987. Learning one subprocedure per lesson. *Artificial Intelligence* 31(1): 1–40.

VanLehn, K. 1989. *Mind Bugs: The Origins of Procedural Misconceptions.* Cambridge, MA: MIT Press.

VanLehn, K., Ball, W., and Kowalski. 1990. Non-Life execution of cognitive procedure. *Cognitive Science* (in press).

Voss, J. F., Greene, T. R., Post, T. A., and Penner, B. C. 1983. Problem solving skill in the social sciences. In G. H. Bower, ed. *The Psychology of Learning and Motivation.* Vol. 17. New York: Academic Press.

Voss, J. F., Tyler, S. W., and Yengo, L. A. 1983. Individual differences in the solving of social science problems. In R. Dillon and R. Schmech, eds. *Individual Differences in Cognition.* New York: Academic Press.

Weisberg, R. W., and Alba, J. W. 1981. An examination of the alleged role of 'fixation' in the solution of several 'insight' problems. *Journal of Experimental Psychology: General* 110(2):169–192.

Weiser, M., and Shertz, J. 1983. Programming problem representation in novice and expert programmers. *International Journal of Man-Machine Studies* 19:391–398.

Zhang, G., and Simon, H. A. 1985. STM capacity for Chinese words and idioms: Chunking and acoustical loop hypotheses. *Memory and Cognition* 13(3):193–201.

15 The Computational Study of Vision

Ellen C. Hildreth and Shimon Ullman

15.1 Introduction

Through vision we derive a rich understanding of what is in the world, where objects are located, and how they are changing with time. Because we obtain this understanding immediately, effortlessly, and without conscious introspection, we can be deceived into thinking that vision should therefore be fairly simple to perform. The computational approach to the study of vision inquires directly into the sort of information processing needed to extract important information from the changing visual image—information such as the three-dimensional (3-D) structure and movement of objects in the scene, or the color and texture of object surfaces. An important contribution that computational studies have made is to show how difficult vision is to perform and how complex are the processes needed to perform visual tasks successfully.

Levels of Analysis

The development of computers with increasing power and sophistication has often stimulated comparisons between computers and the human brain, especially because computers have been applied more and more to tasks that were formerly considered uniquely human capabilities, such as understanding natural language. It is clear, however, that at the level of their hardware, neurons and computer circuits are very different. We can nevertheless attempt to describe the processes that take place in these two systems at a level that is essentially independent of this hardware—this is a description of the tasks that they perform. In much the same way that we can describe the theory of arithmetic independent of the computing device that carries out the arithmetic operations, we can describe the theory of vision independent of the hardware that carries it out, whether it be biological or computer hardware.

This idea of separating the tasks performed by a vision system from the hardware that carries out these tasks was central to the work of

David Marr (1982). Marr argued that there are at least three different levels at which problems in vision can be described, which he labeled the computational theory, algorithm, and mechanism. Theoretical issues include an analysis of how properties of the physical world constrain how problems in vision are solved. An algorithm is a step-by-step procedure that transforms one representation of visual information into the next. Finally the mechanism refers to the details of how a computation is carried out in neural or computer hardware. These three levels of analysis are a useful methodological distinction for studying visual processing, but the distinction between levels such as algorithm and mechanism is often not a sharp one for the brain.

An aspect of computational studies that distinguishes them from other theoretical approaches to the study of vision is the notion that an effective way to analyze the computational strategies used by biological systems to perform complex visual tasks is to build computer vision systems that use similar strategies. The synthesis of machine vision systems allows rigorous testing of whether some strategy that is hypothesized for the biological system really works at solving an important problem in vision. Building machine vision systems often uncovers difficult aspects of a problem and possible solutions that were not realized upon first consideration.

Experimental studies from psychology and the neurosciences provide critical insights into the particular computations that underlie visual processing in biological systems. A given problem typically can be solved in more than one way; there are different choices for how properties of the physical world can constrain its solution and different algorithms, or procedures, that can be used to carry out the solution. Computer implementations of possible strategies can show how the overall behavior of the system depends on the choice of constraints and algorithms, and critical experimental tests can be devised to determine what choices are made in biological systems. Thus a fruitful interaction between computational and experimental approaches can contribute to our understanding of biological vision.

Low-Level and High-Level Vision

Biological vision begins with measurements of the amount of light reflected from surfaces in the environment onto the eye. The retinal image provided by the photoreceptors can be thought of as a large array of continuously changing numbers that represent light intensities. From this array of light measurements the visual system does not achieve an understanding of what is in the scene in a single step. A tenet of computational studies is that vision proceeds in stages, with each stage producing increasingly more useful descriptions of the world. The process of vision can be viewed as the construction of a series of representations of visual information with explicit computation that transforms one representation into the next.

It is not yet known how biological systems represent visual information, but computational studies have suggested several representations that are useful in visual processing (see, for example, Marr 1982, Ballard and Brown 1982, Horn 1986, Fischler and Firschein 1987). Representations proposed for the early stages of vision first capture information that can be extracted simply and directly from the initial image, such as the location and description of significant intensity changes or edges in the image. Subsequent representations capture the local geometry or 3-D shape of visible surfaces in the scene, represented as the orientation or depth of surfaces at each location in the scene. Many familiar visual processes, such as the analysis of movement, binocular stereopsis, surface shading, texture, and color, contribute to the computation of these early visual representations. We refer to these early stages of vision as *low-level* vision. A main goal of low-level visual processes is to recover properties of the surrounding environment, and the representations that they deliver can be evaluated on the basis of their validity, that is, whether the results they deliver are correct and accurate.

Later representations for vision capture information necessary to solve complex tasks such as navigation through the environment, manipulation of objects, and recognition. The visual processes involved in accomplishing these tasks are often referred to as *high-level* vision. Although there is no well-defined boundary between low- and high-level vision, the distinction is often useful. The main difference between low- and high-level visual processes is in the kind of knowledge they use. Low-level vision relies on assumptions regarding the general physical properties of objects, such as continuity and rigidity. High-level tasks, such as recognition, often use some knowledge that we have acquired about specific objects, such as their shape and perhaps the transformations that they may undergo. Additional distinctions between low- and high-level vision and the description of an intermediate domain between them are discussed in section 15.3.

Scope of the Chapter
The next section focuses on three problem areas in which there has been substantial computational work, as well as important interactions between computational work and experimental studies from psychology and the neurosciences. In particular we consider the problems of edge detection, binocular stereo, and the analysis of visual motion. Overall research in computational vision spans a wide range of problems that also include the analysis of texture, color, and the recovery of 3-D shape from image contours and smooth shading. Most early work explored these problems in isolation, whereas recent work has emphasized the integration of multiple visual processes. Reviews of computational work in these areas can be found in a number of recent books (for example, Brady 1981, Ballard and Brown 1982, Marr 1982, Beck, Hope, and Ro-

senfeld 1983, Ullman and Richards 1984, Levine 1985, Horn 1986, Pentland 1986, Brown 1987, Fischler and Firschein 1987, Richards and Ullman 1987). In section 15.3 we explore problems in intermediate and high-level vision and address two major problems. The first problem is the extraction of shape properties of figures and spatial relations among items in the scene. The second is visual object recognition.

15.2 Low-Level Vision

Edge Detection
When the image is first captured by the retinal photoreceptors in the eye, it consists of some 120 million individual pointwise measurements of light intensity. A major problem that arises is how to transform this large and unstructured set of measurements into a more useful representation, that is, a representation that is more concise and more convenient for subsequent processing stages.

In the fields of computer vision and image processing, the dominant suggestion has been to begin the analysis of the incoming image by producing from the intensity array an *edge representation* using a process called *edge detection*. Edges in the image are locations where the light intensity changes significantly from one level to a different one. The main rationale for using an edge representation as the primary representation is that intensity edges are usually physically significant: they correspond to object boundaries and to discontinuities in surface properties, such as spatial orientation or reflectance. The important role of edges is also supported by the fact that for humans a line sketch of an image often conveys most of the essential information, although from the point of view of the underlying intensity distributions, the line sketch and the image are radically different. Similarly in experiments involving pattern recognition by animals (such as the rat, octopus, and goldfish), it has been noted that figures are usually treated as equivalent to a sketch of their outlines (Sutherland 1968). Early perceptual studies by Cornsweet and others (see, for example, Cornsweet 1970) also show that our perception of an image does not directly mimic the initial intensities registered by the eye, but is strongly influenced by the presence of sharp intensity changes, or edges. An example of an edge representation obtained from a natural image, using an edge detection method for computer vision systems proposed by Canny (1986), is shown in Figure 15.1.

It should be mentioned that the operation of edge detection is not the only proposal that has been made concerning the initial representation of the incoming image. A popular alternative has been a local Fourier (or Gabor) decomposition of the image.[1] These alternative suggestions have not yet played as significant a role in computational vision and are not discussed here.

In the following discussion we consider primarily one family of edge-

Figure 15.1 Edge detection. (A) Original image. (B) Edge representation of the same image, produced by the Canny edge-detection algorithm (Canny 1986).

detection schemes that are based on detecting maxima in the rate of change (defined as maxima, or peaks, in the first derivative or zero-crossings in the second) of the image intensities. The reasons for concentrating on this group are first, that such schemes have produced high-quality results that have been used successfully in later stages of visual processing in computer vision systems and second, that interesting possible connections have been proposed between this scheme and edge detection by the human visual system. For reviews of various edge-detection techniques, see, for example, Davis 1975, Fram and Deutsch 1975, Pratt 1978, Ballard and Brown 1982, Torre and Poggio 1986, Fischler and Firschein 1987, and Hildreth 1987.

Differentiation and Smoothing   To produce an edge representation of the image, one needs a more precise definition of what is meant by "significant" intensity changes. One proposed definition is to identify edges as locations in the image where the (directional) derivative of intensity reaches a local maximum in its absolute value. It can be shown that, under quite general conditions, when a signal passes through an optical system, step edges in the incoming intensity distribution (before the optics) give rise to maxima in the first directional derivative of image intensity (after the optics). Locating derivative maxima therefore appears to be a reasonable step toward identifying sharp edges.

The differentiation of a signal, however, raises certain technical difficulties because this operation enhances considerably the high-frequency components of the signal. Because images often contain high-frequency noise, the noise is enhanced by differentiation.[2] To overcome this problem, the differentiation of a signal is usually preceded by a smoothing operation that removes the noisy high-frequency components. It has been shown that optimal results can be obtained by using a smoothing function that has a Gaussian, or close to a Gaussian shape (Shanmugam, Dickey, and Green 1979, Marr and Hildreth 1980, Koenderink 1984, Babaud et al. 1986, Canny 1986, Torre and Poggio 1986). Thus one approach to edge detection is to perform the following steps: (1) smoothing the signal using a Gaussian filter, (2) differentiating the signal, and (3) locating maxima in its directional derivatives.[3]

Mathematically these stages can be summarized (for a one-dimensional signal) as locating maxima in $d / dx(G * I)$, where G is a Gaussian function, and $*$ denotes the filtering, or convolution, operation. Interestingly the same operation can be obtained by performing $(d / dx(G)) * I$. This means that the two successive operations, smoothing and differentiation, can be combined. The image is filtered through a new function, the first derivative of a Gaussian. Maxima in the first derivative of the smoothed image can be detected equivalently by finding locations where the second derivative of the smoothed image crosses zero. If we again use Gaussian smoothing, then mathematically this second scheme corresponds to finding zero-crossings in the signal $(d^2 / dx^2(G)) * I$. To summarize, edges can be found by (1) passing the image through a filter whose shape is the first or second derivative of a Gaussian and (2) locating features such as maxima or zero-crossings in the result of this filtering stage. For the case of one dimension the use of maxima and zero-crossings in the derivatives of Gaussian-filtered images is illustrated in figure 15.2. The figure shows a one-dimensional intensity profile obtained by taking a slice through a natural image, the same profile following Gaussian filtering, and how the edges can be identified by the maxima (or peaks) in the first derivative or zero-crossings in the second.

Peaks and Zero-Crossings in One and Two Dimensions This basic scheme, presented for a one-dimensional signal, has a number of possible extensions to the analysis of two-dimensional images. One alternative uses directional first- or second-derivative operators[4] for performing the two-dimensional differentiation (see, for example, Macleod 1972, Davis 1975, Persoon 1976, Rosenfeld and Kak 1976, Pratt 1978, Haralick 1980, Binford 1981, Nevatia and Babu 1980, Zucker 1987). A second strategy is to evaluate at each location in the image the direction of the intensity gradient, which is the direction along which the intensity changes most rapidly. A one-dimensional analysis of intensity changes is then applied locally in this direction (see, for example, Canny 1986). In a third alternative the image is first passed through a single, nondirectional filter, whose shape is defined by $\nabla^2 G$, the Laplacian of a two-dimensional Gaussian function (the Laplacian is the sum of the two directional derivatives in the horizontal and vertical directions), and then followed by the detection of the zero-crossings in the result of this filtering stage. The $\nabla^2 G$ operator is shown in figure 15.3. It is interesting to note in this regard that under quite general conditions, the zero-crossings representation produced in this manner gives a complete representation of the image; that is, the original image can be reconstructed (up to a single scaling factor) from the zero-crossing contours alone (Curtis and Oppenheim 1987).

Multiple Scales Intensity edges can occur in an image at a variety of scales. Some edges are sharp and close together, others are gradual and well separated. It proved difficult to capture all of the different types of significant intensity changes using only a single fixed operator. An approach that has evolved in computational vision in response to this problem is to analyze the image at a number of different scales (see, for example, Rosenfeld and Thurston 1971, Marr and Hildreth 1980, Mayhew and Frisby 1981, Witkin 1983, Canny 1986). In a coarse-scale edge representation only a limited number of significant, relatively isolated edges would be revealed, whereas a fine-scale (high-resolution) analysis would yield a denser representation of the edges. The resolution or scale of the analysis is determined by the size of the operator

The Computational Study of Vision

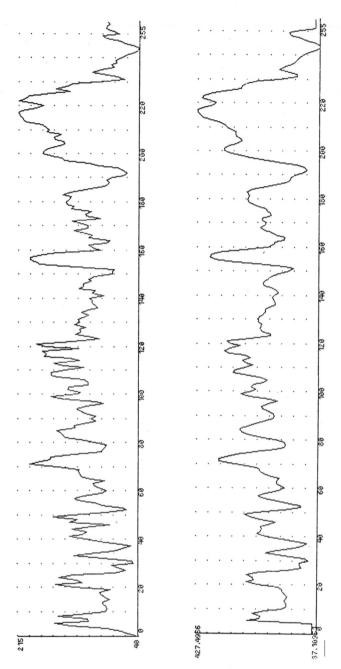

Figure 15.2 Detecting intensity changes. (A) One-dimensional intensity profile obtained by measuring intensities along a horizontal slice of a natural image. (B) The result of smoothing the profile in A. (C) The result of additional smoothing of A. (D, E) The first and second derivatives, respectively, of the smoothed profile shown in C. The vertical dashed lines indicate peaks in the first derivative and zero-crossings in the second derivative that correspond to two significant intensity changes (Hildreth 1987).

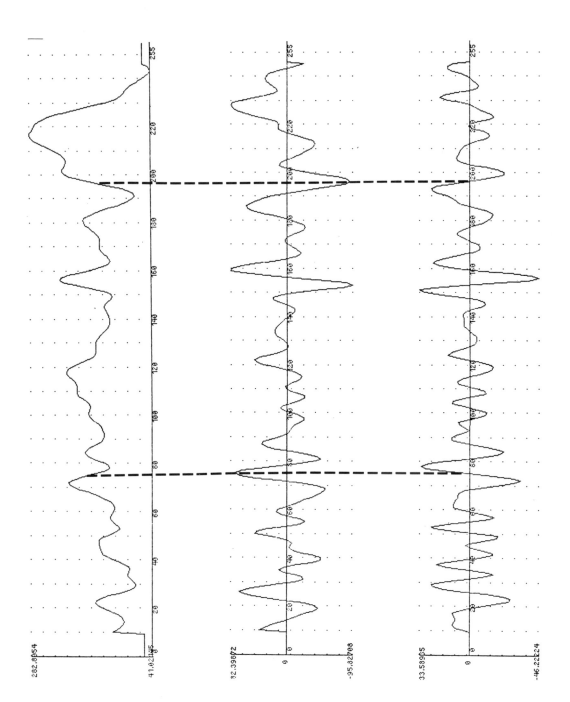

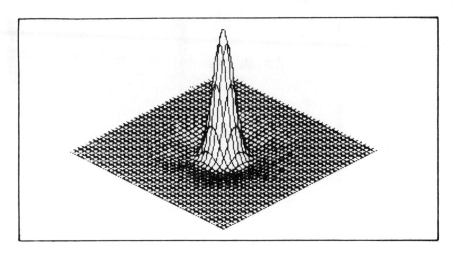

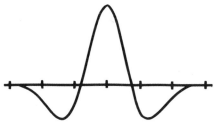

Figure 15.3 The $\nabla^2 G$ operator. (A) Three-dimensional plot of the shape of the two-dimensional operator. (B) A one-dimensional cross-section through the center of the operator.

(such as the value σ of the space constant of the underlying Gaussian in the $\nabla^2 G$ operator). Multiple-scale analysis is therefore achieved by the simultaneous use of a number of operators of different sizes, as shown in figure 15.4.

This general idea of multiple-scale analysis is in agreement with the large body of psychophysical data regarding multiple channels in the visual system. Experiments using techniques such as detection, adaptation, and discrimination suggest that at each location in the visual field, a number of mechanisms analyze the image at a range of different scales (see, for example, Campbell and Robson 1968, Cowan 1977, Graham 1977, Watson and Nachmias 1977, Wilson and Bergen 1979). These mechanisms appear to be sensitive to different ranges of spatial and temporal frequency.

Biological Significance   One question regarding edge representations based on features such as peaks and zero-crossings is their biological relevance. It is known that the appropriate kind of filtering takes place at the level of the retina and the lateral geniculate nucleus. That is, at this level the image can be thought of as being passed through filters, or receptive fields, whose shape can be closely approximated by the

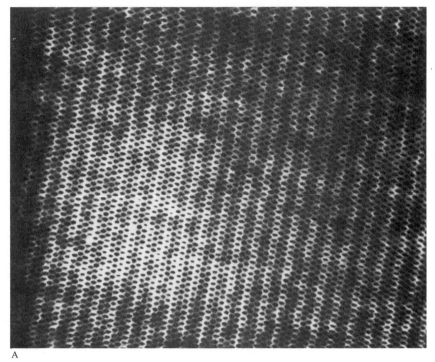

A

Figure 15.4 Multiresolution image analysis. (A) The original image. (B, C) Edge representations obtained at two different scales (Canny 1986).

$\nabla^2 G$ shape. It is not entirely clear, however, what processing takes place beyond this first stage, at the level of the primary visual cortex. It is in fact an instructive point that in spite of the large body of knowledge regarding the anatomy and physiology of the primary visual cortex, relatively little is known about the functions it performs. Many cortical studies are in general agreement with the notion that this area may be involved, among other functions, with the task of edge detection. In particular the so-called cortical simple cells have often been described as edge and bar detectors (see, for example, Hubel and Wiesel 1968). This view is not universally accepted, however (see, for example, DeValois, Albrecht and Thorell 1982), and the exact function of these and other cortical units remains unclear.

A possibility raised by the preceding discussion is that one of the functions of this cortical area may be to construct a number of zero-crossing maps at different scales and then to combine them to construct an edge representation of the incoming image. This point of view regarding the possible function of the primary visual cortex gives rise to specific predictions that can be tested by physiological techniques. Some of these predictions have in fact been tested (Richter and Ullman 1986), and the results appear generally to be compatible with a zero-crossing–based view. Recent psychophysical studies (for example, Watt and Morgan 1983, 1984) provide some support for the use of zero-crossings in

B

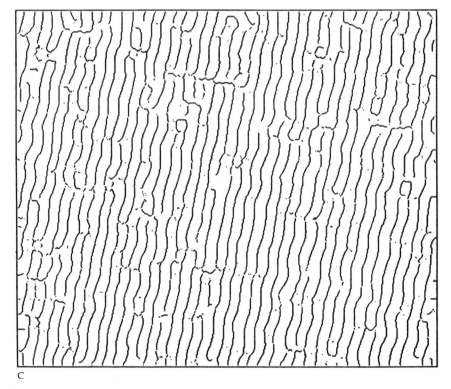

C

human vision, but show that additional primitive features, such as stationary points in an approximation to the second derivative of the image intensities, are essential to account for the ability of the human visual system to detect and localize the positions of significant intensity changes in the image. The experiments performed so far are insufficient to determine conclusively the role of edges in early vision, but they serve to demonstrate that connections are starting to develop between computational theories on the one hand and empirical biological studies of brain mechanisms on the other.

A final comment on edge detection is that even if features such as peaks or zero-crossings in the result of smoothing and differentiating the image are being detected, it should be realized that they constitute only one stage in the analysis of boundaries. Edge representations at different scales must somehow be combined. In addition there are many types of boundaries that humans are sensitive to, but cannot be captured by the zero-crossing scheme or by other intensity-based edge-detection techniques. Examples of such boundaries include texture edges, in which the two sides of the boundary differ in texture rather than in average intensity, and subjective contours, which the visual system fills in from different types of evidence when a physical discontinuity in the image is not present (see figure 15.5). It is interesting to note that recently cells have been found rather early in the visual system, in cortical area V2, that clearly respond to subjective contours (von der Heydt, Peterhans, and Baumgartner 1984).

Binocular Stereo

The left and right eyes obtain two slightly different views of the world, and we use the difference between these two views to recover the distances to surfaces in the environment. In particular there is *disparity* between the positions of corresponding features in the two retinal images, which depends on both where the objects are located in space and where the eyes are focused. Binocular stereo, the process that uses

Figure 15.5 Subjective contours. Examples of boundaries that can be perceived, but cannot be detected directly by an intensity-based edge-detection scheme.

these disparities to recover 3-D information, is a critical component of human vision—it is considered our most accurate system for recovering the distances to surfaces (Westheimer and McKee 1978, 1980, Poggio and Poggio 1984).

Examining the process of stereo vision from a computational perspective, there are three main steps that need to be solved. The first is to extract elements from the images, whose positions will be compared in the two stereo views. The second is to match up these elements in the two views; that is, for each element in the left image an element is located in the right image that corresponds to the same physical feature in the scene. Finally, through a geometric transformation the disparities in position of features in the two images determine the distances to objects in space. It turns out that the second step, referred to as the *stereo correspondence problem,* is one of the most difficult aspects of the stereo process.

When we consider stereo views of a natural scene, such as those shown in figure 15.6a, it might appear that the stereo correspondence problem ought to be straightforward. One could, for example, extract small patches from the left image and look for the most similar patch of image intensities in the right image. This strategy is referred to as *gray-level correlation,* and it formed the basis for early stereo systems developed in computer vision (for review, see Barnard and Fischler 1982) as well as early models of human stereo vision (see, for example, Sperling 1970). Techniques based on matching the image intensities did not work well in practice, primarily for two reasons. First, the image intensities can change significantly between the two views—they undergo photometric and geometric distortions. An example of a photometric change between the two images is a bright highlight that appears in one image but not the other, because of the way the surface catches the light. An example of a geometric change is a rotation of one image relative to the other. Such rotations often occur when the angle of gaze deviates significantly from straight ahead. These distortions can lead to significant errors in stereo methods based on gray-level correlation.

There is a second problem, however, that is more severe—there is tremendous ambiguity in matching features between the two images. Given some patch in one image, there are often many patches in the other that are quite similar. This ambiguity is exacerbated by the wide range of depths contained in a typical scene, from which it follows that there will be a wide range of possible disparities between features in the two images. To solve the stereo correspondence problem, the matching process needs to be constrained to derive a unique matching of features between the two stereo views.

The ambiguity problem is best illustrated with stereo images that consist of random dots, as shown in figure 15.7 (Julesz 1971). The left image is a random array of black and white dots. To construct the right

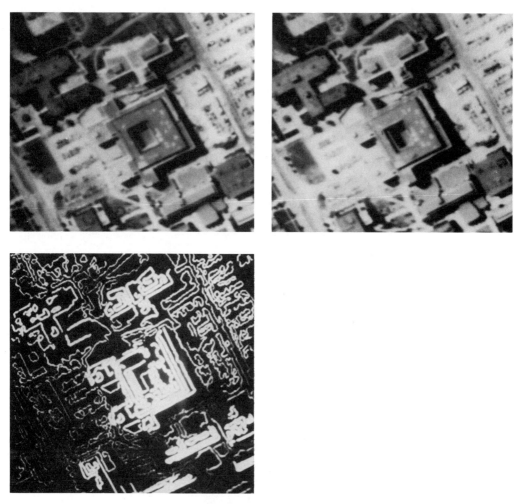

Figure 15.6 Stereo analysis. (A) Aerial stereo photographs of a section of the campus at the University of British Columbia. (B) The disparities computed by the Marr-Poggio-Grimson stereo correspondence algorithm (Grimson 1985) for the images shown in A. Brightness encodes depth, with brighter contours being closer to the viewer.

The Computational Study of Vision

Figure 15.7 A random-dot stereogram with disparities that reveal two depth planes stacked on top of one another

image, patterns of dots from the left image are shifted by different amounts to the left or right in the right image, creating disparity in their positions in the two stereo views. In the case of figure 15.7 a central patch of dots in the left image is shifted to the right in the right image. If the resulting patterns are observed in such a way that the left eye views only the left pattern and the right eye views the right, a perception of 3-D surfaces at different depths results from the relative placement of the dots. The ability to fuse random-dot stereograms to form a perception of depth illustrates two important aspects of stereo vision. First, the features that are matched between the two images must be simple—stereo fusion does not require that we recognize objects in the image and match entire objects between the two stereo views. Second, it illustrates the inherent ambiguity faced by the stereo correspondence process. In principle any dot in the left image could match any dot of the same color in the right image.

To solve the stereo correspondence problem uniquely, it is necessary to constrain the matching process in some way. Computational models of the stereo correspondence process use a variety of such constraints. First, an object in space occupies only a single location at one time, which implies that each feature in the left image matches only a single feature in the right image. This is referred to as the *uniqueness* constraint. Second, because of the nature of stereo projection, features located along a particular line in one image all match with features along a line in the other image. If the eyes are focused at a distance, then these corresponding lines are roughly horizontal and at the same vertical height in the two images. If, however, the eyes are focused at a nearby object, or the angle of gaze deviates significantly from being straight ahead, then these lines have different orientations in the two images. If the positions of the eyes in their orbit are known, then it is possible to determine where the corresponding lines lie in the two images. This facilitates stereo matching because now, given a feature in one image, it is only necessary to search along a single line in the other image for a possible match. Virtually all models of stereo vision assume that the viewing geometry is known. This is referred to as the *epipolar* constraint.

Finally, all models of stereo correspondence assume some form of the constraint that the distance to surfaces in the scene tends to vary slowly across the image (see, for example, Marr and Poggio 1976, 1979, Mayhew and Frisby 1981, Baker 1982, Barnard and Fischler 1982, Medioni and Nevatia 1985, Pollard, Mayhew, and Frisby 1985, Prazdny 1986, Barnard 1987, Hoff and Ahuja 1987). Surfaces are usually smooth, so that the depths of nearby points on the surface are usually similar. Computational models have used this *continuity* constraint in different ways. Some try to match features in the two views in such a way that the variation in depth of the resulting surfaces is minimized (for example, Prazdny 1986, Barnard 1987). Others impose a constant limit on the rate of change of disparity across the image—in other words they do not allow matches to be made that would imply a surface that is too steeply slanted in depth (see, for example, Medioni and Nevatia 1985, Pollard, Mayhew, and Frisby 1985). This latter approach was motivated by psychophysical studies that suggest that in human stereo vision there is a strict limit on the gradient of stereo disparity (see, for example, Tyler 1975, Burt and Julesz, 1980). Finally, some models use a form of this constraint based on the idea that disparities vary slowly along connected edge contours in the image, referred to as *figural* continuity (Mayhew and Frisby 1980, 1981, Baker and Binford 1981, Baker 1982, Medioni and Nevatia 1985, Grimson 1985). These latter models assume that features along continuous contours in the image are likely to lie along contiguous locations on a surface in space and should therefore have similar or smoothly varying disparities. Mayhew and Frisby (1981) present psychophysical evidence that a figural continuity constraint is used in human stereo vision.

Simple strategies for computing stereo correspondence, such as gray-level correlation, work well on random-dot patterns and highly textured natural images, even when the underlying surfaces are quite complex. The need to provide a robust solution for a wide range of natural imagery has proved to be a difficult problem, however, which appears to require a more complex strategy. In search of more successful algorithms, many computational models attempt to incorporate knowledge of human stereo vision. These models in turn provide insight into how these aspects of human vision are useful in solving the stereo correspondence problem.

There are at least three observations regarding human stereo vision that have been incorporated into computational models. First, there is much evidence that the human visual system initially extracts features in the image, such as sharp intensity changes or edges, and it has been suggested that these features may serve as the basic matching elements for stereo correspondence (see, for example, Barlow, Blakemore, and Pettigrew 1967, Marr and Poggio 1979, Mayhew and Frisby 1981). Second, perceptual demonstrations suggest that the human stereo system makes use of the different resolutions of analysis performed by the early stages of vision (see, for example, Felton, Richards, and Smith 1972, Julesz and Miller 1975). Finally, it has been shown that eye movements are critical in fusing two stereo views. If the eyes are fixated at a particular distance, it is only possible to fuse features in the left and right views whose depths fall within a limited range around the fixation distance (known as Panum's fusional area; see, for example, Mitchell 1966, Fender and Julesz 1967). Objects outside of this range are seen as double. One method that can be used to fuse features over a wider range of depths is to perform vergence eye movements, fixating on different depth planes.

Many stereo models incorporate some or all of these factors. For example, most stereo systems match features between the two images, such as sharp intensity changes, edges, or other related features (see, for example, Marr and Poggio 1979, Barnard and Thompson 1980, Mayhew and Frisby 1981, Grimson 1981, 1985, Baker and Binford 1981, Baker 1982, Barnard and Fischler 1982, Medioni and Nevatia 1985, Pollard, Mayhew, and Frisby 1985, Prazdny 1986, Hoff and Ahuja 1987). Some models also assume that the corresponding features in the two eyes are similar to one another in their contrast, orientation in the image, sharpness, and so on, which can also narrow down possible matches (see, for example, Arnold and Binford 1980, Baker and Binford 1981, Baker 1982, Medioni and Nevatia 1985). Stereo correspondence models that match features obtained at multiple resolutions include those proposed by Marr and Poggio (1979), Moravec (1980), Grimson (1981, 1985), Mayhew and Frisby (1981), and Hoff and Ahuja (1987).

The analysis of appropriate matching features in computational models of stereo correspondence has motivated a number of psychophysical studies aimed at determining which features are used in human stereo vision. Mayhew and Frisby (1981) provide evidence that stereo-matching features are extracted after the image has been filtered with a circularly symmetric operator (such as the circular difference-of-Gaussians function), and include the locations of peaks in this filtered image. Bulthoff and Mallot (1987) demonstrate that the human stereo system can derive a 3-D impression by matching smooth variations in shading, but that the sensation of depth is much weaker than that derived in the presence of sharp edge features in the stereo images.

The stereo correspondence model proposed by Marr and Poggio (1979) was presented as a possible model of human stereo vision and has three main components. First, stereo matching takes place independently at different resolutions. Second, within each resolution there is a limit to the amount of disparity over which features can be matched.

At the coarsest scale the algorithm searches over larger distances for matching features, whereas at the finest resolution there is a more severe limit on the distance over which the image is searched for possible matches. Third, the matches established at the coarse resolution guide eye movements that shift the entire images right and left in a way that eventually allows the matching of features at all resolutions. Overall matches at the coarse scale provide a rough idea of where objects are located in depth, and this rough depth map becomes successively refined as matches are established at finer scales. The system incorporates roles for multiresolution analysis and eye movements, which are known to exist in human stereo vision. This algorithm (see also Grimson 1981, 1985) has been implemented in a number of computer vision systems and is one of the most thoroughly tested of existing stereo systems. Figure 15.6b shows the results of this algorithm applied to the two aerial stereo photographs shown in figure 15.6a. The brightness of edge contours represents depth, with brighter contours closer to the viewer. Computer models of this sort serve as a rigorous test for models of human stereo processing.

Other models of stereo correspondence have emerged over the past several years that also attempt to mimic aspects of the human stereo system (see, for example, Mayhew and Frisby 1980, 1981, Pollard, Mayhew, and Frisby 1985). A key aspect of the early model proposed by Mayhew and Frisby (1981), for which they provide psychophysical evidence, is that the locations of image features at multiple spatial resolutions form a combined "signature" that is matched between the left and right views. This differs from Marr and Poggio's (1979) model, in which stereo matching takes place independently at different spatial scales. The model proposed by Pollard, Mayhew, and Frisby (1985), the PMF algorithm, combines the epipolar and uniqueness constraints with a constraint on the disparity gradient. That is, the rate of change of disparity from one image location to the next is restricted to lie within some specified bounds. The PMF algorithm has two stages. In the first every potential match between a pair of features in the left and right images is assigned an initial "strength" that depends on the number of other potential matches within a small neighborhood whose disparities fall within the disparity gradient limit. The second stage is a relaxation procedure, in which matches that are unambiguous or have maximum strengths are used to disambiguate other potential matches. The PMF algorithm was motivated by psychophysical studies that demonstrate the existence of a disparity gradient limit in human stereo vision (see, for example, Tyler 1975, Burt and Julesz 1980). Variations on the use of relaxation procedures for solving the stereo correspondence problem have also been considered by Marr and Poggio (1976), Barnard and Thompson (1980), and Prazdny (1985).

Given the importance of physical constraints in guiding the nature of computational solutions to the stereo correspondence problem, one would expect these constraints to be reflected in the physiological mechanisms underlying binocular combination in biological systems. There has been considerable interest in understanding the neural circuitry that underlies stereo processing in the primate visual system (for review, see Poggio 1984, Poggio and Poggio 1984). In physiological studies by Poggio and his colleagues (Poggio and Fischer 1977, Poggio and Talbot 1981, Poggio 1984), populations of cells were found in cortical areas V1 and V2 of the macaque monkey that respond to the disparity in position of features appearing in the left and right eyes. Some cells respond best when objects appear in front of the point of fixation of the two eyes (NEAR cells), other cells respond best when objects appear behind the fixation point (FAR cells), and a third class responds to objects at depths right around the fixation point. Some of the latter class of cells are excited by disparities around zero (the tuned excitatory cells), whereas others are inhibited by these disparities (tuned inhibitory cells). It was shown recently that these cells respond to disparity in complex random-dot stereograms (Poggio 1984), so their output effectively represents the result of solving a difficult stereo correspondence problem.

Several of the constraints used in computational models are reflected in the neural processes underlying stereopsis. For example, the left and right receptive fields of disparity-sensitive cells are located at roughly the same vertical positions in the two eyes, so that these cells are most active when the two stereo views are in approximate vertical register. (The human stereo system can tolerate large overall vertical disparities between the left and right images, but it appears that much of this disparity is compensated for through vertical eye movements that bring the two images into rough vertical register; only about 4 to 7 arc minutes of vertical disparity can be tolerated at a single eye position (Nielsen and Poggio 1984).) The fact that corresponding features in the two eyes must be located at roughly the same vertical location is analogous to the assumption in computational models that the epipolar geometry is known.

The receptive fields of disparity-sensitive cells are also located at roughly the same horizontal positions in the two eyes. For many of the NEAR and FAR cells, their disparity sensitivity for bar stimuli extends over a range of one degree or more on either side of zero disparity (Poggio and Fischer 1977, Poggio and Talbot 1981, Poggio 1984). Others have a narrower depth-response profile. This overall range is small compared with the actual range of disparity that typically exists for a natural scene. This mechanism effectively constrains the range of search between potential corresponding features in the two retinal images for a given eye position. Vergence eye movements can be used to bring objects over a wider range of depths into roughly corresponding locations on the two eyes. Based on psychophysical evidence from stereoanomalous observers, Richards (1971) proposed that human stereopsis combines the activity of three populations of neurons that are preferentially sensitive to crossed, near zero, and uncrossed disparities. The existence of the three classes of NEAR, FAR, and TUNED disparity-sensitive cells supports this hypothesis. The use of pools of disparity cells with limited disparity range is an explicit component of Marr and Poggio's (1979) stereo model. In addition Marr and Poggio proposed that multiple spatial-frequency channels provide input to these disparity-sensitive mechanisms, with coarser channels feeding mechanisms that are sensitive to larger ranges of disparity. This aspect of the model is supported by physiological studies of binocular mechanisms in the cat (Pettigrew et al. 1968, Ferster 1981), which show a strong correlation between receptive field size and width of disparity tuning curves.

Physiological evidence does not yet address the use of constraints such as smoothness and continuity of disparity information or the use of a disparity gradient limit. These constraints presumably would be reflected in the nature of the interactions between neighboring disparity-sensitive cells. Many of the computational models proposed for the correspondence process incorporate simple, local interactions between nearby disparity mechanisms, which could easily be implemented in parallel over the visual field (see, for example, Marr and Poggio 1976, Barnard and Thompson 1980, Prazdny 1985, Pollard, Mayhew, and Frisby 1985, Poggio and Drumheller 1986). Recent efforts have begun to address the details of the neural circuitry that might underlie the parallel computation of binocular disparity. Koch and Poggio (1987) proposed possible neural implementations of stereo-disparity detectors that yield specific predictions for their behavior that can be tested through physiological experiments.

Finally, we mention some other important aspects of stereo vision that have been addressed in computational and experimental studies, but are not covered in this discussion. One problem is the detection of discontinuities in stereo disparity, which often occur at the locations of object boundaries. Such discontinuities violate the assumptions of smoothness and continuity of disparity and may require specialized mechanisms to detect. A second problem is the filling-in of continuous surfaces between image locations where stereo disparities are initially computed. Human observers perceive continuous surfaces when observing sparse random-dot stereograms. Computational models that initially derive disparity measurements only at the locations of image features, such as edges, also raise the problem of interpolating a dense disparity map between sparse disparity information. A third problem is the transformation between stereo disparity and depth, which is likely to require knowledge about the current viewing geometry, such as the position of the eyes.

The Analysis of Visual Motion

The measurement and use of visual motion is one of the most fundamental abilities of biological vision systems, serving many essential functions. For example, a sudden movement in the scene might indicate an approaching predator or desirable prey. The rapid expansion of features in the visual field can signal an object about to collide with the observer. Discontinuities in motion often occur at object boundaries and can be used to carve up the scene into distinct objects. Motion signals provide input to centers controlling eye movements, allowing objects of interest to be tracked through the scene. Relative movement can be used to infer the 3-D structure and motion of object surfaces, and the movement of the observer relative to the scene, allowing biological systems to navigate quickly and efficiently through the environment.

The pattern of movement in the changing image is not given to the visual system directly, but must be inferred from the changing intensities that reach the eye. The 3-D shape of object surfaces, the locations of object boundaries, and the movement of the observer relative to the scene can in turn be inferred from the pattern of image motion. Typically the overall analysis of motion is divided into these two stages: first, the measurement of movement in the changing two-dimensional (2-D) image and second, the use of motion measurements, for example to recover the 3-D layout of the environment. In the following two subsections we discuss computational studies that address these two aspects of motion analysis.

The Measurement of Motion The measurement of movement may itself be divided into multiple stages and performed in different ways in biological systems. There is evidence that in the human visual system motion may be measured by at least two different processes, termed *short-range* and *long-range* processes (Braddick 1974, 1980). The short-range process analyzes continuous motion or motion presented discretely, but with small spatial and temporal displacements from one moment to the next. The long-range process may then analyze motion over larger spatial and temporal displacements, as in apparent motion. There is evidence that these two processes interact at some stage (see, for example, Green 1983), but initially they may be somewhat independent. This section addresses one fundamental aspect of the short-range measurement of motion, the solution of the *aperture problem.*

Consider the computation of a projected 2-D velocity field, which assigns to each feature in the image a direction and speed of velocity. Figure 15.8a shows an example of the projected velocity field for a 3-D wireframe object that is rotating around a central vertical axis. In both biological and computer vision systems, the first mechanisms for measuring this motion examine only a limited region of the visual image and as a consequence often provide only partial information about the 2-D velocity field, due to the aperture problem (Wallach 1976, Fennema and Thompson 1979, Burt and Sperling 1981, Horn and Schunck 1981, Marr and Ullman 1981, Adelson and Movshon 1982). This problem arises when an oriented pattern in the image, such as an edge contour,

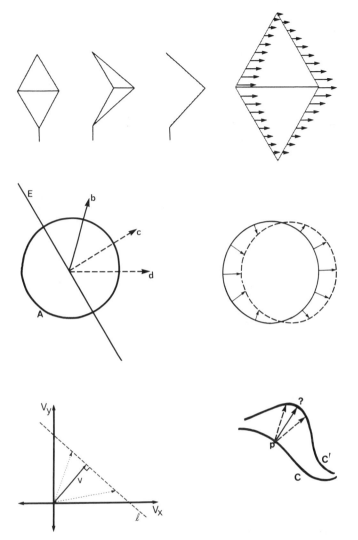

Figure 15.8 The aperture problem. (A) On the left are three views of a wireframe object undergoing rotation around a central vertical axis. On the right the arrows along the contours of the object represent the instantaneous velocities of points along the object's contours at one position in the object's trajectory. (B) An operation that views the moving edge **E** through the local aperture **A** can compute only the component of motion **c** in the direction perpendicular to the orientation of the edge. (C) The circle undergoes pure translation to the right; the arrows represent the perpendicular components of velocity that can be measured from the changing image. (d) The curve **C** rotates, translates, and deforms over time to yield the curve **C'**. The velocity of the point **p** is ambiguous. (E) The vector **v** represents the perpendicular component of velocity at some location in the image. The true velocity at that location must project to the line *l* perpendicular to **v**; examples are shown with dotted arrows.

extends beyond the region of the image analyzed by the initial motion-detection mechanisms. The information provided by such mechanisms is illustrated in figure 15.8b. In this case an extended edge **E** moves across the image, and its movement is observed through a window defined by the circular aperture **A**. Through this window it is only possible to observe the movement of the edge in the direction perpendicular to its orientation. The component of motion along the orientation of the edge is invisible through this limited aperture. Thus it is not possible to distinguish between motions in the directions **b, c,** and **d**. This problem is inherent in any motion-detection operation that examines only a limited area of the image and arises when an oriented pattern extends beyond the region of the image analyzed by the initial motion-detection mechanisms.

As a consequence of the aperture problem, the measurement of motion in the changing image requires two stages of analysis: the first measures components of motion in the direction perpendicular to image features; the second combines these components of motion to compute the full 2-D pattern of movement in the image. In figure 15.8c a circle undergoes pure translation to the right. The arrows along the contour represent the perpendicular components of velocity that can be measured directly from the changing image. These component measurements each provide some constraint on the possible motion of the circle, as illustrated in figure 15.8d. The bold vector **v** represents the local perpendicular component of motion at a particular location in the image. The possible true motions at that location are given by the set of velocity vectors whose endpoint lies along the line *l* oriented perpendicular to the vector **v.** Examples of possible true velocities are indicated by the dotted vectors. The movement of image features such as corners or small spots can be measured directly. In general, however, the first measurements of movement provide only partial information about the true movement of features in the image and must be combined to compute the full pattern of 2-D motion.

The measurement of movement is difficult because in theory there are infinitely many patterns of motion that are consistent with a given changing image. For example, in figure 15.8e the contour **C** rotates, translates, and deforms to yield the contour **C'** at some later time. The true motion of the point **p** is ambiguous. Additional constraint is required to identify a unique solution. In general it may not be possible to recover the 2-D projection of the true 3-D field of motions of points in space from the changing image intensities. Factors such as changing illumination, specularities, and shadows can generate patterns of optical flow in the image that do not correspond to the real movement of surface features. The additional constraint used to measure image motion can yield at best a solution that is most plausible from a physical standpoint.

Many physical assumptions could provide the additional constraint needed to compute a unique pattern of image motion. One possibility is the assumption of pure translation. That is, it is assumed that velocity is constant over small areas of the image. This assumption has been used both in computer vision studies and in biological models of motion measurement (see, for example, Lappin and Bell 1976, Pantle and Picciano 1976, Fennema and Thompson 1979, Anstis 1980, Marr and Ullman 1981, Thompson and Barnard 1981, Adelson and Movshon 1982). Methods that assume pure translation may be used to detect sudden movements or to track objects across the visual field. These tasks may require only a rough estimate of the overall translation of objects across the image. Tasks such as the recovery of 3-D structure from motion require a more detailed measurement of relative motion in the image, and require the use of a more general physical assumption.

Other computational studies have assumed that velocity varies smoothly across the image (Horn and Schunck 1981, Hildreth 1984, Nagel 1984, Nagel and Enkelmann 1984, Anandan and Weiss 1985). The assumption rests on the principle that physical surfaces are generally smooth; that is, variations in the structure of a surface are usually small compared with the distance of the surface from the viewer. When surfaces move, nearby points tend to move with similar velocities. There exist discontinuities in movement at object boundaries, but most of the image is the projection of relatively smooth surfaces. Thus it is natural to assume that image velocities vary smoothly over most of the visual field. A unique pattern of movement can be obtained by computing a velocity field that is consistent with the changing image and has the least amount of variation possible.

The use of the smoothness constraint allows general motion to be analyzed. Surfaces can be rigid or nonrigid, undergoing any movement in space. This assumption also can be embodied in the motion measurement computation in a way that guarantees a unique solution that is often physically correct (Hildreth 1984, Ullman and Yuille 1987). Finally, the velocity field of least variation can be computed straightforwardly using standard computer algorithms (Horn and Schunck 1981, Hildreth 1984, Nagel and Enkelmann 1984), as well as simple analog resistive networks that resemble the properties of neural networks (Poggio, Torre, and Koch 1985, Poggio and Koch 1985). Perceptual studies reveal a similarity between the behavior of a motion measurement computation based on the smoothness assumption and the human perception of motion (Hildreth 1984, Nakayama and Silverman 1988a,b).

The aperture problem in motion measurement can be examined from a physiological perspective. Early movement detectors in biological systems have spatially limited receptive fields and therefore face the aperture problem whenever an extended, oriented pattern moves across their receptive fields. Stimulated by a theoretical analysis of this problem, Movshon and colleagues (1985) sought and found direct physiological evidence for a two-stage motion measurement computation in the primate visual system. Two visual areas that include an abundance of motion-sensitive neurons are cortical areas V1 and MT. MT is the middle temporal area of extrastriate cortex, located in the posterior bank of the superior temporal sulcus (Van Essen and Maunsell 1983). Movshon and colleagues (1985) explored the type of motion analysis taking place in area MT, using visual stimuli that consist of superimposed sinewave gratings, with different orientations and directions of motion. The results of these experiments indicate that the selectivity of neurons in area V1 for direction of movement is such that they could provide only the component of motion in the direction perpendicular to the orientation of image features. Area MT, however, contains a subpopulation of cells, referred to as *pattern* cells, that appear to respond to the 2-D direction of motion of a combined grating pattern, independent of its individual components. These neurons may serve to combine motion components to compute the real 2-D direction of velocity of a moving pattern. These experiments do not yet distinguish between the use of the simple assumption of pure translation, as suggested in the study (Movshon et al. 1985), versus a more general assumption such as smoothness. Stimulus patterns undergoing more complicated motions are required to make such a distinction. If the pattern cells in area MT embody the assumption of smoothness in their computation of motion, one would expect to find direct interaction between pattern cells that analyze nearby areas of the visual field.

The Recovery of 3-D Structure from Motion   When an object moves in space, the motions of individual points on the object differ in a way that conveys information about its 3-D structure. Using 2-D shadow projections of 3-D wireframe objects, such as that shown in figure 18.8a, Wallach and O'Connell (1953) showed that the human visual system can derive the correct 3-D structure of moving objects from their changing 2-D projection alone. Other perceptual studies also demonstrated this remarkable ability (for example, Braunstein 1976, Johansson 1975, Rogers and Graham 1979, Ullman 1979). Relative motion in the image is also created by movement of the observer relative to the environment, and can be used to infer observer motion from the changing image (see, for example, Gibson 1950, Johansson 1971, Lee 1980, Regan, Kaufman, and Lincoln 1986).

Theoretically the two problems of recovering the 3-D structure and movement of objects in the environment and recovering the 3-D motion of the observer from the changing image are closely related. The main difficulty faced by both is that infinitely many combinations of 3-D structure and motion could give rise to any particular 2-D image. To resolve this inherent ambiguity, it is necessary to impose an additional constraint that allows most 3-D interpretations to be ruled out, leaving one that is most plausible from a physical standpoint. Computational studies have used the *rigidity* assumption to derive a unique 3-D structure and motion; they assume that if it is possible to interpret the changing 2-D image as the projection of a rigid 3-D object in motion, then such an interpretation should be chosen (for example, Ullman 1979, 1983, Clocksin 1980, Prazdny 1980, 1983, Longuet-Higgins and Prazdny 1981, Tsai and Huang 1981, Mitiche 1986, Waxman and Ullman 1985, Waxman and Wohn 1987). When the rigidity assumption is used in this way, the recovery of structure from motion requires the computation of the rigid 3-D object that would project onto a given 2-D image. The rigidity assumption was suggested by perceptual studies that described a tendency for the human visual system to choose a rigid interpretation of moving elements (Wallach and O'Connell 1953, Gibson and Gibson 1957, Jansson and Johansson 1973, Johansson 1975, 1977).

Computational studies have shown that the rigidity assumption can be used to derive a unique 3-D structure from the changing 2-D image. Furthermore this unique 3-D interpretation can be derived by integrating image information only over a limited extent in space and in time. For example, suppose that a rigid object in motion is projected onto the image plane by using orthographic projection. Three distinct views of four points on the moving object are sufficient to compute a unique rigid 3-D structure for the points (Ullman 1979). In general if only two views of the moving points are considered or fewer points are observed, there are multiple rigid 3-D structures consistent with the changing 2-D projection. Theoretical results regarding the recovery of a unique 3-D structure under a variety of conditions are summarized by Ullman (1983) and Hildreth and Koch (1987). These theoretical results are important for the study of the recovery of structure from motion in biological vision systems for two reasons. First, they show that by using the rigidity assumption, a unique structure can be recovered from motion information alone. It is not necessary to make further physical assumptions to obtain a unique solution. Second, these results show that it is possible to recover 3-D structure by integrating image information over a small extent in space and in time. This second observation could bear on the neural mechanisms that compute structure from motion; in principle they need only integrate motion information over a limited area of the visual field and a limited extent in time.

Computational studies also provide algorithms for deriving the structure of moving objects. Typically measurements of the positions or velocities of image features give rise to a set of mathematical equations whose solution represents the desired 3-D structure. The algorithms generally derive this structure from motion information extracted over a limited area of the image and a limited extent in time. Testing of these algorithms reveals that although this strategy is possible in theory, it is not reliable in practice. A small amount of error in the image measurements can lead to very different (and often incorrect) 3-D structures.

This behavior is due in part to the observation that over a small extent in space and time, very different objects can induce almost identical patterns of motion in the image (Ullman 1983, 1984a).

This sensitivity to error inherent in algorithms that integrate motion information only over a small extent in space and time suggests that a robust scheme for deriving structure should use image information that is more extended in space or time or both. This conclusion is supported in recent computational studies (for example, Bruss and Horn 1983, Lawton 1983, Ullman 1984a, Adiv 1985, Bolles and Baker 1985, Negahdaripour and Horn 1985, Yasumoto and Medioni 1985, Bharwani, Riseman, and Hanson 1986, Shariat and Price 1986, Subbarao 1986, Waxman and Wohn 1987) that show that consideration of motion information that is more extended in space or time can lead to a stable recovery of structure. The extension in time can be achieved by considering a large number of discrete frames or by observing continuous motion over a significant temporal extent.

With regard to the human visual system, the dependence of perceived structure on the spatial and temporal extent of the viewed motion has not yet been studied systematically, but the following informal observations have been made. Regarding spatial extent, two or three points undergoing relative motion are sufficient to elicit a perception of 3-D structure (Borjesson and von Hofsten 1973, Johansson 1975), although theoretically the recovery of structure is less constrained for two points in motion, and perceptually the sensation of structure is weaker. In addition appropriate visual stimulation in a small region of the peripheral visual field is adequate to elicit a strong sense of self-motion (Johansson 1971). Regarding the temporal extent of viewed motion, Johansson (1975) showed that a brief observation of patterns of moving lights generated by human figures moving in the dark (commonly referred to as biological motion displays) can lead to a perception of the 3-D motion and structure of the figures. Other perceptual studies indicate that the human visual system requires an extended time period to reach an accurate perception of 3-D structure (Wallach and O'Connell 1953, White and Mueser 1960, Doner, Lappin, and Perfetto 1984, Inada et al. 1986). A brief observation of a moving pattern sometimes yields an impression of structure that is "flatter" than the true structure of the moving object. Thus the human visual system is capable of deriving some sense of structure from motion information that is integrated over a small extent in space and time. An accurate perception of structure may, however, require a more extended viewing period.

Most methods compute a 3-D structure from motion only when the changing image can be interpreted as the projection of a rigid object in motion. They otherwise yield no interpretation of structure or yield a solution that is incorrect or unstable. Algorithms that are exceptions to this can interpret only restricted classes of nonrigid motions (see, for example, Bennett and Hoffman 1985, Hoffman and Flinchbaugh 1982,

Koenderink and van Doorn 1986, Subbarao 1986). The human visual system, however, can derive some sense of structure for a wide range of nonrigid motions, including stretching, bending, and more complex types of deformation (Johansson 1975, Jansson and Johansson 1973, Todd 1982, 1984). Furthermore displays of rigid objects in motion sometimes give rise to the perception of somewhat distorting objects (Wallach, Weisz, and Adams 1956, White and Mueser 1960, Braunstein and Andersen 1984, Hildreth 1984, Adelson 1985). These observations suggest that although the human visual system tends to choose rigid interpretations of a changing image, it probably does not use the rigidity assumption in the strict way that previous computational studies suggest.

Ullman (1984a) proposed a more flexible method for deriving structure from motion that interprets both rigid and nonrigid motion. Referred to as the *incremental rigidity scheme,* this algorithm uses the rigidity assumption in a different way from previous studies. It maintains an internal model of the structure of a moving object that consists of the estimated 3-D coordinates of points on the object. The model is continually updated as new positions of image features are considered. Initially the object is assumed to be flat, if no other cues to 3-D structure are present. Otherwise its initial structure may be determined by other cues available, from stereopsis, shading, texture, or perspective. As each new view of the moving object appears, the algorithm computes a new set of 3-D coordinates for points on the object that maximizes the rigidity in the transformation from the current model to the new positions. This is achieved by minimizing the change in the 3-D distances between points in the model. Thus the algorithm interprets the changing 2-D image as the projection of a moving 3-D object that changes as little as possible from one moment to the next. Through a process of repeatedly considering new views of objects in motion and updating the current model of their structure, the algorithm builds up and maintains a 3-D model of the objects. If objects deform over time, the 3-D model computed by the algorithm also changes over time. A parallel model based on Ullman's incremental rigidity scheme was recently proposed by Landy (1986).

Physiological studies have uncovered neurons in higher cortical areas that are sensitive to properties of the motion field that may be relevant to the recovery of the 3-D structure and motion of surfaces in the environment or to the recovery of the motion of the observer relative to the scene. Many studies have revealed neurons sensitive to uniform expansion or contraction of the visual field, a property that is correlated either with translation of the observer forward or backward or, equivalently, motion of an object toward or away from the observer. Such neurons have been found, for example, in the posterior parietal cortex of the monkey (Mottor and Mountcastle 1981, Andersen 1985). Other neurons have been found that are sensitive to global rotations in the visual field (see, for example, Andersen 1985, Sakata et al. 1985). All of these neurons have large receptive fields, so they probably lack the spatial sensitivity required to derive the detailed shape of an object surface from relative motion. A study by Siegel and Andersen (1986) showed that motion processing in area MT of primate visual cortex is critical to the recovery of structure from motion.

15.3 High-Level Vision

The processes we have examined so far belong to the realm of low-level vision. Their goal is primarily to recover properties of the surrounding environment. Such processes can be evaluated on the basis of their validity, that is, whether the results they deliver (such as depth, surface orientation, and so on) are correct and accurate. The low-level processes were also characterized by a bottom-up and parallel mode of processing. *Bottom-up* means that the processing depends on the visual stimulus and not on the task being performed. *Parallel* here means spatial parallelism; that is, the same operations are being performed across the entire visual field or large parts of it.

In high-level vision the descriptions produced by the earlier stages are used for tasks such as recognition, visually guided manipulation, locomotion, and navigation through the environment. At this stage the emphasis is often on usefulness rather than validity. There are, for example, many possible ways to describe the elements in a given image for the purpose of recognition, but some may be more useful than others. The processing here is goal directed (as opposed to bottom-up) and spatially focused (as opposed to spatially uniform).

A further distinction can be made between intermediate and high-level vision. High-level vision uses specific knowledge about objects in the world, such as a catalog of objects stored in long-term memory, whereas intermediate vision does not. The terms *intermediate* and *high-level* vision do not mean to imply a sequential order. It is possible, for example, that recognition tasks may proceed on their own without relying on the prior application of intermediate-level processes. In the following subsection we discuss the area of intermediate vision and in particular the problem of extracting shape properties and spatial relations among objects in the scene from visual information. Then we discuss one of the major problems in high-level vision—visual object recognition.

Intermediate Vision and Visual Routines

The Extraction of Shape Properties and Spatial Relations   The use of visual information often requires the extraction of shape properties of contours and regions and the analysis of spatial relations among items in the image. This analysis plays a role in visual classification and recognition. An example is shown in figure 15.9. The figure on the left is recognized effortlessly and immediately as representing a face, as opposed to the jumbled face figure on the right. In this example the features comprising the face are highly schematic. The eye or nose by themselves, for example, are crude representations of a real eye or nose. It is primarily the spatial relations among the schematic items that make it a face profile. The eye is inside the head boundary, the nose is attached to the boundary, the eye is above the nose and below the eyebrow, and so on. Our ability to recognize objects easily from such a representation demonstrates that we can naturally and effortlessly extract in a single glance spatial relations such as inside, above, or attached to, and then use these relations in recognition tasks.

There is some evidence that the ability to analyze such configurations and to detect certain basic abstract shape properties and spatial relations already exists at a very early age. For example, some studies (Fantz 1961) have suggested that infants as young as one to five weeks of age already make a distinction between "correct" and jumbled schematic faces. At the physiological level neurons were found in the STS area of the macaque visual cortex that respond specifically to faces (Gross, Rocha-Miranda, and Bender 1972). According to some reports (Perret, Rolls, and Caan 1982), these cells often respond to schematic line-drawn faces, but not to scrambled face figures. These findings suggest the existence of mechanisms that respond not only to specific and realistic faces, but to any configuration that has the general overall shape and correct spatial relations among its parts.

The visual analysis of shape and spatial relations also plays an important role in planning actions and manipulating objects. During such activities we often use vision to answer such questions as "Can object A fit into the space between objects B and C?" as shown in figure 15.10.

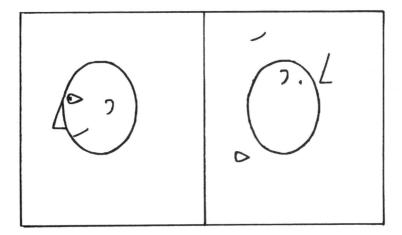

Figure 15.9 Recognizing faces. The figure on the left is perceived immediately as a face profile. The figure on the right contains similar parts in a different spatial arrangement.

The Computational Study of Vision

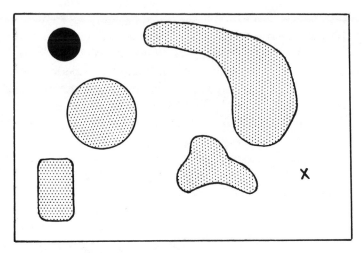

Figure 15.10 Spatial reasoning. It is possible to obtain from visual information answers to questions such as Can the black disk be moved to the location of the cross without colliding with any of the objects in the figure?

These questions may not be posed explicitly, but information about such relations is obtained routinely in our daily activities. Problems of this type do not require recognition because they do not depend on naming the objects or on past familiarity with them. They do, however, require the spatial analysis of shape and relations among objects. In this sense this analysis belongs more to the level termed intermediate vision than to high-level vision.

Properties of Intermediate-Level Vision: Nonuniformity, Open-Endedness, and Task Dependence   The computations involved in extracting shape and spatial relations are also clearly not part of the early visual processes, but must operate at a later, separate stage. As far as we know, the operations involved in the construction of the early visual representations (such as edge detection, the computation of depth, color, motion analysis, and so on) proceed uniformly and in parallel across the entire visual field or a large part of it. In contrast it is not feasible to have at every location an "inside/outside detector," in the same way that orientation of contours is recovered by a dense array of specialized orientation detectors. More generally it is not feasible to extract uniformly and in a bottom-up manner all the possibly relevant shape properties and spatial relations in the image.

The extraction of shape and spatial relations is also more open-ended than the earlier visual processes. That is, different tasks may require the extraction of different shape properties and relations. There does not seem to be a clear bound on the number of properties and relations that can be extracted; new ones can be learned as required by the task. As a result of these properties, the computations involved in intermediate-level vision cannot be entirely bottom-up, but must be task dependent. That is, in viewing the same scene on two different occasions, the processes applied to the scene at this intermediate level of processing may be different, depending on the visual task being accomplished.

The Complexity of Extracting Shape Properties and Spatial Relations
The perception of many shape properties and relations appears to us subjectively to be immediate and effortless. This apparent immediateness is, however, deceiving; the computations required for extracting shape and spatial relations are often quite complicated. In fact in many cases the efficient analysis of shape and spatial relations is still beyond the reach of current computer vision systems.

A simple illustrative example is the perception of inside/outside relations, that is, whether a given location is inside or outside a closed curve. When the curve is not too convoluted, this relation is easy to extract by merely looking at the image. In figure 15.11, the location marked "x" is clearly inside the curve in figure 15.11a, and outside the curve in figure 15.11b. How do we reach this conclusion so effortlessly?

In computer vision a popular method of computing inside/outside relations is the so-called ray-intersection method. A ray is drawn from the location in question to the edge of the image, and the intersections made by the ray with the curve are counted. If the number is even, the point is outside the curve, otherwise it must be inside. This procedure is simple, but clearly insufficient. Consider, for instance, the examples in figure 15.12. In figure 15.12a the number of ray intersections is even, but the point lies inside the curve. This is because the ray-intersection method makes an implicit assumption that the curve in question is isolated in the visual field, an assumption that is violated in this example. In figure 15.12b the number of intersections is odd, therefore the ray-intersection method would conclude that the point lies inside the curve. In this case the error arises because the ray-intersection method incorporates the assumption that the curve is closed. Figure 15.12c is a slight variation on the inside/outside problem. The task is to determine whether any of the points lie inside the closed curve. The

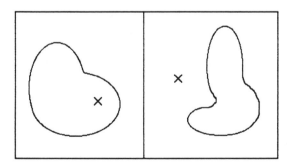

Figure 15.11 Judging inside/outside. The fact that the x lies inside the closed figure in A and outside in B is established effortlessly, by merely looking at the figure.

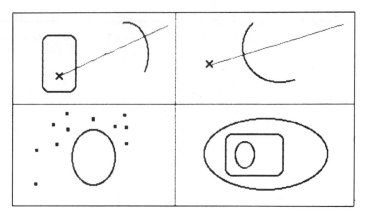

Figure 15.12 Deficiencies of the ray intersection method. (A) The number of intersections is even, but the point lies inside the curve. (B) The number is odd, but the point is not inside a closed region. (C) The task is to determine whether any of the points lies inside the figure. (D) The task is to find a location that is internal to all three curves.

ray-intersection method would require applying the test to all of the individual dots. What our visual system seems to do instead is somehow to inspect the figure and verify that none of the dots lie in its interior. Finally, in figure 15.12d the task is to find an "innermost" location (that is, a point that lies inside all three curves). This task is visually straightforward, but it cannot be solved by any simple application of the ray-intersection method.

The conclusion is that the method used by our own visual system is more powerful and flexible than the ray-intersection method or any other method proposed so far in computational vision. More generally we see that the computation of seemingly simple spatial relations is surprisingly difficult. In addition the problem is complicated by the facts that intermediate-level vision requires the capacity to extract efficiently an essentially unbounded set of properties and relations and that the computations performed must depend on the particular visual task at hand.

Visual Routines   A possible approach to this problem is that the perception of shape properties and spatial relations is achieved by the application of *visual routines* to the early visual representation (Ullman 1984b). These visual routines are sequences of some basic operations that are "wired into" the visual system. Routines for different properties and relations are composed from the same set of basic operations, using different combinations for different tasks. Using a fixed set of basic operations, the visual system can assemble different routines and in this manner extract a large variety of different shape properties and relations. The basic operations themselves are carried out by specialized and highly efficient mechanisms. To understand the perception of spatial relations in general, an important step would be to identify the set of basic operations. To explain how we perceive a particular relation such as *above* or *inside* would require, in this framework, a specification of the particular routine used for establishing the relation in terms of the underlying operations. In the following subsections we describe briefly three basic operations that appear to be useful in visual routines: shifting and indexing, coloring, and boundary tracing.

Shifting and Indexing   The application of visual routines implies a spatial and temporal structuring of the processing. A certain operation is applied at a given location in the visual field, then (perhaps depending on the results of this application) another operation is applied at a new location. *Shifting* is the general operation of moving the focus of processing to a required location. *Indexing* is a particular type of shifting, the shifting of the processing focus to a salient location in the visual field. There is a considerable body of experimental evidence related to the redirecting of the processing focus, the so-called spotlight of visual attention. This body of evidence is reviewed by, for example, Posner (1980) and Treisman and Gelade (1980).

A simple and elegant demonstration that appears to employ shifting and indexing comes from Treisman's experiments with the conjunction of elementary properties (see also Beck and Ambler 1973). Her experiments have shown that certain odd-man-out targets can be detected in a field of distractors in a parallel manner: the time to detect the target does not depend significantly on the number of distractors in the background. For example, a target blue X can be detected in constant time in a field of brown T's and green X's (up to thirty background elements were used in these experiments) on the basis of its unique color. Similarly a target T can be detected in a field of X's in constant time, presumably on the basis of orientation differences. In contrast certain combinations (conjunctions) of elementary properties require sequential search. For example, the target may be a green T in a field of brown T's and green X's. The target in this case matches half the distractors in shape and half in color. The evidence suggests that in this case the processing becomes quite different: the visual system appears to scan the items sequentially in search of the required conjunction. The scan is performed to a large extent internally, rather than by eye movements.

The scan used in the conjunction search is a psychophysical example of the use of a shifting operation. In the parallel-search situation the odd-man-out element is immediately indexable, that is, the processing focus can shift immediately to it without dwelling on other elements. This is therefore an example of an indexing operation. Recently phenomena related to shifting and selective visual attention have also been studied at the physiological level (see, for example, the study by Moran and Desimone (1985) regarding location-specific responses in area V4 of the alert macaque monkey).

Region Coloring and Boundary Tracing   Coloring and tracing are two somewhat similar operations. *Coloring* is the operation of labeling a region with a unique label. Such labeling can be achieved by the bounded activation of a region in the following manner: Starting from a given point, the area around it in the internal representation is somehow activated. This activation spreads outward until a boundary is reached, but it is not allowed to cross the boundary. If the initial point lies inside a closed boundary, the entire region will be colored, or labeled. This labeling can provide, for example, a basis for separating "inside" from "outside" in the tasks considered in figure 15.11 and 15.12. These tasks also often involve an indexing operation: the X is indexed first, and this location serves as the starting point for the coloring operation. Additional stages would be required in all of these examples to complete the inside/outside computations; however, these additions are not considered further here.

Boundary tracing is a similar operation applied to one-dimensional entities in the image, such as contours and boundaries. Starting from a given location on a contour, the contour is traced sequentially in a given direction and labeled. From a computational standpoint such an operation could serve a useful role in the analysis of contours and boundaries by separating them from nearby contours. For a general discussion of coloring and boundary tracing, see Ullman 1984b, and for a psychophysical exploration of boundary tracing, see Jolicoeur, Mackey, and Ullman 1986.

We have considered only a small sample of the problems in intermediate-level vision. On the whole work in this area is only in its infancy, and many questions remain unanswered. The approach discussed is only one of several possible alternatives and has so far been primarily motivated by computational considerations; little is known at present about the processes by which the human visual system extracts abstract shape properties and spatial relations in the image.

Visual Object Recognition

The common view of object recognition is that it requires some sort of matching between the internal representations of an object stored in memory and a similar representation generated from an object in the image. The process of object recognition is therefore different from processes of intermediate and low-level vision in that it is more intimately related to the problems of memory organization, retrieval, expectations, and reasoning.

In this subsection we consider the problem of recognizing objects visually on the basis of their shape. Shape-based recognition is only part of the problem of visual object recognition, because "paths" to recognition other than shape are possible. Objects are sometimes recognized more on the basis of their color or texture than on the basis of their shape. In other instances visual recognition requires certain reasoning processes rather than the identification of a specific shape. We also do not consider here the problem often referred to as the segmentation problem, which has to do with the delineation of the object of interest in an image. Finally, we consider primarily the recognition of individual objects, rather than object classification.

Why is object recognition difficult? According to one approach, termed the *direct* approach (Abu-Mostafa and Psaltis 1987), the problem is primarily one of memory size and efficient parallel matching. To recognize objects, we have to store a large number of object views in memory. In attempting to recognize an object, we must compare the object currently in view with previously stored views of objects and select the one that resembles it most. Models of human associative memory (Willshaw, Buneman, and Longuet-Higgins 1969, Hopfield 1982) have suggested that brain mechanisms can cope efficiently with both of these problems. In large-scale neural networks a large number of patterns can be stored, and a new pattern can be compared simultaneously with all previously stored patterns.

There are, however, at least two problems with the direct approach. First, the set of all possible views of all possible objects is likely to be prohibitively large and at the same time redundant. To recognize, for instance, triangles of any shape, position, and orientation, it clearly is not necessary to store in memory a large number of representative shapes. Second, it should be noted that the comparison used in such schemes between the current image and the images stored in memory is simple, essentially a correlation of the viewed image with previously stored images. In contrast we can recognize objects from novel views that may not be closely similar to any previously stored view by this simple comparison measure.

The alternatives to the direct approach assume that we do not store and compare the input patterns per se. Instead we produce from the image some sort of internal representation of the viewed object and compare it with similar descriptions stored in memory. The hope is that some of the variations in the different appearances of an object will be handled by the description process. That is, an object seen under different viewing conditions, for example, from different viewpoints, will still produce highly similar descriptions. Most of the schemes that have been proposed to date can be classified into three main approaches: the first based on invariant properties, the second on object decomposition into parts, and the third on a process of explicitly compensating for the transformation between the viewed object and the stored model.

The Invariant-Properties Approach   The invariant-properties approach to object recognition assumes that objects have certain invariant properties that are common to all of their views. Formally a property of this type can be thought of as a function from object images to the domain of real numbers. For example, various applications have used the notion of a "compactness measure," defined as the ratio of the object's perimeter length to the square root of its apparent area. Round and compact objects have a low score on this measure, and thin and elongated objects have a high score. Furthermore the measure is unaffected by rotation, translation, and scaling in the image plane. The idea is to define a number of such measures, and collectively they would serve to identify each object unambiguously. The overall recognition process is thus broken down into the extraction of a number of different properties, followed by a final decision stage based on these properties.

In a popular variant of this approach, a property is not expected to be entirely invariant for the different views of an object (or class of objects), but to be restricted to a small interval. Properties of different objects may have partially overlapping ranges, but it is hoped that by defining a number of different properties, it becomes possible to characterize each object uniquely. This leads naturally to the notion of *feature spaces* used extensively in pattern recognition. If n different properties are used, each object can be represented as a point in an n-dimensional space. Recognition and classification then become problems of clustering points in such spaces.

Another approach that belongs to this general class of invariant properties theories is Gibson's theory of high-order invariances (Gibson 1950, 1979). Gibson suggested that invariant properties of objects may be discovered in "high-order" invariances in the optic array. Such invariances were assumed to be based primarily on spatial and temporal gradients of texture density.

The invariant-properties approach has been applied with some success to limited problems, such as the recognition of simple industrial parts under controlled viewing conditions. The approach does not generalize well, however, to more complicated domains. The weakness of the approach seems to be that it is difficult, and often impossible, to find relatively simple properties that are preserved across the different transformations that an object may undergo.

Object Decomposition into Parts A second approach, which replaced invariant properties as the main approach to object recognition, relies on the decomposition of objects into constituent parts. The approach appeals to the intuition that many objects seem to have natural parts. For example, the human body can be divided at some level into a head, torso, arms, and legs. In the decomposition approach these parts are detected, and the recognition of the entire object proceeds on the basis of the constituent parts and their relationships.

There are a number of subclasses within this general approach, the most popular of which has been the "structural description" method. This approach assumes that it would be easier to capture object invariances after their parts have been identified. In particular, simple relations between parts remain invariant across all object views. For example, in the character T one can define two main parts and certain relations (such as "join") that are common to all legal instances of this character.

An early example of a theory of this type applied to human vision is Milner's (1974) model of visual shape recognition. This theory deals primarily with 2-D shapes and uses as basic parts primitive features such as edges and line segments. Marr and Nishihara (1978) proposed a structural description theory applied to 3-D objects. They used as primitive parts elongated volumes called *generalized cylinders.* Recognition proceeds by constructing a description of the object in terms of these cylinders and their relationships. The description produced in this manner is object centered, in the sense that the final description relies on the internal relations among parts and not on their relations relative to the viewer. Additional recent theories of this class applied to human vision include Biederman's (1985) theory of recognition by components and Hoffman and Richards's (1986) "codon" scheme for the description and recognition of image contours.

Although the use of object parts seems to have some clear merits, it also appears that the use of structural descriptions as proposed in most of these schemes has a number of limitations. One is that the decomposition into natural parts is often insufficient to characterize the object in question. In many cases precise shape, rather than the general arrangement of parts, appears to be important. Another problem that appears to limit the applicability of the approach is that many objects do not decompose naturally into the union of clearly distinct parts.

The Alignment Approach   The idea behind the alignment approach is to detect and explicitly compensate for the transformations between an object currently in view and its model stored in memory. This concept has been applied in the past only in simple domains, such as printed character recognition of a known font type (Neisser 1967, ch. 3). In this application it is assumed that a character in view may differ from its ideal prototype stored in memory because it may rotate, translate, and change scale. The first step in the recognition process is therefore to compensate for these transformations. This compensation can be done before the identification of the letter in question. For example, displacement can be compensated for by computing the "center of mass" of the letter and then shifting the letter so that this center always coincides with a fixed location. Size and orientation can also be "normalized" during this first stage. Following the normalization, the remaining differences between the viewed letter and its stored model are small, and a straightforward comparison should suffice to identify the letter correctly.

This general approach has been revived recently and extended in an attempt to apply it to the recognition of complex 3-D objects. The general idea remains the same. The viewed object differs from its stored model because it has undergone a certain transformation such as a change in position and 3-D rotation (in the case of rigid objects). In an alignment approach the first stage is to detect this transformation before the identification of the object. The transformation can then be "undone"; this stage is called the *alignment* stage. Following the alignment, the stored model and viewed object are in close agreement, and the correct model is therefore easier to determine.

Compared with translation, rotation, and scaling in the image, the transformations that the image of a 3-D object can undergo are more complicated to determine and compensate for. A number of recent schemes (for example, Lowe 1986, Ullman 1986, Huttenlocher and Ullman 1987) have been proposed for extending the alignment method to deal with natural objects. The approach appears to offer some advantages, but it has been demonstrated so far in limited domains only.

It must be concluded that in object recognition, which is one of the most fundamental aspects of human vision, theories (as well as experimental work) still have a long way to go. Some combination of an alignment process with part decomposition may offer a promising starting point, but these techniques must be extended and generalized considerably before they will be able to cope successfully with common objects that are recognized efficiently by the human visual system.

Notes

This article describes research done within the Artificial Intelligence Laboratory and the Center for Biological Information Processing (Whitaker College) at the Massachusetts Institute of Technology. Support for the AI Laboratory's artificial intelligence research is provided in part by the Advanced Research Projects Agency of the Department of Defense under Office of Naval Research contract N00014-85-K-0124. Support for this research is also provided by grants from the Sloan Foundation, the National Science Foundation, the McDonnell Foundation, and from the Office of Naval Research Cognitive and Neural Sciences Division.

1. The description of the image using Fourier components is based on the mathematical notion that any periodic function can be expressed as the sum of more elementary functions (sines and cosines), each multiplied by an appropriate scaling factor (see, for example, Bracewell 1978). The set of scaling factors (called the Fourier coefficients) can serve to characterize the function uniquely. The Fourier approach to early vision suggests that the incoming image is divided into regions, and for each region the visual system constructs a representation that resembles a Fourier decomposition.

2. Because the derivative of a sine function $\sin(\omega x)$ is $\omega \cos(\omega x)$ it follows that the effect of differentiation is to enhance periodic components with high spatial frequency (large ω).

3. One can detect maxima in the absolute value of this derivative or, equivalently, maxima or minima (positive or negative *peaks*) in the derivative itself.

4. These operators compute the derivative of the smoothed image along a particular two-dimensional direction.

References

Abu-Mostafa, Y. S., and Psaltis, D. 1987. Optical neural computing. *Scientific American* 256(3):66–73.

Adelson, E. H. 1985. Rigid objects that appear highly non-rigid. *Invest. Ophthalmol. Vision Sci. Suppl.* 26:56.

Adelson, E. H., and Movshon, J. A. 1982. Phenomenal coherence of moving visual patterns. *Nature* 300:523–525.

Adiv, G. 1985. Determining three-dimensional motion and structure from optical flow generated by several moving objects. *IEEE Trans. Pattern Anal. Machine Intell.* PAMI–7:384–401.

Anandan, P., and Weiss, R. 1985 (Oct.). Introducing a smoothness constraint in a matching approach for the computation of optical flow fields. *Proc. IEEE Workshop on Computer Vision: Representation and Control*, Bellaire, MI, pp. 186–194.

Andersen, R. A. 1985. The neurobiological basis of spatial cognition: Role of the parietal lobe. In U. Belugi, N. Kritchevski, J. Stiles-Davis, eds. *Development of Spatial Cognition*. Chicago: Univ. of Chicago Press, pp. 57–80.

Anstis, S. M. 1980. The perception of apparent motion. *Phil. Trans. R. Soc. London Ser. B* 290:153–168.

Arnold, R. D., and Binford, T. O. 1980. Geometric constraints in stereo vision. *SPIE J.* 238:281–292.

Babaud, J., Witkin, A. P., Baudin, M., and Duda, R. O. 1986. Uniqueness of the Gaussian kernel for scale-space filtering. *IEEE Trans. Patt. Anal. Machine Intell.* PAMI-8:26–33.

Baker, H. H. 1982. Depth from edge- and intensity-based stereo. PhD thesis, Univ. of Illinois, Urbana, IL.

Baker, H. H., and Binford, T. O. 1981. Depth from edge- and intensity-based stereo. *Proc. 7th Intern. Joint Conf. on Artif. Intell.*, Vancouver, B.C., pp. 631–636.

Ballard, D. H., and Brown, C. M. 1982. *Computer Vision*. Englewood Cliffs, NJ: Prentice-Hall.

Barlow, Blakemore, C., and Pettigrew, J. D. 1967. The neural mechanism of binocular depth discrimination. *J. Physiol.* 193:327–342.

Barnard, S. T. 1987. A stochastic approach to stereo vision. In Fischler, M. A. and O. Firschein, ed. *Readings in Computer Vision: Issues, Problems, Principles, and Paradigms*. Los Altos, CA: Morgan Kaufmann, pp. 21–25.

Barnard, S. T., and Fischler, M. A. 1982. Computational stereo. *Comput. Surveys* 14:553–572.

Barnard, S. T., and Thompson, W. T. 1980. Disparity analysis of images. *IEEE Trans. Patt. Anal. Machine Intell.* PAMI-2:333–340.

Beck, J., and Ambler, B. 1973. The effects of concentrated and distributed attention on peripheral acuity. *Percept. Psychophys.* 14(2):225–230.

Beck, J., Hope, B., and Rosenfeld, A., eds. 1983. *Human and Machine Vision.* New York: Academic Press.

Bennett, B. M., and Hoffman, D. D. 1985. The computation of structure from fixed axis motion: Nonrigid structures. *Biol. Cybern.* 51:293–300.

Bharwani, S., Riseman, E., and Hanson, A. 1986. Refinement of environmental depth maps over multiple frames. In *Proc. IEEE Workshop on Motion: Representation and Analysis.* New York: IEEE Computer Society, pp. 73–80.

Biederman, I. 1985. Human image understanding: Recent research and a theory. *Comp. Vis. Graph. Image Proc.* 32:29–73.

Binford, T. O. 1981. Inferring surfaces from images. *Artif. Intell.* 17:205–244.

Bolles, R. C., and Baker, H. H. 1985. Epipolar-plane image analysis: a technique for analyzing motion sequences. In *Proc. Third IEEE Workshop on Computer Vision: Representation and Control.* New York: IEEE Computer Society, pp. 168–178.

Borjesson, E., and von Hofsten, C. 1973. Visual perception of motion in depth: Application of a vector model to three-dot motion patterns. *Percept. Psychophys.* 13:169–179.

Bracewell, R. N. 1978. *The Fourier Transform and its Applications.* New York: McGraw-Hill.

Braddick, O. J. 1974. A short-range process in apparent motion. *Vision Res.* 14:519–527.

Braddick, O. J. 1980. Low-level and high-level processes in apparent motion. *Phil. Trans. R. Soc. London Ser. B* 290:137–151.

Brady, J. M., ed. 1981. *Computer Vision.* Amsterdam: North-Holland.

Brady, J. M., and Rosenfeld, A., eds. 1987. *Proceedings of the First International Conference on Computer Vision.* Washington: IEEE Computer Society.

Braunstein, M. L. 1976. *Depth Perception Through Motion.* New York: Academic Press.

Braunstein, M. L., and Andersen, G. J. 1984. A counterexample to the rigidity assumption in the visual perception of structure from motion. *Perception* 13:213–217.

Brown, C., ed. 1987. *Advances in Computer Vision.* New Jersey: Erlbaum.

Bruss, A., and Horn, B. K. P. 1983. Passive navigation. *Comput. Vision Graph. Image Proc.* 21:3–20.

Bulthoff, H. H., and Mallot, H. P. 1987. Interaction of different modules in depth perception. In J. M. Brady, and A. Rosenfeld, eds. *Proc. First International Conference on Computer Vision.* Washington: IEEE Computer Society, pp. 295–306.

Burt, P., and Julesz, B. 1980. A disparity gradient limit for binocular fusion. *Science* 208:615–617.

Burt, P., Sperling, G. 1981. Time, distance, and feature trade-offs in visual apparent motion. *Psych. Rev.* 88:171–195.

Campbell, F. W., and Robson, J. G. 1968. Application of Fourier analysis to the visibility of gratings. *J. Physiol. London* 197:551–556.

Canny, J. 1986. A computational approach to edge detection. *IEEE Trans. Patt. Anal. Machine Intell.* PAMI-8:679–698.

Clocksin, W. F. 1980. Perception of surface slant and edge labels from optical flow: A computational approach. *Perception* 9:253–269.

Cornsweet, T. N. 1970. *Visual Perception.* New York: Academic Press.

Cowan, J. D. 1977. Some remarks on channel bandwidth for visual contrast detection. *Neurosci. Res. Prog. Bull.* 15:492–517.

Curtis, S., and Oppenheim, A. 1987. Reconstruction of multidimensional signals from zero crossings. *J. Opt. Soc. Am.* 4(1):221–231.

Davis, L. S. 1975. A survey of edge detection techniques. *Comp. Graph. Image Proc.* 4:248–270.

DeValois, R., Albrech, D. G., and Thorell, L. G. 1982. Spatial frequency selectivity of cells in macaque visual cortex. *Vis. Res.* 22:545–559.

Doner, J., Lappin, J. S., and Perfetto, G. 1984. Detection of three-dimensional structure in moving optical patterns. *J. Exp. Psychol.: Human Percept. Perform.* 10:1–11.

Fantz, R. L. 1961. The origin of form perception. *Scientific American* 204(5):66–72.

Felton, B., Richards, W., and Smith, A. 1972. Disparity processing of spatial frequencies in man. *J. Physiol.* 225:319–362.

Fender, D., and Julesz, B. 1967. Extension of Panum's fusional area in binocularly stabilized vision. *J. Opt. Soc. Am.* 57:819–830.

Fennema, C. L., and Thompson, W. B. 1979. Velocity determination in scenes containing several moving objects. *Comput. Graph. Image Proc.* 9:301–315.

Ferster, D. 1981. A comparison of binocular depth mechanisms in areas 17 and 18 of the cat visual cortex. *J. Physiol.* 311:623–655.

Fischler, M. A., and Firschein, O., eds. 1987. *Readings in Computer Vision: Issues, Problems, Principles, and Paradigms.* Los Altos, CA: Morgan Kaufman.

Fram, J. R., and Deutsch, E. S. 1975. On the quantitative evaluation of edge detection schemes and their comparison with human performance. *IEEE Trans. Computers* C–24(6):616–628.

Gibson, J. J. 1950. *The Perception of the Visual World.* Boston: Houghton-Mifflin.

Gibson, J. J. 1979. *The Ecological Approach to Visual Perception.* Boston: Houghton-Mifflin.

Gibson, J. J., and Gibson, E. J. 1957. Continuous perceptive transformations and the perception of rigid motion. *J. Exp. Psychol.* 54:129–138.

Graham, N. 1977. Visual detection of aperiodic spatial stimuli by probability summation among narrow band channels. *Vis. Res.* 17:637–652.

Green, M. 1983. Inhibition and facilitation of apparent motion by real motion. *Vis. Res.* 23:861–865.

Grimson, W. E. L. 1981. *From Images to Surfaces: A Computational Study of the Human Early Visual System.* Cambridge: MIT Press.

Grimson, W. E. L. 1985. Computational experiments with a feature based stereo algorithm. *IEEE Trans. Patt. Anal. Mach. Intell.* PAMI-7:17–34.

Gross, C. G., Rocha-Miranda, C. E., and Bender, D. B. 1972. Visual properties of neurons in inferotemporal cortex of the macaque. *J. Neurophysiol.* 35:96–111.

Haralick, R. M. 1980. Edge and region analysis for digital image data. *Comput. Graph. Image Proc.* 12:60–73.

Hildreth, E. C. 1984. *The Measurement of Visual Motion.* Cambridge: MIT Press.

Hildreth, E. C. 1987. Edge detection. In S. Shapiro, ed. *Encyclopedia of Artificial Intelligence.* New York: John Wiley, pp. 257–267.

Hildreth, E. C., and Koch, C. 1987. The analysis of visual motion: From computational theory to neuronal mechanisms. *Ann. Rev. Neurosci.* 10:477–533.

Hoff, W., and Ahuja, N. 1987. Extracting surfaces from stereo images: An integrated approach. In J. M. Brady and A. Rosenfeld, eds. Washington: IEEE Computer Society, pp. 284–294.

Hoffman, D. D., and Flinchbaugh, B. E. 1982. The interpretation of biological motion. *Biol. Cybern.* 42:195–204.

Hoffman, D., and Richards, W. 1986. Parts of recognition. In A. P. Pentland, ed. *From Pixels to Predicates.* Norwood, NJ: Ablex.

Hopfield, J. J. 1982. Neural networks and physical systems with emergent collective computational abilities. *Proc. Nat. Acad. Sci. USA* 79:2554–2558.

Horn, B. K. P. 1986. *Robot Vision.* Cambridge: MIT Press.

Horn, B. K. P., and Schunck, B. G. 1981. Determining optical flow. *Artif. Intell.* 17:185–203.

Hubel, D. H., and Wiesel, T. N. 1968. Receptive fields and functional architecture of monkey striate cortex. *J. Physiology, London* 195:215–243.

Huttenlocher, D. P., and Ullman, S. 1987 (June). Object recognition using alignment. *Proc. Int. Conf. Comp. Vis.*, London, pp. 102–111.

Inada, V. K., Hildreth, E. C., Grzywacz, N. M., and Adelson, E. H. 1986. The perceptual buildup of three-dimensional structure from motion. *Invest. Ophthal. Visual Sci. Suppl.* 27:142.

Jansson, G., and Johansson, G. 1973. Visual perception of bending motion. *Perception* 2:321–326.

Johansson, G. 1971. Studies on visual perception of locomotion. *Perception* 6:365–376.

Johansson, G. 1975. Visual motion perception. *Sci. Am.* 232:76–88.

Johansson, G. 1977. Spatial constancy and motion in visual perception. In W. Epstein, ed. *Stability and Constancy in Visual Perception.* New York: John Wiley.

Jolicoeur, P., Ullman, S., and Mackay, M. 1986. Curve tracing: A possible basic operation in the perception of spatial relations. *Memory and Cognition* 14(2):129–140.

Julesz, B. 1971. *Foundations of Cyclopean Perception.* Chicago: Univ. of Chicago Press.

Julesz, B., and Miller, J. 1975. Independent spatial-frequency-tuned channels in binocular fusion and rivalry. *Perception* 4:125–143.

Koch, C., and Poggio, T. 1987. Biophysics of computational systems: Neurons, synapses and membranes. In G. M. Edelman, W. E. Gall, and W. M. Cowan, eds. *Synaptic Function.* New York: Neurosciences Research Foundation and John Wiley and Sons, pp. 637–697.

Koenderink, J. J. 1984. The structure of images. *Biol. Cybern.* 50:363–370.

Koenderink, J. J., and van Doorn, A. J. 1986. Depth and shape from differential perspective in the presence of bending deformations. *J. Opt. Soc. Am. A* 3:242–249.

Landy, M. S. 1986. A parallel model of the kinetic depth effect using local computations. Mathematical Studies in Perception and Cognition Rep. No. 86–2, Department of Psychology, New York University, New York.

Lappin, J. S., and Bell, H. H. 1976. The detection of coherence in moving random dot patterns. *Vision Res.* 16:161–168.

Lawton, D. T. 1983. Processing translational motion sequences. *Comput. Vision Graph. Image Proc.* 22:116–144.

Lee, D. N. 1980. The optic flow field: The foundation of vision. *Philos. Trans. R. Soc. London B* 290:169–179.

Levine, M. D. 1985. *Vision in Man and Machine.* New York: McGraw-Hill.

Longuet-Higgins, H. C., and Prazdny, K. 1981. The interpretation of moving retinal images. *Proc. R. Soc. London Ser. B* 208:385–397.

Lowe, D. G. 1986. Three-dimensional object recognition from single two-dimensional images. In *Robotics Research Technical Report 202,* Courant Institute of Math. Sciences, New York University, New York.

Macleod, I. D. G. 1972. Comments on techniques for edge detection. *Proc. IEEE* 60:344.

Marr, D. 1982. *Vision*. San Francisco: Freeman.

Marr, D., and Hildreth, E. C. 1980. Theory of edge detection. *Proc. R. Soc. London Ser. B* 207:187–217.

Marr, D., and Nishihara, H. K. 1978. Representation and recognition of the spatial organization of three-dimensional shapes. *Proc. Roy. Soc. London Ser. B* 200:269–291.

Marr, D., and Poggio, T. 1976. Cooperative computation of stereo disparity. *Science* 194:283–287.

Marr, D., and Poggio, T. 1979. A computational theory of human stereo vision. *Proc. R. Soc. London Ser. B* 204:301–328.

Marr, D., and Ullman, S. 1981. Directional selectivity and its use in early visual processing. *Proc. R. Soc. London Ser. B* 211:151–180.

Mayhew, J. E. W., and Frisby, J. P. 1980. The computation of binocular edges. *Perception* 9:69–86.

Mayhew, J. E. W., and Frisby, J. P. 1981. Psychophysical and computational studies towards a theory of human stereopsis. *Artif. Intell.* 17:349–385.

Medioni, G. G., and Nevatia, R. 1985. Segment-based stereo matching. *Comp. Vis. Graph. Image Proc.* 31:2–18.

Milner, P. M. 1974. A model for visual shape recognition. *Psychol. Rev.* 81(6):521–535.

Mitchell, D. E. 1966. Retinal disparity and diplopia. *Vision Res.* 6:441–451.

Mitiche, A. 1986. On kineopsis and computation of structure and motion. *IEEE Trans. Pattern Anal. Machine Intell.* PAMI-8:109–112.

Moran, J., and Desimone, R. 1985. Selective attention gates visual processing in the extrastriate cortex. *Science* 229:782–784.

Moravec, H. P. 1980. Obstacle avoidance and navigation in the real world by seeing a robot rover. *Stanford Artif. Intell. Lab. Memo 340,* Stanford Univ., Stanford, CA.

Motter, B. C., and Mountcastle, V. B. 1981. The functional properties of the light-sensitive neurons in the posterior cortex studied in waking monkeys: Foveal spacing and opponent vector organization. *J. Neurosci.* 1:3–26.

Movshon, J. A., Adelson, E. H., Gizzi, M. S., and Newsome, W. T. 1985. The analysis of moving visual patterns. In C. Chagas, R. Gattas, and C. G. Gross, eds. *Pattern Recognition Mechanisms*. Rome: Vatican Press.

Nagel, H.-H. 1984 (May). Recent advances in image sequence analysis. In *Proc. Premier Colloque Image—Traitement, Synthese, Technologie et Applications*, Biarritz, France, pp. 545–558.

Nagel, H.-H., and Enkelmann, W. 1984 (July). Towards the estimation of displacement vector fields by "oriented smoothness" constraints. *Proc. 7th Int. Conf. on Pattern Recognition*, Montreal, Canada, pp. 6–8.

Nakayama, K., and Silverman, G. H. 1988a. The aperture problem I: Perception of nonrigidity and motion direction in translating sinusoidal lines. *Vis. Res.* 28:739–746.

Nakayama, K., and Silverman, G. H. 1988b. The aperture problem II: Spatial integration of velocity information along contours. *Vis. Res.* 28:747–753.

Negahdaripour, S., and Horn, B. K. P. 1985. Direct passive navigation. *MIT Artif. Intell. Memo 821.*

Neisser, U. 1967. *Cognitive Psychology.* New York: Appleton-Century-Crofts.

Nevatia, R., and Babu, R. 1980. Linear feature extraction and description. *Comp. Graph. Image Proc.* 13:257–269.

Nielsen, K. R. K., and Poggio, T. 1984. Vertical image registration in stereopsis. *Vision Res.* 24:1133–1140.

Pantle, A. J., and Picciano, L. 1976. A multistable display: Evidence for two separate motion systems in human vision. *Science* 193:500–502.

Pentland, A. P., ed. 1986. *From Pixels to Predicates: Recent Advances in Computational and Robotic Vision.* Norwood, NJ: Ablex.

Perret, D. J., Rolls, E. T., and Caan, J. 1982. Visual neurons responsive to faces in the monkey temporal cortex. *Exp. Brain Res.* 47:329–342.

Persoon, E. 1976. A new edge detection algorithm and its applications. *Comp. Graph. Image Proc.* 5:425–446.

Pettigrew, J. D., Nikara, T., and Bishop, P. O. 1968. Binocular interaction on single units in cat striate cortex: Simultaneous stimulation by single moving slits with receptive fields in correspondence. *Exp. Brain Res.* 6:391–410.

Poggio, G. F. 1984. Processing of stereoscopic information in primate visual cortex. In G. Edelman, W. M. Cowan, W. E. Gall, eds. *Dynamic Aspects of Neocortical Function.* New York: Wiley.

Poggio G. F., and Fischer, B. 1977. Binocular interaction and depth sensitivity of striate and prestriate cortical neurons of the behaving rhesus monkey. *J. Neurophysiol.* 40:1392–1405.

Poggio, G. F., and Talbot, W. H. 1981. Mechanisms of static and dynamic stereopsis in foveal cortex of the rhesus monkey. *J. Physiol.* 315:469–492.

Poggio, G. F., and Poggio, T. 1984. The analysis of stereopsis. *Ann. Rev. Neurosci.* 7:379–412.

Poggio, T., and Drumheller, M. 1986. On parallel stereo. *Proc. IEEE Intl. Conf. on Robotics and Automation.*

Poggio, T., and Koch, C. 1985. Ill-posed problems in early vision: From computational theory to analog networks. *Proc. R. Soc. London B* 226:303–323.

Poggio, T., Torre, V., and Koch, C. 1985. Computational vision and regularization theory. *Nature* 317:314–319.

Pollard, S. B., Mayhew, J. E. W., and Frisby, J. P. 1985. PMF: A stereo correspondence algorithm using disparity gradient limit. *Perception* 14:449–470.

Posner, M. I. 1980. Orienting of attention. *Quart J. Exp. Psychol.* 32:3–25.

Pratt, W. 1978. *Digital Image Processing*. New York: John Wiley.

Prazdny, K. 1980. Egomotion and relative depth map from optical flow. *Biol. Cybern.* 36:87–102.

Prazdny, K. 1983. On the information in optical flows. *Comput. Vision Graph. Image Proc.* 22:239–259.

Prazdny, K. 1986. Detection of binocular disparities. *Biol. Cybern.* 52:93–99.

Regan, D. M., Kaufman, L., and Lincoln, J. 1986. Motion in depth and visual acceleration. In K. R. Boff, ed. *Handbook of Perception and Human Performance*. Vol. 2, ch. 19. New York: Wiley.

Richards, W. 1971. Anomalous stereoscopic depth perception. *J. Opt. Soc. Am.* 61:410–414.

Richards, W., and Ullman, S., eds. 1987. *Image Understanding 1985–86*. Norwood, NJ: Ablex.

Richter, J., and Ullman, S. 1986. Nonlinearities in cortical simple cells and the possible detection of zero crossings. *Biol. Cyber.* 53:195–202.

Rogers, B. J., and Graham, M. 1979. Motion parallax as an independent cue for depth perception. *Perception* 8:125–134.

Rosenfeld, A., and Kak, A. 1976. *Digital Picture Processing*. New York: Academic Press.

Rosenfeld, A., and Thurston, M. 1971. Edge and curve detection for visual scene analysis. *IEEE Trans. Comp.* C–20:562–569.

Sakata, H., Shibutani, H., Kawano, K., and Harrington, T. L. 1985. Neural mechanisms of space vision in the parietal association cortex of the monkey. *Vision Res.* 25:453–464.

Shanmugam, K. S., Dickey, F. M., and Green, J. A. 1979. An optimal frequency domain filter for edge detection in digital pictures. *IEEE Trans. Patt. Anal. Machine Intell.* PAMI-1:37–49.

Shariat, H., Price, K. 1986. How to use more than two frames to estimate motion. In *Proc. IEEE Workshop on Motion: Representation and Analysis*. New York: IEEE Computer Society, pp. 119–124.

Siegel, R. M., and Andersen, R. A. 1986. Motion perceptual deficits following ibotenic acid lesions of the middle temporal area (MT) in the behaving Rhesus monkey. *Neuroscience Abstr.* 12:324.8.

Sperling, G. 1970. Binocular vision: A physical and a neural theory. *Am. J. Psychol.* 83:461–534.

Subbarao, M. 1986. Interpretation of image motion fields: A spatiotemporal approach. In: *Proc. IEEE Workshop on Motion: Representation and Analysis.* New York: IEEE Computer Society, pp. 157–165.

Sutherland, N. S. 1968. Outline of a theory of visual pattern recognition in animal and man. *Proc. Roy. Soc. London B* 171:297–317.

Thompson, W. B., and Barnard, S. T. 1981 (Aug.). Lower-level estimation and interpretation of visual motion. *IEEE Computer* pp. 20–28.

Todd, J. T. 1982. Visual information about rigid and nonrigid motion: A geometric analysis. *J. Exp. Psychol.* 8:238–252.

Todd, J. T. 1984. The perception of three-dimensional structure from rigid and nonrigid motion. *Percept. Psychophys.* 36:97–103.

Torre, V., and Poggio, T. 1986. On edge detection. *IEEE Trans. Patt. Anal. Machine Intell.* PAMI-8:147–163.

Treisman, A., and Gelade, G. 1980. A feature integration theory of attention. *Cog. Psychol.* 12:97–136.

Tsai, R. Y., and Huang, T. S. 1981. Uniqueness and estimation of three-dimensional motion parameters of rigid objects with curved surfaces. *Univ. of Illinois Urbana-Champaign, Coordinated Science Laboratory Report* R-921.

Tyler, C. W. 1975. Spatial limitations of human stereoscopic vision. *SPIE J.* 120:36–42.

Ullman, S. 1979. *The Interpretation of Visual Motion.* Cambridge: MIT Press.

Ullman, S. 1983. Computational studies in the interpretation of structure and motion: summary and extension. In J. Beck, B. Hope, and A. Rosenfeld, eds. *Human and Machine Vision.* New York: Academic Press, pp. 459–480.

Ullman, S. 1984a. Maximizing rigidity: the incremental recovery of 3-D structure from rigid and rubbery motion. *Perception* 13:255–274.

Ullman, S. 1984b. Visual routines. *Cognition.* 18:97–159.

Ullman, S. 1986. An approach to object recognition: Aligning pictorial descriptions. *MIT Artif. Intell. Lab. Memo.* 931.

Ullman, S., and Richards, W., eds. 1984. *Image Understanding 1984.* Ablex: Norwood, NJ.

Ullman, S., and Yuille, A. L. 1987. The smoothest velocity field. *MIT Artif. Intell. Memo.*

Van Essen, D. C., and Maunsell, J. H. R. 1983. Hierarchical organization and functional streams in the visual cortex. *Trends Neurosci.* 6:370–375.

von der Heydt, R., Peterhans, E., and Baumgartner, G. 1984. Illusory contours and cortical neurons' responses. *Science* 224:1260–1262.

Wallach, H. 1976. On perceived identity: 1. The direction of motion of straight lines. In H. Wallach, ed. *On Perception*, New York: Quadrangle.

Wallach, H., and O'Connell, D. N. 1953. The kinetic depth effect. *J. Exp. Psych.* 45:205–217.

Wallach, H., Weisz, A., and Adams, P. A. 1956. Circles and derived figures in rotation. *Am. J. Psych.* 69:48–59.

Watson, B. W., and Nachmias, J. 1977. Patterns of temporal interaction in the detection of gratings. *Vis. Res.* 17:893–902.

Watt, R. J., and Morgan, M. J. 1983. The recognition and representation of edge blur: Evidence for spatial primitives in human vision. *Vis. Res.* 23(12):1465–1477.

Watt, R. J., and Morgan, M. J. 1984. Spatial filters and the localization of luminance changes in human vision. *Vis. Res.* 24(10):1387–1397.

Waxman, A. M., and Ullman, S. 1985. Surface structure and three-dimensional motion from image flow kinematics. *J. Robotics Res.* 4:72–94.

Waxman, A. M., and Wohn, K. 1987. Image flow theory: A framework for 3-D inference from time-varying imagery. In C. Brown, ed. *Advances in Computer Vision*. New Jersey: Erlbaum.

Westheimer, G., and McKee, S. P. 1978. Stereoscopic acuity for moving retinal images. *J. Opt. Soc. Amer.* 68:450–455.

Westheimer, G., and McKee, S. P. 1980. Stereoscopic acuity with defocused and spatially filtered images. *J. Opt. Soc. Amer.* 70:772–778.

White, B. W., and Mueser, G. E. 1960. Accuracy in reconstructing the arrangement of elements generating kinetic depth displays. *J. Exp. Psychol.* 60:1–11.

Willshaw, D. J., Buneman, O. P., and Longuet-Higgins, H. C. 1969. Non-holographic associative memory. *Nature* 222:960–962.

Wilson, H. R., and Bergen, J. R. 1979. A four mechanism model for threshold spatial vision. *Vis. Res.* 19:19–32.

Witkin, A. P. 1983. Scale space filtering. In M. A. Fischler, and O. Firschein, eds. *Readings in Computer Vision: Issues, Problems, Principles, and Paradigms*. Los Altos, CA: Morgan Kaufman, pp. 329–332.

Yasumoto, Y., and Medioni, G. 1985. Experiments in estimation of 3-D motion parameters from a sequence of image frames. In *Proc. IEEE Conf. on Computer Vision and Pattern Recognition*. New York: IEEE, pp. 89–94.

Zucker, S. W. 1987. Early orientation selection: Tangent fields and the dimensionality of their support. In M. A. Fischler, and O. Firschein, eds. *Readings in Computer Vision: Issues, Problems, Principles, and Paradigms*. Los Altos, CA: Morgan Kaufman, pp. 333–347.

16 Visual Attention

Alan Allport

16.1 What Is Attention? What Is Attention For?

Issues of attention bear on every area of cognitive science. In addition to the questions that arise within individual cognitive domains, students of attention find themselves confronted, inevitably, by the problems of integration and coordination among different cognitive domains in the overall control of behavior. The latter constitute traditionally the central problems for theories of attention and must be counted surely among the most complex and difficult problems in cognitive science.

Understanding any complex mental function no doubt requires explanation at many different levels. David Marr (1977, 1982), particularly, emphasized the importance of clear, explicit formulation at the level of what he called the *computational theory*, that is, the level at which the overall *purposes* or goals of a given category of cognitive processes are to be specified and at which the internal and environmental *constraints* under which they must operate, and that make those processes possible, are formulated.

What would a computational theory that was adequate to the functions of attention be like? What is the overall *purpose* (or what are the overall *purposes*) of attention, and what are the determining and enabling *constraints* on attentional processes?

Answers to these questions go to the foundations of our current understanding of attention. Many theorists in recent years have been inclined to conceptualize attention—and attentional selectivity—as essentially the consequence of some kind of *system limitation*: the result of limited or insufficient processing resources or processing capacity in the brain. Much of the empirical research on attention, following from this very general orientation, has been concerned with identifying the nature of these system limitations and their functional locus within the architecture of human (and nonhuman) information processing.

One objective of this chapter is to present a somewhat different conception of attention, one that emphasizes the constraints of behavioral coherence and univocal perceptual-motor control in determining the nature of attentional selectivity. It also emphasizes the diversity of attentional functions. Prompted in part by advances in our understanding of information processing in parallel distributed systems (chapter 4), and by related developments in the neurosciences (chapter 8) and in cognitive neuropsychology, I have tried to set out a conceptual framework for the functions of visual attention that offers an alternative to the traditional preoccupation with issues of limited capacity and selectivity of "processing."

As this chapter is at pains to point out, there are many different computational functions of attention. To keep things within manageable bounds, the discussion is confined to certain functions of *visual*[1] attention, in the context of immediate perceptual-motor activities. A large part of the behavioral research on visual attention in recent years has used selective-response measures (often speeded response) to visual stimulation. It seems appropriate therefore to set as our principal, if limited, objective the task of understanding the attentional processes involved in this (actually very large) class of visual motor performance.

The plan of this chapter is as follows: Section 16.2 provides a critical review of the concept of central limited capacity as the causal origin of selective attention. Assumptions underlying the related concepts of "early" versus "late" selection, controlled versus automatic processing, and multiple limited processing resources are also critically examined. Section 16.3 introduces a neurobehavioral perspective on visual-spatial attention, focusing on acquired disturbances of spatial attention and some underlying neurophysiological mechanisms. Section 16.4 returns to the questions with which we began, regarding the purposes of and computational constraints on basic functions of attention. A conceptual framework is presented in which attentional functions of many different kinds contribute to (and are responsible for) both the coherence and continuity of goal-directed behavior and its flexibility and responsiveness to changing events. Finally in section 16.5 a number of experimental paradigms of selective visual response is reviewed in the light of these two contrasted theoretical frameworks.

16.2 Attention and Limited Capacity

Limited Capacity
In the preceding paragraphs two basic questions were posed: What are the fundamental *constraints* on processes of attention, and What are their overall purposes? According to the view of attention that has provided the conceptual framework for the majority of research in that area since the 1950s, the answers to these two foundational questions are apparently clear: (1) The fundamental constraint that underlies all the operations of attention, imposing their essentially *selective* character, is the limited information-processing capacity of the brain. (Thus "If the brain had infinite capacity for information processing, there would

be little need for attentional mechanisms" (Mesulam 1985, p. 125).) (2) Hence, according to the predominant view, the basic function or *purpose* of attentional mechanisms is to protect the brain's limited capacity system (or systems) from informational overload. ("Selection takes place in order to protect a mechanism of limited capacity" (Broadbent 1971).) This conception was articulated in its original and most influential form by Broadbent (1958, 1971, 1982). According to Broadbent, the constraints of limited capacity directly affect the processing of sensory information. Registration of some simple physical characteristics of the sensory input is possible in parallel; on the other hand semantic categorization, or identification of feature combinations, through access to associative memory, is not. Thus in Broadbent's theory, the "limited capacity system" was identified explicitly with a system of perceptual-semantic categorization.[2] Information *not selected* was therefore excluded from semantic categorization or identification, and *selection*, according to this interpretation, was synonymous with selective *processing*, that is, the *shutting out* of nonselected information from further analysis.[3]

Broadbent's original conception of the selective process, his well-known *filter theory* (Broadbent 1958), underwent later modification in that nonselected sensory inputs were no longer supposed to be strictly excluded from the limited capacity systems, but only attenuated in signal strength. Hence "categorization" could sometimes occur even for nonselected stimuli, on the basis of incomplete feature analysis, given a category with sufficiently lowered criterion (Broadbent 1971, 1982). However, the basic concept—of limited central processing capacity as the fundamental causal constraint that imposed the need for selectivity of processing—remained unchanged. Moreover despite other important differences the idea of *limited capacity*, in one form or another, as the basis of attentional limitations has remained a central—in some cases an unquestioned—assumption in otherwise very diverse theoretical approaches to attention (Duncan 1980, Kahneman 1973, Mesulam 1985, Neisser 1967, Norman and Bobrow 1975, Posner 1978, 1982, Schneider, Dumais, and Shiffrin 1984, Shiffrin and Schneider 1977, Treisman 1988, Ullman 1984, and Wickens 1984, among many others).

The idea of a central limited capacity (and of the consequent necessity of restricting processing, beyond some level, to a selected subset of available information) has been linked explicitly by some theorists to intuitive concepts of the limited nature of *consciousness*, or phenomenal awareness. Posner (1982), for example, has invoked "a limited capacity system that might be identified with conscious awareness."[4] For many authors the relationship between these ideas appears to be self-evident. ("Since we are aware of only a small amount of this information [on our retina] at any one time, most of it must be filtered out centrally" (Moran and Desimone 1985).) Any careful reading of the literature can produce dozens of such examples.) The identification of a postulated central "limited-capacity system" with certain ideas of *consciousness* may be responsible at least in part for the extraordinarily widespread, intuitive appeal of the concept of limited capacity. As I have argued elsewhere (Allport 1988), however, this identification does little to clarify the computational basis of the postulated limitation in capacity.

Possibly even more important for the longevity of this idea (of limited processing capacity) has been the belief that no *other* explanation for the selectivity of attention was in fact available. As Broadbent remarked, "The obvious utility of a selection system is to produce an economy in mechanism. If a complete analysis were performed even on neglected messages, there seems *no reason for selection at all*" (1971, p. 147, my italics).

Early versus Late Selection: Underlying Assumptions

Given this general background of ideas, or assumptions, about the causal origins of attention, one issue that has preoccupied students of attention over the past twenty-five years concerns the stage or level of analysis at which the supposed bottleneck of limited capacity was located, and hence—according to the same general assumptions—the level at or before which "selection" must take place. This is the long-running controversy over so-called *early* versus *late* selection.[5]

As outlined, Broadbent originally argued that selective filtering of sensory information must occur at a relatively early stage of analysis, that is, before the stage of perceptual recognition or categorization. Variations on this hypothesis have been put forward by several other authors (for example, Francolini and Egeth 1980, Hoffman 1986, Johnston and Dark 1985, 1986, Kahneman and Treisman 1984, Treisman and Gelade 1980, Ullman 1984, among many others). From quite early on, however, a range of contrary views has also been proposed, again both on empirical and on theoretical grounds, to the effect that a processing bottleneck can be found only at a relatively late stage, if at all, and specifically *after* the level of semantic categorization (see, for example, Coltheart 1984, Deutsch and Deutsch 1963; Duncan 1980, Kantowitz 1974, Keele and Neill 1978, Marcel 1983, Mewhort et al. 1984, Neill 1989, Norman 1968, Pashler 1987, Posner 1978, 1982, Schneider and Shiffrin 1977, Shaffer and LaBerge 1979, Tipper 1985, Tipper and Driver 1988, Allport, Tipper, and Chmiel 1985).

The empirical evidence that has been put forward to support (or to disconfirm) these apparently mutually exclusive sets of hypotheses has been extensively reviewed (see, for example, Allport 1980b, Kahneman and Treisman 1984, Keele and Neill 1978, Johnston and Dark 1986). These empirical arguments are not recapitulated here. We are concerned for the moment with the underlying assumptions that, to some degree, have been common to *both* positions. The fact that, after a quarter-century of energetic experimental research, the controversy, in these terms, over early versus late selection appears still not to have been empirically resolved (or at least that theoretical consensus has not been achieved) suggests that the conceptual framework within which this issue has been formulated requires further critical attention (Allport 1987, Lambert, Beard, and Thompson 1988, Neumann 1987, Pashler and Badgio 1988, van der Heijden 1987).

One important set of assumptions underlying this debate concerns what is supposedly early and what is supposedly late in cognitive processing, including assumptions, implicit or explicit, about a presumed, monotonic ordering of stages of processing. Early selection, according to its conventional characterization, depends solely on the coding of physical, sensory attributes and operates primarily or even exclusively in terms of *spatial location*—hence the popular metaphor of a spatial spotlight of attention. Late selection, according to the same theoretical dichotomy, operates in terms of category membership. An assumption evidently built in to these theoretical alternatives is that the encoding of spatial location and spatial relationships is computed (uniquely?) as an *early* stage in some monotonic hierarchy of stages of visual processing, and that the encoding of categorical identity, or of other "semantic" attributes, occurs (uniquely?) at a *later* stage of processing—either in cascade, following the stage of spatial/sensory encoding, or only after the earlier stage has been completed. Hence, according to this theoretical dichotomy, any operation—in particular any *selective* operation—contingent on spatial/sensory properties or relations is attributed (by definition) to an early stage of processing; any (selective) operation contingent on categorical or other semantic criteria is attributed (by definition) to a late stage of processing.

This set of assumptions appears extraordinarily difficult to reconcile with current neuropsychological evidence concerning the functional architecture of spatial and categorical coding in the brain. This evidence reveals a very high level of parallel modular specialization of perceptual and cognitive function (see section 16.3). In particular there is compelling evidence of the specialization of functionally and neuroanatomically separable, *parallel* systems concerned, respectively, with computing aspects of categorical identity ("What?") and with the computation of spatial relationships ("Where?") (see, for example, Ellis and Young 1988, Levine, Warach, and Farah 1985, Newcombe, Ratcliff, and Damasio 1987, Ungerleider and Mishkin 1982). Furthermore it is evident that the encoding of spatial location and spatial relations in terms of retinotopic and other head- and body-centered coordinates, as well as in terms of environmental relationships, is computationally highly complex (Feldman 1985, Hinton and Parsons 1988, Jeannerod 1987, Zipser 1986). Representation in terms of explicit visual-spatial location can be found from the earliest stages of visual coding through to very late levels of cognitive and even motor processing (see, for example, Goldberg and Segraves 1987, Rolls 1981, 1987). Indeed processes sometimes attributed to early selection may actually take place only *after* the independent processing of figural identity and relative location, namely in the *inte-*

gration of these respective coding domains (see, for example, Coltheart 1980, Pashler and Badgio 1985, Styles and Allport 1986).

Another critical assumption concerns what is meant by selection. In the terms in which much of the controversy over early versus late selection has been conducted, the level at which selection operates has been treated, equivalently, as the level beyond which the processing of "nonselected" (or "rejected") information is (must be?) foreclosed. Clearly if selection is supposed to take place in order to protect a mechanism of limited capacity, it is natural to assume—to take for granted—that selection necessarily *means* selective (that is, exclusive) *processing*. Thus, according to this presumed equivalence, when task instructions to attend to (that is, to respond to or remember) X and to ignore Y are executed with little or no interference (or facilitation) from the presence of Y, especially when Y is semantically related to X, this is liable to be interpreted as evidence ipso facto that Y was excluded from "further processing" of the kind provided by the limited capacity mechanism.

It is often claimed, for example, that in selective report tasks selection cued by sensorily defined attributes, and/or by spatial location, is easier and more efficient than selection based on semantic criteria (Broadbent 1970). Kahneman and Treisman (1984), among others, have suggested that this empirical generalization provides possibly the strongest evidence available in favor of filter theory, or early selection, and hence, they argued, as contrary to late selection: that is, contrary to the "strong automaticity" of stimulus categorization.

In evaluating this conclusion, however, it is important to maintain a distinction between what may be called *selective cueing*—that is, the process (or processes) by which task-relevant information is marked out, or designated, on the basis of some selection cue, for *control of a given response*—and questions of selective *processing*. The efficiency of selective cueing is appropriately indexed, for example, by the presence or absence of response interference resulting from the presentation of task-irrelevant distractors (see, for example, Francolini and Egeth 1980, Kahneman and Treisman 1984). Efficient selective cueing, however, defined in terms of the effective designation (and segregation) of information for the control of a particular action, carries no necessary implications about the level of processing or nonprocessing of the information that has not been thus designated, and still less, any implications about the level or domain of processing in which capacity is limited. These questions are, in this respect, logically independent.[6]

Even if selective cueing based on spatial location (in the "Where?" system) can be shown to be specially effective, or to be distinctive in other ways, this finding would still leave wide open the question of whether perceptual-semantic categorization—computed by the functionally separable "What?" system—is or is not also selective: that is, is dependent or not on the spatial direction of attention. And it would leave wide open also the question of whether perceptual-semantic categorization can occur chronologically before, after, or cotemporaneously with the processes of spatially selective cueing.

Selective cueing in vision may indeed operate preferentially, or particularly efficiently, in the spatial domain. When a selective cue in one representational domain (for example, color or movement) is used to designate a subset of available information in another visual domain (for example, form), this *cross-domain cueing* appears typically to depend on the shared coding of location (Nissen 1985; see also van der Heijden 1986, 1987). On the other hand it is not always true that visual selection based on physical attributes is more efficient than selection based on categorical or "semantic" criteria. For example, Bundesen, Pedersen, and Larsen (1984) found that visual selection (selective report) based on a clearly "physical" attribute (curved versus angular letter shape) was considerably *less* efficient than selection based on alphanumeric category (letter versus digit). Where selection is spatially mediated, an attribute that is represented in terms of its own spatiotopic visual "map" (Maunsell and Newsome 1987, Zeki 1981) should provide an especially effective selection cue. The distinction "curved versus angular" appears unlikely to be represented explicitly in this way.

In summary the controversy over early versus late selection, perceived as mutually exclusive theoretical alternatives, appears to have systematically confused selection in the sense of selective cueing and selection as selective processing. Once this distinction is made clear, it becomes apparent that evidence favoring so-called early selection—that is, evidence favoring selective cueing operating predominantly in the spatial domain—is compatible with a whole range of theoretical options regarding categorical encoding, from strong dependence on spatial attention to independence ("unlimited capacity"?), the position traditionally associated with so-called late selection.

Variations on the Idea of Limited Capacity

Few would deny that attention (in the sense at least of perceptual-motor performance) is limited, or selective. The question at issue is: In what way is this empirical observation (or actually very heterogeneous collection of observations) explained by a theoretical construct of Limited Processing Capacity? If there *is* a limitation on processing capacity that is responsible for the selectivity of attention, what is its computational basis?

Early attempts to identify, experimentally, rate-limiting parameters for the human transmission of information, in information-theoretic terms, resulted in a wide range of different values for different perceptual-motor skills (see, for example, Quastler 1956). Certainly there was no sign that these parameters might converge on some task-independent limit. In any case, when one such task was being performed at around its maximum transmission rate, a second task could in many cases be added to the first and be successfully performed concurrently; hence the limitation on transmission rate of the first task could not have been set by some global, task-independent capacity limit in simple informational terms (see, for example, Allport, Antonis, and Reynolds 1972, Spelke, Hirst, and Neisser 1976). Even more problematic for the idea of an overall global limit on information processing in these terms as the basis for "attentional" limits to human performance is the fact that not all such task-combinations are equally successful or equally possible, despite the use of separate sensory modalities and separate effectors for each pair of tasks. A paradigmatic example was provided by Shaffer (1975), who showed that visually controlled copy-typing can be combined successfully with auditory-vocal shadowing of continuous speech; however, recombining the same types of input and output in reading aloud and audio-typing turns out, even for a highly skilled audio-typist, to be essentially impossible to perform concurrently. This is in spite of identical total amounts of preview and of sequential redundancy in these two different combinations (contra Broadbent 1982).

In this combination of tasks the auditory text provides an optimally compatible specification[7] for the required, vocal output, whereas typing (or writing) is specified most compatibly by the visual text. In this example and in others like it (see, for example, Allport et al. 1972, Hatano, Miyake, and Binks 1977, Spelke, Hirst, and Neisser 1976), it is clear that the brain is able to maintain independent representations of two or more complex and continuously changing messages, in parallel, with minimal crosstalk between them, in the control of separate categories of encoding and action. Representational capacity in the message system or systems, therefore, does not appear to be the primary limiting factor. In contrast when the identical input and output messages are recombined, in the task of simultaneously reading aloud from one (visual) text while typing another text to (auditory) dictation, there is massive crosstalk interference—that is, the channel separation between the two processing streams breaks down—and performance on one (or both) of the individual tasks collapses (Shaffer 1975, Tierney 1973).

Related (though less catastrophic) costs of controlling crosstalk interference can be seen in a wide variety of Stroop-like[8] selective-response tasks, where (again) asymmetries in the direction of interference appear to reflect corresponding asymmetries in the relative compatibility of "wanted" and "unwanted" information sources ("targets" versus "distractors") vis-à-vis the representational domain required for execution of the task (see, for example, Beller 1975, Flowers, Warner, and Polansky 1979, Glaser and Glaser 1982, Greenwald 1970, 1972, McClain 1983, Virzi and Egeth 1985). For example, explicit semantic categorization appears to be cued more directly or compatibly by pictures of objects than by their written names, whereas oral naming is specified more compatibly by a written word than by a corresponding picture (see, for example, Rosch 1975, Seymour 1979). Suppose that a written word is presented, superimposed on the line drawing of an object. The subject can be instructed to respond selectively either to the word or to the pictured object. Glaser and Düngelhoff (1984) found that in a word- or picture-*naming* task, incongruent but related words interfered with the naming of pictures, but not vice versa; in a semantic *categorization* task, on the contrary, incongruent pictures interfered with the response to words, but not vice versa.

Accounts of these asymmetrical effects in terms of a simple time-of-arrival hypothesis can be rejected (see, for example, Neumann 1980, Glaser and Glaser 1982, Glaser and Düngelhoff 1984). The pattern of results in this and many other selective-response tasks can be summarized as follows: (1) When the designated target stimulus provides relatively the *most compatible* information source available for encoding into the representational domain (semantic category, color, name, relative location, and the like) needed for execution of the task, then minimal or zero interference from other, *less* compatible information sources is observed. (2) In contrast when the to-be-ignored distractor information provides an equally,[9] or even more compatible, specification (information source) for encoding into the required domain of representation than does the (task-designated) target information, interference—that is, delay in response, overt crosstalk error, or both—is liable to occur. (3) The extent of interference will then depend further on the availability of other (for example, spatial) cues, enabling effective segregation of target and nontarget information.

The heterogeneous nature of attentional limitations, as illustrated in these examples, and the evident failure to identify, consensually, one unique functional locus for a "processing bottleneck," as implied by Broadbent's theory, motivated two important modifications in the concept of limited capacity."

Automatic and Controlled Processes   One modification, advocated, for example, by Schneider and Shiffrin (1977; Shiffrin and Schneider 1977), involved drawing a distinction between what may be called the message system—all those mechanisms responsible directly for information transmission in perceptual-motor tasks—and a control system that operates on the message system. In Broadbent's (1971) theory it was evidently the message system that was critically limited in capacity. For Shiffrin and Schneider, in contrast, capacity limitations were essentially a property of the control system, where control was conceptualized as some sort of unitary resource of fixed, limited capacity.[10] Shiffrin and Schneider further assumed that *all* attentional selectivity and all forms of distractor interference resulted from competition for (and capture of) the same limited control (or the same controller). According to this view, mental processing can be characterized either on the one hand as *automatic*, that is, not requiring "active control or attention by the subject" and hence (so the theory asserts) capable of running concurrently without interference—without capacity limitations—or on the other hand as nonautomatic or *controlled* and hence *ex hypothesi* tightly capacity limited and generally serial in operation, consequently subject to severe concurrency costs (Shiffrin and Schneider 1977, pp. 155–170).

This dichotomy has been devastatingly criticized by Ryan (1983), specifically as applied to the item-recognition task that Shiffrin and Schneider employed. Virtually every defining attribute of these contrasted operations (automaticity/control), Ryan showed, was violated by existing item-recognition data. In particular he presented evidence that more than one supposedly controlled process, according to Shiffrin and Schneider's criteria, can run concurrently, without mutual interference. In the end, Ryan argued, we are left with just one defining attribute of this dichotomy: controlled processes are load dependent (in the item-recognition task), automatic processes are not. "Because all the other defining attributes fail to distinguish between the operation," Ryan concluded, "one is forced into the conclusion that the net theoretical gain . . . is simply a relabeling of old phenomena. There is no new and independent theory at all; we are left with trivial redescription of the fact that ensemble size is sometimes an important variable in human performance" (Ryan 1983, p. 177). In an important series of experiments Logan (1978a,b, 1979, 1980) showed also that ensemble size effects, as indicators of automaticity/control, can be independent of other measures (concurrent memory-load effects, probe reaction-time) put forward also as indicators of capacity demands.

In the meantime the attempt to apply the same dichotomy (automatic/controlled) to the whole range of dual-task concurrency costs appears to have been, for most practical purposes, abandoned. The enormous empirical diversity of effects, varying apparently with the particular *combinations* of tasks rather than with any supposedly intrinsic characteristics (automatic? controlled?) of the tasks individually, has made it profoundly implausible that any single-factor resource limitation might be able to accommodate them. (For reviews see, for example, Gopher and Sanders 1984, Gopher, Brickner, and Navon 1982, Heuer and Wing 1984, Neumann 1985, 1987, Wickens 1980, 1984. For an alternative concept of automaticity, see Neumann 1984.)

Nevertheless the shift of emphasis toward issues of task preparation and attentional control, inspired by the work of Logan (1978a), Posner (1978), Shiffrin and Schneider (1977) and others at around this time, and away from the earlier focus on the idea of informational limitations in the message system, was important. It still apparently awaited a clear recognition, however, that the limited capacity (in a loose, descriptive sense) of attentional control was what had to be explained, rather than an explanation.

Multiple Resources The principal alternative approach for advocates of capacity or resource limitations as the explanatory basis of attentional limitations has been to postulate a variety of different *specific* resources, as multiple, intervening variables, though sometimes retaining a non-specific *general* resource as well (see, for example, Wickens 1980, 1984, Gopher and Sanders 1984). In their present form at least these approaches appear subject to two complementary and discouraging weaknesses. On the one hand no existing formulation of multiple resource theory is able to account for anything like the existing range of data from dual-task experiments. (For critical reviews of this literature, see Navon 1984, Neumann 1985, 1987.) On the other hand, to the extent that more and more specific resources are postulated to account for each new pattern of interference, the approach becomes increasingly little more than a redescription of the data, lacking in explanatory power.

Heuer (1985a) has pointed out the fundamental similarity between capacity models and factor-analytic models of human performance scores (Spearman 1927), with which they share a number of formal weaknesses, whether as general-factor or as multifactor models. (Formally both approaches offer explanations of global performance-measures in terms of hypothetical variables that have linear or monotonic relations to performance.) In terms of their formal correspondence, it is clear that the concept of multiple resources *in general*, like multiple factors in factor-analytic models, cannot be falsified, since it can be fitted in principle to any set of data. What is fundamentally needed, however, if the metaphor of multiple, limited resources is to have any genuine, explanatory force, is a computational theory of why and in what way certain specifiable functions (or separable subsystems) in the brain are capacity limited, in the sense that multiple-resource theory requires, whereas other computational functions are apparently *not* limited in the same way.

Navon (1984, 1985) has provided an extended and forceful critique of the whole concept of limited "resources," or limited processing capacity, arguing that this concept, albeit intuitively appealing, in practice fails to offer predictions that are either diagnostic or indeed falsifiable. The concept is therefore, Navon has argued, a theoretical "soup stone," excess theoretical baggage, liable if anything only to distract attention from the real need for explanation.

Identifying Specific, Limited Resources The identification of postulated specific resource limitations with specific, functionally separable subsystems, whose ontological status is inferred from quite different experimental paradigms—for example, from the evidence of "doubly dissociated" functional impairments in cognitive neuropsychology (see, for example, Shallice, McLeod, and Lewis 1985)—may provide some constraint on the ad hoc multiplication of resources. Such identification is extraordinarily difficult to establish, however, and can remain a matter of belief, somewhat as in the labeling of factors in factor-analytic approaches.

A number of computationally rather more specific hypotheses has been put forward, regarding different possible forms of *perceptual* (specifically *visual*) capacity limitations dependent on different forms of combinatorial constraint (see, for example, Bergen and Julesz 1983, Treisman and Gelade 1980, Treisman 1986, 1988, Ullman 1984. For a contrasting, connectionist approach, see, for example, Mozer 1988). Treisman's theory, for example, proposes that although individual visual features are encoded spatially in parallel over the visual field, *conjunctions* of visual features can only be securely and accurately encoded in a strictly serial manner, one conjunction at a time.[11] The scope of this hypothesis, however, like that of Bergen and Julesz, is quite specifically confined to the processing of visual stimuli. Clearly such hypotheses are not able to offer any definite predictions about nor provide explanations for the limits of dual-task performance, nor any other supposedly "attentional" issues not directly concerned with visual feature encoding. This is certainly in itself no criticism of such theories; far from it. It is important to recognize, however, insofar as these theories may successfully identify *one* type of attention limitation—they are certainly explicitly presented as theories of "attention"—that *other* theories are still required to account for other kinds of attentional constraint.

This is clearly an important possibility: that different functions of attention owe their origin to quite different computational constraints. Certainly there is no a priori reason to suppose that all of the phenomena attributed, in ordinary language, to "attention" have a common explanation nor (still less) that they derive from a single structural bottleneck, as the either-or controversy over early versus late selection appears implicitly to have assumed.

16.3 Neuropsychology of Spatial Attention

Section 16.3 introduces a somewhat different, neurobehavioral perspective on attentional functions, with emphasis on the functions of *spatial* attention. This section includes a summary overview of neuropsychological data, illustrating the distributed, modular character of cognitive functions, including specifically attentional functions. There follows a brief review of neuropsychological disorders of spatial attention and spatial neglect. Traditionally in the cognitive psychology of attention, studies of the often very dramatic pathologies of spatial attention have played surprisingly little part in either the development or evaluation of attentional theories. Nevertheless, as I try to show, the characterization of these disturbances of spatial attention carries a number of radical implications for the characterization of normal attentional function. Finally, and closely related to this characterization, the section concludes with a short summary of neurophysiological evidence on the modulation of neuronal activity in spatiotopic coding systems, as a function of spatially directed attention.

Neuropsychological Architecture: Distributed Modular Function
Neurophysiological and neuropsychological data reveal a multiplicity of parallel channels and of quasi-modular cognitive subsystems, specialized for different elementary cognitive operations (see, for example, Coltheart 1985, Creutzfeldt 1985, Ellis and Young 1988, Goldman-Rakic 1988, Posner, Petersen, Fox, and Raichle 1988). This distributed multi-channel organization is found not only in perceptual (Barlow 1986) and motor systems (Wise and Evarts 1981) and in perceptual-motor interaction (see, for example, Arbib 1987, Creutzfeldt 1985, Dean 1988) but also in language and other higher cognitive functions (see, for example, Allport, Mackay, Prinz, and Scheerer 1987, Caramazza 1988, Ellis and Young 1988, Petersen, Fox, Posner, Mintun, and Raichle 1988, Shallice 1987). Connectivity between individual subsystems, although very rich and generally reciprocal, is also highly selective. Moreover although some hierarchical relationships between subsystems can be pointed to, particularly within sensory and motor areas, the evidence points to a very large measure of parallelism and of heterarchical (or reciprocal) control. No one subsystem, it appears, could be characterized as uniquely "central."

Similar principles of organization are also evident in attentional functions. Thus different aspects of attentional *set* and executive control can be disturbed selectively by different patterns of frontal injury (Duncan 1986, Eslinger and Damasio 1985, Luria 1966). Using imaging techniques that enable the measurement of local changes in metabolism and regional cerebral blood flow (rCBF) in active humans, Roland and his colleagues have been able to identify a number of different regions of human prefrontal cortex that are activated selectively during different aspects of attentional task preparation and execution (Fuster 1985, Ingvar 1983, Roland 1982, 1985, Roland and Friberg 1985). One of these regions, for example, becomes selectively activated during preparation for Strooplike selective-response tasks, whereas a different, adjacent region appears to be involved in contingent (if-then) *sequencing* of cognitive operations. Using similar techniques, Posner and colleagues (1988) obtained evidence that a region of anterior cingulate cortex, on the medial surface of frontal lobe, is activated specifically in the process of *target detection* in semantic monitoring tasks. However, semantic processing or categorization per se, does not appear to engage either of these anterior attentional systems.

Other subsystems, forming a complex distributed network of cortical and subcortical components, appear to be responsible for the *spatial* direction of attention. The relevant subsystems include posterior parietal cortex, frontal eye fields, posterior cingulate cortex, various thalamic nuclei, basal ganglia, superior colliculus, and midbrain reticular formation (Deuel 1987, Mesulam 1981, Milner 1987, Rizzolatti and Camarda 1987, Vallar and Perani 1987). Injury to individual components of this network can result in highly specific patterns of attentional impairment, affecting selectively the engagement, maintenance, disengagement, and shifting of spatial attention (Posner 1988, Posner, Inhoff, Friedrich, and Cohen 1987, Rafal, Posner, Friedman, Inhoff, and Bernstein 1988). Bilateral lesions of posterior parietal cortex can result in symptoms of *bilateral* peripheral inattention, as well as impairment of visually guided movements of the eyes and of the hand (Pierrot-Deseilligny, Gray, and Brunet 1986). An implication of this neurobehavioral evidence, which would seem difficult to avoid, is that spatial attention is a *distributed* function in which many functionally differentiated structures participate, rather than a function controlled uniquely by a single center. The following subsection provides a very brief overview.

Disturbances of Spatial Attention: Varieties of Spatial Neglect
Disturbances of spatial attention, following injury to different elements of this network and resulting in spatially selective (for example, unilateral) *neglect*, may affect either just one sensory modality or many (see, for example, Chedru 1976, DeRenzi, Gentilini, and Pattacini 1984). In severe, multimodal cases of lateral neglect, the patient appears behaviorally unaware of (or unresponsive to) the presence of objects or events on the neglected side, behaving as though that part of his or her world has effectively ceased to exist. In some patients the symptoms of unilateral neglect may be confined only to *distant* objects in extrapersonal space; in other patients they may be restricted to their own limbs and body surface (Bisiach, Perani, Vallar, and Berti 1986). There are also experimental demonstrations in monkeys of unilateral neglect confined to visual objects in near peribuccal, or biting, space, with normal attention to distant visual objects, and vice versa (Rizzolatti, Gentilucci, and Matelli 1985).

The side or direction of space showing neglect, and so-called extinction under double simultaneous stimulation (DSS), may be defined in terms of a variety of different spatial coordinates: body-centered, gravitational, possibly retinal, and also in terms of external-object–centered coordinates. Thus, for example, left neglect typically affects the left side of individual objects and of perceptual groups of objects, though side of object and side of body-space can interact (Bisiach, Capitani, and Porta 1985, Calvanio, Petrone, and Levine 1987, Gazzaniga and Ladavas 1987, Heilman and Valenstein 1979, Jeannerod and Biguer 1987, Kinsbourne 1977, 1987, Rapcsak, Watson, and Heilman 1987). In some patients symptoms of lateral neglect appear to depend on the side of space (relative to the body midline) to which visual attention is directed; in other patients, on the contrary, what matters appears to be the side of the body on which a manual *action* is to be performed, independent of the direction of gaze (Coslett, Bowers, Fitzpatrick, Hans, and Heilman 1986. See also Joanette, Brouchon, Gauthier, and Samson 1986 for an example of an interaction between unilateral visual neglect, in a target-detection task, and the hand used to indicate target detection.).

There is also evidence suggesting that unilateral neglect can be specific to the orthographic domain, doubly dissociated from neglect affecting nonlinguistic visual space (Bisiach, Meregalli, and Berti 1985, Costello and Warrington 1987, Ellis, Flude, and Young 1987).

The neuropsychological evidence thus indicates extensive specialization of different subsystems and different aspects of spatial attention. Across these different spatial domains, however, the character of the attentional disturbance appears uniformly as a *directional bias*, orienting spatial attention away from the neglected side and *toward* the ipsilesional side (Kinsbourne 1970, 1977, Jeannerod and Biguer 1987). Several features of this characterization deserve emphasis:

Relation to Premotor Organization Rizzolatti and his colleagues have provided a range of evidence, in monkeys as well as in humans, that indicates a close relationship between spatially or directionally specific impairments in premotor control of particular (for example, oculomotor, buccal) effector systems and *corresponding* disturbances of visual-spatial attention, favoring a "premotor" theory of spatial attention (Matelli, Olivieri, Saccani, and Rizzolatti 1983, Rizzolatti, Matelli, and Pavesi 1983, Rizzolatti, Riggio, Dascola, and Umilta 1987). It is also known that covert orienting of visual attention, facilitating behavioral response to stimuli in the attended location (Posner 1980, Posner et al. 1987), is greatly enhanced in normal subjects by premotor eye-movement preparation toward the cued location (Remington 1980, Shepherd, Findlay, and Hockey 1986) and can be antagonized by the voluntary preparation for or peripheral cueing of a saccade in another direction (Maylor 1985, Müller and Rabbitt 1988, Shepherd et al. 1986).

Object-Based Perceptual Representation The observation that lateral neglect and extinction characteristically affects whole objects or coherent subparts of complex objects and groups of objects implies that hierarchical, object-based, structural representations of the presented array have been formed independently of the impaired operations of spatial attention, and that the disordered attention then operates on such a representation. Volpe, LeDoux, and Gazzaniga (1979) reported a pioneering study related to this issue; more recent explorations have been reported by Sieroff and Michel (1987) and Sieroff, Pollatsek, and Posner (1987). Clearly these and related phenomena invite extensive and systematic further research.

Directional Bias Posner and his associates (Posner 1988, Posner et al. 1987, Rafal et al. 1988) have identified the underlying deficits in spatial neglect associated with different neuroanatomical lesion sites, with *directional* impairments in at least three functionally separable components of spatial orienting: disengagement, shifting, and reengagement. The directional bias, favoring stimuli in the (relative) ipsilesional direction and producing dramatic distortions of perceptual space, can be enhanced or diminished by appropriate spatial cueing (Riddoch and Humphreys 1983) and by unilateral vestibular stimulation (Rubens 1985; see also Jeannerod and Biguer 1987). Similar though less extreme lateral biases can be induced in normal subjects, with tachistoscopic presentation in either left or right visual fields (Reuter-Lorenz, Moscovitch, and Kinsbourne 1985). Notice that an interpretation of spatial neglect as a form of pathological orienting-bias differs radically from one that posits merely the *absence* of perceptual processing resources in respect to some part of perceptual space.

Spatial Attention Beyond Sensory Feature Integration Treisman (1988, Treisman and Gelade 1980) has proposed that spatial attention is closely involved in visual feature integration, operating over separate (retinotopic) feature maps. Given that unilateral neglect affects nonsensory, imaginal space (Bisiach and Luzzatti 1978, Bisiach, Capitani, Luzzatti, and Perani 1981) and operates in terms of object-centered (and action-related?) coordinates, it seems clear that the functions of spatial attention that are disturbed in pathological neglect are independent of low-level, sensory feature integration. This conclusion leaves open whether some other function of spatial attention is involved in or necessary for sensory feature integration. The important point is that there are major functions of spatial attention, subject to dramatic disturbances in varieties of spatial neglect, which appear to be entirely separable from processes of visual feature integration.

Attentional Modulation of Neuronal Activity
Over the past decade or more, single-unit recording in monkeys engaged in spatially selective attentional tasks has revealed a consistent pattern of *spatially selective enhancement* of response, in neurons responsive to visual stimulation in the attended region. The effect has been observed in each of the principal brain areas known to be involved directly in overt (for example, oculomotor and postural) spatial orienting or in covert spatial attention, and in which lesions typically evoke symptoms of spatial inattention or neglect. This phenomenon is referred to as the spatially selective enhancement effect (SSEE). Several excellent reviews of the SSEE are available, including Bushnell, Goldberg, and Robinson 1981, Goldberg and Bruce 1985, Robinson and Peterson 1986, and Wurtz, Goldberg, and Robinson 1980.

No evidence of the SSEE has been found in visual area V1. In some systems, including superior colliculus and frontal eye fields, the SSEE appears linked to the preparation of eye movements; in others, particularly in posterior parietal cortex, the SSEE is observed whenever the animal maintains conditional readiness to respond to a given visual location, independent of the modality, or spatial direction, of the intended response. It is suggested that this spatially selective enhancement (increased gain) of visual response provides a mechanism of (spatially selective) *priority assignment* for the potential control of action, which is fundamental to the operation of spatial attention. Within these same spatiotopic coding systems there is no evidence of a complementary process of selective suppression or inhibition affecting nonselected locations. That is, spatial selectivity (in the "Where?" systems) appears to be implemented through a process of *positive priority assignment* rather than through suppression or attenuation of nonselected locations.[12]

There is, however, a very different sort of suppression effect that has been found to follow the engagement of visuospatial attention, namely, the sharply reduced responsiveness of lower-level *oculomotor* systems to visual or other sources of potential command (Fischer 1986, Goldberg, Bushnell, and Bruce 1986, Goldberg and Segraves 1987). Spatial attentional selectivity in this respect evidently acts to suppress extraneous *actions*, not to attenuate the quality of sensory input.

16.4 Toward a Computational Theory of Attention

The data summarized in the preceding section offer a rather different perspective on attentional functions than that provided by the traditional orientation (section 16.2) dominated by issues of central limited capacity and of early versus late selection. The neuropsychological and neurophysiological data point to a multiplicity of attentional functions, dependent on a multiplicity of specialized subsystems. No one of these subsystems appears uniquely "central." I have noted also evidence for a significant interdependence between the orienting of spatial attention and the preparation of action. Within systems responsible for the spatial direction of attention, moreover, there appears singularly little indication of selectivity of *encoding* or representation (limited processing capacity) but clear indication of a process of prioritization (selective enhancement). What is this priority for? These and other unresolved issues, outlined in section 16.2, suggest that our conceptualization of attentional functions—their purposes and constraints—deserves more thorough reappraisal.

Traditional proponents of late selection (as characterized in section 16.2) were faced with an obvious difficulty. If the selectivity of attention was not imposed by capacity limitations (combinatorial constraints and the like) in perceptual-semantic encoding, then *why should attention be limited—or selective—at all?* This was the basis of the a priori objection to late selection put forward by Broadbent (1971), which was quoted earlier. In some cases this question has simply not been addressed. Thus "late selection" appeared sometimes simply as a variant of the original limited-capacity hypothesis, but with the postulated capacity limitation attributed to a later, postsemantic stage of processing. This is to represent attention and attentional selectivity, however, as no more than the consequence of some ultimately arbitrary *system limitation*. ("If the brain had infinite capacity for information processing, there would be little need for attentional mechanisms.")

An alternative approach, advocated here, is to assume that attentional functions have evolved to satisfy a range of positive, biological (or "computational") purposes. Section 16.4 is therefore an attempt to outline what some of these purposes might be and to identify some of the fundamental constraints, both external and internal, that determine them. I focus initially on certain essential attentional functions involved in the perceptual (specifically here, visual) control of action. Later the discussion is widened to outline a more general theoretical framework for the functions of attention.

Attentional Selectivity as Selection-for-Action

Many authors have suggested that the selectivity of attention is in some way related to or dependent on the need for coherent control of *action* (for example, Allport 1980a,b, Keele and Neill 1978, Marcel 1980, 1983, Neill 1989, Neumann 1987, Posner 1978, Shallice 1972, 1978). How, precisely, should this relationship be defined?

Any goal-directed action requires the specification of a unique[13] set of (time-varying) parameters for its execution—parameters that determine the outcome as *this* particular action rather than any other: as this particular vocalic or manual gesture, this particular directional saccade, and so forth. Consider now what is required if these parameters are to be controlled by sensory (say, visual) information.

Suppose that visual information has to guide manual reaching, for example, to grasp a stationary object or to catch a moving one. Clearly, many different objects may be present in the visual field, yet information specific to just *one* of these objects must uniquely determine the spatiotemporal coordinates of the end-point of the reach, the orientation and opening of the hand, and so on. Information about the positions, sizes, and the like of the other objects within view and also available, must not be allowed to interfere with (that is, to produce crosstalk affecting) *these* parameters—though they may need to influence the trajectory of the reach in other ways. Consequently some *selective* process is necessary to map just those aspects of the visual array, specific to the target object, selectively onto appropriate control parameters of the action. I have termed this the functional requirement of *selection-for-action* (Allport 1987, Allport, Tipper, and Chmiel 1985; see also Neumann 1987).

A similar problem is apparent, for example, in the classic task of selectively shadowing (continuously repeating) one of two concurrent speech messages. Only one vocal output sequence is possible at a time.

The computational problem is therefore how to avoid crosstalk interference (or even fusion) in designating *one* auditory input stream to have unique control of the parameters of vocal response. The problem arises independently of any a priori limitation of central processing capacity, from the concrete requirements of coherent and univocal control of action.

The necessary control of action of course includes decisions *not* to perform a given action. The sensory input is clearly able to govern decision processes affecting action at many different levels, including decisions about what category of action and *whether* (as well as when) it is appropriate to release it. Selection among competing sources of control parameters in the sensory input is equally essential for the coherence of action preparation, or action planning, even though no overt action is in fact released or is released only at a later time— including, for example, in later so-called "perceptual reports." The attentional selectivity with which we are concerned is therefore selection for *potential* control of action.

Coordination, Segregation

It is important to recognize that perceptual selection, in the sense of selection-for-action, does not necessarily imply a binary partitioning— a dichotomizing—of information into "selected" and "unselected." Not infrequently, separate concurrently available information sources, sometimes in different spatial locations (or in different modalities), have to be selected for control of different parameters of action at the same time. This can be demonstrated, for example, when subjects are engaged in concurrent, quasi-independent perceptual-motor tasks, such as those described in section 16.2. It is also, and much more commonly, seen when two or more different categories of action are actively coordinated, each under visual control. Every goal-directed action has a range of conditions needed for its successful execution. When the conditions for two or more intended actions conflict, then one or both must be modified sufficiently to enable their continued execution. Failing that, one activity must be given priority while the other is postponed or abandoned.

Take the example of catching a ball while running, perhaps over uneven ground. In this example visual parameters of the approaching ball—time-to-contact (von Hofsten 1987)—must selectively control spatiotemporal parameters of the catching action. At the same time visible features of the terrain have to be characterized as providing suitable footings. Generally more than one potential footing or "stepping stone" is visible at a time; each one affords a different, time-varying value of the control variables needed to modulate aspects of the running action (for example, vertical thrust) so that each individual stride is targeted selectively to land on a specific stepping stone (Warren, Young, and Lee 1986). Clearly, complex coordination between these two constituent activities is needed.[14] Equally clearly, when such coordination is successful, spatially distinct, nonoverlapping sources of information must each be the focus of separate and concurrent processes of visual selection-for-action.

Another important requirement in quasi-independent, concurrent tasks is to keep the streams of information appropriately segregated so as to avoid unwanted crosstalk between them. Limitations in the performance of many concurrent task-combinations can be understood as limitations in the ability to segment and to *keep separate* different processing streams (Allport 1980a,b, 1987, Kinsbourne and Hicks 1978, Navon 1985, Neumann 1987). Some of the evidence favoring this interpretation was referred to briefly in section 16.2.

Visual-Spatial Segmentation and Selection-for-Action

The visual information source that is selected to control a particular set of action parameters may be, spatially and temporally, sharply localized, such as a ball to be caught, possibly one approaching ball among several, or it may be comparatively global, such as an optic flow field, the separation between two physical obstacles defining a passable or impassable gap, and so on (Lee and Young 1985, Warren and Whang 1987).[15] For effective visual-motor control therefore visual selection-for-action must be capable of being focused selectively on any one coherent source of visual information (potential control parameters), however that information might be spatially distributed in the visual array. Very often the appropriate source of control parameters can be characterized as a separable visual "object"—that is, an entity that can be individually named, categorized, avoided, or otherwise independently acted on. (In this sense of the word, for example, a visible "gap," passable or otherwise, can undoubtedly count as a potentially separable, visual object.) This constraint implies that (possibly very complex) processes of perceptual grouping and segmentation may have logically to *precede* the effective focusing of visual selection-for-action.

The segmentation problem is well illustrated in the case of visual selection among one of two (or more) spatially superimposed, outline or moving forms (Rock and Gutman 1981, Neisser and Becklen 1975, Allport, Tipper, and Chmiel 1985). The selective process appears to operate extremely effectively in these conditions, both in phenomenal as well as behavioral terms. It seems clear, however, that shifting or zooming of a notional "attentional spotlight," operating simply in two- or three-dimensional spatial coordinates (Posner 1980, Downing and Pinker 1985, Johnston and Dark 1986), would not be theoretically adequate to account for this kind of visual object-selection.

Many factors are known to influence perceptual segmentation. It is therefore to be expected that these factors will interact very powerfully with the efficiency of attentional selection (Driver and Baylis 1989, Duncan 1984, Kahneman and Henik 1981, Kahneman and Treisman 1984,

Prinzmetal 1981, Treisman 1988). Evidence from the pathology of spatial attention (section 16.3) suggests that perceptual segmentation, guided top down by object-specific (for example, lexical) knowledge, occurs independently of—that is, logically prior to—the impaired attentional process (see, for example, Sieroff, Pollatsek, and Posner 1987).

A Conceptual Framework for Functions of Attention

So far in this discussion I have concentrated on the logic of attentional selectivity in the visual control of action, independently of any possible a priori limitations of processing capacity. Processes of selection-for-action are needed furthermore whether the intended source of control parameters is visual or auditory, internal or external, perceptual or imaginal—that is, wherever alternative, potentially competing information sources are available for the same control variables.

It may be useful at this stage, however, to widen the context of discussion to consider briefly the outlines of a more general *computational theory* of attention, within which these functions of selection-for-action are largely instrumental. We therefore return once more to the foundational questions with which we began: *What is the overall purpose (or what are the overall purposes) of attentional systems, and what are their determining and enabling constraints?*

Multiple Constraints   The following basic ecological constraints impose a number of strong requirements on any attentional motivational system.[16]

· *Unpredictability and time constraint*   First, we are concerned with systems that have to operate in an environment that is, at best, only partly or incompletely predictable. Furthermore it is an environment that can change at any moment extremely rapidly, in ways that may be of critical importance for the organism. If appropriate action is not taken at once, there may be no second chance.

· *Multiple goals*   Second, we are concerned with systems with a very wide range of potential *goals* of action. Priority (importance, urgency) regarding the implementation of different goals must be continuously adjusted, moment by moment, as potential threats or opportunities arise in the environment and as internal conditions (blood-sugar, bladder-pressure, and so on) as well as cognitive variables (plans and subplans, "insights," and so on) change or develop. *Priority assignment* is necessary in that implementation (or protection) of one goal is frequently incompatible with the simultaneous implementation or protection of other concurrently valid goals and may also prejudice the subsequent satisfaction of these other competing goals.

· *Multi-functional systems*   Third, we are concerned with multi-functional organisms (humans and other species, natural or artificial). By this is meant organisms (or robots) whose subcomponents (sense organs, effectors, cognitive subsystems) are not in general uniquely dedicated to particular goals or to particular categories of action. Subcomponents must therefore be selectively engaged and coordinated to implement particular activities and particular goals.

Behavioral Coherence   The primary *purpose* of an attentional system must be to ensure the *coherence* of behavior under these often conflicting constraints. Coherent, goal-directed behavior requires processes of selective *priority assignment* and *coordination* at many different levels (motivational, cognitive, motor, sensory). Together this set of selective and coordinative processes can be said to make up the effective *attentional engagement* (or attentional *set*) of an organism at any moment.[17]

Processes responsible for establishing and maintaining coherent, attentional engagement must involve a number of (logically) separable elements, of which the following represents a minimal, abstractly specified, and certainly incomplete listing:

· selective priority assignment among competing (and cooperating) goals, in a complex, time-varying goal hierarchy, for control of immediate action;
· the engagement and coordination of specific cognitive subsystems to implement current goals;
· selective recruitment (preparation, tuning) of appropriate effectors;
· selective priority assignment among competing available information sources (including *sensory* information sources), for control of specific parameters of action (selection-for-action);
· selective recruitment (preparation, tuning) of appropriate mappings or transformations between different coding domains (see, for example, Hinton 1981).

Maintenance and Shifting of Attentional Engagement   Many—indeed all—perceptually guided activities need time for their completion, that is, for their end-goal to be achieved. The appropriate attentional engagement (or set) has therefore to be *maintained*, or protected in some way during the course of that activity. On the other hand given the unpredictable (that is, incompletely predictable) and potentially dangerous environment that we have taken as one of our fundamental constraints, it is of course vital that such attentional engagement can be diverted or overridden by changing external—or internal—events.

The critical problem for any attentional system (in multifunctional organisms) is therefore how to satisfy two conflicting requirements: the need for continuity of attentional engagement, against the need for its interruptibility. Failure to shift attentional engagement when faced by environmental threats (or opportunities) can of course be fatal to an organism's survival or physical integrity. At the other extreme constant shifting or fragmentation of attentional engagement, triggered by every sensory event of environmental affordance, would make sustained, purposeful activity impossible and result only in behavioral chaos. Between these two equally disastrous extremes lies a range of more or less viable solutions. All of them depend on some means of evaluating, or at least estimating, the relative motivational importance and temporal urgency of the potential threats and affordances *outside* the current attentional engagement, relative to the estimated importance and urgency of the *current* activity or activities. (Both variables—urgency and long-term importance—are needed and should presumably be able to trade off against one another.)

Humans (and other species) appear to have adopted a combination of several different partial solutions to this problem, which can be broadly grouped into three categories: (1) internally generated, *predictive* control of attention shifting, depending on a range of heuristic processes of widely varying levels of sophistication: (2) *externally* elicited shifts of attentional engagement, cued by the detection of more or less complex triggering conditions; and (3) active combinations of (1) and (2), as, for example, in many forms of exploration and search. I should therefore add, as a further indispensable attentional function, continuous (parallel) monitoring of the environment (internal as well as external) for changes relevant to current and long-term goals.

Environmental monitoring may be expected to operate at many different levels. These should include *fast*, relatively crude or approximate systems, operating on rule-of-thumb (that is, associative) criteria, both learned and unlearned, as well as possibly slower and more sophisticated systems, supported also by processes of (discontinuous) predictive search under goal-directed control. Detection of a critical external or internal event must be capable of causing temporary interruption or inhibition of the current attentional engagement and a (rapid) shift of sensory priority assignment (selection-for-action) toward the information source responsible for the interruption—in other words it must be capable of triggering attentional *orienting*. Equally important, sensory-motor orienting must be capable of being inhibited by the competing, higher priority of the current attentional engagement.

Computation of this critical balance of priorities appears to be one of the central problems for any system of intelligent attentional control.

Implications: Multiple Interacting Functions of Attention   One thing that becomes clear—if it were not so already—is that there are many different functions of attention. A theory adequate to some specifiable attentional function or functions may well be quite unsuited to explaining others. Certainly to pursue a general "theory of attention", without first specifying the computational functions that the theory is to account for, would appear to be a likely recipe for disaster. Equally clearly to try to survey the entire range of cognitive operations that can reasonably be described as "attentional"—even if the writer were competent to do so—would be altogether beyond the scope of a single review chapter.

I now return to the mechanisms of visual-spatial selection-for-action. What the preceding discussion also makes clear is that the processes of visual-spatial selection-for-action are instrumental to a number of different, and in principle *competing*, attentional functions or purposes: (1) to implement (and to protect the coherence of) the current attentional engagement; (2) to enable endogenously controlled shifts of perceptual-motor engagement, directed by a variety of different cognitive ("intentional," heuristic) processes; and (3) to enable exogenously elicited, visual-spatial orienting, in particular orienting cued by (spatially compatible) visual events. These different types of control appear to be mediated by a number of functionally (and anatomically) separable—but also in part functionally overlapping—subsystems (Posner et al. 1987, Posner 1988).

Implementation Principles: Parallel Distributed Processing

There is one further source of constraint that may radically affect attentional processes in living organisms. This is that all cognitive processes have to be realized by means of massively parallel computations, in distributed neuronal networks (chapters 4 and 8, Feldman and Ballard 1982). We know very little at present about the possible restrictions, if any, that this imposes on attentional or other cognitive functions (Sejnowski 1986). One possible restriction, however, arises from the so-called binding problem: the problem of representing *what goes with what*—that is, of integrating or linking together appropriate subsets of microfeatures, belonging to one information source or one processing stream, without also creating inappropriate or "illusory" conjunctions among the same and other sets of microfeatures (see, for example, Hinton and Lang 1985, Hinton, McClelland, and Rumelhart 1986, Sejnowski 1986, von der Malsburg 1981, 1985). Put another way, it is the problem of structuring information processing in parallel networks, so as to segregate different subprocesses running concurrently and to avoid unwanted crosstalk between them. Some examples of possible attentional constraints, arising from the problem of restricting crosstalk between concurrent processes, were discussed in section 16.2.

A general theoretical framework for attentional control (attentional engagement) within a parallel interactive system was first outlined by Norman and Shallice (1980). Models of attentional engagement in massively parallel systems have been further developed, for example, by Phaf (1986), and Schneider and Detweiler (1987). In these models as in models of parallel interactive systems for more specialized domains (for example, Mozer 1988), executive control is exercised only *indirectly*, typically through a mechanism of competitive priority assignment. This idea—of indirect *priority assignment*, implemented through the selective modulation (potentiation, tuning, output inhibition, and so on) of units in specific coding pathways—is a recurrent feature of many different theoretical approaches to attention. Neurophysiological evidence of such a process, in the spatial domain, was reviewed in section 16.3. Several students of attention, notably Posner and his associates (Neely 1977, Posner and Snyder 1975; see also Johnston and Dark 1986 and Neill 1989 for recent reviews) have proposed that attentional modulation and the many different phenomena of *priming* in general share common underlying mechanisms.

16.5 Review

Experimental Paradigms of Selective Visual Response
In this chapter I have contrasted two different conceptions of attention and attentional selectivity. The first of these depends on the idea of *limited capacity,* in various forms, as the causal origin of attentional phenomena. The second, contrasting set of assumptions focuses on the necessity of attentional engagement—in particular, in many perceptual-motor activities, the need for what I have called *selection-for-action*—as a condition of behavioral coherence in multifunctional organisms. According to this viewpoint, many phenomena of selective attention in perceptual-motor tasks can be seen to reflect competing processes concerned respectively with the *maintenance* and *shifting* of visual-spatial selection-for-action.

In this concluding section it may be worthwhile therefore to look briefly at some familiar experimental paradigms, the results of which have been taken to support assumptions of limited capacity (and of precategorical, selective processing) and to outline some alternative interpretations. I reviewed in section 16.2 a variety of phenomena of concurrent (dual-task) performance, and Strooplike interference effects in selective response tasks, accounts of which appeared not to require (and were not well suited to) a causal variable of limited capacity.

Probe Reaction Times Reaction time to a secondary probe stimulus (probe RT) has often been presented as a method of assessing the momentary processing capacity demanded by a concurrent primary task. (See, for example, Posner 1978 and Poulton 1981 for reviews.) A well-known difficulty for this general interpretation is that the resulting estimates of capacity demand for the same primary task can vary dramatically, depending on the characteristics of the particular probe task that is used (for example, McLeod 1977, 1978, McLeod and Posner 1984). Equally troublesome, probe RT can also fail to reflect other independent measures of information load in the primary task (Logan 1978b). A different interpretation, following the theoretical orientation suggested here (that is, without appeal to ideas of limited processing capacity), is to think of variations in the latency of response to a probe stimulus in terms of the time costs of attentional *dis*engagement from the primary task and of reorienting of selection-for-action toward the probe (compare LaBerge 1973, Posner 1980, 1988). Where both the primary and the probe tasks share the same response modality or involve a crossover of coding domains (see "Variations on the Idea of Limited Capacity" in section 16.2; see also McLeod and Posner 1984, Virzi and Egeth 1985), they are liable to potential crosstalk in the triggering of speeded responses. In this case the integrity of the primary task will need to be protected by a high level of selective attentional engagement in favor of the primary task, and orienting to the probe stimulus will be correspondingly inhibited. Selection-for-action should presumably be most strongly protected around or preceding the moment of speeded response decision in the primary task: disengagement from the primary task will therefore be particularly delayed during this phase (Posner and Boies 1971, Logan 1978b, McLeod and Posner 1984). In contrast when the combination of primary and probe tasks is such that the risk of crosstalk between them is small, there should not be the same need to protect engagement on the primary task; the S-R mappings for *both* tasks can be maintained in a state of preparedness, concurrently,[18] and the time costs of orienting to the probe stimulus will therefore be minimal, even during the response phase of the primary task (McLeod 1977, McLeod and Posner 1984).

A broadly similar account can be offered in relation to the time costs of self-paced task alternation. Jersild (1927) and Spector and Biederman (1976) found that the time needed to shift between different tasks could vary from *zero* time costs to well over a second in some cases, depending on the extent to which the executive stimuli uniquely indicated the cognitive operations to be performed.

Overlapping Tasks   The systematic delay of response to the second of two executive stimuli (S1 and S2), in the closely related "overlapping tasks" or PRP paradigm (Bertelson 1966, Smith 1967, Kantowitz 1974, Pashler and Johnston 1989), may be interpretable similarly in terms of the time cost of attentional disengagement, orienting, and subsequent reengagement on S2. Evidence that the systematic increase in latency of response to S2 (in the absence of delay in response to S1), represents a genuine *postponement* of R2 "response selection," rather than a process of continuous "capacity sharing" (Pashler 1984, Pashler and Johnston 1989) would appear to be consistent with this interpretation.[19] The elimination of this characteristic pattern of R2 delay, when both tasks are individually highly compatible (Greenwald and Shulman 1973), but otherwise dissimilar from one another (Brebner 1977) is of course strongly congenial to this account.

Delay in responding to S1, which is sometimes observed, may be related to specific patterns of interference between the programming and execution of different movements, including with different hands (for example, Heuer 1985b, 1986, 1987, Heuer and Wing 1984). Heuer's data and his model of "programming-interactions" have a bearing also on the results reported by Brebner (1977).

Priming, Categorical Encoding and Selective Response   In studies of selective response and selective monitoring tasks, certain stimuli (or stimulus attributes) in a visual array are designated by the experimenter as relevant to control a speeded response (*targets*) and others as irrelevant and to-be-ignored (*distractors*). In these paradigms there is extensive evidence that many other dimensions of relevance to the subject's current goals and interests (that is, relevant to "currently active schemata"), in addition to the experimenter's instructions, affect the efficiency of selection-for-action. Interference (omission or slowing of response) caused by the distractors can be greatly increased or decreased, depending on whether distractors or targets are "primed." Johnston and Dark (1986) summarized a range of such results in two empirical generalizations: (1) "All levels of stimulus analysis can be primed for particular stimuli," and (2) "Stimuli conforming to active schemata are easy to attend to, but difficult to ignore." (Or more generally, "Selective attention can be guided by active schemata.")

The results of many different categorization or visual-search experiments with categorically defined targets have been interpreted as showing parallel encoding in terms of semantic category membership (see, for example, Duncan 1980, 1988, Egeth, Jonides, and Wall 1972, Egeth, Folk and Mullin 1989, Fisk and Schneider 1983, Hoffmann 1987, Lambert et al. 1988, Schneider and Shiffrin 1977). With appropriate precueing (consistent mapping), selective report performance can also be based effectively on alphanumeric category (Merikle 1980, Duncan 1983, Bundesen et al. 1984) and on semantic word category (for example, "any animal": Allport 1977). The plausible claim that both sets of results in detection or categorization and in selective report tasks depend on selective priming of the specified target category (Johnston and Dark 1986, Kahneman and Treisman 1984) does not appear to conflict in any way with the assumption that multiple symbolic stimuli can be categorized semantically, in parallel, in respect of the primed category.

Hoffmann (1987) has recently reviewed a number of experimental demonstrations, using arrays of multiple pictured objects, indicating semantic modulation of priority assignment for the selective control of *action*, but based on nonselective semantic encoding. Evidence indicating not only parallel categorization but full symbolic *identification*, in parallel, has been presented by Pashler and Badgio (1985, 1988). Their evidence is based on a task designed to force exhaustive identification, namely, that of naming the highest digit in an array of digits. A variety of experimental manipulations yielded results that argue strongly for the parallel identification of multiple alphanumeric symbols. It is not easy to see how these results are to be reconciled with the hypothesis that conjunctions of alphanumeric features (as in Ps, Rs, and Qs) can be correctly perceived only through serial focusing of attention on each item in turn (Treisman 1988).

When selective report is cued by an extrinsic *spatial* cue on the other hand, selective priority assignment—selective cueing—may operate directly on the spatiotopic visual domain (early selection). As van der Heijden (1987) has pointed out in a review of spatially cued, partial report tasks, evidence to this effect is perfectly consistent with evidence favoring "unlimited capacity" regarding stimulus identification, at least so far as alphanumeric symbols are concerned and within the limitations of visual acuity.

Spatial Selection and Interference   It is often claimed that the amount of interference caused by task-relevant (or semantically related) distractors varies inversely with the spatial separation of target and distractors in the visual array, and this observation has been taken to support the metaphor of a spatial "spotlight" of visual attention (for example, Broadbent 1982, Johnston and Dark 1986). The experiments most often cited in support of this empirical generalization, however, have confounded spatial separation with retinal eccentricity (see, for example, Eriksen and Eriksen 1974, Eriksen and Schultz 1979, Gatti and Egeth 1978). When Hagenaar and van der Heijden (1986) endeavoured to unconfound these two variables, in a spatially separated version of the Stroop color-word task, they found no reliable effect of spatial separation. A related experiment by Eriksen and St. James (1986), however, appears to show such an effect. The issue deserves further investigation.

Other (Gestalt) factors of organization and perceptual grouping, in addition to spatial separation, are known to influence visual selection (Duncan 1984, Kahneman and Henik 1981, Prinzmetal 1981). Driver and Baylis (1989) contrasted a factor of perceptual grouping ("common fate") and spatial proximity directly in a paradigm modeled in other respects on Eriksen and Eriksen (1974). In three experiments they confirmed that, when these variables were directly opposed, perceptual grouping of target and distractors had considerably more influence than their spatial separation. "Far" distractors which were nevertheless perceptually grouped with the target produced more interference than did spatially "near" distractors—a result that runs directly counter to the spotlight hypothesis, in the form in which it is generally proposed, which predicts that visual attention can only be assigned to contiguous regions of the visual array *as a whole*. More sophisticated versions of the hypothesis are needed to accommodate these results. Data reported recently by Lambert (1987) and by Lambert and Hockey (1989) suggest the need for, if anything, more extensive modifications of the original spotlight metaphor.

Spatial Attention and Selective Semantic Processing: The Evidence of Negative Priming   Proponents of early selection maintain that the semantic or categorical processing of symbolic distractors can be strongly modulated, or prevented altogether, through the spatial focusing of attention (Johnston and Dark 1986).[20] This belief evidently rests on experimental demonstrations that the interference caused by semantically related distractors can be reduced or even eliminated when attention is directed away from the distractors. As discussed in relation to the controversy over early versus late selection (section 16.2), however, the absence of semantically based interference does not guarantee in itself the absence of semantic processing; it may indicate only that task-relevant and irrelevant information has been effectively segregated regarding the control of overt action.

The phenomenon of *negative priming*, which has received considerable experimental attention in recent years (Allport, Tipper, and Chmiel 1985, Lowe 1979, 1985, Neill 1977, Neill and Westberry 1987, Tipper 1985, Tipper and Driver 1988, Tipper, MacQueen, and Brehaut 1988), has important bearing on this issue. In the basic experimental paradigm a stimulus appearing as the target for a current selective response is related to—or is categorically identical to—the *distractor* stimulus of the preceding trial. The effect, observed in many different variations of this basic paradigm, appears as an increase in the latency of response to the current selective target, compared with a neutral condition in which previous distractors and current targets are unrelated. That is to say, it is more difficult to select a stimulus, belonging to a given category, for the control of action, if that same category of object was actively ignored on the preceding trial. This categorical, negative priming effect transfers, for example, from a pictured object as distractor on trial n to a written word as target on trial $n + 1$ (Tipper and Driver, 1988), and from a color name as distractor to selective response to a subsequent ink-color (Neill, 1977, Neill and Westberry 1987, Lowe 1979). It also shows transfer between semantically related stimulus categories (Tipper 1985, Allport et al. 1985, Tipper and Driver 1988) and from one response modality to another (for example, from vocal to manual; Tipper et al. 1988). There is some evidence also, from studies of individual differences, that the negative priming effect is strongest in subjects who are "efficient selectors," that is, in those subjects who show typically the smallest interference from simultaneous distractors (Tipper and Baylis 1987, Beech and Claridge 1987, Tipper et al. 1989). As already noted, however, the fact that distractor interference can be reduced or even eliminated in efficient selection-for-action provides at best an insecure basis for inferring that the distractors did not reach semantic levels of encoding. To the contrary the occurrence of the negative priming effect, specific to the conceptual or "categorical" identity of the successfully ignored distractor, provides direct evidence that they did reach semantic levels of encoding.

This argument can be sharpened as follows. Francolini and Egeth (1980) reported an elegant experimental demonstration, often cited in the controversy between so-called early and late selection. Subjects were presented with a circular array of up to six red and black letters or numerals. The subjects' task was to count the number of red items and to ignore the black ones. Vocal RT was measured. When the red items consisted of (Strooplike) numerals whose numerical value conflicted with the actual number of red items to be reported, mean RT was delayed. In contrast when the to-be-ignored, *black* items formed conflicting numerals, there was no interference: RT was unaffected. Francolini and Egeth argued, on the basis of these results, that the symbolic value of the black distractor numerals had simply not been encoded. How secure is this inference? To pursue this question, Driver (1989) repeated Francolini and Egeth's experiments. In doing so, however, he also manipulated the relationship between the to-be-ignored (but conflicting) numeral values on trial n and the number of red target items to be counted on trial $n + 1$, to look for effects of possible negative priming. The results showed significant negative priming not only from the irrelevant number value of the red target items but also, and of equivalent magnitude, from the successfully ignored *black* distractors, although these had caused no detectable interference on the preceding trial.

Since the negative priming effect is specific to the symbolic identity of the distractors on the preceding trial, the results provide direct evidence of categorical identity coding of these distractors. The inference from *no interference* to *no semantic processing* thus appears to be empirically incorrect.

The mechanism of negative priming is still unknown. The simplest suggestion would appear to be that interpretative codes activated by the to-be-ignored stimuli are themselves subject to a direct inhibitory process—that is, their activation is suppressed (Neill, 1979). Other evidence, however, argues against this hypothesis. In particular, when the coding of to-be-ignored distractors is probed not by a subsequent compound stimulus, requiring another *selective* process for control of the response, but by a "simplex" probe stimulus, not requiring selection between task-relevant and irrelevant attributes, the priming effect of a previous distractor reverses to become *facilitatory* (Lowe 1979, Allport et al. 1985). This result appears difficult to reconcile with any simple account of direct suppression or inhibition of activated memory codes. Tipper (1985, Tipper et al. 1988) has proposed instead an inhibitory process that selectively *isolates* active codes, representing the ignored distractors, *from the control of action*. He has suggested that when selection is not required for the simplex probe, this inhibitory process may be released. Priming by ignored distractors thus represents a combination of facilitatory and inhibitory effects. Further clarification of the mechanism (or mechanisms) of negative priming may be expected to add considerably to our understanding of the implementation of visual selection-for-action.

It will be clear that many questions remain to be answered regarding the categorical encoding of successfully "ignored" distractors. The evidence reviewed here certainly cannot be taken as showing that the spatial direction of visual attention (selection-for-action) has no effect on the representation of categorical or symbolic aspects of the to-be-ignored stimuli. What it does, however, is to alter, perhaps radically, the terms in which questions of this kind may be approached. In particular we need to distinguish very carefully between questions of encoding and categorization, and questions of access to the control of action.

Other Issues

The experimental paradigms discussed here are relevant to issues of attentional selectivity in the visual control of immediate action or immediate response. There are of course many other important issues regarding attention, including, for example, the understanding of a great range of executive functions. (In section 16.3 I noted briefly neuropsychological evidence of functional specialization among several different components of executive attentional control.) Different issues, however, involve different experimental paradigms. Different theoretical issues furthermore should be kept carefully distinct and not confused together in favor of a pretheoretical assumption that there is some unitary process, or function, or capacity called "attention."

Many experimental paradigms in cognitive science, for example, appear relevant to questions of selective *memory encoding* of visual information (chapter 17). It may be that visual selection-for-action is a necessary—though certainly not a sufficient—condition for the encoding of visual information into a recoverable engram. Questions of the necessary and sufficient conditions for effective visual memory encoding (visual "selection-for-memory"?), however, go far beyond the scope of this chapter. For the present we can simply note that these are indeed separable questions which must now be set aside.

The same applies to many other issues that are sometimes described in terms of limited capacity, such as, for example, the time costs, or other constraints of visual-imagery generation (Kosslyn, Cave, Provost, and Gierke 1988, Brooks 1968) or maintenance (Phillips 1982) or the generation of random numbers (Baddeley 1966, Wagenaar 1970). We should also perhaps ask ourselves in each case whether the limited capacity that is at issue is simply a redescription of the behavioral phenomenon to be explained, or whether it is intended in some way as an explanation.

Concluding Remarks

In the study of attention, as in other areas of cognitive science, research is shaped by a range of pretheoretical assumptions, implicit or explicit, as to what the subject at issue is about, hence how that area in general is conceptualized and what are the principal empirical questions to be addressed. Thus according to many theorists, and perhaps widely also in ordinary usage, attention has been conceptualized as some unspecified but essentially limited mental energy or resource or capacity. What this resource supposedly enables is *processing*. Or rather, it enables certain sorts of processing ("*further* processing"). *Other* sorts of processing do not need attention.[21]

Unfortunately there is little if any agreement about how these crucially different sorts of processing should be distinguished, nor about how the mysterious, limited resource or capacity (or capacities) is (or are) to be defined; nor yet how exactly—or even approximately—it (or they) is (or are) effectively limited. Yet despite this unhappy state of conceptual disarray, there is a temptation to cling to the underlying intuition, to the effect that attention denotes essentially a limitation (a shortage, a deficiency) or *something*. After all isn't it obvious that attention is intrinsically *limited* (that is, *selective*)? How else could attention be conceptualized?

From these very general initial intuitions it appears to follow that the central empirical questions about attention are questions about the *selectivity of processing*. If we could only establish experimentally where and when processing becomes selective, we might then come to understand the nature of the mysterious capacity limitations that made such selectivity of processing necessary in the first place.

Or have we got the whole issue upside down? These empirical questions about selective processing have proven in practice extraordinarily difficult to resolve. So much so that after thirty years of vigorous but inconclusive experimentation, we may reasonably question the heuristic value of the pretheoretical intuitions that motivated them to begin with.

Much of the experimental research directed at questions of selective visual *processing* (and essentially all of the research reviewed in this chapter) has been concerned in effect with the selective, visual *control of action*. For multifunctional organisms, even for organisms enjoying in principle unlimited perceptual processing capacity, a form of selectivity that is unavoidable is selectivity of perceptual-motor control (selection-for-action). This form of selectivity (which can be studied directly by behavioral methods) should be carefully distinguished from selectivity of "processing", a concept that appears, in general, ill-defined and extraordinarily difficult to operationalize unequivocally in behavioral terms.

Within the domain of perceptual-motor performance (with which this chapter is concerned), it may be a more fruitful heuristic to focus research on a different set of questions regarding the functions of visual attention. These questions are not about processing limitations, or "bottlenecks," but about the mechanisms of attentional *control*: questions about the—multiform—computational mechanisms by which attentional engagement is established, coordinated, maintained, interrupted, and redirected, both in spatial and nonspatial terms, in the preparation and control of action. These, I suggest, are the primary questions for research on visual attention. Already in a number of areas such research is well under way. Its development represents a sufficiently challenging agenda for a future interdisciplinary cognitive science of visual attention.

Notes

1. Theories of selective attention have often considered selectivity in the visual and auditory modalities, and indeed in other senses, as fundamentally equivalent. Neumann, van der Heijden, and Allport (1986) have presented the case for carefully separating theoretical issues (and data) on selective processes within each of these different senses, at the present stage of theoretical development.

2. ". . . our general orientation, that selection takes place in order to protect a mechanism of limited capacity, the P system (serial processing system, or categorizing mechanism)" (Broadbent 1971, p. 178). "The limited capacity system . . . is now thought of as producing *one* of a set of category states" (Broadbent 1971, p. 17). "The occurrence of a category state . . . corresponds to the firing of one of Treisman's dictionary units" (Broadbent 1971, p. 150).

3. Thus "the selection of one ear shuts out most of the information on the other" (Broadbent 1971, p. 140).

4. This identification has been a long-standing feature of Posner's thinking: "The key to understanding the nature of conscious attention is its limited capacity" (Posner 1978, p. 153).

5. "The principal theoretical issue confronting attention research today concerns whether selection is 'early' or 'late' . . ." (Hoffman 1986, p. 221).

6. This distinction was first clearly pointed out, to my knowledge, by van der Heijden (1981). See also Duncan 1985. Toward the end of their review of early versus late selection, Kahneman and Treisman (1984, p. 55) put forward (in small print) a logically similar alternative. If adopted, however, it would appear substantially to undermine their previous arguments for the "nonautomaticity" of categorical encoding, based on the presence or absence (or at least the reduction) of RT interference from semantically relevant distractors, depending on the spatial direction of attention. See section 16.5 for further experimental evidence related to this issue.

7. Pattee (1972, 1977) has developed the distinction between (symbolic, discrete) *indication* and (dynamical, continuous) *specification*, in the control of complex systems. (See Kelso and Kay 1987 for further discussion.) Systems specialized for the analysis of acoustic speech enable uniquely direct or "compatible" access to and specification for the control of vocal articulation (Monsell 1987, Porter 1987). Latency of vocal repetition of an auditory syllable can be as little as 100 ms (Porter and Lubker 1980). In a similar way orthographic input provides an optimally compatible specification for written (typed) output (Greenwald 1972, Ellis 1982).

8. Stroop (1935) first showed that naming a color is delayed by the presence of an irrelevant written color-word.

9. Eriksen and Eriksen (1974) and Shaffer and LaBerge (1979) offer well-known examples of selective interference when both wanted and unwanted stimuli occur in the *same* representational domain, providing in principle equally compatible but conflicting information to control the designated response. See also Hoffmann 1987 and van der Heijden 1981. Virzi and Egeth's (1985) account of Strooplike interference effects, though germane in several respects, would appear to have difficulty with these results. For previous related discussions see Allport 1980a, pp. 135–141, and McLeod and Posner 1984, p. 65.

10. The immediate antecedents of this idea can be traced from Moray 1967 through Kahneman's (1973) notion of nonstructural "processing effort" to Norman and Bobrow's (1975) heroic attempt to provide that idea with a systematic, operational basis. Unfortunately the latter was bought at the expense of confounding, once again, possible limitations of control (processing effort?) and of message capacity ("communication channels", and the like). See Allport 1980b for further commentary.

11. Data presenting various difficulties for Treisman's model have been reported recently, for example, by Allport et al. (1985), Duncan (1988), Duncan and Humphreys (1989), Egeth, Folk, and Mullin (1989), Houck and Hoffman (1986), McLeod, Driver, and Crisp (1988), Pashler (1987), Pashler and Badgio (1988).

12. Other patterns of attentional modulation have been observed in predominantly categorical or identity-coding ("What?") systems, for example in inferotemporal cortex (Desimone and Moran 1987, Moran and Desimone 1985, Richmond, Wurtz, and Sato 1983, Spitzer and Richmond 1987). The interrelations between attentional effects in spatiotopic and identity-coding systems have yet to be studied.

13. The occurrence of fusion or "blend" errors, at many different levels of action control, in these (and other) categories of action (Becker and Jürgens 1979, Stemberger 1985), is evidence that the control parameters may emerge as the resultant of (or as abrupt transitions between) simultaneous, conflicting specifications, but this in no way removes the logical requirement of time-varying uniqueness, if the action is to occur at all.

14. Including coordination with respect to the competing demands for high-resolution vision. As is easily demonstrated, however, foveation of individual stepping stones is not necessary for accurate control of locomotion.

15. Foveation of the selected object in vision is neither necessary nor sufficient for the purpose of selective visual-motor control, though it may considerably enhance its accuracy (see, for example, Biguer, Jeannerod, and Prablanc 1985).

16. Processes responsible for establishing a time-varying goal hierarchy—especially regarding primary "biological" goals—constitute the traditional subject-area of Motivation rather than Attention. The moment-by-moment behavioral *implementation* of goals on the other hand, in particular the multiplicity of instrumental or secondary goals involved in everyday human activity and the selective and coordinative processes needed for their implementation, appears recognizably as a problem of attention. What is important to recognize, however, is not the location of some imaginary boundary between the provinces of attention and motivation but, to the contrary, their essential interdependence. The phenomena and the functions of attention cannot be properly understood unless they are seen in terms of the more general purposes and constraints of behavioral priority assignment in multifunctional organisms.

17. Everyday "slips of action" illustrate, in their remarkable diversity and complexity,

some of the many ways in which attentional engagement can be (temporarily) disturbed (Norman 1981, Reason 1978).

18. S-R preparation for a simple probe RT task can be sufficient on its own to reduce the efficiency of attentional engagement on a primary task (see, for example, Gottsdanker 1980). Appeal to a limited capacity for S-R preparation, however, would appear to be little more than a relabeling of the phenomenon to be explained, rather than an adequate explanation.

19. This interpretation is clearly not to be confused with one of the traditional variants of late selection in which an unexplained processing bottleneck is attributed to a discrete response-selection stage.

20. Thus "Activation of the meaning of an item may . . . be restricted to just those items that are deemed relevant" (Francolini and Egeth 1980). "The involuntary reading of a distant color-word can be prevented by focusing attention on the relevant visual object" (Kahneman and Chajczyk 1983). "Interference from a familiar word seems to occur only if you are looking at it . . . or doing something that is likely to prime that particular word. The process is clearly very much under strategic control and can be stopped . . ." (Broadbent 1982). "Stimuli outside the spatial focus of attention undergo little or no semantic processing" (Johnston and Dark 1986).

21. Different proponents of this idea refer equally vaguely to "central processing", sometimes (pleasantly tautological) to "limited-capacity processing"; more confusedly to "conscious processing." Compare also Johnson-Laird's (1983, 1988) conception of a central "operating system" and other related suggestions of separable subsystems responsible for consciousness. (See Allport 1988 for further critical commentary.)

References

Allport, D. A. 1977. On knowing the meaning of words we are unable to report: The effects of visual masking. In S. Dornic, ed. *Attention and Performance VI*. Hillsdale, NJ: Erlbaum.

Allport, D. A. 1980a. Patterns and actions: Cognitive mechanisms are content-specific. In G. Claxton, ed. *Cognitive Psychology: New Directions*. London: Routledge and Kegan Paul.

Allport, D. A. 1980b. Attention and performance. In G. Claxton, ed. *Cognitive Psychology: New Directions*. London: Routledge and Kegan Paul.

Allport, A. 1987. Selection-for-action: Some behavioral and neurophysiological considerations of attention and action. In H. Heuer and A. F. Sanders, eds. *Perspectives on Perception and Action*. Hillsdale, NJ: Erlbaum.

Allport, A. 1988. What concept of consciousness? In A. J. Marcel and E. Bisiach, eds. *Consciousness in Contemporary Science*. Oxford: Oxford University Press.

Allport, D. A., Antonis, B., and Reynolds, P. 1972. On the division of attention: A disproof of the single channel hypothesis. *Quarterly Journal of Experimental Psychology* 24:225–235.

Allport, A., Tipper, S. P., and Chmiel, N. 1985. Perceptual integration and post-categorical filtering. In M. I. Posner and O. S. M. Marin, eds. *Attention and Performance XI*. Hillsdale, NJ: Erlbaum.

Allport, A., MacKay, D. G., Prinz, W., and Scheerer, E. 1987. *Language Perception and Production: Relations between Listening, Speaking, Reading and Writing*. London: Academic Press.

Arbib, M. A. 1987. Modularity and interaction of brain regions underlying visual-motor co-ordination. In J. L. Garfield, ed. *Modularity in Knowledge Representation and Natural Language Understanding*. Cambridge, MA: MIT Press.

Baddeley, A. D. 1966. The capacity for generating information by randomization. *Quarterly Journal of Experimental Psychology* 18:119–129.

Barlow, H. B. 1986. Why have multiple cortical areas? *Vision Research* 26:81–90.

Becker, W., and Jürgens, R. 1979. An analysis of the saccadic system by means of double step stimuli. *Vision Research* 19:967–983.

Beech, A., and Claridge, G. 1987. Individual differences in negative priming: relations with schizotypal personality traits. *British Journal of Psychology* 78:349–356.

Beller, H. K. 1975. Naming, reading and executing instructions. *Journal of Experimental Psychology: Human Perception and Performance* 1:154–160.

Bergen, J. R., and Julesz, B. 1983. Parallel versus serial processing in rapid pattern discrimination. *Nature* (London) 303:696–698.

Bertelson, P. 1966. Central intermittency twenty years later. *Quarterly Journal of Experimental Psychology* 18:153–163.

Biguer, B., Jeannerod, M., and Prablanc, C. 1985. The role of position of gaze in movement accuracy. In M. I. Posner and O. S. M. Marin, eds. *Attention and Performance XI*. Hillsdale, NJ: Erlbaum.

Bisiach, E., Capitani, E., and Porta, E. 1985. Two basic properties of space representation in the brain. *Journal of Neurology, Neurosurgery and Psychiatry* 48:141–144.

Bisiach, E., Capitani, E., Luzzatti, C., and Perani, D. 1981. Brain and conscious representation of outside reality. *Neuropsychologia* 19:543–551.

Bisiach, E., and Luzzatti, C. 1978. Unilateral neglect of representational space. *Cortex* 14:129–133.

Bisiach, E., Meregalli, S., and Berti, A. 1985. Mechanisms of production-control and belief-fixation in human visuospatial processing: Clinical evidence from hemispatial neglect. Eighth Symposium on Quantitative Analyses of Behavior, Harvard University, Cambridge, MA.

Bisiach, E., Perani, D., Vallar, G., and Berti, A. 1986. Unilateral neglect: Personal and extra-personal. *Neuropsychologia* 24:759–767.

Brebner, J. 1977. The search for exceptions to the psychological refractory period. In S. Dornic, ed. *Attention and Performance VI*. Hillsdale, NJ: Erlbaum.

Broadbent, D. E. 1958. *Perception and Communication*. London: Pergamon.

Broadbent, D. E. 1970. Stimulus set and response set: Two kinds of selective attention. In D. I. Mostofsky, ed. *Attention: Contemporary Theories and Analysis*. New York: Appleton-Century-Crofts.

Broadbent, D. E. 1971. *Decision and Stress*. London: Academic Press.

Broadbent, D. E. 1982. Task combination and selective intake of information. *Acta Psychologica* 50:253–290.

Brooks, L. R. 1968. Spatial and verbal components of the act of recall. *Canadian Journal of Psychology* 22:349–368.

Bundesen, C., Pedersen, L. F., and Larsen, A. 1984. Measuring efficiency of selection from briefly exposed visual displays: A model for partial report. *Journal of Experimental Psychology: Human Perception and Performance* 10:329–339.

Bushnell, M. C., Goldberg, M. E., and Robinson, D. L. 1981. Behavioral enhancement of visual responses in monkey cerebral cortex: I Modulation in posterior parietal cortex related to selective visual attention. *Journal of Neurophysiology* 46:755–772.

Calvanio, R., Petrone, P. N., and Levine, D. N. 1987. Left visual spatial neglect is both environment centered and body centered. *Neurology* 37:1179–1183.

Caramazza, A. 1988. Some aspects of language processing revealed through the analysis of acquired aphasia: The lexical system. *Annual Review of Neuroscience* 11:395–421.

Chedru, F. 1976. Space representation in unilateral spatial neglect. *Journal of Neurology, Neurosurgery and Psychiatry* 39:1057–1061.

Coltheart, M. 1980. Iconic memory and visible persistence. *Perception and Psychophysics* 27:183–228.

Coltheart, M. 1984. Sensory memory: A tutorial review. In H. Bouma and D. G. Bouwhuis, eds. *Attention and Performance, X: Control of Language Processes*. Hillsdale, NJ: Erlbaum.

Coltheart, M. 1985. Cognitive neuropsychology and the study of reading. In M. I. Posner and O. S. M. Marin, eds. *Attention and Performance XI*. Hillsdale, NJ: Erlbaum.

Coslett, H. B., Bowers, D., Fitzpatrick, E., Hans, B., and Heilman, K. M. 1986. Hemispatial hypokinesia and hemisensory inattention in neglect. *Neurology* 36(suppl. 1):344.

Costello, A. D. C., and Warrington, E. K. 1987. The dissociation of visuospatial neglect and neglect dyslexia. *Journal of Neurology, Neurosurgery and Psychiatry* 50:1110–1116.

Creutzfeldt, O. 1985. Multiple visual areas: Multiple sensorimotor links. In D. Rose and V. G. Dobson, eds. *Models of the Visual Cortex*. New York: Wiley.

Dean, J. 1988. The neuroethology of perception and action. In O. Neumann and W. Prinz, eds. *Relations between Perception and Action: Current Approaches*. Berlin: Springer.

DeRenzi, E., Gentilini, M., and Pattacini, F. 1984. Auditory extinction following hemisphere damage. *Neuropsychologia* 22:733–744.

Desimone, R., and Moran, J. 1987. Mechanisms for selective attention in area V4 and inferior temporal cortex of the macaque. *Society for Neuroscience Abstracts* 11:1245.

Deuel, R. K. 1987. Neural dysfunction during hemineglect after cortical damage in two monkey models. In M. Jeannerod, ed. *Neurophysiological and Neuropsychological Aspects of Spatial Neglect*. Amsterdam: North-Holland.

Deutsch, J. A., and Deutsch, D. 1963. Attention: Some theoretical considerations. *Psychological Review* 70:80–90.

Downing, C. J., and Pinker, S. 1985. The spatial structure of attention. In M. I. Posner and O. S. M. Marin, eds. *Attention and Performance XI*. Hillsdale, NJ: Erlbaum.

Driver, J. (1989). On the nonselectivity of "selective seeing": Contrast between interference and priming in selective attention. *Journal of Experimental Psychology: Human Perception and Performance* (in press).

Driver, J., and Baylis, G. C. 1989. Movement and visual attention: the spotlight metaphor breaks down. *Journal of Experimental Psychology: Human Perception and Performance* (in press).

Duncan, J. 1980. The locus of interference in the perception of simultaneous stimuli. *Psychological Review* 87:272–300.

Duncan, J. 1983. Perceptual selection based on alphanumeric class: Evidence from partial reports. *Perception and Psychophysics* 33:533–547.

Duncan, J. 1984. Selective attention and the organization of visual information. *Journal of Experimental Psychology: General* 113:501–517.

Duncan, J. 1985. Visual search and visual attention. In M. I. Posner and O. S. M. Marin, eds. *Attention and Performance XI*. Hillsdale, NJ: Erlbaum.

Duncan, J. 1986. Disorganization of behaviour after frontal lobe injury. *Cognitive Neuropsychology* 3:271–290.

Duncan, J. 1988. Attention and reading: Wholes and parts in shape recognition—A tutorial review. In M. Coltheart, ed. *Attention and Performance XII: The Psychology of Reading*. Hillsdale, NJ: Erlbaum.

Duncan, J., and Humphreys, G. W. 1989. Visual search and stimulus similarity. *Psychological Review* (in press).

Egeth, H. E., Folk, C. L., and Mullin, P. A. 1989. Spatial parallelism in the processing of lines, letters and lexicality. In B. E. Shepp and S. Ballesteros, eds. *Object Perception: Structure and Process*. Hillsdale, NJ: Erlbaum.

Egeth, H. E., Jonides, J., and Wall, S. 1972. Parallel processing of multi-element displays. *Cognitive Psychology* 3:674–698.

Ellis, A. W. 1982. Spelling and writing (and reading and speaking). In A. W. Ellis, ed. *Normality and Pathology in Cognitive Functions*. London: Academic Press.

Ellis, A. W., and Young, A. W. 1988. *Human Cognitive Neuropsychology*. Hillsdale, NJ: Erlbaum.

Ellis, A. W., Flude, B. M., and Young, A. W. 1987. "Neglect dyslexia" and the early visual processing of letters in words. *Cognitive Neuropsychology* 4:465–486.

Eriksen, B. A., and Eriksen, C. W. 1974. Effects of noise letters upon the identification of a target letter in a nonsearch task. *Perception and Psychophysics* 16:143–149.

Eriksen, C. W., and Schultz, D. W. 1979. Information processing in visual search: A continuous flow conception and experimental results. *Perception and Psychophysics*, 25:249–263.

Eriksen, C. W., and St. James, J. D. 1986. Visual attention within and around the field of focal attention: A zoom lens model. *Perception and Psychophysics* 40:225–240.

Eslinger, P. M., and Damasio, A. R. 1985. Severe disturbance of higher cognition after bilateral frontal lobe ablation: Patient EVR. *Neurology* 35:1731–1741.

Feldman, J. A. 1985. Four frames suffice: A provisional model of vision and space. *Behavioral and Brain Sciences* 8:265–289.

Feldman, J. A., and Ballard, D. H. 1982. Connectionist models and their properties. *Cognitive Science* 6:215–254.

Fischer, B. 1986. The role of attention in the preparation of visually guided eye movements in monkey and man. *Psychological Research* 48:251–257.

Fisk, A. D., and Schneider, W. 1983. Category and word search: Generalizing search principles to complex processing. *Journal of Experimental Psychology: Learning, Memory and Cognition* 9:177–195.

Flowers, J. H., Warner, J. L., and Polansky, M. L. 1979. Response and encoding factors in "ignoring" irrelevant information. *Memory and Cognition* 7:86–94.

Francolini, C. N., and Egeth, H. E. 1980. On the non-automaticity of automatic activation: Evidence of selective seeing. *Perception and Psychophysics* 27:331–342.

Fuster, J. M. 1985. The prefrontal cortex, mediator of cross-temporal contingencies. *Human Neurobiology* 4:169–179.

Gatti, S. V., and Egeth, H. E. 1978. Failure of spatial selectivity in vision. *Bulletin of the Psychonomic Society* 11:181–184.

Gazzaniga, M. S., and Ladavas, E. 1987. Disturbances in spatial attention following lesion or disconnection of the right parietal lobe. In M. Jeannerod, ed. *Neurophysiological and Neuropsychological Aspects of Spatial Neglect*. Amsterdam: North-Holland.

Glaser, M. D., and Glaser, W. R. 1982. Time course analysis of the Stroop phenomenon. *Journal of Experimental Psychology: Human Perception and Performance* 8:875–894.

Glaser, W. R., and Düngelhoff, F. J. 1984. The time course of picture-word interference. *Journal of Experimental Psychology: Human Perception and Performance* 10:640–654.

Goldberg, M. E., and Bruce, C. J. 1985. Cerebral cortical activity associated with the orientation of visual attention in the rhesus monkey. *Vision Research* 25:471–481.

Goldberg, M. E., Bushnell, M. C., and Bruce, C. J. 1986. The effect of attentive fixation on eye movements evoked by electrical stimulation of the frontal eye fields. *Experimental Brain Research* 61:579–584.

Goldberg, M. E., and Segraves, M. A. 1987. Visuospatial and motor attention in the monkey. *Neuropsychologia* 25:107–118.

Goldman-Rakic, P. S. 1988. Topography of cognition: Parallel distributed networks in primate association cortex. *Annual Review of Neuroscience* 11:137–156.

Gopher, D., and Sanders, A. F. 1984. "S-oh-R": Oh Stages! Oh resources! In W. Prinz and A. F. Sanders, eds. *Cognition and Motor Processes*. Berlin: Springer.

Gopher, D., Brickner, M., and Navon, D. 1982. Different difficulty manipulations interact differently with task emphasis: Evidence for multiple resources. *Journal of Experimental Psychology: Human Perception and Performance* 8:146–157.

Gottsdanker, R. 1980. The ubiquitous role of preparation. In G. E. Stelmach and J. Requin, eds. *Tutorials in Motor Behavior*. Amsterdam: North-Holland.

Greenwald, A. G. 1970. A double-stimulation test of ideo-motor theory with implications for selective attention. *Journal of Experimental Psychology* 84:392–398.

Greenwald, A. G. 1972. On doing two things at once: Timesharing as a function of ideo-motor compatibility. *Journal of Experimental Psychology* 25:52–57.

Greenwald, A. G., and Shulman, H. G. 1973. On doing two things at once: II. Elimination of the psychological refractory period. *Journal of Experimental Psychology* 101:70–76.

Hagenaar, R., and van der Heijden, A. H. C. 1986. Target-noise separation in visual selective attention. *Acta Psychologica* 62:161–176.

Hatano, G., Miyake, Y., and Binks, M. G. 1977. Performance of expert abacus operators. *Cognition* 5:57–71.

Heilman, K. M., and Valenstein, E. 1979. Mechanisms underlying hemispatial neglect. *Annals of Neurology* 5:116–170.

Heuer, H. 1985a. Some points of contact between models of central capacity and factor-analytic models. *Acta Psychologica* 60:135–155.

Heuer, H. 1985b. Intermanual interactions during simultaneous execution and programming of finger movements. *Journal of Motor Behavior* 17:335–354.

Heuer, H. 1986. Intermanual interactions during programming of finger movements: Transient effects of "homologous coupling." In H. Heuer and C. Fromm, eds. *Generation and Modulation of Action Patterns*. Berlin: Springer.

Heuer, H. 1987. Visual discrimination and response programming. *Psychological Research* 49:91–98.

Heuer, H., and Wing, A. M. 1984. Doing two things at once: Process limitations and interactions. In M. M. Smyth and A. M. Wing, eds. *Psychology of Human Movement*. London: Academic Press.

Hinton, G. E. 1981. A parallel computation that assigns canonical object-based frames of reference. *Proceedings of the 7th International Joint Conference on Artificial Intelligence*, pp. 683–685.

Hinton, G. E., and Lang, K. 1985. Shape recognition and illusory conjunctions. *Proceedings of the Ninth International Joint Conference on Artificial Intelligence*.

Hinton, G. E., McClelland, J. L., and Rumelhart, D. E. 1986. Distributed representations. In D. E. Rumelhart, J. L. McClelland, and the PDP Research Group. *Parallel Distributed Processing: Explorations in the Microstructure of Cognition*. Cambridge, MA: MIT Press.

Hinton, G. E., and Parsons, L. 1988. Scene-based and viewer-centered representations for comparing shapes. *Cognition* 30:1–35.

Hoffman, J. E. 1986. Spatial attention in vision: Evidence for early selection. *Psychological Research* 48:221–229.

Hoffmann, J. 1987. Semantic control of selective attention. *Psychological Research* 49:123–129.

Houck, M. R., and Hoffman, J. E. 1986. Conjunction of color and form without attention. *Journal of Experimental Psychology: Human Perception and Performance* 12:186–199.

Ingvar, D. H. 1983. Serial aspects of language and speech related to prefrontal cortical activity. *Human Neurobiology* 2:177–189.

Jeannerod, M. 1987. *Neurophysiological and Neuropsychological Aspects of Spatial Neglect*. Amsterdam: North-Holland.

Jeannerod, M., and Biguer, B. 1987. The directional coding of reaching movements: A visuomotor conception of spatial neglect. In M. Jeannerod, ed. *Neurophysiological and Neuropsychological Aspects of Spatial Neglect*. Amsterdam: North-Holland.

Jersild, A. T. 1927. Mental set and shift. *Archives of Psychology* no. 89.

Joanette, Y., Brouchon, M., Gauthier, L. and Samson, M. 1986. Pointing with left vs. right hand in left visual field neglect. *Neuropsychologia* 24:391–396.

Johnson-Laird, P. N. 1983. *Mental Models*. Cambridge: Cambridge University Press.

Johnson-Laird, P. N. 1988. A computational analysis of consciousness. In A. J. Marcel & E. Bisiach, eds. *Consciousness in Contemporary Science*. Oxford: Oxford University Press.

Johnston, W. A., and Dark, V. J. 1985. Dissociable domains of selective processing. In M. I. Posner and O. S. M. Marin, eds. *Attention and Performance, XI: Mechanisms of Attention*. Hillsdale, NJ: Erlbaum.

Johnston, W. A., and Dark, V. J. 1986. Selective attention. *Annual Review of Psychology* 37:43–75.

Kahneman, D. 1973. *Attention and Effort*. Englewood Cliffs, NJ: Prentice-Hall.

Kahneman, D., and Chajczyk, D. 1983. Tests of the automaticity of reading: Dilution of Stroop effects by color-irrelevant stimuli. *Journal of Experimental Psychology: Human Perception and Performance* 9:497–509.

Kahneman, D., and Henik, A. 1981. Perceptual organization and attention. In M. Kubovy and B. R. Pomerantz, eds. *Perceptual Organization*. Hillsdale, NJ: Erlbaum.

Kahneman, D., and Treisman, A. M. 1984. Changing views of attention and automaticity. In R. Parasuraman and D. R. Davies, eds. *Varieties of Attention*. New York: Academic Press.

Kantowitz, B. 1974. Double stimulation. In B. Kantowitz, ed. *Human Information Processing: Tutorials in Performance and Cognition*. Hillsdale, NJ: Erlbaum.

Keele, S. W., and Neill, W. T. 1978. Mechanisms of attention. In E. C. Carterette and M. P. Friedman, eds. *Handbook of Perception*. Vol. 9. New York: Academic Press, pp. 3–47.

Kelso, J. A. S., and Kay, B. A. 1987. Information and control: A macroscopic analysis of perception-action coupling. In H. Heuer and A. F. Sanders, eds. *Perspectives on Perception and Action*. Hillsdale, NJ: Erlbaum.

Kinsbourne, M. 1970. The cerebral basis of lateral asymmetries in attention. *Acta Psychologica* 33:193–201.

Kinsbourne, M. 1977. Hemineglect and hemispheric rivalry. In E. A. Weinstein and R. P. Friedland, eds. *Hemi-inattention and Hemispheric Specialization*. New York: Raven Press.

Kinsbourne, M. 1987. Mechanisms of unilateral neglect. In M. Jeannerod, ed. *Neurophysiological and Neuropsychological Aspects of Spatial Neglect*. Amsterdam: North-Holland.

Kinsbourne, M., and Hicks, R. E. 1978. Functional cerebral space: A model for overflow, transfer and interference effects in human performance. A tutorial review. In J. Requin, ed. *Attention and Performance VII*. Hillsdale, NJ: Erlbaum.

Kosslyn, S. M., Cave, C. B., Provost, D. A., and Gierke, S. M. 1988. Sequential processes in image generation. *Cognitive Psychology* 20:319–343.

LaBerge, D. 1973. Identification of two components of the time to switch attention: A test of a serial and a parallel model of attention. In S. Kornblum, ed. *Attention and Performance IV*. New York: Academic Press.

Lambert, A. 1987. Expecting different categories at different locations and spatial selective attention. *Quarterly Journal of Experimental Psychology* 39A:61–76.

Lambert, A. J., Beard, C. T., and Thompson, R. J. 1988. Selective attention, visual laterality, awareness, and perceiving the meaning of parafoveally presented words. *Quarterly Journal of Experimental Psychology* 40A:615–652.

Lambert, A., and Hockey, G. R. J. 1989. Attention and performance with a multi-dimensional visual display. *Journal of Experimental Psychology: Human Perception and Performance* (in press).

Lee, D. N., and Young, D. S. 1985. Visual timing of interceptive action. In D. Ingle, M. Jeannerod, and D. N. Lee, eds. *Brain Mechanisms and Spatial Vision*. Amsterdam: Nijhoff.

Levine, D. N., Warach, J., and Farah, M. 1985. Two visual systems in mental imagery. Dissociation of "what" and "where" in imagery disorders due to bilateral posterior lesions. *Neurology* 35:1010–1018.

Logan, G. D. 1978a. Attention in character-classification tasks: Evidence for the automaticity of component stages. *Journal of Experimental Psychology: General* 107:32–63.

Logan, G. D., 1978b. Attention demands of visual search. *Memory and Cognition* 6:446–453.

Logan, G. D. 1979. On the use of a concurrent memory load to measure attention and automaticity. *Journal of Experimental Psychology: Human Perception and Performance* 5:189–207.

Logan, G. D. 1980. Short-term memory demands of reaction-time tasks that differ in complexity. *Journal of Experimental Psychology: Human Perception and Performance* 6:375–389.

Lowe, D. G. 1979. Strategies, context, and the mechanism of response inhibition. *Memory and Cognition* 7:382–389.

Lowe, D. G. 1985. Further investigations of inhibitory mechanisms in attention. *Memory and Cognition* 13:74–80.

Luria, A. R. 1966. *Higher Cortical Functions in Man*. New York: Basic Books.

Marcel, A. J. 1980. Conscious and preconscious recognition of polysemous words: Locating the selective effects of prior verbal context. In R. S. Nickerson, ed. *Attention and Performance VIII*. Hillsdale, NJ: Erlbaum.

Marcel, A. J. 1983. Conscious and unconscious perception: An approach to the relations between phenomenal experience and perceptual processes. *Cognitive Psychology* 15:238–300.

Marr, D. 1977. Artificial intelligence—a personal view. *Artificial Intelligence* 9:37–48.

Marr, D. 1982. *Vision*. San Francisco: Freeman.

Matelli, M., Olivieri, M. F., Saccani, A., and Rizzolatti, G. 1983. Upper visual space neglect and motor deficits after section of the midbrain commissures in the cat. *Behavioural and Brain Research* 10:263–285.

Maunsell, J. H. R., and Newsome, W. T. 1987. Visual processing in monkey extrastriate cortex. *Annual Review of Neuroscience*. 10:363–401.

Maylor, E. A. 1985. Facilitatory and inhibitory components of orienting in visual space. In M. I. Posner and O. S. M. Marin, eds. *Attention and Performance XI*. Hillsdale, NJ: Erlbaum.

McClain, L. 1983. Stimulus-response compatibility affects auditory Stroop interference. *Perception and Psychophysics* 33:266–270.

McLeod, P. D. 1977. A dual-task response modality effect: Support for multiprocessor models of attention. *Quarterly Journal of Experimental Psychology* 29:651–667.

McLeod, P. D. 1978. Does probe RT measure central processing demand? *Quarterly Journal of Experimental Psychology* 30:83–89.

McLeod, P. D., Driver, J., and Crisp, J. 1988. Visual search for a conjunction of movement and form is parallel. *Nature* (London) 332:154–155.

McLeod, P. D., and Posner, M. I. 1984. Privileged loops from percept to act. In H. Bouma and D. G. Bouwhuis, eds. *Attention and Performance X: Control of Language Processes.* Hillsdale, NJ: Erlbaum.

Merikle, P. M. 1980. Selection from visual persistence by perceptual groups and category membership. *Journal of Experimental Psychology: General* 109:279–295.

Mesulam, M. M. 1981. A cortical network for directed attention and unilateral neglect. *Annals of Neurology* 10:309–325.

Mesulam, M. M. 1985. Attention, confusional states, and neglect. In M. M. Mesulam, ed. *Principles of Behavioral Neurology.* Philadelphia: F. A. Davis.

Mewhort, D. J. K., Marchetti, F. M., Gurnsey, R., and Campbell, A. J. 1984. Information persistence: A dual-buffer model for initial visual processing. In H. Bouma and D. G. Bouwhuis, eds. *Attention and Performance X.* Hillsdale, NJ: Erlbaum.

Milner, A. D. 1987. Animal models for the syndrome of spatial neglect. In M. Jeannerod, ed. *Neurophysiological and Neuropsychological Aspects of Spatial Neglect.* Amsterdam: North-Holland.

Moran, J., and Desimone, R. 1985. Selective attention gates visual processing in the extrastriate cortex. *Science* 229:782–784.

Moray, N. 1967. Where is capacity limited? A survey and a model. *Acta Psychologica* 27:84–92.

Monsell, S. 1987. On the relation between lexical input and output pathways for speech. In A. Allport, D. G. MacKay, W. Prinz, and E. Scheerer, eds. *Language Perception and Production: Relationships between Listening, Speaking, Reading and Writing.* London: Academic Press.

Mozer, M. C. 1988. Early parallel processing in reading: a connectionist approach. In M. Coltheart, ed. *Attention and Performance XII: The Psychology of Reading.* Hillsdale, NJ: Erlbaum.

Müller, H. J., and Rabbitt, P. M. A. 1989. Reflexive and voluntary orienting of visual attention: Time course of activation and resistance to interruption. *Journal of Experimental Psychology: Human Perception and Performance* (in press).

Navon, D. 1984. Resources—a theoretical soup stone? *Psychological Review* 91:216–234.

Navon, D. 1985. Attention division or attention sharing? In M. I. Posner and O. S. M. Marin, eds. *Attention and Performance XI.* Hillsdale, NJ: Erlbaum.

Neely, J. G. 1977. Semantic priming and retrieval from lexical memory: Roles of inhibitionless spreading activation and limited-capacity attention. *Journal of Experimental Psychology: General* 106:226–254.

Neill, W. T. 1977. Inhibition and facilitation processes in selective attention. *Journal of Experimental Psychology: Human Perception and Performance* 3:444–450.

Neill, W. T. 1979. Switching attention within and between categories: Evidence for intracategory inhibition. *Memory and Cognition* 7:283–290.

Neill, W. T. 1989. Ambiguity and context: An activation-suppression model. In D. S. Gorfein, ed. *Resolving Semantic Ambiguity* (in press).

Neill, W. T., and Westberry, R. L. 1987. Selective attention and the suppression of cognitive noise. *Journal of Experimental Psychology: Learning, Memory and Cognition* 13:327–334.

Neisser, U. 1967. *Cognitive Psychology.* New York: Appleton-Century-Crofts.

Neisser, U., and Beklen, P. 1975. Selective looking: Attending to visually superimposed events. *Cognitive Psychology* 7:480–494.

Neumann, O. 1980. *Informations-selektion und Handlungsteuerung.* Doctoral dissertation, Bochum University, FRG.

Neumann, O. 1984. Automatic processing: A review of recent findings and a plea for an old theory. In W. Prinz, and A. F. Sanders, eds. *Cognition and Motor Processes.* Berlin: Springer.

Neumann, O. 1985. Die Hypothese begrenzter Kapazität und die Functionen der Aufmerksamkeit. In O. Neumann, ed. *Perspektiven der Kognitionspsychologie.* Berlin: Springer.

Neumann, O. 1987. Beyond capacity: A functional view of attention. In H. Heuer and A. F. Sanders, eds. *Perspectives on Perception and Action.* Hillsdale, NJ: Erlbaum.

Neumann, O., van der Heijden, A. H. C., and Allport, D. A. 1986. Visual selective attention: Introductory remarks. *Psychological Research* 48:185–188.

Newcombe, F., Ratcliff, G., and Damasio, H. 1987. Dissociable visual and spatial impairments following right posterior cerebral lesions: Clinical, neuropsychological and anatomical evidence. *Neuropsychologia* 25:149–161.

Nissen, M. J. 1985. Accessing features and objects: Is location special? In M. I. Posner and O. S. M. Marin, eds. *Attention and Performance XI.* Hillsdale, NJ: Erlbaum.

Norman, D. A. 1968. Toward a theory of memory and attention. *Psychological Review* 75:522–536.

Norman, D. A. 1981. Categorization of action slips. *Psychological Review* 88:1–15.

Norman, D. A., and Bobrow, D. G. 1975. On data-limited and resource-limited processes. *Cognitive Psychology* 7:44–64.

Norman, D. A., and Shallice, T. 1980. Attention to action: Willed and automatic control of behavior. *University of California San Diego CHIP Report 99.* Published (1985) in R. J. Davidson, G. E. Schwartz, and D. Shapiro, eds. *Consciousness and Self-Regulation.* Vol. 4. New York: Plenum.

Pashler, H. 1984. Processing stages in overlapping tasks: Evidence for a central bottleneck. *Journal of Experimental Psychology: Human Perception and Performance* 10:358–377.

Pashler, H. 1987. Detecting conjunctions of color and form: Reassessing the serial search hypothesis. *Perception and Psychophysics* 41:191–201.

Pashler, H., and Badgio, P. C. 1985. Visual attention and stimulus identification. *Journal of Experimental Psychology: Human Perception and Performance* 11:105–121.

Pashler, H., and Badgio, P. C. 1988. Attentional issues in the identification of alphanumeric characters. In M. Coltheart, ed. *Attention and Performance XII: The Psychology of Reading.* Hillsdale, NJ: Erlbaum.

Pashler, H., and Johnston, J. C. 1989. Chronometric evidence of central postponement in temporally overlapping tasks. *Quarterly Journal of Experimental Psychology* (in press).

Pattee, H. H. 1972. Laws and constraints, symbols and language. In C. H. Waddington, ed. *Towards a Theoretical Biology.* Chicago: Aldine.

Pattee, H. H. 1977. Dynamic and linguistic modes of complex systems. *International Journal of General Systems.* 3:259–266.

Petersen, S. E., Fox, P. T., Posner, M. I., Mintun, M., and Raichle, M. E. 1988. Positron emission tomographic studies of the cortical anatomy of single-word processing. *Nature* 331:585–589.

Phaf, R. H. 1986 April. A connectionist model for attention. Technical Report of Unit of Experimental Psychology, University of Leiden.

Phillips, W. A. 1982. Short-term visual memory. *Philosophical Transactions of the Royal Society of London* B302:295–309.

Pierrot-Deseilligny, C., Gray, F., and Brunet, P. 1986. Infarcts in both inferior parietal lobules with impairments of visually guided eye movements, peripheral visual inattention and optic ataxia. *Brain* 109:81–97.

Porter, R. J. 1987. What is the relation between speech production and speech perception? In A. Allport, D. G. MacKay, W. Prinz, and E. Scheerer, eds. *Language Perception and Production: Relationships between Listening, Speaking, Reading and Writing.* London: Academic Press.

Porter, R. J., and Lubker, J. 1980. Rapid reproduction of vowel-vowel sequences: Evidence for a fast and direct acoustic-motoric linkage in speech. *Journal of Speech and Hearing Research* 23:593–602.

Posner, M. I. 1978. *Chronometric Explorations of Mind.* Hillsdale, NJ: Erlbaum.

Posner, M. I. 1980. Orienting of attention. *Quarterly Journal of Experimental Psychology* 32:3–25.

Posner, M. I. 1982. Cumulative development of attentional theory. *American Psychologist* 37:168–179.

Posner, M. I. 1988. Structures and functions of selective attention. In T. Boll and B. K. Bryant, eds. *Clinical Neuropsychology and Brain Function*. Washington, DC: American Psychological Association.

Posner, M. I., and Boies, S. J. 1971. Components of attention. *Psychological Review* 78:391–408.

Posner, M. I., Inhoff, A. W., Friedrich, F. J., and Cohen, A. 1987. Isolating attentional systems: A cognitive-anatomical analysis. *Psychobiology* 15:107–121.

Posner, M. I., and Snyder, C. R. R. 1975. Attention and cognitive control. In R. L. Solso, ed. *Information Processing and Cognition: The Loyola Symposium*. Hillsdale, NJ: Erlbaum.

Posner, M. I., Petersen, S. E., Fox, P. T., and Raichle, M. E. 1988. Localization of cognitive operations in the human brain. *Science*.

Poulton, E. C. 1981. Human manual control. In V. B. Brooks, ed. *Handbook of Physiology: The Nervous System. Volume 2: Motor Control*. Part 2. Bethesda, MD: American Physiological Society.

Prinzmetal, W. 1981. Principles of feature integration in visual perception. *Perception and Psychophysics* 30:330–340.

Quastler, H. 1956. Studies of human channel capacity. In E. C. Cherry, ed. *Information Theory: Proceedings of Third London Symposium*. London: Butterworth.

Rafal, R. D., Posner, M. I., Friedman, J. H., Inhoff, A. W., and Bernstein, E. 1988. Orienting of visual attention in progressive supranuclear palsy. *Brain* 111:267–280.

Rapcsak, S. Z., Watson, R. T., and Heilman, K. M. 1987. Hemispace-visual field interactions in visual extinction. *Journal of Neurology, Neurosurgery and Psychiatry* 50:1117–1124.

Reason, J. 1978. Actions not as planned: The price of automatization. In G. Underwood and R. Stephens, eds. *Aspects of Consciousness*. Vol. 1. London: Academic Press.

Remington, R. W. 1980. Attention and saccadic eye movements. *Journal of Experimental Psychology: Human Perception and Performance* 6:726–744.

Reuter-Lorenz, P. A., Moscovitch, M., and Kinsbourne, M. 1985. Lateral attention biases on a visual line bisection task: Similarities between the performances of neglect patients and normal subjects. Paper to the International Neuropsychology Society meeting, San Diego, CA.

Richmond, B. J., Wurtz, R. H., and Sato, T. 1983. Visual responses of inferior temporal neurons in awake rhesus monkey. *Journal of Neurophysiology* 50:1415–1432.

Riddoch, M. J., and Humphreys, G. W. 1983. The effect of cueing on unilateral neglect. *Neuropsychologia* 21:589–599.

Rizzolatti, G., and Camarda, R. 1987. Neural circuits for spatial attention and unilateral neglect. In M. Jeannerod, ed. *Neurophysiological and Neuropsychological Aspects of Spatial Neglect*. Amsterdam: North-Holland.

Rizzolatti, G., Gentilucci, M., and Matelli, M. 1985. Selective spatial attention: One center, one circuit, or many circuits? In M. I. Posner and O. S. M. Marin, eds. *Attention and Performance XI*. Hillsdale, NJ: Erlbaum.

Rizzolatti, G., Matelli, M., and Pavesi, G. 1983. Deficits in attention and movement following the removal of postarcuate (area 6) and prearcuate (area 8) cortex in macaque monkeys. *Brain* 106:655–673.

Rizzolatti, G., Riggio, L., Dascola, I., and Umilta, C. 1987. Reorienting attention across the horizontal and vertical meridians: Evidence in favor of premotor theory of attention. *Neuropsychologia* 25:31–40.

Robinson, D. L., and Peterson, S. E. 1986. The neurobiology of attention. In J. E. LeDoux and W. Hirst, eds. *Mind and Brain: Dialogues in Cognitive Neuroscience*. Cambridge, Engl.: Cambridge University Press.

Rock, I., and Gutman, D. 1981. Effect of inattention on form perception. *Journal of Experimental Psychology: Human Perception and Performance* 7:275–285.

Roland, P. E. 1982. Cortical regulation of selective attention in man. *Journal of Neurophysiology* 48:1059–1078.

Roland, P. E. 1985. Cortical organization of voluntary behavior in man. *Human Neurobiology* 4:155–167.

Roland, P. E., and Friberg, L. 1985. Localization of cortical areas activated by thinking. *Journal of Neurophysiology* 53:1219–1243.

Rolls, E. T. 1981. Processing beyond the inferior temporal visual cortex related to feeding, learning, and striatal function: In Y. Katsuki, R. Norgren, and M. Sato, eds. *Brain Mechanisms of Sensation*. New York: Wiley.

Rolls, E. T. 1987. Information representation, processing and storage in the brain: analysis at the single neuron level. In J. P. Changeux and M. Konishi, eds. *Neural and Molecular Mechanisms of Learning*. Berlin: Springer.

Rosch, E. 1975. Cognitive representations of semantic categories. *Journal of Experimental Psychology: General* 104:192–233.

Rubens, A. B. 1985. Caloric stimulation and unilateral visual neglect. *Neurology* 35:1019–1024.

Ryan, C. 1983. Reassessing the automaticity-control distinction: Item recognition as a paradigm case. *Psychological Review* 90:171–178.

Schneider, W., and Detweiler, M. 1987. A connectionist/control architecture for working memory. In G. H. Bower, ed. *The Psychology of Learning and Motivation*. Vol. 21. New York: Academic Press.

Schneider, W., Dumais, S. T., and Shiffrin, R. M. 1984. Automatic and control processing and attention. In R. Parasuraman and D. R. Davies, eds. *Varieties of Attention*. New York: Academic Press.

Schneider, W., and Shiffrin, R. M. 1977. Controlled and automatic human information processing: I. Detection, search and attention. *Psychological Review* 84:1–66.

Sejnowski, T. J. 1986. Open questions about computation in cerebral cortex. In J. L. McClelland, D. E. Rumelhart, and the PDP Research Group. *Parallel Distributed Processing: Explorations in the Microstructure of Cognition*. Vol. 2. Cambridge, MA: MIT Press.

Seymour, P. H. K. 1979. *Human Visual Cognition*. London: Collier Macmillan.

Shaffer, L. H. 1975. Multiple attention in continuous verbal tasks. In P. M. A. Rabbit and S. Dornic, eds. *Attention and Performance V*. New York: Academic Press.

Shaffer, W. O., and LaBerge, D. 1979. Automatic semantic processing of unattended words. *Journal of Verbal Learning and Verbal Behavior* 18:413–426.

Shallice, T. 1972. Dual functions of consciousness. *Psychological Review* 79:383–393.

Shallice, T. 1978. The dominant action system: An information-processing approach to consciousness. In K. S. Pope and J. L. Singer, eds. *The Stream of Consciousness*. New York: Plenum.

Shallice, T. 1987. Impairments of semantic processing: Multiple dissociations. In M. Coltheart, G. Sartori, and R. Job, eds. *The Cognitive Neuropsychology of Language*. London: Erlbaum.

Shallice, T., McLeod, P., and Lewis, K. 1985. Isolating cognitive modules with the dual-task paradigm: Are speech perception and production separate processes? *Quarterly Journal of Experimental Psychology* 37A:507–532.

Shepherd, M., Findlay, J. M., and Hockey, R. J. 1986. The relationship between eye movements and spatial attention. *Quarterly Journal of Experimental Psychology* 38A:475–491.

Shiffrin, R. M., and Schneider, W. 1977. Controlled and automatic human information processing: II. Perceptual learning, automatic attending and a general theory. *Psychological Review* 84:127–190.

Sieroff, E., and Michel, F. 1987. Verbal visual extinction in right/left hemisphere lesion patients and the problem of lexical access. *Neuropsychologia* 25:907–918.

Sieroff, E., Pollatsek, A., and Posner, M. I. 1987. Recognition of visual letter strings following injury to the posterior visual spatial attention system. *Cognitive Neuropsychology* 5:427–449.

Smith, M. C. 1967. Theories of the psychological refractory period. *Psychological Bulletin* 67:202–213.

Spearman, C. 1927. *The Abilities of Man*. New York: Macmillan.

Spector, A., and Biederman, I. 1976. Mental set and mental shift revisited. *American Journal of Psychology* 89:669–679.

Spelke, E., Hirst, W., and Neisser, U. 1976. Skills of divided attention. *Cognition* 4:215–230.

Spitzer, H., and Richmond, B. J. 1987. Visual selective attention modifies single unit activity in inferior temporal cortex. *Society for Neuroscience Abstracts* 11:1245.

Stemberger, J. P. 1985. An interactive activation model of language production. In A. W. Ellis, ed. *Progress in the Psychology of Language*. Vol. 1. Hillsdale, NJ: Erlbaum.

Stroop, J. R. 1935. Studies of interference in serial verbal reactions. *Journal of Experimental Psychology* 18:643–662.

Styles, E. A., and Allport, D. A. 1986. Perceptual integration of identity, location and colour. *Psychological Research* 48:189–200.

Tierney, M. 1973. Dual task performance: the effects of manipulating stimulus-response requirements. B. A. thesis, University of Reading.

Tipper, S. P. 1985. The negative priming effect: Inhibitory effects of ignored primes. *Quarterly Journal of Experimental Psychology* 37A:571–590.

Tipper, S. P., and Baylis, G. C. 1987. Individual differences in selective attention: The relation of priming and interference to cognitive failure. *Personality and Individual Differences* 8:667–675.

Tipper, S. P., and Driver, J. 1988. Negative priming between pictures and words: Evidence for semantic analysis of ignored stimuli. *Memory and Cognition* 16:64–70.

Tipper, S. P., MacQueen, G. M., and Brehaut, J. C. 1988. Negative priming between response modalities: Evidence for the central locus of inhibition in selective attention. *Perception and Psychophysics* 43:45–52.

Tipper, S. P., Bourque, T. A., Anderson, S. H., and Brehaut, J. C. 1989. Mechanisms of attention: A developmental study. *Journal of Experimental Child Psychology* (in press).

Treisman, A. M. 1986. Features and objects in visual processing. *Scientific American* 254:114–124.

Treisman, A. 1988. Features and objects: The fourteenth Bartlett Memorial Lecture. *Quarterly Journal of Experimental Psychology* 40A:201–237.

Treisman, A., and Gelade, G. 1980. A feature integration theory of attention. *Cognitive Psychology* 12:97–136.

Ullman, S. 1984. Visual routines. *Cognition* 18:97–159.

Ungerleider, L. G., and Mishkin, M. 1982. Two cortical visual systems. In D. J. Ingle, M. A. Goodale, and R. J. W. Mansfield, eds. *Analysis of Visual Behavior*. Cambridge, MA: MIT Press.

Vallar, G., and Perani, D. 1987. The anatomy of spatial neglect in humans. In M. Jeannerod, ed. *Neurophysiological and Neuropsychological Aspects of Spatial Neglect*. Amsterdam: North-Holland.

van der Heijden, A. H. C. 1981. *Short-term Visual Information Forgetting*. London: Routledge and Kegan Paul.

van der Heijden, A. H. C. 1986. On selection in vision. *Psychological Research* 48:211–220.

van der Heijden, A. H. C. 1987. Central selection in vision. In H. Heuer and A. F. Sanders, eds. *Perspectives on Perception and Action*. Hillsdale, NJ: Erlbaum.

Virzi, R. A., and Egeth, H. E. 1985. Toward a translational model of Stroop interference. *Memory and Cognition* 13:304–319.

Volpe, B. T., LeDoux, J. E., and Gazzaniga, M. S. 1979. Information processing in an "extinguished" visual field. *Nature* 282:722–724.

von der Malsburg, C. 1981. The correlation theory of brain function. Internal Report 81-2, Dept. Neurobiol., Max-Planck-Institute for Biophysical Chemistry, Göttingen, FRG.

von der Malsburg, C. 1985. Am I thinking assemblies? In G. Palm, ed. *Trieste Meeting on Brain Theory*. Berlin: Springer.

von Hofsten, C. 1987. Catching. In H. Heuer and A. F. Sanders, eds. *Perspectives on Perception and Action*. Hillsdale, NJ: Erlbaum.

Wagenaar, W. A. 1970. Subjective randomness and the capacity to generate information. *Acta Psychologica* 33:233–242.

Warren, W. H., and Whang, S. 1987. Visual guidance of walking through apertures: Body-scaled information for affordances. *Journal of Experimental Psychology: Human Perception and Performance* 13:371–383.

Warren, W. H., Young, D. S., and Lee, D. N. 1986. Visual control of step length during running over irregular terrain. *Journal of Experimental Psychology: Human Perception and Performance* 12:259–266.

Wickens, C. D. 1980. The structure of attentional resources. In R. S. Nickerson, ed. *Attention and Performance VIII*. Hillsdale, NJ: Erlbaum.

Wickens, C. D. 1984. Processing resources in attention. In R. Parasuraman and D. R. Davies, eds. *Varieties of Attention*. New York: Academic Press.

Wise, S. P., and Evarts, E. V. 1981. The role of the cerebral cortex in movement. *Trends in Neurosciences* 4:297–300.

Wurtz, R. H., Goldberg, M. E., and Robinson, D. L. 1980. Behavioral modulation of visual responses in the monkey: Stimulus selection for attention and movement. In J. M. Sprague and A. M. Epstein, eds. *Progress in Psychobiology and Physiological Psychology*. Vol. 9. New York: Academic Press.

Zeki, S. M. 1981. The mapping of visual functions in the cerebral cortex. In Y. Katsuki, R. Norgren, and M. Sato, eds. *Brain Mechanisms of Sensation*. New York: Wiley.

Zipser, D. 1986. Biologically plausible models of place recognition and goal location. In J. L. McClelland, D. E. Rumelhart, and the PDP Research Group. *Parallel Distributed Processing: Explorations in the Microstructure of Cognition*. Vol. 2. Cambridge, MA: MIT Press.

17 Memory

Daniel L. Schacter

It seems, then, that we owe to memory almost all that we either have or are; that our ideas and conceptions are its work, and that our everyday perception, thought, and movement is derived from this source. Memory collects the countless phenomena of our existence into a single whole; and, as our bodies would be scattered into the dust of their component atoms if they were not held together by the attraction of matter, so our consciousness would be broken up into as many fragments as we had lived seconds but for the binding and unifying force of memory. (Hering 1920, p. 75)

There have been many eloquent testimonies to the crucial role that memory plays in mental life, but few can match the sweeping force of Ewald Hering's words in his lecture to the Vienna Academy of Sciences in 1870. For Hering, memory constituted the heart of our sense of personal identity and ability to understand the world in which we exist. Although contemporary students typically describe and analyze memory with prose that is more restrained than Hering's was, most would agree that memory does play the critical role that Hering ascribed to it over one-hundred years ago.

Some years after Hering's lecture, a monograph appeared that represented a key historical event in the psychological study of memory: Hermann Ebbinghaus's (1885) *Uber das Gedächtniss*. In that well-known book, recently celebrated on the one-hundredth anniversary of its publication (Gorfein and Hoffman 1987, Slamecka 1985), Ebbinghaus not only introduced experimental techniques for studying memory—the savings method and the use of nonsense syllables as to-be-remembered materials are the most familiar—he also laid out an experimental agenda that included such problems as repetition effects, remote associations, massed versus distributed practice, and the like. For better or worse Ebbinghaus's methods and agenda exerted a powerful influence on psychological investigations of memory in the years immediately following publication of his monograph (Schacter 1982, ch. 8) and well beyond (Slamecka 1985).

It is virtually impossible to consider the analysis of memory in contemporary cognitive science without acknowledging the legacy of Ebbinghaus. The merits and drawbacks of the Ebbinghausian influence on contemporary psychological analyses of memory have been debated since the early years of memory research (see, for example, Bartlett 1932, Boring 1929, Ogden 1904, Semon 1909), and continue to be discussed today (compare Anderson 1985, Mandler 1985, Schacter 1982, Neisser 1982, Slamecka 1985, Tulving 1983). During the past decade, however, the study of memory has become increasingly characterized by an eclecticism that extends beyond the rather narrow boundaries of what might be called the classical Ebbinghausian tradition and fits well with the general interdisciplinary spirit that characterizes much of cognitive science (see chapter 1). Accordingly this chapter emphasizes the eclectic, interdisciplinary side of contemporary memory research and attempts to acquaint the reader with some of the main concepts and empirical findings of the various subdisciplines that either are or in my view should be important contributors to a cognitive science of memory. I discuss four main perspectives: (1) experimental cognitive psychology, (2) neuropsychology and neurobiology, (3) ecological/evolutionary, and (4) artificial intelligence and parallel distributed processing.

Before proceeding further, it will be useful to say a few words about what I view as the role of what might appear to be "noncognitive" contributors to a cognitive science of memory. It may strike some as strange to see neuropsychology and even neurobiology listed as partners in the interdisciplinary enterprise; after all, these approaches have traditionally been identified with analysis of brain bases of memory, not with understanding at the cognitive level itself. Surely the task of cognitive science does not include specification of the neural underpinnings of memory. However, my conception of the role of neuropsychological and neurobiological analyses in cognitive science does not mandate that cognitive scientists attempt to account for neural phenomena or even make specific reference to brain events in their theoretical formulations. Rather it is based on the idea that memory can be studied at various levels of analysis and that information gathered at certain levels of analysis may profitably inform theoretical developments at another level (see, for example, Schacter 1984, 1986a, Squire 1987). For example, if evidence from neurobiological and neuropsychological studies suggests a need to distinguish between different forms of memory, this evidence ought to be taken into account by cognitive theories. The general point, however, is that relevant evidence from neurobiological and neuropsychological studies should influence theorizing by cognitive scientists *at the cognitive level of analysis;* theoretical descriptions and explanations at the neurobiological level need not be attempted by cognitive scientists. Elsewhere I have suggested that when concepts or findings from one level of analysis in memory research influence thinking at another level, a convergent relation exists between the two subdisciplines (Schacter 1986a). Although we are just beginning to see the emergence of convergent relations among the disciplines that I have identified as contributors to a cognitive science of memory, there are reasons to believe that this trend will accelerate in the future, reasons that I believe become evident in the course of this chapter.

17.1 Approaches to Understanding Memory: Contrasting Viewpoints

The main purpose of this chapter is to provide the reader with an overview of the major issues, investigative strategies, and empirical findings of the various disciplines that contribute to a cognitive science of memory. Accordingly no attempt is made to provide an exhaustive review of data and theory within a particular area. Rather I intend to show that each perspective has unique contributions that complement the contributions of other viewpoints.

Experimental Cognitive Psychology

There can be little doubt that experimental cognitive psychology has generated the largest number of empirical observations and theoretical ideas about memory that are of direct interest to cognitive scientists; accordingly I devote a good deal more attention to developments in this area than in others. It is also the discipline that has been most markedly influenced by the Ebbinghausian tradition, at least at the methodological level. Cognitive analyses of memory were ushered in by the pioneering experiments on short-term memory by Miller (1956), Peterson and Peterson (1959), and Sperling (1960), among others. Shortly thereafter research on organizational processes in long-term memory appeared (see, for example, Mandler 1968, Tulving 1962) that emphasized the importance of active strategic encoding for the recall of various kinds of word lists. The organizational approach challenged the then-predominant associative interference theory (see, for example, Underwood and Ekstrand 1966), which emphasized the importance of relatively automatic and passive formation of stimulus-response bonds. Various versions of associative interference theory had dominated the psychological study of memory since the original formulations of Müller and Pilzecker (1900). Sharp criticisms of this approach were made from time to time, by such investigators as the British psychologist Frederic Bartlett (1932), who proposed that schemas—organized mental structures—play a key role in remembering; the Gestaltists Koffka (1935) and Kohler (1947), whose discussion of the role of configural properties in memory anticipated the main ideas of organizational theory; and the German biologist Richard Semon (1909), whose theory of memory included several critical ideas found in later cognitive theories (see Schacter 1982). For the most part, however, these challenges went unheeded by mainstream experimental psychologists, at least until the advent of organization theory and related cognitive approaches that highlighted the active and constructive nature of mnemonic processes (see, for example, Neisser 1967).

By the late 1960s and early 1970s, the cognitive orientation toward memory had all but eclipsed the behavioristic, S-R–oriented approach exemplified by interference theory, and a number of prominent trends could be clearly identified. A great deal of empirical research had been done on short-term memory, including Sternberg's (1966) famous experimental work on search processes, Murdock's delineation of forgetting functions for different types of material (Murdock 1961, 1962), and Wickens's (1970) studies of release from proactive interference. Research on long-term memory focused heavily on coding processes, as was apparent in numerous experiments that demonstrated that memory performance was improved by use of visual imagery mnemonics (see, for example, Bower 1972, Paivio 1971), and in related studies that revealed the important role of prior knowledge for remembering of new information (see, for example, Bransford and Johnson 1972). Experimental attention began to be paid to the critical importance of retrieval cues in remembering (Tulving and Pearlstone 1966, Tulving and Osler 1968), and studies of knowledge retrieval and semantic memory were initiated (Collins and Quillian 1969). The wealth of empirical information produced by these studies was complemented by the appearance of various new theoretical ideas and models (see, for example, Anderson and Bower 1973, Atkinson and Shiffrin 1968, Waugh and Norman 1965).

This capsule summary of what might be called the "first wave" of cognitive studies of memory touches on only a few of the many issues and problems that were tackled in the 1960s and early 1970s (for thorough coverage the reader is referred to the reviews by Baddeley (1976), Craik (1979), Crowder (1976), and Murdock (1974)). For the bulk of this section, I focus on some of the more salient recent developments in the field, most of which grew directly out of earlier research. Four general topics are considered: working memory, encoding/retrieval interactions, schemas and reconstructive processes, and implicit memory.

Working Memory   During the "first wave" of cognitive memory research, perhaps the most rapid and impressive progress was made within the general area of short-term memory. Not only were reliable experimental techniques devised, but detailed theoretical models of short-term memory were also advanced (see, for example, Atkinson and Shiffrin 1968, Waugh and Norman 1965). These models depicted a limited capacity buffer or store that could hold a small number of items, served as the gateway to a capacity-unlimited long-term store, relied largely on acoustic coding, and was subject to extremely rapid decay unless continuous rehearsal and recycling of information occurred. By the early 1970s, however, serious problems with this view had been delineated (Craik and Lockhart 1972), and the ensuing years witnessed a steady erosion of its plausibility and influence (see Crowder 1982 for a chronicling of the "demise" of the traditional concept of short-term memory).

An alternative conceptualization of short-term memory that emerged during the 1970s and proved exceptionally fruitful is represented by the working memory approach introduced by Baddeley and Hitch (1974) and elaborated further by Baddeley and various colleagues (see Baddeley 1986 for an overview). This approach includes a general model of short-term memory processes, a conceptual emphasis on elucidating the *functions* served by such processes, and experimental techniques for teasing apart the various components of working memory. Consider first the general model adopted by Baddeley's group. The modal model of the 1960s depicted short-term memory as a unitary entity. In contrast Baddeley and Hitch (1974) fractionated working memory into several components. The first is the central executive, a limited-capacity processor that is involved in control and selection functions. This component of the model is the least well studied and most vaguely conceptualized; indeed Baddeley (1986) depicted the central executive as the "area of residual ignorance" (p. 225) in the working memory model. The other two components of the model are depicted as "slave subsystems" of the central executive and are referred to, respectively, as the articulatory loop and the visuospatial scratch pad. The former subsystem is held to be responsible for the temporary storage of speech-based information, the latter for the temporary storage of visual and spatial information. Why distinguish between a central executive and two slave subsystems instead of opting for the apparently simpler alternative of a unitary short-term system? Consideration of a few experimental examples will help to answer this question and will also illustrate the general investigative strategy adopted by Baddeley and his colleagues.

The technique used most frequently by Baddeley's group to investigate working memory involves a dual-task approach. Subjects perform a *primary* task, such as reading, problem-solving, comprehending, or reasoning and at the same time perform a *secondary* task that presumably requires working memory, such as rehearsing and recalling a small set of digits. The critical question is whether performance of the secondary task disrupts performance of the primary task. If such an outcome is observed, it is inferred that some component of working memory is involved in primary task performance. In one of Baddeley and Hitch's (1974) early experiments, the primary task involved comprehension of a spoken prose passage, and the secondary task required subjects to concurrently retain one, three, or six digits. Because language comprehension requires some form of short-term storage, it was expected that the comprehension performance of subjects who were required to retain digits would be impaired relative to that of subjects who were not required to retain any digits (such control subjects typically perform an articulatory suppression task that involves counting from one to six). Baddeley and Hitch found, however, that comprehension performance was impaired only with a concurrent load of six digits; concurrent retention of one or three digits did not affect performance on the comprehension task. Similar results were obtained when the primary task involved reasoning about whether a sentence accurately described the order of two presented letters (for example, *B does not follow A*—BA (true) or *A is preceded by B*—AB (false)). Subjects required more time to make true/false judgments about the sentences with a concurrent load of six digits than in control conditions, but there was no effect of a one- or two-digit load on reasoning performance.

The foregoing pattern of results is difficult to accommodate if one subscribes to the notion of a unitary short-term or working memory. If the short-term storage required by such tasks as reasoning and comprehending taps the same limited-capacity system involved in short-term retention of digits, the addition of any concurrent digit load ought to impair performance. Yet a concurrent load of one or two digits did not affect primary task performance, thereby suggesting that temporary storage of one or two digits is handled by a system or subsystem different from the one involved in primary task performance. According to Baddeley (1986), that subsystem is the articulatory loop. Several other lines of experimentation have provided evidence for the speech-based nature of the articulatory loop. For example, Baddeley, Thomson, and Buchanan (1975) demonstrated that immediate memory for words with one syllable (for example, *wit, hate*) is better than for words with several syllables (for example, *university, opportunity*). Because long words take longer to rehearse than do short words, fewer long words could be retained by a speech-based loop of the kind described by Baddeley. Converging evidence for this point was provided in an ingenious study by Ellis and Hennelley (1980). They observed that the digit spans of Welsh children on standardized intelligence tests were consistently smaller than those of the American children from whom the test norms were obtained. Welsh digits, noted Ellis and Hennelley (1980), contain vowel sounds that take longer to pronounce than do English digits. To investigate the issue, they studied immediate digit recall of Welsh-English bilinguals. All subjects remembered more digits in English than in Welsh. When subvocal rehearsal was prevented with an articulatory suppression task, however, there was no difference between the English and Welsh digit spans. This pattern of results suggests that the initial difference in span lengths was attributable to an overloading of the articulatory loop by the Welsh digits.

Baddeley and associates have also used the concurrent task technique to provide evidence for the subsystem that they call the visuospatial scratch pad—a mental workspace that allows one to manipulate and store temporarily visual and spatial information. In one experiment described by Baddeley (1986), subjects performed a visual tracking task and at the same time performed tasks that required manipulation and storage of either visual or verbal imagery. Baddeley found that the visual but not the verbal imagery task interfered with tracking performance, an outcome consistent with the idea that a visuospatial subsystem of working memory was selectively involved in the tracking and visual imagery tasks. In related experiments Baddeley and Lieberman (1980) required subjects to study a word list either by rote or by using visual imagery mnemonics and to perform at the same time a visual tracking task. They found that performance in the imagery but not rote condition was disrupted by the requirement to perform the tracking task. Additional experiments provided further evidence for a distinct visuospatial subsystem of working memory and suggested that the spatial component of the system is particularly susceptible to disruption by concurrent tasks (see Baddeley 1986 for details).

The foregoing evidence indicates that the general theoretical framework initially put forward by Baddeley and Hitch (1974) has garnered empirical support. Yet there are still significant gaps in the framework, involving principally the rather vaguely specified central executive (see Baddeley 1986, ch. 10, for an attempt to rectify this). As stated previously, however, one of the notable features of the working memory approach is its functional emphasis. The studies discussed, for example, provided useful information concerning the role of working memory in comprehension, reasoning, imagery, and individual differences in digit span. Other studies too have shed light on various functions of working memory, including its role in reading (see, for example, Baddeley, Logie, Nimmo-Smith, and Brereton 1985, Daneman and Carpenter 1980), development (Hitch and Halliday 1983), dementia (Morris 1984), and frontal-lobe syndromes (Baddeley 1986). Thus whatever the ultimate verdict on the theoretical utility of the working memory framework, there can be little doubt that it has proved extremely valuable heuristically.

Encoding/Retrieval Interactions One of the identifying features of a cognitive approach to memory is its emphasis on the concept of *encoding*: the process by which new incoming information is related to and transformed by preexisting knowledge structures. The importance of encoding operations was recognized in the early formulations of Miller (1956) and organizational theorists (Mandler 1968, Tulving 1962) and was assigned a central role in the influential levels of processing framework introduced by Craik and Lockhart (1972). They contended that memory could be viewed as a record of the encoding operations performed on a stimulus and argued further for different "levels" of encoding, with semantic encoding representing the "deepest" level, and nonsemantic encoding representing the "shallowest" level. By this view memory for stimuli analyzed to deep, semantic levels is more robust and durable than memory for stimuli analyzed to shallow, nonsemantic levels. Although the particulars of the levels-of-processing approach have been effectively criticized (see, for example, Baddeley 1978, Nelson 1977), its emphasis on the critical importance of encoding operations for memory performance has had a salutary influence. Numerous experiments have shown clearly that when the traditional sources of variance in memory experiments are held constant—stimulus properties such as word frequency, concreteness, and so forth—variations in the encoding operations performed on to-be-remembered stimuli have large effects on memory performance (see, for example, Craik and Tulving 1975, Matthews 1977, Rogers, Kuiper, and Kirker 1977). Along these same lines it has been demonstrated convincingly that people who possess a great deal of prior knowledge of a particular domain, and can thus encode domain-relevant information in a highly detailed and elaborate manner, exhibit greater retention of domain-related information than do subjects who possess little or no relevant prior knowledge (see, for example, Adelson 1984, Chase and Ericsson 1981, Chiesi, Spillich, and Voss 1979, de Groot 1965).

As important as it is to appreciate the role of encoding operations in memory performance, one of the major lessons of the past decade and more of memory research is that a description of encoding processes alone is not sufficient for a proper understanding of memory. The principal message of this research is that the usefulness of a particular encoding activity depends on and interacts with the conditions that prevail at the time of retrieval. Encoding operations that lead to high levels of memory performance under one set of retrieval conditions may lead to low levels of performance under different retrieval conditions. This critical point was initially made in experiments by Tulving and his colleagues that demonstrated that with certain encoding conditions, retrieval cues that usually lead to high levels of performance—such as a strong associate of a target item or a copy of the item itself—can be surprisingly ineffective (see, for example, Tulving and Osler 1968, Tulving and Thomson 1973, Watkins and Tulving 1975). The general observation that the usefulness of a particular encoding activity depends on the conditions of retrieval has turned out to be quite robust and pervasive. For example, although levels-of-processing research had shown that encoding of the phonemic properties of a word results in poorer memory performance than does semantic encoding (see, for example, Craik and Tulving 1975), subsequent experiments revealed that when a test requires memory for phonemic properties of a word, phonemic encoding produces higher levels of recall and recognition than does semantic encoding (Fisher and Craik 1977, Morris, Bransford, and Franks 1977). Similarly Stein (1978) showed that encoding information about the physical appearance of a to-be-remembered word (whether or not the word possesses a capital letter) results in lower recall than does semantic encoding when semantic retrieval cues are provided on a memory test, but produces higher recall than does semantic encoding when the test probes memory for a word's physical appearance. Another set of experiments revealed that encoding target materials in an elaborate and distinct manner, which is generally believed to yield higher levels of recall and recognition than can routine or nondistinctive encoding (see, for example, Jacoby and Craik 1979), does not necessarily result in superior memory performance. Fisher (1981, Fisher and Craik 1980) found that a highly distinctive encoding aids subsequent recall or recognition only when test cues reinstate those attributes of the encoded target materials that make them distinctive. When encodings are distinctive and appropriate retrieval cues are provided, however, cued recall performance can be strikingly high, with subjects recalling over 90 percent of a 600-word list (Mantyla 1986). Many other examples of encoding/retrieval interactions could be cited (see Tulving 1983 for discussion).

At a general level the conceptual importance of encoding/retrieval interactions is that they highlight the futility of attempting to make global statements about memory that take the form "Study Condition X produces more memorable representations than does Study Condition Y," or "Retrieval Cue A is more effective than Retrieval Cue B." These observations instead encourage a relativistic orientation toward memory. This orientation is represented by Tulving's encoding specificity principle, which asserts that ". . . remembering of events always depends on the interaction between encoding and retrieval conditions, or compatibility between the engram and the cue *as encoded* . . ." (1983, p. 242), and by Morris, Bransford, and Franks's (1977) principle of transfer appropriate processing, which holds that ". . . the value of particular types of acquisition activities must be defined relative to the type of activities to be performed at the time of test" (p. 531). Note that the basic ideas captured by these principles have been incorporated into widely differing models of memory, including Eich's (1982) holographic, distributed CHARM model; Raajimakers and Shiffrin's (1981) probabilistic retrieval model, search of associative memory (SAM); and Morton, Hammersley, and Bekerian's (1985) headed records framework. The fact that these approaches differ radically from one another in numerous respects, yet all subscribe in some form to an encoding/retrieval interaction principle, testifies to the fundamental importance of this general idea.

Schemas, Distortion, and Reconstruction   Most of the experimental studies cited in the previous two subsections can be characterized as "methodologically Ebbinghausian": Subjects typically studied a list of discrete to-be-remembered units, such as familiar words or digits, and were tested with recall or recognition tasks that assessed whether or not they remembered the prior occurrence of a specific unit. Although such an approach permits analysis of the *quantity* of recall or recognition as a function of various experimental manipulations, it does not readily allow for investigation of the *quality* of recollection. As noted previously, Sir Frederic Bartlett (1932) had offered harsh criticisms of this approach, arguing that it allowed for exporation of only a rather narrow domain of literal or rote remembering. In an attempt to broaden the scope of analysis, Bartlett (1932) explored memory for richer and more complex materials, such as stories and folktales. His results revealed that peoples' attempted reproductions of these complex materials were frequently incomplete, distorted, and subject to various kinds of biases and social influence. Based on these observations, Bartlett proposed that remembering is guided by a mental structure, which he called a *schema:* ". . . an active organization of past reactions, or of past experiences, which must always be supposed to be operating in any well-adapted organic response" (1932, p. 201). The general notion is that new, incoming information activates a higher-order body of relevant past knowledge and experience—a schema—and is encoded in terms of the information already present in the schema. At the time of retrieval, when the same schema is activated, recall of a prior experience typically consists of some combination of specific information that was stored about that experience and general information that is contained in the relevant schema. This notion allows for, and even predicts the occurrence of, various kinds of distortions and biases in remembering.

Although Bartlett's notion of a schema is rather fuzzy (Anderson and Bower 1973), and his experimental results have not proved easy to replicate (Alba and Hasher 1983), his approach has exerted a strong theoretical and experimental influence on cognitive research. On the theoretical side a number of investigators have argued that it is necessary to postulate the existence of large-scale or "molar" (Brewer and Nakamura 1984) organizational units, which have been referred to as schemas (see, for example, Mandler 1979, Rumelhart 1980), scripts (Bower, Black, and Turner 1979, Schank and Abelson 1977), or frames (Minsky 1975). Mandler (1979, p. 263) provides a useful summary of the cognitive conception of a schema:

. . . [a schema] is a spatially and/or temporally organized structure in which the parts are connected on the basis of contiguities that have been experienced in space or time. A schema is formed on the basis of past experience with objects, scenes, or events and consists of a set of (usually unconscious) expectations about what things look like and/or the order in which they occur. The parts, or units, of a schema consist of a set of variables, or slots, which can be filled, or instantiated, in any given instance by values that have greater or lesser degrees of probability of occurrence attached to them. Schemata vary greatly in their degree of generality—the more general the schema, the less specified, or the less predictable, are the values that may satisfy them.

On the experimental side Bartlett's work has been partly responsible for increasing investigation of memory for such rich and complex materials as sentences, stories, and real events and has also helped to focus attention on schematic influences on memory for materials (for review see Alba and Hasher 1983, Brewer and Nakamura 1984).

Support for schema-based views has been provided by demonstrations of various types of omissions and distortions in remembering. Three of the major types have been referred to by Alba and Hasher (1983) as *selection, interpretation,* and *integration.* Consider first the notion of selection. According to most schema theories, the only aspects of an event that will be represented are those that are relevant to a schema that is activated at the time of encoding. Therefore the stored representation of an event may be incomplete because a schema appropriate to incoming information is not activated, or because schema-irrelevant details are not encoded. Experimental evidence exists for both types of schema-based selection (see, for example, Bransford and Johnson 1972, Morris, Stein, and Bransford 1979, Pichert and Anderson 1977). Whereas selection is proposed to account for the incompleteness that is characteristic of memory for complex events, distortions and inaccuracies in remembering are attributed in part to a process of *interpretation:* Activated schematic knowledge provides a basis for making inferences and suppositions about the meaning of an event, and such interpretive activities may become part of an event's representation. Various demonstrations of memory for schema-based interpretations and inferences have been provided (see, for example, Johnson, Bransford, and Solomon 1973, Keenan, Baillet, and Brown 1984). Another source of mnemonic distortions is the process of *integration,* whereby various ideas and pieces of information are combined together to form a unified schematic whole. If a particular event or bit of information becomes integrated into a larger schema, it will no longer be accessible as an individual entity, and hence memory for it will be distorted. Perhaps the best-known studies on integration are Bransford and Franks's (1971) demonstration that people claim to remember complex sentences that were never explicitly presented, but could be formed by integrating simpler sentences that were presented, and the work of Loftus and her colleagues (see, for example, Loftus, Miller, and Burns 1978) that suggested that misleading information presented after the occurrence of an event is frequently integrated into the mnemonic representation of the original event.

Although the foregoing studies lend support to schema-based approaches to memory, the results of other studies considerably weaken this support (see Alba and Hasher 1983 for discussion). For instance, it is difficult to obtain evidence for integration in Bransford and Franks's paradigm when experimental procedures are altered slightly (see, for example, James and Hillinger 1977), recent research has called into question whether any integration at all can be demonstrated in the misleading information paradigm (McCloskey and Zarogoza 1985; see also Loftus, Schooler, and Wagenaar 1985), and several studies suggest that schema-based inferences do not occur as frequently or as automatically as schema theories would lead one to expect (see, for example, McKoon and Ratcliff 1981, 1986b, Singer and Ferreira 1983). Moreover findings from a variety of experiments indicate that whether one obtains evidence for the operation of schematic processes depends critically on retrieval conditions (Alba and Hasher 1983). For instance, although performance on recall tasks is consistent with the notion that memory for an event will be poor if an appropriate schema is not activated at the time of study, data from recognition tests do not support this idea (Alba and Hasher 1983). Similarly performance on recognition tests has raised questions about the idea that memory is selective, abstract, and incomplete by revealing considerable retention of schema-irrelevant detail (see, for example, Kintsch and Bates 1977). Finally, it has been shown that information about an event that is not relevant to the schema activated at the time of study and appears to be inaccessible at test can be made accessible by altering the retrieval information that is provided to the subject (Anderson and Pichert 1978). These kinds of results suggest that many different types of information—both schema relevant and schema irrelevant—are represented in memory, and that the accessibility of schema-relevant information depends critically on the nature of available retrieval cues. Such considerations call for revisions in schema theory, with greater emphasis placed on the operation of schematic processes at the time of retrieval (Alba and Hasher 1983).

It should be noted that not all research on distortions of remembering has been pursued within the context of schema theory. For instance, people sometimes mistakenly believe that they have experienced an event when in fact they only imagined it or thought about it. Recent research concerned with the problem of *reality monitoring* (Johnson and Raye 1981) has examined the relation between memory for internally and externally generated experiences and has revealed some important differences between memory for actions and perceptions on the one hand and memory for thoughts and imaginings on the other (see, for example, Anderson 1984, Foley and Johnson 1985, Johnson, Kahan, and Raye 1984). Memories of internally generated thoughts and images tend to contain less sensory and contextual detail than do memories of externally experienced events. A similar finding has emerged from experiments that compared the characteristics of memories for actual events with suggested or "implanted" memories of events that were never experienced (Schooler, Gerhard, and Loftus 1986). In addition to this work on unintentional distortions in remembering, experimental studies have begun to explore intentional distortions of memory, such as those that occur when people attempt to simulate forgetting (Brandt, Rubinsky, and Lassen 1985, Schacter 1986b). Although mnemonic distortions are not well understood, they constitute important phenomena that will have to be encompassed by any complete theory of memory.

Implicit Memory   The studies considered in previous sections address diverse aspects of memory, but they are also tied together by a common feature. In the experiments cited thus far, memory was assessed with recall and recognition tests that make explicit reference to and demand conscious recollection of a specific previous experience. In recent years, however, experimental attention has focused increasingly on a different kind of memory test that does not make explicit reference to any particular previous experience. In this type of test memory for a recent experience is inferred from facilitations of performance, generally known as repetition or direct priming effects, that need not and frequently do not involve any conscious recollection of the prior experience (see chapter 7 for methodological considerations). For example, when required to complete word fragments (for example, –AC–OS– – for LACROSSE) or stems (for example, TAB– – for TABLE) with the first word that comes to mind, subjects tend to provide items from a recently studied list (see, for example, Graf, Mandler, and Haden 1982, Tulving, Schacter, and Stark 1982). Similarly when given an extremely brief (that is, 30-ms) perceptual exposure to a word, subjects identify recently studied words more accurately than new words (see, for example, Jacoby and Dallas 1981, Winnick and Daniel 1970). This kind of memory has been referred to descriptively as *implicit memory*, whereas intentional or deliberate recollection of recent experiences has been referred to as *explicit memory* (Graf and Schacter 1985).

Scattered clinical and experimental observations concerning implicit memory have been made by psychologists, psychiatrists, and neurologists for at least two-hundred years (Schacter 1987a), but only during the past decade have implicit memory phenomena been subject to systematic experimental scrutiny (for review see Richardson-Klavehn and Bjork 1988, Schacter 1987a). This increasing attention has been motivated partly by demonstrations that brain-damaged amnesic patients show intact implicit memory despite profoundly impaired explicit memory; these findings are considered in the next subsection. It is now quite clear, however, that dissociations between implicit and explicit memory can be obtained with normal, non-brain-damaged subjects. In a recent review I identified five types of evidence for implicit/explicit dissociation (Schacter 1987a), which I now summarize briefly.

First, various studies have demonstrated that manipulations of level or type of encoding that have a large influence on explicit memory have little effect or opposite effects on various implicit memory tests (Graf et al. 1982, Graf and Mandler 1984, Jacoby 1983b, Jacoby and Dallas 1981, Schacter 1989b, Schacter and Graf 1986a, Winnick and Daniel 1970). Thus, for example, level of implicit memory performance may be unaffected by semantic versus nonsemantic study tasks that have large effects on explicit memory. Second, it has been shown that changing the presentation modality of target items between study and test (for example, auditory study followed by visual test) substantially lowers implicit memory performance, yet has nonsignificant effects on most explicit memory tests (Graf, Shimamura, and Squire 1985, Jacoby and Dallas 1981, Kirsner, Milech, and Standen 1983, Kirsner and Smith 1974, Roediger and Blaxton 1987, Schacter and Graf 1986a). Similarly study-test changes in various other kinds of physical or surface information that have little influence on explicit memory significantly reduce the level of implicit memory performance (Jacoby and Hayman 1987, Kolers 1976, Roediger and Blaxton 1987, Roediger and Weldon 1987). Third, manipulations of study-test retention interval have differential effects on implicit and explicit memory. Depending on the experimental paradigm and materials that are used, implicit memory can either persist with little change over long delays that impair explicit memory (Jacoby and Dallas 1981, Komatsu and Ohta 1984, Tulving, Schacter, and Stark 1982) or can decay rapidly across brief retention intervals that do not significantly influence explicit memory (Forster and Davis 1984, Graf and Mandler 1984). Fourth, although it has been known for almost a century that proactive and retroactive interference impair performance on explicit memory tests (see, for example, Underwood and Ekstrand 1966), recent evidence indicates that certain interference manipulations do not reduce the level of implicit memory on stem and fragment completion tests (Graf and Schacter 1987, Sloman, Hayman, Ohta, and Tulving 1988). Fifth, it has been reported in several studies that performance on implicit and explicit tests can be statistically independent of one another—that is, success or failure on an implicit memory test is uncorrelated with success or failure on an explicit memory test (Eich 1984, Graf and Schacter 1985, Jacoby and Witherspoon 1982, Schacter, Cooper, and Delaney 1989, Tulving et al. 1982).

Taken together, the foregoing studies constitute solid evidence for a fundamental difference between implicit and explicit memory. It ought to be noted, however, that various similarities between implicit and explicit memory have been established. For example, both forms of memory are influenced by new associations established during a study trial (see, for example, Graf and Schacter 1985, 1987, McKoon and Ratcliff 1979, 1986a, Schacter and Graf 1986a, 1986b), and conditions exist in which the two kinds of memory are affected similarly by levels of processing (Graf and Schacter 1985, Schacter and Graf 1986a, Schacter and McGlynn 1989) and retention interval manipulations (Jacoby 1983a, Schacter and Graf 1986a, Sloman et al. 1988). Nevertheless the evidence for dissociation is impressive, and various theoretical ideas have been proposed in response to it. As argued elsewhere, none of these ideas is entirely satisfactory (Schacter 1987a), but it is worth considering them briefly here (for more detailed discussion, see Jacoby 1983b, Richardson-Klavehn and Bjork 1988, Roediger and Weldon 1987, Schacter 1987a, Tulving 1983, 1985a).

An early idea was that priming or implicit memory is attributable to the temporary activation of preexisting knowledge structures or logo-gens (Kirsner and Smith 1974, Mandler 1980, Morton 1979, Rozin 1976). By contrast performance on explicit memory tests was presumed to depend on new, episodic representations that are established as the result of elaborate processing (Graf and Mandler 1984, Mandler 1980). Although temporary activation likely plays some role in implicit memory (Forster and Davis 1984, Schacter and Graf 1986b), the fact that priming effects can persist across long delays and are influenced by newly acquired associations argues against temporary activation as a general explanation of implicit memory phenomena. Another idea is that different memory systems underlie performance on implicit and explicit memory tests (for example, Tulving 1985a). As will become evident in the discussion of amnesic patients, some implicit/explicit dissociations appear to require the postulation of different memory systems. Taken by themselves, however, the data on priming effects in normal subjects do not provide decisive evidence for multiple memory systems. Functional independence of the kind observed between implicit and explicit memory tests (that is, differential effects of experimental variables on the two types of tests) can also be observed *within* the domain of explicit memory, where there is no need to appeal to the operation of different memory systems (Roediger 1984). Similarly the statistical independence that has been reported between implicit and explicit tasks has also been reported between two implicit tasks (Witherspoon and Moscovitch 1989), thereby suggesting that such evidence does not necessarily imply the existence of multiple memory systems. In contrast to the multiple systems view, a third approach to implicit/explicit dissociations holds that different kinds of processing are demanded by implicit and explicit tests, and that these types of processing are sensitive to specific features of newly established memory representations (see, for example, Moscovitch, Winocur, and McLachlan 1986, Jacoby 1983b, Roediger and Blaxton 1987). At a rather general level these approaches view implicit/explicit dissociations as a special case of the broader principle of encoding/retrieval interactions and thus invoke such ideas as encoding specificity and transfer appropriate processing to account for the dissociations. Although this general emphasis has much to recommend it, some of the specific processing notions that have been put forward are not entirely satisfactory (for discussion see Schacter 1987a).

Despite the apparent conflict between multiple system and processing accounts of implicit/explicit dissociations, there have been recent attempts to integrate the two approaches (Hayman and Tulving 1989, Schacter 1989b). For example, Schacter (1989b) proposed that many implicit memory phenomena depend on *perceptual representation systems* that are distinct from episodic memory. These systems, identified in recent neuropsychological research on perceptual and cognitive deficits (Ellis and Young 1988), are concerned with the representation of structural but not semantic information in various input domains. Schacter presented preliminary data consistent with this hypothesis, but the idea requires further empirical testing (see Schacter et al. 1989).

Summary The preceding four sections covered some, but not all, of the main findings and ideas concerning memory that have recently occupied experimental cognitive psychologists. Other issues of current concern include the role played by emotions and internal states in memory performance (see, for example, Blaney 1986, Bower 1981, Eich 1980, Kihlstrom 1987), remembering of autobiographical episodes (see, for example, Rubin 1986), memory for various kinds of spatial information (see, for example, Light and Zelinski 1983, McNamara 1986, Pezdek, Roman, and Sobolik 1986, Schacter and Nadel 1989), and acquisition of complex knowledge and skills, such as computer programming and text editing (see, for example, Anderson, Farrell, and Sauers 1984, Mayer 1985, Ross 1984). Although the experimental psychology of memory may have at one time been characterized by a rather stifling narrowness, this is clearly no longer the case. In fact one of the major strengths of recent cognitive research has been the ability to document and characterize carefully a host of theoretically stimulating phenomena and to provide general conceptual frameworks that have heuristic value and, in some cases, a modest level of explanatory power. At the same time, however, there is no clear consensus in the field regarding the most appropriate theoretical approach, and no current theory gracefully accommodates all or most of the important empirical facts. This is one reason why theoretical progress in cognitive psychology may be accelerated by incorporating insights from other disciplines concerned with memory.

Neuropsychological and Neurobiological Perspectives
Neuropsychological analyses of memory are based on observations of patients with neurological damage that is restricted to certain areas of the brain. For many years neuropsychological research consisted largely of clinical descriptions and psychometric profiles of memory-impaired patients. More recently a growing number of researchers have attempted to make inferences about the nature of normal memory processes on the basis of empirical studies of patients with memory disorders. The key feature of neuropsychologial impairments that permits the making of such inferences is that they are frequently *selective:* Patients' cognitive function may be entirely normal except for a particular memory process or set of memory processes. Using the logic of double dissociation (Teuber 1955), it is possible to tease apart component processes and systems of memory on the basis of selective breakdowns of function in memory-disordered patients. A double dissociation occurs when patient A performs normally on task X and abnormally on task Y, whereas patient B performs normally on task Y and abnormally on task X. Such a pattern of results provide strong

evidence that different component processes or systems are involved in performing the two tasks and cannot be readily explained by differences in task difficulty or various other factors (for further discussion see Kinsbourne 1987, Shallice 1979). Single neuropsychological dissociations (normal or near-normal performance on one memory task together with impaired performance on another) are subject to alternative interpretations that double dissociation excludes, but nevertheless can provide useful clues regarding component processes and systems of memory (Schacter and Tulving 1982, Squire 1987). I discuss two areas in which neuropsychological evidence provides a basis for fractionating memory into component systems: short-term or working memory, and implicit/explicit dissociations in long-term memory.

Short-Term Memory   Neuropsychologists concerned with memory have concentrated primarily on patients with *global amnesia* or the *amnesic syndrome*, a disorder that results from damage to diencephalic or medial temporal regions of the brain (see, for example, Whitty and Zangwill 1977). Amnesic patients perform relatively normally on standardized tests of intelligence, language, and perception. Yet they have severe difficulties remembering the ongoing events of everyday life (Schacter 1983, Squire 1987) and perform disastrously on laboratory tests that require recall and recognition of study-list materials across retention intervals of as little as a few minutes (for review see Hirst 1982, Squire and Cohen 1984, Weiskrantz 1985).

In contrast to their profoundly impaired ability to remember information across a delay, amnesic patients' immediate memory or memory span generally falls within the normal range. Even a profoundly amnesic patient, such as the famous case of H. M. (Corkin 1984, Milner, Corkin, and Teuber 1968), shows relatively good retention of digits or letters when required to reproduce them immediately after presentation (see also Shallice 1979, Warrington 1982). Although not all amnesic patients perform normally on all kinds of short-term memory tasks (Cermak 1982), the evidence for preserved immediate retention does point to some sort of distinction between processes underlying immediate and long-term memory. Further evidence for this distinction is provided by studies of a different patient population that is typically characterized by lesions to certain regions of the left parietal lobe. These patients exhibit a different pattern of results than those observed in amnesic patients: Immediate retention of verbal materials such as letters and words is seriously impaired, whereas long-term retention of verbal and other kinds of materials is unimpaired (see, for example, Shallice and Warrington 1970, Warrington and Shallice 1972). The importance of the data from this type of patient is twofold. First, in combination with the results from amnesic patients, they reveal a double dissociation between immediate memory and long-term memory, thereby indicating that distinct processes or systems are involved in these two types of remembering. Second, the fact that left parietal patients show normal long-term retention, despite having memory spans of as little as two or three items, indicates that encoding of information into long-term memory need not require the involvement of short-term memory. Thus any model that postulates that storage of new information in long-term memory depends on prior storage in short-term memory, as did the "modal model" of short-term store (see, for example, Atkinson and Shiffrin 1968), is called into question by these observations.

Recent research suggests that the working memory framework advocated by Baddeley and associates may be capable of accommodating the foregoing data. Specifically it has been hypothesized that damage to a particular subsystem of working memory, the articulatory loop, is responsible for short-term memory impairment in some patients (Baddeley 1986). Because the articulatory loop is not thought to be critical for long-term recall (Baddeley 1986), selective damage to it would leave long-term memory unimpaired. Vallar and Baddeley (1984a,b) studied a patient with a short-term memory deficit and provided experimental evidence that her impairment resulted from faulty storage of phonological information in the articulatory loop subsystem. For example, this patient's deficit was restricted to speech-based information, was more pronounced with auditory than visual study, and involved difficulty in verifying complex sentences whose interpretation is thought to require the articulatory loop. More generally the study of patients with short-term memory deficits illustrates how neuropsychological evidence can provide either converging evidence for the validity of a cognitive model or grounds for rejecting particular assumptions of a cognitive model.

Implicit/Explicit Dissociations in the Amnesic Syndrome It has been evident since the earliest clinical observations of the amnesic syndrome that patients possess implicit memory for recent experiences despite their inability to recollect those experiences consciously or explicitly (see, for example, Claparède 1911, Dunn 1845, Korsakoff 1889, Schacter 1987a). During the 1970s and 1980s numerous studies have demonstrated that amnesic patients can show normal or near-normal implicit memory across retention intervals ranging from minutes to days. Although such observations have been made in diverse experimental paradigms (see Parkin 1982, Schacter and Graf 1986b, Shimamura 1986, Squire and Cohen 1984, Weiskrantz 1985), the bulk of recent evidence derives from studies of repetition priming and skill learning.

It was noted earlier that part of the impetus for current research concerning priming effects on implicit memory tests in normal subjects was provided by studies of amnesic patients. One of the most important such studies was reported by Warrington and Weiskrantz (1968, 1974). They found that amnesic patients, like control subjects, tended to complete three-letter test stems (for example, TAB—) with words presented several minutes earlier on a study list (for example, TABLE). Yet the amnesic patients were profoundly impaired when tested with a yes/no recognition test that required them to remember explicitly the prior occurrence of a word on the study list. This striking finding has been confirmed and clarified during the past several years. Graf, Squire, and Mandler (1984) found that amnesic patients exhibit normal priming effects when test stems are given with implicit memory instructions— to write down the first word that comes to mind, but show impaired performance when the same cues are given with explicit memory instructions—to remember a particular study list item. Similar patterns of results have been observed with other familiar, overlearned materials such as highly related paired associates (Shimamura and Squire 1984), linguistic idioms (Schacter 1985b), and categorized word lists (Gardner, Boller, Moreines, and Butters 1973, Graf et al. 1985). Priming effects have also been found in some amnesic patients for newly acquired materials, such as unrelated paired associates (Graf and Schacter 1985, Moscovitch et al. 1986, Schacter and Graf 1986b), but not all amnesic patients show priming for novel information (Cermak et al. 1985, Diamond and Rozin 1984, Schacter and Graf 1986b). Although a number of studies have suggested that priming in amnesic patients is relatively short-lived (Diamond and Rozin 1984, Graf et al. 1984), recent evidence indicates that priming can persist across a one-week retention interval in densely amnesic patients (McAndrews, Glisky, and Schacter 1987).

The second domain of implicit memory in which amnesic patients have exhibited preserved learning ability involves gradual or incremental learning of various skills. This line of research dates to the studies by Milner and her colleagues that demonstrated that the profoundly amnesic patient H. M. could learn new motor skills in a near normal manner: Performance on various motor tasks improved across trials and sessions, even though H. M. did not explicitly remember having previously performed any of the tasks (see, for example, Milner, Corkin, and Teuber 1968). Similar patterns of results have been reported with other amnesic patients on such tasks as puzzle solving (Brooks and Baddeley 1976), reading of mirror-inverted script (Cohen and Squire 1980, Moscovitch et al. 1986), responding to repeated sequential patterns (Nissen and Bullemer 1987), and learning of mathematical rules (Kinsbourne and Wood 1975). Significantly recent research has revealed a double dissociation between skill learning and explicit remembering: Patients suffering from Huntington's disease, a degenerative condition that affects the basal ganglia, perform normally on explicit recognition tests, but have severe difficulty learning new motor skills (Heindel, Butters, and Salmon 1988).

At a rather general level the importance of the foregoing research is to demonstrate unequivocally that recent experiences can influence performance and behavior in the absence of conscious recollection of those experiences (a similar conclusion is suggested by research on *functional amnesia*, in which memory loss is produced by emotional trauma, hypnosis, or other psychological influences; for discussion see Kihlstrom 1987, Schacter and Kihlstrom 1989). This fundamental fact will have to be accommodated by any comprehensive model of memory. One popular interpretive strategy in recent years has been to argue that amnesic patients' preserved learning abilities reflect the operation of a memory system that is neurologically and psychologically distinct from the system that underlies conscious recollection of experiences. For example, Squire and Cohen (1984, Cohen 1984) adopted the distinction made originally in artificial intelligence between procedural and declarative memory (see, for example, Winograd 1975). Procedural memory involves on-line modification of processing operations; knowledge is represented and expressed implicitly as a change in a particular procedure or operation. Declarative memory, on the other hand, involves representation of the *outcome* of a processing operation that is available to conscious recall. The procedural memory system is held to be preserved in amnesic patients, whereas the declarative system is held to be impaired. Mishkin and his colleagues drew a similar distinction between a *habit* system, which is characterized by gradual strengthening of stimulus-response bonds, and a *memory* system, which is characterized by "cognitive" representations of experiences (Mishkin, Malamut, and Bachevalier 1984). Various other similar distinctions have been put forward (for discussion see Cohen 1984, Kinsbourne 1987, Parkin 1982, Schacter 1987a, Shimamura 1986, Squire 1987, Weiskrantz 1987).

The fact that a double dissociation exists between skill learning and explicit recollection supports the general proposition that these abilities are subserved by distinct systems, and the procedural/declarative and habit/memory distinctions would appear to offer reasonable first-approximations concerning the general properties of these systems. What about priming effects? Although it has been contended that both priming and skill learning depend on the procedural system (Cohen 1984, Squire and Cohen 1984; see Squire 1987 for a somewhat different emphasis), Heindel and colleagues (1988) reported a double dissociation between priming and skill learning; Alzheimer patients showed impaired priming and normal motor skill learning, whereas patients with Huntington's disease showed the opposite pattern of results. If double dissociation between skill learning and explicit remembering is taken as evidence for the existence of different memory systems, then the double dissociation between priming and skill learning suggests that these two abilities do not reflect the operation of the same underlying system. As discussed previously with respect to studies of normal subjects, it is possible that priming is based partly on activation of preexisting representations and partly on new perceptual representations that influence performance independently of conscious recollection (see Schacter 1989b for discussion). The sheer variety of situations in which amnesic patients show implicit memory for a recent episode (Schacter, McAndrews, and Moscovitch 1988) also suggests that in some instances priming may reflect the influence of new declarative or episodic representations on verbal or motor response systems together with a failure of these representations to gain access to processes necessary for conscious awareness of remembering (Moscovitch et al. 1986, Schacter 1989a, Weiskrantz 1978).

Studies of Brain-Lesioned Animals   Dissociations between different types of memory tasks have also been observed in neurobiological studies of animal memory. Specifically, studies that have compared the performance of normal animals with that of brain-lesioned animals provide converging evidence for the dissociability of systems underlying gradual acquisition of skills or habits on the one hand and one-trial memory for single episodes on the other. The logic of dissociation employed in these studies is similar to that used in research with patient populations: One looks for selective impairments of specific memory processes, as reflected by single and double dissociations between different types of memory tasks. There are of course questions concerning the validity of inferences about human memory that are drawn from animal research. Nonetheless an advantage of animal studies is that brain lesions are made experimentally and are thus more precisely circumscribed than in the "experiments of nature" on which human neuropsychology depends. Using this approach, various studies have shown that monkeys with lesions to hippocampus and related medial temporal structures perform poorly on various tasks that require memory for a single episode, such as delayed matching and nonmatching to sample (for results and task descriptions, see Malamut, Saunder, and Mishkin 1984, Zola-Morgan and Squire 1984). Yet such animals show normal performance on tasks that require gradual learning of habits and skills, including object and pattern discriminations (Mahut and Moss 1984, Malamut et al. 1984) and motor skills (Zola-Morgan and Squire 1984). Moreover similar dissociations have been observed in hippocampal rats (see, for example, O'Keefe and Nadel 1978, Thomas 1984). Accordingly the convergence of results from human and animal studies lends strong support to the idea that memory for single episodes depends on a neural system that differs fundamentally from the system underlying perceptual and motor skill acquisition. An intriguing and as yet unanswered question concerns whether amnesic animals show priming effects that reflect implicit memory for single episodes (Tulving 1987). One possibility is that even normal animals possess implicit memory only—they can be influenced by a recent event without explicitly remembering its prior occurrence—and that all studies of single-trial retention in animals are priming studies. It seems equally reasonable, however, to maintain that many animals do possess something akin to explicit, conscious remembering in humans (Mishkin et al. 1984, Schacter 1985a, Squire 1987). To the extent that this is so, it ought to be possible to devise experimental paradigms to dissociate priming and remembering in animals.

Frontal Lobe Impairments and the Episodic/Semantic Distinction It is worth mentioning briefly one further area of neuropsychological research that has demonstrated some convergence between human and animal work and also raises an issue not yet touched upon, namely, the relation between episodic and semantic memory. Studies of both humans and animals have revealed that lesions to specific areas of the frontal lobes result in selective impairments of memory for certain kinds of spatiotemporal information. Although frontal lesions generally spare recall and recognition of recently presented items, they disrupt memory for which of two items occurred more recently as well as the ability to perform tasks that require temporal discriminations (for review and discussion, see Milner, Petrides, and Smith 1985, Schacter 1987b, Squire 1987). These findings may bear upon Tulving's (1972, 1983) much-discussed distinction between episodic memory (recollection of contextually specific events) and semantic memory (general knowledge of facts, vocabulary). There has been a good deal of debate as to whether dissociations observed in normal and amnesic subjects provide evidence for or against this distinction; the state of the argument is somewhat ambiguous (see Kinsbourne 1987, McKoon, Ratcliff, and Dell 1986, Roediger and Blaxton 1987, Schacter 1987a, Squire 1987, Tulving 1983, 1986). The data concerning frontal lobe lesions, however, provide clear evidence that one of the key components of episodic memory—temporal information concerning when an item occurred—is mediated by neural processes different from those needed for recall and recognition. If one is willing to identify episodic memory with recollection of spatial and temporal contextual information, and semantic memory with recollection of the items presented during an episode, then it can be argued that the data on frontal lobe lesions support an episodic/semantic distinction (see, for example, Tulving 1987). Drawing the distinction in this way, however, is not entirely satisfying, either. For example, it would lead to the suggestion that frontal lobe patients—who can recall previously studied items relatively normally, but have difficulty remembering their temporal order—have an episodic memory deficit, whereas amnesic patients without frontal damage—who perform disastrously when required to recall previously studied items, but have no special problem with temporal discrimination (Squire 1982)—have a semantic memory deficit. This kind of conceptualization is clearly contrary to the spirit of the episodic/semantic distinction. It is probably more reasonable to hypothesize that remembering of temporal order constitutes one *component* of episodic memory, subserved by certain frontal regions, and that remembering of recently presented items constitutes another component of episodic memory, likely subserved by medial temporal regions.

Ecological and Evolutionary Approaches

The research that has been considered thus far in the chapter addresses diverse aspects of memory. However, two features are shared by virtually all of the cited studies. First, the general goal has been to specify the mechanisms of memory and to delineate broad principles that accommodate many different experimental results. Second, almost all studies have used controlled laboratory experimentation as their sole investigative tool. In recent years a number of researchers have contended that exclusive reliance on these approaches has hindered progress in understanding memory. They have argued for an ecological or naturalistic orientation in which empirical studies examine the role that memory plays in real-life environments, and memory is conceptualized within a broad evolutionary framework. Part of the impetus for this approach has come from mainstream cognitive psychology (see, for example, Neisser 1982), and part from studies of animal learning (see, for example, Rozin and Kalat 1971, Shettleworth 1972). In this subsection I consider briefly some of the contributions to the study of memory that can be made by ecological and evolutionary approaches.

Within cognitive psychology the most visible proponent of an ecological orientation toward memory has been Neisser (1976, 1982). By his view much of the experimental work in mainstream cognitive psychology has concerned itself with artificial phenomena that have little meaning outside of the particular theoretical frameworks and experimental paradigms within which they are pursued. For example, Neisser (1976) points out that once interference theory lost popularity, most of the related experimental phenomena, such as extinction, unlearning, and spontaneous recovery, became meaningless to and were thus ignored by researchers operating in a different conceptual framework. One of the attractions of an ecological approach, according to Neisser, is that observations of naturally occurring memory phenomena ought to be interesting and relevant whatever the prevailing frameworks and paradigms of the day.

There can be little doubt that cognitive psychology must plead guilty to Neisser's charge that it has largely ignored naturalistic observations of memory. In recent years, however, increasing attention has been paid to naturally occurring memory phenomena, partly as a result of Neisser's challenge (see, for example, Harris and Morris 1984, Rubin 1986, Schacter 1983, Zola-Morgan and Oberg 1980). Nevertheless, as Bruce (1985) has pointed out, acknowledgment of the value of naturalistic observations need not imply that laboratory research is inherently useless, nor that attempts to develop general theoretical accounts of memory mechanisms ought to be abandoned. Whereas laboratory research focuses on what Bruce (1985) refers to as *how*-questions (that is, how memory processes operate), ecological research is more concerned with *why*-questions that focus on the functions that memory serves in everyday life. It seems clear that these two approaches ought to complement and enrich one another; they have different insights to offer and need not be mutually exclusive. However, there has not yet been very much interactive exchange between laboratory and ecological approaches.

As part of their emphasis on function and on the importance of the natural environment, ecological approaches are also concerned with questions about the evolution of memory. Because memory abilities have presumably evolved in response to environmental demands, consideration of evolutionary issues should enhance our understanding of the current structure and function of memory. Of course it is difficult to empirically examine evolutionary issues with respect to human memory, so most observations have been provided by ecologically oriented studies of animals (for review and discussion, see Johnston 1981, Rozin and Schull 1989, Shettleworth 1983).

In a recent article Sherry and Schacter (1987) attempted to develop an evolutionary analysis that bears on questions concerning human memory, specifically the issue of multiple memory systems. As a foundation for their analysis, Sherry and Schacter delineated four components of an evolutionary approach to memory. The first is Darwin's principle of natural selection, which states that some elements of heritable variation enhance survival and reproduction more than others do and are thus preserved by evolution. To the extent that memory is subject to natural selection, it should possess features that reflect solutions to environmental problems. Second, for memory to be acted on by natural selection, it must exhibit some *heritable variation*—that is, there must be genetic coding of memory abilities that varies over a population and can be subject to selection. Sherry and Schacter reviewed several lines of evidence indicating that genetic effects on memory have been demonstrated. Third, heritable variation in memory must have consequences for reproduction and survival. Ethological observations suggest that this is so. Animals learn to recognize dangerous predators (Vieth, Curio, and Ernst 1980), remember the outcome of contests that determine social hierarchies (Colgan 1983), and recall information about the distribution and abundance of food (Stephens 1981). The advantages conferred by good memory in these and other situations would be expected to be preserved by selection. The fourth component of an evolutionary approach to memory is the concept of *adaptive specialization* (Rozin and Kalat 1971): a specific memory ability that is formed in response to a particular environmental problem and that differs in structure and function from memory abilities formed in response to other environmental problems. A number of striking adaptive specializations of memory have been studied, including song learning in birds, learning of olfactory orientation cues by salmonoid fish, and learning of stellar orientation by migratory birds (for review, see Rozin and Schull 1989, Sherry and Schacter 1987, Shettleworth 1983). The memory capacities observed in these instances are highly specialized, isolated, and somewhat unusual; in song learning, for example, only certain types of information are admitted to memory, and there are severe temporal restrictions on when it can be retrieved (see, for example, Kroodsma 1982). These kinds of observations support the idea that memory has evolved in response to the demands posed by particular environmental problems.

Sherry and Schacter applied their evolutionary analysis to the problem of multiple memory systems. They argued that multiple systems would be an expected evolutionary outcome when the properties of an existing memory system, as shaped by selection in response to a specific environmental problem, are not compatible with the solution of a new problem: The very features of a memory system that make it adaptive with respect to one environmental problem (for example, song learning) may render it less useful or downright maladaptive with respect to another problem (for example, food storing). Sherry and Schacter referred to this condition as *functional incompatibility* and provided several examples of how functional incompatibility has led to the evolution of multiple memory systems in animals. They also applied this analysis to the previously discussed dissociations observed in humans and argued that evolutionary considerations support a distinction between a system that is involved in gradual habit or skill learning and a system that subserves recall and recognition of single events: The problems handled by one system demand an architecture that is incompatible with effective solution of the problems handled by the other system. In contrast evolutionary analysis provided no strong grounds for supposing that priming effects are handled by a different memory system than the one involved in recall and recognition (but see Schacter 1989b).

At a more general level Sherry and Schacter noted that evolutionary considerations may provide a useful source of information that can help to clarify the theoretical significance of empirically demonstrated dissociations. As acknowledged by several investigators, the mere observation of an experimental dissociation does not specify the nature and theoretical meaning of the dissociation (McKoon et al. 1986, Roediger 1984, Tulving 1983). Once a dissociation has been observed, however, functional and evolutionary considerations can help to guide and shape theoretical formulations. Although evolutionary propositions are themselves difficult to test empirically (see Sherry and Schacter 1987 for discussion), cognitive scientists should not lose sight of the fact that memory is a biological adaptation to significant problems that have been posed by natural environments. Ecological and evolutionary approaches highlight the importance of incorporating such considerations into theoretical conceptualizations of memory.

Artificial Intelligence and Parallel Distributed Processing
Having closed the preceding subsection with a plea to consider biological and ecological constraints on memory, it may seem somewhat

strange to discuss next the role of artificial intelligence (AI) in the understanding of memory; after all, the very name of this approach would appear to place it in opposition to any "naturalistic" orientation. Consistent, however, with the interdisciplinary theme that runs throughout this chapter, I would suggest that AI, like the other disciplines considered, has a particular role in the analysis of memory, but is not itself sufficient to provide a full understanding of memory. Specifically AI can contribute to the understanding of memory both by providing novel conceptual frameworks and ideas and by providing analytical tools for specifying and evaluating theoretical ideas—computer simulations—that complement traditional experimental methodologies.

Consideration of existing literature indicates that a number of ideas developed in AI have helped to shape current conceptualizations of memory. For example, part of the impetus for schema theory was provided by the development in AI of such notions as "frames" (Minsky 1975) and "scripts" (Schank and Abelson 1977). Although Bartlett (1932) had developed the notion of a "schema" many years earlier, the work in AI fleshed out the frame and script ideas in greater detail than Bartlett had ever done with schemas, thus providing for experimental cognitive psychologists a far richer theoretical structure for empirical and conceptual development. Similarly Newell and Simon's (1972) work on production systems provided a basis for the development of Anderson's (1976, 1983) general account of memory and cognition, in which productions—condition/action units that fire when particular conditions are satisfied—play a major role. Another influential idea is the distinction between procedural and declarative knowledge, which emerged from a debate in AI concerning the most useful ways of representing knowledge in computer programs. Winograd (1975) delineated the benefits and drawbacks of each type of representation and in so doing provided a contrast between the characteristics of procedural and declarative knowledge that has since been seized upon by cognitive psychologists and neuropsychologists. Winograd also discussed the general issue of modularity of knowledge representation, a point that was developed further by Minsky (1980) in a theoretical account of memory. Minsky argued for a higher modular "society of mind" in which different types of information are represented in domain-specific divisions that have limited access to one another. This general account presaged the current concern with multiple forms of memory and with modular cognitive organization more generally (see, for example, Fodor 1983, Gazzaniga 1985). A more recent example of a useful AI model of memory is provided by Kolodner's (1983) work on reconstructive retrieval. Although cognitive psychologists have long been aware of the fact that memory retrieval is often reconstructive—involving considerable problem-solving activity, inference making, extended searches for useful cues, and the like (see, for example, Williams and Hollan 1981)—

there have been few attempts to develop explicit theoretical accounts of these reconstructive processes. Kolodner has done just this and has provided a detailed model, in the form of a computer program called CYRUS, that offers several new ideas concerning the nature of reconstructive retrieval.

At present the most influential set of AI-related ideas concerning memory (and cognition more generally) derive from the general class of models known as parallel distributed processing (PDP) models (McClelland and Rumelhart 1986, Rumelhart and McClelland 1986). The basic principles embodied in these models—distributed representation of information, encoding of memory in the strength of connections between units, and learning via gradual changes in connection strengths—are reviewed in detail by Rumelhart in chapter 4. The ascendence of PDP models in cognitive science has occurred rather swiftly during the past five years, but it is interesting to note that an edited volume containing various PDP models of memory had appeared with relatively little fanfare several years earlier (Hinton and Anderson 1981), and some of the work discussed in it extended back a decade or more. Serious attempts to determine whether PDP models can provide a satisfactory account of experimentally established phenomena of human memory have begun only recently, so evaluation of their ability to accommodate actual data is somewhat premature. Nonetheless it is worth noting that PDP models have been applied with reasonable success to data concerning prototype learning, priming effects in word identification, and residual skill-learning abilities in amnesic patients (McClelland and Rumelhart 1986, chs. 17, 25). As PDP proponents themselves acknowledge, however, the models are best suited to situations in which learning is accomplished gradually across trials, through small changes in connection strengths; it is less clear whether they provide a satisfactory account of recall and recognition of single episodes. It is also interesting to consider PDP models in the context of the distinction between implicit and explicit memory. Would a system that operated purely according to PDP principles consciously remember a prior experience or, like the amnesic patient, would such a system merely show implicit effects of a prior experience in performance, without any conscious or explicit recollection? My own guess is that systems depicted by PDP models are largely implicit memory machines: When a new pattern of activation partially matches an existing pattern of activation, the existing pattern is automatically strengthened and affects the response tendencies of the system, without any recollective experience or conscious awareness of a past event. An important future task for PDP models will be to come to grips with the problem of conscious recollection and more generally with the role of consciousness in learning and cognition (Norman 1986).

In summary ideas from AI have been and continue to be influential in shaping theories of human memory, and experimental observations of memory have also been useful for AI researchers (see, for example, Kolodner 1983). Yet it would be naive to ignore the substantial differences in pretheoretical assumptions and methodological approaches that separate AI from experimental disciplines (Lehnert 1984) and that on occasion can lead to intolerance and even hostility between practitioners in the two camps. The emergence of PDP models, however, appears to offer a multidisciplinary point of convergence whereby investigators in AI, cognitive psychology, neuropsychology, and neurobiology can all interact profitably with one another to develop new and perhaps powerful ideas about memory.

17.2 Concluding Comments

The main purpose of this chapter has been to acquaint the reader with some of the findings and ideas of the various disciplines that can contribute to a cognitive science of memory. It should now be evident that each discipline can offer uniquely valuable contributions: experimental cognitive psychology has delineated the characteristics of an impressive range of robust empirical phenomena and offered some general principles to accommodate them; neuropsychology and neurobiology have provided the opportunity to observe sharp dissociations between component processes and systems of memory; ecological and evolutionary approaches have reminded us of the importance of functional considerations in the formulation and evaluation of theoretical ideas; and artificial intelligence has suggested new ways of conceptualizing both the architecture and operation of memory.

If there is one general conclusion that can be extracted from the diverse territory that has been covered, it is that—perhaps paradoxically—chapters such as this ought to be entitled just about anything other than "Memory." This is another way of saying that recent developments in the various relevant disciplines all indicate that memory is not a monolithic entity, but instead comes in numerous varieties or forms: priming studies have demonstrated a striking dissociation between implicit and explicit memory, neuropsychological and neurobiological research have shown that skill learning depends on different neural structures than does remembering of single episodes, evolutionary observations have revealed idiosyncratic adaptive specializations in various animals, and developments in AI have highlighted the differences between procedural and declarative representations. Theoretical interpretation of the relations among the various forms of memory is of course still very much up for grabs; in some cases it may be necessary to appeal to the operation of neurologically distinct memory systems, whereas in other instances the dissociations may be telling us about the relation between memory processes on the one hand and processes underlying conscious awareness on the other (compare Kihlstrom 1987, Moscovitch et al. 1986, Jacoby 1984, Schacter 1989a, Tulving 1985a, 1985b,

Weiskrantz 1978, 1985). Nonetheless further interdisciplinary analyses concerning the nature of and relations among different forms of memory appears to be a highly profitable line to pursue. Such analyses could facilitate development of an adequate taxonomy of memory processes and systems, link observations of modularity in memory with observations of modularity in other domains of cognition (see, for example, Fodor 1983, Gazzaniga 1985, Marr 1982, Shallice 1981), and lay the groundwork for a genuine interdisciplinary understanding of memory that is essential for the development of cognitive science.

Notes

Writing of this chapter was supported by a Biomedical Research Support Grant from the National Institutes of Health. I thank Lynn Cooper, Elizabeth Glisky, John Kihlstrom, Susan McGlynn, Lynn Nadel, Michael Posner, and two anonymous reviewers for useful comments and discussion.

References

Adelson, B. 1984. When novices surpass experts: the difficulty of a task may increase with expertise. *Journal of Experimental Psychology: Learning, Memory, and Cognition* 10:483–495.

Alba, J. W., and Hasher, L. 1983. Is memory schematic? *Psychological Bulletin* 93:203–231.

Anderson, J. R. 1976. *Language, Memory, and Thought.* Hillsdale, NJ: Erlbaum.

Anderson, J. R. 1983. *The Architecture of Cognition.* Cambridge: Harvard University Press.

Anderson, J. R. 1985. Ebbinghaus's century. *Journal of Experimental Psychology: Learning, Memory, and Cognition* 11:436–438.

Anderson, J. R., and Bower, G. H. 1973. *Human Associative Memory.* Washington, DC: V. H. Winston and Sons.

Anderson, J. R., Farrell, R., and Sauers, R. 1984. Learning to program in LISP. *Cognitive Science* 8:87–129.

Anderson, R. C., and Pichert, J. W. 1978. Recall of previously unrecallable information following a shift in perspective. *Journal of Verbal Learning and Verbal Behavior* 17:1–12.

Anderson, R. E. 1984. Did I do it or only imagine it? *Journal of Experimental Psychology: General* 113:594–613.

Atkinson, R. C., and Shiffrin, R. M. 1968. Human memory: A proposed system and its control processes. In K. W. Spence and J. T. Spence, eds. *The Psychology of Learning and Motivation.* Vol. 2. New York: Academic Press.

Baddeley, A. D. 1976. *The Psychology of Memory.* New York: Basic Books, Inc.

Baddeley, A. D. 1978. The trouble with "levels": A re-examination of Craik and Lockhart's framework for memory research. *Psychological Review* 85:139–152.

Baddeley, A. D. 1986. *Working Memory.* Oxford: Clarendon Press.

Baddeley, A. D., and Hitch, G. J. 1974. Working memory. In G. Bower, ed. *Advances in Learning and Motivation.* Vol. 8. New York: Academic Press, pp. 47–90.

Baddeley, A. D., and Lieberman, K. 1980. Spatial working memory. In R. Nickerson, ed. *Attention and Performance VIII.* Hillsdale, NJ: Erlbaum, pp. 521–539.

Baddeley, A. D., Logie, R. H., Nimmo-Smith, M. I., and Brereton, N. 1985. Components of fluent reading. *Journal of Memory and Language* 24:119–131.

Baddeley, A. D., Thomson, N., and Buchanan, M. 1975. Word length and the structure of short-term memory. *Journal of Verbal Learning and Verbal Behavior* 14:575–589.

Bartlett, F. C. 1932. *Remembering.* London: Cambridge University Press.

Blaney, P. H. 1986. Affect and memory: A review. *Psychological Bulletin* 99:229–246.

Boring, E. G. 1929. *A History of Experimental Psychology.* New York: The Century Co.

Bower, G. H. 1972. Mental imagery and associative learning. In L. Gregg, ed. *Cognition in Learning and Memory.* New York: Wiley.

Bower, G. H. 1981. Mood and memory. *American Psychologist* 36:129–148.

Bower, G. H., Black, J. B., and Turner, T. J. 1979. Scripts in memory for text. *Cognitive Psychology* 11:177–220.

Brandt, J., Rubinsky, E., and Lassen, G. 1985. Uncovering malingered amnesia. *Annals of the New York Academy of Sciences* 444:502–503.

Bransford, J. D., and Johnson, M. K. 1972. Contextual prerequisites for understanding: Some investigations of comprehension and recall. *Journal of Verbal Learning and Verbal Behavior* 11:717–726.

Bransford, J. D., and Franks, J. J. 1971. The abstraction of linguistic ideas. *Cognitive Psychology* 2:331–350.

Brewer, W. F., and Nakamura, G. V. 1984. The nature and functions of schemas. In R. S. Wyer and T. K. Srull, eds. *Handbook of Social Cognition.* Hillsdale, NJ: Erlbaum.

Brooks, D. N., and Baddeley, A. D. 1976. What can amnesic patients learn? *Neuropsychologia* 14:111–122.

Bruce, D. 1985. The how and why of ecological memory. *Journal of Experimental Psychology: General* 114:78–90.

Cermak, L. S. ed. 1982. *Human Memory and Amnesia.* Hillsdale, NJ: Erlbaum.

Cermak, L. S., Talbot, N., Chandler, K., and Wolbarst, L. R. 1985. The perceptual priming phenomenon in amnesia. *Neuropsychologia* 23:615–622.

Chase, W. G., and Ericsson, K. A. 1981. Skilled memory. In J. R. Anderson, ed. *Cognitive Skills and their Acquisition.* Hillsdale, NJ: Erlbaum.

Chiesi, H., Spillich, G., and Voss, J. F. 1979. Acquisition of domain-related information in relation to high and low domain knowledge. *Journal of Verbal Learning and Verbal Behavior* 18:257–273.

Claparède, E. 1911. Reconnaissance et moiite. *Archives de Psychologie* 11:79–90. Recognition and 'me-ness.' In D. Rapaport, ed. 1951. *Organization and Pathology of Thought.* New York: Columbia University Press, pp. 58–75.

Cohen, N. J. 1984. Preserved learning capacity in amnesia: Evidence for multiple memory systems. In L. R. Squire and N. Butters, eds. *Neuropsychology of Memory.* New York: Guilford Press, pp. 83–103.

Cohen, N. J., and Squire, L. R. 1980. Preserved learning and retention of pattern-analyzing skill in amnesia: Dissociation of "knowing how" and "knowing that." *Science* 210:207–209.

Colgan, P. 1983. *Comparative Social Recognition.* New York: Wiley-Interscience.

Collins, A. M., and Quillian, M. R. 1969. Retrieval time from semantic memory. *Journal of Verbal Learning and Verbal Behavior* 8:240–247.

Corkin, S. 1984. Lasting consequences of bilateral medial temporal lobectomy: Clinical course and experimental findings in H. M. *Seminars in Neurology* 4:249–259.

Craik, F. I. M. 1979. Human memory. *Annual Review of Psychology* 30:63–102.

Craik, F. I. M., and Lockhart, R. S. 1972. Levels of processing: A framework for memory research. *Journal of Verbal Learning and Verbal Behavior* 11:671–684.

Craik, F. I. M., and Tulving, E. 1975. Depth of processing and the retention of words in episodic memory. *Journal of Experimental Psychology: General* 104:168–294.

Crowder, R. G. 1976. *Principles of Learning and Memory.* Hillsdale, NJ: Erlbaum.

Crowder, R. G. 1982. The demise of short-term memory. *Acta Psychologica* 50:291–323.

Daneman, M., and Carpenter, P. A. 1980. Individual differences in working memory and reading. *Journal of Verbal Learning and Verbal Behavior* 19:450–66.

de Groot, A. D. 1965. *Thought and Choice in Chess.* The Hague: Mouton.

Diamond, R., and Rozin, P. 1984. Activation of existing memories in the amnesic syndrome. *Journal of Abnormal Psychology* 93:98–105.

Dunn, R., 1845. Case of suspension of the mental faculties. *Lancet* 2:588–590.

Ebbinghaus, H. 1885. *Uber das Gedächtnis.* Leipzig: Duncker and Humblot.

Eich, J. E. 1980. The cue-dependent nature of state-dependent retrieval. *Memory and Cognition* 8:157–173.

Eich, J. E. 1982. A composite holographic associative recall model. *Psychological Review* 89:627–661.

Eich, J. E. 1984. Memory for unattended events: Remembering with and without awareness. *Memory and Cognition* 12:105–111.

Ellis, A., and Young, A. 1988. *Human Cognitive Neuropsychology*. London: Erlbaum.

Ellis, N. C., and Hennelley, R. A. 1980. A bilingual word-length effect: Implications for intelligence testing and the relative ease of mental calculation in Welsh and English. *British Journal of Psychology* 71:43–52.

Fisher, R. P. 1981. Interaction between encoding distinctiveness and test conditions. *Journal of Experimental Psychology: Human Learning and Memory* 7:306–310.

Fisher, R. P., and Craik, F. I. M. 1977. The interaction between encoding and retrieval operations in cued recall. *Journal of Experimental Psychology: Human Learning and Memory* 3:701–711.

Fisher, R. P., and Craik, F. I. M. 1980. The effects of elaboration on recognition memory. *Memory and Cognition* 8:400–404.

Fodor, J. A. 1983. *The Modularity of Mind*. Cambridge, MA: MIT Press.

Foley, M. A., and Johnson, M. K. 1985. Confusions between memories for performed and imagined actions: A developmental comparison. *Developmental Psychology* 56:1145–1155.

Forster, K. I., and Davis, C. 1984. Repetition priming and frequency attenuation in lexical access. *Journal of Experimental Psychology: Learning, Memory, and Cognition* 10:680–698.

Gardner, H., Boller, F., Moreines, J., and Butters, N. 1973. Retrieving information from Korsakoff patients: Effects of categorical cues and reference to the task. *Cortex* 9:165–175.

Gazzaniga, M. 1985. *The Social Brain*. New York: Basic Books.

Gorfein, D. J., and Hoffman, R. R., eds. *Memory and Cognitive Processes: The Ebbinghaus Centennial Conference*. Hillsdale, NJ: Erlbaum.

Graf, P., and Mandler, G. 1984. Activation makes words more accessible, but not necessarily more retrievable. *Journal of Verbal Learning and Verbal Behavior* 23:553–568.

Graf, P., Mandler, G., and Haden, P. 1982. Simulating amnesic symptoms in normal subjects. *Science* 218:1243–1244.

Graf, P., and Schacter, D. L. 1985. Implicit and explicit memory for new associations in normal and amnesic subjects. *Journal of Experimental Psychology: Learning, Memory, and Cognition* 11:501–518.

Graf, P., and Schacter, D. L. 1987. Selective effects of interference on implicit and explicit memory for new associations. *Journal of Experimental Psychology: Learning, Memory, and Cognition* 12:45–53.

Graf, P., Shimamura, A. P., and Squire, L. R. 1985. Priming across modalities and priming across category levels: Extending the domain of preserved function in amnesia. *Journal of Experimental Psychology: Learning, Memory, and Cognition* 11:385–395.

Graf, P., Squire, L. R., and Mandler, G. 1984. The information that amnesic patients do not forget. *Journal of Experimental Psychology: Learning, Memory, and Cognition* 10:164–178.

Harris, J., and Morris, P. E. 1984. *Everyday Memory, Actions and Absent-mindedness*. London: Academic Press.

Hayman, C. A. G., and Tulving, E. 1989. Contingent dissociation between cognition and fragment completion: The method of triangulation. *Journal of Experimental Psychology: Learning, Memory, and Cognition* 15:222–248.

Heindel, W. C., Butters, N., and Salmon, D. P. 1988. Impaired learning of a motor skill in patients with Huntington's disease. *Behavioral Neuroscience* 102:141–147.

Hering, E. 1920. Memory as a universal function of organized matter. In S. Butler, ed. *Unconscious Memory*. London: Jonathan Cape.

Hinton, G., and Anderson, J. A. 1981. *Parallel Models of Associative Memory*. Hillsdale, NJ: Erlbaum.

Hirst, W. 1982. The amnesic syndrome: Descriptions and explanations. *Psychological Bulletin* 91:435–460.

Hitch, G. J., and Halliday, M. S. 1983. Working memory in children. *Philosophical Transactions of the Royal Society London B* 302:325–340.

Jacoby, L. L. 1983a. Perceptual enhancement: Persistent effects of an experience. *Journal of Experimental Psychology: Learning, Memory, and Cognition* 9:21–38.

Jacoby, L. L. 1983b. Remembering the data: Analyzing interactive processes in reading. *Journal of Verbal Learning and Verbal Behavior* 22:485–508.

Jacoby, L. L. 1984. Incidental versus intentional retrieval: Remembering and awareness as separate issues. In L. R. Squire and N. Butters, eds. *Neuropsychology of Memory*. New York: Guilford Press, pp. 145–156.

Jacoby, L. L., and Craik, F. I. M. 1979. Effects of elaboration of processing at encoding and retrieval: Trace distinctiveness and recovery of initial context. In L. S. Cermak and F. I. M. Craik, eds. *Levels of Processing and Human Memory*. Hillsdale, NJ: Erlbaum.

Jacoby, L. L., and Dallas M. 1981. On the relationship between autobiographical memory and perceptual learning. *Journal of Experimental Psychology: General* 110:306–340.

Jacoby, L. L., and Hayman, C. G. 1987. Specific visual transfer in word identification. *Journal of Experimental Psychology: Learning, Memory and Cognition* 13:456–463.

Jacoby, L. L., and Witherspoon, D. 1982. Remembering without awareness. *Canadian Journal of Psychology* 36:300–324.

James, C. T., and Hillinger, M. L. 1977. The role of confusion in the semantic integration paradigm. *Journal of Verbal Learning and Verbal Behavior* 16:711–721.

Johnson, M. K., Bransford, J. D., and Solomon, S. K. 1973. Memory for tacit implications of sentences. *Journal of Experimental Psychology* 98:203–205.

Johnson, M. K., Kahan, T. L., and Raye, C. L. 1984. Dreams and reality monitoring. *Journal of Experimental Psychology: General* 113:329–344.

Johnson, M. K., and Raye, C. L. 1981. Reality monitoring. *Psychological Review* 88:67–85.

Johnston, T. D. 1981. Contrasting approaches to a theory of learning. *Behavioral and Brain Sciences* 4:125–173.

Keenan, J., Baillet, S., and Brown, P. 1984. The effects of causal cohesion on comprehension, and memory. *Journal of Verbal Learning and Verbal Behavior* 23:115–126.

Kihlstrom, J. F. 1987. The cognitive unconscious. *Science* 237:1445–1452.

Kinsbourne, M. 1987. Brain mechanisms and memory. *Human Neurobiology* 6:81–92.

Kinsbourne, M., and Wood, F. 1975. Short-term memory and the amnesic syndrome. In D. D. Deutsch and J. A. Deutsch, eds. *Short-Term Memory.* New York: Academic Press, pp. 258–291.

Kintsch, W., and Bates, E. 1977. Recognition memory for statements from a classroom lecture. *Journal of Experimental Psychology: Human Learning and Memory* 3:150–159.

Kintsch, W., Miller, J. R., and Polson, P. G., eds. *Method and Tactics in Cognitive Science.* Hillsdale, NJ: Erlbaum, pp. 21–50.

Kirsner, K., Milech, D., and Standen, P. 1983. Common and modality-specific processes in the mental lexicon. *Memory and Cognition* 11:621–630.

Kirsner, K., and Smith, M. C. 1974. Modality effects in word identification. *Memory and Cognition* 2:637–640.

Koffka, K. 1935. *Principles of Gestalt Psychology.* New York: Harcourt, Brace, & Co.

Kohler, W. 1947. *Gestalt Psychology.* New York: Liveright.

Kolers, P. A. 1976. Reading a year later. *Journal of Experimental Psychology: Human Learning and Memory* 2:554–565.

Kolodner, J. L. 1983. Reconstructive memory: A computer model. *Cognitive Science* 7:281–328.

Komatsu, S. I., and Ohta, N. 1984. Priming effects in word-fragment completion for short- and long-term retention intervals. *Japanese Psychological Research* 26:194–200.

Korsakoff, S. S. 1889. Etude medico-psychologique sur une forme des maladies de la memoire. [Medical-psychological study of a form of diseases of memory.] *Revue Philosophique* 28:501–530.

Kroodsma, D. E. 1982. Learning and the ontogeny of sound signals in birds. In D. E. Kroodsma, E. H. Miller, and H. Ouellet, eds. *Acoustic Communication in Birds.* Vol. 2. New York: Academic Press, pp. 1–23.

Lehnert, W. G. 1984. Paradigmatic issues in cognitive science. In W. Kintsch, J. R. Miller, and P. G. Polson, eds. *Method and Tactics in Cognitive Science*. Hillsdale, NJ: Erlbaum, pp. 21–50.

Light, L. L., and Zelinski, E. M. 1983. Memory for spatial information in young and old adults. *Developmental Psychology* 19:901–906.

Loftus, E. F., Miller, D. G., and Burns, H. J. 1978. Semantic integration of verbal information into a visual memory. *Journal of Experimental Psychology: Human Learning and Memory* 4:19–31.

Loftus, E. F., Schooler, J. W., and Wagenaar, W. A. 1985. The fate of memory: Comment on McCloskey and Zaragoza. *Journal of Experimental Psychology: General* 114:375–380.

Mahut, H., and Moss, M. 1984. Consolidation of memory: The hippocampus revisited. In L. R. Squire and N. Butters, eds. *Neuropsychology of Memory*. New York: Guilford Press, pp. 297–315.

Malamut, B. L., Saunders, R. C., and Mishkin, M. 1984. Monkeys with combined amygdalo-hippocampal lesions succeed in object discrimination learning despite 24-hour interatrial intervals. *Behavioral Neuroscience* 98:759–769.

Mandler, G. 1968. Association and organization: Facts, fancies, and theories. In T. R. Dixon and D. L. Horton, eds. *Verbal Behavior and General Behavior Theory*. Englewood Cliffs, NJ: Prentice-Hall.

Mandler, G. 1985. From association to structure. *Journal of Experimental Psychology: Learning, Memory, and Cognition* 11:464–468.

Mandler, G. 1980. Recognizing: The judgment of previous occurrence. *Psychological Review* 87:252–271.

Mandler, J. M. 1979. Categorical and schematic organization in memory. In C. R. Puff, ed. *Memory Organization and Structure*. New York: Academic Press, pp. 259–299.

Mantyla, T. 1986. Optimizing cue effectiveness: Recall of 500 and 600 incidentally learned words. *Journal of Experimental Psychology: Learning Memory Cognition* 12:66–71.

Marr, D. 1982. *Vision*. San Francisco: W. H. Freeman Co.

Matthews, R. C. 1977. Semantic judgments as encoding operations: The effects of attention to particular semantic categories on the usefulness of interitem relations in recall. *Journal of Experimental Psychology: Human Learning and Memory* 3:160–173.

Mayer, R. E. 1985. Learning in complex domains: A cognitive analysis of computer programming. In G. Bower, ed. *The Psychology of Learning and Motivation*. New York: Academic Press, pp. 89–130.

McAndrews, M. P., Glisky, E. L., and Schacter, D. L. 1987. When priming persists: Long-lasting implicit memory for a single episode in amnesic patients. *Neuropsychologia* 25:497–506.

McClelland, J. L., and Rumelhart, D. E. 1986. *Parallel Distributed Processing, Volume 2*. Cambridge, MA: MIT Press.

McCloskey, M., and Zaragoza, M. 1985. Misleading postevent information and memory for events: Arguments and evidence against memory impairment hypotheses. *Journal of Experimental Psychology: General* 114:1–16.

McKoon, G., and Ratcliff, R. 1979. Priming in episodic and semantic memory. *Journal of Verbal Learning and Verbal Behavior* 18:463–480.

McKoon, G., and Ratcliff, R. 1981. The comprehension processes and memory structures involved in instrumental, inference. *Journal of Verbal Learning and Verbal Behavior* 20:671–682.

McKoon, G., and Ratcliff, R. 1986a. Automatic activation of episodic information in a semantic memory task. *Journal of Experimental Psychology: Learning, Memory, and Cognition* 12:108–115.

McKoon, G., and Ratcliff, R. 1986b. Inferences about predictable events. *Journal of Experimental Psychology: Learning, Memory, and Cognition* 12:82–91.

McKoon, G., Ratcliff, R., and Dell, G. 1986. A critical evaluation of the semantic/episodic distinction. *Journal of Experimental Psychology: Learning, Memory, and Cognition* 12:295–306.

McNamara, T. P. 1986. Mental representations of spatial relations. *Cognitive Psychology* 18:87–121.

Miller, G. A. 1956. The magical number seven plus or minus two: Some limits on your capacity for processing information. *Psychological Review* 63:81–96.

Milner, B., Corkin, S., and Teuber, H. L. 1968. Further analysis of the hippocampal amnesic syndrome: 14-year follow-up study of H. M. *Neuropsychologia* 6:215–234.

Milner, B., Petrides, M., and Smith, M. L. 1985. Frontal lobes and the temporal organization of memory. *Human Neurobiology* 4:137–142.

Minsky, M. 1975. A framework for representing knowledge. In P. H. Winston, ed. *The Psychology of Computer Vision*. New York: McGraw-Hill.

Minsky, M. 1980. K-lines: A theory of memory. *Cognitive Science* 4:117–133.

Mishkin, M., Malamut, B., and Bachevalier, J. 1984. Memories and habits: Two neural systems. In J. L. McGaugh, G. Lynch, and N. M. Weinberger, eds. *Neurobiology of Learning and Memory*. New York: Guilford Press.

Morris, R. G. 1984. Dementia and the functioning of the articulatory loop system. *Cognitive Neuropsychology* 1:143–158.

Morris, C. D., Bransford, J. D., and Franks, J. J. 1977. Levels of processing versus transfer appropriate processing. *Journal of Verbal Learning and Verbal Behavior* 16:519–533.

Morris, C. D., Stein, B. S., and Bransford, J. D. 1979. Prerequisites for the utilization of knowledge in the recall of prose passages. *Journal of Experimental Psychology: Human Learning and Memory* 5:253–261.

Morton, J. 1979. Facilitation in word recognition: Experiments causing change in the logogen models. In P. A. Kolers, M. E. Wrolstad, and H. Bouma, eds. *Processing of Visible Language*. Vol. 1. New York: Plenum, pp. 259–268.

Morton, J., Hammersley, R. H., and Bekerian, D. A. 1985. Headed records: A model for memory and its failures. *Cognition* 20:1–23.

Moscovitch, M. 1982. Multiple dissociations of function in amnesia. In L. S. Cermak, ed. *Human Memory and Amnesia*. Hillsdale, NJ: Erlbaum, pp. 337–370.

Moscovitch, M., Winocur, G., and McLachlan, D. 1986. Memory as assessed by recognition and reading time in normal and memory-impaired people with Alzheimer's disease and other neurological disorders. *Journal of Experimental Psychology: General* 115:331–347.

Müller, G. E., and Pilzecker, A. 1900. Experimentelle Beitrage zur Lehre Vom Gedachtnis. *Zeitschrift for Psychologie* 1:1–300.

Murdock, B. B., Jr. 1961. The retention of individual items. *Journal Experimental Psychology* 61:618–625.

Murdock, B. B., Jr. 1962. The serial position effect of free recall. *Journal of Experimental Psychology* 64:482–488.

Murdock, B. B., Jr. 1974. *Human Memory: Theory and Data*. Potomac, MD: Erlbaum.

Neisser, U. 1967. *Cognitive Psychology*. New York: Appleton-Century-Crofts.

Neisser, U. 1976. *Cognitive and Reality: Principles and Implications of Cognitive Psychology*. San Francisco: W. H. Freeman.

Neisser, U. 1982. Memory: What are the important questions? In U. Neisser, ed. *Memory Observed*. San Francisco: W. H. Freeman. Originally published in M. M. Gruneberg, P. E. Morris, and R. N. Sykes, eds. 1978. *Practical Aspects of Memory*. London: Academic Press.

Nelson, T. O. 1977. Repetition and depth of processing. *Journal of Verbal Learning and Verbal Behavior* 16:151–171.

Newell, A., and Simon, H. A. 1972. *Human Problem Solving*. Englewood Cliffs, NJ: Prentice-Hall.

Nissen, M. J., and Bullemer, P. 1987. Attentional requirements of learning: Evidence from performance measures. *Cognitive Psychology* 19:1–32.

Norman, D. 1986. Reflections on cognition and parallel distributed processing. In J. L. McClelland and D. E. Rumelhart, eds. *Parallel Distributed Processing, Volume 2*. Cambridge, MA: MIT Press, pp. 531–546.

Ogden, R. M. 1904. Memory and the economy of learning. *Psychological Bulletin* 1:177–184.

O'Keefe, J., and Nadel, L. 1978. *The Hippocampus as a Cognitive Map*. Oxford: Clarendon Press.

Paivio, A. 1971. *Imagery and Verbal Processes*. New York: Holt, Rinehart and Winston.

Parkin, A. 1982. Residual learning capability in organic amnesia. *Cortex* 18:417–440.

Peterson, L. R., and Peterson, M. J. 1959. Short-term retention of individual verbal items. *Journal of Experimental Psychology* 58:193–198.

Pezdek, K., Roman, Z., and Sobolik, K. G. 1986. Spatial memory for objects and words. *Journal of Experimental Psychology: Learning, Memory, and Cognition* 12:530–537.

Pichert, J. W., and Anderson, R. C. 1977. Taking different perspectives on a story. *Journal of Educational Psychology* 69:309–315.

Raajimakers, J. G. W., and Shiffrin, R. N. 1981. Search of associative memory. *Psychological Review* 88:93–135.

Richardson-Klavehn, A., and Bjork, R. A. 1988. Measures of memory. *Annual Review of Psychology* 39:475–543.

Roediger, H. L. III. 1984. Does current evidence from dissociation experiments favor the episodic/semantic distinction? *Behavioral and Brain Sciences* 7:252, 254.

Roediger, H. L. III, and Blaxton, T. A. 1987. Retrieval modes produce dissociations in memory for surface information. In D. S. Gorfein and R. R. Hoffman, eds. *Memory and Cognitive Processes: The Ebbinghaus Centennial Conference.* Hillsdale, NJ: Erlbaum.

Roediger, H. L. III, and Weldon, M. S. 1987. Reversing the picture superiority effect. In M. A. McDaniel and M. Pressley, eds. *Imagery and Related Mnemonic Processes; Theories, Individual Differences, and Applications.* New York: Springer-Verlag.

Roger, T. B., Kuiper, N. A., and Kirker, W. S. 1977. Self-reference and the encoding of personal information. *Journal of Personality and Social Psychology* 35:677–688.

Ross, B. H. 1984. Remindings and their effects in learning a cognitive skill. *Cognitive Psychology* 16:371–416.

Rozin, P. 1976. The psychobiological approach to human memory. In M. R. Rosenzweig and E. L. Bennett, eds. *Neural Mechanisms of Learning and Memory.* Cambridge, MA: MIT Press.

Rozin, P., and Kalat, J. W. 1971. Specific hungers and poison avoidance as adaptive specializations of learning. *Psychological Review* 78:459–486.

Rozin, P., and Schull, J. 1989. The adaptive-evolutionary point of view in experimental psychology. In R. C. Atkinson, R. J. Herrnstein, G. Lindzey, and R. D. Luce, eds. *Handbook of Experimental Psychology.* New York: Wiley-Interscience.

Rubin, D. 1986. *Autobiographical Memory.* New York: Cambridge University Press.

Rumelhart, D. E. 1980. Schemata: The building blocks of cognition. In R. J. Spiro, B. C. Bruce, W. F. Brewer, eds. *Theoretical Issues in Reading Comprehension.* Hillsdale, NJ: Erlbaum.

Rumelhart, D. E., and McClelland, J. L. 1986. *Parallel Distributed Processing: Volume 1.* Cambridge, MA: MIT Press.

Schacter, D. L. 1982. *Stranger Behind the Engram: Theories of Memory and the Psychology of Science*. Hillsdale, NJ: Erlbaum.

Schacter, D. L. 1983. Amnesia observed: Remembering and forgetting in a natural environment. *Journal of Abnormal Psychology* 92:236–242.

Schacter, D. L. 1984. Toward the multidisciplinary study of memory: Ontogeny, phylogeny and pathology of memory systems. In L. R. Squire and N. Butters, eds. *Neuropsychology of Memory*. New York: Guilford Press, pp. 13–24.

Schacter, D. L. 1985a. Multiple forms of memory in humans and animals. In N. Weinberger, J. McGaugh, and G. Lynch, eds. *Memory Systems of the Brain: Animal and Human Cognitive Processes*. New York: Guilford Press, pp. 351–379.

Schacter, D. L. 1985b. Priming of old and new knowledge in amnesic patients and normal subjects. *Annals of the New York Academy of Sciences* 444:41–53.

Schacter, D. L. 1986a. A psychological view of the neurobiology of memory. In L. LeDoux and W. Hirst, eds. *Mind and Brain: Dialogues in Cognitive Neuroscience*. Cambridge, Engl.: Cambridge University Press, pp. 265–269.

Schacter, D. L. 1986b. Feeling-of-knowing ratings distinguish between genuine and simulated forgetting. *Journal of Experimental Psychology: Learning, Memory, and Cognition* 12:30–41.

Schacter, D. L. 1987a. Implicit memory: History and current status. *Journal of Experimental Psychology: Learning, Memory and Cognition* 13:501–518.

Schacter, D. L. 1987b. Memory, amnesia, and frontal lobe dysfunction. *Psychobiology* 15:21–36.

Schacter, D. L. 1989a. On the relation between memory and consciousness: Dissociable interactions and conscious experience. In H. L. Roediger and F. I. M. Craik, eds. *Varieties of Memory and Consciousness: Essays in Honor of Endel Tulving*. Hillsdale, NJ: Erlbaum.

Schacter, D. L. 1989b. Perceptual representations systems and implicit memory: Toward a resolution of the multiple memory systems debate. *Annals of the New York Academy of Sciences* (in press).

Schacter, D. L., Cooper, L. A., and Delaney, S. M. 1989. Implicit memory for unfamiliar objects depends on access to structural descriptions. *Journal of Experimental Psychology: General* (in press).

Schacter, D. L., and Graf, P. 1986a. Effects of elaborative processing on implicit and explicit memory for new associations. *Journal of Experimental Psychology: Learning, Memory, and Cognition* 12:432–444.

Schacter, D. L., and Graf, P. 1986b. Preserved learning in amnesic patients: Perspectives from research on direct priming. *Journal of Clinical and Experimental Neuropsychology* 8:727–743.

Schacter, D. L., and Kihlstrom, J. F. 1989. Functional amnesia. In F. Boller and J. Grafman, eds. *Handbook of Neuropsychology*. Amsterdam: Elsevier Publications.

Schacter, D. L., McAndrews, M. P., and Moscovitch, M. 1988. Access to consciousness: Dissociations between implicit and explicit knowledge in neuropsychological syndromes. In L. Weiskrantz, ed. *Thought Without Language*. Oxford: Oxford University Press.

Schacter, D. L., and McGlynn, S. M. 1989. Implicit memory: Effects of elaboration depend on unitization. *American Journal of Psychology* 102:151–181.

Schacter, D. L., and Nadel, L. 1989. Varieties of spatial memory: A problem for cognitive neuroscience. In H. Weingartner and R. Lister, eds. *Cognitive Neuroscience*. New York: Oxford University Press.

Schacter, D. L., and Tulving, E. 1982. Amnesia and memory research. In L. S. Cermak, ed. *Human Memory and Amnesia*. Hillsdale, NJ: Erlbaum, pp. 1–32.

Schank, R. C., and Abelson, R. 1977. *Scripts, Plans, Goals, and Understanding*. Hillsdale, NJ: Erlbaum.

Schooler, J. W., Gerhard, D., and Loftus, E. F. 1986. Qualities of the unreal. *Journal of Experimental Psychology: Learning, Memory, and Cognition* 12:171–181.

Semon, R. W. 1909. *Die Mnemischen Empfindungen*. Leipzig: Wilhelm Engelmann.

Shallice, T. 1979. Neuropsychological research and the fractionation of memory systems. In L. G. Nilsson, ed. *Perspectives on Memory Research*. Hillsdale, NJ: Erlbaum.

Shallice, T. 1981. Neurological impairment of cognitive processes. *British Medical Bulletin* 37:187–192.

Shallice, T., and Warrington, E. K. 1970. Independent functioning of verbal memory stores: A neuropsychological study. *Quarterly Journal of Experimental Psychology* 22:261–273.

Sherry, D. F., and Schacter, D. L. 1987. The evolution of multiple memory systems. *Psychological Review* 94:439–454.

Shettleworth, S. J. 1972. Constraints on learning. *Advances in the Study of Behavior* 4:1–68.

Shettleworth, S. J. 1983. Function and mechanism in learning. In M. D. Zeiler and P. Harzem, eds. *Advances in the Analysis of Behavior*. Vol. 3. New York: Wiley, pp. 1–39.

Shimamura, A. P. 1986. Priming effects in amnesia: Evidence for a dissociable memory function. *Quarterly Journal of Experimental Psychology* 38A:619–644.

Shimamura, A. P., and Squire, L. R. 1984. Paired-associate learning and priming effects in amnesia: A neuropsychological study. *Journal of Experimental Psychology: General* 113:556–570.

Singer, M., and Ferreira, F. 1983. Inferring consequences in story comprehension. *Journal of Verbal Learning and Verbal Behavior* 22:437–448.

Slamecka, N. J. 1985. Ebbinghaus: Some associations. *Journal of Experimental Psychology: Learning, Memory, and Cognition* 11:414–435.

Sloman, S. A., Hayman, C. A. G., Ohta, N., and Tulving, E. 1988. Forgetting and interference in fragment completion. *Journal of Experimental Psychology: Learning, Memory, and Cognition* 14:223–239.

Sperling, G. 1960. The information available in brief visual presentations. *Psychological Monographs* 74(498).

Squire, L. R. 1982. Comparisons between forms of amnesia: Some deficits are unique to Korsakoff's syndrome. *Journal of Experimental Psychology: Learning, Memory, and Cognition* 8:560–571.

Squire, L. R. 1987. *Memory and Brain.* New York: Oxford University Press.

Squire, L. R., and Cohen, N. J. 1984. Human memory and amnesia. In J. McGaugh, G. Lynch, and N. Weinberger, eds. *Proceedings of the Conference on the Neurobiology of Learning and Memory.* New York: Guilford Press, pp. 3–64.

Stein, B. S. 1978. Depth of processing reexamined: The effects of precision of encoding and test appropriateness. *Journal of Verbal Learning and Verbal Behavior* 17:165–174.

Stephens, D. W. 1981. The logic of risk-sensitive foraging preferences. *Animal Behaviour* 29:628–629.

Sternberg, S. 1966. High-speed scanning in human memory. *Science* 153:652–654.

Teuber, H.-L. 1955. Physiological Psychology. *Annual Review of Psychology* 6:267–296.

Thomas, G. J. 1984. Memory: Time binding in organisms. In L. R. Squire and N. Butters, eds. *Neuropsychology of Memory.* New York: Guilford Press, pp. 374–384.

Tulving, E. 1962. Subjective organization in free recall of "unrelated" words. *Psychological Review* 69:344–354.

Tulving, E. 1972. Episodic and semantic memory. In E. Tulving, ed. *Organization of Memory.* New York: Academic Press.

Tulving, E. 1983. *Elements of Episodic Memory.* Oxford: The Clarendon Press.

Tulving, E. 1985a. How many memory systems are there? *American Psychologist* 40:385–398.

Tulving, E. 1985b. Memory and consciousness. *Canadian Psychology* 26:1–12.

Tulving, E. 1986. What kind of a hypothesis is the distinction between episodic and semantic memory? *Journal of Experimental Psychology: Learning, Memory, and Cognition* 12:307–311.

Tulving, E. 1987. Do animals have autobiographical memory? Paper presented at the 28th annual meeting of the Psychonomic Society, Seattle, WA.

Tulving, E., Schacter, D. L., and Stark, H. A. 1982. Priming effects in word-fragment completion are independent of recognition memory. *Journal of Experimental Psychology: Learning, Memory, and Cognition* 8:336–342.

Tulving, E., and Osler, A. 1968. Effectiveness of retrieval cues in memory for words. *Journal of Experimental Psychology* 77:593–601.

Tulving, E., and Pearlstone, Z. 1966. Availability versus accessibility of information in memory for words. *Journal of Verbal Learning and Verbal Behavior* 5:381–391.

Tulving, E., and Thomson, D. M. 1973. Encoding specificity and retrieval processes in episodic memory. *Psychological Review* 80:352–373.

Underwood, B. J., and Ekstrand, B. R. 1966. An analysis of some shortcomings in the interference theory of forgetting. *Psychological Review* 73:540–549.

Vallar, G., and Baddeley, A. 1984a. Fractionation of working memory: Neuropsychological evidence for a phonological short-term store. *Journal of Verbal Learning and Verbal Behavior* 23:151–162.

Vallar, G., and Baddeley, A. 1984b. Phonological short-term store, phonological processing and sentence comprehension: A neuropsychological case study. *Cognitive Neuropsychology* 1:121–141.

Vieth, W., Curio, E., and Ernst, U. 1980. The adaptive significance of avian mobbing, III. Cultural transmission of enemy recognition in blackbirds: Cross-species tutoring and properties of learning. *Animal Behaviour* 28:1217–1229.

Warrington, E. K. 1982. The double dissociation of short- and long-term memory deficits. In L. S. Cermak, ed. *Human Memory and Amnesia*. Hillsdale, NJ: Erlbaum.

Warrington, E. K., and Shallice, T. 1972. Neuropsychological evidence of visual storage in short-term memory tasks. *Quarterly Journal of Experimental Psychology* 24:30–40.

Warrington, E. K., and Weiskrantz, L. 1968. New method of testing long-term retention with special reference to amnesic patients. *Nature* 217:972–974.

Warrington, E. K., and Weiskrantz, L. 1974. The effect of prior learning on subsequent retention in amnesic patients. *Neuropsychologia* 12:419–428.

Watkins, M., and Tulving, E. 1975. Episodic memory: When recognition fails. *Journal of Experimental Psychology: General* 104:5–29.

Waugh, N. C., and Norman, D. A. 1965. Primary memory. *Psychological Review* 72:89–104.

Weiskrantz, L. 1978. A comparison of hippocampal pathology in man and other animals. In Ciba Foundation Symposium 58. *Functions of the Septo-Hippocampal System*. North Holland: Elsevier, pp. 373–387.

Weiskrantz, L. 1985. On issues and theories of the human amnesic syndrome. In N. Weinberger, J. McGaugh, and G. Lynch, eds. *Memory Systems of the Brain: Animal and Human Cognitive Processes*. New York: Guilford Press, pp. 380–415.

Weiskrantz, L. 1987. Neuroanatomy of memory and amnesia: A case for multiple memory systems. *Human Neurobiology* 6:93–106.

Whitty, C. M., and Zangwill, O. 1977. *Amnesia*. London: Butterworths.

Wickens, D. D. 1970. Encoding categories of words: An empirical approach to meaning. *Psychological Review* 77:1–15.

Williams, M. D., and Hollan, J. D. 1981. The process of retrieval from very long-term memory. *Cognitive Science* 5:87–119.

Winnick, W. A., and Daniel, S. A. 1970. Two kinds of response priming in tachistoscopic recognition. *Journal of Experimental Psychology* 84:74–81.

Winograd, T. 1975. Frame representations and the declarative-procedural controversy. In D. G. Bobrow and A. M. Collins, eds. *Representation and Understanding: Studies in Cognitive Science.* New York: Academic Press.

Witherspoon, D., and Moscovitch, M. 1989. Independence between two implicit memory tests. *Journal of Experimental Psychology: Learning, Memory, and Cognition* 15:22–30.

Zola-Morgan, S. M., and Oberg, R. G. E. 1980. Recall of life experiences in an alcoholic Korsakoff patient: A naturalistic approach. *Neuropsychologia* 18:549–557.

Zola-Morgan, S., and Squire, L. R. 1984. Preserved learning in monkeys with medial temporal lesions: Sparing of motor and cognitive skills. *Journal of Neuroscience* 4:1072–1085.

18 Action

Michael I. Jordan and David A. Rosenbaum

For cognitions to be communicated, they must be physically enacted. It follows from this observation that a complete account of the cognitive system must explain how it transmits information to the environment as well as how it takes information in and retains and elaborates it. This fact alone justifies a chapter on action in a handbook of cognitive science, but there are other reasons as well.

One of the effects of the motor system is to move the sensory organs, thereby allowing the organism to acquire information actively. The sensory system in turn allows movements to be carried out efficiently, providing the motor system with the information it needs to correct for and, in some cases, anticipate errors. Noting the intimate connections between perception and action, a number of investigators have suggested that perceptual processing depends on the activation of stored motor routines; this is the so-called *motor theory* of perception (Coren 1986, Liberman, Cooper, Shankweiler, and Studdert-Kennedy 1967). Others have proposed that the planning of actions incorporates representations of anticipated perceptual consequences (Adams 1971, Greenwald 1970, James 1890, Ladefoged, DeClerk, Lindau, and Papçun 1972, Meyer and Gordon 1983). On either view perception and action are viewed as highly interrelated. Thus cognitive science, insofar as it regards perception as one of its core problems, cannot afford to ignore action.

The trend in the study of action, as in perception, is a deepening awareness of the computational complexity of the problems involved. Action is characterized at all levels by a degrees-of-freedom problem—a surplus of options, choices, and potential control variables. There are choice points at the highest levels of planning pertaining to the method of carrying out a task, and there are choices at lower levels about the patterning of muscular innervation. Though in many cases some of the choices are clearly preferable to others, the criteria for making choices are often obscure and may depend on subtle situational variables. This of course is what gives behavior its enormous flexibility. For the theorist the problem is to understand how the system discovers successful patterns of action in the thicket of possibilities.

Our focus in this chapter is on some of the ways in which the complexity of producing actions may be managed. We organize the discussion around three topics. The first is the degrees-of-freedom problem per se—an orientation to motor control originating with Bernstein (1967) that emphasizes the kinematic and dynamical variables of the biomechanical system (see also chapter 19). Next we discuss the *serial order* problem. From one point of view the ability to perform sequences of actions cuts down on degrees of freedom, both because the same set of system elements are being used repeatedly and because of the possibility for "divide-and-conquer" strategies. Sequential performance however, introduces its own complexities. Finally we discuss *learning*. Our point of view on learning is that it too contributes to decreasing the computational load. A system that learns can solve difficult problems in a series of small steps.

18.1 The Degrees-of-Freedom Problem

The degrees of freedom of a system are "the least number of independent coordinates required to specify the position of the system elements without violating any geometrical constraints" (Saltzman 1979). Generally speaking, the larger the number of degrees of freedom in a system, the more difficult it is to make the system behave as desired. Simply counting degrees of freedom, however, oversimplifies the issue. It is the manner in which degrees of freedom *interact* that determines the difficulty of controlling a system. For example, if the n degrees of freedom of a system are independent of one another, then the controlling system need only possess an algorithm that is adequate for the control of a single degree of freedom; the algorithm can be replicated n times to control the ensemble. On the other hand if the degrees of freedom are not independent (that is, if the effects of specifications of values for a particular degree of freedom depend on the values of other degrees of freedom), then a team of independent controllers is no longer adequate, and more complex control algorithms must be considered. Complexity can also vary depending on the form of interactions, according to what the controller is able to represent. For example, certain nonlinear interactions pose particular difficulties for certain classes of controllers. Thus to be somewhat more precise, it is the number, form, and magnitude of the interactions between degrees of freedom, in the context of a particular control architecture, that determine the difficulty of controlling a system.

Another aspect of the degrees-of-freedom problem that is often emphasized is the issue of indeterminacy (Bernstein 1967, Saltzman 1979). Indeterminacies arise when the number of degrees of freedom of the system carrying out some task exceeds the number of degrees of freedom needed to specify the task to be carried out. In such cases there can be multiple solutions to the control problem (that is, the problem of finding specifications of values for the system's degrees of freedom so that it performs the task as desired). There is also an increase in the size of the space of incorrect controls, and there are problems with singularities. Algorithms designed for determinate problems often either break down or undergo a qualitative change in complexity when extended to a corresponding indeterminate problem. Thus an important step in the development of theories of motor control is to characterize the indeterminacies that arise. We know that the motor control system can solve indeterminate problems; otherwise humans would not have the capacity for *motor equivalence*—the ability to achieve the same physical objective in more than one way.

To make these issues more concrete, consider the anatomy of the motor system. The human body has scores of joints, hundreds of muscle groups, and thousands of muscle fibers. At the level of the muscle fibers, the motor control problem is highly indeterminate with respect to most real-world tasks. The large degree of indeterminacy makes the motor control problem intractable at this level, even though the interactions between degrees of freedom are of small magnitude. At the level of the joints the problem would seem to be more tractable. For example, the number of degrees of freedom of the arm is seven—three for the shoulder and two each for the elbow and wrist (ignoring the finger joints, which add many more degrees of freedom). Positioning tasks require the specification of only six values of position and orientation. Thus for such tasks there is only one excess degree of freedom. Motor control at this level is simplified with respect to the issue of indeterminacy. The interactions between degrees of freedom, however, become accordingly much more salient. For example, in the case of an idealized arm, the dynamical equations relating torques to joint-angle variables contain interaction terms whose magnitude can be large enough to exert significant effects on behavior (Bejczy and Lee 1983, Hollerbach and Flash 1982) and whose coefficients are complex nonlinear functions of the arm's configuration (Kahn 1969).

It should be kept in mind that the problem of indeterminacy is not solely anatomical. Because actions have temporal and spatial extent, there are many possible trajectories that can be followed in moving between one position/orientation and another. These trajectories arise from different patterns of efferent signals. To specify such signals, values must be specified for each signal at each moment in time. Thus if this is the level at which we analyze the motor control problem, the number of degrees of freedom the controller must specify depends on the product of the number of anatomical degrees of freedom and the duration of the movement. This value may be greatly in excess of the number of degrees of freedom in the task, unless the task itself specifies an entire trajectory.

Approaching the Degrees-of-Freedom Problem

Let us begin by emphasizing a point that has been implicit in our discussion. The motor control problem can be analyzed at many levels, and it is important to match the level to the specification of the task. This point is particularly important in tasks in which the complex movement trajectories are involved, because such tasks may often have more compact descriptions than the time series of effector positions, and these descriptions can lead to simplified control algorithms. To take an example from Raibert (1986), the task of running can be described as a requirement that the net acceleration of the body over a stride cycle be zero, so that forward movement at a fixed speed with stable posture is maintained. Raibert's insight was that this requirement is achieved by a simple algorithm that ensures that the patterns of body and leg movements have particular even and odd symmetries during the stance phase.

Even if a simple control algorithm that matches the particular task requirements is in operation at a given level, the manner in which other levels participate in action must still be specified, and new aspects of the degrees-of-freedom problem may arise in each transformation between levels. One candidate for a theoretical structure in which both high-level and low-level control can be specified is a hierarchy. In a hierarchy high-level units control lower-level units, which control still lower-level units. (The structure need not be fixed anatomically, but may be reconfigurable and sensitive to task requirements.) Although the low-level units can send feedback to higher-level units, the critical features are that each level exerts descending control only on the units directly beneath it and that a superordinate unit need not know the details of how a subordinate unit organizes its computation (Greene 1972, Simon 1969). The hierarchy helps deal with the problem of indeterminacy by imposing implicit constraints on the kinds of solutions that can be found. Furthermore if the structure of the hierarchy matches the dynamical structure of the system being controlled, then the hierarchy also helps deal with the problem of interactions between degrees of freedom.

Pursuing a hierarchical analysis implies a strategy of partitioning degrees of freedom. Bernstein (1967), a physiologist in the Soviet Union, proposed that connections, physical or physiological, between muscle groups can serve this function. He proposed that there are *synergies* among muscle groups that help reduce the degrees of freedom to be managed. Researchers in the United States have called these hypothesized elements *coordinative structures*. Discussions of synergies and coordinative structures can be found in Easton 1972, Fowler, Rubin, Remez, and Turvey 1981, Greene 1972, Kugler, Kelso, and Turvey 1980, Saltzman 1979, and Turvey 1977. Some of the evidence for them is reviewed in the next section.

A technique for reducing the degrees-of-freedom problem that is common in engineering design is the use of feedback (Melsa and Schultz 1969). Among their other virtues feedback controllers can make do with less-than-perfect compensation for the interactions between the degrees of freedom of a system, as long as the tendency is to move the system in the desired direction, so that errors are corrected over time. Putting a feedback loop around a system defines a new system that is typically easier to control than the original one. For example, in a linear system there are design techniques for choosing fixed feedback gains that result in a closed-loop system having any desired impulse response. For human motor control the delay in the proprioceptive loop is arguably too great for feedback to be useful in the case of rapid, discrete movements (Schmidt 1982). In slower movements and throughout the execution of extended tasks, however, there are several levels of control at which feedback may be important (Albus 1981, Hollerbach 1982).

Another way to reduce or partition degrees of freedom is to introduce cost functions that provide criteria for choosing among actions. The idea is that though there may be a huge number of ways to carry out an action, there is often a rational basis for selecting one method over another, usually on the basis of efficiency. For example, though there are many possible ways to lift a glass, some are less time consuming, energy consuming, or awkward than others. Evaluating the efficiency of possible glass-lifts provides a way of determining which should be used, which correspondingly reduces the degrees of freedom for glass-lifting behavior. Theoretical tools for making such choices have been developed in optimal control theory (Kirk 1970), and the approach has begun to be used in the context of motor control (Hogan 1984, Nelson 1983).

A further approach to the degrees-of-freedom problem, which is discussed more at length in a following section, is to avoid computations by allowing the inherent dynamical characteristics of the limb to determine the trajectory (see also chapter 19). This approach can be used if certain parameters of the limb (for example, muscle stiffnesses) can be tuned, so that the resulting system has dynamical behavior characterized by basins of attraction around points that correspond to desired movement endpoints (or more generally attractors corresponding to desired movement trajectories).[1]

Synergies and Coordinative Structures
Let us return to the first approach to reducing degrees of freedom: the introduction (or discovery) of connections between or among potentially independent elements. Saltzman (1979) illustrated the basic idea as follows. Consider two points in the plane. Each point has two degrees of freedom, corresponding to its Cartesian coordinates, and so the system of two points has four degrees of freedom. If the points are

connected by a line of fixed length, L, the number of degrees of freedom is reduced to three because the line provides an equation of constraint,

$$(x_1 - x_2)^2 + (y_1 - y_2)^2 = L^2,$$

where specification of any three variables constrains the fourth. Saltzman noted that in general the number of degrees of freedom of a system is $(Dn - c)$, where D is the number of dimensions, n is the number of elements, and c is the number of equations of constraint. Such equations need not be limited to algebraic relationships; constraints can also be defined among derivatives or integrals of the variables.

How can an equation of constraint be implemented? One method relies on fixed linkages between muscles, where the activation of one muscle results in the activation or inhibition of other muscles. A number of such connections have been noted (see Fowler et al. 1981, Partridge 1986). When muscles are linked in a hardwired fashion, however, their interactions are relatively inflexible. "Softer" dependencies may also exist in the form of synergies or coordinative structures. Consider, for example, an experiment on speech production by Kelso, Tuller, Vatikiotis-Bateson, and Fowler (1984) (see also Abbs and Gracco 1983). Their subjects repeated the phrase "a baez again" or "a baeb again." Occasionally and unexpectedly a downward force was applied to the jaw and the instantaneous responses of the upper lip and tongue were recorded. Kelso et al. found that during production of "baeb" the upper lip rapidly descended to the lower lip, completing the necessary bilabial stop. During production of "baez," however, the upper lip did not descend to the lower jaw; instead electromyographic activity of the tongue was greater than usual, allowing for completion of the fricative. Kelso and colleagues argued that such data provide evidence for soft linkages between muscle groups because (1) the response was different depending on the phonetic goal and therefore could not be based on a fixed linkage between muscles, (2) the adjustments could not have been based on simple error-correcting feedback because the major effect was not on the perturbed articulator, and (3) the speed of the adjustments was too great to be based on the recomputation of a high-level movement plan.

The Mass-Spring and Virtual-Trajectory Models

Whereas synergies rely on neural links between muscle groups, the physical characteristics of muscles themselves also provide a way of reducing degrees of freedom. In particular the viscoelastic properties of muscle provide a way of generating entire movement trajectories through a few control settings. By analogy with a simple mass-spring system, in which movement results from the relationship $F = k(x - x_0)$, which holds between the spring tension F, the length x, the equilibrium length x_0, and the stiffness k, it has been proposed that limb movement occurs through the selection of length-tension curves for the muscles.

According to one proposal, the thresholds of reflexes are adjusted to select particular length-tension curves (Berkenblit, Fel'dman, and Fucson 1986, Fel'dman 1986). According to another proposal, the stiffnesses of muscle antagonists are specified, which selects pairs of opposing length-tension curves (Polit and Bizzi 1979, Sakitt 1980). The point at which the opposing tensions balance out defines an equilibrium point for the system and thus an endpoint for the limb movement. In either case the limb is brought to the same final position regardless of the limb's starting position, regardless of transient perturbations, and without explicit error-correcting computations based on feedback. This capability is called *equifinality* and demonstrates that entire trajectories can be generated even though the controller is limited to the number of degrees of freedom needed to specify a final postural configuration. If detailed control over the shape of the trajectory is required, however, such a scheme may be insufficient (Delatizky 1982). The general idea can be extended by assuming that the controller specifies a series of intermediate postural equilibrium points during the movement (see chapter 19 and Flash and Hogan 1985, Hinton 1984, Hogan 1985). (For evidence that such intermediate points are actually generated during arm movements, see Bizzi, Accornero, Chapple, and Hogan 1984.) Note, however, that this approach reintroduces one of the problems that the mass-spring model was able to circumvent—the need to specify entire trajectories. Indeed in the work of Hogan (1985) and Flash and Hogan (1985), this problem is solved in a different manner: The path the hand is to follow is specified through an optimality criterion (that the mean square jerk integrated over the path be minimal for all possible choices of paths). This reference path defines a "virtual trajectory," which the limbs are able to follow due to the modulable elastic properties of the muscles. The remaining problem is to specify how virtual trajectories are actually generated. One idea is to reapply the philosophy of the mass-spring model but at a higher level, assuming that the *controller* has inherent dynamics that generate entire trajectories given a simple specification of the desired movement (Bullock and Grossberg 1988). We pursue this idea in the next section.

Attractors
An approach that combines aspects of the mass-spring model and the coordinative-structure idea has been proposed by Saltzman and Kelso (1987) in the form of their *task-dynamics* framework. The basic idea of task dynamics is to formulate movement problems in an abstract, task-based coordinate system in which the equations governing movement are simple (for example, mass-spring dynamics) and uncoupled and are characterized by low-dimensional attractors. By a series of coordinate transformations, these equations are converted into equations appropriate for the underlying physical system. The control problem then is

to ensure that the physical system behaves as specified by the latter equations.

Consider, for example, the problem of moving a manipulator endpoint to a target position. As shown in figure 18.1, Saltzman and Kelso consider a task space with the origin at the target position and the abscissa connecting the initial position of the endpoint and the target position. They then assume that the task space dynamics is of the form

$$M_T\ddot{\mathbf{t}} + B_T\dot{\mathbf{t}} + K_T\mathbf{t} = 0, \tag{1}$$

where $\mathbf{t}$ is the vector of task space coordinates, M_T is a mass matrix, B_T is a damping matrix, and K_T is a stiffness matrix. All of these matrices are assumed to be diagonal, so that the equation reduces to a pair of independent damped mass-spring systems. A mass at position $\mathbf{t}$ would move toward the origin as if connected to each axis by a damped spring. The origin is therefore an attractor point in the four-dimensional state space of positions and velocities.

The dynamical system described by equation 1 can be described in other coordinate systems, in particular, in the system of joint angles of an arm, as shown in figure 18.2. Performing the change of coordinates transforms the equation as follows:

$$M_TRJ\ddot{\phi} + B_TRJ\dot{\phi} + K_TR(\mathbf{x}(\phi) - \mathbf{x_0}) = -M_TR\dot{J}\dot{\phi}, \tag{2}$$

where ϕ is the vector of joint coordinates, R is a rotation matrix that rotates task-space coordinates to the shoulder-centered frame shown in figure 18.2, $\mathbf{x_0}$ is the origin of task space relative to the shoulder, and J is the Jacobian matrix of the manipulator.[2] In this equation the coefficient matrices are no longer diagonal, and furthermore, due to the fact that the Jacobian matrix is a function of the configuration ϕ, the equation is time varying. Thus the equations are not simple in joint coordinates, although they reflect an underlying simplicity in task space.

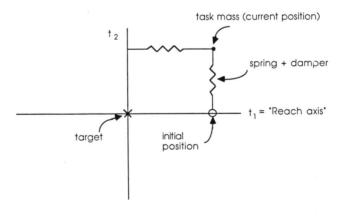

Figure 18.1 The task space for a discrete reaching task. Movement of the task mass toward the target results from the effects of an orthogonal pair of damped mass-spring systems. (Adapted from Saltzman and Kelso 1987.)

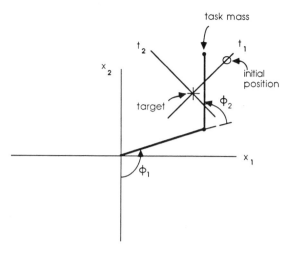

Figure 18.2 A joint-angle description of the reaching task. The task space of figure 18.1 has been rotated and translated within the shoulder-centered (x_1, x_2) coordinate system. (Adapted from Saltzman and Kelso 1987.)

Finally Saltzman and Kelso propose two approaches to controlling an actual arm so that it behaves like equation 2. One approach is to pair terms in equation 2 with terms in the dynamical equation for the real arm and thereby define a state-feedback control law for the arm. The second approach is to actually run equation 2 as an *internal simulation* with coupling terms to the real arm so that the simulation can entrain the arm. (This is our language; Saltzman and Kelso refer to this approach as a *network-coupling* approach.) In either case the endpoint of the real arm should move on an approximately straight line toward the origin of task space as if it were a simple mass attached to a spring. Furthermore if the endpoint of the arm is perturbed from the straight-line trajectory en route to the origin, then it should move back to the x-axis as though it were attached to the axis by a second spring.

A major virtue of task dynamics is that many of the details of trajectory planning and responding to perturbation arise directly from the structure of the dynamical equations and need not be dealt with explicitly by higher levels. Higher levels simply instantiate an invariant (for example, constant coefficient) dynamical organization in the task space. Note that other dynamical forms, such as limit cycles, can also be defined in task space through choice of an appropriate differential equation. It is also possible to add forces in task space through devices such as artificial potential functions (Khatib 1987), leading to a variety of sophisticated behavior, such as obstacle avoidance, with minimal supervisory control. Finally it is important to note that the framework of task dynamics is applicable in the case of excess degrees of freedom (the inverse of the Jacobian matrix in equation 2 becomes a pseudo-inverse). Indeed Saltzman (1986) has demonstrated in simulations of the speech articulators that a step perturbation imposed on one of the articulators tends to be compensated by changes in the other articulators so that a target position is still achieved.

These virtues are not obtained without cost, and the task-dynamic approach requires a large amount of computation at lower levels. Due to the direction in which coordinate transformations are performed, inverses of matrices must be computed, in particular, the inverse of the time-varying Jacobian. When there are excess degrees of freedom, this inverse becomes a pseudoinverse, algorithms for which are computationally expensive for even medium-sized matrices. An alternative to computation, for which the brain seems well suited, is to store pseudoinverse entries in a large memory. However, the number of entries required can be large. For example, with ten degrees of freedom quantized to five levels each, over one billion entries are required to store the pseudoinverse. Such an analysis should not be seen as ruling out task dynamics, because there may may well be simplifications that can be made, but it is nevertheless a serious consideration.

In task dynamics the stability of the system is ensured by choosing differential equations for task space that are known to have particular basins of attraction and limit sets. There are other techniques available for obtaining systems with such behavior. For example, many connectionist networks are nonlinear dynamical systems characterized by attractors. In the case of networks with symmetric connections, it is possible to prove that the state space for the network is partitioned into regions that are basins of attraction with limit points (Cohen and Grossberg 1983, Golden 1986, Hopfield 1982). The positions of the limit points are determined through a learning algorithm. The sequential network discussed in the next section (compare figure 18.4) can be demonstrated empirically to have attractors (Jordan 1989b); if the network learns cyclical trajectories, then those trajectories are limit cycles that partition the state space into basins of attraction.

18.2 Serial Order

Most skilled action involves not just a single movement but rather a *sequence* of movements. This fact would have no particular relevance to our discussion if interactions across time were functionally equivalent to interactions across space. That is, in a sequence of n actions, each of which is composed of m components, we could assume that the controller is forced to deal with a system having mn interacting degrees of freedom. As is well known in linguistics, however, interactions across time tend to be restricted in a variety of ways. Consider, for example, the relationships defining the phonotactics of a language. Sentences can be segmented into component words, and there are strong interactions between values for the phonemic degrees of freedom within a word. Between words these interactions are of a different and more restricted nature, essentially arising indirectly from higher-order syntactic and semantic interactions. Thus the problem of specifying the phonemic structure of a sentence is effectively decoupled into a sequence of independent subproblems, with relationships between the subproblems defining a degrees-of-freedom problem on a higher level.

A difficulty with this classical argument is that it breaks down at the lower levels of skilled behavior. When phenomena nearer the periphery are analyzed, actions do not appear to be performed as separate units; rather the form they take can depend strongly on their temporal context. In speech, for example, the articulatory configuration associated with the production of a given phoneme changes substantially depending on the identity of phonemes nearby in the sequence (Kent and Minifie 1977). Moreover these effects appear across word and clause boundaries. For example, Moll and Daniloff (1971) observed that in phrases such as *Free Ontario* the opening of the velum (muscular tissue that opens to allow air to pass between the pharynx and the nasal cavities) for the nasal /n/ began during the /i/ in *Free*. Such phenomena are referred to as *coarticulation* and are essential in allowing speech to proceed as rapidly as it does. Coarticulation is ubiquitous in speech production and has analogs in other domains as well (compare Gentner, Grudin, and Conway 1981, Olsen and Murray 1976).

In this section we begin by discussing theoretical approaches to serial order with particular emphasis on the problem of context sensitivity. We discuss parallel activation models, which have had some degree of success with this problem. Then we broaden the discussion and turn to other aspects of the serial-order problem where symbolic, hierarchical models have had more success.

Context-Sensitive Allophones

One approach to the problem of context sensitivity is to reintroduce degrees of freedom with higher-order units that explicitly encode for context. This is essentially the idea behind the context-sensitive allophone (Wickelgren 1969)—a phoneme-sized unit that takes into account the left and right context. For example, the context-sensitive allophones for the string *pin* are $\{_\#p_i, _pi_n, _in_\#\}$, where # is a boundary marker. Serial order can be achieved with associative links in a network of such units. Note that the unordered set of context-sensitive allophones implicitly encodes the serial order. Thus there is no problem of ambiguity about which links to follow in the network, as there is in a network of non–context-sensitive units (Lashley 1951).

The proliferation of degrees of freedom in this theory solves the context-sensitivity problem, but introduces other problems. One difficulty is that the approach deals poorly with generalization and rule-governed behavior (Halwes and Jenkins 1971). For example, the rule in English that voiceless stops are unaspirated when they follow /s/ would have to be encoded separately in every relevant context-sensitive allophone. Another problem is that coarticulation effects can depend on noncontiguous phonemes (Benguerel and Cowan 1974, Öhman 1966). The number of context-sensitive allophones needed to account for such phenomena would be unreasonably large. These issues are dealt with more satisfactorily in parallel models, to which we now turn.

Parallel Distributed Processing Models

One approach to accounting for context sensitivity without increasing the number of degrees of freedom is to allow some degree of parallelism (Fowler 1980). An approach that incorporates such parallelism is embodied in the model of typing proposed by Rumelhart and Norman (1982). As shown in figure 18.3, their model is a network with a processing unit for each action in the sequence to be produced. There are inhibitory links from units early in the sequence to units later in the sequence. The inhibition enforces a graded pattern of activation across the units, with the units appearing early in the sequence having the most activation. Each unit pulls the appropriate finger toward a key on the keyboard in proportion to its activation, so that the overall movement of the hand is the vector sum of parallel influences from several future actions. When the activation of a unit reaches a threshold, it is turned off, which disinhibits the remaining units. Rumelhart and Norman have demonstrated that this model can account for a variety of phenomena in typing, including the context-sensitive nature of the movements toward the keys.

This general approach to introducing parallelism into a sequential process is not entirely without problems. One difficulty is that the model provides no general mechanism for dealing with repeated actions. If a

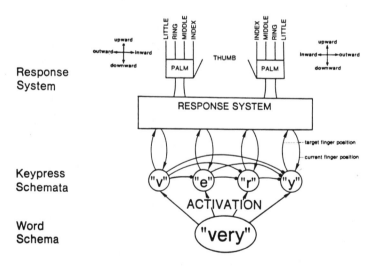

Figure 18.3 A network configured to type the word *very*. (Adapted from Rumelhart and Norman 1982.)

repeated action were represented by separate nodes, one for each token of the repeated type, the total activation for that action would increase, thereby moving its execution forward in time, whether or not that was desirable. Rumelhart and Norman's model has only one node for each type, so that a sequence such as ABCA must be performed as two separate pieces. Interestingly the special-purpose mechanism that the model uses for contiguous repeated actions leads to errors similar to those that typists actually make. (Typists make errors such as AAB → ABB, which Rumelhart and Norman argue results from the transposition of A and a "doubling operator.") Data from speech, however, show that coarticulation can occur across sequences such as ABCA (Benguerel and Cowan 1974), which is not possible in the model. A related difficulty is that there is no way to restrict unwanted parallel interactions. In speech, for example, it is not necessarily the case that the summation of parallel effects on the articulators leads to a correct acoustic output, due to nonlinearities in the mapping from articulatory configuration to acoustic output (Stevens 1972).

Jordan (1989b) has proposed a parallel approach to the serial-order problem that can deal with nonlinear interactions. In the network shown in figure 18.4, an action is a pattern of activation across the output units (the output units can be thought of as representing action features). Sequences of actions are learned as the weights in the network are changed. The external input to the network is a constant *plan* vector, which designates the sequence to be performed. A further input to the network is a *state* vector, which varies in time due to the recurrent connections impinging on the state units. The recurrent connections need only produce discriminable state patterns at each time step, so that with the added discriminability provided by the plan, the remainder of the network can learn to map these patterns to target output

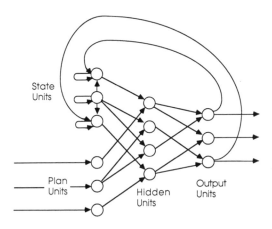

Figure 18.4 A connectionist sequential machine. Sequences are learned as the weights in the network are changed. Different sequences are produced in response to different plan vectors. (From Jordan 1989b.)

patterns at each time step. The idea is to decompose the serial-order problem into two subproblems—how to vary the state vector in time and how to map states to actions. With this approach it is possible to construct networks that can learn arbitrary sequences (although particular sequences are more difficult to learn than others).

In the network in figure 18.4, there is only a single output vector (with three components), so that all actions are a function of the same set of tunable weights. Therefore changes made to the weights due to the learning of a particular action have an automatic effect on other actions in the sequence. This means that context sensitivity arises as a form of generalization that depends on the similarity structure of the states as they change over time and the way in which target patterns are specified to the network (a point to which we return in the section on learning). Jordan (1989a,b) has shown how this approach can be used to model coarticulation in speech production.

The parallel models we have discussed are essentially dynamical approaches to the serial-order problem (see also Grossberg 1978 and Grudin 1981). They are able to deal with some of the criticisms leveled at associationist approaches (Lashley 1951, Halwes and Jenkins 1971). They deal particularly well with context sensitivity, and some of the models treat learning. These models remain simple nonhierarchical models, however, treating interactions on only one level. Sequential phenomena often have interactions at many levels, which are of different kinds and to which different rules apply. These phenomena are suggestive of hierarchies and furthermore suggest symbol structures in which entities can stand for other entities. Whether the parallel distributed processing framework is generally inconsistent with a symbolic view or whether structural phenomena can be accounted for without symbol structures is currently controversial (Fodor and Pylyshyn 1988, McClelland and Kawamoto 1986, Smolensky 1988). In the current context layers or tiers of networks may provide a fruitful point of departure. Higher-level networks could produce outputs to be treated as input plans for lower-level networks, and state vectors at the higher level could depend on the state at lower levels. Furthermore there need be no explicit flow of control; all levels could be active simultaneously, allowing for contextual effects both between and within levels.

One area that is particularly interesting with regard to these issues is the study of speech errors. On the one hand certain aspects of speech errors seem generally consistent with a parallel distributed processing approach; there are similarity effects between units that interact in errors (Fay and Cutler 1977, Fromkin 1971, MacKay 1970) as well as output bias effects, such that when units slip at one level, they tend to form legal strings at the next higher level (Baars, Motley, and MacKay 1975). Other aspects of speech errors, most notably the fact that words that interact are nearly always from the same syntactic category (Garrett 1975), are suggestive of a slot-filling process with restrictions on fillers

(Reich 1977, Shattuck-Hufnagel 1979). To account for these phenomena, Dell (1986) has proposed a hybrid model of speech production. The model has a system of frames with categorized slots that acts as a generative component, and an activation network that is responsible for lexical retrieval. Speech errors are proposed to arise at the interface between these two subsystems.

Hierarchies

A number of authors have proposed that serial ordering is achieved with hierarchically organized plans or programs, a view largely supported by error patterns in spontaneous behavior (Lashley 1951, Gordon and Meyer 1987, MacKay 1982, Rosenbaum et al. 1983). Even if behavioral plans are hierarchically organized, however, the question remains of how such plans actually control production of behavioral sequences. One possibility is that the hierarchy defines the identity and order of commands to the musculature (represented as terminal nodes in the hierarchy), but the commands are issued one after the other without reference to higher levels (figure 18.5b); thus the structure of the plan is hierarchical but its execution is not. Another possibility is that execution as well as structure are hierarchical (figure 18.5a).

The available evidence favors the latter method of control. Collard

(a)

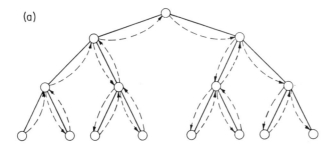

(b)

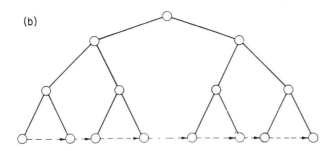

Figure 18.5 Two methods for relying on a hierarchy to control the execution of an action sequence. (A) Readout of terminal nodes (bottom row) as well as nonterminal nodes via a tree-traversal process. (B) Linear readout of terminal nodes only. (Adapted from Rosenbaum, Kenny, and Derr 1983.)

and Povel (1982) and Rosenbaum, Kenny, and Derr (1983) found that latencies of successive keystrokes in the speeded production of memorized sequences increased with the number of superordinate nodes to be traversed to get from one terminal node to the next; the number and types of error also conformed to a tree-traversal model. Rosenbaum (1985) also showed that the main features of an influential set of results reported by Sternberg, Monsell, Knoll, and Wright (1978) could be accounted for by appealing to a tree-traversal process. Sternberg and colleagues showed that the time to produce a brief burst of highly prepared responses increased with the length of the sequence. This was true both for the latency of the first response and the latencies of subsequent responses (interresponse times). From the perspective of a tree-traversal model, one expects longer sequences to be more deeply nested than shorter sequences. Therefore the effect of sequence length on initiation time can be accounted for, provided that initiation of the sequence awaits activation of the root of the tree, that the distance from the root of the tree to the leftmost terminal node (corresponding to the first response) increases with sequence length and that traversing extra nodes takes extra time. The increase of interresponse times with sequence length can similarly be explained by assuming that the mean number of superordinate nodes between terminal nodes increases with the length of the sequence.

The overall success of the tree-traversal model suggests that execution of rapid response sequences is achieved through hierarchical decoding processes. This conclusion is appealing because similar processes are known to characterize performance in other domains of cognition, most notably verbal recall (see, for example, Reitman and Rueter 1980). As in these other domains relying on hierarchies minimizes the load on peripheral memory structures, which have limited storage capacities. Another advantage of hierarchical control is that hierarchies are convenient structures for the application of transformational rules, such as repetition, mirroring, and transposition (Greeno and Simon 1974, Restle 1970). By applying such rules at various levels, selected spans of behavior can be transformed, allowing for a large number of structures that must be stored in long-term memory.[3]

Parameters and Extended Action Sequences

Just as transformational rules may be applied to all or part of a motor program, it may also be possible to apply abstract parameters that define the specific form the program will take. This possibility was noted as long ago as 1932, when Bartlett advocated the view that plans for motor activities are represented schematically. The view has since been endorsed by a number of authors (Arbib 1981, Pew 1974, Schmidt 1975).

Recent experiments have provided evidence about the way abstract parameters may be applied to motor programs. The experiments have shown that when a parameter can apply to an entire program, it can be specified in a single processing operation. In one experiment (Rosenbaum, Gordon, Stillings, and Feinstein 1987), subjects were asked to produce one of two possible utterances in response to one of two possible signals. In each condition the two possible utterances contained one, two, or three syllables, and differed with respect to a single vowel. In the three-syllable condition, the choice was /gibidi/ versus /gubudu/, in the two-syllable condition the choice was /gibi/ versus /gubu/, and in the one-syllable condition the choice was /gi/ versus /gu/. The reaction signals were a high-pitched tone and a low-pitched tone. In the compatible mapping conditions the high-pitched tone was mapped to the /i/ sequences, and the low-pitched tone was mapped to the /u/ sequences, whereas in the incompatible mapping conditions the mapping was reversed. As seen in figure 18.6, it took longer for subjects to start speaking in the incompatible condition than in the compatible condition. There was also an effect of the number of syllables, but the interaction between compatibility and number of syllables was not statistically significant. This result supports the hypothesis that the choice of vowel occurred only once and applied to all the syllables in the forthcoming utterance. Note that the increase of choice reaction time with the number of syllables also corroborates the tree-traversal

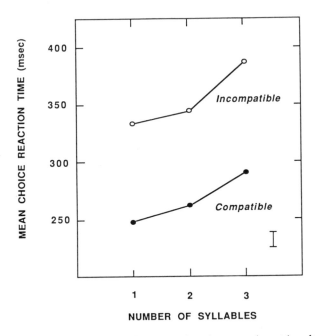

Figure 18.6 Results of choice reaction time experiment in which subjects responded to one of two possible signals with utterances of one, two, or three syllables to which the signals were compatibly or incompatibly mapped. See text for details. (From Rosenbaum, Gordon, Stillings, and Feinstein 1987.)

model. The model predicts that the time to initiate a sequence should increase with its complexity. Because the choice of vowel apparently occurred only once, it may have occurred before the first descent from the top of the tree; thus the choice of vowel applied *distributively* to the entire sequence. Other experiments have confirmed this interpretation and demonstrated the generality of the distributive assignment method (Inhoff, Rosenbaum, Gordon, and Campbell 1984). Distributive assignment is appealing because of its efficiency: If a number of subprograms take the same parameter value, it is desirable for all the subprograms to receive that value simultaneously.

For the distributive assignment method to work with particular parameters, those parameters must exist as autonomous functional entities. Such autonomy allows for another kind of efficiency: It allows programs to be *edited* for successive productions. To see why this is desirable, consider the possible fates that could await motor programs. One possibility is that they are lost from memory, in which case subsequent actions that require either the same or similar programs must be programmed "from scratch." Another possibility is that the programs are saved, in which case they are available for later productions. Pursuing the latter possibility, if the program needed at a given time is similar but not identical to a recently saved program, it is desirable to be able to edit just those aspects of the saved program that distinguish it from the new one needed. Not only does this minimize the number of changes to be made; it also allows extended motor sequences to be represented in memory as a single program with instructions about its needed changes.

If editing is used, programs that differ from recently used programs should take longer to assemble than programs that are identical to recently used programs. This prediction was confirmed by Rosenbaum, Weber, Hazelett, and Hindorff (1986), who showed that when response sequences are performed from memory and aspects of the sequence vary in successive production cycles, the rate of performance is slower than when the identical sequence is performed over and over again. The latter result is obtained even when subtle aspects of the responses, such as stress levels of individual syllables, vary in successive production cycles. Qualitatively similar results have been reported by Barmack (1970) for eye movements and by Bock (1982) for syntactic organization in sentence production. Relatedly Miller (1986) has noted that motor perseveration is a sign of *dyspraxia*, a deficit in the high-level control of movement. Collectively these results support the hypothesis that programs are normally retained after being executed and are edited to generate similar, subsequent response sequences. It is likely that this is a general property of systems that engage procedural knowledge, for even when people solve series of similarly structured problems, their speed of performance increases (Luchins 1942).

18.3 Learning

The difficulty of the task of executing actions is largely ameliorated by the fact that the system can learn from experience. The system can find solutions to difficult control problems by constructing successive approximations to the solutions over repeated trials rather than having to produce the solution outright. This cuts down on the complexity of the computation required for any given performance at the expense of more sophisticated processes of memory and integration over trials. Another virtue of learning, typically emphasized in the literature on the subject, is that it allows the system to deal with changing or underspecified environments.

The literature on learning is vast, and we accordingly must restrict our treatment of it in this section. We discuss some recent computational approaches to the problem of sensorimotor learning and focus on the kinds of information that a learning process might reasonably be expected to need, how this information can be acquired, and how it can be used to improve performance. Readers desiring a broader and more historical approach to the subject should consult Adams (1984) or Schmidt (1982).

Consider a child learning to make speech sounds. We can assume that the environment provides targets y_i^*, which are acoustic tokens from the language being learned. These targets could be patterns of energy in frequency bands, for example. The problem for the child is that there is no one to provide the patterns of motor outflow x_i^* that map into the acoustic targets. These motor patterns must be discovered through experience. Note that the problem reduces to one of inverting a function: If we denote by f the function that maps articulatory to acoustic to auditory patterns, then the problem is to find a solution x_i^* such that $f(x_i^*) = y_i^*$. The difficulty is that we cannot assume that the function f or its inverse (if it exists) are known a priori. This point is more clear in a large variety of other sensorimotor tasks, such as shooting baskets. There the targets y_i^* can be taken to be the visual patterns of balls passing through hoops, and the problem is to discover motor patterns x_i^* that achieve these desired visual results. The function f, which includes the physics of basketballs, is clearly not known a priori. Note finally that even if there is a priori knowledge, it must be malleable because there is simply too much maturational change for a fixed model to be useful.

In control-systems terminology the problem we are discussing involves the adaptation of the *feedforward* component of a system. As shown in figure 18.7, a control system may include both a feedforward component, which transforms the reference signal y^* to a signal x, and a feedback component, which compares the reference signal y^* to the output y of the controlled system or *plant* (the traditional term used in

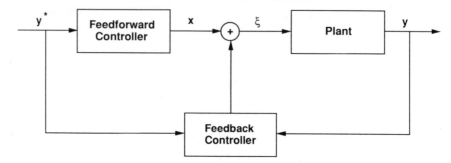

Figure 18.7 A control system with feedback and feedforward controllers. The feedforward controller is described by the function g, and the plant is described by the function f.

control theory for any system being controlled). The signals from the feedforward controller and the feedback controller are summed to form a signal ξ, which is the control input to the plant. The feedforward adaptation problem we are considering can be seen in figure 18.7 by ignoring the feedback term, that is, by letting $\xi = \mathbf{x}$.

Note that it is also possible to consider algorithms that adapt the feedback controller. Indeed the major thrust of adaptive control theory (Gupta 1986) is to do just that. Our neglect of this theory is based on the fact that in humans response to feedback is quite slow relative to the high-precision, rapid movements that can be made, and there seems to be more to gain by pursuing feedforward approaches, considering human abilities to plan and predict. This orientation is consistent with current trends in human motor control (Schmidt 1982, Hollerbach 1982).

It should be emphasized that all of the various approaches to learning that we discuss are of recent origin, and so it is difficult to make judgments about their relative strengths and weaknesses. In principle all of the approaches solve the sensorimotor learning problem that we posed, and all make reasonable requirements with respect to a priori knowledge and the amount of computation needed on a learning trial. Few of the approaches, however, have been tested on a wide range of sufficiently difficult problems. Also it should be kept in mind that learning is probably not a single entity, and it is possible that several of the mechanisms we discuss may have some role in a complete theory.

Finally, we offer a word on notation. In systems theory a distinction is often made between systems with or without memory (Vidyasagar 1973). A system is memoryless if the system function depends only on the instantaneous value of its input. If the function depends as well on past time values of its input, then the system is said to have memory. In this section a symbol such as $\mathbf{y}^*$ denotes the instantaneous value of a vector variable, when an algorithm is applied to a memoryless problem. For systems with memory certain of the algorithms we discuss apply only when the input signal contains not only the current value of some vector, but a finite number of past values of the vector as well.

In such a case the symbol **y*** is taken to represent an *mn*-dimensional vector constructed by stacking subvectors **v**(1), **v**(2), . . . , **v**(*n*), where **v** is an *m*-dimensional vector representing the instantaneous configuration of the underlying system. For other algorithms past values of a signal **v** are not used; rather the velocity and acceleration vectors $\dot{\mathbf{v}}$ and $\ddot{\mathbf{v}}$ are assumed to be available. In this case **y*** is formed by stacking **v**, $\dot{\mathbf{v}}$, and $\ddot{\mathbf{v}}$. This ambiguity in notation allows us to ignore certain differences between algorithms and present the basic ideas in a uniform mathematical framework.

Reinforcement Learning

One approach to learning with a long history in psychology is that of *reinforcement learning* (Bower and Hilgard 1966; Bush and Estes 1959, Mowrer 1960, Thorndike 1911). Recently there has been renewed interest in reinforcement learning algorithms (Barto and Anandan 1985, Fu 1970, Sutton 1984, Widrow, Gupta, and Maitra 1973, Williams 1987), and there has been some discussion of the application of such algorithms to control problems (Barto and Epstein 1983, Mendel and McLaren 1970, Widrow, Gupta, and Maitra 1973).

In the reinforcement learning paradigm there is a set of possible responses, which we denote as $\{x_1, x_2, . . . , x_n\}$. Associated with the *i*th response is a probability p_i of selecting that response as an output x on a given trial. Once a response is selected and transmitted to the environment, a scalar evaluation or reinforcement signal is computed as a function of the response and the state of environment. The reinforcement signal is then used in changing the selection probabilities for future trials: If reinforcement is high, the probability of selecting a response is increased, otherwise the probability is decreased. Typically the probabilities associated with the remaining (unselected) responses are also adjusted in some manner, so that the total probability sums to one. An example of such an algorithm is given by the following pair of equations (Fu 1970), in which the variables are indexed by the time step k. For the selected action x_i the update rule is

$$p_i(k + 1) = (1 - \alpha)p_i(k) + \alpha r(k),$$

where α is a learning rate between zero and one, and $r(k)$ is the reinforcement, also between zero and one. For the unselected actions x_j, where $j \neq i$, $j = 1, 2, . . . , n$, the rule is

$$p_j(k + 1) = (1 - \alpha)p_j(k) + \frac{\alpha}{n - 1} (1 - r(k)).$$

Note that if the probabilities sum to one on the *k*th time step, then they continue to do so on the $(k + 1)$th time step.

In a feedforward controller it is necessary to be able to produce different outputs based on the input; thus the reinforcement learning paradigm needs to be augmented to allow the selection probabilities to depend on an input vector $\mathbf{y}^*$. Mendel and McLaren's (1970) proposal is to partition the input space into a mutually exhaustive set of non-overlapping regions and maintain a different set of probabilities for each region. Within each region a reinforcement learning algorithm is used to adjust the probabilities.

Another approach, discussed by Barto and Epstein (1983), is to consider *associative* reinforcement learning algorithms, in which the response probabilities are a parameterized function of the input vector. The reinforcement signal is used to alter the parameters, thereby indirectly changing the response probabilities. Although the algorithms they discuss are restricted to two responses and use probability distribution functions that depend on a linear function of the input, Barto and colleagues have shown elsewhere that *networks* of computational elements using such algorithms are able to produce vector outputs and learn nonlinear mappings (see, for example, Barto and Anderson 1985).

Reinforcement learning algorithms are able to learn in situations in which very little instructional information is available from the environment. In particular such algorithms need make no comparison between the input goal (the vector $\mathbf{y}^*$) and the result obtained (the vector $\mathbf{y}$) to find a control signal that achieves the goal. When such a comparison can be made, however, reinforcement learning is still applicable, but will be slower than other algorithms that make use of such information (the reinforcement signal can be defined as a function of the error $\mathbf{y}^* - \mathbf{y}$, with larger reinforcement corresponding to a smaller error vector). Although we have suggested that in cases such as speech acquisition, where there is a strong imitative component, a comparison with a goal vector is feasible (note that we are *not* suggesting that the control solution $\mathbf{x}^*$ is available for comparison), the question is empirical and as yet unresolved (Adams 1971): Does feedback during learning serve to strengthen or weaken the action just emitted or to provide structural information about how to change the action just emitted into a more suitable action? The discussion in the next two sections may provide some insight into this classical issue, because it describes several attempts to provide algorithms by which the second alternative could be realized.

Direct Inverse Modeling

The goal of sensorimotor learning, as we have formulated the problem, is to find control signals so that the actual outcome $\mathbf{y}$ matches the desired outcome $\mathbf{y}^*$. Thus referring back to figure 18.7, the system must configure itself so that the composition of the feedforward controller and the plant is the identity transformation. The feedforward controller should therefore be an inverse of the plant. One approach to learning this inverse is to build an inverse model directly by observing the input/output behavior of the plant. This approach is represented by the recent work of An, Atkeson, and Hollerbach (1985), Grossberg and Kuperstein (1986), Kuperstein (1988), Miller (1987), Raibert (1978), and Widrow and Stearns (1985). A closely related approach has been proposed by Kawato, Furukawa, and Suzuki (1987).

Suppose that the feedforward controller is an associative device that depends on a vector of adaptable parameters $\mathbf{w}$. Thus we have $\mathbf{x} = g(\mathbf{w}, \mathbf{y}^*)$, where g represents the input/output behavior of the feedforward controller. On successive learning trials the system chooses a random vector $\mathbf{x}'$ as input to the plant, observes the output $\mathbf{y}$, assigns $\mathbf{y}^* = \mathbf{y}$, and then associates $\mathbf{y}^*$ to $\mathbf{x}'$ in the controller by changing the parameters $\mathbf{w}$. Depending on the form of the function g, there are many methods available for changing the parameters. One popular method, which is commonly used in associative memories, is gradient descent on an error surface that is a function of the difference between the controller's actual output $\mathbf{x}$ and the given test vector $\mathbf{x}'$. Consider the error measure E defined by

$$E = \tfrac{1}{2} (\mathbf{x}' - \mathbf{x})^{\mathrm{T}}(\mathbf{x}' - \mathbf{x}),$$

where the superscript T denotes the transpose operation.[4] This function is a quadratic surface around the test vector $\mathbf{x}'$ and goes to zero when $\mathbf{x} = \mathbf{x}'$, that is, when the controller is producing the desired output. The gradient descent[5] learning rule is then obtained by using the chain rule

$$
\begin{aligned}
\Delta \mathbf{w} &= -\alpha\, \nabla_{\mathbf{w}} E \\
&= -\alpha \nabla_{\mathbf{w}} \tfrac{1}{2}(\mathbf{x}' - \mathbf{x})^{\mathrm{T}}(\mathbf{x}' - \mathbf{x}) \\
&= \alpha\, \frac{\partial \mathbf{x}}{\partial \mathbf{w}}^{\mathrm{T}} (\mathbf{x}' - \mathbf{x}),
\end{aligned}
\tag{3}
$$

where $(\partial \mathbf{x}/\partial \mathbf{w})^{\mathrm{T}}$ is the transpose of a matrix of partial derivatives, and α is a learning rate. Note that the matrix $(\partial \mathbf{x}/\partial \mathbf{w})^{\mathrm{T}}$ depends only on the structure of the controller input/output function g, and it is therefore available to the system. As the error measure goes to zero, the controller is able to take an input $\mathbf{y}^*$ into an output $\mathbf{x}$ that, when applied to the plant, produces $\mathbf{y} = \mathbf{y}^*$. For the full inverse mapping to be approximated, experience with a variety of vectors is necessary. The process can be aided if g has continuity properties to allow generalization or interpolation.

The associative approach to building an inverse model has been proposed by Kuperstein (1988) and Widrow and Stearns (1985), both of whom use the least mean squares algorithm of Widrow and Hoff (1960), which is a gradient descent learning rule. Kuperstein uses this approach to model the learning of the mapping from retinal coordinates to hand positions. After a phase during which the mapping is learned, it is possible to command the hand to move to the position where the eyes are focused.

There are other approaches to learning an inverse model. An, Atkeson, and Hollerbach (1985) have proposed a nonassociative approach in which knowledge of the structure of the differential equations of the plant (a robot arm in their case) is used. The problem then reduces to estimating the inertial terms in these equations, and An and colleagues have shown that a linear estimation scheme can do this in a small number of trials. This approach has the advantage that if these terms are estimated correctly, even on a restricted set of test trajectories, then the inverse model will be correct for all other trajectories. There is no need to randomly explore the space of trajectories. A disadvantage is that the structure of the differential equations may not always be known, particularly when the plant includes a dynamical system external to the body.

Finally it is also possible to simply store the vectors x' in a table indexed by y^*, so as to limit the amount of computation involved in using the feedforward controller. A problem with such tables is that they can be very large, given reasonable assumptions about the quantization and dimensionality of the indexing variables. One way to lessen this problem is to use hash coding (Albus 1981, Miller 1987). Another approach is to combine the use of tables with knowledge of the structure of the differential equations of the plant. In work with a robot arm Raibert (1978) proposed such a hybrid approach in which certain of the variables (the positions and velocities) were used as indexes into a table of parameters, and other variables (the accelerations) were combined with the parameters in the resulting linear computation of the torques.

One drawback with the various direct inverse modeling approaches as we have presented them so far is that there is no mechanism for goal-directed learning. That is, there is no way to improve on a particular target y^*. On a given trial if an incorrect output y is produced, then that output is treated as an input to the controller and associated to the corresponding test vector x' that produced it. This will be useful on some future trial if that y is the target, but it is not necessarily of help with respect to the current target y^*.

One approach to goal-directed learning is to have the error correction inherent in the *feedback* controller aid the learning process. This is the approach taken by Kawato and colleagues (1987). Their feedforward controller is an associative memory, and learning proceeds by gradient descent. Rather than associating the output from the plant to a randomly chosen input to the plant, however, they associate the target y^* to an input to the plant which is the sum of the feedforward contribution and the feedback contibution (ξ in figure 18.7). To see how this approach works, consider first the initial situation where the feedforward signal is zero. On the first trial the input to the plant is given by the feedback signal alone (in the simplest case this would be given by K $(y^* - y)$, where K is a gain matrix). In general this feedback signal is sufficient for the output of the plant to come close to the goal trajectory, but it does not constitute a solution **x**. This input ξ, however, can still be stored away in the associative memory and thereby be used as the feedforward contribution on the next trial. The feedback then brings the resulting output even closer to the target. Thus the process moves successively closer to a solution.

Another approach to goal-directed learning is to make do with an incorrect model and instead change particular feedforward commands corresponding to particular desired output trajectories. Atkeson and McIntyre (1986) propose updating the particular feedforward command after each trial by incorporating the feedback command (as in Kawato et al. 1987) and a further term, which is an estimate of the difference between the current command and the correct command **x***. This estimate is made by applying the (inaccurate) inverse model to the current output **y** and the desired output **y***. If the model is not too inaccurate, then this further term should speed learning.

A problem yet to be addressed within the direct inverse modeling framework is the problem of indeterminacy or excess degrees of freedom. In the case of excess degrees of freedom, there are many control signals that yield the same plant output, which implies that the relationship between data seen at the input and the output of the feedforward controller is one to many. For the feedforward controller to model an inverse of the plant, the learning process must select one of the possible outputs corresponding to each input. Such a selection mechanism, however, is not automatically provided for within the direct inverse modeling approach. In particular the learning rule in equation 3 averages over the various possible outputs, which yields an incorrect result in the case of a nonlinear plant. One solution to this problem is to define an error measure in terms of the output of the plant, rather than the output of the controller, so that correctness can be directly assessed. This leads to an alternative, indirect approach to learning an inverse model that makes use of a *forward* model of the plant.

Forward Modeling

The final approach to sensorimotor learning that we discuss involves using a forward model of the plant to construct the feedforward controller (Jordan 1989a, Jordan and Rumelhart 1989). As in the previous section let us assume that the feedforward controller has the form $\mathbf{x} = g(\mathbf{w}, \mathbf{y}^*)$, where **w** is a vector of adjustable parameters. Let us now consider a quadratic error surface based not on the output of the controller but rather on the output of the plant. That is, let

$$E = \tfrac{1}{2}(\mathbf{y}^* - \mathbf{y})^{\mathrm{T}}(\mathbf{y}^* - \mathbf{y}),$$

which is minimal when $\mathbf{y} = \mathbf{y}^*$, that is, when the plant is producing the desired response. Given that **y** is a function of **w**, that is, $\mathbf{y} = f(g(\mathbf{w}, \mathbf{y}^*))$, we can base a learning rule on the gradient of this error surface by using the chain rule as follows:

$$\Delta \mathbf{w} = -\alpha \, \nabla_{\mathbf{w}} E$$

$$= -\alpha \, \nabla_{\mathbf{w}} \tfrac{1}{2} (\mathbf{y}^* - \mathbf{y})^{\mathrm{T}} (\mathbf{y}^* - \mathbf{y})$$

$$= \alpha \, \frac{\partial \mathbf{y}}{\partial \mathbf{w}}^{\mathrm{T}} (\mathbf{y}^* - \mathbf{y}) \tag{4}$$

$$= \alpha \left(\frac{\partial \mathbf{y}}{\partial \mathbf{x}} \frac{\partial \mathbf{x}}{\partial \mathbf{w}} \right)^{\mathrm{T}} (\mathbf{y}^* - \mathbf{y})$$

$$= \alpha \, \frac{\partial \mathbf{x}}{\partial \mathbf{w}}^{\mathrm{T}} \frac{\partial \mathbf{y}}{\partial \mathbf{x}}^{\mathrm{T}} (\mathbf{y}^* - \mathbf{y}).$$

As before the first matrix depends only on the structure of the function g and is therefore available to the learner, as is the vector $\mathbf{y}^* - \mathbf{y}$, which is obtained by comparing the desired output of the plant with the actual output. On the other hand the middle matrix $\partial \mathbf{y}/\partial \mathbf{x}$ is not available a priori. It is a matrix that relates small changes in the components of $\mathbf{x}$ to small changes in the components of $\mathbf{y}$ and depends on the nature of the plant. Note, however, that these are all *forward* derivatives (as compared with the matrix $\partial \mathbf{x}/\partial \mathbf{y}$), and are readily obtained by differentiation if a forward model of the plant can be found.[6]

The proposal then is to first learn a forward model of the plant. The model is of the form $h(\mathbf{v}, \mathbf{x})$, where $\mathbf{v}$ is a vector of adjustable parameters, and a parameter estimation scheme is used so that the model comes to approximate the input/output behavior of the plant. In Jordan and Rumelhart 1989, the model is implemented as a multilayer connectionist network, and parameter estimation is achieved by using the backpropagation algorithm (LeCun 1985, Parker 1985, Rumelhart, Hinton, and Williams 1986). (Backpropagation is an algorithm for computing gradients in a layered connectionist network with nonlinear units.) After the forward model is learned, it is possible to learn the controller. Again backpropagation is used, with the gradient now being computed with respect to the underlying parameters $\mathbf{w}$. Given a target $\mathbf{y}^*$, the controller produces a vector $\mathbf{x}$, which leads to an output $\mathbf{y}$. The error vector $\mathbf{y}^* - \mathbf{y}$ is propagated back through the (now fixed) connections of the model, which multiplies by the estimated Jacobian matrix of the plant, computing the vector $(\partial \mathbf{y}/\partial \mathbf{x})^{\mathrm{T}} (\mathbf{y}^* - \mathbf{y})$. This vector is then propagated down into the controller so as to multiply by the remaining matrix $(\partial \mathbf{x}/\partial \mathbf{w})^{\mathrm{T}}$. (Note that this procedure, as given by equation 4, is analogous to the learning rule in equation 3, with the error $\mathbf{x}' - \mathbf{x}$ replaced by the term $(\partial \mathbf{y}/\partial \mathbf{x})^{\mathrm{T}} (\mathbf{y}^* - \mathbf{y})$.)

To summarize, once the forward model of the plant has been learned, all of the terms in equation 4 are available to the system and can be computed in a single pass using the backpropagation algorithm. The system essentially uses the forward model to find out how to change the parameters of the controller so as to perform gradient descent in the "distal" error measure E. Jordan and Rumelhart have demonstrated this algorithm in the inverse kinematic problem of positioning a six-degree-of-freedom planar manipulator and in a two-degree-of-freedom inverse dynamics problem.

The forward modeling approach is the most complex approach we have considered, requiring a model of the plant that must be learned separately from the feedforward controller, as well as a differentiation procedure (for example, backpropagation) so that the forward model can be used in the learning of control signals. There are, however, advantages to offset the complexity. First, once the forward model is learned, the algorithm is inherently goal directed, given that it works directly to minimize the error between the goal y^* and the actual output y. Second, indeterminate motor learning problems can be solved using the forward modeling approach; indeed it is possible to add additional terms to the error functional to resolve the indeterminacy in a principled manner (Jordan 1989a). Finally, it may be useful for other reasons to have a forward model of the plant. Such a model allows the system to predict the result it expects, given the output it has produced. This ability allows the system to notice its own errors, as well as to learn through "mental practice" (MacKay 1982, Singer 1980).

Discussion

The currently dominant psychological theory of motor learning is schema theory (Schmidt 1975, 1982). It is interesting to consider this theory in light of the work discussed previously. According to schema theory, four kinds of information are available after a movement—the movement outcome, the response specification (control signal), the initial conditions, and a proprioceptive signal. Learning a motor program involves changing a "recall schema" in such a way that the movement outcome and initial conditions can be used on future trials to retrieve the corresponding response specifications. The schema concept is invoked to deal with two issues that were problematic for earlier theories—how the system can produce novel control signals for novel situations, and how the system avoids a massive storage problem. These problems are lessened in schema theory because the schema is an abstraction of the observed data points, and it is able to interpolate as needed.

These properties of a schema are embodied in the feedforward controllers that we have discussed. In the associative approach, for example, learning proceeds by changing the parameters of a continuous function g. The function g is an abstraction of the data points, and the continuity provides interpolation. (The gradient descent rules we have discussed are an iterative approach to nonlinear least-squares regression.) In fact if we let y represent the movement outcome and x' be the corresponding response specification, then the learning of a recall schema is essentially the same as the direct inverse modeling approach.

Action

Indeed, like the unadorned version of that approach, schema theory provides no account of goal-directed learning. The recall schema simply learns the relationship between actual outcomes and response specifications, and no mechanism is provided by which the schema can be changed so as to provide a more correct control signal with respect to the *currently* desired movement outcome. This problem was addressed to some degree in the theory that preceded schema theory—Adams's (1971) closed-loop theory. In that theory the movement outcome ("knowledge of results") was treated as the input to a problem-solving process that led to a varied response on the next trial. This process, however, was never made explicit in the theory. The issue has perhaps been overlooked because both of these theories were designed to address data from discrete, single-degree-of-freedom movements. In such movements the problem of converting from knowledge of results to a change in the response specification is not particularly difficult. In tasks with many degrees of freedom, however, this conversion is arguably the most difficult part of the learning process.

Schema theory also proposes a "recognition schema," which learns associations from movement outcomes and initial conditions to proprioceptive feedback. This schema is used for error recognition after fast movements and provides a reference signal for a servomechanism during slow positioning tasks. The recognition schema and an "error-labeling" schema, which maps to predicted movement outcomes, act somewhat like a forward model. They are able to serve as a substitute for external information about the movement outcome, and thereby provide an input for the learning of the recall schema. These schemata, however, are not used directly in making changes to the recall schema, as in the forward modeling approach.

In terms of relating the approaches that we have discussed to experimental data, there is clearly much to be gained from making comparisons with schema theory. One example of such data, which has been taken as strong support for schema theory, is the relationship between the amount of learning in a task and the amount of variability during practice. In some tasks it is more beneficial to experience repeated trials in the neighborhood of a target than at the target itself (Shapiro and Schmidt 1981). This is a result that would be predicted by the forward modeling approach, because variable experience yields a forward model that is correct over a larger domain, which in turn provides better derivative information for learning the controller. The estimation procedures of An and colleagues would also benefit from varied experience. It is less clear how the other direct inverse modeling approaches would fare with this datum. Kawato and colleagues' model would seem to learn most from experience with a specific target. Finally, reinforcement learning would not appear to predict the result, because the overall probability of reward for the correct output would be lower in the variable practice condition.

18.4   Toward an Integration

In preceding sections we organized our discussion of computational issues in the study of action around the three topic areas of degrees of freedom, serial order, and learning. For the most part our discussion has treated these problems separately, reflecting the separate histories of research in these areas. In this section we illustrate why an integrated treatment of these problems would be desirable by describing some recent work that takes a limited step in this direction (Jordan 1989a).

Let us reconsider the problem of context sensitivity. The notion that the same action can have different forms depending on the context implies that there are excess degrees of freedom somewhere in the system. We can model the situation by considering a *task space*, in which actions appear as points, and an *articulatory space*, which maps into task space through a many-to-one function f. (Task space corresponds to vectors $\mathbf{y}^*$ in the previous section, and articulatory space corresponds to vectors $\mathbf{x}$). In articulatory space actions are the inverse images of points in task space and are regions rather than points, due to the assumption that f is many-to-one. We also assume that a task is specified to the system as a sequence of points $\mathbf{y}_1^*, \mathbf{y}_2^*, \ldots , \mathbf{y}_n^*$ to be followed in task space. As shown in figure 18.8, the learning problem facing the system is to find a trajectory in articulatory space passing through the regions in the specified order (where the regions are defined implicitly as inverse images of the target points). Clearly this requirement is fulfilled by many possible trajectories. If we add the constraint that values of articulatory degrees of freedom should change little over time,

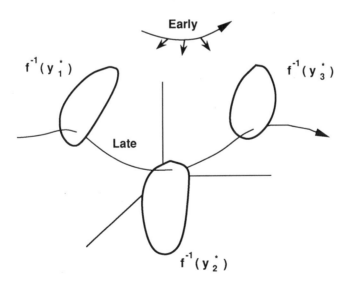

Figure 18.8 A representation of articulatory space. The three regions are the inverse images of points in task space (not shown). Also shown are a trajectory early in learning, with the transformed error vectors computed during the steps of a learning trial, and a trajectory late in learning.

however, then certain trajectories are to be preferred to others. This constraint represents an interaction between the serial nature of the task and the existence of excess degrees of freedom—the fact that an action appears in a temporal context of other actions imposes implicit constraints on possible configurations of degrees of freedom to realize the action.

The problem we have described can be formulated as a problem in optimal control theory, but its solution in terms of a control law is complicated by the nature of the constraints on the trajectories (they appear as inverse images of an unknown function f). It is accordingly difficult to see how the system could generate preferred trajectories on the fly, particularly given the need to anticipate future actions. However, if we include a role for learning, then the problem becomes somewhat easier. Referring to figure 18.8, let us suppose that the short trajectory represents an attempt made by the system on an early learning trial. At each time step we assume that learning proceeds by (1) a comparison in task space between the target action and the actual action, thereby generating an error vector, (2) a transformation of the error vector into articulatory space, and (3) an updating of the trajectory based on the transformed error vector. The overall effect of these steps is to pull the trajectory toward the region corresponding to the currently specified target point. For the system to move toward preferred trajectories, it is possible to bias the adjustments made at a particular point on the trajectory by the adjustments made at nearby points. Metaphorically we can imagine attaching springs along the trajectory to bias the learning process toward solutions in which the articulatory variables change little over time.

The computations we have described can be performed in the parallel distributed processing network shown in figure 18.9. This network consists of the sequential network shown in figure 18.4 composed with an additional layered network. This additional network connects the output units (which encode articulatory space) to a set of units that encode task space, and it serves as a forward model of the function f. In learning to imitate a target sequence, errors are generated at the task units between actual and desired outputs and are propagated back through the previously-learned connections of the forward model and down into the sequential network, where the weights are changed. This process implements the three steps described in the previous paragraph and occurs for each action in the sequence. Furthermore the fact that adjustments for each action are made to the same set of underlying weights means that adjustments automatically tend to bias one another, the form of the bias depending on the similarities between the patterns on the input units of the sequential network at nearby points in time. (Jordan (1989a) also discusses a method that generates additional errors directly at the articulatory units based on the time-rate of change of

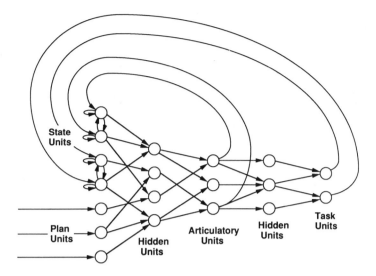

Figure 18.9 The connectionist sequential machine of figure 18.4 augmented with a layered network that serves as a forward model. The articulatory units are the output units of the network. (From Jordan 1989a.)

their activations.) Thus the sequential network is biased to find articulatory representations that are sensitive to their temporal context.

The results of a simulation of such a network are shown in Figure 18.10. The network has six output units for the six articulatory degrees of freedom of the "hand" being controlled, and four task units for the four Cartesian coordinates of the endpoints. The task for the system is to learn to touch the indicated positions in a specified order, using either finger, with the choice of finger based on a simple distance comparison. As shown in figure 18.10, the network finds a solution that both meets the nonlinear endpoint constraints and makes use of the excess degrees of freedom to anticipate future actions. Anticipation is achieved by a nonlinear compensation between the translational degrees of freedom and the joint angles of the finger touching the target; furthermore the joint angles of the unconstrained finger show parallel anticipation of the following configuration. Finally, simulations also demonstrate that the solution found by the network is an attractor, in particular a stable limit cycle. When the system is perturbed by adding transient noise to the activations of the articulatory units, it returns to the learned sequence, demonstrating the stability of the solution.

Although preliminary, these results suggest that it may be useful to consider integrated treatments of degrees-of-freedom problems. In particular learning appears to be a powerful way to introduce constraints that reduce degrees of freedom. Finally, it is worth pointing out that excess degrees of freedom are not always best thought of as a problem

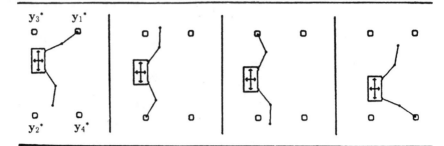

Figure 18.10 A six-degree-of-freedom (two translational and four joint angles) system that has learned a sequential positioning problem, moving an end effector through the sequence y_1^*, y_2^*, y_3^*, y_4^*. (From Jordan 1989a.)

in the pejorative sense of the term. Rather excess degrees of freedom can allow flexibility and responsiveness to contextual variables. Computations that reduce degrees of freedom may only make sense when we consider the larger context in which a problem is posed (Fowler and Turvey 1978).

18.5 Conclusions

The study of action has a long history, yet a computational approach to the area is still in its infancy. There have been promising developments, and current research in the area is an interesting confluence of ideas from such disciplines as psychology, linguistics, control theory, robotics, and physics. In this chapter we have emphasized the unified nature of the study of action by treating various problems that arise as instances of a general degrees-of-freedom problem. In taking this approach, we have been influenced by several authors, including Albus (1981), Bernstein (1967), Greene (1972), Norman and Shallice (1986), Saltzman (1979), and Turvey (1977). Our perspective has been that the major problem for an action system is to control relationships between interacting systems of degrees of freedom. These degrees of freedom may appear at a variety of levels of analysis and may refer to both spatial and temporal aspects of behavior. We believe that this perspective provides a useful framework for discussion and will allow meaningful comparisons to be made as computational theories continue to be developed.

Notes

Preparation of this chapter was supported in part by the Air Force Office of Scientific Research, Bolling, AFB, through grant AFOSR-87-030, National Science Foundation grants BNS-8408634, and BNS-8710933, and a Research Career Development Award K04-NS00942 from the National Institutes of Neurological and Communicative Diseases and Stroke (to David A. Rosenbaum). We thank Chris Atkeson, Heather Jane Barnes, Andrew Barto,

Emilio Bizzi, Vijaykumar Gullipalli, Robert Jacobs, Larry Parsons, Brian Pinette, Michael Posner, Elliot Saltzman, Michael Seymour, and an anonymous reviewer for helpful comments.

1. A basin of attraction is a region in state space such that trajectories that start in the region approach a limit set contained in the region over time. For example, a linear mass-spring system with damping is a system with a single attractor point and a basin of attraction that includes the entire state space (in this example the state space is two-dimensional: one dimension for position and one for velocity).

2. The Jacobian matrix is a matrix that relates small changes in endpoint position to small changes in joint-angle configuration. That is, it is the matrix whose i, jth entry is the partial derivative $\partial x_i/\partial \theta_j$; where x_i is the ith endpoint position coordinate, and θ_j is the jth joint angle.

3. Knoll and Sternberg (1987) observed that the tree-traversal model may not account for some of the detailed aspects of the results of Sternberg and colleagues (1978). However, the model developed by Sternberg and colleagues to account for their results was specifically designed to do so. Moreover their model does not account for as large a range of phenomena as the tree-traversal model does.

4. The vector notation used here should not obscure the fact that this error measure is simply the sum of squares: $E = \frac{1}{2} \Sigma_{i=1}^n (x_i' - x_i)^2$, where the subscript i picks out the ith component of the vector.

5. The gradient denoted by $\nabla_w E$, is simply the vector of partial derivatives of E with respect to the components of $\mathbf{w}$. It points in the direction of steepest ascent of E. The negation sign in the learning rule changes the search to gradient *descent*.

6. The matrix $\partial \mathbf{y}/\partial \mathbf{x}$ is referred to as the Jacobian matrix of the plant function f. (Compare with note 2, in which f is the forward kinematic function of a manipulator.)

References

Abbs, J. H., and Gracco, V. L. 1983. Sensorimotor actions in the control of multimovement speech gestures. *Trends in Neuroscience* 6:393–395.

Adams, J. A. 1971. A closed-loop theory of motor learning. *Journal of Motor Behavior* 3:111–149.

Adams, J. A. 1984. Learning of movement sequences. *Psychological Bulletin* 96:3–28.

Albus, J. S. 1981. *Brains, Behavior, and Robotics*. Peterborough, NH: BYTE Books.

An, C. H., Atkeson, C. G., and Hollerbach, J. M. 1985. Estimation of inertial parameters of rigid body links of manipulators. *Proceedings of the 24th Conference on Decision and Control*, Fort Lauderdale, FL.

Arbib, M. A. 1981. Perceptual structures and distributed motor control. In V. B. Brooks, ed. *Handbook of Physiology—The Nervous System II*. Bethesda, MD: American Physiological Society.

Atkeson, C. G., and McIntyre, J. 1986. Robot trajectory learning through practice. *IEEE Conference on Robotics and Automation*, San Francisco, CA.

Attneave, F., and Benson, B. 1969. Spatial coding of tactual stimulation. *Journal of Experimental Psychology* 81:216–222.

Baars, B. J., Motley, M. T., and MacKay, D. G. 1975. Output editing for lexical status from artificially elicited slips of the tongue. *Journal of Verbal Learning and Verbal Behavior* 14:382–391.

Barmack, D. 1970. Dynamic visual acuity as an index of eye movement control. *Vision Research* 10:1377–1391.

Barlett, F. C. 1932. *Remembering*. London: Cambridge University Press.

Barto, A. G., and Anandan, P. 1985. Pattern-recognizing stochastic learning automata. *IEEE Transactions on Systems, Man, and Cybernetics* 15:360–375.

Barto, A. G., and Anderson, C. W. 1985. Structural learning in connectionist systems. *Proceedings of the Seventh Annual Conference of the Cognitive Science Society*. Hillsdale, NJ: Erlbaum.

Barto, A. G., and Epstein, S. 1983. Adaptive networks and sensorimotor control. *Proceedings of the Second Workshop on Visuomotor Coordination in Frog and Toad: Models and Experiments*, Mexico City, pp. 105–158.

Bejczy, A. K., and Lee, S. 1983. Robot arm dynamic model reduction for control. *IEEE Conference on Decision and Control*, San Antonio, TX.

Benguerel, A. P., and Cowan, H. A. 1974. Coarticulation of upper lip protusion in French. *Phonetica* 30:41–55.

Berkenblit, M. B., Fel'dman, A. G., and Fucson, O. I. 1986. Adaptability of innate motor patterns and motor control. *Behavioral and Brain Sciences* 9:585–638.

Bernstein, N. 1967. *The Coordination and Regulation of Movements*. London: Pergamon.

Bizzi, E., Accornero, N., Chapple, W., and Hogan, N. 1984. Posture control and trajectory formation during arm movement. *Journal of Neuroscience* 4:2738–2745.

Bock, J. K. 1982. Toward a cognitive psychology of syntax: Information processing contributions to sentence formulation. *Psychological Review* 89:1–47.

Bower, G. H., and Hilgard, E. R. 1966. *Theories of Learning*. New York: Appleton-Century-Crofts.

Bullock, D., and Grossberg, S. 1988. Neural dynamics of planned arm movements: Emergent invariants and speed-accuracy properties during trajectory formation. *Psychological Review* 95:49–90.

Bush, R. R., and Estes, W. K., eds. 1959. *Studies in Mathematical Learning Theory*. Stanford, CA: Stanford University Press.

Cohen, M. A., and Grossberg, S. 1983. Absolute stability of global pattern formation and parallel memory storage by competitive neural networks. *IEEE Transactions on Systems, Man, and Cybernetics* 13:815–825.

Collard, R., and Povel, D-J. 1982. Theory of serial pattern production: Tree traversals. *Psychological Review* 85:693–707.

Coren, S. 1986. An efferent component in the visual perception of direction and extent. *Psychological Review* 93:391–410.

Delatizky, J. 1982. Final position control in simulated planar arm movement. *Neuroscience Abstracts* 8:283–292.

Dell, G. S. 1986. A spreading-activation theory of retrieval in sentence production. *Psychological Review* 93:283–321.

Easton, T. A. 1972. On the normal use of reflexes. *American Scientist* 60:591–599.

Fay, D., and Cutler, A. 1977. Malapropisms and the structure of the mental lexicon. *Linguistic Inquiry* 8:505–520.

Fel'dman, A. G. 1986. Once more on the equilibrium-point hypothesis (λ model) for motor control. *Journal of Motor Behavior* 18:17–54.

Flash, T., and Hogan, N. 1985. The coordination of arm movements: An experimentally confirmed mathematical model. *Journal of Neuroscience* 5:1688–1703.

Fodor, J. A., and Pylyshyn, Z. W. 1988. Connectionism and cognitive architecture: A critical analysis. *Cognition* 28:3–71.

Fowler, C. A. 1980. Coarticulation and theories of extrinsic timing. *Journal of Phonetics* 8:113–133.

Fowler, C. A., Rubin, P., Remez, R. E., and Turvey, M. T. 1981. Implications for speech production of a general theory of action. In B. Butterworth, ed. *Language Production. Volume 1: Speech and Talk*. London: Academic Press, pp. 373–420.

Fowler, C. A., and Turvey, M. T. 1978. Skill acquisition: An event approach with special reference to searching for the optimum of a function of several variables. In G. Stelmach, ed. *Information Processing in Motor Control and Learning*. New York: Academic Press.

Fromkin, V. A. 1971. The nonanomalous nature of anomalous utterances. *Language* 47:27–52.

Fu, K. S. 1970. Stochastic automata as models of learning systems. In J. M. Mendel and K. S. Fu, eds. *Adaptive, Learning, and Pattern Recognition Systems*. New York: Academic Press.

Garrett, M. F. 1975. The analysis of sentence production. In G. H. Bower, ed. *The Psychology of Learning and Motivation*. New York: Academic Press.

Gentner, D. R., Grudin, J., and Conway, E. 1981. Finger Movements in Transcription Typing. Tech. Rep. 8001. University of California, Center for Human Information Processing, San Diego, CA.

Golden, R. M. 1986. The "brain-state-in-a-box" neural model is a gradient descent algorithm. *Journal of Mathematical Psychology* 30:73–80.

Gordon, P. C., and Meyer, D. E. 1987. Control of serial order in rapidly spoken syllable sequences. *Journal of Memory and Language* 26:300–321.

Greene, P. H. 1972. Problems of organization of motor systems. *Progress in Theoretical Biology* 2:303–338.

Greeno, J. G., and Simon, H. A. 1974. Processes for sequence production. *Psychological Review* 81:187–197.

Greenwald, A. G. 1970. Sensory feedback mechanisms in performance control: With special reference to the ideo-motor mechanism. *Psychological Review* 7:73–99.

Grossberg, S. 1978. A theory of visual coding, memory, and development. In R. Rosen and F. Snell, eds. *Progress in Theoretical Biology*. Vol. 5. New York: Academic Press.

Grossberg, S., and Kuperstein, M. 1986. *Neural Dynamics of Adaptive Sensory-Motor Control: Ballistic Eye Movements*. Amsterdam: North-Holland.

Grudin, J. T. 1981. *The Organization of Serial Order in Typing*. Doctoral dissertation, University of California, San Diego, CA.

Gupta, M. 1986. *Adaptive Methods for Control System Design*. New York: IEEE Press.

Halwes, T., and Jenkins, J. J. 1971. Problem of serial order in behavior is not resolved by context-sensitive associative memory models. *Psychological Review* 78:122–129.

Hinton, G. E. 1984. Parallel computations for controlling an arm. *Journal of Motor Behavior* 16:171–194.

Hogan, N. 1984. An organising principle for a class of voluntary movements. *Journal of Neuroscience* 4:2745–2754.

Hogan, N. 1985. The mechanics of multi-joint posture and movement control. *Biological Cybernetics* 53:1–17.

Hollerbach, J. M. 1982. Computers, brains, and the control of movement. *Trends in Neuroscience* 5:189–193.

Hollerbach, J. M., and Flash, T. 1982. Dynamic interactions between limb segments during planar arm movement. *Biological Cybernetics* 44:67–77.

Hopfield, J. J. 1982. Neural networks and physical systems with emergent collective computational abilities. *Proceedings of the National Academy of Sciences* 79:2554–2558.

Inhoff, A. W., Rosenbaum, D. A., Gordon, A. M., and Campbell, J. A. 1984. Stimulus-response compatibility and motor programming of manual response sequences. *Journal of Experimental Psychology* 10:724–733.

James, W. 1890. *The Principles of Psychology*. New York: Dover.

Jordan, M. I. 1989a. Indeterminate motor skill learning problems. In M. Jeannerod, ed. *Attention and Performance, XIII*. Hillsdale, NJ: Erlbaum.

Jordan, M. I. 1989b. Serial order: A parallel, distributed processing approach. In J. L. Elman and D. E. Rumelhart, eds. *Advances in Connectionist Theory: Speech*. Hillsdale, NJ: Erlbaum.

Jordan, M. I., and Rumelhart, D. E. 1989. Supervised learning with a distal teacher. *Cognitive Science* (in press).

Kahn, M. E. 1969. *The Near-Minimum Time Control of Open-Loop Articulated Kinematic Chains*. Stanford Artificial Intelligence Memo No. 106. Stanford University, Stanford, CA.

Kawato, M., Furukawa, K., and Suzuki, R. 1987. A hierarchical neural-network model for control and learning of voluntary movement. *Biological Cybernetics* 57:169–185.

Kelso, J. A. S., Holt, K. G., Kugler, P. N., and Turvey, M. T. 1980. On the concept of coordinative structures as dissipative structures: II. Empirical lines of convergence. In G. E. Stelmach and J. Requin, eds. *Tutorials in Motor Behavior*. Amsterdam: North-Holland, pp. 49–70.

Kelso, J. A. S., Tuller, B., Vatikiotis-Bateson, E., and Fowler, C. A. 1984. Functionally specific articulatory cooperation following jaw perturbations during speech: Evidence for coordinative structures. *Journal of Experimental Psychology: Human Perception and Performance* 10:812–832.

Kent, R. D., and Minifie, F. D. 1977. Coarticulation in recent speech production models. *Journal of Phonetics* 5:115–117.

Khatib, O. 1987. A unified approach for motion and force control: The operational space formulation. *IEEE Journal of Robotics and Automation* 3:43–54.

Kirk, D. E. 1970. *Optimal Control Theory*. Englewood Cliffs, NJ: Prentice-Hall.

Knoll, R. L., and Sternberg, S. 1987. *Local Invariance in Hierarchical Models of Sequence Production*. Paper presented at the Annual Meeting of the Psychonomic Society. Seattle, WA.

Kugler, P. N., Kelso, J. A. S., and Turvey, M. T. 1980. On the concept of coordinative structures as dissipative structures: I. Theoretical lines of convergence. In G. E. Stelmach and J. Requin, eds. *Tutorials in Motor Behavior*. Amsterdam: North-Holland, pp. 49–70.

Kuperstein, M. 1988. Neural model of adaptive hand-eye coordination for single postures. *Science* 239:1308–1311.

Ladefoged, P., DeClerk, J., Lindau, M., and Papçun, G. 1972. An auditory-motor theory of speech production. *UCLA Working Papers in Linguistics* 22:48–75.

Lashley, K. S. 1951. The problem of serial order in behavior. In L. A. Jeffress, ed. *Cerebral Mechanisms in Behavior*. New York: Wiley.

LeCun, Y. 1985. A learning scheme for asymmetric threshold networks. *Proceedings of Cognitiva 85*, Paris, France.

Liberman, A. M., Cooper, F. S., Shankweiler, D. P., and Studdert-Kennedy, M. G. 1967. Perception of the speech code. *Psychological Review* 74:431–461.

Luchins, A. S. 1942. Mechanization in problem solving. *Psychological Monographs* 54 (248).

MacKay, D. G. 1970. Spoonerisms: The structure of errors in the serial order of speech. *Neuropsychologia* 8:323–350.

MacKay, D. G. 1982. The problem of flexibility, fluency, and speed-accuracy trade-off in skilled behavior. *Psychological Review* 89:483–506.

McClelland, J. L., and Kawamoto, A. H. 1986. Mechanisms of sentence processing: Assigning roles to constituents. In J. L. McClelland and D. E. Rumelhart, eds. *Parallel Distributed Processing: Volume 2*. Cambridge, MA: MIT Press.

Melsa, J. L., and Schultz, D. G. 1969. *Linear Control Systems*. New York: McGraw-Hill.

Mendel, J. M., and McLaren, R. W. 1970. Reinforcement-learning control and pattern recognition systems. In J. M. Mendel and K. S. Fu, eds. *Adaptive Learning and Pattern Recognition Systems*. New York: Academic Press.

Meyer, D. E., and Gordon, P. C. 1983. Speech production: Motor programming of phonetic features. *Journal of Memory and Language* 24:3–26.

Miller, N. 1986. *Dyspraxia and its Management*. London: Croom Helm.

Miller, W. T. 1987. Sensor-based control of robotic manipulators using a general learning algorithm. *IEEE Journal of Robotics and Automation* 3:157–165.

Moll, K. L., and Daniloff, R. G. 1971. Investigation of the timing of velar movements during speech. *Journal of the Acoustical Society of America* 50:678–684.

Mowrer, O. H. 1960. *Learning Theory and Behavior*. New York: Wiley.

Nelson, W. 1983. Physical principles for economies of skilled movements. *Biological Cybernetics* 46:135–147.

Norman, D. A., and Shallice, T. 1986. Attention to action: Willed and automatic control of behavior. In R. J. Davidson, G. E. Schwartz, and D. Shapiro, eds. *Consciousness and Self-Regulation: Advances in Research, Volume IV*. New York: Plenum Press.

Öhman, S. E. G. 1966. Coarticulation in VCV utterances: spectrographic measurements. *Journal of the Acoustical Society of America* 39:151–168.

Olsen, R. A., and Murray, R. A., III. 1976. Finger motion in typing texts of varying complexity. *Proceedings 6th Congress of the International Ergonomics Association*, San Francisco, CA.

Parker, D. 1985. *Learning-logic*. Tech. rep. TR-47. Cambridge, MA: MIT Sloan School of Management.

Partridge, L. 1986. Frogs solve Bernstein's problem. *Behavioral and Brain Sciences* 9:619–620.

Pew, R. W. 1974. Human perceptual-motor performance. In B. H. Kantowitz, ed. *Human Information Processing: Tutorials in Performance and Cognition*. Hillsdale, NJ: Erlbaum, pp. 1–39.

Polit, A., and Bizzi, E. 1978. Processes controlling arm movements in monkeys. *Science* 201:1235–1237.

Rabbitt, P. M. A., Vyas, S. M., and Fearnley, S. 1975. Programming sequences of complex responses. In P. M. A. Rabbitt and S. Dornic, eds. *Attention and Performance V*. London: Academic Press.

Raibert, M. H. 1978. A model for sensorimotor control and learning. *Biological Cybernetics* 29:29–36.

Raibert, M. H. 1986. Symmetry in running. *Science* 231:1292–1293.

Reich, P. A. 1977. Evidence for a stratal boundary from slips of the tongue. *Forum Linguisticum* 2:211–217.

Reitman, J. S., and Rueter, H. H. 1980. Organization revealed by recall orders and confirmed by pauses. *Cognitive Psychology* 12:554–581.

Restle, F. 1970. Theory of serial pattern learning: Structural trees. *Psychological Review* 77:481–495.

Rosenbaum, D. A., Kenny, S., and Derr, M. A. 1983. Hierarchical control of rapid movement sequences. *Journal of Experimental Psychology: Human Perception and Performance* 9:86–102.

Rosenbaum, D. A. 1985. Motor programming: A review and scheduling theory. In H. Heur, U. Kleinbeck, and K-M. Schmidt, eds. *Motor Behavior: Programming, Control, and Acquisition*. Berlin: Springer-Verlag, pp. 1–33.

Rosenbaum, D. A., Gordon, A. M., Stillings, N. A., and Feinstein, M. H. 1987. Stimulus-response compatibility in the programming of speech. *Memory and Cognition* 15:217–224.

Rosenbaum, D. A., Weber, R. J., Hazelett, W. M., and Hindorff, V. 1986. The parameter remapping effect in human performance: Evidence from tongue twisters and finger fumblers. *Journal of Memory and Language* 25.

Rumelhart, D. E., Hinton, G. E., Williams, R. J. 1986. Learning internal representations by error propagation. In D. E. Rumelhart and J. L. McClelland, eds. *Parallel Distributed Processing: Volume 1*. Cambridge, MA: MIT Press.

Rumelhart, D. E., and Norman, D. A. 1982. Simulating a skilled typist: A study of skilled cognitive-motor performance. *Cognitive Science* 6:1–36.

Sakitt, B. 1980. A spring model and equivalent neural network for arm posture control. *Biological Cybernetics* 37:227–234.

Saltzman, E. L. 1979. Levels of sensorimotor representation. *Journal of Mathematical Psychology* 20:91–163.

Saltzman, E. L. 1986. Task-dynamic coordination of the speech articulators: A preliminary model. In H. Heuer and C. Fromm, eds. *Generation and Modulation of Action Patterns. Experimental Brain Research Series* 15:129–144. New York: Springer-Verlag.

Saltzman, E. L., and Kelso, J. A. S. 1987. Skilled actions: A task-dynamic approach. *Psychological Review* 94:84–106.

Schmidt, R. A. 1975. A schema theory of discrete motor skill learning. *Psychological Review* 82:225–260.

Schmidt, R. A. 1982. *Motor Control and Learning.* Champaign, IL: Human Kinetics Publishers.

Shapiro, D. C., and Schmidt, R. A. 1981. The schema theory: Recent evidence and developmental implications. In J. A. S. Kelso and J. E. Clark, eds. *The Development of Movement Control and Coordination.* New York: Wiley.

Shattuck-Hufnagel, S. 1979. Speech errors as evidence for a serial-ordering mechanism in sentence production. In W. E. Cooper and E. C. T. Walker, eds. *Sentence Processing: Psycholinguistic Studies Presented to Merrill Garrett.* Hillsdale, NJ: Erlbaum.

Simon, H. A. 1969. *The Sciences of the Artificial.* Cambridge, MA: MIT Press.

Singer, R. N. 1980. *Motor Learning and Human Performance.* 3rd ed. New York: Macmillan.

Smolensky, P. 1988. On the proper treatment of connectionism. *Behavioral and Brain Sciences* 11:1–74.

Sternberg, S., Monsell, S., Knoll, R. L., and Wright, C. E. 1978. The latency and duration of rapid movement sequences: Comparisons of speech and typewriting. In G. E. Stelmach, ed. *Information Processing in Motor Control and Learning.* New York: Academic Press, pp. 117–152.

Stevens, K. N. 1972. The quantal nature of speech: Evidence from articulatory-acoustic data. In E. E. David, Jr. and P. B. Denes, eds. *Human Communication: A Unified View.* New York: McGraw-Hill.

Sutton, R. S. 1984. *Temporal Aspects of Credit Assignment in Reinforcement Learning.* Doctoral dissertation, University of Massachusetts, Amherst, MA.

Thorndike, E. L. 1911. *Animal Intelligence.* Darien, CT: Hafner.

Turvey, M. T. 1977. Preliminaries to a theory of action with reference to vision. In R. Shaw and J. Bransford, eds. *Perceiving, Acting, and Knowing: Toward an Ecological Psychology.* Hillsdale, NJ: Erlbaum.

Vidyasagar, M. 1978. *Nonlinear Systems Analysis.* Englewood Cliffs, NJ: Prentice-Hall.

Wickelgren, W. A. 1969. Context-sensitive coding, associative memory, and serial order in (speech) behavior. *Psychological Review* 76:1–15.

Widrow, B., Gupta, N. K., and Maitra, S. 1973. Punish/reward: Learning with a critic in adaptive threshold systems. *IEEE Transactions on Systems, Man and Cybernetics* 5:455–465.

Widrow, B., and Hoff, M. E. 1960. Adaptive switching circuits. *Institute of Radio Engineers, Western Electronic Show and Convention, Convention Record, Part 4*, pp. 96–104.

Widrow, B., and Stearns, S. D. 1985. *Adaptive Signal Processing*. Englewood Cliffs, NJ: Prentice-Hall.

Williams, R. J. 1987. *Reinforcement-Learning Connectionist Systems*. Tech. Rep. NU-CCS-87-3. Northeastern University, College of Computer Science, Boston, MA.

19 Geometrical and Mechanical Issues in Movement Planning and Control

E. Bizzi and F. A. Mussa-Ivaldi

In the previous chapter, Jordan and Rosenbaum dealt with complex questions such as the degree-of-freedom problem, sequential execution of actions, and acquisition of motor skills. A common thread in their review is an attempt at understanding how the central nervous system (CNS) might decrease the "computational" complexity of these high-level planning functions.

To a certain extent the same approach dominates this chapter. We describe a view of motor control that represents one way to simplify the execution of arm trajectories. This view is based on a novel understanding of geometrical and mechanical properties of muscles. Given that one of the main tasks of the CNS in executing movements is the generation of torques at the joints, then the theory and the experimental evidence summarized in this chapter provide a plausible and perhaps relatively simple solution to this complex problem.

Although the theme of reducing "computational loads" runs through both chapters, there are of course substantial differences. For instance, we believe that because the physical interaction with the environment is one of the objectives of motor control, "mechanics" has a fundamental role in shaping both CNS planning and the execution of movements. In a sense by subscribing to this point of view, we part company with a distinguished tradition in physiological thinking that views motor control almost entirely as processing neural "signals." If physical interaction with the environment is the principal objective of the motor apparatus, then planning and execution are likely to be influenced by the interactions between the effector and the environment.

From this point of view action systems are different from perceptual systems because in the latter direct physical interactions with the environment are limited to the transformation of some forms of energy (light, sound, heat, and the like) into a single form (electric neural signals) that is suitable for information processing. Thus the specific mechanisms by which photons are converted into neural impulses have little relevance to understanding the process of edge detection, not to mention the ability to perform object recognition.

Although the emphasis on the role of mechanics may not be considered a stunning revelation, the fact remains that physiological thinking in the area of motor control has focused almost entirely on the processing of neural "signals." Research has too often ignored the motor system's interface with the environment as well as the interactions among the degrees of freedom within the arm itself. Our purpose in this chapter is to show how a different approach, based on the analysis of geometrical and mechanical features of the motor system, can provide new insights about the central organization of voluntary movements.

Focusing our attention on the planning and execution of arm movements in humans and in robot manipulators, we address three critical issues: Section 19.1 deals with the question concerning which representation or "coordinate system" is used to express the sequence of positions assumed by the arm. Specifically it has been suggested (Bernstein 1935, Morasso 1981, Flash and Hogan 1985) that movements are planned by the CNS in terms of spatial coordinates and then transformed in joint or muscle coordinates. In contrast with this view other investigators (Soechting and Laquaniti 1981, Soechting and Ross 1984, Hollerbach et al. 1986) have supported the hypothesis that movements are directly planned in terms of joint-related variables.

A second controversial issue, discussed in section 19.2, regards the representation of movement dynamics or more specifically the derivation of the torques necessary to accomplish a given planned trajectory. This is an issue that has been central in robotics research and that has recently attracted considerable interest among investigators of biological motor control, especially those who deal with multijoint movements.

The dynamics of a multijoint system are in fact characterized by complex nonlinear equations that contain terms of interaction between different joints. Two different approaches to the dynamics problem have been proposed in robotics. One solves the equations explicitly (Hollerbach 1980, Luh et al. 1980). The second prestores the solutions in lookup tables indexed in one of three ways: (1) by joint positions only (Raibert and Horn 1978), (2) by joint positions and velocities (Raibert 1978), (3) by joint positions, velocities, and accelerations (Albus 1975).

The third issue, discussed in the remaining sections, is the relevance of the muscle mechanical properties with respect to the problem of computing dynamics, as well as to the representation of movement trajectories.

19.1 Hand versus Joint Coordinates in the Planning of Movements

The fact that humans and robots share similar environments provides a common ground for the study of motor planning. For a computer scientist the steps involved in planning the trajectory of a robot arm from point A to point B unravel in the following way: first, a desired trajectory of the manipulator end-point in environment-based (for example, cartesian) coordinates is established; second, this trajectory is transformed into the intrinsic geometry of the manipulator as a sequence of joint motions (joint coordinates).

All humans and most robots are endowed with skeletal systems: either bones and articulations or kinematic chains of rigid links with rotational or sliding joints. In either case the geometrical properties of the skeleton are characterized by a complex, noneuclidean metric.[1] For example, to execute a displacement of the hand of one centimeter from right to left, the corresponding displacement of the shoulder will be larger if the starting position of the hand is closer to the chest. In 1935 Bernstein noted that our ability to control movements is independent of movement scale or position. He concluded that at higher levels of motor control, representations of space are used instead of representation of joints or muscles.

What are the practical consequences of this hypothesis? Let us consider the following experimental situation: a subject is asked to move the hand toward a target. This task specifies not a trajectory for the arm but merely a location in space that, given a starting position, can be reached through a wide variety of paths. If movements are conceived at a planning stage as displacements of the skeletal segments, one would expect that the hand trajectory is obtained from some simple and invariant pattern of joint motions. Going from an initial to a final set of joint angles, the simplest solution is a monotonic change in joint angles for the whole duration of the movement. This choice would result in a predictable and significant curvature of the hand path between starting and final positions. In contrast, if movements of the hand are planned in hand coordinates, an invariant shape of the hand movement—that is, a straight line—would be seen in conjunction with a more complex description of joint motion.

When this experiment was actually carried out (Morasso 1981), it was found that trajectories were remarkably invariant if described in hand coordinates with respect to a fixed frame in the environment. Regardless of movement direction and of the location of the targets, the hand followed almost straight paths with simple unimodal velocity profiles (figure 19.1). In contrast when the same movements were represented in joint coordinates, joint angles were characterized by more complex trajectories, with different velocity profiles in different regions of the workspace and in some cases with joint reversals during a single movement. Hence the outcome of this experiment is in agreement with Bernstein's hypothesis: The planning of movements appears to be expressed in a geometrical representation consistent with the metric of the environment rather than with the metric of the musculoskeletal system.

The same conclusion was reached by Flash and Hogan (1985) in their study of multijoint arm trajectories. The kinematic features of point-to-point arm movements were derived from a single optimization principle expressing the idea that trajectories from initial to final positions are

Geometrical and Mechanical Issues in Movement Planning and Control

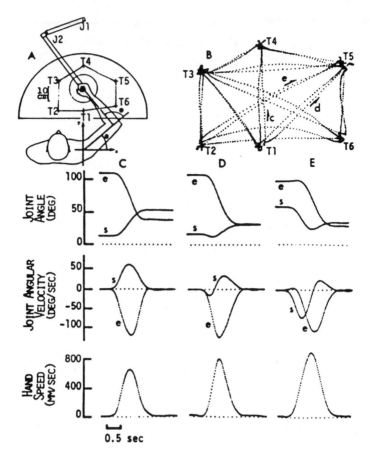

Figure 19.1 (A) Plan view of a seated subject grasping the handle of the two-joint hand-position transducer (designed by N. Hogan). The right arm was elevated to shoulder level and moved in a horizontal work space. Movement of the handle was measured with potentiometers located at the two mechanical joints of the apparatus (J1, J2). A horizontal semicircular plate located just above the handle carried the visual targets. Six visual target locations (T1 through T6) are illustrated as crosses. The digitized paths between targets and the curved path were obtained by moving the handle along a straight edge from one target to the next and then along a circular path; movement paths were reliably reproduced. (B) A series of digitized handle paths (sampling rate, 100 Hz) performed by one subject in different parts of the movement space. The subject moved his hand to the illuminated target and then waited for the appearance of a new target. Targets presented in random order. Arrows show direction of some of the hand movements. (C, D, E) Kinematic data for three of the movements, the paths of which are shown in (B). Letters show correspondence, for example, data under (C) are for path c in (B); e, elbow joint, s, should, angles measured as indicated in (A). (From Bizzi and Abend 1983, modified from Morasso 1982.)

chosen to be maximally smooth (Hogan 1984). In mathematical terms this is equivalent to requiring the chosen trajectory to minimize the mean-square amplitude of the jerk (that is, the rate of change of acceleration) associated with the motion of the hand (Flash 1983, Flash and Hogan 1985).

Recent studies by Georgopoulos and colleagues (1982, 1983) based on recording single neurons from the parietal cortex of monkeys may also be interpreted as supporting the idea of planning in spatial or hand coordinates. The experiment consisted of recording activity from individual cortical cells as the monkey executed movements from a fixed location to a set of targets placed around the starting point. The results indicated that the curves relating the frequency of discharge of a cell to the direction of movement were characterized by a single maximum, corresponding to the "preferred direction" of the cell. The average direction of a cell ensemble (defined as the weighted sum of all the preferred directions with the weights given by the cell activities) was found to be in good agreement with the direction of hand movements.

It is tempting to speculate that these signals may represent the physiological underpinnings of trajectory planning in spatial coordinates. An alternative hypothesis, however, has recently been suggested (Mussa-Ivaldi 1988). According to this view, it is also possible to interpret Georgopoulos's results as evidence that cortical cells encode muscle activations instead of hand-movement directions.

In contrast to the views of Morasso and Hogan, other investigators have suggested that movement planning occurs in joint coordinates. For instance, Soechting and Laquaniti (1981) found a constancy in the ratio of elbow-to-shoulder-joint velocities as the hand approached a set of targets located in the sagittal plane. These researchers concluded that the planning of arm movements is done in joint coordinates. Work of Hollerbach and colleagues (1986) supports the idea of motor planning in joint rather than hand coordinates on a different basis. Hollerbach and colleagues suggest that straight hand trajectories can be obtained using joint interpolation by introducing delays between the onsets of movements in different joints (staggered joint interpolation). In this hypothesis the motion of each joint is still characterized as a monotonic change from the initial to the final angle. By controlling the delays between the joint motions, it is possible to introduce some curvature in the joint-space trajectories, and in many cases this is sufficient to generate straight hand movements.

However, we still favor planning in hand coordinates for the following reasons: (1) During the execution of planar hand trajectories (Morasso 1981), reversals of joint motions (both of shoulder and elbow) have been observed for certain movements. These reversals are necessary to maintain the hand on a straight path as movements occur in certain regions. More precisely to obtain straight hand movements in the horizontal plane, the shoulder must invert its motion as the forearm becomes orthogonal to the trajectory, and the elbow must invert its motion as the hand passes through the point of minimum normal distance from the shoulder. It is evident that such joint reversals cannot be accounted for by the staggering joint interpolation because the model assumes monotonic joint motions. (2) Even neglecting the previous problem, different delays are required for obtaining straight hand trajectories with different directions and in different regions of the workspace. Given an arbitrary hand movement, computing the appropriate delays seems to be a task similar in complexity to that of deriving the inverse kinematics by traditional methods. For this reason, although the staggering mechanism is competent to obtain some degree of joint coordination, it does not seem to provide an appropriate representation for planning movements of the hand within the environment.

19.2 The Problem of Dynamics in Natural and Artificial Systems

The major goal of dynamics is to derive the motion of a system, given the forces acting on it. In movement planning, however, whether for natural or for artificial systems, the task is reversed. For example, given a desired motion of the arm, the problem is to find the forces that the actuators must generate to achieve this motion. This is called the inverse dynamics problem. In a single-joint situation it may appear rather simple. For example, if $\theta(t)$ is the desired time course of the elbow angle, and I and B are respectively the forearm inertia and the elbow joint viscosity, then the torque $T(t)$ that the muscles generate is simply given by

$$T = I\,\theta'' + B\,\theta'. \tag{1}$$

Here primes indicate derivatives with respect to time.

When dealing with multijoint arm movements, these equations assume a more complex form. First of all, joint angles and torques are vectors instead of scalar variables.[2] Hence with N angular degrees of freedom,[3] the configuration of the arm is given by the array $\boldsymbol{\theta} = [\theta_1, \ldots, \theta_N]$, the joint torque is a vector $\mathbf{T} = [T_1, \ldots, T_N]$, and similar definitions hold for joint velocity, $\boldsymbol{\theta}'$, and acceleration $\boldsymbol{\theta}''$. Consequently inertia and viscosity in the multijoint arm are matrices relating acceleration and velocity vectors to torque vectors.

Other problems arise from the fact that the multijoint inertia changes at different arm configurations, that is, $\mathbf{I}=\mathbf{I}(\boldsymbol{\theta})$, and from the presence of dynamic interactions between moving links. In other words the equivalent of equation 1 for a multijoint arm is

$$\mathbf{T} = \mathbf{I}(\boldsymbol{\theta})\,\boldsymbol{\theta}' + \mathbf{c}(\boldsymbol{\theta}, \boldsymbol{\theta}') + \mathbf{B}\,\boldsymbol{\theta}'. \tag{2}$$

where $\mathbf{c}(\boldsymbol{\theta}, \boldsymbol{\theta}'')$ is a vector of centripetal and coriolis torques expressing nonlinear interaction terms between different joints. Hollerbach and

Flash (1982) have shown that significant interaction torques are present in human arm movements, even at fairly moderate speeds. Hence the interaction torques cannot be neglected in a computational approach based on the explicit solution of the inverse dynamics problem.

Traditionally in the field of robotics, two alternative approaches are used to transform the planned joint trajectory into the appropriate joint torques. One method, based on solving on-line the inverse dynamics equations, involves reducing the number of basic operations (sums and multiplications) to a bare minimum. Significant savings are offered by recursive methods, which have been applied both to the Newton-Euler (Luh et al 1980) and the Lagrangian (Hollerbach 1980) formulations of dynamics. The other method involves obtaining the desired torques from look-up tables indexed by the desired motion of the manipulator.

Although there is a significant technological difference between explicit computation and the use of look-up tables, the two methods are to some degree conceptually equivalent because by definition any function is a correspondence between sets of values (that is, a look-up table). The look-up table approach, in its most extreme interpretation, corresponds to a complete ignorance of the structure of a function. For example, in the case of the inverse dynamics equations (equation 2), all the kinematic variables, θ, θ', θ'', can be used as indexes. As a result the computational problem is entirely reduced to retrieval from memory (plus of course some interpolation).

The obvious drawback of tabular approaches is that they need very large amounts of memory. Furthermore changes in the controlled system, such as in the applied loads or in the effective limb size, may require the reestablishment of entirely new tables. The equally obvious advantage of tabular approaches is the reduction of computing time and the possibility of implementing associative learning schemes, although for the latter purpose some knowledge of the structural properties of the controlled system seems to be necessary for successful learning (Atkeson 1986).

The opposite extreme to unstructured tabular approaches is reached when a function is decomposed into much simpler functions such as sums and products. Eventually these basic functional units are the look-up tables, or truth tables, implemented by the logical gates within a computer (AND, NOT, and so on). Then the association between input and output must be carried out in a sequence of steps, and as the memory requirement decreases, the computation time increases. There are also intermediate strategies for solving the inverse dynamics problem. For example, Raibert and Horn (1978) suggested storing only configuration-dependent elements, such as inertia and gravity, and computing the remaining parts of the dynamics equations.

What is the relevance of these approaches with respect to biological motor control? It is evident that the choice of a computational method

Geometrical and Mechanical Issues in Movement Planning and Control

in the field of robotics depends on the trade-offs between memory and processing time compatible with the available computer hardware. This consideration alone is sufficient to undermine the analogy between natural and artificial algorithms.

A more fundamental question, however, is whether or not inverse dynamics must be "computed" at all by the CNS. To answer this question, one must consider the mechanical properties of the controlled system. Conventional robot arms are mostly operated by torque motors, that is, by actuators that transform an input control signal into an output torque. Hence the inverse dynamics problem (equation 2) is a "natural" way to relate planning to execution because the solution (a torque vector) is immediately related to the effects of control signals.

In contrast biological motor systems are operated by muscles that are characterized by tunable viscoelastic properties. It follows that the control signals—that is, the activities of motoneurons—do not specify joint torques independently of joint angles and velocities, but instead specify a functional relation among these variables. We show in the following sections that this fact has important consequences for the organization of biological algorithms and in particular for the solution of the inverse dynamics problem.

19.3   Muscle Mechanical Properties

Recent experimental work has focused on the role of the muscle's mechanical properties in the control of posture and movement. Feldman (1966) and others (Cooke 1979, Bizzi et al. 1976, Kelso 1977, Kelso and Holt 1980, Nichols and Houk 1976, Rack and Westbury 1969) have suggested that a muscle is mechanically analogous to a spring. In other words the muscle is characterized by a set of integrable functions between length and tension at steady state. Neural input selects a particular function (length-tension curve) out of this set. Then for any given value of muscle activation, the position at which the length-dependent forces due to opposing muscles are equal defines an equilibrium position and a stiffness of a joint.

It must be stressed that the dependence of muscle force on muscle length implies that alpha motoneuronal activity can be interpreted as commanding either a limb position or a force. If the CNS commands a limb position, then the stiffness specifies a force given by the difference between the actual and the commanded positions. If the CNS commands a force, then the compliance (that is, the inverse of the stiffness) specifies the position given by the difference between the actual and the commanded force. A question of long-standing interest in the neurophysiology of motor control (Evarts 1966) has been whether a descending command specifies a position or a force. If the characteristics of muscles are such that force and length are functionally related, then their control is obtained from a common principle: the modulation of length-tension curves. In this case there is no need to postulate separate mechanisms for generating motions and forces (Feldman 1966, 1974, Hogan 1985a, b).

Experimental studies of visually triggered head and arm movements in trained monkeys (Bizzi et al. 1976, Polit and Bizzi 1979) have shown that a final head and forearm position is indeed an equilibrium point between opposing springlike forces. Also these investigations showed that monkeys can execute single-joint pointing movements of the forearm and briefly maintain (1 s) the forearm in a new equilibrium position in the complete absence of visual as well as proprioceptive feedback from forearm muscles and joints (Polit and Bizzi 1979). These findings imply a functional relation between the descending commands to the relevant muscles and the equilibrium position of the forearm.

Furthermore recent experimental evidence (Bizzi et al. 1984) indicates that the transition from one arm posture to another is achieved by the CNS's adjustment of the relative intensity of neural signals directed to each of the opposing muscles. The result is that the equilibrium point defined by their interaction moves toward either flexion or extension of the limb. According to this result, a single-joint arm trajectory is obtained through neural signals that specify a series of equilibrium positions for the limb.

Experimental data supporting this view are shown in figure 19.2. For a 60° movement of the forearm lasting 600 ms, the torque produced by the alpha motoneuronal activity did not reach steady state until 400 ms after the onset of muscle activation (Bizzi et al. 1984). In these experiments a target specifying a 60° forearm movement was presented, and the arm was held at the initial position for various durations. It was found that the initial acceleration after release of the forearm increased gradually with the duration of the holding period, reaching a steady-state value no sooner than 400 ms after the onset of electromyographic (EMG) activity. Equivalently the torque generated in response to alpha motoneuronal activity during the holding period at the initial position increased gradually, reaching a peak of 448 ms (average value) after the onset of EMG activity. These results demonstrate that the CNS had programmed a slow, gradual shift of the equilibrium position instead of a sudden, discontinuous transition to the final position.

The same conclusion is supported by experiments based on forcing the forearm to a target position through an assisting torque pulse applied at the beginning of a forearm movement. The goal of this experiment was to move the limb ahead of the equilibrium position with an externally imposed displacement in the direction of the target. It was found that the forearm, after being forced by the assisting pulse to the target position, returned to a point between the initial and the final position before moving to the endpoint. This outcome results from the

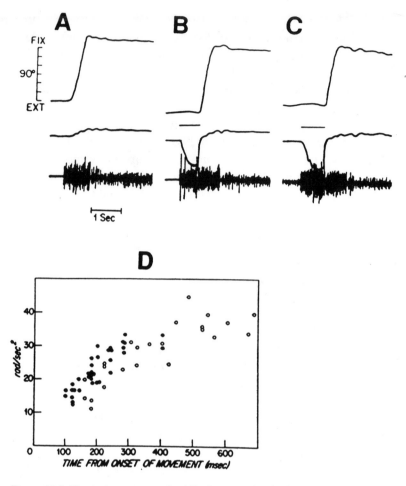

Figure 19.2 The torque generated while the arm of a deafferented monkey was held at the initial position after a target had been presented. The upper trace shows arm position, the middle trace shows torque, and the lower trace shows flexor (biceps) EMG. The bar beneath the arm trace represents duration of the holding torque. (A) Control movement without a holding torque. (B, C) Two movements in which the buildup of isometric tension can be observed. Position scale representing angular excursion equals 60°. (D) Plot of acceleration immediately following release versus holding time. The abscissa shows time in milliseconds; the ordinate shows radians per second squared. Solid circles represent a deafferented animal. (Modified from Bizzi et al. 1984.)

fact that a restoring force is generated by the elastic muscle properties. Because the same response was also observed in deafferented monkeys (Bizzi et al. 1984), reflex feedback is not essential to the generation of restoring forces. Taken together, these results suggest that alpha motoneuronal activity specifies a series of equilibrium positions throughout the movement. Note that if muscles merely generated force, or if the elastic properties were negligible, we would not have seen the return motion of the limb.

The sequence of static equilibrium positions encoded during movement by the motorneuronal activity has been defined as a "virtual trajectory" (Hogan 1984), to be distinguished from the actual trajectory followed by the limb. The virtual trajectory is a consequence of known length-tension relationships derived under static conditions. By contrast the actual trajectory is the result of the interactions between the elastic forces and other dynamic components such as limb inertia, muscle velocity-tension properties and joint viscosity. It should be also stressed that the forearm movements studied by Bizzi and colleagues (1984) were performed at moderate speed. It is conceivable that for very fast movements, the shift in the equilibrium point may be more steplike or may even reach a point beyond the intended equilibrium point (Hogan 1984). Then the shift should amount to a pulse-step command of the type known to control eye movements (Robinson 1970) and fast limb movements (Desmedt and Godaux 1978).

19.4 Implications of the Virtual Trajectory and Generalization to Multijoint Posture and Movements

In this section we discuss some of the implications of the moving equilibrium hypothesis in a computational perspective. To this end we start with a more formal definition of the concept of virtual trajectory. A detailed discussion of related control issues can be found in Hogan 1985a, b.

Let us first consider the case of a simple one-dimensional system characterized by a length l, a tension f, and a control input u. Such a system is said to have tunable springlike properties when at steady state, the force is a function of length and input,

$$f = f(l,u), \tag{3}$$

and when this function can be integrated with respect to l to obtain the elastic energy stored in a change of length. Note that this definition does not require linearity of the length-tension relation. The stiffness is defined locally about a given position and at constant input as $k = df/dl$. The equilibrium position of the system is given by the condition $f(l,u) = 0$. A stable equilibrium position is characterized by negative stiffness (that is, the forces about the equilibrium are attractive). By contrast a positive stiffness would imply an unstable equilibrium similar to the equilibrium of a ball on the top of a hill.

When the input is a continuous function of time $u(t)$, the static equilibrium condition becomes

$$f_e(l, u(t)) = 0 \qquad (4)$$

Here the subscript e is used to indicate that f_e is not the total force acting on the system, but only its elastic component; during movement the total force contains in addition inertial and viscous components. Equation 4 defines implicitly a unique map from $u(t)$ to l,

$$l_e(t) = l(u(t)), \qquad (5)$$

with $l_e(t)$ and $u(t)$ satisfying equation 4, provided that the stiffness k at each equilibrium position $l_e(t)$ is not zero.[4] The function $l_e(t)$ is the virtual trajectory of the system given the input function $u(t)$. A few important features of the virtual trajectory concept are highlighted by this simple unidimensional example. In particular:

· This concept is not a computational hypothesis but a direct consequence of the muscle's springlike properties.
· It can be regarded as a map from a control input (u) to a length (l_e).
· This map is provided by an algebraic rather than a differential equation.[5]

The extension of the virtual trajectory to a multidimensional system is straightforward. Let us consider, for example, a serial arrangement of n limb segments connected by rotational joints. For the purposes of the discussion that follows, it makes no difference whether each joint has one or more degrees of freedom. In robotics notation joints with multiple degrees of freedom are often represented as assemblies of elements with one degree of freedom connected by segments of zero length (Paul 1981). The configuration of this system is the array of joint angles $\boldsymbol{\theta} = [\theta_1, \ldots, \theta_n]^T$, and the net torque is the array of joint torques $\mathbf{T} = [T_1, \ldots, T_n]^T$. Furthermore the limbs are driven by a set of m muscles with $m > n$ (that is, there are more muscles than joints). Collectively the muscles are characterized by a length array $\mathbf{l} = [l_1, \ldots, l_m]^T$, by a force array $\mathbf{f} = [f_1, \ldots, f_m]^T$, and by an array of input activations $\mathbf{u} = [u_1, \ldots, u_m]$. If each muscle has tunable springlike properties, the overall muscle behavior is characterized by the vector equivalent of equation 3, namely

$$\mathbf{f} = \mathbf{f}(\mathbf{l}, \mathbf{u}). \qquad (6)$$

The n-dimensional joint-torque vector is obtained from the m-dimensional muscle-tension vector by multiplying the latter by the matrix of moment arms $\mathbf{u}$. The elements of the matrix $\mathbf{u}$, μ_{ij}, are the partial derivatives $\partial l_i / \partial \theta_j$. The relation $\mathbf{l} = \mathbf{l}(\boldsymbol{\theta})$, which uniquely defines the muscle length array as a function of the joint configuration, is in general nonlinear. Therefore the matrix of moment arms is also a function of joint configuration $\boldsymbol{\theta}$. Hence by using equation 6 to express muscle forces, the net joint-torque vector becomes

$$\mathbf{T} = \boldsymbol{\mu} \ (\boldsymbol{\theta})^{\mathrm{T}}\mathbf{f} = \boldsymbol{\mu} \ (\boldsymbol{\theta})^{\mathrm{T}} \ \mathbf{f}(\mathbf{l} \ (\boldsymbol{\theta}), \ \mathbf{u}) = \mathbf{T} \ (\boldsymbol{\theta}, \ \mathbf{u}). \tag{7}$$

When the input array is a function of time $\mathbf{u}(t)$, the static equilibrium condition $\mathbf{T} = 0$ defines implicitly the joint virtual trajectory as a function of $\mathbf{u}(t)$:

$$\boldsymbol{\theta}_e(t) = \boldsymbol{\theta}(\mathbf{u}(t)) \quad \text{such that} \quad \mathbf{T}_e(\boldsymbol{\theta}_e(t), \ \mathbf{u}(t)) = 0. \tag{8}$$

These equations are analogous to equations 5 and 4. From the fundamental theorem on implicit functions, the necessary and sufficient condition for the existence and uniqueness of the virtual trajectory, $\boldsymbol{\theta}_e(t) = \boldsymbol{\theta}(\mathbf{u}(t))$, is that the determinant of the joint stiffness matrix $\mathbf{R}$, whose elements are $R_{ij} = \partial T_i/\partial\theta_j$ $(i, j = 1, \ldots, n)$, doesn't vanish[6] at any equilibrium point.

This condition is equivalent to the requirement of nonzero stiffness in one-dimensional systems: a negative joint-stiffness determinant corresponds to stable equilibrium, whereas a positive determinant implies unstable equilibrium. Note, however, that the requirement of a nonzero joint-stiffness determinant is much less stringent than a requirement on individual muscle stiffness or on each joint-stiffness term. As we show in the next section, there is experimental evidence that the multijoint elastic forces during posture are always attractive, indicating that the condition for the virtual trajectory is satisfied.

As for one-dimensional systems, the muscle's springlike properties allow one to map the input $\mathbf{u}$ (motoneuron firing rates) into the equilibrium arm configuration. Hence the virtual trajectory, together with the joint stiffness, is a summary of all the inputs involved in the execution of a movement. The virtual trajectory accounts for the net mechanical effect of a whole pattern of activations and can be derived from actual movements, from the arm's mechanical properties (such as net stiffness, viscosity, and inertia), and from the response to external perturbations.

An important consequence of the concept of a virtual trajectory is that it can be used to avoid the computation of inverse dynamics. The inertial and viscous components of the dynamics equation (equation 2) can be considered as "perturbing torques" that make the arm deviate from the virtual trajectory. At low speeds and accelerations the difference between actual and virtual trajectory is small and can be neglected by the motor controller. As the speed of the movement increases, however, limb inertia and viscosity are expected to cause larger deviations from the virtual trajectory. These deviations can be corrected by increasing the stiffness and by modifying the virtual trajectory itself.

Another feature of the springlike properties is that they provide stability to the planned movements (Hogan 1985). In a computational approach based on the solution of inverse dynamics, problems arise when an external perturbation (such as the arm's hitting of an obstacle) causes a deviation from the preprogrammed path. If this happens, the dynamics must be recomputed or some special servo-control mechanisms must be provided. In contrast if movement is obtained by shifting the equilibrium position defined by elastic actuators, a deviation from the intended path simply results in larger restoring forces without need of computation or of particular control schemes (McKeon et al. 1984).

Traditionally in motor control, behaviors such as maintaining posture, generating movements, and generating forces have been considered separate domains requiring different control schemes. However, in this chapter we show that these apparently diverse behaviors derive from a common framework. In particular we consider the ability to maintain posture a precondition for executing successful limb movements. This is also our point of view in section 19.5, in which we analyze multijont posture.

19.5 Analysis of Multijoint Posture and Movement

The idea that posture results from the coordination of neural inputs to agonist and antagonist muscles has recently been extended to the multijoint case. To deal with this more complex situation, a new experimental approach to the study of posture and movement was developed (Mussa-Ivaldi et al. 1985). This approach was based on measuring the net springlike behavior of the multijoint arm by displacing the hand (see figure 19.3) in several directions. Each time the restoring forces were determined at steady state before the onset of any voluntary reaction.

The hand stiffness in the vicinity of equilibrium is a matrix that was estimated by analyzing the force and displacement vectors. The hand stiffness was represented as an ellipse characterized by three parameters: magnitude (the total area derived from the determinant of the stiffness matrix); orientation (the direction of maximum stiffness); and shape (the ratio among maximum and minimum stiffness). This representation captures the main geometrical features of the elastic-force field associated with a given hand posture and provides an understanding of how the arm interacts with the environment.

We tested the hand stiffness of four subjects while they maintained the hand in a number of workspace locations. The results are shown in figure 19.4. The stiffness ellipses measured at given hand positions are shown along with a schematic display of the corresponding arm configurations. A remarkable feature of these data is the similarity between the different subjects with respect to stiffness shape and orientation. By contrast the stiffness magnitude varies considerably. This graphical representation provides a "gestalt" and affords a qualitative understanding of the way in which the hand may interact with external forces that could change its posture.

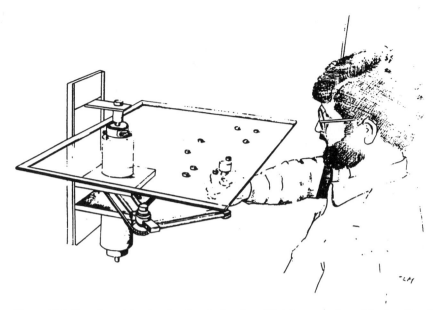

Figure 19.3 Experimental setup for the study of multijoint arm posture. The handle of the manipulandum was displaced by two servo-controlled torque motors. The hand location was derived from signals generated by two potentiometers mounted on the rotation axes of the manipulandum. (Modified from Mussa-Ivaldi et al. 1985.)

Describing hand posture as an oriented stiffness ellipse helps us to determine which elements of motor behavior require accurate coordination of neural signals and which result from the arm biomechanical design. To address this issue, Mussa-Ivaldi and colleagues (1987) measured the postural stiffness in four different conditions: with no load (normal posture), and with a 10-N force applied at each of the following directions: 0°, 45°, 90°. These forces were applied to elicit different patterns of contraction in different sets of muscles and thus to test how variations in neural input affect the parameters of postural stiffness measured at a given location.

This procedure generated a surprising result: there were large changes in stiffness amplitude but only small changes in orientation and shape. To a first approximation, this result means that the parameter of orientation and shape are predominantly dependent on musculoskeletal geometrical properties, that is to say, the biomechanical design of the arm.

One way to affect the stiffness shape and orientation is to change the configuration of the arm while the hand remains in a given position. This finding suggests that an effective strategy for modifying all parameters of the postural stiffness may be to combine variations of neural input to the muscles with variations of configuration of the "extra," or redundant, degrees of freedom of the limb. Changes in configuration will also have a relevant effect on other components of motor impedance. Indeed changing arm configuration is the only way the CNS can

Geometrical and Mechanical Issues in Movement Planning and Control

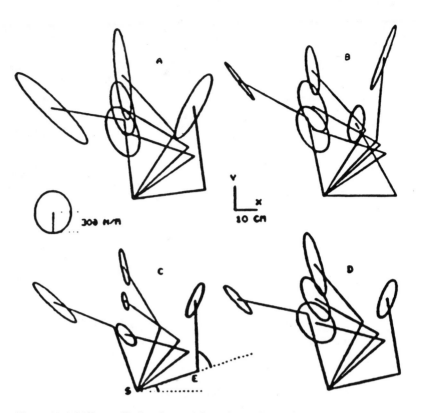

Figure 19.4 Stiffness ellipses obtained from four subjects during the postural task. Each ellipse has been derived by regression on about 60 force and displacement vectors. The upper arm and the forearm are indicated schematically by two line segments and the ellipses are placed on the hand. The calibration for the stiffness is provided by the circle to the left, which represents an isotropic hand stiffness of 300 N/m.

change the endpoint inertia of the limb (Hogan 1985a, 1985b). From this point of view, it can be seen that the configuration of the limb should be regarded as one of the "commanding inputs" available to the CNS for controlling posture. Redundancy of the musculoskeletal system is usually regarded as a problem to be overcome by the CNS in coordinating limb movements (Bernstein 1937); instead the results reported here show that it may also offer alternative ways to control postural dynamics.

To sum up, the experimental evidence indicates that the equilibrium position of the hand is established by the coordinated interaction of elastic forces generated by the arm muscles (Mussa-Ivaldi et al. 1985). According to the equilibrium trajectory hypothesis, which was tested first in the context of single-joint movements (see section 19.3), the multijoint arm trajectory is achieved by gradually shifting the arm equilibrium between the initial and final positions. In this control scheme the hand tracks its equilibrium point, and torque is not an explicitly computed variable.

Evidence supporting this hypothesis in the context of multijoint hand movements has been obtained by combining observations of hand movements with computer simulation studies. A model developed by Flash (1987) has successfully captured the kinematic features of measured planar arm trajectories. As shown by Morasso (1981), planar hand movements between pairs of targets are characterized by approximately straight hand paths. If the same movements are analyzed at a finer level of detail, however, the paths present certain degrees of inflection and curvature, depending on the direction of movement and on the workspace location. In the simulation Flash made the assumption that the hand equilibrium trajectories (but not necessarily the actual trajectories) are invariantly straight. In addition she assumed that the equilibrium trajectory has a unimodal velocity profile, regardless of the target locations in the workspace.

To test this hypothesis, the arm dynamics were simulated (equation 2), obtaining the driving torques **T** from the difference between actual and equilibrium positions multiplied by the stiffness. It must be stressed that the stiffness parameters used in the simulation of movements were derived from experimentally measured postural stiffness values. In particular the observation (Mussa-Ivaldi et al. 1985, 1987) that the shape and the orientation of the hand stiffness are insensitive to changes in the net force output provided the evidence for assuming that these parameters may not change when the hand moves through the locations at which the field was measured.

The result of the simulation was that with straight equilibrium trajectories, the actual movements were slightly curved. Moreover, the direction of curvature in different workspace locations and with different movement directions, was in good agreement with the experimentally observed movements (figure 19.5). This result suggests that during movement planning the CNS ignores the dynamics of the arm (that is, its inertial and viscous properties): the desired trajectory is directly translated into a sequence of static postures. Then when the movement is executed, the inertial and viscous forces act as perturbations, causing deviations of the actual path with respect to the planned path.

A directly testable consequence of the equilibrium trajectory hypothesis is the built-in stability of movements: if, during the execution of a hand trajectory, an unpredicted disturbance displaces the hand from the planned path, then, according to the equilibrium trajectory hypothesis, the muscle's elastic properties generate without delay a force attracting the hand toward the original path. This prediction was experimentally confirmed by McKeon and colleagues (1984). They asked subjects to perform pointing movements between two targets while gripping the handle of a two-link manipulandum similar to that shown in figure 19.3. A clutch mounted on the inner joint of the manipulation was used to brake the inner link under computer control. As the clutch was activated at the onset of a movement, the hand trajectory was restricted to a circular path with radius equal to the length of the outer

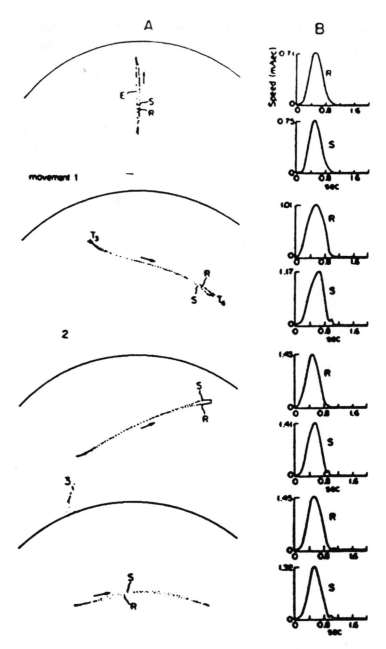

Figure 19.5 Comparison between measured (R) and simulated (S) trajectories, with the assumption that the hand equilibrium trajectory (E) is a straight segment with unimodal velocity profile and that at each location the hand stiffness is proportional to the stiffness measured during posture. (Modified from Flash 1987.)

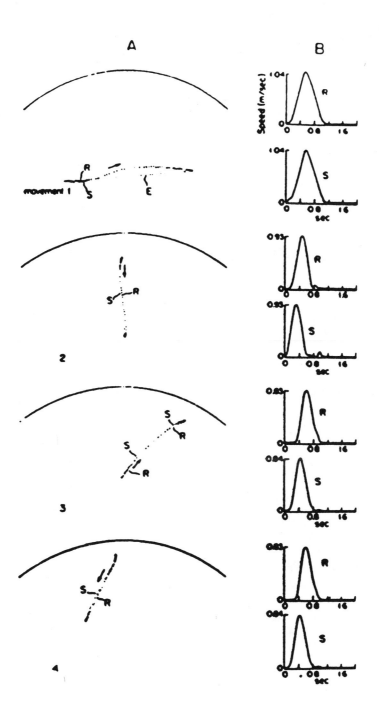

Geometrical and Mechanical Issues in Movement Planning and Control

link of the manipulandum. While the clutch was engaged, handle force was found to be always strongly oriented so as to restore the hand to the unconstrained path (determined from other trials without the activation of the clutch) and not to the end-point of the path.

The success of the simulation in capturing the kinematic details of measured arm movements is important as a step in providing us with a new intellectual frame for understanding trajectory formation in the multijoint context. This work indicated a planning strategy whereby the motor controller may avoid complex computational problems such as the solution of inverse dynamics. According to the equilibrium trajectory hypothesis, the muscle's springlike properties are responsible for generating the necessary joint torques, thus implicitly providing an approximated solution of the inverse dynamics problem. As the approximation becomes inadequate at higher speeds and acceleration, the stiffness can be increased and the equilibrium trajectory can be modified on the basis of the difference between actual and planned path. The task of the CNS is then to transform the planned trajectory into a different sequence of equilibrium positions and stiffnesses.

19.6 Concluding Remarks

In this chapter we have described a new view of the execution of arm trajectories. We began by reviewing the current debate on whether trajectory planning is represented in hand or joint coordinates. From this issue we moved to the main focus of this chapter: the ways in which the CNS generates the forces necessary to move the arm along the intended trajectory. There is little doubt that this process is one of the major research problems in motor neurophysiology and perhaps one of the toughest. In this chapter we have stressed that the difficulty of understanding how the CNS derives the appropriate torques is compounded by the presence of torques that depend on the multisegmental nature of the biological arm and its motion.

Faced with these seemingly impossible hurdles, the neuroscientist might find solace in the thought that after all, these problems have been made easier by the advent of artificial intelligence and robotics. In these domains various solutions have been proposed, and in general a satisfactory level of motor performance has been achieved. As pointed out in section 19.2, however, it is not easy to translate the results of robotics into the operations of the biological motor controller. Although at a certain level of abstraction we can all agree that both artificial and natural systems must successfully perform something akin to the inverse dynamics, we believe intuitively that this line of thinking is not satisfactory; something is missing. At the very least what is missing is a biological theory capable of explaining how torques are generated in the context of the biological actuators, the reflexes and ultimately the distributed nature of the neural hardware. This chapter's goal was to present such a theory.

The foundations of this theory are spelled out in section 19.3, in which the elastic behavior of muscles is described, together with an explanation of single-joint movement and posture. The main lesson from all the single-joint experiments is that movement is nothing more than a series of sequentially implemented postures. To use the terminology of this chapter, movement derives from shifting the equilibrium point between agonist and antagonist length-tension curves. Although it is easy to understand these experimental results in the context of single-joint motion, it is the multijoint case that poses the most difficult challenge for this theory. It is the latter case that we have tackled in the last two sections by describing in detail the biomechanical characteristics of multijoint posture.

Finally, we conclude by reporting that the scheme proposed for the single-joint motion is also plausible for multijoint movements. Modeling and experimental evidence (McKeon et al. 1984) support the hypothesis of a moving equilibrium point and provide for the first time a way to generate forces at the joints that do not depend on computing "inverse dynamics."

Notes

This research was supported by National Institute of Neurological Disease and Stroke Research Grant NS09343, National Institute of Arthritis, Metabolism and Digestive Diseases Grant AM26710.

1. The term "metric" refers to the measure of distances in space. Euclidean geometries are characterized by a constant metric: the length of a segment is the same regardless of its location in space. In contrast, in a noneuclidean geometry the measure of length depends on the considered location of space.

2. Here we use the term vector simply to indicate an array of components. In a more rigorous mathematical context, however, the array of joint angles is not a vector because the basic properties of vector spaces do not apply to finite joint rotations.

3. Note that the upper arm has seven degrees of freedom, if one neglects the motion of the shoulder girdle and the fingers.

4. This is a direct consequence of a fundamental theorem on implicit functions. For two variables, x and y, this theorem can be stated as follows: Let $F(x,y)$ be a function continuous with its first partial derivatives in a region R of the plane x,y, and let the following conditions be satisfied: $F(x^0,y^0) = 0$ at a point $P^0=(x^0,y^0)$ in R, and the partial derivative $\partial F/\partial y$ is different from zero at the pont P^0. Then the expression $F(x,y) = 0$ can be solved for y, that is, a single-valued function $y=f(x)$ can be defined in the vicinity of P^0.

5. In general for a dynamic system, a map of the form $\mathbf{x}' = \boldsymbol{\sigma}(\mathbf{x}, \mathbf{u},t)$ is defined. This map allows to derive the future time course of the system state $\mathbf{x}(t)$, that is, the actual trajectory, given the input function $\mathbf{u}(t)$ *and the initial value of the state*, $\mathbf{x}_0$ at some time t_0, $\mathbf{x}_0=\mathbf{x}(t_0)$. Because the state equation is a differential equation, its solution depends on the arbitrary

selection of the initial conditions. In contrast the virtual trajectory, being the result of an algebraic equation, does not contain arbitrary terms. Actually the virtual trajectory defines the initial conditions for the state equations because the system is at static equilibrium (equation 5) before the onset of a movement.

6. The theorem of implicit functions mentioned in note 5 is immediately generalized to a system of n equations,

$$F_i(X_1, \ldots, X_m, Y_1, \ldots, Y_n) = 0; \quad i=1, \ldots, n,$$

by requiring that at a solution point $P^0 = (X_1^0 \ldots, X_m^0, y_n^0)$ the functional (or jacobian) determinant DF/Dy is different from zero. Then the n equations can be solved for Y_i, that is, n functions $Y_i = f_i(X_1, \ldots, X_n)$ can be defined in the vicinity of P^0.

References

Albus, J. S. 1975. *A New Approach to Manipulator Control: The Cerebellar Model Articulation Controller (CMAC)*. J. Dynamics Sys. Meas. Control 97:220–227.

Atkeson, C. G. 1986. *Roles of Knowledge in Motor Learning*. Ph.D. dissertation, Dept. of Brain and Cognitive Sciences, MIT, Cambridge, MA.

Bernstein, N. 1935. The problem of the interrelation of coordination and localization. *Arch. Biol. Sci.* 38:15–59. Reprinted in Bernstein, N. 1967. *The Coordination and Regulation of Movements*. Oxford: Pergamon Press.

Bizzi, E., and Abend, W. 1983. Posture control and trajectory formation in single- and multi-joint arm movements. In J. E. Desmedt, ed. *Motor Control Mechanisms in Health and Disease*. New York: Raven Press, pp. 31–45.

Bizzi, E., Polit, A., and Morasso, P. 1976. Mechanisms underlying achievement of final head position. *J. Neurophysiol.* 39:435–444.

Bizzi, E., Accornero, N., Chapple, W., and Hogan, N. 1984. Posture control and trajectory formation during arm movement. *J. of Neurosci.* 4:2738–2744.

Cooke, J. D. 1979. Dependence of human arm movements on limb mechanical properties. *Brain Res.* 165:366–369.

Desmedt, J. E., and Godaux, E. 1978. Ballistic skilled movements: Load compensation and patterning of the motor commands. *Prog. Clin. Neurophysiol.* 4:21–55.

Evarts, E. V. 1966. Pyramidal tract activity associated with a conditioned hand movement in the monkey. *J. Neurophysiol.* 29:1011–1027.

Feldman, A. G. 1966. Functional tuning of the nervous system during control of movement or maintenance of a steady posture. II. Controllable parameters of the muscles. III. Mechanographic analysis of the execution by man of the simplest motor task. *Biophysics* 11:565–578, 766–775.

Feldman, A. G. 1974. Control of the length of a muscle. *Biofizika* 19:749–753.

Flash, T. 1983. Organizing principles underlying the formation of hand trajectories. Ph.D. dissertation, Harvard/MIT Division of Health Sciences and Technology, Cambridge, MA.

Flash, T., and Hogan, N. 1985. The coordination of arm movements: An experimentally confirmed mathematical model. *J. Neurosci.* 5:1688–1703.

Flash, T. 1987. The control of hand equilibrium trajectories in multi-joint arm movements. *Biol. Cybern.* 57:257–274.

Georgopoulos, A. P., Kalaska, J. F., Caminiti, R., and Massey, J. T. 1982. On the relations between the direction of two-dimensional arm movements and cell discharge in primate motor cortex. *J. Neurosci.* 2:1527–1537.

Georgopoulos, A. P., Kalaska, J. F., Caminiti, R., and Massey, J. T. 1983. Spatial coding of movement: A hypothesis concerning the coding of movement direction by motor cortical populations. In J. Massion, J. Paillard, W. Schultz and M. Wiesendanger, eds. *Neural Coding of Motor Performance. Exp. Brain Res.* [Suppl] 7:327–336.

Hogan, N. 1984. An organizing principle for a class of voluntary movements. *J. Neurosci.* 4:2745–2754.

Hogan, N. 1985a. The mechanics of multi-joint posture and movement control. *Biological Cybernetics* 53:1–17.

Hogan, N. 1985b. Impedance control: An approach to manipulation. Part I: Theory. Part II: Implementation. Part III: Application. *ASME J. Dyn. Sys. Meas. Cont.* 107:1–24.

Hollerbach, J. M. 1980. A recursive lagrangian formulation of manipulator dynamics and a comparative study of dynamics formulation complexity. *IEEE Trns. Syst. Man and Cybern.* 11:730–736.

Hollerbach, J. M., and Flash, T. 1982. Dynamic interaction between limb segments during planar arm movements. *Biol. Cybern.* 44:67–77.

Hollerbach, J. M., Moore, S. P., and Atkeson, C. G. 1986. Workspace effect in arm movement kinematics derived from joint interpolation. In G. Gantchev, B. Dimitrov and P. Gatev, eds. *Motor Control.* New York: Plenum Press.

Kelso, J. A. S. 1977. Motor control mechanisms underlying human movement reproduction. *J. Exp. Psychol.* 3:529–543.

Kelso, J. A. S., and Holt, K. G. 1980. Exploring a vibratory system analysis of human movement production. *J. Neurophysiol.* 43:1183–1196.

Luh, J. Y. S., Walker, M. W., and Paul, R. P. 1980. On-line computational scheme for mechanic manipulators. *Trans. ASME J. Dyn. Syst. Meas. and Control* 120:69–76.

McKeon, B., Hogan, N., and Bizzi, E. 1984 (Oct. 10–15). Effect of temporary path constraint during planar arm movements. *Abstr. 14th Ann. Conf. Soc. for Neurosci.* Anaheim, CA, 337.

Morasso, P. 1981. Spatial control of arm movements. *Exp. Brain Res.* 42:223–227.

Mussa-Ivaldi, F. A. 1988. Do neurons in the motor cortex encode movement direction? An alternative hypothesis. *Neurosci. Lett.* 91:106–111.

Mussa-Ivaldi, F. A., Hogan, N., and Bizzi, E. 1985. Neural, mechanical, and geometric factors subserving arm posture in humans. *J. of Neurosci.* 10:2732–2743.

Mussa-Ivaldi, F. A., Hogan, N., and Bizzi, E. 1987. The role of geometrical constraints in the control of multi-joint posture and movement. *Soc. for Neurosci. Abst.* 13:347.

Nichols, T. R., and Houk, J. C. 1976. Improvement in linearity and regulation of stiffness that results from actions of stretch reflex. *J. Neurophysiol.* 39:119–142.

Paul, R. P. 1981. *Robot Manipulators: Mathematics, Programming and Control.* Cambridge, MA: MIT Press.

Polit, A., and Bizzi, E. 1979. Characteristics of the motor programs underlying arm movements in monkeys. *J. Neurophysiol.* 42:183–194.

Rack, P. M. H., and Westbury, D. R. 1969. The effects of length and stimulus rate on tension in the isometric cat soleus muscle. *J. Physiol.* 204:443–460.

Raibert, M. H. 1978. A model of sensorimotor control and learning. *Biol. Cybern.* 29:29–36.

Raibert, M. H., and Horn, B. K. P. 1978. Manipulator control using the configuration space method. *Industrial Robot* 5:69–73.

Robinson, D. A. 1970. Oculomotor unit behavior in the monkey. *J. Neurophysiol.* 33:393–404.

Soechting, J. F., and Laquaniti, F. 1981. Invariant characteristics of a pointing movement in man. *J. Neurosci.* 1:710–720.

Soechting, J. F., and Ross, B. 1984. Psychophysical determination of coordinate representation of human arm orientation. *Neurosci.* 13:595–604.

Assessment

20 Cultural Cognition

Roy G. D'Andrade

The main contribution of anthropology to cognitive science over the past three decades has been the development of a deeper understanding of the nature of symbolic representation. A major part of this work has focused on classification and natural language. There has also been a significant amount of research on the relation between culturally constituted symbolic representations and other cognitive processes, such as perception, memory, and reasoning.

In the area of classification anthropologists and linguists have identified ways in which terminological systems are organized and have developed an understanding of the constraints and limits on such terminological structures. Initial work in this area used the notion of *features* or *attributes* as the basic building blocks out of which terminological systems are constructed. Although later work has used a more schema-oriented approach, it is important to note that schemas themselves are typically formulated in terms of a special kind of organization of featurelike elements (see, for example, chapter 13).

20.1 The Problem of Definition

There is some controversy about how to formulate definitions. A number of alternative models have been presented in linguistics, psychology, and anthropology. At present there is agreement that the so-called classical view of meaning as an if-and-only-if relation between the item to be defined and a conjunctively connected class of features or attributes is insufficient to describe the semantics of natural language (Lakoff 1987; see also chapter 13). Perhaps the most complete metalanguage for the description of meanings has been developed by Langacker (1986, 1987). In Langacker's theory the unit to be defined, whether a grammatical particle, word, phrase, or sentence, has two basic parts: a *base* and a *profile*. The base is the background object, relation, or event that is differentiated by the profile; for example, the term *pediatrician* has as its base being a doctor and as its profile the caretaking of children, whereas the term *mother* has as its base being a woman and as its profile the giving birth to a child.

Langacker has developed a set of concepts and a method of using diagrams for describing the way predications are built up, which permit one to identify relatively subtle aspects of meaning. Consider the meanings of *go*, *away*, and *gone*, as in

(a) You have been here long enough—please *go* now.

(b) California is very far *away*.

(c) By the time I arrived, she was already *gone*.

The time process designated by *go* is diagrammed in figure 20.1(a), taken directly from Langacker 1986. Time is one salient domain for this verb and is indicated by the arrow in the diagram. The diagram for *go* displays only four states out of a continuous series. There are two major participants, represented by circles. One of these Langacker calls the *trajector* (tr), the other the *landmark* (lm). The heavy lines connecting the trajector and the landmark within each state mark the distance of the trajector relative to the landmark. In the initial state the trajector is in the neighborhood of the landmark (represented by the ellipse). The trajector's position changes from state to state over time, and in the final state it lies outside the neighborhood of the landmark.

For *away* time is not an active domain. Figure 20.1(b) shows a single configuration for *away* that is identical to the final state of *go*. Thus the process designated by *go* results in the locative state of being *away*. The analysis for *gone* is more complex. As diagrammed in figure 20.1(c), *gone* matches *away* in profiling (the dark lines) a single locative arrangement in which the trajector is outside the neighborhood of the landmark. However, these two terms differ in their base; for *away* the base is just a spatial region, whereas for *gone* the base is the entire process diagrammed for *go*. That is, something is *gone* because it is the result of the process of *going*.

This brief discussion gives some indication of the complexity of relations to be found in the construction of lexical meaning. Profile and

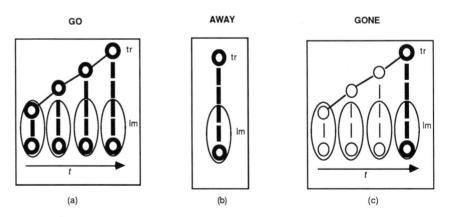

Figure 20.1

Assessment

base, trajector and landmark are complex relational terms needed in the analysis of a word like *gone*. These relationships are basically cognitive and psychological rather than set-theoretical in nature. Because they are a basic part of the semantics of natural language, such cognitive processes must be frequently used and highly practiced, and one might expect to find them in many areas of intellective functioning.

The way in which the word *gone* builds on the structure of *go*, which in turn is built on the structure of increasing "awayness" across time, exemplifies a major characteristic of human semantics; the chunking of structures into cognitive units that serve as the parts of more complex structures. An early finding in the field of cognitive psychology was that humans operate under severe limitations with respect to information processing (Miller 1956). Anthony Wallace extended Miller's finding to cultural terminological systems (Wallace 1961). In a survey of kin-term systems and other lexical sets in which every item is in direct contrast with every other item, such as an alphabet, a phonemic system, pieces of game, verb case systems, and so on, Wallace found that the number of items in such systems ranges from 14 to 50, limited to a number smaller than the number of items that can be discriminated by 2^6 binary bits of information.

The limitations of short-term memory also appear to affect both the depth and width of folk taxonomic systems. Rarely do folk taxonomies exceed more than five hierarchical levels. Also rarely do the terms that fall directly under any one node exceed the 50-item limit, a result that is expectable from the size constraints (Berlin, Breedlove, and Raven 1966, 1973).

20.2 Polysemy

Related to the controversy about the way in which meanings are constructed is the issue of *polysemy*—that is, the multiple senses of a single term. Human language is marked by extensive polysemy. Rarely does any word have only *one* sense. In anthropology the issue of polysemy has been frequently discussed with respect to kinship terms. In many cultures the basic kin terms (*mother, father, son, daughter*) have at least two senses. One sense is *genealogical*, involving biological parentage. Another sense is *role designating*—behaviorally a *father* is someone who provides basic support and guidance for ego. The two senses contrast in the following sentences:

Sam never met his father.

Jim wasn't the father he wanted to be.

A common approach to the problem of polysemy has been to try to reduce the meanings of terms to one sense. Other senses of a term are then taken to be derivable from the basic sense, or as metaphorical extensions of the basic sense. One way to do this is to take the most abstract sense as the basic or primary meaning. For the term *father* one might posit an upper-level sense defined as "the male responsible for the reproduction of offspring" and then treat both the genealogical and role-designating senses as contextually defined specifications of being "responsible for reproduction of offspring." An opposing tactic is to order the terms with respect to some kind of logical, temporal, or physical priority and take the most prior sense as the basic or primary sense. For the term *father* one might argue that the genealogical sense is temporally and logically prior to the role-designating sense, and hence the genealogical sense is the basic or primary sense, whereas the role-designating sense is given by context.

A major drawback of this kind of argument is that there is no principled reason to accept any particular way of deciding which sense is basic or primary as the *right* method. However, analysis of the relations between senses have proved valuable. Empirically it has been found that the different senses of terms tend to be interrelated in complex ways, by abstraction; by logical, spatial, or temporal priority; and by culturally based associations (Lakoff 1987).

20.3 Paradigmatic Classes

The simplest kinds of lexical classes are those that are created by the very features or attributes that characterize the items of the class. One such type is a *contrast set*. A contrast set is composed of a set of terms that are alike with respect to base attributes, but differ with respect to profile attributes; for example, the terms *chop, slice, grate, chip, fillet, mince* are all ways of cutting up an object, but vary in the manner in which the object is cut.

In some special domains the profiling attributes on which a contrast set of terms differ are orthogonal or cross-cutting, resulting in *paradigmatic sets*. Paradigmatically organized sets of terms are not frequent in the lexicon of natural languages. They are found mainly in the lexical domains of kin terms, pronouns, and verb inflections. In some instances alternative paradigmatic analyses using different selections of attributes can be constructed for the same terms. In such cases similarity judgments can be used to determine which analysis corresponds best to the psychological distinctions made by native speakers (Romney and D'Andrade 1962, Wexler and Romney 1972). Similarity judgments can also be used by themselves as a method to investigate the semantic structure of lexical domains (see, for example, Fillenbaum and Rapaport 1971).

An interesting empirical finding about paradigmatic sets is that, based on the space defined by the attributes, it is the case that the great majority of terms are conjunctively or relationally defined and are *not* disjunctive in nature (a term is disjunctive when an *or* is needed to link its defining attributes). To illustrate this, consider the attributes by which sibling terms can be distinguished (Nerlove and Romney 1967).

One dimension is the gender of the sibling, as in English, in which *brother* refers to a male sibling and *sister* refers to a female sibling. Another dimension is the *relative age* of the sibling: in some languages there are just two sibling terms, one for *older* sibling, one for *younger* sibling. A third dimension is the *cross/parallel* relation between the sex of the speaker and the sex of the sibling: in some languages there are just two sibling terms, one for sibling of the *same sex* as the speaker, one for sibling of the *opposite sex* as the speaker. These three binary attributes define a space of eight kin types. Nerlove and Romney collected from ethnographic and linguistic sources the sibling kin-term systems for 245 distinct cultural groups. They found that only four of the 245 systems had any disjunctive terms. (An example of a disjunction sibling term is one in which the term refers to *either* younger brother *or* sister.) Out of the very large number of logically possible systems (4,140), only 12 major types actually occurred. No language makes use of a system that distinguishes all eight kin types with separate terms. The English type, which only distinguishes gender of sibling, was not frequent, occurring in only 21 of the 245 societies. The most frequent system is one in which both gender of sibling and relative age are distinguished, creating a four-term system.

The attribute composition of terminological categories has implications for the way in which information may be cognitively integrated. For example, consider how judgments might be affected by the attributes found in a paradigmatic analysis of American kin terms. Four dimensions can be used to partition American kin terms—*direct* versus *collateral*, *ascending* versus *descending*, *male* versus *female*, and *first* versus *second* versus *own generation* (see table 20.1). Suppose respondents are presented with pairs of kin terms and asked to select the term that refers to the relative with whom one expects to have the greater *solidarity*. To the extent that respondents are reacting to kin categories as if they were simply made up of these attributes, it should be possible to predict the degree of solidarity ascribed to each kind of kin solely from knowledge of the degree of solidarity found for each of the attributes. In a test of this hypothesis, undergraduates were given a questionnaire containing randomized lists of all possible pairs of the fifteen American consanguineal kin terms and asked to check for each pair the relative "you would expect to be the warmer, friendlier, and more trustworthy person" (see D'Andrade 1989a). Respondents were told they should make the rating on the basis of "how people generally expect kin to be." The solidarity score for each kin term for each respondent was calculated by counting the number of times the term was checked. Mean solidarity scores for each kin term are presented in table 20.1 To derive solidarity weights for each of the attributes, the mean for all terms containing that attribute was computed. The difference between the attribute mean and the grand mean of all the kin terms constitutes the solidarity weight for that feature. To compute the pre-

Table 20.1 Observed and Predicted Solidarity Scores for American Kin Terms (predicted scores)

Generation	Direct		Collateral	
	Male	Female	Male	Female
Second				
Ascending	grandfather 5.6 (6.1)	grandmother 8.3 (8.1)		
Descending	grandson 4.5 (4.1)	granddaughter 5.9 (6.1)		
First				
Ascending	father 9.9 (10.1)	mother 12.7 (12.1)	uncle 3.6 (3.9)	aunt 6.3 (5.9)
Descending	son 8.4 (8.1)	daughter 9.7 (10.1)	nephew 2.0 (1.9)	niece 3.6 (3.9)
Own	brother 9.5 (9.2)	sister 10.8 (11.2)	cousin 4.1 (4.0)	

dicted solidarity value for each kin from its attributes, the attribute scores are simply added together with a constant for the grand mean of all the solidarity scores. The predicted score for *nephew*, for example, consists of the sum of the weight for a male (-1.0), descending (-1.0), first generation ($+1.3$), collateral (-3.1), plus the grand mean constant (5.7), yielding a predicted score of 1.9.

The predicted scores for the fifteen kin terms are presented in parentheses by the actual scores. The fit between the two sets of scores is relatively good ($r = 0.91$). Even the discrepancies between the observed and predicted scores appear to be neatly patterned. In every case the ascending female terms and the descending male terms have slightly higher solidarity scores than predicted by the attribute weights, whereas the ascending male terms and the descending female terms have lower solidarity scores than predicted. It would seem that respondents agree that one can expect a little more solidarity from senior female kin and junior male kin than either sex or generation alone would predict.

Paradigmatic attributes can also be used to predict the ease with which children learn appropriate definitions. Using data from a study by Haviland and Clark (1974) of children's definitions of American consanguineal kin, it was found that the number of children who could define correctly different kin terms could be predicted using the same procedure described above. It was found that more children learn *lineal* earlier than *collateral* terms and *ascending* earlier than *descending* terms. *First-generation* terms are learned earlier than *own-generation* terms, which are learned earlier than *second-generation* terms. Finally, there is a very slight tendency to learn *female* before *male* terms. Overall the Pearson correlation between observed and predicted frequencies was 0.89.

These results support the hypothesis that attributes have an *independent* effect on how one judges the classes constructed out of these attributes and on how easily the definitions of these classes are learned. Although there are undoubtedly cases in which there are strong interaction effects between attributes (consider the kin term *mother-in-law*, for example, which would probably have a much worse observed solidarity score than if predicted solely from its attributes), the evidence here is that for consanguineal kin terms, each attribute acts as an independent force. More generally the proposition being presented here is that, given a category, judgments about it—how much people like it, what it costs, and so on—can often be predicted by simply summing or averaging the values of the various attributes that characterize that category (Anderson 1981). This makes for cognitive efficiency, in that the judgments about a large number of categories can potentially be generated from a smaller number of attributes.

20.4 Taxonomy

Folk taxonomies are another kind of semantic structure that have been extensively investigated by anthropologists. A taxonomic relation, in which A *is a kind of* B, is created whenever A is a subset of B, and A has all the attributes of B as well as additional attributes that distinguish it from B. For example, a *cottage* is a kind of *house,* a *ponderosa* is a kind of *pine*, and a *cousin* is a kind of *relative.*

Folk taxonomies in the plant domain have been extensively investigated. A series of generalizations about the structure of this kind of hierarchical system have been proposed (Berlin, Breedlove, and Raven 1966, 1973, Conklin 1962), along with various modifications (Brown 1977, Dougherty and Keller 1985, Hunn 1976, 1985, Randall 1976, Weirzbicka 1984). The basic findings are that folk biological taxonomies are based on the identification of generic taxa. Generic taxa correspond appoximately to biological genera, which form natural groupings with many attributes in common. Generics often consist of related species that exhibit a strong family resemblance, but cannot be defined by some necessary and sufficient set of attributes. Berlin and colleagues call these generics *basic-level categories.* In a recent study of Jivaro folk ornithology, for example, Boster, Berlin and O'Neill (1986) found that not only do Jivaroan bird generics generally correspond to scientific generics, but also that there is a strong overall degree of correspondence between Jivaroan and scientific systems of classification.

In general folk taxonomies rarely exceed five levels. The five levels are designated *unique beginner, life form, generic, specific,* and *varietal.* Unique beginner (for example, *plant*) refers to the largest inclusive grouping of taxa and is often unlabeled linguistically by a single term. Life-form taxa (for example, *tree*) are invariably few in number (5 to 10). The generic taxa (for example, *oak*) are more numerous (approximately

500). Sometimes unusual generics (for example, *cacti, cassowary, platypus*) are not included in any lexically distinct life form. Specific and varietal taxa are generally less numerous than generics, typically forming small sets of a few members within a single generic. Specific and varietal taxa are commonly labeled in binomial (for example, *white pine*) or trinomial (for example, *American golden plover*) form. These generalizations hold not only for folk taxonomies of plants and animals, but appear to be general for other domains. For example, Brown and colleagues (1976) found the same structure for cultural artifacts (American automobiles and Finnish winter vehicles), religious figures (Thai spirits), and partonomies (Huastic body parts).

Using the notion of generics, Rosch (1975) extended Berlin's generalizations to include a wide range of phenomena. Rosch used the term *basic object* to refer to genericlike classes, that is, classes that are composed of intrinsically distinct objects that have many attributes in common, many motor movements in common, and strong similarity in shape. Rosch found that, presented with taxonomies consisting of a life form, generics, and specifics (for example, life form, *tool*; generics, *hammer, saw, screwdriver*; specifics, *ball-peen hammer, hack hand saw, Phillips screwdriver*), subjects could list many more attributes and more motor movements for generics than for life forms, but could not list significantly more attributes and motor movements for specifics than for generics. Rosch found, however, that for the categories of *trees, fish,* and *birds*, subjects could *not* list more attributes for generics than for life forms. To explain this finding, Rosch argues that for normal urban Americans *tree, fish,* and *bird* are psychologically basic-level objects. With respect to shapes Rosch found that figure outlines of specifics of the same generic were much more similar in form than generics of the same life form and that the basic level is also the most inclusive level at which an average shape of an object can be recognized.

Rosch proposed that where there are different exemplars of the same category (different generics of some life form or different specifics of some generic), people form a *prototype* (clearest case, best example) that serves to define that category, and nonprototype members can be ordered from better to worse as examples of the category. Rosch (1975) showed that subjects are able to make reliable ratings of "goodness of example," and that such ratings predict reaction time in categorization tasks and also the order in which subjects list examples of a category. Uyeda and Mandler (1980) replicated Rosch's ratings for 28 categories on a different sample of subjects and found that their ratings correlated with a Spearmans r of 0.87 with Rosch's ratings, a mean Spearman r of 0.55 with Battig and Montague's (1969) norms for production frequency, and a mean Spearman r of 0.20 with Kucera and Francis's norms of word frequency.

Although findings about prototype phenomena appear to be robust, it is important to note that Rosch (1973) was unable to obtain similar results for certain other types of categories, such as categories of action (*walking, eating,* and so forth). The hypothesis, derived from Rosch's work, that people categorize by computing similarity distances between the object to be categorized and various prototypes and then place the object in the category belonging to the closest prototype has encountered objections because there is evidence that in some cases a prototype will be most similar to a particular exemplar that is not categorized under the same term as the prototype. For example, most informants judge a *paper cup* to be more like a *glass* than a *cup*, although they say a *paper cup* is a kind of *cup* not a kind of *glass*. (Kronenfeld et al. 1985, Ripps 1975, Werner 1985; see also chapter 13).

Although Berlin's folk taxonomy formulations have proved valuable to enthnobiological study, and his generalizations about the differences between generics, life forms, and specifics have been validated in a number of studies, various problems have arisen. First, it has been pointed out that folk taxonomies are unlike true scientific taxonomies in that the folk taxonomic relation is not always mutually exclusive (D'Andrade 1976). For example, American informants will say that although some *oaks* are *bushes, oaks,* are really *trees*. One answer to this problem is to say that the folk taxonomic relation is defined on the prototypic forms of the term, not every exemplar. Another solution is to say that the taxonomic relation does not really hold between life forms and generics, but does hold between generics and specifics (Hunn 1985). A third solution is to say that the problem is in the application of concept of taxonomic relation, which should be restricted more than it presently is. Wierzbicka (1984), for example, argues that the taxonomic relation should be limited to cases in which the superordinate category forms, in Langacker's terminology, the base of the subordinate category. Thus an *oak* is really a kind of *tree*, because being a *tree* serves as the base of the term *oak*. The term *bush* on the other hand does not typically serve as a base domain for plant terms. A *hawthorne* or *lilac* may grow in a bushlike form, but being a *bush* is not the base of their definition. Some supporting evidence for this is that if one asks informants to list kinds of *trees*, informants produce a reasonably lengthy sets of terms. However, if one asks informants for kinds of *bushes* they produce very short lists.

Wierzbicka (1984) has extended her semantic analysis of superset/subset relations to a number of other kinds of relationships. She distinguishes the true taxonomic *kind of* relation from the relationship found between terms like *bike* and *toy* or between *gun* and *weapon*, which she argues are not relations between two kinds of *things*, but relations between a *kind of thing* and a *functional class*. She argues that the superset/subset connections between functionals and things is not as tight as the taxonomic relation between things and things, in that things like knives can be either weapons or toys or silverware, depending on context.

In addition to these two relationships, Wierzbicka distinguishes other types of superset relations. Wierzbicka points out that superordinate terms such as *furniture, cutlery, clothing,* and *fruit* are *collections* of objects defined partly by function and partly by unity of place. *Furniture,* for example, is made up of objects used to furnish a house or place of residence and to contrast with the *fittings* of a house. Other collective terms such as *leftovers, groceries,* and *refreshments* are even more ad hoc collections, defined partly by function, place, or common fate. Terms such as *vegetable, drugs, medicines,* and *dyes* can be distinguished from collectives by the fact that they basically refer to *uses* of a certain kind of stuff, not to a kind of thing. This fact offers an explanation for Rosch's discovery that in the case of the biological taxonomies (birds, trees, and fish), there was little difference in number of ascribed attributes between the basic-level terms and the superordinates, because for biological classes the superordinates were the same kinds of thing as the basic-level objects. According to this argument, what Rosch found was not that there are intrinsic conceptual differences between different levels of a taxonomy, but rather that there are conceptual differences between terms that refer to kinds of things in the world versus terms that refer to functions of things or collections and uses of things. This is not to deny the point made by Dougherty (1978) that the salience of different taxonomic levels varies by culture and subcultural interests.

Other objections to the use of taxonomic models have been made on ethnographic grounds. Randall (1976) pointed out that just because an ethnographer can elicit by careful questioning a large, extensive, taxonomic tree, this does not mean that informants actually use any such cognitive schema. Rather, Randall argued, the available evidence indicates that informants actually use "dwarf trees"—small networks consisting of a basic object and it attributes. Hunn (1985) pointed out that biological taxonomies only lexicalize a very small portion of the total number of available plant and animal taxa, and that what is lexicalized are the plants and animals that have some special importance to people. For Hunn terms like *bush* are *residual categories,* constructed to refer to a large number of taxa that are not worth distinguishing further. Hunn argues that the taxonomic system developed by Berlin is a compromise between the Linnean hierarchical model and what Hunn (1985) calls the *natural core model,* which treats folk biological domains as "composed of a general purpose, polythetic core of taxa surrounded by special-purpose, monothetic concepts in peripheral position."

This research on taxonomies supports the generalization that humans are opportunistic information processors who in constructing systems of symbols will make use of any kind of structure that will help to communicate information of interest. Because there are always tradeoffs between consistency and generality in categorization, phenomena such as polysemy and the mixture of terms for kinds of things, functions, uses, and collections within a single hierarchical system represent compromises between the need to have symbols that are defined by simple consistent formulations and the need to organize great varieties of experience by means of a limited number of symbols. As Rosch (1978) argued, the problem is one of understanding the human "cognitive economy"—that is, how to best partition a world in which the salient properties of objects are imperfectly correlated to arrive at the classes that keep the number of terms to a minimum yet maximize the information potentially offered by these properties.

20.5 More on Features

Semantic analyses have not been restricted to nouns. Talmy (1978), for example, has carried out an extensive analysis of the distinctions carried by *grammatical* particles such as *a, the, in, across, -ed* (past tense), *-s* (plural), and so forth in contrast to the distinctions carried by *open lexical* items, such as *tree, write, angry*, and so on. Talmy finds that grammatical particles are preponderantly relativistic and topological and exclude fixed or metrically Euclidean distinctions. For example, many languages inflect nouns to specify the *uniplex* or *multiplex* character of the object, but no language has noun inflections that specify the particular color or size of an object. Deitics such as *this* or *that* specify the location of an object by setting up a *partition* that divides a space into region and then *locate* some *entity* at a *point* or *region* that is on the *same* or *different* side as the speaker. The specifications of *this* or *that* appear to be truly topological, in that the partitions and regions set up by using such terms are "rubber-sheet geometry"—they have no metric constraints and may apply to the most concrete or the most abstract spaces. Prepositions, like verb inflections and various deitics, also have topological rather than metric or absolute specifications, as Talmy (1978, p. 9) states:

An illustrative case here are the twenty-odd motion related prepositions in English, such as *through* or *into*, which together subdivide the domain of "paths considered with respect to reference-objects." This domain covers a great and varied range, but any particular "path" falls within the purview of one or another preposition, associated there with other "paths." The associations are often language-specific and sometimes seem arbitrary or idiosyncratic. Thus . . . classed together by *through* are such dissimilar cases as a straightforward liquid-parting course (walking through water) and a zig-zag obstacle-avoiding course (walking through timber). The question arises why such distinctions should be effaced by the grammatical system, while they are observed by the lexical and other cognitive systems. Why are grammatical elements— say, such prepositions—not a large and open class marking indefinitely many distinctions? One may speculate that the cognitive function of such classification lies in rendering contentful material manipulable—i.e., amenable to transmission, storage, and processing—and that its lack would render content an ineffective agglomeration.

Talmy's hypotheses that the construction of a complete cognitive representation in language requires two distinct classes of terms, one which is closed, topological and relativistic, whereas the other is open and can contain almost any combination of features, would be interesting to test with various artificial languages such as the first-order predicate calculus, Loglan, and Lisp.

Considerable work has been done on the semantics of English prepositions. Linder (1981), using Langacker's concepts of *landmark* and *trajector*, has made an extensive analysis of the prepositions *up* and *out*. A similar analysis of *over* has been carried out by Brugman (1981). These analyses support Talmy's hypothesis that grammatical elements are defined by relatively few criteria and that these criteria are relational and topological in character.

Prepositions are extensively polysemic. Each of the senses is a specific *image-schema*—that is, a schematic pictorial representation—and may include metaphorical extensions of this image-schema. Lakoff (1987), for example, discusses how one spatial sense of *over*, as in

The plane flew over the hill.

is transformed into the metaphorical sense found in

He was passed over for promotion.

The spatial sense of the first sentence can be represented by the relation between a landmark and a trajector, as in figure 20.2. The arrow represents the path of the trajector. The trajector has a horizontal path and is *up* from the landmark with no contact between them. The metaphorical sense of being *passed over for promotion* is based on the metaphorical equivalences *control is up* and *choosing is touching*. Using these equivalences, the hearer infers that the person was not contacted by whoever is in control and therefore not chosen for promotion (Lakoff 1987).

Another kind of semantic organization, discussed by Fillmore (1977), consists of a set of terms that involve the same basic schema. (Fillmore sometimes uses the terms *scene* and *scenario* to refer to what are here called *schemas*.) Fillmore uses as an example terms that refer to the schema of a commercial event. Elements of this schema are the *buyer*, the *seller*, the *price*, and the transfer of *money* to the seller and of *goods* to the buyer. There is a large class of terms that use this event in their

```
===========>  trajector

       Λ     landmark
```

Figure 20.2

definition. *Sell, buy, borrow, rent, lease, purchase, charge, embezzle, defraud, haggle, bid, tip, ransom, refund, pension, allowance, tuition, salary, alimony, reward,* and so on each involve different aspects of the same underlying notion of a commercial transaction.

A point that Fillmore has made is that because such schemas are highly simplified representations of the world, the application of a particular term to a specific situation that does not reasonably fit that term's base schema results in odd or inappropriate use (Fillmore 1975, 1977). As Fillmore (1975, pp. 128–129) put it,

How old does an unmarried man have to be before you can call him a bachelor? Is someone who is professionally committed to the single life properly considered a bachelor? (Is it correct to say of Pope John XXIII that he died a bachelor?) If so, is bachelorhood a state one can enter? That is, if a man leaves the priesthood in middle life, can we say that he became a bachelor at age 47? When we say of a divorced man or a widower that he is a bachelor, are we speaking literally or metaphorically? How can we tell? Would you call a woman a widow who murdered her husband? Would you call a woman a widow whose divorce became final on the day of her husband's death? Would you call a woman a widow if one of her three husbands died but she had two living ones left?

. . . According to the prototype theory of meaning, these concepts are defined in the context of a simple world in which men typically marry around a certain age, they marry once, they marry exclusively, they stay married until one partner dies. Men who are unmarried at the time they could be married are called bachelors. Women whose husbands have died are called widows.

A nice example of the way in which the schema-based presuppositions of a term create unconscious inferences has been described by Sweetser (1987). She begins by presenting evidence that the way people define the term *lie* is based on simplified schema or folk theory of discourse and interaction. The basic assumptions of this folk theory are the maxims

(1) Try to help, not harm.

(2) Knowledge is a beneficial thing.

These two maxims entail

(3) Try to inform others; don't misinform.

Further assumptions are

(4) Normally people obey the rules.

(5) People's beliefs normally have adequate justification.

(6) Adequately justified beliefs are normally true.

The result of this set of assumptions—this folk theory of discourse interaction—is that if somebody tells you something, normally that something is true. What then is a *lie?* Research by Coleman and Kay (1981) found that of the three prototypic conditions of lying,

(a) Speaker believes statement is false.

(b) Speaker intends to deceive hearer by making the statement.

(c) The statement is false in fact.

that when respondents were given various combinations of these statements, condition (a) was strongest in producing a judgment that the speaker was lying, and (c) was weakest. This makes sense given the folk theory Sweetser outlines, because if the speaker believes the statement is false, and if most belief is justified, then it would be the case that the statement is false in fact. Furthermore because to be beneficial one should not misinform, one would not give a false statement unless one wanted to deceive. Therefore (b) and (c) follow from (a) and the folk model. Sweetser also points out that when the prototypic assumptions do not hold, a special sense of *lie* is created, as in a *social lie*, in which the speaker wants to be beneficial, but believes the truth would not be beneficial and so says what is intended to be beneficial but not true.

A similar type of analysis has been carried out by Kay (1986) on linguistic *hedges*. Kay finds that certain hedges are defined relative to folk schemas or folk models of language itself. The term *loosely speaking*, for example, is defined with reference to a folk theory of language that portrays words as referring to a world that is independent of our talk and that can be more or less faithful to the nonlinguistic facts they represent (an intensional theory of reference). In the sentence

Loosely speaking, the first human beings lived in Kenya.

loosely speaking serves as a pragmatic hedge, indicating that what is being referred to as the *first human beings* and *Kenya* are only approximate fits to the actual objects. *Loosely speaking* takes a Fregean view of language. In contrast the hedge *technically speaking*, as in the expression

The movers have come for your furniture, which technically includes TV sets.

assumes a very different theory of language, one in which there is a body of experts who have the power to fix particular words to particular objects and events (a causal theory of reference). This theory is like the baptismal-causal theories of Kripke and Putnam, in which a word refers to what it does not because of some sense or intention that it has, but because someone once stipulated that henceforth this word would designate some particular type of object. Thus the underlying referential semantics of English are not frozen, but are manipulable by ordinary speakers using appropriate hedges.

20.6 Cultural Models

The material presented on the analysis of natural-language symbols indicates that an adequate account of symbolic representation requires more than just features or attributes. Not only is there a need to have a theoretical vocabulary that deals with complex relations, such as the relation between base and profile, but this vocabulary must also deal with complex objects such as simple worlds and folk theories. Recognition of this fact has led to a shift in the focus of anthropological investigations from feature analyses to *cultural models*. A cultural model is a cognitive schema that is intersubjectively shared by a social group. Because cultural models are intersubjectively shared, interpretations made about the world on the basis of a cultural model are experienced as obvious facts of the world. For those who know baseball, a wild pitch that flies over the head of the catcher is obviously a *ball*. A further consequence of the intersubjectivity of cultural models is that much of the information relevant to a cultural model need not be made explicit, because what is obvious need not be stated. If an announcer says that the pitch was *wild*, he need not say that it was a ball.

To circumvent the limits of short-term memory, cognitive schemas may be organized hierarchically, in that the parts of any one schema can often be unpacked into further complex subparts. One consequence of such hierarchical structure is that certain cultural models have a wide range of application because they serve as parts of many other cultural models. Thus the culture model of *money* is found as a part of a great many cultural models, such as the models of *buying, interest, banking, inflation, salary,* and so forth. Knowing a culture requires at least knowing the cultural models that are widely used as parts of other cultural models.

An important characteristic of many cultural models is the fact that informants usually cannot produce an organized description of the entire model. They can use the model, but rarely produce a good description of it. The model is like a well-learned set of procedures rather than a declarative body of recountable fact. Most cultural models, however, are not purely procedural because informants can describe partially how the model operates when asked specific questions about it.

In psychology one of the best-known examples of a cultural model is the *restaurant script* (Schank and Abelson 1977). The restaurant script is dependent on a sociocultural institution—that is, the existence of a particular kind of business that sells cooked food. The script concept is intended to refer to stereotyped sequences of events. Event sequences, however, are just one type of organization of elements. As Casson (1983) has pointed out in a summary of the use of schema theory in anthropology, there are schemas that are cultural *object* models (plants, animals, manufactured objects, persons, kinsmen, occupations, ethnic identities, personality descriptors, illnesses, and emotions have all been studied, for example), *orientation* models, (such as cognitive maps for cities), or even spatial mnemonic devices such as the "method of loci," as well as *event* models, such Frake's (1975) study of how to enter a Yakan house.

Quinn and Holland (1987) have reviewed the cultural-model approach, placing it within the general framework of cognitive anthropology. They stress the shift from previous work in semantic analysis toward greater diversity in methodological techniques, more reliance on native intuitions in formulating the model with subsequent testing the adequacy of the model on different kinds of data, and greater reliance on the analysis of natural discourse. They also point to the convergence between anthropologists and linguists in the study of cultural models (Quinn and Holland 1987, p. 24):

> Understandably linguists are most concerned with the important implications of underlying cultural models for their theories of word definition, metaphor, polysemy, hedging, and other linguistic phenomena. Anthropologists tend to orient their analyses in the opposite direction, treating linguistic usages as clues to the underlying cultural model, and working toward a more satisfactory theory of culture and its role in nonlinguistic tasks such as reasoning, problem solving, and evaluating the behavior of others. But the different questions which draw linguists and anthropologists should not obscure the common insight . . . that culturally shared knowledge is organized into prototypical event sequences enacted in simplified worlds. That much of such cultural knowledge is presumed by language use is as significant a realization to anthropologists as to linguists. For the latter, these cultural models promise the key to linguistic use, while for the former, linguistic usage provides the best available data for reconstruction of cultural models.

Quinn and Holland discuss the relation between what they term, following Lakoff (1987), *image schemas* and *proposition schemas*. Basically image schemas are abstract visual representations, whereas proposition schemas are abstract language-based representations. Although there may be cultural models that are based solely on one or the other of these two forms of representation, they conclude that most cultural models include both forms.

An important process in the construction of schemas of all types, including cultural models, is the use of analogy and metaphor. Lakoff and Johnson (1983), in pointing out the pervasiveness of metaphor in ordinary talk, raised the question concerning why it is that certain things are used as metaphors and other things are metaphorized. They suggest that metaphors generally carry structure from physical world models into nonphysical domains, perhaps because physical world structures are well formed and experientially universal, although this is not always the case (Holland 1982). Quinn and Holland (1987) point out that physical world models, because they are things that can be seen and have spatial properties, allow the construction of image schemas that can be transferred to nonphysical domains. Thus, for example, *marriage* can be conceptualized as a *manufactured object* and hence more or less likely to *fall apart*. Even more specifically there is a question of why one kind of physical object rather than another is used as the source of metaphor. According to Quinn and Holland (1987, p. 30),

. . . the classes from which speakers select metaphors they consider to be appropriate are those which capture aspects of the simplified world, and the prototypical events unfolding in this world, constituted by the cultural model. Chosen metaphors not only highlight particular features of the cultural model; as we have discussed, they also point to entailments among these elements. Thus, one husband's metaphor of marriage as a "do-it-yourself project" at once suggests for the him the durable quality of something made in this manner—"it was very strong because it was made as we went along"—and implies, additionally, the craft and care and effort which must go into such a thing to make it well. Speakers often favor just such metaphors, which allow two or more related elements of the source domain to be mapped onto a corresponding set of related elements in the cultural model [Quinn 1985], and comment upon that relation to be made. At the same time, other metaphors which fail to reflect, or even contradict, aspects of the cultural model in the target domain to which they are mapped, are likely to be rejected. Quinn [1985] gives an anecdotal example in which marriage was likened to an ice-cream cone which could be eaten up fast or licked slowly to make it last longer—a metaphor in such clear violation of our understanding of marriage as an enduring relationship that it bothered and offended members of the wedding at which it was voiced.

A number of detailed analyses of cultural models are presented in Holland and Quinn's 1987 book, *Cultural Models in Language and Thought*. An example of a cultural model that is described in detail is the Western folk model of the mind (D'Andrade 1987). Unlike marriage or the restaurant script this model is unrelated to any specific social institution, although it is widely used in ordinary discourse. It is a *folk* model in that it contrasts with a *scientific* model, which is something only experts (psychologists, psychiatrists, cognitive scientists, and the like) are expected to know about. A comparison of this western cultural model with the model of the mind described by Lutz (1985) for the people of Ifaluk, a small Micronesian atoll, indicates that both models have the same overall framework, although there are important differences in detail.

The cultural models discussed so far have been purely conceptual in nature. In contrast to these purely conceptual models, some cultural models are *physically realized*. For example, Frake (1985) has described the way in which the medieval *compass rose*, the 32-point compass found printed on many old maps, was used to calculate tides—apparently its major use. The operation of the compass rose is based on the fact that tides are related to the position of the moon in the sky. Tide times may vary quite a bit from place to place along any particular sea coast, but the relation between the position of the moon and the high tide for any specific place along the coast always remains constant. The compass rose was used to calculate the time of high and low tides from a knowledge of the time of the last full moon and the time of high tide relative to moon's position for a specific place along some coast by using the compass rose as a clock in which each of the 32 points divides the day into 45-minute intervals. Each day the tides rise and fall approximately 48 minutes later than they did the day before—close to the 45-minute intervals of the compass rose—so that given knowledge of the number of days since the last full moon, one could count around the compass to the current position of the moon relative to the time for high tide at that location.

The problem of coordinating the basic cognitive operations involved in the use of physically realized models, such as the compass rose, with the physical world has been addressed in a recent paper by Hutchins 1988. Even such an extremely simple physical device as a *checklist* has a complex *mediating structure*. Suppose one has to perform a complete ordered sequence of actions to do something (say, start an airplane), and one has a printed checklist of these actions. For the checklist to work, first, the printed list of actions must correspond to the user's descriptions of the actions that must be taken to actually start the plane. Second, the user must invoke a sequential execution strategy to determine which step is next. (One simple way to do this is to start reading at the top of the list and place a mark next to each item when it is performed.) Third, the user must then read and understand at some level the printed instructions, constructing a representation of the instructions that maps onto the relevant task world. Finally, the user must coordinate his or her actions with this representation of the task environment. Thus what might at first look like a simple device, in fact turns out to be a complex set of mediations and coordinations.

Hutchins points out that the *internalization* and *automatization* of the device like a checklist involves the gradual transfer of control from the different coordinating structures. For a checklist one first learns the list and in doing the task, remembers the instruction seriatim. After the list has been thoroughly learned, one recalls one task representation after another rather than remembering the verbal instructions of the list. Finally, when the checklist is fully automated, one directly recalls the actions to be taken and their associated environmental changes. At that point the mediating structure has become unconscious, and all that one is aware of is the task environment and the need to do one thing and then the need to do the next.

For Hutchins all cultural models, whether embodied in artifacts or as image and propositional schemas, are mediating structures (1988, pp. 13–14):

In this view, what we learn and what we know, and what our culture knows for us in the form of artifacts and social organizations are these hunks of mediating structure. Thinking consists of bringing these structures into coordination with each other such that they can shape (and be shaped by) each other. The thinker in this world is a very special medium that provides coordination among many structured media, some internal, some external, some embodied in artifacts, some in ideas, and some in social relationships.

20.7 Color

The relation between systems of classification, perception, and memory has been most thoroughly investigated for the domain of color. Color is a practical area for such cross-cultural research because color terms are a distinct part of every language and because well-standardized yet rich stimulus materials, such as the Munsell color chips, are available and easily transportable to field research settings. Using such materials permits controlled comparison between the ranges of color terms for languages as different as English and Zuni (Lenneberg and Roberts 1956). As a result color chips have been the primary materials for testing the Sapir-Whorf hypothesis, which states that language differences in the way objects are categorized are paralleled by cognitive differences in the perception and memory of such objects.

In their landmark study of the Sapir-Whorf hypothesis, Brown and Lenneberg (1954) found that high-saturation color chips with short agreed-upon names were most accurately remembered. Using a different array of chips, however, which varied by hue, but had the same level of saturation and brightness, Lenneberg (1961) found that chips that did *not* have short names were more accurately remembered. This array, the Farnsworth-Munsell array, does not generally include good examples of the so-called *focal* colors (real red, green, yellow, and so on). Because it is primarily the focal colors that have short names, the chips that elicited short focal-color terms were bad examples of the focal colors and so were inaccurately remembered.

Lantz and Stefflre (1964) reestablished the potential of the Sapir-Whorf hypothesis using a different linguistic variable called *communication accuracy,* which measures the degree to which a speaker of a language can describe a chip within an array so that other speakers of the same language can correctly select that same chip from the array. Using the Farnsworth-Munsell array, communication accuracy was found by Lantz and Stefflre to correlate strongly with accuracy of recognition. Stefflre, Castillo Vales, and Moreley (1966) extended the study of communication accuracy to Spanish and Yucatec Mayan speakers and found the same strong correlation between communication accuracy and recognition accuracy. They also found that mistakes in memory are systematically distorted in that when subjects misremembered which chip they had seen, they tended to select a chip in the direction of the median chip selected as typical of that chip's description. For example, a chip that is called "rose" may not be as good as example of the color rose as some other chip. When trying to select from memory this "rose-but-not-the-best-rose" chip, subjects will tend to err in the direction of the "best-rose" chip.

Research emphasis shifted in the late 1960s from how language influenced perception and memory to how the bedrock of color experience is so inescapably what it is that languages naturally conform to it. In *Basic Color Terms* Berlin and Kay (1969), using Munsell's 320-chip array of varying hue and brightness at maximal saturation, found that speakers of different languages agreed closely on the best exemplars for basic color terms, and that while languages had varying numbers of basic color terms, these terms pattern across cultures in a Guttman scalelike order. Rosch (Heider 1972), using a 160-Munsell array, found that the chips universally selected as best exemplars of basic color terms (focals) were more accurately remembered, regardless of naming. Lucy and Shweder (1979) found, however, that in a simple matching test the focal color chips were easier to find in a randomized array, indicating that the chips were not equal in discriminability. In a specially created array, in which the discriminability of chips was controlled, it was found that focality did not correlate with accuracy of recognition, but that communication accuracy did. Garro (1986) and Lucy and Shweder (1988) found in later work that under certain conditions *both* focality and communication accuracy correlate with recognition.

In their original study Lucy and Shweder also developed a purely classificatory measure of how accurately the terminological system used by American subjects selected the target chips. To do this, they first elicited descriptions for each of the target chips and then worked out the most frequent labels for each chip. A different sample of subjects was then used to determine the likelihood that the target chip would be identified as the best example of its own labels. It was found that the target chips varied considerably in the degree to which subjects' labels for these chips allowed others to correctly select the chip from just the label, and that accuracy of memory correlated strongly with this measure of accuracy of labeling (r values of 0.55 and 0.69 for 5-second and 30-second delay periods).

Kay and Kempton (1984) carried out a test of the Sapir-Whorf perceptual hypothesis comparing American speakers of English to Tarahumara speakers using specific color chips in the blue-green area. Tarahumara differs from English in having only one basic-level term for the whole blue and green color region. Kempton and Kay used three chips differing only in hue, with the middle and one end chip falling on the same side of the English blue-green boundary, whereas the middle and the other chip were actually closer together with respect to hue. They found that American speakers of English, compared with

Tarahumara speakers, were more likely to select as the most different the chip that has a different English color name, whereas Tarahumara speakers more often selected on the basis of actual similarity in hue.

In another ingenious experiment Kay and Kempton devised an apparatus in which three chips are arranged in a container with a sliding top so that the subject can see either of two pairs of the three chips but not all three at once. The chips selected for this experiment were the same as the chips selected for the first experiment, in which two chips fall on one side of the name boundary, and one falls on the other. The subject then was asked, "Tell me which is bigger: the difference in greenness between the two chips on the left or the difference in blueness between the two chips on the right." The central chip, which is intermediate in hue between the other two, was in view at all times.

With this apparatus American subjects see more accurately that there is a greater difference between the two chips on the same side of the green-blue boundary than the two chips on different sides of the boundary. The effect is like a perceptual illusion, because as soon as the sliding cover is taken off, and all three chips are seen simultaneously, the difference between the two chips with the same color name appears to be the smaller. Although formally the same judgment is involved in both experiments, the use of the apparatus apparently blocks the application of different names to the chips, thereby blocking the Sapir-Whorf labeling effect on the perception of similarity.

Overall the conclusion to be drawn from these experiments is that classification systems have strong effects on memory, but that the effects depend greatly on the nature of the set of objects used in the memory test. Items that have descriptive labels that allow them to be accurately selected out of a particular set of objects will be remembered better than less accurately labelable items. Other factors, however, such as the degree to which items fit a prototype of some sort, may also affect memory. Finally, an effect of naming on perception appears to be demonstrable, but occurs only in cases in which there is considerable difficulty in discriminating between objects.

20.8 Emotion

The cross-cultural study of emotion is like the cross-cultural study of color in that it also involves problems concerning potential universals of experience and the cognitive effects of different lexically coded systems of categorization. Although there is evidence that the facial patterns that are postulated to express the basic emotions are universally lexically differentiated (Ekman 1971), exactly what is meant when a speaker of a non-Western language uses a particular term to refer to a particular facial expression remains controversial. Anthropologists (for example, Gerber 1975, 1985, Levy 1985, Lutz 1982, 1985, Poole 1994) who have studied discourse about emotion ethnographically, have found that emotion terms often are defined with reference to complex, culturally stereotyped scenarios. Because these complex scenarios are often culturally idiosyncratic, emotion terms are often difficult to translate exactly from one language to another, although partial synonyms can usually be found (Wierzbicka 1986).

A major question here is the degree to which the different cultural organizations of emotion terms affect perception and memory. In languages that do not distinguish between *fear* and *shame*, what do people feel when something *frightening* happens to them? And do they have the same feeling when something *shameful* happens to them? Feelings appear to be difficult to tell apart, which makes them good candidate material for the study of the effect of linguistic categorization on nonlinguistic processes.

Cultural understandings about emotions do more than segment the domain of basic affects. Because culturally defined eliciting situations and behavior responses are included as part of the definition of emotions, emotion terms can convey covert cultural ideologies. Gerber (1985) analyzes some of the cultural ideology carried by Samoan emotion terms. Thus the major term *alofa*, best translated by the English term *love*, has the following basic cultural scenario: an old person, hot, tired, and perhaps ill, is seen walking down the road carrying a heavy load. This makes one feel *alofa*, which prompts one to provide help, perhaps by taking the burden or by offering a cool drink and a place to rest. The emphasis in *alofa* is on caring, giving, and obligation, rather than the characteristics of intimacy, physical affection, and the appreciation of individual uniqueness found in the English term *love*. *Alofa* is the normal feeling toward kin, and the behaviors that express and are prompted by this feeling are the behaviors that are morally correct and socially obligatory. A good child works for his or her parents and thereby expresses *alofa*. The emotions thought to be similar to *alofa* are feelings of peacefulness, absence of angry thoughts, forgiveness, humility, generosity, and agreeableness. *Alofa* is thought to be the way good people feel. The cultural ideology in Samoa, an ideology that strengthens obligations to elders and kin, is readily apparent to most Americans, because they have been raised in a very different reality-defining system.

There is an interesting relation between emotion terms and colors: a series of studies of the association between emotion terms and Munsell color chips in four different cultures (D'Andrade and Egan 1974, Kieffer 1974, Johnson, Johnson, and Baksh 1986) has found that similar chips out of various arrays tend to be chosen by informants as the best examples of translations of the English emotion terms *happy*, *sad*, *angry*, and *frightened* in all four cultures. There is also considerable agreement among all four cultures on which color chips are *good*, *bad*, *strong*, and *weak*. This is not to say there are no cultural differences (see Johnson et al. 1986). However, the cultural differences seem to be small compared with the very general similarity in emotional response to colors.

20.9 Reasoning and Cultural Models

Another important area of research in the relation between culture and cognition is the study of reasoning or inference. There is a general position in cognitive science that treats the problem of reasoning as a problem that can potentially be solved by the use of some variety of *logic* (see chapter 1). The particular kind of logic is not the issue here. Whether the sentential calculus, Venn diagrams, first-order predicate calculus, modal logics, multivalued logics, nonmonotonic logics, or probability theory are used, the overall strategy is the same. The content of the problem, typically a verbal formulation of some kind, is *recoded* into a set of variables and a set of specially defined operators. Along with the rules for recoding content into form go certain rules of transformation by which one can change one well-formed expression into a different well-formed expression. These transformations are "truths" that depend on the *form* of the expression alone, not on the *content* of the original sentence or proposition. This transformational capacity allows the construction of various kinds of computational strategies by which conclusions can be derived from premises—thereby modeling the effects if not the process of reasoning.

The possibility of modeling reasoning with a logic system has made the creation of such systems an attractive strategy for cognitive scientists. However, there are two important drawbacks to such a strategy. The first of these involves the implausibility of the hypothesis that people actually use formal systems in reasoning. The second drawback involves the computational problems that emerge when trying to construct a logical system of any complexity that can actually reach task-relevant conclusions.

The implausibility of logical inference as a description of how people actually reason is indicated by the fact that the *content* of propositions strongly affects how well people reason (Johnson-Laird 1983; see also chapter 12). Because logic operates on a formal representation of a problem in which all the content has been recoded into variables and logical connectives, if people use logic to solve a problem and fail, this can only be because either they are unable to represent the problem correctly or they are unable to find a sequence of inferences to reach the desired conclusion. But it is a fact that people fail on problems that they understand quite well and that have logical forms that, based on their performance on problems with the same logical form but different content, they should be able to solve easily. The classical example of this type of problem is the Wason problem (Wason 1969). Simpler examples of this type of content-affected problem can be created using modus tollens in the ordinary sentential calculus (D'Andrade 1989b). Modus tollens has the following form:

If p then q. Not q. Therefore not p.

American undergraduate students, when given modus tollens problems, are generally unable to solve them when the content is arbitrary, that is, when no well-formed cultural schema links p and q. An example of modus tollens with arbitrary content is

GIVEN: If Roger is a musician, then Roger is a Bavarian.

SUPPOSE: Roger *is not* a Bavarian.

THEN:

(a) It must be the case that Roger is a musician.

(b) Maybe Roger is a musician, maybe he isn't.

(c) It must be the case that Roger is not a musician.

No widely shared cultural schema links someone's being a musician with someone's being a Bavarian, which leaves the subject who tries to solve this problem more dependent on logical form alone. Only 53 percent of a sample of 50 undergraduates gave the correct answer to this problem (D'Andrade 1989b).

Subjects do much better when the problem contains a well-formed cultural schema linking p and q. For example, given the following problem,

GIVEN: If this rock is a garnet, then it is a semiprecious stone.

SUPPOSE: This rock *is not* a semiprecious stone.

THEN:

(a) It must be the case that this rock is a garnet.

(b) Maybe this rock is a garnet, and maybe it isn't.

(c) It must be the case that this rock is not a garnet.

96 percent of an undergraduate sample gave the correct answer. For this problem there is a well-shared cultural schema linking something being a garnet and something being semiprecious—that is, garnets *are* semiprecious stones. Other examples of modus tollens problems with well-formed schematic links between p and q, which have been tested on University of California, San Diego undergraduates, are

If Tom was born in San Diego, Tom is a native Californian. (86-percent correct)

If Janet lives in San Cristóbal, then Janet lives in Mexico. (80-percent correct)

If Bill cut himself, then Bill would be bleeding. (77-percent correct)

If it is raining, then the roof is wet. (68-percent correct)

If John bought a present, then John spent some money. (65-percent correct)

Examples of problems that lack well-formed schematic linkages between p and q and that subjects had more difficulty solving are

If Janet went to town, then Janet brought home some bread. (57-percent correct)

If Roger drank Pepsi, then Tom sat down. (53-percent correct)

If James is a watchman, then James likes candy. (51-percent correct)

If D is true, then E is true. (E is false.) (45-percent correct)

If Harold is a politician, then Harold is from New York (40-percent correct)

If J is true, then K is true (not K is true). (33-percent correct)

Sample sizes for these results range from 30 to 50.

It is not the case that people *always* have difficulty reasoning with arbitrary content. People do seem to be able to reason correctly with certain very simple logical forms irrespective of content. For example, when presented with the following modus ponens problem:

GIVEN: If James is a watchman, then James likes candy.

SUPPOSE: James *is* a watchman.

THEN:

(a) It must be the case that James likes candy.

(b) Maybe James likes candy, maybe he doesn't.

(c) It must be the case that James does not like candy.

Ninety-six percent of an undergraduate sample gave the correct answer—although the content of the problem is the same as the modus tollens problem, which only 51 percent of another sample were able to solve. In general people seem to be able to solve modus ponens problems no matter how bizarre the content (D'Andrade 1989a,b). In solving modus ponens problems, people act like true logicians for whom only form counts. Logical forms other than modus ponens that people seem to be able to use effectively no matter what the content are

Not not p. Therefore p.

P or q. Not p. Therefore q.

These findings raise the question How do people reason when *not* using logical forms? Although a long way from a full answer, work on reasoning carried out in natural settings has given some clues. An examination of legal disputes among the Trobriand Islanders (Hutchins 1980) indicates that connectives such as *and, if-then, not, or* and so forth are apparently culturally universal and of central importance in reasoning. The conceptual materials that these universal connectives organize into larger structures are typically made up of parts of cultural models. Furthermore the connectives *and, if-then, not,* and so forth are understood *not* in terms of truth-table relations but rather in terms of various kinds of temporal and causal contingencies. What appears to be the case is that people manipulate mental models whose content consists of ordinary representations of the world in such a way that they can compute whether certain things could or could not happen (D'Andrade 1989b, Johnson-Laird 1983).

The representations that are mentally manipulated in reasoning are often surprisingly concrete and particular. For example, in a study of the missionaries and cannibals puzzle, Hutchins and Levin (1981) found that subjects were less likely to detect that they had attempted illegal moves when they imagined events taking place on the river bank away from them compared with imagined events on their side of the river (the subject's point of view with respect to the river was determined by the subject's use of deixis in their verbal protocols, for example, "they *go* to the *other* side, then I *bring* them back *here*.") It is as if events that are imagined to occur on the subject's side of the river are closer and hence easier to see than events that are imagined to occur on the other side of the river. Similarly it is said that chess players prefer to play with familiarly shaped chess sets, and that they complain if they have to use unusually shaped pieces because they say such pieces are harder to manipulate mentally. Preferred mental models appear to be those that are most familiar and best understood.

Work on reasoning by Americans about marriage has yielded a similar pattern of concrete imaginings and has shown further that reasoning in ordinary discourse frequently uses complex analogies (Quinn 1987). The frequent use of analogic thinking and linguistic metaphors in natural discourse is, I believe, more than an embellishment. Metaphor and analogy permit the use of auxiliary structures that can be used as supplemental models in reasoning. According to Collins and Gentner (1987, p. 243),

Analogies are powerful ways to understand how things work in a new domain. We think this is because they enable people to construct a structure mapping that carries across the way the components in a system interact. This allows people to create a new mental models that they can then run to generate predictions about what should happen in various situations in the real world.

Metaphor and analogy are not the only ways new structures are introduced into problems to aid in reaching a solution. As an illustration let us examine the problem-solving routines used by a modern ship to find its location along a familiar and well-mapped coast (Hutchins 1989). The basic technique is to find two landmarks on the coast that correspond to two identifiable points on a chart, determine the direction of the lines of sight from the ship to the landmarks, and then compute the point of intersection of the two lines on the chart. The ship must be located at the point in space that corresponds to the point on the chart where the lines intersect. To actually compute the position of a ship the direction of the line of sight from the ship to the landmarks is measured with a compass. These measurements are represented by a number from 0 to 360. When these measurements are plotted on a chart, the information represented by the number is converted back to a direction and brought into coordination with the chart.

A close look at the actual process of navigations shows that many distinct cultural structures are involved (Hutchins 1989). The landmarks have names ("Pt. Loma Light," "Dive Tower"), and to find a named landmark, one must learn to associate the names with the appearances of the landmarks in the world. (The navigating crew's inexperience with local landmarks may have been the cause of the Exxon Valdez disaster in Prince William Sound.) Determining the direction of the landmark from the ship is accomplished with a tool that combines a telescopic sight and a compass. When the hairline in the sight is aligned with a landmark, the direction of the line of sight can be read where the hairline intersects the compass scale. The numbers that are read from the scale are relayed by phone to the chart table, where they are recorded as digits in a log book. The plotter then aligns an index on a plotting tool with a scale (like the one on the compass) at the appropriate number. The plotting tool is aligned with the symbol of the landmark on the chart and oriented so that the directional circle on the tool is in alignment with the directional frame of the chart. Finally, a line that depicts the directional relationship of the ship to the landmark is drawn on the chart.

When the person sighting a landmark aligns the sighting device with the landmark, a representational state has been constructed. The information captured in that representational state is moved across a number of representational structures, each taking a different form. What begins as an alignment of a hairline with a scale becomes a spoken string of digits, then a written string of digits, then an alignment of an index with a scale, and finally a line on a chart.

These navigational procedures are often carried out by more than one person. When navigating near hazards such as land and ship traffic, a ship must frequently update its information about current position and projected future positions. This need for frequent updates means that a lot of computation must be done in a short time, more in fact than any one individual could do. In the United States Navy, under time pressure the task is performed by a six-person team. When a group does the computations there is no need for all the team members to know the entire procedure. Novice navigators can participate in the team performance, doing small pieces of the task, such as sighting landmarks, long before they know the uses to which the information they provide are put. They simply need to be able to find the named landmarks in the world, align the sighting device and read the numbers on command. In fact there is no need for any of the members of the team to know the entire procedure. Each member simply needs to know his or her part of the job and to have his or her actions triggered by conditions produced by other team members. The computational procedures and the social organization in the form of division of labor are similar kinds of cultural artifacts. Both are ways of organizing sequential behavior of a computational system.

The ubiquity of systems composed of many minds raises a number of interesting questions. What are the information-processing properties of groups of human minds? How are those properties affected by changes in the organization of the activities of the minds that constitute them? How is cognition distributed? Why are knowing, reasoning, and remembering distributed the way they are? What are the consequences of this distribution for the properties of individual minds? A complete theory of cultural cognition will require a theory of distributed processing that permits understanding of multiactor systems—what George Miller has called the "many-mind problem."

Coordination of structures is not unique to navigation. Consider the following excerpt from a natural conversation:

When we were talking she wouldn't look at me. I think she is mad at me. Maybe she expected me to be more help in getting everything cleaned up.

There are three distinct cultural models or structures being coordinated here. First, there is the model of the world of gesture and bodily movement. A "landmark" is noticed—the direction of a person's gaze. This landmark is lined up with an internal state that is part of a different cultural model concerning the operation of invisible feelings and thoughts in the mind through a coordinating proposition that *angry people either stare or look away to hide their anger*. This model of the mind in turn is coordinated with a causal account model consisting of a general event structure about how disconfirmed expectations about assistance in reaching goals give rise to angry feelings toward the perceived source of frustration. In this simple example we see again how inference can be done by coordinating models so that one can read from one structure to another. The mappings are not analogic or metaphorical but causal and temporal.

The general argument here is that most ordinary reasoning is done not by recoding propositions into logical forms but by manipulating propositional content according to the constraints of a cultural or idiosyncratic model so that different cultural models are coordinated with each other. As Simon says in *The Science of the Artificial* (1985, p. 153, emphasis added),

Problem Solving as a Change in Representation
That representation makes a difference is a long-familiar point. We all believe that arithmetic has become easier since Arabic numeral and place notation replaced Roman numerals. . .
That representation makes a difference is evident for a different reason. All mathematics exhibits in its conclusions only what is already

implicit in its premises. . . . Hence all mathematical derivation can be viewed simply as change in representation, making evident what was previously true but obscure.

This view can be extended to all of problem solving—solving a problem simply means representing it so as to make the solution transparent. *If problem solving could actually be organized in these terms, the issue of representation would indeed become central.*

The claim here is that this is precisely what cultural models often do effectively—they coordinate with each other in ways that make the solution transparent.

20.10 Final Remarks

People are good at learning complex conceptual structures. They are poor at mental manipulation of uninterpreted symbols and poor at extended search in decision trees. These strengths and weaknesses interact in a complicated way with cultural models. First, because people are good at learning complex conceptual structures, they can learn a great number of cultural models and the ways in which these structures are to be aligned with each other.

It is of interest that humans like to bedevil themselves by challenging themselves to do things they do not do very well, such as jumping over bars placed seven feet in the air, or hitting rapidly flying small balls with thin bats, or running across fields when lots of people are trying to knock them down, and so on. These tasks are called *games*. Cognitive games, such as chess or the Tower of Hanoi or various word and logic puzzles, are examples of culturally learned solutions to the problem of how to entertain ourselves by making ourselves do cognitive tasks we are not good at. A number of these games require extended search, which is partially what makes them so difficult for us. Typically they do not have obvious transformations to other kinds of representation that make the solutions directly apparent. It is therefore a matter of some irony that when cognitive scientists began to try to simulate human reasoning, they took as exemplary tasks either cognitive games of the highly specialized symbol-manipulation problems found in math and logic. Neither choice gives a very representative sample of the cognitive tasks that people do frequently or do well.

The overall point is not just that people reason using mental models rather than formal logical systems; this point has been made effectively by Johnson-Laird. The point here is that much of the reasoning that people do depends on *cultural* models, and that these cultural models are *more* than just some kind of package of information about the world.

The argument that much of the reasoning people do depends on cultural models has been presented. One objection that readers of an earlier version of this review had to this claim is that many of the examples seem to be *personal* models. Propositions that not looking at someone can be an indication of anger, that failed hopes give rise to anger, that getting cut leads to bleeding, or that raining makes roofs wet, are, according to some critics, things we learn out of personal experience, not beliefs taught by the culture.

It is reasonable to assume that these propositions are, in large measure, learned from personal experience along with a certain amount of "guided discovery" (D'Andrade 1981). Saying that something is a cultural model, however, is not contradicted by saying that something is a personal model. What makes something a cultural model is not whether or not the model is true, or whether the model was learned through untutored experience, but whether the model is *intersubjectively shared, used,* and *sanctioned*—that is, whether the members of a culture expect everyone to know the model, and if they do not, sanction them because it is considered important to know how to use the model. What makes something a cultural model is the use of it, not how it is learned.

Much more problematic is the claim that cultural models are more than packages of information about the world. There is a relatively well-established notion that culture and personal experience provide the *content* of what people think about, whereas the way in which this content is manipulated depends on various universal *psychological processes*. According to this position, the way the mind works is psychology, the content on which it works is culture and idiosyncratic experience. Here culture is *inert,* dependent on a mental machinery that manipulates it.

If culture is nothing more than inert content to be manipulated by some universal machinery, there is little of interest that those who study culture might contribute to cognitive science except perhaps to show how the working of the universal mental machinery limits the content of culture. The argument here is not that the working of the universal machine does not limit the content of culture—the research on how the limits of short-term memory affect systems of classification demonstrates that it does. Nor is the argument here that no universal machine exists—clearly there are universal generalizations to be made about how the mind works. One would not expect the Chinese to solve algebra problems in a different way than Americans do if they learned the *same* algebra.

What then *is* the argument? The argument here is that to some extent cultural models are actually little *machines*. They are software *programs,* not just *data*. Of course the brain contains a more general mental machine that runs these little cultural machines, just as there is a more general program that runs a specific Fortran program. But the little programs are also important, because without them the general program, which does various universal procedures such as *search, chunk, store,* and *recall,* would have to work very hard to do very little.

In what sense then are cultural models little programs? Perhaps the program aspect of cultural models is easiest to see in physical cultural models like the compass rose. One learns as part of the understanding the compass rose how to compute high and low tide for different days at various locations. Learning the model is learning a little program. The program aspect of cultural models is also easy to see in things like algebra, in which learning consists of putting together various transformational and interpretational procedures that make it possible to solve certain kinds of problems. The program aspect of structures like the model of the mind may be more difficult to see. Part of the model of the mind contains the propositions that what one *perceives* affects what one *thinks*, which affects one's *feelings*, which affects what one *wants*, which affects the things one *aims for* (D'Andrade 1987). This causal sequence is in itself a little computational device, *a small production system* that attaches one thing to another. Culture also contains integrative procedures that coordinate different cultural models, permitting the complex computations illustrated in the example of ship navigation. The study of cultural cognition then is the study of cultural information and cultural programs that interact with the more general programs of intelligent systems.

Whatever benefits the study of cultural cognition comes to have for different cognitive science enterprises, the study of cultural cognition itself will undoubtedly benefit from future advances in cognitive science. Much of what has been found out about cultural classification and cultural cognition was directly stimulated by work in cognitive psychology and artificial intelligence, as well as linguistics. This trend is likely to continue. One reason for this is that the materials that cognitive scientists use to test out their models are typically taken from culture; for example, chess, syllogisms, verb forms, the diagnosis of disease, theorem proving, story understanding, and so on. As the tasks studied by cognitive scientists become more representative of the things people do in ordinary life, the models of cognitive science will undoubtedly become an increasingly valuable tool for the study of culture.

On the other hand it is difficult to predict how useful the study of cultural cognition will be to the various parts of the cognitive science enterprise. At present little that is known about cultural cognition is of great relevance to model building in artificial intelligence, for example. However, it is possible that this will change. Parallel distributed process models bring new computational problems to the fore. The problem of developing a program that has good common sense continues to plague the field. It may be that knowledge about the solution that humans developed to the problem of becoming intelligent will prove to be of practical and theoretical value. The human solution was to develop culture. It may be that the way in which culture is organized and transmitted to produce intelligence will also prove to be a good way to model intelligence.

References

Anderson, N. 1981. *Foundations of Information Integration Theory*. New York: Academic Press.

Battig, W. F., and Montague, W. E. 1969. Category norms for verbal items in 56 categories: A replication and extension of the Connecticut category norms. *Journal of Experimental Psychology Monographs* 80:3, part 2.

Berlin, B., Breedlove, D., and Raven, P. H. 1966. Folk taxonomies and biological classification. *Science* 154:273–275.

Berlin, B., Breedlove, D., and Raven, P. H. 1973. General principles of classification and nomenclature in folk biology. *American Anthropologist* 75:214–242.

Berlin, B., and Kay, P. 1969. *Basic Color Terms*. Berkeley: University of California Press.

Boster, J., Berlin, B., and O'Neill, J. 1986. The correspondence of Jivaroan to Scientific Ornithology. *American Anthropologist* 88:569–583.

Brown, C. 1977. Folk botanical life-forms: Their universality and growth. *American Anthropologist* 79:317–342.

Brown, C., Kolar, J., Torrey, B., Truon-Quan, T., and Volkman, P. 1976. Some general principles of biological and non-biological folk classification. *American Ethnologist* 3:73–85.

Brown, R., and Lenneberg, E. 1954. A study in language and cognition. *Journal of Abnormal and Social Psychology* 49:73–85.

Brugman, C. 1981. *The Story of Over*. M.A. thesis, University of California, Berkeley, CA.

Casson, R. 1983. Schemata in cognitive anthropology. *Annual Review of Anthropology* 12:429–462.

Coleman, L., and Kay, P. 1981. Prototype semantics: The English verb 'lie.' *Language* 57:26–44.

Collins, A., and Gentner, D. 1987. How people construct mental models. In D. Holland and N. Quinn, eds. *Cultural Models in Language and Thought*. New York: Cambridge University Press, pp. 243–265.

Conklin, H. C. 1962. Lexicographic treatment of folk taxonomies. In F. Householder and S. Saporta, eds. *Indiana University Research Center in Anthropology, Folklore, and Linguistics, Publication 21. Problems in Lexicography*. Bloomington: University of Indiana Press, pp. 119–141.

D'Andrade, R. 1976. A propositional analysis of U.S. American beliefs about illness. In K. Basso and H. Selby, eds. *Meaning in Anthropology*. Albuquerque: University of New Mexico Press, pp. 155–180.

D'Andrade, R. 1981. The cultural part of cognition. *Cognitive Science* 5:179–195.

D'Andrade, R. 1987. A folk model of the mind. In D. Holland and N. Quinn, eds. *Cultural Models in Language and Thought*. New York: Cambridge University Press, pp. 112–148.

D'Andrade, R. 1989a. Some propositions about the relation between culture and human cognition. In J. Stigler, G. Herdt, and R. Shweder, eds. *Cultural Psychology: The Chicago Symposia*. Cambridge, Engl.: Cambridge University Press.

D'Andrade, R. 1989b. Culturally based reasoning. In A. Gellatly and D. Rogers, eds. *Cognition and Social Worlds*. Oxford, Engl.: Oxford University Press.

D'Andrade, R., and Egan, M. 1974. The colors of emotion. *American Ethnologist* 1:49–63.

Dougherty, J. 1978. Salience and relatively in classification. *American Ethnologist* 5:66–80.

Dougherty, J., and Keller, C. 1985. Taskonomy: A practical approach to knowledge structures. In J. Dougherty, ed. *Directions in Cognitive Anthropology*. Urbana: University of Illinois Press, pp. 161–174.

Ekman, P. 1971. Universals and cultural differences in facial expressions of emotion. In J. Cole, ed. Lincoln: University of Nebraska Press, pp. 207–283.

Fillenbaum, S., and Rapaport, A. 1971. *Structures in the Subjective Lexicon*. New York: Academic Press.

Fillmore, C. 1975. An alternative to checklist theories of meaning. In C. Cogen, H. Thomson, G. Thurgood, K. Whilster, and J. Wright, eds. *Proceedings of the First Annual Meeting of the Berkeley Linguistics Society*. Berkeley: Berkeley Linguistic Society, pp. 123–131.

Fillmore, C. 1977. Topic in lexical semantics. In R. Cole, ed. *Current Issues in Linguistic Theory*. Bloomington: Indiana University Press, pp. 76–138.

Frake, C. 1975. How to enter a Yakan house. In. M. Sanches and B. Blount, eds. *Socio-cultural Dimensions of Language Use*. New York: Academic Press, pp. 25–40.

Frake, C. 1985. Cognitive maps of time and tide among Medieval seafarers. *Man* 20:254–270.

Garro, L. 1986. Language, memory, and focality: A reexamination. *American Anthropologist* 88:128–136.

Gerber, E. 1975. *The Cultural Patterning of Emotion in Samoa*. Ph.D. dissertation, University of California, San Diego.

Gerber, E. 1985. Rage and obligation: Samoan emotion in conflict. In G. White and J. Kirkpatrick, eds. *Person, Self, and Experience*. Berkeley: University of California Press, pp. 121–167.

Haviland, S. and Clark, E. 1974. "This man's father is my father's son": A study of acquisition of English kin terms. *Journal of Child Language* 1:23–47.

Heider, E. 1972. Universals in color naming and memory. *Journal of Experimental Psychology* 93:10–20.

Holland, D. 1982. Conventional metaphors in human thought and language. *Reviews in Anthropology* 9:287–297.

Hunn, E. 1976. Toward a perceptual model of folk biological classification. *American Ethnologist* 3:508–524.

Hunn, E. 1985. The utilitarian factor in folk biological classification. In J. Dougherty, ed. *Directions in Cognitive Anthropology.* Urbana: University of Illinois Press, pp. 117–140.

Hutchins, E. 1980. *Culture and Inference: A Trobriand Case Study.* Cambridge: Harvard University Press.

Hutchins, E. 1988. Mediation and automatization. In *Institute for Cognitive Science Technical Report 8704.* University of California, San Diego, CA.

Hutchins, E. 1989. The technology of team navigation. In J. Galegher, R. Kraut, and C. Egedo, eds. *Intellectual Teamwork: Social and Technical Bases of Cooperative Work.* Hillsdale, NJ: Erlbaum.

Hutchins, E., and Levin, J. A. 1981. Point of view in problem solving. In *CHIP Technical Report, 105.* University of California, San Diego, CA.

Johnson, A., Johnson, O., and Baksh, M. 1986. The colors of emotions in Machiguenga. *American Anthropologist* 88(3):674–681.

Johnson-Laird, P. 1983. *Mental Models.* Cambridge: Harvard University Press.

Kay, P. 1986. Linguistic competence and folk theories of language: Two English hedges. In D. Holland and N. Quinn, eds. *Cultural Models in Language and Thought.* New York: Cambridge University Press, pp. 67–77.

Kay, P., and Kempton, W. 1984. What is the Sapir-Whorf hypothesis? *American Anthropologist* 86:65–79.

Kieffer, M. 1974. *Color and Emotion: Synesthesia in Tzutujil Mayan and Spanish.* Ph.D. dissertation, University of California, Irvine, CA.

Kronenfeld, D., Armstrong, J., and Wilmoth, S. 1985. Exploring the internal structure of linguistic categories: An extensionist semantic view. In J. Dougherty, ed. *Directions in Cognitive Anthropology.* Urbana: University of Illinois Press, p. 110.

Lakoff, G. 1987. *Woman, Fire, and Dangerous Things: What Categories Reveal about the Mind.* Chicago: University of Chicago Press.

Lakoff, G., and Johnson, M. 1983. *Metaphors We Live By.* Chicago: University of Chicago Press.

Langacker, R. 1986. Cognitive grammar. *Cognitive Science* 10:1–40.

Langacker, R. 1987. *Foundations of Cognitive Grammar.* Stanford: Stanford University Press.

Lantz, D. and Stefflre, V. 1964. Language and cognition revisited. *Journal of Abnormal and Social Psychology* 69:472–481.

Lenneberg, E. 1961. Color naming, color recognition, color discrimination: A reappraisal. *Perceptual and Motor Skills* 12:375–382.

Lenneberg, E., and Roberts, J. 1956. The language of experience; A study in methodology. *International Journal of Linguistics, Memoir No. 13.*

Levy, R. L. 1985. Emotion, knowing, and culture. In R. Shweder and R. LeVine, eds. *Culture Theory: Essays on Mind, Self, and Emotion.* Cambridge: Cambridge University Press, pp. 214–237.

Linder, S. 1981. A lexico-semantic analysis of verb-particle constructions with UP and OUT. Ph.D. dissertation, University of California, San Diego, CA.

Lucy, J., and Shweder, R. 1979. Whorf and his critics: Linguistic and non-linguistic influences on color memory. *American Anthropologist* 81:581–615.

Lucy, J., and Shweder, R. 1988. The effect of incidental conversation on memory for focal colors. *American Anthropologist* 90(4):923–931.

Lutz, C. 1982. The domain of emotion words on Ifaluk. *American Ethnologist* 9:113–128.

Lutz, C. 1985. Ethnopsychology compared to what: Explaining behavior and consciousness among the Ifaluk. In G. White and J. Kirkpatrick, eds. *Person, Self, and Experience.* Berkeley: University of California Press, pp. 35–79.

Miller, G. A. 1956. The magical number seven plus or minus two: Some limits on your capacity for processing information. *Psychological Review* 63:81–96.

Nerlove, S., and Romney, A. K. 1967. Sibling terminology and cross-sex behavior. *American Anthropologist* 69:1249–1253.

Poole, F. J. P. 1984. Coming into social being: Cultural images of infants in Bimin-Kuskusmin folk psychology. In G. White and J. Kirkpatrick, eds. *Person, Self, and Experience.* Berkeley: University of California Press, pp. 183–242.

Quinn, N. 1985. American marriage through metaphors: A cultural analysis. In *North Carolina Working Papers in Culture and Cognition No. 1.* Durham, NC: Duke University Department of Anthropology.

Quinn, N., and Holland, D. 1987. Introduction. In D. Holland and N. Quinn, eds. *Cultural Models in Language and Thought.* New York: Cambridge University Press, pp. 3–40.

Quinn, N. 1987. Convergent evidence for a cultural model of American marriage. In D. Holland and N. Quinn, eds. *Cultural Models in Language and Thought.* New York: Cambridge University Press, pp. 173–192.

Randall, R. 1976. How tall is a taxonomic tree? Some evidence for dwarfism. *American Ethnologist* 3:543–553.

Ripps, L. 1975. Inductive judgements about natural categories. *Journal of Verbal Learning and Verbal Behavior* 14:665–681.

Romney, A. K., and D'Andrade, R. 1962. Cognitive aspects of English kin terms. *American Anthropologist* 66:146–170.

Rosch, E. 1973. On the internal structure of perceptual and semantic categories. In T.

Moore, ed. *Cognitive Development and the Acquisition of Language*. New York: Academic Press, pp. 123–142.

Rosch, E. 1975. Cognitive representations of semantic categories. *Journal of Experimental Psychology* 104:192–233.

Rosch, E. 1978. Principles of categorization. In E. Rosch and B. Lloyd, eds. *Cognition and Categorization*. Hillsdale, NJ: Erlbaum, pp. 27–48.

Schank, R., and Abelson, R. 1977. *Scripts, Plans, Goals, and Understanding: An Inquiry into Human Knowledge Structures*. Hillsdale, NJ: Erlbaum.

Simon, H. 1985. *The Science of the Artificial*. 2nd ed. Cambridge: MIT Press.

Stefflre, V., Castillo Vales, V., and Moreley, L. 1966. Language and cognition in Yucatan: A cross-cultural replication. *Journal of Personality and Social Psychology* 4:112–115.

Sweetser, E. 1987. The definition of *lie:* An examination of the folk models underlying a semantic prototype. In D. Holland and N. Quinn, eds. *Cultural Models in Language and Thought*. New York: Cambridge University Press, pp. 43–66.

Talmy, L. 1978. The relation of grammar to cognition—a synopsis. In D. Waltz, ed. *Proceedings of TINLAP-2 (Theoretical Issues in Natural Language Processing)*. Champaign Coordinated Science Laboratory, University of Illinois, pp. 3–23.

Uyeda, K., and Mandler, G. 1980. Prototypicality norms for 28 semantic categories. *Behavioral Research Methods and Instrumentation* 12:587–595.

Wason, P. 1969. Regression in reasoning. *British Journal of Psychology* 60:471–480.

Wallace, A. F. C. 1961. On being just complicated enough. *Proceedings of the National Academy of Sciences* 47:458–464.

Werner, O. 1985. Folk knowledge without fuzz. In J. Dougherty, ed. *Directions in Cognitive Anthropology*. Urbana: University of Illinois Press, pp. 73–90.

Wexler, K., and Romney, A. K. 1972. Individual variations in cognitive structures. In. R. Shepard and S. Nerlove, eds. *Multidimensional Scaling Vol. II*. New York: Seminar Press, pp. 73–92.

Wierzbicka, A. 1984. Apples are not a "kind of fruit": The semantics of human categorization. *American Ethnologist* 11:313–328.

Wierzbicka, A. 1986. Human emotions: Universal or culture specific? *American Anthropologist* 88:584–594.

21

Some Philosophical Issues in Cognitive Science: Qualia, Intentionality, and the Mind-Body Problem

Gilbert Harman

21.1 Mind-Body

This chapter is concerned with one of the most basic philosophical issues that arise in and around cognitive science, namely, whether science can in principle account for the relation between mind and body. A few other issues, with references to recent literature, are mentioned in section 21.5.

Science can tell us a great deal about vision. Light is reflected from an object and travels through space until it reaches the retina. Photons are absorbed and neurons fire, sending signals into the brain, signals that depend on the relative frequencies of the impinging light at various places on the retina and the relative intensity of this light on various places. Patterns are teased out of these data, and the patterns discerned on one retina are related to patterns on the other. Further processing occurs until, to make a long story short, at a key point there is a conscious visual experience accompanied by beliefs about the environment.

Although we have an increasingly better understanding of various stages in this sequence (Marr 1982), we do not know at what precise point the cascades of neuronal firing have an effect on consciousness and belief, nor do we know exactly how this effect is accomplished. Indeed it may be questioned whether we will ever be able to understand how mental phenomena can emerge from purely physical processes (Popper and Eccles 1977).

Nevertheless it is widely believed that mental phenomena are a special kind of physical phenomena. Crude behaviorism represents one form this opinion can take, holding that mental phenomena are behavioral dispositions or tendencies. In this view a pain in the big toe consists in a set of dispositions to favor the big toe in certain ways, including the disposition to act in ways that might remove the toe from extremes of temperature or pressure and the disposition to complain about the big toe. Similarly the belief that it is going to rain consists in dispositions to act as if it was going to rain, for example, the disposition to stay indoors or under cover and the disposition to take an umbrella or wear a raincoat on going out (Morris 1946).

Behaviorism of this simple sort seems to be too crude. The suggested analyses do not work. You can believe that it will rain without having a disposition to take an umbrella when you go out, because you may want to get wet. You may have a pain in your toe without having a disposition to complain or move your toe, because you may be a super spartan who does not want to give any sign of what you are feeling (Putnam 1980).

Many critics would object more controversially that behaviorism takes too external a view of the mental. According to these critics, mental states and processes are not behavioral dispositions, they are the internal states and processes that are responsible for relevant behavioral dispositions.

Now it seems clear that states and processes in the brain are responsible for behavioral dispositions. So the only way in which mental states and processes can be responsible for behavioral dispositions is for them to be the very same as the underlying physical states and processes that are responsible for those behavioral dispositions. If X = Z, and Y = Z, then X = Y. If pain equals what is responsible for pain behavior, and (to oversimplify matters) the firing of C-fibers equals what is responsible for pain behavior, then pain equals the firing of C-fibers (Lewis 1966).

A *type-type identity theory* holds that every type of mental experience, such as pain, is identical to a corresponding type of physical experience, such as the firing of C-fibers (Place 1956, Smart 1959). It is controversial whether this is an overly strong thesis, because of its implication that the physical basis for any type of mental event, such as pain, must be the same in different creatures. A weaker *functionalism* allows that pain might be the firing of C-fibers in people and a different event in other creatures. Functionalism holds that mental events of a certain sort are to be identified as those underlying events, whatever they are, that function in the relevant way. If the firing of C-fibers is responsible for pain behavior in people, but some other sort of event is responsible for pain behavior in cats, then the pain in people can be identified with the firing of their C-fibers, and pain in cats can be identified with the other sort of event (Putnam 1967).

According to functionalism, it does not matter what mental states and processes are made of any more than it matters what a carburetor or heart or a chess king is made of (Sellars 1954, Fodor 1968). What makes something a carburetor is not what color or shape it is or what it is made of but its function and the way it attains that function. A carburetor is a part of an engine that mixes the fuel with air before the mixture is exploded to power the engine. (A complete description of the way it attains this function would distinguish motors that use carburetors from motors that use a fuel injection system.) Any device that achieves its function in the relevant way counts as a carburetor, no matter what it is made of or what it looks like. A bodily organ is a heart if it functions in the relevant way to pump blood; it does not have to be heart shaped or made of a given material. There can be an artificial heart made of metal or plastic; similarly psychophysical functionalism allows for an artificial mind made of silicon.

To understand the nature of a given sort of mental state is to understand how that state functions. Desires function to specify a creature's goals. Beliefs function as its representation of the world. Perception functions to provide such representations of the immediate environment. Pain functions to warn of damage or extremes of pressure or temperature (Armstrong 1968).

An important aspect of functional notions is that they are defined in relation to a whole system of interdependent functions. To understand what a heart is, you have to understand its function as a pump, which requires understanding what the function of the circulation of blood is in relation to other functional processes. To understand what a carburetor is, you have to know how an internal combustion engine works; you need to see how the functioning of the carburetor fits in with the rest of the process. To understand what a king in chess is, you have to understand the role of the king in relation to the roles of the other pieces in chess—pawn, queen, rook, knight, and bishop. Similarly to understand how beliefs function, you have to understand how beliefs function in relation to desires, intentions, perception, emotion, and inference, given that a creature acts in ways that promise to achieve its goals given its beliefs (Harman 1973, Lycan 1987).

This is one reason why crude behaviorism must fail. A particular belief taken by itself cannot be identified with particular behavioral dispositions, because the relevant behavioral dispositions are determined by various beliefs taken together plus various desires and other mental states. Whether you are disposed to take your umbrella with you depends on not just your belief that it will rain but also your desire not to get wet, your perception of the umbrella in the corner, your further belief that umbrellas are good for keeping rain off, and so on.

Functionalism holds that mental states and events are precisely those states and events inside the head that have the relevant functions. Clearly this is to suppose that there are internal states and events that have such functions. Unlike crude behaviorism, functionalism is committed to a positive claim about internal processes.

So functionalism goes beyond crude behaviorism in at least two different ways. First, functionalism supposes that behavioral dispositions are the result of interactions between various mental states, where crude behaviorism assigns behavioral dispositions to individual mental states of belief or desire one by one. Second, functionalism attributes mental states and events to a creature only if there are appropriately functioning internal states, whereas crude behaviorism is willing to attribute mental states and beliefs given the relevant behavioral dispositions, no matter what internal states are responsible for these dispositions.

Must functionalism suppose that *all* beliefs and other psychological states are explicit functional states? Most people believe that the number of the earth's moons is less than twenty, also that the number of the earth's moons is less than ten. Although these are different beliefs, it is doubtful that they are realized in two distinct functional states, at least in people who have never contemplated these particular propositions.

One possible functionalist response is to hold that, strictly speaking, people do not normally believe that the number of the earth's moons is less than twenty until they actually consider this proposition and explicitly accept it. Until then the proposition is only implicit in what they actually believe. Or if that does violence to our ordinary ways of talking about belief, an equivalent response would be to allow such implicit beliefs to count as full-fledged beliefs, but to distinguish explicit functional beliefs from beliefs that are merely implicit in explicit beliefs (Harman 1978).

But then is it clear that all beliefs are either realized in explicit functional states or implicit in such explicit beliefs? Most people believe that giraffes do not wear overcoats in the wild. Is this belief implicit in their explicit functional beliefs? It is hard to find explicit functional beliefs that strictly *imply* this proposition (Dennett 1975). To take a different example, Ullman (1979) proposed that the processing responsible for the visual perception of motion involves the tacit assumption that most objects seen are rigid. This is not the proposal that the acceptance of this proposition plays a functional role in visual perception, nor is it the proposal that the proposition is implied by other propositions whose explicit acceptance plays a functional role in visual perception. The point is rather to claim that the relevant processes will yield appropriate representations of visual motion only if the objects seen tend to be rigid (Dennett 1986).

Consideration of these and other examples raises the possibility that beliefs and other psychological states are never themselves functional states, but are always tacit or implicit in other sorts of states and processes that cannot be identified with commonsense psychological states. This is the viewpoint of what I call *complex behaviorism*, which agrees in part with functionalism in holding that dispositions cannot be assigned to mental-event states taken one by one, but also agrees in part with crude behaviorism in rejecting the claim that mental states and processes must themselves play a real functional role instead of merely being implicit in other sorts of underlying states and processes (Dennett 1987).

Dennett (1983) claims that we can use attributions of mental states to people to predict and understand what they are doing without supposing that these states are functionally realized, just as we can attribute a center of gravity to a device and use that attribution to predict and understand the stability of the device without having to suppose that its center of gravity is made of a special material or has any other special intrinsic character.

So three possible answers to the mind-body problem are the type-type identity theory, psychophysical functionalism, and complex behaviorism. All three offer roughly the same answer to our question about the transition between the physical stimulation of the retina and the neurological processes that result on the one hand, and the ensuing visual experience and beliefs about the environment on the other hand. How can purely physical events and processes give rise to mental events and processes? Mental states and events result when the physical events and processes produce the relevant behavioral dispositions. Complex behaviorism identifies the mental states and events with the dispositions. The identity theory and functionalism identify the mental states and events with the physical causes of the dispositions.

We must now consider whether such identifications of mind and matter have any prospect of accounting for what is distinctively mental in mental states and experiences.

21.2 Intentionality

One important feature of mental states and experiences is that they can have content. They can represent things as being a certain way. Visual experience represents a large red tomato. A pain in the foot represents a disturbance as located in the foot. Fear that the boss is watching represents the boss as watching.

Certainly there are aspects of mental states that go beyond their content. Fear that the boss is watching and hope that the boss is watching may have the same representational content—that the boss is watching—but they are distinct attitudes toward that content. However, the content of a state is one of its important aspects.

The technical term *intentionality* is sometimes used in talking about the way in which mental states and experiences can be about something (Rosenthal 1986, Dennett 1987). Anything that a belief or experience is about counts as an *intentional object* of that belief or experience, and the way in which a belief or experience represents things constitutes its *intentional content*. One reason to use the qualification "intentional" is to allow for the possibility that the intentional object of an experience or mental state does not exist or that the intentional content of a mental state or experience is not true. You may hallucinate a pink lobster, worship a false god, and search for the fountain of youth; you can believe things that are not true; a white tie may look red to you in certain light; and the disturbance that causes the pain in your foot may actually be located in your back.[1]

Mental states and experiences have a nonderivative or "original"

Some Philosophical Issues in Cognitive Science

intentionality that contrasts with the derivative intentionality of a description expressed in language or a picture in a book (Haugeland 1981). The intentional contents of linguistic descriptions are due to the use of linguistic descriptions to express the speakers' thoughts and produce corresponding thoughts in audiences. The intentional contents of linguistic descriptions and therefore derivative from the intentional contents of the thoughts that the descriptions express and call to mind. But those thoughts do not have merely derivative content in this sense.

States of a computer can have intentional content, but it is controversial whether a computer can have states with the sort of original intentionality that mental states have. Some philosophers argue that we can attribute intentionality to the states of a computer only if and when the computer is used to produce something that we can interpret as meaningful. If we use the computer to perform some calculation and print out the result, then the printed out result has content that derives from the use we make of the printout; this in turn gives content to the internal representation of the answer in the computer and to the intermediate representations that arise in the course of the computer's processing.

On the other hand a computer might control a robot or other machinery without ever printing out results for human beings to read. The computer's procedures for doing this might well involve the use of inner representations of the task at hand, the resources to be used, the states of the environment, and so forth. Would these representations have the sort of nonderivative intentionality that mental states and experiences have?

Consider a simpler example (Dennett 1981). A thermometer measures temperature by the amount of bending in a bimetalic strip of metal attached to an indicator of the temperature in degrees Celsius. Here there is derivative intentionality: The position of the indicator indicates that the temperature is 15° because the position of indicator can communicate such information to a human being. On the other hand if the same sort of bimetalic strip is used in a thermostat controlling an air conditioner, a sufficient curving in the strip will open an electrical contact and turn off the air conditioner. The opening of the electrical contact in this way has the intentional content that the room is now cool enough, but not because of any message to a human operator. The relevant states of the thermostat do not have derivative content in the way in which the relevant states of the thermometer have derivative content.

This is not to suggest that a thermostat has beliefs about the temperature or even that it has any real awareness of the temperature, only that there is a clear sense in which it has states with nonderivative intentional content.

Some philosophers would object that there is still an important sense in which the thermostat has derivative content: All that is meant by attributing content to the opening of electrical contact is that we find it useful or attractive to interpret the thermostat this way. It has content only from a third-person perspective, whereas mental states and experiences have content from a first-person perspective. Your mental states and experiences have content for you and not just for observers of you. The opening of the electrical contact has no content for the thermostat in this view (Searle 1980, 1983).

But this is not obviously correct. Even if the opening of the electrical contact has no content for the thermostat, it does have content for the temperature control system that includes the air conditioner and the thermostat, because the opening of the electrical contact turns off the air conditioner. Furthermore the content does in a sense have a first-person perspective, because the content is not just that it is cool somewhere but "cool enough near me (the air conditioning system) that I can stop cooling the air."

The states in an air conditioning system have intentional content because of the way the states function to keep the room within a particular range of temperatures. Similarly the more complex representations used in a computer controlling a robot might have intentional content because of the way these representations function. This leaves open whether the intentionality of mental states and processes involves anything further.

Searle (1980) argues that mental intentionality involves more than the sort of intentionality that can be attributed to components in an intentional system such as an air conditioner or a robot. Suppose we have a complete functional specification of the internal processes responsible for the behavior of a speaker of Chinese in the form of a computer simulation. The instructions in this program are translated into English so that they can be followed by people who know only English and no Chinese. When English speakers follow these instructions, they start with Chinese input, which they process by forming various representations and performing operations on those representations in accordance with their instructions, until finally they are led to react as a speaker of Chinese would to the input given. Searle observes that being able to follow such instructions would not be sufficient to provide English speakers with an understanding of Chinese. While the English speakers followed the instructions, they would make use of various representations that had intentional content in the functional sense without these representations having any true mental intentionality. Furthermore in Searle's view if we replace the English speakers with an appropriately programmed computer controlling a robot speaker of Chinese, the robot would have no more understanding of Chinese than the English speakers. The mental life of the robot would be as blank as that of the thermostatically controlled air conditioner, even though in both cases we can attribute intentionality to internal states on the basis of functional considerations.

That is Searle's view. Others have thought that Searle's conclusion must be mistaken: A robot whose behavioral dispositions are sufficiently similar to a person's will have a similar mental life, especially if there is a sufficient functional similarity between the robot and a person. In this view the difference between the thermostatically controlled air conditioner and a person is therefore merely one of degree (Dennett 1981, Bennett 1964, 1976).

If the robot's behavioral dispositions were sufficiently similar to those of a person, there would seem to be just as much reason to suppose the robot has a mental life as to suppose this of the person. Searle (1980) uses his Chinese room argument to deny this. He argues that if a large robot had the relevant behavioral dispositions because it contained a room with an English-speaking person who ran around inside following the instructions of the program that simulated a Chinese speaker, that would not be enough for the person to understand Chinese and, according to Searle, it would not be enough for the large robot that contained the person to understand anything either. So, according to Searle, by parity of reasoning we must deny that a computer-controlled robot could understand anything.

What justifies attributing a mental life to other people if behavioral dispositions are not sufficient? Searle (1983) answers that you reason by analogy with your own case. You know directly that you have a mental life and you have reason to think that this is connected with your having a functioning brain of such and such a sort. Because other people have functioning brains of the relevant sort, you are justified in supposing that they have a mental life like yours. The trouble with the imagined robot, according to Searle, is that its brain (that is, its computer) would not be made of the right sort of stuff. So Searle ends up with a type-type identity theory.

Again that is Searle's view. Defenders of behaviorism, functionalism, and interpretivism reject Searle's Chinese room argument. They argue that a robot that is functionally isomorphic to a Chinese speaker will understand Chinese, even if it turns out that the internal processing is carried out by one or more English speakers running around inside the robot, carrying out the instructions in an internal program. The little people inside do not understand Chinese, but the system to which they contribute does. Searle thinks the system reply is clearly wrong, but others disagree. In fact it is not clear how different ordinary people are from Chinese rooms staffed by hoards of dumb little creatures. Our brains work as they do because they are full of tiny little organisms (brain cells) that stupidly follow certain limited principles!

21.3 Qualia

Let us turn to a related issue. Consider what it is like to see the world in color. Now imagine what it would be like to have the same experiences but with different colors, green replacing red, blue replacing orange, and so on throughout the spectrum. Finally, suppose Alice sees the world in the first way, and Bert sees the world in the second way. If this has always been true for Alice and Bert, there may be no easy way to discover it. They will use color terms in the same way for the same external things, calling grass green and ripe tomatoes red even though ripe tomatoes look to Alice the way fresh grass looks to Bert, and vice versa. The difference between them need not be reflected in their behavioral dispositions or the functional characteristics of the states that arise from looking at fresh grass. The difference may lie only in the quality of their visual experiences.

This line of thought forms the basis of a controversial objection to functionalism and complex behaviorism: Because such views cannot distinguish Alice's experience from Bert's, it is claimed that they cannot account for the most important aspect of experience, namely, its qualitative character. This objection is sometimes called the objection from *inverted qualia*, whereas Searle's objection is a form of the objection from *absent qualia* (Fodor and Block 1972), because Searle argues that it is all blank inside the robot—no qualia of any sort at all.

It turns out to be very difficult to assess the inverted-qualia objection, because it is unclear what qualia are supposed to be—qualities of experience or qualities of experienced objects. The issue is quite complicated. But it seems to me that proponents of the inverted-qualia objection are faced with a dilemma. If qualia are supposed to be qualities of experienced objects, then functionalism and complex behaviorism can deny the possibility of inverted qualia without embarrassment. On the other hand if qualia are supposed to be qualities of experience, there is no reason to think that they are of any mental or psychological significance. The apparent power of the qualia objection rests on not clearly distinguishing these two possibilities. Let me explain.

Are Alice and Bert supposed to be aware of their qualia? When they look at a nice ripe tomato, what qualities are they aware of? In the first instance they are aware of certain features of the tomato. They are not obviously presented with simple features of their experience. The quality that Alice would describe as "red" is presented to her as a feature of the tomato, not as a feature of her experience. Similarly the quality that Bert would describe as "red" is presented to him as a feature of the tomato.

This suggests taking qualia to be qualities of the (presented) tomato. On this interpretation of the qualia objection, we are to suppose that Alice's experience presents her with a tomato possessing feature X and Bert's experience presents him with a tomato presenting feature Y instead. When the two of them look at grass, the opposite is true; Alice's experience presents her with grass possessing feature Y, and Bert's experience presents him with grass possessing feature X.

This interpretation fits in with the thought that tomatoes look to Alice

Some Philosophical Issues in Cognitive Science

the way grass looks to Bert, and vice versa. To say that tomatoes look a certain way to Alice is to say that her experience presents tomatoes as having a certain feature, namely, the feature that Bert's experience presents grass as having.

But then there is a further consequence. If this is a situation of normal perception in the sense that Alice and Bert both take the environment to be as they perceive it to be, then Alice believes that the tomato has the feature that it looks to her to have, and Bert believes the tomato has the feature that it looks to him to have. So they have different beliefs about the tomato. Bert thinks the tomato is Y and not X, and Alice thinks the tomato is X and not Y.

Moreover because they use the word *red* to express their beliefs, Alice means X by *red* and Bert means Y. So a consequence of this interpretation of the inverted-qualia objection, is that Alice and Bert mean different things by the word *red*, even though they use these terms in exactly the same way in talking about objects in the world! But this is absurd. Something has gone wrong.

It seems we must agree that Alice and Bert mean the same thing by the word *red*. Furthermore because their words are used to express their beliefs, they have the same beliefs about the color of the tomato. But isn't it still possible that the tomato looks different to Bert from the way it looks to Alice? No. This is not possible because of the functional connection between perceptual experience and belief. Normally one trusts the way things look—one takes the way things look to be a good guide to the way they are. If the way a ripe tomato looks to Alice leads her to the same belief that the way a ripe tomato looks to Bert leads him to, then the tomato must look the same to each, because in the normal case they form their beliefs by simply accepting the way things look as the way things are.

So to summarize this part of the dilemma I see, if qualia are taken as properties of the presented object of experience, we can accept the possibility of inverted qualia despite similar dispositions and functional states only if we are prepared to allow for "inverted meanings" despite similar usage of color words. Or to put the point the other way round, because the meanings of color words are determined by what objects in the world these words are applied to, there cannot be inverted qualia in this first sense.

On the other hand if qualia are taken to be features of particular experiences (rather than features of the presented objects of particular experiences), then it is question begging to assume that they are relevant to experience qua experience. Consider low-level physical properties of particular experiences. Suppose that red light falling on Alice's retina causes physical events X, and green light falling on her retina causes physical events Y, whereas this is reversed for Bert: red light causes physical events Y in his eye, and green light causes physical events X (Lycan 1973, Shoemaker 1982). It begs the question to suppose that a mere physical difference must make a relevant mental difference, because that is precisely the issue between the type-type identity theory on the one hand and functionalism and complex behaviorism on the other hand.

If qualia are supposed to be features of particular experiences of which we are aware (as opposed to physical features of which we are normally unaware), then the difficulty is that we just don't seem to be aware of the right features. Alice may be aware of such intentional features of her experience as that it is the experience of seeing a ripe red tomato. But she is not obviously aware of those features of her experience by virtue of which it is an experience with that intentional feature. In other words she is not obviously aware of any "mental paint" that leads her experience to be a representation of a nearby tomato.

If it is objected that the red Alice is aware of must be a feature of something mental because she can be aware of it even when there is no physical tomato before her (if she is having a hallucination, for example), that is just a version of the fallacious "argument from illusion" for the infamous sense datum theory of perception. (The sense datum theory holds that tomatoes and grass are perceived only indirectly via the direct perception of mental representations.) This reasoning looks attractive only if you fail to notice that the object of awareness is an intentional object, which need not exist (Anscombe 1965, Quine 1960, Armstrong 1961, 1968). In the case of hallucination Alice is aware of something red, but the red thing is a nonexistent physical thing rather than an existent mental thing.

The fallacy in the argument from illusion can be brought into the open by considering an analogous argument concerning Ponce de Leon's search for the fountain of youth. "He was definitely looking for something. But nothing in the world can be identified with what he was looking for. So he must have been looking for something mental." This is obviously wrong. The object of his search was a real physical fountain of youth. Alas, there is no such thing. Similarly what Alice sees or seems to see when she hallucinates is the redness of a tomato. Maybe there is no redness in the world before her, but that does not mean she sees mental redness. It only means that she is seeing (or seeming to see) something that does not exist.

So any apparent plausibility to the inverted qualia objection must be because of confusing the redness of the presented apple with a feature of experience that represents that redness. If that confusion is avoided, there is no reason at all to suppose that Alice and Bert are in any way aware of relevant features of their experiences. Their experiences may well have inverted physical features with respect to each other, but it begs the question to suppose that such an inversion has any experiential significance.[2]

The experience of pains and other sensations may seem at first to involve the awareness of intrinsic qualities of experience, but here too it is important to distinguish qualities of the intentional object of experience from qualities of the experience itself (Armstrong 1962). When you have a pain in your leg, you are aware of features of something in your leg, but your experience is not in your leg. If anywhere it is in your head.

So-called objectless emotions might be thought to be cases in which you are aware of intrinsic qualities of your experience that cannot be qualities of the object of experience. But these are really examples of experiences with *indefinite* objects. The content of an objectless fear might be roughly expressed in words as *something bad is going to happen*.

Therefore there is no force to the inverted-qualia objection against functionalism and complex behaviorism.

21.4 Subjective-Objective

We must still briefly consider a last worry about all three of these views, type-type identity theory, functionalism, and complex behaviorism, indeed a worry about cognitive science in general. The worry is that any scientific approach to the mind must view mental states from the outside, from an objective third-person point of view. But it seems that there are important aspects of mental life that cannot be understood from that perspective and that can only be understood from a subjective first-person perspective. For example, although an objective third-person account of neural events, functional relations, and behavioral dispositions may give a complete characterization of certain aspects of pain, it cannot indicate how pain feels. Someone who does not know what pain feels like will still not know after reading a completely functional account of pain. Similarly a person blind from birth may know everything objective about visual perception, including all the behavioral and functional facts, without having the faintest idea what it is like to see the color red (Dilthey 1910, Nagel 1974, 1986, Jackson 1982, 1986).

I think that this is right, but it does not mean that cognitive science cannot account for what is distinctively mental in mental states and experiences. Notice that a similar point can be made in connection with the theory of meaning. It seems that the meaning of a word in a language is determined by the way that word is used (Sellars 1954, Harman 1987). But a completely objective description of the use of any given word may not be sufficient to indicate what the term means. For example, the use of certain words might be explained via the role they play in immediately recognizable implications in the language and in immediately recognizable inconsistencies, where we might say that two sentences immediately exclude each other if it is immediately obvious that they are inconsistent with each other (Harman 1986). Now consider a one-place sentential operator N whose use is explained as follows: "For every sentence A, N(A) and A immediately exclude each other, and each is immediately implied by anything that immediately excludes the other." What does that operator mean? Supposing that it is a negation operator, is it ordinary (classical) negation or some special (for example, intuitionistic) negation? The answers to these questions are not evident if you are given only this sort of description of use.

On the other hand if you can translate a word into your own way of talking, for example, if you know that N can be translated into your language as *not* (or as *it is not the case that*), then you know what it means. In fact it seems that no matter what you know about the objective facts of usage, you will not understand a term until you learn how to use it yourself or how to translate it into your language (Quine 1960). So the empathetic understanding that is needed for full psychological understanding is similar to the need for translation in semantics. A person blind from birth cannot understand what it is to see something red because there is no way to translate that experience into something with which the blind person is familiar.

To repeat, this is not an argument against type-type identity theory, functionalism, complex behaviorism, or cognitive science in general. The point is rather that these views do not imply that you can acquire a full understanding of another person's mental life simply by coming to know that person's behavioral dispositions and the underlying causal or functional explanation of those dispositions. These views are compatible with their being a further understanding that can be achieved only by imagining what it is like to experience things as the other person does. We gain this sort of understanding only by coming to be able to translate another person's experience into our own, just as we gain a further understanding of another person's word when we figure out how to translate it into our words.

Can science ever tell us how the various neural activities of the eye and brain can give rise to visual experience? Perhaps it can by telling us about how these activities function in response to the environment to give a person information about the environment that can be used in deciding how to act. It may someday be able to tell us all about the underlying neural activities and the complex behavioral dispositions that these activities give rise to. Such an account could specify what makes states and processes mental states and processes, even though what it says would be insufficient to tell a blind person what it is like to see something red.

21.5 Some Other Philosophical Issues

This chapter has been concerned with some of the issues centering around the mind-body problem. There are other relevant aspects to this problem. For example, there are questions about free will (Dennett 1984, Strawson 1986).

Furthermore the mind-body problem is not the only way in which current philosophy connects with cognitive science. For example, philosophical epistemology is concerned with perception, memory, and reasoning. Goldman (1986) provides a good account of the subject that locates it in relation to work in psychology and artificial intelligence. Harman (1986) discusses a number of issues in reasoning and belief revision. Holland and colleagues (1986) develop accounts of covariation detection and scientific reasoning. Planning, intention, and practical reasoning are taken up by Bratman (1987) and Wilson (1989). Stich and Nisbett (1980) and Cohen (1981) discuss whether psychological experiments by Kahneman, Tversky, and others (Kahneman et al. 1982, Nisbett and Ross 1980) demonstrate instances of human failure or irrationality.

There are also philosophical questions of methodology. In particular Fodor (1980) and Stich (1983) argue that explanations in cognitive science are or should be conceived purely "syntactically," or "solipsistically," that is, without reference to an organism's environment. Harman (1988) argues on the contrary that cognitive activities cannot be understood without seeing how they function in the life of an organism that interacts with its environment.

A related methodological question concerns the relation between cognitive science and ordinary views. Commonsense folk psychology holds that people act from their beliefs and their desires, that is, they act to satisfy their desires in the light of their beliefs, they form plans and intentions that they then attempt to carry out. How does this picture fit in with cognitive science? Will a mature cognitive science refer to desires, beliefs, and other familiar psychological states? A number of philosophers have argued that an adequate cognitive science must abandon such notions as desire and belief. See Paul Churchland 1979, 1981, Patricia Churchland 1986, Stich 1983, and (for an argument on the other side) Baker 1987. This view conflicts with the type-type identity theory and with the psychophysical functionalism discussed in this chapter, and implies that there are no such things as beliefs and desires unless a complex behavioristic view is correct as in Dennett 1987.

Finally, there is philosophy of language and philosophical logic, which blend into linguistic semantics. LePore 1987 contains a number of survey articles and position papers with many references to other recent work.

Notes

The preparation of this paper was supported in part by research grants to Princeton University from the James S. McDonnell Foundation and the National Science Foundation (under NSF grant number IST8503968).

1. Some accounts of intentionality explain content or meaning in terms of *possible* (that is, not necessarily actual) objects, situations, or worlds. See chapter 6.

2. Similarly in discussing imagery, it is important not to confuse properties of what is imagined with properties of the experience of imagination. People rotate images in the sense that they imagine things rotating (Shepard and Metzler 1971). It does not follow that people rotate mental representations that serve as the vehicles of their imagery (Pylyshyn 1981). People can imagine scanning a scene (Kosslyn 1983), and perhaps that is to scan the imagined scene. But it is important not to confuse the imagined scene with a postulated mental representation of that scene. To scan an imagined scene is not necessarily to scan a mental picture. It may be merely to imagine scanning a scene.

References

Anscombe, G. E. M. 1965. The intentionality of sensation: A grammatical feature. In R. J. Butler, ed. *Analytical Philosophy*. 2nd series. Oxford: Blackwell. Reprinted in Anscombe, G. E. M. 1981. *Metaphysics and the Philosophy of Mind: Collected Philosophical Papers, Volume II*. Minneapolis: University of Minnesota Press, pp. 3–20.

Armstrong, D. M. 1961. *Perception and the Physical World*. London: Routledge and Kegan Paul.

Armstrong, D. M. 1962. *Bodily Sensations*. London: Routledge and Kegan Paul.

Armstrong, D. M. 1968. *A Materialist Theory of the Mind*. London: Routledge and Kegan Paul.

Baker, L. R. 1987. *Saving Belief: A Critique of Physicalism*. Princeton, NJ: Princeton University Press.

Bennett, J. 1964. *Rationality*. London: Routledge and Kegan Paul.

Bennett, J. 1976. *Linguistic Behaviour*. Cambridge, Engl.: Cambridge University Press.

Bratman, M. 1987. *Intention, Plans, and Practical Reason*. Cambridge, MA: Harvard University Press.

Churchland, P. M. 1979. *Scientific Realism and the Plasticity of Mind*. Cambridge, Engl: Cambridge University Press.

Churchland, P. M. 1981. Eliminative materialism and the propositional attitudes. *Journal of Philosophy* 78:67–90.

Churchland, P. S. 1986. *Neurophilosophy: Toward a Unified Science of the Mind/Brain*. Cambridge, MA: MIT Press.

Cohen, L. J. 1981. Can human irrationality be experimentally demonstrated? *Brain and Behavioral Sciences* 4:317–331.

Dennett, D. C. 1975. Brain writing and mind reading. In K. Gunderson, ed. *Language, Mind, and Meaning: Minnesota Studies in the Philosophy of Science, VII*. Minneapolis: University of Minnesota Press.

Dennett, D. C. 1981. True believers. In A. F. Heath, ed. *Scientific Explanation*. Oxford: Oxford University Press. Reprinted in Dennett 1987.

Dennett, D. C. 1983. Intentional systems in cognitive ethology: The "Panglossian paradigm" defended. *Behavioral and Brain Sciences* 6:343–390. Reprinted in Dennett 1987.

Dennett, D. C. 1984. *Elbow Room*. Cambridge, MA: MIT Press.

Dennett, D. C. 1986. Remarks in discussion in Pylyshyn, Zenon, and Demopoulos, eds. *Meaning and Cognitive Structure: Issues in the Computational Theory of Mind*. Norwood, NJ: Ablex.

Dennett, D. C. 1987. *The Intentional Stance*. Cambridge, MA: MIT Press.

Dilthey, W. 1910. *Der Aufbau der geistegen Welt in der Geisteswissenshaften*. Reprinted as *Gessammelte Schriften*. Vol. 7. Leipzig and Berlin: Teubner, 1927. Selections translated in H. P. Rickman, ed. *Meaning in History*. London: Allen, 1961.

Fodor, J. A. 1968. *Psychological Explanation*. New York: Random House.

Fodor, J. A. 1980. Methodological solipsism considered as a research strategy in cognitive psychology. *Behavioral and Brain Sciences* 3:63–73.

Fodor, J. A., and Block, N. 1972. What psychological states are not. *Philosophical Review* 81:159–181.

Goldman, A. I. 1986. *Epistemology and Cognition*. Cambridge, MA: Harvard University Press.

Harman, G. 1973. *Thought*. Princeton, NJ: Princeton University Press.

Harman, G. 1978. Is there mental representation? In C. W. Savage, ed. *Perception and Cognition: Issues in the Foundations of Psychology. Minnesota Studies in the Philosophy of Science*. Vol. 9. Minneapolis: University of Minnesota Press, pp. 57–64.

Harman, G. 1986. *Change in View*. Cambridge, MA: MIT Press.

Harman, G. 1987. (Nonsolipsistic) conceptual role semantics. In E. LePore, ed. *New Directions in Semantics*. London: Academic Press, pp. 55–81.

Harman, G. 1988. Wide functionalism. In. S. Schiffer and S. Steele, eds. *Cognition and Representation*. Boulder, CO: Westview Press, pp. 11–20.

Haugeland, J. 1981. *Mind Design*. Cambridge, MA: MIT Press.

Holland, J. H., Holyoak, K. J., Nisbett, R. E., and Thagard, P. R. 1986. *Induction: Processes of Inference, Learning, and Discovery*. Cambridge, MA: MIT Press.

Jackson, F. 1982. Epiphenomenal qualia. *Philosophical Quarterly* 32:127–132.

Jackson, F. 1986. What Mary didn't know. *Journal of Philosophy* 83:291–295.

Kahneman, D., Soliv, P., and Tversky, A. 1982. *Judgment under uncertainty: Heuristics and Biases*. New York: Cambridge University Press.

Kosslyn, S. 1983. *Ghosts in the Mind's Machine*. New York: Norton.

LePore, E. 1987. *New Directions in Semantics*. London: Academic Press.

Lewis, D. 1966. An argument for the identity theory. *Journal of Philosophy* 63:17–25.

Lycan, W. G. 1973. Inverted spectrum. *Ratio* 15:315–319.

Lycan, W. G. 1987. *Consciousness*. Cambridge, MA: MIT Press.

Marr, D. 1982. *Vision*. Cambridge, MA: MIT Press.

Morris, C. 1946. *Signs, Language, and Behavior*. New York: Braziller.

Nagel, T. 1974. What is it like to be a bat? *Philosophical Review* 83:435–450.

Nagel, T. 1986. *The View from Nowhere*. New York: Oxford University Press.

Nisbett, R., and Ross, L. 1980. *Human Inference: Strategies and Shortcomings of Social Judgment*. Englewood Cliffs, NJ: Prentice-Hall.

Place, U. T. 1956. Is consciousness a brain process? *British Journal of Psychology* 47:44–50.

Poppler and Eccles. 1977. *The Self and Its Brain*. London: Routledge and Kegan Paul.

Putnam, H. 1967. Psychological predicates. In W. H. Capitan and D. D. Merrill, eds. *Art, Mind, and Religion*. Pittsburgh: University of Pittsburgh Press, pp. 37–48.

Putnam, H. 1980. Brains and behavior. In N. Block, ed. *Readings in the Philosophy of Psychology*. Vol. 1. Cambridge, MA: Harvard University Press.

Pylyshyn, Z. 1981. The imagery debate: Analog media versus tacit knowledge. In N. Block, ed. *Imagery*. Cambridge, MA: MIT Press, pp. 151–206.

Quine, W. V. 1960. *Word and Object*. Cambridge, MA: MIT Press.

Rosenthal, D. 1986. Intentionality. *Midwest Studies in Philosophy* 10:151–184.

Searle, J. 1980. Minds, brains, and programs. *Behavioral and Brain Sciences* 3:417–457.

Searle, J. 1983. *Intentionality, an Essay in the Philosophy of Mind*. Cambridge, Engl.: Cambridge University Press.

Sellars, W. 1954. Reflections on language games. *Philosophy of Science* 21:204228.

Shepard, R. N., and Metzler, S. 1971. Mental rotation of three dimensional objects. *Science* 171:701–703.

Shoemaker, S. 1982. The inverted spectrum. *Journal of Philosophy* 79:357–381.

Smart, J. J. C. 1959. Sensations and brain processes. *Philosophical Review* 68:141–156.

Stich, S. 1983. *From Folk Psychology to Cognitive Science*. Cambridge, MA: MIT Press.

Stich, S., and Nisbett, R. 1980. Justification and the psychology of human reasoning. *Philosophy of Science.* 47:188–202.

Strawson, G. 1986. *Freedom and Belief.* Oxford: Clarendon Press.

Ullman, S. 1979. *The Interpretation of Visual Motion.* Cambridge, MA: MIT Press.

Wilson, G. 1989. *The Intentionality of Human Action.* Revised ed. Los Angeles: University of California Press.

Author Index

Note: Italicized page numbers indicate illustrations.

Subject Index

Note: Italicized page numbers indicate illustrations.

Artificial intelligence (AI) (cont.)
and computer simulation, 29–31
and parallel distributed processing, 707–710
research in, 4
Association structures
expert/novice, 564, 565
Associative structures, use of, 4
Associative interference theory, 685–686
Asymmetric transfer, 557
Attention, 651–654
and behavioral coherence, 652
bias, 277
construct of, 250
engagement, 652–653
focus, 40
and limited capacity, 632–642
selective, 648–649
state, 445
Attractors, in task-dynamics framework, 733–736
Attributes, 795
independent effect of, 801
Attributive descriptions, 447
Aufgabe, 11
Augmented transition networks, 190
Autoencoding, of pattern set, 155
Automatic processes, vs. controlled, 639–640
Automatization, 101, 555
Automaton(a)
components of, 166–167
types of, 167
Autonomy, in computer architecture, 108–109
Availability, 521
Available state, 536

Backpropagation, 752
learning procedure, 153–156
Backup strategy, and search process, 537–539
Backward chaining, 455, 538
Baptismal-causal theories, 808
Base, in lexical meaning, 795–797
Basic Color Terms (Berlin and Kay), 814
Basic-level categories, 801
Basic object, 802
Bayesian inference, theory of, 5
Behavior
automatic, 101

controlled, 101
determination of, 97–98
Behavioral indeterminacy claim, 82–85
Behaviorism
and cognitive performance, 3
dominance of, 161
Best-match, 147–148, 186
Between-subjects experimental design, 248
Binding theory, 182
consequences of, 183
principles of, 182
Binocular stereo, 593–601
Biology, and language acquisition, 364–365
Biological motor displays, 608
Blackboard control structure, 69
Body, 454
Boltzmann methods, 42
Bottom-up, defined, 610
Bootstrapping
correlational, 377–378
into language, 377–379
prosodic, 378
semantic, 378–379
Boundary conditions, need for, 37
Boundary technique, *421–422*
Boundary tracing, 616
Brain
anatomical techniques for, 320–338
architecture, 303
cognition, 301–356
computation, 134–136
laminar organization of, 312–315, *313*
lesions, 703–704
medial view of, *308*
physiological techniques for, 320–338
Brain systems
and correlations between neurons, 308–310
reciprocal connections between, 308

Cardinality, 241
Case markings, and *wh*-questions, 171–172
Categorical encoding, and selective response, 657–658
Categorical grammar, 195–196
Categories, 273
exclusivity of, 28

scope of, 28
of structural organization, 305, *306*
Categorization, and induction, 515–521
Causal analysis, 521
in larger discourse units, 284–285
Causal effects, isolating, 248–249
c-command, 182
Cell, receptive field of, 341
Centering theory, 447
Central executive, concept of, 118, 687
Central nervous system (CNS)
and inverse dynamics, 776
and movement planning, 769–770
and positions/forces, 776
Cf (forward-looking center), 447
Change operators, vs. inference rules, 18–19
Checklist, as mediating structure, 812
"Chomsky hierarchy," 363
Chopping rules, 173–174
Chunking, 111
central role of, 125
and EPAM model, 126
as form of tuning, 543
Soar's, 115
Chunks, 9, 271
as unit of measurement for memory capacity, 567
Church's theorem, 227
Circumscription, theory of, 455
Classical computational architecture, 57
Classical view
of computers and cognition, 56–61
of concepts, 502–503
objections to, 61–62
Classification systems, effect of memory, 815
Clue words, 443
Clustering, 259
Coarticulation, 737
Code, 256
Coding categories
derivation of, 24
strategies for developing, 23
"Codon" scheme, 619
Cognition
architecture of, 96–99
and the brain, 301–356
classical view of, 56–61
invariance in laws of, 38–43

"standard" model of, 9–10
stimulus-independence of, 77–78
symbolic architectures for, 93–131
Cognitive architecture, 72
adequate theory of, 126–128
algorithms and, 72–78
hidden connections in, 125–126
known functions of, 102–103
levels of, 57
nature of, 102–109
requirements on, 99–101
uses of, 120–126
Cognitive behavior, form of simple, 123–125
Cognitive economy, 805
Cognitive mechanisms, neurobiological constraints on, 339–341
Cognitive neuroscience, as interdisciplinary, 344
Cognitive penetrability, 81–82
Cognitive performance, as kind of program, 253
Cognitive processes, experiments on human, 253–255
Cognitive research, methods of, 20–38
Cognitive science
computational methodologies in, 62–78
defined, 2
disciplines contributing to, 2–7
domain of, 85–86
experimental methods in, 245–300
goals of, 1–2
influence of computing on, 51
and language acquisition, 361–371
methodology in, 844
philosophical issues in, 831–848
role of architecture in, 93–99
Cognitive Science, 32
Cognitive Science Society, 6
Cognitive social psychology, 6–7
Cognitive truth, notion of, 227
Coindexing, 181
Collaborative Activation-based Production System (CAPS), 30
Color, in cross-cultural research, 813–815
Coloring, defined, 616
Columns, in brain organization, *314–315*
Communication accuracy, 813
Compactness measure, 618

Context-sensitive allophones, 737–738
Context-sensitive grammars, 164–165
Context units
  in sequential performance, *154*
  in sequential recognition, *155*
Contextual information, 375–377
Continuity constraint, 597
Contrast rule, 506
Contrast set, 798
Control
  analysis of, in LFG, 189
  flow of, 67
  hierarchy of, 68
  phenomenon of, 368
Control of action, selective, visual, 662
Control structures, 10, 11–12
  classes of, 11
  distinctions in, 68–69
Control system, 747–746
Controlled behavior, 101
Controlled experiments, 247–249
Converging evidence, 252
Conversationally relevant descriptions, 447
Cooccurrence restrictions, 169, 171
Coordinate conjunction, 192–193
Coordinates, hand vs. joint, in movement planning, 770–774, *772*
Coordination
  of attentional system, 652
  of categories of action, 649
  as conjunction of constituents, 196
Coordinative structures, and synergies, 730–732
Core, 509–510
Correlational studies, 246–247
Correspondence, levels of, 70–72
Cover story, varying, and difficulty, 555
Credit assignment problem, 544
Creoles, 366
Cross-domain cueing, 637
Crosstalk interference, 638
Crude behaviorism, 831–833
  and functionalism, 833–834
c-structure, 186
Cue phrases, 443–444
Cue specificity, 265
Cued recall, 265, 292
Cultural cognition, 795–830
  study of, 825
Cultural models, 809–813
  as little programs, 824–825

use of, 823–824
Cultural Models in Language and Thought (Holland and Quinn), 811
Culture, as inert, 824
Cyclic node, vs. bounding node, 200
CYRUS, 709

Decision cycle, Soar's, 116
Decision heuristics, 521
Declarative memory, 702
  Act*'s, 112
  storage in, 115
Declarative sentences, focus on, 214
Decoding hypothesis, 66
Decoding productions, 118
Decomposition, as goal, 255
Deep dyslexics, 412
Deep structure, 170
Defining properties, failure to specify, 503
Definition, problem of, 795–797
Degrees-of-freedom problem, 728–736
  approaching, 730–731
  integrated treatment of, 757–758
Deixis, 460
  types of, 448
  use of, 448
Delta rule, 141
Demonstrations, defined, 342
Demonstratives, 228
Density of data, as theme, 37
Dependencies, in memory structure, 104
Dependent variable, 247
Derivational theory of complexity, 190
Descriptive formalism, and functional architecture, 73
Designation, as core idea of computing, 55
Designed languages, 216–219
Development, and general learning, 108
Developmental changes, causes of, 382–390
Developmental psycholinguistics, 365–371
  and innate constraints, 370–371
  and productivity, 367–386
  and structure dependence, 368–370
Difference reduction heuristics, 538
Differentiation, and edge detection, 586–587
Digital computer, 94–96, *95*

Images
  and node-link structures, 20
  vs. propositions, 19–20
Imaging techniques, 326–330
Immediate focus, 447
Impasse, 12, 550
  in Soar, 117
Implicature, theory of, 457
Implicit memory, 695–698
Incremental recognition techniques,
    456–457
Incremental reference evaluation,
    concept of, 450
Incremental rigidity scheme, 609
Independence, doctrine of, 303
Independent variable, 247
Indeterminacy
  and degrees-of-freedom problem,
    729
  and direct inverse modeling, 751
Indexicals, 228, 230
Indexing, as type of shifting, 615
Induction
  categorization as form of, 516
  in concept learning, 273
Inductive inference, defined, 516
Inference, 226–228, 475. *See also*
    Reasoning
  content-specific rule of, 476
Inference rules, vs. change operators,
    18–19
Inferential capacity, as systematic,
    62
Information, minimizing loss of, 26–
    27
Information processing abilities, 383–
    384
Inner environment, invariants of, 39–
    40
Input units
  defined, 138
  in sequential recognition, *155*
Inputs
  Act*'s vs. Soar's, 119
Insight problems, 527
Instantiation, 547
Integration, process of, 693
Intelligence, and adaptivity, 43
Intelligent systems
  architecture of, 7–14
  kinds of, 39–40
Intended recognition, notion of, 455
Intentional content, 835
Intentional object, 835

Intentionality, 835–838
  derivative, 836
  and functionalism, 837
  of language and thought, 207
  "original," 835
Interaction
  Act*'s vs. Soar's, 117–119
  and combination, 37–38
Intercoder reliability, 28
Interference, 259
  defined, 657
  and spatial selection, 658
Intermediate level, theories of, 6
Intermediate-level vision
  properties of, 612–613
  and visual routines, 610–616
Intermediate states, 78
Internal simulation, 735
Interpretation
  Act*'s vs. Soar's, 115–117
  basic loop of, *106*
  process of, 693
Interpretation function, 240
Interpretivism, 177
Interrupt mechanism, 107
  Act*'s vs. Soar's, 119
Interrupting questions, as perfor-
    mance measure, 289–290
Intonation, and discourse structure,
    444–445
Intransitive clauses, types of, 185
Introspection, 21
Intrusion errors, 266
Intuition, 41
Invariants, empirically observed, 40–
    41, 617–618
Inverse dynamics problem, 774
Inverted meanings, 840
Ion channels, 320, *322*
IPSPs (inhibitory postsynaptic poten-
    tials), 304
ISAAC system, 17
Island constraints, 180, 199
  formulation of, 173–174
Isomorphic problems, 555

Judgment tasks, 268–269
  in language processing, 279–280
Judgment times, 258

Katz-Postal hypothesis, 176–177
"Keyhole recognition," 452
Knowledge, as built into processor,
    136

Knowledge level, 8, 38, 57, 60, 96, 97–98
Knowledge-based learning tasks, 276–278
Knowledge-lean problem solving, 528–529, 530–544

Lagrangian formulations, 775
Landmark (lm), 796–797
Language. *See also* Designed language; Human language
and thought, 360
uniqueness of, 15–18
Language acquisition
and cognitive science, 361–371
course of, 379–382
input to, 372–377
stages of, *364*
Language development, crosslinguistic studies of, 366
Language learnability, study of, 163
Language processing
characterizing studies of, 279
experimental methods for, 278–294
Language research, key issues in, 278–279
Language stimuli, in reception tasks, 283–286
Language universals, and linguistics, 362
Language and Perception (Miller and Johnson-Laird), 5
Laplacian, defined, 587
Late selection, vs. early, 634–637
Lateral geniculate nucleus (LGN), 308
Layers, in brain systems, 312–315, *313*
Learnability theory, 363
Learning
and action, 745–754
in connectionist systems, 148–152
effects of, 38
and generalization, 153–154
and innateness, 360–361
mechanisms for, 42
and memory, experimental methods for, 263–278
and problem solving, 530
during problem solving, 541–544
Learning rule, 147
Learning techniques
annealing, 42
Boltzmann methods, 42

Learning theories, and expert problem solving, 529
Length-tension curve(s), 732–733
and neural input, 776
Lesions, 320–326, *338*
animal models of, 323–324
human studies of, 320–323
microlesions, 324–326, *338*
reversible, 324–326
Letter detectors, 403
Letter identification, and word identification, 403–416, *404*, *405*
Level I rules, 370
Levels, physiological, 304
Levels of analysis, 302–303
Levels of investigation, 302–320
Levels of organization, 303–304
Lexical decision task, 289
Lexical entry, 412
Lexical-Functional Grammar (LFG), 186–190
Lexical lookup route, 412
Lexical meaning, construction of, 759–796
Lexical rules, in LFG, 188
Lexical semantics, 209
Limbic system, structures in, *308*
Limited capacity, 632–634
as cause of attentional phenomena, 655
variations on, 637–642
Linear bounded automation, 167
Linear plan formation, 454
Linguistic competence, vs. performance, 197
Linguistic hedges, 808
Linguistic representations, 472–475
Linguistics, and cognitive science, 5
List structures, interpretation of, 17–18
LMS puzzle, 532–533
and means-end analysis, 539–*540*
Local focusing, 446
Local networks, *314*
brain system's, 315–316
Localist representational system, 138
Logic
and cognitive science, 36–37
elements, scoping of, 177
equivalence, problem of, 235
form (LF), 177
properties, emergence of from meanings, 483
process, of motion, 602

Models (cont.)
  as representation of knowledge, 485–488
  source of, 487–488
Model-theoretic semantics, 207–243
  challenge of, 215
Modification, *513*
Modifier attachment, as phrase-level problem, 445
Modularity, 359–360, 424. *See also* Task specificity
  and scale problem, 156
Modus tollens, 818–819
Molecules, function of, 319–320, *321, 322*
Motion
  measurement of, 602–606
  recovery of 3-D structure from, 606–610
Motor equivalence, defined, 729
Motor organs, and inner/outer environments, 41
Motor system, Soar's, 118
Motor theory, of perception, 727
"Move α," 181
Movement planning, geometrical and mechanical issues in, 769–792
Moving window technique, 417–420, *418*
Multifunctional systems, 651–652
Multijoint movement, analysis of, 782–788
Multijoint posture, analysis of, 782–788
Multiple resources, 641
Multiple scales, in visual analysis, *587–590*
Muscle mechanical properties, 776–779

Name-matching task, 257–*258*
Nativism
  Chomsky's, 163, 172
  as psychological question, 197
Natural core model, 804
Naturalistic observation, 246
The Nature of Explanation (Craik), 469
Navigational procedures, cultural structure in, 820–822
Necker cube, 143–145, *144*
Negative evidence, *364*, 373–374
  defined, 373
  role of, 363

Negative priming, evidence of, 658–661
Negative transfer, 269, 557–558
N-methyl-D-aspartic acid (NMDA) receptors, 325
Network models, 12–13
Network-coupling approach, 735
Neural networks, models of, 341–343
Neuronal activity, attentional modulation of, 646–647
Neurons, *317*
  classes of, 318
  electrical signaling in, 320, *322*
  as elementary unit, 316
  sources of, 340–341
Neurophysiology, 3
Neuropil, 315
Neuropsychological architecture, and distributed modular function, 643–644
Neuroscience and cognitive science, 6
Newton-Euler formulations, 775
NOAH system, 453
Nominal-kind concepts, 503
Nonlinguistic cognitive development, 386
Nonmonotonic logics, 37, 476
Nonnatural meaning, theory of, 451
Nonterminal vocabulary, 164
Nonuniformity, and intermediate vision, 612
Notation, in systems theory, 746–747
Noun phrases, modification relations in, 449–450
Novice, defined, 560

Objects
  decomposition into parts approach, to object recognition, 618–619
  models, 809
  perceptual representation, 645
Observables, theory and, 249–253
Old Zealandish, syntax of, 217–219
On-line performance measures, 286–294
"100-step program" constraint, 135
Open lexical items, 805
Operations
  Act* vs. Soar, 114–115
  and operands, 119
Operator selection, in schema-driver problem solving, 552
Operator subgoaling, 538
Operators, 453

Plan units, in sequential performance, *154*
Plan vector, *739*
PLANNER, 476
Plant, 745, *746*
Plasticity
  of computers, 54–55
  in connectivity, 340
Plot units, 441
PMF algorithm, 599
Polysemy, 797–798
Positive evidence, 372–373
Positive priority assignment, 647
Positron emission tomography (PET), 320, *338*
  and blood flow, *331*
  use of, 327
Possible worlds, as situations, 239–240
Possible-worlds semantics, 231–235
  adding parameter to, 233–235
Power law, of practice, 101, 554
Predictability, 424
  effect of, 429
  and lexical access, 426
Presupposition, 216
Primary visual cortex, function of, 591
Priming, and selective response, 657–658
Principle of Compositionality, 208
Priority assignment, 651
  of attentional system, 652
  indirect, 654–655
"PRO," 181–182
  dual classification of, 183
Proactive interference, 270
Probabilities
  estimating, 518–521
  and probability theory, 519
Probe reaction times (probe RT), 655–656
  as performance measure, 288
Problem classification, expert/novice, 563–564
Problem environments, 39
Problem schema, 545
Problem solving
  by analogy, 556–557, 559–560
  as change in representation, 822–823
  and cognitive skill acquisition, 527–579
  operators, Act*'s vs. Soar's, 116
  standard theory of, 552–553

Problem space, 8, 531
  use of in Soar, 117
Procedural memory, 702
Proceduralization, 543
Processes, methods of invoking, 69
Processing units, in connectionist system, 138
Processor, in classical view, 56
Production compilation, Act*'s, 115
Production match
  context-dependent nature of, 113
  recognition nature of, 113–114
Production memory, Act*'s vs. Soar's, 112
Production systems
  control cycles of, 69
  forms of interpretation inherent in, 116–117
  as recognition-based architectures, 119
  as representation for prototypes, 514
Production tasks, in language processing, 280–282
Productions, 10–11
  Act*'s vs. Soar's, 112
  parts of, 10
  strength of, 115
Productivity, of thought and reasoning, 57
Profile, in lexical meaning, 795–797
Program, defined, 71
Projection rules, 175
Pronominals, 182–183
Pronouns
  and definite descriptions, 445–448
  and referents, 445–446
Properties, as basic (primitives), 237
Property lists, 17
Proposition schemas, 810
Propositional representations, 488–489
Propositional scoring systems, 292–293
Propositions, vs. images, 19–20
Prosodic information, 375
Protection, in computer architecture, 109
Protocol analysis, 78
  as technique, 21–27
  typical procedures in, 22–24
Protocols, computer-aided encoding of, 24
Prototype(s)
  in categorization, 802–803

defined, 505
on-line computation of, 508–509
representations for, 514–515
Prototype-core distinction, 509–510
PRP paradigm, 656
Pseudoinverse, 735–736
Pseudopassive, 185
Pseudoword-superiority effect, 406–407
Psycholinguistics, 3, 5
Psychological processes, characterizing, 255–259
Psychological reality, 197
Psychometrics, 3
Pure translation, assumption of, 605, 606
Pushdown automaton, 167
p.w. proposition, 234

Qualia, 838–842
absent, 839
inverted, 839
Question answering, as performance measure, 291

Rapid pattern matching, 147–148
Rapid serial visual presentation (RSVP), 286–287
Rasters, 20
Ray-intersection method, 613–614
Reaction time (RT), 260
as measure, 83
READER, 29–31
Reading time, as performance measure, 286–287
Reality monitoring, problem of, 694
Real-time demand, 107–108
Real-time requirement, production systems as responsive to, 119
Real-world categories, learning tasks for, 276
Reasoning
and cultural models, 817–823
and mental models, 475–484
theories of, 475–477
Recall confusions, 265
Recall orders, 566
Recall pauses, 566
Recall schema, 753–754
Recall structure and semantic relatedness, 566
Recall tasks, 265–266
Recall tests, 264

Reception tasks, in language processing, 282–286
Recognition, 41
Recognition response, 147
Recognition schema, 754
Recognition tasks, 266–268
accuracy in, 267
speed in, 267–278
Recognition tests, 264
Recognize-act cycle, 69, 116
Recognition-memory tests, as performance measure, 291–292
Reconstruction, and schemas, 691–694
Recording STM contents, as verbalization, 25
Reentrancy, 187
Referential descriptions, 447
Reflex arc, as systems concept, 306, 309
Refractoriness, rule of, 11
R-expressions, 182–183
Regional blood flow, as imaging technique, 329, 331, 338
Register architecture, and Turing machine, 74
Register-transfer level, 96–97
Regression, 418
Regularity effect, 413
Reinforcement learning, 747–748
Relational grammar, 184–186
Relations, as basic (primitives), 237
Relative-frequency information, and estimating probabilities, 519
Relaxation, 143
Relaxation procedures, and stereo-correspondence problems, 599
Reliability
as property, 106
in protocol analysis, 24
types of, in context analysis, 28
"Remarks on Nominalization" (Chomsky), 178
Repair, 550
Repeating back, as performance measure, 286
Representation
of external world, 104
forms of, 472
levels of in LFG, 186
Representational capacity, as systematic, 62
Representational types, analyzing, 256–259